WORLD LITERATURE CRITICISM

1500 to the Present

WORLD LITERATURE CRITICISM

1500 to the Present

*A Selection of
Major Authors from
Gale's Literary
Criticism Series*

1

Achebe-Cather

JAMES P. DRAPER, Editor

Gale Research Inc. · DETROIT · LONDON

STAFF

James P. Draper, *Editor*

Laurie DiMauro, Tina Grant, Paula Kepos, Jelena Krstović, Daniel G. Marowski, Roger Matuz, James E. Person, Jr., Joann Prosyniuk, David Segal, Joseph C. Tardiff, Bridget Travers, Lawrence Trudeau, Thomas Votteler, Sandra L. Williamson, Robyn V. Young, *Contributing Editors*

Catherine Falk, Grace Jeromski, Michael W. Jones, Andrew M. Kalasky, David Kmenta, Marie Lazzari, Zoran Minderović, Sean René Pollock, Mark Swartz, *Contributing Associate Editors*

Jennifer Brostrom, David J. Engelman, Andrea Gacki, Judith Galens, Christopher Giroux, Ian A. Goodhall, Alan Hedblad, Elizabeth P. Henry, Christopher K. King, Kyung-Sun Lim, Elisabeth Morrison, Kristin Palm, Susan M. Peters, James Poniewozik, Eric Priehs, Bruce Walker, Debra A. Wells, Janet Witalec, Allyson J. Wylie, *Contributing Assistant Editors*

Jeanne A. Gough, *Permissions & Production Manager*

Linda M. Pugliese, *Production Supervisor*
Paul Lewon, Lorna Mabunda, Maureen Puhl, Camille Robinson, Jennifer VanSickle, *Editorial Associates*
Donna Craft, Brandy C. Johnson, Sheila Walencewicz, *Editorial Assistants*

Victoria B. Cariappa, *Research Manager*

Maureen Richards, *Research Supervisor*
Mary Beth McElmeel, Tamara C. Nott, *Editorial Associates*
Andrea B. Ghorai, Daniel J. Jankowski, Julie K. Karmazin, Robert S. Lazich, *Editorial Assistants*

Sandra C. Davis, *Permissions Supervisor (Text)*
Maria L. Franklin, Josephine M. Keene, Michele M. Lonoconus, Denise M. Singleton, Kimberly F. Smilay, *Permissions Associates*
Rebecca A. Hartford, Shalice Shah, Nancy K. Sheridan, *Permissions Assistants*

Margaret A. Chamberlain, *Permissions Supervisor (Pictures)*
Pamela A. Hayes, *Permissions Associate*
Amy Lynn Emrich, Karla Kulkis, Nancy M. Rattenbury, Keith Reed, *Permissions Assistants*

Mary Beth Trimper, *Production Manager*
Mary Winterhalter, *Production Assistant*

Arthur Chartow, *Art Director*
C. J. Jonik, *Keyliner*
Kathleen A. Hourdakis, Mary Krzewinski, *Graphic Designers*

∞™ This book is printed on acid-free paper that meets the minimum requirements of American National Standard for Information Sciences— Permanence Paper for Printed Library Materials, ANSI Z39.48-1984.

ISBN 0-8103-8361-6 (6-volume set)
A CIP catalogue record for this book is available from the British Library
Printed in the United States of America

Published simultaneously in the United Kingdom
by Gale Research International Limited
(An affiliated company of Gale Research Inc.)

Table of Contents

Introduction xxv

Chinua Achebe 1930-
Widely considered the finest Nigerian novelist, Achebe was the first African writer to attract international attention with his classic work *Things Fall Apart*. His novels are among the first in English to present an intimate and authentic rendering of African culture **1:1**

Edward Albee 1928-
Best known for his first full-length drama, *Who's Afraid of Virginia Woolf?*, Albee was initially classified as an absurdist. He generally defies this term, however, by dismissing the absurdist sense of inescapable determinism and offering, instead, solutions to the conflicts he creates.. **1:16**

Louisa May Alcott 1832-1888
Alcott is best known for her sentimental yet realistic depictions of nineteenth-century American domestic life. Her most famous novel, *Little Women*, has been a staple for generations of readers since its publication in 1868 .... **1:35**

Hans Christian Andersen 1805-1875
Andersen is known as the author of such well-loved stories as "The Little Mermaid" and "The Ugly Duckling." By drawing on folklore and personal experience for his fairy tales, Andersen expanded the scope of the genre.......................... **1:52**

Sherwood Anderson 1876-1941
Anderson was among the first American authors to explore the influence of the unconscious upon human behavior. His most famous work, a collection of stories titled *Winesburg, Ohio*, is based on his time growing up in Clyde, Ohio **1:70**

Matthew Arnold 1822-1888
As one of the most influential poets of the later Victorian period, Arnold wrote elegiac verse expressing a sense of modern malaise. Such poems as "Dover Beach" and "The Forsaken Merman" mark some of the finest of the era **1:88**

Margaret Atwood 1939-
Atwood's acclaimed novels and poems explore the relationship between humanity and nature, unsettling aspects of human behavior, and power as it pertains to gender and political roles. For the latter, she has earned a distinguished reputation among feminist writers and readers... **1:106**

W. H. Auden 1907-1973
A modernist whose rejection of Romantic tenets was summarized in a single line ("Poetry makes nothing happen"), Auden spawned the "Oxford Group" or "Auden Generation" of writers. His work remains highly influential.................... **1:123**

Jane Austen 1775-1817
As a supreme prose stylist, Austen has secured a lasting place in English literature. She penned such widely-read classics as *Pride and Prejudice*, *Sense and Sensibility*, *Emma*, and *Persuasion*.. **1:142**

James Baldwin 1924-1987
One of the most important American writers of the twentieth century, Baldwin—author of *Go Tell It on the Mountain*—is considered an eloquent and impassioned critic of racial and sexual discrimination in American society............................ **1:159**

Honoré de Balzac 1799-1850
One of the greatest French novelists of the nineteenth century, Balzac wrote *La comédie humaine*, a collection of more than ninety novels and short stories that provide a comprehensive portrait of French society in his day............ 1:177

Charles Baudelaire 1821-1867
One of the world's greatest lyric and prose poets, Baudelaire is acclaimed for controversial poems chronicling his spiritual obsessions and depicting beauty amidst the poverty, amorality, and filth he believed characterized urban Paris.. 1:195

Simone de Beauvoir 1908-1986
In addition to her feminist theories, Beauvoir is esteemed for her documentation of left-wing intellectualism and existentialism. She is best known for her nonfiction work *The Second Sex*, a study of women's status throughout history, although her novels also achieved acclaim.............. 1:212

Samuel Beckett 1906-1989
The plotless scenario and seemingly senseless dialogue of Beckett's experimental masterpiece, *Waiting for Godot*, inspired the term "Theater of the Absurd" and helped shape the focus of contemporary drama.............. 1:226

Aphra Behn 1640?-1689
As the first English woman to earn a living solely by writing, Behn was known for her quick wit and her advocacy of women's rights.............. 1:244

Saul Bellow 1915-
The author of *The Victim* and *The Adventures of Augie March*, Bellow often depicts conflicts between New World and Old World values and addresses the question of what it is to be human in an increasingly impersonal and mechanistic world.............. 1:260

Ambrose Bierce 1842-1914?
Bierce's stories, which typically involve mental deterioration and bizarre forms of death, express the terror of existence in a meaningless universe. His penchant for horror led to his distinction as "the wickedest man in San Francisco.".......... 1:278

William Blake 1757-1827
A visionary poet and artist, Blake was once ridiculed as a madman but is now revered as a genius. His best-known work is "The Tyger": "Tyger! Tyger! burning bright / In the forests of the night / What immortal hand or eye / Could frame thy fearful symmetry?".............. 1:295

Heinrich Böll 1917-1985
One of Germany's most popular and prolific authors, Böll gained international fame as a chronicler of the Federal German Republic. He was awarded the Nobel Prize in 1972.............. 1:313

Jorge Luis Borges 1899-1986
Among the foremost literary figures to have written in Spanish, Borges is best known for his esoteric short stories in which he blended fantasy and realism to address complex philosophical problems.............. 1:330

James Boswell 1740-1795
One of the most colorful figures in eighteenth-century English literature, Boswell is esteemed for his inimitable conversational style and pictorial documentation of life in such nonfiction works as *London Journal* and *The Life of Samuel Johnson*.............. 1:345

Ray Bradbury 1920-
Bradbury has written short stories, novels, dramas, screenplays, poetry, and nonfiction, but he is best known as the science fiction author who wrote *The Martian Chronicles*.............. 1:362

Bertolt Brecht 1898-1956
Brecht's imagination, artistic genius, and profound grasp of the nature of drama establish him as a chief innovator of modern theatrical techniques. His great talent in the medium allowed him to exploit his stage sense to promote his political and humanistic concerns 1:380

Charlotte Brontë 1816-1855
In her highly acclaimed *Jane Eyre: An Autobiography*, Brontë challenged the

nineteenth-century stereotypical view of women as submissive, dependent beings. For her originality in form and content, Brontë is regarded by many as a forerunner of feminist novelists 1:397

Emily Brontë 1818-1848
One of the most important yet elusive figures in English literature, Brontë led a brief and circumscribed life but left behind a literary legacy that includes some of the most passionate and inspired writing in Victorian literature 1:414

Rupert Brooke 1887-1915
Considered England's foremost young poet at the time of his death, Brooke is best known today for his war poetry and for his personal mystique as the embodiment of idealized youth 1:432

Gwendolyn Brooks 1917-
Brooks, a major contemporary poet, is best known for her sensitive portraits of urban blacks. Her early works avoided overt statements about race and racism but, with the advent of the Black Power movement, she began to explore the marginality of black life in her poetry and to recognize the rage and despair among many black people as her own 1:448

Elizabeth Barrett Browning 1806-1861
One of the most celebrated English poets, Browning is remembered for a collection of love poems written to her husband, poet Robert Browning. The best-known selection from *Sonnets from the Portuguese* is Sonnet XLIII, which contains the often-quoted line "How do I love thee? Let me count the ways." 1:465

John Bunyan 1628-1688
Bunyan is recognized as a master of allegorical prose, and his conception and technique are often compared to those of John Milton and Edmund Spenser. He is chiefly remembered for his religious classic *Pilgrim's Progress* 1:479

Edmund Burke 1729-1797
As the founder of modern Anglo-American conservatism, Burke is considered by many to be the most important and influential English statesman and political writer of the eighteenth century 1:495

Robert Burns 1759-1796
Admired for his fervent championship of the innate freedom and dignity of humanity, Burns is regarded as the national poet of Scotland 1:514

William S. Burroughs 1914-
An innovative and controversial author of experimental fiction, Burroughs is best known for *Naked Lunch*, a surreal account of his fourteen-year addiction to morphine and other drugs 1:531

Samuel Butler 1835-1902
Novelist Butler, one of the most renowned English authors of the late-Victorian period, created scathing portraits of Victorian family life and pungent satires of English society 1:548

Lord Byron 1788-1824
English poet Byron—author of the epic *Don Juan*—was enormously popular during his life until the press vilified him, alleging that he maintained an incestuous relationship with his sister 1:565

Albert Camus 1913-1960
One of the most important literary figures of the twentieth century, Camus is known for his consistent and passionate exploration of his major theme: the belief that people can attain happiness in an apparently meaningless world. This theme is captured in such famous works as *The Myth of Sisyphus* and *The Stranger* 1:582

Karel Čapek 1890-1938
In such science-fiction works as *Rossum's Universal Robots* and *War with the Newts*, Čapek satirized a host of social, economic, and political systems and warned against the dehumanizing aspects of modern civilization 1:598

Truman Capote 1924-1984
With the popular and controversial *In Cold Blood*, a psycho-biographical investigation of a mass murder, Capote became a leading practitioner of New Journal-

ism, popularizing a genre that he called the nonfiction novel. He was an intriguing public figure as well as a writer, serving as the model for the character Dill in Harper Lee's *To Kill a Mockingbird* and playing the role of an eccentric millionaire in a screen adaptation of Neil Simon's *Murder by Death* 1:615

Lewis Carroll (Charles Lutwidge Dodgson) 1832-1898
The creator of the well-loved Alice in Wonderland, Carroll wrote novels that continue to be embraced by children and adults alike 1:633

Willa Cather 1873-1947
Cather is best known for her novels *O Pioneers!* and *My Antonia*. Both are regarded as evocative, realistic portrayals of pioneer life written in celebration of the courageous endurance of the early Midwestern settlers and the natural beauty of the prairie landscape 1:651

Miguel de Cervantes 1547-1616
Cervantes has had an inestimable impact on the development of modern fiction through his novel *Don Quixote*. Viewed as one of the most enduring masterpieces of world literature, the hilarious adventures of the deranged gentleman-turned-knight Quixote and his companion, Sancho Panza, assume archetypal importance for what they reveal of the human mind and emotions, Golden Age Spanish society, and the compass of earthly existence 2:667

John Cheever 1912-1982
Dubbed "the Chekhov of the exurbs," Cheever chronicled the psychic unrest of suburban life in such highly regarded short stories as "The Swimmer," "The Enormous Radio," and "The Housebreaker of Shady Hill" and such novels as *The Wapshot Chronicle* and *Bullet Park* 2:687

Anton Chekhov 1860-1904
The most significant Russian author of the literary generation succeeding Leo Tolstoy and Fyodor Dostoyevsky, Chekhov is revered for his stylistic innovations in fiction and drama and for his depth of insight into the human condition 2:704

Jean Cocteau 1889-1963
Viewing himself as a creative and misunderstood social outcast, Cocteau made alienation a central theme of his work 2:721

Samuel Taylor Coleridge 1772-1834
The intellectual stalwart of the English Romantic movement, Coleridge is best known for three poems: "The Rime of the Ancient Mariner," "Kubla Kahn," and "Christabel." His fame and influence were marred by health problems and a lifelong dependence on opium 2:740

William Congreve 1670-1729
Congreve is recognized as the greatest comic dramatist of the Restoration. The wit of such plays as *Love for Love* and *The Way of the World* continues to engage audiences 2:758

Joseph Conrad 1857-1924
Conrad is best known as the author of *Heart of Darkness*, the story of a man's symbolic journey into his own inner being and the basis for Francis Ford Coppola's 1979 film *Apocalypse Now* 2:777

Hart Crane 1899-1932
A lyric poet in the Romantic visionary tradition, Crane has been compared to William Blake, Samuel Taylor Coleridge, and Charles Baudelaire 2:793

Stephen Crane 1871-1900
One of America's foremost realistic writers, Crane made his mark as the progenitor of American Naturalism. In such works as *The Red Badge of Courage* and *Maggie: A Girl of the Streets*, he espoused his view of "life as warfare," depicting hardship on the battlefield and in the slums 2:811

E. E. Cummings 1894-1962
Conformity, mass psychology, and snobbery were frequent targets of Cummings's humorous and sometimes scathing satirical poetry: "the Cambridge ladies who live in furnished souls / are unbeautiful and have comfortable minds. . . . the Cambridge ladies do not care, above Cambridge if sometimes in its box of sky lavender and cornerless the / moon rattles like a fragment of angry candy" 2:829

Robertson Davies 1913-
The author of such novels as *Fifth Business* and *The World of Wonders*, Davies is a prominent figure in Canadian literature. He often directs his satirical humor toward Canadian provincialism, which he perceives as a hindrance to Canada's cultural development... **2:846**

Daniel Defoe 1660?-1731
The "father of the English novel," Defoe was sentenced to three days in the pillory and a prison term for his writings satirizing Tory leaders and high churchmen; he later served as a secret agent and political propagandist for the Tories....... **2:862**

Walter de la Mare 1873-1956
De la Mare's poetry and fiction blend mystical experiences with ordinary objects and events, exploring such romantic concerns as dreams, death, and the fantasy worlds of childhood.. **2:883**

Charles Dickens 1812-1870
One of the best-known writers in all of literature, Dickens created such memorable characters as Ebenezer Scrooge, Little Nell, and Miss Havisham. He achieved popularity with an early work, *Posthumous Papers of the Pickwick Club*, and went on to produce such time-honored classics as *Oliver Twist*, *A Christmas Carol*, *The Personal History of David Copperfield*, *Bleak House*, *Great Expectations*, and *Little Dorrit* **2:895**

Emily Dickinson 1830-1886
Dickinson's forthright examination of her philosophical and religious skepticism, unorthodox attitude toward her gender, and original style of writing have facilitated her reputation as one of the greatest American poets. This distinction came posthumously; few of Dickinson's poems were published during her lifetime..... **2:913**

John Donne 1572-1631
One of the most accomplished—and controversial—poets of the seventeenth century, Donne composed such famous works as "Death Be Not Proud," "Hymn to God My God in My Sicknesse," and "A Valediction: Forbidding Mourning." Such poems focused on religion, love, death, and spirituality: "Moving of th' earth brings harms and fears, / Men reckon what it did and meant; / But trepidation of the spheres, / Though greater far, is innocent. / Dull sublunary lovers' love / (Whose soul is sense) cannot admit / Absence, because it doth remove / Those things which elemented it." **2:929**

John Dos Passos 1896-1970
Called "the greatest writer of our time" by Jean-Paul Sartre, Dos Passos was a master novelist and chronicler of twentieth-century American life. His commitment to leftist political causes and his later shift to a conservative stance inform his best known works, *Manhattan Transfer* and *U. S. A.*..................................... **2:949**

Fyodor Dostoyevsky 1821-1881
In such novels as *Crime and Punishment* and *The Brothers Karamazov*, Dostoyevsky attained profound philosophical and psychological insights that anticipated important developments in twentieth-century thought, including psychoanalysis and existentialism. His work also influenced the thoughts and themes of many modern writers, including Franz Kafka.. **2:969**

Frederick Douglass 1817?-1895
Author of one of the most compelling antislavery documents produced by a fugitive slave, *Narrative of the Life of Frederick Douglass*, Douglass was an important spokesman for the abolition of slavery... **2:987**

Arthur Conan Doyle 1859-1930
Despite his numerous historical works, Doyle is known chiefly as the writer of detective novels and as the creator of one of the most famous literary characters of all time, Sherlock Holmes.. **2:1004**

Theodore Dreiser 1871-1945
Dreiser was one of the principal American exponents of literary Naturalism at the turn of the century. With such novels as *Sister Carrie* and *An American Tragedy*, he led the way for a generation of writers seeking to present a detailed and realistic portrait of American life... **2:1022**

John Dryden 1631-1700

Regarded as the father of modern English poetry and criticism, Dryden dominated literary life in England during the last four decades of the seventeenth century.. 2:1040

W. E. B. Du Bois 1868-1963

Although he wrote the famous *The Souls of Black Folk* as well as numerous essays, novels, poems, and histories, Du Bois is generally remembered as a pioneering civil rights activist in the twentieth century.. 2:1060

Alexandre Dumas, père 1802-1870

Regarded as one of the world's greatest storytellers, Dumas penned two of the most widely read novels in literary history, *The Count of Monte Cristo* and *The Three Musketeers* 2:1077

Paul Laurence Dunbar 1872-1906

Considered America's first great black poet, Dunbar is best known for his dialect verse and as the first black author in America to earn a living from his pen 2:1096

George Eliot 1819-1880

Upon their publication, Eliot's early novels received high praise. When it was revealed that George Eliot was the pseudonym of a woman, Mary Ann Evans, the works were duly condemned, as were *The Mill on the Floss* and *Silas Marner*. Today, however, the latter books are regarded as classics, and Eliot is revered as the most learned and respected novelist of the later Victorian period........... 2:1115

T. S. Eliot 1888-1965

Throughout his career, Eliot strongly advocated the development of a "historical sense," which he stated was "nearly indispensable to anyone who would continue to be a poet beyond his twenty-fifth year." Consequently, awareness and affirmation of his literary and cultural heritage is one of the most prominent features of such epic poems as *The Waste Land* and *Four Quartets*, as well as Eliot's shorter verse, including "The Love Song of J. Alfred Prufrock." The last-named work contains the famous lines: "In the room the women come and go / talking of Michaelangelo." 2:1133

Ralph Ellison 1914-

One of the most influential and accomplished American authors of the twentieth century, Ellison is best known for his masterpiece *Invisible Man*, the story of an unnamed black youth's quest for identity in a hostile world................................. 2:1152

Ralph Waldo Emerson 1803-1882

A founder of the Transcendental movement, which embodied a distinctly American philosophy based on optimism, individuality, and mysticism, essayist and poet Emerson was one of the most influential literary figures of the nineteenth century 2:1168

William Faulkner 1897-1962

Faulkner's work often explores exploitation and corruption in the American South. Such novels as *The Sound and the Fury*, *Light in August*, *Absalom, Absalom!*, and *As I Lay Dying* are regarded as classics of American literature and earned the author a Nobel Prize. In his acceptance speech for the award, Faulkner stated that the fundamental theme of his fiction is "the human heart in conflict with itself" 2:1185

Henry Fielding 1707-1754

Instrumental in the development of the English novel, Fielding sought to depict the natural world in such a way that would "laugh mankind out of their favourite follies and vices." 2:1201

F. Scott Fitzgerald 1896-1940

Fitzgerald's best-known stories of the Jazz Age, including *The Great Gatsby* and *Tender is the Night*, examine an entire generation's search for the elusive American dream of wealth and happiness 2:1219

Gustave Flaubert 1821-1880

The most influential French novelist of the nineteenth century, Flaubert is remembered primarily for the stylistic precision and dispassionate rendering of psychological detail found in his masterpiece, *Madame Bovary* 2:1237

E. M. Forster 1879-1970
Forster is best remembered as the author of *Howards End*, *A Passage to India*, and other novels of manners depicting Edwardian society and British morality. His works are highly esteemed for their realistic renderings of conservative English culture 2:1256

Anne Frank 1929-1945
Frank is known throughout the world for the diary she did not live to see published. *Anne Frank: The Diary of a Young Girl* documents Frank's adolescence, most of which was spent in the tiny upper quarters of a house in Amsterdam where she and her Jewish family hid from Nazi troops during World War II 2:1272

Robert Frost 1874-1963
Pulitzer Prize-winning poet Frost commented on social and political issues and described scenes of natural beauty in his explorations of humanity's constant struggle against chaos and bewilderment 2:1286

Carlos Fuentes 1928-
A novelist who is chiefly concerned with establishing a viable Mexican identity in his work, Fuentes uses the past thematically and symbolically to comment on contemporary concerns and to project his own vision of Mexico's future 2:1307

John Galsworthy 1867-1933
Galsworthy's relatives provided him with the basis for the characters in his "Forsyte Chronicles," a well-known series of stories centering on upper middle-class English life 2:1325

Federico García Lorca 1898-1936
Hailed as one of Spain's most important poets, García Lorca drew upon all elements of Spanish life and culture to create poetry at once traditional, modern, personal, and universal. He sought to liberate language from its structural constraints and bring out the musicality inherent in the Spanish language 2:1337

Gabriel García Márquez 1928-
García Márquez's stories feature an imaginative blend of history, politics, social realism, fantasy, magic, and surrealism. Using these techniques, García Márquez obscures the customary distinctions between illusion and reality 3:1355

André Gide 1869-1951
All of Gide's works in some way reflect his emotional struggles, and critics agree that one aspect of his genius was his ability to translate the contradictions and complexities of his nature into art.. 3:1373

Allen Ginsberg 1926-
The opening lines of Ginsberg's "Howl" are among the most well-known in American poetry: "I saw the best minds of my generation destroyed by madness, starving / hysterical naked, / dragging themselves through the negro streets at dawn looking for an / angry fix." 3:1390

Johann Wolfgang von Goethe 1749-1832
In addition to his career as a highly distinguished writer, Goethe was an established scientist, artist, musician, and philosopher. He is considered Germany's greatest writer and a genius of the highest order 3:1408

Nikolai Gogol 1809-1852
Progenitor of the Russian Naturalist movement, novelist Gogol explored many aspects of Russian life in the epic novel *Dead Souls* and is often cited as a major inspiration to such prominent authors as Fyodor Dostoyevsky and Franz Kafka... 3:1426

William Golding 1911-1991
The winner of the Nobel Prize in 1983, Golding is among the most popular and influential post-World War II British authors. He is best known for his novel *Lord of the Flies* 3:1443

Oliver Goldsmith 1728?-1774
The author of *The Vicar of Wakefield* and *She Stoops to Conquer*, novelist and dramatist Goldsmith neglected his studies at Dublin's Trinity College and was frequently reprimanded for infractions of regulations, such as his participation in a riot, growing from a protest of another student's arrest, during which several people were killed.. 3:1461

Maxim Gorky 1868-1936
Gorky's brutal yet romantic portraits of Russian life and sympathetic depictions of the working class had an inspirational effect on the oppressed people of his native land 3:1480

Günter Grass 1927-
Grass's Danzig trilogy graphically captures the reactions of many German citizens to the rise of Nazism and the horrors of war. Inspired by Surrealism and German Expressionism, Grass utilizes black humor, satire, and wordplay in his fiction, prompting comparisons to James Joyce, Laurence Sterne, and François Rabelais 3:1499

Thomas Gray 1716-1771
English poet Gray achieved immediate critical and popular acclaim with his "Elegy Written in a Country Churchyard," a poem admired for, in the words of Alfred, Lord Tennyson, its "divine truisms that make us weep." 3:1517

Graham Greene 1904-1991
A popular and prolific novelist, Greene engaged his readers with his terse style and vivid descriptive passages, as in his most famous novel *The Power and the Glory*, in which a priest is jailed overnight for drunkenness in a Mexican province that has outlawed Catholicism 3:1535

Thomas Hardy 1840-1928
Although it is regarded as a classic, Hardy's *Tess of the d'Urbervilles* was denounced upon publication as immoral, anti-Christian, and unduly pessimistic. When his following novel, *Jude the Obscure*, garnered a similar response, Hardy ceased writing fiction and turned instead to poetry and drama 3:1556

Bret Harte 1836?-1902
American short story writer Harte achieved immense popularity for his nostalgic portrayals of the mining camps and ethnic groups of California during the Gold Rush of 1849 .... 3:1574

Nathaniel Hawthorne 1804-1864
Along with Edgar Allan Poe, Hawthorne is viewed as one of the principal architects of the modern American short story. In addition, his best-known novel, *The Scarlet Letter*, is acknowledged as a classic of American literature 3:1592

H. D. (Hilda Doolittle) 1886-1961
H. D.'s early free verse poetry was the inspiration for Ezra Pound's formulation of Imagism. Although her later poetry transcended the principles of Imagist verse to include mythological, occult, and religious themes as well as psychoanalytic concepts and symbolism, she is often called "the perfect Imagist." 3:1610

Joseph Heller 1923-
Heller's works combine a comic vision of modern society with serious moral overtones. His best-known novel, *Catch-22*, is regarded as a post-World War II classic 3:1628

Ernest Hemingway 1899-1961
Despite his tendency to generate controversy at every turn, Hemingway is regarded as one of the greatest writers of the twentieth century. He is remembered as much for his extravagant lifestyle as for such acclaimed novels as *The Sun Also Rises*, *A Farewell to Arms*, and *For Whom the Bell Tolls* 3:1646

O. Henry (William Sydney Porter) 1862-1910
One of the most popular short story writers of the twentieth century, O. Henry began his literary career after serving five years in prison on embezzlement charges 3:1664

Hermann Hesse 1877-1962
Best known as the author *Siddhartha*, *Demian*, and *Steppenwolf*, Hesse attained a huge, cult-like readership among the youth of the 1960s, who readily identified with his rebellious, passionately spiritual heroes and their struggle to transcend the materialism of society through art, mysticism, and love 3:1683

Gerard Manley Hopkins 1844-1889
Hopkins, a crafter of both poetry and poetic theory, is known for religious poetry cast in a meter he termed "sprung rhythm." 3:1701

Langston Hughes 1902-1967
Called "the Poet Laureate of Harlem," Hughes articulated the frustrations of African-Americans in the poem "A Dream Deferred": "What happens to a dream deferred?/ Does it dry up/ like a raisin in the sun?/ Or fester like a sore—/And then run?/ Does it stink like rotten meat?/ Or crust and sugar over—/ like a syrupy sweet?/ Maybe it just sags/ like a heavy load./ Or *does it explode?* " 3:1718

Victor Hugo 1802-1885
French novelist and poet Hugo completed his best-known work, the novel *Les misérables*, while in exile due to his uncompromising opposition to Louis Napoleon's dictatorial ambitions.. 3:1738

Aldous Huxley 1894-1963
English novelist Huxley is best known for *Brave New World*, in which he forecasts a horrific world civilization resulting from new technologies and political manipulation... 3:1758

Henrik Ibsen 1828-1906
A pioneer of modern theater, Ibsen left his native Norway in 1864. He believed that only by distancing himself from his homeland could he obtain the perspective necessary to write truly Norwegian drama 3:1774

Eugène Ionesco 1912-
A prominent dramatist associated with the Theater of the Absurd, Rumanian-born Ionesco explores the human condition in such darkly comic dramas as *Rhinoceros*.. 3:1796

Washington Irving 1783-1859
The author of such famous and well-loved stories as "Rip Van Winkle" and "The Legend of Sleepy Hollow," Irving is considered the first professional writer in the United States 3:1814

Shirley Jackson 1919-1965
In works that often contain elements of conventional gothic horror, Jackson chronicled the evil underlying human nature. Her classic short story "The Lottery" portrays a village gathering for an annual drawing that ends with a ritual sacrifice.. 3:1833

Henry James 1843-1916
One of the greatest novelists to write in the English language, James was a leading advocate of Realism in American literature 3:1853

Robinson Jeffers 1887-1962
An American poet whose prophetic admonitions against modern civilization and human introversion have attracted both critical censure and widespread admiration, Jeffers is best known for writing long narrative poems in which he contrasted the strength and enduring beauty of nature with a tragic vision of human suffering and inconsequence 3:1871

Samuel Johnson 1709-1784
Johnson ranks as the major literary figure of the late eighteenth century and is perhaps the most often-quoted writer in the English language after Shakespeare 3:1886

Ben Jonson 1572?-1637
One of the greatest writers and theorists of English literature, Jonson is remembered for his poetry as well as his satirical comedies... 3:1905

James Joyce 1882-1941
One of the most important literary figures of the twentieth century, Irish novelist Joyce redefined the limits of language and recreated the form of the modern novel in such seminal works as *Ulysses* and *Portrait of the Artist as a Young Man* 3:1923

Franz Kafka 1883-1924
Kafka's fiction has been variously described as autobiographical, psychoanalytic, Marxist, religious, Existentialist, Expressionist, and Naturalist. In his works, Kafka

gave literary form to the disorder of the modern world, turning his private nightmares into universal myths **3:1939**

John Keats 1795-1821
A key figure of the English Romantic movement, Keats wrote such poetic standards as "La Belle Dame Sans Merci" and his collection of odes. The final lines of "Ode on a Grecian Urn" are among literature's best-known: " 'Beauty is truth, truth beauty,'—that is all / Ye know on earth, and all ye need to know.".......... **3:1953**

Jack Kerouac 1922-1969
The chief literary figure and spokesman of the 1950s cultural phenomenon known as the Beat Movement, Kerouac depicted the world-weary yet optimistic attitude of his generation in the novel *On the Road*, a loosely-structured, fictionalized account of the wanderings and reckless adventures of Kerouac and his friends **3:1971**

Ken Kesey 1935-
As a member of the "Merry Pranksters," Kesey traveled around the United States during the 1960s promoting experimental drug use and social revolt. His best-known novel, *One Flew over the Cuckoo's Nest*, focuses on alienated and nonconformist individuals confined in a mental institution who attempt, through love, hope, rebellion, and humor, to overcome their limitations and to retain their sanity and self-respect.. **3:1990**

Rudyard Kipling 1865-1936
Creator of many of the world's best-loved short stories, Kipling also wrote poetry and novels. He is best known for *The Jungle Books*, which depict the adventures of Mowgli, a boy abandoned by his parents and raised by wolves **3:2006**

Charles Lamb 1775-1834
A well-known literary figure in nineteenth-century England, Lamb is chiefly remembered today for his "Elia" essays, a sequence renowned for its witty, idiosyncratic treatment of everyday subjects **3:2024**

D. H. Lawrence 1885-1930
One of the most original English writers of the twentieth century, Lawrence explored human nature through frank discussions of sex, psychology, and religion. His work defied not only the conventional artistic norms of his day but also the political, social, and moral values. Lawrence's last major novel, *Lady Chatterley's Lover*, was subjected to an obscenity trial in England before it was vindicated as a work of literature... **3:2041**

Harper Lee 1926-
Novelist Lee's story of racial prejudice in the American South, *To Kill a Mockingbird*, achieved immediate popularity and acclaim, winning a Pulitzer Prize and prompting a film adaptation that received an Academy Award............................ **4:2059**

C. S. Lewis 1898-1963
An accomplished and influential literary scholar, logician, Christian polemicist, and writer of fantasy literature, Lewis attributed his Christian conversion to a conversation in which novelist J. R. R. Tolkien convinced him that to believe in the God of Christianity was to enter the enjoyment of a myth grounded in reality... **4:2075**

Sinclair Lewis 1885-1951
A brilliant satirist, Lewis wrote fiction that vengefully attacked what he saw as the dullness and smug provincialism of much of American life **4:2096**

Vachel Lindsay 1879-1931
Poet Lindsay often found that critics ignored his concern for beauty and democracy, focusing instead on his spirited public readings. The strong rhythmic quality of much of his poetry nearly requires that it be chanted aloud **4:2115**

Jack London 1876-1916
The author of *The Call of the Wild*, London incorporated socialism, mysticism, Darwinian determinism, and Nietzschean theories of race into his many stories of adventure... **4:2133**

Robert Lowell 1917-1977
One of the most influential and widely acclaimed American poets of the midtwentieth century, Lowell experimented with a wide range of verse forms and

styles, seeking through artistic expression to order and make meaning of experience, particularly the dark and chaotic aspects of his own life and the world around him 4:2150

Bernard Malamud 1914-1986
Malamud is one of the most prominent figures in Jewish-American literature. Despite his emphasis on his faith, in such well-known works as *The Natural* and *The Assistant* he stressed human compassion over religious dogma.................. 4:2171

Thomas Mann 1875-1955
Best known as the author of *Death in Venice* and *The Magic Mountain*, Mann is one of the foremost German novelists of the twentieth century. Though his fiction typically reveals a somber and cerebral fascination with death, his works often display a deep, often humorous sympathy for humanity............................. 4:2192

Katherine Mansfield 1888-1923
An early practitioner of stream-of-consciousness narration, Mansfield is one of few authors to attain prominence exclusively for short stories. Her works remain among the most widely read in world literature.. 4:2210

Christopher Marlowe 1564-1593
Recognized as the first English dramatist to reveal the full potential of blank verse poetry, and as one who made significant advances in the genre of English tragedy through keen examinations of Renaissance morality, Marlowe is the author of such renowned plays as *Doctor Faustus*; *Tamburlaine, Parts I and II*; *The Jew of Malta*; and *Edward II* 4:2229

Andrew Marvell 1621-1678
One of the last seventeenth-century English metaphysical poets, Marvell is noted for his intellectual, allusive poetry, rich in metaphor and unexpected twists of thought and argument. His best lyric poetry, such as "To His Coy Mistress" and "The Garden," is characterized by ambiguity, complexity, and a thematic irresolution that many critics believe both define his talent and account for his appeal 4:2248

W. Somerset Maugham 1874-1965
One of the world's most prolific and popular authors, Maugham wrote such novels as *Of Human Bondage* and *Cakes and Ale; or, The Skeleton in the Cupboard* 4:2268

Guy de Maupassant 1850-1893
Considered one of the finest short story writers of all time and a champion of the realistic approach to writing, Maupassant created a narrative style outstanding in its austere power, simplicity, and vivid sensuousness 4:2287

Carson McCullers 1917-1967
One of the most enduring authors of the American Southern literary tradition, McCullers is best known for writing *The Heart Is a Lonely Hunter*, *The Ballad of the Sad Café*, and *The Member of the Wedding* 4:2305

Claude McKay 1889-1948
Jamaican-born American poet McKay was a forerunner of the militant spirit behind the Harlem Renaissance and the civil rights movement, evidenced in his poem "If We Must Die": "If we must die, O let us nobly die. . ./ Like men we'll face the murderous, cowardly pack,/ Pressed to the wall, dying, but fighting back!" 4:2322

Herman Melville 1819-1891
A major nineteenth-century American literary figure, Melville is best known as the author of *Moby-Dick*, the classic tale of a sea captain's monomaniacal quest to destroy a white whale that he views as the embodiment of all earthly malignity and evil 4:2340

Arthur Miller 1915-
American dramatist Miller insisted that "the individual is doomed to frustration when once he gains a consciousness of his own identity," a sentiment reflected in two of his most famous works, *Death of a Salesman* and *The Crucible* 4:2359

Henry Miller 1891-1980
Miller's novel *Tropic of Cancer* has been censured for its bawdy humor, obscene

language, and explicit sexual content; some critics, however, praise Miller for shocking his readers out of complacency by attacking the repression of the individual in a society bedeviled by technology **4:2376**

John Milton 1608-1674
Recognized as one of the greatest writers in the English language, Milton is best known for *Paradise Lost*, an epic poem recounting the Biblical story of humanity's fall from grace. This work and its sequel, *Paradise Regained*, are celebrated for their consummate artistry and searching consideration of God's relationship with the human race **4:2394**

Yukio Mishima 1925-1970
Known for his unorthodox views and eccentric personal life, Mishima, a Japanese short story writer and dramatist, wrote works that are characterized by a preoccupation with aggression and violent eroticism. **4:2413**

Molière 1622-1673
Molière is widely recognized as the greatest comic writer of seventeenth-century France and as one of the foremost dramatists in world literature. In such masterpieces as *Tartuffe*, *Don Juan*, and *The Misanthrope* he set precedents that completely altered the focus and purpose of comedy, introducing realism to the French stage and elevating comic drama from farcical buffoonery to an important form for social and religious criticism **4:2432**

Michel de Montaigne 1533-1592
The inventor of the essay form as a literary genre, Montaigne raised introspection to the level of art in his monumental work *The Essays*, a collection of more than three hundred pieces that treat myriad subjects from the trivial to the profound, ranging from the author's attitude towards radishes to his feelings about God **4:2451**

Toni Morrison 1931-
One of the most important American novelists of the twentieth century, Morrison won the Pulitzer Prize for *Beloved*, the story of a former slave's daughter who returns from the grave to seek revenge for her brutal death **4:2469**

Vladimir Nabokov 1899-1977
Nabokov, one of the outstanding literary stylists of the twentieth century, is best known for his novel *Lolita*. The novel's focus on a middle-aged man's sexual desires for a 12-year-old girl was subject to much controversy upon publication, but Nabokov drew unified praise for his ability to evoke both repugnance and sympathy in the reader **4:2483**

Pablo Neruda 1904-1973
Poet Neruda is noted for his innovative techniques and influential contributions to major developments in modern poetry, both in his native Chile and abroad **4:2502**

Joyce Carol Oates 1938-
Prizewinning author Oates depicts the decline of American society in novels and short stories that focus on the evils Americans must face: rape, incest, murder, mutilation, child abuse, and suicide **4:2520**

Flannery O'Connor 1925-1964
A Roman Catholic short story writer from the Bible-belt South whose stated purpose was to reveal the mystery of God's grace in everyday life, O'Connor depicted spiritually and physically grotesque characters engaged in shocking, often violent, behavior in the quest for salvation **4:2539**

Eugene O'Neill 1888-1953
Nobel Prize-winner O'Neill is generally considered America's foremost dramatist. In such plays as *The Iceman Cometh* and *Long Day's Journey into Night*, he examined the implacability of an indifferent universe, the materialistic greed of humanity, and the problems of discovering one's true identity **4:2556**

George Orwell 1903-1950
Celebrated English author of the novels *Animal Farm* and *Nineteen Eighty-Four*, Orwell is significant for his unwavering commitment, both as an individual and as an artist, to personal freedom and social justice **4:2572**

xvi

John Osborne 1929-

As one of Britain's Angry Young Men, Osborne encouraged social and political awareness. His landmark drama, *Look Back in Anger*, initiated a new era in British theater that emphasized aggressive social criticism, authentic portrayals of working-class life, and anti-heroic characters.. 4:2590

Wilfred Owen 1893-1918

Owen's realistic protest poems of World War I sought to present the grim realities of battle and its effects on the human spirit: "My subject is War, and the pity of war. I am not concerned with Poetry. The Poetry is in the Pity. Yet these elegies are to this generation in no sense consolatory. They may be to the next. All a poet can do is warn.".. 4:2603

Boris Pasternak 1890-1960

Russian novelist Pasternak ignited a political and artistic controversy with *Doctor Zhivago*, an epic portrayal of the Russian Revolution and its consequences..... 4:2621

Alan Paton 1903-1988

One of the earliest proponents of racial equality in his native South Africa, Paton is best known for his novel *Cry, the Beloved Country*. In this and other works he confronted the horrors of apartheid.. 4:2640

Octavio Paz 1914-

Mexican writer Paz has earned international acclaim for poetry and essays in which he seeks to reconcile divisive and opposing forces in contemporary life, stressing that language and love can provide means for attaining unity............. 4:2657

Samuel Pepys 1633-1703

As a highly placed civil servant and tireless man-about-town in Restoration London, Pepys observed and recorded in his diary the goings-on of his age, providing a unique record of what it was like to be alive in the early years of the reign of Charles II 4:2677

Harold Pinter 1930-

A major figure in contemporary drama, Pinter explores the meticulously preserved social pretenses of his characters and the subconscious desires or neuroses they repress... 4:2695

Luigi Pirandello 1867-1936

Italian dramatist Pirandello described his works as representing a "theater of mirrors" in which the audience sees what passes on stage as a reflection of their own lives... 4:2713

Sylvia Plath 1932-1963

An important American poet of the post-World War II era, Plath became widely known following her suicide and the posthumous publication of *Ariel*, a collection containing her most vivid and acclaimed verse.. 4:2700

Edgar Allan Poe 1809-1849

Poe made himself known not only as a superlative author of poetry and fiction, but also as a literary critic whose level of imagination and insight had been unapproached in American literature 4:2749

Alexander Pope 1688-1744

One of the most forceful poetic satirists of all time, Pope is best known as the author of *The Dunciad*, a harsh, satirical attack on London writers; *An Essay on Criticism*, a treatise on literary theory and poetic versification; and the mock-heroic poem *The Rape of the Lock*, a charming, slightly irreverent depiction of English high society 5:2767

Ezra Pound 1885-1972

Pound is credited with creating some of modern poetry's most enduring and inventive verse in such volumes as *Ripostes*, *Cathay*, and *Hugh Selwyn Mauberley*. These works display Pound's efforts to "resuscitate the dead art" and "make it new" by combining stylistic elements from the verse of Provençal and Tuscan troubadours, French and Oriental poets, and the Pre-Raphaelites with Imagistic principles expounded by T. E. Hulme, Ernest Fenellosa, and Ford Madox Ford.. 5:2786

Marcel Proust 1871-1922

Although the brilliance of Proust's achievement is now seldom disputed, in the past his novel *Remembrance of Things Past* was frequently the subject of critical controversy.. 5:2804

Alexander Pushkin 1799-1837

Censorship remained a lifelong problem for Russian poet Pushkin, who was exiled for his allegedly "revolutionary" verse. The poet despaired: "the devil prompted my being born in Russia with a soul and with talent." 5:2821

Thomas Pynchon 1937-

Best known for such novels as *The Crying of Lot 49* and *Gravity's Rainbow*, Pynchon is regarded as one of the most eminent literary stylists in contemporary American fiction. Living amidst the chaos of modern existence that is mirrored in the fragmented structure of his novels, Pynchon's protagonists typically undertake vague yet elaborate quests to discover their identities and to find meaning and order in their lives. 5:2838

François Rabelais 1494?-1553

A Renaissance monk, physician, and scholar, Rabelais has long been praised for his *Gargantua and Pantagruel*, a multivolume narrative comprising comedy, satire, myth, and humanist philosophy... 5:2856

Ayn Rand 1905-1982

An exceptionally powerful writer, Rand is best known for promoting a philosophy of capitalism and extreme individualism as exemplified in her most popular novels, *The Fountainhead* and *Atlas Shrugged*.. 5:2874

Samuel Richardson 1689-1761

Celebrated for such works as *Clarissa*, *Pamela*, and *The History of Sir Charles Grandison*, Richardson is considered the originator of the modern English novel. His detailed exploration of his characters' motives and feelings, accomplished through his subtle use of the epistolary method, added a new dimension to the art of fiction.. 5:2889

Arthur Rimbaud 1854-1891

Although Rimbaud's writing career was brief and his output small, his development of the prose poem and innovative use of the unconscious as a source of literary inspiration was highly influential, anticipating the freedom of form characteristic of much contemporary poetry.. 5:2906

Christina Rossetti 1830-1894

Rossetti is ranked among the finest English poets of the nineteenth century. Rather than grapple with the social problems that preoccupied many writers of her era, Rossetti chose to explore the themes of love and death, and her works are praised for their simple diction and consummate stylistic technique............. 5:2927

Dante Gabriel Rossetti 1828-1882

Equally renowned as a painter and poet, Rossetti was an acknowledged master of the sonnet form as well as the leader of the Pre-Raphaelite Brotherhood, a group of artists and writers who sought to emulate the purity and simplicity of the Italian Proto-Renaissance school of art.. 5:2944

Philip Roth 1933-

One of the most prominent and controversial writers in contemporary literature, Roth draws heavily on his Jewish-American upbringing and his life as a successful author to explore such concerns as the search for self-identity and conflicts between traditional and contemporary moral values. Taking the form of a profane, guilt-ridden confession, Roth's best-known novel, *Portnoy's Complaint*, relates Alexander Portnoy's struggle with his sexual fetishes and his constant state of war with his overbearing mother.. 5:2960

Jean-Jacques Rousseau 1712-1778

Recognized today as one of the greatest thinkers of the French Enlightenment, Rousseau suffered periods of madness and paranoia following public condemnation of his works and his banishment from France.. 5:2977

Saki (H. H. Munro) 1870-1916

A popular and respected master of the short story, English writer Saki memorialized a comfortable world of upper-class English tea parties and weekends in the country that his characters may humorously deride but in which they never completely lose faith 5:2996

J. D. Salinger 1919-
In his popular novel *The Catcher in the Rye*, Salinger presented a classic depiction of adolescent angst through the perspective of Holden Caulfield, the novel's sensitive and alienated teenage protagonist 5:3013

George Sand 1804-1876
Sand was the pseudonym of Amandine Aurore Lucile Dupin Dudevant, one of France's most celebrated, prolific, and controversial authors, who wrote nearly sixty novels, a lengthy autobiography, numerous essays, twenty-five plays, and approximately 20,000 letters; she wrote effortlessly, as she said, "much as another might garden." 5:3033

Carl Sandburg 1878-1967
One of the most popular poets of the twentieth century, Sandburg celebrated the history, landscape, and "common people" that make up the American experience 5:3049

William Saroyan 1908-1981
Saroyan is probably best known for his plays *The Time of Your Life* and *My Heart's in the Highlands*. The son of Armenian immigrants, Saroyan wrote of the lighter side of the immigrant experience in America, revealing his appreciation of the American dream and his awareness of the strengths and weaknesses of American society 5:3069

Jean-Paul Sartre 1905-1980
French philosopher Sartre, one of the leading proponents of existentialism, wrote dramas, novels, essays, and short stories that examine virtually every aspect of the human endeavor to achieve total freedom 5:3085

Sir Walter Scott 1771-1832
Scott is celebrated as the author of the *Waverley Novels*, a multivolume series that includes such time-honored classics as *Ivanhoe* and *Rob Roy* 5:3103

Robert W. Service 1874?-1958
During the early twentieth century, Service was one of North America's most popular poets, and his work is still widely read. He is best known for his playfully rhythmic verses that celebrate the spirit of the Yukon, particularly "The Shooting of Dan McGrew" and "The Cremation of Sam McGee," which mythologize the adventure and masculine vigor of life during the Klondike Gold Rush at the turn of the century 5:3119

Anne Sexton 1928-1974
A Confessional poet who admired Robert Lowell and Sylvia Plath, Sexton began writing as a form of therapy for depression. Her poetry details the emotional turmoil that eventually led to her suicide 5:3134

William Shakespeare 1564-1616
Considered the most important dramatist in the history of English literature, Shakespeare occupies a unique position in the pantheon of great world authors; his work continues to sustain critical attention and elicit popular approval on a scale unrivaled by that accorded to writers of the period—or, for that matter, of any other time 5:3151

Bernard Shaw 1856-1950
Dramatist Shaw succeeded in revolutionizing the English stage, instituting a theater of ideas grounded in realism, and was, during his lifetime, equally famous as an iconoclastic and outspoken figure 5:3184

Mary Wollstonecraft Godwin Shelley 1797-1851
Shelley's reputation rests chiefly on what she once called her "hideous progeny," the novel *Frankenstein*, which depicts a seemingly godless universe where science and technology have gone awry, suggesting a powerful metaphor for the modern age 5:3202

Percy Bysshe Shelley 1792-1822
Shelley was one of the early nineteenth century's most controversial literary fig-

ures. His *Prometheus Unbound* and *Adonais* are recognized as leading expressions of radical thought during the Romantic age.. 5:3221

Richard Brinsley Sheridan 1751-1816
Irish dramatist Sheridan displayed a talent for sparkling dialogue and farce in his most popular comedies *The Rivals* and *The School for Scandal*.......................... 5:3240

Upton Sinclair 1878-1968
Best known for his controversial novel *The Jungle*, in which he exposed the unsanitary working conditions of the meat-packing industry and the squalid living conditions of the workers, Sinclair is generally regarded as the most prominent of the "muckrakers," a group of early twentieth-century American journalists and writers who sought to initiate social and political reforms by illuminating their country's worst excesses and abuses 5:3258

Isaac Bashevis Singer 1904-1991
An internationally renowned figure, Singer is widely considered the foremost Yiddish writer of the twentieth century. In 1978, Singer was awarded the Nobel Prize in Literature for his "impassioned narrative art which, with roots in a Polish-Jewish cultural tradition, brings universal human conditions to life.".................................. 5:3281

Aleksandr Solzhenitsyn 1918-
Best known as the author of *One Day in the Life of Ivan Denisovich* and *The Gulag Archipelago*, Solzhenitsyn confronts in his writing the oppressive actions of the former Soviet Union as well as the political and moral problems of the West. Although Soviet authorities frequently banned his works, Solzhenitsyn received the 1970 Nobel Prize for what the Nobel committee termed "the ethical force with which he has pursued the indispensable traditions of Russian literature." 5:3298

Wole Soyinka 1934-
Nobel Prize-winner Soyinka is one of Africa's finest writers. He incorporates traditional Yoruban folk-drama with European dramatic forms to create works that are considered rewarding, if demanding, reading.. 5:3316

Edmund Spenser 1552?-1599
Known as "the poet's poet" for his delight in the pure artistry of his craft, Spenser is admired for his epic allegorical poem *The Faerie Queene*, which, though unfinished, is indisputably a masterwork of English literature...................................... 5:3334

Gertrude Stein 1874-1946
One of the most controversial and influential literary figures of the Modernist era, poet and novelist Stein violated convention, allowing the reader to experience language and ideas in provocative new ways.. 5:3353

John Steinbeck 1902-1968
When he was honored in 1962 with the Nobel Prize in literature, the awards committee praised American novelist Steinbeck for his "sympathetic humor and sociological perception" as well as his "instinct for what is genuinely American, be it good or bad." 5:3372

Stendhal 1783-1842
The quintessential egoist, French novelist Stendhal depicted the individual's lifelong quest for self-knowledge and romance; despite his reputation as a womanizer, he wrote in later years that he was "sad to have nothing to love.".............. 5:3390

Laurence Sterne 1713-1768
Sterne is the author of one of the most eccentric and influential works in Western literature, *Tristram Shandy*, which features profoundly odd characters and an unpredictable style that digresses rather than progresses...................................... 5:3409

Wallace Stevens 1879-1955
Integrating such European influences as Symbolism, Imagism, and Romanticism into his distinctly American idiom, Stevens created a poetic language that is praised for its originality, intricacy, and vibrancy 5:3427

Robert Louis Stevenson 1850-1894
Beloved by young and adult readers alike, Stevenson is best known for *Treasure Island*, *Kidnapped*, and *Dr. Jekyll and Mr. Hyde*, colorful tales of adventure that feature fast-paced action, strong plots, and well-drawn characters 5:3441

Bram Stoker 1847-1912
Irish writer Stoker is best known as the author of *Dracula*, one of the most famous
horror novels of all time 6:3461

Tom Stoppard 1937-
A leading contemporary dramatist, Stoppard garnered widespread acclaim with
his first major play, *Rosencrantz and Guildenstern Are Dead*, which depicts the
absurdity of life through two characters who have "bit parts" in a play not of their
making and who are only capable of acting out their dramatic destiny.............. 6:3479

Harriet Beecher Stowe 1811-1896
Stowe stirred the conscience of America and the world with her famous novel,
Uncle Tom's Cabin, which relates the experiences of the virtuous slave Uncle
Tom and his three successive owners. Its strong humanitarian tone, melodramatic plot, religious themes, and controversial antislavery message combined to
make *Uncle Tom's Cabin* one of the most popular and influential novels of the
nineteenth century.. 6:3496

August Strindberg 1849-1912
Strindberg, one of the greatest dramatists in modern literature, has been called
the "father of expressionism"; his *The Dream Play* and the trilogy *To Damascus*
are recognized as forerunners of Surrealism and the theater of the absurd 6:3513

Jonathan Swift 1667-1745
Irish satirist Swift wrote numerous barbed essays, poems, and pamphlets. His
works include *A Modest Proposal*, in which he ironically suggested that the Irish
poor combat starvation by eating their children, and *Gulliver's Travels*, a political
satire in which he chronicled one man's journeys to several strange lands 6:3531

Algernon Swinburne 1837-1909
An accomplished poet of Victorian England and a symbol of rebellion against
conservative values, Swinburne's poems—with their explicit and often pathological sexual themes—shocked readers during his day and have since achieved critical acclaim... 6:3550

Alfred, Lord Tennyson 1809-1892
Tennyson's elegiac work, *In Memoriam*, earned him the title of Poet Laureate
of England, succeeding William Wordsworth. The success of that work, and Tennyson's place at the forefront of English literature, was secured when Queen Victoria declared that she valued *In Memoriam* next to the Bible as a work of consolation.. 6:3568

William Makepeace Thackeray 1811-1863
Thackeray is best known for his novel *Vanity Fair*, a satiric panorama of early
nineteenth-century English society, generally regarded as a masterpiece 6:3590

Dylan Thomas 1914-1953
Viewing the act of writing as a process of self-discovery, Thomas sought in both
his poetry and his prose to explore the mysteries of his own existence and to
communicate his discoveries, asserting: "I do not want to express only what other
people have felt. I want to rip something away and show what they have never
seen." 6:3608

Henry David Thoreau 1817-1862
In one of the finest prose works in American literature—*Walden; or, Life in the
Woods*—Thoreau advocated a simple, self-sufficient way of life in order to free
the individual from self-imposed social and financial obligations, insisting on
every person's right to independent thinking 6:3624

J. R. R. Tolkien 1892-1973
Set in an enchanted world called Middle-earth, Tolkien's epic fantasy/romance
trilogy of novels *The Lord of the Rings* tells of a timeless struggle between good
and evil, embodied in such magical beings as wizards, dwarves, elves, orcs, trolls,
and hobbits, the small furry-footed creatures with human qualities that Tolkien
introduced in his first novel, *The Hobbit; or, There and Back Again*.................... 6:3642

Leo Tolstoy 1828-1910
Tolstoy's *War and Peace* has often been called the greatest novel ever written.
This massive work combines a chronicle of the interrelated histories of several

families over the course of a generation with an epic depiction of the military struggle between Russia and Napoleonic France in the early decades of the nineteenth century **6:3659**

Anthony Trollope 1815-1882
Victorian novelist Trollope is remembered for his lively and humorous portrayal of middle-class life in an English cathedral town in *Barchester Towers*, the second in the series of six Barsetshire novels **6:3677**

Ivan Turgenev 1818-1883
The first Russian author to achieve widespread international fame, Turgenev is regarded as his country's premier nineteenth-century novelist **6:3694**

Mark Twain (Samuel Langhorne Clemens) 1835-1910
As the author of *Tom Sawyer* and *The Adventures of Huckleberry Finn*, Twain is considered the father of modern American literature. His vernacular narrative style and satirical observations concerning human folly and social injustice led to widespread denunciation of his works as coarse and improper upon their initial publication **6:3712**

Sigrid Undset 1882-1949
Norwegian writer Undset is a dominant figure among Scandinavian novelists and one of the foremost literary proponents of Christian ethics and philosophy. Her major works, *Kristin Lavransdatter* and *The Master of Hestviken*, are skillfully rendered portrayals of medieval Norwegian life and have been praised as exemplary models of historical fiction **6:3730**

John Updike 1932-
Best known for his "Rabbit" series that began with *Rabbit, Run*, novelist Updike typically examines the domestic life of the American middle class and its attendant rituals: marriage, sex, and divorce **6:3747**

Voltaire 1694-1778
A principal figure of the French Enlightenment who tirelessly promoted freedom of speech and thought as well as his faith in humanity's ability to perfect itself, Voltaire is recognized today as a leading world philosopher **6:3766**

Kurt Vonnegut, Jr. 1922-
A sharp satirist of modern society, Vonnegut is widely acclaimed for such novels as *Slaughterhouse Five* and *Cat's Cradle*, which emphasize the futility of war, the destructive power of technology, and the human potential for irrationality and evil **6:3784**

Robert Penn Warren 1905-1989
The first Poet Laureate of the United States and a recipient of Pulitzer prizes for both fiction and poetry, Warren is one of the most distinguished figures in American literature. The tenor of his writing conveys a passionate allegiance to his Southern heritage, and he often relied on dialect to render authentic characterizations and impart the local color of the rural South **6:3802**

Evelyn Waugh 1903-1966
During a career that spanned four decades, Waugh produced overtly Roman Catholic works, most notably *Brideshead Revisited*. The satirical nature of his writing was highly controversial **6:3818**

John Webster 1580?-1634?
The two major works of English dramatist Webster, *The White Devil* and *The Duchess of Malfi*, are more frequently revived on stage than any plays of the Jacobean period other than Shakespeare's **6:3835**

H. G. Wells 1866-1946
Wells is best known as one of the progenitors of modern science fiction. His pioneering works in this genre—including such novels as *The Time Machine*, *The Island of Dr. Moreau*, *The Invisible Man*, and *The War of the Worlds*—are classics that have profoundly influenced the course of twentieth-century science fiction and foretold such developments as chemical warfare, atomic weapons, and world wars **6:3854**

Eudora Welty 1909-
Welty is chiefly known as a Southern writer, but the transcendent humanity por-

trayed in her stories places her beyond regional classification, and she is widely regarded as one of the foremost fiction writers in America..................................... 6:3878

Edith Wharton 1862-1937

Wharton's fiction exposes the cruel excesses of aristocratic society in the United States. Her works reflect concern for the status of women in society as well as for the moral decay she observed underlying the propriety of the upper classes.. 6:3895

Phillis Wheatley 1753?-1784

Commonly referred to as America's first black author, Wheatley was the first African-American to have published a collection of poems in the United States. (Another black writer, Jupiter Hammon, published a single broadside poem in 1761, pre-dating Wheatley's first appearance in print.) While popular during her day, *Poems on Various Subjects, Religious and Moral* is now of more historical than literary interest... 6:3914

Walt Whitman 1819-1892

Whitman's poetry collection, *Loaves of Grass*, is hailed as a hallmark of American literature. With this volume, Whitman pioneered a vision of humanity based on egalitarian and democratic ideals. The jubilance with which he wrote is vivid in "Song of Myself:" "I celebrate myself, and sing myself, / And what I assume you shall assume, / For every atom belonging to me as good belongs to you."....... 6:3932

Oscar Wilde 1854-1900

Renowned for his intelligence, wit, and charm, Wilde cultivated an extravagant persona that was both admired and burlesqued by his contemporaries. Today he is best known as the author of such works as *The Importance of Being Earnest* and *The Picture of Dorian Gray*.. 6:3950

Thornton Wilder 1897-1975

Pulitzer Prize-winning author Wilder is admired for *Our Town* and *The Skin of Our Teeth*, dramas traditional in their promotion of Christian morality, community, and family and unorthodox in their theatrical technique.. 6:3968

Tennessee Williams 1911-1983

One of the most important American dramatists of the post-World War II era, Williams is lauded for his compassionate understanding of the spiritually downtrodden. His prize-winning plays include *A Streetcar Named Desire*, *Cat on a Hot Tin Roof*, *The Glass Menagerie*, and *The Night of the Iguana*.................................... 6:3987

William Carlos Williams 1883-1963

Believing that language is a reflection of character, American poet Williams concentrated on recreating American idioms in verse, and his poetry is often praised for its vivid imagery... 6:4009

Thomas Wolfe 1900-1938

Wolfe is considered one of the foremost American novelists of the twentieth century. In his four major novels—*Look Homeward, Angel*, *Of Time and the River*, *The Web and the Rock*, and *You Can't Go Home Again*—he took the facts of his own life and wove them into an epic celebration of spiritual fulfillment in America.. 6:4025

Virginia Woolf 1882-1941

Woolf is one of the most prominent literary figures of the twentieth century. Her novels are noted for their subjective exploration and delicate poetic quality, while her essays are commended for their perceptive observations on nearly the entire range of English literature, as well as many social and political concerns of the early twentieth century.. 6:4043

William Wordsworth 1770-1850

Wordsworth is considered the greatest and most influential English Romantic poet. Asserting in the Preface to his *Lyrical Ballads* that poetry should employ "language really used by men," Wordsworth challenged the prevailing eighteenth-century notion of formal poetic diction and thereby profoundly affected the course of modern poetry.. 6:4060

Richard Wright 1908-1960

Wright's acclaimed *Native Son* was one of the first works to portray—often in graphic, brutal accounts—the dehumanizing effects of racism on blacks. Focusing on Bigger Thomas, a young black chauffeur who accidentally kills a white woman, Wright attacked racial injustice in America, as he continued to do in *Black Boy* 6:4078

William Butler Yeats 1865-1939
Although his interest in Irish politics and his visionary approach to poetry often confounded his contemporaries and set him at odds with the intellectual trends of his time, Yeats is remembered for poetic achievements that place him at the center of modern literature 6:4095

Emile Zola 1840-1902
As the founder and principal theorist of Naturalism, French novelist Zola succeeded in documenting a historical period with great detail and accuracy. Nonetheless, his works offer a highly personal vision expressed with emotion and artistry 6:4114

Acknowledgments **6**:4135

WLC Author Index **6**:4159

WLC Nationality Index **6**:4167

WLC Title Index **6**:4169

Introduction

A Comprehensive Information Source
on World Literature

World Literature Criticism, 1500 to the Present (WLC) presents a broad selection of the best criticism of works by major writers of the past five hundred years. Among the authors included in WLC are sixteenth-century Spanish novelist Miguel de Cervantes and English dramatist William Shakespeare; seventeenth-century English poet John Milton and dramatist Aphra Behn; eighteenth-century Anglo-Irish novelist Jonathan Swift, English essayist Samuel Johnson, and French Enlightenment masters Jean-Jacques Rousseau and Voltaire; acclaimed nineteenth-century writers Jane Austen, William Blake, Emily Brontë, Lewis Carroll, Charles Dickens, Fyodor Dostoyevsky, Frederick Douglass, Gustave Flaubert, Edgar Allan Poe, Mary Shelley, Robert Louis Stevenson, William Wordsworth, and Emile Zola; and major twentieth-century authors W. H. Auden, James Baldwin, Albert Camus, Arthur Conan Doyle, Ralph Ellison, F. Scott Fitzgerald, Ernest Hemingway, James Joyce, Franz Kafka, Toni Morrison, Sylvia Plath, J. D. Salinger, Gertrude Stein, John Steinbeck, Virginia Woolf, and Richard Wright. The scope of WLC is wide: more than 225 writers representing dozens of nations, cultures, and time periods.

Coverage

This six-volume set is designed for high school, college, and university students, as well as for the general reader who wants to learn more about literature. WLC was developed in response to strong demand by students, librarians, and other readers for a one-stop, authoritative guide to the whole spectrum of world literature. No other compendium like it exists in the marketplace. About 95% of the entries in WLC were selected from Gale's acclaimed Literary Criticism Series and completely updated for publication here. Typically, the revisions are extensive, ranging from new author introductions to wide changes in the selection of criticism. A few entries—about 5%— were prepared especially for WLC in order to furnish the most comprehensive coverage possible.

Inclusion Criteria

Authors were selected for inclusion in WLC based on the advice of leading experts on world literature as well as on the recommendation of a specially formed advisory panel made up of high school teachers and high school and public librarians from throughout the United States. Additionally, the most recent major curriculum studies were closely examined, notably Arthur N. Applebee, *A Study of Book-Length Works Taught in High School English Courses* (1989); Arthur N. Applebee, *A Study of High School Literature Anthologies* (1991); and Doug Estel, Michele L. Satchwell, and Patricia S. Wright, *Reading Lists for College-Bound Students* (1990). All of these resources were collated and compared to produce a reference product that is strongly curriculum driven. To ensure that WLC will continue to meet the needs of students and general readers alike, an effort was made to identify a group of important new writers in addition to the most studied authors.

Scope

Each author entry in *WLC* presents a historical survey of critical response to the author's works. Typically, early criticism is offered to indicate initial responses, later selections document any rise or decline in literary reputations, and retrospective analyses provide modern views. Every endeavor has been made to include seminal essays on each author's work along with commentary providing current perspectives. Interviews and author statements are also included in many entries. Thus, *WLC* is both timely and comprehensive.

Organization of Author Entries

Information about authors and their works is presented through ten key access points:

- The **Descriptive Table of Contents** guides readers through the range of world literature, offering summary sketches of authors' careers and achievements.

- In each author entry, the **Author Heading** cites the name under which the author most commonly wrote, followed by birth and, where appropriate, death dates. Uncertain birth or death dates are indicated by question marks. Name variations, including full birth names when available, are given in parentheses in the caption below the **Author Portrait**.

- The **Biographical and Critical Introduction** contains background information about the life and works of the author. Emphasis is given to four main areas: 1) biographical details that help reveal the life, character, and personality of the author; 2) overviews of the major literary interests of the author—for example, novel writing, autobiography, poetry, social reform, documentary, etc.; 3) descriptions and summaries of the author's best-known works; and 4) critical commentary about the author's achievement, stature, and importance. The concluding paragraph of the **Biographical and Critical Introduction** directs readers to other Gale series containing information about the author.

- Every *WLC* entry includes an **Author Portrait**. Many entries also contain **Illustrations**—including holographs, title pages of works, letters, or pictures of important people, places, and events in the author's life—that document the author's career.

- The **List of Principal Works** is chronological by date of first book publication and identifies the genre of each work. For non-English-language authors whose works have been translated into English, the title and date of the first English-language edition are given in brackets beneath the foreign-language listing. Unless otherwise indicated, dramas are dated by first performance rather than first publication.

- **Criticism** is arranged chronologically in each author entry to provide a useful perspective on changes in critical evaluation over the years. Most entries contain a detailed, comprehensive study of the author's career as well as book reviews, studies of individual works, and comparative examinations. To ensure timeliness, current views are most often presented, but not to the exclusion of important early pieces. For the purpose of easy identification, the critic's name and the date of the critical work are given at the beginning of each piece of criticism. Unsigned criticism is preceded by the title of the source in which it appeared. Within the criticism, titles of works by the author are printed in boldface type. Publication information (such as publisher names and book prices) and certain numerical references (such as footnotes or page and line references to specific editions of works) have been deleted at the editor's discretion to provide smoother reading of the text.

■ Critical essays are prefaced by **Explanatory Notes** as an additional aid to readers of *WLC*. These notes may provide several types of valuable information, including: 1) the reputation of the critic; 2) the importance of the work of criticism; 3) the commentator's approach to the author's work; 4) the purpose of the criticism; and 5) changes in critical trends regarding the author. In some cases, **Explanatory Notes** cross-reference the work of critics within an entry who agree or disagree with each other.

■ A complete **Bibliographical Citation** of the original essay or book follows each piece of criticism.

■ An annotated list of **Sources for Further Study** appears at the end of each entry and suggests resources for additional study. These lists were specially compiled to meet the needs of high school and college students. Additionally, most of the sources cited are available in typical small and medium-size libraries.

■ Many entries contain a **Major Media Adaptations** section listing important non-print treatments and adaptations of the author's works, including feature films, TV mini-series, and radio broadcasts. This feature was specially conceived for *WLC* to meet strong demand from students for this type of information.

Other Features

WLC contains three distinct indexes to help readers find information quickly and easily:

■ The **Author Index** lists all the authors appearing in *WLC*. To ensure easy access, name variations and changes are fully cross-indexed.

■ The **Nationality Index** lists all authors featured in *WLC* by nationality. For expatriate authors and authors identified with more than one nation, multiple listings are offered.

■ The **Title Index** lists in alphabetical order all individual works by the authors appearing in *WLC*. English-language translations of original foreign-language titles are cross-referenced to the foreign titles so that all references to a work are combined in one listing.

Citing *World Literature Criticism*

When writing papers, students who quote directly from *WLC* may use the following general forms to footnote reprinted criticism. The first example is for material drawn from periodicals, the second for material reprinted from books:

Gary Smith, "Gwendolyn Brooks's 'A Street in Bronzeville,' the Harlem Renaissance and the Mythologies of Black Women," *MELUS*, Vol. 10, No. 3 (Fall 1983), 33-46; excerpted and reprinted in *World Literature Criticism, 1500 to the Present*, ed. James P. Draper (Detroit: Gale Research, 1992), pp. 459-61.

Frederick R. Karl, *American Fictions, 1940/1980: A Comprehensive History and Critical Evaluation* (Harper & Row, 1983); excerpted and reprinted in *World Literature Criticism, 1500 to the Present*, ed. James P. Draper (Detroit: Gale Research, 1992), pp. 541-46.

Acknowledgments

The editor wishes to acknowledge the valuable contributions of the many librarians, authors, and scholars who assisted in the compilation of *WLC* with their responses to telephone and mail inquiries. Special thanks are offered to the members of *WLC*'s advisory board, whose names are listed opposite the title page.

Comments Are Welcome

The editor hopes that readers will find *WLC* to be a useful reference tool and welcomes comments about the work. Send comments and suggestions to: Editor, *World Literature Criticism, 1500 to the Present*, Gale Research Inc., Penobscot Building, Detroit, MI 48226-4094.

WORLD LITERATURE CRITICISM

1500 to the Present

Chinua Achebe

1930-

(Born Albert Chinualumogu Achebe) Nigerian novelist, short story writer, poet, essayist, editor, and author of children's books.

INTRODUCTION

*A*chebe is one of the most important figures in contemporary African literature. His novels, which chronicle the colonization and independence of Nigeria, are among the first works in English to present an intimate and authentic rendering of African culture. His major concerns, according to Abiola Irele, involve "the social and psychological conflicts created by the incursion of the white man and his culture into the hitherto self-contained world of African society, and the disarray in the African consciousness that has followed." Critics praise Achebe's innovative and successful fusion of folklore, proverbs, and idioms from his native Ibo tribe with Western political ideologies and Christian doctrines. Margaret Laurence noted: "Chinua Achebe's careful and confident craftsmanship, his firm grasp of his material and his ability to create memorable and living characters place him among the best novelists now writing in any country in the English language."

The son of Ibo missionary teachers, Achebe was born in Nigeria in 1930. He attended Church Mission Society in Ogidi and Government College in Umuahia before obtaining his Bachelor of Arts degree from Ibadan University in 1953. He began working for the Nigerian Broadcasting Company a year later. Dissatisfied with the political situation in Lagos, he resigned in 1966 and moved to Eastern Nigeria, now devoting all his time to writing poetry, short stories, and juvenilia. Poems written during this period were collected in *Beware, Soul Brother and Other Poems* (1971) and in *Christmas in Biafra and Other Poems* (1973). In the early 1970s Achebe accepted a visiting professorship at the University of Massachusetts and later at the University of Connecticut. While in the United States, he taught literature, founded and edited the literary magazine *Okike: A Nigerian Journal of New Writing*, and continued to write novels. In 1976 he returned to Nigeria and began teaching at the University of Nigeria-Nsukka.

Achebe's first novel, *Things Fall Apart* (1958), is considered a classic of contemporary African fiction for its realistic and anthropologically informative portrait of Ibo tribal society before colonization. Set in the village of Umuofia in the late 1880s, when English missionaries and bureaucrats first appeared in the region, this book traces the conflict between tribal and Western customs through Okonkwo, a proud village leader, whose refusal to adapt to European influence leads him to murder and suicide. Arthur Ravenscroft noted: "*Things Fall Apart* is impressive for the wide range of what it so pithily covers, for the African flavour of scene and language, but above all for the way in which Achebe makes that language the instrument for analyzing tragic experience and profound human issues of very much more than local Nigerian significance." *No Longer at Ease* (1960), set in the Nigerian city of Lagos during the late 1950s, details the failure of Obi Okonkwo, the grandson of Okonkwo from *Things Fall Apart,* to successfully combine his traditional Ibo upbringing with his English education and affluent life-style. While *No Longer at Ease* was less universally praised than *Things Fall Apart,* some critics defended its stylistic weaknesses as a deliberate attempt to demonstrate the consequences of one culture's dilution by another.

In his third novel, *Arrow of God* (1964), Achebe returned to Umuofia to describe life in the village during the 1920s. This book centers on Ezeulu, the spiritual leader of the region, who sends his son Oduche to a missionary school to discover Western secrets. Upon his return, Oduche attempts to destroy a sacred python, setting in motion a chain of events in which Ezeulu is stripped of his position as high priest and imprisoned by the English. Critics noted a change of thematic direction in Achebe's next novel, *A Man of the People* (1966). Here, focusing on the tribulations of a teacher who joins a political organization endeavoring to remove a corrupt bureaucrat from office, Achebe condemned the widespread graft and abuse of power among Nigeria's leadership following its independence from Great Britain. Adrian A. Roscoe commented: "Achebe's first three novels showed the author as teacher. . . . From instructing his society to lashing it with satire; from portraying with a touching nostalgia the beauty of a vanishing world to savagely pillorying what is succeeding it—*A Man of the People* indeed marks a new departure."

Anthills of the Savannah (1988), Achebe's first novel in two decades, garnered widespread acclaim as his most accomplished work of fiction. In this book, according to Nadine Gordimer, "22 years of harsh experience, intellectual growth, self-criticism, deepening understanding and mustered discipline of skill open wide

a subject to which Mr. Achebe is now magnificently equal." Set in Kangan, an imaginary West African nation, *Anthills of the Savannah* is about three childhood friends who become leaders in their country's government. Ikem is the editor-in-chief of the state-owned newspaper; Sam is a military leader who becomes President of Kangan; and Chris serves as Sam's Minister of Information. Their friendship ends tragically when Sam fails in his attempt to be elected President-for-Life and begins to suppress his opposition. Ikem is murdered by Sam's secret police for publishing several articles denouncing the government; Sam's corpse is later discovered in a shallow grave on the palace grounds following a military coup; and Chris is killed in a street riot. In *Anthills of the Savannah,* Achebe examined the ways in which individual responsibility and power are often exploited to the detriment of an entire society. He also emphasized the roles of women and the urban working class while retaining the use of Ibo proverbs and legends to enhance his themes. Ben Okri stated: "All those who have inundated Achebe with critical analysis, and who spoke of him as the grandfather of African literature before he was 36, have [*Anthills of the Savannah*] to wrestle with for some time to come. Chinua Achebe has found new creative fire."

Achebe's most recent work, *Hopes and Impediments: Selected Essays* (1988), a collection of fourteen political essays and speeches, has been praised as "brilliant." In addition to a controversial essay attacking Joseph Conrad's *Heart of Darkness* as "racist," it also contains a tribute to James Baldwin as well as biting commentaries about post-colonial Africa and the social forces that have shaped it. Critic Joe Wood noted: "Though Mr. Achebe sometimes fails to pursue his ideas with rigor [in *Hopes and Impediments*], . . . his thoughts always pack a provocative wallop."

Recognized as perhaps the finest living Nigerian novelist, Achebe is credited with helping launch the field of modern African literature. His novels are praised for their balanced examination of contemporary Africa and are often the standards by which other African works are judged. Critics note, however, that Achebe's writing reverberates beyond the borders of Nigeria and beyond the arenas of anthropology, sociology, and political science. As literature, it deals with universal qualities. And, as Douglas Killam observed: "Achebe's novels offer a vision of life which is essentially tragic, compounded of success and failure, informed by knowledge and understanding, relieved by humour and tempered by sympathy, embued with an awareness of human suffering and the human capacity to endure. . . . Sometimes his characters meet with success, more often with defeat and despair. Through it all the spirit of man and the belief in the possibility of triumph endures."

(For further information about Achebe's life and

works, see *Black Writers; Contemporary Authors*, Vols. 1-4; *Contemporary Authors New Revision Series*, Vols. 6, 26; *Contemporary Literary Criticism*, Vols. 1, 3, 5, 7, 11, 26, 51; *Children's Literature Review*, Vol. 20; Major 20th-Century Writers; and *Something about the Author*, Vols. 38, 40. For related criticism, see the entry on Nigerian Literature in *Twentieth-Century Literary Criticism*, Vol. 30.)

CRITICAL COMMENTARY

G. D. KILLAM
(essay date 1971)

[In the following excerpt, Killam discusses theme, setting, and characterization in Achebe's novels.]

Chinua Achebe is Nigeria's best-known novelist, and possibly the best-known writer of fiction in black Africa. He has written four novels which are widely read in Africa and are now achieving an audience in Europe and North America. Achebe attracted considerable attention when the publication of his fourth book, *A Man of the People*—the closing scenes of which describe a military take-over from a corrupt civil regime in a West African country—coincided with the first military coup in Nigeria, in January, 1966. Yet his reputation rests principally on his first novel, *Things Fall Apart*, published in 1958, the first novel by a Nigerian writer to have serious claim to consideration as literature.

Things Fall Apart is about Iboland, in the eastern region of present-day Nigeria, in the period between 1850-1900; that is, the period just prior to and after the arrival of white men in this part of West Africa. The setting is Umuofia and Mbanta, the two principal villages in a union called the "nine villages". Okonkwo, the hero of the novel, a great wrestler in his youth, is, when we meet him, a renowned warrior, celebrated in songs at religious festivals, and one of the most wealthy, powerful, and influential people in Umuofia. The language of Okonkwo and the other villagers is expressed in the idiom of the Ibo villages as Achebe transmutes it into modern English. The conflict in the novel, vested in Okonkwo, derives from the series of crushing blows which are levelled at traditional values by an alien and more powerful culture, causing, in the end, the traditional society to fall apart. Thus the significance of the title of the book taken from Yeats's *The Second Coming*:

Turning and turning in the widening gyre

The falcon cannot hear the falconer;
Things fall apart; the centre cannot hold;
Mere anarchy is loosed upon the world.

Things Fall Apart is a vision of what life was like in Iboland between 1850 and 1900. Achebe makes a serious attempt to capture realistically the strains and tensions of the experiences of Ibo people under the impact of colonialism. It is not wholly true, however, to say that the novel is written consistently from their point of view. Achebe is a twentieth-century Ibo man, and recognizes the gulf which exists between his present-day society and that of Ibo villagers sixty years ago, sixty years which have seen remarkable changes in the texture and structure of Ibo society. Achebe is able to view objectively the forces which irresistibly and inevitably destroyed traditional Ibo social ties and with them the quality of Ibo life. His success proceeds not from his interest in the history of his people and their folklore and legend in an academic sense, but from his ability to create a sense of real life and real issues in the book and to see his subject from a point of view which is neither idealistic nor dishonest.

Things Fall Apart is written in three parts: the first and most important is set in Umuofia before the coming of the white man—before his existence is even known. The second part dramatizes Okonkwo's banishment to Mbanta, the village of his mother's people, for sins committed against the Earth Goddess, and describes, mostly through reports, the coming of the white man to the nine villages, the establishment of an alien church, government, and trading system, and the gradual encroachment of these on the traditional patterns of tribal life. The third section and the shortest brings the novel swiftly to a close, dramatizing the death of the old ways and the death of Okonkwo.

Okonkwo is a character of intense individuality, yet one in whom the values most admired by Ibo peoples are consolidated. He is both an individual and a type. The first paragraphs of the book indicate the deftness and certainty with which Achebe establishes not

Principal Works

Things Fall Apart (novel) 1958

"The Sacrificial Egg" (short story) 1959; published in periodical Atlantic Monthly

No Longer at Ease (novel) 1960

The Sacrificial Egg and Other Stories (short stories) 1962

"Where Angels Fear to Tread" (essay) 1962; published in periodical Nigeria Magazine

Arrow of God (novel) 1964

Chike and the River (juvenilia) 1966

A Man of the People (novel) 1966

Beware, Soul Brother and Other Poems (poetry) 1971

How the Leopard Got His Claws [with John Iroa-ganachi] (juvenilia) 1972

Christmas in Biafra and Other Poems (poetry) 1973

Girls at War and Other Stories (short stories) 1973

Morning Yet on Creation Day (essays) 1975

Don't Let Him Die: An Anthology of Memorial Poems for Christopher Okigbo [coeditor with Dubem Oka-for] (anthology) 1978

The Drum (juvenilia) 1978

The Flute (juvenilia) 1978

The Trouble with Nigeria (essays) 1983

African Short Stories [coeditor with C. L. Innes] (anthology) 1984

Anthills of the Savannah (novel) 1988

Hopes and Impediments: Selected Essays (essays) 1988

only the character but the ethical and moral basis of his life and, by extension, the ethical and moral basis of the life of the clan. (pp. 514-16)

In the second and third parts of the novel the critical social conflict takes place. These sections present the social and psychological effects and the tragic consequences which result from the clash between traditional Ibo society and British Christian imperialism. In the second section, as well, the relationship between Okonkwo and his refractory son Nwoye is delineated in such a way as to transmute the broader cultural conflict to the personal level. (p. 521)

The third part of the novel begins by describing Okonkwo's return to Umuofia after his seven years of exile, a return less auspicious than he hoped it would be. Again Achebe emphasizes the heroic stature of Okonkwo: he has withstood reversals of fortune and personal calamities which would have crushed a less resilient spirit. "It seemed to him as if his *chi* might be making amends for past disasters!" (p. 526)

The novel is in fact a structure of ironies—irony

of the tragic kind which shows an exceptional man who sees his best hopes and achievements destroyed through an inexorable flow of events which he is powerless to restrain, tragic irony suggested and supported by a carefully integrated pattern of minor ironies throughout the work: the accidental shooting which brings about his exile; the irony of the appeal of Christianity to Nwoye, Okonkwo's first-born, in whom he had placed his hopes; the irony contained in the persistent comment by Okonkwo that his daughter Ezinma ought to have been born a male child. And there is the more general irony made explicit in the closing paragraph of the book, but implicit in the encounter between the Africans and Europeans throughout the second and third parts: that Christianity, seen as a "civilizing agent", acts as a catalyst in destroying a civilization which heretofore had strength and cohesion.

Achebe's second novel, *No Longer at Ease,* is set in the present (1960) and has as its hero Obi Okonkwo, the grandson of Okonkwo in *Things Fall Apart.* The novel opens with Obi on trial for accepting bribes when a Civil Servant, and the book takes the form of long flashback which leads up to the trial. The novel tells of Obi's return from England where he has recently completed his B.A. degree. Filled with idealism, Obi is determined to assist in ridding his country of corruption and to help create a better nation. A second and parallel plot concerns Obi's affair with Clara, a nurse with whom he falls in love on the boat returning them to Nigeria. Clara is *"osu"* among the Ibo, a descendant of cult slaves, and according to tradition she must live apart from the free-born.

The novel records Obi's professional, social, and moral decline. He begins well enough on his return: he is appointed Scholarship Secretary at the Federal Ministry of Education. He resists attempts at bribing him. The relationship with Clara is at first a happy one. But a series of conflicting and simultaneous demands are made on him which undermine his security and eventually his integrity. (pp. 530-31)

The novel reveals the pressures placed upon a young man like Obi, the wide gulf between his idealism which is based on his western education, and the actuality of his status as an individual within a complex and contradictory society in which the old values maintain sway and influence. Thus the significance of the title, taken from a line of T. S. Eliot's "Journey of the Magi":

We returned to our places, these Kingdoms,
But no longer at ease here, in the old dispensation,
With an alien people clutching their gods.
I should be glad of another death.

The novel closes with Obi's conviction, and Achebe writes:

Everybody wondered why. The learned judge, as we have seen, could not comprehend how an educated young man and so on and so forth. The British Council man, even the men of Umuofia, did not know. And we must presume that, in spite of his certitude, Mr. Green did not know either.

The questions posed in the closing paragraph of the novel are rhetorical. The novel has offered implicitly, and in dramatic form, the answers to them.

The book is an attempt by Achebe at writing modern tragedy and it is in this regard that the novel's most serious limitation is revealed. There is an element of the *roman à thèse* in the novel which proceeds not from Achebe's attempt to create a modern tragedy but from the need he seems to have felt to define what he is going to do and then deliberately to illustrate this. At the interview for appointment to the Civil Service post a discussion takes place between Obi and the chairman on the nature of tragedy, and concludes with this speech by Obi:

> 'Real tragedy is never resolved. It goes on hopelessly for ever. Conventional tragedy is too easy. The hero dies and we feel a purging of the emotions. A real tragedy takes place in a corner, in an untidy spot, to quote W. H. Auden. The rest of the world is unaware of it. Like that man in *A Handful of Dust* who reads Dickens to Mr. Todd. There is no release for him. When the story ends he is still reading. There is no purging of the emotions for us because we are not there.'

Here Achebe momentarily loses his objectivity and breaks the dramatic pattern of the novel by obtruding himself between his book and his readers.

Achebe's third book, *Arrow of God*, is set in the period between that of *Things Fall Apart* and *No Longer at Ease*. The locale is Umuaro and the other villages which form a union of six villages. Achebe presents this area as the center of the values and experience of the people of the novel. As in *Things Fall Apart* the presence of white men suggests a world and peoples outside Umuaro, but the significance is in the power and influence of white men as they shape the day-to-day destinies of the Umuaro villagers.

The principal character in the novel is Ezeulu, chief priest of Ulu—a god created to supersede the older village deities at the time when the six villages banded together for protection against the slave raids. When we meet him Ezeulu's power is supreme. A powerful, forceful, and noble character, Ezeulu resembles Okonkwo in the first novel but experiences none of the inner doubts and uncertainties of the latter. Yet though his power and influence are secure, they need to be protected from outside pressures which threaten to undermine them. Against a carefully developed plot which describes Umuaro's history through a series of births,

deaths, marriages, ceremonies, Achebe displays the pressures brought to bear on Ezeulu which lead to tragic consequences at both the individual and social levels. (pp. 533-35)

The Man of the People marks a change in Achebe's approach to novel-writing. In his first three books he explored in various ways the results of the confrontation between Africa and Europe and centered his novels in the stories of heroes whose lives end tragically, partly because of flaws in their natures which cause them to make miscalculations at critical moments, and partly because they are caught up in historical circumstances which they are powerless to control and which overwhelm them. Achebe's approach in these books is insistently ironic but it is irony of a tragic kind. In *A Man of the People*, which presents situations and events exactly contemporary with its writing, Achebe employs the irony of the satirist in order to ridicule and condemn the moral and political situations which the book describes and which determine its pattern.

The novel tells, in the first person, the story of Odili, a university graduate and teacher, and of his involvement with Chief the Honourable M. A. Nanga, M.P., and with the political life of the country. Scornful of Nanga's fraudulent political behavior, Odili is nearly overwhelmed by Nanga's charm and seduced to Nanga's opportunistic way of thinking and acting. But when Nanga steals his mistress from him, Odili, mostly from motives of revenge but partly because of a political idealism which reasserts itself, joins a rival political party which contests the election, receives a brutal beating from Nanga's hired thugs, and sees the leader of his party—a close personal friend—murdered. The novel closes with a military take-over of the country, with Odili, now happily married, determined to found a school to honor the martyred leader of the party he has served.

Achebe achieves balance and proportion in his theme of political corruption by showing both the absurdity of much of the behavior of the principal characters and the destructive consequences of that behavior to the commonwealth. Of the chief characters, Odili, Nanga, and Odili's father are the most successful, and for different reasons. Odili's motives are never entirely disinterested: capable of idealism and a desire to rid the country of political corruption, he nevertheless acts often out of self-interest and spite in his dealings with his protagonist, Nanga. He is not a stereotyped character of a kind familiar in novels treating this theme.

Nanga is a compelling character. In Achebe's words,

> Chief Nanga was a born politician; he could get away with almost anything he said or did. And as long as men are swayed by their hearts and stomachs and not their heads the Chief Nangas of this world

will continue to get away with anything. He had that rare gift of making people feel—even while he was saying harsh things to them—that there was not a drop of ill will in his entire frame. I remember the day he was telling his ministerial colleague over the telephone in my presence that he distrusted our young university people and that he would rather work with a European. I knew I was hearing terrible things but somehow I couldn't bring myself to take the man seriously. He had been so open and kind to me and not in the least distrustful. The greatest criticism a man like him seemed capable of evoking in our country was an indulgent: 'Make you no min' am.'

This is of course a formidable weapon which is always guaranteed to save its wielder from the normal consequences of misconduct as well as from the humiliation and embarrassment of ignorance. For how else could you account for the fact that a Minister of Culture announced in public that he had never heard of his country's most famous novel and received applause—as indeed he received again later when he prophesied that before long our great country would produce great writers like Shakespeare, Dickens, Jane Austen, Bernard Shaw and—raising his eyes off the script—Michael West and Dudley Stamp.

The character of Odili's father is presented as both a type and an individual, one who embodies attitudes typical of the generality of Nigerians of his generation, yet capable of independent and at times noble action.

The appropriateness of the language Achebe uses is as evident here as in the earlier books. Here, too, he makes use of "pidgin", the *lingua franca* of West Africa. Used generally as the language of extravagant and sometimes grotesque comic presentation, "pidgin" has, as Achebe shows, a close correlation to the sentiments of the common man and can be used to reflect serious as well as comic considerations.

A Man of the People attracted considerable attention when it was published because the closing actions it describes coincided with the military coup which took place in Nigeria in January, 1966. The novel had, and perhaps still has, topicality. There is no necessary correlation between topicality and art: a novel achieves the status of art when it transcends the local and particular circumstances which inspire it. Achebe is aware of this and has stated that "the writer's duty is not to beat the morning's headlines in topicality, it is to explore the depth of the human condition." (pp. 539-41)

G. D. Killam, "Chinua Achebe's Novels," in *The Sewanee Review,* Vol. LXXIX, No. 4, Autumn, 1971, pp. 514-41.

CHARLES R. LARSON
(essay date 1972)

[An American critic, novelist, and editor, Larson is a leading scholar of Third World literature. He is the author of *American Indian Fiction* (1978), the first book-length study of novels by native Americans. In the excerpt below, he offers a close reading of Achebe's first novel, *Things Fall Apart,* labeling it "the archetypal African novel."]

Chinua Achebe's *Things Fall Apart* was published in England in 1958, two years before Nigerian independence. The price of the book was fifteen shillings, which placed it out of reach for the average Nigerian whose annual income in those days did not exceed seventy-five dollars. Achebe's novel, however, had been written not for a Nigerian reading audience nor even for an African reading audience, but, to a large extent, for readers outside of Africa. However, in 1960, when Nigeria became independent, the educational system began to reflect a sense of growing national pride; and in 1964, . . . *Things Fall Apart* became the first novel by an African writer to be included in the required syllabus for African secondary school students throughout the English-speaking portions of the continent. By 1965, Achebe was able to proclaim that his novel in a paperbacked reprint edition priced at a more moderate five shillings had the year before sold some 20,000 copies within Nigeria alone.

In the seven years during which this spectacular change had taken place, Chinua Achebe became recognized as the most original African novelist writing in English. He wrote and published three additional novels (*No Longer at Ease,* 1960; *Arrow of God,* 1964; and *A Man of the People,* 1966), and he became one of the first African writers to build up a reading audience among his fellow Africans. So famous and popular did he become within his own country, that by the time Achebe published his fourth novel it could no longer be said that he was writing for a non-African audience. *Things Fall Apart* during this time became recognized by African and non-African literary critics as the first "classic" in English from tropical Africa. So far did Achebe's influence extend that by the late 1960's his impact on a whole group of younger African novelists could also be demonstrated. (pp. 27-8)

Things Fall Apart has come to be regarded as more than simply a classic; it is now seen as the archetypal African novel. The situation which the novel itself describes—the coming of the white man and the initial disintegration of traditional African society as a consequence of that—is typical of the breakdown all African societies have experienced at one time or another as a result of their exposure to the West. And, moreover, individual Africans all over the continent may identify with the situation Achebe has portrayed. (p. 28)

Although *Arrow of God* is in some ways probably artistically superior to *Things Fall Apart,* it is fated to run a second place in popularity to Achebe's first work. [*Things Fall Apart*] may also be regarded as archetypal because of Achebe's reshaping of a traditional Western literary genre into something distinctly African in form and pattern. (p. 29)

Achebe's dialogue in *Things Fall Apart* is extremely sparse. Okonkwo [the protagonist] says very little at all; not of any one place in the novel may it be said that he has an extended speech or even a very lengthy conversation with another character. And as for authorial presentations of his thoughts, they are limited to two or three very brief passages. Indeed, Achebe relies for the development of his story usually on exposition rather than the dramatic rendering of scene, much as if he were telling an extended oral tale or epic in conventional narrative fashion—almost always making use of the preterit. Again and again the reader is told something about Okonkwo, but he rarely sees these events in action. (pp. 40-1)

I have . . . noted the strong aversion that many Western critics have toward the anthropological overtones present in African fiction, except for the anthropologist, of course, who is looking for this kind of thing. This aversion of the literary critics, however, is no doubt due to their equation of the anthropological with the local colorists at the end of the last century and the beginning of this one. However, in a work such as *Things Fall Apart,* where we are not presented with a novel of character, the anthropological is indeed important. Without it there would be no story. The only way in which Achebe can depict a society's falling apart is first by creating an anthropological overview of that culture, and it should be clear that it is not going to Okonkwo's story that Achebe is chronicling as much as the tragedy of a clan. It is the village of Umuofia, which has been sketched in so carefully, which he will now show as falling apart, crumbling from its exposure to Western civilization. (pp. 43-4)

The piling up of ethnological background, I suggest, is often the equivalent of atmospheric conditioning in Western fiction. Achebe's anthropological passages are what Hardy's descriptive passages are for him—equivalent to Hardy's evocation of atmosphere and mood. Indeed, it is extremely difficult to find a passage of pure description of a natural setting anywhere in Anglophone African writing of the first generation. There is very little that can be related to "landscape painting" in English fiction except for the anthropological passages. (p. 44)

The concluding chapter of *Things Fall Apart* is one of the highlights of contemporary African fiction. In less than three pages, Achebe weaves together the various themes and patterns he has been working with throughout much of his novel. Technically, the most significant aspect of this final chapter is Achebe's sudden shifts in point of view. (p. 57)

The shifting point of view back and forth between an African and a Western viewpoint symbolizes the final breakup of the clan, for *Things Fall Apart,* in spite of the subtitle on the first American edition, *The Story of a Strong Man,* is only in part Okonkwo's story, and, as we have noted, as the book progresses, the story becomes increasingly that of a village, a clan. Achebe clearly indicates this in the final paragraph of his novel where he reduces Okonkwo's story to nothing more than a paragraph in a history book, for history is facts and not individuals, and the history of the coming of the white man to Africa is not the story of the pacification of individuals but of entire tribes of people and even beyond that. . . . Achebe has moved throughout his book away from the individual (Okonkwo) to the communal (Umuofia) and beyond that to the clan. And in the last paragraph, the extension is even further beyond the Ibo of Southeast Nigeria to that of the *Primitive Tribes of the Lower Niger,* ergo, the entire African continent.

The conclusion to *Things Fall Apart* has often been considered over-written, anti-climactic, unnecessarily didactic. . . . Certainly it can be argued that Achebe takes pains to make his message clear, but I feel that the shift to the District Commissioner's point of view strengthens rather than weakens the conclusion. It seems impossibile for any one to read Achebe's last chapter without being noticeably moved, and if it is didactic in the sense of tying things up a little too nicely, then I would have to insist that this was Achebe's intention from the beginning and not merely an accident because of his background of oral tradition. . . . Achebe has written . . . [that] the novelist in an emergent nation cannot afford to pass up a chance to educate his fellow countrymen. . . . [Furthermore], contemporary African literature and other forms of African art have inherited a cultural inclination toward the didactic which in regard to African tradition may be called functionalism.

The ending of *Things Fall Apart* also illustrates the dichotomy of interpretations which cultural backgrounds impose upon a reader. Most Western readers of Achebe's novel seem to interpret the story of Okonkwo's fall as tragic if not close to pure tragedy in classical terms. They cite Okonkwo's pride, his going against the will of the gods (for instance, breaking the Week of Peace, and killing Ikemefuna), and interpret the ending as tragic and inevitable, citing, usually, a parallel to Oedipus. Achebe's own feelings about Okonkwo and the conclusion to the novel, however, would tend to indicate a rather different interpretation. The most obvious clue is Achebe's title, *Things Fall Apart,* taken from William Butler Yeats's poem, "The Second Coming." Although Yeats's title may be applied ironically to Achebe's story, the indications are that Achebe views the new dispensation as something inevitable, perhaps even desirable. His criticism is clearly of the old way of life which is unsatisfactory now that the West has arrived. This interpretation is supported by several comments Achebe has made about his novel. . . . Lack of adaptability . . . is what Achebe implies led to the collapse of traditional Ibo society. (pp. 59-61)

Of the three major divisions of the book, only the trajectory of Parts II and III resembles the traditional Western well-made novel with conflict—obstacles to be overcome by the protagonist. Part I is especially loose, incorporating as it does section after section of anthropological background. The effect is, of course, to re-create the entire world of day-to-day existence in traditional Ibo society, and Achebe takes pains to make certain that the major stages of life are included: birth, marriage, and death. In the symbiosis which results, Umuofia, rather than Okonkwo, becomes the main character of *Things Fall Apart,* and the transformation it undergoes is archetypal of the entire breakdown of traditional African cultures under exposure to the West.

The novel itself, as I stated at the beginning, must also be regarded as archetypical for the form and patterns Achebe has given it. If we compare the novel very briefly with Joyce Cary's *Mister Johnson* it is readily evident that *Things Fall Apart* is not a story about a character as is Cary's novel and as I feel we tend to regard Western novels as being. For example, Achebe could never have called his novel *Okonkwo,* though it could have been given the name of Okonkwo's village if Achebe had thought that the situation did not extend beyond that one locale within Nigeria. Okonkwo himself does not alter at all throughout the novel. He is the same at the ending as he is at the beginning of the story. Thus, *Things Fall Apart,* because of its emphasis on community rather than individuality, is a novel of situation rather than of character, and this is undoubtedly its major difference from the traditional Western genre, which in the twentieth century, at least, has emphasized the psychological depiction of character. (pp. 62-3)

Let it simply be noted here that the situational plot is indeed the most typical narrative form one encounters in contemporary African fiction. The reason for this is that by and large the major theme of African writing to date has been the conflict of Africa with the

Cover of a paperback edition of *Things Fall Apart.*

West, whether this is shown in its initial stages, as in Achebe's *Things Fall Apart,* or at any one of several different later stages. All four of Achebe's novels are examples of the situational plot, for what happens is ultimately more significant for the group than for the individual whom Achebe uses to focus the situation. The significance, then, is felt by the village, the clan, the tribe, or the nation. (pp. 63-4)

Things Fall Apart does not necessarily give the impression that the story is "plotless" in spite of the fragmentary nature of many of the substories or tales. . . . Achebe's use of the proverb can act as a serious counterpart for the more continuous surface progression of the story. . . . The other unities which he relies on to give form and pattern to the story are the traditional oral tale or tale within a tale—a device no longer in favor with contemporary Western novelists, yet a convention at least as old as the "Man in the Hill" episode in Fielding's *Tom Jones.* The use of the leitmotif and its associations with stagnancy in Umuofia, masculinity, land, and yam also act as connective links throughout the narrative. It is because of these unities and others, which are vestiges of his own traditional culture, that Achebe's *Things Fall Apart* deserves its position in the forefront of contemporary African writing. Achebe has widened our perspective of the novel and illustrated how a typically Western genre may be given a healthy injection of new blood once it is reshaped and formed by the artist whose vision of life and art is different from our own. (pp. 64-5)

Achebe has increased the importance of dialogue in [*Arrow of God*]—especially dialogue which makes use of materials drawn from traditional oral literature such as the proverb. Hardly a page of his story passes without the presence of a proverb or two; sometimes there will be as many as half-a-dozen, piled one upon another. . . . The use of these oral examples is a primary means of characterization, and it is the adults in Achebe's novel who make the greatest use of these materials—giving the impression of great wisdom. The majority of the proverbs in *Arrow of God* are spoken as dialogue rather than as a part of authorial commentary. The unique aspect of Achebe's characterization, then, is his use of oral literary materials—far more frequently than almost all other African writers. (pp. 150-52)

Achebe's European characters in *Arrow of God* are generally a little less convincing than they could be, for, in truth, they are examined only from the outside, are stereotyped and one-dimensional, efficient little machines meant to do a job in the British Foreign Service, and, necessarily, I suppose, are in too many ways typical of the men who were in the colonial service. (p. 153)

Almost all—if not all—of Achebe's characters in *A Man of the People* are stereotypes, because with this novel Achebe moved into a new area: satire. In many ways the novel is his weakest so far, and I am convinced that its popularity with the African reading audience bears little correlation to its literary merits, however, the novel accomplishes exactly what it set out to do—satirize life in Nigeria in the mid-1960's. Many of the situations satirized can only be appreciated by someone who lived in Nigeria during those years: political corruption, the increasing bureaucracy, the postal strike, the census, the means of communication, the daily news media.

It probably is not fair to criticize Achebe's cardboard characters in *A Man of the People,* since satire rarely is built on believeable characters. Even the fact that the story is told in the first person results in no great insight into Achebe's narrator, Odili Samalu, or any of the other characters. The thin story thread is more reminiscent of the novels of Cyprian Ekwensi than of Achebe's earlier works. . . . When the story line gets out of control, Achebe conveniently draws his political morality to an end by having the nation succumb to a military coup. In spite of the de-emphasis on character development, there is certainly more dialogue

than Achebe has ever used before, especially in dialects such as Pidgin English, as a means of characterization. The conversation at times is witty, but the whole affair—Odili's entering politics because he has lost his girl—is unconvincing and rather overdrawn. Everybody gets satirized, however, educated and uneducated Africans, the British and the Americans, even the Peace Corps. . . . *A Man of the People* should be acknowledged for exactly what it is: an entertainment, written for Africans. Achebe no longer tries to explain the way it is, to apologize for the way things are, because this is exactly the point: this is the way things are. The characters are ineffectual, and Achebe's satire itself will be short-lived. The story and the characters have none of the magnitude or the nobility of those in *Things Fall Apart* or *Arrow of God.* (pp. 153 55)

Charles R. Larson, "Chinua Achebe's 'Things Fall Apart': The Archetypal African Novel" and "Characters and Modes of Characterization: Chinua Achebe, James Ngugi, and Peter Abrahams," in his *The Emergence of African Fiction,* revised edition, Indiana University Press, 1972, pp. 27-65, 147-66.

PRAFULLA C. KAR

(essay date 1981)

[Here, Kar examines Achebe's use of the African past to delineate its present condition. This essay was originally a lecture delivered at the Post-Graduate Department of English and the Centre for Commonwealth Literature and Research, the University of Mysore, in September 1981.]

The concept of the Vanishing African is similar to the concept of the "Vanishing American" which Leslie Fiedler discusses in great detail in his mythopoetic approach to American history and culture. Fiedler tries to salvage the pre-lapsarian image of the American Adam from the labyrinth of history in order to create a sustaining myth surrounding a changing culture. The image of the vestigial American in his Edenic state of exclusiveness is systematically corroded through centuries of "progress" and "enlightenment" in the wake of scientific and technological advance. The enigmatic nature of Crèvecoeur's "new man" continues to haunt the memory of the modern American writer who is searching for his ancient roots in the debris of history. The idea of the loss of the self is almost a recurrent idea in all literature, particularly in the literature of the twentieth century. To the African writer of today this idea has a deeper psychological and emotional significance. Africa has been going through quick changes through certain accidents in history, and in the midst of social, economic and political turmoil the image of the traditional African will necessarily change. It is gradually losing its distinct shape and colour and tends to become amorphous. The contemporary African writer is deeply, and perhaps obsessively, concerned with the changing image of the African as he struggles desperately to cope with a fast changing society. Chinua Achebe is perhaps the most sensitive writer in Africa today who tries to capture the sense of this mutation in the African character during the colonial period and after. But Achebe's vision of change occurring in Africa is more philosophical than historical. Although he deals in great detail with the impact of colonialism on the African character, he is more concerned with a broad, comprehensive and dynamic idea of history as a transforming process. In this regard he may be compared with Faulkner whose depiction of the decay of the old South is governed by a philosophical conception of culture in transformation. Faulkner is inclined to believe that the Civil War only quickened the process of change from an agrarian society to an industrial one, but it did not start the process; the process was a part of the subtle linear movement of history from one stage to another. There was something inexorably deterministic about the way the American south was slowly dying, a process which suggests that a new order was in the offing. Similarly, Achebe seems to believe that the British administration and the Western missionaries in Africa acted as mere catalysts in accelerating transformation of old Africa, a process which was under way before the Westerners arrived. . . . Achebe is more concerned with broad philosophical questions concerning the nature of change when a culture tries to shed its superfluities and transform itself than with specific changes occurring as a result of Africa's colonial experience. He seems to believe that the African in his primitive, agrarian and blissful state taking pride in his religion, numerous gods, folklore, magic and rituals no longer exists now; it is transformed into a myth and an archetype which are slowly passing into the ancestral memory of the race. This transformation of reality into myth is a part of the general shift of culture . . . Achebe's evocation of the image of the archetypal African has both elements of pathos and celebration, and as a creative writer he is impulsively attracted to its power. That is why, the past in its haunting quality of magic and power, remains in his consciousness as a seminal force to be invoked as a talisman. Achebe, [in his essay **"The Role of the Writer in a New Nation"**] asks a vital question concerning the responsibility of the African writer in a changing milieu:

> . . . how does a writer re-create this past? When I think of this I always think of light and glass. When white light hits glass one of two things can happen. Either you have an image which is faithful if somewhat unexciting or you have a glorious spectrum which though beautiful is really a distortion. Light from the past passes through a kind of glass to reach

us. We can either look for the accurate though somewhat unexciting image or we can look for the glorious technicolor.

This is a very pertinent question, involving the integrity of a writer. Achebe, as is made clear above, prefers the "unexciting image" to the "distorted" "technicolor."

In his delineation of the African past, Achebe tries to re-create the sense of it by evoking its magic and rituals. In the past, the African lived in a world where the social life, religious life and aesthetic life were integrated as one indivisible unit. The individuals were a part of the group and believed in a general code of conduct derived from the group. This aspect of life in Africa has been exaggerated in much of the African writing now, and there is a tendency to be sentimental about the African past. Achebe is opposed to this tendency, and, therefore, he tries to give an accurate, though unexciting, image of the archetypal African in his native surrounding before his encounter with an alien culture. In *Things Fall Apart* and *Arrow of God,* the novels dealing with the pre-colonial Africa, he examines the nature of the traditional African without trying to idealise it. He makes this point clear in the essay . . . from which the above passage is quoted. He remarks:

> The credibility of the world he is attempting to recreate will be called to question and he will defeat his own purpose if he is suspected of glossing over the inconvenient facts. We cannot pretend that our past was one long, technicolor idyll. We have to admit that like other people's pasts ours had its good as well as its bad sides.

This is an important statement, and in the context of the background of *Things Fall Apart* and *Arrow of God,* it gives us another dimension to the nature of reality represented in the two novels. . . . Before the English missionaries and the government came to be entrenched on the African soil, the traditional society was already giving out slow symptoms of change. The idea of closely knit, harmonious, integrated social order was being wrecked from within, by a centrifugal impulse challenging the very idea of order. . . . [In *Things Fall Apart*] Okonkwo is caught in the midst of this subterranean change trying to affect the structure of reality already established as a unifying frame of reference. He is like Faulkner's Quentin Compson in *The Sound and The Fury.* Quentin's problems stem from his inability to stop the flow of time. He had the vision of the south as an unspoiled Eden almost in an abstract, Puritanical sense, a vision that became increasingly difficult to sustain because of the quick changes in the South. He commits suicide as the "last romantic" of the aristocratic South. The death of Quentin symbolises the death of the old South. Similarly, Okonkwo's tragedy springs from his refusal to compromise with the change that is slowly coming over Africa. . . . The title of the novel taken from Yeats's "Second Coming" suggests an apocalyptic and ironic vision. In "Second Coming" Yeats is celebrating the second coming of Christ in the form of an animal "slouching towards Bethlehem to be born", an idea of a disruptive order taking over the already existing one. Achebe must have chosen this title to present a similar view of change occurring in Africa. The dominance of the centripetal over the centrifugal, Achebe seems to suggest, represents an inevitable movement of history, and when Okonkwo refuses to accept the Christian missionaries and the British administration, he, in a way, obstructs the flow of history and, in the process, is swallowed. His tragedy, like Quentin Compson's, stems from his refusal to "grow", to lose his "innocence" in the "rite of passage."

In Okonkwo's death Achebe symbolises the death of traditional Africa. But again, like Faulkner's vision of the South, Achebe's has a curious mixture of irony and ambivalence. Achebe could never have saved Okonkwo from death, since his death could be seen as the logical conclusion of a chain of events having the inevitability of a Greek tragedy. Okonkwo has the inadequacies of a primitive man, is like a caterpillar who refuses to become a butterfly. He believes that his physical strength can win everything for him; his stress on emotional, not intellectual, life limits him as an individual. His instinct for the group, ironically, hinders his growth as an individual. . . . When Okonkwo kills the messenger of the British administration he invites troubles for himself, not by his act of revenge but, by trying to check the natural flow of events. This makes him a tragic character who becomes a victim of both an error of judgment and an unknown deterministic force operating from outside.

Okonkwo's friend Obierika, who is like Horatio to Hamlet, acts as a foil, a counterforce to the former's conception of reality. His conception of change sweeping through the entire Africa is based on a broad, philosophical awareness, a conception which could be taken as Achebe's own. . . . [Obierika suggests] that it is impossible to drive out the white man from Africa, and even if he is physically removed, he will leave behind him a symbolic trait, a kind of scar that can never be wiped out. . . . That they have "fallen apart" and will never act "like one" implies that the society has already passed from the *Gemeinschaft* to the *Gesselschaft* stage by an imperceptible movement of history. An act of suicide, Obierika says, is a kind of sacrilege and they must make sacrifices to "cleanse the desecrated land." So, Okonkwo's death by suicide is taken not as a triumph over forces of disintegration but a vile act to be purged off.

In *Arrow of God* the transition has already passed and the new culture is solidly entrenched on the African soil. The kind of African which Okonkwo represents is already a part of ancient history. The facade of traditional culture is still present in the setting of *Arrow of God,* but its inner force and vitality is lost. The characters in this novel are more open in their attitudes to the changing scene, and some of them even try to reap benefits from the new reality. Ezeulu, the Chief Priest of Umuaro, is very different from Okonkwo in character, attitude and response to the changing cultural scene. He seems to have accepted the fact of the inevitability of change and tries to modify his traditional vision of reality to suit the needs of change. He wields considerable power in the community by his position as the Chief Priest, but Achebe makes it clear in the novel that within the apparent stability and cohesiveness in the community, there exist disruptive elements which threaten that stability from within. Nwaka, Ezeulu's opponent in the novel represents such a force. He not only questions Ezeulu's special prerogatives as the Chief Priest, but also the very existence of the god that Ezeulu has forced them to accept. He is a man of self-interest begotten by an individualistic and competitive society. The structure of reality presented by Achebe in this novel demonstrates that the culture is at the beginning of transformation, not by the impact of any external force, but more importantly, by a subtle inner mechanism from within, which is accelerated by the coming of Christian missionaries and Western administration. Ezeulu seems to recognise this change, and his deliberate delaying of the harvest to take revenge on a recalcitrant community can be seen as precipitating the movement to its logical step of liquidation of the community. He even tries to benefit from the new order and sends one of his sons to the Christian missionaries to be a convert, a step which represents Ezeulu's somewhat eclectic approach to reality and makes him a little advanced over Okonkwo. He compares the world to a Mask dancing in which one has to turn round and round to have the full view of the dance:

> I want one of my sons to join these people and be my eye there. If there is nothing in it you will come back. If there is something there you will bring home my share. The world is like a Mask dancing. If you want to see it well you do not stand in one place. My spirit tells me that those who do not befriend the white man today will be saying had we known tomorrow.

This is a significant point and expresses Ezeulu's intuitive understanding of the dynamics of cultural change, and it suggests that he has moved a long way from where Okonkwo had stood. But, ironically, Ezeulu is defeated by the same forces he seems to be friendly with. His defeat can be taken as the defeat of a man who is not properly formed in intellect, is not properly balanced.

Ezeulu is the link between Okonkwo on the one hand and Obi Okonkwo and Chief Nanga on the other. In Obi Okonkwo and Chief Nanga, the protagonists of *No Longer at Ease* and *Man of the People* respectively, the image of the African is pushed to its farthest limits. In these characters there is no vestige of the traditional African. They even do not seem to understand the roles played by their ancestors in the evolution of their culture. They are beneficiaries of a changed system, but they too are defeated at the end. Their defeat can be explained in terms of their divided status, which means they have left their native culture without being able to grasp another. They suffer the fate of intermediaries, dangling between two cultures. Obi Okonkwo, essentially a good man, educated in England and having illusions of doing good to his country after his return from England, is caught in a terrible maelstrom of change sweeping through his country and is pushed into an extreme situation in which he is unable to decide his fate and finally commits an act which he cannot accept himself in his own code of morality. (pp. 149-57)

But Chief Nanga is a much different man. He is shrewd, Machiavellian and extremely opportunistic. In him the image of the African has reached the extreme limits. He is more or less like Jason Compson of Faulkner's novel, a character who adopts a new code of values and tries to benefit from it. . . . Chief Nanga succeeds for a time, but by the same logic of history he too is defeated. Achebe seems to sing the dirge over the death of the African character in the fall of Nanga when a military coup takes over the country and a seeming peace is restored. Achebe is intensely nostalgic about the African past and is deeply sad at the loss of the African character, but like a philosopher of history he accepts the change with detachment and mute resignation. The change that has come over the entire country after independence is the logical result of the subtle process in the mechanism of culture trying to adapt itself to the psychology of change. . . . The epigraph which he attaches to *No Longer at Ease* suggests his broad, philosophical and almost tragic sense of loss which is irreparable. The lines are taken from Eliot's poem "The Journey of the Magi." They are as follows:

> We returned to our places, these Kingdoms,
> But no longer at ease here, in the old dispensation,
> With alien people clutching their gods.
> I should be glad of another death.

The vision here is ironic and tragic. Like Ulysses dissatisfied with his own country after his return from adventures, Obi Okonkwo, the grandson of the protagonist of *Things fall Apart* may be thinking of fresh territories, but he has forfeited his rights for adventure since he is now a mixed man combining two diametrically opposed cultures but without having any clear conception of either. Achebe's own dilemma and the dilemma of the African writer is implicit in this epigraph. (pp. 157-58)

Prafulla C. Kar, "The Image of the Vanishing African in Chinua Achebe's Novels," in *The Colonial and the Neo-Colonial Encounters in Commonwealth Literature,* edited by H. H. Anniah Gowda, Prasaranga, University of Mysore, 1983, pp. 149-59.

NEAL ASCHERSON
(essay date 1988)

[In the excerpt below, Ascherson reviews *Anthills of the Savannah.*]

In this decade of African catastrophe, it is hard to reconstruct the optimism and certainties of the emergent African political class thirty years ago, and of their liberal-minded European sympathizers. Independence seemed the happy-ever-after conclusion, even to those territories—the Portuguese domains, Rhodesia-Zimbabwe—that were destined to fight long, bitter wars before they could claim to "govern themselves." Instead, so often although not everywhere, independence set off a degenerative process: freedom became corruption, while democracy collapsed into autocracy, "life-presidencies," and finally military dictatorship; the country people faced starvation brought by crop failure and mismanagement while the town people withered in colossal, spreading slums where the AIDS pandemic is beginning to reap its harvest.

Who or what is to blame? For a time, it was fashionable to blame "neo-colonialist exploitation," real and ruthless enough indeed. Later, in a Europe still clinging to the tatters of fond hopes, there emerged a wry defense of corruption as no more than the modern form of traditional African clientship relations, something "natural" and not to be judged by European standards of public life. Patronizing and even racist, this explanation too was less than a half-truth.

In [*Anthills of the Savannah*], . . . Chinua Achebe says, with implacable honesty, that Africa itself is to blame, and that there is no safety in excuses that place the fault in the colonial past or in the commercial and political manipulations of the First World. The first postcolonial leaders, for all their European educations and sophistication, utterly failed to meet their responsibility. And by the time that they began to understand the scale of their failure, their own brief period of hegemony was beginning to fall apart as power passed into the hands of more limited and infinitely more ferocious men, usually military. During the years of open political contest, the first "independence" generation recklessly allowed the distinction between power and force to be blurred, until those whose trade was force began in increasing numbers to drive their tanks across that line.

The "Kangan" of *Anthills of the Savannah* is more or less Achebe's own Nigeria. That country is today governed by General Babangida, among the least oppressive and most enlightened of Africa's military rulers. But as I write, the newspapers report that there is little popular enthusiasm for the slow return to civilian rule that he intends. Civilian politicians have discredited themselves. A diplomat in Lagos is quoted as saying: "Who could stand over Babangida's murdered body and proclaim liberty? Answer: nobody!"

At the beginning of the novel, the reader meets four members of Kangan's elite, "the cream of our society and the hope of the black race." Chris Oriko is Commissioner for Information, Ikem Osodi is a poet and the restless, rebellious editor of the *National Gazette*. Beatrice Okoh, lover of Chris, is a strong and independent young woman, an intellectual with a first-class English degree from London who is a senior civil servant. The fourth character is Sam, otherwise "His Excellency," the new military ruler of Kangan. Sam, Chris, and Ikem were all at school together at "Lord Lugard College," one of those little black Etons peculiar to the old British Empire. His schoolmates, in fact, helped Sam into power, considering him to be a slightly slow-witted but basically decent fellow who would clear up the mess left behind by the corrupt civilian government that preceded him.

As the novel opens, they are discovering how wrong they were. Sam—"not very bright, but not wicked," in Ikem's original estimate—is turning himself into a "Great African Leader." He is no longer Sam but "H. E." His cabinet (the novel's first pages describe a cabinet meeting with murderous satire) is already reduced to a pack of nervous toadies, jostling to throw doubts on each others' loyalty. At some moments, H. E. luxuriates in his own sense of achievement. . . . But he can banish only for a few minutes his gnawing humiliation over the recent referendum to make him President for Life; he has failed to gain the necessary majority, and failed because the people of the distant, dry savannah province of Abazon boycotted the poll. He has punished them by denying them water during a disastrous drought. Now a delegation from Abazon has had the impudence to arrive unlicensed in the capital to petition him for aid. Who put them up to it? H. E. suspects a plot, possibly by those classmates who still secretly think they are much better than he is. Trouble is brewing in Kangan.

After this introduction, the novel slows and broadens out as Achebe explores more deeply the character and meditations of Chris, reluctant to abandon what remains of his influence over the political scene, of Beatrice as she treads warily along the fringe of H.

E.'s set of cronies, and of Ikem. It is Ikem whose shift from meditation to action provides the theme of the book. But all three of them share something "Russian," both in their thoughts and in their relation to the social and political setting; their fears are the fears of Herzen's "superfluous" people, and their sense of privilege, guilt, and impotence constantly reminded me of the novels of Turgenev. . . .

In [*Anthills of the Savannah*], Achebe's characters are obsessed with the problem of "the people"; they act in their name, and yet are painfully aware that they have lost contact with them. In a very Russian way, they debate the nature of "the people," at times confident that the humility and good nature of the masses will save the nation from its leaders, at others fearing that the goodness has been turned to evil and cruelty, which any revolution would release as a tide of dark savagery. (p. 3)

Language at once unites and divides the poor and the powerful. Chris, Ikem, and their British-educated friends talk sophisticated London English among themselves. But at intimate moments—loving, teasing, trying to express something special to their country—they resort to the vivid West African version of pidgin English which is the nation's real lingua franca. Much of the novel's dialogue is in pidgin, as when the two drivers try to thank Ikem for defending the cause of the poor. . . .

H. E. orders Chris to fire Ikem from the *National Gazette*, on the grounds that he is suspected by the "State Research Council" (security police) of having organized the delegation of protest from Abazon. Chris refuses, but Ikem is removed anyway. He addresses an incandescent student rally at the university, as the Abazon leaders are arrested; incautiously, he answers a question about a rumor that H. E. will put his own head on the coinage with a jest that the ruler is "inciting the people to take his head off." Next day, the tamed *National Gazette* leads with the headline: "EX-EDITOR ADVOCATES REGICIDE!" Within hours, Ikem is dead, murdered by security police after a raid on his house. Chris manages to gather a few foreign correspondents in order to tell them the truth, then goes into hiding. A few days later, in ragged disguise, he boards a bus heading for the North and the arid, rebellious province of Abazon.

A bus! Chris Oriko has not ridden a bus since before he left for Britain as a student. The people he meets in the office, at cocktail parties, at any gathering of the elite have no idea what it means to travel on a bus. This becomes Chris's own pilgrimage to the people, a liberation from the "Mercedes class" registered by Achebe in one of those curious, spreading, raftlike sentences he uses—much as Tolstoy used them—to describe a change in the heart. . . .

But this is also the journey of Chris Oriko to his own death. On the borders of Abazon, the bus is stopped by a drunken mob celebrating news on the radio from the capital: there has been another *coup d'état* and Sam, "His Excellency," has been kidnapped. His chief of staff proclaims with unconvincing outrage that the abductors will be found, but it is "H. E." who is soon found in a shallow grave. Chris never learns this. Attempting to save a young girl in the crowd from a police sergeant bent on rape, he is shot dead.

In their very different ways, the three boys from Lord Lugard College have all expiated the sin that two of them recognized but one did not: that "failure to re-establish vital inner links with the poor and dispossessed." The three murders, senseless as they are, represent the departure of a generation that compromised its own enlightenment for the sake of power—even the power of bold opposition enjoyed by Ikem Osodi. They are succeeded by altogether cruder and less inhibited men: the inner, African danger that they all underestimated. (p. 4)

It is the courage of this complex novel to cast Africans, even in this wretched decade, always as subjects and never as the objects of external forces. It is a tale about responsibility, and the ways in which men who should know better betray and evade that responsibility. Women, in Achebe's novel, do not betray. Not only the figure of Beatrice Okoh but the main female characters here show a "priestess-like" strength and calm. They endure, angrily enough, the "Desdemona complex" that tempts their men to make fools of themselves with white women; they are the bearers of traditional morals and perceptions to which they coax their erratic, ambitious men to return. They pick up the pieces after male disasters. They are left to mourn.

And yet this is neither a solemn work nor an entirely pessimistic one. It has wonderful satiric moments and resounds with big African laughter. Legend and tradition have their places here, as characters recount old myths of creation or new parables about the abuses of power. The question of how deep and lasting are the wounds to the "heart of the people" is left open. But Achebe emphasizes that the strength of the human race is its unpredictability: "man's stubborn antibody called surprise. Man will surprise by his capacity for nobility as well as for villainy."

All that can be done is to understand what cannot be done, that all total solutions fail and that therefore "we may accept a limitation on our actions but never, under no circumstances, must we accept restriction on our thinking."

That is the conclusion of a young student leader, at a gathering to mourn Ikem and to give a name (Amaechina: may-the-path-never-close) to his fatherless baby. Ikem himself, with Chinua Achebe perhaps speaking through him, has already found his way to the humility of liberalism. "Experience and intelligence," he says, "warn us that man's progress in freedom will be piecemeal, slow and undramatic. Revolution may be necessary for taking a society out of an intractable stretch of quagmire but it does not confer freedom, and may indeed hinder it." (pp. 4, 6)

Neal Ascherson, "Betrayal," in *The New York Review of Books*, Vol. XXXV, No. 3, March 3, 1988, pp. 3-4, 6.

CHERRY CLAYTON
(essay date 1988)

[In the following excerpt, Clayton declares *Hopes and Impediments* to be a work of a "new and superior order." In an unexcerpted portion of the essay, the critic also reviews J. M. Coetzee's *White Writing: On the Culture of Letters in South Africa*.]

The critical work represented in the selected essays of the South African novelist J. M. Coetzee and the Nigerian author Chinua Achebe is of a new and superior order, mobilizing the best creative and critical energies of two writers as committed to their craft as they are to exposing what Achebe calls the "monster of racist habit". In both cases the critique of a "white" culture (whether European, American, or South African)—its assumptions, blind spots, abuses of language, logic or humanity—is based on a scrupulous examination of evidence, as it emerges within early travel writing, anecdotes, or the work of individual authors who appear to be transmitting the "truth" of a continent and its indigenous peoples, but are often perpetuating Western conceptual grids. The result, as they see it, is the entrenching of dehumanizing myths. The pervasiveness and harm of such myths are driven home with a new force by two highly intelligent writers with insight, humour and moral passion.. . . .

Like Coetzee, Achebe is both rooted in his own culture and critical of it, though he has a richer and more dynamic culture to draw on, which may partly account for his less cerebral, but vigorous, humane and humorous voice. The "essays" in *Hopes and Impediments* are often the texts of occasional talks, and thus they gain the fuller dimension of personality, and the cutting edge of a spoken denunciation, counterargument, and reiteration of principle and belief which the genre offers. The collection begins with a convincing demonstration of Joseph Conrad's racism, and the ways in which *Heart of Darkness* has been appropriated by teachers and critics. Anyone who has not yet quietly removed *Heart of Darkness* from their undergraduate syllabus and substituted *Things Fall Apart* will do so after reading this essay. But perhaps the best idea would be to go on teaching *Heart of Darkness* with Achebe's essay as accompaniment.

Though Achebe's revelation of certain offensive tones and assumptions is unanswerable, his real concern, shown throughout these essays, is to address racism as such, as a habit of mind which cannot conceive of the African as an equal, and uses Africa as a giant projection screen for its own Western fantasies and flaws. Like Coetzee, he sees the imaginative annexation of a territory, without an eye for the "recognizable humanity" within it, as deeply culpable and artistically distorting. In reply to this skewed perspective, he enlists many of the values he defines in Igbo art: an "outward, social and kinetic quality", together with a space for the private and contemplative. His own inclusive and life-enhancing definitions of art clearly draw on traditions within Nigerian cultural life: "Even if harmony is not achievable in the heterogeneity of human experience, the dangers of an open rupture are greatly lessened by giving to everyone his due in the same forum of social and cultural surveillance."

Achebe's emphasis on human beings as creatures who find their fulfilment not in individualism, consumerism, or an ideal of free, uncluttered space, but in "a presence—a powerful, demanding presence limiting the space in which the self can roam uninhibited . . . an aspiration by the self to achieve spiritual congruence with the other", is healthy and corrective. This belief is the core of his critique of some Western writers and

of his appraisal of undervalued or misunderstood African writers, such as Amos Tutuola, of whose novel *The Palm-Wine Drinkard* he offers a vigorous and illuminating reading.

The collection begins with his analysis of Conrad and ends with a tribute to James Baldwin. Along the way there are speeches on broad topics, such as **"The Truth of Fiction"** and **"Thoughts on the African Novel"**, a personal tribute to Christopher Okigbo, and passing reflections on the present needs of his own society. Despite the more glaring practical deficiencies operating within his own modernizing society, he still values a literary culture and sees its role as crucial:

> Literature . . . gives us a second handle on reality; enabling us to encounter in the safe, manageable dimensions of make-believe the very same threats to integrity that may assail the psyche in real life; and at the same time providing through the self-discovery which it imparts a veritable weapon for coping with these threats whether they are found within problematic and incoherent selves or in the world around us.

It is in this valuing of "benevolent" fictions, which know themselves as fictions, and the discrediting of the "malignant fiction" of racism, which is fiction masquerading as truth, that Achebe and Coetzee are united directing their considerable eloquence.

Cherry Clayton, "Uprooting the Malignant Fictions," in *The Times Literary Supplement,* No. 4460, September 23-29, 1988, p. 1043.

SOURCES FOR FURTHER STUDY

Bruchac, Joseph. "Achebe As Poet." *New Letters* 40, No. 1 (October 1973): 23-31.

Brief discussion of *Christmas in Biafra and Other Poems.*

Busby, Margaret. "Bitter Fruit." *New Statesman* 114, No. 2948 (25 September 1987): 34.

Appraises *Anthills of the Savannah,* noting: "Reading *Anthills of the Savannah* is like watching a master carver skillfully chiselling away from every angle at a solid block of wood. . . . True, there are occasional slips, lines one might wish less awkward, but the overall effect is undeniably powerful."

Evalds, Victoria K. "Chinua Achebe: Bio-Bibliography and Recent Criticism, 1970-75." *A Current Bibliography on African Affairs* 10, No. 1 (1977-78): 67-87.

Comprehensive bio-bibliography of Achebe. Contains brief summary of criticism on his works.

Gordimer, Nadine. "A Tyranny of Clowns." *The New York Times Book Review* (February 21, 1988): 1, 26.

Positive review of *Anthills of the Savannah,* noting that "it is a work in which 22 years of harsh experience, intellectual growth, self-criticism, deepening understanding, and mustered discipline of skill open wide a subject to which Mr. Achebe is now magnificently equal."

Rogers, Philip. "Chinua Achebe's Poems of Regeneration." *Journal of Commonwealth Literature* 10, No. 3 (April 1976): 1-9.

Discussion of *Beware, Soul Brother.* Contends that the themes of death and rebirth found in the poems mirrors war-torn Nigeria of the 1970s.

Tucker, Martin. *Africa in Modern Literature: A Survey of Contemporary Writing in English.* New York: F. Ungar, 1967, 316 p.

Offers summary overviews of and commentary on Achebe's major works.

Edward Albee

1928-

(Full name Edward Franklin Albee, III) American dramatist, poet, short story writer, scriptwriter, and dramatist.

INTRODUCTION

Best known for his first full-length drama, *Who's Afraid of Virginia Woolf?* (1962), Albee is among the United States's most acclaimed and controversial contemporary dramatists. Although initially characterized either as a realist or an absurdist, Albee usually combines elements from the American tradition of social criticism established by such playwrights as Arthur Miller, Tennessee Williams, and Eugene O'Neill with aspects of the Theater of the Absurd as practiced by Samuel Beckett and Eugène Ionesco. While Albee often portrays alienated individuals who suffer as a result of unjust social, moral, or religious strictures, he usually offers solutions to conflicts rather than conveying an absurdist sense of inescapable determinism. According to Allan Lewis, Albee "writes plays that grip an audience, that hold with their elusiveness, their obscurity, their meaning; and he has functioned in the true role of the playwright—to express the human condition dramatically and metaphorically."

Albee was the adopted child of Reed and Frances Albee, heirs to the multi-million dollar fortune of American theater manager Edward Franklin Albee I. He began attending the theater and writing poetry at the age of six, wrote a three-act sex farce when he was twelve, and attempted two novels while a teenager. Many critics suggest that the tense family conflicts of Albee's dramas derive from his childhood experiences. After attending several private and military schools and enrolling briefly at Trinity College in Connecticut, Albee achieved limited success as an author of poetry and fiction before turning to drama. Although he remained associated with off-Broadway theater until the production of *Who's Afraid of Virginia Woolf?*, he first garnered critical and popular acclaim for his one-act dramas, which prompted comparisons to the works of Tennessee Williams and Eugène Ionesco. His first one-act play, *The Zoo Story* (1959), is a satire set in New York City in which a young homosexual attempts to force conversation on a reticent conservative. After intimidating the man into defending himself with a knife, the homosexual purposely impales himself on its blade. While most reviewers regarded *The Zoo Story* as an absurdist condemnation of the artificiality of American values and the failure of communication, others described the work as an allegory of Christian redemption in which the young man martyrs himself to demonstrate the value of meaningful communication. Albee's next one-act drama, *The Death of Bessie Smith* (1960), revolves around the demise of black blues singer Bessie Smith, who died after being refused treatment at a Southern hospital that catered exclusively to white patients. Although initially interpreted as an indictment of Southern racism, Albee's ambiguous portrayal of the tensions that the incident provokes between a nurse, an intern, and an orderly have led many critics to regard *The Death of Bessie Smith* as an attack on dehumanizing American social values.

Albee's next major one-act plays, *The Sandbox* (1960) and *The American Dream* (1961), are generally viewed as expressionistic or burlesque satires of middle-class family values. In *The Sandbox,* a domineering Mommy and an emasculated Daddy tire of Grandma, the play's only sympathetic character, and abandon her on a beach to be collected by a handsome young man who symbolizes death. *The American Dream* focuses on similar Mommy and Daddy characters who, long ago, had adopted a son who later died as a result of the severe punishments they had inflicted upon him for failing to fulfill their ideal of "the American Dream." The vacuous, opportunistic twin brother of their deceased child confronts the parents, who recognize in him their "American Dream." Although faulted as defeatist and nihilistic, *The American Dream* was commended for its savage parody of traditional American values. Albee commented: "Is the play offensive? I certainly hope so; it was my intention to offend—as well as amuse and entertain."

Albee's most acclaimed drama, *Who's Afraid of Virginia Woolf?*, has generated popular and critical notoriety for its controversial depiction of marital strife. This play depicts the alternately destructive and conciliatory relationship between George and Martha, a middle-aged history professor and his wife, during a late-night party in their living room with Nick, George's shallow colleague, and Honey, his spouse. As the evening proceeds, George and Martha alternately attack and patronize their guests before Martha seduces Nick with the intent of hurting her husband; George retaliates by announcing the death of their nonexistent son, whom they had created to sustain their relationship. The conclusion suggests that George and Martha may be able to reappraise their relationship based on the intimacy, which was both feared and sought all evening, that arises from their shared sorrow.

Although faulted as morbid and self-indulgent, *Who's Afraid of Virginia Woolf?* was honored with two Antoinette Perry Awards and a New York Drama Critics Circle Award. Variously interpreted as a problem play in the tradition of August Strindberg, a campus parody, or a latent homosexual critique of conventional relationships, the drama has generated a wide array of critical analyses. When Albee failed to receive the Pulitzer Prize because one trustee objected to the play's sexual subject matter, drama advisors John Gassner and John Mason Brown publicly resigned. *Who's Afraid of Virginia Woolf?* has since been assessed as a classic of American drama for its tight control of form and command of both colloquial and abstruse dialogue.

While several of Albee's plays written since 1962 have failed commercially and elicited scathing reviews for their abstract classicism and dialogue, many scholars have commended his commitment to theatrical experimentation and refusal to pander to commercial pressures. *Tiny Alice* (1964) addresses the crisis of faith arising from the human tendency to represent the metaphysical with symbols that necessarily limit and attenuate. The action of this play surrounds a Catholic lay brother who struggles to believe in a supreme entity that he cannot intellectually comprehend. Although many critics considered the drama incomprehensible for the manner in which it deviates from realism with respect to setting, character portrayal, and internal time, Richard Gilman praised *Tiny Alice* as "far and away the most significant play on Broadway [in 1965]," commending its "scenes that break down the walls of reticence and safety that mark the commercial theater." In *A Delicate Balance* (1966), a troubled middle-aged couple examine their relationship during a prolonged visit by two close friends. While the husband comes to realize that avoidance of love and compassion can lead to remorse and self-contempt, his wife remains oblivious, and their guests eventually feel compelled to leave. While garnering approval for its synthesis of dramatic elements, this drama was widely faulted for lacking action and cohesive ideas. When *A Delicate Balance* was awarded the Pulitzer Prize, most regarded the decision as a belated attempt by the Pulitzer committee to honor Albee for *Who's Afraid of Virginia Woolf?*.

Albee has stated that in his abstract, interrelated one-act plays *Box* and *Quotations from Chairman Mao Tse-Tung* (1968), he attempted to apply "musical form to dramatic structure." *Box*, which involves no physical action or movement, is a monologue on the decline of Western civilization delivered by an unseen woman whose voice issues from the back and sides of the theater while a bright light illuminates a large cube that has been interpreted as a cage, a womb, or a coffin. In *Quo-*

tations from *Chairman Mao Tse-Tung,* the same cube encompasses a steamship deck upon which Chairman Mao reads from a book of aphoristic quotations while an elderly woman recites doggerel verse written by nineteenth-century poet Will Carleton and another woman relates a personal anecdote. Like *Box,* this play addresses the deterioration of Western culture, but its inherent meaning is conveyed through random associations resulting from contrapuntal dialogue. In *All Over* (1971), Albee returned to the predominantly realistic mode of his earlier plays to examine the vicious resentments and rivalries that result among the mistress, best friend, and family of an old man near death. Although most critics faulted the play's characters as lacking dramatic urgency, Richmond Crinkley called *All Over* "a beautiful and exciting piece of theater," and Harold Clurman commented: "Listening attentively . . . [to] this largely verbal play, one comes to recognize that it contains not only feeling but pathos all the more poignant for its severe repression."

In *Seascape* (1975), which Brendan Gill described as "a short, wryly witty, and sometimes touching play about discovery," Albee depicted a middle-aged couple who are accosted on a beach by a pair of intelligent lizard-like creatures that have been driven from the sea by the processes of evolution. The four characters discuss topics of mutual understanding, including the purpose of existence, before concurring that human and alien creatures should aid and inspire one another to shape the conditions of life. Although regarded by some critics as pretentious, *Seascape* was commended for its originality and intriguing dialogue and earned Albee a second Pulitzer Prize. In his one-act plays *Listening: A Chamber Play* (1977) and *Counting the Ways: A Vaudeville* (1977), Albee returns to the experimental forms of *Box* and *Quotations from Chairman Mao Tse-Tung. Listening,* adapted from Albee's radio play of the same title, blends four voices to achieve the effect of a chamber quartet. The protagonists of this drama meet by a fountain pool and exchange observations and insults until one character drives another to commit suicide. *Counting the Ways* is a comic play consisting of twenty-one scenes that reflect the divergent moods of married life. In this work, a couple known as He and She question their love for one another before concluding that their bond depends on faith. Thomas P. Adler commented that "this entertaining 'diversion'—for that seems an apt classification—can delight with its considerable charm and wit and occasional beauties of language."

In his next play, *The Lady from Dubuque* (1980), Albee posited that reality is a subjective phenomenon open to multiple interpretations. This drama concerns a woman dying of an unspecified disease who vents her pain and hostility on her friends and husband prior to the arrival of an ambiguous, commanding woman who alternately evokes the images of archetypal mother and angel of death. While this play closed after only twelve performances, Gerald Clarke deemed it Albee's "best work since *Who's Afraid of Virginia Woolf?*," and Otis Guernsey included it in *The Best Plays of 1979-1980. The Man Who Had Three Arms* (1983) also failed financially. Although Albee denied any autobiographical intent, critics dismissed this play for what they perceived as a self-pitying portrayal of himself; his dramas had been poorly received since the early 1960s. This play centers on Himself, a man who acquired wealth and fame after growing a third arm that later disappeared. Addressing the audience from a lecture podium, Himself alternately pleads for sympathy and attacks his audience for his loss of prominence. Although most reviewers concurred with the contention of Clive Barnes that this play contains "a freefall of writing, some of it remarkably good, all of it dangerously unedited, and most of it sadly bitter," Gerald Weales deemed *The Man Who Had Three Arms* "a great deal more substantial than its reception and very brief run suggests."

Albee described his stylized drama *Finding the Sun* (1983) as "pointillist in manner." This play counterbalances characters, in one example contrasting a young man's forthcoming freedom with an old man's awareness of his impending death. Linda Ben-Zvi commented: "There is much that is strong and theatrical about the piece. It plays well . . . thanks in large measure to the vivid personalities that Albee has created." In his recent *Marriage Play* (1987), which Dana Rufolo-Hörhager praised as "a resonant, poetical, and cleanly hewn work," Albee returned to the themes of his earlier plays to portray the ambivalent relationship between a cynical woman and her detached husband. According to Jeanne Luere, *Marriage Play* "comes alive onstage and arrests the audience through starkly contrasting visual elements to depict the couple's sometimes warm, sometimes cool reaction to each other's physical presence."

(For further information about Albee's life and works, see *Authors in the News,* Vol. 1; *Concise Dictionary of American Literary Biography, 1941-1968; Contemporary Authors,* Vols. 5-8; *Contemporary Authors Bibliographical Series,* Vol. 3; *Contemporary Authors New Revision Series,* Vol. 8; *Dictionary of Literary Biography,* Vol. 7: *Twentieth-Century American Dramatists;* and *Major 20th-Century Writers.*)

CRITICAL COMMENTARY

RUBY COHN
(essay date 1969)

[An American critic and educator, Cohn has published numerous works on modern drama, including several studies of Samuel Beckett. In the following excerpt, she surveys Albee's works through *A Delicate Balance*.]

Like European Absurdists, Albee has tried to dramatize the reality of man's condition, but whereas Sartre, Camus, Beckett, Genet, Ionesco, and Pinter present that reality in all its alogical absurdity, Albee has been preoccupied with illusions that screen man from reality. For the Europeans, absurdity or non-sense *is* metaphysical reality; for Albee, the world "makes no sense because the moral, religious, political and social structures man has erected to 'illusion' himself have collapsed." In Albee's drama, however, illusion is still present, and the action often dramatizes the process of collapse, so that we, the audience, arrive at a recognition of the reality behind illusion. In successive plays, Albee's vision of reality grows more complex, and it cannot be contained by mere words; instead, metaphor, gesture, and rhythm depict reality obliquely.

The Zoo Story already announces the suggestive indirection of subsequent works. Significantly, the method of indirection is explained by an outsider who has suffered at the hands of the Establishment. Early in *The Zoo Story*, Jerry, the near-tramp, informs Peter, the conformist: "I took the subway down to the Village so I could walk all the way up Fifth Avenue to the zoo. It's one of those things a person has to do; sometimes a person has to go a very long distance out of his way to come back a short distance correctly." The only purpose of Jerry's long walk is to accommodate his methodology. Jerry could have gone to New York City's Central Park Zoo by the cross-town bus, but, deliberately indirect, he chose the circuitous route. On Fifth Avenue, a street of many sights, Jerry apparently noticed nothing, though he has remarkable powers of observation. That luxury-laden avenue is simply the "distance out of his way to come back a short distance correctly" to the zoo. Through Jerry's explanation, indirection and animality enter Albee's play. Jerry couples these two themes to introduce his dog story, the verbal climax of the play: "THE STORY OF JERRY AND THE DOG! . . . What I am going to tell you has something to do with how sometimes it's necessary to go a long distance out of the way in order to come back a short distance cor-

rectly." By the time we hear the dog story, we are familiar with Jerry's "out of the way" dialogue, and we should be ready to see in the dog story an analogue for the zoo story.

In *The Zoo Story* Peter, who "look[s] like an animal man," becomes the dog, friend-enemy to Jerry. Jerry views Peter as he does the dog—with sadness and suspicion; Jerry tickles Peter as he tempts the dog—into self-revelation; Jerry forces Peter to defend his premises as the dog defends *his* premises; Jerry hopes for understanding from the dog ("I hoped that the dog would . . . understand") and from Peter ("I don't know what I was thinking about; of course you don't understand"); as the dog bit Jerry, Peter stabs Jerry. (pp. 6-7)

[Jerry punch-baits Peter] into using the knife. Since Peter is a defensive animal only, not an attacker, Jerry "impales *himself* on the knife" (my italics). Though Jerry cries like a "fatally wounded animal," he dies like a man—talking. (p. 8)

Albee's *Zoo Story* generalizes that men are animals; beneath the illusion of civilization, they may use words and knives instead of fangs and claws, but they still can kill.

Beyond this, however, *The Zoo Story* suggests another meaning in man's search for God. Albee himself has pointed out the influence upon *The Zoo Story* of *Suddenly Last Summer* by Tennessee Williams; Albee's play, like that of Williams, contains a search for God climaxed by violence. Like the Old Testament Jeremiah, whose cruel prophecies were a warning kindness to his people, Jerry may have educated Peter in his relation to God. Like his namesake, Jerry lapses into prophetic language: "And it came to pass that . . . " "So be it!" Before the dog story, Jerry exclaims, "For God's sake." (p. 9)

This undercurrent of divine suggestion is climaxed by the final words of the play. Toward the beginning Peter reacted to Jerry's unconventional life story with "Oh, my; oh, my." And Jerry sneered, "Oh, your what?" Only after the impalement is Jerry's question answered—by Peter's whispered repetitions: "Oh my God, oh my God, oh my God," and these are the only words Peter speaks while Jerry dies, thanking Peter in biblical phrases: "I came unto you . . . and you have comforted me." After Jerry's revelation of Peter's animal nature, and Peter's subsequent departure according to Jerry's instructions, "OH MY GOD!" is heard offstage as a *howl*—the final proof of Peter's animality,

Principal Works

The Zoo Story (drama) 1959
The Death of Bessie Smith (drama) 1960
Fam and Yam (drama) 1960
The Sandbox (drama) 1960
The American Dream (drama) 1961
*Bartleby (opera) 1961
Who's Afraid of Virginia Woolf ? (drama) 1962
†The Ballad of the Sad Café (drama) 1963
Tiny Alice (drama) 1964
A Delicate Balance (drama) 1966
‡Malcolm (drama) 1966
§Everything in the Garden (drama) 1967
Box (drama) 1968
Quotations from Chairman Mao Tse-Tung (drama) 1968
All Over (drama) 1971
Seascape (drama) 1975
Counting the Ways: A Vaudeville (drama) 1977

‖Listening: A Chamber Play (drama) 1977
The Lady from Dubuque (drama) 1980
#Lolita (drama) 1981
Finding the Sun (drama) 1983
The Man Who Had Three Arms (drama) 1983
Marriage Play (drama) 1987

*This drama is an adaptation of Herman Melville's short story "Bartleby the Scrivener."
†This drama is an adaptation of a novel by Carson McCullers.
‡This drama is an adaptation of a novel by James Purdy.
§This drama is an adaptation of a play by Giles Cooper.
‖This drama was first produced as a radio play.
#This drama is an adaptation of a novel by Vladimir Nabokov.

but also of his humanity, since he howls to his God. (pp. 9-10)

Because life is lonely and death inevitable, Jerry seeks to master them in a single deed of ambiguous suicide-murder; he stages his own death, and by that staging, he punctures Peter's illusion of civilization, converting Peter into his apostle who will carry the message of man's caged animality—the zoo story. Jerry's death brings us to dramatic definition of humanity—bounded by animal drives but reaching toward the divine. Though this definition is at least as old as Pascal, Albee invests it with contemporary significance through his highly contemporary idiom—an idiom manipulated in tense theatrical rhythms. (p. 10)

In *The American Dream,* . . . the caricature of contemporary America often depends, in production, on elaborate set and props. In *The American Dream* Mommy and Daddy spout the clichés of middle-class America, and the implication is that such clichés lead to the death of Grandma, who represents the vigorous old frontier spirit. Grandma resembles Jerry in her independence, but age has made her crafty, and she has learned to roll with the punches. In both *The American Dream* and *The Sandbox* it is Mommy who delivers the punches, and yet she does not literally kill Grandma.

Of the relationship between these two plays, Albee has written: "For *The Sandbox,* I extracted several of the characters from *The American Dream* and placed them in a situation different than, but related to, their predicament in the longer play." *The Sandbox* is named for the grave of Grandma, the first-generation

American, and *The American Dream* is named for the third-generation American, a grave in himself; in both plays, murderous intention is lodged in the middle generation, especially Mommy. In *The Sandbox* Mommy and Daddy deposit Grandma in a child's sandbox, as Hamm relegates his legless parents to ashbins in Beckett's *Endgame.* Half-buried, Grandma finds that she can no longer move, and she accepts her summons by the handsome Young Man, an Angel of Death.

[In *The American Dream*], Albee places a family in the American grain, with its areas for senior citizens, and its focus on money. When Mommy was eight years old, she told Grandma that she was "going to mahwy a wich old man." Sterile, Mommy and Daddy have purchased a baby from the Bye-Bye Adoption Service, which puns on Buy-Buy. Mommy seems to spend her life shopping, when she isn't nagging Daddy or Grandma. In *The Sandbox* Mommy and Daddy carry Grandma to *death,* but in *The American Dream* Mommy makes Grandma's *life* impossible. (pp. 11-12)

[The] American Dream leads but to the grave, and Grandma, accepting her fate, goes out in style—escorted by a handsome swain whose gallantry substitutes for feeling. (pp. 13-14)

[The] play ends with Grandma's aside: "Everybody's got what he wants . . . or everybody's got what he thinks he wants." The American family accepts its illusion of sex and success.

In *The Death of Bessie Smith* Albee avoids sentimentality by keeping the sympathetic titular protagonist offstage. The play is based on a newspaper account of the death of the Negro blues singer; its documentary origin is unique in Albee's works. But his Bessie Smith is a presence rather than a character. The most sustained character, in contrast, is a voluble young Nurse who lashes out against her invalid Father, her Intern suitor, and her Negro Orderly. Lacking Jerry's self-proclaimed kindness and Mommy's hypocritical conformity, the dialogue of the Nurse is unrelievedly vicious, and yet she is not responsible for the death of Bessie Smith.

In the eight scenes of the play Albee attempts to counterpoint two story threads—the trip north of blues-singer Bessie Smith and the Nurse's sadistic control of a southern hospital. However, the Nurse story overshadows that of Bessie Smith, who is known only through the dialogue of her chauffeur-companion, Jack. As in some Brecht plays, the sympathetic Negroes have names—Jack, Bernie, Bessie Smith—whereas the white world is typecast—Nurse, Father, Intern, light-skinned Orderly, Second Nurse. The Nurse is the only coherent character in the play, and she coheres through her verbalization of scorn and conformity. (p. 15)

In the two longest of the eight scenes (sixth and last) the cynical, reactionary Nurse and her liberal Intern suitor engage in a thrust-and-parry dialogue. At his rare dialectical best, the Intern is able to be as cruel as the Nurse. Though ideologically opposed to her, he desires her—a desire inflamed by her taunts. When his sneer about her chastity evokes her threat to "fix" him, he stares at her admiringly: "You impress me. No matter what else, I've got to admit that." But she also arouses his sadism: "I just had a lovely thought . . . that maybe sometime when you are sitting there at your desk opening mail with that stiletto you use for a letter opener, you might slip and tear open your arm . . . then you could come running into the emergency . . . and I could be there when you came running in, blood coming out of you like water out of a faucet . . . and I could take ahold of your arm . . . and just hold it . . . just hold it . . . and watch it flow . . . just hold on to you and watch your blood flow. . . ."

The death of Bessie Smith occurs between the last two scenes of the play. In the brief seventh scene the Second Nurse refuses hospital admission to Bessie Smith, injured in the automobile accident: "I DON'T CARE WHO YOU GOT OUT THERE, NIGGER. YOU COOL YOUR HEELS!" Similarly, when Jack brings Bessie Smith to the central hospital in the last scene, the First Nurse refuses admission to the singer. (pp. 16-17)

In *The Death of Bessie Smith* nurses do not tend the sick; they sit at hospital admissions desks, refusing care to the injured. The First Nurse says she is sick of things, and Albee implies that Bessie Smith dies of such sickness. The Nurse speaks of her letter opener in the Intern's ribs, of a noose around his neck, but it is Bessie

Smith who dies violently. The Nurse likes Negro blues, but she will not lift a finger to save a Negro blues singer; rather she mocks dead Bessie Smith, singing until the Intern slaps her. Albee indicts the whole South for the murder of Bessie Smith . . . nevertheless, the singer's story remains fragmentary, and we are left with a more vivid impression of the verbal duel of Nurse and Intern—gratuitous skirmishing in this loosely constructed, morally earnest play.

The Intern exhibits more spirit than Peter in *The Zoo Story* or Daddy in *The American Dream.* In his thrust-and-parry exchange with the Nurse we can almost hear George and Martha of *Who's Afraid of Virginia Woolf ?* In that play, as in Albee's shorter plays, murderous dialogue leads obliquely to murder. As the shadow of death lay over the sun-drenched afternoon of *The Zoo Story,* death lies like a sediment in Martha's gin, Nick's bourbon, Honey's brandy, and mainly George's "bergin." Though George claims that "musical beds is the faculty sport" in New Carthage, the sport that commands our attention is verbal fencing in the most adroit dialogue ever heard on the American stage.

Popular taste has often cloaked unpopular themes, and Albee has used the popular taste for punch lines to expose an anatomy of love. Although there are four characters, the play's three acts focus on the relationship of George and Martha, who express their love in a lyricism of witty malice. Act I, "Fun and Games," rises toward a dissonant duet: Martha chants about George's failures as he tries to drown her voice in the party refrain, "Who's afraid of Virginia Woolf ?" Toward the end of the Act III "exorcism" George and Martha reach "a hint of communion." Two of the three acts thus close on views of the togetherness of George and Martha, and during the three acts each is visibly tormented by the extended absence of the other. However malicious they sound, they *need* one another—a need that may be called love.

George and Martha have cemented their marriage with the fiction of their child. Outwardly conformist, they privately nourish their love upon this lie. Yet George's play-long preoccupation with death hints that such lies must be killed before they kill. George and Martha's distinctive love-duet is played against a background of death. In Act I George tells Martha "murderously" how much he is looking forward to their guests. Once Nick and Honey are on the scene, George shoots Martha with a toy gun, and then remarks that he might really kill her some day. In Act II Nick and George exchange unprovoked confessions; Nick reveals intimacies about his wife and her father, but George's anecdotes play upon death. He tells of a fifteen-year-old boy who accidentally shot his mother; then, when the boy was being taught to drive by his father, he swerved to avoid a porcupine; he crashed into a tree and killed his father. Later in Act II Martha summarizes George's novel about a boy who accidentally kills both his parents. Martha's father had forbidden George to publish the novel, and George had protested, "No, Sir, this isn't a novel at all . . . this is the truth . . . this really happened . . . TO ME!" George reacts to Martha's narration with a threat to kill her, and he grabs her by the throat. Athletic Nick, who resembles the American Dream both in physique and in lack of feeling, tears George from Martha, and she accuses her husband softly, "Murderer. Mur . . . der . . . er." But George's murder is only a theatrical performance.

While Nick and Martha disappear upstairs, drunken Honey voices her fear of having children, and George needles her: "How you do it? Hunh? How do you make your secret little murders stud-boy doesn't know about, hunh?" With Honey's unknowing help, George proceeds to plan the "secret little murder" of his child of fantasy. George and Martha declare "total war," and George vows "to play this one to the death." But death takes only their fantasy son, who, by George's account, swerves his car to avoid a porcupine, and crashes into a tree. George's imaginary child and his perhaps imaginary father—both absent from the stage—die in precisely the same way. (pp. 17-19)

The sado-masochistic marriage of George and Martha is sustained through their verbal dexterity and their imaginary child. Far from a *deus ex machina*, the child is mentioned before the arrival of Nick and Honey; George warns Martha not to "start in on the bit about the kid." By that time they have been sparring in their recurrent pattern, Martha cutting George with his lack of professional success and George striking at Martha's age, drinking, and promiscuity. (p. 20)

In the destruction of illusion, which may lead to truth, "snap" becomes a stage metaphor—sound, word, and gesture. Martha snaps her fingers at George and plays variations on the theme of snapping; she rhymes snap with crap, then uses snap as a synonym for the cipher she claims George has become. In Act III when George announces the death of their son, he pays her in kind. Entering from the garden with a bunch of snapdragons, George begins the game he calls "Bringing Up Baby": "Flores; flores para los muertos. Flores." Soon he throws snapdragons—*his* flowers for the dead—at Martha, one at a time, stem first, spear-like, phallic, as he echoes her "snaps" at him. St. George slew the dragon; Albee's George slays with snapdragons. (p. 21)

After the departure of Nick and Honey, the dialogue narrows down to monosyllables until George hums the title refrain, and Martha admits that *she* is afraid of Virginia Woolf—a woman afflicted with a madness that drove her to suicide.

Martha's fear is understandable. Whatever will

they do, now that their bean bag is dead, their illusion exorcized? Since Albee once planned to give the Act III title, "The Exorcism," to the entire play, we know the importance he attaches to it. To exorcize is to drive out evil spirits, and in New Carthage the evil spirits are the illusion of progeny—Honey's "hot air" pregnancy and Martha's imaginary son. These are comparable illusions, but they differ in causes and effects. Honey seems to have forced Nick into a marriage which "cured" her of the illusion of pregnancy. During marriage her "delicacy" is the apparent reason that they have no children. Without truth or illusion, they live in a vacuum of surface amenities, a mishmash of syrupy Honey and trivial Nicks. But when Martha indulges in an idealized biography of her son (before George kills him), Honey announces abruptly, "I want a child." She repeats this wish just before Martha shifts from the son as ideal biography to the son as weapon against George. Though Honey's conversion is sudden (and scarcely credible), it seems to be sustained.

For George and Martha, the exorcism is less certain, less complete, and infinitely more involving. The marriage of Nick and Honey kills their illusion, but the illusion of George and Martha is born in wedlock, perhaps because they could have no real children, and Martha "had wanted a child." Martha's recitation indicates that the conception of the child—intellectual rather than biological—may have originated as a game, but the lying game expressed their need. Since we never see George and Martha alone at their game—as we see Genet's Maids—we do not know whether it is played soft or hard, though it probably varies between Martha's penchant for sentimentality and George's probing thrusts. Until this *Walpurgisnacht* when magic runs rampant, the couple seems to have kept private both tender and taunting use of the son, even though Keeping-It-Private may be another game.

Uninteresting in themselves, Nick and Honey function as foils and parallels of George and Martha: the syllabic similarity of the names, the parallel fantasies of the women, the opposing professions of the men, and the cross-couples advancing the plot. Without Nick, Martha's adultery would not have driven George to murder their son; without Honey, George could not have accomplished the murder. Albee's insistence upon Truth versus Illusion emphasizes that George kills Illusion, but it is problematical whether Truth will succeed, and Albee deliberately leaves it problematical, refusing Martha the easy conversion of Honey. Unless the Act III title, "The Exorcism," is ironic, however, George and Martha may rebuild their marriage on the base of Truth, though their gifts seem more destructive than constructive. The lasting impression of the play is not of exorcizing but of exercising the wits of George and Martha.

In *Who's Afraid of Virginia Woolf?* Albee reaches a pinnacle of mastery of American colloquial idiom. Since colloquialism is usually associated with realism, the play has been viewed as realistic psychology. But credible motivation drives psychological drama, and Albee's motivation is designedly flimsy: Why does George stay up to entertain Martha's guests? Why, for that matter, does she invite them? And why do Honey and Nick allow themselves to be "gotten"? The play coheres magnetically only if we accept the *Walpurgisnacht* as a *donnée;* these four people are together to dramatize more than themselves.

Tiny Alice . . . interweaves human and divine love (and hatred) so that the strands are virtually inseparable. In an interview Albee claimed that *Tiny Alice* is a mystery play in two senses of the word: "That is, it's both a metaphysical mystery and, at the same time, a conventional 'Dial M for Murder'-type mystery." But the one murder in *Tiny Alice*—the Lawyer's shooting of Julian—takes place before our eyes, bereft of detective-story mystery. Instead, the mystery of what is happening onstage dissolves into the larger mystery of what happens in the realm of ultimate reality. Governing both is a conception of mystery as that which is hidden from human understanding. (pp. 22-6)

Common to . . . analogues [Duerrenmatt's *The Visit of the Old Lady,* Strindberg's *A Dream Play,* and T. S. Eliot's *The Cocktail Party*] of *Tiny Alice* is a questioning protagonist who is traumatically shocked into a deeper perception of reality. This dramatic movement was already present in *The Zoo Story* and *Who's Afraid of Virginia Woolf?* Rather than a potpourri, then, Albee's *Tiny Alice* reflects his own search for kindred spirits. Like T. S. Eliot's Webster, moreover, all these authors are "much possessed by death / And [see] the skull beneath the skin."

Albee's questing protagonist is Brother Julian, who claims to be "dedicated to the reality of things, rather than the appearance," but who has to be violently shocked—mortally wounded—before he recognizes reality, and even then he tries to rearrange it into familiar appearance. Using the disjunctive technique of Absurdism and the terminology of Christianity, Albee drapes a veil of unknowing over a mystery of wide relevance. Thus, the play is nowhere in place and time, though the flavor is vaguely contemporary and American. The three stage settings are fantastic, and Miss Alice's millions are counted in no currency. Time moves with the imprecision of a dream, and yet it is, as the Lawyer claims, "the great revealer." Except for pointed references to Julian's "six blank years," Albee obscures the *passing* of time; the Lawyer says that Miss Alice's grant is a hundred million a year for twenty years, and after Julian is shot, the Lawyer offers the Cardinal "two billion, kid, twenty years of grace for no work at all." The play may thus have lasted twenty years between the twelve "tick's" in the Lawyer's

opening gibberish and Julian's dying question, "IS IT NIGHT . . . OR DAY? . . . Or does it matter?"

Of the five characters, two have names, two are named by their function, and one—Butler—bears the name of his function. Albee has denied the suggestion that Alice stands for Truth and Julian for Apostasy, but he cannot expunge such associations for us. Named or unnamed, however, all characters are locked into their functions: Brother Julian into service to his God, the Cardinal into service to his church, and the castle trio into service to their deity, knowable only as the mouse in the model. Servants of Tiny Alice, they appear to master the rest of the world. Like the trio in Sartre's *No Exit,* they are bound in an eternal love-hate triangle, but *their* mission is to deliver victims to Tiny Alice, at once a reduced truth and a small obscene aperture into an aspect of being. (Tiny Alice is homosexual slang for a tight anus.)

Julian, a lay brother, is Albee's Christian hero in this modern mystery play. John Gielgud, creator of the role, commented, "The wonderful relief that I had about this part was that I was *supposed* to keep wondering what it was all about." So pervasive is Julian's bewilderment that some critics have suggested the entire play takes place in Julian's mind. But Albee is working on a larger stage. As in medieval mystery plays, we are involved in the conflict within a tempted soul, but we are aware too of our world in which that conflict resonates. Rather than Virtue versus Vice, Albee's Julian is torn between Truth and Illusion, between a desire for the real and his irrepressible imagination. (pp. 27-9)

As in earlier Albee plays, thrust-and-parry dialogue leads obliquely to murder. The master verbal fencer of *Tiny Alice,* the Lawyer, shoots Julian, but Miss Alice is the principal agent of his undoing, and she, as the Lawyer remarks, was "never one with words." Rather, she acts through surprises: the old hag turns into a lovely woman; unprompted, she confesses to Julian her carnal relations with the Butler and the Lawyer; abruptly, she inquires into Julian's sex life; before marrying and abandoning Julian, she alternates a mysterious prayer with an address to "someone in the model." She cradles the wounded Julian, making "something of a Pietà." At the end she is cruel and kind; her last words are "Oh, my poor Julian"; yet she leaves him.

Miss Alice's seduction of Julian is accomplished through deeds rather than words, but Julian himself translates the erotic into a highly verbal mysticism. He defends his loquacity to Miss Alice, "Articulate men often carry set paragraphs." In each of the play's three acts Julian indulges in a rhapsodic monologue that does not sound like a set paragraph, since the rhythms are jagged. The cumulative effect is apocalyptic, but Julian's apocalypse is sexually rooted, *lay* brother that he is (Albee's pun). In Act I Julian describes a perhaps hallucinatory sexual experience with a woman who occasionally hallucinated as the Blessed Virgin. Not only does Julian speak of ejaculation; he speaks *in* ejaculations. Julian's mistress with an illusory pregnancy recalls the illusion-ridden women of *Virginia Woolf;* as the imaginary child of that play is an evil spirit to be exorcised, the imaginary pregnancy of the hallucinating woman of *Tiny Alice* proves to be a fatal cancer. And even as Julian confesses to Miss Alice what he believes to be his struggle for the real, she tempts him with her own desirability—very beautiful and very rich.

In Julian's Act II monologue about martyrdom he shifts his identity—a child, both lion and gladiator, then saint and the hallucinating self of the Act I monologue. While Julian describes this eroto-mystical, multi-personal martyrdom, Miss Alice shifts her attitude, first urging Julian to marry her, then spurring him to sacrifice himself to Alice, whom she invokes in the third person.

In Act III Julian, who left the asylum because he was persuaded that hallucination was inevitable and even desirable, embarks on his final hallucination which ends in his real death. Abandoned and dying, Julian recollects (or imagines) a wound of his childhood, as Miss Alice in her prayer recollected (or imagined) being hurt in *her* childhood. Alternately a child and the hallucinating woman who called for help, Julian is forced to face himself in death—the prototypical existential confrontation. (pp. 30-1)

Even puzzled audiences have been involved in Julian's plight, which the Butler describes: "Is walking on the edge of an abyss, but is balancing." Albee's next play, *A Delicate Balance,* is named for that perilous equilibrium. Like *Virginia Woolf,* the play presents a realistic surface; as in *Virginia Woolf,* a love relationship in one couple is explored through the impact of another couple. There is enough talking and drinking to convey the impression of a muted, diluted *Virginia Woolf.* And yet *A Delicate Balance,* like *Tiny Alice,* is death-obsessed symbolism.

Each of the six characters of *A Delicate Balance* "is walking on the edge of an abyss, but is balancing"; a middle-aged marriage is balancing too, until a make-shift home in a "well-appointed suburban house" is threatened by both family and friends. In Friday night Act I, terror-driven friends seek refuge in the family home; in Saturday night Act II, the master of the house, Tobias, assures his friends of their welcome, but his daughter Julia reacts hysterically to their presence. In Sunday morning Act III, the friends know that they are not welcome, know that they would not have welcomed, and they leave. The delicate balance of the home is preserved.

The play begins and ends, however, on a different

delicate balance—that of the mind of Agnes, mistress of the house, wife of Tobias, mother of Julia, sister of Claire. In convoluted Jamesian sentences she opens and closes the play with doubts about her sanity; at the beginning she also extends these doubts to an indefinite "you"—"that each of you wonders if each of *you* might not . . ." As we meet the other members of the family, we can understand the wonder: Claire the chronic drunk, Julia the chronic divorcée, and Tobias who heads the house. Though Agnes starts and finishes the play on her doubts about sanity, each of the acts dramatizes the precarious stability of the other members of the family: first Claire, then Julia, and finally Tobias. In each case the balance is preserved, a little more delicate perhaps for being threatened.

Each member of the family contributes to the atmosphere of emptiness, but no one exists in a vacuum; they are bound by love. In Claire's words to Tobias, "You love Agnes and Agnes loves Julia and Julia loves me and I love you . . . Yes, to the depths of our self-pity and our greed. What else but love?" Claire's definition may be brushed by modern psychology, but Albee's plays are never reducible to psychology. If Agnes is responsible for Claire's continuous drinking and Julia's four marriages, she is also concerned "to keep in shape." Blaming the others for their faults, she describes such blame as the "souring side of love" in this drama about the limits of love. (pp. 36-8)

As in other Albee plays, death lurks in the dialogue of *A Delicate Balance,* but death is not actualized in this drama; violence is confined to a single slap, a glass of orange juice poured on the rug, and an ineffectual threat with a gun. In words, however, Claire urges Tobias to shoot them all, first Agnes, then Julia, and herself last. Agnes suggests that Claire kill herself, and Claire in turn asks Agnes, "Why don't you die?" It is this sisterly exchange between Claire and Agnes that inspires Tobias to his digressive monologue, his cat story. Because his cat inexplicably stopped liking him, Tobias first slapped her and then had her killed. Out of the depths of his self-pity and greed, he had her killed.

A Delicate Balance is itself in most delicate balance between the cruel kindness of its surface and dark depths below, between a dead child and a new dawn, between ways of living and ways of loving. Albee has posed his equilibrium discreetly, without the symbolic histrionics of *Tiny Alice,* without the coruscating dialogue of *Virginia Woolf.*

Happy endings are not for Albee; nor does he strain, like Eugene O'Neill and Arthur Miller, for tragedy. Rather, Albee shares with Absurdist writers, in his words, "an absorption-in-art of certain existentialist and post-existentialist philosophical concepts having to do, in the main, with man's attempts to make sense for himself out of his senseless position in a world which makes no sense—which makes no sense because

George (Richard Burton) and Martha (Elizabeth Taylor) in the 1966 screen version of *Who's Afraid of Virginia Woolf?*

the moral, religious, political and social structures man has erected to 'illusion' himself have collapsed." In successive plays Albee has dramatized man's several attempts to make sense *of* himself and *for* himself.

Albee has been moving away from political and social structures toward moral and religious illusion. Thus, the greedy, conformist American family of *The American Dream* differs markedly from the greedy, love-bound family of *A Delicate Balance,* as apocalyptic Jerry of *The Zoo Story* differs markedly from apocalyptic Julian of *Tiny Alice.* Common to several of Albee's plays is the existentialist view of an Outsider who suffers at the hands of the Establishment—social, moral, or religious—which announces itself in "peachy-keen" clichés that indict those who mouth them—Peter, Mommy, the Nurse, Nick. Albee has moved from this American anti-American idiom into the metaphysical suggestiveness of *Tiny Alice* and *A Delicate Balance,* and his language accommodates both colloquialism and convolution, both excruciating specificity and horrifying generality.

The shadow of death darkens all Albee's plays,

growing into the night of *Tiny Alice* and *A Delicate Balance.* Man's mortality is the subject of both plays, and the drama arises from man's terror. Transitional, *Virginia Woolf* touches on the fear in human love without illusion. *Tiny Alice* probes the heroism of human illusion about the divine. *A Delicate Balance* returns to a shrunken earth; the house appointed for all living is shaken by the living dead, but accident and brinkmanship salvage the equilibrium.

Like the Absurdists whom he defends, Albee is anguished because men die and they cannot make themselves happy with illusion. He absorbs this condition into art by counterpointing interrogation and repetition, familiar phrase and diversified resonance, repartee and monologue, minute gesture and cosmic sweep, comic wit and a sense of tragedy. The Albeegory is that distinctive allegorical drama in which ideas are so skillfully blended into people that we do not know how to divorce them or how to care about one without the other. (pp. 39-44)

Ruby Cohn, in her *Edward Albee,* University of Minnesota Press, Minneapolis, 1969, 48 p.

C. W. E. BIGSBY

(essay date 1975)

[A Scottish critic and educator, Bigsby has written extensively about twentieth-century American drama. In the following excerpt, he evaluates Albee's career.]

Few playwrights can have been so frequently and mischievously misunderstood, misrepresented, overpraised, denigrated, and precipitately dismissed [as Edward Albee]. Canonized after the performance of his first play, *The Zoo Story* [produced Off-Broadway], he found himself in swift succession billed as America's most promising playwright, leading dramatist, and then, with astonishing suddenness, a "one-hit" writer with nothing to his credit but an ersatz masterpiece patched together from the achievements of other writers. The progression was essentially that suggested by George in *Who's Afraid of Virginia Woolf?*, "better, best, bested." (p. 1)

To read the bulk of criticism that Albee's work has inspired is to discover the depths to which abstruse pedantry and the Ph.D. industry can go. And, worse still, a number of sizable red-herrings have been dragged across the path of audience and reader alike by those who wish to see his work as an expression of a particular dramatic movement or pathological condition. (p. 2)

There is no doubt that the Broadway production of *Who's Afraid of Virginia Woolf?* provided the basis for Albee's amazing popular reputation; less obviously, but equally certainly, it was also the primary reason for the suspicion with which some reviewers and critics approached his work. For there was a sense in which the move to Broadway seemed a betrayal of the nascent values of Off-Broadway—a confession that he was a mere entertainer with a talent for simulating seriousness. . . . Yet *Who's Afraid of Virginia Woolf?* is by no means conventional Broadway fare. The single claustrophobic set, the excoriating language, the disconcerting emotional and theatrical power, were remote from the usually bland products of the Great White Way. And Albee's decision to use some of the profits from the production to encourage new American dramatists merely underlined his continuing concern with experiment.

The success of *Who's Afraid of Virginia Woolf?* established Albee's reputation around the world, and the curious assaults on the play as epitomizing some presumed decadence either in the state of the American theatre or in his personal sensibility only served to promote considerable interest in him by the media. He became a public figure, . . . in other words, the Famous American Playwright, whom he had satirized in an early sketch. And now, public and reviewers alike expected him to repeat his early success. His failure to do so lead to a curious sense of betrayal in the minds of some people, as the man singled out to take on the burden formerly carried by O'Neill, Miller, and Williams began an apparently eccentric series of experiments which seemed ill-adapted to one now widely regarded as a Broadway writer. The truth was that Albee has remained at heart a product of Off-Broadway, claiming the same freedom to experiment and, indeed, fail, which is the special strength of that theatre. The difficulty is that he continues to offer his plays to a Broadway audience who, even given their tolerance for anything which can be officially ratified as "art," find his refusal to repeat the formula of *Who's Afraid of Virginia Woolf?* increasingly perverse. The animus directed at Albee in recent years thus comes, at least in part, from his failure to realize expectations formed by his first Broadway success as well as, partly, from genuine failures of craft and slackness of artistic control.

What he in fact chose to do was to alternate new works of his own with adaptations of the work of Carson McCullers, James Purdy, and Giles Cooper respectively. But while the choice of these particular works (*The Ballad of the Sad Café, Malcolm, Everything in the Garden*) was entirely explicable in terms of his own thematic concerns, the decision to lend his talents to such a project was not. He had early voiced a suspicion of the whole process of adaptation which has, unfortunately, proved more than justified by his own efforts in that direction. (pp. 4-6)

His original plays tell a different story. Though all of them are, I think, flawed in some important respect, they offer clear evidence of Albee's commitment to extending his range as a writer. They stand as proof of his fascination with the nature of theatricality and of his determination to trace those social and psychological concerns which have provided the focus for so much American drama to their root in metaphysical anguish. . . . If he is to be regarded as a social critic, as a number of writers have suggested, then he is what he himself has described as "a demonic social critic," intent on establishing the connection between a collapse of social structure and the failure of nerve on an individual level. And though his work has revealed a considerable stylistic diversity, it is legitimate to talk of his central concerns in this way, for thematically there is a unity to his work which links his first Off-Broadway play to his latest Broadway offering.

His heroes have all failed in some fundamental way. They have betrayed the values to which, even now, they are capable of pledging a belated allegiance.

They are liberal humanists who have allowed themselves to become detached from a reality which disturbs them and hence from those individuals who are the expression of their commitment to a vision of private and public responsibility. They have sold out; not for wealth or success, but for an untroubled existence—to preserve their own innocence. Unwilling to recognize that pain is a natural corollary of a free existence, they have blunted their moral convictions with alcohol and a sterile intellectualism, as George has done in *Who's Afraid of Virginia Woolf?*; or they have embraced the spurious consolation offered by religious determinism, as Julian has done in *Tiny Alice*; or they have simply permitted the slow disintegration of human responsibilities, as Tobias has done in *A Delicate Balance.* The consequence of such a drift toward moral extinction is clear enough in the apocalyptic imagery of *Who's Afraid of Virginia Woolf?*, *Box, Quotations from Chairman Mao Tse-Tung,* and *All Over.* The action of the first of these takes place in a town which is pointedly called New Carthage and which is likened to two other cities destroyed by their hedonism and capitalist frenzy, Penguin Island and Gomorrah. The action of the last is concerned with the final collapse of structure in the moment of death.

Albee's work is characterized by an overwhelming sense of loss which, though doubtless rooted in the details of his own painful childhood, becomes an image, firstly, of the loss by America of the principles which had been invoked by its founders, and, secondly, of the inevitable process of deprivation which is the basis of individual existence. The problem which he sets himself is that of formulating a response to this sense of loss which involves neither a self-pitying despair nor capitulation to those facile illusions endorsed by Madison Avenue, the Church, or simply the conventional wisdom of contemporary society. The solution which he advances is essentially a New Testament compassion, a liberal commitment to the Other. That is to say, he attacks a social system which fails in its primary duty of creating a communal responsibility and presents characters who must strip themselves of all pretense if they are to survive as autonomous individuals and accept their responsibility toward other people.

Albee's work is a prophecy and a warning. Nor should the splendid articulateness of the dialogue or the brilliant wit, which is a mark of so many of his plays, be seen as detracting from the seriousness of his diagnosis. For they are themselves a part of the evidence—the means deployed by a sophisticated society to evade the pain of real communication and the menace of a world slipping towards dissolution. (pp. 6-8)

Albee has brought to the theatre not merely a magnificent command of language, a control of rhythm and tone which has never been rivaled in America, but also a sensitivity to dramatic tradition and particularly to the achievements of European dramatists, which gives his work a dimension all too often lacking in American writers. . . . [Though] one can indeed detect in his work elements of Ionesco's style, Strindberg's obsessive misogyny, Eliot's suburban metaphysics, and Miller's liberal *angst,* this is to say no more than that Albee has shown an awareness of the achievement of other writers and a commitment to examining the nature of theatrical experiment. It is surely as much a mistake to regard *Who's Afraid of Virginia Woolf?* as simply a modern version of Strindberg's *A Dance of Death* as it is to see *Tiny Alice* as only a transcribed version of *The Cocktail Party.* The Influence is there; the voice is Albee's. The gulf between eclecticism and impersonation is the gulf between honesty and fraud, a receptive imagination and an impoverished sensibility. The Byzantine complexity of *Tiny Alice,* the fascinating blend of strict structure and free form in *Quotations from Chairman Mao Tse-Tung,* and even the misguided attempt to adapt the "surreal" imagination of James Purdy all provide evidence of his refusal to limit his talent or to accept conventional notions of theatrical propriety. If Albee is not what he seemed when he first burst upon the scene at the beginning of the sixties, if he was never the absurdist he was taken to be nor the man summoned to redeem Broadway, he was in some ways much more. He was a serious artist with the courage to refuse the blandishments of the commercial theatre. He was a writer who offered genuine gifts, including a mastery of words, a musician's sense of rhythmic structure, an undeniable ability to create dramatic metaphors of compelling power, and, most important of all, a stunning integrity which permits no compromise with his artistic objectives. If this latter has at times led him into misjudgments on a considerable scale, it is also the guarantee that Albee will remain, not merely a dramatist of international reputation, but also, and in ways which early reviewers could not really appreciate, one of the mainstays of American drama over the next decade. (pp. 8-9)

C. W. E. Bigsby, in an introduction to *Edward Albee: A Collection of Critical Essays,* edited by C. W. E. Bigsby, Prentice-Hall, Inc., 1975, pp. 1-9.

GARETH LLOYD EVANS
(essay date 1977)

[A Welsh educator and author, Evans was an authority on English drama. In the following excerpt, he analyzes Albee's use of language in order to determine the influences on his work.]

[The] most brilliantly effective user of the American

language in drama is Edward Albee. He has achieved as much fame in England as have Miller and Williams. In his case there might seem to be a special relationship with European drama for he has frequently been dubbed an 'absurd' dramatist. The claim of his alleged affiliation to this essentially European cult was based largely on the play *The Zoo Story.* On the evidence, however, of a more substantial and longer work—*Who's Afraid of Virginia Woolf?*—the claim seems to have an uncertain validity.

Absurdism, in so far as it relates to drama, has two main aspects—the point of view expressed in and by the play, and the method and means of expression. (p. 196)

The language of an 'absurd' play is just as distinctive as the vision which one senses or observes in it. Indeed what marks off Pinter, Ionesco, Beckett, in particular, from their non-absurdist colleagues is the amount of attention the language they use demands (because of its uniqueness) from the playgoer and the critic. To a very high degree, the language is the focus of the vision. To try and separate meaning and speech in an absurd play is to enter far into misrepresentation or into bafflement. In absurd drama language is used poetically, in the sense that however much it may seem to be a naturalistic version of real speech, closer examination shows that it is using the resources of poetry, to a degree. (p. 197)

An absurd play is . . . an image of human existence. It uses the sense-data provided by the so-called everyday world . . . but, in the long run, the spatial boundaries of an absurd play are not to be found in 'real' life, but in an inexplicable universe and a relentless eternity.

Edward Albee, in *The Zoo Story,* seems to partake of some of the characteristics of absurdism. The language is apparently inconsequential at times; the relationships are unsure or inexplicable; motivations both for speech and action seem governed less by rational processes than by a meaningless spontaneous reflex, the 'meaning' is elusive and, like so many absurd plays, there is 'no beginning, no middle, no end'.

This seems a formidable collection of evidence, but it may be suggested that, qualitatively, it is spurious. Almost every item seems too mechanically arrived at, contrived by a 'clever' writer. All the figures are correct, but the answer is not the right one. There are two main reasons for placing doubt on the claim for Albee's absurdism.

The first is the absence of the characteristic absurdist vision. This is absent from all of his plays, including the chief candidate for acceptance—*The Zoo Story.* In that play the frenzy, the change of mood, the menace, seem to be less an attribute of character than an exercise of quixotic theatricality. Apart from this,

we find ourselves eventually wondering whether this sort of episode happens often in Central Park—in other words the play is less an image than a brilliant piece of quasi-naturalistic guignol.

The second arises from the degree of 'naturalism' which is present in Albee's plays and which, finally, separates him from the absurdists. Both the degree and its extent is rooted in Albee's sensitive, almost nervy feeling for contemporary American society. He is a superb demonstrator and explicator of certain aspects of Americanism. In order to align him with Pinter we would have to say that in Pinter we find the best mirror of certain aspects of British society today—and nothing else.

It is Albee's commitment to a surgical analysis of certain aspects of American society which debars him from acceptance as a complete and pure absurd dramatist. It is easy to see why he has been associated with these dramatists, because some details of attitude which he takes up towards his society are reminiscent of the typical absurdist vision. *The American Dream, Who's Afraid of Virginia Woolf?, The Zoo Story,* in particular, exhibit the meaninglessness of certain habits of behaviour, speech, *mores,* cults, myths. Again, all three plays, to a degree, brilliantly dissect certain sterile usages of speech. *The Zoo Story,* especially, is redolent of Pinter's concern with human isolation and the dark wastes of non or partial communication. It might be said that Albee's apparent preoccupation with an inability to beget children (in *The American Dream* and *Virginia Woolf*) as an image of sterile futility is, in itself, an 'absurdist' point of view.

But, in all this, there is not the characteristically absurdist miasma of menace, sometimes terror, the sense of unfathomable contexts behind the immediate world of the play, the implacable atmosphere of amorality, the curiously paradoxical use of language in a 'poetic' fashion to demonstrate, often, the futility of language itself. Indeed it is in the use of language that we can find the distance from European absurdism and the closeness to Americanism. In Albee, too, is perhaps the clearest proof, if not the deepest, that the American language is not the same thing as the English language.

He is amazingly versatile in his deployment of language forms and styles, but there are two broad areas in which he excels—they occupy . . . extreme positions from one another. The one may be called literary/dramatic—an eloquent, rhetorical, philosophically inclined mode, the other is demotic/dramatic—in which the usages of contemporary American speech are employed with exciting variety and effect. In *The Zoo Story* he uses both types, in *Who's Afraid of Virginia Woolf?* he concentrates, though not exclusively, on the second, *A Delicate Balance* is almost monopolized by the first. His handling of the demotic/dramatic is much surer, and the results are decidedly more dramatically and theatrically credible than his attempts in the other mode. There, echoes of Eliot, traces even of Charles Morgan and a ghostly assembling of literary forefathers petrify the drama. . . . (pp. 197-99)

Albee is revealed as a dramatist of stature in his use of his 'alternative' language. He owes something to Miller in his deployment of certain characteristics of American speech but, in the long run, his is a more precise and searching mode. The most obvious affinity to Miller is in the use of repetition, but the effect is different. With Miller we feel that repetition is used in order to heighten the effect of the language—to take it one degree over naturalistic statement. With Albee we are aware that the repetitions fit more closely into the matrix of characterization; indeed they are often used, as in *Virginia Woolf,* self-consciously by characters with that kind of brittle, conscious verbosity apparent when the scotch-on-the-rocks set has reached the cocktail hour and its tongue is becoming loose. (p. 200)

One of the most conspicuous characteristics of absurdist writing is the extent to which dialogue—often using repetition—mirrors emptiness and futility. That emptiness separates and isolates the participants

Still photograph from a production of *Quotations from Chairman Mao Tse-Tung.*

in the dialogue as certainly as a thousand miles of ocean. . . . The emptiness is, largely, imposed upon the participants, first and foremost by the nature of existence, but also by the particular situation and by their respective personalities. The crucial factor, however, is the first one—the strong sense of a blank force beyond control.

Albee very rarely gives this impression. The gaps and emptiness that fall between his characters when they speak habitually convey the impression that they could be filled but, more often, they are filled almost as soon as we are aware of them—not by words, but often as efficaciously in the circumstances. Albee, unlike the absurdists, is less dominated by 'mal d'existence' than beguiled by 'mal de psychologie'. His silences and gaps are filled very quickly by material which comes straight out of the personality of the participants, goaded by the situation or event. (pp. 200-01)

Albee's métier as a dramatist of society and man's self-created tensions within it, and his versatility with words are shown, too, in his remarkable manipulation of the language of situation. Again, he uses repetition, but with a very much greater sense of using a technique; at times he reminds one of the Restoration penchant for drawing attention to the very fabric of language and to the cleverness with which it is spun. *Virginia Woolf,* again, provides the best evidence. (p. 202)

Albee, generally, seems to be very much more deliberately conscious of the technicalities of using words and takes more delight in employing them for dramatic and theatrical effect than other twentieth-century American dramatists. He seems to have a fastidiousness in his make-up which impels him to look at and to listen to the way his countrymen speak with a rare attention to detail. . . .

In his deployment of American speech Albee, especially in *The Zoo Story* and *Virginia Woolf,* shows that same compulsion towards the rhetorical . . . [noticeable] in Miller and Williams and which seems to be a characteristically American predisposition. Albee seems more aware than his colleagues of its dangers—of sentimentality and sententiousness—and he attempts to disguise these in different ways. In *A Delicate Balance* where he uses a sophisticated language which has the flavour of the more cerebral long speeches in *A Family Reunion,* he tries to moderate the effects by the occasional use of an idiomatic phrase. (p. 203)

Albee, like Miller and Williams, is at his best when he is not attempting to create a 'literary' language. The American penchant for over-dramatization, over-explicit statement, sentimentality of expression, overcomes them all when they try to invent a poetry of language. All three, but particularly Albee, succeed when they exploit the resources of American spoken speech, not when they try to make one up. This can be put in another way. When American dramatists, either consciously or unconsciously, try to achieve an English classicism they fail. When they write out of the dialect or dialects of their own American tribe, they succeed. (p. 204)

Gareth Lloyd Evans, "American Connection—O'Neill, Miller, Williams and Albee," in his *The Language of Modern Drama,* J. M. Dent & Sons Ltd., 1977, pp. 177-204.

LILIANE KERJAN
(essay date 1989)

[In the following excerpt, Kerjan observes the evolution of theme in Albee's later works.]

[The] sad smiles of a man, the curt sneers of a woman and the withdrawal of a child in *Listening,* the pains of reminiscence and acceptance in *Counting the Ways,* the fragility of protocol and the relativity of all values in *The Lady from Dubuque* may sound like a familiar story.

However, if the themes and the situations are not unheard of, the recent works [of Edward Albee] offer other compensations: songs simplified, new arrangements, operatic duets, a *capella* melodies; like Capote's chameleons, Albee's wolves are music lovers. George once explained that "Martha's tastes in liquor have come down, simplified over the years . . . crystallised." And for the sheer pleasure of cocktail-drinkers and metaphor-lovers, George adds:

> You would not believe it! We'd go into a bar . . .
> you know a whisky, beer and bourbon bar . . . and
> what she'd do would be, she'd screw up her face,
> think real hard and come up with brandy Alexan-
> ders, crème de cacao frappée, gimlets, flaming punch
> bowls . . . seven layer liqueur things. But the years
> have brought to Martha a sense of the essentials: al-
> cohol, pure and simple.

If the cook in *Listening* only declares that he prepares "food," if the guests in *The Lady from Dubuque* confess they will take "a last little night crap," in *Counting the Ways* we are given more food for our thought, and quite tellingly, in terms of desert. Hungrily. He wonders what happened to the Crème Brûlée. As it is, "there is no Crème Brûlée", she says, for if you "unfocus your eyes . . . and day dream, think . . . your caramel will scorch, or worse: will blacken, become hard, burned and awful!" What else then? Your last order has to be an "Idiot's Delight." Pure and simple.

Albee's three recent plays, two short plays and a full length work, have been more acclaimed by literary critics than by the general public as troubling plays, showing great theatrical skill and commanding attention. *The Lady from Dubuque* (1980), described by Albee as "perfectly straightforward and clear," an indication of his willingness to abandon esoteric theorizing, has been considered by many as a return to the living-room wars or to the home-base of *Who's Afraid of Virginia Woolf?* simply because it deals with fictitious parents and children, choices of different realities, games of love and death. Furthermore, this two-act drama about three interwoven suburban couples suddenly visited by the little old lady from Dubuque and her black male companion is also a return to themes that have preocupied Albee in *Tiny Alice* and *All Over.* But there is more to it: the play concerns a duality of vision illustrated in black and white by the visitors challenging both plausibility and fantasy, it concerns self definition and our commitment to others, order and disorder, gains and losses.

The progress of the work is in itself interesting. For eighteen years, Albee had been regularly announcing the play then called "The Substitute Speaker," while constantly putting it aside to write other plays. If *The Sandbox* momentarily borrowed characters from *The American Dream,* here in a somewhat similar mechanism, Albee wrote *A Delicate Balance, Seascape* and *All Over* on the permanent background of *The Lady from Dubuque* which harbors the main line of each play: invasion, confrontation, death. In its original form, one of the wives died in the first act and her husband dressed up like her, assumed her identity, thus becoming the substitute speaker. One can immediately imagine reactions such as those expressed by the well-known essay "The Play that Dare not Speak its Name;" however, this plot and title were abandoned but substitution remains the central motif. In the final version, the wife is dying at the end of Act II, the crescendos of her pain, like those of Big Daddy in *Cat on a Hot Tin Roof,* marking the rhythm of the play, a play focused on the agony and adjustment of the dying and the living. Over the years, the play has undergone considerable rewriting in Albee's mind; "Originally, it was about how much anguish people will allow us to demonstrate before they destroy us. Now it says our identity is created by other people's needs for our identity to exist. Our existence depends on our usefulness." In actual fact, both ideas are still developed in the play for when Sam, sobbing too loudly, interfering too often, voices his revolt too aggressively, he is put to sleep, tied up and eventually slapped by his companions. More important, though, is the creation of our existence by the precise needs of others, each of us being the receptacle of someone's expectations and ultimately the agent, which here no longer means the dream. (pp. 99-101)

The play is another of those initiations between midnight and dawn, between the comfort of bourbon and the domesticity of breakfast, one of those voyages of transition between life and death since "Samsday precedeth Doomsday." Above all, it is an exploration not so much of saving lies but of adjustment at a decisive point. The choice between black and white and the two act structure establish the worth as a double game between being and nothingness. (p. 102)

As the masculine lead, Sam is given the persuasive, pathetic interrogation "Dear great God, woman, who are you!?", "intense" and "whispered," haunting men in *Tiny Alice* and *Listening,* and Elisabeth the voicing of the final truth: "All the values (are) relative save one . . . Who am I? All the rest is semantics," and the restatement of the dream of the Voice in *Box-Mao-Box* [the interrelated plays *Box* and *Quotations from Chairman Mao*] about the end of the world: on a beach at sunset, by a driftwood fire, with the sea-gulls in the distance and the light of the explosion in a beautiful silence: "No time to be afraid." It is the moment when the dying person lets loose her moorings to drift into another environment, that Albee chooses to privilege; hence two realities in *The Lady from Dubuque:* Sam having lost contact with his beloved Jo remains bereaved in ordinary reality, Jo moving to her own plane into "a better kind of reality to die with," both equally true and artificial.

Another way then for Albee to explore "survival-kits" and existential fears in an articulate opposition, which should reach his public, one of his preoccupations since he is always upset when people resist the emotions of his plays. This might also explain what he considered as a major change in the course of the writing—to have the actors address some of their remarks to the audience as co-conspirators with a double aim, to objectify and to involve. A device basically relevant to the theater he had already used in *The American Dream* and *The Sandbox,* and obliquely referring to the Chinese boxes he particularly enjoys.

She and He will also look at the audience, talk to the audience in *Counting the Ways* (1977), while debating a private dilemma "Do you love me?" as well as public issues: the old questions about civilization and veneer. She and He form a loving couple living in domestic quietness: he reads and smokes his pipe; she reads, cooks and arranges flowers. In a naturalistic costume and make-up they are presented in a clear white light, a minimal set of bare chairs, one table with no sharp angles, no clutter. Pure and simple then.

On a similar topic, the itinerary of love, Shepard and Chaikin wrote *Savage/Love,* [David] Mamet *Sexual Perversity.* With *Counting the Ways,* a vaudeville of 21 scenes interrupted by brief black-outs and an Entre-Scène where the actors identify themselves, Albee composes a delicate piece, for *Counting the Ways* is a book of hours using the basic elements of illumination: the initial, the miniature and the border. As Ruskin af-

firmed in a memorable phrase "Illumination is only writing made beautiful," this is playwriting made beautiful by the elucidation of dainty, subdued emotions born from delight, fear and speculation. For this couple in their fifties, what are the facets of love? Children forgotten, the corruption of love-making, the discovery that generally speaking, in poems and papers, love means sex. Albee will replace his favourite declensions by a progressive diet of abstinence: king-size bed, twin beds, separate rooms—single coffin. But one can joke about it, parodying Auden's line "Thousands have lived without love, but none without water," to make it "Thousands have lived without love but none without Crème Brûlée."

The central metaphor of the vaudeville is sustained by vermilion roses, vermilion being the original colour of miniators. Roses will wilt if left alone, they will be oracles to count the ways of love. In scene 7, the man slowly depetals a flower but after a number of petals, he suddenly pops the remainder of the rose into his mouth and chews it. In scene 9, the woman picks up the petals and relates them one by one to the stem, never reaching a decision. The careful symmetry of diction and design tells more about the couple, their vulnerability, their mutual dependence than any direct conversation. Typical of Albee's style, a variation is introduced: the two extra roses brought to replace the mutilated stem conjure up two attitudes. He just watches them objectively, remembering some poetry and his youth; she suggests putting them in water on a table between their beds. Two faces of reality, two choices—romantic flight or practicality—two illustrations of replacement, of loss and gain. (pp. 102-04)

Listening, set in the semi-circular patio of an overgrown garden opens with a man contemplating an empty fountain-pool and its arresting Italianate marble-head, above, in the center. The circularity and symmetry of the structure, the void, the in/out interplay appear immediately just as the ambivalence of interpretation since the tutelary head of the fountain could be "Monster or God . . . monster probably." Clearly the past and present are to be confronted in this old park reminiscent of Verlaine's poem, and inevitably the past is equated with graceful design, harmony "clipped and trained and planned," with exchange and effusiveness, with vital sources: the fountain-bowl then was full, lovers were making love then, whereas the present is dry and impersonal although there remains some shy expectation in this man waiting for a woman who soon enters with a girl.

Their silhouettes reveal a couple in their fifties and a grown up child, the man good-looking and a bit flamboyant, the woman plain and ample, the girl pretty and fragile in a lovely pastel. In short, the archetype of Albee's couples and families as he indicates the man will be "defensive," "puzzled," "offended," "gentle," the woman "sarcastic," "abrupt" and "cold," the girl close to hysteria or fenced in her quiet intensity. No longer a private home but an institution: he is the cook, she is a nurse, the girl is a patient.

Albee's titles are often catching. On comparable grounds David Storey called his play *Home* and Beckett *Play,* for a work where the response to light is immediate—not the eye with Albee, but the ear. The sound of finger-snaps starts the Girl, the man remembers the sounds of footsteps on the patio and the sudden silence of the grass: the play is called *Listening* all the more so as it was commissioned as radio-play. Starting with the assumption that plays are music for voices (he himself being the Voice in the tape sent from New York to the BBC), Albee considers that many of his works, among them *The Zoo Story, A Delicate Balance,* and *All Over* "would work just as well if they were not staged." Reduced to an outline by the author, Albee said "the play is just another of those things about people's failure to communicate. It's about three people who talk but who don't say anything." Indeed, what matters is not primarily what is said but the testing of the sounds, the sounds of the words and, more provocatively "the sound of an idea" as the Girl puts it. What matters is the balance between emotion and abstraction, the shape of the play with its triangle inside the circle and its curves and rhythms. Twenty sequences punctuated by the Voice, recurrent lines: "You don't listen," "You don't pay attention," with a double receiver, the protagonists and the audience, echoes of meetings, a Roman long-drawn metaphor compose the poem. "My work is a matter of fundamental sounds . . . made as fully as possible and I accept responsibility for nothing else," Beckett once declared. Here the refusal to listen may prove fatal: we are made to believe that the woman can hear the Girl's pupils widen, yet she will not move when the Girl cuts her wrists and dies sitting with her blood all over the bottom of the pool, over the half-blue egg, the mouse-bones and the feather inside the basin.

A story of multiple betrayals, blurred memories and failed possibilities, *Listening* is not the first case of brutal lack of compassion which leads to both physical and spiritual murder of the sensitive and the vulnerable. The temptation to self-pity and confession is cut short, but the man has to express his long frustration: "Reveal yourself " when the woman refuses to admit or renew their past intimacy. It is also not Albee's first exploration of the ambiguous frontier between humanity and animality. The Girl successively plays insect, butterfly and praying mantis, serpent sucking air and venomous adder: "She *is* an animal, isn't she?" asks the man with "admiration" and "tenderness"; she was slowly humanizing to become eventually the best listener and questioner of the trio, before she bleeds to death. *Listening* betrays Albee's obsessions concerning

sexuality, the feminine body, the destructive force of women. The cook, totally baffled, finally appeals to "God or monster," addressing not the marble divinity of the fountain but the woman facing him and rejecting both girl and man. (pp. 104-06)

In these three plays, Albee is concerned with man's attempt to relate himself to the terms of his existence and, as in his previous works, he recognizes the crisis of identity; nowadays he tends to accentuate the central struggle towards acceptance, finally implying the recognition of one's fears and limitations as well as the other's needs and uncertainties. The recent plays therefore rely more and more on compassion, on love and sharing, acceptance of the other ultimately leading to acceptance of one's own self. Flipping the coin of love, Albee is now able to show one positive side and to demonstrate it gently in a subdued voice, unheard of previously. This in turn implies a re-evaluation of love, no longer a deal or a business contract but a maturing process. Starting as in his first play *The Zoo Story* with the individual's attempts to relate to another individual—no animal mentioned here, except briefly some Dubuque dog named Dignity—, the picture broadens and the suffering pilgrim will gradually accept strangers for what they are and the outside world as it is.

No lies, no nonsense. People are facing reality with no mythology, no escapist strategies. The characters only drink "a little," Jo is not on heroin in spite of the pain: reality is explored without the filters of alcohol, drugs or fiction-writing. In that context, one cannot fail to be struck by the genuine efforts of Albee's protagonists: they take care, they try hard to respond, they reconsider. Indeed they can still be wolves at first, but ultimately they grow human and share experiences in common. The audience invited to get involved as co-conspirator learns something, becomes part of the experience, enters into complicity achieving a necessary catharsis; Albee has not abandoned the teaching emotion. What remains is a growing awareness of the needs of human beings and a protocol of manners restored.

Not that everything has become "peachy-keen;" isolation still exists and solitude. But the main purpose of the plays might be to repeat the demonstration, shortened and simplified, that communication is not impossible. It may be minimal, it will be difficult, it can be disturbed, but if it fails, indirectly provoking the other's death, it is because partners refuse it deliberately. Has Albee abandoned the image of the zoo as a valid transposition of the human world? Although *Listening* replaces it by another strong poetic equivalence, the dishevelled, deserted garden of a mental home, Albee's present tendency would be to remain in the seemingly naturalistic space of a living-room, reproducing an average reality, to the point that he jokingly promised that Attila, the Hun, "will be sitting around playing games, drinking and smoking" in a living room in his first historical play.

Strong emotions and violence have always been Albee's forte and still are with a suicide *à la Pétrone,* some grapping in the presence of the karate expert and a couple on the verge of fracturing, howling their pain. If the emphasis is obviously put on the anguish, the loss, the teaching emotion privileges not so much the destruction but the quality of trust and true relationship, up to the point though it may be. It seems that the period when Albee was concerned with social illusion and metaphysical lies is over. In the recent plays we are no longer confronted with evanescent deities or imaginary "bean bags" but with the sweet and sour reality: no coating, no sugar-crust to embellish the cream, no raspberries left even to top the desert. No illusion to survive on and no substitute speaker.

No clutter, a minimal set but careful visual effects; a Bauhaus feeling, Florentine curves, elegant, pure and simple: formal order as the last vision. Why then these significant objects hidden at the bottom of the dried-up fountain—another allusion to Tennessee Williams—, the broken crockery to materialize the mess? Yet Albee relies less and less on those transpositions so that articulate speech and poetry always predominate. Minimal families restricted to couples—the Girl in *Listening* may or may not be their daughter—secondary characters still unconvincing. At unexpected moments, humor—Sam trapped in a logical chain of remarks ending up in setting off his visitor's blackness, Sam offering his gadgets for punks and junkies—a stereo, three TV sets—to get rid of the intruders, just like Shepard in *True West* making use the same incongruity has Austin, the scenario-writer, steal all kinds of toasters in the neighborhood; humor to relieve the tension

since we must keep in mind that two of these three plays end up with the death of a lovely young woman.

Today could such titles as "Albee, Playwright in Protest" be chosen? Who would have imagined Albee writing a vaudeville? Could we include him now in the Theater of the Absurd or in a survey of the theater of revolt? Twenty years ago, Albee declared: "The only thing that bothers me about these student demonstrations is that they don't seem to be for anything, they are against things. There was a time when social and political protest used to be in favor of something, not just in opposition." Albee is now building more than he destroys.

One can no longer say that American drama in the eighties is dominated by Edward Albee; worse even, some of his commissioned works, screenplays for Hollywood, have not yet been produced, that in spite of his constant dedication, in spite of a clarity he has undoubtedly gained. His compelling power is intact, his ambition has not changed: "The characters of my plays are interested in teaching characters about self-knowledge. The audience too eventually." With great coherence, unfailing patience and inventiveness, Albee continues to explore various dramatic forms, here a radio-play and a vaudeville, next a historical play. One of his projects for a full-length play is called *Quitting,* but Albee is not. More concerned than many others by the development and progress of theater as an art form, more concerned now by positive demonstrations of intellectual honesty, Albee works at it with a serenity never achieved by O'Neill or Williams. (pp. 106-08)

Liliane Kerjan, "Pure and Simple: The Recent Plays of Edward Albee," in *New Essays on American Drama,* edited by Gilbert Debusscher and Henry I. Schvey, Editions Rodopi B.V., 1989, pp. 99-110.

SOURCES FOR FURTHER STUDY

Amacher, Richard E. *Edward Albee.* Rev. ed. Boston: Twayne Publishers, 1982, 219 p.

> Studies Albee's plays through *The Man Who Had Three Arms.* Amacher states: "By using a combination of *explication de texte* and Aristotelian part-whole analysis, I have aimed to give the reader as complete a sense of the play as it is possible for him to have without his actual reading it and seeing it in the theater."

———, and Rule, Margaret. *Edward Albee at Home and Abroad: A Bibliography.* New York: AMS Press, 1973, 95 p.

> Indexes nearly one thousand entries for the first decade of Albee's work, 1958-1968. Except for reviews, works in English are annotated.

Bigsby, C. W. E., ed. *Edward Albee: A Collection of Critical Essays.* Englewood Cliffs, N. J.: Prentice-Hall, Inc., 1975, 180 p.

> Twenty-one critical essays that "represent something of the range and variety of opinion which Albee's work has inspired."

Debusscher, Gilbert. *Edward Albee: Tradition and Renewal,* translated by Anne D. Williams. Brussels: American Studies Center, 1967, 94 p.

> Contends that Albee is a nihilist and praises his treatment of the theme of solitude.

Giantvalley, Scott. *Edward Albee: A Reference Guide.* Boston: G. K. Hall & Co., 1987, 459 p.

Comprehensive index of academic criticism, reviews, interviews, books, and articles from other countries, most of which are annotated.

Paolucci, Anne. *From Tension to Tonic: The Plays of Edward Albee.* Carbondale: Southern Illinois University Press, 1972, 143 p.

Views language as "Albee's most significant contribution to the American stage." Discusses *Virginia Woolf, Tiny Alice, Box* and *Mao,* and *All Over* in individual chapters.

Louisa May Alcott

1832-1888

(Also wrote under pseudonyms Flora Fairfield, A. M. Barnard, Cousin Tribulation, A. M., Abba May Alcott, and A. M. daughter of Amos Bronson Alcott) American novelist, short story and fairy tale writer, poet, essayist, editor, and dramatist.

INTRODUCTION

Alcott is best known for her sentimental yet realistic depictions of nineteenth-century domestic life. Her *Little Women* series attracted young and old readers alike and remains popular today. Alcott's continuing popular appeal is generally attributed to her believable characterizations and simple, charming writing style, reflected in her adage: "Never use a long word when a short one will do as well." The twentieth century has seen increased attention given to Alcott's canon, with literary critics noting in particular her prevalent feminist and psychosexual themes. Alcott scholar Madeleine B. Stern noted that "today . . . [Louisa May] is viewed as an experimenting, complex writer, and her work has become fertile ground for the exploration both of literary historians and psychohistorians."

Alcott, the second of four daughters, was born in Germantown, Pennsylvania, and raised in Boston and Concord, Massachusetts. Her father, Amos Bronson Alcott, was a noted New England Transcendentalist philosopher and educator who worked only sporadically throughout Louisa May's life. Her mother, Abigail May Alcott, was descended from the witch-burning Judge Samuel Sewall and the noted abolitionist Colonel Joseph May. Although severely impoverished, Alcott's childhood was apparently happy. Taught by her father, Alcott was deeply influenced by his transcendentalist thought and experimental educational philosophies. Ralph Waldo Emerson's personal library of classics and philosophy was available for use to the young Alcott, and Henry David Thoreau taught her botany. Margaret Fuller, James Russell Lowell, and Julia Ward were only a few of Alcott's intellectually influential neighbors and friends. Women's rights and educational reform—important social reform issues of nineteenth-century America—were two of Alcott's pet causes that often appear as themes in her novels.

Bronson Alcott founded several schools, but all of them failed, forcing Abigail and her daughters to undertake the financial support of the family. Later, Alcott often remarked that her entire career was inspired by her desire to compensate for her family's early discomfort. Alcott taught school, took in sewing, and worked briefly as a domestic servant. At age sixteen she began writing, convinced that she could eventually earn enough money to alleviate the family's poverty. In 1851, her first poem was published in *Peterson's Magazine* under the pseudonym Flora Fairfield, bringing Alcott little money but a great deal of confidence. It was during the ensuing years that Alcott published, as A. M. Barnard, a number of sensational serial stories, which were both popular and lucrative.

In 1862, Alcott went to Washington, D.C. to serve as a nurse to soldiers wounded in the American Civil War. It was a shortlived experience, however, for she contracted typhoid within a month, from which she nearly died. Her health, undermined by the long illness and by mercury poisoning from her medication, was never fully recovered. Alcott later recounted her experiences as a nurse in her popular *Hospital Sketches* (1863) which was originally published in the periodical *Commonwealth.* Her first novel, *Moods* (1864), pronounced immoral by critics, sold well nonetheless, and its success encouraged Alcott to continue writing. In 1865, Alcott traveled through Europe as a companion to a wealthy invalid and wrote for periodicals. While abroad, she was offered the editorship of *Merry's Museum,* an American journal featuring juvenile literature. She accepted the position and became the journal's chief contributor.

The turning point of Alcott's career came with the publication of *Little Women; or, Meg, Jo, Beth, and Amy* (1868-69). An autobiographical account of nineteenth-century family life, the novel traces the development of Alcott, depicted as Jo March, and her three sisters. The work was an immediate success and established Alcott as a major author. She published four sequels to *Little Women* entitled *Good Wives* (volume two of *Little Women*), *Little Men: Life at Plumfield with Jo's Boys* (1871), *Aunt Jo's Scrap Bag* (1872-82), and *Jo's Boys and How They Turned Out* (1886). Alcott was regarded as a celebrity and was easily able to support her family with her earnings.

Alcott's literary career can be divided into three periods. The first phase, spanning the 1840s to the late 1860s, is characterized by the lurid, sensational short stories that were published anonymously and pseudonymously in various New England periodicals. Critics generally agree that the characters in these early efforts are well drawn and colorful and that the plots are intricate and tightly woven. Most of these tales feature a mysterious, vengeful woman bent on manipulation and destruction. Alcott also included ghosts, opium eaters, and mercenaries in these serials. These melodramatic stories were extremely popular and provided Alcott with a steady income as she worked on lengthier pieces.

The publication of *Moods* inaugurated Alcott's most profitable and popular period. The *Little Women* books, which were the most successful series of their time, illustrate the struggles between adolescence and maturity. *Little Women* depicts the March family with a strong sense of realism and represents New England manners and customs with documentary accuracy. Critics have noted that its organization, in which each chapter comprises a well-rounded episode with a moral commentary, succeeds as a study of adolescent psychology. In particular, commentators praise Alcott's insightful characterization, which they regard as the essential reason for the book's enduring popularity.

From 1875 onward, as her health deteriorated, Alcott primarily produced popular juvenile literature. Most of her later works, particularly *Work: A Story of Experience* (1873) and *Rose in Bloom* (1876), depict heroines who have acquired inner strength through personal hardship and achieved personal satisfaction through careers and without marriage. In general, these works provoked mixed reviews. Most critics applaud the feminist tone reflected in these later pieces, but consider their characters and plots to be weak.

Henry James called Alcott the "novelist of children . . . the Thackeray, the Trollope, of the nursery and the schoolroom . . . ," and other contemporaries remarked that her spirited, wholesome stories were destined to become American classics. The twentieth century, however, witnessed a change in the critical assessment of Alcott's works. Although still popular with an adolescent audience, Alcott's *Little Women* has been criticized for its blatant moralizing. In 1920, Katharine Fullerton Gerould carried the criticism further, calling the March girls "underbred" and "unworldly." Gerould found the novel dated and sentimental and attacked the work for its "inexcusable amount of love-making." She insisted that Alcott wrote as one who had never loved. Both *Little Women* and *Little Men* have been faulted by some early-twentieth-century scholars for poor structure and organization. Specifically, critics charged that the works resemble collections of single sketches and lack the unity of integrated novels. More recent critics, however, value this method of construction and maintain that it mirrors the adolescent point of view. The last two decades have seen a renewed interest in Alcott's melodramatic early work. The noted Alcott critic Madeleine Stern has reprinted two collections of these colorful stories and introduced them to a new audience.

Alcott remains an enduring figure in American literature. Although some regard her portrayals of nineteenth-century domestic life as dated, she is remembered for her sympathetic and realistic depictions of the maturing adolescent. Her most popular work, *Little Women*, was instrumental in changing the focus of juvenile literature to include sensitive, not merely formulaic, portrayals of young adults.

(For further information about Alcott's life and works, see *Children's Literature Review*, Vol. 1; *Concise Dictionary of American Literary Biography, 1865-1917*; *Dictionary of Literary Biography*, Vols. 1, 42; *Nineteenth-Century Literature Criticism*, Vol. 6; and *Yesterday's Authors of Books for Children*, Vol. 1.)

CRITICAL COMMENTARY

G. K. CHESTERTON

(essay date 1907)

[Remembered primarily for his detective stories, Chesterton was also a biographer, essayist, novelist, poet, journalist, dramatist, and critic. Here, in an essay first published in 1907, he ranks Alcott with Jane Austen and states that *"Little Women* was written by a woman for women. . . . "]

Little Women was written by a woman for women— for little women. Consequently it anticipated realism by twenty or thirty years; just as Jane Austen anticipated it by at least a hundred years. For women are the only realists; their whole object in life is to pit their realism against the extravagant, excessive, and occasionally drunken idealism of men. . . . There is, indeed, a vast division in the matter of literature (an unimportant matter), but there is the same silent and unexplained assumption of the feminine point of view. There is no pretence, as most unfortunately occurred in the case of another woman of genius, George Eliot, that the writer is anything else but a woman, writing to amuse other women, with her awful womanly irony. Jane Austen did not call herself George Austen; nor Louisa Alcott call herself George Alcott. These women refrained from that abject submission to the male sex which we have since been distressed to see; the weak demand for masculine names and for a part in merely masculine frivolities; parliaments, for instance. These were strong women; they classed parliament with the public-house. But for another and better reason, I do not hesitate to name Miss Alcott by the side of Jane Austen; because her talent, though doubtless inferior, was of exactly the same kind. There is an unmistakable material truth about the thing; if that material truth were not the chief female characteristic, we should most of us find our houses burnt down when we went back to them. To take but one instance out of many, and an instance that a man can understand, because a man was involved, the account of the quite sudden and quite blundering proposal, acceptance, and engagement between Jo and the German professor under the umbrella, with parcels falling off them, so to speak, every minute, is one of the really human things in human literature; when you read it you feel sure that human beings have experienced it often; you almost feel that you have experienced it yourself. There is something true to all our own private diaries in the fact that our happiest moments have happened in the rain, or under some absurd impediment of absurd luggage. The same is true of a hundred other elements in the story. The whole affair of the children acting the different parts in *Pickwick*, forming a childish club under strict restrictions, in order to do so; all that is really life, even where it is not literature. And as a final touch of human truth, nothing could be better than the way in which Miss Alcott suggests the borders and the sensitive privacy of such an experiment. All the little girls have become interested, as they would in real life, in the lonely little boy next door; but when one of them introduces him into their private club in imitation of *Pickwick*, there is a general stir of resistance; these family fictions do not endure being considered from the outside.

All that is profoundly true; and something more than that is profoundly true. For just as the boy was an intruder in that club of girls, so any masculine reader is really an intruder among this pile of books. There runs through the whole series a certain moral philosophy, which a man can never really get the hang of. For instance, the girls are always doing something, pleasant or unpleasant. In fact, when they have not to do something unpleasant, they deliberately do something else. A great part, perhaps the more godlike part, of a boy's life, is passed in doing nothing at all. Real selfishness,

Principal Works

Flower Fables (fairy tales) 1855

"Pauline's Passion and Punishment" [as A. M. Barnard] (short story) 1862; published in newspaper Frank Leslie's Illustrated Newspaper

Hospital Sketches (letters and sketches) 1863

Moods (novel) 1864; also published as Moods [revised edition], 1882

Little Women; or, Meg, Jo, Beth, and Amy. 2 vols. (novel) 1868-69; also published as Little Women and Good Wives, 1871

An Old-fashioned Girl (novel) 1870

Little Men: Life at Plumfield with Jo's Boys (novel) 1871

Aunt Jo's Scrap Bag. 6 vols. (short stories) 1872-82

Work: A Story of Experience (novel) 1873

Eight Cousins; or, The Aunt-Hill (novel) 1875

Rose in Bloom (novel) 1876

A Modern Mephistopheles (novel) 1877

Under the Lilacs (novel) 1878

Jack and Jill: A Village Story (novel) 1880

Jo's Boys and How They Turned Out (novel) 1886

Louisa May Alcott: Her Life, Letters, and Journals (letters and journals) 1889

Comic Tragedies (drama) 1893

Behind a Mask: The Unknown Thrillers of Louisa May Alcott (short stories) 1975

Plots and Counterplots: More Unknown Thrillers of Louisa May Alcott (short stories) 1976

which is the simplest thing in the world to a boy or man, is practically left out of the calculation. The girls may conceivably oppress and torture each other; but they will not indulge or even enjoy themselves—not, at least, as men understand indulgence or enjoyment. . . . But two things are quite certain; first, that even from a masculine standpoint, the books are very good; and second, that from a feminine standpoint they are so good that their admirers have really lost sight even of their goodness. (pp. 164-66)

G. K. Chesterton, "Louisa Alcott," in his *A Handful of Authors: Essays on Books & Writers,* edited by Dorothy Collins, Sheed and Ward, 1953, pp. 163-67.

KATHARINE FULLERTON GEROULD
(essay date 1920)

[Gerould is one of the best-known of Alcott's twentieth-century detractors. In the following excerpt, she agrees that Alcott's perception of New England is accurate and well-represented but finds fault with the "inexcusable amount of love-making" in the novels as well as with the "blatant" moral tone she perceives throughout Alcott's works.]

The astounding result of re-reading Miss Alcott at a mature age is a conviction that she probably gives a better impression of mid-century New England than any of the more laborious reconstructions, either in fiction or in essay. The youth of her characters does not hinder her in this; for childhood, supremely, takes life ready-made. Mr. [William Dean] Howell's range is wider, and he is at once more serious and more detached. Technically, he and Miss Alcott can be compared as little as [Gustave Flaubert's] *Madame Bovary* and the *Bibliothèque Rose.* Yet, although their testimonies often agree, his world does not "compose" as hers does. . . . Miss Alcott is content to be typical. All her people have the same background, live in the same atmosphere, profess the same ideals. Moreover, they were ideals and an atmosphere that imposed themselves widely during their period. Mr. Howells gives us modern instances in plenty, but nowhere does he give us clearly the quintessential New England village. It is precisely the familiar experiences of life in that quintessential village that Miss Alcott gives us, with careless accuracy, without *arrière-pensée* [a hidden motive]. (pp. 184-85)

[What] strikes one on first re-reading her, is the extraordinary success with which she has given us our typical New England. Some of her books, obviously, are less successful in this way than others—*Under the Lilacs,* for example, or *Jack and Jill,* where . . . there is an inexcusable amount of love-making. There is an equally inexcusable amount of love-making, it is interesting to remember, in much of the earlier Howells. But for contemporary record of manners and morals, you will go far before you match her masterpiece, *Little Women.* What Meg, Jo, Beth, Amy, and Laurie do not teach us about life in New England at a certain time, we shall never learn from any collected edition of the letters of Emerson, Thoreau, or Hawthorne.

The next—and equally astounding—result of re-reading Miss Alcott was [that her characters] . . . were, in some ways, underbred. Bronson Alcott (or shall we say Mr. March?) quotes Plato in his family circle; but his family uses inveterately bad grammar. "Don't talk about 'labelling' Pa, as if he was a pickle-bottle!"—thus Jo chides her little sister for a malapropism. Bad grammar we might expect from Jo, as a wilful freak; but should we expect the exquisite Amy (any little girl will tell you how exquisite Amy is supposed to be) to write to her father from Europe, about buying gloves in Paris, "Don't that sound sort of elegant and rich?"

The bad grammar, in all the books, is constant. And yet, I know of no other young people's stories, anywhere, wherein the background is so unbrokenly and sincerely "literary." Cheap literature is unsparingly satirized; Plato and Goethe are quoted quite as everyday matters; and "a metaphysical streak had unconsciously got into" Jo's first novel. In *The Rose in Bloom*, Miss Alcott misquotes Swinburne, to be sure, but she does it in the interest of morality. . . . (pp. 185-87)

Breeding is, of course, not merely a matter of speech. . . . Miss Alcott's people are, as the author herself says of them, unworldly. They are even magnificently so; and they score the worldly at every turn. (p. 188)

Granted their unworldliness, their high scale of moral values, where, then, is the trace of vulgarity that is needed to make breeding bad? They pride themselves on their separation from all vulgarity. "My mother is a lady," Polly reflects, "even if "—even if she is not rich, like the Shaws. The March girls are always consoling themselves for their vicissitudes by the fact that their parents are gentlefolk. Well, they are underbred in precisely the way in which, one fancies, the contemporaries of Emerson in Concord may well have been underbred. It is the "plain-living" side of the "high thinking." They despised externals, and, in the end, externals had their revenge. Breeding, as such, is simply not a product of the independent village. . . . The villagers have not—and who supposes that Bronson Alcott and Thoreau had it?—the gift of civilized contacts. A contact, be it remembered, is not quite the same thing as a relation. Manners are a natural growth of courts. Recall any mediaeval dwelling of royalty; then imagine life lived in those cramped chambers, in the perpetual presence of superiors and inferiors alike—and lived informally!

In Miss Alcott's world, all that is changed. According to the older tradition, a totally unchaperoned youth would mean lack of breeding. Here, on the contrary, all the heroines are unchaperoned, while the match-making mamma is anathema. . . . The reward of the unchaperoned daughter is to make a good match. In that rigid school, conventions are judged—and nobly enough, Heaven knows!—from the point of view of morals alone (of absolute, not of historic or evolutionary morals) and many conventions are thereby damned. . . . "Underbred" is very likely too strong a word; yet one does see how the social state described

in *Little Women* might easily shock any one brought up in a less provincial tradition. There is too much love-making, for example. Though sweethearting between five-year-olds is frowned on, sweethearting between fifteen-year-olds is quite the thing. In real life, it would not always be safe to marry, very young, your first playmate. Any one who has lived in the more modern New England village knows perfectly well that people still marry, very young, their first playmates, and that disaster often results. Nor can Una always depend on the protection of a lion that is necessarily invisible. Granted that Jo's precocious sense was right, and that it would have been a mistake for her to marry Laurie; which of us believes that, in real life, she would not have made the mistake? (pp. 188-90)

The whole tissue of the March girls' lives is a very commonplace fabric. You know that their furniture was bad—and that they did not know it; that their aesthetic sense was untrained and crude—and that they did not care; that the simplicity of their meals, their household service, their dress, their every day manners (in spite of the myth about Amy) was simplicity of the common, not of the intelligent, kind. You really would not want to spend a week in the house of any one of them. Nor had their simplicity in any wise the quality of austerity. Remember the pies that the older March girls carried for muffs (the management whereof was one of the ever unsolved riddles of my childhood).

No: in so far as breeding is a matter of externals, one must admit that there is some sense in calling Miss Alcott's people underbred. Perhaps we do not choose to call breeding a matter of externals. In that, we should perfectly agree with Miss Alcott's people themselves; and to that we shall presently come. For what is incontrovertible is that Miss Alcott's work is a genuine document. (p. 191)

There are not, I believe, any other books in the world so blatantly full of morality—of moral issues, and moral tests, and morals passionately abided by—and at the same time so empty of religion. The Bible is never quoted; almost no one goes to church; and they pray only when very young and in extreme cases. The only religious allusion, so far as I know, in *Little Women*, is the patronizing mention of the Madonna provided for Amy by Aunt March's Catholic maid. And even then, you can see how broad-minded Mrs. March considers herself, to permit Amy the quasi-oratory; and Amy does not attempt to disguise the fact that she admires the picture chiefly for its artistic quality. (pp. 192-93)

The New English literary tradition seems to be fairly clear: either passion must be public, or, if it is private, it must be thwarted. There is a good deal of public passion—for philanthropy, for education, and whatnot—in the books, after all. There is no private passion at all: though the books brim with sentiment, Miss Alcott writes as one who had never loved. It would be difficult to find, anywhere, stories so full of lovemaking and so empty of emotion. (p. 195)

Katharine Fullerton Gerould, "Miss Alcott's New England," in her *Modes and Morals,* Charles Scribner's Sons, 1920, pp. 182-98.

MADELEINE B. STERN

(essay date 1949)

[In the following excerpt, Stern elucidates reasons for *Little Women*'s enduring popularity. Calling the novel "far more than a picture of childhood," she praises Alcott's depictions of adolescent psychology and claims that *Little Women*'s episodic organization "results in a mighty architecture" of structure.]

[Louisa May Alcott's] muse was, first and foremost, domestic. She unlatched the door to one house, and her readers speedily discovered that it was their own house that they entered. She unroofed every dwelling in the land by unroofing the home of the four March girls. *Little Women* is great because it is a book on the American home, and hence universal in its appeal. As long as human beings delight in "the blessings that alone can make life happy," as long as they believe, with Jo March, that "families are the most beautiful things in all the world," the book will be treasured. It is a domestic drama, indeed, and Louisa Alcott knew, as her representative did, that when she wrote of her own home "something got into that story that went straight to the hearts of those who read it." Like Jo, the author had "found her style at last." The jolly larks, the plays and tableaux, the sleigh rides and skating frolics are enjoyed not by an isolated heroine, but by a family. The poverty, the domestic trials, . . . are the troubles and the joys of family life. The omissions indicate as notably as the actual content the writer's contributions to the domestic novel. (pp. 476-77)

To the domestic novel the author made still another contribution in *Little Women.* While her glorification of family life is universal in its appeal, her details offer a local flavor that gives the work a documentary value. . . . By its documentary value alone, *Little Women,* as an index of New England manners in the mid-century, would be accorded a place in literary history. It is the great merit of the book that it is at once a documentary account of a given locality and a universal delineation of any American home. By those two contributions, the one local, the other universal, the author raised the domestic novel from the state of trite in-

sipidity in which it had remained so long, and carved for herself a niche in American letters.

Louisa Alcott added no less to juvenile literature than to the domestic novel. *Little Women* is far more than a "picture of a happy childhood." . . . The author's knowledge of adolescent psychology reveals itself in twofold form throughout the work, for it consisted first of an appeal to adolescents, the skill of making them laugh or cry, and secondly of an ability to describe adolescents, to catch and transfix the varied emotions and thoughts of the young. (pp. 477-78)

Louisa Alcott remembered her adolescence and recorded it before the memory faded. . . . *Little Women* runs the gamut of the adolescent heart and mind, and supplies a case book of adolescent psychology far surpassing any text on the subject.

By combining her local and universal contributions to the domestic novel with her knowledge of adolescent psychology, Louisa Alcott cleared the ground of juvenile literature and wrote a best-seller for the generations. The means whereby she arrived at such an end are less apparent than the end itself. She forgot none of the varied techniques she had tried when she sat down to produce a girls' book. . . . She remembered her apprenticeship in the short story, and the method she evolved in *Little Women* is therefore episodic. Each chapter in turn is granted almost invariably to one of the sisters, so that Meg's married life alternates with Amy's experiences abroad or Jo's tussles with herself at home. This segmental structure results in a mighty architecture when it houses human beings, for the author knew that "our lives are patchwork." . . . [The] episodic technique requires a short attention span for young readers and at the same time gives the effect of verisimilitude in the lives of human beings which do indeed resemble patchwork. (pp. 478-80)

[Realism] provided the finest grist for [Louisa Alcott's] mill. (p. 480)

The use of "good strong words, that mean something," the grammar that is as natural as it is unpolished aided her in producing that "mannerless manner" by which verisimilitude is achieved. She was well aware of the value of never using a long word when a short one would do as well. Her defenses of impure English were not written until later, but they were practised in *Little Women.* It is better to "let children write their own natural letters . . . than to make them copy the Grandisonian style." (p. 481)

The author was less successful in her attempts at repeating her characterizations of adolescence [in her later works following *Little Women*]. By reason of her hearty good will and honest realism, Polly, of *An Old-Fashioned Girl,* narrowly escapes being a "little prig in a goody story-book." She is at once a symbol of the old-fashioned virtues and a genuine little girl who heartily enjoys a coast down the mall, dolls' dresses, and Grandma Shaw's stories. The March girls were individuals who never deteriorated into symbols. Once the writer converted Polly into "Sweet P.," "Polly Peacemaker," she ran the risk of weakening the verisimilitude of her character. . . . The boys of *Little Men* . . . lack the three-dimensional qualities of the March girls. . . . To each the author endowed one glaring fault awaiting correction by the Plumfield methods; hence the reader is likely to think of Ned as the braggart, Stuffy as the glutton, Tommy as the mischievous youth, and Dan as the wild boy rather than as fully rounded individuals. Nan . . . was modeled from the mold of Jo March, but she lacks Jo's completeness and becomes a mere symbol of the tomboy. The symbols continue to pursue the readers of *Eight Cousins,* where the characterizations were touched off boldly with broad strokes, each of the *dramatis personae* possessing one distinguishing trait adumbrated in the beginning and continually stressed. . . . Louisa Alcott was never to repeat the more minute characterizations of *Little Women.* Bab of *Under the Lilacs* . . . is simply another Nan, the tomboy who inherits Jo March's gallantry and allows Ben to win the archery contest. Jack of *Jack and Jill* is a symbol of pluck rather than a plucky adolescent; Merry Grant is a representative of household art rather than an artistic girl. Jo's Boys continue to be the stereotypes of *Little Men* . . . . The author had no time to add full-length portraits to her gallery of adolescents or to complete with minute touches the sketches too broadly painted in her *Little Women* Series. (pp. 482-84)

So aware was the author of the means of titillating the minds of her readers that when she could no longer invent fresh incidents she repeated the old to delight them. Where Amy March had nearly met her death after a fall through the ice, Rob of *Jo's Boys* . . . narrowly escapes hydrophobia because of Ted's wilfulness. Where Laurie had asked to pull forever in the same boat with his beloved, Tom expresses the wish to go on cycling with his angel. . . . As the years drew on, the author found it impossible to resist the temptation of repeating her themes with or without variation. She knew her public and she catered to their demands. . . . Children, she believed, were "good critics . . . , and to suit them was an accomplishment that any one might be proud of." Suit them she did, and she will continue to suit them as long as their tastes remain unchanged. (p. 484)

From all the authors whose influence she acknowledged, Louisa Alcott took only what she could apply to her own purposes—from Bunyan, the picturesque progress of an Everyman from the Slough of Despond to the Celestial City; from Dickens, a few obvious and sentimental characterizations; from Carlyle, a simple and a single doctrine; from Thoreau, a flowery

fairyland and its gardener; from Emerson, a lofty ethic; from Parker, exaltation of strength of character. She selected precisely such material as would be intelligible to youthful readers. When she borrowed from Hawthorne, however, the author found that she was borrowing from writings composed in an intellectual twilight, haunted by shadows and the ghosts of shadows. By no amount of literary skill could such material be worked into wholesome tales for *Harper's Young People* or *St. Nicholas.* Hence it is that Hawthorne's influence is most apparent in a book written neither for nor about children, but in a book issued anonymously in the No Name Series of Roberts Brothers, that freed the author from fulfilling her obligations to her young public and from adding fresh laurels to her reputation as a juvenile writer.

[This book,] *A Modern Mephistopheles,* is less interesting, however, as a demonstration of Hawthorne's influence upon Louisa Alcott than as an instance of what the successful author wrote when she pleased herself instead of her admirers. It is, indeed, the only book written after 1868 that gives any indication of what Louisa Alcott might have become had she not devoted herself to juvenile literature. The result is disappointing. Instead of using her journalistic skill to report the domestic life of her day, or incorporating in the novel her observations of adolescents, she reverted to the sensationalism of her early career, combining with it a verbose intellectuality based upon her readings in Hawthorne and Goethe. *A Modern Mephistopheles* is a bookish and spurious attempt at "literature," a study, almost in abstract, of good contending with evil, of crime and the punishment consequent upon it.

The characters of the novel are pegs upon which the author hung her theme, artificial puppets lacking all reality. Felix Canaris, the Adonis who sells his liberty and his love for fame, the young Bacchus who revels in "olives and old wine," surely never lived in Concord; Jasper Helwyze, the Sybarite with a Mephistophelian love of power, who believes "in nothing invisible and divine," whose god is intellect and who studies the subtle evil of men's minds, bears little resemblance to any human being. Olivia, the mellow beauty, and Gladys, the artless, "white-souled" girl, are contrasting symbols rather than contrasting women.

When Louisa Alcott wrote anonymously she borrowed as much from the effusions of "A. M. Barnard" (the pseudonym she had frequently used in her own thrillers), as from Hawthorne or Goethe, for *A Modern Mephistopheles* follows not only in its characterizations but in its episodes the pattern of the penny dreadfuls. Mesmerism is substituted for more obvious violence, and hashish, enclosed in a "*bonbonnière* [candy box] of tortoise-shell and silver" takes the place of opium. The style itself is reminiscent of the mannerisms of "A. M. Barnard," for it is peppered with exotic descriptions of "lustrous silks sultanas were to wear," of "odorous woods and spices, . . . with fragrance never blown from Western hills," of "skins mooned and barred with black upon the tawny velvet, that had lain in jungles, or glided with deathful stealthiness along the track of human feet." . . . The ghost of "A. M. Barnard" had not been laid.

Yet it must be admitted that the threads of these sensational phrases and themes have been woven upon a more mature framework than any used by "A. M. Barnard." The plot itself, consisting of "the contest between good and evil," the struggle between the world, the flesh and the devil, on the one hand, and virtue on the other is, as it was designed to be, a modern debate between the body and soul. (pp. 494-96)

Louisa Alcott will be remembered first for her accurate depiction of the domestic life of the nation in *Little Women* especially, but also in *An Old-Fashioned Girl, Eight Cousins,* and *Jack and Jill.* She will be remembered secondly for her studies of adolescent psychology exhibited in the three-dimensional characters of the March girls, and thirdly for her astounding ability to appeal to youthful readers revealed in the *Little Women* Series. Her contribution to the domestic novel has a value at once universal and local, to be treasured by adult readers as well as by an adolescent public, for the household which she chose to delineate is indeed a "microcosm of the world outside." It is and ever will be valid that "the incidents of any life truly set forth in their human interest will take hold of humanity as with a spell." Louisa Alcott's translation of the incidents of family life to the domain of literature will take hold of humanity as long as family life abides. Her twofold contribution to the more limited field of juvenile literature, her characterization of adolescence and her ability to appeal to adolescents, will likewise be cherished as long as youth endures. (p. 497)

Madeleine B. Stern, "Louisa M. Alcott: An Appraisal," in *The New England Quarterly,* Vol. XXII, No. 4, December, 1949, pp. 475-98.

ELIZABETH JANEWAY

(essay date 1968)

[In the excerpt below, Janeway comments on the equality between Jo and Laurie in *Little Women*. Jo, Janeway argues, "is a unique creation: the one young woman in 19th-century fiction who maintains her individual independence . . . and gets away with it."]

[*Little Women*] is dated and sentimental and full of

preaching and moralizing, and some snobbery about the lower classes that is positively breathtaking in its horror: that moment, for instance, when old Mr. Laurence is improbably discovered in a fishmarket, and bestows his charity on a starving Irish woman by hooking a large fish on the end of his cane, and depositing it, to her gasping gratitude, in her arms. It is as often smug as it is snug, and its high-mindedness tends to be that peculiar sort that pays. . . .

Its faults we can see in a moment. . . . *Little Women* does harp on our nerves, does play on our feelings, does stack the cards to bring about undeserved happy outcomes here and undeserved come-uppance there. But that is not the whole story, and couldn't be, or there wouldn't be all those girls with their noses in the book right now, and all those women who remember the supreme shock of the moment when Jo sold her hair; when Beth was discovered on the medicine chest in the closet with scarlet fever coming on; when Meg let the Moffats dress her up; when Amy was packed off, protesting and bargaining, to Aunt March's stiff house.

No, *Little Women* does manipulate life, but it is also *about* life, and life that is recognizable in human terms today. Miss Alcott preached, and the conclusions she came to are frequently too good to be true; but the facts of emotion that she started with were real. She might end by softening the ways to deal with them, but she began by looking them in the eye. Her girls were jealous, mean, silly and lazy; and for 100 years jealous, mean, silly and lazy girls have been ardently grateful for the chance to read about themselves. If Miss Alcott's prescriptions for curing their sins are too simple, it doesn't alter the fact that her diagnoses are clear, unequivocal and humanly right. When her girls are good, they are apt to be painful; but when they are bad, they are bad just the way we all are, and over the same things. . . .

This general background of human interest makes *Little Women* still plausible, but it is hardly enough to keep it a perennial classic. The real attraction is not the book as a whole, but its heroine, Jo, and Jo is a unique creation: the one young woman in 19th-century fiction who maintains her individual independence, who gives up no part of her autonomy as payment for being born a woman—and who gets away with it. Jo is the tomboy dream come true, the dream of growing up into full humanity with all its potentialities instead of into limited femininity: of looking after oneself and paying one's way and doing effective work in the real world instead of learning how to please a man who will look after you, as Meg and Amy both do with pious pleasure. (So, by the way, does Natasha [in Leo Tolstoy's "War and Peace"]). It's no secret that Jo's story is the heart of *Little Women* . . . (p. 42)

[The relationship between Laurie and Jo] has always been that of two equals, which in 19th-century America (and in some places today) implies two equals of the same sex. Twice at least Laurie suggests that they run off together, not for lovemaking, but for adventure; very much in the manner and mood in which [Mark Twain's] Tom Sawyer and Huck Finn plan to run away from comfort and civilization. Again when Jo speaks to her mother about the possibility of marriage to Laurie, Mrs. March is against it "because you two are too much alike." So they are, and so—with no explanations ever given—Jo refuses Laurie, and the reader knows she is right, for Jo and Laurie are dear friends, competitors and not in the least a couple. It is worth noting that the two other adored 19th-century heroines who say "No" to the hero's proposal give way in the end, when circumstances and the hero have changed: Elizabeth Bennet and [Charlotte Brontë's] Jane Eyre. But Jo says "No" and does not shift.

The subtlety of Miss Alcott's character drawing (or self knowledge, if you will) comes through here, for Jo is a tomboy, but never a masculinized or Lesbian figure. She is, somehow, an idealized "New Woman," capable of male virtues but not, as the Victorians would have said, "unsexed." Or perhaps she is really archaic woman, re-created out of some New-World-frontier necessity when patriarchy breaks down. For Jo marries (as we all know! Who can forget that last great self-indulgent burst of tears when Professor Bhaer stops, under the umbrella, and asks "Heart's dearest, why do you cry?"). Yes, Jo marries and becomes, please note, not a sweet little wife but a matriarch: mistress of the professor's school, mother of healthy sons (while Amy and Laurie have only one sickly daughter), and cheerful active manager of events and people. For this Victorian moral tract, sentimental and preachy, was written by a secret rebel against the order of the world and woman's place in it, and all the girls who ever read it know it. (pp. 44, 46)

Elizabeth Janeway, "Meg, Jo, Beth, Amy and Louisa," in *The New York Times Book Review*, September 29, 1968, pp. 42, 44, 46.

SARAH ELBERT

(essay date 1984)

[In the excerpt below, Elbert examines major themes in *Little Women*.]

[*Little Women*] develops three major themes: domesticity, the achievement of individual identity through work, and true love. The same motifs appear in *Little Men, Jo's Boys, Eight Cousins, Rose in Bloom* and *An Old Fashioned Girl*. None has been out of print since

first written. Together they comprise a fictional record of liberal feminist ideology, process, and programs from 1867 through 1886 in America.

From the outset Alcott established the centrality of household democracy, underscoring the importance of "natural" cooperation and mutual self-sacrifice within family life. The March cottage shelters the four sisters and their parents, all of whom love and depend upon one another. Even the family poverty, so reminiscent of Louisa's own, serves to reinforce democratic practice in the family. With the help of Hannah, who worked as a maid for Mrs. March in better days and now considers herself a "member of the family," all the women work together to accomplish household chores, making the most of meager means by sharing everything.

The virtues of mutual self-sacrifice and domestic cooperation, however, must be proven to the March girls before they can recognize how important such virtues are to their self-realization. Independent-minded and childishly selfish, the girls must learn how to shape their individualities in harmony with the interests of the family. In an important episode Alcott describes the tactics used by Mrs. March to win her daughters to a higher social standard.

After listening to Jo, Meg, Beth, and Amy pine for the "vacations" enjoyed by wealthier friends, Marmee agrees to release them from domestic duties for one week. She allows them to structure their time in any way they please. On the first morning, the neat inviting cottage is suddenly a different place. Meg, coming down to a solitary breakfast, finds the parlor "lonely and untidy," because "Jo had not filled the vases, Beth had not dusted, and Amy's books lay about scattered." Before long, selfishness produces more domestic disasters, which increase alarmingly as the week progresses. Jo gets sunburnt boating too long with Laurie, and headachy from spending hours devouring her cherished novels. "Giving out" her ordinary sewing chores, Meg falls to "snipping and spoiling" her clothes in an attempt to be fashionable. Amy sketches lazily under a hedge and getting drenched by a summer rain, ruins her best white frock. Beth makes a mess out of her doll's closet, leaves the mess, and goes off to practice some new music. By the end of the day, she is left with "the confusion of her closet" and, "the difficulty of learning three of four songs at once." All these small troubles make the girls grumpy and ill-tempered.

The experiment, however, is far from over. Excessive attention to self-pleasure produces a scarcity of necessities, including food. Emulating the little red hen, Mrs. March decides that those who do not work shall not eat. She gives Hannah a holiday, and the maid leaves with these parting words: "Housekeeping ain't no joke." Unable to rely on the experience and counsel of Hannah and their mother, the girls produce a breakfast featuring "boiled tea, very bitter, scorched omelette, and biscuits speckled with saleratus." Jo caters a luncheon for friends, only to discover that she can't make anything "fit to eat" except "gingerbread and molasses candy." So she sails off to purchase "a very young lobster, some very old asparagus, and two boxes of acid strawberries." She boils the asparagus for an hour until the heads are "cooked off" and the stalks "harder than ever." She undercooks the lobster and the potatoes, and sprinkles salt instead of sugar on the strawberries.

In the midst of this culinary chaos, Beth discovers that her canary, Pip, is dead from lack of water and food. Her sisters, and the assembled guests, including Laurie, try to help, but to no avail. Amy proposes that they warm the bird in an oven to revive him. "Overcome with emotion and lobster," sickened by the death of her bird, Beth rebels. "He's been starved," she says of her bird, "and he shant be baked, now he's dead . . . and I'll never have another bird . . . for I am too bad to own one."

Returning home to find her daughters miserable over the death of Pip and their failures as homekeepers, Mrs. March easily persuades them to admit that "it is better to have a few duties, and live for others." This experiment, she says, was designed to show you "what happens when everyone thinks only for herself. Now you know that in order to make a home comfortable and happy," everyone in it must contribute to the family welfare. Marmee has also proven to the girls that domestic work is real work, giving women a "sense of power and independence better than money or fashion." She has shown them that home life becomes a "beautiful success" only if work alternates with leisure, independence with cooperation and mutual concern.

Although this episode deals almost exclusively with girls, Alcott integrated men into her vision of cooperative family life. Men too should benefit from and participate in this family experience, but only on the grounds that they respect the independence and equal authority of women within the home.

Accepting, even glorifying the importance of women's domestic work, Alcott emphasizes that men are homeless without women. Since the ability to create a home and sustain a family supercedes fame and money as evidence of success and civilization, it follows that women have already proved themselves in the world; thus their ability to extend their sphere is unquestioned in *Little Women*. Homeless men, despite wealth, wages and worldly experience, are motherless children. Meg's suitor, John Brooke, is attracted to the March cottage in large part because he is a lonely young man who has recently lost his mother. Laurie is motherless, which excuses most of his faults, and Mr. Laurence, his grandfather, has neither wife, daughter, or granddaughter. Mr. March alone has a proper home

and knows his place in it, returning from the war to augment, but not supercede, Marmee's authority. He wholly accepts the female abundance around him, tending the flock of his tiny parish and leaving domestic arrangements to his womenfolk.

The question of whether men can be integrated into domestic life on feminist terms first appears in the relationship between young Laurie and the March sisters. Laurie starts out right. The gift of food is an excellent way to gain acceptance into an alien tribe. Meg, Jo, Beth and Amy, having given up their Christmas breakfast for a starving German immigrant family, are happily surprised by a compensatory feast sent over by the Laurences. Mrs. March has encouraged her daughters to pack up their hot muffins, buckwheat cakes, bread and cream early Christmas morning and deliver the meal to the hungry Hummels. After a full day spent giving gifts to Marmee and then performing a homemade opera for their friends, a fashionable supper of "ice cream actually two dishes of it, pink and white, cake and fruit and distracting French bon-bons" is exactly what the unfashionable March girls crave. Three huge bouquets of hothouse flowers complete the Laurence boy's offerings. Under the guise of rewarding their self-sacrifice, he is courting them.

Laurie and Jo reverse the gift-giving and also their sexual personnas when Jo visits her new friend on his home ground, the "Palace Beautiful," as the girls call the mansion next door. Having spied "a curly black head leaning on a thin hand at the upper window," Jo throws up a snowball and promises to visit Laurie. She suggests a visit from girls, because her sex ordinarily is "quiet and likes to play nurse." Laurie does not want boys to visit, he tells Jo, because "they make such a row and my head is weak." "I am not quiet and nice," she says, "but I'll come."

In a moment, appearing "rosy and quite at her ease" in Laurie's parlor, Jo unpacks a maternal abundance of gifts, including Meg's blancmange, decorated with Amy's "pet" geranium leaves, and a basket of Beth's kittens to amuse the sick "sister." Jo's gift is her own womanly touch; she brushes the hearth, straightens books and bottles, and plumps Laurie's pillows. He has been observing the March sisters through their parlor window, "where the flowers are," and when the lamps are lit he can see them around the table with Marmee. It is this shy confession, coupled with the "hungry, solitary look in his eyes," that turns Jo from boy to little woman to foster mother in a twinkling. Skeptical readers are warned away from any other interpretation of the unchaperoned visit by Alcott's firm assertion that Jo "had been so simply taught that there was no nonsense in her head, and at fifteen, she was as innocent and frank as any child."

A boy's acceptance of motherly abundance entices an innocent young girl to treat him as her sister and also make him, as Jo says, her "boy" or foster-son. An adult romance, emerging out of this familiar relationship, is fraught with incestuous complications. The worst one, from Jo's viewpoint, is that such frozen domestic roles preclude female independence within marital union; democratic households cannot be incestuous.

Alcott advances ideas about the place of men in the family that emerged out of her domestic experiences with her parents, despite her belief in universal laws of progress and democracy. On the whole, she does not paint a compelling picture of marital equality in *Little Women.* Instead she presents the possibility of educating and parenting a new generation of little men and little women. In the second part of *Little Women* Alcott describes the married life of John and Meg Brooke. Theirs is no ideal egalitarian marriage, but then John Brooke was not raised by Marmee. The single wage-earner for his family, John provides a domestic servant but does not share domestic chores himself, except for disciplining his son in the evening. Meg is totally dependent upon his income both for household and personal expenses. Careful of her household accounting, she nevertheless often behaves like an impulsive child. On one occasion, she is tempted by a length of lovely violet silk while shopping with an old friend, Sallie Moffet. The silk costs fifty dollars, an enormous sum to the young couple. When Meg tells John that she has bought the silk, he responds only that "twenty-five yards of silk seems a good deal to cover one small woman, but I've no doubt my wife will look as fine as Ned Moffet's when she gets it on." Meg is overwhelmed with remorse at her own selfishness. Sallie generously buys the silk, whereupon Meg uses the fifty dollars to buy a new overcoat for her husband.

In a chapter called "On the Shelf," Meg's docility appears as her greatest virtue and her most serious domestic flaw. Docility is a fine quality in a daughter, even a sister, Alcott admits, but dangerous in a wife. Meg becomes dowdy and dependent, isolated in her little cottage with two small children. John spends more time away from home, provoking Marmee to confront Meg, but not her son-in-law, reminding her that "it's mother who blames as well as mother who sympathizes."

Mother shares her domestic secret: a good marriage is based on mutuality of interests and responsibilities. Marmee herself learned this as a young wife, when after a hard time caring for her children, she welcomed father's help. Now, she says, he does not let business distract him from domestic details, and she remembers to interest herself in his pursuits. "We each do our part alone in many things, but at home we work together, always." Marmee's advice is heeded; Meg pays more attention to the niceties of her dress, tries to

talk about current affairs, and cedes to her husband some measure of child management.

According to Alcott, the reform of domestic life required restoration of a mutuality that had vanished with the separation of home and work. Yet of all the domestic advice presented in *Little Women,* this lesson carries the least conviction. Mr. March is the minister of a small parish and presumably home a great deal. John Brooke, on the other hand, is a clerk, far removed from his home and children. As we shall see, Alcott can only offer model domesticity in utopian settings where cooperative communities reappear in feminist forms.

When Louisa finished writing part two of *Little Women,* she suggested "Wedding marches" as a possible title. She changed it, however to "Birds Leaving the Nest," or "Little Women Grow Up," because she did not wish to suggest that marriage should be the focal event for growing girls. Instead she argues that girls who take trial flights from secure homes will find their own paths to domestic happiness. They might choose independent spinsterhood or some form of marital bonds that range from partial to complete "household democracy." For Alcott, sisterhood and marriage, though often contradictory, are equally valuable possibilities for women. Fully realized sisterhood becomes a model for marriage, not simply an alternative to it. Together, marriage and sisterhood guarantee that individual identity and domesticity will be harmonious.

Meg, the eldest and most "docile daughter," does not attain Alcott's ideal womanhood. Democratic domesticity requires maturity, strength, and above all a secure identity that Meg lacks. Her identity consists of being Marmee's daughter and then John's wife. Yet she and John are well matched. Neither really wants sexual equality in the dovecote. When Meg leaves home to work as a governess she accepts a three-year engagement period, dreaming that she will have much to learn while she waits. But John says, "You have only to wait; I am to do the work." Alcott accepts the limitations of temperament and circumstance in Meg, as she does in all her characters. In *Little Men,* however, Meg's widowhood grants her the circumstances to develop a stronger side of her character.

Fashion provides a counterpoint to feminism in *Little Women.* Jo's strong sense of self is established in part by her rejection of fashion, which she perceives as a sign of dependency and sexual stereotyping. Amy, on the other hand, struggles against her burden of vanity, which has its positive side in her "nice manners and refined way of speaking." Amy must learn that appearances can be deceiving, whereas Jo must learn that appearances do count in the larger world. Meg's vanity may be one reason she is linked to Amy in the game of "playing mother," wherein Meg and Jo watch over their sisters "in the places of discarded dolls." Jo obviously rejects Amy early in their lives. Amy's flat nose, her chief "trial," as she says, is supposedly the result of careless Jo's dropping her baby sister onto a coal-hod.

Jo's lack of vanity about clothes at first conceals her pride both in her writing talent and in her exclusive relationship to Laurie. Laurie enjoys Jo's vivid imagination; it gives color and vivacity to his own lonely childhood. Keeping Amy out of pleasurable excursions with Laurie is one of Jo's main "faults." Left at home once too often, Amy burns a collection of Jo's painstakingly written fairy tales as revenge. Furious, Jo leaves her behind again when she and Laurie go skating. Amy follows behind and is almost killed by falling through the thin ice. Penitent, Jo vows to curb her temper and cherish Amy. Accepting the fact that she is not the only independent and talented member of the family is part of Jo's growing up.

Her notion that she is "the man of the family" is a more serious problem in the story. In a strange way this too plays itself out around fashion. Jo has her first serious encounter with Laurie at a neighborhood dance, where she is uncomfortably dressed up to accompany Meg on their first "grown up" social expedition. Meg's woes arise from her desire for fashionable frippery; she dances in overly tight high-heeled slippers that cripple her before the dance is over. Jo wears sensible shoes, but cannot dance because "in maroon, with a stiff gentlemanly linen collar and a white chrysanthemeum or two for her only ornament," she is pledged to hide the scorched back of her "poplin" gown. Therefore she must stand quietly or hide in a corner in penance for her habit of standing too near the fire. The Laurence boy is shy, a stranger to the neighborhood who has spent much of his childhood in a Swiss boarding school. He wears two "nice pearl colored gloves" and dances well, volunteering to polka with Jo in the privacy of a hall. Jo is suddenly aware that the gentility she rejects as too "lady-like" can be quite acceptable when it is "gentlemanly," or in other words, gender-free. Her regret at having only one good glove (the other is stained with lemonade) signals her growth from tomboyhood to womanhood in the feminist sense of the term. Jo is somewhat confused, having made a cause celebré out of being a sloppy, rough boy who clumps about in unlaced boots. Now she finds herself attracted by Laurie's "curly black hair, brown skin, big black eyes, handsome nose, fine teeth, small hands and feet." She observes her new model closely: "Taller than I am," says Jo, and "very polite for a boy, altogether jolly." Finding her sartorial model in the opposite sex, Jo decides she can grow up to be a splendid woman with neatly laced boots and clean linen. She does not want Laurie as a sweetheart; she wants to adopt both him and his air of freedom and elegant comfort.

Meg can easily sympathize with Amy. Both love pretty things and are well regarded by wealthy relatives who appreciate their social graces and attention to niceties of dress. Mr. Laurence buys Meg her first silvery silk dress, a seemingly harmless and generous act. But because she is always dependent upon someone else's generosity, poor Meg must forego her next silk gown five years later. Meg elicits the reader's sympathy, however, while Amy's tastes seem symptoms of a selfish, superficial character.

First of all, Amy is too young to care about jewelry or fashionable frocks in the first half of *Little Women.* Nevertheless, she cares a great deal for them; she covets a schoolmate's carnelian ring, and preens and postures in front of her friends while exaggerating her family's lost wealth and status. Amy's pretensions lead her into trouble in the famous incident of the "pickled limes." Fashionable little school-girls have allowances, but Amy has none. As a result she has gone in debt to chums who treat her to the current delicacy—pickled limes. Meg then gives Amy a quarter, and the delighted girl purchases a bag of limes.

Mr. Davis, the school master, has forbidden treats in his classroom. Discovering that Amy has hidden limes in her desk, he calls her to the front of the room and humiliates her with "several tingling blows on her little palm." The author suggests that this incident might mark the beginning of Amy's maturation. Instead, Marmee and Jo rescue Amy by giving her a vacation from school. A small lecture by Marmee on the "power of modesty" does not alter the fact that Amy has had her burden lightened.

Later, at a charity fair, Amy is unfairly treated by rich and envious girls. This time she tries to "love her neighbor" and modestly allows her trinkets to be sold by a rival. Once again, this time augmented by Laurie and his friends (who have been commandeered by Jo) the family sails to Amy's rescue. They buy back Amy's trinkets and all the bouquets (provided by the Laurences' gardener) on sale at Amy's unfashionable booth. If this were not enough, Amy's Aunt Carrol, hearing of her niece's delicate manners, talented fancy work, and Christian forbearance at the charity fair, rewards her with a trip to Europe as her companion. Poor Jo, who engineered the rescue, is left behind, too unfashionable and forthright to be patronized. . . . It is precisely because Jo is indeed more substantial that the author grants Amy a free holiday in Europe and eventually a wealthy indulgent husband.

Amy and Laurie grow up together in Europe. Both are fashionable, inclined to indolence and coquetry. Both have talent, Amy for painting and Laurie for music, but only enough to please friends in polite salons. Neither is put to the test of earning a living. Both are also inclined toward "illusion" in dressing themselves and appreciating each other's refined taste. Their growing up, however, does require a degree of honesty:

Alcott's frontispiece for the first volume of *Little Women.*

they admit that "talent isn't genius and you can't make it so."

Despite the sniping and competition for parental love, social approval, and material rewards, Amy and Jo share one great loss that matures them both. The central tragedy of *Little Women,* one that generations of readers remember, is Beth's death in the final part of the book. Loving home the best, gentle Beth never wants to leave it; perhaps she would never have done so. She grows more fragile each year, and in her last months confides to Jo feeling that she was never intended to live long. Her short speech is also her longest in the novel:

> I'm not like the rest of you; I never made any plans about what I'd do when I grew up; I never thought of being married, as you all did. I couldn't seem to imagine myself anything but stupid little Beth, trotting about at home, of no use anywhere but there. I never wanted to go away and the hard part now is the leaving you all. I'm not afraid, but it seems as if I should be homesick for you even in heaven.

Jo's maturation is sealed by her grief over Beth's decline. The chapter entitled "Valley of the Shadow" sketches a household that revolves around Beth's room for one year. Everyone, including Beth, knows she is dying. Jo writes a long poem to her sister in which she acknowledges that true sisterhood is born in shared domestic experiences, and that such loving ties cannot be severed:

> Henceforth, safe across the river,
> I shall see forevermore
> Waiting for me on the shore.
> Hope and faith, born of my sorrow,
> Guardian angels shall become,
> And the sister gone before me
> By their hands shall lead me home.

Wasted away, suffering with "pathetic patience," Beth's death releases her parents and sisters to "thank God that Beth was well at last." Beth's self-sacrifice is ultimately the greatest in the novel. She gives up her life knowing that it has had only private, domestic meaning. Only the March family knows and loves her sweet "household spirit."

Nobody mourns Beth more than Jo, her opposite in temperament as well as her partner in the bonds of sisterhood. Beth is shy and Jo is as frank and fearless as her fictional heroes. Beth never has any plans, and Jo is full of plots and dreams. Their commonality lies in the simple fact that both of them value their sororal relationship above any other unions.

When Meg becomes engaged and Jo feels she is about to lose her "best friend," Laurie declares that he will stand by Jo forever. Jo gratefully shakes his hand, saying "I know you will, and I'm ever so much obliged; you are always a great comfort to me, Teddy." But Laurie turns out to be a boy, not Jo's sister after all. Jo's rejection of Laurie's suit is her first grown-up act, and her trip to New York to become a writer is her first flight into the world. Beth's death, through which she escapes the awful problem of growing up, triggers Jo's maturation. She does leave home to go "across the river." Jo's journey is the only fully complete one in *Little Women* and it involves her learning to tell true love from romantic fancy. She must do so in order to reproduce her lost sisterhood in a new, feminist domestic union.

The ability to distinguish true love from romantic fancy is a prerequisite for a woman's growing up in *Little Women.* True love involves mutual self-sacrifice and self-control, and requires the kind of man who can make the household the center of his life and work. Romance, on the other hand, is inherently selfish, passionate, and unequal.

Ultimately all the surviving heroines are paired off in true love. Jo, however, proves closest to Alcott's ideal because she rejects Laurie Laurence. At one point

Jo tells Laurie that they are unsuited to one another because both have strong wills and quick tempers. Unpersuaded and unreasonable, the spoiled young man presses his suit, forcing her to tell him a harder truth: she does not love him as a woman loves a man, and never did, but simply feels motherly toward him.

Jo does not want to be an adoring adornment to a fashionable man's home. Nor will she give up her "scribbling" to satisfy Laurie. She knows he would hate her writing, and that she "couldn't get on without it." Laurie shared the secret of Jo's pseudononymous stories in the past, but he really views her writing as just another glorious lark. Laurie's proposal reveals just how much "scribbling" really means to Jo. If merely saving her "pathetic family" from poverty were her only motivation, she might marry Laurie and enrich them all. She might even produce leisured, graceful literature under his patronage. But she won't be patronized and she won't concede. "I don't believe I shall every marry," she declares. "I am happy as I am, and love my liberty too well to be in any hurry to give it up for any mortal man."

Laurie stubbornly refuses to believe her, even though she has made perfectly clear that, like Louisa Alcott, she prefers "paddling her own canoe." Laurie insists that Jo has some unknown romantic rival in mind who will induce her to give up her foolish notions of independence and "live and die for him." Exasperated, her limited patience turns to defiance. "Yes, I will live and die for him," she declared, "if he ever comes and makes me love him in spite of myself, and you must do the best you can." We do not know if Jo really means that she would yield to a "great romance," or is merely angry enough to tell Laurie that his worst "envious" fantasy is what he deserves. Possibly, Jo also recognizes passions in herself, however hard she struggles to keep them under control. She certainly experiences more than "moods;" she has genuine emotional depth and active fantasies, which she usually transforms into tragi-comic family operas or melodramatic stories.

In the nineteenth-century world of *Little Women,* there are only two alternatives following the sexual equality of childhood: romantic love or rational affection. With considerable regret Jo chooses the latter, because she must forego forever the equality she once knew with Laurie, her exuberant companion in childhood. Jo's decision, as Alcott knew, presents the reader with a bitter pill, for nearly everyone wants Laurie to win Jo. Yet the author has her heroine firmly reject any "silliness" from the start. She enjoys being Laurie's chum, plays at being his mother, but is never tempted to be his domestic companion.

It is precisely because Alcott makes Laurie such an irresistible boy-man that the reader must take Jo's refusal seriously. The youthful sweet surrogate sister develops into a handsome, passionate suitor. Moreover, Jo is physically attracted to Laurie, and frequently observes his handsome face, curly hair, and fine eyes. She hates it when he briefly ruins his romantic looks with a collegiate pose. The reader as well as Jo feels the power of Laurie's sexuality and the power he tries to exert over her. Yet if he calls her "my girl," meaning his sweetheart, she calls him "my boy," meaning her son.

Jo's refusal is not prompted by love for a rival suitor. In New York she works as a governess to children in her boardinghouse and scribbles away for the penny-dreadful newspapers. Soon she encounters Friedrick Bhaer helping a serving maid. Bhaer's life, unlike Laurie's, is not the stuff of romance. Forty-years old, "learned and good," he is domestic by nature and darns his own socks. He loves flowers and children and reads good literature. Moreover, he insists that Jo give up writing blood-and-thunder tales and learn to write good fiction. He gives her his own copy of Shakespeare as a Christmas present. . . . Bhaer is a man Jo can love and marry.

A mature adult capable of raising his two orphaned nephews, he does not need Jo to mother him, although she is drawn to do so. Bhaer is more attracted to her youth and independent spirit. Nevertheless, he bestows his affection upon her by appreciating both her Old World "gemutlichkeit" and her American self-reliance. In a way he is Santa Claus, giving gifts despite his poverty to friends and servants alike. In one scene Bhaer buys oranges and figs for small children while holding a dilapidated blue umbrella aloft for Jo in the rain. Unlike Father March, who is a fragile invalid, Father Bhaer is a strapping, generous man.

There is no end to his domesticity or his capacity for cooperative self-sacrifice. Matching his paternal benevolence to Jo's maternal abundance, Bhaer does the shopping for both himself and Jo. As Alcott describes him, he "finished the marketing by buying several pounds of grapes, a pot of rosy daisies, and a pretty jar of honey, to be regarded in the light of a demijohn. Then, distorting his pockets with the knobby bundles, and giving her the flowers to hold, he put up the old umbrella and they travelled on again." Contrast this fulgent account of a man who understands the "household spirit" with Laurie, who cannot even direct the maids to plump his pillows properly, or with John Brooke, who magisterially sends the meat and vegetables home to Meg (no knobby bundles in his pockets!).

Meanwhile, Laurie has returned from Europe with Amy, and they tell the story of their Swiss romance. Laurie has found a perfect mate in Amy, who will be very good at giving orders to their servants, having practised in her imagination for years. Theirs will also be an equal marital partnership, though somewhat different from that of Jo and Fritz, and very different from the frugal conventions of Meg and John.

Jo, the last sister to leave home, might never have accepted Professor Bhaer's proposal were it not for Beth's death. Fritz has found a poem of Jo's expressing the deep love and devotion she feels for Meg, Amy, and Beth. We are "parted only for an hour, none lost," she writes, "one only gone before." Tenderly Bhaer declares: "I read that, and I think to myself, she has a sorrow, she is lonely, she would find comfort in true love. I haf a heart full for her."

Bhaer has all the qualities Bronson Alcott lacked: warmth, intimacy, and a tender capacity for expressing his affection—the feminine attributes Louisa admired and hoped men could acquire in a rational, feminist world. As Marmee says, he is "a dear man." He touches everyone, hugs and carries children about on his back. Bronson, despite all his genuine idealism and devotion to humanity, was emotionally reserved and distant. Fritz Bhaer loves material reality, is eminently approachable, and values all the things that Bronson Alcott rejects, such as good food, warm rooms, and appealing domestic disorder, even though he is a "bacheldore" when Jo meets him.

Bhaer's love for Jo gives him courage to conquer the barriers between them, including his poverty and age, his foreignness and his babbling, unromantic self. They decide to share life's burdens just as they shared the load of bundles on their shopping expedition. Jo hopes to fulfill "woman's special mission" of which is "drying tears and bearing burdens," so that nobody will ever again call her unwomanly. She resolutely adds the feminist postscript: "I'm to carry my share Friedrich and help to earn the home. Make up your mind to that, or I'll never go." She has her family duty and her work to keep her busy, while Fritz goes west to support his nephews before he can marry. The marriage contract they arrange is very different from that of Meg and John at the end of *Little Women*, part one. (pp. 153-64)

True love is not denied at the end of *Little Women;* it is linked, as Fritz Bhaer put it, "to the wish to share and enlarge that so happy home." (p. 166)

Sarah Elbert, in her *A Hunger for Home: Louisa May Alcott and "Little Women,"* Temple University Press, 1984, 278 p.

ELAINE SHOWALTER

(essay date 1988)

[Showalter is an American educator. In the following excerpt, she surveys Alcott's literary career.]

Alcott's professional writing life really began after 1862 when she made the daring decision to volunteer as a nurse in a Civil War army hospital. (p. xviii)

Although the work was backbreaking and miserably paid, and the spectacle of suffering much more traumatic than she had anticipated, she was exhilarated by the city of Washington and the challenge of important work: "Though often homesick, heartsick, and worn out, I like it," she wrote in her journal. But after only six weeks of duty, she caught typhoid fever and was brought home in delirium by her father. (p. xix)

The illness took a lifelong toll on Alcott; she never recovered from the poisonous side effects of mercury medication, and permanently lost the stamina and health of her youth. Yet she was able to draw on her war experiences to write about "men and reality" as she had intended. *Hospital Sketches* (1863) was her first literary success; the little volume "never made much money, but it showed me my 'style' "—a mixture of humor, realism, and pathos. During the next several years, she was finally able to give up other work, developing her literary skills by writing in several different modes. In 1862 she wrote the first of her sensation tales in order to win a hundred-dollar prize offered by *Frank Leslie's Illustrated Newspaper.* (pp. xx-xxi)

In contrast, her much-revised Emersonian novel *Moods* (1864), inscribed to "Mother, my earliest patron, kindest critic, and dearest reader," drew criticism for its frank representation of marriage and divorce. To speak freely of marriage caused trouble, Alcott noted: "My next book shall have no *ideas* in it, only facts, and the people shall be as ordinary as possible; then critics will say it is all right."

In 1865-66, Alcott went to Europe for the first time, not as a journalist, but as the companion to a wealthy young invalid, Anna Weld. The trip might have been a turning point for her; it was her first extended absence from her parents, and she had long dreamed of traveling abroad. Instead she chafed at the restrictions of her job, and often felt lonely, homesick, and bored. (p. xxi)

The trip to Europe was Alcott's farewell to adventure and romance. She returned home in July to Marmee's welcoming arms, but also to new financial obligations and family debts. **"Behind a Mask,"** which she wrote in August 1866, suggests her rage at servitude, and the bitterness with which she faced the prospects of eternal repression and pretense. Her last sensation story, **"A Modern Mephistopheles, or The Fatal Love Chase"** (1867), was rejected by her publishers as too lurid. A full-length novel about a girl who sells her soul to the devil in exchange for a life of adventure, it powerfully mirrored many of her own temptations, and her fascination with the idea of a female Faust. Alcott never published the story, the manuscript of which is in Houghton Library at Harvard; ten years later she would use the title for a different novel, one that editors and biographers have often confused with her unpublished thriller.

After several years of rising income, Alcott earned $1000 in 1867 and saw a secure future: "I want to realize my dream of supporting the family and being perfectly independent." In the interests of this quest for financial stability, she began to make the literary compromises that would plague her for the rest of her career. Early in 1868, she accepted the editorship of a girls' magazine, *Merry's Museum,* to which she contributed stories, poems, and advice under the diminishing pseudonym of "Aunty Wee." She also set out to prepare a new edition of *Hospital Sketches* and her war stories: "By taking out all Biblical allusions, and softening all allusions to rebs, the book may be made 'quite perfect,' I am told. Anything to suit customers." Soon after, at the request of her publishers, Roberts Brothers, she set aside her own literary projects to write a "girls' story." *Little Women*—a book she had not particularly wanted to write—ironically made her not only famous, but famous for womanly goodness. Money came pouring in, pilgrims came to see the famous author, and Bronson found new celebrity as the Father of the Little Women.

Despite fame and prosperity, Alcott's maturity found her increasingly "porcupiny," sick, and embittered. Celebrity seekers invaded her privacy, and she never felt pride in her work. "When I had youth," she wrote, "I had no money; now I have the money, I have no time; and when I get the time, if I ever do, I shall have no health to enjoy life." The demands of her readers for more books like *Little Women* tied her to a particular domestic style she found maddeningly restrictive, while her family's constant needs kept her at the grindstone of literary production. Anna's husband died in 1870, leaving the widow with two small sons; and Louisa rushed back from a European vacation to churn out books for their support.

Yet Alcott's feminist interests entered her work even under the guise of conventional plots; in 1868 she had joined the New England Woman Suffrage Association, and women's rights are an issue in much of her writing in the next decade. *An Old-Fashioned Girl* (1870) and *Little Men* (1871), which continued the story of the March family, presented lively independent girls and described communities that took them seriously. In 1872, Alcott carried the theme further in *Work,* a feminist novel she had begun ten years earlier. Two other novels for girls, *Eight Cousins* (1875) and *Rose in Bloom* (1876), also took a feminist perspective on women's education, dress reform, physical education for girls, and women's work. In the second book, the heroine Rose offers a spirited defense of feminist ideals: "We've got minds and souls as well as hearts; ambition and talents as well as beauty and accomplishments; and we want to live and learn as well as love and be loved. I'm sick of being told that is all a woman is fit for! I won't have anything to do with love until I

prove that I am something beside a housekeeper and a baby-tender!" Alcott also published several collections of stories and sketches for her insatiable readers, including the temperance stories of *Silver Pitchers* and six volumes of *Aunt Jo's Scrap-Bag.*

In 1877, eager for a way out of the role of domestic novelist, Alcott published *A Modern Mephistopheles,* another Faustian fantasy, in Roberts Brothers' anonymous No Name Series. As Eugenia Kaledin and Judith Fetterley have suggested, the novel's plot of a writer who sells his soul for fame by publishing poetry that is not his own reflected Alcott's feeling that she had made her own "Faustian pact" of inauthenticity for the sake of financial success. By the end of the decade, as she nursed Abba through the final illness, the quality of her writing noticeably declined, although the quantity of her production stayed high. *Under the Lilacs* (1878) and *Jack and Jill* (1879) were feeble and moralistic recyclings of her earlier work. Although she had always intended to write the story of her mother's life, she burned many of Abba's diaries after her mother's death instead, perhaps unable to face the realities she had learned to evade after so many years. (pp. xxii-xxiv)

Meanwhile, Bronson remained a steady responsibility. In August 1879 Alcott endowed a School of Philosophy for her eighty-year-old father at Concord. While Bronson basked in the attention and acclaim, his daughter, as usual, did all the work: "The town swarms with budding philosophers, and they roost on our steps like hens waiting for corn. Father revels in it, so we keep the hotel going, and try to look as if we liked it. If they were philanthropists, I should enjoy it; but speculation seems a waste of time when there is so much real work crying to be done." She had put her own celebrity to work for the women's suffrage movement, writing frequent letters of endorsement for the *Woman's Journal,* attending women's congresses, and leading the campaign for the vote in Concord. While the philosophers roosted and clucked, she "drove about and drummed up women to my suffrage meeting," and became the first woman in Concord to register as a voter.

Alcott's last years were devoted to the care of [her niece] Lulu and her father. Mothering the little girl came as a pleasure and gave meaning to a life which seemed to have lost direction: "I see now why I lived. To care for May's child and not leave Anna all alone." Lulu's arrival gave her the excuse for the first time to establish her own home in Boston's Louisville Square. But ill health made it difficult for her to be patient and playful, and severe attacks of vertigo, headaches, dyspepsia, rheumatism, insomnia, and nervous prostration made it impossible for her to write. She unsuccessfully sought help from a variety of quacks, homeopathic physicians, and mind-cure specialists, but never could confront the emotional conflicts that expressed themselves in these physical forms.

During her last years, her literary productivity finally began to decline; *Jo's Boys* had [to] be put aside while she rested. Instead she wrote down in *Lulu's Library* the simple stories she had told her niece: "Old ladies come to this twaddle when they can do nothing else," she told her publisher. In 1881, having bought the copyright of *Moods* from the publisher for one dollar, she issued a revised and moralistic version of the earlier text, in which the heroine repents of her adulterous longings and goes back to her husband. To the last, Alcott tried to believe that her self-sacrifice would be rewarded, and that any success she had won had come because "my ambition was not for selfish ends but for my dear family." Yet somehow there was never time for the rest, pleasure, and travel she desired. "Shall never live my own life," she wrote bleakly in her journal.

Jo's Boys, which she finally managed to finish in 1886, completed the saga of the March family, and the real family seemed to follow its literary destiny. After a long decline, Bronson Alcott died on March 4, 1888, and the weary Louisa wondered, "Shall I ever find time to die?" Two days later, the slowly accumulating effects of mercury poisoning from her Civil War treatment finally took her life. At their joint funeral, the minister suggested that Bronson had needed his dutiful daughter's help even in heaven. (pp. xxv–xxvi)

Elaine Showalter, in an introduction to *Alternative Alcott* by Louisa May Alcott, edited by Elaine Showalter, Rutgers University Press, 1988, pp. ix–xliii.

SOURCES FOR FURTHER STUDY

Bedell, Madelon. *The Alcott's: Biography of a Family.* New York: Clarkson N. Potter, 1980, 400 p.
  Extensive history of the Alcott family.

The Horn Book, Special Number XLIV, No. 5 (October 1968): 158 p.
  Special issue commemorating the centennial of the publication of *Little Women.* The issue contains essays from several Alcott critics, including Cornelia Meigs and Lavinia Russ.

MacDonald, Ruth K. *Louisa May Alcott.* Boston: Twayne, 1983, 111 p.
  Monograph study of Alcott's life and works, including a discussion of her "influence on the tradition of children's literature."

Marsella, Joy. *The Promise of Destiny: Children and Women in the Short Stories of Louisa May Alcott.* Westport, Conn.: Greenwood Press, 1983, 166 p.
  Examines *Aunt Jo's Scrap Bag* as "an analysis of women's roles, female destiny in the affirmation of the family, the duty of the maiden aunt, and the noble ends for the single woman."

Stern, Madeleine [B]. Introduction to *Behind a Mask: The Unknown Thrillers of Louisa May Alcott,* by Louisa May Alcott, edited by Madeleine [B.] Stern, pp. vii–xxxiii. New York: William Morrow and Co., 1975.
  Excellent introduction to the pseudonymous works of Alcott. Stern traces each story's origin, the periodical in which each piece first appeared, and the critical reception each received.

Stern, Madeleine B. *Critical Essays on Louisa May Alcott.* Boston: G. K. Hall and Co., 1984, 295 p.
  Collection of excerpts from previously published critical reviews and studies of Alcott's works.

Hans Christian Andersen

1805-1875

(Also wrote under pseudonym Villiam Christian Walter) Danish fairy tale writer, poet, short story writer, novelist, travel writer, autobiographer, and dramatist.

INTRODUCTION

Andersen is perhaps the foremost writer of fairy tales in world literature. Known for such stories as "The Little Mermaid," "The Steadfast Tin Soldier," and "The Ugly Duckling," he expanded the scope of the fairy tale genre by creating original stories drawn from a wealth of folklore and personal experience that reveal his boundless imagination. Though Andersen hoped for greater success as a dramatist than as a children's writer and wrote a number of dramas and novels, none of these works achieved the popularity of his fairy tales. Andersen utilized the simple premise and structure of the fairy tale to transform his ideas about human nature into allegories that are written in a conversational language children can understand and enjoy. "I seize an idea for older people," he wrote, "and then tell it to the young ones, while remembering that father and mother are listening and must have something to think about." Many critics believe that Andersen's genius lay in his ability to see nature, events, people, and objects with childlike curiosity and imagination, and to infuse his subjects with traits never before attributed to them. A master craftsman, Andersen created a body of literature that is loved by readers of all ages throughout the world.

Andersen's childhood experiences greatly influenced his literary perspective and are reflected in his fairy tales. He was born in Odense, Denmark, to a poor shoemaker and his superstitious, uneducated wife. His father, a religious man who had hoped for a more fulfilling career, encouraged his son to aspire to a better life by telling him glamorous stories about the theater and opera and by sending him to school at an early age. The elder Andersen also encouraged his son's vivid imagination; he read to the boy from the comedies of Ludvig Holberg, *The Arabian Nights,* and the fairy tales of Jean de La Fontaine, and he built him a puppet the-

52

ater. Andersen was a shy child: instead of playing with other children, he wrote puppet dramas and designed costumes for his characters. In 1819, three years after his father's death, Andersen moved to Copenhagen to pursue an acting career. As a young boy without references, he was denied admittance to the Royal Theater and was rejected by Copenhagen's opera company. However, Jonas Collin, a director of the Royal Theater, was impressed by the promise Andersen showed as a writer. Collin took Andersen into his home, sent him to grammar school, and supported him until he passed the entrance exams to the University of Copenhagen. He was Andersen's confidant, critic, and friend, and Andersen remained closely connected with the Collin family throughout his life.

Andersen's initial works were inspired by William Shakespeare and Sir Walter Scott; his pseudonym at that time, Villiam Christian Walter, was adopted in homage to the two writers. Although his first works were virtually ignored, Andersen won recognition in 1829 for *Fodreise fra Holmens Canal til østpynten af Amager i aarene,* the chronicle of an imaginary journey through Copenhagen. He traveled to Germany in 1831 and then to Italy in 1833. During his stay in Italy, Andersen began his *Eventyr, fortalte for børn* (1835-44; *Fairy Tales Told for Children*), tales that would later be recognized as among his most significant works. By 1835, when his *Eventyr,* or "Wonder Stories," was published, Andersen was well-known in Denmark for his travel books, plays, and a novel, *Improvisatoren* (1845; *The Improvisatore; or, Life in Italy*). Early critical reception of *Eventyr* was generally negative, and at first, Andersen agreed with his detractors, calling his tales *smaating,* or trifles. However, he soon realized that these short works were the perfect outlet for his messages to the world, so he continued to write stories in this vein. Andersen also discovered that his tales commanded his greatest audience and could bring him the international fame he craved. His popularity increased in Europe and America, and he traveled extensively throughout Germany, Holland, and England. Andersen was unpopular in Denmark, however, and it was not until his health began to fail that he was acknowledged by his native country as its most universally popular and prominent author.

Andersen's fairy tales fall into two general groups: twelve adaptations of traditional Danish folktales and one hundred forty-four original creations. In his adaptations, Andersen frequently integrated plots from more than one source. "The Tinder Box," for example, is based on a combination of an old Danish tale, "The Spirit of the Candle," and an episode from the *Arabian Nights.* Andersen himself divided his original tales into two distinct classes: *eventyr* and *historier.* The *eventyr* are fairy tales in which a supernatural element contributes to the outcome of the narrative. "The

Little Mermaid," for example, is set in a kingdom beneath the sea and tells the story of a mermaid who drinks a magical potion brewed by a sea-witch in hopes that she will be metamorphosed into a human. Andersen's *historier* are stories that do not employ a supernatural element. Frequently, the *historier* starkly portray poverty and suffering, leaving readers disturbed when good is not necessarily rewarded at a story's conclusion. The *historier* also often reveal their author's strong moral and religious attitudes: Andersen had a childlike faith in God and perceived death as a reward for a difficult life. This perception is perhaps most vividly portrayed in "The Little Match Girl," a grim story in which an impoverished child dies from exposure on Christmas Eve when no one will buy her matches. The child is finally freed from her suffering when her deceased grandmother arrives to lead her to heaven. Although many of Andersen's *historier* and fairy tales end unhappily, most critics concur that his underlying attitude in his stories is positive. Andersen often offered an optimistic approach to otherwise distressing situations and invested many of his tales with a mischievous sense of humor. Of all his stories, his semi-autobiographical sketches are considered his most enduring. Stories like "The Little Mermaid," "The Nightingale," and "The Steadfast Tin Soldier" reflect in part Andersen's own unrequited love affairs in varying degrees of melancholy and satire. "The Ugly Duckling," the story of a homely cygnet who becomes the most beautiful of all swans, is probably Andersen's best-loved and most popular work of this type. Just as the snubbed cygnet becomes a beautiful swan, so Andersen became the pride of Denmark and its international literary representative.

In general, Andersen's works have been consistently well received. Georg Brandes, one of the first prominent critics to recognize Andersen's literary significance, especially commended Andersen's use of conversational language, which he claimed distinguished the author from other children's writers and prevented his stories from becoming outdated. Later, such Danish critics as Elias Bredsdorff and Erik Haugaard praised the uncluttered structure of Andersen's tales. Some twentieth-century commentators have considered Andersen's work maudlin and overly disturbing for small children. Nevertheless, he is usually recognized as a consummate storyteller who distilled his vision of humanity into a simple format that has proved universally popular. His fairy tales remain the enduring favorites of children and adults throughout the world.

(For further information about Andersen's life and works, see *Children's Literature Review,* Vol. 6; *Nineteenth-Century Literature Criticism,* Vol. 7; *Short Story Criticism,* Vol. 6; and *Yesterday's Authors of Books for Children,* Vol. 1.)

CRITICAL COMMENTARY

HORACE E. SCUDDER

(essay date 1875)

[Scudder was Andersen's first American champion, intervening on behalf of the Danish fairy tale writer to secure payment for the sale of Andersen's works in the United States. In the following excerpt, he discusses Andersen's contribution to the fairy tale genre.]

It is customary to speak of Andersen's best known short stories as fairy tales; wonder-stories is in some respects a more exact description, but the name has hardly a native sound. Andersen himself classed his stories under the two heads of *historier* and *eventyr;* the historier corresponds well enough with its English mate, being the history of human action, or, since it is a short history, the story; the eventyr, more nearly allied perhaps to the German *abenteuer* than to the English *adventure,* presumes an element of strangeness causing wonder, while it does not necessarily demand the machinery of the supernatural. When we speak of fairy tales, we have before our minds the existence, for artistic purposes, of a spiritual world peopled with beings that exercise themselves in human affairs, and are endowed in the main with human attributes, though possessed of certain ethereal advantages, and generally under orders from some superior power, often dimly understood as fate; the Italians, indeed, call the fairy *fata.* In a rough way we include under the title of fairies all the terrible and grotesque shapes as well, and this world of spiritual beings is made to consist of giants, ogres, brownies, pixies, nisses, gnomes, elves, and whatever other creatures have found in it a local habitation and name. The fairy itself is generally represented as very diminutive, the result, apparently, of an attempted compromise between the imagination and the senses, by which the existence of fairies for certain purposes is conceded on condition they shall be made so small that the senses may be excused from recognizing them.

The belief in fairies gave rise to the genuine fairy tale, which is now an acknowledged classic, and the gradual elimination of this belief from the civilized mind has been attended with some awkwardness. These creations of fancy—if we must so dismiss them—had secured a somewhat positive recognition in literature before it was finally discovered that they came out of the unseen and therefore could have no life. (pp. 598-99)

It may be accepted as a foregone conclusion that with a disbelief in fairies the genuine fairy tale has died, and that it is better to content ourselves with those stories which sprang from actual belief, telling them over to successive generations of children, than to seek to extend the literature by any ingenuity of modern skepticism. There they are, the fairy tales without authorship, as imperishable as nursery ditties; scholarly collections of them may be made, but they will have their true preservation, not as specimens in a museum of literary curiosities, but as children's toys. Like the sleeping princess in the wood, the fairy tale may be hedged about with bristling notes and thickets of commentaries, but the child will pass straight to the beauty, and awaken for his own delight the old charmed life.

It is worth noting, then, that just when historical criticism, under the impulse of the Grimms, was ordering and accounting for these fragile creations,—a sure mark that they were ceasing to exist as living forms in literature,—Hans Christian Andersen should have come forward as master in a new order of stories, which may be regarded as the true literary successor to the old order of fairy tales, answering the demands of a spirit which rejects the pale ghost of the scientific or moral or jocular or pedantic fairy tale. Andersen, indeed, has invented fairy tales purely such, and has given form and enduring substance to traditional stories current in Scandinavia; but it is not upon such work that his real fame rests, and it is certain that while he will be mentioned in the biographical dictionaries as the writer of novels, poems, romances, dramas, sketches of travel, and an autobiography, he will be known and read as the author of certain short stories, of which the charm at first glance seems to be in the sudden discovery of life and humor in what are ordinarily regarded as inanimate objects, or what are somewhat compassionately called dumb animals. When we have read and studied the stories further, and perceived their ingenuity and wit and human philosophy, we can after all give no better account of their charm than just this, that they disclose the possible or fancied parallel to human life carried on by what our senses tell us has no life, or our reason assures us has no rational power.

The life which Andersen sets before us is in fact a dramatic representation upon an imaginary stage, with puppets that are not pulled by strings, but have their own muscular and nervous economy. The life

Principal Works

Ungdoms-Forsøg [as Villiam Christian Walter] (novel) 1822

Fodreise fra Holmens Canal til østpynten af Amager i aa-rene 1828 og 1829 (travel essay) 1829

Eventyr, fortalte for børn. 2 vols. (fairy tales) 1835-44

   [Fairy Tales Told for Children, 1845]

Improvisatoren (novel) 1835

   [The Improvisatore; or, Life in Italy, 1845]

Kun en spillemand (novel) 1837

   [Only a Fiddler!, 1845]

De to baronesser (novel) 1838

   [The Two Baronesses, 1848]

Billedbog uden billeder (short stories) 1840

   [Picture Book without Pictures, 1847]

En digters bazar (poetry, short stories, and travel essays) 1842

   [A Poet's Bazaar, 1846]

I Sverrig (travel sketches) 1851

[Pictures of Sweden, 1851]

Mit Livs Eventyr (autobiography) 1855; revised edition, 1859

   [The Story of My Life, 1871; revised edition, 1877]

At voere eller ikker voere (novel) 1857

   [To Be or Not To Be, 1857]

I Spanien (travel essays) 1863

   [In Spain, 1864]

Lykke-Peer (novel) 1870

   [Lucky Peer, 1871]

Samlede voerker. 15 vols. (fairy tales, short stories, travel essays, novels, and poetry) 1876-80

Eventyr og historier. 5 vols. (short stories) 1894-1900

The Complete Andersen. 6 vols. (fairy tales and short stories) 1942-48

Hans Christian Andersen's Fairy Tales (fairy tales) 1950

---

which he displays is not a travesty of human life, it is human life repeated in miniature under conditions which give a charming and unexpected variety. By some transmigration, souls have passed into tin-soldiers, balls, tops, beetles, money-pigs, coins, shoes, leap-frogs, matches, and even such attenuated individualities as darning-needles; and when, informing these apparently dead or stupid bodies, they begin to make manifestations, it is always in perfect consistency with the ordinary conditions of the bodies they occupy, though the several objects become by this endowment of souls suddenly expanded in their capacity. Perhaps in nothing is Andersen's delicacy of artistic feeling better shown than in the manner in which he deals with his animated creations when they are brought into direct relations with human beings. The absurdity which the bald understanding perceives is dexterously suppressed by a reduction of all the factors to one common term. For example, in his story of **"The Leap-Frog,"** he tells how a flea, a grasshopper and a leap-frog once wanted to see which could jump highest, and invited the whole world "and everybody else besides who chose to come," to see the performance. The king promised to give his daughter to the one who jumped the highest, for it was stale fun when there was no prize to jump for. The flea and the grasshopper came forward in turn and put in their claims; the leap-frog also appeared, but was silent. The flea jumped so high that nobody could see where he went to, so they all asserted that he had not jumped at all; the grasshopper jumped in the king's face, and was set down as an ill-mannered thing; the leap-frog, after reflection, leaped into the lap of the princess, and thereupon the king said, "There is nothing above my daughter; therefore to bound up to her is the highest jump that can be made: but for this, one must possess understanding, and the leap-frog has shown that he has understanding. He is brave and intellectual." "And so," the story declares, "he won the princess." The barren absurdity of a leap-frog marrying a princess is perhaps the first thing that strikes the impartial reader of this abstract, and there is very likely something offensive to him in the notion; but in the story itself this absurdity is so delightfully veiled by the succession of happy turns in the characterization of the three jumpers, as well as of the old king, the house-dog, and the old councilor "who had had three orders given him to make him hold his tongue," that the final impression upon the mind is that of a harmonizing of all the characters, and the king, princess, and councilor can scarcely be distinguished in kind from the flea, grasshopper, leap-frog, and house-dog. After that, the marriage of the leap-frog and princess is quite a matter of course.

The use of speaking animals in story was no discovery of Andersen's, and yet in the distinction between his wonder-story and the well-known fable lies an explanation of the charm which attaches to his work. The end of every fable is *hoec fabula docet,* and it was for this palpable end that the fable was created. The lion, the fox, the mouse, the dog, are in a very limited way true to the accepted nature of the animals which they represent, and their intercourse with each other is governed by the ordinary rules of animal life, but the actions and words are distinctly illustrative of some morality. The fable is an animated proverb. The animals are made to act and speak in accordance with some intended lesson, and have this for the reason of their being. The lesson is first; the characters, created afterward, are, for purposes of the teacher, disguished as animals; very little of the animal appears, but very much of the lesson. The art which invented the fable was a modest handmaid to morality. In Andersen's stories, however, the spring is not in the didactic but in the imaginative. He sees the beetle in the imperial stable stretching out his thin legs to be shod with golden shoes like the emperor's favorite horse, and the personality of the beetle-determines the movement of the story throughout; egotism, pride at being proud, jealousy, and unbounded self-conceit are the furniture of this beetle's soul, and his adventures one by one disclose his character. Is there a lesson in all this? Precisely as there is a lesson in any picture of human life where the same traits are sketched. The beetle, after all his adventures, some of them ignominious but none expelling his self-conceit, finds himself again in the emperor's stable, having solved the problem why the emperor's horse had golden shoes. "They were given to the horse on my account," he says, and adds, "the world is not so bad after all, but one must know how to take things as they come." There is in this and other of Andersen's stories a singular shrewdness, as of a very keen observer of life, singular because at first blush the author seems to be a sentimentalist. The satires, like **"The Emperor's New Clothes"** and **"The Swiftest Runners,"** mark this characteristic of shrewd observation very cleverly. Perhaps, after all, we are stating most simply the distinction between his story and the fable when we say that humor is a prominent element in the one and absent in the other; and to say that there is humor is to say that there is real life.

It is frequently said that Andersen's stories accomplish their purpose of amusing children by being childish, yet it is impossible for a mature person to read them without detecting repeatedly the marks of experience. There is a subtle undercurrent of wisdom that has nothing to do with childishness, and the child who is entertained returns to the same story afterward to find a deeper significance than it was possible for him to apprehend at the first reading. The forms and the incident are in consonance with childish experience, but the spirit which moves through the story comes from a mind that has seen and felt the analogue of the story in some broader or coarser form. The story of **"The Ugly Duckling,"** is an inimitable presentation of Andersen's own tearful and finally triumphant life; yet no child who reads the story has its sympathy for a moment withdrawn from the duckling and transferred to a human being. Andersen's nice sense of artistic limitations saves him from making the older thought obtrude

itself upon the notice of children, and his power of placing himself at the same angle of vision with children is remarkably shown in one instance, where, in **"Little Klaus and Big Klaus,"** death is treated as a mere incident in the story, a surprise but not a terror.

Now that Andersen has told his stories, it seems an easy thing to do, and we have plenty of stories written for children that attempt the same thing, sometimes also with moderate success; for Andersen's discovery was after all but the simple application to literature of a faculty which has always been exercised. The likeness that things inanimate have to things animate is constantly forced upon us; it remained for Andersen to pursue the comparison further, and, letting types loose from their antitypes, to give them independent existence. The result has been a surprise in literature and a genuine addition to literary forms. It is possible to follow in his steps, now that he has shown us the way, but it is no less evident that the success which he attained was due not merely to his happy discovery of a latent property, but to the nice feeling and strict obedience to laws of art with which he made use of his discovery. Andersen's genius enabled him to see the soul in a darning-needle, and he perceived also the limitations of the life he was to portray, so that while he was often on the edge of absurdity he did not lose his balance. Especially is it to be noted that these stories, which we regard as giving an opportunity for invention when the series of old-fashioned fairy tales had been closed, show clearly the coming in of that temper in novel-writing which is eager to describe things as they are. Within the narrow limits of his miniature story, Andersen moves us by the same impulse as the modern novelist who depends for his material upon what he has actually seen and heard, and for his inspiration upon the power to penetrate the heart of things; so that the old fairy tale finds its successor in this new realistic wonder-story, just as the old romance gives place to the new novel. In both, as in the corresponding development of poetry and painting, is found a deeper sense of life and a finer perception of the intrinsic value of common forms. (pp. 599-602)

Horace E. Scudder, "Andersen's Short Stories," in *The Atlantic Monthly,* Vol. XXXVI, No. CCXVII, November, 1875, pp. 598-602.

GEORG BRANDES
(essay date 1883)

[An esteemed Danish literary critic and biographer, Brandes was the first prominent scholar to write extensively on Andersen. According to Elias Bredsdorff, Brandes was "the first scholar altogether who realised that Andersen's tales gave him an important and unique place in world literature and who saw that the tales themselves merited serious critical discussion." The following excerpt is from an essay that initially appeared in Danish in Brande's *Det moderne gjennembruds maend* (1883). Here, Brandes favorably assesses Andersen's tales, admiring in particular his ability to write as a child might think.]

[In Andersen's stories we find that the] construction, the position of the words in individual sentences, the entire arrangement, is at variance with the simplest rules of syntax. "This is not the way people write." That is true; but it is the way they speak. To grown people? No, but to children; and why should it not be proper to commit the words to writing in the same order in which they are spoken to children? In such a case the usual form is simply exchanged for another; not the rules of abstract written language, but the power of comprehension of the child is here the determining factor; there is method in this disorder, as there is method in the grammatical blunder of the child when it makes use of a regular imperfect for an irregular verb. . . . [Andersen] has the bold intention to employ oral speech in a printed work, he will not write but speak, and he will gladly write as a school-child writes, if he can thus avoid speaking as a book speaks. (p. 2)

Happy, indeed, is Andersen! What author has such a public as he? . . . His stories are numbered among the books which we have deciphered syllable by syllable, and which we still read to-day. There are some among them whose letters even now, seem to us larger, whose words appear to have more value than all others, because we first made their acquaintance letter by letter and word by word. (p. 4)

The starting-point for this art is the child's play that makes everything out of everything; in conformity with this, the sportive mood of the artist transforms playthings into natural creations, into supernatural beings, into heroes, and, *vice versa,* uses everything natural and everything supernatural—heroes, sprites, and fairies—for playthings, that is to say, for artistic means which through each artistic combination are remodelled and freshly stamped. The nerve and sinew of the art is the imagination of the child, which invests everything with a soul, and endows everything with personality; thus, a piece of household furniture is as readily animated with life as a plant, a flower as well as a bird or a cat, and the animal in the same manner as the doll, the portrait, the cloud, the sunbeam, the wind, and the seasons. . . . This is the way a child dreams, and this is the way a poet depicts to us the dream of a child. The soul of this poetry, however, is neither the dream nor the play; it is a peculiar, ever-childlike, yet at the same time a more than childlike faculty, not only for putting one thing in the place of another (thus, for making constant exchange, or for causing one thing to live in another, thus for animating all things), but also a faculty for being swiftly and readily reminded by one thing of another, for regaining one thing in another, for generalizing, for moulding an image into a symbol, for exalting a dream into a myth, and through an artistic process, for transforming single fictitious traits into a focus for the whole of life. . . . A form that for any one else would be a circuitous route to the goal, a hindrance and a disguise, becomes for Andersen a mask behind which alone he feels truly free, truly happy and secure. His child-like genius, like the well-known child forms of antiquity, plays with the mask, elicits laughter, awakens delight and terror. Thus the nursery story's mode of expression, which with all its frankness is masked, becomes the natural, indeed, the classic cadence of his voice, that but very rarely becomes overstrained or out of tune. The only disturbing occurrence is that now and then a draught of whey is obtained instead of the pure milk of the nursery story, that the tone occasionally becomes too sentimental and sickly sweet (**"Poor John," "The Poor Bird," "Poor Thumbling"**), which, however, is rarely the case in materials taken from folk-lore tales, as **"The Tinder-Box," "Little Claus and Big Claus,"** etc., where the naïve joviality, freshness, and roughness of the narrative, which announces crimes and murders without the slightest sympathetic or tearful phrase, stand Andersen in good stead, and invest his figures with increased sturdiness. Less classic, on the other hand, is the tone of the lyric effusions interwoven with some of the nursery stories, in which the poet, in a stirring, pathetic prose gives a bird's-eye view of some great period of history (**"The Thorny Path of Honor," "The Swan's Nest"**). In these stories there seems to me to be a certain wild flight of fancy, a certain forced inspiration in the prevailing tone, wholly disproportionate to the not very significant thought of the contents; for thought and diction are like a pair of lovers. Thought may be somewhat larger, somewhat loftier, than diction, even as the man is taller than the woman; in the opposite case there is something unlovely in the relation. With the few exceptions just indicated, the narrative style of Andersen's nursery stories is a model of its kind. (pp. 5-8)

Now what is there in plants, in animals, in the child, so attractive to Andersen? He loves the child because his affectionate heart draws him to the little ones, the weak and helpless ones to whom it is allowable to speak with compassion, with tender sympathy, and because when he devotes such sentiments to a hero,—as in *Only a Fiddler,*—he is derided for it. . . . but when he dedicates them to a child, he finds the natural resting-place for his mood. It is owing to his genuine democratic feeling for the lowly and neglected that Andersen, himself a child of the people, continually introduces into his nursery stories (as Dickens, in his novels), forms from the poorer classes of society, "simple folk," yet endowed with the true nobility of the soul. . . . The poor are as defenseless as the child. Furthermore, Andersen loves the child, because he is able to portray it, not so much in the direct psychologic way of the romance,—he is by no means a direct psychologist,—as indirectly, by transporting himself with a bound into the child's world, and he acts as though no other course were possible. . . . He seldom introduces the child into his nursery stories as taking part in the action and conversation. He does it most frequently in the charming little collection *A Picture-Book without Pictures* where more than anywhere else he permits the child to speak with the entire simplicity of its nature. In such brief, naïve child-utterances as those cited in it there is much pleasure and entertainment. . . . Yet his child forms are comparatively rare. The most noteworthy ones are little Hjalmar, little Tuk, Kay and Gerda, the unhappy, vain Karen in **"The Red Shoes,"** a dismal but well-written story, the little girl with the matches and the little girl in **"A Great Sorrow,"** finally Ib and Christine, the children in **"Under the Willow-Tree."** Besides these real children there are some ideal ones, the little fairy-like Thumbling and the little wild robber-maiden, undoubtedly Andersen's freshest child creation, the masterly portrayal of whose wild nature forms a most felicitous contrast to the many good, fair-haired and tame children of fiction. (pp. 23-5)

An author like Andersen, who has so great a repugnance to beholding what is cruel and coarse in its nakedness, who is so deeply impressed by anything of the kind that he dare not relate it, but recoils a hundred times in his works from some wanton or outrageous deed with the maidenly expression, "We cannot bear to think of it!" Such an author feels content and at home in a world where everything that appears like egotism, violence, coarseness, vileness, and persecution, can only be called so in a figurative way. It is highly characteristic that almost all the animals which appear in Andersen's nursery stories are tame domestic animals. This is, in the first place, a sympton of the same gentle and idyllic tendency which results in making almost all Andersen's children so well-behaved. It is, furthermore, a proof of his fidelity to nature, in consequence of which he is so reluctant to describe anything, with which he is not thoroughly familiar. It is finally an interesting phenomenon with reference to the use he makes of the animals, for domestic animals are no longer the pure product of nature; they remind us, through ideal association, of much that is human; and, moreover, through long intercourse with humanity and long education they have acquired something human, which in a high degree supports and furthers the effort to personify them. These cats and hens, these ducks and turkeys, these storks and swans, these mice and that unmentionable insect "with maiden's blood in its

body," offer many props to the nursery story. They hold direct intercourse with human beings; all that they lack is articulate speech, and there are human beings with articulate speech who are unworthy of it, and do not deserve their speech. Let us, therefore, give the animals the power of speech, and harbor them in our midst.

On the almost exclusive limitation to the domestic animal, a double characteristic of this nursery story depends. First of all, the significant result that Andersen's animals, whatever else they may be, are never beastly, never brutal. Their sole faults are that they are stupid, shallow, and old-fogyish. Andersen does not depict the animal in the human being, but the human in the animal. In the second place, there is a certain freshness of tone about them, a certain fulness of feeling, certain strong and bold, enthusiastic, and vigorous outbursts which are never found in the quarters of the domestic animal. Many beautiful, many humorous and entertaining things are spoken of in these stories, but a companion piece to the fable of the wolf and the dog—the wolf who observed the traces of the chain on the neck of the dog and preferred his own freedom to the protection afforded the house dog—will not be found in them. The wild nightingale, in whom poetry is personified, is a tame and loyal bird. "I have seen tears in the Emperor's eyes; that is the real treasure to me," it says. "An emperor's tears have a peculiar power!" Take even the swan, that noble, royal bird in the masterly story, **"The Ugly Duckling,"** which for the sake of its cat and its hen alone cannot be sufficiently admired,—how does it end? Alas! as a domestic animal. This is one of the points where it becomes difficult to pardon the great author. (pp. 26-7)

Andersen prefers the bird to the four-footed animal. More birds than mammals find place with him; for the bird is gentler than the four-footed beast, is nearer to the plant. The nightingale is his emblem, the swan his ideal, the stork his declared favorite. It is natural that the stork, that remarkable bird which brings children into the world,—the stork, that droll, long-legged, wandering, beloved, yearningly expected and joyfully greeted bird, should become his idolized symbol and frontispiece.

Yet plants are preferred by him to birds. Of all organic beings, plants are those which appear most frequently in the nursery story. For in the vegetable world alone are peace and harmony found to reign. Plants, too, resemble a child, but a child who is perpetually asleep. There is no unrest in this domain, no action, no sorrow, and no care. Here life is a calm, regular growth, and death but a painless fading away. Here the easily excited, lively poetic sympathy suffers less than anywhere else. Here there is nothing to jar and assail the delicate nerves of the poet. Here he is at home; here he paints his *Arabian Nights' Entertainments* beneath a burdock leaf. Every grade of emotion may be experienced in the realm of plants,—melancholy at the sight of the felled trunk, fulness of strength at the sight of the swelling buds, anxiety at the fragrance of the strong jasmine. Many thoughts may flit through our brain as we follow the history of the development of the flax, or the brief honor of the fir-tree on Christmas evening; but we feel as absolutely free as though we were dealing with comedy, for the image is so fleeting that it vanishes the moment we attempt to render it permanent. Sympathy and agitation gently touch our minds, but they do not ruffle us, they neither rouse nor oppress us. A poem about a plant sets free twofold the sympathy to which it lays claim; once because we know that the poem is pure fiction, and again because we know the plant to be merely a symbol. Nowhere has the poet with greater delicacy invested plants with speech than in **"The Fir-Tree," "Little Ida's Flowers,"** and in **"The Snow Queen."** (pp. 28-9)

Yet a step farther, and the fancy of the poet appropriates all inanimate objects, colonizes and annexes everything, large and small, an old house and an old clothes-press **("The Shepherdess and the Chimney Sweep"),** the top and the ball, the darning needle and the false collar, and the great dough men with bitter almonds for their hearts. After it has grasped the physiognomy of the inanimate, his fancy identifies itself with the formless all, sails with the moon across the sky, whistles and tells stories like the wind, looks on the snow, on sleep, night, death, and the dream as persons.

The determining element in this poetic mind was, then, sympathy with all that is childlike, and, through the representation of such deep-seated, elementary, and constant spiritual conditions as those of the child, the productions of this imagination are raised above the waves of time, spread beyond the boundaries of their native land and become the common property of the divers classes of society. (pp. 29-30)

The most marked trait in Andersen's mode of viewing life, is that which gives the ascendency to the heart, and this trait is genuinely Danish. Full of feeling itself, this method of contemplation takes every opportunity to exalt the beauty and significance of the emotions. It overleaps the will (the whole destiny of the Flax, in the story of its life, comes from without), does combat with the critique of the pure reason as with something pernicious, the work of the Devil, the witch's mirror, replaces pedantic science with the most admirable and witty side-thrusts **("The Bell," "A Leaf From the Sky"),** describes the senses as a tempter, or passes them over as unmentionable things, pursues and denounces hardheartedness, glorifies and commends goodness of heart, violently dethrones coarseness and narrowness, exalts innocence and decorum, and thus "puts everything in its right place." The key-note of its

earnestness is the ethic-religious feeling coupled with the hatred felt by geniality for narrowness, and its humorous satire is capricious, calm, in thorough harmony with the idyllic spirit of the poet. (pp. 33-4)

Andersen writes a grotesque, irregular prose, full of harmless mannerisms, and whose poetry is a luxuriant, gushing, rapturous conceit. It is this fantastic element which makes Andersen so foreign to the French people whose rather gray poetry wholly lacks the bright-hued floral splendor found among the Northern people and attaining its highest beauty in Shakespeare's *Midsummer Night's Dream,* a splendor which may be detected throughout Andersen's nursery stories, and which imparts to them their finest perfume. And as the fantastic caprice of this element is Norse-Danish, its idyllic key-note is purely Danish. No wonder that the earliest and most original of these nursery stories were written during the reign of Frederich VI and bear the stamp of his day. We recognize this monarch in all the fatherly, patriarchal old kings represented in them; we find the spirit of the age in the complete lack of social, to say nothing of political satire, that we detect in them. (pp. 34-5)

The romance is a species of poetic creation which demands of the mind that would accomplish anything remarkable in it, not only imagination and sentiment, but the keen understanding, and the cool, calm power of observation of the man of the world; that is the reason why it is not altogether suited to Andersen, although it is not wholly remote from his talent. In the entire scenery, the background of nature, the picturesque effect of the costumes, he is successful; but where psychological insight is concerned, traces of his weakness may be detected. He will take part for and against his characters; his men are not manly enough, his women not sufficiently feminine. I know no poet whose mind is more devoid of sexual distinctions, whose talent is less of a nature to betray a defined sex, than Andersen's. Therefore his strength lies in portraying children, in whom the conscious sense of sex is not yet prominent. The whole secret lies in the fact that he is exclusively what he is,—not a man of learning, not a thinker, not a standard bearer, not a champion, as many of our great writers have been, but simply a poet. A poet is a man who is at the same time a woman. Andersen sees most forcibly in man and in woman that which is elementary, that which is common to humanity, rather than that which is peculiar and interesting. I have not forgotten how well he has described the deep feeling of a mother in **"The Story of a Mother,"** or how tenderly he has told the story of the spiritual life of a woman in **"The Little Sea-Maid."** I simply recognize the fact that what he has represented is not the complicated spiritual conditions of life and of romance, but the element of life; he rings changes on single, pure tones, which amid the confused harmonies and disharmonies of life, appear neither so pure nor so distinct as in his books. Upon entering into the service of the nursery story all sentiments undergo a process of simplification, purification, and transformation. The character of man is farthest removed from the comprehension of the poet of childhood, and I can only recall a single passage in his stories in which a delicate psychological characteristic of a feminine soul may be encountered, and even this appears so innocently that we feel inclined to ask if it did not write itself. (pp. 36-7)

The drama is a species of poetic production that requires the faculty for differentiating an idea and distributing it among many characters; it requires an understanding of conscious action, a logic power to guide this, an eye to the situation, a passion for becoming absorbed and overwhelmed in the inexhaustible study of individual, many-sided characters. Therefore it is that the drama is still farther removed from the genius of Andersen than the romance, and that his lack of capacity for the dramatic style increases with mathematical exactness in the same ratio as each variety of dramatic art is removed from the nursery story, and consequently from his gifts. He naturally succeeds best with the nursery-story comedy; although, to be sure, it possesses little more of comedy than the name. It is a mixed species, and if it were put to the test of the Spanish story, it would be recognized as a bastard. In the comedy of special situations he is happy with respect to the poetic execution of single scenes (**"The King's Dream"**), but singularly unfortunate in the execution of the idea as a whole (**"The Pearl of Good Fortune"**). The comedy proper is not poorly suited to his gifts. . . . In stories of this kind character delineation comes easier to him than in the grave drama, for in them he walks directly in the footsteps of Holberg, so strikingly does his talent accord in a single direction with that of this early Northern dramatist. (p. 38)

In his descriptions of travel very naturally a large number of his best qualities come to light. Like his favorite, the migratory bird, he is in his element when he travels. He observes with the eye of a painter, and he describes like an enthusiast. Yet even here two faults are apparent: one is that his lyric tendency at times runs away with him, so that he chants a hymn of praise instead of giving a description, or exaggerates instead of painting . . . ; the other, that the underlying, personal, egotistical element of his nature, giving evidence that his innermost personality lacks reserve, occasionally obtrudes itself in a most disturbing manner.

The latter tendency characterizes with especially marked force the style of his autobiography. The criticism that can with justice be made on his *The Story of My Life* is not so much that the author is throughout occupied with his own private affairs (for that is quite natural in such a work); it is that his personality is scarcely ever occupied with anything greater than itself, is never absorbed in an idea, is never entirely free from the ego. The revolution of 1848 in this book affects us as though we heard some one sneeze; we are astonished to be reminded by the sound that there is a world outside of the author. (pp. 39-40)

Thus the nursery story remains his sole individual creation, and for it he requires no patent, since no one is likely to rob him of it. . . . Andersen's nursery story has its individual character, and his theories are comprised in the law it obeys, whose boundaries it may not overstep without bringing to light a monster. Everything in the world has its law, even that species of poetry which transcends the laws of nature. (pp. 40-1)

The form of fancy and the method of narration in the nursery story admit the treatment of the most heterogeneous materials in the most varied tones. Within its province may be found sublime narratives, as **"The Bell"**; profound and wise stories, as **"The Shadow"**; fantastically bizarre, as **"The Elfin Mound"**; merry, almost wanton ones, as **"The Swineherd,"** or **"The Leap Frog"**; humorous ones, as **"The Princess on the Pea,"** **"Good Humor,"** **"The False Collar,"** **"The Lovers"**; also stories with a tinge of melancholy, as **"The Constant Tin Soldier"**; deeply pathetic poetic creations, as **"The Story of a Mother"**; oppressively dismal, as **"The Red Shoes"**; touching fancies, as **"The Little Sea-Maid"**; and those of mingled dignity and playfulness, as **"The Snow Queen."** Here we encounter an anecdote like **"A Great Sorrow,"** which resembles a smile through tears, and an inspiration like **"The Muse of the Coming Age,"** in which we feel the pinion strokes of history, the heart-throbs and pulse-beats of the active, stirring life of the present, as violent as in a fever, and yet as healthy as in a happy moment of enthusiastic inspiration. In short, we find everything that lies between the epigram and the hymn.

Is there, then, a boundary line which limits the nursery story, a law which binds it? If so, where does it lie? . . . The nursery story, which unites unbridled freedom of invention with the restraint its central idea impresses upon it, must steer between two rocks: between the luxuriance of style that lacks ideas, and dry allegory; it must strike the medium course between too great fulness and too great meagreness. This, Andersen most frequently succeeds in doing, and yet not always. Those of his stories that are based on materials derived from folklore, as **"The Flying Trunk,"** or those that may be classed with the fairy-tale proper, as **"Thumbling,"** do not attract grown people as they do children, because the story in such instances conceals no thought. In his **"Garden of Paradise"** everything preceding the entrance to the garden is masterly, but the Fairy of Paradise herself seems to me to be invested with little, if any, beauty or charm. (pp. 41-3)

The first duty of the nursery story is to be poetic, its second to preserve the marvellous element. Therefore, it is first of all necessary that the order of the legendary world be sacred to it. What in the language of legendary lore is regarded as a fixed rule, must be respected by the nursery story, however unimportant it may be in relation to the laws and rules of the real world. Thus it is quite inappropriate for the nursery story, as in Andersen's **"The Dryad,"** to part its heroine from her tree, to let her make a symbolic journey to Paris, to go to the "bal Mabille," etc., for it is not more impossible for all the kings of the earth to place the smallest leaf on a nettle than it is for legendary lore to tear a dryad away from its tree. But in the second place, it lies in the nature of the nursery story form that its outline can frame nothing that, in order to obtain its poetic rights, requires a profound psychological description, an earnest development, such as would be adapted either to the nature of the drama or the romance. (pp. 44-5)

[Andersen] has the genuine gift for creating supernatural beings, in modern times so rare. How deeply symbolical and how natural it is, for instance, that the little sea-maid, when her fish-tail shrivelled up and became "the prettiest pair of white feet a little girl could have," should feel as though she were treading on pointed needles and sharp knives at every step she took! How many poor women tread on sharp knives at every step they take, in order to be near him whom they love, and are yet far from being the most unhappy of women! (p. 47)

Georg Brandes, "Hans Christian Andersen," in his *Creative Spirits of the Nineteenth Century,* translated by Rasmus B. Anderson, Thomas Y. Crowell Company, 1923, pp. 1-53.

ROBERT LYND

(essay date 1922)

[Lynd was an Irish journalist and author. In the following excerpt from an essay originally published in 1922, he explores the moral content and realistic denouements of Andersen's fairy tales.]

Hans Andersen, indeed, was in many respects more nearly akin to the writers of tracts and moral tales than to the folklorists. He was a teller of fairy-tales. But he domesticated the fairy-tale and gave it a townsman's home. In his hands it was no longer a courtier, as it had been in the time of Louis XIV, or a wanderer among cottages, as it has been at all times. There was never a teller of fairy-tales to whom kings and queens mattered less. He could make use of royal families in the most charming way, as in those little satires, **"The Princess and the Pea"** and **"The Emperor's New Clothes."** But his imagination hankered after the lives of children

such as he himself had been. He loved the poor, the ill treated, and the miserable, and to illuminate their lives with all sorts of fancies. His miracles happen preferably to those who live in poor men's houses. His cinder-girl seldom marries a prince: if she marries at all it is usually some honest fellow who will have to work for his living. In Hans Andersen, however, it is the exception rather than the rule to marry and live happily ever afterwards. The best that even Hans the cripple [in **"The Cripple"**] has to look forward to is being a schoolmaster. There was never an author who took fewer pains to give happy endings to his stories. (p. 156)

[In] his fairy-tales Hans Andersen has always appealed to men and women as strongly as to children. We hear occasionally of children who cannot be reconciled to him because of his incurable habit of pathos. A child can read a fairy-tale like "The Sleeping Beauty" as if it were playing among toys, but it cannot read **"The Marsh King's Daughter"** without enacting in its own soul the pathetic adventures of the frog-girl; it cannot read **"The Snow Queen"** without enduring all the sorrows of Gerda as she travels in search of her lost friend; it cannot read **"The Little Mermaid"** without feeling as if the knives were piercing its feet just as the mermaid felt when she got her wish to become a human being so that she might possess a soul. Even in **"The Wild Swans,"** though Lisa's eleven brothers are all restored to humanity from the shapes into which their wicked stepmother had put them, it is only after a series of harrowing incidents; and Lisa herself has to be rescued from being burned as a witch. Hans Andersen is surely the least gay of all writers for children. He does not invent exquisite confectionery for the nursery such as Charles Perrault, having heard a nurse telling the stories to his little son, gave the world in "Cinderella" and "Bluebeard." To read stories like these is to enter into a game of make-believe, no more to be taken seriously than a charade. The Chinese lanterns of a happy ending seem to illuminate them all the way through. But Hans Andersen does not invite you to a charade. He invites you to put yourself in the place of the little match-girl who is frozen to death in the snow on New Year's Eve after burning her matches and pretending that she is enjoying all the delights of Christmas. He is more like a child's Dickens than a successor of the ladies and gentlemen who wrote fairy-tales in the age of Louis XIV and Louis XV. He is like Dickens, indeed, not only in his genius for compassion, but in his abounding inventiveness, his grotesque detail, and his humour. He is never so recklessly cheerful as Dickens with the cheerfulness that suggests eating and drinking. He makes us smile rather than laugh aloud with his comedy. But how delightful is the fun at the end of **"Soup on a Sausage Peg"** when the Mouse King learns that the only way in which the soup can be made is by stirring a pot of boiling water with his own tail! And what child does not love in all its bones the cunning in **"Little Claus and Big Claus,"** when Big Claus is tricked into killing his horses, murdering his grand-mother, and finally allowing himself to be tied in a sack and thrown into the river?

But Hans Andersen was too urgent a moralist to be content to write stories so immorally amusing as this. He was as anxious as a preacher or a parent or Dickens to see children becoming Christians, and he used the fairy-tale continually as a means of teaching and warning them. In one story he makes the storks de-cide to punish an ugly boy who had been cruel to them. 'There is a little dead child in the pond, one that has dreamed itself to death; we will bring that for him. Then he will cry because we have brought him a little dead brother.' That is certainly rather harsh. **"The Girl Who Trod on the Loaf "** is equally severe. As a result of her cruelty in tearing flies' wings off and her waste-fulness in using a good loaf as a stepping-stone, she sinks down through the mud into hell, where she is tor-mented with flies that crawl over her eyes and, having had their wings pulled out, cannot fly away. Hans An-dersen, however, like Ibsen in *Peer Gynt,* believes in re-demption through the love of others, and even the girl who trod on the loaf is ultimately saved. 'Love begets life' runs like a text through **"The Marsh King's Daughter."** His stories as a whole are an imaginative representation of that gospel—a gospel that so easily becomes mush and platitude in ordinary hands. But Andersen's genius as a narrator, as a grotesque inventor of incident and comic detail, saves his gospel from com-monness. He may write a parable about a darning-needle, but he succeeds in making his darning-needle alive, like a dog or a schoolboy. He endows everything he sees—china shepherdesses, tin soldiers, mice, and flowers—with the similitude of life, action, and conver-sation. He can make the inhabitants of one's mantel-piece capable of epic adventures, and has a greater sense of possibilities in a pair of tongs or a doorknocker than most of us have in men and women. His is a cre-ator of a thousand fancies. He loves imagining elves no higher than a mouse's knee, and mice going on their travels leaning on sausage-skewers as pilgrims' staves, and little Thumbelina, whose cradle was 'a neat pol-ished walnut-shell . . . blue violet-leaves were her mattresses, with a rose-leaf for a coverlet.' His fancy

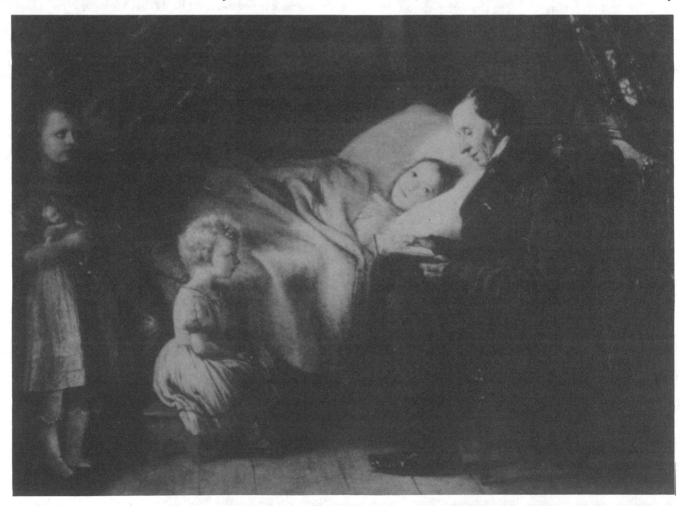

Painting by Jerichau-Baumannsborn of Andersen reading aloud to the children of his friend
Madame Baumann.

never becomes lyrical or sweeps us off our feet, like Shakespeare's in *A Midsummer Night's Dream.* But there was nothing else like it in the fairy-tale literature of the nineteenth century. And his pages are full of the poetry of flights of birds. More than anything else one thinks of Hans Andersen as a lonely child watching a flight of swans or storks till it is lost to view, silent and full of wonder and sadness. Edmund Gosse, in *Two Visits to Denmark,* a book in which everything is interesting except the title, describes a visit which he paid to Hans Andersen at Copenhagen in his old age, when 'he took me out into the balcony and bade me notice the long caravan of ships going by in the Sound below—"they are like a flock of wild swans," he said.' The image might have occurred to any one, but it is specially interesting as coming from the mouth of Hans Andersen, because it seems to express so much of his vision of the world. He was, above all men of his century, the magician of the flock of wild swans. (pp. 158-60)

Robert Lynd, "Hans Andersen," in his *Essays on Life and Literature,* J. M. Dent & Sons Ltd., 1951, pp. 155-60.

PAUL V. RUBOW
(essay date 1947)

[Rubow was a Danish critic who wrote *H. C. Andersens Eventyr* (1927), a scholarly discussion of the literary genres in Andersen's fairy tales. In the following excerpt, he studies Andersen's depictions of his native Denmark in his fairy tales and discusses the author's craftsmanship.]

To most of us, Hans Andersen (1805-1875) is the typical Danish writer. That may be a mistake, for others have as much of the native blood in their veins. But he was happy enough to live and write in an age when feeling for the national features in landscape and character was developed as never before. Denmark had been discovered, and the great writers and poets from the first decades of the century had revealed the thousand secrets of the language. Especially from the poets he had learned to describe and impart the visible world by suggestion. He wove into his novels, poems, and fairy tales—a whole picture of his country. At first his conception of nature was rather ordinary. But after his travels in France and Italy he used his own eyes, and later he got to know his own country very well. He describes in a way which is never partial all strata of society and many different types of men: the fashionable world which attracted him without blinding him (for after all he was a writer of fairy tales), the scholar, the artist, the young officer, the clerk, the watchman in the street, the little girl selling matches, the prisoner in his

cell. He knows the countryside too, as well as the town. You will find Fyen, the island of his childhood, in such tales as **"The Travelling Companion"** and **"The Buckwheat,"** Zealand in his tales from manor houses such as **"The Ugly Duckling"** and **"The Happy Family"**; and Jutland, which he discovered as early as the 'thirties and which during the 'fifties became the main country, in **"A Story from the Dunes"** and **"The Bishop of Borglum."** Instead of the empty landscape of the traditional fairy tales he inserted the real countryside with sun and wind, the indigenous nature and climate: 'It was lovely in the country—it was summer! The wheat was yellow, the oats were green, the hay was stacked in the green meadows, and the stork went strutting about . . . ' Instead of the roses, lilies, and fig-trees of the popular fairy tales we have a complete Danish flora including pease-blossom, burdock, and many weeds. The poet knew the secret of each flower as he shows in such tales as **"The Snow Queen,"** where the orange lily, the convolvulus, the hyacinth, the buttercup, and the white narcissus in turn tell their dreams. Andersen is a specialist in the seasons. **"The Snow Queen"** is like a whole mythus of the birth and death of the year, and of the intervention in human destiny by an animated nature. Each month has its own description: in January 'the panes are pasted with snow, and it falls in heaps from the roofs'; in March the moss shines fresh on the trunks of the trees; in July the evening sky gleams like gold and the moon is up between dusk and dawn; in October the King of the Year paints from his big colour-pot. (pp. 92-3)

A very important feature in [Andersen's] tales is the narrator. Andersen took over this anonymous character from the popular tale. He is an intermediary between the reader and the experience. In some of the shorter tales his presence is felt everywhere, in others he hangs back discreetly. But in all cases it is he who gives to the tale its definite form. Without him Andersen's art would be too subjective for the small genre. In the first tales, like **"The Goloshes of Fortune,"** he is an actor who is very much alive. Note, for instance, the beginning of this tale where the two fairies talk together in the anteroom of a Copenhagen home, giving us the theme of the story, then the quick changing of scene when, almost unprepared, we are put back three hundred years in time, then again Copenhagen interiors, interrupted by an animal fable, and in the next moment an Italian scene. In conclusion the life and death of the theme are discreetly touched upon. But in the tales from the 'forties, Andersen's great time, these living mimics are replaced by the tragic and the comic masks. On a small scale he now produces the great art. The many sentimental asides, the playful, satirical tricks from his first period are now gone. He realized his ideal and created in his tales a universal poetry. He condensed the stuff of tragedy into a nut-shell and wrote

"The Story of a Mother" and "The Little Match Girl." He wrote tales that are comedies in miniature such as "The Top and the Ball" and "The Shepherdess and the Chimney-Sweep." On the same scale he wrote such stories of life as "The Ugly Duckling" and "The Fir Tree." Already in his first period he had been able to re-cast the burlesque heroic poem in the vest-pocket size of "The Steadfast Tin Soldier." It was his ambition to translate all the beautiful, but heavy poetry of the world into a form that was short, rich, and clear. He tackled the greatest subjects when he dared to write about the closed book of fate, about pity, ambition, and even about love, of which he knew little.

Later, in another and larger group of tales and stories, the narrator shows another face. Late in the 'fifties, he disguises himself as a divinely inspired bard. Like Ossian on the heath, he lets the elements sound in his work without mediating. He has sung "The Wind Tells of Valdemar Daae and His Daughters," this wonderful tragedy of fate in prose (it is called prose), the most original work of fiction in our literature. He also wrote "The Last Dream of the Old Oak" that tells about his unstilled longing for love and about the fettered strength of his soul.

But most of the stories in his great collection are the popular tales. Starting from the two types of popular tales we can divide Andersen's work into two similar main types.

In one group he simply re-tells the tales which tradition has brought him, often in a language closely related to the popular one. These are tales such as "The Tinder-Box," "Little Claus and Big Claus," "The Princess and the Pea," "The Swineherd," "What Father Does," and "The Emperor's New Clothes"—that is to say some of the best known and beloved of all. It holds good of all these tales that Andersen sticks to humorous models. They are old rogue's stories. He has renewed them in a style close to the original. He retains all essential features down to the component of popular formulas. Before he became a writer of tales he had written comical stories in the manner of the medieval *fabliaus* and of La Fontaine and the Danish poets Wessel and Baggesen.

Another group consists of the serious tales: "The Little Mermaid," "The Travelling Companion," "The Snow Queen," and others. Here Andersen uses his models quite freely or works entirely on his own. The point is that the serious popular tales have roots in a mystical conception of the world and use an apparatus of magic requisites which he could not lightly transfer into his own poetry. Here he describes a milieu, dresses up the real or fantastic figures and animates the supernatural elements that had in the course of time lost their original meaning.

He knew this job. That, in a certain sense, is his secret. He was a primitive soul to whom the surrounding world was alive. Andersen was not an orthodox Protestant; as a religious man he was a rationalist. But that is of no import. At the bottom of the world which Science described to him lay, according to his holy conviction, the *fairy tale*. To him dead things were alive.

Hans Andersen is the greatest illusionist of literature. This is due to his kinship with the child's mind, his faculty of daydreaming. Happy are those who are able to see motives in everything. One sometimes sees a child getting bored with his toy and going to another child who is playing with another. The first child takes away the second one's toy. Then the second child will take two sticks and play with them. The first child will look to see what he is doing and does not understand it. He lacks the gift of illusion, and that cannot be borrowed. Early childhood is the proper age of illusion. Boyhood is more one-sided, boys early acquire a certain maidenlike hardness and narrowness. Youth means a sort of revenge for the productive mind. This age has a passion for tragedy. Manhood again is poor in imagination and vegetative meditation. Poets often dry up in the real working years of life—unless (like Kierkegaard or Andersen) they 'escape when they are going to be men'. The old, when they are not completely withered in the struggle of life, become poetic again and play with their tools, arbitrary remembrance replacing imagination.

In Hans Andersen there was something of a youth, an aunt, and a child. He has the spiritual intensity and power of imagination of early childhood. He has the child's gift of imitation. His tales are full of mimics, of limited gestures and speeches, including an immense store of animal sounds. Another childish feature is his impetuosity. He is said to have been hysterical as children sometimes are. And he was a great dreamer and visionary in the manner of little folks. He lets his scholar ask the Shadow who has been in the Anteroom of Poetry: 'Did all the gods of antiquity walk through the great halls? Did the old heroes fight there? Did sweet children play there and tell you their dreams?'

However, dreams alone do not suffice. I have mentioned that Andersen's tales build on the popular tales. It is even certain that the book of tales would never have been created had he not from the start retained a humble attitude towards the popular art of story-telling. His heroes and heroines can be followed back to the primitive tales that were once the common property of all European peoples. The child-hero, whom Andersen first introduced in his novels, but only made something of in his tales, is an inheritance from the brave prince or the innocent Cinderella of the popular tales. The child-hero in the serious tales has morals and right on his side in Andersen's version as with the old story-tellers. But in the merry tales the hero is a rogue, even though sometimes a sympathetic rogue like Little Claus.

Andersen's enchanted world is also anchored in the popular tales. The world of the old tales is magic and ceremonial. Its characters are stiff like dolls, the plot is like a formula. The people live up to their definition: the good by their goodness, the cunning by their artfulness, the stupid by their stupidity. They are known by their deeds. The hero is one with his action. The three lives of three brothers are told in perfectly parallel terms. The characters and the plot are reiterated from one tale to another. After overcoming various obstacles the hero wins the princess, who is often bewitched or ill, the old king gladly gives half his kingdom away, the stepmother persecutes her stepdaughter, and so on. The characters behave in a similar way under similar circumstances. When the princess carries a secret she pretends to be dumb. When a man has lost his wife, he marries for his daughter's sake a widow who is wicked and has a daughter who is also wicked, and the two wicked women chase away the real daughter. When a man is in distress an unknown person appears to help him, but demands as a reward that which his wife carries under her girdle; the man thinks it is the keys, while in reality it is the child. When two young lovers die, two red roses grow on their graves, and on the grave of a virgin grows a pale lily.

All this is found in Hans Andersen's tales as well. But he uses the supernatural with caution. In **"The Travelling Companion"** or **"The Wild Swans"** he still sticks to tradition. John gets three feathers from the swan's wing and a small bottle. He puts a big tub of water by the bridal bed, and when the princess comes to the bed he pushes her into the water and dips her three times, having thrown the feathers and the contents of the bottle into it; then she is transformed. Elisa throws eleven shirts over the swans and eleven beautiful princes stand before her. But in his later tales the supernatural is balanced against the profoundly human. In **"The Story of a Mother"** the Night and the Lake and the Thorn-Bush are personifications that extend beyond the real world—but the mother's love is a natural force stronger than they. Andersen also favoured a form of conclusion like that of **"The Little Match Girl"** or **"A Story from the Dunes"**: the great ecstasy of release from mortal misery precedes the moment of death and is followed by a description of the immensity and inclemency of the surrounding world.

I have tried to give glimpses into Hans Andersen's workshop. It is a curious shop, for Andersen is in a way the hero of all his tales, just as he is in another sense the narrator of all of them. Yet it is not a purely subjective and arbitrary world he creates. As he has inherited strong traditions from the story-tellers of the past, so he employs a technique that must force from us a deep admiration. Looking closer at his work we find that his small poetic creations are actually very complicated. There is a firmness of form, even though it is wound about with the vines of imagination. It is a very national work, but a work that has its roots in an international kind of literature. Behind the picture of nineteenth century Denmark there is a huge rock-like pre-world. This is the reason why Andersen has been able to conquer the whole globe from his native country. His tales contain palaces built by imagination—but built on rock. He has revived the lost age, the childhood we no longer remember. His poetic book of tales, first and foremost to Danes, but then to the whole world, is the key of a wonderland whose enchanted tracts look like those of the real world—only they are richer. (pp. 94-8)

Paul V. Rubow, "Hans Andersen and His Fairy Tales," in *Life and Letters and the London Mercury,* Vol. 53, April-June, 1947, pp. 92-8.

JOHN GRIFFITH
(essay date 1984)

[In the excerpt below, Griffith illuminates Andersen's handling of love and sexuality in his fairy tales.]

[Andersen] wrote love-stories by the dozen—**"The Little Mermaid," "Thumbelina," "The Steadfast Tin Soldier," "The Shepherdess and the Chimney Sweep," "The Sweethearts"** and **"The Bog King's Daughter"** are perhaps the most famous. Through them all runs one story, the basic Andersen fantasy. The central character is small, frail, more likely to be female than male—above all, *delicate,* an embodiment of that innocence which is harmlessness, that purity which is incapacity for lust. He/she is usually incapable of ordinary motion, physically unsuited to pursuit and consummation: the tin soldier has only one leg, the mermaid has no legs at all, Thumbelina is carried from place to place as if she were crippled. Andersen's imagination is much taken with *statues* as the emblem of chaste erotic feeling: the tin soldier and his ballerina are inanimate figurines, the shepherdess and the chimney sweep are made of porcelain, the little mermaid falls in love with a marble statue before she ever sees the prince in the flesh. (It is fitting that Copenhagen has immortalized the little mermaid herself as a statue.) In another story, **"Psyche,"** the hero creates a statue of the girl he loves, the pristine symbol of his devotion. The girl herself rejects him.

Andersen's ideal lovers are often rejected. A few of the folk-tales he retold—such as **"The Tinderbox"**—end with the hero married and living happily ever after; but the stories he made up himself do not.

Usually something prevents marriage—rejection, mis-understanding, snobbery, fate. At the end of **"The Bog King's Daughter,"** the heroine steps out onto a balcony on her wedding night and just disappears. Andersen doesn't care very much if love is satisfied in this world, since the conclusion his fantasy really works toward is splendid, mystical death—the launching out of the soul into the infinite, leaving troublesome flesh behind. "It is lovely to fly from love to love, from earth into heaven," says Andersen, describing the death of the hero in **"The Ice Maiden."** "A string snapped, a mournful tone was heard. Death's kiss of ice was victorious against corruption." Similarly, the little mermaid leaves her body behind and becomes a daughter of the air. The tin soldier and the ballerina die together in flames, he melting into a tin heart and she reduced to a bright spangle. The shepherdess and the chimney sweep "loved each other until they broke." Thumbelina dons white wings and flies away with her fairy-lover, who is "almost transparent, as if he were made of glass." The bog king's daughter becomes "one single beautiful ray of light, that shot upward to God."

Physical sensuality in these stories tends to be pictured as grasping, slimy, and disgusting. Thumbelina is coaxed, abducted, clutched at by a toad and her son, a fat black mole, and an ugly insect before she flies away to the fairy-king; the shepherdess is pursued by a satyr who had "a long beard, . . . little horns sticking out of his forehead and the legs of a goat." The princess in **"The Bog King's Daughter"** is shudderingly embraced by an "ancient king; a mummy, black as pitch, glittering like the black slugs that creep in the forest." Frequently the physical ordeal Andersen's lovers must go through in pursuit of transcendent love is a descent into dark, close, filthy places—the tin soldier floats down a gutter into a sewer and is swallowed by a fish; the shepherdess and the chimney sweep have to creep up and down a chimney flue; the ball and the top met in a garbage bin where "all kinds of things were lying: gravel, a cabbage stalk, dirt, dust, and lots of leaves that had fallen down from the gutter."

Andersen's sharpest vision of sensual horror is in **"The Little Mermaid."** There the heroine, smitten with love for a human prince, sets out to find what she must do to make him love her in return. The grotesque ordeal Andersen contrives for her is a direct fantasy-enactment of the idea that, in order to be a wife, a girl must submit to rape. She must "divide her tail," and the experience is an excruciating one. She has to travel down to a terrible forest in the deepest part of the ocean, through polyps "like snakes with hundreds of heads," with "long slimy arms, and they had fingers as supple as worms" that reach out to grab her as she "held both her hands folded tightly across her breast" and hurries past.

At last she came to a great, slimy open place in the middle of the forest. Big fat eels played in the mud, showing their ugly yellow stomachs. . . . Here the witch . . . sat letting a big ugly toad eat out of her mouth, as human beings sometimes let a canary eat sugar candy out of theirs. The ugly eels she called her little chickens, and held them close to her spongy chest.

The witch tells her that if the prince is to love her, she must lose her tail with a sensation of having her body pierced by a sword. "The little mermaid drank the potion, and it felt as if a sword were piercing her body. She fainted and lay as though she were dead."

Nowhere else in classic children's literature is there so terrified a vision of sex, seen through the eyes of innocence. The scene in **"The Ice Maiden"** where Rudy accepts death as his lover is calm by comparison:

He threw his arms around her and looked into her marvelous clear eyes for a second. Only for a second! And how is one to describe, to tell in words, what he saw in that fraction of a moment? What was it that overpowered him—a ghost? Or was it a bit of life that exists in death? Had he been lifted upward or had he been plunged into a deep, death-filled world of ice?

When she kisses him, "the eternal coldness penetrated his backbone and touched his forehead." Here, as elsewhere, Andersen compresses into one scene the contradictory ideas that death is erotic, and that one can escape eroticism by dying. Something of that same paradox is present in another Andersen story, **"The Garden of Eden,"** which posits sex as original sin. A young prince falls from innocence by kissing the lips of a beautiful naked woman, and death is both the reward and punishment for his action.

A fearful clap of thunder was heard, deeper, more frightening than any ever heard before. The fairy vanished and the garden of Eden sank into the earth: deep, deep down. The prince saw it disappear into the dark night like a far distant star. He felt a deathly coldness touch his limbs; his eyes closed, and he fell down as though he were dead.

This troubled view of sex is important even in Andersen stories which are not explicitly about erotic subjects, for it explains his obsession with innocence in many forms. *Innocence* is the watchword in Andersen's fantasies. No virtue rates so high with him as child-like purity, by which he means freedom from adult desire, ambition, and thought. He found inspiration of a sort in folk-tales, because they often begin with heroes who are simple, humble and childlike. But he had to change the folk-tale pattern in order to bring out his personal fantasies. The traditional folk-tale shows its protagonist's growth and happiness directly; he gets money, love and power—as for instance in Andersen's own retelling of **"The Tinderbox,"** in which a soldier seizes a princess, kills her father, and ascends to the throne; or **"Little Claus and Big Claus,"** in which an under-dog-hero kills his rival and gets rich. The stories that Andersen made up himself turn this pattern inside out. Like folk-tale heroes, Andersen's start poor—but his stories demonstrate that the poor in spirit are blessed. Like them, Andersen's heroes hurl themselves into life—but discover that they would do better to die and be with God. In an Andersen story, it is better to be the peasant girl who can hear the nightingale than the chamberlain who cannot (**"The Nightingale"**); better to be little Gerda, who trusts and believes and wants to stay at home, than Kay, who "gets a piece of the Devil's glass in his eye" and questions and criticizes and explores (**"The Snow Queen"**).

In story after story, Andersen makes fun of and punishes people who care about money and power and artifice and prestige and critical judgment; he celebrates the humble and long-suffering and credulous and sentimental. His attitude belongs partly to Christian asceticism, and partly to nineteenth-century Romantic primitivism, sentimentalism, and anti-intellectualism, and no doubt takes many of its forms and phrases from those philosophies. But for Andersen personally the value of innocence is closely tied to his nightmarish view of sex, a fact which is easily discernible in several of his most famous stories. For him, to be innocent is, first and foremost, to expunge or repress one's sexual urges.

One especially graphic case in point here is his tale **"The Red Shoes,"** a story Andersen found to be a particular favorite in the Puritan strongholds of Scotland, Holland, and the United States. Read in the loosest, most abstract terms, the story is a parable on the idea that pride goeth before a fall: a pretty girl, preoccupied with beauty and finery, shows her vanity, is punished for it, and learns her lesson. But given the concrete details of Andersen's personal fantasy, the story vibrates with sexual panic, celebrating innocence that is won through the repression of sexuality.

Andersen records that **"The Red Shoes"** was inspired by a memory from his youth: "In *The Fairy Tale of My Life*, I have told how I received for my confirmation my first pair of boots; and how they squeaked as I walked up the aisle of the church; this pleased me no end, for I felt that now the whole congregation must know that my boots are new. But at the same time my conscience bothered me terribly, for I was aware that I was thinking as much about my new boots as I was about our Lord." Out of that bothersome conscience came Andersen's story, with the new boots transformed to red shoes, and Andersen, the boy wearing them, transformed to a pretty girl named Karen.

What Andersen consciously thinks of as an emblem of pride and vanity, he unconsciously imbues with sexual significance in a number of ways. First, he gives his heroine the name of his scandalous half-sister, the one who disappeared into the red-light districts of Copenhagen and later embarrassed her brother by turning up with a common-law husband. Shoe and foot-symbolism tends to be sexual in many uses—the Old Testament and other folk-literatures often say "feet" as a euphemism for sexual organs, and foot-fetishism is a common neurotic device for expressing forbidden interest in the genitals. That **"The Red Shoes"** emanates from Andersen's memory of a ritual of puberty, and of his flaunting the new boots he had for that occasion, also helps to place it psychologically. Andersen emphasizes the sexual quality by making Karen's shoes red, the traditional color of unruly passion, and by making them dancing shoes, with a power to catch her up and carry her away against her conscious will: "Once she had begun, her feet would not stop. It was as if the shoes had taken command of them . . . her will was not her own." Giving herself over to their excitement, she faces the debility Andersen associated with sexual excess: "You shall dance in your red shoes until you become pale and thin. Dance till the skin on your face turns yellow and clings to your bones as if you were a skeleton."

She must first acquire the red shoes against her mother's wishes; it is a man who sets them doing their fearful, orgiastic dancing, an old soldier with "a marvelously long beard that was red with touches of white in it." When he touches them, they begin dancing.

The shoes "grow fast" to Karen's feet and will not come off—they are part of her body. The only way she can purge their evil is to cut off the offending members. "Do not cut off my head," she begs the executioner, "for then I would not be able to repent. But cut off my feet!" He does as she asks, and she becomes like Andersen's other acceptable lovers: crippled. For a time thoughts of the lost sexuality still linger—she sees the red shoes dancing before her when she tries to go to church. Finally, in an agony of contrition and self-reproach, she wins God's mercy, and He sends His sunshine: "The sunshine filled Karen's heart till it so swelled with peace and happiness that it broke. Her soul flew on a sunbeam up to God; and up there no one asked her about the red shoes."

"The Red Shoes" is a harrowing, gothic little tale, to be sure, and that may help to explain its popularity. Actually, it doesn't succeed very well in advancing the dry moral idea that we should be humble and love God better than ourselves. What the solid events of the story convey is rather the idea that there is something we are tempted to do with our feet, but old ladies and ministers and angels don't want us to do it. If we refuse to listen to their warnings, a leering old man will touch our feet and set them working and we won't be able to stop. Then we'll be glad to have the grown-ups chop them off, and to be allowed to die and go to God. I suppose there is more than one way to say what that fantasy means; but any description which fails to account for the evocative image of the red-bearded man touching the girl's feet and setting them dancing uncontrollably has hardly done it justice.

Andersen himself was aware—at least partly—of the psychological links between his inhibited sexuality and his artistic creativity, his wish for fame as an artist, and his longing for death. The story **"Psyche"** shows clearly that he believed that his pursuit of ideal beauty and immortality through art and religion sprang from sexual longings that he could not allow himself to fulfill.

"Psyche" is the story of a young artist, poor and unknown, who strives for perfection in his art, but cannot produce anything that satisfies him. His worldly friends tell him he is too much the dreamer: "You have not tasted life. You ought to take a big healthy swallow and enjoy it." They invite him to join them in their orgies and he is excited—"his blood ran swiftly through his body, his imagination was strong." But he cannot bring himself to go with them—he feels "within himself a purity, a sense of piety" that stops him, and turns him toward working in clay and marble instead, as a superior alternative to physical lust. "What he wanted to describe [in his sculpture] was how his heart sought and sensed infinity, but how was he to do it?"

The answer is that he sees a girl, just in passing, and falls in love. At first he makes no attempt to approach her; he turns his attention to a mental image he has of her, as she becomes "alive in his mind." He sets to work on a statue of her, made from marble he has to dig out from heaps of "broken glass," "discarded vegetables," "the tops of fennel and the rotten leaves of artichokes." With these materials—a fantasy-image snatched from a passing glimpse of a beautiful girl, and white marble extracted from the filth of ordinary life—the artist constructs an image of perfect beauty.

He wants to believe that he now has what his friends have—only better. "Now I know what life is," he rejoices. "It is love! It is to be able to appreciate loveliness and to delight in beauty. And what my friends call 'life' is nothing but empty vanity, bubbles from the fermentation of the dregs, instead of the pure wine, drunk at the altar to consecrate life." But despite this brave speech, he finds that his feelings for the statue are rooted in those "dregs" of erotic passion. He desires not just the idea of beauty, but the girl herself. "Soon both God and his tears were forgotten; instead he thought of his Psyche, who stood before him, looking as if she had been cut out of snow and blushing in the light of the dawn. He was going to see her: the living, breathing girl who stepped so lightly, as if she walked on air, the girl whose innocent words were music."

His attempt to make love to the girl is a disaster. "He grabbed her hand and kissed it, and he thought it was softer than a rose petal and yet it inflamed him. He was so excited, so aroused, that he hardly knew what he was saying; words gushed out of his mouth and he could no more control their flow than the crater can stop the volcano from vomiting burning lava. He told her how much he loved her." Contemptuously she spurns him.

His lust aroused, the young artist yields to his friends' coaxing and spends a riotous night with some beautiful peasant girls. Andersen's metaphors convey the sexual excitement, release, and disappointment he feels: "The flower of life . . . bloomed, bent its head, and withered. A strange, horrible smell of corruption blended itself with the odor of roses, it lamed his mind and blinded his sight. The fireworks of sensuality were over and darkness came." Sickened with guilt, he buries the beautiful statue, enters a monastery, and begins a lifelong struggle to suppress the "unclean, evil thoughts" that spring up inside. "He punished his body, but the evil did not come from the surface but from deep within him." He dies at last, his body and bones rot away, and the centuries pass over the unmarked grave of the statue which his love inspired him to make. At last, workmen digging a grave in a convent unearth the statue. No one knows the name of its creator. "But his gain, his profit from his struggle, and his search, the glory that proved the godliness within him, his Psyche, will never die. It will live beyond the name of its creator. His spark still shines here on earth and is admired, appreciated, and loved."

What Andersen says in this elaborate parable is that the erotic hunger which other men feed with "a big healthy swallow of life"—"not only the bread, but the baker woman"—has for him been diverted to a hunger for ideal beauty and fame and spirituality. But he can find no satisfaction in these ideals; he goes to his grave cursing "the strange flames that seemed to set his body on fire." The statue he has made is beautiful, perfect, and his own, a product of his imagination inspired by passion. But there is no primary gratification to be had from it—only highly theoretical pleasure in the hope that this embodied fantasy would constitute a "gain, his profit from his struggle and his search, the glory that proved the godliness within him."

Andersen's stories are like the artist's statue—minded from the "dregs" and "filth" of ordinary life, with energy that might otherwise have been spent in sensual revels. Their substance is the stuff of desire, the drive for love and power; but the art that shapes them is self-doubt and anxiety and troubled conscience. So they become in the end monuments to chastity and innocence, a marble statue in a nun's grave: no abiding satisfaction to their creator, but still something to be admired by others, "his spark that still shines here on earth and is admired, appreciated, and loved." Thus, finally, and by a most circuitous route, is the desire for love and eminence to be fulfilled, for Andersen. (pp. 82-8)

John Griffith, "Personal Fantasy in Andersen's Fairy Tales," in *Kansas Quarterly*, Vol. 16, No. 3, Summer, 1984, pp. 81-8.

SOURCES FOR FURTHER STUDY

Auden, W. H. "Grimm and Andersen." In his *Forewords and Afterwords*, pp. 198-208. New York: Random House, 1942.
  Contrasts fairy tales by Andersen with those by the Brothers Grimm. Auden praises what he considers Andersen's originality in shaping the fairy tales into a literary form.

Bredsdorff, Elias. *Hans Christian Andersen: The Story of His Life and Work, 1805-75*. New York: Charles Scribner's Sons, 1975, 376 p.
  Authoritative, well-organized biography, offering criticism of Andersen's stories.

Grønbech, Bo. *Hans Christian Andersen*. Boston: Twayne Publishers, 1980, 170 p.
  Biographical and critical study surveying Andersen's life and works.

Robb, Nesca A. "Hans Andersen." In her *Four in Exile*, pp. 120-53. London: Hutchinson & Co., 1948.
  Analyzes contrasting elements in Andersen's tales, finding that his fairy-tale world "holds no rose-coloured image of human nature, but shows it with all its too-familiar burden of weaknesses and sins."

Sale, Roger. "Written Tales: Perrault to Andersen." In his *Fairy Tales and After: From Snow White to E. B. White*.
  Discerns flaws in Andersen's fairy tales, concluding that Andersen's understanding and representation of a child's world were frequently clouded by "false rhetoric."

Spink, Reginald. *Hans Christian Andersen and His World*. London: Thames and Hudson, 1972, 128 p.
  Thoroughly researched biographical study. Spink provides the reader with a pictorial glimpse of Andersen, including caricatures, reproductions of title pages, and various other illustrations.

Sherwood Anderson

1876-1941

(Full name Sherwood Berton Anderson; also wrote under pseudonym Buck Fever) American short story writer, novelist, autobiographer, essayist, editor, poet, and dramatist.

INTRODUCTION

*A*nderson, one of the most original early twentieth-century writers, was among the first American authors to explore the influence of the unconscious upon human behavior. A writer of brooding, introspective works, his "hunger to see beneath the surface of lives" was best expressed in the bittersweet stories which form the classic *Winesburg, Ohio: A Group of Tales of Ohio Small Town Life* (1919). This, his most important book, exhibits the author's characteristically simple prose style and his personal vision, which combines a sense of wonder at the potential beauty of life with despair over its tragic aspects. The style and outlook of *Winesburg, Ohio* and of Anderson's three other short story collections—*The Triumph of the Egg* (1921), *Horses and Men* (1923), and *Death in the Woods, and Other Stories* (1933)—were influential in shaping the writings of Ernest Hemingway, William Faulkner, Thomas Wolfe, John Steinbeck, and many other American authors.

Born in Ohio to an out-of-work harness maker and a washerwoman, Anderson was raised in the small town of Clyde, which later served as the model for Winesburg. There, while coming to hate the self-sacrificing drudgery to which his mother was reduced and the irresponsibility of his alcoholic father, Anderson first learned the art of telling stories while listening to his father tell the entertaining anecdotes for which he was known. Attending school infrequently, Anderson took a number of temporary jobs to help his impoverished family, working as a newsboy, a housepainter, a field worker, and a "swipe," or stablehand. These experiences, along with the awkward sexual initiation described in his *Memoirs* (1941), later provided thematic and incidental material for his fiction. After a stint in the U.S. Army during the Spanish-American War, he married, became an advertising copywriter in Chicago, and then went on to manage his own paint factory, the Anderson Manufacturing Company, in Elyria, Ohio. His commercial success, however, did not satisfy his awakening artistic aspirations, and he spent his spare time—and a fair amount of company time—writing fiction.

Scholars have noted that the year 1912 marked a watershed in Anderson's artistic and professional life. In November of that year, overworked and beset by various worries, Anderson suffered a mental breakdown; as best as can be determined from the conflicting accounts in his writings, he suddenly walked out of his office in the midst of dictating a letter and was discovered four days later many miles away, babbling incoherently and amnesic. Shortly afterward, his marriage and business failed, and he returned to Chicago to resume work in advertising. There he met such writers of the Chicago Renaissance as Floyd Dell, Carl Sandburg, Theodore Dreiser, Ben Hecht, and Burton Rascoe, who read his early fiction and encouraged him. Although Anderson's first published short story, "The Rabbit Pen," appeared in William Dean Howells's *Harper's* magazine, most of his early stories were printed in *Masses, Little Review, Seven Arts,* and other "little" magazines. Anderson attained recognition as an important new voice in American literature with the appearance of *Winesburg, Ohio* in 1919. Some critics denounced the book as morbid, depressing, and overly concerned with sex; others, however, praised it for its honesty and depth, comparing Anderson's accomplishment with that of Anton Chekhov and Fedor Dostoevski in its concern with the buried life of the soul. Commentators noted that Anderson achieved a fusion of simply stated fiction and brooding psychological analysis—"half tale and half psychological anatomizing" was H. L. Mencken's description—which reveals the essential loneliness and beauty of ordinary people living out their lives during the twilight days of agrarian America in a fading Ohio town.

Anderson's style was shaped during the 1920s by the works of Gertrude Stein, particularly her *Three Lives,* while his personal philosophy reflected that of D. H. Lawrence. In such stories as " 'Unused' " and "The New Englander" he attempted to write with the simple, repetitive verbiage and rhythms of Stein and to develop Lawrence's beliefs concerning the psychologically crippling effects of sexual repression. Exploring the psychological undercurrents of life in industrialized America, Anderson wrote some of his strongest works in the 1920s, although he was compelled to continue working in advertising until 1922. That year he received *Dial* magazine's first annual Dial Award for his accomplishment in *The Triumph of the Egg,* and the cash award enabled Anderson to leave advertising and to devote himself to full-time writing.

In 1927, with the earnings from his novel *Dark Laughter* (1925)—the only commercially successful work of his lifetime—Anderson settled in the town of Marion, Virginia, where he bought two weekly newspapers that he wrote for and edited. He spent much of the rest of his life in rural southwestern Virginia among the small-town people with whom he had always felt a warm kinship, occasionally publishing collections of his newspaper columns and essays on American life. His final collection of fiction, *Death in the Woods,* appeared in 1933 during the Great Depression and sold poorly. He wrote little during the last few years of his life, declaring that writing was a dead art in America and that the future for artistic achievement lay in motion pictures. While on a cruise to South America in 1941, Anderson died of peritonitis after accidentally swallowing part of a wooden toothpick at a shipboard banquet. He is buried just outside Marion, with his chosen epitaph inscribed upon his gravestone: "Life, not death, is the great adventure."

Critics agree that Anderson's short stories best convey his vision of life, which is often despairing but tempered by his folksy, poignant tone and sense of wonder. In addition to "Hands," "The Untold Lie," and "Sophistication" from *Winesburg, Ohio,* commentators place the stories "The Egg," "Death in the Woods," "I'm a Fool," "The Man Who Became a Woman," and "I Want to Know Why" among his best tales and among the best works of American short fiction. Exemplifying Anderson's innovative form, these stories capture the essence of people divided by insensitivity, convention, circumstance, and personal weakness, who are joined but briefly by love, sympathy, and shared moments of spiritual epiphany. "In Anderson, when all is said and done," wrote Henry Miller, "it is the strong human quality which draws one to him and leads one to prefer him sometimes to those who are undeniably superior to him as artists."

Scholars of Anderson's work have found the author to be a much more complex writer than his simple stories suggest. He was long called a leader in "the revolt from the village" in American literature, an often-quoted appellation given him by Carl Van Doren in a 1921 essay. But while Anderson examined the troubled, darker aspects of provincial life, he saw the small town as an essential and admirable part of America, and he attacked Sinclair Lewis and Mencken for their incessant satirical gibes at village vulgarity. Hostile reviewers of his works called him "Sherwood Lawrence" and tended to portray him as a writer obsessed with sex, though the next generation of American writers made his treatment of sexual relations seem tame by comparison. And some critics and readers who had early enjoyed Anderson's books found them in later years stylistically and thematically adolescent and repetitive: reviewing *Death in the Woods* for *New Republic* in 1933, T. S. Matthews spoke for many critics when he wrote that he was "so used to Anderson now, to his puzzled confidences, his groping repetitions, his occasional stumblings into real inspiration that perhaps we tend to underrate him as an American phenomenon. Or perhaps we no longer overrate him"—a thesis later developed, independently, by Lionel Trilling in one of the most important negative assessments of Anderson. Anderson's many critical admirers and defenders include Alfred Kazin, Malcolm Cowley, and Paul Rosenfeld who, while describing Anderson in a 1922 essay, coined for his friend the widely quoted sobriquet "a phallic Chekhov." Dreiser spoke for many of Anderson's readers when in 1941 he wrote: "Anderson, his life and his writings, epitomize for me the pilgrimage of a poet and dreamer across this limited stage called Life, whose reactions to the mystery of our beings and doings here . . . involved tenderness, love and beauty, delight in the strangeness of our will-less reactions as well as pity, sympathy and love for all things both great and small."

For his simple, impressionistic style and his frequent acknowledgement that he was puzzled by life's basic questions—an unfashionable admission to make during the intellectually self-assured Jazz Age and the politically opinionated climate of the Great Depression—Anderson has often been dismissed as a primitive minor talent who was of more value as a literary catalyst than as an artist in his own right. But the continued popularity of his works has led critics to reexamine them more closely, and Anderson has regained recognition as an important American author.

(For further information about Anderson's life and works, see *Contemporary Authors,* Vols. 104, 121; *Dictionary of Literary Biography,* Vols. 4, 9, 96; *Dictionary of Literary Biography Documentary Series,* Vol. 1; *Major 20th-Century Writers; Short Story Criticism,* Vol. 1; and *Twentieth-Century Literary Criticism,* Vols. 1, 10, 24.)

CRITICAL COMMENTARY

SHERWOOD ANDERSON

(essay 1924)

[In the excerpt below from an essay first published in 1924, Anderson discusses his concept of literary realism.]

There is something very confusing to both readers and writers about the notion of realism in fiction. As generally understood it is akin to what is called "representation" in painting. The fact is before you and you put it down, adding a high spot here and there, to be sure. No man can quite make himself a camera. Even the most realistic worker pays some tribute to what is called "art." Where does representation end and art begin? The location of the line is often as confusing to practicing artists as it is to the public. (p. 71)

Easy enough to get a thrill out of people with reality. A man struck by an automobile, a child falling out at the window of a city office building. Such things stir the emotions. No one, however, confuses them with art.

This confusion of the life of the imagination with the life of reality is a trap into which most of our critics seem to me to fall about a dozen times each year. Do the trick over and over and in they tumble. "It is life," they say. "Another great artist has been discovered."

What never seems to come quite clear is the simple fact that art is art. It is not life.

The life of the imagination will always remain separated from the life of reality. It feeds upon the life of reality, but it is not that life—cannot be. Mr. John Marin painting Brooklyn Bridge, Henry Fielding writing *Tom Jones,* are not trying in the novel and the painting to give us reality. They are striving for a realization in art of something out of their own imaginative experiences, fed to be sure upon the life immediately about. A quite different matter from making an actual picture of what they see before them.

And here arises a confusion. For some reason—I myself have never exactly understood very clearly—the imagination must constantly feed upon reality or starve. Separate yourself too much from life and you may at moments be a lyrical poet, but you are not an artist. Something within dries up, starves for the want of food. Upon the fact in nature the imagination must constantly feed in order that the imaginative life remain significant. The workman who lets his imagination drift off into some experience altogether disconnected with reality, the attempt of the American to depict life in Europe, the New Englander writing of cowboy life—all that sort of thing—in ninety-nine cases out of a hundred ends in the work of such a man becoming at once full of holes and bad spots. The intelli-

---

Principal Works

Windy McPherson's Son (novel) 1916

Winesburg, Ohio: A Group of Tales of Ohio Small Town Life (short stories) 1919

Poor White (novel) 1920

The Triumph of the Egg: A Book of Impressions from American Life in Tales and Poems (short stories and poetry) 1921

Horses and Men (short stories) 1923

Many Marriages (novel) 1923

A Story Teller's Story: The Tale of an American Writer's Journey through His Own Imaginative World and through the World of Facts, with Many of His Experiences and Impressions among Other Writers (autobiography) 1924

Dark Laughter (novel) 1925

The Modern Writer (essays) 1925

Sherwood Anderson's Notebook (sketches) 1926

Tar: A Midwest Childhood (autobiography) 1926

Beyond Desire (novel) 1932

Death in the Woods, and Other Stories (short stories) 1933

Kit Brandon (novel) 1936

Memoirs (unfinished memoirs) 1942

---

gent reader, tricked often enough by the technical skill displayed in hiding the holes, never in the end accepts it as good work. The imagination of the workman has become confused. He has had to depend altogether upon tricks. The whole job is a fake.

The difficulty, I fancy, is that so few workmen in the arts will accept their own limitations. It is only when the limitation is fully accepted that it ceases to be a limitation. Such men scold at the life immediately about. "It's too dull and commonplace to make good material," they declare. Off they sail in fancy to the South Seas, to Africa, to China. What they cannot realize is their own dullness. Life is never dull except to the dull.

The writer who sets himself down to write a tale has undertaken something. He has undertaken to conduct his readers on a trip through the world of his fancy. If he is a novelist his imaginative world is filled with people and events. If he have any sense of decency as a workman he can no more tell lies about his imagined people, fake them, than he can sell out real people in real life. The thing is constantly done but no man I have ever met, having done such a trick, has felt very clean about the matter afterward.

On the other hand, when the writer is rather intensely true to the people of his imaginative world,

when he has set them down truly, when he does not fake, another confusion arises. Being square with your people in the imaginative world does not mean lifting them over into life, into reality. There is a very subtle distinction to be made and upon the writer's ability to make this distinction will in the long run depend his standing as a workman.

Having lifted the reader out of the reality of daily life it is entirely possible for the writer to do his job so well that the imaginative life becomes to the reader for the time real life. Little real touches are added. The people of the town—that never existed except in the fancy—eat food, live in houses, suffer, have moments of happiness and die. To the writer, as he works, they are very real. The imaginative world in which he is for the time living has become for him more alive than the world of reality ever can become. His very sincerity confuses. Being unversed in the matter of making the delicate distinction, that the writer himself sometimes has such a hard time making, they call him a realist. The notion shocks him. "The deuce, I am nothing of the kind," he says. "But such a thing could not have happened in a Vermont town." "Why not? Have you not learned that anything can happen anywhere? If a thing can happen in my imaginative world it can of course happen in the flesh and blood world. Upon what do you fancy my imagination feeds?"

My own belief is that the writer with a notebook in his hand is always a bad workman, a man who distrusts his own imagination. Such a man describes actual scenes accurately, he puts down actual conversation.

But people do not converse in the book world as they do in life. Scenes of the imaginative world are not real scenes.

The life of reality is confused, disorderly, almost always without apparent purpose, whereas in the artist's imaginative life there is purpose. There is determination to give the tale, the song, the painting Form—to make it true and real to the theme, not to life. Often the better the job is done the greater the confusion.

I myself remember with what a shock I heard people say that one of my own books, *Winesburg, Ohio,* was an exact picture of Ohio village life. The book was written in a crowded tenement district of Chicago. The hint for almost every character was taken from my fellow-lodgers in a large rooming house, many of whom had never lived in a village. The confusion arises out of the fact that others besides practicing artists have imaginations. But most people are afraid to trust their imaginations and the artist is not.

Would it not be better to have it understood that realism, in so far as the word means reality to life, is always bad art—although it may possibly be very good journalism?

Which is but another way of saying that all of the

so-called great realists were not realists at all and never intended being. Madame Bovary did not exist in fact. She existed in the imaginative life of Flaubert and he managed to make her exist also in the imaginative life of his readers.

I have been writing a story. A man is walking in a street and suddenly turns out of the street into an alleyway. There he meets another man and a hurried whispered conversation takes place. In real life they may be but a pair of rather small bootleggers, but they are not that to me.

When I began writing, the physical aspect of one of the men, the one who walked in the street, was taken rather literally from life. He looked strikingly like a man I once knew, so much like him in fact that there was a confusion. A matter easy enough to correct.

A stroke of my pen saves me from realism. The man I knew in life had red hair; he was tall and thin.

With a few words I have changed him completely. Now he has black hair and a black mustache. He is short and has broad shoulders. And now he no longer lives in the world of reality. He is a denizen of my own imaginative world. He can now begin a life having nothing at all to do with the life of the red-haired man.

If I am to succeed in making him real in this new world he, like hundreds of other men and women who live only in my own fanciful world, must live and move within the scope of the story or novel into which I have cast him. If I do tricks with him in the imaginative world, sell him out, I become merely a romancer. If, however, I have the courage to let him really live he will, perhaps, show me the way to a fine story or novel.

But the story or novel will not be a picture of life. I will never have had any intention of making it that. (pp. 72-8)

Sherwood Anderson, "A Note on Realism," in his *Sherwood Anderson's Notebook,* Boni & Liveright, 1926, pp. 71-8.

ALFRED KAZIN
(essay date 1942)

[An American literary critic, Kazin is best known for his essay collection *On Native Grounds* (1942), a study of American prose writing since the era of William Dean Howells. In the following excerpt from that work, Kazin examines Anderson's career and his place in American literary history.]

[Anderson's] great subject always was personal freedom, the yearning for freedom, the delight in freedom; and out of it he made a kind of left-handed mysticism,

a groping for the unnamed and unrealized ecstasy immanent in human relations, that seemed the sudden revelation of the lives Americans led in secret. If Sinclair Lewis dramatized the new realism by making the novel an exact and mimetic transcription of American life, Anderson was fascinated by the undersurface of that life and became the voice of its terrors and exultations. Lewis turned the novel into a kind of higher journalism; Anderson turned fiction into a substitute for poetry and religion, and never ceased to wonder at what he had wrought. He had more intensity than a revival meeting and more tenderness than God; he wept, he chanted, he loved indescribably. There was freedom in the air, and he would summon all Americans to share in it; there was confusion and mystery on the earth, and he would summon all Americans to wonder at it. He was clumsy and sentimental; he could even write at times as if he were finger-painting; but at the moment it seemed as if he had sounded the depths of common American experience as no one else could.

There was always an image in Anderson's books—an image of life as a house of doors, of human beings knocking at them and stealing through one door only to be stopped short before another as if in a dream. Life was a dream to him, and he and his characters seemed always to be walking along its corridors. Who owned the house of life? How did one escape after all? No one in his books ever knew, Anderson least of all. Yet slowly and fumblingly he tried to make others believe, as he thought he had learned for himself, that it was possible to escape if only one laughed at necessity. That was his own story, as everything he wrote—the confession in his *Memoirs* was certainly superfluous— was a variation upon it; and it explained why, for all his fumbling and notorious lack of contemporary sophistication, he had so great an appeal for the restive postwar generation. For Anderson, growing up in small Ohio villages during the eighties and nineties at a time when men could still watch and wait for the new industrial world to come in, enjoyed from the first—at least in his own mind—the luxury of dreaming away on the last margin of the old prefactory freedom, of being suspended between two worlds. Unlike most modern American realists even of his own generation, in fact, Anderson always evoked in his books the world of the old handicraft artisans, the harness makers and Civil War veterans like his father, the small-town tailors and shoemakers, the buggy and wagon craftsmen of the old school. (pp. 210-11)

It was certainly on the basis of his experiences in this world that Anderson was able ever after to move through the world that Chicago now symbolized as if he, and all his characters with him, were moving in puzzled bliss through the interstices of the great new cities and factories. No other novelist of the time gave so vividly the sense of *not* having been brought up to the constraints, the easy fictions, the veritable rhythm, of modern commercial and industrial life. It was as if he had been brought up in a backwater, grown quaint and self-willed, a little "queer," a drowsing village mystic, amidst stagnant scenes; and the taste of that stagnance was always in his work. A certain sleepy inarticulation, a habit of staring at faces in wondering silence, a way of groping for words and people indistinguishably, also crept into his work; and what one felt in it was not only the haunting tenderness with which he came to his characters, but also the measureless distances that lay between these characters themselves. They spoke out of the depths, but in a sense they did not speak at all; they addressed themselves, they addressed the world around them, and the echoes of their perpetual confession were like sound-waves visible in the air.

"I would like to write a book of the life of the mind and of the imagination," Anderson wrote in his *Memoirs*. "Facts elude me. I cannot remember dates. When I deal in facts, at once I begin to lie. I can't help it." The conventional world for him was a snare, a cheat that fearful little men had agreed among themselves to perpetuate; the reality lay underground, in men and women themselves. It was as if the ageless dilemma of men caught by society found in him the first prophet naïve enough, and therefore bold enough, to deny that men need be caught at all. His heroes were forever rebelling against the material, yet they were all, like Anderson himself, sublimely unconscious of it. The proud sons who rebel against their drunkard fathers, like Windy McPherson's son, sicken of the riches they have gained, but they never convince one that they have lived with riches. The rebels against working-class squalor and poverty, like Beaut McGregor in *Marching Men*, finally do rise to wealth and greatness, but only to lead men—as Anderson, though a Socialist in those early years, hoped to lead them—out of the factory world itself into a vague solidarity of men marching forever together. The business men who have revolted against their families, like John Webster in *Many Marriages*, make an altar in their bedrooms to worship; the sophisticated artists, like Bruce Dudley in *Dark Laughter*, run away from home to hear the laughter of the triumphantly unrepressed Negroes; the ambitious entrepreneurs, like Hugh McVey in *Poor White*, weep in despair over the machines they have built. And when they do escape, they all walk out of the prison house of modern life, saying with inexpressible simplicity, as Anderson did on the day he suddenly walked out of his paint factory in Ohio: "What am I going to do? Well, now, that I don't know. I am going to wander about. I am going to sit with people, listen to words, tell tales of people, what they are thinking, what they are feeling. The devil! It may even be that I am going forth in search of myself."

"I have come to think," he wrote in *A Story-Teller's Story*, "that the true history of life is but a history of moments. It is only at rare moments that we live." In those early days it was as if a whole subterranean world of the spirit were speaking in and through Anderson, a spirit imploring men to live frankly and fully by their own need of liberation, and pointing the way to a tender and surpassing comradeship. . . . Out of his wandering experiences at soldiering and laboring jobs, at following the race horses he loved and the business career he hated, he had become "at last a writer, a writer whose sympathy went out most to the little frame houses, on often mean enough streets in American towns, to defeated people, often with thwarted lives." Were there not people, people everywhere, just people and their stories to tell? Were there not questions about them always to be asked—the endless wonderment, the groping out toward them, the special "moments" to be remembered? (pp. 212-14)

Between the people he saw and the books he read, Anderson saw the terrible chasm of fear in America—the fear of sex, the fear of telling the truth about the hypocrisy of those businessmen with whom he too had reached for "the bitch-goddess of success"; the fear, even, of making stories the exact tonal equivalent of their lives; the fear of restoring to books the slackness and the disturbed rhythms of life. For Anderson was not only reaching for the truth about people and "the terrible importance of the flesh in human relations"; he was reaching at the same time for a new kind of medium in fiction. As he confessed explicitly later on, he even felt that "the novel form does not fit an American writer, that it is a form which had been brought in. What is wanted is a new looseness; and in *Winesburg* I had made my own form." Significantly enough, even such warm friends of the new realism as Floyd Dell and H. L. Mencken did not think the *Winesburg* stories stories at all; but Anderson, who had revolted against what he now saw as the false heroic note in his first work, knew better, and he was to make the new readers see it his way.

For if "the true history of life was but a history of moments," it followed that the dream of life could be captured only in a fiction that broke with rules of structure literally to embody moments, to suggest the endless halts and starts, the dreamlike passiveness and groping of life. What Gertrude Stein had for fifteen years, working alone in Paris, learned out of her devotion to the independent vision of modern French painting, Anderson now realized by the simple stratagem of following the very instincts of his character, by groping through to the slow realization of his characters on the strength of his conviction that all life itself was only a process of groping. The difference between them (it was a difference that Gertrude Stein's pupil, Ernest Hemingway, felt so deeply that he had to write a parody of Anderson's style, *The Torrents of Spring,* to express his revulsion and contempt) was that where Miss Stein and Hemingway both had resolved their break with the "rules" into a formal iconoclastic technique, a conscious principle of design, Anderson had no sense of design at all save as life afforded him one. Although he later listened humbly enough to Gertrude Stein in Paris—she had proclaimed him one of the few Americans who could write acceptable sentences—he could never make one principle of craft, least of all those "perfect sentences" that she tried so hard to write, the foundation of his work. Anderson was, in fact, rather like an older kind of artisan in the American tradition—such as Whitman and Albert Pinkham Ryder—artisans who worked by sudden visions rather than by any sense of style, artisans whose work was the living grammar of their stubborn belief in their own visions. (pp. 214-15)

Anderson did not merely live for the special "moments" in experience; he wrote, by his own testimony, by sudden realizations, by the kind of apprehension of a mood, a place, a character, that brought everything to a moment's special illumination and stopped short there, content with the fumbling ecstasy it brought. It was this that gave him his interest in the "sex drive" as a force in human life (it had so long been left out), yet always touched that interest with a bold, awkward innocence. He was among the first American writers to bring the unconscious into the novel, yet when one thinks of how writers like Dorothy Richardson, Virginia Woolf, and James Joyce pursued the unconscious and tried to trace some pattern in the fathomless psychic history of men and women, it is clear that Anderson was not interested in contributing to the postwar epic of the unconscious at all. What did interest him was sex as a disturbance in consciousness, the kind of disturbance that drove so many of his heroes out of the world of constraint; but once he had got them out of their houses, freed them from convention and repression, their liberation was on a plane with their usually simultaneous liberation from the world of business. It was their loneliness that gave them significance in Anderson's mind, the lies that they told themselves and each other to keep the desperate fictions of conventionality; and it was inevitably the shattering of that loneliness, the emergence out of that uneasy twilit darkness in which his characters always lived, that made their triumph and, in his best moments, Anderson's own.

The triumph, yes; and the agony. It is a terrible thing for a visionary to remain a minor figure; where the other minor figures can at least work out a minor success, the visionary who has not the means equal to his vision crumbles into fragments. Anderson was a minor figure, as he himself knew so well; and that was his tragedy. For the significance of his whole career is that though he could catch, as no one could, the inex-

pressible grandeur of those special moments in experience, he was himself caught between them. Life was a succession of moments on which everything else was strung; but the moments never came together, and the world itself never came together for him. It was not his "mysticism" that was at fault, for without it he would have been nothing; nor was it his special way of groping for people, of reaching for the grotesques in life, the homely truths that seemed to him so beautiful, since that was what he had most to give—and did give so imperishably in *Winesburg,* in stories like **"I'm a Fool,"** in parts of *Poor White* and *Dark Laughter,* and in the autobiographical *Tar.* It was rather that Anderson had nothing else in him that was equal to his revelations, his tenderness, his groping. He was like a concentration of everything that had been missed before him in modern American writing, and once his impact was felt, the stammering exultation he brought became all. That was Anderson's real humiliation, the humiliation that perhaps only those who see so much more deeply than most men can feel; and he knew it best of all. (pp. 215-16)

"If you love in a loveless world," he wrote in *Many Marriages,* "you face others with the sin of not loving." He had that knowledge; he brought it in, and looked at it as his characters looked at each other; but he could only point to it and wonder. "There is something that separates people, curiously, persistently, in America," he wrote in his last novel, *Kit Brandon.* He ended on that note as he had begun on it twenty-five years before, when Windy McPherson's son wondered why he could never get what he wanted, and Beaut McGregor led the marching men marching, marching nowhere. The brooding was there, the aimless perpetual reaching, that indefinable note Anderson always struck; but though no writer had written so much of liberation, no writer seemed less free. He was a Prospero who had charmed himself to sleep and lost his wand; and as the years went on Anderson seemed more and more bereft, a minor visionary whose perpetual air of wonder became a trance and whose prose disintegrated helplessly from book to book. Yet knowing himself so well, he could smile over those who were so ready to tell him that it was his ignorance of "reality" and of "real people" that crippled his books. What was it but the reality that was almost too oppressively real, the reality beyond the visible surface world, the reality of all those lives that so many did lead in secret, that he had brought into American fiction? It was not his vision that was at fault, no; it was that poignant human situation embodied in him, that story he told over and again because it was his only story—of the groping that broke forth out of the prison house of life and . . . went on groping; of the search for freedom that made all its substance out of that search, and in the end left all the supplicators brooding, suffering, and overwhelmed. Yet if he had not sought so much, he could not have been humiliated so deeply. It was always the measure of his reach that gave others the measure of his failure. (p. 217)

Alfred Kazin, "The New Realism: Sherwood Anderson and Sinclair Lewis," in his *On Native Grounds: An Interpretation of Modern American Prose Literature*, Reynal & Hitchcock, 1942, pp. 205-26.

HORACE GREGORY
(essay date 1949)

[Gregory was an American poet and critic. Below, he offers an overview of Anderson's work.]

As one reads Anderson's stories and autobiographies, three older writers come to mind: one is Herman Melville, another Mark Twain, and the third George Borrow. (p. 7)

Anderson's liking for Borrow has an instinctive rightness beyond anything he could have learned through a conventional education. Borrow showed what a writer could do while ignoring the conventional rules for writing autobiographies and novels. This was a valuable lesson that Anderson never forgot; he became, as Thomas Seccombe wrote of Borrow, not a "matter-of-fact," but a "matter-of-fiction" man. He did not allow Borrow to influence him directly, and in matters of style, in which Borrow was notoriously uneven, Anderson greatly improved upon him. The choice of Borrow as one of his models placed Anderson on the side of those who see and feel things from the ground up, from the pavement of a city street, from the grasses of a field, from the threshold of a house. This view is always an independent view that refuses to become housebroken.

Anderson's debt to Mark Twain is less veiled than that to Borrow, for Mark Twain's *Huckleberry Finn* is literally close to an American time and place that Anderson knew. . . . The people of Anderson's boyhood in the Middle West were but a single generation beyond Tom Sawyer and Huckleberry Finn, and there was an unbroken continuity between the two generations. Huckleberry Finn's skepticism concerning the virtues of church-going was of a piece with the world that Anderson knew, a world whose enjoyment was of the earth. Anderson's affinity to Mark Twain was as "natural," as unstudied as Anderson's memories of growing up and coming of age. Equally natural was the example of perspective taken from Borrow, choosing the life of the out-of-doors as the true center of worldly experience.

With Melville, Anderson's affinities are of a far less conscious order; they belong to the inward-looking, darkened "nocturnal" aspects of Anderson's heritage. The affinities to Twain and Borrow are of daylight character; they are clear and specific, and are sharply outlined within the lively scenes that Anderson created, but his kinship with Melville belongs to that diffused and shadowy area of his imagination which Paul Rosenfeld named as mysticism. . . . It was once fashionable to call such "mysticism" Freudian, because it touched upon the emotions of adolescent sexual experience. In Anderson those emotions are transcended in **"Death in the Woods,"** and whatever "mysticism" may be found within them, including the expression of mystery and awe, is of an older heritage than are the teachings of Freud in America. . . . The diffused affinity that Anderson has with Melville is not a facile one, for Anderson made it one of his few rules to stand aside from "literary precedent," to re-create scenes of action in terms of his own experience rather than to lean upon experiences gained from reading the works of others. The kinship of Anderson's writings with *Moby Dick* embraces that side of Anderson's imagination which is "non-realistic," and which converts what is outwardly the simple telling of a story into a series of symbolic actions. The fluttering, "talking" quality of Wing Biddlebaum's "slender expressive fingers, forever active," in **"Hands,"** is endowed with the mystery that Anderson makes his readers feel. (pp. 8-10)

If the "real Anderson" is seen more clearly in legendary episodes of the autobiographies than when he employs too consciously the pronoun "I," how vividly, how memorably he moves before the reader in his major novel, *Poor White*. (p. 15)

Poor White belongs among the few books that have restored with memorable vitality the life of an era, its hopes and desires, its conflicts between material prosperity and ethics, and its disillusionments, in a manner that stimulates the historical imagination. The book belongs to the period, those years between the middle 1870's and the first ten years of the present century, that gave Thorstein Veblen's *The Theory of the Leisure Class* . . . its air of immediate reference. It was in *Poor White* that the ideas, the talk overheard in Anderson's boyhood, bore fruit. (pp. 16-17)

Anderson did not reach the accomplishment of *Poor White* without preparation; in writing *Winesburg, Ohio* he had begun to discover his style, and in the last chapters of the book he had really found it. He records the importance of that discovery in his *Memoirs*, how the book came to life in a series of stories while he was living in a Chicago rooming house. But *Poor White* also has behind it *Windy McPherson's Son* and more particularly, *Marching Men*, which, Anderson afterwards wrote, should have been a poem. The book was not a poem, but a novel that failed to accomplish its intentions, and yet foreshadowed the kind of novel *Poor White* became. In theory *Marching Men* is a good idea for a book; it embraces the problem of labor leadership in America and the spectacle of American workingmen marching together to redress industrial wrong. But the good idea in the novel remained too theoretical to take on the semblance of life; its hero "Beaut" McGregor, the tall, awkward, red-haired miner's son who becomes a lawyer, and afterwards a leader of workingmen, is too thinly drawn; he is an unindividualized type, whose eventual failure as a leader of men is not felt by the reader. And the entire book is punctuated by fictional clichés. . . . The only scene in *Marching Men* that comes to life is irrelevant to the historical and social themes of the book—and that is the passionate recital of the woman problem by a minor character, a barber. In the barber's speech on his unhappy marriage and his relationship to women the accents of the future Anderson are heard; the barber's theme is expanded in *Many Marriages,* and is heard with greater clarity in *Dark Laughter.* It is sounded fitfully in Anderson's first novel, *Windy McPherson's Son.*

A too broad, too loose fictional method of writing cultural (and industrial) history begins in *Windy Mc-Pherson's Son,* grows into a more clearly discerned view of Anderson's world in *Marching Men,* and then achieves a justly proportioned design in *Poor White.* (pp. 18-20)

Poor White, a tribute to a cultural past, does not, of course, resemble the costume historical novel in any of its features: it is as plotless as though Anderson had wisely taken to heart Mark Twain's warning to the readers of *Huckleberry Finn*—"persons attempting to find a plot in it will be shot." And he drew as much from the example of Mark Twain's kind of plotlessness (which never, however, permitted a story to lack action and incident) as from the examples provided by the stories in Gertrude Stein's *Three Lives.*

No novel of the American small town in the Middle West evokes in the minds of its readers so much of the cultural heritage of its milieu as does *Poor White;* nor does Anderson in his later novels ever recapture the same richness of association, the ability to make memorable each scene in the transition from an agrarian way of living to a twentieth-century spectacle of industrial conflict with its outward display of physical comfort and wealth.

One of Anderson's critics has remarked on his ability to write at his best only when the impulse to write urgently moved him, and that statement has an enlightening truth within it for anyone examining his short stories. In these he held to his position of being one whose concern for prose was like a poet's concern for verse: he was a story-teller who desired only to gratify his need to talk and to charm his listeners, with no thought of pecuniary reward. But if his standards

seem often those of one who perpetuates the folk tale in its simplicity, he is also the artist, who with a limited number of brush strokes leaves his style, the impress of his personality, along with the image of an undraped figure, or a landscape, upon his canvas. And if one finds the impact of any style of plastic art in Anderson's stories, it is the style of Renoir and Pissaro, of late Impressionism. For often there seems to be light and air between his sentences, as in **"The American County Fair,"** for example, and the same loose Impressionistic strokes introduce the reader to scenes in **"The Egg"** and **"The Man Who Became a Woman."** It is in seeming at times to wander away from his story that Anderson so often relaxes and lures his readers, and within the details of an Impressionistic haze of light and color that he often creates an "artlessness" that conceals his art.

In Anderson's stories, from the early pieces which became parts of a series in *Winesburg, Ohio,* to his masterpiece **"Death in the Woods,"** one sees the particulars of people, rather than the types that one finds in his novels. The first edition of *The Triumph of the Egg: A Book of Impressions from American Life in Tales and Poems* (its subtitle is not to be ignored) is illustrated by photographs of grotesques in clay by Tennessee Mitchell. The grotesques, nearly burlesque portrait heads of the people in the book, are in spirit with the stories told about these people, for their individuality is carried upward, slightly off the earth, into a higher register of fancy. Since Anderson's view is always from the earth upward, in the story of **"The Egg"** the flight of fancy takes off from a child's-eye-view level, and we are warned early in the story that a grotesque humor will be released: we are told, "Grotesques are born out of eggs as out of people." . . . From the child's-eye-view through which Anderson presents it, the story has the authenticity of a fable, an air of candor which saves it from falling into bad taste, and the high spirit in which it is told rescues it from a mawkish concern over the spectacle of repeated failure, for the grotesque man is no more successful as a restaurant-keeper and panic-stricken salesman than he was as a chicken-farmer. It is the kind of story that having been told once cannot be told again; it is the story that makes the entire book, *The Triumph of the Egg,* memorable, and all the other stories and verses in the volume grow pale beside it; these others seem to have been written with less urgency of impulse, and though no less lyrical in tone, are thin and diffused. The book is in fact The Triumph of the Egg.

Anderson's ventures into the higher registers of fancy (which make it strange to think of him as a realist, as he was once classified) did not end with *The Triumph of the Egg*—the ventures had actually begun in **"Hands,"** the first of the *Winesburg* stories, and indeed the prelude to *Winesburg* was called **"The Book of the Grotesque."** As the image, the theme, and the fear of being grotesque matured in Anderson's imagination, some of the most clearly inspired of his stories were possessed by it. The fears of being strange and, similarly, the painful, half-comic experiences of "growing up," pervade the stories and sketches of *Horses and Men.* The book is literally of horses and men, and no American writer of Anderson's generation or any other has caught the colors, the lights and shadows, the spirit of the race track as well as he; the race track is Anderson's milieu quite as the American county fair is, and among those who write of sports, he is in the company of Ring Lardner and Ernest Hemingway. But here also his view of the scene is a characteristic upward glance, the view of country boys in **"I'm a Fool"** and **"The Man Who Became a Woman."** The boys are grooms' helpers, "swipes," and they follow the circuit of race track activities with the same delight with which their younger brothers would try to enter the world of the traveling wild west show or circus. The influence of George Borrow's attraction to gypsy life is active here, but Anderson translates it wholly into American sights and scenes.

Yet all this is finally only the happy choice of a decor for what he really has to say, and in **"The Man Who Became a Woman"** what is said touches upon the fears, the mysteries of adolescence—the fear of the boy (now grown to a man) on discovering that he is

"strange," is not wholly masculine, and underlying this, the fear of sterility and death. With a touch as sure as that of D. H. Lawrence, and with none of the mechanical features of overt psychological fiction, Anderson uses, with deceptive simplicity, the scenes in the bar-room and the hayloft, and the incident of the boy's fall, naked, into the shell of bones which was once the carcass of a horse, as the means to tell his story. None of Anderson's stories, with the exception of **"Death in the Woods,"** is a better example of his skill in giving the so-called common experiences of familiar, everyday life, an aura of internal meaning. In this story there is also the fear of Negro laughter, a fear which enters at extended length into two of his later novels, *Dark Laughter* and *Beyond Desire.* In **"The Man Who Became a Woman,"** that particular fear is made more convincing, more appropriate than in the novels; the boy's innocence, his lack of experience, do much to justify his fear, and the fear properly belongs to the immature, the unpoised, the ignorant.

"I'm a Fool" is done with the same turning of light upon common experience—the telling of an awkward, grotesque, foolish lie. Again it is part of the painful experience of growing up, a boyish shrewdness that failed of its desires; it is the image of the concealed, the fatal mistake made by the glib, the young, the un-

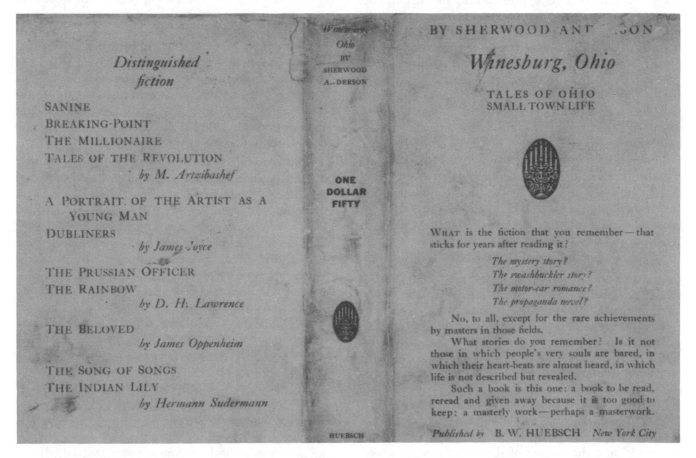

Dust jacket of Anderson's *Winesburg, Ohio.*

worldly, who parade their candor and innocence wherever they walk and breathe.

"Death in the Woods," Anderson's masterpiece among his shorter stories, is of a different temper and key than the colorful, high-spirited narratives of *Horses and Men.* It is a story which, as Anderson realized, demanded perfection of its kind: he rewrote it several times; it had originally been an episode in *Tar,* and had continued to haunt Anderson's imagination. The strong, initial impulse to write it was not enough, for the story, beyond any other story that Anderson wrote, was the summing up of a lifetime's experience, and in its final version it became Anderson's last look backward into the Middle West of his childhood. It was the last of his *Mid-American Chants,* the book of verses in prose, the last of the prose poems in *A New Testament,* and though its external form is plainly that of a story, its internal structure is that of poetry; it has the power of saying more than prose is required to say, and saying it in the fewest words. But of more importance than the phonetic art of the story is the interplay of those prose rhythms of which Anderson had become a master, and the control of its central theme. (pp. 22-7)

["Death in the Woods"] contains the kind of poetry that we associated with Wordworth—the recollection of youthful experience, the figures of common speech, the instinctive dignity and life of the poor, the moonlit rural scene—done with the simplicity that Wordsworth sought and attained. It is for this reason (among others) that the story transcends its regional atmosphere, and becomes the universal story that it is. One can think of it, and not inappropriately, as a story that applies to the years of cold and famine in postwar twentieth-century Europe; it has that kind of universality, one that makes possible analogies in life as well as literature. In writing it Anderson's transcendental note was clearly sounded. The note transcends, in more than one meaning of the verb, the writers from whom Anderson drew inspiration—his own contemporaries, Gertrude Stein, Dreiser, D. H. Lawrence, as well as the writers who came before him in revolt against the Puritan New England tradition—and places him not too far from the figures of Thoreau and Emerson.

To enter that dangerous ground which lies between prose and poetry, and to emerge at last, as Anderson does in **"Death in the Woods,"** unscarred by its pitfalls, is a considerable accomplishment, one that has been achieved by few writers in America, and of this small number most are writers whose books provide larger scenes of action than are witnessed in any of Anderson's short stories or novels. It was his contribution and perhaps his destiny, to limit the size of his canvas, to give those who read him a view whose depth, like that of a picture, is greater than the span of the frame around it, and that is one of the reasons why Anderson's best stories have the penetrating quality of Ishmael's gaze in the opening chapters of *Moby Dick.* (pp. 27-8)

Horace Gregory, in an introduction to *The Portable Sherwood Anderson,* edited by Horace Gregory, Viking Penguin, 1949, pp. 1-31.

IRVING HOWE
(essay date 1951)

[A longtime editor of the leftist magazine *Dissent* and a regular contributor to *The New Republic*, Howe is one of America's most repected literary critics and social historians. In the following excerpt, he describes the role of the "grotesque" in Anderson's *Winesburg, Ohio*.]

Winesburg is a book largely set in twilight and darkness, its backgrounds heavily shaded with gloomy blacks and marshy grays—as is proper for a world of withered men who, sheltered by night, reach out for that sentient life they dimly recall as the racial inheritance that has been squandered away. Like most fiction, *Winesburg* is a variation on the theme of reality and appearance, in which the deformations caused by day (public life) are intensified at night and, in their very extremity, become an entry to reality. From Anderson's instinctively right placement of the book's central actions at twilight and night comes some of its frequently noticed aura of "lostness"—as if the most sustaining and fruitful human activities can no longer be performed in public communion but must be grasped in secret. (p. 98)

Misogyny, inarticulateness, frigidity, God-infatuation, homosexuality, drunkenness—these are symptoms of their recoil from the regularities of human intercourse and sometimes of their substitute gratifications in inanimate objects, as with the unloved Alice Hindman who "because it was her own, could not bear to have anyone touch the furniture of her room." In their compulsive traits these figures find a kind of dulling peace, but as a consequence they are subject to rigid monomanias and are deprived of one of the great blessings of human health: the capacity for a variety of experience. That is why, in a sense, "nothing happens" in *Winesburg.* For most of its figures it is too late for anything to happen, they can only muse over the traumas which have so harshly limited their spontaneity. Stripped of their animate wholeness and twisted into frozen postures of defense, they are indeed what Anderson has called them: grotesques.

The world of *Winesburg,* populated largely by these back-street grotesques, soon begins to seem like a buried ruin of a once vigorous society, an atrophied remnant of the egalitarian moment of 19th-century America. Though many of the book's sketches are placed in the out-of-doors, its atmosphere is as stifling as a tomb. And the reiteration of the term "grotesque" is felicitous in a way Anderson could hardly have been aware of; for it was first used by Renaissance artists to describe arabesques painted in the underground ruins, *grotte,* of Nero's "Golden House."

The conception of the grotesque, as actually developed in the stories, is not merely that it is an unwilled affliction but also that it is a mark of a once sentient striving. In his introductory fantasy, **"The Book of the Grotesque,"** Anderson writes: "It was the truths that made the people grotesques . . . the moment one of the people took one of the truths to himself, called it his truth, and tried to live his life by it, he became a grotesque and the truth he embraced a falsehood." There is a sense . . . in which these sentences are at variance with the book's meaning, but they do suggest the significant notion that the grotesques are those who *have* sought "the truths" that disfigure them. By contrast the banal creatures who dominate the town's official life, such as Will Henderson, publisher of the paper for which George Willard works, are not even grotesques: they are simply clods. The grotesques are those whose humanity has been outraged and who to survive in Winesburg have had to suppress their wish to love. Wash Williams becomes a misogynist because his mother-in-law, hoping to reconcile him to his faithless wife, thrusts her into his presence naked; Wing Biddlebaum becomes a recluse because his wish to blend learning with affection is fatally misunderstood. Grotesqueness, then, is not merely the shield of deformity; it is also a remnant of misshapen feeling, what Dr. Reefy in **"Paper Pills"** calls "the sweetness of the twisted apples." (pp. 99-101)

The grotesques rot because they are unused, their energies deprived of outlet, and their instincts curdled in isolation. As Waldo Frank has noticed in his fine study of *Winesburg,* the first three stories in the book suggest this view in a complete theme-statement [see excerpt dated 1941]. The story, **"Hands,"** through several symbolic referents, depicts the loss of creativity in the use of the human body. The second story, **"Paper Pills,"** directly pictures the progressive ineffectuality of human thought, pocketed in paper pellets that no one reads. And the third story, **"Mother,"** relates these two themes to a larger variant: the inability of Elizabeth Willard, *Winesburg's* mother-figure, to communicate her love to her son. "The form of the mother, frustrate, lonely, at last desperate," Frank writes, "pervades the variations that make the rest of the book: a continuity of variation swelling, swirling into the corners and crannies of the village life; and at last closing in the mother's death, in the loss forever of the $800 which

Elizabeth Willard had kept for twenty years to give her son his start away from Winesburg, and in the son's wistful departure." In the rupture of family love and the consequent loss of George Willard's heritage, the theme-statement of the book is completed.

The book's central strand of action, discernible in about half the stories, is the effort of the grotesques to establish intimate relations with George Willard, the young reporter. At night, when they need not fear the mockery of public detection, they hesitantly approach him, almost in supplication, to tell him of their afflictions and perhaps find health in his voice. Instinctively, they sense his moral freshness, finding hope in the fact that he has not yet been calloused by knowledge and time. To some of the grotesques, such as Dr. Reefy and Dr. Parcival, George Willard is the lost son returned, the Daedalus whose apparent innocence and capacity for feeling will redeem Winesburg. To others among the grotesques, such as Tom Foster and Elmer Cowley, he is a reporter-messenger, a small-town Hermes, bringing news of a dispensation which will allow them to reenter the world of men. But perhaps most fundamentally and subsuming these two visions, he seems to the grotesques a young priest who will renew the forgotten communal rites by which they may again be bound together. To Louise Trunnion he will bring a love that is more than a filching of flesh; to Dr. Parcival the promise to "write the book that I may never get written" in which he will tell all men that "everyone in the world is Christ and they are all crucified"; to the Reverend Curtis Hartman the willingness to understand a vision of God as revealed in the flesh of a naked woman; to Wash Williams the peace that will ease his sense of violation; and to Enoch Robinson the "youthful sadness, young man's sadness, the sadness of a growing boy in a village at the year's end [which can open] the lips of the old man."

As they approach George Willard, the grotesques seek not merely the individual release of a sudden expressive outburst, but also a relation with each other that may restore them to collective harmony. They are distraught communicants in search of a ceremony, a social value, a manner of living, a lost ritual that may, by some means, re-establish a flow and exchange of emotion. Their estrangement is so extreme that they cannot turn to each other though it is each other they really need and secretly want; they turn instead to George Willard who will soon be out of the orbit of their life. (pp. 101-03)

The burden which the grotesques would impose on George Willard is beyond his strength. He is not yet himself a grotesque mainly because he has not yet experienced very deeply, but for the role to which they would assign him he is too absorbed in his own ambition and restlessness. The grotesques see in his difference from them the possibility of saving themselves, but actually it is the barrier to an ultimate companionship. George Willard's adolescent receptivity to the grotesques can only give him the momentary emotional illumination described in that lovely story, **"Sophistication."** . . . For George this illumination is enough, but it is not for the grotesques. They are a moment in his education, he a confirmation of their doom. (p. 104)

Irving Howe, "The Book of the Grotesque," in his *Sherwood Anderson,* William Sloane Associates, 1951, pp. 91-109.

MALCOLM COWLEY
(essay date 1960)

[A prominent American critic, Cowley has written widely about American authors Nathaniel Hawthorne, Walt Whitman, and Ernest Hemingway. Here, he discusses the creative and mechanistic processes of Anderson's writing.]

Anderson made a great noise . . . when he published *Winesburg, Ohio* in 1919. The older critics scolded him, the younger ones praised him, as a man of the changing hour, yet he managed in that early work and others to be relatively timeless. There are moments in American life to which he gave not only the first but the final expression.

He soon became a writer's writer, the only story teller of his generation who left his mark on the style and vision of the generation that followed. Hemingway, Faulkner, Wolfe, Steinbeck, Caldwell, Saroyan, Henry Miller . . . each of these owes an unmistakable debt to Anderson, and their names might stand for dozens of others. (p. 1)

After finding his proper voice at the age of forty, Anderson didn't change as much as other serious writers; perhaps his steadfastness should make us thankful, considering that most American writers change for the worse. He had achieved a quality of emotional rather than factual truth and he preserved it to the end of his career, while doing little to refine, transform, or even understand it. Some of his last stories—by no means all of them—are richer and subtler than the early ones, but they are otherwise not much different or much better.

He was a writer who depended on inspiration, which is to say that he depended on feelings so deeply embedded in his personality that he was unable to direct them. He couldn't say to himself, "I shall produce such and such an effect in a book of such and such a length"; the book had to write or rather speak itself while Anderson listened as if to an inner voice. In his business life he showed a surprising talent for planning and manipulation. "One thing I've known always, instinctively," he told Floyd Dell, "—that's how to handle people, make them do as I please, be what I wanted them to be. I was in business for a long time and the truth is I was a smooth son of a bitch." He never learned to handle words in that smooth fashion. Writing was an activity he assigned to a different level of himself, the one on which he was emotional and unpractical. To reach that level sometimes required a sustained effort of the will. He might start a story like a man running hard to catch a train, but once it was caught he could settle back and let himself be carried—often to the wrong destination.

He knew instinctively whether one of his stories was right or wrong, but he didn't always know why. He could do what writers call "pencil work" on his manuscript, changing a word here and there, but he couldn't tighten the plot, delete weak passages, sharpen the dialogue, give a twist to the ending; if he wanted to improve the story, he had to wait for a return of the mood that had produced it, then write it over from beginning to end. . . . Sometimes, in different books, he published two or three versions of the same story, so that we can see how it grew in his subconscious mind. One characteristic of the subconscious is a defective sense of time: in dreams the old man sees himself as a boy, and the events of thirty or forty years may be jumbled together. Time as a logical succession of events was Anderson's greatest difficulty in writing novels or even long stories. He got his tenses confused and carried his heroes ten years forward or back in a single paragraph. His instinct was to present everything together, as in a dream. (pp. 3-4)

His earliest and perhaps his principal teacher was his father, "Irve" Anderson, who used to entertain whole barrooms with tales of his impossible adventures in the Civil War. A great many of the son's best stories, too, were told first in saloons. Later he would become what he called "an almighty scribbler" and would travel about the country with dozens of pencils and reams of paper, the tools of his trade. "I am one," he said, "who loves, like a drunkard his drink, the smell of ink, and the sight of a great pile of white paper that may be scrawled upon always gladdens me"; but his earlier impulse had been to speak, not write, his stories. The best of them retain the language, the pace, and one might even say the gestures of a man talking unhurriedly to his friends.

Within the oral tradition, Anderson had his own picture of what a story should be. He was not interested in telling conventional folk tales, those in which events are more important than emotions. American folk tales usually end with a "snapper"—that is, after starting with the plausible, they progress through the barely possible to the flatly incredible, then wait for a laugh. Magazine fiction used to follow—and much of it still does—a pattern leading to a different sort of snapper, one that calls for a gasp of surprise or relief instead of a guffaw. Anderson broke the pattern by writing stories that not only lacked snappers, in most cases, but even had no plots in the usual sense. The tales he told in his Midwestern drawl were not incidents or episodes, they were *moments,* each complete in itself.

The best of the moments in *Winesburg, Ohio,* is called **"The Untold Lie."** The story, which I have to summarize at the risk of spoiling it, is about two farm hands husking corn in a field at dusk. Ray Pearson is small, serious, and middle-aged, the father of half a dozen thin-legged children; Hal Winters is big and young, with the reputation of being a bad one. Suddenly he says to the older man, "I've got Nell Gunther in trouble. I'm telling you, but keep your mouth shut." He puts his two hands on Ray's shoulders and looks down into his eyes. "Well, old daddy," he says, "come on, advise me. Perhaps you've been in the same fix yourself. I know what everyone would say is the right thing to do, but what do you say?" Then the author steps back to look at his characters. "There they stood," he tells us, "in the big empty field with the quiet corn shocks standing in rows behind them and the red and yellow hills in the distance, and from being just two indifferent workmen they had become all alive to each other."

That single moment of aliveness—that epiphany, as Joyce would have called it, that sudden reaching out of two characters through walls of inarticulateness and misunderstanding—is the effect that Anderson is trying to create for his readers or listeners. There is more to the story, of course, but it is chiefly designed to bring the moment into relief. Ray Pearson thinks of his own marriage, to a girl he got into trouble, and turns away from Hal without being able to say the expected words about duty. Later that evening he is seized by a sudden impulse to warn the younger man against being tricked into bondage. He runs awkwardly across the fields, crying out that children are only the accidents of life. Then he meets Hal and stops, unable to repeat the words that he had shouted into the wind. It is Hal who breaks the silence. "I've already made up my mind," he says, taking Ray by the coat and shaking him. "Nell ain't no fool. . . . I want to marry her. I want to settle down and have kids." Both men laugh, as if they had forgotten what happened in the cornfield. Ray walks away into the darkness, thinking pleasantly now of his children and muttering to himself, "It's just as well. Whatever I told him would have been a lie." There has been a moment in the lives of two men. The moment has passed and the briefly established communion has been broken, yet we feel that each man has revealed his essential being. It is as if a gulf had opened in the level Ohio cornfield and as if, for one moment, a light had shone from the depths, illuminating everything that happened or would ever happen to both of them.

That moment of revelation was the story Anderson told over and over, but without exhausting its freshness, for the story had as many variations as there were faces in his dreams. Behind one face was a moment of defiance; behind another, a moment of resignation (as when Alice Hindman forces herself "to face bravely the fact that many people must live and die alone, even in Winesburg"); behind a third face was a moment of self-discovery; behind a fourth was a moment of deliberate self-delusion. This fourth might have been the face of the author's sister, as he describes her in a chapter of *Sherwood Anderson's Memoirs.* Unlike the other girls she had no beau, and so she went walking with her brother Sherwood, pretending that he was someone else. "It's beautiful, isn't it, James?" she said, looking at the wind ripples that passed in the moonlight over a field of ripening wheat. Then she kissed him and whispered, "Do you love me, James?"—and all her loneliness and flight from reality were summed up in those words. Anderson had that gift for summing up, for pouring a lifetime into a moment. (pp. 5-8)

Those moments at the center of Anderson's often marvelous stories were moments, in general, without a sequel; they existed separately and timelessly. That explains why he couldn't write novels and why, with a single exception, he never even wrote a book in the strict sense of the word. A book should have a structure and a development, whereas for Anderson there was chiefly the flash of lightning that revealed a life without changing it.

The one exception, of course, is *Winesburg, Ohio,* and that became a true book for several reasons: because it was conceived as a whole, because Anderson had found a subject that released his buried emotions, and because most of the book was written in what was almost a single burst of inspiration, so that it gathered force as it went along. (p. 11)

All the stories were written rapidly, with little need for revision, each of them being, as Anderson said, "an idea grasped whole as one would pick an apple in an orchard." He was dealing with material that was both fresh and familiar. The town of Winesburg was based on his memories of Clyde, Ohio, where he had spent most of his boyhood and where his mother had died at the same age as the hero's mother. The hero, George Willard, was the author in his late adolescence, and the other characters were either remembered from Clyde or else, in many cases, suggested by faces glimpsed in the Chicago streets. Each face revealed a moment, a mood, or a secret that lay deep in Anderson's life and for which he was finding the right words at last.

As the book went forward, more and more of the faces—as well as more streets, buildings, trades, and landscapes—were carried from one story to another, with the result that Winesburg itself acquired a physical and corporate life. Counting the four parts of **"God-liness,"** each complete in itself, there would be twenty-five stories or chapters in all. None of them taken separately—not even **"Hands"** or **"The Untold Lie"**—is as effective as the best of Anderson's later work, but each of them contributes to all the others, as the stories in later volumes are not expected to do. There was a delay of some months before the last three chapters—**"Death,"** **"Sophistication,"** and **"Departure"**—were written with the obvious intention of rounding out the book. First George Willard is released from Winesburg by the death of his mother; then, in **"Sophistication,"** he learns how it feels to be a grown man; then finally he leaves for the city on the early-morning train, and everything recedes as into a framed picture. "When he aroused himself and looked out of the car window," Anderson says, "the town of Winesburg had disappeared and his life there had become but a background on which to paint the dreams of his manhood."

In structure the book lies midway between the novel proper and the mere collection of stories. Like several famous books by more recent authors, all early readers of Anderson—like Faulkner's *The Unvanquished* and *Go Down, Moses,* like Steinbeck's *Tortilla Flat* and *The Pastures of Heaven,* like Caldwell's *Georgia Boy*—it is a cycle of stories with several unifying elements, including a single background, a prevailing tone, and a central character. These elements can be found in all the cycles, but the best of them also have an underlying plot that is advanced or enriched by each of the stories. In *Winesburg* the underlying plot or fable, though hard to recognize, is unmistakably present, and I think it might be summarized as follows:

George Willard is growing up in a friendly town full of solitary persons; the author calls them "grotesques." Their lives have been distorted not, as Anderson tells us in his prologue, by their each having seized upon a single truth, but rather by their inability to express themselves. Since they cannot truly communicate with others, they have all become emotional cripples. Most of the grotesques are attracted one by one to George Willard; they feel that he might be able to help them. In those moments of truth that Anderson loves to describe, they try to explain themselves to George, believing that he alone in Winesburg has an instinct for finding the right words and using them honestly. They urge him to preserve and develop his gift. "You must not become a mere peddler of words," Kate Swift the teacher insists, taking hold of his shoulders. "The thing to learn is to know what people are thinking about, not what they say." Dr. Parcival tells him, "If something happens perhaps you will be able to write the book I may never get written." All the grotesques hope that George Willard will some day speak what is in their hearts and thus re-establish their connection with

mankind. George is too young to understand them at the time, but the book ends with what seems to be the promise that, after leaving Winesburg, he will become the voice of inarticulate men and women in all the forgotten towns.

If the promise is truly implied, and if Anderson felt he was keeping it when writing **"Hands"** and the stories that followed, then *Winesburg, Ohio* is far from the pessimistic or destructive or morbidly sexual work it was one attacked for being. Instead it is a work of love, an attempt to break down the walls that divide one person from another, and also, in its own fashion, a celebration of small-town life in the lost days of good will and innocence. (pp. 11-15)

Malcolm Cowley, in an introduction to *Winesburg, Ohio,* by Sherwood Anderson, revised edition, The Viking Press, 1960, pp. 1-15.

JOHN UPDIKE
(essay date 1984)

[A perceptive observer of the human condition and an accomplished literary stylist, Updike is one of America's most distinguished men of letters. While best known as a novelist, he is also a frequent contributor of reviews and essays to various periodicals. In the following excerpt, he considers the bittersweet quality for which *Winesburg, Ohio* is noted.]

Sherwood Anderson's *Winesburg, Ohio* is one of those books so well known by title that we imagine we know what is inside it: a sketch of the population, seen more or less in cross section, of a small Midwestern town. It is this as much as Edvard Munch's paintings are portraits of the Norwegian middle class around the turn of the century. The important thing, for Anderson and Munch, is not the costumes and the furniture or even the bodies but the howl they conceal—the psychic pressure and warp underneath the social scene. Matter-of-fact though it sounds, *Winesburg, Ohio* is feverish, phantasmal, dreamlike. Anderson had accurately called this collection of loosely linked short stories *The Book of the Grotesque;* his publisher, B. W. Huebsch, suggested the more appealing title. The book . . . remains his masterpiece.

"The Book of the Grotesque" is the name also of the opening story, which Anderson wrote first and which serves as a prologue. A writer, "an old man with a white mustache . . . who was past sixty," has a dream in which "all the men and women the writer had ever known had become grotesques." . . . Another writer, an "I" who is presumably Sherwood Anderson, breaks in and explains the old writer's theory of grotesqueness. . . . Having so strangely doubled authorial personae, Anderson then offers twenty-one tales, one of them in four parts, all "concerning," as the table of contents specifies, one or another citizen of Winesburg; whether they come from the old writer's book of grotesques or some different set to which the younger author had access is as unclear as their fit within the cranky and fey anthropological-metaphysical framework set forth with such ungainly solemnity.

"Hands," the first tale, "concerning Wing Biddlebaum," introduces not only its hero, a pathetic, shy old man on the edge of town whose hyperactive little white hands had once strayed to the bodies of too many schoolboys in the Pennsylvania town where he had been a teacher, but also George Willard, the eighteen-year-old son of the local hotelkeeper and a reporter for the *Winesburg Eagle.* He seems a young representative of the author. There is also a "poet," suddenly invoked in flighty passages like:

> Let us look briefly into the story of the hands. Perhaps our talking of them will arouse the poet who will tell the hidden wonder story of the influence for which the hands were but fluttering pennants of promise.

A cloud of authorial effort, then, attends the citizens of Winesburg, each of whom walks otherwise isolated toward some inexpressible denouement of private revelation. Inexpressiveness, indeed, is what is above all expressed: the characters, often, talk only to George Willard, and then only once; their attempts to talk with one another tend to culminate in a comedy of tongue-tied silence. (p. 95)

For Anderson, society scarcely exists in its legal and affective bonds, and dialogue is generally the painful imposition of one monologue upon another. At the climax of the unconsummated love affair between George Willard and Helen White that is one of *Winesburg, Ohio*'s continuous threads, the two sit together in the deserted fairground grandstand and hold hands:

> In that high place in the darkness the two oddly sensitive human atoms held each other tightly and waited. In the mind of each was the same thought. "I have come to this lonely place and here is this other," was the substance of the thing felt.

They embrace, but then mutual embarrassment overtakes them and like children they race and tumble on the way down to town and part, having "for a moment taken hold of the thing that makes the mature life of men and women in the modern world possible."

The vagueness of "the thing" is chronic, and only the stumbling, shrugging, willful style that Anderson made of Stein's serene run-on tropes affords him half a purchase on his unutterable subject, the "thing" troubling the heart of his characters. Dr. Reefy, who at-

tends and in a sense loves George Willard's dying mother, compulsively writes thoughts on bits of paper. He then crumples them into little balls—"paper pills"—and shoves them into his pocket only to eventually throw them away. "One by one the mind of Dr. Reefy had made the thoughts. Out of many of them he formed a truth that arose gigantic in his mind. The truth clouded the world. It became terrible and then faded away and the little thoughts began again." What the gigantic thought was, we are not told.

Another questing medical man, Dr. Parcival, relates long tales that at times seem to George Willard "a pack of lies" and at others to contain "the very essence of truth." As Thornton Wilder's *Our Town* reminded us, small-town people think a lot about the universe (as opposed to city people, who think about one another). The agonizing philosophical search is inherited from religion; in the four-part story **"Godliness,"** the author, speaking as a print-saturated modern man, says of the world fifty years before: "Men labored too hard and were too tired to read. In them was no desire for words printed upon paper. As they worked in the fields, vague, half-formed thoughts took possession of them. They believed in God and in God's power to control their lives. . . . The figure of God was big in the hearts of men." The rural landscape of the Midwest becomes easily confused in the minds of its pious denizens with that of the Bible, where God manifested himself with signs and spoken words. Jesse Bentley's attempt to emulate Abraham's offered sacrifice of Isaac so terrifies his grandson David that the boy flees the Winesburg region forever. Anderson writes about religious obsession with cold sympathy, as something that truly enters into lives and twists them. To this spiritual hunger sex adds its own; the Reverend Curtis Hartman breaks a small hole in the stained-glass window of his belltower study in order to spy on a woman in a house across the street as she lies on her bed and smokes and reads. "He did not want to kiss the shoulders and the throat of Kate Smith and had not allowed his mind to dwell on such thoughts. He did not know what he wanted. 'I am God's child and he must save me from myself,' he cried." One evening he sees her come naked into her room and weep and then pray; with his fist he smashes the window so all of it, with its broken bit of a peephole, will have to be repaired.

There are more naked women in *Winesburg, Ohio* than one might think. **"Adventure"** shows Alice Hindman, a twenty-seven-year-old spinster jilted by a lover a decade before, so agitated by "her desire to have something beautiful come into her rather narrow life" that she runs naked into the rain one night and actually accosts a man—a befuddled old deaf man who goes on his way. In the following story, **"Respectability,"** a fanatic and repulsive misogynist, Wash Williams, recalls to George Willard how, many years before, his mother-in-law, hoping to reconcile him with his unfaithful young wife, presented her naked to him in her (Dayton, Ohio) parlor. George Willard, his chaste relation to Helen White aside, suffers no lack of sexual invitation in Winesburg's alleys and surrounding fields. Sherwood Anderson's women are as full of "vague hungers and secret unnamable desires" as his men. The sexual quest and the philosophical quest blend: of George Willard's mother, the most tenderly drawn woman of all, the author says, "Always there was something she sought blindly, passionately, some hidden wonder in life. . . . In all the babble of words that fell from the lips of the men with whom she adventured she was trying to find what would be for her the true word." *Winesburg, Ohio* is dedicated to the memory of Anderson's own mother, "whose keen observations on the life about her first awoke in me the hunger to see beneath the surface of lives."

The author's hunger to see and express is entwined with the common hunger for love and reassurance and gives the book its awkward power and its limiting strangeness. The many characters of *Winesburg, Ohio,* rather than standing forth as individuals, seem, with their repeating tics and uniform loneliness, aspects of one enveloping personality, an eccentric bundle of stalled impulses and frozen grievances. There is nowhere a citizen who, like Thomas Rhodes of Spoon River, exults in his material triumphs and impenitent rascality, nor any humbler type, like "real black, tall, well built, stupid, childlike, good looking" Rose Johnson of Stein's fictional Bridgepoint, who is happily at home in her skin. Do the Winesburgs of America lack such earthly successes; does the provincial orchard hold only, in Anderson's vivid phrase, "twisted apples"? No, and yet Yes, must be the answer; for the uncanny truth of Anderson's sad and surreal picture must awaken recognition within anyone who, like this reviewer, was born in a small town before highways and development filled all the fields and television imposed upon every home a degraded sophistication. The Protestant villages of America, going back to Hawthorne's Salem, leave a spectral impression in literature: vague longing and monotonous, inbred satisfactions are their essence; there is something perilous and maddening in the accommodations such communities extend to human aspiration and appetite. As neighbors watch, and murmur, lives visibly wrap themselves around a missed op-

portunity, a thwarted passion. The longing may be simply the longing to get out. The healthy, rounded apples, Anderson tells us, are "put in barrels and shipped to the cities where they will be eaten in apartments that are filled with books, magazines, furniture, and people." George Willard gets out in the end, and as soon as Winesburg falls away from the train windows "his life there had become but a background on which to paint the dreams of his manhood."

The small town is generally seen, by the adult writer arrived at his city, as the site of youthful paralysis and dreaming. Certainly Anderson, as Malcolm Cowley has pointed out, wrote in a dreaming way, scrambling the time and logic of events as he hastened toward his epiphanies of helpless awakening, when the citizens of Winesburg break their tongue-tied trance and become momentarily alive to one another. Gertrude Stein's style, so revolutionary and liberating, has the haughtiness and humor of the *faux-naïve;* there is much genuine naïveté in Anderson, which in even his masterwork flirts with absurdity and which elsewhere weakens his work decisively. *Winesburg, Ohio* describes the human condition only insofar as unfulfillment and restlessness—a nagging sense that real life is elsewhere—are intrinsically part of it. Yet the wide-eyed eagerness with which Anderson pursued the mystery of the meager lives of Winesburg opened Michigan to Hemingway, and Mississippi to Faulkner; a way had been shown to a new directness and a freedom from contrivance. Though *Winesburg, Ohio* accumulates external facts—streets, stores, town personalities—as it gropes along, its burden is a spiritual essence, a certain tart sweet taste to life as it passes in America's lonely lamplit homes. A nagging beauty lives amid this tame desolation; Anderson's parade of yearning wraiths constitutes in sum a democratic plea for the failed, the neglected, and the stuck. "On the trees are only a few gnarled apples that the pickers have rejected. . . . One nibbles at them and they are delicious. Into a little round place at the side of the apple has been gathered all of its sweetness." Describing a horse-and-buggy world bygone even in 1919, *Winesburg, Ohio* imparts this penetrating taste—the wine hidden in its title—as freshly today as yesterday. (pp. 96-7)

John Updike, "Twisted Apples," in *Harper's,* Vol. 268, No. 1606, March, 1984, pp. 95-7.

SOURCES FOR FURTHER STUDY

Anderson, David D., ed. *Critical Essays on Sherwood Anderson.* Boston: G. K. Hall & Co., 1981, 302 p.

> Collection of reviews and essays by noted critics. In his introduction, Anderson provides an insightful overview of the most important critical and bibliographic writings on the writer's life.

Appel, Paul P., ed. *Homage to Sherwood Anderson (1876-1941).* Mamaroneck, N.Y.: Paul P. Appel, 1970, 212 p.

> Compiles reviews, reminiscences, and essays about Anderson by noted men and women of letters such as Theodore Dreiser, Gertrude Stein, and Henry Miller, as well as some of the author's previously unpublished letters and his essay "The Modern Writer."

Burbank, Rex. *Sherwood Anderson.* Twayne Publishers, 1964, 159 p.

> Analysis and evaluation intended as an introduction to Anderson's career and works.

Rideout, Walter B., ed. *Sherwood Anderson: A Collection of Critical Essays.* Englewood Cliffs, N.J.: Prentice-Hall, 1974, 177 p.

> Reprints sixteen important essays on Anderson's work. Contributors include Rideout, Lionel Trilling, Gertrude Stein, Waldo Frank, and several others. A helpful bibliography is included.

Rosenfeld, Paul. Introduction to *The Sherwood Anderson Reader,* by Sherwood Anderson, pp. vii-xxviii. Boston: Houghton Mifflin, 1947.

> Biographical essay and insightful critical interpretation of Anderson's works.

Townsend, Kim. *Sherwood Anderson.* Boston: Houghton Mifflin, 1987, 370 p.

> Critical biography focusing on Anderson's relationships with friends and colleagues and the ways in which he incorporated personal experiences into his fiction.

Matthew Arnold

1822-1888

English poet, lecturer, and critic.

INTRODUCTION

*A*rnold was one of the most influential authors of the later Victorian period in England. His elegiac verse often expresses a sense of modern malaise, and critics rank such poems as "Dover Beach" and "The Forsaken Merman" with the finest of the era. While Arnold is well known today as a poet, in his own time he asserted his greatest influence through his prose writings. As a social critic, he denounced materialism and called for a renewal of art and culture. His forceful literary criticism, which is based on his humanistic belief in the value of balance and clarity in literature, significantly shaped modern theory; T. S. Eliot stated, for example, that "the valuation of the Romantic poets, in academic circles, is still very largely that which Arnold made." In his effort to establish high artistic standards, Arnold sought to deter the loss of faith that he perceived among his contemporaries and expressed so eloquently in his verse.

Arnold was the eldest son of Dr. Thomas Arnold, an influential educator who became headmaster of Rugby School in 1828. Arnold attended Rugby and Balliol College, Oxford, where he was known as a dandy. At Oxford he met Arthur Hugh Clough, who became his close friend and correspondent and whose death Arnold mourned in his well-known pastoral elegy, "Thyrsis." Even Arnold's early poetry, such as the privately issued *Alaric at Rome* (1840), had the brooding tone that was to become characteristic of his mature work. After the publication of *The Strayed Reveller and Other Poems* (1849), Arnold was appointed inspector of schools, a position that he held, with the exception of his ten years as Professor of Poetry at Oxford, for the rest of his life. In the eight years following the publication of *The Strayed Reveller,* Arnold published the bulk of his poetry, including *Poems* in 1853. That volume contains his famous preface outlining the reasons for deleting from the collection the title poem from his earlier book, *Empedocles on Etna and Other Poems* (1852). Arnold declared that "Empedocles on Etna" did not fulfill the requirements of a good poem and therefore did not qualify as meaningful art. In his emphasis on the purpose of poetry in the preface, Arnold indicated the direction that his writing and thought were to take.

Arnold's election to the position of Professor of Poetry at Oxford in 1857 marked the beginning of his transition from poet to literary, educational, and theological critic. *On Translating Homer* (1861), based on lectures he delivered at Oxford, and *The Popular Education of France; With Notices of That of Holland and Switzerland* (1861), a study made for the education commission, mark his turn toward prose. His first volume of *Essays in Criticism* (1865) advances Arnold's belief in the scope and importance of literary criticism: he describes it as "a disinterested endeavor to learn and propagate the best that is known and thought in the world, and thus to establish a current of fresh and true ideas." After the publication of *Culture and Anarchy: An Essay in Political and Social Criticism* in 1869, Arnold's interests tended increasingly towards social criticism and centered on the issue of the deterioration of faith in the modern world. In *Literature and Dogma: An Essay towards a Better Apprehension of the Bible* (1873), Arnold proposed a new approach to scripture. He contended that the Bible had been misread as prose and therefore taken literally, while it should have been read as poetry and taken figuratively. *God and the Bible: A Defense of Literature and Dogma* (1875) and *Last Essays on Church and Religion* (1877) are also concerned with the importance of religion and faith in an age of skepticism. Arnold toured America in 1883. Later, he published the lectures he had delivered there as *Discourses in America* (1885). Arnold's most noted writings, *Essays in Criticism, second series,* were published posthumously in 1888. The essays are generally considered Arnold's tour de force; in them he gave final expression to his belief that the humanities are an essential and nurturing force for society. With this conviction, he implicitly elevated the status of criticism from an intellectual pastime to a creative occupation with vital repercussions.

Many critics have viewed the pervasively melancholy tone of Arnold's verse as a reflection of the dilemma of the Victorian, who, in the words of Arnold's

"The Scholar-Gypsy," published in *Poems,* is caught between "two worlds, one dead / The other powerless to be born." Though not overtly didactic, Arnold, in his poetry as in his prose, often concerned himself with the diagnosis of the maladies of his time. Many critics have particularly applauded Arnold's awareness of and sensitivity to the spirit of the day. Stylistically, Arnold's poetry is subtle and unadorned, particularly in comparison with that of the Romantics and his Victorian contemporaries. Although he strove to achieve a classical sense of balance and unity in his works, some critics feel that Arnold sacrificed meaning and depth to attain this goal. Furthermore, he has been accused of lacking the breadth of true poetic imagination. Perhaps due to the elegiac tone of his verse, Arnold was not a popular poet in his day. However, many of his poems—most notably "The Scholar-Gypsy," "Empedocles on Etna," "Thyrsis," and "Dover Beach"—are still studied and respected as some of the best verse of the Victorian period.

Ironically, while Arnold's poetry has been labeled passionless, his critical writings have been termed overly poetic and emotional. Critics maintain that Arnold's overriding concern with structure is in many ways responsible for the more obvious flaws in his critical arguments. Moreover, many commentators have faulted what they consider Arnold's inattention to scholarship, citing his devaluation of Geoffrey Chaucer, Percy Bysshe Shelley, and Alfred, Lord Tennyson as evidence of his narrow critical perspective. Perhaps Arnold's greatest accomplishment as a prose writer is his crisp and simple writing style, marked by such enduring catch-phrases as "high seriousness" and "Grand Style." Although critics have argued that Arnold's use of such terms reinforces the fact that his criticism is too simplistic, it has also been suggested that through this technique the scholar-poet made criticism accessible to the average reader.

Today, Arnold is remembered for more than just his numerous insightful and critically acclaimed poems. As a literary critic, he played a significant role in clearing the way for twentieth-century literature and critical theory.

(For further information about Arnold's life and works, see *Dictionary of Literary Biography,* Vols. 32, 57 and *Nineteenth-Century Literature Criticism,* Vols. 6, 29.)

CRITICAL COMMENTARY

HENRY JAMES
(essay date 1865)

[James was an American-born English novelist, short story writer, critic, essayist, and playwright. Below, he praises Arnold's willingness to take the "high ground" in criticism and his seriousness in approaching his subject.]

Mr. Arnold's *Essays in Criticism* come to American readers with a reputation already made,—the reputation of a charming style, a great deal of excellent feeling, and an almost equal amount of questionable reasoning. . . .

Mr. Arnold's style has been praised at once too much and too little. Its resources are decidedly limited; but if the word had not become so cheap, we should nevertheless call it fascinating. This quality implies no especial force; it rests in this case on the fact that, whether or not you agree with the matter beneath it, the manner inspires you with a personal affection for the author. (p. 206)

His Preface is a striking example of the intelligent amiability which animates his style. His two leading Essays were, on their first appearance, made the subject of much violent contention, their moral being deemed little else than a wholesale schooling of the English press by the French programme. Nothing could have better proved the justice of Mr. Arnold's remarks upon the "provincial" character of the English critical method, than the reception which they provoked. (p. 207)

For Mr. Arnold's critical feeling and observation, used independently of his judgment, we profess a keen relish. He has these qualities, at any rate, of a good critic, whether or not he have the others,—the science and the logic. It is hard to say whether the literary critic is more called upon to understand or to feel. It is certain that he will accomplish little unless he can feel acutely; although it is perhaps equally certain that he will become weak the moment that he begins to "work," as we may say, his natural sensibilities. The best critic is probably he who leaves his feelings out of account, and relies upon reason for success. If he actually possesses delicacy of feeling, his work will be delicate without detriment to its solidity. The complaint of Mr. Arnold's critics is that his arguments are too sentimental. . . . [Sentiment] has given him, in our opinion, his greatest charm and his greatest worth. Hundreds of other critics

have stronger heads; few, in England at least, have more delicate perceptions. (p. 208)

We may here remark, that Mr. Arnold's statement of his principles is open to some misinterpretation,—an accident against which he has, perhaps, not sufficiently guarded it. For many persons the word *practical* is almost identical with the word *useful*, against which, on the other hand, they erect the word *ornamental*. Persons who are fond of regarding these two terms as irreconcilable, will have little patience with Mr. Arnold's scheme of criticism. They will look upon it as an organized preference of unprofitable speculation to common sense. But the great beauty of the critical movement advocated by Mr. Arnold is that in either direction its range of faction is unlimited. It deals with plain facts as well as with the most exalted fancies; but it deals with them only for the sake of the truth which is in them, and not for *your* sake, reader, and that of your party. It takes *high ground*, which is the ground of theory. It does not busy itself with consequences, which are all in all to you. (p. 211)

Some of the parts in these *Essays* are weak, others are strong; but the impression which they all combine to leave is one of such beauty as to make us forget, not only their particular faults, but their particular merits. If we were asked what is the particular merit of a given essay, we should reply that it is a merit much less common at the present day than is generally supposed,—the merit which pre-eminently characterizes Mr. Arnold's poems, the merit, namely, of having a *subject*. Each essay is *about* something. . . . If we were questioned as to the merit of Mr. Arnold's book as a whole, we should say that it lay in the fact that the author takes high ground. The manner of his *Essays* is a model of what criticisms should be. . . . [Mr. Arnold] says a few things in such a way as that almost in spite of ourselves we remember them, instead of a number of things which we cannot for the life of us remember. There are many things which we wish he had said better. . . . [But] Mr. Arnold's excellent spirit reconciles us with his short-comings. . . . [His] supreme virtue is that he speaks of all things seriously, or, in other words, that he is not offensively clever. The writers who are willing to resign themselves to this obscure distinction are in our opinion the only writers who understand their time. That Mr. Arnold thoroughly understands his time we do not mean to say, for this is the privilege of a very select few; but he is, at any rate, profoundly conscious of his time. This fact was clearly ap-

Principal Works

Alaric at Rome (poetry) 1840

* The Strayed Reveller and Other Poems (poetry) 1849

Empedocles on Etna and Other Poems (poetry) 1852

Poems (poetry) 1853

Poems, second series (poetry) 1855

Merope [first publication] (drama) 1858

On Translating Homer (lectures) 1861

The Popular Education of France; With Notices of That of Holland and Switzerland (essay) 1861

Essays in Criticism (criticism) 1865

†New Poems (poetry) 1867

On the Study of Celtic Literature (criticism) 1867

Culture and Anarchy: An Essay in Political and Social Criticism (essay) 1869

Friendship's Garland: Being the Conversations, Letters, and Opinions of the Late Arminus, Baron von Thunder-Ten-Tronckh (humorous letters) 1871

Literature and Dogma: An Essay towards a Better Apprehension of the Bible (essay) 1873

God and the Bible: A Defense of Literature and Dogma (essay) 1875

Last Essays on Church and Religion (essays) 1877

Mixed Essays (essays) 1879

Irish Essays and Others (essays) 1882

Discourses in America (lectures) 1885

Essays in Criticism, second series (criticism) 1888

Letters of Matthew Arnold, 1848-1888 (letters) 1895

*This work includes the poem "The Forsaken Merman."

†This work includes the poems "Dover Beach" and "Thyrsis."

---

parent in his poems, and it is even more apparent in these *Essays*. It gives them a peculiar character of melancholy,—that melancholy which arises from the spectacle of the old-fashioned instinct of enthusiasm in conflict (or at all events in contact) with the modern desire to be fair,—the melancholy of an age which not only has lost its *naïveté*, but which knows it has lost it. (pp. 212-13)

Henry James, "Arnold's 'Essays in Criticism'," in *The North American Review*, Vol. CI, No. CCVIII, July, 1865, pp. 206-13.

A. E. DYSON
(essay date 1957)

[In the following excerpt, Dyson evaluates Arnold's "The Scholar-Gypsy" as a mirror of the Victorian predicament: "to desire with the heart what is rejected by the head, to need for the spirit what was excluded by the mind."]

The Scholar Gipsy confronts the joyful illusions of an earlier age with the melancholy realism of the nineteenth century, and . . . in this confrontation, with its complex emotional tensions, the really moving quality of the poem is to be found. Arnold was as aware of the difficulties of 'belief' as any Victorian, and as determined as George Eliot to live and think 'without opium'. (p. 258)

In *The Scholar Gipsy* Arnold's attitude to the gipsy is closely analogous to that of an adult towards a child. He appreciates and even envies its innocence, but realizes that no return to such a state is possible for himself. The child loses its 'innocence' not by some act of sin, nor by a defect of intellect, but merely by gaining experience and developing into an adult. The realities of adult life turn out to be less agreeable, in many respects, than childish fantasies, but there can be no question of thinking them less true.

The gipsy, like a child, is the embodiment of a good lost, not of a good temporarily or culpably mislaid. When Arnold contrasts the gipsy's serenity with the disquiets and perplexities of his own age, he is not satirizing the nineteenth century, or renouncing it, or criticizing it, or suggesting a remedy. He is, rather, exploring its spiritual and emotional losses, and the stoic readjustment which these will entail for it. (pp. 259-60)

The scholar gipsy embodies . . . the optimistic but chimerical hopes of an earlier age. He waits for 'the spark from Heaven to fall' . . . , but he waits in vain: the spark does not fall, as the nineteenth century has discovered for itself. . . . This realization is in the rhythms and tone of the poem, which is reflective and melancholy in the elegiac mode, not filled with dynamic hope. The gipsy is committed to a discredited art, and so exiled from Oxford. In [stanza] 8, as he looks down on the lighted city at night, he looks not as a presiding deity but as a long superseded ghost from the past. His very nature forbids him to enter, since one touch of Victorian realism would reveal him for the wraith he is. . . . The situation is not unlike that of the young Jude gazing eagerly towards the lights of that same city—not to Oxford itself, however, but to the ideal city which his childish dreams have superimposed. The scholar gipsy turns away from the real Oxford, and seeks his 'straw' in 'Some sequester'd grange'. His place is with the primitive, the uncultured, the unintellectual. Only so can he survive at all, so late in history.

In *Literature and Dogma* and *God and the Bible* Arnold insists that he is writing not for those who are still happy with their Christian illusions (the Victorian version of 'simple faith'), but only for those highly serious few who still value the illusions whilst being unable honestly to accept them. The scholar gipsy would not have been one of the readers Arnold had in mind: he would have been one of the happier (though perhaps less honest) band who enjoyed the faith of earlier ages simply because they had not been intellectually awakened to reality in Oxford. The gipsy is essentially outside Oxford; and his exclusion, though it tells against the happiness of Oxford, tells even more against the acceptability of the gipsy. (p. 261)

The Victorian predicament, in so far as Arnold represents it, was a tragic one—to desire with the heart what was rejected by the head, to need for the spirit what was excluded by the mind. . . . [This] is the tradition in which *The Scholar Gipsy* stands. (p. 262)

When Tennyson's head had assimilated honest doubts to the edge of scepticism, his 'heart stood up and answered "I have felt" '. When Strauss had undermined the historicity of the Bible, he tried to reinstate it as a myth. Matthew Arnold, also, tried to find an emotional cure for the loss of faith. In his case, it took the form of an attempt to substitute culture and poetry for religion, and to find a few axioms that could be made real on the moral pulses. But when it came to the trail, his head gained the day, honesty won the victory over expediency. *The Scholar Gipsy* is a poem of unbelief. Arnold did not discover anything adequate to replace the hopes of the earlier world. (p. 265)

A. E. Dyson, "The Last Enchantments," in *The Review of English Studies*, n.s., Vol. VIII, No. 31, 1957, pp. 257-65.

━━━━━━━

W. STACY JOHNSON
(essay date 1961)

[In the excerpt below, Johnson examines Arnold's use of such literary devices as interior dialogue and epic simile in "Balder Dead," "Sohrab and Rustum," and other poems.]

Whether it takes the form of soliloquy, of monologue, or of dialogue, virtually all of Arnold's best poetry involves, . . . what he calls in his Preface of 1853 the "dialogue of the mind with itself." This process, Ar-

nold asserts, had commenced by the time of the historical Empedocles, and apparently it continues in the minds of modern men; for, unlike a Platonic dialogue, the conversation of inner voices does not often conclude with the wisdom of one master voice. Arnold's dialogue between disillusioned Tristram and faithful Iseult and his contrast between the songs of Empedocles and those of Callicles make these several voices seem to represent the several sides of a dialogue, as it were, within the poet's own mind, just as the opposites of land and sea do in **"The Forsaken Merman"** and **"Dover Beach."** But, perhaps because literal dialogue can so easily be reduced to unsettled debate on points of philosophy and religion, as it is in Clough's "Dipsychus," or to simple preaching, as it begins to be in the first act of **"Empedocles,"** the dialogue of the poet's mind with itself is often represented less strikingly in the speeches of his characters than in contrasts implied by the more indirect and symbolic means.

In Arnold's narrative poetry, too, the inner tensions are realized by contrasts in imagery and setting, along with the speeches that reveal the differences between Sohrab and Rustum or between Balder and his fellows. Although the weaker narratives, like **"Saint Brandan,"** amount at last to fairly single-minded moralities, the most successful of Arnold's poetic tales involve these contrasts and are essentially double visions. The voice of the narrator does not intrude upon the stories as it does sometimes in **"Tristram"**—where the pronouns *I, we,* and *you* introduce the author's and the reader's points of view and where, in the third part, a moralizing *I* comments directly on the poem—but it describes actions and settings so as to reveal differences not only between several people's lives but also between several ways of viewing their lives.

The views implied, the messages carried, in **"The Neckan"** and **"Saint Brandan"** are comparatively simple: each of these short narratives versifies a folk tale which shows that there may be divine grace given to one who is apparently lost. The first piece is another version of the tale that Arnold tells in **"The Forsaken Merman,"** but now the story is rendered almost as a ballad, and in the third person; and, although the words of the sea-creature are again plaintive, his attitude, that of his wife, and the implicit attitude of the narrator are much less painfully ambivalent than those in the better poem. . . . A quatrain added to ["The Neckan"] in 1869 . . . takes emphasis away from the miracle to make this point explicit:

He said: 'The earth hath kindness,
    The sea, the starry poles;
Earth, sea, and sky, and God above—
    But, ah, not human souls!'

The mood of these lines is almost directly opposed to that of **"Dover Beach,"** where the earth is seen to lack the sympathy that human love may provide.

But this poem is not, like **"Dover Beach,"** qualified by any imagery in contrast to its message: it never makes us feel strongly why the earth and his mate are so attractive to the neckan, and so it realizes only one side of the contrast between the natural and the human orders. The difference, however, between **"The Neckan"** and some other less impressive poems is that the Christian God now seems to be on the side of this lonely creature who is more human than the human beings in his sadness, not that of the smug priest, the horrified knights and ladies and the weeping wife. And that difference, after all, helps to give interest to this rather tight and limited version of the pathetic story.

"Saint Brandan," too, Arnold's verse rendering of the Celtic legend about Judas on the iceberg, carries some interest as evidence of the poet's desire to make the most of the most humane elements in religion. It is a crisply told tale of the Saint's vision on the "sea without a human shore," a vision of the archtraitor momentarily relieved from his torment each Christmas eve because of one good deed done in his lifetime. But these stanzas, which include dialogue within the narrative (and Judas' narrative within his speech), are less dramatic than parabolic, are simple and fanciful rather than complex and serious. (pp. 118-20)

It is not so easy to sum up the sense of his longer narrative **"The Church of Brou,"** a poem that lacks the richness of Arnold's greatest verse tales but one that has, nevertheless, some fine passages, especially in the last part. . . . Like **"The Neckan,"** **"The Church of Brou"** must suffer by comparison with the larger work it resembles; but the contrast is not now so distinct or even so extreme. (p. 121)

"Balder Dead," a poem obviously comparable with **"Sohrab and Rustum"**—Arnold compared the two and preferred **"Balder,"** although his readers have rarely done so—brings more complication into its storytelling than **"Sohrab"** and departs somewhat more from its source in its ordering of events and use of narrative detail. If it is not quite so fine a poem as the more celebrated work, **"Balder"** nevertheless makes a better narrative, with its beginning *in medias res,* its omens and foreshadowings, journeys and quests. It adapts a Homeric manner and an ultimately Virgilian tone to another kind of classical material, the Norse, dealing with an heroic society and with the death of a hero: **"Balder"** begins as **"Sohrab and Rustum"** ends, with the death of and the mourning for a mighty father's mighty son. But **"Balder"** makes more use of dialogue between characters, so that it is rather more vigorous and less stately in its diction and movement. (p. 122)

In fact, **"Balder"** is a poem of polarities, of ironies and even of paradoxes. It is filled with a visionary knowledge of the future—the knowledge that Frea possesses and Odin, and finally Balder too—which makes its action seem inevitably futile, and yet the gods are apparently fated to will and act against the decrees of fatality. Its central figure is the ideal hero of a Valhalla to whose heroic code he is opposed. And its imagery again and again contrasts the value of heavenly warfare with the value of heavenly rest.

To the tensions implicit within this dark story the narration gives emphasis, especially in its use of imagery. First, there is a contrast between epic characters, setting, and movement, all of which are magnified and formal, and the details that give a specific, even personal, quality to the poem. This contrast is enforced almost always by the Homeric similes, which Arnold introduces with reference neither to Homer nor to the Edda. Hoder's touch on Hermod's arm is like the touch of honeysuckle brushing across a tired traveler's face (surely English honeysuckle and an English traveler), and the road to Hell is blocked by a maiden just as a mountain pass is blocked by cattle. (pp. 122-23)

But it is not only through the epic similes, with their yoking of heroic events and pastoral or domestic terms, that the Eddic story takes on its new dimensions. Images and themes that are symbolic and recurrent in Arnold's poetry, those of light and shadow, of battle in life and repose in death, are embodied in the settings and metaphors of this poem, and they again express duality, tension, or dialogue between contrasting attitudes. The most striking contrast, perhaps, is that between the dark and the sunlit places. There is daylight in Heaven, and none in the place of obscure spirits; Odin would, on entering Hell, "set the fields of gloom ablaze with light," did not Frea insist that he could not rightly violate Hela's darkness. Both Thok's iron wood and Hela's world are dark, cold regions, and their shadows are associated with the dreary and morbid. And yet the brilliance of Odin's Asgard is a harsh brilliance, one that is not at last so clearly preferable to the peaceful gloom of Hela. (pp. 123-24)

The final paradox of the poem has to do with the nature of death. Within the hall where heroes live after their valiant deaths, a god has died, only to find rest in his underworld and to anticipate a new life. The name of the poem and its first lines introduce us to the subject of life in death—we never see Balder *alive,* literally, but he is quite as alive in another sense as any of the gods— and the titles of its parts remind us of it. Like **"Tristram"** and **"The Church of Brou,"** the narrative has a threefold division, with sections called **"Sending,"** **"Journey to the Dead,"** and **"Funeral."** The task that Hermod is sent upon is the recovery of Balder from the realm of ghosts, the mythical quest of Orpheus, but his journey is to be vain, for the guile of Lok the enemy, who caused Balder's downfall by giving blind Hoder the mistletoe to throw at him, prevents the gods from meeting Hela's demand that all things grieve for Balder before he be returned to life. And so the god's funeral, with his ship a pyre sent blazing out to sea, is for Asgard final, if not for Balder. The most nearly invincible of the gods, after Odin himself, seems at last to be subject to death's power, and not only in the body but in his mind and will. Arnold's version of the story, filled with forebodings and ominous signs of a Götterdämmerung, suggests some promise too, through Balder's vision of a new Heaven and a new earth, but it concludes literally in darkness and withdrawal, not only with life in death but with a sense of death in life—or, rather, with a melancholy sense of how imperfect, in the world as it is, both energy without peace and peace without energy must be.

Balder's vision of peace and wholeness, then, the Arnoldian vision, is only that, a vision of the longed-for future. Even the god's acceptance of his death cannot make us forget the contrast, the opposition, at the heart of the poem between darkness and light, between the pathetic picture of life as essentially passive, resigned at best to the inevitable, and the picture of an heroic existence as a series of quests or battles which the gods delight to watch if not to enter. (pp. 125-26)

The paradox of **"Balder Dead,"** that the pagan Hell offers peace with gloom and the heroic Heaven weariness with glory, is very closely related to an ironic quality of **"Sohrab and Rustum,"** in which two images of human existence are even more clearly opposed one to the other. Partly because **"Sohrab and Rustum"** has a somewhat less complex plot and partly, perhaps, because it ends with the narrator's description of a scene rather than a character's speech, the effect of the work is more formal and "poetic"; but in its exploiting of the subject, involving a conflict of father and son, and in its extensive use of imagery both Homeric and symbolic, **"Sohrab"** finally achieves, if less rapidity, then an even more moving effect of pathos than **"Balder Dead."**

Implicit in Arnold's Persian material is the psychological significance of a son's search for his father and the battle between the two, followed by reconciliation. No doubt the poet's own feelings as the son of a famous father are reflected in his choice of this story about Sohrab's defeat by Rustum (Sohrab is in effect defeated by his filial piety, for it is his father's name that vanquishes him). . . . Just as it is possible for the action in the poem to occur because father and son do not recognize each other, so it is possible for Arnold to narrate the action, and the death of the young warrior, because he has not fully recognized Sohrab and Rustum, because the conflict does not have to be presented as a distinct and personal irreconciliation of old earnestness and young enthusiasm.

Even so, the death of Sohrab is painful, and the fair amount of skill Arnold displays in using narrative devices of irony (Rustum's "Be as a son to me," for instance) and fore-shadowing (as in the initial scene between Sohrab and the paternal Peran-Wisa, who pre-

dicts "danger or death") might not be enough to make the finest poetry of this pattern that is so painfully resolved—at least, not according to the critical doctrine that led Arnold to withdraw his **"Empedocles."** The most striking parts of the poem, striking because of their conjunction with the narrative, are those metaphorical and symbolic passages that once more transform violence into beauty and death into peace; one is likely to remember these pictures rather than the intermittent dialogue or the details of the main action. (pp. 127-28)

"Sohrab and Rustum" makes somewhat more extensive use of the Homeric simile than **"Balder,"** again with the effect of adding immediacy and pathos to the military events of the poem; at the same time, the similes provide relief from and dramatic contrast to the tension which gradually builds up all the way through the first half of the poem. And so the imagery, rather like that of the *Iliad*, often evokes scenes basically unlike those of camp and battle, recalling either peaceful settings from nature or domestic life. (pp. 128-29)

Perhaps the two most striking epic similes are those which compare the dying Sohrab with a flower, first with a hyacinth and then with a violet—similes that may remind us of the deaths both of Gorgythion in the *Iliad*, whose head droops in death like a poppy, and of Euryalus in the *Aeneid*. The device works well for Arnold as it has for Homer and Virgil, and the images are strangely beautiful. They are, of course, in extreme contrast with the literal scene, for they draw our attention from the plain which has become a scene of death to the cultivated garden, where flowers are destroyed merely by carelessness. Both similes occur after the tension of the conflict has been suddenly relaxed, while Sohrab is slowly dying, and they do not follow the tendency that has made the earlier images reflect the minds of actors within the poem, leaping to pictures of cranes and eagles, Caucasus mountains and Persian deserts; the feeling of the similes becomes less subjective now as it becomes less violent. (p. 130)

The sense of death as consummation is yet more beautifully embodied in the water imagery of the poem. The whole scene, the challenge, the fierce battle, and the death of Sohrab, has taken place by the river Oxus, which is alluded to again and again, even in the midst of the fighting. (p. 131)

Just as the metaphors are fine only in the context of the narrative, however, [the poem's final] passage of description gains its power from the terrible and finally pathetic events that precede it. We know that the old warrior has defeated himself in defeating his enemy, and we have seen a poignant outcome of the conflict between generations. With the change of mood from urgent vigor to quiet grief, from heroic to elegiac, the poem concludes in what might be called a brief comment of the narrator's—but a comment made by indirection—which reveals another way of viewing this action. Now a new contrast is implied, between the story of two human lives reaching their climax in the battle of ignorant forces on a darkling plain and the imaging forth of human life as essentially a natural flowing of waters toward their consummation in the ultimate and inevitable sea. (pp. 132-33)

In **"Sohrab and Rustum,"** as in **"Balder Dead,"** the contrasts are implicit in action, speech, and setting: the dialogue of the mind with itself is represented but does not become a debate. The narrator of **"Balder"** makes no specific comment on the Eddic values that his transcription of the story must reveal when the inhabitants of Hell are described as women, cowards, and old men who had the misfortune to die in bed rather than in battle; but the final mood of Balder is comment enough. . . . Arnold is like some other Victorian poets in drawing largely from mythical and legendary materials for his narrative poems, and his plotting of these materials is less masterly than Tennyson's or even Morris's; in his ability to translate legendary scenes into not only contemporary terms but timeless human situations, however, he far surpasses Morris and easily rivals Tennyson. **"Balder Dead"** is infused with a moving quality that the more truly Eddic "Sigurd the Volsung" rarely achieves, and **"Tristram and Iseult"** is a more beautiful poem than any of the *Idylls.* One might go so far, indeed, as to compare the death of Balder favorably with the more thrilling but very slightly stagy death of Arthur.

Although narrative invention is not his *forte* and his production of strictly narrative verse is slight, Arnold can, in the last of **"Tristram"** and especially in **"Balder Dead"** and **"Sohrab and Rustum,"** add even to good stories a heightening and enriching quality that is peculiarly his own; a quality of pathos deep and genuine and touched at best with a sense of the dignity of human suffering. His double vision, of men and gods as heroic forces, and of Nature or Fate as the single dominant principle in the life of the world, reflects two sides, two voices, of his imagination: voices that can fairly be represented if not perfectly reconciled in the action and imagery of these poems, in the one voice of the narrator. (pp. 133-34)

W. Stacy Johnson, in his *The Voices of Matthew Arnold: An Essay in Criticism,* Yale University Press, 1961, 146 p.

RENÉ WELLEK
(essay date 1965)

[In the following excerpt, Wellek asserts that Arnold's advocacy of a critical spirit involving the free exchange of ideas suggests a valuable lesson for modern criticism.]

The position of Matthew Arnold . . . as the most important English critic of the second half of the 19th century seems secure. His eminence is due not only to his literary criticism but also to his standing as a poet and general critic of English society and civilization. (p. 155)

Arnold is, first of all, a very important apologist for criticism. Criticism, of course, means for him not simply literary criticism but rather the critical spirit in general, the application of intelligence to any and all subjects. Arnold is an eloquent advocate of "disinterestedness," curiosity, flexibility, urbanity, a free circulation of ideas. . . . Arnold's ideal of "disinterestedness" must not be understood as Olympian aloofness or escape to the ivory tower. It is easy to show that Arnold himself was deeply absorbed in the problems of his age and was not above engaging in polemics and even losing his temper. But "disinterestedness" surely means for him something quite specific: a denial of immediate political and sectarian ends, a wide horizon, an absence of prejudice, serenity beyond the passions of the moment. . . . [Arnold] had the gentleman-scholar's dread of pedantic learning and disparages his own erudition with some mock humility. But while one should admit that he was no Sainte-Beuve, Dilthey, or Croce (he was, after all, a poet and a busy inspector of schools), he read Greek and Latin, German and French (and some Italian), and knew enough for a critic who does not even pretend to be a professional literary historian or classical philologist. Arnold's advocacy of the critical spirit, of an atmosphere conducive to the free exchange of ideas, his praise of objectivity, disinterestedness, and curiosity (properly understood) are valuable and sound even today. (pp. 156-57)

Contrary to the usual opinion, Matthew Arnold is . . . primarily a historical critic who works with a historical scheme in his mind. Society is often conceived as an independent, fixed, given force that even genius cannot change. (p. 161)

Yet Arnold does not think merely in terms of genius versus age, individual versus society, poet versus current or staple of ideas. He just as often thinks in collectivist terms of race and the march of history. He is preoccupied almost as much as Taine with racial theories. All his writings play variations on the contrasts appearing among the Latin, Celtic, and Germanic races, or in that between the Hebraic and the Greek spirit. But the distinction between national spirit (*Volksgeist*) and race is not clear to him. He sketches the history of France in terms of the conflict between Gaul, Latin, and Teuton. His lectures *On the Study of Celtic Literature* turn upon the concept of race. . . . He confidently assigns to the Celts (with whom he sometimes includes the French) specific literary characters: a turn for style, a turn for melancholy, and a turn for natural magic, while he denies them other literary abilities, such as a sense of over-all form. He never raises the obvious question whether these qualities could not be found elsewhere in the world where there were no Celts—in the Orient, for instance—and he never seems to doubt the cogency of his argument that the occurrence of these qualities in English literature is a proof of Celtic nature in the English. (pp. 161-62)

The contradictions in Arnold's concept of poetry and its limitations—the alternatives of mere didacticism or soulful religious seriousness—are connected with Arnold's lack of clarity on such central problems of poetics as the relation between content and form, between totality and local detail. Arnold (like his time in general) has a feeble grasp of the difference between art and reality. Imagination, illusion, the special world of art, mean little to him. In some sense he acknowledges the unity of form and content, but mostly he conceives of the subject of poetry as something given and fixed, something capable of being judged as poetic or unpoetic outside a work of art. Form just as often is conceived of as a hard vessel into which the poet pours his content. Even reality is often seen as something given and fixed, either good or bad for the artist, and art often means only artifice, technique, virtuosity. The poet, Arnold assumes, should deal with a beautiful world, but, unfortunately, he is not always able to do so. (p. 167)

Arnold is well aware of the central importance of totality and unity in art. The idea of "totality" appears early in his critical vocabulary: the 1853 **"Preface"** makes much of the "grandiose effect of the whole," the "total-impression" (Arnold spells the term with a hyphen) and of *architectonice,* something suggested to him by Goethe's reflections on dilettantism. The ancients are contrasted with the moderns on this point. "They regarded the whole, we regard the parts." These terms recur in later essays and are varied by the addition of such phrases as the "spirit which goes through her [George Sand's] work as a whole," or "a supreme total effect," or "the *symmetria prisca* of the Greeks," or "composition," or "grouping" used in a painter's sense. These terms are used to express standards of judgment. (pp. 170-71)

Arnold's more celebrated proposal to use "touch-

stones," "infallible touchstones," "short passages, even single lines" as a norm for judging poetry is an obvious contradiction of the insight into unity, an atomistic principle that may be used to justify the most willful and erratic prejudices. Arnold himself, however, warns against a mechanical application of the touchstones. "These few lines, if we have tact and can use them, are enough even of themselves to keep clear and sound our judgments about poetry, to save us from fallacious estimates of it, to conduct us to a real estimate." But he admits that it is not easy to apply such lines to other poetry. "Of course we are not to require this other poetry to resemble them; it may be very dissimilar." The touchstones enumerated in **"The Study of Poetry"** are eleven passages, three each from Homer, Dante, and Milton, two from Shakespeare, all in a tone of sadness, melancholy, or resignation. . . . They are, no doubt, all fine passages but, as specimens of great poetry, extremely limited in range. They are not always representative of their authors and often hardly comprehensible outside of their context. (p. 171)

Arnold's stereotyped phrases and formulas are unfortunately the best remembered side of his criticism. He knew it himself and treated his pet phrases with proper irony. . . . The range and variety of Arnold's criticism belie such a superficial indictment. It seems necessary to survey his essays in an attempt to rank them and to point out some of their virtues and shortcomings. (p. 173)

The two first essays in [*Essays in Criticism*], **"The Function of Criticism at the Present Time"** and **"The Literary Influence of Academies,"** are Arnold's most formal and most eloquent pleas for criticism and the critical spirit. The whole volume clearly shows the influence of Sainte-Beuve; not only are the essays on the two Guérins and on Joubert suggested by Sainte-Beuve's essays on these writers: they are also (as is the essay on Marcus Aurelius) portraits in Sainte-Beuve's sense: deft blends of biography, liberal quotation, and psychological observation. Arnold has been blamed for wasting his energy on three minor French writers, but he wanted to paint unknown figures as part of his program of arousing "curiosity," and he was drawn to them by sympathetic interest in the religious and contemplative temper of his sitters. (pp. 173-74)

The essay on Heine, which has been much admired, seems to me the least satisfactory of the literary essays in the volume. Arnold, from a perspective which is French in its sources, considers Heine the follower and heir of Goethe, on whom "incomparably the largest portion of Goethe's mantle fell." The emphasis on Heine as the "brilliant soldier in the Liberation War of humanity" is quite speciously linked up with Goethe's very differently meant saying about himself that he had been the Liberator of the Germans. The admiration for Heine's "culture" . . . seems excessive if one knows

Heine's gross simplifications of German philosophy, while the condescending attitude to his morals strikes one as unpleasantly smug. (p. 174)

Arnold's newly found certainty and authority are most boldly and memorably expressed in the series of essays devoted to the English romantic poets. . . . (p. 177)

Arnold's preference for Wordsworth is admirably defended. The anthology shows in detail that he loved the pastoral, serene Wordsworth above the speculative and mystical. The protest against the attempt to extract a philosophy of nature and ethics from Wordsworth is perfectly defensible if one remembers Arnold's desire to dismiss Wordsworth's *formal* philosophy. But one should not forget that Arnold actually values Wordsworth for the cognitive element in him, for "seeing into the life of things." Arnold, however, does not quite recognize the intellectual subtlety and profundity of Wordsworth's poetry and overstates his "provincialism" and lack of book learning. (pp. 177-78)

The preference for Byron as the second greatest poet is harder to defend. . . . Byron seems to Arnold "an ordinary nineteenth-century English gentleman, with little culture and with no ideas." But in spite of all these reservations Arnold exalts Byron as "the greatest natural force, the greatest elementary power" in English poetry since Shakespeare. His admiration has mainly political motives: Byron is an enemy of cant and Philistinism, a great fighter in the war for the liberation of mankind. Byron, Arnold feels strongly, is fundamentally sincere in spite of all his theatrical preludings. . . . Arnold's anthology shows clearly what he liked in Byron: descriptive and narrative passages, rhetorical reflections. But any defense of Byron as a poet must be based largely on *Don Juan* and *The Vision of Judgment*. Arnold gives only small fragments of the satires and thus cannot present a persuasive argument for Byron's importance as a poet. (p. 178)

Keats stands highest among these poets in Arnold's eyes. . . . He acknowledges that Keats' passion for the Beautiful was "an intellectual and spiritual passion." He emphasizes, however, Keats' "natural magic," in which "he ranks with Shakespeare." He underscores, excessively to my mind, the idea that Keats was not ripe for "moral interpretation." He admires rightly the great odes for their "rounded perfection," but does not think *Hyperion* a success. Keats, though greatly admired, is seen too much as a mere promise.

Shelley is criticized as a man and hardly as a writer. But there are scattered passages that concern his work. To say that the pieces by Shelley in Palgrave's *Golden Treasury* are "a gallery of his failures" shows a complete lack of appreciation even for the best in Shelley, and to prefer the translations, the "delightful Essays and Letters," to the poetry seems puzzling. (p. 179)

[However] much we may disagree with Arnold's ranking of the poets and ages, he accomplished the main task of a practical critic: the sifting of the tradition, the arrangement or rearrangement of the past, the discrimination among currents, major and minor. The table of the English poets was fixed by Arnold for a long time to come. But Arnold's defense of the critical spirit, his theory of criticism with its emphasis on the real estimate, and even his discussion of the concept of poetry (limited as it is by his didacticism) were a great contribution to English criticism. Arnold, almost single-handedly, pulled English criticism out of the doldrums into which it had fallen after the great Romantic Age. (p. 180)

René Wellek, "Arnold, Bagehot, and Stephen," in his *A History of Modern Criticism, 1750-1950: The Later Nineteenth Century,* Yale University Press, 1965, pp. 155-90.

JAMES DICKEY
(essay date 1966)

[In the following excerpt from an essay first published in 1966 in *Master Poems of the English Language*, Dickey provides an interpretation of "Dover Beach."]

"Dover Beach" has been called the first modern poem. If this is true, it is modern not so much in diction and technique—for its phrasing and its Miltonic inversions are obvious carryovers from a much older poetry—but in psychological orientation. Behind the troubled man standing at the lover's conventional moon-filled window looking on the sea, we sense—more powerfully because our hindsight confirms what Arnold only began to intuit—the shift in the human viewpoint from the Christian tradition to the impersonal world of Darwin and the nineteenth-century scientists. The way the world is seen, and thus the way men live, is conditioned by what men know about it, and they know more now than they ever have before. Things themselves—the sea, stars, darkness, wind—have not changed; it is the perplexed anxiety and helplessness of the newly dispossessed human being that now come forth from his mind and transmute the sea, the night air, the French coast, and charge them with the sinister implications of the entirely alien. What begins as a rather conventional—but very good—description of scenery turns slowly into quite another thing: a recognition of where the beholder stands in relation to these things; where he *really* stands. It is this new and comfortless knowledge as it overwhelms for all time the old and does away with the place where he thought he stood, where his tradition

From a December 1857 letter written by Arnold to his brother Thomas. Arnold's discussion
of Pope's poetry as "adequate . . . to Pope's age" echoes the views he expressed in the first
lecture he delivered as Professor of Poetry at Oxford.

told him he stood, that creates the powerful and melancholy force of the poem.

In statement, **"Dover Beach"** goes very easily and gravely, near prose and yet not too near. It has something of the effect of overheard musing, though it is addressed, or half-addressed, to someone present. Its greatest technical virtue, to my mind, is its employment of sound-imagery, particularly in the deep, sustained vowels of lines like "Its melancholy, long, withdrawing roar." The lines also seem to me to *break* beautifully: " . . . on the French coast, the light / Gleams, and is gone." I have tried many times to rearrange Arnold's lines, and have never succeeded in doing anything but diminish their subtlety, force, and conviction.

The one difficulty of the poem, it seems to me, is in the famous third strophe wherein the actual sea is compared to the Sea of Faith. If Arnold means that the Sea of Faith was formerly at high tide, and he hears now only the sound of the tide going out, one cannot help thinking also of the cyclic nature of tides, and the consequent coming of another high tide only a few hours after the present ebb. In other words, the figure of speech appears valid only on one level of the comparison; the symbolic half fails to sustain itself. Despite the magnificence of the writing in this section, I cannot help believing that it is the weakest part of the poem when it should be the strongest; the explicitness of the comparison seems too ready-made. Yet I have the poem as it is so deeply in memory that I cannot imagine it changed, and would not have it changed even if I knew it would be a better poem thereby.

In the sound of waves rolling pebbles, an eternal senseless motion, unignorable and meaningless, Arnold hears—as we ever afterwards must hear—human sadness, the tears of things. It links us to Sophocles and to all men at all times who have discovered in such a sound an expression of their own unrest, and have therefore made of it "the eternal note of sadness." Yet our sadness has a depth that no other era has faced: a certainty of despair based upon our own examination of empirical evidence and the conclusions drawn by our rational faculty. These have revealed not God but the horror and emptiness of things, including those that we cannot help thinking beautiful: that *are* beautiful. By its direct, slow-speaking means, the poem builds toward its last nine lines, when the general resolves into the particular, divulging where *we* stand, what these things mean to *us.* The implication is that if love, morality, constancy, and the other traditional Western virtues are not maintained without supernatural sanction, there is nothing. The world that lies before us in such beauty that it seems to have come instantaneously from God's hand does not include, guarantee, or symbolize the qualities that men have assumed were also part of it. It is beautiful and impersonal, but we must experience it—and now suffer it—as persons. Human affection is revealed as a completely different thing than what we believed it to be; as different, in fact, as the world we were mistaken about. It is a different thing but also a new thing, with new possibilities of terror, choice, and meaning. The moment between the lovers thus takes on the qualities of a new expulsion from Eden: they tremble with fear but also with terrible freedom; they look eastward. The intense vulnerability of the emotional life takes place in an imperiled darkness among the sounds of the sea and against the imminence of violence, wars, armies blundering blindly into each other for no reason. Yet there is a new, fragile center to things: a man and a woman. In a word, it is love in what we have come to call the existential predicament. Nearly a hundred years ago, Arnold fixed unerringly and profoundly on the quality that more than any other was to characterize the emotion of love in our own century: desperation. (pp. 235-38)

James Dickey, "Arnold: 'Dover Beach'," in his *Babel to Byzantium: Poets & Poetry Now,* Grosset & Dunlap, 1971, pp. 235-38.

CLYDE DE L. RYALS
(essay date 1988)

[In the excerpt below, Ryals examines various thematic aspects of Arnold's verse, maintaining that contrary to the commonly held critical perception, Arnold's poetry displays irony.]

Irony is a term not often associated with the poetry of Matthew Arnold. Instead critics like Lionel Trilling more often speak of Arnold's "sincerity"; and even when they perceive a certain irony in his work, it is to his prose and not to his poetry that they look. Douglas Bush, for example, in his book on Arnold, allows that "although he was to become a master of irony in prose, he rarely approached it in verse." Yet almost every contemporary account that we have about the man, from early youth to the time of his death, testifies to his

playfulness, his posturings, his poses. Many of his friends and family were surprised that he was even capable of the seriousness that they discovered in his first published volume of poems. And later, when his seriousness was no longer to be questioned, his readers were often amazed by the frivolity that frequently seemed to invade his work. In his autobiography the philologist Max Mueller noted that Arnold "trusts . . . to *persiflage,* and the result was that when he tried to be serious, people could not forget that he might at any time turn round and smile, and decline to be *au grand serieux.*" Jest and seriousness, artless openness and dissimulation—these seem to have been the characteristics of Arnold the man. The same qualities define his poetry, which is to say, the poet is an ironist.

In Arnold's world all is in a state of change. Characterized by an endless process of creation and decreation, nature in its plentitude is always in a state of becoming, everything being both itself and something else. In this world the individual, seeing that A is both A and $A > B$, faces contradictions on all sides; and this perception engenders the most contradictory impulses within himself, the desire for, simultaneously, both fixity and fluidity, involvement and detachment, subjectivity and objectivity, bondage and freedom. Further, the self recognizes its own instability, its essential nothingness. "I am nothing," Arnold wrote to his friend Arthur Clough, "and very probably never shall be anything—but there are characters which are truest to themselves by never being anything, when circumstances do not suit." And speaking of his poems to his sister Jane, Arnold urged: "Fret not yourself to make my poems square in all their parts. . . . The true reason why parts suit you while others do not is that my poems are fragments—i.e. that I am fragments . . . ; the whole effect of my poems is quite vague & indeterminate . . . ; & do not plague yourself to find a consistent meaning." His was, he confessed to Clough, a chameleon personality: "I can go thro: the imaginary process of mastering myself and see the whole affair as it would then stand, but at the critical point I am too apt to hoist up the mainsail to the wind and let her drive." For like Goethe, he was quite willing to believe that in most matters "there is no certainty, but alternating dispositions." Yes, "this little which we are / Swims on an obscure much we might have been." One cannot "talk of *the* absolutely right but of *a* promising method with ourselves." " 'Hide thy life,' said Epicurus, and the exquisite zest there is in doing so can only be appreciated by those who, desiring to introduce some method into their lives, have suffered from the malicious pleasure the world takes in trying to distract them till they are as shatter-brained and empty-hearted as the world itself " (*Letters* 1:62-63). Years later Arnold was to claim the chameleon personality as the ideal critic: "The critic of poetry should have the finest tact, the nicest moderation, the most free, flexible, and elastic spirit imaginable; he should be indeed the 'ondoyant et divers,' the *undulating and diverse* being of Montaigne.''

An undulating and diverse being—such a one is, in Arnold's view, an ironist, not a traditional ironist of local, verbal, and corrective ironies but a Romantic Ironist, whose way of regarding the world requires an artistic mode correspondent to his world-view. A literary work in this mode avoids closure and determinate meanings; deconstructs the invented fictional world that it pretends to offer; mirrors its author and itself to the end that it represents only itself and its maker; is permeated by a sense of play; and permits transcendence to the creative self of its own image and representational system, thereby allowing the self to hover above the work and glorify in its own self-activity. In brief, works of Romantic Irony forego meaning for metaphysical and aesthetic play.

In his poetry Arnold presents a number of varying positions all of which are deemed of equal value. Let us consider the matter of fate, for example, in *The Strayed Reveller and Other Poems* (1849). Poem after poem deals with characters as victims of fate, yet in almost every case the working of fate is called into question. **"Mycerinus"** considers whether there is a ''Force'' that makes all ''slaves of a tyrannous necessity,'' or whether the gods are ''mere phantoms of man's self-tormenting heart'' (ll. 42, 25). The chorus in the **"Fragment of an 'Antigone'"** praises both those who flee from fate and those who observe its dictates. The eager response of **"To a Republican Friend"** is mitigated in **"Continued"** by the ''Uno'erleaped Mountains of Necessity, / Sparing us narrower margin than we deem.'' The laborer in **"The World and the Quietist"** is granted a sense of omnipotence although his and others' actions are limited by how ''Fate decreed.'' The speaker in **"Written in Emerson's Essays"** contends that ''the will is free'' so ''Gods are we, bards, saints, heroes, if we will''; but the last line of the poem asks whether this be ''truth or mockery'' (the manuscript reading being the more decisive ''O barren boast, O joyless Mockery''). The colloquist in **"Resignation"** staunchly maintains that persons ''who await / No gifts from chance, have conquered fate'' (ll. 247-248), while also freely admitting that fate thwarts our expectations of life (ll. 271-278).

This same ambivalence about fate marks the poems of Arnold's later volumes as well. The initial lyrics of the **"Switzerland"** series assume that the relationship with Marguerite is doomed to fail, and subsequent ones impute the lovers' parting to ''a God [who] their severance ruled'' (**"To Marguerite—Continued,"** l. 22) because for ''durability . . . they were not meant'' (**"The Terrace at Berne"** ll. 43-44). The workings of fate are inexorable: ''I knew it when my life was young;

/ I feel it still, now youth is o'er'' (ll. 49-50). Communication on the deeper levels of sensibility is impossible because that which seals the lips ''hath been deep-ordained,'' yet occasionally there come moments when we talk openly and sincerely (**"The Buried Life,"** ll. 29, 87). Arnold's speakers are forever questioning whether they are free or determined, and they conclude, hopefully but questioningly, with the possibility that they are both: ''Ah, *some* power exists there, which is ours?'' (**"Self-Deception,"** l. 27).

Arnold's views of nature are likewise contradictory. In **"Quiet Work," "Lines Written in Kensington Gardens," "A Summer Night,"** and **"The Youth of Man"** nature is the great moral exemplar, teaching ''toil unsevered from tranquillity'' (**"Quiet Work"**). In **"In Harmony with Nature," "The Youth of Nature," "Self-Dependence,"** and **"A Wish,"** on the other hand, nature is shown to be a distinct realm of being that mankind cannot possibly emulate and would not wish to if it could: ''Nature and man can never be fast friends'' (**"In Harmony with Nature"**). No attempt is made to come down on either side of the question, as Arnold presents not certainties but possibilities. Here it is not a matter of either / or but of both / and.

We may say the same of Arnold's many verses dealing with love. In poems like **"Dover Beach"** and **"The Buried Life"** love is regarded as redemptive, whereas in the Marguerite poems and *Tristram and Iseult* it is shown to be a snare and delusion. While love alone appears able to fill the void in which ''we mortal millions live alone'' (**"To Marguerite—Cont."**), passion, or the love that engenders it, is too unstable, too transient to provide a firm basis for life.

Arnold favors situations that are intrinsically ironic. Mycerinus, the good king, is condemned to an early death while his father, who spurned justice, lived long and happily. Homer, though blind, saw much (**"To a Friend"**). Shakespeare, the greatest of poets, ''didst tread on earth unguessed at'' (**"Shakespeare"**). The Duke of Wellington, the leader of conservative forces, sponsored revolution but in accordance with law (**"To the Duke of Wellington"**). The strayed reveller ''enswines'' himself in Circe's palace, the enchantress having ''lured him not hither'' (l. 97).

From basically ironic situations Arnold develops, even in his earliest poems, narratives of more complex irony. In **"A Memory Picture"** lovers' promises are made to be broken and ''new made—to break again'' (l. 38). The Modern Sappho waits for her lover whose attention is now focused on another but who, ''as he drifts to fatigue, discontent, and dejection / Will be brought, thou poor heart, how much nearer to thee!'' The New Sirens argue that, ''only, what we feel, we know'' (l. 84). Yet since feeling is evanescent and ignorance the way of life, the speaker, eschewing roses and lilies for cypress and yew, approaches love from a new point of view: "Shall I seek, that I may scorn her / Her I loved at eventide?" (ll. 271-272). In similar fashion the speaker of **"The Voice"** hears a compelling voice that issues "a thrilling summons to my will" and makes "my tossed heart its life-blood spill" yet to which his will ultimately remains unshaken and his heart unbroken. On the other hand, the speaker of **"To Fausta,"** in full realization that joys flee when sought and that dreams are false and hollow, nevertheless may go in pursuit of them. The gipsy child has "foreknown the vanity of hope, / Foreseen [his] harvest—yet proceed-[s] to live" (**"To a Gipsy Child by the Sea-shore,"** ll. 39-40). The busy world is made aware of its power only when reminded of the vanity of its busyness, just as Darius was most mindful of his power when made aware of the one check to it (**"The World and the Quietist"**).

A number of the early poems dramatize Arnold's perception that each moment is a watershed "whence, equally, the seas of life and death are fed" (**"Resignation,"** l. 260). This is particularly true of the verses dealing with moral problems, the point of which is that the arguments are about as good on one side as another. In the **"Fragment of an 'Antigone'"** the chorus is right in its praise of Antigone, who in respect for universal law buried her brother in violation of the civil law and with disregard to her lover; but Haemon is also right in his claim that Antigone preferred a corpse to her lover. No wonder then that the chorus is forced to conclude that praise is due both him who "makes his own welfare his unswerved-from law" (l. 8) and him who "dares / To self-selected good / Prefer obedience to the primal law" (ll. 28-30). In **"The Sick King in Bokhara"** the vizier is right in his respect for the law and its demand that the individual follow it unswervingly, yet the king is surely not wrong to heed the claims of conscience and seek to mitigate the punishment of the moolah. In **"The Forsaken Merman"** Arnold shows Margaret as both right and wrong in her return to land: a wife and mother, she has obligations in the sea-world to her family, which she leaves desolate; but a human, she also has responsibilities in the land-world, where she must fulfil her religious duties among her kind.

Such poems, which are dramatizations of irony, reflect the young poet's embrace of irony as a cosmic view. In the modern world certainty is rarely if ever possible. What is required in confronting such a world, Arnold evidently believes, is an ironic posture that permits toleration of indeterminancy. Thus whether the poet sees deeply or widely—possibilities entertained in, respectively, **"The Strayed Reveller"** and **"Resignation"**—is not easily determined and both alternatives should be entertained. Thus whether the universe is of divine or purely physical origin one should be prepared (**"In Utrumque Paratus"**) or, to use a favorite term of Arnold's, resigned.

Critics have frequently elaborated on Arnold's stoic resignation and his supposedly bleak view of life. But as his Empedocles says, one need not despair if one cannot dream (*Empedocles on Etna*, I.ii.423-426). Life is still worth living even though one has "foreknown the vanity of hope" (**"To a Gipsy Child"**). Often the poet's stoic attitude seems no more than that, an attitude, a posture, a pose. Where Mycerinus was a stoic posing as a reveller, Arnold not infrequently appears to be a reveller posing as a stoic. As a poet he is always exploring possibilities with a tentativeness, a drawing back that does not permit conclusiveness. In his work as in his letters there are constant oscillations as he explores options that receive, even at the moment he seems to embrace them, only provisional assent. The narrator's "It may be" in his examination of Mycerinus' inner self well expresses the poet's own qualified positions; and his explorations are not experiments in despair but, frequently, playful exercises "not of mere resigned acquiescence, not of melancholy quietism, but of joyful activity." As he told Clough, "composition seems to keep alive in me a *cheerfulness*—a sort of Tüchtigkeit, or natural soundness and valiancy." Even in his apparently darkest poems there is something of Mycerinus' "clear laughter . . . ringing through the gloom" (l. 113), issuing from the poet's playful acceptance of the ironic fact that man is born with desires that cannot be fulfilled:

> Why each is striving, from of old,
> To love more deeply than he can?
> Still would be true, yet still grows cold?
> —Ask of the Powers that sport with man!
> They yoked in him, for endless strife,
> A heart of ice, a soul of fire;
> And hurled him on the Field of Life,
> An aimless unallayed Desire.
>
> (**"Destiny"**)

The "sport" of the gods can be the poet's, and the poet's serious play is illustrative of the belief Arnold shared with Schiller that "lofty thought lies oft in childish play" (**"Thekla's Answer"**).

The poems of *Empedocles on Etna and Other Poems* (1852) portray characters playing out their roles in complex dramas of undefined irony. Let us look, for example, at **"The Church of Brou."** To memorialize her dead husband and their love for each other the duchess erects a church and inside it an ornate tomb on the top of which are effigies of the pair lying side by side and in which she too is eventually buried. Centuries pass as the dead lovers are left alone in their church undisturbed except for Sunday services. The meaning of their memorial is now forgotten as people after mass visit the tomb "and marvel at the Forms of stone, / And praise the chiselled broideries rare" until they part and "the princely Pair are left alone / In the Church of Brou" (ll. 36-40). Here in this lonely sepulchre there is no life, only the silent art of glass and stone. Wishing them well the narrator apostrophizes: "So sleep, for ever sleep, O marble Pair!" (III.16) And then momentarily indulging in the dream of eternal love that might have been theirs or what at the instant might be his, he considers two possibilities of their awaking: first, when the western sun shines through the stained glass and throws a dazzling array of colors throughout the church and they will say, *"What is this? we are in bliss—forgiven— / Behold the pavement of the courts of Heaven!"*; or second, when the autumn rains come and the moon occasionally shines out and through the windows of the clerestory illuminates the "foliaged marble forest" and they will say, *"This is the glimmering verge of Heaven, and these / The columns of the heavenly palaces!"* (III. 30-31, 41-42). This is of course but a fancy, and even in the fancy the lovers would be deluded because it is not in heaven but in the church of Brou wherein the putatively awakened pair find themselves. The fact is that they continue to lie under "the lichen-crusted leads above" on which there is but the dream of listening to "the rustle of the eternal rain of love." In the long run, art serves as neither a memorial nor a transformation; it remains but beautiful forms at which to marvel.

In poem after poem Arnold recalls us to the fact that what we witness in his verse is not life but art. The action of *Empedocles on Etna* centers on the Sicilian philosopher, but the last word is given to Callicles, who undercuts the poem by stating explicitly that what we have just witnessed is not the proper subject matter for poetry—"Not here, O Apollo! / Are haunts meet for thee" (II.421-422)—and in effect saying pretty much what Arnold himself said in his *Preface* to the 1853 *Poems* when he explained why he was not reprinting the poem. The poet is likewise separated from the poem in the **"Stanzas in Memory of the Author of 'Obermann',"** wherein after praising the author and his book the poet bids farewell to both, although leaving "half of my life with you" (l. 123). In such verses the poet, like God, is both in and out of his creation, subjective and objective, immanent and transcendent. He "moves, but never moveth on" (**"The Hayswater Boat"**).

Although doubleness and dividedness are commonplaces of Victorian literature, the degree of self-reflexivity in Arnold is uncommon. Arnold is always splitting himself up into various "selves"—the best self and the ordinary self, the buried self and the masked self. On the one hand modern life, with its constant claims and banalities calling us out of ourselves, necessitates this. On the other hand the ennui of solitude and the fear that there is no real self at all compel such a separation. "Two desires" toss the poet about: "One drives him to the world without / And one to solitude" (**"Stanzas in Memory of the Author of 'Obermann',"** ll. 93-96). "And I," puzzles the speaker of **"A Summer Night,"**

I know not if to pray
Still to be what I am, or yield and be
Like the other men I see."

(ll. 34-36)

The answer is clearly that he will have to be both.

The inadequacy of language, its inability to permit one to delve into oneself and express what is there or what is lacking, in part mandates the answer. Arnold perhaps best explores the deficiences of language in **"The Buried Life,"** in which the speaker and his beloved, though engaging in a "war of mocking words," cannot communicate openly. Love is apparently too weak to open the heart and let it speak, yet the desire remains to apprehend the buried life and to share it with another. After investigating the impossibility of such communication the speaker, seemingly unmindful of the presence of his beloved, then says that it is possible:

When a belovéd hand is laid in ours,
....
The eye sinks inward, and the heart lies plain
And what we mean, we say, and what we would, we know

(ll. 78, 86-87)

This seems to be but hypothetical, however, since the nature and destiny of the buried self are not revealed. Further, in looking into his beloved's eyes he sees himself mirrored there: his eye sinks inward and he becomes aware of the flow of his life and thinks he knows where his life rose and where it goes.

What the speaker discovers about the buried life is that which in fact cannot be said. Silence is all that is possible in consideration of the great questions of life. Thus the models Arnold held up for emulation can be both superhuman—like Shakespeare and the poet of **"Resignation"**—or subhuman—like the gipsies of "Resignation" and the gipsy child—but they have one trait in common: they do not or cannot break their silence to offer any counsel. It is each person's own impossible struggle to find the right words. Man has the letters God has given him to "make with them what word he could." Different civilizations have combined them in different ways and "somewhat was made." But man knows that "he has not yet found the word God would," and if only he could achieve the right words in the right order, then he would be relieved of a terrible oppression and at long last breathe free (**"Revolutions"**). But this will never happen: human language belongs to the phenomenal world and it can never encompass the noumenal world to speak God's word. The poet, Arnold knows, can never fully replicate or represent anything. That is why it must always be admitted "that the singer was less than his themes." No, even the best of poets—"who have read / Most in themselves—have beheld / Less than they left unrevealed" (**"The Youth of Nature"** ll. 89, 104-106). The truth is that the buried self cannot be expressed because without the proper words it cannot be apprehended.

To attempt to view their inner being from various perspectives Arnold's heroes don masks and play roles, just as Arnold did when he assumed the role of dandy in the late 1840s. And with their roles and masks they not only view themselves but also become spectators watching others watching themselves watch others. To refuse to engage in this kind of dramatic play is, in the mid-nineteenth century at any rate, to admit to inelasticity, to be spiritually moribund: "only death / Can cut his oscillations short, and so / Bring him to poise" (*Empedocles* II.232-234). Poise, peace, rest, calm—those qualities which speaker after speaker claims to desire—are, Arnold knows, the attributes of death:

> 'Tis death! and peace, indeed, is here
>
> ....
>
> But is a calm like this, in truth,
> The crowning end of life and youth,
> And when this boon rewards the dead,
> Are all debts paid, has all been said?
> ("**Youth and Calm**," ll. 1-8)

The answer is a ringing no:

> *Calm's not life's crown, though calm is well.*
> 'Tis all perhaps which man acquires,
> But 'tis not what our youth desires.
>
> (ll. 23-25)

In Arnold's world there is always more to say; there are always visions to be revised.

After 1852 most of Arnold's better poems were written in the elegiac mode. Elegy was a congenial mode for him because it allowed for the irony of reversal: Lycidas is dead and we lament his loss as we celebrate his talents; but Lycidas is not dead, he lives on in another state. As Arnold employed it, his poems in this mode call into question the meaning of their opening parts. We see this clearly in "**The Scholar-Gipsy.**" The poem begins by building up the myth of the scholar-gipsy to the point where the narrator himself asserts the living reality of the young Oxonian of two hundred years ago: "Have I not passed thee?" (l. 123). But then this assertion in the form of a question is almost immediately denied: "But what—I dream / . . . / thou from earth art gone / Long since, and in some quiet churchyard laid" (ll. 131, 136-137). The scholar is indeed dead, and the verbs associated with him change to the past tense. This is however but momentary, for while talking of how the scholar fled with his powers unsullied and undiverted to the world, the speaker again resurrects him and speaks of him in the present tense: "Thou waitest for the spark from heaven" (l. 171). It is an imaginative recovery as the speaker grants him "an immortal lot" because he "imagine[s] thee exempt from age" (ll. 157-158). But immortal lot or not, the scholar is still apparently subject to the ills which afflict mortals living nowadays. And so if he is ever to encounter the divine spark, the scholar must flee the infection of modern life to which present-day mortals are subject and like the Tyrian trader establish his enterprise elsewhere.

The poem complicates itself still further by purportedly dealing with two quests—the speaker's for the scholar-gipsy and the scholar's for some kind of revelation—that are in fact one and the same. Although the scholar quests for the secret knowledge of nature which can be gained only by nonrational means, he himself is already the embodiment of that knowledge, as the poet makes him a kind of nature-spirit who in the first part of the poem can be perceived only by the simple and untutored or those, like poets, who live imaginatively, and who near the end of the poem is granted life "On some mild pastoral slope" listening "with enchanted ears" to nightingales (ll. 216-220). In sum, the scholar is the object of his own quest. And the speaker, questing for the scholar and the secret possessed by him, locates within himself the imaginative insight that the scholar embodies, which is to say that the speaker is the object of his own quest.

If all the elements seem to cancel each other out, what finally are we left with? In the end we are left with the poet himself who, in the elaborate simile concluding the poem, reminds us that this is not a transcription of life with its sick hurry or of nature with its pale pink convolvulus but art—a poem, a making, over which looms the figure of the poet himself. In the end we see that the imaginative donnée of the poem is not the scholar-gypsy and his quest or modern life with its ills or meaning of any kind; rather, its imaginative donnée is Romantic Irony, which permits the poet to rise above his finite subject matter to a realm of aesthetic consciousness.

The coda of *Sohrab and Rustum* serves also to recall the reader from the poem to the poet. In this narrative of ironic situations in which two persons longing for union are frustrated in that desire and come together only through conflict, when one slays the other, the dead son is transformed into art: first when he makes himself known by the vermilion seal, which is compared to "some clear porcelain vase" painstakingly made by a Chinese workman for the emperor, and second when there is erected over his grave a giant pillar which also serves as a seal not only of the son but of the father too in that those who see it say, *"Sohrab, the mighty Rustum's son, lies there, / Whom his great father did in ignorance kill"* (ll. 792-793). In the end Arnold makes of the concluding symbol of the Oxus the same use as Rustum made of the tomb erected for his son. It "seals" the narrative into art and reminds the reader of its maker, saying in effect: *"Sohrab and Rustum,* poema, Matthew Arnold fecit." Its composition was an exercise in the development of aesthetic consciousness and as a result the consciousness of the poet, like the winding River Oxus, spirals toward its "luminous home" (l. 890).

Arnold's twistings and turnings in his memorial poems are remarkable in the **"Stanzas in Memory of Edward Quillinan."** While his friend was alive, the speaker wished him health, success, and fame—qualities that are their own reward, "leave no good behind," and "oftenest make us hard, / Less modest, pure, and kind." But the dead man did not receive them and thus he was "a man unspoiled." Implicit in the tribute is the notion that Quillinan is therefore better dead than alive: "Alive, we would have changed his lot, / We would not change it now."

In **"Haworth Churchyard,"** the elegy for Charlotte Brontë and prematurely for Harriet Martineau, Arnold followed the usual elegiac reversal of awakening when the poem was first published in 1855:

> Sleep, O cluster of friends,
> Sleep!—or only when May,
> Brought by the west-wind, returns
> Back to your native heaths,
> And the plover is heard on the moors,
> Yearly to behold
> The opening summer, the sky,
> The shining moorland—to hear.
> The drowsy bee, as of old,
> Hum o'er the thyme, the grouse
> Call from the heather in bloom!
> Sleep, or only for this
> Break your united repose.
>
> (ll. 112-124)

When the poem appeared in revised form in 1877, Arnold added an Epilogue, which is nothing less than a palinode. Denying the possibility of a May awakening, the Muse angrily shakes her head and says that this shall not be: these "unquiet souls" will not awaken but will remain "in the dark fermentation of earth," "the never idle workshop of nature," "the eternal movement" of the universe of becoming, and there "ye shall find yourselves again!" (ll. 125-128).

With even less cordiality Arnold elegizes Heinrich Heine in **"Heine's Grave."** Heine too was an ironist but he lacked love and charm, and his irony was in consequence bitter. Properly situated in Montmartre Cemetery in Paris and not in Naples' bay or among Ravenna's pines or by the Avon's side, where poets like Virgil, Dante, and Shakespeare belong, Heine's grave reeks of a kind of poison distilled from the harshness and malignity of his life. Once the poet had admired the dead man, but it was necessary that he part from Heine lest he be infected by his mocking laughter. Obviously Arnold has come to re-bury Heine and not to

praise him. Yet near the end of his elegy, after 198 lines of mocking derision of the German writer, the poet decides not thus to take leave of him but "with awe / Hail, as it passes from earth / Scattering lightnings, that soul!" (ll. 203-205). At the very end however the poet returns to himself as he asks "the Spirit of the world" to grant that "a life / Other and milder be mine" and that his work be made "a beat of thy joy!" (ll. 225-226, 232). Evidently what Arnold repudiates in Heine is not his irony but his lack of playfulness and joy, characteristic of a higher irony.

In **"Thyrsis"** Arnold is again critical of the subject to be elegized. Clough-Thyrsis was a "too quick despairer" who deserted the landscape of the scholar-gipsy's haunts by his own will, and because of the storms of which "he could not wait their passing, he is dead" (ll. 61, 50). Seemingly Thyrsis, out of silly impatience, had willed his own death, leaving the speaker here alone in these fields that "our Gipsy-Scholar haunts, outliving thee" (l. 197). Yes, the scholar-gipsy remains "a wanderer still; then why not me?" (l. 200). Why not indeed? And so the speaker and the scholar go off, as fellow questers, seeking for the light of truth and apparently putting Thyrsis, the deserter, out of mind. This is, however, an elegy in memory of his friend, and Arnold cannot afford to leave the matter at this point. Adding three final stanzas to the poem, he allows that Thyrsis too was bound on a like quest though in foreign territory. Further, he gives Thyrsis the last word. But addressed to the poet, it urges him to wander on in his quest, thereby in the end returning the focus of the poem to the poet himself who hovers above the work.

From this hasty survey of Arnold's poetry we see many of the conflicts that the poet faced and found unresolvable. He was well aware of "wandering between two worlds" (**"Stanzas from the Grande Chartreuse"** l. 85) and being caught between at least "two desires" (**"Stanzas in Memory of the Author of 'Obermann' "**) and that it was impossible for him to take either side or bring them into accord. So much about Arnold has long been clear. But what has not been clear is the degree to which Arnold exhibits his conflicts ironically—so as to transcend them. Far from being the poet of "sincerity" Arnold is self-conscious, playful, problematic, and equivocal. His is, in sum, the art of the Romantic Ironist that presents a self always in process and always relishing and extolling its own self-activity. (pp. 91-101)

Clyde de L. Ryals, "Romantic Irony in Arnold's Poetry," in *Victorian Poetry*, Vol. 26, Nos. 1-2, Spring-Summer, 1988, pp. 91-102.

SOURCES FOR FURTHER STUDY

Allott, Kenneth, ed. *Matthew Arnold.* Athens: Ohio University Press, 1976, 353 p.

A collection of essays by ten scholars exploring such issues as Arnold's attitude toward religion, his social and political thought, and his relationship to Johann Wolfgang von Goethe and Arthur Hugh Clough.

Baum, Paul F. *Ten Studies in the Poetry of Matthew Arnold.* Durham, N.C.: Duke University Press, 1958, 139 p.

Explications of eight of Arnold's poems, including "Dover Beach," "Tristram and Iseult," "Thyrsis," and the Marguerite poems.

Gottfried, Leon. *Matthew Arnold and the Romantics.* Lincoln: University of Nebraska Press, 1963, 277 p.

Appraises the full range of Arnold's critical reaction to the major Romantic poets.

Jump, J. D. *Matthew Arnold.* London: Longmans, Green, and Co., 1955, 185 p.

Assessment of Arnold from three perspectives: "The Man," "The Poet," and "The Critic."

Miller, J. Hillis. "Matthew Arnold." In his *The Disappearance of God,* pp. 212-69. Cambridge, Mass: The Belknap Press, 1963.

Studies Arnold's poetry and poetic theory as a reflection of the nineteenth century's struggle with godlessness.

Trilling, Lionel. *Matthew Arnold.* New York: Norton, 1939, 465 p.

A sympathetic and insightful analysis of Arnold's concepts. This work is considered the definitive critical biography of Arnold.

Margaret Atwood

1939-

(Full name Margaret Eleanor Atwood) Canadian novelist, poet, short story writer, critic, and author of books for children.

INTRODUCTION

*I*nternationally acclaimed as a novelist, poet, and short story writer, Atwood has emerged as a major figure in Canadian letters. Using such devices as irony, symbolism, and self-conscious narrators, she explores the relationship between humanity and nature, unsettling aspects of human behavior, and power as it pertains to gender and political roles. Her authorial voice has sometimes been described as formal and emotionally distant, but her talent for allegory and intense imagery informs an intellectual and sardonic style popular with both literary scholars and the reading public. Atwood has also been instrumental as a critic. She has helped define the identity and goals of contemporary Canadian literature and has earned a distinguished reputation among feminist writers for her exploration of women's issues.

Atwood was born in Ottawa and grew up in suburban Toronto, a metropolitan area that appears in many of her stories and novels. As a child she spent her summers at her family cottage in a wilderness region of Quebec, where her father, a forest entomologist, conducted research. She first began to write while in high school, contributing poetry, short stories, and cartoons to the school newspaper. As an undergraduate at the University of Toronto, Atwood met the critic Northrop Frye, who introduced her to the poetry of William Blake. Influenced by Blake's contrasting mythological imagery, Atwood wrote the poems collected in her first volume, *Double Persephone* (1961). While this work demonstrated her penchant for using metaphorical language, it was her second volume of poetry, *The Circle Game* (1966), that garnered widespread critical recognition. The winner of the 1967 Governor General's Award, Canada's highest literary honor, *The Circle Game* established the major themes of Atwood's poetry: the inconsistencies of self-perception, the paradoxical nature of language, Canadian identity, and the conflicts between humankind and nature. Sherrill Grace commented: "[Atwood] is constantly aware of opposites—self/other, subject/object, male/female, nature/man—and of the need to accept and work within them." Atwood explored the meaning of art and literature in the volume *The Animals in That Country* (1968). Presenting the poet as both performer and creator, she questioned the authenticity of the writing process and the effects of literature on both the writer and the reader. Although all of her verse explores the uniqueness of the Canadian psyche, it was in *The Journals of Susanna Moodie* (1970) that Atwood devoted her attention to what she calls the schizoid, double nature of Canada. Centered on the narratives of a Canadian pioneer woman, *Journals* examines why Canadians came to develop ambivalent feelings toward their country. Atwood further developed this dichotomy in *Power Politics* (1971), in which she explored the relationship between sexual roles and power structures by focusing on personal relationships and international politics.

In addition to her numerous collections of poetry, Atwood earned widespread attention for *Survival: A Thematic Guide to Canadian Literature* (1972), a seminal critical analysis of Canadian literature that served as a rallying point for the country's cultural nationalists. In *Survival* Atwood argued that Canadians have always viewed themselves as victims, both of the forces of nature that confronted them as they settled in wilderness territory and of the colonialist powers that dominated their culture and politics. She proposed that Canadian writers should cultivate a more positive self-image by embracing traditions of Native Americans and French Canadians, rather than identifying with Great Britain or the United States.

Atwood addressed feminist concerns through satire and irony in the novels *The Edible Woman* (1969), *Surfacing* (1972), *Life before Man* (1979), and *Bodily Harm* (1982). These works feature intelligent and independent women in search of meaning and self-identity in the midst of unsettling situations. Atwood's first novel, *The Edible Woman,* is about Marian MacAlpin, who rebels against her upcoming marriage after realizing that her fiancé is "ordinariness raised to perfection" and that the role of wife is fixed and limiting. *Surfacing,* frequently hailed as a classic of contemporary feminist literature, traces a young woman's struggle to accept her past and overcome spiritual alienation. The story of an unnamed free-lance artist who journeys to the wilderness of Quebec to investigate her father's disappearance, *Surfacing* focuses on the dichotomous nature of family relationships, cultural heritage, and self-perception. In her next novel, *Life before Man,* Atwood dissected the relationships between three characters: Elizabeth, a married woman who mourns the recent death of her lover; Elizabeth's husband, Nate, who is unable to choose between his wife and his lover; and Lesje, Nate's lover, who works with Elizabeth at a museum of natural history. All three characters are emotionally isolated from one another and are unable to take responsibility for their feelings as their relationships deteriorate. In *Bodily Harm,* Atwood further explored themes of miscommunication and deception in social actions. The protagonist of this novel, Rennie Wilford, is a Toronto journalist who specializes in light, trivial pieces for magazines. Following a partial mastectomy, which causes her lover to abandon her, Rennie attempts to avoid her disappointment and dissatisfaction by taking an assignment on the Caribbean island of St. Antoine, where she becomes embroiled in local political disputes. While developing serious subject matter and focusing on troubled characters struggling for survival, these works feature detached humor and penetrating, ironic insights into the human condition and contradictions in contemporary life.

The title of Atwood's first collection of short fiction, *Dancing Girls* (1977), refers to the leading characters in the stories—women who obligingly accept the roles assigned to them by male-dominated society rather than following their own desires. This volume, which is considered more pessimistic in outlook than Atwood's earlier works, contains pointed observations concerning patriarchal social systems and emotionally withdrawn males. The protagonists of these short stories are intelligent, urbane, and alienated from their social environment. Sometimes this alienation emerges as psychosis, such as the schizophrenia experienced by Louise in "Polarities." Commentators note that several of the stories in this volume reflect the theories of psychologist R. D. Laing, who regarded schizophrenia as an understandable reaction to irrational conditions created by modern society. Louise, hospitalized for psychotic behavior, is portrayed as being fundamentally in touch with reality, while her ostensibly "normal" friend Morrison is dismayed by his own moral shortcomings. As in most of Atwood's short stories, the female is depicted as intuitive, life-affirming, and allied with nature, while the male stands for violence, oppression, and artifical values.

Atwood turned to speculative fiction with her novel *The Handmaid's Tale* (1986). In this work she created the dystopia of Gilead, a future America in which Fundamentalist Christians have imposed dictatorial rule. Here, in a world polluted by toxic chemicals and nuclear radiation, most women are sterile; those who are able to bear children are forced to become Handmaids, official breeders who enjoy some privileges yet remain under constant surveillance. Almost all other women have been deemed expendable, except those who embrace the repressive religious hierarchy run by men. Although Atwood's strong feminist beliefs were evident in her previous novels, *The Hand-*

maid's Tale is the first of her works to be dominated by feminist concerns. Barbara Holliday wrote: "[Atwood] has been concerned in her fiction with the painful psychic warfare between men and women. [But] in *The Handmaid's Tale*, a futuristic satire, she casts subtlety aside, exposing woman's primal fear of being used and helpless." Many critics favorably compare *The Handmaid's Tale* with George Orwell's *1984* and other distinguished dystopian novels for its disturbing extension of contemporary trends and its allegorical portrait of political extremism.

While *The Handmaid's Tale* focuses on an imagined future, Atwood's next novel, *The Cat's Eye* (1990), explores how misconceptions about the past can influence people's present lives. The story of Elain Risley, a prominent artist who returns to her childhood home in Toronto, *The Cat's Eye* traces Elain's discovery that her childhood relationships were often manipulative and that her memories of past events have not always been accurate or honest. Considered by many an allegorical exploration of the realities confronting individuals at the approach of the twenty-first century, this work reveals the implications of evil and redemption in both a personal and social context. In *The Cat's Eye*, as in all her works, Atwood forgoes specific political or moral ideologies, concentrating instead on the emotional and psychological complexities that confront individuals in conflict with society.

(For further information about Atwood's life and works, see *Contemporary Authors*, Vols. 49-52; *Contemporary Authors New Revision Series*, Vol. 3; *Contemporary Literary Criticism*, Vols. 2, 3, 4, 8, 13, 15, 25, 44; *Dictionary of Literary Biography*, Vol. 53: *Canadian Writers since 1960*; and *Major 20th-Century Writers*.)

CRITICAL COMMENTARY

TOM MARSHALL

(essay date 1978)

[A Canadian poet, short story writer, novelist, and critic, Marshall is noted for his investigation of such topics as Canadian landscape and history and the inherent sadness of human relationships. In the following excerpt, he praises Atwood's Canadian consciousness and her ability to explore universal issues in a regionalistic context.]

Atwood is a swimmer. The familiar Canadian "underwater" motif, the notion of the self and Canada itself trapped underwater like Atlantis, occurs in the first poems of her first full collection and is repeated throughout her work, reaching a kind of climax in the novel *Surfacing*. The notions of inner order and outer space, garrison and wilderness, the issue of perspective and of the ways of seeing also recur, as they do in the work of Avison, Page and numerous other writers. Like Al Purdy and others, she has a concern for ancestors and for evolution, even for the geological past. There is the familiar Canadian identification with animals and a sense of fierce native gods. There is both social satire and an interest in the metaphysics of landscape, as in the work of P. K. Page. . . . , [But] Atwood utilizes Canadian traditions in an apparently more conscious way than most writers of her generation. She taps Canadian culture's most important concerns. And she brings to traditional materials her own sensibility, her own way of saying things: the famous cool, apparently detached tone, the canny disposition of loaded words in short, punchy lines without much heightening of rhythm. It is a style highly distinctive both in its limitations and its strengths. Atwood attempts, for better and/or worse, and certainly to her immediate advantage with readers, to clarify what is complex and difficult, to get right to what she regards as the essential point.

Metaphysics and metaphor: the search for ways in which to find one's whole self, to find identity with one's body, one's instincts, one's country—in this emotional pioneering Atwood moves to the centre of national concerns. (pp. 154-55)

The Journals of Susanna Moodie enlarges upon the national theme; as a poem sequence it enlarges Atwood's scope and is highly successful, indeed an advance on her two earlier books [*The Circle Game* and *The Animals in That Country*], which were uneven though often striking. In the person and experience of Susanna Moodie the poet finds an appropriate objective correlative for her own thoughts and emotions. The book is both personal and objective, both nationalist and universal in its metaphysical enquiry. . . .

Procedures for Underground presents family poems, the deep well of childhood memories, the bush, Canada under water, the descent into the earth to recover the wisdom of the spirits of place, alienation in cities, travel, and marriage. It is a quieter book of individual poems with a quieter and, for some, a more enduring appeal than the one that follows. *Power Politics*

Principal Works

Double Persephone (poetry) 1961

The Circle Game (poetry) 1966

The Animals in That Country (poetry) 1968

The Edible Woman (novel) 1969

The Journals of Susanna Moodie (poetry) 1970

Procedures for Underground (poetry) 1970

Power Politics (poetry) 1971

Surfacing (novel) 1972

Survival: A Thematic Guide to Canadian Literature (criticism) 1972

You Are Happy (poetry) 1974

Lady Oracle (novel) 1976

Selected Poems (poetry) 1976

Dancing Girls, and Other Stories (short stories) 1977

Two-Headed Poems (poetry) 1978

Up in the Tree (children's book) 1978

Life before Man (novel) 1979

True Stories (poetry) 1981

Bodily Harm (novel) 1982

Second Words: Selected Critical Prose (criticism) 1982

Bluebeard's Egg (short stories) 1983

Murder in the Dark: Short Fictions and Prose Poems (short stories) 1983

Interlunar (poetry) 1984

The Handmaid's Tale (novel) 1986

Selected Poems II: Poems Selected and New, 1976-1986 (poetry) 1987

The Cat's Eye (novel) 1990

is, as they say, something else again—an account of grim sexual warfare that restores all the Atwood bite and mordant humour. It makes surreal black comedy out of the historic difficulties of women and the destructive games, projections and illusions of modern lovers in a world built on war and the destruction of the environment. But in *You Are Happy,* which can be regarded as a kind of sequel, the Atwood protagonist moves forward toward a new country of relationship without false hopes, promises, defences, evasions, mythologies. The singularity, the uniqueness of things, of people, in the flux: this is something nameless, beyond language, as in *Surfacing.* One gives oneself to the flux. (p. 157)

Her first two novels, *The Edible Woman* and *Surfacing,* are enlargements upon the themes of her poems. In each of them a young woman is driven to rebellion against what seems to be her fate in the modern technological "Americanized" world and to psychic breakdown and breakthrough. But they are quite different in tone and style.

The Edible Woman is delightfully, wickedly funny. It is feminist, certainly, but it provides a satirical account of the absurd ways of Canadian men *and* women. It is kindly in its irony: never so fierce in its assault as is *Power Politics.* There is anger but there is also good humour. The major characters are satirized—they represent various undesirable ways of existing in the modern consumer society—but they are also seen sympathetically as human beings, even the pompous Peter and the pathetic Lothario Leonard. They are not grotesque caricatures like David and Anna in *Surfacing.* (p. 158)

[*The Edible Woman*] is a largely successful comic novel, even if the mechanics are sometimes a little clumsy, the satirical accounts of consumerism a little drawn out. It is skilfully written, shifting easily from first to third person and back again to convey the stages of Marian's mental travels, her journey into self-alienation and out again. Of Atwood's three novels it is least a poet's novel. . . .

Surfacing introduces a young woman far more fearful, desperate, and alienated from her true self than Marian McAlpin. The atmosphere is correspondingly tense and eerie, for this is a psychological ghost story like *The Turn of the Screw,* in which the ghosts, the young woman's parents, are lost parts of herself that she must recover. She has been unable to feel for years, even though she had a good childhood, much of it spent on an island in northern Quebec. She believes (as the reader does for much of the book) that she has been married and divorced, abandoning a child. Her encounter with the gods of place and, apparently, with the corpse of her drowned father when she returns to the scene of her childhood reveals the truth—that she had in fact had a traumatic abortion—and this drives her to a healing madness, a descent to animal simplicity and a rejection of the destructive, mechanical "civilization" that has wounded her and of all its works, even words. (p. 159)

The first-person point of view combined with the evocative description of setting makes it possible for Atwood to get away with a certain shallowness of characterization; only the narrator seems at all complex. But this is not something that interferes with the powerful flow of the novel as one reads it.

Still, it is evident here, as it is more seriously in *Lady Oracle,* the third novel, that characterization is not Atwood's strong point. And it is revealing that much of her fiction, including her shorter fiction, employs the first person. Everything must be filtered through the mind of the Atwood protagonist, who is usually supposed to be both shrewd and confused, a combination that is possible but which tends in certain cases to put some strain on the reader's credulity. In this respect *The Edible Woman* is a more balanced novel than *Surfacing,* and yet it is *Surfacing,* the poet's novel, that more powerfully engages the reader's emotions.

In *Surfacing* the repeated imagery of bottled, trapped and murdered animals builds powerfully to the key scene in which the father's corpse and the aborted foetus are encountered. . . . In *Lady Oracle,* however, a similar patterning of images, metaphors, and ideas fails to compensate for the fuzzy personality of the narrator, even if this last is part of the author's point. Nor is there the power of language found in the latter part of *Surfacing.* Indeed, the female-picaresque *Lady Oracle* is decidedly thinner than the other novels and lacking in over-all shape or focus, even if it is in places very interesting and enjoyable and even if it offers some rewarding insights into the need for and nature of art and the fantasy life. It is just that all of this seems too intellectually worked out, too far removed from any very deeply felt or imagined experience of the kind that "stood in," so to speak, for any very searching exploration of human character in *Surfacing.* Though a serious emotional resonance seems quite clearly intended, it is not achieved, mainly because recurrent poetic imagery is finally no substitute for depth of characterization. This is the major limitation of Atwood the novelist. Also, the reader may suspect that Atwood is indulging herself a little in this book, even to the extent of succumbing somewhat to the old-style "woman's fiction" she parodies. . . . (pp. 160-61)

It is in *Surfacing,* where a considerable emotional power is allowed to develop (as in *The Journals of Susanna Moodie,* another excursion into "large darkness" and out again), that Atwood's vision and gifts may be seen to best advantage. Here she has given the theme of quest into darkness and the journey to wholeness, a theme that she shares in recent Canadian fiction with Klein, LePan, Watson, Cohen, and MacEwen, its most overtly Canadian expression, and this is no doubt one reason for her considerable success at a time when this great and universal theme has a special significance for a rapidly developing and "surfacing" Canadian consciousness. (p. 161)

Tom Marshall, "Atwood Under and Above Water," in his *Harsh and Lovely Land: The Major Canadian Poets and the Making of a Canadian Tradition,* University of British Columbia Press, 1978, pp. 154-61.

LINDA W. WAGNER

(essay date 1981)

[Wagner, an American educator and critic, is the author of numerous studies on major twentieth-century writers. In the following excerpt, she pro-

vides a thematic and formalistic analysis of Atwood's poetry.]

For Margaret Atwood, life is quest, and her writing—particularly her poetry—is the charting of that journey. Atwood's journey is seldom geographical. . . . Atwood does not dwell on location, physical presence, details of place. Her search is instead a piercing interior exploration, driving through any personal self-consciousness into regions marked by primitive responses both violent and beautiful. Atwood is interested in the human condition, a condition which exists independent of sex; and she plays a variety of games in order to explore that condition fully.

The strategies Atwood uses in her poems are similar to those of her fiction: personae described in terms of such basic biological functions as eating and sleeping; myriad patterns of disguise, whether literal or anthropomorphic; duality presented as separation, as in relationships between lovers (the hints of Jungian traits suggest that Atwood's "males" could represent the rational side of her female characters as well as their own selves); praise for life simplified, closer and closer to the natural; and a stark diction and rhythm, meant to be as far from the "literary" as Atwood's own ideal life is from the conventionally "feminine."

Whether the Atwood persona is a Circe, a Lady Oracle, a Susanna Moodie, a Marian MacAlpin, or the unnamed heroine of *Surfacing* she is a questioning and often bitter woman, at first resisting the passions that eventually lead her to knowledge. She pits accepted roles of womanliness, with all their final ineffectuality, against those of outraged non-conformity. . . . (pp. 81-2)

Ironically, given the tools of the writer, Atwood finds that the most significant knowledge comes without words. . . . Atwood's poetry and fiction teem with characters who fail, consistently and harshly, in expressing themselves; and she often comments on the ineffectuality of purely rational knowledge. . . .

By her 1974 collection, *You Are Happy,* however, Atwood has stopped lamenting and instead shows her acceptance of the nonverbal. . . . One learns because one senses in the blood/heart/hands—centers of touch and emotion rather than intellect. And one is happy, without qualification, only when she, or he, has accepted that resolution of the quest. Self-knowledge must go deeper than fragile, temporal self. It must include an other. . . . (p. 82)

Atwood's progression to this new and apparently satisfying resolution is clearly drawn through her first six books of poetry. While the poems of *The Circle Game* in 1966 appeared to be direct, cutting in their perceptions, the personae of those poems never did make contact, never did anything but lament the human condition. . . . Relationships in these poems are sterile if not destructive. . . . The lovers in **"Spring in the Igloo"** are touching the edge of drowning; the lover in **"Winter Sleepers"** has already gone down. The female persona in **"A Sibyl"** admits her "bottled anguish" and "glass despair."

Even in this first collection, however, the problem as Atwood sees it is more than personal. There are complex reasons why love between a man and a woman is tenuous—cultural, philosophical, anthropological reasons, many of which grow from mistaken values in modern living. Because contemporary people judge in terms of technology and scientific progress, they value "improvements," devices, the urban over the rural, the new over the timeless. Much of Atwood's first collection is filled with her arguments against these attitudes. . . . (p. 83)

This dissatisfaction with the modern milieu, and the ethos it has spawned, leads Atwood first to the immediate move away from urban life. . . . **"Pre-Amphibian"** reinforces that tactic, and in the three-part poem **"Primitive Sources"** she studies ancient beliefs about god-systems, magic, and other devices for understanding the process of life—and a sentient human being's place in it. (p. 84)

Although most of the attention in the poems of *The Circle Game* falls on personae other than the female character, the book can easily be read as her portrait. The collection opens with **"This Is a Photograph of Me,"** which describes the landscape surrounding the lake in which the heroine has recently drowned. In Atwood's wry directions to the viewer lies her admission of the long and difficult process that "surfacing" is to be. First one must realize the need to surface. Identity comes after that, and full definition much later. . . . As the last lines [of **"This Is a Photograph of Me"**] imply, part of that full definition must also come from the viewer/reader/lover. Attention in *The Circle Game* tends to be given more regularly to the male persona— he may be disappointing but he is the authority, the determinant. Atwood is not yet able to draw her female characters as if they had distinctive qualities. They are instead mirrors, listeners, watchers. . . . Atwood's eventual development from woman as pupil to the authoritative protagonist of *Lady Oracle* illustrates well the journey to self-definition.

That Atwood has excluded so many of these poems first published in *The Circle Game* from her 1976 *Selected Poems* suggests that—for all their thematic accuracy—she finds them less satisfying as poems than some later work. Perhaps the very directness and flat diction that in the sixties appeared to be strengths had grown comparatively uninteresting, for Atwood later set her direct statements in more metaphorical contexts, and often avoided making statements at all, unless they were ironic. She also began the search for poetic personae other than the woman-lover of the poems in *The Circle Game.*

In *The Animals in That Country* she wrote about anthropomorphic characters who seemed to represent the human types already drawn in her early poems. Metaphor suffuses these poems. . . . The young feminine persona remains submissive, coerced into action, dissatisfied with what choices do exist—and with her decisions about those choices. Repeatedly, she wrongs herself, whether she takes in **"A Foundling"** or blurs into the obliging lover ("more and more frequently the edges / of me dissolve and I become / a wish"). (pp. 85-7)

Her experiments here with varying rhythms and tones probably equipped her to catch the ambivalent persona of the book-length sequence of poems, *The Journals of Susanna Moodie (1970).* Her achievement in this collection is to present a protagonist believable in her conflicts. Through Moodie/Atwood, we experience hope, anguish, fear, joy, resignation, and anger. It may be more important for the thematic development of Atwood's poetry that we experience the paradox of Canadian nationalism. Like Atwood, Moodie wrote enthusiastically about life in Canada yet her journals also showed her real fear of the wild, the primitive, the untamed. (p. 87)

The character of Susanna Moodie becomes a perfect mask for the journey to self-exploration that Atwood attempts. Her statement "Whether the wilderness is / real or not / depends on who lives there" sounds much like Atwood's later surfacer. **"Looking in a Mirror"** and **"The Wereman"** repeat this theme of unwitting metamorphosis, identity shaped by the wilderness and its arduous living. Not all changes are negative, however; and one of the results of this acrid confrontation with natural forces is an acceptance of dream knowledge. . . .

Published in the same year as the Susanna Moodie collection, Atwood's *Procedures for Underground* has as central persona a pioneer woman, whose memories seem to be given voice as she looks at old photographs. Her family, the old cabin, hard winters, her husband—she speaks with a spare wisdom, moving easily between fact and dream, myth and custom. In **"Procedures for Underground"** she speaks as a Persephone who has gone below, been tested, learned "wisdom and great power," but returns to live separate, feared, from her companions. Knowledge of whatever source is the prize for Atwood's persona, and many of the poems in the collection play with the definition of truth, fact, knowledge, the "search for the actual." In some of the poems Atwood moves to present-day Canada and continues the theme of search through the sexual power conflict that is to be the subject of her 1971 *Power Politics.* (p. 88)

Power Politics is Atwood's comic scenario of the themes she had treated with relative sombreness in *Susanna Moodie* and *Underground.* If the former was an exploration of a sentient woman character, caught in and finally able to acknowledge "the inescapable doubleness of her own vision," then *Procedures for Underground* is a survival manual for the kind of learning that a perceptive woman would have to undertake. Handicapped as she is (with her head resting in her "gentle" husband's sack), she must make use of emotion, dream, the occult, the primitive, even the animal to find her way. In *Power Politics* the assumption that any woman's protective male *is* her handicap becomes a given, and the fun in the book comes through Atwood's myriad inventive descriptions of the power struggle—as politics, war, physical waste, innuendo, sly attack. (pp. 88-9)

One of the changes Atwood made in choosing work for *Selected Poems* was to omit many of the poems in *Power Politics* that were titled as if for stage directions: **"He reappears," "He is a strange biological phenomenon," "He is last seen."** By emphasizing instead poems about the two people in the relationship, and often the woman, she manages to reverse the expected power positions. In *Selected Poems* the male ego is less often central. The collection as represented in the 1976 book thus meshes more closely with Atwood's earlier poems, in which the female persona often moves independently on her search for self-awareness, although in her omissions Atwood has deleted some poems important to thematic strains. **"Small Tactics,"** for example, a seven-part sequence in *Power Politics,* relates the war games described in this collection to those of **"The Circle Game,"** but here the feminine voice laments, "Let's go back please / to the games, they were / more fun and less painful." . . . More often, in [*Selected Poems*], the woman is wise and loving, ready to admit her own necessary anger, but not misshapen by it. (p. 90)

Atwood's reasons for deleting [the] powerful poem [**"He is last seen"**] with its important recognition of dual emotions remain unexplained, but the poem does picture the male as dominant—decisive, aggressive—in ways that tend to contrast with the transformation and Circe poems of *You Are Happy.* In tone, however, in the strong balance of antipathy and desire, it leads [towards the poems of *You Are Happy*] with its somewhat richer diction and more varied rhythms.

The ironically generous central persona of *You Are Happy* is Atwood's fully-realized female—maker, poet, lover, prophet—a Circe with the power to change all men into animals, all men except Odysseus. Her capacity to control and yet give marks her as truly royal; her sometimes coy reluctance to accept praise suggests her basic awareness of the futility of bucking convention. Her powers may be dramatic, as the poems of

"Songs of the Transformed" indicate, but they are limited to the physical, and fragile compared to the "wrecked words" Circe laments. Powerful as she is, Circe still cannot create words, and it is words for which her people beg. (pp. 92-3)

Circe differs from Atwood's earlier protagonists in that she is more aware of inhibiting mythologies. Her great understanding—of individuals as well as of patterns and cultural expectations—sharpens her perception but does not make her less vulnerable. (p. 93)

As Odysseus' dissatisfaction [with Circe] grows (his basic greed is impossible to satisfy), he thinks often of Penelope, and Circe realizes the wife's power to draw him back. . . . At the base of reality is the word. Despite omens and auguries, fire signs and bird flights, happenings return to the word, as Odysseus did:

> You move within range of my words
> you land on the dry shore
> You find what there is . . .

Atwood changes the image of conquering male into the image of man lured by a subtler power. Verbal magic bests physical force; feminine wiles and words convince the male persona—no matter what the circumstance—that "you are happy." The ambivalence of the opening poem, **"Newsreel: Man and Firing Squad"** suggests the transitory and often indefinable quality of any happiness. One learns to say *No* to the most unpleasant of life's experiences; one counters fate and myth with strategy; one develops powers of his or her own kind and value, and for the poet, those powers are verbal. . . .

Atwood's poems suggest that the range of human promise is wide, that exploring that range—for woman, man, artist, or lover—should be a primary life experience: "To learn how to live," "to choose," "to be also human," and as culmination, "to surface." (p. 94)

Linda W. Wagner, "The Making of 'Selected Poems', the Process of Surfacing," in *The Art of Margaret Atwood: Essays in Criticism,* edited by Arnold E. Davidson and Cathy N. Davidson, Toronto: House of Anansi Press, 1981, pp. 81-94.

LEE BRISCOE THOMPSON
(essay date 1981)

[In the following excerpt, Thompson offers a detailed survey of Atwood's short story collection *Dancing Girls*, a volume that collects individual pieces spanning the years 1964 to 1977.]

Two-headed poems; polarities, mythic reversals: it may be from Margaret Atwood's own delight in oppositions

Original manuscript page of Atwood's *The Handmaid's Tale*.

and strong contradictions that critics often take their cue. One notices, at any rate, a tendency for commentators to deplore or dwell exclusively upon the clinical chill, the frightening detachment in Atwood's poetry, at the same time as they often criticize her fiction, particularly *The Edible Woman* and *Lady Oracle*, as shallow, flippant, frivolous, with silly protagonists, in a phrase, "not the essential Atwood." The poetry is seen as cold, strange, mythical, ritualistic, while the prose is considered comparatively warm, full of common touches and ordinary bumblers; one intense and austere, the other almost frothy, rambling, diffused; one humourless, the other marked by considerable (to some tastes, too much) humour. This polarized view, while rarely pushed and almost always obliged to ignore *Surfacing* or term it a "poetic novel," implies a schizophrenia, a two-headedness of the poet, two separate and distinct psyches joined only at the body level for the mechanical purposes of writing and never overlapping territories.

For this interpretation there is reinforcement in Atwood's own analysis of her endeavours in verse and fiction. Interviewed for *The New York Times* by novelist Joyce Carol Oates, Atwood was reminded that "You work with a number of different 'voices' in your poetry and prose," and asked, "Have you ever felt that the discipline of prose evokes a somewhat different 'personality' (or consciousness) than the discipline of poetry?" Atwood replied, "Not just a 'somewhat different' personality, an almost totally different one. Though readers and critics, of course, make connections because the same name appears on these different forms, I'd make a bet that I could invent a pseudonym for a reviewer and that no one would guess it was me." She explained, further, that "Poetry is the most joyful form, and prose fiction—the personality I feel there is a curious, often bemused, sometimes disheartened observer of society." The appended remark, like a T. S. Eliot footnote, raises more questions than it answers. Poetry joyful? She must mean in its tight, rich creation, its soarings and plunges, its sophisticated levels of "naming." And the narrators of many of her fictions are indeed puzzled, uncertain, frequently demoralized. In this they stand contrasted to the assured tone of some of her poetic personae. But to argue that a reader is prompted to connect the fiction and poetry solely by the appearance of Atwood's name on both is to overlook or pay insufficient attention to importantly congruent elements which unify the genres. In so saying, Atwood underrates the organic quality of her writing. (pp. 107-08)

Nevertheless Atwood's idea of two voices has a superficial validity, in that pulse readings of *Lady Oracle, Edible Woman,* and many of Atwood's short pieces undeniably detect a somewhat sunnier, more 'ordinary' approach to the universe than the bulk of Atwood's poetry. John Metcalf has pointed to the short story as the literary form closest to poetry by virtue of its intensity, brevity, and striving for a single effect. Assuming that

is correct, one could then regard Atwood's short fiction, specifically her 1977 volume, *Dancing Girls,* as a visible bridge between the dominant 'voices' of her poetry and her long fiction. There are bemused fictive narrators, it is true, but there are also the characteristics of the poetry, especially the madness, the heightened consciousness, the mythic elements. Rather than speak in a voice utterly different from that of her verse, the short stories share the non-rational attributes of the poetry, and mingle the qualities of the mundane (minuets) and the poetic/mythic (madness) which have been misrepresented by some as exclusive to prose and poetry respectively.

The fourteen stories which appear in the Canadian version of *Dancing Girls* are resistant to glib systematization in that their original, individual publication spans fourteen years, from 1964 through 1977. Let us for convenience retain the loose terms "minuet" and "madness" to refer to the headsets which Atwood has suggested dominate her writing of prose and poetry. One is inclined to set in the "minuets" category: **"The War in the Bathroom," "The Man from Mars," "Rape Fantasies," "The Grave of the Famous Poet," "Hair Jewellery," "Training," "Lives of the Poets," "The Resplendent Quetzal," "Dancing Girls,"** and perhaps **"A Travel Piece"** and **"Giving Birth."** Eleven out of fourteen: only **"Polarities," "When It Happens,"** and **"Under Glass"** seem to commit themselves totally and immediately to the world of madness, in the dance metaphor a "danse macabre." Under examination, however, one finds that even these categories within categories, these voices within a genre, fluctuate and transform themselves. In the work of a lover of metamorphoses, surely this is to be expected.

"The War in the Bathroom" is a week in the life of a typical Atwood character—rootless, alienated, meticulous, relentlessly self-analytic, keeping madness at bay only by a series of rituals and inventories. Using the first person narration throughout, the story presents a deliberately ambiguous relationship between the narrator and the "she" whose slightest movements are described. Is it a mind-body split we are overhearing? A spontaneous, self-indulgent persona fused with a disciplined, self-denying persona? The reader rummages for signals among the domestic details, the small joys and sorrows, coming up with only indirect evidence of time (modern, with supermarkets, fridges, apartments, and current products) and place (somewhere North American, far enough north to have snow) and no concrete bearings on the situation. But the narrator is not doing much better than the reader, carefully cataloguing everything to achieve the illusion of control. The minuet is reinforced by small standards ("I draw the line at margarine"), the madness by paranoia (suspicions of a checkout girl, of the German woman). The unsettling duality on the narrator's side of the apartment wall becomes echoed on Tuesday, the second day of the "diary" by the emergence of two voices in the next-door communal bathroom, one high and querulous, the other an urgent whisper, like daylight and nighttime selves. The narrator assumes that it is one person rather more swiftly than even the hearing of single footsteps would explain; this encourages the reader to notice that the puzzling and parallel "I-she" split is clarifying along lines of "she" doing all the physical action and "I" doing all the cerebral action and direction. "Perhaps she is a foreigner," the narrator guesses of the dual voices by Friday, forging yet another link between Atwood's poetry and fiction. On all fronts, one is a stranger confronted by foreigners, an alien subtly warring with aliens.

Actually the major war in this story focusses not on the enigmatic voices (whose secret is resolved before the week is up) but on a consumptive old man, a fellow tenant of the apartment block. The narrator takes an excessive and cruel dislike to him on account of his compulsively regular schedule in the bathroom, despite—possibly because of—her(?) own compulsiveness. (One is tempted to comparisons with such poems as "Roominghouse, Winter" and must fight the impulse to wander into a lengthy digression on bathrooms in Atwood's work.) The story concludes on the same terms as almost all of Atwood's poetry and fiction, the view of life as a series of small, uncertain battles on the fringe of madness: "For the time being I have won."

"The Man from Mars" presents a mother and daughter team much like the one in *Lady Oracle:* a fragile, dainty mom trying to manipulate a King Kong daughter. And like the fat Joan in *Lady Oracle,* Christine fits a dominant pattern of Atwoodian women: manless, acutely self-aware, inclined to animal imagery in her description of herself and others, making a wry, running commentary upon life in general and in particular. The narrator, while in the third person, concentrates on Christine's point of view. And the gothic combinations of pursuit, flight, and terror which play such large parts in *Lady Oracle, Surfacing,* and some of the poetry turn up here as the centre both hilarious and horrible of the story.

The title is a tip-off to the transitional quality of the tale: the foreigner again, here explicitly identified as about as alien as the common stock of metaphors permits: a Martian, a creature from other worlds. With that starting point, the movement of the story is rhythmic: the less-than-attractive Christine, whose life is so dull that she dreads the end of the school year; the slide into a magic, slightly mad phase, as she is mysteriously, hotly pursued by the "person from another culture"; the escalation of mystery into nightmare as she begins to brood over blood-drenched visions of assault and murder. The recession into mediocrity, the removal of the Martian/mystery/madness, finds Christine re-

membering her now romanticized pursuer and, when he is proclaimed "nuts," countering defensively that there is "more than one way of being sane." Graduation with mediocre grades is followed by a tolerable career and an adequate little life. Near the conclusion the Vietnamese conflict makes for a flickering revival of exoticism and Christine finds "the distant country becoming almost more familiar to her than her own" (a characteristic Atwood reversal). Predictably, however, the mood threatens again to become madness (shades of the poem "It Is Dangerous to Read Newspapers"); the new nightmare visions provoke a deliberate retreat into the mundane, out of graphic modern television into genteel nineteenth-century novels and a carefully nondescript, domesticated final view. A certain control has been regained but only to the tenuous degree familiar throughout Atwood's writings.

The title story, **"Dancing Girls"**, autobiographically set in the United States in the 1960s with a female grad student protagonist from Toronto, aligns itself with **"The War in the Bathroom"** in its boarding-house cheapness and with **"The Man from Mars"** in Ann's "encountering" another alien male, an Arab neighbour. Ann and her landlady, while staunchly defending the prosaic side of life, are acutely aware of and fascinated by the exotic and alien: Turkish Lelah with her gypsy earrings and gold tooth, the tattooed Arab with his noisy partying, dancing girls, and vacuumed-up dirt. Indeed, these polarities give Atwood a chance to voice the chagrin Canadians so often feel at the American view that "You're not, like, foreign." Parallel to the paradoxical approach-avoidance Atwood's characters experience regarding Gothic pursuers is the web of contradictory responses concerning aliens and alienation. One wants, simply, to be different—but not too different; the balance is rarely managed; hence the metaphor of the dance. And in a deft pirouette, Atwood casts the sober landlady and her sort as "cold, mad people" in the eyes of the amazed, terrified, and pursued alien. A wistful conclusion underscores the longing of so many of Atwood's creatures, from pioneer to highrise dweller, for escape, for gentle, green spaces, for a world where human contact is no longer measured out in razors in the bathroom or hair in the drain.

Four of the short stories in this collection concentrate on late stages of what Chaucer called the "olde daunce," the minuet between the sexes, and one finds again polarities of vulnerability and insensitivity, control and chaos, humour and rage. The war dance is cast, typically for this writer, as trivial guerilla warfare rather than overt bloodshed: surface minuet and subliminal massacre; it is this observance of the properties, this staying miserably within the rules of the dance floor, that gives the impact of a particularly Canadian truth.

"The Grave of the Famous Poet" and **"Hair Jewellery"** speak through the predominant Atwood voice, first person *very* singular female. **"The Grave of the Famous Poet"** involves the imminent split-up with an as-usual nameless "him." There is an emphasis on alienation, contrasted with the man and woman's joint purpose of a literary pilgrimage in England. The story ties itself closely to Atwood's poetry in its clinical tone, its emphasis on victimhood, emotional paralysis, traps and helplessness. **"Hair Jewellery,"** dealing with similar circumstances, handles it somewhat differently. The diction is more formal, its self-consciousness the trademark of the literary academic (Atwood *and* her character), the analysis and delivery more amusing. Speaking of her preference for the safety of unrequited love, the narrator explains to her lover of long ago:

> If, as had happened several times, my love was requited, if it became a question of the future, of making a decision that would lead inevitably to the sound of one's beloved shaving with an electric razor while one scraped congealed egg from his breakfast plate, I was filled with panic. . . . What Psyche saw with the candle was not a god with wings but a pigeonchested youth with pimples, and that's why it took her so long to win her way back to true love. It is easier to love a daemon than a man, though less heroic.
> You were, of course, the perfect object. No banal shadow of lawnmowers and bungalows lurked in your melancholy eyes, opaque as black marble, recondite as urns, you coughed like Roderick Usher, you were, in your own eyes and therefore in mine, doomed and restless as Dracula. Why is it that dolefulness and a sense of futility are so irresistible to young women?

She fluctuates, as we have seen elsewhere, between the mundane world of Filene's bargain basement and the Gothic horrors of such moments as the boyfriend's hand on her throat and announcement that he is the Boston Strangler. But in this story, the sequel to terror is regularly ironic humour and then wistful, romantic melancholy, a posture with implicit self-mockery. One realizes at the last the appropriateness of the title **"Hair Jewellery"**—memorial jewellery made from the hair of the dear departed—for the story presents just such dusty, obsolete, romantic kitsch, with all the right macabre undertones.

"The Resplendent Quetzal" carries on the basically humane tone of **"Hair Jewellery,"** but offers this time a bit of insight into both dance partners' steps. The story makes use of dramatic, mythic, poetic effects from the very first line: "Sarah was sitting near the edge of the sacrificial well." However, Atwoodian *reductio* operates throughout; here, "Sarah thought there might be some point to being a sacrificial victim if the well were nicer, but you would never get her to jump into a muddy hole like that." Her husband, Edward, exhibits the same vacillation between fantasies of the mythic past and glum realization of modern mediocrity; his vi-

sion of himself, "in the feathered costume of the high priest, sprinkl[ing] her with blood drawn with thorns from his own tongue and penis," becomes debased to a Grade Six special project with scale models of the temples, slides, canned tortillas and tamales. Atwood tells of an abrupt reversal of roles near the end. Yet, even in the intense scene of ritual sacrifice of the doll baby, practical Sarah has noted wrinkles in her skirt and the likelihood of more flea bites. A moment of potential reconciliation or at least the introduction of strangers arises:

> Sarah took her hands away from her face, and as she did so Edward felt cold fear. Surely what he would see would be the face of someone else, someone entirely different, a woman he had never seen before in his life. Or there would be no face at all. But (and this was almost worse) it was only Sarah, looking much as she always did.

The still point at the centre of the dance between the mundane and the mad has been reached again.

The fourth of the stories about deteriorated romance is **"The Lives of the Poets,"** which opens with Julia speaking but, as she realizes her lack of control, shifts quickly into third person. Starting with the indignities of an actual, boring nosebleed, the tale alternates complexly through relationships not only between lovers but also between a person and his environment, a writer and his audience, words and the mind, reality and metaphor, before coming to a closing drenched in symbolic blood. In the midst of increasing emotional pain, Julia humorously anatomizes the small idiocies of the visiting poet's lot. Once more Atwood's conclusion combines the self-deprecating wit of an edible woman with the raging, apocalyptic visions of many of her poetic personae:

> They park the virtuous car and she is led by the two young men into the auditorium, grey cinderblock, where a gathering of polite faces waits to hear the word. Hands will clap, things will be said about her, nothing astonishing, she is supposed to be good for them, they must open their mouths and take her in, like vitamins, like bland medicine. No. No sweet identity, she will clench herself against it. She will step across the stage, words coiled, she will open her mouth and the room will explode in blood.

The story which best fits the critical stereotype of Atwood's "bubbleheaded/ladies' magazine fiction" (vs. her "serious poetry") is probably **"Rape Fantasies."** Agreed, its lower-middle-class diction, full of babbling asides and slang, is far removed from the fine intuitions of the *Power Politics* voices. And the subject matter, the dynamics of a female office/lunch room and the "girls'" revelations of their extremely unimaginative rape fantasies, hardly seems in the same league as the mythic patterns of *You Are Happy* or the multiple metaphors of *The Journals of Susanna Moodie.* Nevertheless, when the intellectual snobberies are put aside (and appropriately so, since that is one of Atwood's satiric targets here), the narrator does demonstrate an admirable sense of humour, appreciation of the ridiculous, and considerable compassion. For once in Atwood the cutting edge seems thoroughly dulled by the sheer zaniness of the monologue.

One imaginary rapist is "absolutely covered in pimples. So he gets me pinned against the wall, he's short but he's heavy, and he starts to undo himself and the zipper gets stuck. I mean, one of the most significant moments in a girl's life, it's almost like getting married or having a baby or something, and he sticks the zipper." She ends up drawing him out and referring him to a dermatologist. In another incarnation, she and the rapist are both slowed down by ferocious head-colds, which make the would-be assault "like raping a bottle of LePage's mucilage the way my nose is running." The cheerful remedy here is conversation, Neo-Citran and Scotch, plus the Late Show on the tube. . . . As the reader is introduced to these and other alternatives, it becomes apparent that the naïve narrator's innocent premise is the power of the word. "Like, how could a fellow do that to a person he's just had a long conversation with, once you let them know you're human, you have a life too, I don't see how they could go ahead with it, right?" That we see so easily the flaws in this simplistic and determined optimism serves to underscore a subtle counterpoint Atwood strikes throughout her writing—the actually severe limitations of language, and the doubtfulness of real communication. The sunny normalcy of this lady's world view glosses over a chaotic realm even she must tentatively acknowledge: "I mean, I know [rape] happens but I just don't understand it, that's the part I really don't understand."

What is also noteworthy is that this story explicitly draws men into the circle of victimhood that Atwood tends to populate with women. Rapists, yes, but failed rapists; they are betrayed by their jammed flies, their sinuses, their gullibility, their pimples, their inadequacies. And one sees that the filing clerk's rape fantasies are actually scenarios of kinship, friendship with and support of other mediocre, in fact worse-off, human beings.

"A Travel Piece" also operates in a chatty, colloquial (here third-person) voice, with a heavy measure (even for Atwood) of run-on sentences and comma splices presumably bespeaking a slightly mindless protagonist skimming on the surface of life. The story is less successful than **"Rape Fantasies"** in that we, like Annette, never quite penetrate to the reality of her being. But the juxtaposition of her everlasting calm/numbness with the increasingly dramatic events has a definitely surreal power, and demonstrates ably

Dust jacket of Atwood's *The Handmaid's Tale.*

Atwood's skill at combining minuets and madness, the mundane and the bizarre. Drifting in a life raft after a plane crash, surrounded by masks and bloody markings which it is increasingly hard to remember are merely plastic sandwich trays and lipstick donned for protection against the sun,

> Annette feels she is about to witness something mundane and horrible, doubly so because it will be bathed not in sinister blood-red lighting but in the ordinary sunlight she has walked in all her life. . . . she is . . . stuck in the present, with four Martians and one madman, waiting for her to say something.

Annette's predicament, in Atwood's work, is not all that unusual.

"Training" too concerns itself with emotional paralysis and human inadequacies, but here the reader becomes far more involved. The story centres on the unorthodox relationship of a healthy teenaged boy and a nine-year-old cerebral palsy victim confined to a wheelchair. Jordan's cages are explicit: the uncontrolled body, the "metal net" of machinery upon which she must depend; "that mind trapped and strangling."

Rob's are subtler: his overachieving medical family and their and everyone else's expectations for him; feeling the "bumbling third son in a fairy tale, with no princess and no good luck." Superficial antitheses are set up— the "crips" or the "spazzes" vs. the "norms." Then the distinctions are gradually demolished. Rob feels abnormal regarding his sexuality; the possibility of the healthy person failing to cope with reality introduces madness ("Real life would be too much for him, he would not be able to take it. . . . He would go crazy. He would run out into the snow with no galoshes, he would vanish, he would be lost forever.") And steady-eyed Jordan, meanwhile, comes to represent the honest, psychologically whole person. In the grotesqueries of the compelling conclusion, the polarized worlds are poignantly united in the "danse macabre": the wheelchair square dancers "danced like comic robots. They danced like him."

"Giving Birth," which with **"Training"** and **"Dancing Girls"** comprise the only previously unpublished material in the collection, has been taken by some critics as autobiographical evidence of a mellowing of the formidable Atwood as a result of motherhood. In fact, one reviewer has summarized the story as "good reading for many parents, past or prospective;" another, less pleased, considers it "a mass magazine approach to a lesson in childbirth, tinged, of course, with female chauvinist irony." Sniffs a third, it will have appeal only for those who have "been there."

Certainly the story *is* a detailed account of one birthing experience, told with Atwood's remarkable clarity and precision and having some fun with prenatal classes and maternity fads. It is also correct to say that most readers will notice a warmth and positivity, a wholeness, that is very scarce in Atwood's writings. Nor is the male figure here a nebbish; both the narrator's mate and the pregnant woman's companion, "A.," are supportive, helpful, reasonable, in no way threatening. But Atwood's concerns in the collection have not been abandoned in this, the last story. Split and multiple personalities have appeared elsewhere, and in **"Giving Birth"** one has not only the complications of the narrator differentiating herself from but obviously in some respects coinciding with Jeannie, but also the fluctuating presence of Jeannie's mysterious brown alter ego. There is "pain and terror" as well, an undercurrent of fear, a consideration of death, the need for talismans against the Evil Eye, cages of conventional thought, descent into a "dark place," the "tubular strange apparatus like a science fiction movie," the screams. " 'You see, there was nothing to be afraid of,' A. says before he leaves [after the birth], but he was wrong."

Most important, **"Giving Birth"** tackles yet again Atwood's intense interest in the relationship between language and the body. The story opens with contemplation upon the title phrase and its true meaning. Numerous explanations are discarded; "Thus language muttering in its archaic tongues of something, yet one more thing, that needs to be re-named." The narrator abandons that struggle for the moment, but almost at once resumes it in the form of naming the universe with her child—dog, cat, bluejays, goldfinches, winter. The young daughter "puts her fingers on my lips as I pronounce these words; she hasn't yet learned the secret of making them, I am waiting for her first word; surely it will be miraculous, something that has never yet been said. But if so, perhaps she's already said it and I, in my entrapment, my addiction to the usual, have not heard it." This compares remarkably closely with the considerations of several selections in the recent *Two-Headed Poems,* but also traces its lineage to pieces from *The Journals of Susanna Moodie, Power Politics, The Animals in That Country,* and *Circle Game.* The struggle of birth gives the relationship between flesh and the word a focus, but offers no answers: "indescribable, events of the body . . . ; why should the mind distress itself trying to find a language for them?" When, in the middle of a contraction, a nurse speaks of pain, "*What pain?* Jeannie thinks. When there is no pain she feels nothing, when there is pain, she feels nothing because there is no *she.* This, finally, is the disappearance of language." In a surreal postpartum illusion Jeannie sees the watery fragility of a solid building and is overwhelmed by the enormity of her maternal perception that "the entire earth, the rocks, people, trees, everything needs to be protected, cared for, tended." But that technically mad anxiety is counterbalanced by the normalcy of her baby, "solid, substantial, packed together like an apple. Jeannie examines her, she is complete, and in the days that follow Jeannie herself becomes drifted over with new words, her hair slowly darkens, she ceases to be what she was and is replaced, gradually, by someone else." As with Rob in **"Training,"** too much "reality" might have driven Jeannie permanently insane; protective metamorphosis is a necessity.

The justice of this view is demonstrated by a look at the three short stories one may clearly designate as tales of madness rather than mundane minuets: **"Polarities," "Under Glass,"** and **"When It Happens."** Least successfully realized of the three (and arguably of the entire collection), **"When It Happens"** anticipates the apocalypse with an unruffled certainty and overlay of domestic chores which serves to heighten the atmosphere of insanity. Agreed, the characters, Mrs. Burridge and her husband Frank, are too cardboard and plodding to infuse the contrast of the mundane and the mad (personal and global) with real terror. But the closing intimation of bloody destruction, restrainedly expressed as "the burst of red," juxtaposed with Mrs. Burridge's final housewifely gesture of adding cheese to the shopping list, does play its part in the cumulative effect of *Dancing Girls.*

From the first semi-insane paragraph of **"Under Glass,"** it is clear that this female narrator is holding herself and her universe together with only the flimsiest of threads. She notes with satisfaction that, on this good day, "the trees come solidly up through the earth as though they belong there, nothing wavers. I have confidence in the grass and the distant buildings, they can take care of themselves. . . ." Her identification with the plant world is intimate, speaking as she does from the start of "all of us [greenhouse plants and the narrator] keeping quite still." "Today, however . . . I walk on two legs, I wear clothes," she explains, making a distinction between the human and the natural very near to that of the *Surfacing* narrator. Similarly, it is abundantly clear where her real allegiances lie, how strained her human "affiliation."

As in **"When It Happens,"** the narrator of **"Under Glass"** maintains an impeccably "normal" surface and a deranged interior. The story moves quickly from her vegetarian fantasies into her relationship with a man, the description of which dazzles with its authenticity and all the fancy footwork of the sexual dance. A favourite: "I'm annoyed with him for some reason, though I can't recall which. I thumb through my cardfile of nasty remarks, choose one: You make love like a cowboy raping a sheep." And closer to the bone: "I steer my course so he will have to go through all the puddles. If I can't win, I tell him, neither can you. I was saner then, I had defences."

From contemplation of self as "something altogether different, an artichoke" through her abrupt self-admonition, "None of that," to moving a moment later "about the room in a parody of domesticity," the narrator dances among animal, vegetable, and human incarnations. References abound to animals in zoos, "under glass," hunted, huddled, hiding. Her death fantasy is crazily followed by visions of ducks and a line of cartoon dancing mice. Angered, she uses animal and plant images, serene and "doing nothing," to get a grip on her rage. Estranged from her lover, she feels "bloodless as a mushroom," finds "he's too human." Turning her metaphoric tables when she wants a reconciliation with him, she sees her lover's face as "a paper flower dropped in water," spreading tendrils, becoming "inscrutable as an eggplant." The couple appear to have made up their differences by the conclusion of the story but Atwood inexorably slows the action from the normal, mundane pace of the purposefully departing narrator ("I ponder again his need for more glasses and consider buying him a large bath towel") to the motionless, insane world under glass, the dream of no more dancing, the longing for annihilation or zerodom:

I find myself being moved, gradually, station by station, back towards the 7-B greenhouse. Soon I will be there: inside are the plants that have taught themselves to look like stones. I think of them; they grow silently, hiding in dry soil, minor events, little zeros, containing nothing but themselves; no food value, to the eye soothing and round, then suddenly nowhere. I wonder how long it takes, how they do it.

"Polarities" is the story whose titular metaphor competes most strongly with dance for control of the entire collection. It begins with an excerpt from a Margaret Avison poem which complements the other Margaret's survival ethic of "beyond truth, tenacity":

> Gentle and just pleasure
> It is, being human, to have won from space
> This unchill, habitable interior. . . .
> ("New Year's Poem")

The obvious introductory contrast is between no-nonsense, brisk Louise and shambling, slothful Morrison, a false effect the omniscient narrator begins reversing almost immediately. Louise's progression into complete madness is handled in slyly paradoxical fashion, for her vision of Blakean wholeness looks remarkably reasonable, a sort of metropolitan yin and yang, in comparison with those "sane" friends who eagerly tuck her away in the loony bin and violate her privacy. Like the aphorisms and short poems in her notebooks, "which were thoroughly sane in themselves but which taken together were not," Louise's understanding is frequently perfect, as in her fine assessment of Morrison, even when her total picture is askew. "Morrison is not a complete person. He needs to be completed, he refuses to admit his body is part of his mind. He can be in the circle possibly, but only if he will surrender his role as a fragment and show himself willing to merge with the greater whole." Morrison, rather impressive in his awareness and swift comprehension, interprets Louise correctly in turn: "she's taken as real what the rest of us pretend is only metaphorical."

All these polarities, then: of wholeness and partiality, exposure and retreat, the mind-body split, interchangeable madness and sanity, energy and the inert, decorating apartments and facing the void, zoos and asylums, living colour and glacial whiteness, chosen and involuntary isolation, inclusion and exclusion, the dream of the "unchill, habitable interior" and the reality of Morrison's "chill interior, embryonic and blighted." Morrison, the American, the actual and metaphoric outsider, can understand but not change; the reader's position, Atwood suggests by the act of writing, is less bleak.

Travels through these tales make quite unworkable the Atwoodian notion that her poetry and fiction are expressed in two entirely different, stylistically unrelated, philosophically dissimiliar voices. Two voices there are, and more, but they are found throughout her work and come from a remarkably unified consciousness. It may be that Atwood's theory is subtly related to her own two public faces: mythic Margaret, the fox-woman, laconic even at readings, reserved, cool, detached, distant, vs. earth-mother Maggie on the farm, folksily recommending Aussie french fries and chatting about Jess's cute tricks. Behind the promotional masks, however, Atwood seems to have no confusion about who she is, and reading her stories and poems, her audience has no doubt about the quality of her dance. Proceeding from a single, powerful sensibility, *Dancing Girls* is a virtuoso performance. (pp. 109-22)

Lee Briscoe Thompson, "Minutes and Madness: Margaret Atwood's 'Dancing Girls'," in *The Art of Margaret Atwood: Essays in Criticism,* edited by Arnold E. Davidson and Cathy N. Davidson, Toronto: House of Anansi Press, 1981, pp. 107-22.

AMIN MALAK

(essay date 1987)

[In the following excerpt, Malak examines how Atwood infuses the conventions of the dystopian genre with her own distinctive artistry in *The Handmaid's Tale*.]

One of [*The Handmaid's Tale*'s] successful aspects concerns the skillful portrayal of a state that in theory claims to be founded on Christian principles, yet in practice miserably lacks spirituality and benevolence. The state in Gilead prescribes a pattern of life based on frugality, conformity, censorship, corruption, fear, and terror—in short, the usual terms of existence enforced by totalitarian states, instance of which can be found in such dystopian works as Zamyatin's *We,* Huxley's *Brave New World,* and Orwell's *1984.* (pp. 9-10)

What distinguishes Atwood's novel from those dystopian classics is its obvious feminist focus. Gilead is openly misogynistic, in both its theocracy and practice. The state reduces the handmaids to the slavery status of being mere "breeders." . . . The handmaid's situation lucidly illustrates Simone de Beauvoir's assertion in *The Second Sex* about man defining woman not as an autonomous being but as simply what he decrees to be relative to him: "For him she is sex—absolute sex, no less. She is defined and differentiated with reference to man and not with reference to her; she is the incidental, as opposed to the essential. He is the Subject, he is the Absolute—she is the Other." This view of man's marginalization of woman corroborates Foucault's earlier observation about the power-sex correlative; since man holds the sanctified reigns of power in society, he rules, assigns roles, and decrees after social, religious,

and cosmic concepts convenient to his interests and desires.

However, not all the female characters in Atwood's novel are sympathetic, nor all the male ones demonic. The Aunts, a vicious élite of collaborators who conduct torture lectures, are among the church-state's staunchest supporters; these renegades turn into zealous converts, appropriating male values at the expense of their feminine instincts. One of them, Aunt Lydia, functions, ironically, as the spokesperson of antifeminism; she urges the handmaids to renounce themselves and become non-persons: "Modesty is invisibility, said Aunt Lydia. Never forget it. To be seen—to be *seen*—is to be—her voice trembled—penetrated. What you must be, girls, is impenetrable. She called us girls." On the other hand, Nick, the Commander's chauffeur, is involved with the underground network, of men and women, that aims at rescuing women and conducting sabotage. Besides, Atwood's heroine constantly yearns for her former marriage life with Luke, presently presumed dead. Accordingly, while Atwood poignantly condemns the misogynous mentality that can cause a heavy toll of human suffering, she refrains from convicting a gender in its entirety as the perpetrator of the nightmare that is Gilead. Indeed, we witness very few of the male characters acting with stark cruelty; the narrative reports most of the violent acts after the fact, sparing the reader gory scenes. Even the Commander appears more pathetic than sinister, baffled than manipulative, almost, at times, a Fool.

Some may interpret Atwood's position here as a non-feminist stance, approving of women's status-quo. In a review for the *Times Literary Supplement,* Lorna Sage describes *The Handmaid's Tale* as Atwood's "revisionist look at her more visionary self," and as "a novel in praise of the present, for which, perhaps, you have to have the perspective of dystopia." It is really difficult to conceive Atwood's praising the present, because, like Orwell who in *1984* extrapolated specific ominous events and tendencies in twentieth-century politics, she tries to caution against right-wing fundamentalism, rigid dogmas, and misogynous theosophies that may be currently gaining a deceptive popularity. The novel's mimetic impulse then aims at wresting an imperfect present from a horror-ridden future: it appeals for vigilance, and an appreciation of the mature values of tolerance, compassion, and, above all, for women's unique identity.

The novel's thematics operate by positing polarized extremes: a decadent present, which Aunt Lydia cynically describes as "a society dying . . . of too much choice," and a totalitarian future that prohibits choice. Naturally, while rejecting the indulgent decadence and chaos of an anarchic society, the reader condemns the Gilead regime for its intolerant, prescriptive set of values that projects a tunnel vision on reality and eliminates human volition: "There is more than one kind of freedom, said Aunt Lydia. Freedom to and freedom from. In the days of anarchy, it was freedom to. Now you are being given freedom from. Don't underrate it." As illustrated by the fears and agonies that Offred endures, when human beings are not free to aspire toward whatever they wish, when choices become so severely constrained that, to quote from Dostoyevsky's *The Possessed*, "only the necessary is necessary," life turns into a painfully prolonged prison term. Interestingly, the victimization process does not involve Offred and the handmaids alone, but extends to the oppressors as well. Everyone ruled by the Gilead regime suffers the deprivation of having no choice, except what the church-state decrees; even the Commander is compelled to perform his sexual assignment with Offred as a matter of obligation: "This is no recreation, even for the Commander. This is serious business. The Commander, too, is doing his duty."

Since the inhabitants of Gilead lead the precarious existence befitting victims, most try in varied ways to cope, endure, and survive. This situation of being a victim and trying to survive dramatizes Atwood's major thesis in her critical work *Survival: A Thematic Guide to Canadian Literature,* in which she suggests that Canada, metaphorically still a colony or an oppressed minority, is "a collective victim," and that "the central symbol for Canada . . . is undoubtedly Survival, *la Survivance.*" Atwood, furthermore, enumerates what she labels "basic victim positions," whereby a victim may choose any of four possible options, one of which is to acknowledge being a victim but refuse "to accept the assumption that the role is inevitable." This position fully explains Offred's role as the protagonist-narrator of *The Handmaid's Tale.* Offred's progress as a maturing consciousness is indexed by an evolving awareness of herself as a victimized woman, and then a gradual development toward initiating risky but assertive schemes that break the slavery syndrome. Her double-crossing the Commander and his Wife, her choice to hazard a sexual affair with Nick, and her association with the underground network, all point to the shift from being a helpless victim to being a sly, subversive survivor. This impulse to survive, together with the occasional flashes of warmth and concern among the handmaids, transmits reassuring signs of hope and humanity in an otherwise chilling and depressing tale.

What makes Atwood's book such a moving tale is its clever technique in presenting the heroine initially as a voice, almost like a sleepwalker conceiving disjointed perceptions of its surroundings, as well as flashing reminiscences about a bygone life. As the scenes gather more details, the heroine's voice is steadily and imperceptively, yet convincingly, transfigured into a full-roundedness that parallels her maturing comprehension of what is happening around her. Thus the vic-

tim, manipulated and coerced, is metamorphosed into a determined conniver who daringly violates the perverted canons of Gilead. Moreover, Atwood skilfully manipulates the time sequence between the heroine's past (pre-Gilead life) and the present: those shifting reminiscences offer glimpses of a life, though not ideal, still filled with energy, creativity, humaneness, and a sense of selfhood, a life that sharply contrasts with the alienation, slavery, and suffering under totalitarianism. By the end of the novel, the reader is effectively and conclusively shown how the misogynous regime functions on the basis of power, not choice; coercion, not volition; fear, not desire. In other words, Atwood administers in doses the assaulting shocks to our sensibilities of a grim dystopian nightmare: initially, the narrative voice, distant and almost diffidently void of any emotions, emphasizes those aspects of frugality and solemnity imposed by the state, then progressively tyranny and corruption begin to unfold piecemeal. As the novel concludes, as the horror reaches a climax, the narrative voice assumes a fully engaged emotional tone that cleverly keeps us in suspense about the heroine's fate. This method of measured, well-punctuated revelations about Gilead connects symbolically with the novel's central meaning: misogynous dogmas, no matter how seemingly innocuous and trustworthy they may appear at their initial conception, are bound, when allowed access to power, to reveal their ruthlessly tyrannical nature.

Regardless of the novel's dystopian essence, it nevertheless avoids being solemn; on the contrary, it sustains an ironic texture throughout. We do not find too many frightening images that may compare with Oceana's torture chambers: the few graphic horror scenes are crisply and snappily presented, sparing us a blood-curdling impact. (Some may criticize this restraint as undermining the novel's integrity and emotional validity.) As in all dystopias, Atwood's aim is to encourage the reader to adopt a rational stance that avoids *total* "suspension of disbelief." This rational stance dislocates full emotional involvement in order to create a Brechtian type of alienation that, in turn, generates an ironic charge. This rational stance too should not be total, because Atwood does want us to care sympathetically about her heroine's fate; hence the emotional distance between reader and character must allow for closeness, but up to a point. Furthermore, Atwood is equally keen on preserving the ironic flair intact. No wonder then that she concludes *The Handmaid's Tale* with a climactic moment of irony: she exposes, in a hilarious epilogue, the absurdity and futility of certain academic writings that engage in dull, clinically sceptic analysis of irrelevancies and inanities, yet miss the vital issues. . . . The entire "Historical Notes" at the end of the novel represents a satire on critics who spin out theories about literary or historical texts without genuinely recognizing or experiencing the pathos expressed in them: they circumvent issues, classify data, construct clever hypotheses garbed in ritualistic, fashionable jargon, but no spirited illumination ever comes out of their endeavours. Atwood soberly demonstrates that when a critic or scholar (and by extension a reader) avoids, under the guise of scholarly objectivity, taking a moral or political stand about an issue of crucial magnitude such as totalitarianism, he or she will necessarily become an apologist for evil; more significantly, the applause the speaker receives gives us a further compelling glimpse into a distant future that still harbours strong misogynous tendencies.

While the major dystopian features can clearly be located in *The Handmaid's Tale,* the novel offers two distinct additional features: feminism and irony. Dramatizing the interrelationship between power and sex, the book's feminism, despite condemning male misogynous mentality, upholds and cherishes a man-woman axis; here, feminism functions inclusively rather than exclusively, poignantly rather than stridently, humanely rather than cynically. The novel's ironic tone, on the other hand, betokens a confident narrative strategy that aims at treating a depressing material gently and gradually, yet firmly, openly, and conclusively, thus skilfully succeeding in securing the reader's sympathy and interest. The novel shows Atwood's strengths both as an engaging story-teller and a creator of a sympathetic heroine, and as an articulate craftswoman of a theme that is both current and controversial. As the novel signifies a landmark in the maturing process of Atwood's creative career, her self-assured depiction of the grim dystopian world gives an energetic and meaningful impetus to the genre. (pp. 11-15)

Amin Malak, "Margaret Atwood's 'The Handmaid's Tale' and the Dystopian Tradition," in *Canadian Literature,* No. 112, Spring, 1987, pp. 9-16.

SOURCES FOR FURTHER STUDY

Atwood, Margaret. *Margaret Atwood: Conversations.* Princeton: Ontario Review Press, 1990, 276 p.

> Compilation of twenty-one interviews spanning the years 1972 through 1989 in which Atwood discusses the development of her writing.

Davey, Frank. "Margaret Atwood." In *Profiles in Canadian Literature,* Vol. 2, edited by Jeffrey M. Heath, pp. 57-64. Toronto: Dundurn Press, 1980.

> Concise critical survey of Atwood's writing. The book includes a biographical chronology, bibliography, and a selection of quotes by and about the author.

Davidson, Arnold E., and Davison, Cathy N., eds. *The Art of Margaret Atwood: Essays in Criticism.* Toronto: House of Anansi Press, 1981, 304 p.

> Collection of thirteen essays, including studies of Atwood's place in the Canadian literary tradition, her relationship to feminism, and her use of myth and allegory. Also includes an annotated primary bibliography and a checklist of criticism through 1980.

Grace, Sherrill. *Violent Duality: A Study of Margaret Atwood.* Montreal: Véhicule Press, 1980, 154 p.

> Critical survey of Atwood's work, focusing on the theme of duplicity.

The Malahat Review, No. 41 (January 1977): 223 p.

> Special issue devoted to Atwood, edited by Linda Sandler. Articles include an interview with the author, as well as essays and poems by many notable Canadian authors, including Al Purdy, Susan Musgrave, Jane Rule, and George Woodcock.

Rosenberg, Jerome H. *Margaret Atwood.* Boston: Twayne, 1984, 184 p.

> Critical survey of Atwood's works.

W. H. Auden

1907-1973

(Full name Wystan Hugh Auden) English-born American poet, critic, essayist, dramatist, editor, translator, and librettist.

INTRODUCTION

Auden is one of the preeminent poets of the twentieth century. His poetry centers on moral issues and evidences strong political, social, and psychological orientations. In his work, Auden applied conceptual and scientific knowledge to traditional verse forms and metrical patterns while assimilating the industrial countryside of his youth. He thereby created an allegorical landscape rife with machinery, abandoned mines, and technological references. Commentators agree that Auden's canon represents a quest for a systematic ideology in an increasingly complex world. This search is illuminated in its early stages by the teachings of Sigmund Freud and Karl Marx and later by philosopher Søren Kierkegaard and theologian Reinhold Niebuhr. Auden's poetry is versatile and inventive; ranging from terse, epigrammatic pieces to booklength verse, it incorporates the author's vast knowledge and displays his efforts to discipline his prodigious talent. Affirming Auden's influence on twentieth-century poetry, Seamus Heaney commented: "Auden was an epoch-making poet on public themes, the register of a new sensibility, a great sonneteer, a writer of perfect light verse, a prospector of literature at its most illiterate roots and a dandy of lexicography at its most extravagant reaches."

Auden was born and raised in heavily industrial northern England. His father, a prominent physician whose knowledge extended into the mythology and folklore of his Icelandic ancestry, and his mother, a strict Anglican, both exerted strong influences on Auden's poetry. Auden's early interest in science and engineering earned him a scholarship to Oxford University, where his fascination with poetry caused him to change his field of study to English. His attraction to science never waned, however, and scientific references are frequently found in his poetry. While at Oxford, Auden became familiar with modernist poetry, particularly that of T. S. Eliot, which was to influence his early writing. It was also at Oxford that Auden became the pivotal member of a group of writers that included Stephen Spender, C. Day Lewis, and Louis MacNeice, a collective variously labeled the "Oxford Group" or the "Auden Generation." These authors adhered to various communist and anti-fascist doctrines and expressed in their writings social, political, and economic concerns, all of which are evident in Auden's work of the 1930s.

In 1928, Auden's first book, *Poems,* was privately printed by Stephen Spender. During the same year, T. S. Eliot accepted Auden's verse play *Paid on Both Sides* for publication in his magazine *Criterion.* This play, along with many poems from the 1928 collection, appeared in an early revision of Auden's *Poems* that was published on Eliot's urging in 1930. Critics noted that these early poems display the influences of Thomas Hardy, Laura Riding, Wilfred Owen, and Edward Thomas and commended the collection for its ability, in M. D. Zabel's words, to "evoke a music wholly beyond reason, extraordinarily penetrating and creative in its search for significance behind fact." Stylistically, these poems are fragmentary and terse, relying on concrete images and colloquial language to convey Auden's political and psychological concerns. In his next volume, *The Orators: An English Study* (1932), Auden implemented modernist and surrealist techniques to detail and satirize fascism and the stagnation of British life and institutions, although much of the work consists of private allusions, jokes, and references to his friends. Despite its abstruseness, *The Orators* was praised for its adventurous experimentation with literary styles and lively and original use of English verse and prose. During the next few years, the pieces Auden published in periodicals and anthologies evidenced a gradual change in his verse style. Many of these poems are collected in the 1936 volume *Look, Stranger!* (published in the United States as *On This Island*), in which Auden's development of a highly disciplined style is expressed in the volume's dedication to Erika Mann: "Since the external disorder, and extravagant lies, / . . . What can truth treasure, or heart bless, / But a narrow strictness?" These poems are written in an intensely formal style that appears to eschew Romantic idealism and modernism and is seemingly intended to offset contemporary chaos. The change in Auden's approach prompted Gavin Ewart to comment: "Mr. Auden's verse has undergone a considerable simplification and a more severe formal discipline, emerging both concise and emotive, in the political poems of very great powers and in the love poems . . . of very great sympathy and tenderness."

Auden's poems from the second half of the 1930s evidence his many travels during this period of political turmoil. "Spain," one of his most famous and widely anthologized pieces, is based upon his experiences in that country during the civil war. *Letters from Iceland* (1937), a travel book written in collaboration with MacNeice, contains Auden's poem "Letter to Lord Byron." This long epistle to the author of *Don Juan* derives from that work the metaphor of the journey for artistic growth and displays Auden's mastery of ottava rima, a stanza of eight lines of heroic verse with a rhyme scheme of *abababcc. Journey to War,* a book about China written with Christopher Isherwood in 1939, features Auden's sonnet sequence and verse commentary "In Time of War." The first half of the sequence recounts the history of humanity's move away from rational thought, while the second half addresses the moral problems faced by humankind on the verge of another world war.

Auden left England in 1939 and became a citizen of the United States. His first book as an emigrant, *Another Time* (1940), contains some of his best-known poems, among them "September 1, 1939," "Musée des Beaux Arts," and "Lay Your Sleeping Head, My Love." *Another Time* also contains elegies to A. E. Housman, Matthew Arnold, and William Butler Yeats, from whose careers and aesthetic concerns Auden was beginning to develop his own artistic credo. A famous line from "In Memory of W. B. Yeats"—"Poetry makes nothing happen"—presents Auden's complete rejection of romantic tenets. Auden's increasing concentration on ethical concerns in *Another Time* points to his reconversion to Christianity, which he had abandoned at age 15. His reconversion was influenced by his disillusionment with secular political solutions, his reading of the works of Kierkegaard, and his personal friendships with Niebuhr and theological writer Charles Williams. These concerns are central to *The Double Man* (1941) and *For the Time Being* (1944). *The Double Man* contains "New Year Letter," a long epistolary poem outlining Auden's readings of Christian literature, while *For the Time Being* features two allegorical pieces, the title poem and *The Sea and the Mirror: A Commentary on Shakespeare's "Tempest,"* that present in prose and verse the author's views on art and life. The poem *For the Time Being* is a rendering of the Nativity that utilizes technical language derived from modern science and psychology in order to rationalize Christian faith. Even more ambitious is *The Sea and the Mirror,* considered by many critics to be Auden's best extended poem. Taking characters from *The Tempest, The Sea and the Mirror* represents, according to Herbert Greenberg, "Auden's conception of the true function of art; both mimetic and paradigmatic, its purpose is not only to show us as we truly are but also, by its example of order, to suggest that we might be different and better."

Auden's next volume, *The Collected Poetry*

(1945), in which he revised, retitled, or excluded many of his earlier poems, helped solidify his reputation as a major poet. *The Age of Anxiety: A Baroque Eclogue* (1947), winner of the Pulitzer Prize for poetry, features four characters of disparate backgrounds who meet in a New York City bar during World War II. Written in the heavily alliterative style of Old English literature, the poem explores the attempts of the protagonists to comprehend themselves and the world in which they live. The characters fail to attain self-realization and succumb to their immediate desires rather than adhering to a spiritual faith. Auden's next major work, *Nones* (1951), includes another widely anthologized piece, "In Praise of Limestone," and the first poems of the "Horae Canonicae" sequence. This sequence, and another entitled "Bucolics," are contained in *The Shield of Achilles* (1955), for which Auden received the National Book Award. These works, though less overtly Christian in content, are serene meditations on human existence informed by the philosophy of Martin Heidegger, historical events of the Christian church, and elements of nature. *Homage to Clio* (1960), in similar fashion, begins the sequence "Thanksgiving for a Habitat," which appeared in its entirety in *About the House* in 1965. In these poems, Auden expressed the conflict between the private and public spheres of an artist's life.

In his later years, Auden wrote three more major volumes—*City without Walls and Many Other Poems* (1969), *Epistle to a Godson and Other Poems* (1972), and the posthumously published *Thank You, Fog: Last Poems* (1974). All three works are noted for their lexical range and humanitarian content. Auden's penchant for altering and discarding poems has prompted the publication of several anthologies since his death. The 1976 *Collected Poems* is faithful to Auden's last revisions, while *The English Auden: Poems, Essays, and Dramatic Writings, 1927-1939* (1977) includes the original versions of Auden's early writings as well as portions of his dramatic and critical pieces. Included in *The English Auden* is an uncompleted work, *The Prolific and the Devourer*, an epigrammatic piece written in the manner of Blaise Pascal and William Blake.

Auden's career has undergone much re-evaluation through the years. While some critics contend that he wrote his finest work when his political sentiments were less obscured by religion and philosophy, others defend his later material as the work of a highly original and mature intellect. Many critics echo the assessment of Auden's career by the National Book Committee, which awarded him the National Medal for Literature in 1967: "[Auden's poetry] has illuminated our lives and times with grace, wit and vitality. His work, branded by the moral and ideological fires of our age, breathes with eloquence, perception and intellectual power."

(For further information about Auden's life and works, see *Contemporary Authors*, Vols. 9-12, 45-48 [obituary]; *Contemporary Authors New Revision Series*, Vol. 5; *Contemporary Literary Criticism*, Vols. 1, 2, 3, 4, 6, 9, 11, 14, 43; *Dictionary of Literary Biography*, Vols. 10, 20; *Major 20th-Century Writers*; and *Poetry Criticism*, Vol. 1.)

CRITICAL COMMENTARY

RANDALL JARRELL
(essay date 1941)

[Jarrell was an acclaimed American literary critic and poet. He is perhaps best known for his war poems and his often acerbic reviews of the literary works of his contemporaries. In the following excerpt, he analyzes the "general position" Auden made for himself in his early poems and compares it with the attitude evident in his later poems.]

The date is *c.* 1930, the place England. Auden (and the group of friends with whom he identifies himself) is unable or unwilling to accept the values and authority, the general world-picture of the late-capitalist society in which he finds himself. He is conscious of a profound alienation, intellectual, moral, and aesthetic—financial and sexual, even. Since he rejects the established order, it is necessary for him to find or make a new order, a myth by which he and his can possess the world. Auden synthesizes (more or less as the digestive organs synthesize enzymes) his own order from a number of sources: I. Marx—communism in general. 2. Freud and Groddeck: in general, the risky and non-scientific, but fertile and imaginative, side of modern psychology. 3. A cluster of related sources: the folk, the blood, intuition, religion and mysticism, fairy tales, parables, and so forth—this group includes a number of semi-Fascist elements. 4. The sciences, biology particularly: these seem to be available to him because they have been only partially assimilated by capitalist culture, and because, like mathematics, they are practically incapable of being corrupted by it. 5. All sorts of

Principal Works

Poems (poetry) 1928; revised editions, 1933, 1960, 1965

Paid on Both Sides: A Charade (verse drama) 1930; published in periodical Criterion

The Ascent of F6: A Tragedy in Two Acts (drama) 1931

The Orators: An English Study (poetry) 1932; revised edition, 1967

The Dance of Death (drama) 1934

The Dog beneath the Skin; or, Where Is Francis? (drama) 1936

Look, Stranger! (poetry) 1936; also published as On This Island, 1937

Letters from Iceland [with Louis MacNeice] (poetry) 1937; revised edition, 1969

Spain (poetry) 1937

The Oxford Book of Light Verse [editor] (anthology) 1938

Selected Poems (poetry) 1938

Journey to a War [with Christopher Isherwood] (poetry) 1939; revised edition, 1973

Another Time (poetry) 1940

Some Poems (poetry) 1940

The Double Man (poetry) 1941; also published as New Year Letter, 1941

The Rocking-Horse Winner (radio play) 1941

Three Songs for St. Cecilia's Day (poetry) 1941

For the Time Being (poetry) 1944

The Collected Poetry of W. H. Auden (poetry) 1945

The Age of Anxiety: A Baroque Eclogue (poetry) 1947

Collected Shorter Poems, 1930-44 (poetry) 1950

The Enchafed Flood (essays and criticism) 1950

Nones (poetry) 1951

Mountains (poetry) 1954

The Shield of Achilles (poetry) 1955

The Old Man's Road (poetry) 1956

A Gobble Poem (poetry) 1957

Selected Poetry (poetry) 1959; revised edition, 1971

Homage to Clio (poetry) 1960

W. H. Auden: A Selection (poetry) 1961

The Dyer's Hand, and Other Essays (criticism) 1962

The Common Life (poetry) 1964

Selected Essays (essays and criticism) 1964

About the House (poetry) 1965

The Cave of the Making (poetry) 1965

Half-Way (poetry) 1965

The Platonic Blow (poetry) 1965

Collected Shorter Poems, 1927-57 (poetry) 1966

Marginalia (poetry) 1966

Portraits (poetry) 1966

A Selection by the Author (poetry) 1967

Collected Longer Poems (poetry) 1968

Selected Poems (poetry) 1968; revised edition, 1979

Two Songs (poetry) 1968

City without Walls and Many Other Poems (poetry) 1969

A Certain World: A Commonplace Book (annotated personal anthology) 1970

Academic Graffiti (poetry) 1971

Epistle to Godson and Other Poems (poetry) 1972

Selected Poems [with Leif Sjoeberg] (poetry) 1972

Forewords and Afterwords (essays and criticism) 1973

Thank You, Fog: Last Poems (poetry) 1974

Collected Poems (poetry) 1976

The English Auden: Poems, Essays and Dramatic Writings, 1927-1939 (poetry) 1977

---

boyish sources of value: flying, polar exploration, mountain-climbing, fighting, the thrilling side of science, public-school life, sports, big-scale practical jokes, "the spies' career," etc. 6. Homosexuality: if the ordinary sexual values are taken as negative and rejected, this can be accepted as a source of positive revolutionary values.

Auden is able to set up a We (whom he identifies himself with—rejection loves company) in opposition to the enemy They; neither We nor They are the relatively distinct or simple entities one finds in political or economic analyses, but are tremendous clusters of elements derived from almost every source: Auden is interested in establishing a dichotomy in which one side, naturally, gets all the worst of it, and he wants this *all the worst* to be as complete as possible, to cover everything from imperialism to underlining too many words

in letters. A reader may be indifferent to some or most of Their bad points, but They are given so many that even the most confirmed ostrich will at some point break down and consent to Auden's rejection. Auden wants a total war, a total victory; he does not make the political mistake of taking over a clear limited position and leaving to the enemy everything else. Sometimes his aptitude for giving all he likes to Us, all he doesn't like to Them, passes over from ingenuity into positive genius—or disingenuousness. I am going to treat this We-They opposition at the greatest length—a treatment of it is practically a treatment of Auden's early position; and I shall mix in some discussion of the sources of value I have listed.

Auden begins: The death of the old order is inevitable; it is already economically unsound, morally corrupt, intellectually bankrupt, and so forth. We—the

Future, They—the Past. (So any reader tends to string along with Us and that perpetual winner, the Future.) Auden gets this from Marxism, of course; but never at any time was he a thorough Marxist: it would have meant giving up too much to the enemy. He keeps all sorts of things a Marxist rejects, and some of his most cherished doctrines—as the reader will see—are in direct contradiction to his Marxism. At the ultimate compulsive level of belief most of his Marxism drops away (and, in the last few years, *has* dropped away); his psychoanalytical, vaguely medical beliefs are so much more essential to Auden—"son of a nurse and doctor, loaned a dream"—that the fables he may have wanted to make Marxist always turn out to be psychoanalytical. But Marxism as a source of energy, of active and tragic insight, was invaluable; it was badly needed to counteract the passivity, the trust in Understanding and Love and God, that are endemic in Auden. Marxism has always supplied most of the terror in his poetry; in his latest poems all that remains is the pity—an invalid's diet, like milk-toast.

Obviously They represent Business, Industrialism, Exploitation—and, worse than that, a failing business, an industrialism whose machines are already rusting. Auden had seen what happened to England during a long depression, and he made a romantic and beautifully effective extension of this, not merely into decadence, but into an actual breakdown of the whole machinery, a Wellsish state where commerce and transportation have gone to pieces, where the ships lie "long high and dry," where no one goes "further than railhead or the end of pier," where the professional traveler "asked at fireside . . . is dumb." The finest of these [is **"Poem XXV"**] in *Poems*: history before the event, one's susceptible and extravagant heart tells one. (Incidentally, this vision is entirely nonMarxist.) Here Auden finds a symbol whose variants are obsessive for him, reasonably so for the reader, another machine's child: *grass-grown pitbank, abandoned seam, the silted harbors, derelict works*—these, and the wires that carry nothing, the rails over which no one comes, are completely moving to Auden, a boy who wanted to be a mining engineer, who "Loved a pumping-engine, / Thought it every bit as / Beautiful as you." The thought of those "beautiful machines that never talked / But let the small boy worship them," abandoned and rusting in the wet countryside—the early Auden sees even his machines in rural surroundings—was perhaps, unconsciously, quite as influential as some political or humanitarian considerations.

Auden relates science to Marxism in an unexpected but perfectly orthodox way: Lenin says somewhere that in the most general sense Marxism is a theory of evolution. Auden quite consciously makes this connection; evolution, as a source both of insight and image, is always just at the back of his earliest poems. (This,

along with his countryishness—Auden began by writing poetry like Hardy and Thomas—explains his endless procession of birds and beasts, symbols hardly an early poem is without.) ["**Poem IV**" in the same collection] is nothing but an account of evolution—by some neo-Hardyish *I* behind it—and a rather Marxist extension of it into man's history and everyday life. The critical points where quantity changes into quality, the Hegelian dialectic, what Burke calls neo-Malthusian limits—all these are plain in the poem. There are many examples of this coalition of Marxism and biology; probably the prettiest is ["**Poem IX**"] a poem with the refrain, "Here am I, here are you: / But what does it mean? What are we going to do?" The *I* of the poem is supposed to be anonymous and typical, a lay-figure of late capitalism; he has not retained even the dignity of rhetoric, but speaks in a style that is an odd blank parody of popular songs. He has finally arrived at the end of his blind alley: he has a wife, a car, a mother-complex, a vacation, and no use or desire for any. All he can make himself ask for is some fresh tea, some rugs—this to remind you of Auden's favorite view of capitalism: a society where everyone is sick. Even his instincts have broken down: he doesn't want to go to bed with Honey, all the wires to the base in his spine are severed. The poem develops in this way up to the next to the last stanza: "In my veins there is a wish, / And a memory of fish: / When I lie crying on the floor, / It says, 'You've often done this before.' " The "wish" in the blood is the evolutionary will, the blind urge of the species to assimilate the universe. He remembers the fish, that at a similar impasse, a similar critical point, changed over to land, a new form of being. Here for the millionth time (the racial memory tells the weeping individual) is the place where the contradiction has to be resolved; where the old answer, useless now, has to be transcended; where all the quantitative changes are over, where the qualitative leap has to occur. The individual remembers all these critical points because he is the product of them. And the individual, in the last stanza, is given a complete doom. . . . But his bankruptcy and liquidation are taken as inevitable for the species, a necessary mode of progression; the destructive interregnum between the old form and the new is inescapable, as old as life. The strategic value in Auden's joining of Marxism and evolution, his constant shifting of terms from one sphere to the other, is this: the reader will tend to accept the desired political and economic changes (and the form of these) as themselves inevitable, something it is as ludicrous or pathetic to resist as evolution.

When compared with the folkish Us, They are complicated, subtle in a barren Alexandrian-encyclopedia way. They are scholarly introspective observers, We have the insight and natural certainty of the naive, of Christ's children, of fools, of the third sons in fairy stories. They are aridly commercial, financial, distributive; We represent real production, the soil. They are bourgeois-respectable or perverted; We are folk-simple, or else consciously Bohemian so as to break up Their system and morale—there is also a suggestion of the prodigal son, of being reborn through sin. They represent the sterile city, We the fertile country; I want to emphasize this, the surprisingly *rural* character of most of Auden's earliest poems, because so far as I know everyone has emphasized the opposite. They are white-collar workers, executives, or idlers—those who neither "make" nor "do"; We are scientists, explorers, farmers, manual laborers, aviators, fighters and conspirators—the real makers and doers. Auden gets Science over on Our side by his constant use of it both for insight and images, by his admiration of, preoccupation with the fertile adventurous side of it; he leaves Them only the decadent complexity of Jeans or "psychological" economics.

Since Auden has had to reject Tradition, he sets up a new tradition formed of the available elements (available because rejected, neglected, or misinterpreted) of the old. There are hundreds of examples of this process (particularly when it comes to appropriating old writers as Our ancestors); the process is necessary partly to reassure oneself, partly to reassure one's readers, who otherwise would have to reject Our position because accepting it necessitated rejecting too much else. One can see this working even in the form of Auden's early poetry: in all the Anglo-Saxon imitation; the Skeltonics; the Hopkins accentual verse, alliteration, assonance, consonance; the Owens rhymes; the use of the fairy story, parable, ballad, popular song—the folk tradition They have rejected or collected in Childs. Thus Auden has selected his own ancestors, made from the disliked or misprized his own tradition.

In *The Orators* Auden shows, by means of the regular Mendelian inheritance chart, that one's "true ancestor" may be neither a father nor a mother, but an uncle. (His true ancestor wasn't the Tradition, but the particular elements of it most like himself.) This concept is extremely useful to Auden in (1) family, (2) religious, and (3) political relations. (1) By this means he acquires a different and active type of family relationship to set up against the inertia of the ordinary bourgeois womanized family. (2) God is addressed and thought of as Uncle instead of Father: God as Uncle will help revolutionary Us just as naturally and appropriately as God as Father would help his legitimate sons, the Enemy. This Uncle has a Christ-like sacrificial-hero representative on earth, who is surrounded with a great deal of early-Christian, secret-service paraphernalia. This hero is confused or identified with (3) the political leader, a notably unpolitical sort of fantasy-Hitler, who seems to have strayed into politics with his worshipers only because he lives in an unreligious age. There is

hardly more politics in early Auden than in G. A. Henty; what one gets is mostly religion, hero-worship, and Adventure, combined with the odd Lawrence-Nazi folk-mysticism that serves as a false front for the real politics behind it—which Auden doesn't treat.

When Auden occasionally prays to this Uncle he asks in blunt definite language for definite things: it is a personal, concrete affair. In his later poetry Auden is always praying or exhorting, but only to some abstract eclectic Something-Or-Other, who is asked in vague exalted language for vague exalted abstractions. Once Auden wanted evils removed by revolutionary action, and he warned (*it is later than you think*). Today—when he is all ends and no means, and sees everything in the long run—he exhorts (*we all know how late it is, but with Love and Understanding it is not too late for us to . . .*) or prays (*Thou knowest—O save us!*). Most of this belongs to the bad half of what Burke calls secular prayer: the attempt, inside any system, to pray away, exhort away, legislate away evils that are not incidental but essential to the system. Auden used to satirize the whole "change of heart" point of view; "do not speak of a change of heart," he warned. He had a deceived chorus sing vacantly: "Revolutionary worker / I get what you mean. / But what you're needing / 'S a revolution within." He came to scoff, he remained to pray: for a general moral improvement, a spiritual rebirth, Love. Remembering some of the incredible conclusions to the later poems—*Life must live,* Auden's wish to *lift an affirming flame*—the reader may object that this sort of thing is sentimental idealism. But sentimental idealism is a necessity for someone who, after rejecting a system as evil, finally accepts it—even with all the moral reservations and exhortations possible. The sentimentality and idealism, the vague abstraction of such prayers and exhortations, is a *sine qua non:* we can fool ourselves into praying for some vague general change of heart that is going to produce, automatically, all the specific changes that even we could never be foolish enough to pray for. When Auden prays for anything specific at all; when he prays against the organization of the world that makes impossible the moral and spiritual changes he prays for, it will be possible to take the prayer as something more than conscience-and face-saving sublimation, a device ideally suited to make action un-urgent and its nature vague. (pp. 326-32)

Just how did Auden manage to change from almost-Communist to quite-liberal? He did *not* switch over under stress of circumstance; long before any circumstances developed he was making his Progress by way of an old and odd route: mysticism. In Auden's middle period one finds a growing preoccupation with a familiar cluster of ideas: All power corrupts; absolute power corrupts absolutely. Government, a necessary evil, destroys the governors. All action is evil; the will is evil; life itself is evil. The only escape lies in the avoidance of action, the abnegation of the will. I don't mean that Auden wholly or practically accepted all this—who does? But he was more or less fascinated by such ideas (completely opposed to Marxism; fairly congenial with a loose extension of psychoanalysis), and *used* them: If all government is evil, why should we put our trust in, die for a choice of evils? If all action is evil, how can we put our faith in doing anything? If the will itself is evil, why select, plan, do? Life is evil; surely the contemplation of ideal ends is better than the willing and doing of the particular, so-often-evil means.

The reader may object that the method of change I suggest is too crude. But let me quote against him the changer: "The windiest militant trash / Important Persons shout / Is not so crude as our wish . . . " What is the mechanism of most changes of attitude?—the search for any reasons that will justify our believing what it has become necessary for us to believe. How many of us can keep from chorusing with Bolingbroke, *God knows, my son, by what bypaths and indirect crook'd ways I met this*—position? Marxism was too narrow, tough, and materialistic for the Essential Auden, who would far rather look dark with Heraclitus than laugh with Democritus. Auden's disposition itself (Isherwood says that if Auden had his way their plays would be nothing but choruses of angels); the fact that he was never a consistent or orthodox Marxist; the constant pressure of a whole society against any dangerous heresy inside it; Auden's strong "medical" inclinations, his fundamental picture of society as diseased, willing itself to be diseased (a case to be sympathized with, treated, and talked to *à la* Groddeck); his increasing interest in metaphysics and religion; the short-range defeatism, the compensatory long-range optimism that kept growing during the interminable defeat of the '30's; these, and more, made Auden's change inevitable. (p. 333)

These earliest poems are soaked in Death: as the real violence of revolutionary action and as a very comprehensive symbol. Death is Their necessary and desired conclusion; often poems are written from Their increasingly desperate point of view. Death belongs to Us as martyrs, spies, explorers, tragic heroes—with a suggestion of scapegoat or criminal—who die for the people. It belongs to Us because We, Their negation, have been corrupted by Them, and must ourselves be transcended. But, most of all, it is a symbol for *rebirth*: it is only through death that We can leave the old for good, be finally reborn. I have been astonished to see how consistently most of the important elements of ritual (purification, rebirth, identification, etc.) are found in the early poems; their use often seems unconscious. The most common purification rituals (except that of purification by fire) are plain. There is purification through decay: physical and spiritual, the rotting-away of the machines and the diseased perversions of the men. There are constant glaciers, ice, northern explora-

tion—enough to have made Cleanth Brooks consider the fundamental metaphorical picture of the early poems that of a new ice age. There is purification by water: in the second poem in *On This Island* a sustained flood-metaphor shifts into parent-child imagery. There is some suggestion of purification through sin. There is mountain-climbing: from these cold heights one can see differently, free of the old perspectives; one returns, like Moses, with new insights. This is akin to the constantly used parable of the fairy-tale search, the hero's dangerous labors or journey. And the idea of rebirth is plainest of all, extending even to the common images of ontogenetic or phylogenetic development; of the foetus, new-born infant, or child; of the discontinuities of growth. The *uncle* is so important because he is a new ancestor whom We can identify ourselves with (Auden recommends "ancestor worship" of the true ancestor, the Uncle); by this identification We destroy our real parents, our Enemy ancestry, thus finally abolishing any remaining traces of Them in us. These ideas and their extensions are worth tracing in detail, if one had the space. Here is a quotation in which rebirth through death is extremely explicit; seasonal rebirth and the womb of the new order are packed in also. Auden writes that love

> Needs death, death of the grain, our death,
> Death of the old gang; would leave them
> In sullen valley where is made no friend,
> The old gang to be forgotten in the spring,
> The hard bitch and the riding-master,
> Stiff underground; deep in clear lake
> The lolling bridegroom, beautiful, there.

I want my treatment of Auden's early position to be suggestive rather than exhausting, so I shall not carry it any further; though I hate to stop short of all the comic traits Auden gives the Enemy, wretched peculiarities as trivial as saying *I mean* or having a room called the Den. The reader can do his own extending or filling in by means of a little unusually attractive reading: Auden's early poems. My own evaluation of Auden's changes in position has been fairly plain in my discussion. There are some good things and some fantastic ones in Auden's early attitude; if the reader calls it a muddle I shall acquiesce, with the remark that the later position might be considered a more rarefied muddle. But poets rather specialize in muddles—and I have no doubt which of the muddles was better for Auden's poetry: one was fertile and usable, the other decidedly is not. Auden sometimes seems to be saying with Henry Clay, "I had rather be right than poetry"; but I am not sure, then, that he is either. (pp. 335-37)

Randall Jarrell, "Changes of Attitude and Rhetoric in Auden's Poetry," in *The Southern Review*, Louisiana State University, Vol. VII, No. 2, Autumn, 1941, pp. 326-49.

JUSTIN REPLOGLE

(essay date 1969)

[In the following excerpt, Replogle explores the meter, diction, and syntax of Auden's poetry.]

Auden's dazzling prosodic skill is acknowledged by everybody. Admirers talk about his mastery of nearly every metrical and stanzaic practice known to English poetry (and of several unknown), while detractors gleefully emphasize the same point as proof that Auden, the Good Gray Academic Poet, is a huge museum of outmoded prosody. Since more than anything else, rhythmical effects are peculiar to individual works, in one giant generalization I will pass over practices that may produce the most exciting effects in each poem: Auden's rhythmical skill, it seems to me, is almost completely traditional or an extension of practices introduced by his recent predecessors. Though his prosody is one of his great accomplishments, close analysis will show that he relies heavily on the rhythmical expectations established during centuries of English poetic development. His prosodic practices reveal what is obviously true of his temperament, that his own aesthetic excitement almost never comes from *avant-garde* art. Like most other admirers of past poetry, he clearly gets great pleasure from the skill with which a performer handles familiar technical devices. This has always been one of the most important sources of aesthetic delight in all the arts. Until expectations have been established by witnessing a great many similar performances, no reader can respond with excitement to an extraordinarily skillful exhibition. Auden's own habits show that he, like all good readers, responds aesthetically to a skillful performance quite apart from the performer's subject. This is part of what he means by poetry being a game. Like all the other arts it is a performing art, with the creator as performer. Every knowledgeable reader knows about the relative difficulty of certain practices (rules, Auden likes to call them), and will respond emotionally when a poet's skill makes difficulties seem easy. Even modern Romantic critics like Kenneth Rexroth or Karl Shapiro, while they deplore "rules," would surely understand and approve of Auden when he says, " . . . the formal structure of the poem 'I Remember, I Remember' [by Phillip Larkin], in which the succession of five-line stanzas is regular but the rhyming is not, being used both within the stanza and as a link across the stanza break, gives me great pleasure as a device, irrespective of the poem's particular contents." If that is not all art is, it is that as well. And just such a taste for prosodic technique for

its own sake is, I think, the best general explanation of Auden's own practice.

Whatever its traditional roots, though, Auden's prosody conforms to the main stream of twentieth-century practice by freely using prose and speech rhythms. In his syllable-stress poems, his general practice is enough like that of his metrical predecessors to be passed over without comment. But his prose or speech rhythms deserve special attention, since they play a large part in creating one of his characteristic voices. Of course the pleasing struggle between metrical rhythms and those of speech and prose has always caused a good bit of the excitement in English poetry. And Auden's poetry contains all the varieties of this struggle: poems where syllable-stress rhythm dominates, poems where syllable-stress and speech rhythm are about equally powerful, poems where speech rhythms are played off against strong-stress patterns learned from Hopkins and Anglo-Saxon literature, and poems where speech or prose rhythms nearly obscure metrical patterns. In a great many poems, especially after 1940, foot and stress patterns succumb to their much stronger opponent. Speech or prose rhythms prevail, and no one exceeds Auden's virtuosity in running these across the most unlikely meters. One of the most unlikely, for instance, is in a playful monologue in *For the Time Being.* Here an extremely colloquial speech rhythm ("For having reasoned—'Woman is naturally pure / Since she has no moustache' ") flows through ten-line stanzas of intricately patterned four- and five-foot lines (4,5,5,4,5,5,5,4,5,5) rhyming abcacbddff. This rigorous stanza design in no way aids the colloquial speech. Quite the opposite. Its formidable demands make speech more difficult. Its creator is the poet who believes art to be partly a game. His aesthetic delight arises from self-imposed rules made increasingly difficult, and most knowledgeable readers will respond to this with a similar pleasure.

Whether accompanied by formal patterns or not, Auden's speech rhythms nearly always have heavy stresses. Unlike Pound (who consciously explored the far reaches of rhythmical flatness), Auden's speech rhythms usually have stresses as strong as (and sometimes stronger than) his metrical rhythms. Because of this it is not always possible to decide what formal pattern governs some of the later poems. Is Auden counting syllables, feet, or stresses? Some lines, for instance, in the acknowledged syllabic poem **"In Praise of Limestone,"** are syllabic anomalies and seem to be governed by stresses. (Counting elided vowels as single syllables will not explain away all the syllabic deviations.) In contrast, foot and stress poems sometimes appear to be governed by syllable count. The cause of all this is not Auden's faulty ear, but that he hears something more pre-emptive than line pattern. Whatever their formal shape, many poems after 1940 contain an unmistakably similar voice, with its own strong speech rhythm. In various poems this same voice runs across lines that are technically six feet, five feet, four feet, three feet, even two feet, or syllabic. (It even appears in the prose included in poetry volumes.) The line unit, almost never dominant in these, often eludes the ear, and sometimes even analysis. In a given poem Auden may theoretically be writing thirteen-syllable lines, but he is mostly listening to a speech voice that sometimes may use fourteen or fifteen syllables or speak in six-stress units. The rhythms of this voice are so outstandingly distinctive that surely the voice itself can be singled out for identification. The voice rhythms are used by both Poet and Antipoet for all sorts of verse—high, low, or middle style—and I am tempted to guess that both voice and rhythms owe something originally to Marianne Moore. (Auden says he read her poetry for the first time in 1935.) Though short syllabic lines can often be heard (that is, the reader can hear or feel the proper number of syllables instead of stresses or feet) in long lines of the sort Miss Moore likes, the syllable count itself is often an intellectual rather than an auditory game. What the reader hears is not a repeated number of syllables but a distinctive speech rhythm. This is just what the reader hears in Auden's syllabic poems as well, and to my ear the voice in these poems sounds similar to that in Miss Moore's poetry, as though when he borrowed her prosody he also borrowed part of her voice (perhaps the one is nearly the sole cause of the other). I say this only as a descriptive aid. When speech rhythms dominate in Auden they often create a distinctive voice. The voice first became distinctive in the late 1930's and early 1940's. Originally it sounded something like Miss Moore's poetic voice, and Auden used it in both syllabic and nonsyllabic poems and in prose. But no amount of abstract description can classify this voice as well as a few illustrations. Here is the voice:

> . . .to become a pimp
> Or deal in fake jewelery or ruin a fine tenor voice
> For effects that bring down the house could happen. . . .
>
> **("In Praise of Limestone")**

> To manage the Flesh,
> When angels of ice and stone
> Stand over her day and night who make it so plain
> They detest any kind of growth, does not encourage. . . .
>
> **("Mountains")**

> To practise one's peculiar civic virtue was not
> So impossible after all; to cut our losses
> And bury our dead was really quite easy. . . .
>
> (The Narrator in *For The Time Being*)

> To break down Her defences
> And profit from the vision

> That plain men can predict through an
> Ascesis of their senses,
> With rack and screw I put Nature through
> A thorough inquisition. . . .
>
> (The First Wise Man in *For The Time Being*)

> As long as there were any roads to amnesia and anaesthesia still to be explored, any rare wine or curiosity of cuisine as yet untested, any erotic variation as yet unimagined . . . there was still a hope. . . .
>
> (Simeon in *For The Time Being*)

The formal line patterns here (each different, the last prose) all quickly capitulate to the overpowering speech stresses of a voice nearly identical in each passage. This voice appears in a great many poems after 1940 and is an important and obtrusive feature of Auden's style, one created largely by rhythm. So powerful is this rhythm in creating a distinctive voice, that by the time of *Homage to Clio* it makes sense to say that in all of Auden the Grand Persona speaks in two distinct voices (used in variation by all his speakers), one created by dominant metrical, the other by dominant speech, rhythm. Poet and Antipoet make their speeches out of both. Despite the vast number of shared features these voices have (diction, imagery, and so forth) rhythm alone makes them very unlike. For instance:

> Within a shadowland of trees
> Whose lives are so uprightly led
> In nude august communities,
> To move about seems underbred. . . .
>
> **("Reflection in a Forest")**
> . . . .
> Out of a gothic North, the pallid children
> Of a potato, beer-or-whiskey
> Guilt culture, we behave like our fathers and come
> Southward into a sunburnt otherwhere. . . .
>
> **("Good-bye to the Mezzogiorno")**
>
> (pp. 182-86)

A large part of all English poetry depends on evocative diction for much of its effect, and without it Auden must use something else to give verbal excitement to what otherwise would be flat sentences of direct conceptual statement. Since the most obvious thing he does is to animate concepts, his poetry is filled with the moving, dancing ideas that animate allegories small as an epithet and large as a volume, and set in motion all the related verbal practices that attend them. This way of intensifying language has been very much out of fashion (at least in theory) since Coleridge labeled it Fancy and called it a lesser thing than Imagination, and Auden has suffered at the hands of critics who, knowingly or not, share this preference, probably more common now than in Coleridge's time. Auden himself has accurately described Fancy as a "conscious process" involving in its analogical method a "one to one correspondence . . . grasped by the reader's reason," while Imagination, he says, is a process emphasizing the "less conscious side of artistic creation . . . the symbolic rather than the decorative or descriptive value of images." A symbol "is an object or event . . . felt to be more important than the reason can immediately explain . . . " Whatever he may prefer in his theoretical prose, in poetry Auden employs the resources of Fancy: embellishment, decoration, invention, ornament. A great many twentieth-century readers respond to these words as Kenneth Rexroth does, when he says that "Bad poetry always suffers from the same defects: synthetic hallucination and artifice. Invention is not poetry. . . . Poetry is vision, the pure act of sensual communion and contemplation." That "invention" and "ornament" have such pejorative associations again shows how much twentieth-century readers are fashioned by the nineteenth-century tastes they so often deplore. For of course Dr. Johnson thought Rexroth's "bad poetry" the very best sort: " 'A work more truly poetical,' " he said of *Comus,* " 'is rarely found; allusions, images and descriptive epithets embellish almost every period with lavish decoration!' " This is not the place to engage in lengthy polemics or to assess the caprices of changing fashions. But if some doubtful reader of Auden is put off by the very nature of his poetry (no one would claim it is everywhere successful, of course), he should recall that all poets must make their artifacts out of either conceptual or emotive diction, and there is no reason a priori to believe one better than the other. (pp. 195-96)

Syntax, more than anything else, creates an oratorical voice. A 1939 poem opens with "Not as that . . . Napoleon, rumour's dread and centre, / Before whose riding all the crowds divide. . . ." This period runs on until the eighth line, a truly Miltonic postponement of subject and verb. Only slightly less imposing are the opening lines

Will you turn a deaf ear
. . . .
Yet wear no ruffian badge
Nor lie. . . .

By "oratorical" syntax I mean the syntax in just such lines as these. With their lengthy periods, declarative and declamatory questions, and such miscellaneous formulations as "Yet . . . Nor," such sentences are almost never used by two individuals speaking to each other, but only by speakers addressing much larger audiences. The syntax shows what even the meaning of the words may try to deny. For instance, one Auden speaker talks like this:

And since our desire cannot take that route which is straightest,
Let us choose the crooked, so implicating these acres,
These millions in whom. . . .

Auden pretends that this is a lover speaking to his beloved, the "my darling" of a previous stanza. But we never doubt that these sonorities (astounding between two lovers) are meant for the ears of some vast public who will find such constructions appropriate. "Consider this and in our time," another speaker begins, clearly from the podium, and even in middle-style poems speakers usually adopt such oratorical voices. "Here on the cropped grass of the narrow ridge I stand," though a traditional first line for English meditative poetry, is, however traditional, far too theatrical to be put to an individual in conversation or in a letter to a friend. Letter or conversation demand "I am standing here on the cropped grass of a narrow ridge"—at least. (Even "cropped" alone probably makes the sentence "literary" and oratorical.) One familiar generalization, then, is: the more periodic and inverted the syntax, the more consciously patterned, the higher the oratory.

A majority of Auden's poems have a voice at some level of oratory, whatever their subject or other stylistic feature. "To-day no longer occupied like that, I give,"; "Deaf to the Welsh wind now, I hear." Whether appropriate to the subject or not, voices ringing out in these periods produce the emotional effects a poet with conceptual diction cannot get from his words alone, and the handy, and usually lengthy, inverted sentences make possible a wide variety of rhythmical complexity. Looked at this way, one of Auden's problems in the 1930's can be described as a syntax—or voice—problem. His oratorical syntax enabled him to create emotional voices and excellent rhythms, but its very existence automatically created a persona sometimes too sententious and formal for the occasion. If he wanted to bring his Poet down off the Parnassian peaks, Auden had to rebuild his syntax. The syntax of conversational speech generally runs to short sentences with a subject-verb-object arrangement or no clear grammatical arrangement, not to oratorical inversions and lengthy periods grammatically polished. Swinging from one extreme to the other, for a time in the late 1930's Auden's Poetic speakers came forth in . . . exaggerated short declarative statements. . . . They reached a degree of compulsiveness in **"In Time of War"** that added another eccentric manner to that already mannered work:

They wondered why the fruit had been forbidden;
It taught them nothing new. They hid their pride,
. . . .
They knew exactly what to do outside.
They left. . . .

Along with this new syntax came some of the choppy rhythms always threatened by short sentences with parallel structure. Auden was already a master of rhythms that could be made from oratorical speech, but he had not learned how to make this new style work. To get some kind of rhythmical flow across these maddeningly short and similar sentences, he began sticking them together with that weakest of connectives, "and."

In the first 112 lines (eight sonnets), "and" turns up forty-four times at the head of a line. In *Another Time* he tried occasionally to remedy matters by pasting the oratorical "O" onto these nonoratorical sentences: "O in these quadrangles where Wisdom honours herself." Sometimes that helped; sometimes it simply made the speech an incongruous mixture. But the excessively simple syntax began to fade. A higher oratory returns in *Another Time* and remains in the later poetry. Thus most of Auden's poetry could be described as fundamentally oratorical (the major cause, I suspect, of the peculiar belief that he is our most pedagogical poet).

But not all his poems, even the Poetic ones, have high oratory in them. Among the exceptions are those late poems where Auden again tries to develop a plain, nonoratorical voice:

> The sailors come ashore
> Out of their hollow ships,
> Mild-looking middle-class boys. . . .

A poem that begins like this is certainly not a declamation from some high podium. But if it is not high oratory it is certainly not conversation either. It might accurately be called low oratory, part of the long tradition of poetic speech that presents the illusion of informality and conversation, but in reality always aims at a large audience from a public platform, which if low is always there.

Yet if much of his poetry is oratorical, Auden certainly knew how to write the syntax of face-to-face talk, informal and personal: "The fact is, I'm in Iceland"; "You must admit, when all is said and done"; "I don't know whether / You will agree, but"; "And then a lord—Good lord, you must be peppered [with fan mail]." It must be clear by now that nonoratorical syntax and other colloquial features are the very things that often separate the Antipoet's voice from that of the Poet. I say "often" because while the Poet nearly always orates, the Antipoet does not always use the syntax of face-to-face talk. A good share of his syntax is oratorical too—parodied oratory. He mocks the Poet's style:

> For in my arms I hold
> The Flower of the Ages,
> And the first love of the world.
> . . . .
> The didactic digit and dreaded voice
> Which imposed peace on the pullulating
> Primordial mess. Mourn for him now,
> Our lost dad. . . .

I have remarked in various contexts that Auden never found a comfortable style for his Poetic voice. He dared not let it become too ornate. The Antipoet would burlesque it. Neither could he seem to lower it with ease, even though he obviously had a knack for writing colloquial speech. Now we can speculate about the cause (the stylistic cause, at least) of Auden's problem. Apparently he could not separate certain kinds of speech from certain kinds of speakers. Colloquial voices seem to be so firmly part of Auden's joking, farcical sense of life's foolishness that he can seldom speak colloquially without being comic. In other words, the Poet cannot borrow the Antipoet's vernacular idiom without getting the rest of his mocking, comic behavior as well. However informal he may be, the Poet cannot maintain sobriety and speak conversationally at the same time, so Auden's Poetic voice, even at its least formal, fails to be completely informal and always sounds a bit stiff. On the other side, Auden's Antipoetic self cannot speak formally without self-parody, self-mockery. Only when Poet and Antipoet are combined in the speakers of the middle-style and high comic poems can Auden successfully combine oratory with the most unbuttoned conversational syntax, sobriety with horseplay, and all with an emotive and intellectual profundity. These speakers mock themselves and their style, but their very self-contradictions and incongruities are the poem's intellectual and emotional message. (pp. 203-07)

Justin Replogle, in his *Auden's Poetry,* University of Washington Press, 1969, 258 p.

AUSTIN WARREN
(essay date 1981)

[An American educator, Warren is best known for literary criticism that focuses on religious and philosophical concerns. In the following excerpt, he surveys Auden's poetry.]

Auden's periods [in his poetic career] I make out to be five. His earliest group, by which he made his immediate reputation, both in England and in the United States, comprised *Poems* 1927-1932 and *The Orators.* The early work of Auden, collected in the Random House *Poems* of 1934, was acclaimed by Eliot in England, by Cleanth Brooks (*Modern Poetry and the Tradition*), and by Randall Jarrell. It was this first running of Auden's genius which immediately established his reputation and remains his most striking. All Auden's subsequent shifts of attitude and poetic style were attacked by some, led by Jarrell, his inveterate and severe critic, as the defalcations of a Lost Leader.

This early poetry is undeniably obscure; Auden, an Oxford man with a more or less close circle around him, his so-called Group, was, it seemed, in lieu of an established audience whom he could address, engaging in private talk addressed only to his friends. Recently, however, we have been told on the authority of his literary executor, Edward Mendelson, that these early poems were almost as obscure to his friends as to others: that he wrote them only for himself and by his own strange method of composition, which Isherwood has plausibly described. We may suppose something of both.

It is in detail that the poems are obscure, not in drift, attitude, tone. When I try to figure out the exact meaning of a line I am often baffled; but the general sense is one of impending Judgment. A justly famous poem begins with the line, in that alliterative New Old-English style of his, "Doom is dark, and deeper than any sea-dingle." The comfortable age of European and British civilization, Victorian, Edwardian, Georgian, is forever gone—the days comfortable, that is, for the landed gentry, the upper middle class, and the privileged intellectuals. The First World War, in which the fathers and schoolmasters of Auden's generation fought, ended all that; and now some new World War is felt to be imminent.

Auden's early (1932) ambitious work, *The Orators,* is a puzzler. Like his later Long Poems it is a mixture, an assemblage, of verse and art-prose, with, in its case, a larger proportion of prose than verse. Its coherence is loose, and its degree of obscurity, both in intent and in detail, large. Its author called it, in retrospect, "a fair notion, fatally injured in the treatment," and for many years refused to reprint it; and when, in 1966, he did reissue it, he said that his name, as author, "seems a pseudonym for someone else, someone talented but near the border of sanity, who might well, in a year or two, become a Nazi." The work ends with a set of odes, one of which, the fifth, he included in the *Collected Poems* of 1945 under the apt title, **"Which Side Am I Supposed to Be On?"**

About this poem, which has fascination for me as a critic and exegete, [Monroe] Spears and [John] Fuller have suggestive and useful things to say. The former thinks the title contrasts speechmakers and others articulate with men of action, doers; further, that the work itself as "An English Study," as Auden subtitles it, is not only a study of the English upper classes but a manual of English rhetoric, with examples of the argument, exposition, the letter, and the diary—which it most certainly is. The latter, John Fuller, characterizes the work as literary *avant-garde* (i.e., in the mode of Stein and Joyce and, especially, of the surrealists) and thinks it contains a few fragments of automatic writing—suggestions worth pondering.

But what was the "fair notion" and how was it "fatally injured"? In my judgment, the "fair notion" is, as Spears suggests, the contrast of sayers and doers, and, I will add, the neurotic young literary man's then vast preference for the doers. It is also the eternally recurrent warfare between young and old, and is the ve-

W.H. Auden, 1938.

hicle in which one clever and mildly "angry" young man can express his hostility, and pitying disdain, toward outmoded old statesmen, country gentlemen, and school administrators—all talkers—and his sympathy for the young, "my pupils," who are called upon to act, to fight, doctrinally and also literally, against the Old Order, the Establishment.

The notion is fatally injured (I opine) because the action proposed can certainly be read as either Fascist or Communist: there may even have been a brief time during which Auden himself hesitated between positions, clearer of the need to attack than of the enemy's identity. And the central figure of the Airman remains ambiguous: a neurotic, vaguely modeled on T. E. Lawrence but partly also, I suspect, a version of Auden himself. Is he a Strong Man or a Weak (in terms of Isherwood's distinction in *Lions and Shadows*)? His *Journal* strikes me as that of a neurotic who cannot clearly distinguish between his sickness and his sin on the one hand, his health and virtue on the other—a self-analytical, highly articulate adolescent with daydreams of political and military leadership.

While Auden was writing this "Poem," he was himself a young schoolmaster, and as such (he was an excellent teacher, with a keen interest in pedagogy) he had divided loyalties, partly seeing the need of authority, partly feeling on the side of the young revolters; so, in every way, the thematics and tone of his "Poem" are ambiguous to the point of incoherence, reaching beyond the celebrated principle of "irony." A brilliant example is the opening "Address," with its Groddeckian, and Audenian, diatribe against psychosomatic ills, which suddenly comes to an end as the speaker orders the arrest of all neurotics and leaves the room, leaving the reader with a plausible doctrine undercut.

Literarily, *The Orators* is full of interest. Especially engaging are the riddles, the litany (modeled on its Anglican prototype) in "Argument," Section II, and the catalogues (modeled on Ecclesiastes, Whitman's *Song of Myself,* and poems from the Old English *Exeter Book*) in "Statement," Sections I and II, but also in the opening "Address." The catalogue, a list of Types, each accompanied by a pungent, picturesque, physiological particularism, is central to cerebral Auden from youth to age; but what he later learns to control and proportion is here a conscious stylistic Euphuism. For example, in the "Address," he speaks thus of one neurotic type: "With odd dark eyes like windows, a lair for engines, suffering more and more from cataract or deafness, leaving behind them diaries full of incomprehensible jottings, complaints less heard than the creaking of a wind pump on the moor." But *The Orators* is a repertory of literary experiments, both in prose and in verse, like that of Joyce. It is the one real Modernist poem Auden wrote. It both shows what a skillful Modernist he might have been, and is a monument to a road not hereafter taken—indeed tacitly rejected.

Then comes the second, still English, period of *Poems 1933-1938,* which was also exciting but less obscure, less private, more meditative—the period of his brilliant pieces in verse, the critical portraits of Melville, Henry James, Freud, Matthew Arnold, Edward Lear, Rimbaud, and Yeats, also of **"Crisis"** ("Where do they come from?") and **"Oxford"** and—what I would without much hesitation choose as his finest single poem—the **"Musée des Beaux Arts,"** a comment on Brueghel's *Icarus:*

> About suffering they were never wrong,
> The Old Masters: how well they understood
> Its human position; how it takes place
> While someone is eating or opening a window or
>   just walking dully along
>   . . . .
> the expensive delicate ship that must have seen
> Something amazing, a boy falling out of the sky,
> Had somewhere to get to and sailed calmly on.

The poems of this period made an especial appeal to me in the 1940s, and still deeply appeal—these sensitive, subtle, evocative, and not too obscure poems which distill the essence of an author's personality or the personality of a place into a criticism which is also a poem. I could easily think this Auden's best period,

but I hesitate, remembering my own professional bias as that of biographer and literary critic.

The third period (1940-1948), the first after Auden's migration to America, is the period of his Long Poems. First comes the *New Year Letter* (also called *The Double Man*), followed by *For the Time Being* (A Christmas Oratorio), *The Sea and the Mirror,* and *The Age of Anxiety* (1947). After this, for whatever reason (he never explained his abstinence), Auden wrote no more Long Poems, though he substituted for them groups of poems, the literary equivalent of orchestral suites.

Milton was the author, as every schoolboy used to know, of Minor Poems, such as "Il Penseroso" and "Lycidas," and of Major Poems, such as *Paradise Lost.* And Virgil too wrote both the *Aeneid* and the *Eclogues* and *Bucolics;* so we might go on. The postulate certainly is that, in middle life, a major poet must write major poems—*major* meaning, to start with, long, but, less superficially, poems which have to be long because they concern themes not to be essayed unless they can be given the space for appropriate development, and because a large poetic personality, at its maturity, needs such space for expression of its opulence.

So Auden had to write Long (i.e., intentionally Major) Poems. And he did. They did not wholly satisfy his on the whole best, certainly most rigorous, critics, Bayley and Frazer; and they do not satisfy me. The consensus is that *The Sea and the Mirror* is the best of them; I register my dissent, voting for the last written, *The Age of Anxiety.* Indeed, to my finding, these Long Poems become progressively better.

New Year Letter, in Hudibrastic tetrameter couplets, contains quotable lines, most of them in the first section, which recites the Honor Roll of past poets, the Tribunal which aspirant Auden, when he presumes to write, must face: Dante, "self-educated" William Blake, Rimbaud, Dryden, Catullus, Tennyson, Baudelaire, Hardy, and Rilke, "whom *die Dinge* bless." The second section, on sin and the wiles of Satan, reminds me of C. S. Lewis' *Screwtape Letters,* without, from the dates of the two works, any indebtedness. The third concerns America, industrialism, the need for a Just City (Auden's standard phrase for his political ideal, which is neither an Eden nor a Utopia). To this didactic poem, an epistle, Auden appended pages of notes, quotations from the impressive reading on which, so to speak, his poem had been based—his prooftexts. This, Auden's first poem since his conversion to Christianity, gives evidence of a clever convert's intelligence and zeal.

The Hudibrastic couplets do not fit the poem; heroics would, I think, have been better. Perhaps this is as good a place as any to remark on the unpredictability of Auden's success in matching verse forms and meter with subject matter and tone. In all the bulk of his criticism, Auden never attempts, as Eliot does in writing about his earlier plays, to discuss matters so ultimately technical. The verse forms interested Auden, the virtuoso craftsman, and so did his ideas, but these two often ran on separate tracks—not always, or at his best, but often.

Certainly he is never given to "imitative form," so urged by *Understanding Poetry.* Without his ever pronouncing a doctrinal position, his theory and his practice seem rather on the side of Yvor Winters and John Crowe Ransom (in *The New Poetry*): decay and limpness are not to be echoed but rather portrayed by crispness of mind and metrical regularity.

For the Time Being, an Oratorio, is an intelligent, up to its date, Christian poem, dramatizing—with interspersed lyrics and a prose speech by Herod, wittily conceived of as a Liberal—the cycle of Christmas. It is too bright, too little brooding. The Christian paradoxes of the Incarnation, familiar to any reader of Christian theology of the great tradition, and the Christian poetry of Baroque poets such as Crashaw, not being freshened up, sound tired. Auden's most overtly religious poem does not compare favorably when ranged against the poems of deeply religious men like George Herbert, Gerard Manley Hopkins, Charles Péguy, and T. S. Eliot—or the novels of Georges Bernanos. He is intelligent, and he has sincerely adopted the Christian position; but he has adopted it as, on the whole, the best available solution of the world's mysteries—not been adopted, gripped, seized by it.

The Sea and the Mirror is a kind of commentary on Shakespeare's *The Tempest,* that final play commonly interpreted as his farewell to his art, and a play ever attractive to his fellow artists, Henry James among them. Auden's work, formally hard to classify, is half a closet drama, half a philosophical poem on the theme of the artist's relation to experience, life, people—at once his subject and his audience.

The first part presents the characters in *The Tempest* as they are about to depart the enchanted isle, each given a speech. It is, on one level, a virtuoso display of Auden's technical powers at his craft, the magic of his wand; on another level, it is an exhibition of the unresolved struggle between Prospero and his "wicked" brother Antonio, who returns (a recalcitrant ego or experiential reality), not to be reconciled, absorbed within Prospero's art.

The second section, Caliban's speech, a prose epilogue to the closet drama, is a disquisition on the relation of the artist and his audience. Addressed to the audience, it points out what great art cannot do: it can satisfy neither the lowbrow, who wants something sentimental and nostalgic, nor the highbrow, who desires abstract philosophical ideals.

One curious feature of Caliban's speech, its style, is seen by commentators, myself included, as a parodic imitation of Henry James's late manner. Caliban's is, says Spears, a "faintly ridiculous style"; says John Fuller, it "partakes of the smiling drone of the unnerving bore." Both are correct, I think: Caliban's speech is far too long, and so full of subtle distinctions and ironies and illustrative examples that the reader finally gives up trying to follow the argument and just enjoys the rich Audenian satire and detail. Though by what reasoning Auden makes Caliban speak ripe Jamesian language, I cannot work out, I know that the author of **"At the Grave of Henry James"** was a lover of the Master who could recite whole pages from his works. I also know that we parody only styles, and persons, loved, and that love is quite compatible with seeing the ridiculous side of loved objects—for example, the prolixity and the incapacity for the simple of the old James.

The Age of Anxiety I think the most characteristic of Auden's talents and their range, and the most central. It does not prove anything, and happily does not try to: written after Auden had long been a Christian, it has nothing tendentiously Christian about it, yet nothing incompatible with the Christian faith. The final meditation, by Malin, Canadian and a medical man, like Auden's father, and the character nearest to representing Auden's own point of view, is Christian, but undoctrinal.

The poem has a satisfying formal structure. It is a modern version of the traditional pastoral scheme, as we find it in Theocritus and in *The Shepheardes Calender:* "the singing contest; an elegy; love-songs and laments, with courtship of a shepherdess; a dirge; formal, 'artificial' diction and meter" (Spears). There is a melange of styles: lyrics, sung to the accompaniment of the jukebox; interspersed announcements and commercials from the radio of the New York bar in which four "lonelies" find themselves gathered by chance on one All Souls' Eve during the Second World War. All the verse is encased in a continuum of prose, the most flexible and civilized prose Auden ever wrote—not Jamesian, indeed not mannered at all, just well-bred, flexible yet urbane. It is conversational without being sloppy or repetitious; it is modulated prose without any eccentricity or special hallmark. Auden has almost as many prose styles as styles in verse; in prose, too, he is virtuoso. But the prose in *The Age of Anxiety* is quintessential Audenic prose.

The prose encasement, or links, offers one continuum. The alliterative verse, after the Old English model, provides another; and, unlike the prose, which is modern, contemporary, this neo-archaic verse provides aesthetic distancing from the material—the characters and themes—of the poem. Its choice was a masterly stroke on Auden's part. His Norse heritage, or whatever, makes him a "natural" as a reviver; and his unflagging inventiveness in this seemingly limited verse form removes it from ever being boring. The disparity between matter and form is not really ironic: the sadness of Old English lyrics has something in common with the sadness of the anxious "lonelies" gathered in the bar. But there is a counterpoint.

What is baroque about this eclogue? Auden uses this word in no strict literary-historical sense, any more than Spears does when he speaks of Caliban's speech as baroque. Both mean a style which is intentionally artificial, ostentatiously artful—still more, one given to profuse ornamentation, to rich and lavish and redundant use of detail, illustration, specificity. These latter traits are reminiscent of Dickens, with whom Bayley and the Italian critic Carlo Izzo find Auden, a Dickens lover, to have such an overlap. In a loose sense, both Dickens and Henry James write baroque, and so often does Auden, even when he does not, as here, so name his work.

The characters in *The Age of Anxiety* are four: three men, old, middle-aged, and young, and one woman, an English Jewess of uncertain age. She is a disillusioned Romantic who nostalgically dreams of the English countryside, either real or fictive. The young man, the only American among them, has his memories of his typical American boyhood and his fears about his future—fears that, once the glamor of his uniformed youth is over, he may turn out to be as commonplace as his boyhood friends.

Auden is not a dramatic poet. The characters all speak alike, in Old English Audenese. They are distinguished by their type traits of sex and age, by their symbolic memories, and, most of all, by their attitudes. Medieval allegory and its eighteenth-century diminution into personification are both forms natural to cerebral-minded Auden. An instinctive generalizer, he is hence attracted to types—of character and of situation. He is the conceptual in search of the illustrative concrete, not the particularizer who broadens out.

According to some commentators, the four characters represent Jung's four epistemological types: Malin, Thought; Rosetta, Feeling; Quant, Intuition; and Emble, Sensation—and their very names have been given emblematic significance. Though I do not find this reading very convincing, it points in the right general direction. The ancestral writers who come most to mind are Langland and Spenser, most of all in the interior sections of the poem, "The Seven Ages" of man and "The Seven Stages" of life. The former, fairly easy to follow, reminds one vaguely of the shorter parallel sequence in Pope's *Essay on Man*. The latter, the obscurest part of the poem, John Fuller explains as a physiological allegory, each landscape corresponding to some part of the human body (e.g., the city represents the brain).

About the Long Poems, my feelings, in the mid-forties and now, are mixed. None of them, I judge, is an unqualified success. Yet to have written them augments the stature of Auden. Not afraid to fail, he is the greater poet for having attempted them. That very courage sets him apart from minor poets who are partly so because they are perfectionists. Greatness takes risks, is willing to be imperfectly large rather than impeccably small.

The fourth period (1948-1957) comprises the autumnal poetry of the much (and justly) lauded **"In Praise of Limestone,"** that *paysage moralisé,* the fine suites **"Bucolics"** and **"Horae Canonicae," "The Shield of Achilles,"** and a modern Horatian ode which I much admire, **"Under Sirius,"** a stanzaic and rhymed poem combining wit and magic.

And period five (1958-1973) is that of the poet's premature old age (poets early become aged eagles). *About the House,* later called *Thanksgiving for a Habitat,* one of Auden's groups of poems, belongs to this last period. And there are other fine shorter pieces such as **"The Horatians"** and **"Ode to the Medieval Poets"** and **"On the Circuit"** and **"Old People's Home."** Many occasional poems, verse epistles, and greetings remind us of the eighteenth-century poets, not only Dryden and Pope but Prior, Shenstone, and all the rest. (pp. 467-75)

From a fine, perceptive, and just essay on "Auden's Last Poems," those of his sixties, written by Robert Bloom for the 1974 *Harvard Advocate* Auden issue, let me quote two comparative judgments. The last poems "are deeply personal . . . yet not confessional, not embarrassingly intimate, as Lowell, or Snodgrass, or Plath can be, nor historically autobiographical, like Yeats." And again: Auden, in his old age and its poems, offers "the example of a man using all his powers to sustain a civilized existence in the midst of twentieth-century horror, brutality, fanaticism, and anarchy without resorting to the moaning of Eliot, the theatrics of Yeats, or the exotic, enigmatic oracularism of Stevens." These judgments, out of Bloom's context of delicate specificities in the perception of Auden's poetry, and his fine choice of passages to quote sound, in their brevity, melodramatically crude; yet only crude contrasts like these can give one what one is always in danger of losing, amid distinctions and discriminations—one's ultimate critical bearings.

Unfamiliar with these post-*Age of Anxiety* poems of Auden's till a year or two ago, I am more and more coming to admire them—for their civilized urbanity, so wondrously blended with the personal voice, the "I" never stridently assertive yet never merely the socially disciplined mask. The chasm between I-poetry and we-poetry or communal poetry sometimes, often, seems unbridgeable. Yet here it is done, in a community of independent and individual voices voluntarily collaborating. The achievement is a poetry of a maturely wise old age. (pp. 475-76)

Austin Warren, "The Poetry of Auden," in *The Southern Review,* Louisiana State University, Vol. 17, No. 3, Summer, 1981, pp. 461-78.

EDWARD CALLAN
(essay date 1983)

[In the following excerpt, Callan appraises Auden's career.]

In the forty-four years between his first volume, *Poems,* 1930, and his final collection, *Thank You, Fog!,* published some months after his sudden death in September 1973, W. H. Auden produced a body of poems, plays, opera libretti, and criticism unmatched in the twentieth century. He wrote rapidly, and sometimes he was slipshod; but his best and most characteristic work achieved what good artists are commonly remembered for: the highlighting of some facet of truth that was always there, but outside the circle of our recognition until brought into focus by their art.

At one time or another Auden sought to reach a variety of audiences and tastes, from popular to highbrow. He could range widely in tone from shrill name-calling in a political broadside—"Beethameer, Beethameer, bully of Britain,/With your face as fat as a farmer's bum" . . . —to erudite bookish allusion that assumed everyone who read Auden had also read Freud (and as time went on, Goethe and Kierkegaard, too). As his choices for *The Oxford Book of Light Verse* (1937) attest, he liked all sorts of light verse, and in his own includes ballads, blues, limericks, clerihews, and cabaret songs—forms attuned in some degree to the tinselled social atmosphere of the twenties in which he grew up. But the things that most excited his imagination had an intellectual reach; and if the term *intellectual* implies an aptitude for thought coupled with a well-stocked, witty, and logical mind, Auden was an intellectual. He particularly respected books by "thinkers"—R. G. Collingwood and A. N. Whitehead as well as Freud, Jung, and Groddeck in his earlier years in England where his reputation as a poet was first established in the 1930s; and Paul Tillich, Reinhold Neibuhr, Simone Weil, and Hannah Arendt, as well as Kierkegaard and other existentialists in his later years in America.

He valued books for their language as well as for their ideas, and he had a special passion that increased with age for dictionaries, crossword puzzles, and linguistic oddities of all sorts. He was pleased when his usage was cited in dictionaries—a pleasure given him by several entries in the unabridged *Webster's Third* (1961) where, for example, the instance cited for *egoist* in the sense of *egocentric* is his, and the instance given of *abrupt* as a verb is "let brazen bands abrupt their din" from *The Age of Anxiety* (1947). His playful late poem, **"A Bad Night: A Lexical Exercise"** exhumes gnarled dialect words like *hirple, glunch,* and *sloomy;* but even his earliest verse employed unusual words—typically with the clinical air of a detached observer. At nineteen, for example, he wrote a poem on lovers' partings ("Consider if you will how lovers stand") that brought surprise to this genre with words like *suction, heartburn, clinically-minded,* and *ligatured*—this last in a laconic phrase of the kind that became his early hallmark: "Have ligatured the ends of a farewell." (pp. 3-4)

Although it may have become so in old age, Auden's youthful fascination with words was not a sterile one. The first quality in his work that proclaims him an artist—the marked ability to give to "airy nothing/A local habitation and a name"—is manifest in his effective figurative use of clinical terms like "ligatured"; and in the comic extravagance of a metaphorical line like: "Or hum of printing presses turning forests into lies," to depict the partisan slant of mass-circulation English dailies in the thirties. But his gift for imaginative "naming" went beyond verbal marksmanship. It enabled him to discover a poetic mythology for the times. (p. 4)

The range of Auden's poetic imagery, and the scope of the several technical vocabularies he from time to time employed show him remarkably aware of twentieth-century intellectual trends, and more attuned to discoveries in the natural sciences than either Eliot or Yeats. One may encounter in his poetry on the one hand, technical terms from the specialized vocabularies of existentialist thinkers like Jaspers, Heidegger, Kierkegaard, and Buber; and on the other, precise images from various natural sciences—from the chemistry of cellular division, for example, in **"Meiosis"**; from paleontology in **"Winds"**; and from microbiology in **"A New Year Greeting"** (a humorous *tour de force* first published in *Scientific American*). Given the wide range of his interests, there is little to be gained from approaching Auden's art—as was once commonly done—by comparing it with the work of his Oxford contemporaries in "The Auden Group": Louis MacNiece, Cecil Day Lewis, and Stephen Spender, none of whom grew and changed to the extent that he did, or continued to deploy new technical equipment to meet the challenge of new themes. Auden is more aptly classed in the company of Pope and Wren whose names recall an age. (pp. 7-8)

Whatever their deeper differences, both Pope and Auden were committed to their craft; and both were primarily occasional poets. Pope wrote *The Rape of the*

Lock in the hope of mending a family quarrel, and his other more memorable works are in such traditional occasional forms as the verse essay and the epistle. Auden also wrote many letters in verse, including the two long works *Letter to Lord Byron* and *New Year Letter,* a number of shorter verse letters in *Letters from Iceland,* and the title poem in *Epistle to a Godson.* Pope wrote few elegies and a great number of epitaphs. Auden wrote few epitaphs: one of them for a favorite cat, Lucinda, that he and Chester Kallman owned in Ischia, but none of them for specific people. However, he often turned to the elegy as an occasional form. A remarkable proportion of the poetry of his later years is elegiac including memorial poems for his housekeeper at Kirchstetten, Frau Emma Eiermann, and for his New York doctor, David Protetch, M.D. Several of his elegies, including **"In Memory of W. B. Yeats," "At the Grave of Henry James,"** and **"In Memory of Sigmund Freud,"** are among his better known occasional poems.

Auden represented himself not in the high Romantic manner as a lover of the Muse—an *amateur*—but as a professional who could produce verse for a play, a libretto, an epistle, or an elegy as the occasion demanded. In the English cricketing terms of his day he was a "Player," as professionals were then called, not one of the amateur "Gentlemen." At a time when some literary theorists found traditional forms suspect, he preferred to believe that a poet's first duty was to master the technical elements of his craft. For more than forty years he commanded a greater variety of poetic forms than any poet writing in English. Readers who have sampled his poetry from time to time may well recall a cluster of ballads; various sonnets and sonnet sequences; instances of the villanelle, ballade, and canzone; a number of sestinas—four of them in "Kairos and Logos"; and sustained passages of terza rima and of alliterative verse. Some of the more complex stanza forms in the poems of his middle years—those employed in **"Streams"** and **"In Transit,"** for example— are derived from elaborate courtly metrical forms whose names he brought back into the general vocabularly: the Welsh englyn, and the Skaldic drott-kvaett; and in his sixties he perfected other syllabic forms, derived ultimately from Greek prosody, but more immediately based on Goethe's hexameters and Horace's Sapphics and Alcaics. He imposed on himself even stricter limitations than those inherent in the traditional forms he adopted. (pp. 9-11)

[There] was a strong utopian strain in Auden's work of the early 1930s welcomed by a generation struggling out from the quagmire of war and depression. Many among his contemporaries nursing a sense of betrayal by their elders whose policies had led to the mass slaughter of the 1914-18 war were delighted by the irreverent vision he set before them of England's ruling caste beguiled by its native forms of oratory: the

lies of press lords; the dubious rhetoric of pulpit and political platform; and the vapid talk above the old school tie. The poetry of Wilfred Owen had linked the patrician rhetoric of these elders—*Dulce et decorum est pro patria mori* [Horace: "It is sweet and fitting to die for one's country"]—to the slaughter in the trenches, and it was to Owen's banner that Auden rallied with lines like the one about "printing presses turning forests into lies." Many among Auden's contemporaries also welcomed the fresh combination of qualities in his verse that gave rise to the term *Audenesque:* a clinical air, clipped phrase, sharp ironical eye, and deft control of line and rhythm. Such verse seemed designed to probe the infected spots on the body politic like a surgical scapel. Auden was soon a newspaper celebrity in England at a time when the growing Fascist power in Germany, Italy, and Spain seemed to outweigh all other dangers, so much so that from 1931 onward it brought socialists and liberals into an alliance with the Communist Party in a Popular Front against Fascism.

The Popular Front rallied to the Republican cause during the Spanish Civil War—a war that presented intellectuals in the West with a crisis of conscience comparable to that faced by Americans during the Vietnam War thirty years later—and Auden's widely heralded intention to serve in an ambulance unit that resulted in a short visit to the Spanish war zone in 1937, together with his subsequent journey, in 1938, to the Sino-Japanese war front, seemed to set him on the high road to a poetry grafted to political Romanticism. In retrospect, Auden saw in his politically oriented poetry of the mid-thirties a departure from the true line of his poetic development. He also felt on looking back that the public acclaim given him and his fellow poets in the thirties was undeserved. In the second half of life he turned the search light of his art on the Romantic obsession with oracular truth within, not only in the realm of politics but in the realm of poetry, where so many of the Romantic poets, including some older contemporaries he had admired, like W. B. Yeats and D. H. Lawrence, had fancied that they had discovered truth anew within themselves.

Auden's misgivings about the Romantic imagination were not apparent in his writings until 1937-38, when he was thirty years old and already fairly widely acclaimed as the leader of a new and politically oriented poetic movement, consisting mainly of his friends, C. Day Lewis, Stephen Spender, and Louis MacNeice. Then, partly through a re-examination of his own personal values and of his public role as a poet, he began to question the conventional Romantic assumption that the artist-genius was more than commonly privy to the truth and that his creative imagination was geared exclusively to the service of freedom. This questioning first becomes evident in his sonnet sequence from China in *Journey to a War* (1938). His later American work expresses a conviction that Romanticism's deification of the imaginative original genius spawned the modern totalitarian dictator, whether of the Left or of the Right.

By 1940 he had come to recognize, perhaps with the aid of Kierkegaard's categories, that an analogous urge for the creation of perfect order marked both artist and tyrant—the one in the aesthetic sphere, the other in the political. He felt that the artist, habituated to shaping or discarding his materials at will, was by cast of mind inclined to seek tyrannical solutions in civil affairs—a weakness he had begun to diagnose in himself. Conversely, he felt that tyrants like Hitler or Stalin who sought to mould human societies to utopian ideals were artists out of their spheres. For, in pursuit of civil order, tyrants display the quality of ruthlessness with which the poet, for aesthetic reasons, liquidates unsound rhymes or removes whole stanzas to some other part of his design. (pp. 14-16)

Now that Auden's work is complete it can be seen that his long identification with the *avant garde* of the thirties is not the whole measure of his art. His perspective changed with time, but he continued to illuminate in his poetry obscure areas of individual human freedom necessarily circumscribed in each life by ties to nature and to history; and he scorned W. B. Yeats for reviving outmoded cyclic theories in which, as in Greek religion, nature and history were confused. He regarded formal restrictions in art and natural limitations in life as both circumscribing and nurturing liberty by contributing to creative ingenuity. As he put it in an essay on Valéry where he also says it is more becoming in poets to talk of versification than of mysterious voices: "The formal restrictions of poetry teach us that the thoughts which arise from our needs, feelings, and experiences are only a small part of the thoughts of which we are capable." . . . This is the theme of his **"Ode to Terminus"** honoring the Roman god of limits and boundaries whom he thanks "for giving us games and grammar and metres." . . . The couplet from his **"In Memory of W. B. Yeats,"** now inscribed on Auden's memorial in the Poets' Corner of Westminster Abbey,

In the prison of his days

Teach the free man how to praise, . . .

is but one instance of the type of analogy he liked to draw between vitality arising from imposed restraint in the making of a poem and from natural limitations in the life of a free man. (pp. 16-17)

Auden's conception of man's responsibility for Nature's freedom—less common perhaps among poets than among physicists—sets him apart from those poets among his contemporaries more immediately concerned with social and political ideologies, and . . . it certainly set him apart from W. B. Yeats. The difference is fundamental. Therefore simplistic charts of his changes of attitude toward questions of politics or religion help little toward the enjoyment of his later, more philosophical, poems that are so frequently concerned with the nature of man and the origins of creativity. Having thought as a schoolboy that his future lay in mining engineering, in time he came to regard his choice of a poetic vocation as providential—given his life circumstances. (p. 20)

As there is no way back to lost innocence in science, so there is no way back in art; not even in the particular case of Auden's art. He was not simply a poet of the thirties. The significance of his work, early and late, transcends local loyalties. His perennial themes were consciousness and the human condition; and no other writer has so consistently chosen for theme the gap between the world of consciousness where the responsibilities of freedom begin and the unconscious natural world where necessity rules. His works in prose explore this theme also; and a measure of the qualities of mind he brought to criticism was his capacity for turning such occasional pieces as reviews and introductions into essays of permanent value. But his reputation as an artist rests, ultimately, on the poetry; and—apart from a Romantic emphasis on the spirit where Auden would include the flesh—what Sir Herbert Grierson said of seventeenth-century metaphysical poetry—that it was a poetry inspired by a philosophical conception of "the role assigned to the human spirit in the great drama of existence"—applies to Auden's poetry three centuries on. (pp. 266-67)

Edward Callan, in his *Auden: A Carnival of Intellect,* Oxford University Press, Inc., 1983, 299 p.

SOURCES FOR FURTHER STUDY

Brophy, James D. *W. H. Auden.* Columbia Essays on Modern Writers, edited by William York Tindall, No. 54. New York: Columbia University Press, 1970, 48 p.

Isolates and describes the principal verse forms of Auden's poetry.

Buell, Frederick. *W. H. Auden as a Social Poet.* Ithaca, N. Y.: Cornell University Press, 1973, 196 p.

Discusses the formation of Auden's social vision during the 1930s.

Carpenter, Humphrey. *W. H. Auden: A Biography.* Boston: Houghton Mifflin Co., 1981, 495 p.

In-depth study of Auden's life and literary works. Carpenter notes of the biography: "It is not a book of literary criticism. I have not usually engaged in a critical discussion of Auden's writings. But I have tried to show how they often arose from the circumstances of his life, and I have also attempted to identify the themes and ideas that concerned him."

Fuller, John. *A Reader's Guide to W. H. Auden.* New York: Farrar, Straus & Giroux, 1970, 288 p.

Commentary on Audon's poetry and drama aimed "to help the reader with difficult passages and to trace some of the sources and allusions, since despite the now happily increasing volume of Auden criticism, there is still nothing quite as systematic or as detailed as the reader would like." Includes a comprehensive index of poems and references to the main treatment of each poem in the text.

Mendelson, Edward. *Early Auden.* New York: Viking Press, 1981, 407 p.

Book-length history and interpretation of Auden's work up to 1939.

Spears, Monroe K., ed. *Auden: A Collection of Critical Essays.* Englewood Cliffs, N. J.: Prentice-Hall, 1964, 184 p.

Claiming that most critical assessments of Auden are "unsatisfactory," Spears has collected thirteen essays, including criticism by Christopher Isherwood, Stephen Spender, and Edmund Wilson, that are not "representative" but that seem "both illuminating and likely to retain some permanent value."

Jane Austen

1775-1817

English novelist.

INTRODUCTION

*A*s a supreme prose stylist, Austen has secured a lasting place in English literature. Although her first novel was not published until she was thirty-five, she wrote three volumes of juvenilia before she was eighteen, and *Sense and Sensibility* (1811) was completed before her twenty-second birthday. Her career is generally divided into an early and a late period, the former encompassing the juvenilia, as well as *Sense and Sensibility, Pride and Prejudice* (1813), and *Northanger Abbey* (1818), the latter including *Emma* (1816), *Mansfield Park* (1814), and *Persuasion* (1818). They are separated by a hiatus of eight years. There is a remarkable consistency in the work of the early and late periods, marked by a certain mellowing of tone in the later works.

Austen began writing while she was still living at her childhood home at Steventon Rectory in Hampshire, England. Her life at Steventon, though sheltered from the world at large, gave her an intimate knowledge of a segment of English society—the landed gentry—that was to provide the materials for most of her fiction. Austen had already begun to produce stories, dramas, and short novels by 1787, and in 1795 she began writing *Elinor and Marianne,* an early version of her first published novel, *Sense and Sensibility.* One year later, she started *First Impressions,* the work that eventually became *Pride and Prejudice.* When Austen finished *First Impressions* in 1797, her father submitted it to a London publisher. Although the publisher rejected it, the story remained a popular favorite among the circle of relations and acquaintances with whom Austen shared her writings. Scholars have suggested that she was still working intermittently on *First Impressions* when she moved to Bath in 1801 and continued to work on the text until 1805 when, following the deaths of both her father and a close friend, she appears to have given up writing for almost five years. In 1809, after a difficult period of traveling and staying with various relatives, Austen settled once again in Hampshire at Chawton Cottage, a location close to her former home at Steventon. There she resumed writing and in 1809 or 1810 began revising the manuscript of *Sense and Sensibility* for publication. By the time the novel appeared in 1811, Austen was recasting *First Impressions* into *Pride and Prejudice*. On January 28, 1813, *Pride and Prejudice* was published anonymously in London.

Austen's novels are peopled with characters of her own social class: the ladies and gentlemen of the landed gentry. Her plots involve the intricacies of courtship and marriage between members of this class. Although she wrote about the people she knew best, she illuminated in their characters the follies and failings of men and women of all times and classes. Austen's concept of narrative perspective is unique and innovative. In each of her works there is a central character through whose eyes we view the world of the novel. This technique is used to greatest effect in *Emma,* where we see the world of Highbury and its intrigues through Emma's eyes. Austen's genius emerges as we begin to note the flaws in Emma's perception: her inability, through her own pride and penchant for self-deception, to comprehend the situation around her.

A perennial favorite of readers and critics alike, *Pride and Prejudice* is often regarded as Austen's consummate achievement. The plot revolves around a series of misunderstandings between Elizabeth, a lively young middle-class woman with a satirical temperament, and Darcy, an unconsciously arrogant and enormously wealthy upper-class young man who becomes her suitor. Initially offended by Darcy's apparently haughty manner, Elizabeth determines "to be uncommonly clever in taking so decided a dislike to him." Darcy, however, finds himself reluctantly drawn to Elizabeth despite the "inferiority of her connections" and the "want of propriety" displayed by her son-in-law-hunting mother, officer-chasing younger sisters, and kind but indolent and cynical father. Elizabeth is taken entirely by surprise when Darcy proposes. Her prejudice against him and the sense that he is lowering himself, which he communicates during his proposal, cause her to summarily reject his offer of marriage. The two part for a time, but not before Darcy writes a letter explaining his past conduct and absolving himself of most of the offenses with which Elizabeth charged him. The remainder of the novel traces the series of events that eventually leads to their reconciliation. When Darcy renews his offer of marriage, he does so with the knowledge that his pride had made him arrogant and insensitive; Elizabeth accepts him, recognizing that her precipitous judgment had led her to mistake his real character. In their union both find happiness and a better understanding of themselves.

The critical history of *Pride and Prejudice* is in most respects indistinguishable from that of Austen's writings as a whole, despite the novel's long-standing popularity with readers and the tendency of critics to rank it (with *Emma* and *Mansfield Park*) as the author's finest work. During Austen's lifetime, both her anonymous mode of publication and quiet life prevented her from being widely known: approximately fifteen early reviews of her works have been uncovered, including only three on *Pride and Prejudice.* B. C. Southam has pointed out, however, that while the critical press granted limited attention to the work when it first appeared, *Pride and Prejudice* was "remarkably well-received" in light of the harsh treatment granted most novels. Anonymous articles in the *British Critic* and the *Critical Review* praised Austen's characterization and her portrayal of domestic life. Additional early commentary exists in the diaries and letters of such prominent contemporary readers as Mary Russell Mitford and Henry Crabb Robinson, both of whom admired the work's characters, realism, and freedom from the trappings of Gothic fiction. After the initial reviews of the novel, however, little substantial criticism appeared during the first half of the nineteenth century. Influential articles on Austen by Sir Walter Scott in 1815 and Archbishop Richard Whateley in 1821 are important primarily for their analysis of the general qualities of her fiction rather than from their insight into individual novels. Scott recorded in a journal entry on *Pride and Prejudice* his respect for Austen's ability to render "commonplace things and characters interesting."

The publication in 1870 of the first major biography of Austen, by her nephew James Edward Austen-Leigh, inspired a number of important articles on the novelist by such critics as Margaret Oliphant and Richard Simpson. Modern scholars, however, have come to see the attempts of Austen's family and her legions of staunch admirers (christened "The Janeites" by Rudyard Kipling) to portray her as a benign and pious "spinster aunt" as ultimately inhibiting the progress of serious Austen criticism. Southam has contended that despite occasional outbursts of interpretive acumen in the late Victorian era, the majority of criticism presented only "a sentimental portrait of Jane Austen as a kind of Sunday writer, an amateur genius, a gentlewoman who surprised her family and herself with the success of her books." Thus, while both Austen's life and works received increasing attention at the end of the nineteenth century—including a lengthy discussion of characterization, narrative perspective, and satire in *Pride and Prejudice* by George Saintsbury—it remained for twentieth-century critics to explore in depth such facets of the novel as its structure, language, irony, and sociology. Scholars generally agree that modern Austen criticism began with the publication in 1939 of Mary Lascelles's *Jane Austen and Her Art*, the first comprehensive study of the author and her works. In her analysis of *Pride and Prejudice*, Lascelles explored its carefully detailed and deliberately plotted structure, contesting the notion that Austen was an unconscious, "natural" artist.

For all their wit and good humor, Austen's works are deeply concerned with the moral values in life, and her satire is at its finest when aimed at the snobbish and presumptuous. Despite her claim that she was working merely on a "little piece of ivory," Austen brought genius and consummate craftsmanship to her work, producing prose masterpieces that remain among the best literary mirrors of their age.

(For further information about Austen's life and works, see *Nineteenth-Century Literature Criticism*, Vols. 1, 13, 19, 33.)

CRITICAL COMMENTARY

REGINALD FARRER
(essay date 1917)

[In the following examination of *Emma*, Farrer identifies the study of character as the central concern in the novel.]

Emma is the very climax of Jane Austen's work; and a real appreciation of *Emma* is the final test of citizenship in her kingdom. For this is not an easy book to read; it should never be the beginner's primer, nor be published without a prefatory synopsis. Only when the story has been thoroughly assimilated, can the infinite delights and subtleties of its workmanship begin to be appreciated, as you realise the manifold complexity of the book's web, and find that every sentence, almost every epithet, has its definite reference to equally unemphasised points before and after in the development of the plot. Thus it is that, while twelve readings of *Pride and Prejudice* give you twelve periods of pleasure repeated, as many readings of *Emma* give you that pleasure, not repeated only, but squared and squared again with each perusal, till at every fresh reading you feel anew that you never understood anything like the widening sum of its delights. But, until you know the story, you are apt to find its movement dense and slow and obscure, difficult to follow, and not very obviously worth the following.

For this is *the* novel of character, and of character alone, and of one dominating character in particular. And many a rash reader, and some who are not rash, have been shut out on the threshold of Emma's Comedy by a dislike of Emma herself. Well did Jane Austen know what she was about, when she said, 'I am going to take a heroine whom nobody but myself will much like.' And, in so far as she fails to make people like Emma, so far would her whole attempt have to be judged a failure, were it not that really the failure, like the loss, is theirs who have not taken the trouble to understand what is being attempted. Jane Austen loved tackling problems; her hardest of all, her most deliberate, and her most triumphantly solved, is Emma.

What is that problem? No one who carefully reads the first three opening paragraphs of the book can entertain a doubt, or need any prefatory synopsis; for in these the author gives us quite clear warning of what we are to see. We are to see the gradual humiliation of self-conceit, through a long self-wrought succession of disasters, serious in effect, but keyed in Comedy throughout. Emma herself, in fact, *is never to be taken seriously.* And it is only those who have not realised this who will be 'put off' by her absurdities, her snobberies, her misdirected mischievous ingenuities. Emma is simply a figure of fun. To conciliate affection for a character, not because of its charms, but in defiance of its defects, is the loftiest aim of the comic spirit; Shakespeare achieved it with his besotted old rogue of a Falstaff, and Molière with Celimène. It is with these, not with 'sympathetic' heroines, that Emma takes rank, as the culminating figure of English high-comedy. And to attain success in creating a being whom you both love and laugh at, the author must attempt a task of complicated difficulty. He must both run with the hare and hunt with the hounds, treat his creation at once objectively and subjectively, get inside it to inspire it with sympathy, and yet stay outside it to direct laughter on its comic aspects. And this is what Jane Austen does for Emma, with a consistent sublimity so demure that indeed a reader accustomed only to crude work might be pardoned for missing the point of her innumerable hints, and actually taking seriously, for example, the irony with which Emma's attitude about the Coles' dinner-party is treated, or the even more convulsing comedy of Emma's reflexions after it. But only Jane Austen is capable of such oblique glints of humour; and

---

Principal Works

Sense and Sensibility (novel) 1811

Pride and Prejudice (novel) 1813

Mansfield Park (novel) 1814

Emma (novel) 1816

Northanger Abbey, and Persuasion (novels) 1818

Lady Susan (novel) 1871

The Watsons (unfinished novel) 1871

Love & Friendship, and Other Early Works (juvenilia) 1922

Sanditon. Fragment of a Novel (unfinished novel) 1925

Jane Austen's Letters to her Sister Cassandra and Others [edited by R. W. Chapman] (letters) 1932

Volume the First (juvenilia) 1933

Volume the Third (juvenilia) 1951

---

only in *Emma* does she weave them so densely into her kaleidoscope that the reader must be perpetually on his guard lest some specially delicious flash escape his notice, or some touch of dialogue be taken for the author's own intention.

Yet, as Emma really does behave extremely ill by Jane Fairfax, and even worse by Robert Martin, merely to laugh would not be enough, and every disapproval would justly be deepened to dislike. But, when we realise that each machination of Emma's, each imagined piece of penetration, is to be a thread in the snare woven unconsciously by herself for her own enmeshing in disaster, then the balance is rectified again, and disapproval can lighten to laughter once more. For this is another of Jane Austen's triumphs here—the way in which she keeps our sympathies poised about Emma. Always some charm of hers is brought out, to compensate some specially silly and ambitious naughtiness; and even these are but perfectly natural, in a strong-willed, strong-minded girl of only twenty-one, who has been for some four years unquestioned mistress of Hartfield, unquestioned Queen of Highbury. Accordingly, at every turn we are kept so dancing up and down with alternate rage and delight at Emma that finally, when we see her self-esteem hammered bit by bit into collapse, the nemesis would be too severe, were she to be left in the depths. By the merciful intention of the book, however, she is saved in the very nick of time by what seems like a happy accident, but is really the outcome of her own unsuspected good qualities, just as much as her disasters had been the outcome of her own most cherished follies.

In fact, Emma is intrinsically honest (it is not for nothing that she is given so unique a frankness of outlook on life); and her brave recognition of her faults, when confronted with their results, conduces largely to

the relief with which we hail the solution of the tangle, and laugh out loud over 'Such a heart, such a Harriet'! The remark is typical, both of Emma and of Emma's author. For this is the ripest and kindliest of all Jane Austen's work. Here alone she can laugh at people, and still like them; elsewhere her amusement is invariably salted with either dislike or contempt. *Emma* contains no fewer than four silly people, more or less prominent in the story; but Jane Austen touches them all with a new mansuetude, and turns them out as candidates for love as well as laughter. Nor is this all that must be said for Miss Bates and Mr Woodhouse. They are actually inspired with sympathy. Specially remarkable is the treatment of Miss Bates, whose pathos depends on her lovableness, and her lovableness on her pathos, till she comes so near our hearts that Emma's abrupt brutality to her on Box Hill comes home to us with the actuality of a violent sudden slap in our own face. But then Miss Bates, though a twaddle, is by no means a fool; in her humble, quiet, unassuming happiness, she is shown throughout as an essentially wise woman. For Jane Austen's mood is in no way softened to the second-rate and pretentious, though it is typical of *Emma* that Elton's full horror is only gradually revealed in a succession of tiny touches, many of them designed to swing back sympathy to Emma; even as Emma's own bad behaviour on Box Hill is there to give Jane Fairfax a lift in our sympathy at her critical moment, while Emma's repentance afterwards is just what is wanted to win us back to Emma's side again, in time for the coming catastrophe. And even Elton's 'broad handsome face,' in which 'every feature works,' pales before that of the lady who 'was, in short, so very ready to have him.' 'He called her Augusta; how delightful!'

Jane Austen herself never calls people she is fond of by these fancy names, but reserves them for such female cads or cats as Lydia Bennet, Penelope Clay, Selina Suckling, and 'the charming Augusta Hawkins.' It is characteristic, indeed, of her methods in *Emma*, that, though the Sucklings never actually appear, we come to know them (and miss them) as intimately as if they did. Jane Austen delights in imagining whole vivid sets of people, never on the stage, yet vital in the play; but in *Emma* she indulges herself, and us, unusually lavishly, with the Sucklings at Maple Grove, the Dixons in Ireland, and the Churchills at Enscombe. As for Frank, he is among her men what Mary Crawford is among her women, a being of incomparable brilliance, moving with a dash that only the complicated wonderfulness of the whole book prevents us from lingering to appreciate. In fact, he so dims his cold pale Jane by comparison that one wonders more than ever what he saw in her. The whole Frank-Jane intrigue, indeed, on which the story hinges, is by no means its most valuable or plausible part. But Jane Fairfax is drawn in dim tones by the author's deliberate purpose.

She had to be dim. It was essential that nothing should bring the secondary heroine into any competition with Emma. Accordingly Jane Fairfax is held down in a rigid dullness so conscientious that it almost defeats another of her *raisons d'être* by making Frank's affection seem incredible.

But there is very much more in it than that. Emma is to behave so extremely ill in the Dixon matter that she would quite forfeit our sympathy, unless we were a little taught to share her unregenerate feelings for the 'amiable, upright, perfect Jane Fairfax.' Accordingly we are shown Jane Fairfax always from the angle of Emma; and, despite apparently artless words of eulogy, the author is steadily working all the time to give us just that picture of Jane, as a cool, reserved, rather sly creature, which is demanded by the balance of emotion and the perspective of the picture. It is curious, indeed, how often Jane Austen repeats a favourite composition; two sympathetic figures, major and minor, set against an odious one. In practice, this always means that, while the odious is set boldly out in clear lines and brilliant colour, the minor sympathetic one becomes subordinate to the major, almost to the point of dullness. (pp. 23-7)

Reginald Farrer, "Jane Austen," in *The Quarterly Review*, Vol. 228, No. 452, July, 1917, pp. 1-30.

VIRGINIA WOOLF

(essay date 1929)

[An English novelist, essayist, and short story writer, Woolf was an important practitioner of the stream-of-consciousness novel. In the excerpt below, she comments on Austen's styles, characterization, theme, and narrative viewpoint in *Pride and Prejudice*.]

The novels which make us live imaginatively, with the whole of the body as well as the mind, produce in us the physical sensations of heat and cold, noise and silence, one reason perhaps why we desire change and why our reactions to them vary so much at different times. Only, of course, the change must not be violent. It is rather that we need a new scene; a return to human faces; a sense of walls and towns about us, with their lights and their characters after the silence of the wind-blown heath.

After reading the romances of Scott and Stevenson and Mrs. Radcliffe, our eyes seem stretched, their sight a little blurred, as if they had been gazing into the distance and it would be a relief to turn for contrast to a strongly marked human face, to characters of extrav-

agant force and character in keeping with our romantic mood. Such figures are most easily to be found in Dickens, of course, and particularly in *Bleak House* where, as Dickens said, "I have purposely dwelt upon the romantic side of familiar things." (p. 269)

In Dickens the characters are impressive in themselves but not in their personal relations. Often, indeed, when they talk to each other they are vapid in the extreme or sentimental beyond belief. One thinks of them as independent, existing forever, unchanged, like monoliths looking up into the sky. So it is that we begin to want something smaller, more intense, more intricate. Dickens has, himself, given us a taste of the pleasure we derive from looking curiously and intently into another character. He has made us instinctively reduce the size of the scene in proportion to the figure of a normal man, and now we seek this intensification, this reduction, carried out more perfectly and more completely, we shall find, in the novels of Jane Austen.

At once, when we open *Pride and Prejudice,* we are aware that the sentence has taken on a different character. Dickens, of course, at full stride is as free-paced and far-stretched as possible. But in comparison with this nervous style, how large-limbed and how loose. The sentence here runs like a knife, in and out, cutting a shape clear. It is done in a drawing-room. It is done by the use of dialogue. Half a dozen people come together after dinner and begin, as they so well might, to discuss letter-writing. Mr. Darcy writes slowly and "studies too much for words of four syllables". Mr. Bingley, on the other hand (for it is necessary that we should get to know them both and they can be quickest shown if they are opposed) "leaves out half his words and blots the rest". But such is only the first rough shaping that gives the outline of the face. We go on to define and distinguish. Bingley, says Darcy, is really boasting when he calls himself a careless letter-writer because he thinks the defect interesting. It was a boast when he told Mrs. Bennet that if he left Netherfield he would be gone in five minutes. And this little passage of analysis on Darcy's part, besides proving his astuteness and his cool observant temper, rouses Bingley to show us a vivacious picture of Darcy at home. "I don't know a more awful object than Darcy, on particular occasions, and in particular places; at his own house especially, and of a Sunday evening, when he has nothing to do."

So, by means of perfectly natural question and answer, everyone is defined and, as they talk, they become not only more clearly seen, but each stroke of the dialogue brings them together or moves them apart, so that the group is no longer casual but interlocked. The talk is not mere talk; it has an emotional intensity which gives it more than brilliance. Light, landscape—everything that lies outside the drawing-room is arranged to illumine it. Distances are made exact; arrangements accurate. It is one mile from Meryton; it is Sunday and not Monday. We want all suspicions and questions laid at rest. It is necessary that the characters should lie before us in as clear and quiet a light as possible since every flicker and tremor is to be observed. Nothing happens, as things so often happen in Dickens, for its own oddity or curiosity but with relation to something else. No avenues of suggestion are opened up, no doors are suddenly flung wide; the ropes which tighten the structure, since they are all rooted in the heart, are so held firmly and tightly. For, in order to develop personal relations to the utmost, it is important to keep out of the range of the abstract, the impersonal; and to suggest that there is anything that lies outside men and women would be to cast the shadow of doubt upon the comedy of their relationships and its sufficiency. So with edged phrases where often one word, set against the current of the phrase, serves to fledge it (thus: "and whenever any of the cottagers were disposed to be quarrelsome, discontented, or *too poor*") we got down to the depths, for deep they are, for all their clarity.

But personal relations have limits, as Jane Austen seems to realize by stressing their comedy. Everything, she seems to say, has, if we could discover it, a reasonable summing up; and it is extremely amusing and interesting to see the efforts of people to upset the reasonable order, defeated as they invariably are. But if, complaining of the lack of poetry or the lack of tragedy, we are about to frame the familiar statement that this is a world which is too small to satisfy us, a prosaic world, a world of inches and blades of grass, we are brought to a pause by another impression which requires a moment further of analysis. Among all the elements which play upon us in reading fiction there has always been, though in different degrees, some voice, accent or temperament clearly heard, though behind the scenes of the book. "Trollope, the novelist, a big, blustering, spectacled, loud-voiced hunting man"; Scott, the ruined country gentleman, whose very pigs trotted after him, so gracious was the sound of his voice—both come to us with the gesture of hosts, welcoming us, and we fall under the spell of their charm or the interest of their characters.

We cannot say this of Jane Austen, and her absence has the effect of making us detached from her work and of giving it, for all its sparkle and animation, a certain aloofness and completeness. Her genius compelled her to absent herself. So truthful, so clear, so sane a vision would not tolerate distraction, even if it came from her own claims, nor allow the actual experience of a transitory woman to color what should be unstained by personality. For this reason, then, though we may be less swayed by her, we are less dissatisfied. It may be the very idiosyncrasy of a writer that tires us of him. Jane Austen, who has so little that is peculiar,

does not tire us, nor does she breed in us a desire for those writers whose method and style differ altogether from hers. Thus, instead of being urged as the last page is finished to start in search of something that contrasts and completes, we pause when we have read *Pride and Prejudice.*

The pause is the result of a satisfaction which turns our minds back upon what we have just read, rather than forward to something fresh. Satisfaction is, by its nature, removed from analysis, for the quality which satisfies us is the sum of many different parts, so that if we begin praising *Pride and Prejudice* for the qualities that compose it—its wit, its truth, its profound comic power—we shall still not praise it for the quality which is the sum of all these. At this point, then, the mind, brought to bay, escapes the dilemma and has recourse to images. We compare *Pride and Prejudice* to something else because, since satisfaction can be defined no further, all the mind can do is to make a likeness of the thing and, by giving it another shape, cherish the illusion that it is explaining it, whereas it is, in fact, only looking at it afresh. To say that *Pride and Prejudice* is like a shell, a gem, a crystal, whatever image we may choose, is to see the same thing under a different guise. Yet, perhaps, if we compare *Pride and Prejudice* to something concrete, it is because we are trying to express the sense we have in other novels imperfectly, here with distinctness, of a quality which is not in the story but above it, not in the things themselves but in their arrangement.

Pride and Prejudice, one says, has form; *Bleak House* has not. The eye (so active always in fiction) gives its own interpretation of impressions that the mind has been receiving in different terms. The mind has been conscious in *Pride and Prejudice* that things are said, for all their naturalness, with a purpose; one emotion has been contrasted with another, one scene has been short, the next long; so that all the time, instead of reading at random, without control, snatching at this and that, stressing one thing or another, as the mood takes us, we have been aware of check and stimulus, of spectral architecture built up behind the animation and variety of the scene. It is a quality so precise it is not to be found either in what is said or in what is done; that is, it escapes analysis. It is a quality, too, that is much at the mercy of fiction. Its control is invariably weak there, much weaker than in poetry or in drama because fiction runs so close to life the two are always coming into collision. That this architectural quality can be possessed by a novelist, Jane Austen proves. And she proves, too, that far from chilling the interest or withdrawing the attention from the characters, it seems on the contrary to focus it and add an extra pleasure to the book, a significance. It makes it seem that here is something good in itself, quite apart from our personal feelings.

Not to seek contrast but to start afresh—this is the impulse which urges us on after finishing *Pride and Prejudice.* We must make a fresh start altogether. Personal relations, we recall, have limits. In order to keep their edges sharp, the mysterious, the unknown, the accidental, the strange subside; their intervention would be confusing and distressing. The writer adopts an ironic attitude to her creatures, because she has denied them so many adventures and experiences. A suitable marriage is, after all, the upshot of all this coming together and drawing apart. A world which so often ends in a suitable marriage is not a world to wring one's hands over. On the contrary, it is a world about which we can be sarcastic; into which we can peer endlessly, as we fit the jagged pieces one into another. Thus, it is possible to ask not that her world shall be improved or altered (that our satisfaction forbids) but that another shall be struck off, whose constitution shall be different and shall allow of the other relations. People's relations shall be with God or nature. They shall think. They shall sit, like Dorothea Casaubon in *Middlemarch,* drawing plans for other people's houses; they shall suffer like Gissing's characters in solitude; they shall be alone. *Pride and Prejudice,* because it has such integrity of its own, never for an instant encroaches on other provinces and, thus, leaves them more clearly defined. (pp. 271-73)

Virginia Woolf, "Phases of Fiction, Part 2," in *The Bookman,* New York, Vol. LXIX, No. 3, May, 1929, pp. 269-79.

DAVID CECIL

(lecture date 1935)

[Cecil is highly acclaimed for his work on the Victorian era. In the following excerpt from the text of a 1935 lecture, he examines the nature of Austen's artistry.]

The most successful writer is he who obeys most strictly the laws which govern the art of his choice. And of all those who have chosen the novel none has been more careful to keep its laws than Jane Austen. It is this that gives her her advantage over other English novelists. She was not the most talented, she did not write about the most sensational topics; but as a master of her craft she outshines them all. And when we turn to analyse our admiration for her it is the triumphs of her craft that first strike us.

To begin with we notice that she obeys the first rule of all imaginative composition, that she stays within the range of her imaginative inspiration. . . . Now Jane Austen's imaginative range was in some re-

spects a very limited one. It was, in the first place, confined to human beings in their personal relations. . . . Her view was further limited by the fact that in general she looked at [her characters] in one perspective, the satiric. Jane Austen was a comedian. Her first literary impulse was humorous; and to the end of her life humour was an integral part of her creative process; as her imagination starts to function a smile begins to spread itself across her features. And the smile is the signature on the finished work. It is the angle of her satiric vision, the light of her wit that gives its peculiar glitter and proportion to her picture of the world. (pp. 7-9)

There are no adventures in her books, no abstract ideas, no romantic reveries, no death scenes. Nor does she give much space to the impressions of the senses. . . . But satire, like Blake's tear, is an intellectual thing, a critical comment on life. And the impressions of the senses are conveyed not by critical comment but by direct record. To interpolate many such records into a comedy will disperse its comic atmosphere. Jane Austen avoided them.

She avoided jarring characters too. Two-thirds of her dramatis personae are regular comic character-parts like Mr Collins or Mrs Allen. And even those figures with whom she is most in sympathy, even her heroines, are almost all touched with the comic spirit. (pp. 10-11)

The nature of her talent imposed a third limitation on her; it made her unable to express impulsive emotion directly. She surveyed her creatures with too detached an irony for her to identify herself with them sufficiently to voice their unthinking gushes of feeling. On the few occasions she tried she becomes self-conscious, unreal and, incredible to relate, rather absurd. . . . She traces brilliantly the effect of emotion, the way it heats a situation, modifies character; but she expresses it only by implication. (p. 12)

Jane Austen's natural range was further bounded by the limitations imposed by circumstances. . . . The world of Jane Austen's experience was a very small one. She was a woman in an age when women were forbidden by convention from moving in any society except that in which they were born: and the class she was born in, that of the smaller English gentry, was the one most enslaved to convention. But she kept to it. Her stories all take place in England, all in one class. (p. 13)

She is not only true to the rules of literary art in general; she is also true to the particular laws that govern the art of the novel. The novelist has a more complex task than the poet. For he sets out to give a picture of the world as it is. . . . Now Jane Austen's imagination was, as we have seen, a comedian's imagination. Her problem is to draw a true picture of life which should also amuse us. And in the masterpieces of her maturity, in *Emma* and *Persuasion,* she succeeds perfectly. She paints the surface of English life with a meticulous and Dutch accuracy. . . . (pp. 14-15)

Comedy is also implicit in the manner in which she tells her story. Her irony, her delicate ruthless irony, is of the very substance of her style. It never obtrudes itself; sometimes it only glints out in a turn of phrase. But it is never absent for more than a paragraph; and her most straightforward piece of exposition is tart with its perfume. (p. 17)

The writer has to devise a form for his inspiration which will at once please us as an artistic pattern and give us a convincing impression of disorderly reality. In addition to reconciling fact and imagination he must reconcile fact and form. It is a hard task: and, it cannot be said that Jane Austen always succeeded in it. In *Northanger Abbey* and *Sense and Sensibility* she sacrifices fact to form. The character of Edward Ferrars, the eccentric conduct of General Tilney, these are too palpably pieces of machinery invented to fit the exigencies of the plot. In *Mansfield Park* she sacrifices form to fact. The original design of the book obviously intended Henry Crawford to fill the rôle of villain. But as she works Jane Austen's creative power gets out of control, Henry Crawford comes to life as a sympathetic character; and under the pressure of his personality the plot takes a turn, of which the only logical conclusion is his marriage with the heroine, Fanny. Jane Austen was not one to be put upon by her creatures in this way. In the last three chapters she violently wrenches the story back into its original course: but only at the cost of making Henry act in a manner wholly inconsistent with the rest of his character.

At her best, however, she keeps the balance between fact and form as no other English novelist has ever done. . . . Her stories are meticulously integrated; not a character, not an episode but makes its necessary contribution to the development of the plot. Only, we do not notice it. The scaffolding is so artfully overlaid with the foliage of her invention that it seems a free growth. . . . The picture she presents to us seems no calculated composition but rather a glimpse of life itself; life caught at a moment when its shifting elements have chanced to group themselves into a temporary symmetry. *Emma* and *Pride and Prejudice* are as logically constructed as a detective story; yet they give us all the sense of spontaneous life we get from a play of Chekhov.

Persuasion is less impeccably designed: Mrs. Smith, like Edward Ferrars, is a bit of lifeless machinery. But it is its author's greatest formal achievement. For in it she gives her story not only a dramatic but also a spiritual unity. Its subject is love, the constant love renounced from an unwise prudence, that Anne Elliot feels for Wentworth. And every episode of the story refers to this subject. The rash happy marriage of the Crofts, the love, enduring through hardship, of the Harvilles, the inconstancy of Benwick and Louisa Musgrove—all these, by contrast or similarity, illustrate Anne's situation: now in the major key, now in the minor, now simply, now with variations, they repeat the main theme of the symphony. Even the tender autumnal weather in which most of the action takes place echoes and symbolises the prevailing mood of the story. Such singleness of structure gives *Persuasion* an emotional concentration unattainable by any other means. (pp. 18-22)

The absorbing, searching interest she awakes in the mind—so that one turns to her again and again and always finds something new to think about—is one only stirred by works of major art. Her books . . . have a universal significance.

This is due in the first place to the sheer strength of their author's talent; to the fact that she is endowed in the highest degree with the one essential gift of the novelist, the power to create living characters. (p. 23)

Jane Austen also realises the psychological organism that underlies speech and manner. She is not content just to dash down her intuitive impressions of people; her lucid knife-edged mind was always at work penetrating beneath such impressions to discern their cause, discover the principles of her subject's conduct, the peculiar combination of qualities that go to make up his individuality. And she shows us surface peculiarities always in relation to these essentials. The consequence is she does not need to present man involved in major catastrophes. (pp. 24-5)

Nothing escapes her, nothing baffles her, nothing deceives her. However slight its manifestation, however muffled by convention or disguised by personal charm, unfailingly she detects the essential quality of character. (p. 26)

Such penetration enabled her to elucidate far more complex characters than most novelists. The young ladies who play the chief rôles in her stories are more intricately conceived than those of any English novelist before George Eliot. (pp. 26-7)

Like all great comedians, she satirises in relation to a universal standard of values: her books express a general view of life. It is the view of that eighteenth-century civilisation of which she was the last exquisite blossom. One might call it the moral-realistic view. (p. 32)

Not one of her characters, however farcical or however delightful, but is brought to trial before the triple bar of taste, sense and virtue; and if they fail to give satisfaction on any one of these counts, smiling but relentless she passes sentence on them. Her sense of justice is exquisite and implacable; neither pity nor anger can make it swerve from its course; she is never vindictive and never sentimental; she makes no exceptions in deference to public opinion or to her personal feelings. (p. 36)

[Jane Austen's] graceful unpretentious philosophy, founded as it is on an unwavering recognition of fact, directed by an unerring perception of moral quality, is as impressive as those of the most majestic novelists. Myself I find it more impressive. If I were in doubt as to the wisdom of one of my actions I should not consult Flaubert or Dostoievsky. The opinion of Balzac or Dickens would carry little weight with me: were Stendhal to rebuke me, it would only convince me I had done right: even in the judgment of Tolstoy I should not put complete confidence. But I should be seriously upset, I should worry for weeks and weeks, if I incurred the disapproval of Jane Austen. (p. 43)

David Cecil, in his *Jane Austen,* Cambridge at the University Press, 1935, 43 p.

ELIZABETH JENKINS
(essay date 1938)

[In the following excerpt from her highly regarded biographical and critical study of Austen, Jenkins comments on characterization, realism, structure, and comic irony in *Pride and Prejudice.*]

The depth, the perspective of impression conveyed by *Pride and Prejudice* is so intense that when one re-reads the book one is astonished by its brevity. The people in the story are so distinctly present to one's mind that one searches in vain for the actual passage of description that made them so.

There is none; and in this lies the most characteristic aspect of Jane Austen's art, and the one most difficult to discuss and understand. What Macaulay said of Milton might with more aptness be said of her: 'There would seem at first sight to be no more in his words than in other words. But they are words of enchantment. No sooner are they pronounced, than the past is present, and the distant, near. . . . Change the structure of the sentence . . . and the whole effect is destroyed. The spell loses its power, and he who should hope to conjure with it would find himself as much mistaken as Cassim in the Arabian tale, when he stood saying Open Wheat, Open Barley, to the door which obeyed no sound but Open Sesame.' (pp. 154-55)

The structure of *Pride and Prejudice* explains what [Austen meant by saying to her niece] Anna Austen that two or three families in a small area was the very thing to work upon and just the situation she liked herself. She did not mean it to be inferred that a pleasant round of gossip and intrigue and an absence of any-

thing of external interest were all that she herself felt fitted to cope with; but that, for her method of establishing conviction, it was essential to keep the threads of the story converging upon a single point and to show the various characters, not only as she saw them, or as two of them saw each other, but as each of them appeared to his or her acquaintance as a whole.

In *Pride and Prejudice* this interlacing of the characters forms, as it were, the steel structure upon which the work, with its amazing buoyancy, is sprung. Every important fact in the story is shown to be the inevitable consequence of something that has gone before. The fact that Bingley, pliable as he was, should be deterred by Darcy from his courtship of Jane Bennet is at first surprising; and Darcy's explanation is that Bingley was very modest, and really believed Darcy's representation of Jane's indifference; which, added Darcy, he genuinely believed himself. He saw that Jane liked Bingley, but he did not believe her to be in love, and therefore liable to be injured except in a worldly sense by Bingley's withdrawal. We then remember what Charlotte Lucas had said, very early in Jane and Bingley's acquaintance, when Elizabeth had remarked to her that though Jane was falling in love with Bingley, her serenity and self-control were such that Elizabeth did not think anyone else would be able to notice it. (p. 156)

The suddenly brought about marriage of Charlotte and Mr. Collins, which is in its way one of the most interesting things in the book, is led up to before the reader has any suspicion of what is to happen. At the Netherfield Ball, before Mr. Collins has made his famous proposal to Elizabeth, he exacerbates her almost beyond endurance by his pertinacious attentions; as she has refused to dance with him, she is not able, in the etiquette of the day, to accept another partner; therefore she has to sit and endure Mr. Collins, who says he had rather sit by her than dance with anybody else. Her only moments of relief are when Charlotte Lucas comes to them and kindly diverts some of Mr. Collins' conversation to herself.

The difference between the meretricious, dishonest Wickham and his father, who had been the trusted steward and lifelong friend of old Mr. Darcy, is explained in a single statement. The elder Wickham had had an extravagant wife.

The celestial brightness of *Pride and Prejudice* is unequalled even in Jane Austen's other work; after a life of much disappointment and grief, in which some people would have seen nothing but tedium and emptiness, she stepped forth as an author, breathing gaiety and youth, robed in dazzling light. The penetration, the experience, the development of a mature mind, are latent in every line of the construction, in every act and thought; but the whole field of the novel glitters as with sunrise upon morning dew. The impression cannot be wholly analysed and accounted for, but it is

A sketch of Steventon Rectory, Austen's childhood
home.

worth while noting that in this book there are no people who are thrown in upon themselves by an unsympathetic atmosphere, like Fanny Price; no one who is labouring under a painful secret like Jane Fairfax; no one whose natural frame of mind is one of stormy light and shade, like Marianne Dashwood; no one whose life has been radically altered by a killing past of unhappiness like Anne Elliot; there is disappointment in the book, and agitation, and acute distress, but the characters are all, even Wickham's, of an open kind, despite their individual variety.

Much of the novel's charm is created by the relationship of the two sisters; the idea that we have here something of the relationship of Jane and Cassandra is inescapable, particularly in such a passage as: 'I was uncomfortable enough—I was very uncomfortable—I may say, unhappy. And with no one to speak to of what I felt, no Jane to comfort me, and say that I had not been so very weak and vain and nonsensical as I knew I had! Oh, how I wanted you!' Cassandra Austen is to us something of a sybil; she is a veiled presence whose face we never see. Her sister is always talking to her; and we listen to her sister's voice and watch the changing expression of her face, but we never see the person to whom Jane is turned. . . . In acknowledging one of her letters, Jane declared her to be 'one of the finest comic writers of the age.' Would Cassandra but read her own letters through five times, she might get some of the pleasure out of them that her sister did. Jane sent delighted thanks for the 'exquisite piece of workmanship' which had been brought into Henry's breakfast-room among the other letters.

Now a letter from Jane Bennet would never have ranked as an exquisite piece of workmanship. A partial sister could not have described her as one of the first comic writers of the age. If she had been, Mr. Bingley would not have fallen in love with her. (pp. 157-58)

'Mild' and 'steady' are words used in describing

her; her very beauty was of the reposeful cast; she was not so light nor so used to running as Elizabeth; she was the sooner out of breath when they pursued Mr. Bennet across the paddock. In every respect she forms the ideal contrast to her mercurial sister, whose face, Miss Bingley said, was too thin, and whose eyes enchanted Mr. Darcy with 'their shape and colour, and the eyelashes, so remarkably fine.'

Of the young men, Bingley and Wickham sustain the sense of gaiety and open good humour which is a part of the novel's atmosphere. Bingley is simple, modest, easily led; but with a disposition to be pleased. (p. 159)

The character of Wickham, though so base, is not of a kind to cloud the brilliant surface of the mirror. A curious degree of sexual attraction often goes with a lively, unreliable disposition, which may either be somewhat superficial but perfectly well-meaning, or, driven by circumstances which it has not the strength to withstand, become that of a scoundrel. Wickham was well on the way to being a scoundrel; but his sexual fascination was so great that Elizabeth Bennet, who was normally of a very critical turn of mind, saw at first absolutely nothing in him but what made him seem the most charming man she had ever met. Even Mrs. Gardiner thought him delightful and only warned Elizabeth against him because he was not in the position to support a wife. (p. 160)

Elizabeth Bennet has perhaps received more admiration than any other heroine in English literature. Stevenson's saying, that when she opened her mouth he wanted to go down on his knees, is particularly interesting because it is the comment of a man on a woman's idea of a charming woman. Not less significant is Professor Bradley's: 'I am meant to fall in love with her, and I do'. She is unique. The only girl between whom and herself there is any hint of resemblance is Benedict's Beatrice. The wit, the prejudice against a lover, the warm and generous indignation against the ill usage of a cousin or a sister, remind us, something, one of the other. She attacks the mind in two ways:

. . . when she moves you see
Like water from a crystal over-filled,
Fresh beauty tremble out of her, and lave
Her fair sides to the ground.

She is also completely human. Glorious as she is, and beloved of her creator, she is kept thoroughly in her place. She was captivated by Wickham, in which she showed herself no whit superior to the rest of female Meryton. She also toyed with the idea of a fancy for Colonel Fitzwilliam, who was much attracted by her. But Colonel Fitzwilliam had made it clear that he had no intentions at all, and, agreeable as he was, she did not mean to be unhappy about him.' Above all there is her prejudice against Darcy, and though their first encounter was markedly unfortunate, she built on it every dislike it could be made to bear; her eager condemnation of him and her no less eager remorse when she found that she had been mistaken, are equally lovable.

The serious side of her nature is perhaps nowhere better indicated than in the chapter where Charlotte Lucas secures and accepts Mr. Collins' proposal and then has to tell Elizabeth that she has done so. (pp. 160-61)

It is a scene between two young women, both of them normal, pleasant and good; the conversation is of the briefest; in it the more remarkable of the two speaks only twice, and less than a dozen words in all; but what a world of thought and feeling, experience and philosophy it conjures up! (pp. 161-62)

The character of Fitzwilliam Darcy has been said to have no counterpart in modern society. The error is a strange one. Darcy's uniting gentle birth with such wealth is indeed an anachronism. To-day death duties would have felled the Pemberley woods and the estate passed into the hands of ales and stout. But Darcy's essential character is independent of circumstances. He had the awkwardness and stiffness of a man who mixes little with society and only on his own terms, but it was also the awkwardness and stiffness that is found with Darcy's physical type, immediately recognizable among the reserved and inarticulate English of to-day. That his behaviour in the early part of the book is owing to a series of external circumstances rather than to his essential character is very carefully shown, and we have a further proof of how easy it was to misunderstand him: when he and Elizabeth were becoming reconciled to each other at Lambton, and Elizabeth had suddenly to give him the news of Lydia's elopement, he was quite silent and took an abrupt departure. She thought his behaviour owing to his redoubled disgust at her family; it was really consternation at a state of affairs for which, as one who had failed to expose Wickham to society, he thought himself partially responsible.

That his character was actually quite different from what it appeared to be on the surface is of course revealed by his behaviour once the shock of Elizabeth's abuse has made him realize how it struck other people. It is a piece of extremely subtle characterization that when Elizabeth first met Lady Catherine, she thought that she and Mr. Darcy were alike, and after she had fallen in love with Darcy, she wondered how she could ever have imagined a resemblance. We do not, however, doubt that the resemblance was there. It was a family likeness, accentuated on the one hand by a harsh and arrogant nature and on the other by a shy and uncommunicative one. This view of Darcy is borne out by the drawing of his sister. Georgiana Darcy was a very well-meaning girl, but she was so extremely shy that society was an agony to her; and though for her brother's sake she was longing to please Elizabeth and Mrs. Gardiner, it was all that her gentle, pleasant governess could do to guide her through the occasion of their call as became the lady of Pemberley.

That some of his real nature had been, if unconsciously, perceived by Elizabeth before their reconciliation is proved by one of Jane Austen's rare and very beautiful touches of sensibility. It occurs when Elizabeth and her party are being taken round Pemberley by the housekeeper and arrive at the picture-gallery. 'In the gallery were many family portraits, but they could have little to fix the attention of a stranger. Elizabeth walked on in quest of the only face whose features would be known to her. At last it arrested her—and she beheld a striking resemblance of Mr. Darcy, with such a smile over the face, as she remembered to have sometimes seen when he looked at her.'

It is true that in an attempt to see whether Darcy's character would stand the test of time, it is necessary to see how it would appear were he denuded of his wealth; but from the point of view of his position in the work of art that presents him to us, the background of Pemberley, that Derbyshire landscape with its trees in the variegated beauty and the stillness of summer, is truly harmonious. (pp. 162-63)

There is such intense psychological interest in Jane Austen's work that it is possible, strange as it may seem, to forget for a moment that they are primarily creations of comedy; not only are they so in the broader sense, by which one implies that in the development of the plot a character which begins with a mistaken attitude to life is brought back to the angle of normality, and reformed in the process, but Jane Austen's own attitude to the various characters is largely satirical, in however mildly luminous a degree; there is none of her figures whom she treats in a consistently serious manner. Most important of all, she has comic portraits whose effect is that of 'straight' comedy, though their foundation is of the most brilliant and subtle excellence. Mr. Bennet is one of the most remarkable figures in the whole range of English comedy. Dean Swift is one of the few English masters of irony; it is not perhaps too much to say that Mr. Bennet is another. Of every other one of Jane Austen's male characters we may say that they are men as they appear to women; and that they are so is no reflection upon her powers. Man's aspect as he appears to women is after all as important, neither more nor less, as his aspect as he appears to men. But Mr. Bennet is the unique exception; he might have been drawn by a man, except that it is difficult to think of a man who could have drawn him so well. It is relatively easy to be witty at somebody else's expense; but to create the character of a genuinely witty man is, one would say, for a woman, next door to impossible. Male characters of unconscious humour, women, with their capacity for acute observation, achieve very well. George Eliot was highly successful in this genre, so was Fanny Burney; even Emily Brontë relaxed her sternness over the delineation of old Joseph; Jane Austen herself is of course inimitable; but Mr. Bennet was something extraordinary even for her. To detach his remarks from their context is to deprive them of half their subtlety and force: as, for instance, his reply to the endless maunderings of Mrs. Bennet on the subject of the entail in Mr. Collins's favour.

> ' "How anyone could have the conscience to entail away an estate from one's own daughters, I cannot understand, and all for the sake of Mr. Collins, too! Why should *he* have it more than anybody else?"

> ' "I leave it to yourself to determine," said Mr. Bennet.'

One can appreciate the full aroma of that only after having read the twenty-three chapters that precede it.

Of Mrs. Bennet and Mr. Collins, those two creations of unconscious humour, the only method of doing justice to them would be to repeat every word uttered by either; but it is one of the remarkable aspects of Jane Austen's comedy that though such characters are brilliantly funny, one can at the same time see them in relation to every aspect of ordinary life. (pp. 164-65)

The distinguishing of novelists as 'subjective' and 'objective' is essentially misleading, since a purely objective presentation of a character is, to a human being, an impossibility; but the degree to which novelists appear to be either is sometimes very marked. In the last four of Jane Austen's works we are insensibly drawn in to believing that her rendering of the characters of Mrs. Bennet and Mrs. Norris and Miss Bates and Mary Musgrave gives us the actual scientific truth about those characters. It is impossible, almost, to have any other opinion of them than that held by Jane Austen herself. She makes none of those violent assaults upon our prejudice and our imagination which the writer makes who is eminently subjective; she seems to leave us quite free to form our own judgement on the most mature of her masterpieces, but really the guiding is there, only it is so firm and skilful that we have not the opportunity to perceive it, excepting just now and again. (pp. 165-66)

Elizabeth Jenkins, in her *Jane Austen: A Biography*, 1938. Reprint by Victor Gollancz Ltd., 1968, 286 p.

D. W. HARDING
(essay date 1940)

[In the excerpt below, Harding discusses intention and theme in Austen's works.]

The impression of Jane Austen which has filtered through to the reading public down from the first-hand critics, through histories of literature, university courses, literary journalism and polite allusion, deters many who might be her best readers from bothering with her at all. How can this popular impression be described? In my experience the first idea to be absorbed from the atmosphere surrounding her work was that she offered exceptionally favourable openings to the exponents of urbanity. (p. 346)

I was given to understand that her scope was of course extremely restricted, but that within her limits she succeeded admirably in expressing the gentler virtues of a civilized social order. She could do this because she lived at a time when, as a sensitive person of culture, she could still feel that she had a place in society and could address the reading public as sympathic equals; she might introduce unpleasant people into her stories but she could confidently expose them to a public opinion that condemned them. Chiefly, so I gathered, she was a delicate satirist, revealing with inimitable lightness of touch the comic foibles and amiable weaknesses of the people whom she lived amongst and liked.

All this was enough to make me quite certain I didn't want to read her. And it is, I believe, a seriously misleading impression. Fragments of the truth have been incorporated in it but they are fitted into a pattern whose total effect is false. And yet the wide currency of this false impression is an indication of Jane Austen's success in an essential part of her complex intention as a writer: her books are, as she meant them to be, read and enjoyed by precisely the sort of people whom she disliked; she is a literary classic of the society which attitudes like hers, held widely enough, would undermine. (pp. 346-47)

Look at the passage in *Northanger Abbey* where Henry Tilney offers a solemn reprimand of Catherine's fantastic suspicions about his father:

> 'Dear Miss Morland, consider the dreadful nature of these suspicions you have entertained. What have you been judging from? Remember the country and the age in which we live. Remember that we are English, that we are Christians. Consult your own understanding, your own sense of the probable, your

own observation of what is passing around you. Does our education prepare us for such atrocities? Do our laws connive at them? Could they be perpetrated without being known, in a country like this, where social and literary intercourse is on such a footing, and where roads and newspapers lay everything open?'

Had the passage really been as I quote it nothing would have been out of tone. But I omitted a clause. The last sentence actually runs: 'Could they be perpetrated without being known, in a country like this, where social and literary intercourse is on such a footing, where every man is surrounded by a neighbourhood of voluntary spies, and where roads and newspapers lay everything open?' 'Where every man is surrounded by a neighbourhood of voluntary spies'—with its touch of paranoia that surprising remark is badly out of tune both with 'Henry's astonishing generosity and nobleness of conduct' and with the accepted idea of Jane Austen. (pp. 347-48)

Why is it that, holding the view she did of people's spying, Jane Austen should slip it in amongst Henry Tilney's eulogies of the age? By doing so she achieves two ends, ends which she may not have consciously aimed at. In such a speech from such a character the remark is unexpected and unbelievable, with the result that it is quite unlikely to be taken in at all by many readers; it slips through their minds without creating a disturbance. It gets said, but with a minimum risk of setting people's backs up. The second end achieved by giving the remark such a context is that of off-setting it at once by more appreciative views of society and so refraining from indulging an exaggerated bitterness. (p. 348)

[The] eruption of fear and hatred into the relationships of everyday social life is something that the urbane admirer of Jane Austen finds distasteful; it is not the satire of one who writes securely for the entertainment of her civilised acquaintances. And it has the effect for the attentive reader, of changing the flavour of the more ordinary satire amongst which it is embedded. (p. 350)

To speak of this aspect of her work as 'satire' is perhaps misleading. She has none of the underlying didactic intention ordinarily attributed to the satirist. Her object is not missionary; it is the more desperate one of merely finding some mode of existence for her critical attitudes. To her the first necessity was to keep on reasonably good terms with the associates of her everyday life; she had a deep need of their affection and a genuine respect for the ordered, decent civilisation that they upheld. And yet she was sensitive to their crudenesses and complacencies and knew that her real existence depended on resisting many of the values they implied. The novels gave her a way out of this dilemma. This, rather than the ambition of entertaining a posterity of

urbane gentlemen, was her motive force in writing. (p. 351)

She found, of course, that one of the most useful peculiarities of her society was its willingness to remain blind to the implications of a caricature. She found people eager to laugh at faults they tolerated in themselves and their friends, so long as the faults were exaggerated and the laughter 'good-natured'—so long, that is, as the assault on society could be regarded as a mock assault and not genuinely disruptive. (p. 352)

Caricature served Jane Austen's purpose perfectly. Under her treatment one can never say where caricature leaves off and the claim to serious portraiture begins. Mr. Collins is only given a trifle more comic exaggeration than Lady Catherine de Bourgh, and by her standards is a possible human being. Lady Catherine in turn seems acceptable as a portrait if the criterion of verisimilitude is her nephew Mr. Darcy. And he, finally, although to some extent a caricature, is near enough natural portraiture to stand beside Elizabeth Bennet, who, like all the heroines, is presented as an undistorted portrait. The simplest comic effects are gained by bringing the caricatures into direct contact with the real people, as in Mr. Collins' visit to the Bennets and his proposal to Elizabeth. But at the same time one knows that, though from some points of view caricature, in other directions he does, by easy stages, fit into the real world. He is real enough to Mrs. Bennet; and she is real enough to Elizabeth to create a situation of real misery for her when she refuses. Consequently the proposal scene is not only comic fantasy, but it is also, for Elizabeth, a taste of the fantastic nightmare in which economic and social institutions have such power over the values of personal relationships that the comic monster is nearly able to get her. (pp. 352-53)

The social group having such ambivalence for her, it is not surprising if her conflict should find some outlets not fully within her conscious control. To draw attention to these, however, is not to suggest that they lessen the value of her conscious intention and its achievements.

The chief instance is the fascination she found in the Cinderella theme, the Cinderella theme with the fairy godmother omitted. For in Jane Austen's treatment the natural order of things manages to reassert the heroine's proper pre-eminence without the intervention any human or quasi-human helper. In this respect she allies the Cinderella theme to another fairy-tale theme which is often introduced—that of the princess brought up by unworthy parents but never losing the delicate sensibilities which are an inborn part of her. This latter theme appears most explicitly in *Mansfield Park,* the unfinished story of *The Watsons,* and, with some softening, in *Pride and Prejudice.* The contrast between Fanny Price's true nature and her squalid home at Portsmouth is the clearest statement of the idea, but in the first four of the finished novels the heroine's final position is, even in the worldly sense, always above her reasonable social expectations by conventional standards, but corresponding to her natural worth.

To leave it at this, however, would be highly misleading. It is the development which occurs in her treatment of the Cinderella theme that most rewards attention. In *Northanger Abbey, Sense and Sensibility* and *Pride and Prejudice* it is handled simply; the heroine is in some degree isolated from those around her by being more sensitive or of finer moral insight or sounder judgment, and her marriage to the handsome prince at the end is in the nature of a reward for being different from the rest and a consolation for the distresses entailed by being different. (p. 355)

To put the point in general terms, the heroine of these early novels is herself the criterion of sound judgment and good feeling. She may claim that her values are sanctioned by good breeding and a religious civilisation, but in fact none of the people she meets represents those values so effectively as she does herself. (p. 356)

[In *Mansfield Park* Jane Austen's] emphasis is on the deep importance of the conventional virtues, of civilised seemliness, decorum, and sound religious feeling. These become the worthy objects of the heroine's loyalties; and they so nearly comprise the whole range of her values that Fanny Price is the least interesting of all the heroines. For the first time, Jane Austen sets the heroine in submissive alliance with the conventionally virtuous people of the story. . . . (p. 357)

Whether or not Jane Austen realised what she had been doing, at all events the production of *Mansfield Park* enabled her to go on next to the extraordinary achievement of *Emma,* in which a much more complete humility is combined with the earlier unblinking attention to people as they are. The underlying argument has a different trend. She continues to see that the heroine has derived from the people and conditions around her, but she now keeps clearly in mind the objectionable features of those people; and she faces the far bolder conclusion that even a heroine is likely to have assimilated many of the more unpleasant possibilities of the human being in society. And it is not that society has spoilt an originally perfect girl who now has to recover her pristine good sense, as it was with Catherine Morland, but that the heroine has not yet achieved anything like perfection and is actually going to learn a number of serious lessons from some of the people she lives with.

Consider in the first place the treatment here of the two favourite themes of the earlier novels. The Cinderella theme is now relegated to the sub-heroine, Jane Fairfax. Its working out involves the discomfiture of

the heroine, who in this respect is put into the position of one of the ugly sisters. Moreover the Cinderella procedure is shown in the light of a social anomaly, rather a nuisance and requiring the excuse of unusual circumstances.

The associated theme of the child brought up in humble circumstances whose inborn nature fits her for better things is frankly parodied and deflated in the story of Harriet Smith, the illegitimate child whom Emma tries to turn into a snob. . . .

Thus the structure of the narrative expresses a complete change in Jane Austen's outlook on the heroine in relation to others. And the story no longer progresses towards her vindication or consolation; it consists in her gradual, humbling self-enlightenment. (p. 359)

We cannot say that in *Emma* Jane Austen abandons the Cinderella story. She so deliberately inverts it that we ought to regard *Emma* as a bold variant of the theme and a further exploration of its underlying significance for her. In *Persuasion* she goes back to the Cinderella situation in its most direct and simple form, but develops a vitally important aspect of it that she had previously avoided. This is the significance for Cinderella of her idealised dead mother. (p. 360)

Now one of the obvious appeals of the Cinderella story, as of all stories of wicked step-mothers, is that it resolves the ambivalence of the mother by the simple plan of splitting her in two: the ideal mother is dead and can be adored without risk of disturbance; the living mother is completely detestable and can be hated whole-heartedly without self-reproach.

In her early novels Jane Austen consistently avoided dealing with a mother who could be a genuinely intimate friend of her daughter. Lady Susan, of the unfinished novel, is her daughter's enemy. In *Northanger Abbey* the mother is busy with the household and the younger children. In *Sense and Sensibility* she herself has to be guided and kept in hand by her daughter's sounder judgment. In *Pride and Prejudice* she is Mrs. Bennet. In *Mansfield Park* she is a slattern whom the heroine only visits once in the course of the novel. In *Emma* the mother is dead and Miss Taylor, her substitute, always remains to some extent the promoted governess. This avoidance may seem strange, but it can be understood as the precaution of a mind which, although in the Cinderella situation, is still too sensitive and honest to offer as a complete portrait the half-truth of the idealised dead mother.

But in *Persuasion* she does approach the problem which is latent here. She puts her heroine in the Cinderella setting, and so heightens her need for affection. And then in Lady Russell she provides a godmother, not fairy but human, with whom Anne Elliot can have much the relationship of a daughter with a greatly loved, but humanly possible, mother. Jane Austen then goes on to face the implications of such a relationship—and there runs through the whole story a lament for seven years' loss of happiness owing to Anne's having yielded to her godmother's persuasion. (pp. 360-61)

The attempt to suggest a slightly different emphasis in the reading of Jane Austen is not offered as a balanced appraisal of her work. It is deliberately lopsided, neglecting the many points at which the established view seems adequate. I have tried to underline one or two features of her work that claim the sort of readers who sometimes miss her—those who would turn to her not for relief and escape but as a formidable ally against things and people which were to her, and still are, hateful. (p. 362)

D. W. Harding, "Regulated Hatred: An Aspect of the Work of Jane Austen," in *Scrutiny,* Vol. VIII, No. 4, March, 1940, pp. 346-62.

IAN WATT
(essay date 1957)

[Watt is one of the most significant contributors to the study of the novel form in the twentieth century. In the following excerpt, he discusses theme and technique in Austen's works.]

[Both Jane Austen and Fanny Burney] followed Richardson—the Richardson of the less intense domestic conflicts of *Sir Charles Grandison*—in their minute presentation of daily life. At the same time Fanny Burney and Jane Austen followed Fielding in adopting a more detached attitude to their narrative material, and in evaluating it from a comic and objective point of view. It is here that Jane Austen's technical genius manifests itself. She dispensed with the participating narrator, whether as the author of a memoir as in Defoe, or as letterwriter as in Richardson, probably because both of these roles make freedom to comment and evaluate more difficult to arrange; instead she told her stories after Fielding's manner, as a confessed author. Jane Austen's variant of the commenting narrator, however, was so much more discreet that it did not substantially affect the authenticity of her narrative. Her analyses of her characters and their states of mind, and her ironical juxtapositions of motive and situation are as pointed as anything in Fielding, but they do not seem to come from an intrusive author but rather from some august and impersonal spirit of social and psychological understanding.

At the same time, Jane Austen varied her narrative point of view sufficiently to give us, not only editorial comment, but much of Defoe's and Richardson's psychological closeness to the subjective world of the characters. In her novels there is usually one character whose consciousness is tacitly accorded a privileged status, and whose mental life is rendered more completely than that of the other characters. In *Pride and Prejudice* . . . , for example, the story is told substantially from the point of view of Elizabeth Bennet, the heroine; but the identification is always qualified by the other role of the narrator acting as dispassionate analyst, and as a result the reader does not lose his critical awareness of the novel as a whole. The same strategy as regards point of view is employed with supreme brilliance in *Emma* . . . , a novel which combines Fielding's characteristic strength in conveying the sense of society as a whole, with something of Henry James's capacity for locating the essential structural continuity of his novel in the reader's growing awareness of the full complexity of the personality and situation of the character through whom the story is mainly told: the unfolding of Emma Woodhouse's inner being has much of the drama of progressive revelation with which James presents Maisie Farange or Lambert Strether.

Jane Austen's novels, in short, must be seen as the most successful solutions of the two general narrative problems for which Richardson and Fielding had provided only partial answers. She was able to combine into a harmonious unity the advantages both of realism of presentation and realism of assessment, of the internal and of the external approaches to character; her novels have authenticity without diffuseness or trickery, wisdom of social comment without a garrulous essayist, and a sense of the social order which is not achieved at the expense of the individuality and autonomy of the characters.

Jane Austen's novels are also the climax of many other aspects of the eighteenth-century novel. In their subjects, despite some obvious differences, they continue many of the characteristic interests of Defoe, Richardson and Fielding. Jane Austen faces more squarely than Defoe, for example, the social and moral problems raised by economic individualism and the middle-class quest for improved status; she follows Richardson in basing her novels on marriage and especially on the proper feminine role in the matter; and her ultimate picture of the proper norms of the social system is similar to that of Fielding although its application to the characters and their situation is in general more serious and discriminating.

Jane Austen's novels are also representative in another sense; they reflect the process whereby . . . women were playing an increasingly important part in the literary scene. The majority of eighteenth-century novels were actually written by women, but this had long remained a purely quantitative assertion of dominance; it was Jane Austen who completed the work that Fanny Burney had begun, and challenged masculine prerogative in a much more important matter. Her example suggests that the feminine sensibility was in some ways better equipped to reveal the intricacies of personal relationships and was therefore at a real advantage in the realm of the novel. (pp. 296-98)

Ian Watt, "Realism and the Later Tradition: A Note," in his *The Rise of the Novel: Studies in Defoe, Richardson and Fielding,* University of California Press, 1957, pp. 290-302.

SUSAN MORGAN

(essay date 1980)

[In the following excerpt, Morgan considers the positive role of the imagination in *Emma*.]

Emma is not a book about mature understanding replacing immature fancy. Nor is it about a girl's fear of involvement in life being overcome. It is about the powers of the individual mind, the powers of sympathy and imagination, and about how these powers can find their proper objects in the world outside the mind. The heroine insists that life be interesting and tries to make it so. She makes the child's demand that she be entertained. But the source of that demand is her imagination. Emma's demand is valid; the largeness of her claims on life gives her greatness, in spite of her faults. The claim of the novel is that life is interesting, that fact can be as delightful as fiction, that imagination need not be in conflict with reality.

At the end of the novel Emma marries Mr. Knightley and is assured of happiness. For Mr. Knightley, who sees her lovingly and clearly, she is "faultless in spite of all her faults." But Emma can no longer think of herself as first because there is someone else in the world. And that someone else is not Mr. Knightley. It is Jane Fairfax. Jane must leave Highbury without ever satisfying that wish to know her which the author has so deliberately created. *Emma* celebrates the joys of close family connections, well-known scenes, "very old friends." It is a story in which the ideal of a lover has turned out to be a relative and neighbor since childhood, in which the idyll of perfect happiness is to be lived without leaving home. But Highbury is not a closed world. And Jane is our promise that there are interesting people yet to become acquainted with. Austen can send her heroine out from the proven delights of her own mind into the world of other people because she has provided someone worth making that journey for.

What Emma learns by the end of the story has

been present for the reader throughout in the narrative technique. The leap which takes writer and reader into the minds of characters is impossible in life but common in novels. Austen is the first writer in English fiction to make this privileged perspective a major technique. She uses "free indirect speech" to see into a character and to see from that character's point of view. Certainly, as [Wayne] Booth has pointed out, seeing into Emma provides sympathy for her as well as knowledge of her faults:

> By showing most of the story through Emma's eyes, the author insures that we will travel with Emma rather than stand against her . . . the sustained inner view leads the reader to hope for good fortune for the character with whom he travels, quite independently of the qualities revealed.

This inside view has become necessary because of Austen's sense of difficulties of perception, her conviction that there is a space between an inner and outer view. What people or characters in books say and do is not enough to know them by. There are, of course, acts that by themselves condemn the doers. But villains are rare and easily judged. Austen concerns herself with the more difficult and more subtle problem of how to understand those around us and ourselves. Morality in *Emma,* as in all Austen's novels, is not a code, or norm, or principle, which one can live and die by. Instead, it is a way of seeing which includes within its definition some sort of candor or affection. Judgment is seldom conclusive, never infallible. So we understand best and judge best when aided by sympathy and imagination. Austen lets us understand Emma by allowing us, for a little while, to live in her mind.

Austen called Emma a character "whom no one but myself will much like," but it is clear that the joy and pleasure of the book depend upon caring about Emma. Certainly, the external events are not gripping. There are no abductions or seductions, no rapes or near rapes, no murders or stray babies, no stirring adventures, no dark deeds, no characters beneath contempt or even above reproach. There are a few gypsies who wander in and scare Harriet, but they seem a little silly in the environs of Highbury and are soon dispatched. In fact, they remind us that it is not Harriet's rescue from them but her rescue on the dance floor which actually matters. Not only does nothing out of the way happen—very little happens at all. There are some dinners, a couple of parties, one secret engagement, and even a few marriages. We do learn by hearsay of trips, a death, and a birth. In *Emma* the lack of large-scale events is a prominent fact. This is characteristic of Austen. Nonetheless, *Emma* is an extreme case. Less happens in this novel than in any of her others. It is the only one set all in one place, and Emma the only heroine who is never away from home.

Emma is also extreme in the decency of its characters. Austen was never directly interested in villains, but in all her other novels there is at least one man and one woman who are wicked. We do hear about Mrs. Churchill, and the Eltons are both crude and cruel. But they do not compare, at least in their actions, to Isabella Thorpe and General Tilney, Wickham and Lady Catherine de Bourgh, Willoughby and Lucy Steele, Henry Crawford and Mrs. Norris, or Mr. Elliot and Mrs. Clay. Some of these people do horrible things. The Eltons are probably capable of meanness beyond their public cruelty to Harriet or their excruciating officiousness to Jane Fairfax. And Mrs. Churchill could have swooped down like Lady Catherine if Austen had wished to advance her story by external conflict, by having the not-so-nice people get in the way of the nice. But Highbury is an idyll, and its evil characters are ineffectual.

The only character whose actions provide obstacles to the deserved happiness of others is Emma herself. Her snobbery damages Robert Martin as Lady Catherine had tried to damage Elizabeth Bennet, and she flirts as self-indulgently as Mary Crawford. We side with Elizabeth and Fanny, and with farmer Martin and Jane. Still, by what Booth calls that "stroke of good fortune," Emma is the heroine. We don't turn a page to see Robert Martin get his girl or even to see Mr. Knightley get his, but just to see more of Emma.

Emma's power to interest the reader is inseparable from her power to interest herself. Emma will always love herself. In thinking of what she learns it is clear that the aim is not to relinquish her self-love. It is al-most the end of the story when Emma makes that wonderful remark to Mr. Knightley that "I always deserve the best treatment, because I never put up with any other." Emma's love of herself is part of what makes her creative and part of why she asks so much of her world. . . . In *Emma* loving oneself is the necessary condition for morality and imagination. This had already been true for heroes. Austen has transformed the idea of the heroine in English fiction by making it true of Emma.

When Mr. Knightley tells her that Robert Martin has at last got Harriet, Emma is relieved and grateful that her interference had in the end not been irretrievable. She vows humility and circumspection: "Serious she was, very serious in her thankfulness, and in her resolutions; and yet there was no preventing a laugh, sometimes in the very midst of them." Without that laugh Emma's joy in her world would have shrunk. For Harriet's fluctuating heart is comical. Emma is not too reformed to appreciate that. Early in the novel, after the pain of telling Harriet Mr. Elton's true intentions, Emma had made a similar resolution, of "being humble and discreet, and repressing imagination all the rest of her life." But Emma has done no such thing. For imagination, like tenderness, belongs to the strong people. To repress it would be to repress the power of the self to reach out and make significant "all those little matters on which the daily happiness of private life depends." (pp. 38-43)

Susan Morgan, in her *In the Meantime: Character and Perception in Jane Austen's Fiction,* University of Chicago Press, 1980, 210 p.

SOURCES FOR FURTHER STUDY

Halperin, John, ed. *Jane Austen: Bicentenary Essays.* Cambridge: Cambridge University Press, 1975, 334 p.

A collection of critical essays published in commemoration of the two-hundreth anniversary of Austen's birth. The contributors include well-known Austen scholars, and the essays offer a variety of topics and approaches to her work.

Jenkins, Elizabeth. *Jane Austen.* New York: Grosset & Dunlap, 1948, 410 p.

A biographical and critical study noted for its thorough and detailed examination of Austen's life and works.

Parrish, Stephen M., ed. *Emma,* by Jane Austen. A Norton Critical Edition. New York: W. W. Norton & Co., 1972, 460 p.

An authoritative text of the novel, including background materials, letters, and excerpts from contemporary reviews and modern criticism.

Rubenstein, E., ed. *Twentieth-Century Interpretations of "Pride and Prejudice": A Collection of Critical Essays.* Twentieth-Century Interpretations, edited by Maynard Mack. Englewood Cliffs, N.J.: Prentice-Hall, 1969, 120 p.

Reprints a selection of important essays about Austen.

Southam, B. C., ed. *Critical Essays on Jane Austen.* New York: Barnes & Noble, 1969, 206 p.

Essay collection.

Wright, Andrew H. *Jane Austen's Novels: A Study in Structure.* Rev. ed. London: Chatto & Windus, 1967, 210 p.

Explores Austen's narrative technique and style.

James Baldwin

1924-1987

(Full name James Arthur Baldwin) American novelist, essayist, dramatist, nonfiction and short story writer, poet, scriptwriter, and author of children's books.

INTRODUCTION

*B*aldwin is recognized as one of the most important writers in post-World War II American literature. In his works he exposed racial and sexual polarization in American society and challenged readers to confront and resolve these differences. Baldwin's influence and popularity reached their peak during the 1960s, when he was regarded by many as the leading literary spokesman of the civil rights movement. His novels, essays, and other writings attest to his premise that the black American, as an object of suffering and abuse, represents a universal symbol of human conflict.

Much of Baldwin's work is based on his unhappy childhood and adolescence. He was born and raised in Harlem under very trying circumstances. His stepfather, an evangelical preacher, struggled to support a large family and demanded the most rigorous religious behavior from his nine children. According to John W. Roberts, "Baldwin's ambivalent relationship with his stepfather served as a constant source of tension during his formative years and informs some of his best mature writings. . . . The demands of caring for younger siblings and his stepfather's religious convictions in large part shielded the boy from the harsh realities of Harlem street life during the 1930s." As a youth Baldwin read constantly and even tried his hand at writing. He once noted, "For me writing was an act of love. It was an attempt—not to get the world's attention—it was an attempt to be loved. It seemed a way to save myself and to save my family. It came out of despair. And it seemed the only way to another world." During the summer of his fourteenth birthday he underwent a dramatic religious conversion, partly in response to his emerging sexuality and partly as a further buffer against the omnipresent temptations of drugs and crime. Baldwin served as a junior minister for three years at the

Fireside Pentecostal Assembly, but gradually he lost his desire to preach as he began to question blacks' acceptance of Christian tenets that had, in essence, been used to enslave them.

Shortly after his conversion, Baldwin was accepted at De Witt Clinton High School, a predominantly white, Jewish school in the Bronx. This new environment was also a cause of Baldwin's reassessment and eventual rejection of his religious stance. Soon after he was graduated in 1942, Baldwin was compelled to find work in order to help support his brothers and sisters. He took a job in the defense industry in Belle Meade, New Jersey, and there, not for the first time, he was confronted with racism, discrimination, and the debilitating regulations of segregation. Baldwin's disagreeable experiences in New Jersey were closely followed by his stepfather's death, after which Baldwin determined to make writing his sole profession. He moved to Greenwich Village and began to write a novel, supporting himself by performing a variety of odd jobs. In 1944 he met author Richard Wright, who helped him obtain the 1945 Eugene F. Saxton fellowship. Despite the financial freedom the fellowship provided, Baldwin was unable to complete his novel that year. Moreover, he found the social and cultural tenor of the United States increasingly stifling. Eventually, in 1948, he moved to Paris, using funds from a Rosenwald Foundation fellowship to pay his passage. Most critics believe that this journey abroad was fundamental to Baldwin's development as a writer.

"Once I found myself on the other side of the ocean," Baldwin told the *New York Times,* "I could see where I came from very clearly, and I could see that I carried myself, which is my home, with me. You can never escape that. I am the grandson of a slave, and I am a writer. I must deal with both." Through some difficult financial and emotional periods, the young author undertook a process of self-realization that included both an acceptance of his heritage and an admittance of his homosexuality. Robert A. Bone noted that Europe gave Baldwin many things: "It gave him a world perspective from which to approach the question of his own identity. It gave him a tender love affair which would dominate the pages of his later fiction. But above all, Europe gave him back himself. The immediate fruit of self-recovery was a great creative outburst. First came two [works] of reconciliation with his racial heritage. *Go Tell It on the Mountain* (1953) and *The Amen Corner* (1955) represent a search for roots, a surrender to tradition, an acceptance of the Negro past. Then came a series of essays which probe, deeper than anyone has dared, the psychic history of this nation. They are a moving record of a man's struggle to define the forces that have shaped him, in order that he may accept himself."

Baldwin was hailed by critics as a major novelist and a worthy successor to Ralph Ellison and Richard Wright following the publication of his semiautobiographical novel *Go Tell It on the Mountain.* The book dramatizes the events leading to the religious confirmation of John Grimes, a sensitive Harlem youth struggling to come to terms with his confusion over his sexuality and his religious upbringing. At the core of the novel is a family's legacy of brutality and hate, augmented by the destructive relationship between John and his stepfather, a fundamentalist preacher whose insecurities over his own religious commitment result in his abusive treatment of John and his emotional neglect of the family. Baldwin earned unanimous praise for his skillful evocation of his characters' squalid lives and for his powerful language, which some critics likened to a fire-and-brimstone oratory.

While most critics regarded *Go Tell It on the Mountain* as a cathartic novel in which Baldwin attempted to resolve the emotional anguish of his adolescence, others viewed his next work, *Giovanni's Room* (1956), as the one in which he openly confronted his homosexuality. The novel was controversial, because Baldwin was one of the first black writers to openly discuss homosexuality in his fiction. *Giovanni's Room,* which is set in Paris, is the story of an ill-fated love affair between a white American student and an Italian bartender. Many critics were outraged by Baldwin's blunt language and his polemic topic, though some reviewers echoed David Littlejohn's assessment that the work is "certainly one of the most subtle novels of the homosexual world." Baldwin continued his investigation of racial and sexual politics in the novel *Another Country* (1962), which provoked even more debate. Although it received largely negative reviews due to Baldwin's candid depiction of sexual relations, some commentators considered *Another Country* superior to *Giovanni's Room* in terms of thematic scope and descriptive quality.

Baldwin's fiction of the late 1960s and early 1970s was primarily influenced by his involvement in the civil rights movement. *Tell Me How Long the Train's Been Gone* (1968) centers on two brothers and different attempts to escape the ghetto; one finds success in the entertainment industry, while the other is nearly destroyed by racism and violence. *If Beale Street Could Talk* (1974) further examined blacks living in a hostile environment. In *Just above My Head* (1979), Baldwin returned to his earlier themes of religion and sexuality in a complex story of a homosexual gospel singer. Although these works were best-sellers, they signalled for most critics a decline in Baldwin's creative talents due to his reliance on didacticism. In a 1985 interview, Baldwin discussed his erratic literary position: "The rise and fall of one's reputation. What can you do about it? I think that comes with the territory. . . . Any real artist will never be judged in the time of his time; whatever judgment is delivered in the time of his time cannot be trusted."

Because Baldwin sought to inform and confront whites, and because his fiction contains interracial love affairs, he quickly came under attack from writers of the Black Arts Movement, who called for a literature exclusively by and for blacks. Baldwin refused to align himself with the movement; he continued to call himself an "American writer" as opposed to a "black writer" and continued to confront the issues facing a multi-racial society. Eldridge Cleaver, in his book *Soul on Ice,* accused Baldwin of a hatred of black people and a "shameful, fanatical fawning" love of whites. What Cleaver saw as complicity with whites, Baldwin saw rather as an attempt to alter the real daily environment with which black Americans have been faced all their lives.

Although Baldwin is best known as a novelist, his nonfiction works have also received substantial critical acclaim. The essay "Everybody's Protest Novel," published in 1949, introduced him to the New York intelligentsia and generated controversy for its attack on authors of protest fiction, including Richard Wright, who, Baldwin maintained, perpetuated rather than condemned negative racial stereotypes. While Baldwin viewed this piece as an exploration of the thematic options that black writers could follow, Wright considered it a personal affront and subsequently terminated his professional alliance with Baldwin. Nevertheless, critics praised Baldwin for his perceptive analysis of protest literature and for his lucid prose. He earned additional praise for the essays collected in *Notes of a Native Son* (1955) and *Nobody Knows My Name: More Notes of a Native Son* (1961). In these volumes, Baldwin optimistically examined the condition of race relations in the United States and abroad In essays that range from poignant autobiographical remembrances to scholarly literary and social criticism. He also used personal experience to address the problems artists face when drawn to political activism. Critics viewed Baldwin's next nonfiction work, *The Fire Next Time* (1963), as both a passionate plea for reconciliation between the races and as a manifesto for black liberation. As racial tensions escalated in the mid-1960s, Baldwin's vision of America turned increasingly bitter and his prose more inflammatory. After the publication of *No Name in the Street* (1972), Baldwin was faulted for abandoning his deft powers of persuasion in favor of rhetoric and was accused by some of racism. One of Baldwin's last nonfiction works, *The Evidence of Things Not Seen* (1985), is about the Atlanta child murders, which claimed the lives of more than twenty black children and adolescents between 1979 and 1981. In this treatise, Baldwin combined straight reportage with an examination of the tragedy, perceiving the murders as a prelude to an apocalyptic confrontation between black and white society.

In addition to his numerous books, Baldwin was one of the few black authors to have had more than one of his plays produced on Broadway. Both *The Amen Corner,* another treatment of storefront pentecostal religion, and *Blues for Mister Charlie* (1964), a drama based on the racially motivated murder of Emmett Till in 1955, had successful Broadway runs and numerous revivals. Fred L. Standley commented that in both plays, "as in his other literary works, Baldwin explores a variety of thematic concerns: the historical significance and the potential explosiveness in black-white relations; the necessity for developing a sexual and psychological consciousness and identity; the intertwining of love and power in the universal scheme of existence as well as in the structures of society; the misplaced priorities in the value systems in America; and the responsibility of the artist to promote the evolution of the individual and the society." In *The Black American Writer: Poetry and Drama,* Walter Meserve offered remarks on Baldwin's abilities as a playwright: "Essentially, Baldwin is not particularly dramatic, but he can be extremely eloquent, compelling, and sometimes irritating as a playwright committed to his approach to life." Meserve added, however, that although the author was criticized for creating stereotypes, "his major characters are the most successful and memorable aspects of his plays. People are important to Baldwin, and their problems, generally embedded in their agonizing souls, stimulate him to write. . . . A humanitarian, sensitive to the needs and struggles of man, he writes of inner turmoil, spiritual disruption, the consequence upon people of the burdens of the world, both White and Black."

At the time of his death from stomach cancer late in 1987, Baldwin was still working on two projects—a play, *The Welcome Table,* and a biography of Martin Luther King, Jr. Although he lived primarily in France, he had never relinquished his United States citizenship and preferred to think of himself as a "commuter" rather than as an expatriate. The publication of his collected essays, *The Price of the Ticket: Collected Nonfiction, 1948-1985* (1985), and his subsequent death sparked reassessments of his career and commentary on the quality of his lasting legacy. "Mr. Baldwin has become a kind of prophet, a man who has been able to give a public issue all its deeper moral, historical, and personal significance," remarked Robert F. Sayre. . . . " [One mark of his achievement] is that whatever deeper comprehension of the race issue Americans now possess has been in some way shaped by him. And this is to have shaped their comprehension of themselves as well." Perhaps the most telling demonstration of the results of Baldwin's achievement comes from other black writers. Orde Coombs, for instance, concluded that "[because] he existed we felt that the racial miasma that swirled around us would not consume us, and it is not too much to say that this man saved our lives, or at least, gave us the necessary ammunition to face what we knew would continue to be a hostile and condescending world." Playwright and poet Amiri Baraka offered similar thoughts in his eulogy to Baldwin. "This man traveled the earth like its history and its biographer," Baraka said. "He reported, criticized, made beautiful, analyzed, cajoled, lyricized, attacked, sang, made us think, made us better, made us consciously human. . . . He made us feel . . . that we could defend ourselves or define ourselves, that we were in the world not merely as animate slaves, but as terrifyingly sensitive measurers of what is good or evil, beautiful or ugly. This is the power of his spirit. This is the bond which created our love for him." In a posthumous tribute for the *Washington Post*, Juan Williams wrote: "The success of Baldwin's effort as the witness

is evidenced time and again by the people, black and white, gay and straight, famous and anonymous, whose humanity he unveiled in his writings. America and the literary world are far richer for his witness. The proof of a shared humanity across the divides of race, class and more is the testament that the preacher's son, James Arthur Baldwin, has left us."

(For further commentary about Baldwin's life and works, see *Black Literature Criticism*, Vol. 1; *Black Writers; Concise Dictionary of American Literary Biography, 1941-1968; Contemporary Authors*, Vols 1-4, 124; *Contemporary Authors Bibliographical Series*, Vol. 1; *Contemporary Authors New Revision Series*, Vol. 3; *Contemporary Literary Criticism*, Vols. 1, 2, 3, 4, 5, 8, 13, 15, 17, 42, 50; *Dictionary of Literary Biography*, Vols. 2, 7, 33; *Dictionary of Literary Biography Yearbook: 1987*; and *Something about the Author*, Vol. 9.)

CRITICAL COMMENTARY

DAVID LITTLEJOHN

(essay date 1960)

[In the following excerpt, Littlejohn examines *Go Tell It on the Mountain, Giovanni's Room*, and *Another Country*, asserting that each work is "a staving off of death, a matter of survival" for Baldwin.]

James Baldwin has followed the traditional pattern of the Man of Letters, the Man of Letters with a message, in utilizing almost every means of verbal expression to convey his warnings. But almost anyone so committed to directness of statement is likely to find the odd exigencies of theater more a hindrance than a help. One can tell the truth in novels, especially novels like Baldwin's, more or less directly; one must tell the truth in social essays. But a play is made up fundamentally of the lies of other people's lives. The truth is never in the parts, but in the sum, never stated, but experienced. In *The Amen Corner* . . . , a play derived, to some degree, from the same childhood experience as *Go Tell It on the Mountain,* Baldwin was able to attain something of the stark sincerity of that memoir-novel, despite an excess of rhetoric over plot. But his more ambitious attempt, *Blues for Mister Charlie,* betrays serious imaginative disability.

The play was obviously intended as an explosive race-war document . . . , "an attempt," as one reviewer put it, "to give the Caucasians in the audience a

white inferiority complex." With some Caucasians the attempt succeeded all too easily, and reviewers paid pious acknowledgments to the justice of Baldwin's anger. But it is an essay in artless bullying, not a play. Its wicked South is faked, its white villains are flat collages of prejudice-clichés—and this despite Baldwin's professed moral experiment (in the wake of the Medgar Evars murder), his generous attempt to imagine a Southern lynch-killer as a human being. There are playable, even moving moments, bits of ritual drama ("Blacktown" talks to "Whitetown"), intriguing shifts back and forth in time. But the dialogue, for the most part, is hopeless: faked banter, faked poetry, doctrinaire racism, dated slang, all conflated with artificial violence and obscenity. The play rarely comes to life, enough life to hurt a serious listener, because Baldwin lacked either the skill or the patience to imagine completely the place, the story, or the people. . . . Baldwin is no playwright—he has difficulty imagining anyone not Baldwin. It provides a perfect example of the relinquishing of judgment by an undiscerning and intimidated white audience. (pp. 72-4)

Each of James Baldwin's three novels [*Go Tell It on the Mountain, Giovanni's Room,* and *Another Country*] has been written out of some personal necessity of the author's, a necessity which it describes, conveys, and, hopefully, enables the author to transcend. Everything he writes—when he writes well—bears this sense of an inner necessity, of the whole of himself told

Principal Works

Go Tell It on the Mountain (novel) 1953

The Amen Corner (drama) 1955

Notes of a Native Son (essays) 1955

Giovanni's Room (novel) 1956

Nobody Knows My Name: More Notes of a Native Son (essays) 1961

Another Country (novel) 1962

The Fire Next Time (essays) 1963

Blues for Mister Charlie (drama) 1964

Going to Meet the Man (short stories) 1965

Tell Me How Long the Train's Been Gone (novel) 1968

No Name in the Street (essays) 1972

One Day, When I Was Lost (screenplay) 1972

If Beale Street Could Talk (novel) 1974

The Devil Finds Work (criticism) 1976

Little Man, Little Man: A Story of Childhood (juvenile fiction) 1976

Just above My Head (novel) 1979

The Evidence of Things Not Seen (nonfiction) 1985

Jimmy's Blues: Selected Poems (poetry) 1985

The Price of the Ticket: Collected Nonfiction, 1948-1985 (essays) 1985

and overcome. From no other contemporary author does one get such a sensation of writing as life; it is all so open and desperate and acute, minute by minute and word by word. The captivation of the reader, the feeling of rightness comes from Baldwin's absolute honesty, from his yielding, however unwillingly, to necessity. A reader *feels* the desperation—if the man had not written this book, and written it so, he could not have survived. Each book is a renewed effort to stay alive and upright through the finding and placing of perfect words. Each book is a staving off of death, a matter of survival.

If this is the case, it can scarcely be considered illegitimate or extra-literary prying to regard the novels as essentially about him, the man, James Baldwin. Autobiographical exactness, after all, is the very source of their sting, their astringent modern taste. It is not anti-literary, therefore, or anti-poetic, to talk of *James Baldwin's* family, or experience, or pain, in these novels, rather than John's or David's. It is no more nasty to write of his inversion than of Proust's. When a writer makes it so clear that he is not lying, one should do him the honor of believing him.

There is more than one kind of honesty in writing, of course. A self-dissolving symbolist may tell truth as well as a self-displaying realist, and Baldwin's honesty is only his, the latest variety: the need to tell "all" the truth, with no pretenses, no fictions, no metaphors—the quality one associates with his best essays. Such a need (cf. Mailer, Genet) may ultimately render unusable all the standard props of fiction. In this new, needful, stripped-bare kind of nervous truth, one tells far more than is customarily told, in order to stay this side of insanity. Baldwin allows himself, for example, none of Ellison's objectivity, very little of his distance from his fictions. Like Richard Wright, ultimately, he is probably more a symbolic Negro than a typical one; but, again, like Richard Wright, he is no less useful, or even less necessary, for that.

Each novel, for Baldwin, has been a stage; a stage to be lived through, transformed into words, then exorcised and transcended. The next novel begins a new stage, and the process goes on. This does not, of course, mean that he will ever reach the shores of fulfillment and rest. It seems, in fact, highly unlikely, unless he should begin to lie.

Go Tell It on the Mountain was the first stage, Baldwin's baptism of fire. It is the testament of his coming to terms with, his defining and transcending, the experience of his boyhood—his family, his religion, his Harlem youth. (The story is told again in **"Notes of a Native Son"**; it is told a third time, far less honestly, in *The Fire Next Time.*) The telling was necessary for Baldwin, in the same way that telling *Look Homeward, Angel* was necessary for Thomas Wolfe. *Go Tell It on the Mountain* has, in fact, much the same kind of effect as Wolfe's great novel, the effect of autobiography-as-exorcism, of a lyrical, painful, ritual exercise whose necessity and intensity the reader feels. The impact on a reader, in books of this sort, appears to be in direct relation to the amount of truth the author is able to tell himself. At the end of *Go Tell It on the Mountain,* the hero, John, has "come through"; one presumes that Baldwin had as well. (pp. 119-21)

Baldwin is as unafraid of glorious prose as he is of honest prose, and the book is woven out of both. But the strength, at last, is that of his own personal necessity, a necessity that the reader can vicariously share. It is the strength of a harrowing prayer, simple and felt, of a small tragic truth that enlarges the heart. The book is carven with love. Because of its peculiar kind of necessary, very personal truth, it remains one of the few, the very few, essential Negro works.

Giovanni's Room served its purpose too, I suspect. Baldwin's personal uncertainties are not limited to the racial, religious, and familial. (pp. 123-24)

It is certainly one of the most subtle novels of the homosexual world, not as poetic and outspoken as Genet's, not as trashy as John Rechy's; but the emotions are more to be observed than to be shared. It has something of the lyrical allusiveness of *Go Tell It on the Mountain,* of its squeezing, sonnetlike smallness—

Giovanni's room is the perfect symbolic setting, as cluttered and oppressively closed as one of Pinter's settings. But the effect, on the whole, is slight. (p. 124)

Another Country, and the sick truths it tells Americans about themselves, had to wait for the emergence of a new style: a style one may designate as New York-1960's. . . . It is used, at its shrillest, most wide-open, by Baldwin, Edward Albee, LeRoi Jones, Norman Mailer, Lenny Bruce, *The Realist,* the new Grove Press novelists, some of the Jewish Establishment journalists and critics (*The New York Review, The New Leader, Partisan Review*), and probably by hundreds of New Yorkers whose names we will never know. It has correspondences with softer manifestations like pop art, Jules Feiffer, [Mike] Nichols and [Elaine] May, *A Hard Day's Night.* Jane, Vivaldo's "beat chick" in *Another Country,* is a splendid specimen: she is brittle, bitchy, fresh from the shrink, with sex like broken glass; a frenzied neurotic with every nerve bare and bleeding loud, first cousin to Lula in [Jones's] *The Dutchman.*

This style almost entirely carries the book, a style of screaming, no-holds-barred verbal violence. The revolving sequence of events, the inter-ringing figures of the sex dance (everyone mixing with everyone else), even, ultimately, the characters in the dance themselves, white and black, homo-, hetero-, and bi-sexual, exist primarily to provide voices and vehicles for the screamy exchanges, the ear-piercing insults, the excruciating displays of mutual torment. (pp. 125-26)

The race war, as depicted in this novel, is a difficult thing to understand. First of all, Baldwin has almost entirely excluded "average" people, the simple white American bourgeoisie or lower orders, whose prejudice is so obvious and so stupid it bores even more than it disgusts him. The few representatives of *that* world, the upstairs world, who foolishly drop into the plot are usually dissolved into steam with single drops of acid. (A pair of white heterosexual liberals, the Silenskis, so square they are married and have children and make money, degenerate into the crudest samples of sick America before the book is through, despite Baldwin's obvious efforts to be fair. Their racial liberality, it develops, is as fragile as their sexual assurance. So much for "normal" people.)

So all we have left to fight the race war are a few outlaw blacks and highly emancipated whites. In such a context the war loses its social relevance (except perhaps symbolically), and takes on the dimensions of a private duel. But the issues are no less clear. "Somewhere in his heart the black boy hated the white boy because he was white. Somewhere in his heart Vivaldo had hated and feared Rufus because he was black." Baldwin tries, or at least the top of his mind tries, to keep the sides equal, and the fighting fair. The white combatants, Leona, Vivaldo, especially Eric, are created with affection and care: these are no evil, ill-

understood Wrighteous puppets. But the Negroes have all the trumps. It is *they,* always, who carry the whip, and no white lover, friend, or reader dares to deny them the right. (pp. 126-27)

At their most intense, these race-war combats always transmute into sex combats—which illustrates Baldwin's theory of the fundamentally sexual character of racism. This aspect of the novel, however, is even more unsettled and unsettling, because of the case Baldwin is trying to make for inversion. (p. 128)

The over-lyrical poeticizing of homosexual love is one of the real flaws of the book. Surely Genet's pictures, or even Baldwin's in *Giovanni's Room,* of the foul *and* fair of inversion, are more just. (pp. 129-30)

Another Country has, in its frantic new writer's world called New York, much of the same necessity, the same quality of desperate exorcism as Baldwin's earlier works. But things here are less under control. Almost all of the thinking, the non-imaginative thinking of Baldwin's essays is sandwiched into the fiction, bearing a suggestion that the man is now writing more from his ideas than his imagination. The piercing one-note tone of repetitiousness of so much of this long book supports this dissatisfying notion. Another dangerous sign is the confusion of narrative authority, very like the confusions of self-identity which mar so many of Baldwin's latest and weakest essays. His own opinions mingle with those of his characters, subjectivity jars with objectivity in such a way as to indicate that the author is unaware of the difference: i.e., that James Baldwin, through the 1950's the sole master of *control* in American prose, in the 1960's has begun to lose control.

What is there to salvage and prize? A number of things. More often than not, between the explosions, *Another Country* reminds the reader that James Baldwin is still one of the genuine stylists of the English language. (p. 130)

He is the most powerful and important American essayist of the postwar period, perhaps of the century. **"Notes of a Native Son"** and *Nobody Knows My Name* will maintain their place among the small collection of genuine American classics. They have already been adopted as standard texts and models of style in American college courses; and this is not just a "vogue," an offshoot of the Civil Rights movement. Two such books would sustain any reputation, as long as men can tell the true from the false. (pp. 135-36)

Baldwin has shown more concern for the painful exactness of prose style than any other modern American writer. He picks up words with heavy care, then sets them, one by one, with a cool and loving precision that one can feel in the reading. There are no bright words in his best essays, no flashes, allusions, delusions, no Tynanesque "brilliance." His style is like stripped conversation, saying the most that words can *honestly* say. If it hurts, if it ties one down and hammers its words on one's mind, it is simply the effect of his won't-let-go rigor. There is good and bad prose, there is moral and immoral.

This does not of course imply that the style is flat, because it is not like champagne. Baldwin is fully aware of the ambiguities and ironies implicit in his subjects (primary among them the sick paradox that calls itself America), and he weaves these same ambiguities and ironies into his prose. He is also drivingly and constantly self-critical, which is why his writing is so strong and clear, his thinking so often unassailable. His paragraphs work like a witty colloquy of two sharp minds. Baldwin's and his critic's, one within the other: the devastating qualifiers, the cool understatements, the parentheses, the litotes, the suggestions and quiet parallels display the double mind of the self-critic at work.

Writing like this can be more harrowing, more intense than *any* of the works we are considering [elsewhere in the book]. As Baldwin himself admits, Negro literature "is more likely to be a symptom of our tension than an examination of it," and this includes his own three novels, his plays, and his stories. The exhilarating exhaustion of reading his best essays—which in itself may be a proof of their honesty and value—demands that the reader measure up, and forces him to learn. (pp. 136-37)

David Littlejohn, in his *Black on White: A Critical Survey of Writing by American Negroes,* Viking, 1966, pp. 119-37.

ROBERT A. BONE

(essay date 1965)

[Bone is a distinguished literary critic and an authority on African-American literature. In the following excerpt, he surveys theme and plot in *Go Tell It on the Mountain, Giovanni's Room,* and *Another Country.*]

Go Tell It on the Mountain (1953) is the best of Baldwin's novels, and the best is very good indeed. It ranks with Jean Toomer's *Cane,* Richard Wright's *Native Son,* and Ralph Ellison's *Invisible Man* as a major contribution to American fiction. For this novel cuts through the walls of the storefront church to the essence of Negro experience in America. This is Baldwin's earliest world, his bright and morning star, and it glows with metaphorical intensity. Its emotions are his emotions; its language, his native tongue. The result is a prose of unusual power and authority. One senses in Baldwin's first novel a confidence, control, and mastery of style which he has not attained again in the novel form. (p. 5)

Baldwin sees the Negro quite literally as the bastard child of American civilization. In Gabriel's double involvement with bastardy, we have a re-enactment of the white man's historic crime. In Johnny, the innocent victim of Gabriel's hatred, we have an archetypal image of the Negro child. Obliquely, by means of an extended metaphor, Baldwin approaches the very essence of Negro experience. That essence is rejection, and its most destructive consequence is shame. But God, the Heavenly Father, does not reject the Negro utterly. He casts down only to raise up. This is the psychic drama which occurs beneath the surface of John's conversion. . . .

This quality of Negro life, unending struggle with one's own blackness, is symbolized by Baldwin in the family name, *Grimes.* One can readily understand how such a sense of personal shame might have been inflamed by contact with the Christian tradition and transformed into an obsession with original sin. (p. 8)

Given this attack on the core of the self, how can the Negro respond? . . . There is . . . the path of self-hatred and the path of self-acceptance. Both are available to Johnny within the framework of the church, but he is deterred from one by the negative example of his father.

Consider Gabriel. The substance of his life is moral evasion. A preacher of the gospel, and secretly the father of an illegitimate child, he cannot face the evil in himself. In order to preserve his image as the Lord's anointed, he has sacrificed the lives of those around him. His principal victim is Johnny, who is not his natural child. In disowning the bastard, he disowns the "blackness" in himself. Gabriel's psychological mechanisms are, so to say, white. Throughout his work Baldwin has described the scapegoat mechanism which is fundamental to the white man's sense of self. To the question, Who am I?, the white man answers: I am *white,* that is, immaculate, without stain. I am the purified, the saved, the saintly, the elect. It is the *black* who is the embodiment of evil. Let him, the son of the bondwoman, pay the price of my sins.

From self-hatred flows not only self-righteousness but self-glorification as well. . . . When the Negro preacher compares the lot of his people to that of the children of Israel, he provides his flock with a series of metaphors which correspond to their deepest experience. The church thus offers to the Negro masses a ritual enactment of their daily pain. It is with this poetry of suffering, which Baldwin calls the power of the Word, that the final section of the novel is concerned.

The first fifteen pages of Part III contain some of Baldwin's most effective writing. As John Grimes lies before the altar, a series of visionary states passes through his soul. Dream fragments and Freudian sequences, lively fantasies and Aesopian allegories, combine to produce a generally surrealistic effect. Images of darkness and chaos, silence and emptiness, mist and cold—cumulative patterns developed early in the novel—function now at maximum intensity. These images of damnation express the state of the soul when thrust into outer darkness by a rejecting, punishing, castrating father-figure who is the surrogate of a hostile society. The dominant emotions are shame, despair, guilt, and fear. (pp. 8-9)

On these harsh terms, Baldwin's protagonist discovers his identity. . . . To the question, Who am I?, he can now reply: I am he who suffers, and yet whose suffering on occasion is "from time set free." And thereby he discovers his humanity, for only man can ritualize his pain. We are now very close to that plane of human experience where art and religion intersect. What Baldwin wants us to feel is the emotional pressure exerted on the Negro's cultural forms by his exposure to white oppression. And finally to comprehend that these forms alone, through their power of transforming suffering, have enabled him to survive his terrible ordeal.

Giovanni's Room (1956) is by far the weakest of Baldwin's novels. There is a tentative, unfinished quality about the book, as if in merely broaching the subject of homosexuality Baldwin had exhausted his creative energy. Viewed in retrospect, it seems less a novel in its own right than a first draft of *Another Country*. The surface of the novel is deliberately opaque, for Baldwin is struggling to articulate the most intimate, the most painful, the most elusive of emotions. The characters are vague and disembodied, the themes half-digested, the colors rather bleached than vivified. We recognize in this sterile psychic landscape the unprocessed raw material of art.

And yet this novel occupies a key position in Baldwin's spiritual development. Links run backward to *Go Tell It on the Mountain* as well as forward to *Another Country*. The very furniture of Baldwin's mind derives from the storefront church of his boyhood and adolescence. When he attempts a novel of homosexual love, with an all-white cast of characters and a European setting, he simply transposes the moral topography of Harlem to the streets of Paris. When he strives toward sexual self-acceptance, he automatically casts the homosexual in a priestly role. (p. 10)

At the emotional center of the novel is the relationship between David and Giovanni. It is highly symbolic, and to understand what is at stake, we must turn to Baldwin's essay on André Gide. Published toward the end of 1954, about a year before the appearance of *Giovanni's Room,* this essay is concerned with the two sides of Gide's personality and the precarious balance which was struck between them. On the one side was his sensuality, his lust for the boys on the Piazza d'Espagne, threatening him always with utter deg-

radation. On the other was his Protestantism, his purity, his otherworldliness—that part of him which was not carnal, and which found expression in his Platonic marriage to Madeleine. As Baldwin puts it, "She was his Heaven who would forgive him for his Hell and help him to endure it." It is a drama of salvation, in which the celibate wife, through selfless dedication to the suffering artist, becomes in effect a priest.

In the present novel, Giovanni plays the role of Gide; David, of Madeleine.

Possessing the power to save, David rejects the priestly office. Seen in this light, his love affair with Giovanni is a kind of novitiate. The dramatic conflict of the novel can be stated as follows: does David have a true vocation? Is he prepared to renounce the heterosexual world? When David leaves Giovanni for Hella, he betrays his calling, but ironically he has been ruined both for the priesthood and the world.

It is Giovanni, Baldwin's doomed hero, who is the true priest. For a priest is nothing but a journeyman in suffering. . . . It is a crucial distinction for all of Baldwin's work: there are the relatively innocent—the *laity* who are mere apprentices in human suffering—and the fully initiated, the *clergy* who are intimate with pain. Among the laity may be numbered Americans, white folks, heterosexuals, and squares; among the clergy, Europeans, Negroes, homosexuals, hipsters, and jazz-men. (p. 11)

The patterns first explored in *Giovanni's Room* are given full expression in *Another Country*. Rufus is a Negro Giovanni—a journeyman in suffering and a martyr to racial oppression. Vivaldo and the other whites are mere apprentices, who cannot grasp the beauty and the terror of Negro life. Eric is a David who completes his novitiate, and whose priestly or redemptive role is central to the novel. There has been, however, a crucial change of tone. In *Giovanni's Room,* one part of Baldwin wants David to escape from the male prison, even as another part remains committed to the ideal of homosexual love. In the later novel, this conflict has been resolved. Baldwin seems convinced that homosexuality is a liberating force, and he now brings to the subject a certain proselytizing zeal.

Another Country (1962) is a failure on the grand scale. It is an ambitious novel, rich in thematic possibilities, for Baldwin has at his disposal a body of ideas brilliantly developed in his essays. When he tries to endow these ideas with imaginative life, however, his powers of invention are not equal to the task. The plot consists of little more than a series of occasions for talk and fornication. Since the latter is a limited vehicle for the expression of complex ideas, talk takes over, and the novel drowns in a torrent of rhetoric.

The ideas themselves are impressive enough. At the heart of what Baldwin calls the white problem is a moral cowardice, a refusal to confront the "dark" side of human experience. The white American, at once over-protected and repressed, exhibits an infuriating tendency to deny the reality of pain and suffering, violence and evil, sex and death. He preserves in the teeth of human circumstance what must strike the less protected as a kind of willful innocence. (p. 12)

By projecting the "blackness" of his own being upon the dark skin of his Negro victim, the white man hopes to exercise the chaotic forces which threaten to destroy him from within.

The psychic cost is of course enormous. The white man loses the experience of "blackness," sacrificing both its beauty and its terror to the illusion of security. In the end, he loses his identity. For a man who cannot acknowledge the dark impulses of his own soul cannot have the vaguest notion of who he is. (pp. 12-13)

There are psychic casualties on the Negro side as well. No human personality can escape the effects of prolonged emotional rejection. The victim of this cruelty will defend himself with hatred and with dreams of vengeance, and will lose, perhaps forever, his normal capacity for love. Strictly speaking, this set of defenses, and the threat of self-destruction which they pose, constitutes the Negro problem.

It is up to the whites to break this vicious circle of rejection and hatred. They can do so only by facing the void, by confronting chaos, by making the necessary journey to "another country." What the white folks need is a closer acquaintance with the blues. . . .

What dramatic materials are employed to invest these themes with life? A Greenwich Village setting and a hipster idiom. . . . A square thrown in for laughs. A side trip to Harlem (can we be *slumming?*). A good deal of boozing, and an occasional stick of tea. . . . Five orgasms (two interracial and two homosexual) or approximately one per eighty pages, a significant increase over the Mailer rate. Distracted by this nonsense, how can one attend to the serious business of the novel?

In one respect only does the setting of *Another Country* succeed. Baldwin's descriptions of New York contain striking images of malaise, scenes and gestures which expose the moral chaos of contemporary urban life. The surface of his prose reflects the aching loneliness of the city with the poignancy of a Hopper painting. (p. 13)

At the core of Baldwin's fiction is an existentialist psychology. . . . Sexual identity—all identity—emerges from the void. Man, the sole creator of himself, moves alone upon the face of the waters. . . .

[Eric holds a] pivotal position in the novel. Through his commitment to Yves, he introduces an element of order into the chaos of his personal life. This precarious victory, wrested in anguish from the heart of darkness, is the real subject of *Another Country*. Images of chaos proliferate throughout the novel. (p. 15)

Eric is the first of Rufus' friends to face his demons and achieve a sense of self. He in turn emancipates the rest.

From this vantage point, one can envision the novel that Baldwin was trying to write. With the breakdown of traditional standards—even of sexual normality—homosexuality becomes a metaphor of the modern condition. . . . The homosexual becomes emblematic of existential man.

What actually happens, however, is that Baldwin's literary aims are deflected by his sexual mystique. Eric returns to America as the high priest of ineffable phallic mysteries. His friends, male and female, dance around the Maypole and, *mirabile dictu,* their sense of reality is restored. . . .

For most readers of *Another Country*, the difficulty will lie in accepting Eric as a touchstone of reality. . . . [Few] will concede a sense of reality, at least in the sexual realm, to one who regards heterosexual love as "a kind of superior calisthenics." . . . To most, homosexuality will seem rather an invasion than an affirmation of human truth. Ostensibly the novel summons us to reality. Actually it substitutes for the illusions of white supremacy those of homosexual love. (p. 16)

The drama of reconciliation is enacted by Ida and Vivaldo. Through their symbolic marriage, Ida is reconciled to whites; Vivaldo, to women. This gesture, however, is a mere concession to majority opinion. What Baldwin really feels is dramatized through Rufus and Eric. Rufus can neither be fully reconciled to, nor fully defiant of, white society. No Bigger Thomas, he is incapable of total hate. Pushed to the limits of endurance, he commits suicide. Similarly, Eric can neither be fully reconciled to women, nor can he surrender to the male demi-monde. So he camps on the outskirts of Hell. In the case of Rufus, the suicidal implications are overt. With Eric, . . . Baldwin tries to persuade us that Hell is really Heaven. (pp. 16-17)

Coupled with these racial sentiments are manifestations of sexual Garveyism. Throughout the novel, the superiority of homosexual love is affirmed. Here alone can one experience total surrender and full orgastic pleasure; here alone the metaphysical terror of the void. Heterosexual love, by comparison, is a pale—one is tempted to say, white—imitation. In many passages hostility to women reaches savage proportions. . . . (p. 17)

In *Another Country,* the sharp outlines of character are dissolved by waves of uncontrolled emotion. The novel lacks a proper distancing. One has the impression of Baldwin's recent work that the author does not know where his own psychic life leaves off and that of his characters begins. What is more, he scarcely cares to know, for he is sealed in a narcissism so engrossing that he fails to make emotional contact with his characters. If his people have no otherness, if he repeatedly violates their integrity, how can they achieve the individuality which alone will make them memorable? (p. 18)

Properly regarded, *Another Country* will be seen as the celebration of a Black Mass. The jazzman is Baldwin's priest; the homosexual, his acolyte. The bandstand is his altar; Bessie Smith his choir. God is carnal mystery, and through orgasm, the Word is made flesh. Baldwin's ministry is as vigorous as ever. He summons to the mourners' bench all who remain, so to say, hardened in their innocence. Lose that, he proclaims, and you will be saved. To the truly unregenerate, those stubborn heterosexuals, he offers the prospect of salvation through sodomy. With this novel doctrine, the process of inversion is complete. (p. 19)

[Baldwin] has already devoted two novels to his sexual rebellion. If he persists, he will surely be remembered as the greatest American novelist since Jack Kerouac. The future now depends on his ability to transcend the emotional reflexes of his adolescence. So extraordinary a talent requires of him no less an effort. (p. 20)

Robert A. Bone, "The Novels of James Baldwin," in *Tri-Quarterly,* No. 5, Winter, 1965, pp. 3-20.

KENETH KINNAMON

(essay date 1974)

[The essay below is excerpted from Kinnamon's introduction to his *James Baldwin: A Collection of Critical Essays.* Here, he illuminates the blend of social and psychological elements in Baldwin's work.]

A decade ago James Baldwin, more than any other author, seemed to liberal white Americans to personify as well as to articulate the outrage and anguish of black Americans struggling to put an end to racial oppression and to achieve their civil and human rights. . . . Though as Northern as Martin Luther King was Southern, James Baldwin preached a more secular and apocalyptic but not really dissimilar sermon: the redemptive force of the love of a prophetic, interracial few could, even at that late date, yet prevail over the bigotry of the white majority, and so "end the racial nightmare, and achieve our country, and change the history of the world." If these brave words today seem both naïve and anachronistic, the reason is partly the nation's re-

cent habit of giving more publicity than credence to its seers, of lavishing attention while withholding belief. (p. 1)

A proper understanding of Baldwin and his work must take into account a complicated amalgam of psychological and social elements sometimes thought to be antithetical. If, like most major black writers, Baldwin has extracted from his private ordeal the symbolic outline of his race's suffering, he has done so without obscuring the uniqueness of his personal experience. (p. 2)

However much he may revile the historical role of Christianity in the enslavement of black people, *The Fire Next Time* attests that [Baldwin] has never forgotten the compensatory values of his [adolescent] religious experience: "In spite of everything, there was in the life I fled a zest and a joy and a capacity for facing and surviving disaster that are very moving and very rare." And for good or ill, Baldwin's work is of a kind in which the didactic—even homiletic—element is of the essence. (p. 3)

Out of Baldwin's experience have emerged certain recurring themes in his writing, the most important of which is the quest for love. On a personal level, the search is for the emotional security of a love of which the protagonist has always been deprived. In his brilliant first novel, *Go Tell It on the Mountain,* the theme develops with autobiographical clarity, as is also the case in the related short story **"The Outing"** or such essays as **"Notes of a Native Son," "The Black Boy Looks at the White Boy," "Down at the Cross,"** and **"No Name in the Street."** But elsewhere the search for love is equally imperative. David finds it in *Giovanni's Room* but loses it again because of his failure to commit himself totally. The interracial and bisexual bedhopping of *Another Country* constitutes a frenzied effort to realize love in the loveless city of New York. It falls to Leo Proudhammer of *Tell Me How Long the Train's Been Gone* to articulate the poignant paradox of Baldwin's love theme: "Everyone wishes to be loved, but, in the event, nearly no one can bear it. Everyone desires love but also finds it impossible to believe that he deserves it." If the search for love has its origin in the desire of a child for emotional security, its arena is an adult world which involves it in struggle and pain. Stasis must yield to motion, innocence to experience, security to risk. This is the lesson that the black Ida inculcates in her white lover Vivaldo in *Another Country,* and it saves Baldwin's central fictional theme from sentimentality.

Similarly, love as an agent of racial reconciliation and national survival is not for Baldwin a vague yearning for an innocuous brotherhood, but an agonized confrontation with reality, leading to the struggle to transform it. It is a quest for truth through a recognition of the primacy of suffering and injustice in the American past. In racial terms, the black man as victim of this past is in a moral position to induce the white man, the oppressor, to end his self-delusion and begin the process of regeneration. . . . Baldwin wrote in 1962 in **"My Dungeon Shook,"** ["This] is what [integration] means: that we, with love, shall force our brothers to see themselves as they are, to cease fleeing from reality and begin to change it." By 1972, the year of *No Name in the Street,* the redemptive possibilities of love seemed exhausted in that terrible decade of assassination, riot, and repression, of the Black Panthers and Attica. Social love had now become for Baldwin more a rueful memory than an alternative to disaster. Violence, he now believes, is the arbiter of history, and in its matrix the white world is dying and the third world is struggling to be born. In his fiction, too, this shift in emphasis is apparent. Though love may still be a sustaining personal force, its social utility is dubious. (pp. 5-6)

Whether through the agency of love or violence, Baldwin is almost obsessively concerned with the writer's responsibility to save the world. As an essayist, he assumes the burden not only of reporting with eloquent sensitivity his observations of reality, but also of tirelessly reminding us of the need to transform that reality if Armageddon is to be averted. Over and over he concludes an essay by enlarging the perspective to a global scale. . . . Introducing the theme of self-examination in *Nobody Knows My Name,* he asserts that "one can only face in others what one can face in oneself. On this confrontation depends the measure of our wisdom and compassion. This energy is all that one finds in the rubble of vanished civilizations, and the only hope for ours." . . . Two of the simplest expressions of his faith in the possibility of change are the concluding challenges of the speeches entitled **"In Search of a Majority"** and **"Notes for a Hypothetical Novel"**: "The world is before you and you need not take it or leave it as it was when you came in" and "We made the world we're living in and we have to make it over." *Nobody Knows My Name* concludes with an account of Baldwin's friendship with Norman Mailer, another writer who emphasizes the social value of the literary perspective: "For, though it clearly needs to be brought into focus, he has a real vision of ourselves as we are, and it cannot be too often repeated in this country now, that, where there is no vision, the people perish." The possibility of just such a perishing is pursued further in *The Fire Next Time,* and the possibility has become a probability in *No Name in the Street,* where Baldwin speaks of "the shape of the wrath to come" and the setting of the white man's sun. (pp. 6-7)

James Baldwin has always been concerned with the most personal and intimate areas of experience and also with the broadest questions of national and global destiny—and with the intricate interrelationships between the two. Whatever the final assessment of his literary achievement, it is clear that his voice—simultaneously that of victim, witness, and prophet—has been among the most urgent of our time. (p. 7)

Keneth Kinnamon, in an introduction to *James Baldwin: A Collection of Critical Essays,* edited by Keneth Kinnamon, Prentice-Hall, 1974, pp. 1-8.

JAMES BALDWIN WITH QUINCY TROUPE
(interview date 1987)

[Troupe, an American poet, editor, educator, and nonfiction writer, is founding editor of *Confrontation: A Journal of Third World Literature.* Among his works are *Embryo* (1972) and *Skulls along the River* (1984). The excerpt below is taken from a November 1987 interview with Baldwin. Here, Baldwin discusses such issues as fame and his thoughts about other prominent black American writers.]

[Baldwin]: It's difficult to be a legend. It's hard for me to recognize *me.* You spend a lot of time trying to avoid it. It's really something, to be a legend, unbearable. The way the world treats you is unbearable, and especially if you're black. It's unbearable because time is passing and you are not your legend, but you're trapped in it. Nobody will let you out of it. Except other people who know what it is. But very few people have experienced it, know about it, and I think that can drive you mad; I know it can. I know it can.

You have to be lucky. You have to have friends. I think at bottom you have to be serious. No one can point it out to you; you have to see it yourself. That's the only way you can act on it. And when it arrives it's a great shock.

[Troupe]: *To find out?*

It's a great shock to realize that you've been so divorced. So divorced from who you think you are—from who you really are. Who you think you are, you're not at all. . . . I don't know who I thought I was. I was a witness, I thought. I was a very despairing witness though, too. What I was actually doing was trying to avoid a certain estrangement perhaps, an estrangement between myself and my generation. It was virtually complete, the estrangement was, in terms of what I might have thought and expected—my theories. About what I might have hoped—I'm talking now in terms of one's function as an artist. And the country itself, being black and trying to deal with that.

Why do you think it occurred. That estrangement between your generation and the country?

Baldwin strongly advocated civil rights in both his literature and in practice. Here, with civil rights leader Bayard Rustin, he attends a press conference urging President John F. Kennedy to send troops into Alabama after a series of racial incidents in the state.

Well, because I was right. That's a strange way to put it. I *was* right. I was right about what was happening in the country. What was about to happen to all of us really, one way or the other. And the choices people would have to make. And watching people make them and denying them at the same time. I began to feel more and more homeless in terms of the whole relationship between France and me, and America and *me* has always been a little painful, you know. Because my family's in America I will always go back. It couldn't have been a question in my mind. But in the meantime you keep the door open and the price of keeping the door open was to actually be, in a sense, victimized by my own legend.

You know, I was trying to tell the truth and it takes a long time to realize that you can't—that there's no point in going to the mat, so to speak, no point in going to Texas again. There's no point in saying this again. It's been said, and it's been said, and it's been said. It's been heard and not heard. You are a broken motor.

A broken motor?

Yes. You're a running motor and you're repeating, you're repeating, you're repeating and it causes a breakdown, lessening of will power. And sooner or later your will gives out—it has to. You're lucky if it is a physical matter—most times it's spiritual. See, all this involves hiding from something else—not dealing with how lonely you are. And of course, at the very bottom it involves the terror of every artist confronted with what he or she has to do, you know, the next work. And everybody, in one way or another, and to some extent, tries to avoid it. And you avoid it more when you get older than you do when you're younger; still there's something terrifying about it, about doing the work.

O.K. Let's change the subject and talk about some writers. Amiri Baraka?

I remember the first time I met Amiri Baraka, who was then Leroi Jones. I was doing *The Amen Corner* and he was a student at Howard University. I liked him right away. He was a pop-eyed little boy poet. He showed me a couple of his poems. I liked them very much. And then he came to New York a couple of years later. He came to New York when I came back to New York from Paris. And by this time I knew the business. I'd been through the fucking business by that time. I was a survivor.

And I remember telling him that his agent wanted him to become the young James Baldwin. But I told him you're not the young James Baldwin. There's only one James Baldwin and you are Leroi Jones and there's only one Leroi Jones. Don't let them run this game on us, you know? You're Leroi Jones, I'm James Baldwin. And we're going to need each other. That's all I said. He didn't believe it then but time took care of that.

He believes it now?

Yes he knows it now.

What person has hurt you the most recently?

Ishmael Reed.

Why?

Because he is a great poet and it seemed to be beneath him. His anger and his contempt for me, which was both real, and not real. He ignored me for so long and then he called me a cock sucker, you know what I mean? It's boring. But I always did say he was a great poet, a great writer. But that does not mean I can put up with being insulted by him everytime I see him, which I won't.

What do you think about Toni Morrison?

Toni's my ally and it's really probably too complex to get into. She's a black woman writer, which in the public domain makes it more difficult to talk about.

What do you think are her gifts?

Her gift is in allegory. *Tar Baby* is an allegory. In fact all her novels are. But they're hard to talk about in public. That's where you get in trouble because her books and allegory are not always what they seem to be about. I was too occupied with my recent illness to deal with *Beloved.* But, in general, she's taken a myth, or she takes what seems to be a myth, and turns it into something else. I don't know how to put this—*Beloved* could be about the story of truth. She's taken a whole lot of things and turned them upside down. Some of them—you recognize the truth in it. I think that Toni's very painful to read.

Why?

Because it's always, or most times, a horrifying allegory; but you recognize that it works. But you don't really want to march through it. Sometimes people have a lot against Toni, but she's got the most believing story of everybody, this rather elegant matron, whose intentions really are serious, and according to some people, lethal . . .

We were talking once about the claustrophobia among writers. You said you prefer actors and painters to writers.

Yes. Well, first of all, when I was coming up there weren't any writers that I knew. Langston Hughes was far away. The first writer I met was Richard Wright and he was much older than me. And the people I knew were people like Beauford Delaney and the women who hung out with him; it was a whole world that was not literary. That came later; then it wasn't literary. It came later in Paris, with Sartre and others. But there was something else. And in Paris it had nothing whatsoever to do with race for one thing. It was another kind of freedom there altogether. It had nothing to do with literature. But when I looked back on it years and years later, looked back at myself on the American literary scene, I could see what almost happened to me was an attempt to make myself fit in, so to speak, to wash myself clean for the American literary academy.

You mean they wanted you scrubbed and squeaky clean?

Exactly. You have to be scrubbed and squeaky clean and then there's nothing left of you. Let me tell you a story.

When Ralph Ellison won the National Award in '52 for *Invisible Man,* I was up for it the next year, in 1953, for *Go Tell It on the Mountain.* But at the same time, I was far from scrubbed. I didn't win. Then, years later, someone who was on the jury told me that since Ralph won it the year before they couldn't give it to a Negro two years in a row. Now, isn't that something? . . .

Once, after I published *Go Tell It on the Mountain* and *Giovanni's Room,* my publisher, Knopf, told me I was "a Negro writer" and that I reached "a certain audience." "So," they told me, "you cannot afford to alienate that audience. This new book will ruin your career because you're not writing about the same things and in the same manner as you were before and we won't publish this book as a favor to you."

As a favor to you?

So I told them, "Fuck you." My editor, whose name I won't mention here, is dead now, poor man. I told them that I needed a boat ticket. So I took a boat to England with my book and I sold it in England before I sold it in America. You see, whites want black writers to mostly deliver something as if it were an official version of the black experience. But the vocabulary won't hold it, simply. No true account really of black life can be held, can be contained, in the American vocabulary. As it is, the only way that you can deal with it is by doing great violence to the assumptions on which the vocabulary is based. But they won't let you do that.

And when you go along, you find yourself very quickly painted into a corner; you've written yourself into a corner—because you can't compromise as a writer. By the time I left America in 1948 I had written myself into a corner as I perceived it. The book reviews and the short essays had led me to a place where I was on a collision course with the truth; it was the way I was operating. It was only a matter of time before I'd simply be destroyed by it. And no amount of manipulation of vocabulary or art would have spared me. It's like I think that Al Murray and Ralph Ellison are totally trapped. It's sad, because they're both trapped in the same way, and they're both very gifted writers.

But you can't do anything with America unless you are willing to dissect it. You certainly cannot hope to fit yourself into it; nothing fits into it, not your past, not your present. *The Invisible Man* is fine as far as it goes until you ask yourself who's invisible to whom? You know, what is this dichotomy supposed to do? Are we invisible before each other? And invisible why, and by what system can one hope to be invisible? I don't know how anything in American life is worthy of this sacrifice. And further, I don't see anything in American life—for myself—to aspire to. Nothing at all. It's all so very false, so shallow, so plastic, so morally and ethically corrupt.

James Baldwin and Quincy Troupe, in an interview in *The Village Voice,* Vol. XXXIII, No. 2, January 12, 1988, p. 36.

AMIRI BARAKA

(essay date 1987)

[Baraka, an American dramatist, poet, novelist, essayist, and critic, rose to prominence as a controversial and influential voice in the Black Power movement of the 1960s and 1970s. In the following excerpt from a eulogy he delivered at Baldwin's funeral on December 8, 1987, at the Cathedral of St. John the Divine in New York City, he praises the author as a gifted man of letters and an inspiring leader.]

First of all, Jimmy Baldwin was not only a writer, an international literary figure, he was a man, spirit, voice—old and black and terrible as that first ancestor.

As man, he came to us from the family, the human lives, names we can call David, Gloria, Lover, George, Samuel, Barbara, Ruth, Elizabeth, Paula . . . and this extension is one intimate identification as he could so casually, in that way of his, eyes and self smiling, not much larger than that first ancestor, fragile as truth always is, big eyes popped out like righteous monitors of the soulful. The Africans say that big ol' eyes like that means someone can make things happen! And didn't he?

Between Jimmy's smile and grace, his insistent elegance even as he damned you, even as he smote what evil was unfortunate, breathing or otherwise, to stumble his way. He was all the way live, all the way conscious, turned all the way up, receiving and broadcasting, sometime so hard, what needed to, would back up from those two television tubes poking out of his head!

As man, he was my friend, my older brother he would joke, not really joking. As man, he was Our friend, Our older or younger brother, we listened to him like we would somebody in our family—whatever you might think of what he might say. We could hear it. He was close, as man, as human relative, we could make it some cold seasons merely warmed by his handshake, smile or eyes. Warmed by his voice, jocular yet instantly cutting. Kind yet perfectly clear. We could make it sometimes, just remembering his arm waved in confirmation or indignation, the rapid-fire speech, pushing out at the world like urgent messages for those who would be real.

This man traveled the earth like its history and its biographer. He reported, criticized, made beautiful, analyzed, cajoled, lyricized, attacked, sang, made us think, made us better, made us consciously human or perhaps more acidly pre-human.

He was spirit because he was living. And even past this tragic hour when we weep he has gone away, and why, and why we keep asking. There's mountains of evil creatures who we would willingly bid farewell to—Jimmy could have given you some of their names on demand—we curse our luck, our oppressors—our age, our weakness. Why and Why again? And why can drive you mad, or said enough times might even make you wise!

Yet this why in us is him as well. Jimmy was wise from asking whys giving us his wise and his whys to go with our own, to make them into a larger why and a deeper Wise.

Jimmy's spirit, which will be with us as long as we remember ourselves, is the only truth which keeps us sane and changes our whys to wiseness. It is his spirit, spirit of the little black first ancestor, which we feel those of us who really felt it, we know this spirit will be with us for "as long as the sun shines and the water flows." For his is the spirit of life thrilling to its own consciousness.

When we saw and heard him, he made us feel good. He made us feel, for one thing, that we could defend ourselves or define ourselves, that we were in the world not merely as animate slaves, but as terrifyingly sensitive measurers of what is good or evil, beautiful or ugly. This is the power of his spirit. This is the bond which created our love for him. This is the fire that terrifies our pitiful enemies. That not only are we alive but shatteringly precise in our songs and our scorn. You could not possibly think yourself righteous, murderers, when you saw or were wrenched by our Jimmy's spirit! He was carrying it as us, as we carry him as us.

Jimmy will be remembered, even as James, for his *word.* Only the completely ignorant can doubt his mastery of it. Jimmy Baldwin was the creator of contemporary American speech even before Americans could dig that. He created it so we could speak to each other at unimaginable intensities of feeling, so we could make sense to each other at yet higher and higher tempos.

But that word, arranged as art, sparkling and gesturing from the page, was also man and spirit. Nothing was more inspiring than hearing that voice, seeing that face, and that whip of a tongue, that signification that was his fingers, reveal and expose, raise and bring down, condemn or extol!

It was evident he loved beauty—art, but when the civil rights movement pitched to its height, no matter his early estheticism and seeming hauteur, he was our truest definer, our educated conscience made irresistible by his high consciousness.

Jimmy was a "civil rights leader" too, *at the same time!,* thinkers of outmoded social outrage. He was in the truest tradition of the great artists of all times. Those who understand it is beauty *and truth* we seek, and that indeed one cannot exist without and as an extension of the other.

At the hot peak of the movement Jimmy was one of its truest voices. His stance, that it is *our* judgement of the world, the majority of us who still struggle to survive the beastiality of so-called civilization (the slaves), that is true and not that of our torturers, was a dangerous profundity and as such fuel for our getaway and liberation!

He was our consummate complete man of letters, not as an unliving artifact, but as a black man we could touch and relate to even there in that space filled with black fire at the base and circumference of our souls. And what was supremely ironic is that for all his estheticism and ultra-sophistication, there he was now demanding that we get in the world completely, that we comprehend the ultimate intelligence of our enforced commitment to finally bring humanity to the world!

Jimmy's voice, as much as Dr. King's or Malcolm X's, helped shepherd and guide us toward black liberation.

Let us hold him in our hearts and minds. Let us make him part of our invincible black souls, the intelligence of our transcendence. Let our black hearts grow big world-absorbing eyes like his, never closed. Let us one day be able to celebrate him like he must be celebrated if we are ever to be truly self-determining. For Jimmy was God's black revolutionary mouth. If there is a God, and revolution His righteous natural expression. And elegant song the deepest and most fundamental commonplace of being alive. (pp. 27, 29)

Amiri Baraka, "We Carry Him as Us," in *The New York Times Book Review,* December 20, 1987, pp. 27, 29.

DARRYL PINCKNEY
(essay date 1988)

[In the following excerpt, Pinckney recalls the impact of Baldwin's work on his own ideas about race and literature and reflects upon the author's career.]

Go Tell It on the Mountain, its pages heavy with sinners brought low and prayers groaning on the wind, scared me when I read it as a teen-ager. I was afraid that around any corner in the story of how Johnny Grimes, "frog eyes," came to be saved I ran the risk of exposure. It spoiled my wistful identification with *The Catcher in the Rye,* which all my friends were soaking up at the time. None of them had read *Go Tell It on the Mountain,* though, as did everyone else in the late 1960s, they knew what the name James Baldwin stood for. I was left alone with the book, as if it had been the little box at the bottom of the exam form that only I, as a black, was asked to pencil in. I thought I was better than Johnny, sweeping dust from a worn-out rug on his birthday, but I wasn't sure that the trap of Harlem, 1935, was as long ago and far away as I wanted to believe.

The name James Baldwin had been around the house for as long as I could remember, and meant almost as much as that of Martin Luther King. *The Fire Next Time,* my parents tell me, had an explosive effect unlike anything else since *Native Son* or *Invisible Man,* and in part led to a settling of accounts and an opening of new ones. Some old-timers thought he was too far out, others were jealous of this storefront preacher's Jamesian overlay—"slimy" was my grandfather's word—but

Baldwin's prophetic voice was irresistible. It brought an intense moment of unity among Freedom Riders, professionals spawned by the GI Bill, the Blue Vein Circle that considered itself slandered by E. Franklin Frazier's exposé, *Black Bourgeoisie,* and the many who did not think Frazier had gone far enough. In retrospect, Baldwin's cry that blacks were of two minds about integration into a burning house seems hopeless since the power of a minority to threaten a majority with moral collapse depends on how much the majority cares. The climate of the times—perilous sit-ins and voter registration drives, murders and marches, songs of toil and deliverance—had everything to do with the sensation created by *The Fire Next Time.* Of course in those pre-Selma days no one believed that we'd ever have to walk alone.

Baldwin gave expression to the longings of blacks in exalted prose. He was embraced, in the tradition of Negro Firsterism, even by those who never sat down with a book, as *our* preeminent literary spokesman, whether he liked it or not. Neither athlete nor entertainer, but nevertheless a star. I do not know why it became fashionable among militants to dismiss him as absent without leave from the struggle, or as too moderate, conciliatory, a honky lover. He was, it seemed, always there, and he arrived on the stage in the apocalyptic mood. He filled my mind as the single enduring image of the black writer, an example to dwell upon beyond admiration or envy.

It helped that he had a genius for titles, for the phrase at once biblical and bluesy. I was drawn without hesitation to *Tell Me How Long the Train's Been Gone,* and at a time, I must admit, when I was ashamed to request a book from the library that had the word *Negro* or *Black* on the spine, as if there were something Baptist and loud about the connection between me and such a text. I didn't have to be embarrassed to say his name because James Baldwin was more than all right. One day I spotted **"An Open Letter to My Sister, Miss Angela Davis,"** in this paper. I read it over and over, as if it were a poem—"For, if they take you in the morning, they will be coming for us that night"—and was very moved to find joined the two living souls who, because I looked up to them, relieved my fear that I was an Uncle Tom.

For a long time I thought of my being black as an extracurricular activity. Baldwin's novels represented time off from the reading list: I took to them as romances, in the privacy of my room. *Another Country* was the steamiest book I'd ever sneaked off the shelf. There was something illicit in the vulnerability of his black male characters, given the smoky deviations by which his prodigals acted out their torment, and I vaguely expected to uncover in his interracial plots some clue to my own social inhibitions. When no black character appeared in the Paris of *Giovanni's Room,* I knew that he had broken the rules. (p. 8)

He had a way of sometimes signing off at the end of a work—"Istanbul, December 10, 1961"—and that, not the labor of composition, said, to me, that there was indeed a door somewhere to the outside. Wherefore wilt thou run, my son, seeing that thou hast no tidings?

James Baldwin was born into the black church and he came into the world with his subject matter. He was a boy evangelist, a dreamer in school—"I read books like they were some kind of weird food"—a malcontent in the defense plants of New Jersey, then, with the teeth marks still on his throat, an escapee to France, and from these unlikely beginnings he projected a career. "I wanted to prevent myself from becoming *merely* a Negro, or even, merely a Negro writer." He held fast to the steady view, to a premise profound in its simplicity: the conditions under which black Americans lived were unnatural. Out of the fundamental distortions of black life he spun the essays in *Notes of a Native Son,* a work triumphant in the clarity of its paradoxes.

Harlem was central to his journey. He described in celebrated essays and in the stories of *Going to Meet the Man* not a slum, but a ghetto, an unfathomable valley where wasted sharpies, toil-blasted women, idle old men, and sanctified girls stood corralled. "Only the Lord saw the midnight tears." He knew about street corners, teen-age pregnancy, and drug addiction, the urban equivalents of the chain gang. Baldwin's Harlem was a desolate landscape, completely severed from the cultural glories of its past. Though in *Nobody Knows My Name* he was haunted by the South as the source of his "inescapable identity," the Old Country remained opaque, erotic in his polemics, almost fable-like in his fiction, and fathers like Deacon Grimes revealed themselves as kinsmen to Bigger Thomas only when restored to the suffocation of the tenements. He wrote out of the black urban experience of his generation. Harlem was not a capital, not even a metaphor for claustrophobia. It was the real thing.

The journey out of Egypt was his great theme—that, and the search for identity, the necessary shedding of spiritual burdens along the road, the white world as the wilderness. The early essays are an unequalled meditation on what it means to be black in America. Baldwin came of age as a writer during the cold war. He spent his youth, unlike Wright or Ellison, not in radical politics, but in religion. The pulpit was always present in his work, and this legacy guided a vivid literary imagination that made for his high style, for his arresting lyricism of despair. The refinement of gut feeling and the bravery of his ambivalence were entirely original. I do not think I am alone when I say that for young blacks Baldwin's candor about self-hatred was both shocking and liberating. A message slid under the cell door.

He conceived of race relations as a drama of confession and absolution. He asked questions of the future and dared to believe that to hate and fear white people, to despise black people and the black ghetto, gave to the butch and criminal elite an easy victory. If there were no acceptable version of himself as a black man he would have to invent one, and demystify whites in the process. "No one in the world—in the entire world—knows more—knows Americans better or, odd as this may sound, loves them more than the American Negro. This is because he has had to watch you, outwit you, deal with you, and bear you, and sometimes even bleed and die with you, ever since we got here, that is, since both of us, black and white, got here—and this is a wedding." People, he argued, do not wish to become worse, they want to become better, but don't know how. Eventually he was made to pay the price for his gamble that they, the motley millions, worried as much about us as we, the new day a-coming, did about them; for his insistence on loaded values like love in an age of dubious cool.

Baldwin once warned us that the second generation has no time to listen to the first, but we were caught up in the long, hot summer and then yonder came the blues in the form of the southern strategy of the Nixon campaign, the beginning of the end. The right made quick business of the revolution, as we liked to call it, because those doomed creatures, white liberals, already had been intimidated, purged, told where to go. On our side of the cameras, ideological patricide became the order of the day, and extra dustbins were conjured up to accommodate the gentlemen who failed the how-black-and-bad-are-you test. Someday someone will assess what damage, if any, was done to Baldwin—and to us—by the attacks on him as an apologist for the Jews.

The denunciation of Baldwin in Eldridge Cleaver's *Soul on Ice* precipitated a crisis of inspiration. Where are those Sentas of Black Power who ran around the school lockers with this manifesto of extreme violence and vulgarity? Cleaver equated intellectuality with homosexuality and declared them crimes against the people, worse than "baby-rape." Perhaps, given the bitterness and frustration of those days, the venality of benign neglect, Baldwin would have come to distrust the worth of the intellectual life, the uses of the reflective voice, but I can't help wondering if he didn't take Cleaver's indictment seriously because of the "merciless tribunal" he convened in his own head. The evasive response in *No Name in the Street,* the capitulation in his saying that Cleaver did what he felt he had to do, caused me to think of him as defenseless, adrift, lacking the blustering, self-protecting ego of the important American writer. In any case, today we know where the dude Cleaver is at. As for Baldwin, the baroque sense of grievance was replaced by sermon, and maybe I'm wrong but I think the change in tone came about because he was forced by his volatile constituents to keep up with events as they saw them. His need to be political, in the popular sense, undermined his literary gift.

"Some escaped the trap, most didn't. Those who got out always left something of themselves behind." He often said that he was a commuter, not an expatriate, and maybe the gestures of the engaged writer were part of a larger compulsion to get back home, to honor where he came from, to prove that he had not forgotten. The later novels, *If Beale Street Could Talk* and *Just Above My Head,* place emphasis on the black family as refuge, on reconciliation and belonging, but they are as immobile as urns, as if in them he hoped to lay down his burden of being different, the smart black youth who feared his father and wrote his way out of poverty into the bohemian life. "Nothing is ever escaped," he said early on. But he was not a home boy; he was an elevated extension of ourselves.

It is impossible to read his memoir of Richard Wright without suffering a chill. Baldwin was young and very aware of his own promise, a reminder that before St. Paul de Vence he had his share of crummy rooms. Wright, in exile, sat alone, isolated from other blacks, mocked. "I could not help feeling: *Be careful. Time is passing for you, too, and this may be happening to you one day.*" Then Wright was gone and Baldwin noted the will in the lesson: "Well, he worked up until the end, died, as I hope to do, in the middle of a sentence, and his work is now an irreducible part of the history of our swift and terrible time." I thought of this passage after I read *The Evidence of Things Not Seen,* his report on the Wayne Williams trial in Atlanta, which made it a hard book to face in the first place. The flow of startling insights and connections had dried up. "The auction block is the platform on which I entered the Civilized World. Nothing that has happened since, from South Africa to El Salvador, indicates that the Western world has any real quarrel with slavery." It was a performance *sopra le righe.*

One heard exhaustion when he, still a striking apparition, murmured rhymes at audiences during his last appearances around town, and everyone remembered that back in the kingdom of the first person his work had the grace and melancholy of obsolete beauty, like a Palladian dance hall uptown improbably at rest between empty lots.

> There's not a breathing of the common wind
> That will forget thee.

Among writers, black or white, he had few peers, among those who bore witness none. He was buried from St. John the Divine as a hero of the folk. The drums sounded and one missed him immediately. Against great odds he lived out the life of a brilliant innocent, and went the luckless distance for us all. The first time I met him I had with me a book that was meant to serve the sad function of showing Manhattan how interesting I thought I was. It was a volume from Leslie Marchand's edition of Byron's journals that Mr. Baldwin found himself asked to sign, and sometimes I think his smile as he wrote across the title page said: number got. (pp. 8, 10)

Darryl Pinckney, "On James Baldwin (1924-1987)," in *The New York Review of Books*, Vol. XLIV, Nos. 21 & 22, January 21, 1988, pp. 8, 10.

SOURCES FOR FURTHER STUDY

Bloom, Harold, ed. *James Baldwin.* New York: Chelsea House, 1986, 164 p.

Reprints significant criticism of Baldwin's literary works. Included are such essays as Marion Berghahn's "Images of Africa in the Writings of James Baldwin," C. W. E. Bigsby's "The Divided Mind of James Baldwin," and Stephen Adams's "*Giovanni's Room:* The Homosexual as Hero."

Porter, Horace A. *Stealing the Fire: The Art and Protest of James Baldwin.* Middletown, Conn.: Wesleyan University Press, 1989, 220 p.

Studies Baldwin's genesis as a writer, focusing on his earliest essays and novels, particularly *Notes of a Native Son, Go Tell It on the Mountain,* and *Giovanni's Room.*

Standley, Fred L., and Burt, Nancy V., eds. *Critical Essays on James Baldwin.* Boston: G.K. Hall, 1988, 312 p.

Reprints selected criticism of Baldwin's works. Essays include: Richard K. Barksdale, "Temple of the Fire Baptized"; Leslie A. Fiedler, "A Homosexual Dilemma"; Joyce Carol Oates, "A Quite Moving and Very Traditional Celebration of Love"; Keith E. Byerman, "Words and Music: Narrative Ambiguity in 'Sonny's Blues' "; and Julius Lester, "Some Tickets Are Better: The Mixed Achievement of James Baldwin."

Standley, Fred L., and Pratt, Louis H., eds. *Conversations with James Baldwin.* Jackson: University Press of Mississippi, 1989, 297 p.

Collection of 27 interviews with Baldwin conducted between 1961 and 1987. Interviewers include David Frost, Henry Louis Gates, Jr., and Studs Terkel.

Sylvander, Carolyn Wedin. *James Baldwin*. New York: Frederick Ungar Publishing Co., 1980, 181 p.
> Critical and biographical study of Baldwin's life and works up to the publication of *Just above My Head* (1979). Bibliography.

Weatherby, W. J. *James Baldwin: Artist on Fire*. New York: Donald I. Fine, 1989, 412 p.
> Full-length biography by one of Baldwin's longtime friends.

Honoré de Balzac

1799-1850

(Born Honoré Balzac; also wrote under pseudonyms Lord R'hoone and Horace de Saint-Aubin) French novelist, short story and novella writer, dramatist, essayist, and editor.

INTRODUCTION

*B*alzac is one of the greatest French novelists of the nineteenth century. His importance rests on his vast work *La comédie humaine* (1895-98), which consists of more than ninety novels and stories. Critics generally concur that his genius lies in his accurate use of observation and detail, his inexhaustible imagination, and his authentic portraits of men, women, and their physical environments. Considered an early exponent of realism, Balzac is praised for providing a comprehensive portrait of French society in his day.

Balzac led a solitary childhood and received little attention from his parents. He lived with a wet nurse until the age of three, and at eight was sent to board at the Oratorian College at Vendôme. In 1884 his family moved from Tours to Paris, where Balzac completed his studies. He received his law degree in 1819; however, to his parents' disappointment, he announced that he intended to become a writer. From 1819 to 1825 Balzac experimented with literary forms, including verse tragedy and, later, sensational novels and stories, which he wrote under various pseudonyms. He considered these works to be stylistic exercises; they were conscious efforts to learn his craft, as well as his only means of support. At one point in his career he abandoned writing to become involved in a series of unsuccessful business ventures. Later, he returned to writing, but despite eventual renown, money problems continued to haunt him throughout his life.

Le dernier Chouan; ou, La Bretagne en 1800 (1829; *The Chouans*) was Balzac's first critically successful work and the first to appear under his own name, to which he added, in 1831, the aristocratic particle *de*. The novel *Physiologie du mariage; ou, Méditations de philosophie éclectique sur le bonheur et le malheur conjugal* (*The Physiology of Marriage*) and the collection of short stories *Scènes de la vie privée,* both published in 1830, further enhanced his reputation. These works also enhanced his appeal to female readers, who valued his realistic and sympathetic portraits of women as vital members of society. In 1832 Balzac received a letter from one of his female admirers signed *l'Étrangère* (the Stranger). The writer expressed her admiration for *Scènes de la vie privée* and chided Balzac for the ironic tone in his newest work, *La peau de chagrin* (1831). Later she revealed her identity as Madame Hanska, the wife of a wealthy Polish count. Balzac and Madame Hanska carried on an extended liaison through letters and infrequent visits. For nine years after her husband's death in 1841, she refused to remarry; her marriage to Balzac just five months before his death came too late to ease his financial troubles.

Commentators on Balzac rarely fail to note his flamboyant lifestyle and eccentric working habits. He never completed a work before sending it to the printer; instead, he sent a brief outline and scrupulously composed the entire work on successive galley proofs. To be free of distractions, he began working at midnight and continued, with only brief interruptions, until midday, fueled by tremendous quantities of strong black coffee.

After several months of this solitary, exhausting routine he would cease working and plunge into a frenzy of social activity, hoping to be admitted to the milieu of Parisian aristocracy. Balzac's ostentatious dress, extensive collection of antiques, outlandish printer's bills, and unsuccessful business schemes kept him perenially short of money. Many critics believe that the pressure of mounting debts pushed him to write faster and thus contributed to the creation of *La comédie humaine.*

La comédie humaine, written between 1830 and 1850, is considered to be his finest achievement. His preface to the 1842 collection outlines the goal of his writings. He refers to himself as "secretary to French society," and expresses his desire to describe and interpret his era. Balzac considered it possible to classify social species as the naturalists had classified zoological species. By organizing his stories into groups that depict the varied classes and their milieu, Balzac reveals his belief that environment determines an individual's development. *La comédie humaine* includes three main sections: *Études analytiques, Études philosophiques,* and the bulk of his work, *Études de moeurs,* which he further divided into *Scènes de la vie de province, Scènes de la vie parisienne, Scènes de la vie politique, Scènes de la vie militaire, Scènes de la vie de campagne,* and *Scènes de la vie privée,* a title he had previously used for a collection of short stories. Balzac intended to portray all levels of contemporary French society, but he did not live to complete the task.

Despite the great length and ambitious scope of *La comédie humaine,* most critics agree that the work should be approached as a whole. Many praise Balzac's technique of using the same characters in several novels, depicting them at different stages in their lives. For some critics, this strengthens the versimilitude of Balzac's fictional world and enabled Balzac to explore the psychology of individual characters more fully than would have been possible in a single novel. Henry James considered Balzac's portraits of people to be his greatest talent. His best–known characters are monomaniacs, victims of a consuming passion, such as Goriot's obsessive love for his daughters in *Le père Goriot: Histoire parisienne* (1835; *Old Goriot*), and the miser Grandet's love for money in *Eugénie Grandet* (1837?; *Eugenia Grandet; or, The Miser's Daughter: A Tale of Everyday Life in the Nineteenth Century*). In each of Balzac's memorable portraits, the essential characteristics of an individual are distilled into an embodiment and a reflection of an entire class. Balzac's accurate rendering of detail is generally attributed to his acute powers of observation; however, many critics, notably Charles Baudelaire and George Saintsbury, have emphasized other aspects of his work. They note that while he observed and recorded a wide variety of social milieus with objectivity and accuracy, his work also reveals a profound creative and imaginative power. Modern critics concur, finding Balzac's work to be a blend of acute observation and personal vision.

The morality of Balzac's works has long been debated. According to Ferdinand Brunetière, "Balzac brought about a revolution in the novel . . . by doing artistic work with elements reputed unworthy of art." In his effort to achieve a complete representation of society, Balzac included in his world not only virtue, faithfulness, and happiness, but also squalor, misery, chicanery, sexual perfidy, and greed. Many nineteenth-century readers and critics found his work to be depressing, and, more frequently, they considered his representation of life immoral. Others contended that Balzac was a realist and merely depicted society as he saw it.

Modern critical interest in Balzac attests to his enduring importance. His influence on the development of the novel in France is unsurpassed. Many critics contend that his use of the genre as social commentary steered the novel toward realism, and Balzac is now considered one of the world's greatest novelists. His ability to blend realistic detail, acute observation, and visionary imagination is considered his greatest artistic gift.

(For further information about Balzac's life and works, see *Nineteenth-Century Literature Criticism,* Vol. 5 and *Short Story Criticism,* Vol 5.)

CRITICAL COMMENTARY

HONORÉ DE BALZAC
(essay date 1842)

[In the following excerpt from his celebrated 1842 preface to the first edition of his collected works, Balzac defines the scope, theoretical basis, and purpose of his vast work.]

In giving the general title of *The Human Comedy* to a work begun nearly thirteen years since, it is necessary to explain its motive, to relate its origin, and briefly sketch its plan, while endeavoring to speak of these matters as though I had no personal interest in them. (p. li)

The idea of *The Human Comedy* was at first as a dream to me, one of those impossible projects which we caress and then let fly; a chimera that gives us a glimpse of its smiling woman's face, and forthwith spreads its wings and returns to a heavenly realm of phantasy. But this chimera, like many another, has become a reality; has its behests, its tyranny, which must be obeyed.

The idea originated in a comparison between Humanity and Animality.

It is a mistake to suppose that the great dispute which has lately made a stir, between Cuvier and Geoffroi Saint-Hilaire, arose from a scientific innovation. Unity of structure, under other names, had occupied the greatest minds during the two previous centuries. As we read the extraordinary writings of the mystics who studied the science in their relation to infinity, such as Swedenborg, Saint-Martin, and others, and the works of the greatest authors on Natural History—Leibnitz, Buffon, Charles Bonnet, etc., we detect in the *monads* of Leibnitz, in the *organic molecules* of Buffon, in the *vegetative force* of Needham, in the correlation of similar organs of Charles Bonnet—who in 1760 was so bold as to write, "Animals vegetate as plants do"—we detect, I say, the rudiments of the great law of Self for Self, which lies at the root of *Unity of Plan*. There is but one Animal. The Creator works on a single model for every organized being. "The Animal" is elementary, and takes its external form, or, to be accurate, the differences in its form, from the environment in which it is obliged to develop. (pp. li-lii)

I, for my part, convinced of this scheme of nature long before the discussion to which it has given rise, perceived that in this respect society resembled nature. For does not society modify Man, according to the conditions in which he lives and acts, into men as manifold as the species in Zoölogy! The differences between a soldier, an artisan, a man of business, a lawyer, an idler, a student, a statesman, a merchant, a sailor, a poet, a beggar, a priest, are as great, though not so easy to define, as those between the wolf, the lion, the ass, the crow, the shark, the seal, the sheep, etc. Thus social species have always existed, and will always exist, just as there are zoölogical species. If Buffon could produce a magnificent work by attempting to represent in a book the whole realm of zoölogy, was there not room for a work of the same kind on society? But the limits set by nature to the variations of animals have no existence in society. When Buffon describes the lion, he dismisses the lioness with a few phrases; but in society a wife is not always the female of the male. There may be two perfectly dissimilar beings in one household. The wife of a shopkeeper is sometimes worthy of a prince, and the wife of a prince is often worthless compared with the wife of an artisan. The social state has freaks which Nature does not allow herself; it is nature *plus* society. The description of social species would thus be at least double that of animal species, merely in view of the two sexes. Then, among animals the drama is limited; there is scarcely any confusion; they turn and rend each other—that is all. Men, too, rend each other; but their greater or less intelligence makes the struggle far more complicated. . . . Buffon found that life was extremely simple among animals. Animals have little property, and neither arts nor sciences; while man, by a law that has yet to be sought, has a tendency to express his culture, his thoughts, and his life in everything he appropriates to his use. Though Leuwenhoek, Swammerdam, Spallanzani, Réaumur, Charles Bonnet, Müller, Haller and other patient investigators have shown us how interesting are the habits of animals, those of each kind are, at least to our eyes, always and in every age alike; whereas the dress, the manners, the speech, the dwelling of a prince, a banker, an artist, a citizen, a priest, and a pauper are absolutely unlike, and change with every phase of civilization.

Hence the work to be written needed a threefold form—men, women, and things; that is to say, persons and the material expression of their minds; man, in short, and life. (pp. lii-liv)

But how could such a drama, with the four or five thousand persons which a society offers, be made interesting? How, at the same time, please the poet, the phi-

Principal Works

Le dernier Chouan; ou, La Bretagne en 1800 (novel) 1829; also published as Les Chouans: ou, La Bretagne en 1799, 1834

[The Chouans, 1890]

Physiologie du mariage; ou, Méditations de philosophie éclectique sur le bonheur et le malheur conjugal (novel) 1830

[The Physiology of Marriage, 1904]

Scènes de la vie privée (short stories) 1830; also published as Scènes de la vie privée [enlarged edition] (novella and short stories) 1832

La peau de chagrin (novel) 1831

[The Wild Ass's Skin, 1895-98]

La recherche de l'absolu (novel) 1834; published in Études de moeurs au XIXe siècle; also published as Balthazar Claës; ou, La recherche de l'absolu, 1839

[Balthazar; or, Science and Love, 1859; also published as The Quest of the Absolute, 1888]

Le père Goriot: Histoire parisienne (novel) 1835

[Daddy Goriot; or, Unrequited Affection, 1860; also published as Old Goriot, 1895-98]

Le lys dans la vallée (novel) 1836

[The Lily of the Valley, 1891]

Eugénie Grandet (novel) 1837?; published in Études de moeurs au XIXe siècle

[Eugenia Grandet; or, The Miser's Daughter: A Tale of Everyday Life in the Nineteenth Century, 1843]

Histoire de la grandeur et de la décadence de César Birotteau, parfumeur (novel) 1838

[History of the Grandeur and Downfall of César Birotteau, 1860; also published as The Rise and Fall of César Birotteau, 1912]

Béatrix; ou, Les amours forcés (novel) 1839

[Béatrix, 1895-98]

[A Great Man of the Provinces in Paris, 1893]

La femme de trente ans (novel) 1842; published in Oeuvres complètes de M. de Balzac: La comédie humaine

[A Woman of Thirty, 1895-98]

[Modeste Mignon, 1888]

*Histoire des parens [sic] pauvres: La cousine Bette et Les deux musiciens (novels) 1847; also published as Les parents pauvres. 12 vols. 1847-48

[Poor Relations, 1880]

Théâtre (dramas) [first publication] 1853

La Rabouilleuse (novella) 1858; published in Les célibataires

[A Bachelor's Establishment, 1895-98]

Les paysans [completed by Madame Hanska] (novel) 1863; published in Oeuvres complètes de H. de Balzac

[The Peasantry, 1895-98]

Balzac's Contes Drôlatiques: Droll Stories Collected from the Abbeys of Touraine (short stories) 1874

Splendeurs et misères des courtisanes (novel) 1879; published in Oeuvres complètes de H. de Balzac: Édition définitive

[A Harlot's Progress, 1895-98; also published as Splendors and Miseries of a Courtesan (date unknown)]

Oeuvres complètes de Honoré de Balzac. 40 vols. (novels, novellas, short stories, dramas, letters, and essays) 1912-40

*This work includes the novels La cousine Bette and Le cousin Pons.

---

losopher, and the masses who want both poetry and philosophy under striking imagery? Though I could conceive of the importance and of the poetry of such a history of the human heart, I saw no way of writing it; for hitherto the most famous story-tellers had spent their talent in creating two or three typical actors, in depicting one aspect of life. It was with this idea that I read the works of Walter Scott. Walter Scott, the modern troubadour, or finder (*trouvère—trouveur*), had just then given an aspect of grandeur to a class of composition unjustly regarded as of the second rank. . . . Walter Scott raised to the dignity of the philosophy of History the literature which, from age to age, sets perennial gems in the poetic crown of every nation where letters are cultivated. He vivified it with the spirit of the past; he combined drama, dialogue, portrait, scenery, and description; he fused the marvelous with truth—the two elements of the times; and he brought poetry into close contact with the familiarity of the humblest speech. But as he had not so much devised a system as hit upon a manner in the ardor of his work, or as its logical outcome, he never thought of connecting his compositions in such a way as to form a complete history of which each chapter was a novel, and each novel the picture of a period.

It was by discerning this lack of unity, which in no way detracts from the Scottish writer's greatness, that I perceived at once the scheme which would favor the execution of my purpose, and the possibility of executing it. Though dazzled, so to speak, by Walter Scott's amazing fertility, always himself and always original, I did not despair, for I found the source of his genius in the infinite variety of human nature. Chance is the greatest romancer in the world; we have only to study it. French society would be the real author; I should only be the secretary. By drawing up an inventory of vices and virtues, by collecting the chief facts of the passions, by depicting characters, by choosing the principal incidents of social life, by composing types out of a combination of homogeneous characteristics, I might perhaps succeed in writing the history which so many historians have neglected: that of Manners. By patience and perseverance I might produce for France in the nineteenth century the book which we must all regret that Rome, Athens, Tyre, Memphis, Persia, and India have not bequeathed to us; [a] history of their social life. . . . (pp. liv-lvi)

The work, so far, was nothing. By adhering to the strict lines of a reproduction a writer might be a more or less faithful, and more or less successful painter of types of humanity, a narrator of the dramas of private life, an archaeologist of social furniture, a cataloguer of professions, a registrar of good and evil; but to deserve the praise of which every artist must be ambitious, must I not also investigate the reasons or the cause of these social effects, detect the hidden sense of this vast assembly of figures, passions, and incidents? And finally, having sought—I will not say having found—this reason, this motive power, must I not reflect on first principles, and discover in what particulars societies approach or deviate from the eternal law of truth and beauty? In spite of the wide scope of the preliminaries, which might of themselves constitute a book, the work, to be complete, would need a conclusion. Thus depicted, society ought to bear in itself the reason of its working. (pp. lvi-lvii)

As to the intimate purpose, the soul of this work, these are the principles on which it is based.

Man is neither good nor bad; he is born with instincts and capabilities; society, far from depraving him, as Rousseau asserts, improves him, makes him better; but self-interest also develops his evil tendencies. Christianity, above all, Catholicism, being—as I have pointed out in the *Country Doctor* (*Le Médecin de Campagne*)—a complete system for the repression of the depraved tendencies of man, is the most powerful element of social order.

In reading attentively the presentment of society cast, as it were, from the life, with all that is good and all that is bad in it, we learn this lesson—if thought, or if passion, which combines thought and feeling, is the vital social element, it is also its destructive element. In this respect social life is like the life of man. Nations live long only by moderating their vital energy. Teaching, or rather education, by religious bodies is the grand principle of life for nations, the only means of diminishing the sum of evil and increasing the sum of good in all society. Thought, the living principle of good and ill, can only be trained, quelled, and guided by religion. The only possible religion is Christianity. . . . Christianity created modern nationalities, and it will preserve them. Hence, no doubt, the necessity for the monarchical principle. Catholicism and Royalty are twin principles. (pp. lvii-lviii)

I write under the light of two eternal truths—Religion and Monarchy; two necessities, as they are shown to be by contemporary events, towards which every writer of sound sense ought to try to guide the country back. (p. lviii)

Some persons may, perhaps, think that this declaration is somewhat autocratic and self-assertive. They will quarrel with the novelist for wanting to be an historian, and will call him to account for writing politics. I am simply fulfilling an obligation—that is my reply. The work I have undertaken will be as long as a history; I was compelled to explain the logic of it, hitherto unrevealed, and its principles and moral purposes. (p. lix)

Now every one who, in the domain of ideas, brings his stone by pointing out an abuse, or setting a mark on some evil that it may be removed—every such man is stigmatized as immoral. The accusation of immorality, which has never failed to be cast at the courageous writer, is, after all, the last that can be brought when nothing else remains to be said to a romancer. If you are truthful in your pictures; if by dint of daily and nightly toil you succeed in writing the most difficult language in the world, the word *immoral* is flung in your teeth. Socrates was immoral; Jesus Christ was immoral; they both were persecuted in the name of the society they overset or reformed. When a man is to be killed he is taxed with immorality. . . .

When depicting all society, sketching it in the immensity of its turmoil, it happened—it could not but happen—that the picture displayed more of evil than of good; that some part of the fresco represented a guilty couple; and the critics at once raised the cry of immorality, without pointing out the morality of another portion intended to be a perfect contrast. . . . [The] time for an impartial verdict is not yet come for me. (p. lx)

Some persons, seeing me collect such a mass of facts and paint them as they are, with passion for their motive power, have supposed, but wrongly, that I must belong to the school of Sensualism and Materialism—two aspects of the same thing—Pantheism. But their misapprehension was perhaps justified—or inevitable. I do not share the belief in indefinite progress for society as a whole; I believe in man's improvement in himself. (p. lxii)

A sure grasp of the purport of this work will make it clear that I attach to common, daily facts, hidden or patent to the eye, to the acts of individual lives, and to their causes and principles, the importance which historians have hitherto ascribed to the events of public national life. The unknown struggle which goes on in a valley of the Indre between Mme. de Mortsauf and her passion is perhaps as great as the most famous of battles (*Le Lys dans la Vallée*). In one the glory of the victor is at stake; in the other it is heaven. The misfortunes of the two Birotteaus, the priest and the perfumer, to me are those of mankind (*Le Curé de Tours* and *Histoire de la Grandeur et de la Décadence de César Birotteau, Parfumeur*). La Fosseuse (*Médecin de Campagne*) and Mme. Graslin (*Curé de Village*) are almost the sum-total of woman. We all suffer thus every day. (pp. lxiii-lxiv)

It was no small task to depict the two or three thousand conspicuous types of a period; for this is, in fact, the number presented to us by each generation, and which *The Human Comedy* will require. This crowd of actors, of characters, this multitude of lives, needed a setting—if I may be pardoned the expression, a gallery. Hence the very natural division, as already known, into *Scenes of Private Life*, of *Provincial Life*, of *Parisian*, *Political*, *Military*, and *Country Life*. Under these six heads are classified all the studies of manners which form the history of society at large, of all its *faits et gestes*, as our ancestors would have said. These six classes correspond, indeed, to familiar conceptions. Each has its own sense and meaning, and answers to an epoch in the life of man. . . . After being informed of my plan, [the young writer Felix Davin] said that the *Scenes of Private Life* represented childhood and youth and their errors, as the *Scenes of Provincial Life* represented the age of passion, scheming, self-interest, and ambition. Then the *Scenes of Parisian Life* give a picture of the tastes and vice and unbridled powers which conduce to the habits peculiar to great cities, where the extremes of good and evil meet. Each of these divisions has its local color—Paris and the Provinces—a great social antithesis which held for me immense resources.

And not man alone, but the principal events of life, fall into classes by types. There are situations which occur in every life, typical phases, and this is one of the details I most sought after. I have tried to give an idea of the different districts of our fine country. My work has its geography, as it has its genealogy and its families, its places and things, its persons and their deeds; as it has its heraldry, its nobles and commonalty, its artisans and peasants, its politicians and dandies, its army—in short, a whole world of its own.

After describing social life in these three portions, I had to delineate certain exceptional lives, which comprehend the interests of many people, or of everybody, and are in a degree outside the general law. Hence we have *Scenes of Political Life*. This vast picture of society being finished and complete, was it not needful to display it in its most violent phase, beside itself, as it were, either in self-defence or for the sake of conquest? Hence the *Scenes of Military Life*, as yet the most incomplete portion of my work, but for which room will be allowed in this edition, that it may form part of it

when done. Finally, the *Scenes of Country Life* are, in a way, the evening of this long day, if I may so call the social drama. In that part are to be found the purest natures, and the application of the great principles of order, politics, and morality.

Such is the foundation, full of actors, full of comedies and tragedies, on which are raised the *Philosophical Studies*—the second part of my work, in which the social instrument of all these effects is displayed, and the ravages of the mind are painted, feeling after feeling; the first of this series, *The Magic Skin*, to some extent forms a link between the *Philosophical Studies* and Studies of Manners, by a work of almost Oriental fancy, in which life itself is shown in a mortal struggle with the very element of all passion.

Besides these, there will be a series of *Analytical Studies*, of which I will say nothing, for one only is published as yet—*The Physiology of Marriage*.

In the course of time I purpose writing two more works of this class. First, the Pathology of Social Life, then an Anatomy of Educational Bodies, and a Monograph on Virtue. In looking forward to what remains to be done, my readers will perhaps echo what my publishers say, "Please God to spare you!" I only ask to be less tormented by men and things than I have hitherto been since I began this terrific labor. (pp. lxiv-lxvii)

The vastness of a plan which includes both a history and a criticism of society, an analysis of its evils, and a discussion of its principles, authorizes me, I think, in giving to my work the title under which it now appears—*The Human Comedy*. Is this too ambitious? Is it not exact? That, when it is complete, the public must pronounce. (p. lxvii)

Honoré de Balzac, "Author's Introduction," in his *The Works of Honoré de Balzac: The Magic Skin, The Quest of the Absolute and Other Stories, Vol. I-II*, edited by William P. Trent, translated by Ellen Marriage, Thomas Y. Crowell Co., Inc., 1900, pp. li-lxvii.

CHARLES BAUDELAIRE
(essay date 1859)

[A poet whose collection *Les fleurs du mal* (1857) is considered one of the great works of French poetry, Baudelaire was also an important critic. In the following excerpt from an essay first published in French in 1859, he comments on Balzac's extraordinary vitality, suggestiveness, and power of observation.]

I have often been astonished that Balzac's chief title to fame should be to pass for an observer; it had always seemed to me that his principle merit was that of being a visionary, and an impassioned visionary. All his characters are endowed with the zest for life with which he himself was animated. All his fabrications are as intensely colored as dreams. From the highest ranks of the aristocracy to the lowest dregs of society, all the actors in his *Comédie* are more eager for life, more energetic and cunning in their struggles, more patient in misfortune, more greedy in pleasure, more angelic in devotion than they are in the comedy of the real world. In a word, everyone in Balzac has genius—even the doormen. Every living soul is a weapon loaded to the very muzzle with will. This is actually Balzac himself. And as all beings of the exterior world presented themselves to his mind's eye in strong relief and with a striking grimace, he has made their forms convulsive, he has blackened their shadows and heightened their highlights. His prodigious taste for detail, which stems from an inordinate ambition to see everything and to guess everything as well as to make others see everything and guess everything, forced him, moreover, to give greater emphasis to the main lines in order to maintain the perspective of the whole. He sometimes makes me think of those etchers who are never satisfied with the biting and who tranform the main scratches on the plate into veritable ravines. This amazing natural bent has led to marvelous results. But this bent is generally considered a weakness in Balzac. Properly speaking, it is really one of his virtues. But who can boast of being so fortunately endowed and of being able to apply a method that will allow him to clothe the most commonplace things with the splendor of imperial purple? Who can do that? Now, to tell the truth he who does not succeed in doing that, accomplishes very little. (p. 170)

Charles Baudelaire, "Théophile Gautier," in his *Baudelaire as a Literary Critic*, translated by Lois Boe Hyslop and Francis E. Hyslop, Jr., The Pennsylvania State University Press, University Park, 1964, pp. 149-78.

OSCAR WILDE

(essay date 1886)

[Wilde, an English playwright, poet, novelist, essayist, and writer of short fiction, was known for his brilliant wit and idealistic dedication to art. In the excerpt below from an essay that first appeared in *Pall Mall Gazette* in 1886, he lauds the characterization in Balzac's works, declaring that a "course of Balzac reduces our living friends to shadows, and our acquaintances to the shadows of shades."]

Many years ago, in a number of *All the Year Round*, Charles Dickens complained that Balzac was very little read in England, and although since then the public have become more familiar with the great masterpieces of French fiction, still it may be doubted whether the *Comédie Humaine* is at all appreciated or understood by the general run of novel-readers. It is really the greatest monument that literature has produced in our century, and M. Taine hardly exaggerates when he says that, after Shakespeare, Balzac is our most important magazine of documents on human nature. Balzac's aim, in fact, was to do for humanity what Buffon had done for the animal creation. As the naturalist studied lions and tigers, so the novelist studied men and women. Yet he was no mere reporter. Photography and proces-verbal were not the essentials of his method. Observation gave him the facts of life, but his genius converted facts into truths, and truths into truth. He was, in a word, a marvellous combination of the artistic temperament with the scientific spirit. The latter he bequeathed to his disciples; the former was entirely his own. The distinction between such a book as M. Zola's *L'Assommoir* and such a book as Balzac's *Illusions Perdues* is the distinction between unimaginative realism and imaginative reality. . . . [Balzac] was of course accused of being immoral. Few writers who deal directly with life escape that charge. His answer to the accusation was characteristic and conclusive. "Whoever contributes his stone to the edifice of ideas," he wrote, "whoever proclaims an abuse, whoever sets his mark upon an evil to be abolished, always passes for immoral. If you are true in your portraits, if by dint of daily and nightly toil, you succeed in writing the most difficult language in the world, the word immoral is thrown in your face." The morals of the personages of the *Comédie Humaine* are simply the morals of the world around us. They are part of the artist's subject-matter, they are not part of his method. If there be any need of censure it is to life not to literature that it should be given. Balzac, besides, is essentially universal. He sees life from every point of view. He has no preferences and no prejudices. He does not try to prove anything. He feels that the spectacle of life contains its own secret. . . .

And what a world it is! What a panorama of passions! What a pell-mell of men and women! It was said of Trollope that he increased the number of our acquaintances without adding to our visiting lists; but after reading the *Comédie Humaine* one begins to believe that the only real people are the people who have never existed. Lucien de Rubempré, le Père Goriot, Ursule Mirouët, Marguerite Claës, the Baron Hulot, Mdme. Marneffe, le Cousin Pons, De Marsay—all bring with them a kind of contagious illusion of life. They have a fierce vitality about them: their existence is fervent and fiery-coloured: we not merely feel for them, but we see them—they dominate our fancy and defy scepticism. A steady course of Balzac reduces our living friends to shadows, and our acquaintances to the shadows of shades. (pp. 29-30)

Oscar Wilde, "Balzac in English," in his *The Artist as Critic: Critical Writings of Oscar Wilde,* edited by Richard Ellmann, W. H. Allen, 1970, pp. 29-32.

HENRY JAMES
(essay date 1913)

[Regarded as one of the greatest English novelists, the American-born James is also known as a short story writer, essayist, critic, and playwright. His novels include *Portrait of a Lady* (1881) and *The Ambassadors* (1903). In the following excerpt from a 1913 essay, he discusses Balzac's talent for depicting the social conditions affecting the lives of his characters.]

In reading [Balzac] over, in opening him almost anywhere to-day, what immediately strikes us is the part assigned by him, in any picture, to the *conditions* of the creatures with whom he is concerned. Contrasted with him other prose painters of life scarce seem to see the conditions at all. He clearly held pretended portrayal as nothing, as less than nothing, as a most vain thing, unless it should be, in spirit and intention, the art of complete representation. "Complete" is of course a great word, and there is no art at all, we are often reminded, that is not on too many sides an abject compromise. The element of compromise is always there; it is of the essence; we live with it, and it may serve to keep us humble. The formula of the whole matter is sufficiently expressed perhaps in a reply I found myself once making to an inspired but discouraged friend, a fellow-craftsman who had declared in his despair that there was no use trying, that it was a form, the novel, absolutely too difficult. "Too difficult indeed; yet there is one way to master it—which is to pretend consistently that it isn't." We are all of us, all the while, pretending—as consistently as we can—that it isn't, and Balzac's great glory is that he pretended hardest. He never had to pretend so hard as when he addressed himself to that evocation of the medium, that distillation of the natural and social air, of which I speak, the things that most require on the part of the painter preliminary possession—so definitely require it that, terrified at the requisition when conscious of it, many a painter prefers to beg the whole question. He has thus, this ingenious person, to invent some *other* way of making his characters interesting—some other way, that is, than the arduous way, demanding so much consideration, of presenting them to us. They are interesting, in fact, as subjects of fate, the figures round whom a situation closes,

in proportion as, sharing their existence, we feel where fate comes in and just how it gets at them. In the void they are not interesting—and Balzac, like Nature herself, abhorred a vacuum. Their situation takes hold of us because it is theirs, not because it is somebody's, any one's, that of creatures unidentified. Therefore it is not superfluous that their identity shall first be established for us, and their adventures, in that measure, have a relation to it, and therewith an appreciability. There is no such thing in the world as an adventure pure and simple; there is only mine and yours, and his and hers—it being the greatest adventure of all, I verily think, just to *be* you or I, just to be he or she. To Balzac's imagination that was indeed in itself an immense adventure—and nothing appealed to him more than to show *how* we all are, and how we are placed and built-in for being so. (pp. 134-35)

Henry James, "Honoré de Balzac," in his *Literary Criticism: French Writers, Other European Writers, The Prefaces to the New York Edition,* The Library of America, 1984, pp. 31-151.

ERNST ROBERT CURTIUS
(essay date 1950)

[Curtius was an eminent German philologist, scholar, and critic. In the following excerpt from a 1950 essay, he rejects traditional academic approaches to Balzac, emphasizing the magical appeal of the French novelist's work.]

[In writing my *Balzac* (1923), I wished] to explore Balzac's work in all its greatness and depth. I thought that up until then Balzac had been unfairly treated and imperfectly appreciated by literary history.

It was Balzac's misfortune to have displeased not only a Sainte-Beuve but also the so-called *critique universitaire,* that is, the professors who write histories of literature. According to them, he had spoiled his novels with pretentious didacticism. His psychology was inadequate. He lacked emotional refinement. He knew no moderation and had no taste. He was totally devoid of any feeling for nature. He was a robust and vulgar genius. Worst of all, he had no style. All this added up to an impressive number of gross defects. But after they had been duly noted, one could afford to be lenient and acknowledge a few merits as well.

I found the injustice and incomprehension of these judgments exasperating. I was imbued with the sense of Balzac's unique greatness. His work seemed to me a world whose structure must be investigated. Here was a mystery to be unraveled. I thought I should discover it in a visionary experience that could be traced to Balzac's childhood. He had been vouchsafed an illumination that transported him to the spheres of the angels. He saw "the celestial powers ascending and descending, handing one another the pails of gold." The presentiment of a continuity pervading all things flashed through his mind. He felt within himself a nameless power that could find no outlet. We know that there are two philosophical novels by Balzac—*Louis Lambert* and *La Peau de Chagrin*—whose heroes, while living in a shabby Parisian garret, compose a treatise on the will, a *Théorie de la Volonté*. The critics like to count this among the abstruse chimeras which, they say, disfigure Balzac's work. And yet it must have been a very personal and central concern with Balzac. For Louis Lambert and Raphael de Valentin bear autobiographical traits. What they term will is assuredly not the faculty of willing but an all-pervasive *fluidum*, an essence, which can be condensed but also dissipated. It is the life force. Balzac did not write the Theory of the Will, but its formulas are, after all, the mere skeleton of a total vision of man and the world that could only be unfolded through artistic creation. Today, we would not speak of will but of libido in Jung's sense. A system of psychic energy can be derived from the *Comédie Humaine;* indeed, the entire work may be seen as a grandiose representation of the transformations and symbols of the libido. The talisman that Raphael de Valentin acquires from a mysterious antiquary, that piece of shagreen leather endowed with magical powers which fulfills its possessor's boldest wishes—but only at the expense of his vital energy—this talisman was a poetic

symbol for the libido—a fairy-tale symbol. And just as the theory of the libido led Jung to the deciphering of alchemy, so too an alchemical novel found a place in the *Comédie Humaine: La Recherche de l'Absolu*. The theory of energy proved to me to be the magic word that one had to know in order to understand the whole and the true Balzac. Now his work revealed a surprising unity which I had previously only dimly suspected but never grasped. It was a discovery that excited and elated me. I am as convinced of its truth today as I was then, and I may say that it has received recognition. But my scholarly research has since been directed toward very different fields. I have remained an admirer and a reader of Balzac, but not a Balzac scholar. So that if I am asked to say something about Balzac today, I find myself in a peculiar position. A new encounter with Balzac means to me virtually a new encounter with myself.

My first contacts with French literature had been tentative and contradictory. While still in the last year at the Gymnasium, I had been lucky enough to see the great Coquelin in the role of Cyrano de Bergerac. At that time Rostand's play seemed to me to be one of the summits of poetry. . . . Later, as a young student in Berlin, I heard Yvette Guilbert sing French folk songs. For me it was the captivating voice of *La France*, a summons that penetrated to my innermost being.

But then, when I began to study French literature, I became confused. On my first vacation I took along a volume of Corneille, and Flaubert's *Madame Bovary*. Corneille I found merely dull, but the novel, which had been recommended to us in the course, revolted me. What? This collection of disgusting, stupid, sordid human beings was supposed to be interesting? Suicide by arsenic was the end of the matter? What kind of a country, what kind of a people was it where such a thing could be produced? Not so much as a spark of grandeur, love, beauty, strength? And I was expected to admire it? At nineteen, I could not do so.

But a year later I became acquainted with the work of Balzac, and then everything changed. I was passionately carried away. I felt I was in the grip of a powerful magic. Countless readers on every level have had the same experience. Balzac's world casts its spell over everyone.

When I speak of magic and enchantment, I have something very specific in mind. Even at the outset of Balzac's literary career a critic observed that the word *fascination* occurred frequently in his work and that it was admirably suited to describe the effect that this author had on the reader. Fascination, in its original sense, is the power possessed by certain people of subduing animals with their eyes. It is a sort of magnetism that emanates from a person: an inexplicable but most real phenomenon. And how is this effect to be understood? Balzac himself was magnetically attracted by the promises of life. He was filled with an insatiable desire for beauty, pleasure, power, knowledge, wealth, fame, love, passion. "Je veux vivre avec excès," says one of his typical characters. To all of them he imparted this boundless craving for life. "All of them," writes Baudelaire, "are endowed with the ardent vitality that animated the man himself " [see excerpt dated 1859].

Balzac's life and creation always proceed at the highest temperatures, and he transmits his own fervor to the receptive reader. Our sense of life is heightened, our existence is intensified when we see the world through Balzac's eyes. This is the source of the fascination that emanates from him.

Balzac's limitless craving encompasses the realm of the mind as well as that of the senses and the soul. He reaches for the fruits of the tree of knowledge and of the tree of experience. He wants the whole, the unconditional—*La Recherche de l'Absolu.* When I look for something comparable, all I can find is Faust's striving. Not that I would maintain that Balzac was dependent on Goethe. It is only a matter of elucidating through comparisons a basic element in Balzac's intellectual makeup. In the gallery of archetypal figures created by the European mind, we find the hero, the saint, and the sage. We find the sensualist, seeking the absolute in sexual love: that is Don Juan. But Faust wants more: he lusts after magic, after Helen, after power over time and space, "insatiable at every moment." Let us not forget that Faust belongs to the sect of the alchemists. This infinity of desire is a psychological configuration known only to modern Europe: not to classical Antiquity nor to the Orient, despite the splendors of the *Thousand and One Nights.* It is in this world of the Faustian soul that Balzac must be viewed—this great modern genius to whom Europe's classical tradition meant nothing.

The Faustian element in Balzac, the insatiable and infinite desire for all of life's fulfillments, is only another aspect of what I have called energy, will, libido. It is the mainspring of his artistic activity, the motor of his imagination. He projects it upon all of reality. With Balzac desire becomes a creative principle.

French literature of the nineteenth century depicts life in predominantly dark colors. (pp. 189-93)

Balzac is the only great Frenchman of the last century who affirms the world: this modern world in its immeasurable abundance, its prose and its poetry, its reality and its spirituality. Balzac loves his century. The enormous edifice of the *Human Comedy* was to have been capped by a "Philosophical and Political Dialogue on the Perfections of the Nineteenth Century," which was to have been preceded by a "Monograph on Virtue." We cannot have any idea of the content of these books. It was not permitted Balzac to complete his gigantic task. Destiny granted him only a brief span of

fifty-one years. If we consider that he wrote his first fully valid work, *Les Chouans,* at the age of thirty, it leaves barely twenty years for the labor of a lifetime.

Balzac developed slowly and matured late. He loses ten years in professional and literary experiments that are a series of failures. But when he has found himself, his production bursts forth with unparalleled power and abundance. And in this fever of creation its inner meaning becomes clear to him. In the summer of 1833 he is suddenly struck with the idea of consolidating all his novels into a vast, coherent system, into a cosmos. He receives this idea in a state of illumination accompanied by a high degree of exaltation. It overwhelms him so completely that he dashes across half of Paris to see his sister and inform her that he is quite simply on the verge of becoming a genius. What went on in Balzac at that moment? A psychological breakthrough has taken place, an illumination that is integration at the same time. This means that an insight that had long been present as a vague intuition now enters the consciousness with precise outlines. Balzac feels that all the works he has already produced have an organic connection and that they are thus parts of a comprehensive whole. And this whole exhibits a purposeful order. It was a spiritual event which has its analogy in physical nature: a process of crystallization, a rapid conversion of the fluidum into a regular structure. Balzac preserved the insight of that day in the phrase: "Il ne suffit pas d'être un homme; il faut être un système." To be a system means: to apprehend one's own creation as a purposefully ordered continuity. (pp. 194-95)

I have said that Balzac's experience in the summer

First corrected proof-sheet of a page of *Une Ténébreuse affaire.*

of 1833 was accompanied by a state of exaltation. He realized that he was a genius. What does that mean? An integrative experience such as his releases the awareness of a hitherto unknown energy and power. The creative person feels that he is being raised to a higher potency. He can organize, plan, control. In the same year, 1833, he writes to his beloved: "I wish to dominate the intellectual world of Europe; two more years of patience and labor, and I shall walk on the heads of all those who would tie my hands and clog my flight." And in 1844: "Four men (in the nineteenth century) will have had immense lives: Napoleon, Cuvier, O'Connell, and I wish to be the fourth. The first lived the life of Europe; he inoculated armies upon himself! The second embraced the globe. The third incorporated a people. I shall have carried an entire society in my head!"

Balzac does not compare himself with, say, the great reputations of contemporary literature. No doubt he did not recognize any standard that he and they might have in common. The names he mentions seem disparate: the emperor elevated by legend to mythical grandeur; the great naturalist, founder of comparative anatomy and paleontology; finally, the emancipator of Ireland. What they have in common, in Balzac's view, is the range, the total character of their effective energy. They master a whole: whole armies, a whole people, the whole globe. They are individuals who bear an entirety within themselves. And this is precisely what Balzac can quite rightly attribute to himself. What a tremendous feeling of power was alive in him! One is reminded of the late Nietzsche. But Balzac's self-confidence is free from hubris.

In order to organize his work into a totality, Balzac invented the device of having his characters reappear in different books. He begins to use this device in 1834. He then arranged the novels in various groups; in 1842 he at last chose the collective title of *Comédie Humaine* and discussed his intentions in an introduction [see excerpt dated 1842]. A new and final plan for a system was drawn up in 1845. According to this design the *Comédie Humaine* was to consist of 137 works, of which 87 had been completed, 50 more sketched out or planned. In the few years still remaining to him Balzac wrote yet another half-dozen novels.

After Balzac had conceived and designed his creation as a system of novels, he proceeded to fit his earlier works into this system as well. The critics have found fault with him for this, maintaining that the systematization was an afterthought and artificial, and that it simulated a unity which did not exist. Marcel Proust, one of the greatest modern admirers of Balzac, has refuted these reproaches. According to him, the unity of Balzac's work is all the more convincing and genuine for having dawned upon its creator only after the event. Precisely because Balzac was not aware of it

at first, it is a vital, not a logical unity. The separate parts tended of their own accord to form a whole. Even in the unfinished state in which we possess it Balzac's cycle of novels gives a total picture of humanity. I look in vain in the history of European literature for something to compare with it. Balzac's uniqueness stands out all the more clearly when we compare him with his imitators. (pp. 195-96)

[There] have been numerous attempts to create a human comedy of our age in the form of a series of novels in many volumes. They are equipped with all the current psychological and sociological innovations. Only one thing is missing: the impalpable essence of life. They are necropolises, inhabited by shadows whose names one can scarcely remember, let alone their destinies. They will have been long forgotten when Balzac's work is still alive.

All the imitators of Balzac have copied only the external features of his work. Its inner impulse they have not understood. They have taken Balzac to be a realist, and our unthinking literary histories in part still disseminate this belief today. From them we learn that literature consists of so-called currents that succeed one another. In the nineteenth century we have first Romanticism, then Realism. The latter continues in intensified form as Naturalism and is then replaced by Symbolism, which unfortunately cannot be satisfactorily defined. Such is the conventional scheme. It is grotesque. But it is explained by the fact that we divide world literature according to languages, nations, and centuries, and parcel it out in small pieces. Thus all perspective is lost. The reproduction of daily reality is not an artistic conquest of the nineteenth century. It can be found in Hellenistic poetry, in the novel of the Roman imperial age, in the Icelandic sagas of the twelfth century, but also in Chaucer, in Rabelais, in Cervantes, in Fielding. Realism in the plastic arts begins as early as the cave paintings of the Neolithic period. There are realistic tendencies in all ages and zones. There are dozens, if not hundreds, of realisms of different kinds, different styles, different techniques. Literary scholarship—like art history—will gradually learn to distinguish them.

The effort toward the faithful rendering of nature can correspond to the most diverse of motives. The realism of the Neolithic cave paintings is magical: it is intended to guarantee success in hunting. Late Gothic art or Spanish art of the seventeenth century displays the figures of saints with horrible traces of physical degradation—but only in order to make sanctity comprehensible in human terms to the beholder or the worshipper. That would be a sacral realism. There is satirical realism: sturdy in Hogarth, caustic in George Grosz. There are many other kinds besides. . . . Flaubert's realism has complex psychological roots. It is the reaction of a disillusioned romantic who had sought refuge in extravagant dreams and fantasy worlds. He takes his revenge, as it were, in an emotional negation of all of life's values. "L'éternelle misère de tout"—that is the sum he draws from human existence. That is his perspective. He believes it to be an objective statement—as though there were an objective truth about life. Flaubert wants us to see it through his eyes. His realism is a nihilism. In this world there is nothing constructive, no elevating purpose, no faith and no hope. The hallucinations of Flaubert's St. Anthony culminate in the self-annihilating wish to dissolve into matter: "descendre jusqu'au fond de la matière—être la matière!" It is the cruel logic of psychopathy that leads to this outcry. In Flaubert there is a conflict between the desires and the realities of life that ends in an irreconcilable dichotomy. In Balzac it is the reverse: a boundless imagination of desire that succeeds in penetrating all of reality and assimilating it.

Flaubert finds life senseless and compiles a catalogue of human stupidity. He gathers incriminating evidence against man and the world. *Bouvard et Pécuchet* is a heap of such material which never received a definitive artistic form. Balzac has a burning interest in life and conveys his ardor to us as Flaubert conveys his disgust. Flaubert turns his back on reality. About the France of his period we learn little from the books of this realist, and nothing favorable. How very different with Balzac! He once summed up his aim as an artist in the phrase, he wanted to express his century—"exprimer mon siècle." And how graphically his epoch stands before us.

We know the role that money played in Balzac's life. Even at the peak of success he was often scarcely able to evade his creditors. He earned a great deal, but he spent even more. He was a collector of art; he loved luxury. He knew the part money plays in life from intimate personal experience. And he was the first to depict it. His work tells us what income people had. The miser is an ancient figure of comedy. But Balzac's Grandet is the first whose fortune we can see being made and whose profits we can audit. Financial operations on the largest and the smallest scale occupy a place in Balzac that seemed previously to have been reserved for grand passions. The sordid usurer is a member of the cast of the *Human Comedy* no less than the important banker who influences international politics. In Balzac's time industry was still in its infancy, as was modern transportation. No machines, no technology existed as yet. Balzac himself had been a printer. He can describe the business of printing and the manufacture of paper from firsthand observation. In another novel we follow the rise of a perfume manufacturer; we witness his bankruptcy, but also his rehabilitation on the Paris stock exchange. He dies a martyr to commercial honesty, assured of the palms of heaven. "This is the death of the just," says the priest at his deathbed. So the career of a Parisian merchant becomes a modern drama, ready to view with the martyr tragedies of the seventeenth century.

But in Balzac one can also study the judicial system, the methods of the police, the psychology of the criminal, the election of a deputy. Ministers and tribunes of the people betray state secrets to us. Prostitution is analyzed as well as administrative affairs. We enter the salons of the aristocracy but also the student's garret, the artist's studio, the editor's office. Balzac presents a sociology of Paris. We come to know every aspect of public life. But Balzac also shows us the mysteries of Paris. One of his novels bears the characteristic title, *L'Envers de l'Histoire contemporaine.* We are introduced to a small group of people, sorely tried by fate, who have banded together to practice active Christian charity. Their breviary is the *Imitatio Christi.* It is a genuine touch of Balzac that we should also be precisely informed of their bank account. Mystery in all its forms possessed a magical attraction for Balzac. The *Human Comedy* is full of people who carry a secret around with them. There are artists ignorant of their parentage but whose destiny is guided by an unknown hand. There is the galley slave, Vautrin, who turns up under the most varied names and disguises and in the most diverse milieux to play the role of Providence in the lives of young men. Balzac shows us secret societies in the heart of modern Paris but also secret dramas like the story of the girl with the golden eyes, about which Hofmannsthal has said:

> This is the magnificent and unforgettable tale in which sensuality grows out of mystery, the Orient uncloses its heavy-lidded eyes amidst the insomnias of Paris, adventure is entwined with reality, the flower of the soul blossoms on the brink of ecstasy and death, and the present is illumined by such a torch that it lies before us like the great ages of ancient dreams. . . . The story of Henry de Marsay and the girl with the golden eyes. The story whose beginning is a description of Paris, an immense portrait in words, a vast pile, a tower built of pale light and deepest darkness; and whose ending is an Oriental poem in which the stupefaction of the most profound lust mingles with the odor of blood and an indefinable something soars beyond sense into the unnameable; whose beginning might have been from the hand of Dante, whose end from the *Thousand and One Nights,* and which, as a whole, could be by none other than the man who wrote it.

And Hofmannsthal concludes: "I do not know what cravings of the imagination could possess a reader which the books of this man might not satisfy."

If Hofmannsthal cites Dante and the *Thousand and One Nights* for comparison, he also invokes Shakespeare in order to suggest the poetic wealth of Balzac's imgination.

The fact is that Balzac cannot be fitted into any of the literary movements and revolutions of the nineteenth century. He never drew up a program, never wanted to found a school. The inner law of his work and of his person is self-development, realization of the vision that he carried within him. Nothing is further from his intentions than the break with the past proclaimed by Romanticism. The roots of Balzac's spiritual world are embedded in the venerable traditions of the French mind. Rabelais is for him one of the greatest of geniuses, Racine perfection itself, the *Fables* of La Fontaine sacred relics of mankind. But he reveres with the same enthusiasm a Montesquieu, a Diderot, a Buffon. He regards himself as an heir, never as a rebel. He cherishes a boundless admiration for France's classical centuries, but also for the France of the cathedrals, of the mediaeval builders' corporations, of the Gothic.

The *Comédie Humaine* is not merely a portrait of the present, like Zola's cycle of novels. Balzac's work has an historical dimension as well. Balzac was born on the threshold of the nineteenth century, in the midst of the tremendous historical drama that France enacted before the world between 1789 and 1815. Some of his most gripping works present scenes from the Revolution and the Napoleonic era. But in the *Comédie Humaine* we also find novels set in the seventeenth, sixteenth, and fifteenth centuries. Only one story, *Les Proscrits,* goes back even further, to the early years of the fourteenth century. It shows us Dante as an exile in Paris and describes a lecture at the Sorbonne by the celebrated Scholastic philosopher Siger de Brabant. We know that this willful thinker, who was condemned as a teacher of heresy even in his own lifetime, receives a tribute in Dante's *Paradiso* that puzzles the interpreters to this day. What was it about this material that attracted Balzac? And why did he classify this novel among his *Études philosophiques,* which loom over the massif of the *Études de Moeurs* like the interpretation over the realm of facts? There is a precinct in the *Comédie Humaine* that has never become popular, but has always had a particular attraction for certain minds, even as Balzac himself set the greatest store by it. These are the novels in which he represents the mystical and magical thinking of an original religious revelation, for which his authorities are Jacob Böhme, Swedenborg, and Saint-Martin. On his own authority he assigned Siger de Brabant a place in this Mystery-Christianity. This, I believe, is the meaning of the story, or at least one of its meanings.

For of course it means much more. After all, in Balzac everything is related to everything else. It is not by chance that in 1831, on the threshold of his career, Balzac invokes Dante, the creator of the mediaeval synthesis, and a master of Christian philosophy. They are images that rise before him because they symbolize his own vocation. The poet who summons past and pres-

ent to the bar of his justice and the intrepid spirit who proclaims Eternal Christianity as a thinker are symbols, interpreters; they are powerful patrons. Balzac was profoundly shaken by the Revolution of 1830. Apocalyptic visions tormented him. From the same period dates the wonderful legend *Jésus-Christ en Flandre,* which culminates in the vision of a rejuvenated Church and ends with the words: "To believe is to live! I have just seen the funeral of a monarchy; the Church must be defended!" The historical frame of the legend refers back to the fifteenth century. It is the century in which the *Imitatio Christi* was composed. Here, as in the Dante novella, Balzac is seeking a connection with the Catholic Middle Ages.

Balzac's interpretation of Catholicism contains gnostic and heterodox elements that are fed, in part, by murky sources. He personally tended toward an esoteric form of Christianity not recognized by the Church and for which he cites dubious witnesses. But even where, venturing on the track of Swedenborg and Saint-Martin, he loses himself in fantasy and ecstasy, a genuine mystical longing is unmistakable. He has been touched by the spiritual powers of Christianity. He confessed the conviction, moreover, that active *caritas* was the remedy for the ills of the time. And he powerfully exemplified this belief in novels like *Le Curé de Village* and *Le Médecin de Campagne.* His apostolic priest figures have become models for the social Catholicism of the nineteenth and twentieth centuries. All of Balzac's work places itself at the service of a political, social, and religious reform of France. (pp. 197-203)

[Balzac] was a great affirmer. He lived in the euphoria of creation. In his titanic consciousness as a creator he compared himself to Napoleon. Power, fame, dominion, authority, legitimacy—these to him were forms of human greatness. To these he gave admiration. His political convictions are not to be measured by the yardstick of strict adherence to party dogmas. Balzac was carried away by greatness in all its forms. For he was akin to it himself.

Greatness—no other word will serve in determining Balzac's rank. If we survey the broad landscape of European literature, we shall find only a few figures to whom we attribute unqualified greatness: Homer, Dante, Shakespeare. (pp. 204-05)

One of the most remarkable occurrences in the history of the French mind is the break which it effected in the sixteenth century with the Middle Ages, and that means with its great Gothic past. This break is located between Rabelais and Ronsard. If anything is evident, it is that Rabelais stems from Gothic France. The Renaissance elements in him, which are usually emphasized, are all on the surface. The rupture with the Gothic world involved a loss of substance of immeasurable extent. It is the price which France paid for its Classicism: for refinement, elegance, rationality, style, form. When once these qualities have been inbred, they shape the instincts. One seeks to reproduce them and, wherever possible, even to improve upon them—irrespective of all disjunctions in style. Thus sublime essences are engendered like the poetry of a Valéry. But the substance of Gothic France lived on underground. The historical eruptions of the Great Revolution, Napoleon, and the July Revolution loosened the soil. I can do no more than allude here to this transformed substance that emerges once again to the light simultaneously in Michelet, in Auguste Comte, in Balzac—and finally in Rodin. Is there any more impressive testimony to Balzac's greatness than Rodin's marble, from which the visionary Balzac gazes out at us? Than Balzac, as Rilke says, "in the ecstasy of vision, foaming with creation; in his superabundant fertility, founder of generations, lavisher of destinies?" Balzac's creative power can rival that of the greatest. (pp. 207-08)

Today we are revising the evaluations of the nineteenth century in every field. More than a century seems to separate 1900 and 1950. At the Paris World's Fair in 1900 an exhibition of modern French paintings was presented. But it lacked Monet, Degas, Puvis de Chavannes, Renoir, Cézanne. Instead, paintings by artists whose very names have been forgotten today were admired. With literature it is not very different. Around 1900, it was obligatory to admire Sully Prudhomme. In 1901 he was awarded the first Nobel prize for literature. Who knows anything about him today? Who still admires the sonnets of Hérédia? Who still considers Marcel Prévost and Paul Adam important novelists? And what of the great names in French criticism of the period—Faguet, Lemaître, Brunetière, Lanson?

Balzac, too, must be viewed differently in 1950 than in 1900 or even in 1920. It is a long time since Zola has been set beside him. Do people still put him on a level with Stendhal and Flaubert? I do not believe that they will long continue to do so. I believe I sense a shift in critical emphasis. In the field of literary criticism I find no problem so interesting as that of the order of rank and its changes. It is a very delicate task, which requires us not only to consult our own personal sense of values but to keep an eye out for signs of the weather. If I look at Balzac from this perspective, I notice that he has continually increased in stature over the last three decades. Time has brought out new aspects in him. We must bear in mind that since 1919 the entire situation of the French novel has been altered by the appearance of Proust. The advent of a new artist of genius also throws the art of the past into a new light. This is a regularly established process. Literary criticism does not take it sufficiently into account. But in 1936 a critic like Thibaudet had already drawn a portrait of Balzac that was seen through Proust. He found in Monsieur de Charlus a heightened Vautrin, and he calls Proust "le plus balzacien des écrivains français

après Balzac," as Saint-Simon had been "le plus balzacien des écrivains avant Balzac." Proust is the most comprehensive and subtle intelligence ever to manifest itself in the medium of the French novel; an intelligence that was simultaneously intuition in Bergson's sense. For that reason it is doubly significant that Proust's art should have an affinity with Balzac and not with Stendhal or Flaubert. It was Paul Morand who remarked that only through Proust was one of Balzac's greatest novels, *Les Illusions Perdues,* discovered for the present day. And whoever reads Morand's wonderful novella, *Parfaite de Saligny,* will realize that this modern Frenchman follows in the line of Balzac's great tragic novellas—I am thinking of *El Verdugo* or *La Fille aux yeux d'or.* Moreover, in both Proust and Morand, elements recur which the democratic nineteenth and the socialistic twentieth centuries have charged to the great Balzac as improprieties: his need for luxury and his so-called snobbishness. Both are expressions of an aesthetic sense for which Baudelaire found the poetic formula: *Luxe, calme et volupté.*

It is remarkable that it has always been the poets who have understood Balzac most profoundly: Baudelaire, Browning, Hofmannsthal. Among contemporaries: Gottfried Benn. This influence of Balzac, in range and in depth, would also pose a problem for criticism, were criticism willing to recognize it. These poets respond to Balzac as to a related element. From this phenomenon we may gather that an inexhaustible poetic substance inheres in Balzac. But it tells us something else besides. These poets are completely distinct from one another. But in each of them we find the utmost refinement of soul and intellect. This means that Balzac receives the tribute of the European elite. Yet the same Balzac also speaks to the mass of readers. Stendhal wrote for "the happy few." In order to appreciate Flaubert, one must be initiated into the subtleties of artistic form. Balzac writes neither for intellectuals nor for aesthetes. Nevertheless, they too render him admiration. He is perhaps the only writer of the nineteenth century who bridges the gap between the elite and the masses. This too is a seal of greatness. Balzac as a Frenchman contains all mankind. That is why he could become the property of all mankind.

Balzac's greatness was still in dispute at the end of the nineteenth century and beyond. But today, a century after his death, it is emerging ever more forcefully. And it will grow, from century to century. (pp. 208-10)

E. R. Curtius, "New Encounter with Balzac," in his *Essays on European Literature,* translated by Michael Kowal, Princeton University Press, 1973, pp. 189-210.

V. S. PRITCHETT
(essay date 1964)

[Acknowledged as a master of the short story, Pritchett is also an esteemed literary critic. In the excerpt below, he praises Balzac's ability, exemplified by the novels *Le cousin Pons* and *La cousine Bette*, to identify with his time.]

The small house on the cliff of Passy hanging like a cage between an upper and lower street, so that by a trick of relativity, the top floor of the Rue Berton is the ground floor of the Rue Raynouard, has often been taken as a symbol of the life of Balzac. . . . Two houses in one, a life with two front doors, dream and reality; the novelist, naïve and yet shrewd, not troubling to distinguish between one and the other. Symbol of Balzac's life, the house is a symbol of the frontier life, the trapdoor life of the great artists, who have always lived between two worlds. . . . At this house in the worst year of his life, the least blessed with that calm which is—quite erroneously—supposed to be essential to the novelist, Balzac wrote [*Le Cousin Pons*] and *La Cousine Bette,* respectively the best constructed and the most fluent and subtle of his novels. (pp. 327-28)

Balzac is certainly the novelist who most completely exemplifies the "our time" novelist, but not by his judgments on his society. He simply *is* his time. He is identified with it, by all the greedy innocence of genius. The society of rich peasants brought to power by revolution and dictatorship, pushing into business and speculation, buying up houses and antiques, founding families, grabbing at money and pleasure, haunted by their tradition of parsimony and hard work, and with the peasant's black and white ideas about everything, and above all their weakness for fixed ideas, is Balzac himself. He shares their illusions. Like them he was humble when he was poor, arrogant when he was rich. As with them, his extravagance was one side of the coin; on the other was the face of the peasant miser. The cynic lived in a world of romantic optimism. We see the dramatic phase of a century's illusions, before they have been assimilated and trodden down into the familiar hypocrisies. To us Balzac's preoccupation with money appears first to be the searching, scientific and prosaic interest of the documentary artist. On the contrary, for him money was romantic; it was hope and ideal. It was despair and evil. It was not the dreary background, but the animating and theatrical spirit. (pp. 329-30)

[In *Le Cousin Pons,*] Balzac examined the dossier of human nature with the quizzical detachment of some nail-biting, cigar-stained Chief of Police who is going rapidly up in the world; who has seen so many cases; who thanks heaven that he does not make the moral law and that a worldly Church stands between himself and the Almighty. Passion, even when it is a passion for the best food, always becomes—in the experience of the Chief of Police—a transaction; Pons trades the little errands he runs on behalf of the family for the indispensable surprises of the gourmet. In the pursuit of that appetite he is prepared to ruin himself where other men, more voluptuously equipped by nature, will wreck themselves in the capture and establishment of courtesans. Sex or food, money or penury, envy or ambition—Balzac knows all the roads to ruin. If only men and women were content with their habits instead of craving the sublimity of their appetites.

But *Pons* is a type. He is a poor relation. (pp. 334-35)

Look at the delightful Pons. His character has so many departments. He is an old man, an ugly man, an outmoded but respected musician, a dandy survived from an earlier period, a collector of antiques, a poor man, a careful man, a simple man who is not quite so simple. . . . Pons is the kind of character who, inevitable, becomes fantastic in the English novel simply because no general laws pin him down. He would become a static "character." Instead Balzac takes all these aspects of Pons and mounts each one, so that Pons is constructed before our eyes. We have a double interest: the story or plot, which is excellent in suspense, drama and form—this is one of Balzac's well-constructed novels, as it is also one of the most moving—and the exact completion, brick by brick, of Pons and his circle. There are the historical Pons—he is an *incroyable* left-over from the Directoire—the artistic Pons, the financial Pons, the sociable Pons, the moral Pons, and in the end Pons dying, plundered, defiant, a man awakened from his simplicity and fighting back, the exquisitely humble artist turned proud, sovereign and dangerous in his debacle. Pons is a faceted stone, and part of the drama is the relation of each facet with the others. . . . We have the portrait of a man who in every trait suggests some aspect of the society in which he lives. The history of his time is explicit in him. Yet he is not a period piece. A period piece is incapable of moral development and the development of a moral theme is everything in the novels of Balzac, who facilitates it by giving every character not merely a time and place, but also an obsession. (pp. 335-36)

Balzac is the novelist of our appetites, obsessions and our *idées fixes*, but his great gift is his sense of the complexity of the human situation. He had both perceptions, one supposes, from his peasant origins, for among peasants, as he was fond of saying, the *idée fixe* is easily started; and their sense of circumstance overpowers all other consideration in their lives. A character in Balzac is thus variously situated in history, in money, in family, class and in his type to begin with; but on top of this, Balzac's genius was richly inventive in the field least exploited by the mass of novelists: the field of probability. (pp. 337-38)

I do not know that I would put anything in *Le Cousin Pons* above the first part of *La Cousine Bette,* though I like Pons better as a whole. Pons is the old bachelor. Bette is the old maid. The growth of her malevolence is less subtly presented than the course of Pons's disillusion, because Balzac had the genius to show Pons living with a man even simpler than himself. One sees two degrees of simplicity, one lighting the other, whereas Bette stands alone; indeed it may be complained that she is gradually swamped by the other characters. She is best in her obscurity, the despised poor relation, the sullen peasant, masculine, counting her humiliations and her economies like a miser, startling people with her bizarre reflections. . . . Bette is a wronged soul; and when her passion does break, it is, as Balzac says, sublime and terrifying. Her advance to sheer wickedness and vengeance is less convincing, or, rather, less engrossing. It is a good point that she is the eager handmaid and not the igniting cause of ruin; but one draws back, incredulously, before some of her plots and lies. Acceptable when they are naïve, they are unacceptable when they fit too efficiently the melodramatic intrigue of the second part of the book. But the genius for character and situation is here again. (p. 339)

No one has surpassed Balzac in revealing the great part played by money in middle-class life; nor has anyone excelled him in the portraits of the parvenu. Henry James alone, coming at the zenith of middle-class power, perceived the moral corruption caused by money; but money had ripened. It glowed like a peach that is just about to fall. Balzac arrived when the new money, the new finance of the post-Napoleonic world was starting on its violent course; when money was an obsession and was putting down a foundation for middle-class morals. In these two novels about the poor relation, he made his most palatable, his least acrid and most human statements about this grotesque period of middle-class history. (p. 340)

V. S. Pritchett, "Poor Relations," in his *The Living Novel & Later Appreciations,* revised edition, Random House, 1964, pp. 327-40.

CHARLES ROSEN
(essay date 1987)

[Rosen is a noted American scholar and concert pianist. In the following excerpt, he argues that revision significantly improved the text of Balzac's story "The Unknown Masterpiece."]

It is a convenient and pleasing Romantic myth that the true work of art springs full-blown from the unconscious mind. Revision comes from the conscious intellect or will, and this, as Wordsworth wrote, "is the very littleness of life, . . . relapses from the one interior life that lives in all things." Some years ago, a novelist— Muriel Spark, I believe—was asked how she was able to write so many books in such a short space of time. She replied, "I write very fast and I never correct." This is the ideal. Few writers are so fortunate. Most revise and, as they do so, create more problems than they resolve.

One of Balzac's most interesting tales, **"Le Chef d'oeuvre inconnu" ("The Unknown Masterpiece"),** deals imaginatively and succinctly with revision. It was a subject close to the author's heart: his books generally went through several versions before and after publication. However, no work of his was more completely or profoundly rewritten than **"Le Chef d'oeuvre inconnu."**

The scene is laid in Paris in 1612, and the central figure is an invention of Balzac's, a demonic personality who might have stepped out of the fantastic tales of E. T. A. Hoffmann: the old Frenhofer, the greatest painter of the age (all of Balzac's important characters possess their qualities in the superlative degree, and no moderately talented artist could play a significant role in his work—even Wenceslas Steinbock in *La Cousine Bette,* when he loses his talent, becomes obsessively and spectacularly incapable and the hopelessly mediocre Pierre Grassou sees his work sold under the names of Rembrandt, Rubens, and Titian, becomes the favorite painter of the bourgeoisie, and enters the Academy). The two other painters in the tale are historical: the young Nicholas Poussin, just starting out as an artist, visits the atelier of the already established Franz Porbus, and meets Frenhofer there. For ten years Frenhofer has been working on one painting, a life-size portrait of a nude woman lying on a velvet couch—"but what are ten years," he says, "when it is a question of wrestling with Nature? We do not know how long it took Lord Pygmalion to make the only statue that walked."

Frenhofer will show no one the picture: to finish

it, he says, he needs a model of absolutely perfect beauty. Poussin has such a mistress, the young and modest Gillette, who adores him. He persuades her with difficulty to pose in the nude for Frenhofer, who will in return allow him to view the unknown masterpiece. Alone in his studio with Gillette, Frenhofer compares his painting to the living form of the girl, and decides that it is finished, more beautiful than reality. . . .

Lost in admiration of his own work, Frenhofer does not comprehend that his ten years of revision have destroyed his painting, and Poussin loses his mistress, for Gillette cannot forgive his having sacrificed her deeply felt modesty simply to see a picture.

This moral tale of the terrifying effects of revision underwent wholesale revision after its 1831 printing in a periodical, *L'Artiste,* and its reappearance with some corrections in book form the same year. Six years later, in 1837, Balzac republished it, considerably enlarged and with a different ending as part of the seventeenth volume of his *Etudes philosophiques.* In this version, definitive except for some retouching in Balzac's own copy of *La Comédie humaine,* the old painter, observing the reaction of his fellow artists, realizes the disaster, and throws the two younger painters out in a blind rage. That night he burns all his pictures and dies mysteriously.

The additions of 1837 are largely discussions of the theory of painting, in which Balzac ascribes to his seventeenth-century artists the ideas current in the 1830s: the supremacy of the colorist over the draftsman, for example. The anachronism is compounded in the reader's mind by the development of art since Balzac's day, by the suspicion that Frenhofer's superposition of colors, his multitude of bizarre lines, his chaos of tones and indecisive nuances, might be found more sympathetic today than the banal life-size nude on a velvet couch. It is more significant, however, that the isolated foot that comes out of this chaos would have had a charm already in Balzac's time precisely because it is a fragment, and Balzac's description brings out this charm magnificently:

> This foot appeared there like the torso of some Venus in Parian marble risen from the debris of a city destroyed by fire.

Perhaps the most extraordinary textual change made in 1837 is an apparently small one. Frenhofer's refusal to display his picture to anyone else is a parallel to Gillette's reluctance to pose in the nude for anyone except her lover. Before yielding he expresses his resistance with passion:

> The work I keep under lock and key is an exception in our art; it is not a canvas, it's a woman! a woman with whom I weep, I laugh, I talk and think. Do you want me to abandon ten years' happiness as one

takes off a coat? To cease in a single moment, being father, lover and God? This woman is not a creation, but a creature.

This is the version of 1831. In 1837 the final sentence was altered:

> This woman is not a creature, but a creation.

It is wonderful to be able to reverse the terms in this way, and the sentence still makes sense with no change of context. It is clear that for this to happen, the meaning of the words have shifted but then, as Lichtenberg once wrote, whoever decreed that a word must have a fixed meaning?

Placed so near to "creation" in both versions "creature" means not only a living being but one created, and Frenhofer's admission that he enjoyed playing God brings us to the first woman, Eve. A "creature" implies a living being, and "creation" only something made. What is imposed by the contrast is woman against portrait, the experience of life against the object. The two are fused ambiguously in both versions of this passage, but their opposition is the theme of **"The Unknown Masterpiece."** Poussin loses his mistress for the sake of the portrait; Frenhofer has made his portrait the substitute for a woman, and his ten years of happiness destroy his work.

The two versions can act only as a paradox—or different paradoxes. To make sense of both, the meaning of "this woman" must shift. In "not a creation, but a creature," we have "this portrait of a woman is alive"; in "not a creature, but a creation," it changes to "this woman is something I have made." What is disconcerting about the revision is the alteration of values. In the 1831 version, the living being takes precedence over the made object. (p. 22)

The change from 1831 to 1837 is, when you come to think of it, a parallel to the story. Both Frenhofer and Poussin allow the work of art to take precedence over the living being: Eve becomes not a creature, but a thing; the work becomes a fetish. The variant of 1837 reveals a moral deterioration of the author that reflects the tale, as if Balzac were corrupted by his subject (it is significant that the earlier version is not only more humane but more directly effective, the later version more subtly insidious).

Another variant reveals the same process. Poussin endeavors to persuade Gillette to pose nude for Frenhofer, and assures that her modesty will not be violated. In the periodical version, he says:

> *Il ne verra pas la femme en toi, il verra la beauté: tu es parfaite!*
> (He will not see the woman in you, he will see beauty: you are perfect.)

In the first edition in book form a month later, we find:

Il ne pourra voir que la femme en toi. Tu es si parfaite!
(He will only be able to see the woman in you. You are so perfect.)

In the first version "woman" is physical, sexual, and vulnerable: the woman in Gillette will be protected from the gaze of Frenhofer. In the second, woman has become a concept, abstract and general. This suggests the way revision in Romantic art moves away from direct experience to a mediated reflection.

In the case of **"The Unknown Masterpiece,"** however, there is no point in judging one version superior to the other. It is clear that a perception of the richness of meaning in these passages depends on a comparison of the different states of the text—the meanings may be implicit in each individual version, but they are more easily revealed when one version is superimposed over the other. In this sense, Frenhofer's "masterpiece" is less an allegory of the dangers of revi-

sion than an image of a critical edition with all the variant readings displayed to the reader—above all when we reflect that we would probably have preferred the magical appearance of Frenhofer's disaster to the more banal work he thought he had painted and that Porbus and Poussin all too reasonably expected to see.

Balzac's description of the picture does not correspond to the ordinary process of revision, in which the difficulties are smoothed away and the original awkwardness covered over. In the chaos of colors, tones, and decisive nuances we seem to see all of the different versions superimposed. The different variant states of **"The Unknown Masterpiece"** constitute a more profound and original work than any individually published text. (pp. 22, 24)

Charles Rosen, "Romantic Originals," in *The New York Review of Books,* Vol. XXXIV, No. 20, December 17, 1987, pp. 22, 24-31.

SOURCES FOR FURTHER STUDY

Brunetière, Ferdinand. *Honore de Balzac.* Translated by Robert Louis Sanderson. Philadelphia: J. B. Lippincott, 1906, 316 p.

> Exhaustive analysis of Balzac's oeuvre.

Faguet, Emile. *Balzac.* Translated by Wilfrid Thorley. 1918. Reprint. New York: Haskell House Publishers, 1974, 264 p.

> Appreciative critical study of Balzac's ideas, style, and technique.

Marceau, Felicien. *Balzac and His World.* Translated by Derek Coltman. New York: The Orion Press, 1966, 548 p.

> Perceptive guide to the characters and themes of *La comedie humaine.*

Maurois, Andre. *Prometheus: The Life of Balzac.* Translated by Norman Denny. London: The Bodley Head, 1965, 573 p.

> Clear and accurate biography of Balzac.

Pritchett, V. S. *Balzac.* New York: Alfred A. Knopf, 1973, 272 p.

> Covers the principal aspects of Balzac's private and professional life.

Zweig, Stefan. *Balzac.* Translated by William Rose and Dorothy Rose. New York: The Viking Press, 1946, 404 p.

> A warm and sympathetic biography that demonstrates Zweig's high regard and affection for Balzac, whom he considered to be "the greatest writer of his age." This work, expected to be his *magnum opus,* was left unfinished at the time of Zweig's death.

Charles Baudelaire

1821-1867

French poet, critic, translator, essayist, novelist, diarist, and dramatist.

INTRODUCTION

*O*ne of the world's greatest lyric and prose poets, Baudelaire is acclaimed for controversial poems in which he chronicled his personal and spiritual obsessions and sought to depict beauty amidst the poverty, amorality, and filth of urban Paris. His best-known collection of poetry, *Les fleurs du mal* (1857; *The Flowers of Evil*), scandalized readers with its depictions of unconventional sexuality, physical and psychological morbidity, and moral corruption; it was a critical and popular failure during his lifetime. However, later poets of the Symbolist, Decadent, and Modernist movements embraced Baudelaire's startling language and subject matter, and he is hailed today as the first poet to depict human life from a distinctly modern perspective.

Baudelaire was born in Paris to financially secure parents. His father, who was thirty-four years older than his mother, died when Baudelaire was six years old. Afterward Baudelaire grew very close to his mother, and he later remembered their relationship as "ideal, romantic . . . as if I were courting her." When Madame Baudelaire married Jacques Aupick, a military officer, in 1828, Baudelaire became deeply resentful. Initially he had excelled in school, but as he grew older he increasingly neglected his studies in favor of a dissipated, rebellious lifestyle. In 1841 the Aupicks sent him to India, hoping that his experiences abroad would reform him. During his travels he began writing poetry and composed the first poems that would be included in *The Flowers of Evil.* When Baudelaire returned to France in 1842, he received a large inheritance and began to lead the hedonistic life of a Parisian dandy. In Baudelaire's view, the dandy was one who glorified the ego as the ultimate spiritual and creative power—a heroic individualist rebelling against society. At this time, Baudelaire fell in love with Jeanne Duval, a

French woman of African descent who inspired Baudelaire's "Black Venus" cycle of love poems in *The Flowers of Evil.* He also began to experiment with opium and hashish, a practice he later documented in his 1860 volume *Les paradis artificiels: Opium et haschisch* (*Artificial Paradises: On Hashish and Wine as a Means of Expanding Individuality*), which also contains his translation of Thomas De Quincey's *Confessions of an English Opium Eater* and his own "Poème du haschisch" ("Hashish Poem").

In 1844 Baudelaire's mother obtained a court order blocking his inheritance, and thereafter he supported himself by his writing, much of it art criticism. During this time, he established friendships with such painters as Eugène Delacroix and Gustave Courbet. In 1846 he first read the works of Edgar Allan Poe, whose critical writings stressed technical perfection and the creation of an absolute beauty. Baudelaire found confirmation of his own artistic philosophy in the works of Poe, whom he regarded as his "twin soul." Determined to gain recognition for Poe in Europe, Baudelaire devoted several years to translating his works. These translations were widely acclaimed and are considered among the finest in French literature. In 1855 Baudelaire published several poems in the journal *Revue des deux mondes;* two years later his collected poems were published as *The Flowers of Evil.* Upon publication of this volume, Baudelaire was denounced by critics as immoral, and even his close friend, the critic Charles Sainte-Beuve, refused to praise the book. Subsequently, Baudelaire and his publisher were prosecuted and convicted of offenses against religion and public morality. Six poems deemed obscene were published later the same year in Belgium as *Les épaves.* These poems had scandalized Paris with their detailed eroticism and graphic depiction of lesbianism and vampirism. *The Flowers of Evil* was reissued in 1861 and 1868 with some poems added and others reworked, but the ban on the suppressed poems was not lifted in France until 1949. After the publication of the 1861 edition, Baudelaire's publisher went bankrupt, and in an attempt to regain both his reputation and his financial solvency, Baudelaire traveled to Belgium on a lecture tour. The tour was a failure, and in 1866 Baudelaire returned to Paris, where he suffered a debilitating stroke. Having recently reconciled with his mother, he remained in her care until his death in 1867.

In *The Flowers of Evil,* Baudelaire discussed—in candid terms—erotic love, the underclasses and lowlife of Paris, and, above all, his own moral, psychological, and spiritual conflicts. His exploration of spiritual issues and concern for salvation have prompted some critics to label him a religious writer, while others deny that any definite belief can be perceived in his works. Most agree, however, that Baudelaire firmly believed that individuals are inherently evil and that a type of salvation can be found in the creation and contemplation of art. For Baudelaire, the function of poetry was to create beauty from even the most unpleasant aspects of human existence. According to Geoffrey Brereton, the reader of *The Flowers of Evil* "must pass through eye-splitting perspectives of pink and black, rooms of incredible dilapidation tenented by moustached harpies, fungous alleys haunted by cats, boudoirs rancid with rotting flowers, the whole evening tour of tawdry vice." Baudelaire, in his own words, sought to depict "the horror and ecstasy of life." He also explored in his poetry the perplexities of a soul both sinful and repentant; he once wrote that "in all men, at all times, there are two simultaneous Postulations, one towards God, the other towards Satan." Organized in six sections—"Spleen and Ideal," "Parisian Scenes," "Wine," "Flowers of Evil," "Revolt," and "Death"—*The Flowers of Evil* juxtaposes an ideal of perfect beauty with the knowledge of the futility of such an ideal.

This sense of hopelessness culminates for Baudelaire in the mood of spiritual torpor and hellish despair he termed "spleen." In "Spleen," Baudelaire described the mood by picturing an internal landscape in which "earth is changed into a humid dungeon / In which Hope, like a bat / Flits to and fro, beating the walls with its timid wing." Baudelaire expanded on this theme in the prose poems collected posthumously in *Petits poèmes en prose: Le spleen de Paris* (1869), considered by many critics to be the first work ever in this genre. Many of these poems take the form of parabolic vignettes in which Baudelaire illustrates the crushing effect of misery, poverty, and tedium on the citizens of Paris. In "Le vieux saltimbanque," he portrays the suffering of an aging entertainer against the background of a crowd seeking temporary diversion at a carnival. Although these poems, like those of *The Flowers of Evil,* evince Baudelaire's desire for escape from life's cycle of despair and ennui, some critics contend that they also celebrate the common people by depicting their heroic endurance in the face of suffering.

Although Baudelaire was widely condemned in his lifetime as a "sick poet" by critics appalled by the unrelenting pessimism of his work as well as its explicit sexual content, he was championed after his death by writers such as Algernon Charles Swinburne and Joris Karl Huysmans, who lauded his stylistic innovation and individualism. By breaking with the Parnassian and Romantic poetic traditions of seeking beauty only in *objects d'art* and nature, Baudelaire significantly broadened the subject matter of future poetry; he also was a seminal influence on both the Symbolist and Decadent movements of the late nineteenth century. The former group was inspired by his idea, expressed in his famous poem "Correspondances," that the poet unveils the true nature or essence of existence masked by the outward appearance of objects; the latter group drew on his devotion to revealing the beauty in corruption and to the doctrine of aestheticism or "art for art's sake." Contemporary critics consider Baudelaire a poet of strong moral vision, arguing that his subjects of Satanism, hedonism, and corruption evidence his agonizingly acute awareness of the conflict between sensual pleasure and spiritual redemption. His perceptiveness and candor in writing of both his personal mis-

ery and that of the world around him have exerted a profound influence on every generation of poets to succeed him, leading many critics to observe that the grim vision of life proffered by much of modern literature is a tradition that began with Baudelaire.

(For further information about Baudelaire's life and works, see *Nineteenth-Century Literature Criticism*, Vols. 6, 29 and *Poetry Criticism*, Vol. 1.)

CRITICAL COMMENTARY

ANDRÉ GIDE

(essay date 1917)

[Gide is regarded as one of the most influential thinkers and writers of the twentieth century. In his fiction as well as his criticism, he stressed autobiographical honesty, unity of subject and style, modern experimental techniques, and sincere confrontation of moral issues. The following essay originally appeared as a preface to a 1917 edition of *The Flowers of Evil*.]

One suspects that one of Baudelaire's most ingenious paradoxes was to have dedicated his *Fleurs du mal* to Théophile Gautier, to offer this cup, all overflowing with emotion, music, and thought, to the most dry, least musical, least meditative artisan that our literature has ever produced. Was he deluding himself? He was a critic with too lucid a vision not to be sensitive to the poverty of those *Émaux et camées*, which owed their reputation not to what they are but to what they claim to be. The *Fleurs du mal* are dedicated to what Gautier claimed to be: magician of French letters, pure artist, impeccable writer—and this was a way of saying: Do not be deceived: what I venerate is the art and not the thought, my poems will have merit not because of their movement, passion, or thought, but because of their form.

Form, that justification for the work of art, is what the public never perceives until later. Form is the secret of the work. Baudelaire never takes for granted that harmony of contours and sounds in which the art of the poet is displayed; he achieves it through sincerity; he conquers it; he imposes it. Like every unaccustomed harmony, it was shocking at first. For many long years, and I would be tempted to say: even until now, certain misleading appearances of this book have hidden its most radiant treasures, while, at the same time, it protected them. Certain gestures, certain harsh tones,

certain subjects of the poems, and, as I think, some affectation, an amused satisfaction in being misunderstood, deluded his contemporaries and many of those who came later. Without doubt, Baudelaire is the artist about whom the most nonsense has been written, who has been ignored the most unjustly. I know of certain manuals of French literature of the nineteenth century in which he is not even mentioned.

The fact that in the eyes of certain persons the figure of Gautier has long appeared and still appears more important than that of Baudelaire is explained by the very simple attitude (oversimple or simplified) of Gautier, from which he did not for a moment swerve, thanks to which he held on to that place in the limelight which he had acquired right at the very first; it is also explained by the cordial banality of his face, which suddenly opens up when we encounter it and never means anything more than what it first promised. Whereas we glimpsed a disconcerting complexity in Baudelaire, a cabal of strange contradictions, antagonisms almost absurd, which could be taken for pretense, the more easily because he was capable of pretense as well.

I should not swear that Baudelaire, elsewhere so perspicacious, was not somewhat mistaken about his own merit, about what constituted his value. He worked, not always consciously, at that misunderstanding which isolated him from his period; he worked at it all the more because this misunderstanding was already taking shape in him. His private notes, published posthumously, are painfully revealing in this respect; to be sure, Baudelaire felt his essential originality, but he did not succeed in defining it clearly to himself. As soon as this artist of incomparable ability speaks of himself, he is astonishingly awkward. Irreparably he lacks pride to the point where he reckons incessantly with fools, either to astonish them, to shock

Principal Works

La fanfarlo (novel) 1847
[La fanfarlo, 1986]

Histoires extraordinaires [translator; from the short stories of Edgar Allan Poe] (short stories) 1856

Les épaves (poetry) 1857

Les fleurs du mal (poetry) 1857; also published as Les fleurs du mal [revised editions], 1861 and 1868
[The Flowers of Evil, 1909]

Nouvelles histoires extraordinaires [translator; from the short stories of Edgar Allan Poe] (short stories) 1857

Adventures d'Arthur Pym [translator; from the novel The Narrative of Arthur Gordon Pym by Edgar Allan Poe] (novel) 1858

*Les paradis artificiels: Opium et haschisch (autobiography and poetry) 1860
[Artificial Paradises: On Hashish and Wine as a Means of Expanding Individuality, 1971]

Curiosités esthétiques (criticism) 1868

L'art romantique (criticism) 1869

Petits poèmes en prose: Le spleen de Paris (poetry) 1869
[Poems in Prose from Charles Baudelaire, 1905; also published as Paris Spleen, 1947 and The Parisian Prowler, 1989]

†Journaux intimes (diaries) 1887
[Intimate Journals, 1930]

Lettres: 1841-1866 (letters) 1905

Oeuvres complètes de Charles Baudelaire. 19 vols. (poetry, criticism, essays, novel, letters, journals, autobiography, and translations) 1922-63

The Letters of Charles Baudelaire (letters) 1927

Baudelaire on Poe (criticism) 1952

The Mirror of Art: Critical Studies (criticism) 1955

Baudelaire as a Literary Critic (criticism) 1964

Art in Paris, 1845-1862: Salons and Other Exhibitions Reviewed by Charles Baudelaire (criticism) 1965

Selected Writings on Art and Artists (criticism) 1986

*This work includes Baudelaire's translation of Thomas De Quincey's *Confessions of an English Opium Eater.*

†This work includes the diaries "Fusées" ("Skyrockets") and "Mon coeur mis á nu" ("My Heart Laid Bare").

them, or after all to inform them that he absolutely does not reckon with them.

"This book has not been written for my wives, my daughters, or my sisters," he says, speaking of the *Fleurs du mal.* Why warn us? Why this sentence? Oh, simply for the pleasure of affronting bourgeois morals with these words "my wives" slipped in, as if carelessly; he values them, however, since we find in his private journal: "This cannot shock my wives, my daughters, nor my sisters."

This ostentatious pretense, which came to shelter Baudelaire's fervor, antagonized certain readers, the more violently because some of his early admirers were most enthusiastic about this very pretense. He especially felt the need of taking cover from his admirers.

People thought they were completely rid of him when they buried these feints along with the romantic devices. He reappears, stripped of disguise, rejuvenated. He went about it in such a way that we understand him much better today than they did in his day. Now he quietly converses with each one of us. Certainly he begs and obtains from each reader a sort of connivance, almost a collaboration; in this way his power is proved.

"He was the first," says Laforgue, "to recount himself in the restrained mode of the confessional, without assuming an inspired air." In this respect he calls to mind Racine; Baudelaire's choice of words is perhaps more disquieting and of more subtle preten-sion; I claim that the sound of his voice is the same; instead of giving the greatest possible sonority to their inspiration, in the manner of Corneille or Hugo, each of them speaks in a whisper, with the result that we listen to them at length.

What a disquieting sincerity the kindred spirit, attentive to this discreet song, soon discovers! With Baudelaire, antithesis, born from personal contradictions, is no longer merely exterior and verbal, a technique as it is in Hugo; rather it is honest. It blossoms spontaneously in this catholic heart, which experiences no emotion without having the contours fade immediately, without having its opposite reflected like a shadow, or better, like a reflection in the duality of this heart. Thus everywhere in his verses, there is sorrow mingled with joy, confidence with doubt, gaiety with melancholy, and he seeks uneasily a measure of love in the horrible.

However, the anguish of Baudelaire is of a still more secret nature. At this point I seem to lose sight of his poetry: but where does one find the source and the prompting of so faithful a melody, if not in the soul of the poet?

We are often told that there is nothing new in man. Perhaps; but all that is in man has probably not been discovered. Yes, trembling, I convince myself that many discoveries are still to be made, and that the outlines of the psychology of the past, according to which we judge, think, and even act, have acted up to now, will soon appear more artificial and out of date than do the outlines of the chemistry of the past, now that radium has been discovered. If chemists have now come to the point of speaking to us of the decomposition of simple bodies, why should "we psychologists" not be tempted to envisage the decomposition of simple feelings? A simple way of considering feelings is what allows anyone to believe in simple feelings.

I shall not go so far as to say that Baudelaire felt as clearly as did Dostoevsky, for example, the existence—opposite to that force of cohesion which keeps the individual consistent with himself, through which, as Spinoza said, "the individual tends to persist in his being"—the existence of another force, centrifugal and disintegrating, through which the individual tends to be divided, dissociated, through which he tends to risk, gamble, and lose himself. But it is not without a shiver of recognition and terror that I read these several sentences from his private journal: "In a mature man, the impulse toward productive concentration must replace that toward wasting his forces." Or again: "Concerning the vaporization and the centralization of the self. Everything lies in this." Or: "In every man there are always two *simultaneous* [the whole interest of the sentence lies in this word] postulations: one toward God and the other toward Satan." Are these not traces of that infinitely precious radium in contact with which the old theories, laws, conventions, and the pretensions of the soul are all volatilized?

I shall not affirm that these fragments which I have just isolated are the only ones in his prose work; at least, it can be said that they have left a perceptible imprint on his entire poetic work.

And none of all this is sufficient to make of Baudelaire that incomparable artist whom we praise. Quite to the contrary, the admirable fact is, that in spite of all this, he has remained that artist. As Barbey d'Aurevilly said magnificently in that fine article which consoles us for the silence of Sainte-Beuve: "The artist has not been too defeated." (pp. 256-60)

André Gide, in a preface to "Fleurs du Mal," translated by Blanche A. Price, in his *Pretexts: Reflections on Literature and Morality*, edited by Justin O'Brien, Meridian Books, Inc., 1959, pp. 256-60.

T. S. ELIOT

(essay date 1930)

[An American-born British writer, Eliot is perhaps best remembered as the author of *The Waste Land*

(1922). In the following excerpt from a 1930 essay, he discusses Baudelaire's stylistic prowess and the influence of Christianity on the theme of good and evil in his writing.]

It was once the mode to take Baudelaire's Satanism seriously, as it is now the tendency to present Baudelaire as a serious and Catholic Christian. . . . I think that the latter view—that Baudelaire is essentially Christian—is nearer the truth than the former, but it needs considerable reservation. When Baudelaire's Satanism is dissociated from its less creditable paraphernalia, it amounts to a dim intuition of a part, but a very important part, of Christianity. Satanism itself, so far as not merely an affectation, was an attempt to get into Christianity by the back door. Genuine blasphemy, genuine in spirit and not purely verbal, is the product of partial belief, and is as impossible to the complete atheist as to the perfect Christian. It is a way of affirming belief. This state of partial belief is manifest throughout the *Journaux Intimes.* What is significant about Baudelaire is his theological innocence. He is discovering Christianity for himself; he is not assuming it as a fashion or weighing social or political reasons, or any other accidents. He is beginning, in a way, at the beginning; and being a discoverer, is not altogether certain what he is exploring and to what it leads; he might almost be said to be making again, as one man, the effort of scores of generations. His Christianity is rudimentary or embryonic. . . . His business was not to practise Christianity, but—what was much more important for his time—to assert its *necessity.* (pp. 373-74)

[Baudelaire] was one of those who have great strength, but strength merely to *suffer.* He could not escape suffering and could not transcend it, so he *attracted* pain to himself. But what he could do, with that immense passive strength and sensibilities which no pain could impair, was to study his suffering. And in this limitation he is wholly unlike Dante, not even like any character in Dante's Hell. But, on the other hand, such suffering as Baudelaire's implies the possibility of a positive state of beatitude. (pp. 374-75)

From the poems alone, I venture to think, we are not likely to grasp what seems to me the true sense and significance of Baudelaire's mind. Their excellence of form, their perfection of phrasing, and their superficial coherence, may give them the appearance of presenting a definite and final state of mind. In reality, they seem to me to have the external but not the internal form of classic art. . . . Now the true claim of Baudelaire as an artist is not that he found a superficial form, but that he was searching for a form of life. In minor form he never indeed equalled Théophile Gautier, to whom he significantly dedicated his poems: in the best of the slight verse of Gautier there is a satisfaction, a balance of inwards and form, which we do not find in Baudelaire. He had a greater technical ability than Gautier, and yet the content of feeling is constantly bursting the receptacle. His apparatus, by which I do not mean his command of words and rhythms, but his stock of imagery (and every poet's stock of imagery is circumscribed somewhere), is not wholly perdurable or adequate. His prostitutes, mulattoes, Jewesses, serpents, cats, corpses, form a machinery which has not worn very well; his Poet, or his Don Juan, has a romantic ancestry which is too clearly traceable. Compare with the costumery of Baudelaire the stock of imagery of the *Vita Nuova* . . . , and you find Baudelaire's does not everywhere wear as well as that of several centuries earlier. . . . (pp. 375-76)

To say this is only to say that Baudelaire belongs to a definite place in time. Inevitably the offspring of romanticism, and by his nature the first counter-romantic in poetry, he could, like any one else, only work with the materials which were there. It must not be forgotten that a poet in a romantic age cannot be a "classical" poet except in tendency. If he is sincere, he must express with individual differences the general state of mind—not as a *duty*, but simply because he cannot help participating in it. For such poets, we may expect often to get much help from reading their prose works and even notes and diaries; help in deciphering the discrepancies between head and heart, means and end, material and ideals.

What preserves Baudelaire's poetry from the fate of most French poetry of the nineteenth century up to his time, and has made him . . . the one modern French poet to be widely read abroad, is not quite easy to conclude. It is partly that technical mastery which can hardly be over-praised, and which has made his verse an inexhaustible study for later poets, not only in his own language. (p. 376)

[His] invention of language, at a moment when French poetry in particular was famishing for such invention, is enough to make of Baudelaire a great poet, a great landmark in poetry. Baudelaire is indeed the greatest exemplar in *modern* poetry in any language, for his verse and language is the nearest thing to a complete renovation that we have experienced. But his renovation of an attitude towards life is no less radical and no less important. In his verse, he is now less a model to be imitated or a source to be drained than a reminder of the duty, the consecrated task, of sincerity. From a fundamental sincerity he could not deviate. The superficies of sincerity . . . is not always there. . . . [Many] of his poems are insufficiently removed from their romantic origins, from Byronic paternity and Satanic fraternity. The "satanism" of the Black Mass was very much in the air; in exhibiting it Baudelaire is the voice of his time; but I would observe that in Baudelaire, as in no one else, it is redeemed by *meaning something else*. He uses the same paraphernalia, but cannot limit its symbolism even to all that of which he is conscious. . . .

Baudelaire is concerned, not with demons, black masses, and romantic blasphemy, but with the real problem of good and evil. It is hardly more than an accident of time that he uses the current imagery and vocabulary of blasphemy. In the middle nineteenth century . . . , an age of bustle, programmes, platforms, scientific progress, humanitarianism and revolutions which improved nothing, an age of progressive degradation, Baudelaire perceived that what really matters is Sin and Redemption. It is a proof of his honesty that he went as far as he could honestly go and no further. To a mind observant of the post-Voltaire France . . . , a mind which saw the world of *Napoléon le petit* more lucidly than did that of Victor Hugo, a mind which at the same time had no affinity for the *Saint-Sulpicerie* of the day, the recognition of the reality of Sin is a New Life; and the possibility of damnation is so immense a relief in a world of electoral reform, plebiscites, sex reform and dress reform, that damnation itself is an immediate form of salvation—of salvation from the ennui of modern life, because it at last gives some significance to living. It is this, I believe, that Baudelaire is trying to express; and it is this which separates him from the modernist Protestantism of Byron and Shelley. It is apparently Sin in the Swinburnian sense, but really Sin in the permanent Christian sense, that occupies the mind of Baudelaire.

Yet . . . , the sense of Evil implies the sense of good. Here too, as Baudelaire apparently confuses, and perhaps did confuse, Evil with its theatrical representations, Baudelaire is not always certain in his notion of the Good. The romantic idea of Love is never quite exorcised, but never quite surrendered to. In **"Le Balcon"** . . . , there is all the romantic idea, but something more: the reaching out towards something which cannot be had *in*, but which may be had partly *through*, personal relations. (pp. 377-79)

[In] the adjustment of the natural to the spiritual, of the bestial to the human and the human to the supernatural, Baudelaire is a bungler compared with Dante; the best that can be said, and that is a very great deal, is that what he knew he found out for himself. In his book, the *Journaux Intimes*, and especially in **"Mon coeur mis à nu,"** he has a great deal to say of the love of man and woman. . . . Baudelaire has perceived that what distinguishes the relations of man and woman from the copulation of beasts is the knowledge of Good and Evil (of *moral* Good and Evil which are not natural Good and Bad or puritan Right and Wrong). Having an imperfect, vague romantic conception of Good, he was at least able to understand that the sexual act as evil is more dignified, less boring, than as the natural, "life-giving," cheery automatism of the modern world. (pp. 379-80)

[Baudelaire's] human love is definite and positive, his divine love vague and uncertain: hence his insistence upon the evil of love, hence his constant vituperations of the female. In this there is no need to pry for psychopathological causes, which would be irrelevant at best; for his attitude towards women is consistent with the point of view which he had reached. Had he been a woman he would, no doubt, have held the same views about men. He has arrived at the perception that a woman must be to some extent a symbol; he did not arrive at the point of harmonising his experience with his ideal needs. The complement, and the correction to the *Journaux Intimes,* so far as they deal with the relations of man and woman, is the *Vita Nuova,* and the *Divine Comedy.* . . . But—I cannot assert it too strongly—Baudelaire's view of life, such as it is, is objectively apprehensible, that is to say, his idiosyncrasies can partly explain his view of life, but they cannot explain it away. And this view of life is one which has grandeur and which exhibits heroism; it was an evangel to his time and to ours. (p. 381)

T. S. Eliot, "Baudelaire," in his *Selected Essays,* Harcourt Brace Jovanovich, Inc., 1950, pp. 371-81.

P. MANSELL JONES
(essay date 1952)

[In the following excerpt, Jones provides a thematic overview of *The Flowers of Evil.*]

As we pass from **"Au Lecteur"** to **"Bénédiction"** [in *Les fleurs du Mal*] we perceive the antithesis from which the tragic interest of the entire series draws its strongest effects—the judgment of man in error under the curse. the magnification of art as a supernatural and vicarious grace. That the artist has a chance of redemption through pleading the cause of mankind in the anguish of its predicament is the positive implication of his task. And this faith is the intermittent rainbow against that 'thick shadow of cloud and fire of molten light' in which Swinburne found the poems to be steeped.

[The subsection] "Spleen et idéal" elaborates and diversifies this fundamental contrast to the extent of two-thirds of the whole collection. In **"Bénédiction"** the position of the poet in society is contrasted with his divine function. The poet belongs to the spiritual order to which, when his arduous work is done, he returns. (p. 31)

The romantic cliché of the poet's fate, misunderstood and victimized in an indifferent society, is developed with unexampled ferocity; though, characteristically, it is the intimate hostilities that are emphasized. The mother's lamentations at having given birth to a

poet are almost as harsh as the threats of his harpy-fingered wife. The rhythmic vituperation rises to a stridency that verges on the melodramatic but to evaporate in the notably fine stanzas of the close. Redemption through suffering, the price of ransom, is, however precarious its credal foundations, a note struck never more impressively than when, as here, hope can dictate chords of such clear perfection as to dissolve the orchestrated din of mockeries and aspersions. The poem is not a masterpiece; it strains one's suspension of disbelief more, I think, in its virulent denunciations than in its soaring finale. . . .

Most of the pieces in this subsection ["Spleen et Idéal"] symbolize the spiritual task of the artist. In **"Les phares"** the theme is illustrated from the work of great painters who, like beacons aflame on citadels, pass on the cry of humanity.

The light five-stanzaed **"Élévation"** which followed **"Bénédiction"** in the first edition sings of the joyous ascension of the spirit uninhibited by notions of retribution or reward, with a purity of timbre we should not miss in Baudelaire's orchestration. Its implication of intuition into the language of flowers and mute things leads by clear design to the sonnet, **"Correspondances"**. . . . Itself a fascinating meditation in fourteen lines rather than a perfect sonnet, this compact repository of mystical reveries, analogies and synaesthesia concentrates a considerable number of ingredients in Baudelaire's thought. Here (to use a favourite image of his) many influences are condensed as in a phial of perfumes, whence they spread out again with effects covering the whole field of modern poetry. (p. 32)

Originality is more flagrantly achieved in another sonnet, **"La géante."** Here the author's plethoric sensuality is powerfully symbolized in the huge female figure which, lying across the countryside seems, under the spell of the long rhythms which trace her outlines, to become the ample nonchalant naked Earth herself and to prefigure the lure to which the poet will succumb in body and spirit: the obverse of his mystical aspirations and their contamination.

Unlike Leconte de Lisle Baudelaire has no statuesque fixation. Soon he is crying out against the abuse of 'that frightful word, "plastic' "', which makes his flesh creep; nor do themes of abstract beauty satisfy him for long. Two pieces seem arranged to cut through this pictorialism with a singular blend of novelty and premonition. (pp. 34-5)

[The] pieces inspired by Jeanne Duval are not mere exhibitions of corruption; still less are they crude records of debauchery. They are involved in a metaphysique of the conscience—eddies in the vortex of an *âme en peine* [soul in pain] round which the series whirls, from which it rebounds and into which it plunges again. (p. 36)

Distraught power, a desperate sincerity and an impulse of provocation went into the making of many of these pieces, the more interesting of which escape crudity through the intimations they give of a mind at work in reactions of abhorrence and misery—but a mind in fundamental error. The inescapable fury of animal desire is not merely an outrage committed on the flesh; the intimacy is damned in its inception and the pleasure of union is derived from the conviction of its iniquity. . . . At times it would seem as if the sexual relationship was conceived as *the* original sin, redeemed, if at all, by the law of procreation. . . . (pp. 36-7)

Never since Villon had a major French poet declared so emphatically that the wages of sin is the putrescence of wasted flesh and carious bone. And the question, as I have suggested, is not whether the lesson is driven home with sufficiently revolting detail—few things in literature can equal that notorious *tour de force,* **"Une La charogne,"**—but whether the antithesis is not at times so abruptly juxtaposed that the mind of the common reader registers *truquage*—shock for shock's sake—even when he may notice the moral so many offended critics seem to have missed? (p. 37)

Considered together the pieces inspired by the Black Venus make a remarkable group. Baudelaire's introspection is a lucid, not a saving grace. But the vitality of his treatment has extracted an astonishing variety of moods out of the liaison and has transmuted them, through the expert manipulation of complex resources, into a set of love poems as distinctive as if they had been written before Romanticism had begun to abuse the theme of the *femme fatale.* . . .

Of all his associations [Baudelaire's romantic liaison with Marie Daubrun] seems to have been the most beneficent to the poet. To **"L'Invitation"** some critics seem to prefer the equally perfect, though even less personal, **"Chant d'Automne"**. . . . But while the pieces known to have been inspired by Marie are free from dross, they are not all euphoric. **"L'Irréparable"** is one of the most disquieting of the collection. . . . [This] mysterious and powerful poem is built up of two elements: the conviction of the irremissible felt by a soul smitten with remorse and a set of images and formulae precisely related to a play of which Marie was the principal interpreter. The perfect fusion of these images used as symbols with the favourite reversible form produces a strange fascination. (p. 42)

[Finally,] the Ideal withdraws, while Spleen progressively invades all avenues and contaminates all feelings. It is remarkable how much interest romanticism has extracted from the analysis of ennui; and even more remarkable that Baudelaire could have extended

the field of morbid interest so as to make it almost his own. What appears from [the final pieces in the book] is the variety of treatment applied to *taedium vitae* [boredom of life] experienced in its many forms: moral paralysis, reaction from excesses, claustrophobia of the void which is a cell, a vault, the dropped lid of asphyxiation, the weight of dead bodies on wounded limbs. . . .

As with all French poetry of the mid-nineteenth century—apart from the persistent virtuosity with which Hugo in exile challenged Ronsard—line and stanza are insufficiently varied to satisfy our restless taste for protean forms. (p. 43)

[The] two pieces in octosyllabic quatrains, **"L'Héautontimorou-ménos"** and **"L'Irrémédiable"** revert to the more sinister vein. . . . [These] pieces reflect the most intense preoccupation with their author's sombre predicament. (p. 44)

The series of about [twenty poems] that compose the "Tableaux Parisiens" are very unequal in value. The uninitiated should not be put off by the first two or identify the climax with the last of all—pedestrian pieces of moralizing, in the manner of Sainte-Beuve, amongst the earliest of those collected and obviously immature. They do however contribute to the greater objectivity of this phase; and many in the subsequent sections could find their place under the same rubric. The three central poems show an acute sense of types of personal tragedy involved in the social order. Baudelaire was not even a 'Socialiste mitigé' (a phrase scribbled against a stanza which he suppressed). What criticism of society he indulges in shows a sense of wrongs more deeply interfused than social injustices. It is not the social or even the moral order that is wrong but the vindictiveness of the mysterious order of the universe—and this order is not branded as Satanic. The pariahs of society and the pariah poet himself are the victims, not of God's vengeance, but of his inscrutable law. From the pathos of his own plight Baudelaire reacts in a superb effort of compassion: he is the founder of the modern order of pariah poets, the order that feeds on destitution to-day.

"Le Cygne" is a poem of exile. Formally it is perhaps the most original piece in the collection, combining a number of classical, romantic and modern themes in a quasi-symphonic arrangement. Though some commentators ignore the musical character of the composition, this aspect seems inescapable, based as it is on an expert use of recurrent motifs, not regularly disposed, their discords of tempo, tone and imagery resolving into the harmonies and psychological unity of a new kind of incantatory poem, a prototype for much Symbolist experimentation. (pp. 45-6)

The poem is arranged in two movements. The second picks up the theme of Paris through whose contemporary transformation the earlier scene re-emerges. The incidents are distanced and recur, as it were, in the depths of reverie or meditation. . . . (pp. 46-7)

The three poems, **"Le Cygne," "Les Sept Vieillards," "Les Petites Vieilles,"** are each dedicated to Victor Hugo and owe a degree of their impulsion to his example. (p. 47)

Less than thirty poems are distributed under the rubrics, "Le Vin," "Fleurs du Mal," "Révolte," [and] "La Mort." But they contain some significant additions to the presentation of the poet's philosophy interspersed with a few of the most perfect examples of his art. . . . [This] section reveals, along with the temerity, the *limits* of Baudelaire's genius: it delimits his actual achievement as that of a major, not a great, poet. For all his fascination with human error, the range of evils analysed in his work is narrow: they are predominantly, though not exclusively, sexual. And they are regarded as *secret* sins, sins against the self or against God, not as sins against society. Even when they are felt to be sins against the *other*, they are still not envisaged as sins against society. Adultery, the social form of sexual transgression . . . , is of no interest to Baudelaire. In this alone his inferiority to Racine is such as to differentiate him as a great introspective from a great dramatist and, for all the maturity he demands of his readers, to prompt the question whether he himself had time to survive his 'stormy' adolescence?

But whatever else they reveal or lack, few of these pieces fail to bear witness to that vigilance of the judgment already differentiated. Indeed the most celebrated poem in this group, **"Un Voyage à Cythère,"** is at once the most brilliant and the most realistic sermon in verse he ever extemporized on the text, 'The wages of sin is death'—if one can use the word 'extemporized' of a theme he returned to so often. (pp. 50-1)

"Révolte" comprises three short pieces which might, for the little they add to the total effect, have been distributed among the rest. Presumably intended to mark an essential attitude, they lack the strength to demonstrate it distinctively as compared with its expression elsewhere in the collection. The first, in which God is conceived as a tyrant, indifferent to the torments of the martyred, is addressed to the supreme Martyr who is reminded of the successful days of his mission and of the desertion he suffered at the end. Did Christ feel remorse? (p. 51)

["**Les Litanies de Satan**"] are a version, showing some slight novelty of form, of the romantic apotheosis of the Devil as patron saint of exiles and outcasts. Though the language is not free from clichés, nothing Baudelaire wrote could lack originality of phrase. . . .

The final section on Death is, if not one of the richest, at least one of the most attractive of the groups. It is composed of five sonnets, simple in structure but

of subtle charm, followed by the longest and, many think, the greatest of all Baudelaire's poems. The first sonnet, **"La Mort des Amants,"** is one of his most perfect trifles—if a thing so perfect can be called a trifle. Worked, as it were, in soft colours on shot silk yet free from languorousness, touched but not steeped in the sheen of luxury, it illustrates the significance of that self-sufficing objective so fondly characterized as writing a poem for the poem's sake. (p. 52)

The lightness which characterizes these sonnets is not absent from the finale. **"Le Voyage"** is a poem, not of death, but of departure. Not an escapist poem either, but a piece of inspired meditation on the fatuity of escapism. Anything but a poem written for its own sake, it is full of restrained irony at the illusions of restless *déplacement* [displacement]. Baudelaire professed a hatred of direct moralizing; but meditation on the fruits of desire and activity is one of the strengths of his collection. **"Le Voyage"** is a poem which conforms to the definition, a 'criticism of life'.

A noble exhilaration carries the quatrains on with a fine swing of controlled rapture toward the unknown. . . . The famous envoy constitutes a supreme achievement in its fusion of strange serenity of feeling with mastery of the long, nervous, solemn yet exultant rhythm. . . . (p. 53)

P. Mansell Jones, in his *Baudelaire*, Bowes & Bowes, 1952, 63 p.

JEAN PRÉVOST
(essay date 1953)

[Prévost was a French novelist, critic, and essayist esteemed for his lively style and lucid thought. In the following excerpt from his 1953 study *Baudelaire: Essai sur l'inspiration et la création poétiques*, he discusses Baudelaire's poetry, particularly the themes of death, evil, and love in *The Flowers of Evil*.]

Baudelaire certainly does not have the extreme variety of subjects, of themes, and of tones found in Victor Hugo. But his poetical themes are broader and more numerous than those of Lamartine, for example: The *Fleurs du mal* offers horizons of an amplitude seldom equalled in any other single volume. There would have been scant, if any, gain in the book's being two or three times larger; if Baudelaire, for sheer mass, equalled Hugo, he would be hardly tolerable. Under the variety of topics, an extreme suppleness of form, a distinctive unity of tone and of feeling is perceptible, with the same tension and the same will. Baudelaire's contemporaries did not fail to notice it, when they mockingly compared him to Boileau, and Sainte-Beuve, unjust as he was in his estimate of the poet's greatness, nevertheless saw his deliberate attempt to transform and transpose. Different as Baudelaire may be from Pascal, aesthetic impressions akin to those produced by the *Pensées* are frequently experienced by those who reread the *Fleurs du mal.* Each of them in his own realm probes our feelings and our thoughts with a very acute knife, cutting narrow and deep furrows into the quick. Both are anatomists rather than contemplators of life; in a few words, they reach straight to the bone, and strip it of all flesh.

Listing the themes of Baudelaire's poetry would not be enough. First and foremost one must ask how the poet *wants* to transform that theme, and to which others he wishes to marry it. A survey of the simple themes, or of those which seem simple at first, could be made fast enough. Again like Pascal, and like all those who load their thought and their looks with passion,

Baudelaire feels, sees, understands through antitheses. The most important picture of Baudelairean themes can only be had through contrasting touches.

Naturally it happens that the poet receives or undergoes dreams which he has not organized; even if he has perhaps provoked them through hashish or laudanum, he has not organized their visions. Let us consider the poem **"Rêve parisien"**: nothing appears clearer or simpler, provided we do not look for sources too high or too far, in the clouds or in regions beyond the spirit, of what the poet actually found in a precise craftsmanship and in the resources of his art. That weird vision owes little or nothing to De Quincey, E. A. Poe, Novalis, or Gautier, whose vision was distorted (in the case of the first two through intoxication). Baudelaire is clearcut, even when he describes what is vague.

In **"Rêve parisien,"** the poet sees nothing but his hotel-room. But the perspectives are distorted: the tables, the door, the shelves, the plinths, the plaster moldings on the ceiling, the mantelpiece become prestigious structures. To a vague and magnifying perception, all that shines becomes metal if it is very small, a sheet of water if it is larger. Thus the mirror on the wall can be in turn huge polished glass and a waterfall rushing down from the sky; a few bottles around a wash basin are enough to suggest a colonnade around a garden pond; the little vault of the fireplace, above a metal plate which vaguely shines, becomes an arch or a tunnel above an ocean. The lines on the ruled paper are turned into rivers which come down from the sky; the small fragment of sky which can be seen from the window is projected afar, into the infinite, and instead of standing upright, appears to stretch horizontally; it is a boundless sea, weirdly contained on its sides. And if nothing vegetal appears in that vision, it is because the poet does not have the slightest bunch of flowers in his room; he is honest and refuses to alter anything in that perception so simply and vastly distorted.

It must be distorted a second time, or rather it must be given a shape at last, and pass from a false perception into a work of art. Then only, along with the customary rhymes which associate the images ("crise" and "cristallise," "féeries" and "pierreries," "diamant" and "firmament"), images will appear which have been borrowed from Baudelaire's predecessors, in poetry, or perhaps in painting and engraving. For every sight which he contemplates or interprets, the poet is prepared by all the images he has seen, all the words he has heard.

"La Chambre double," one of the prose poems, with similar simplicity describes another aspect, a humbler one, of the reveries provoked by intoxication. This time, the phial of laudanum is mentioned; it interposes only a happy mist between reality and the poet's eye; it makes the shape of the furniture and the settling more harmonious; its sole task of hallucination, a very modest one, is to spread a veil of muslin between the windows and the bed. The loved woman is dreamt; she is scarcely believed to be present; even the dream seems to wonder about its own presence. The vision as a whole does not create objects, but merely transposes values and invests every commonplace object with an appearance of beauty.

The same "moral message" emerges from **"Rêve parisien"** and **"La Chambre double"**—that which is also proposed by Thomas De Quincey's confessions. The dream which has been voluntarily caused by the dreamer and to which he submits must be followed by a desolate awakening, a bleak and frozen return to earth. . . . But if Baudelaire knew, underwent passively, and recorded the dreams caused by artificial paradises, his dreams are vastly different. These, more vaporous and subtle than the others, are impervious to change and are not followed by that forlorn awakening; they emerge at the mind's highest peak of lucidity.

The idea of death, on which the *Fleurs du mal* ends, remains more real and more religious than that of God for the poet. Even in that idea, which might appear to be monolithic and without any diverse hues, similar to the mat black of painters, he finds contrasts. He consents to rest in **"La Fin de la journée,"** but seems to have doubts about doing so in **"Le Squelette laboureur"**; with exaltation, he affirms survival in **"La Mort des amants"**; he denies it in **"Le Mort joyeux,"** which sounds like a challenge to fear and to faith. The vague hope of a glorious blossoming transfigures the end of **"Bénédiction"** and of **"La Mort des artistes"**; but **"Le Rêve d'un curieux"** tells us that even our thirst for the beyond must be frustrated.

The man for whom nature was monotonous and narrow, and who saw the world through a few artists rather than in its original nudity, vaguely expected from death something which no longer would look like what was known, which would not be our shadow or our reflection on things, but a novel sensation. **"Le Voyage"** thus truly deserves to be the final poem of the book, the one in which the stages of the poet's life are, one after the other, most clearly marked: memoirs, in a word, but at the same time the memoirs of all of us. Once again, this time all encompassed in one poem, the world as he has seen it unrolls before our eyes; life, like the sea, wearies us with its monotonous and dazzling brightness. Let us close our eyes, first to rest them, then to implore wildly for newness, "du nouveau." Spiritual flame has extinguished the sumptuous spectacle of nature, and the sun is now only an inner one:

If the sky and the sea are black like ink,
  Our hearts which you well knew are filled with
    bright rays!

That enchanted and disappointed review of human things sacrifices everything to a last hope, the only one which life cannot take away. The world, so lovely in its images, has shrunk and wilted; love is a stain which obstinately lingers; the lightness of departures, full of fresh hopes when one set out at the dawn of one's life, appears madness to him whose dreams have regularly foundered on rocky reefs. Even the splendor of the Orient, not unlike the grey sadness of our cities, fails to conceal the powerless human misery. The only folly which comes up to our mad expectations is that of opium. One hope alone will restore to the poet the cheerful joy of his earlier departure; in the midst of the vain tumult of old temptations, it will blow like an off-shore breeze, the only chance of freshness; death is the only certitude left to man, and the poet attempts to make it the only hope.

Along with poems in which Baudelaire yearns for the good or for nothingness, there are some in which complacency in plunging into evil is triumphant. His conscientious examinations now appeal to God, now to the Devil. So exacting, so perfect in playing his part is the latter, that he ceases to be the enemy and becomes the object of a desolate cult.

In **"L'Horreur sympathique,"** the misery of the unhappy libertine is relieved by his pride. There, as in **"Le Rebelle,"** the soul agrees to persist in its evil incarnation. The damned one in **"Le Rebelle"** is content with saying: "I do not want." The libertine in **"Horreur sympathique"** refuses to moan; he wants neither the brightness nor the certainty promised to the elect by faith; on the contrary, he is "avide de l'obscur et de l'incertain." What matters it to him if he is expelled from Paradise? At last, he will confess his pride and his taste for Inferno. The two poems are close to each other: the taste for Inferno is but a fierce taste for freedom; in spite of all hopes, in spite of all the rewards promised to docile submission, I want to choose what appeals to me, "to prefer myself to my happiness."

"L'Irrémédiable" shows another voluptuous aspect of evil, another pride: no longer that of independence, but of lucidity. Yes, I have seen myself, I have gazed clearsightedly at all the evil that is in me, and here I am, God of myself, fully aware of my good and of my evil. In its first part, the poem is a series of comparisons, borrowed from Vigny's "Eloa," Poe, and De Quincey. These comparisons which all bring the reader back to the poet recall the pieces entitled **"Spleen,"** in which the soul, melting in melancholy images of the world, seems to surrender. But the Devil appears, and the poet's admiration for that character who "always does well all that he does" gives a clearer outline to despair. Thus the second half of the poem is introduced, in which the mournful joy of lucidity will give itself free play:

Unique relief and glory—
Conscience in Evil.

Examination of conscience does not necessarily constitute an exercise toward virtue for Baudelaire. A particular examination impels to energy and hard work; a general examination leads to despair, and to the acceptance of that despair. The Socratic "Know thyself," basis of all virtues, here becomes awareness of and consent to evil; the monastic meditation which leads to good resolutions is utilized against laziness, but it accepts and it exalts the vast realm of sins. We do not have to judge it from the point of view of a moralist, but from that of a lover of poetry. Bound as it was to the constant quest for new and adequate translation into words, it made the poet more acutely aware of his own particular being. It led him to borrow the language of religion for very secular descriptions, to merge into one the two desires to know himself and to judge himself. When he observes man, he starts with himself; lyricism and lucidity are thus married.

It appears that once at least Baudelaire experienced romantic passion of the kind which transfigures the loved one into an angelic creature. Most of the poems sent to "La Présidente," as she was called by her friends, or written for her, seem like the rites of a cult. The poet occasionally offered the same fervor to Berthe or to Marie, "the child, the sister," but then without pretending to lower himself before them. Does he find in this experience the great "romantic love," and are not those poems as beautiful as the great love elegies by Musset, Lamartine, or Hugo, closely allied to them in their inspiration?

For the romantics, passion is an exchange. The words and the feelings of the loved woman appear to occupy the first place there. She is almost like Dante's Beatrice or Petrarch's Laura, the inspirer, she to whom the poet owes his genius. The inspirer is aware of her role and of her mission, so that her beauty seems but a paltry thing compared to the loftiness of her mind or the impulses of her heart.

Not so with Baudelaire. "La Présidente," for him, is not a living goddess but a nearly mute idol. He calls her Angel, but praises chiefly the merits of a filly in her: splendid eye, beauty, blooming and contagious health. Curiously enough, the confessions in the *Journals* and the other love poems in *Les Fleurs du mal* evince an enduring taste, first instinctive and then reasoned, for the thin, much painted, rather sad-looking type of woman. Does he offer his adoration to this healthy and plump woman precisely because she is not "his type," because he can sympathize with that healthy and overflowing vigor without feeling any desire for it? Doubtless this woman, whom he had long known, a good partner at smoking and hashish parties, the mistress of several of his friends, held little mystery for him at the time when he decided to make her his idol. Biography allows us to see in that "love" only a poetical raw material, a pretext for sonnets; the written work confirms it. From his idol, he received only one confidence, out of which he made the stanzas of **"Confession."** He succeeded there in hiding the extreme banality of the avowal under the description of a Paris night and a simple and faultless rhythm. We owe it to his genius to imagine that, by himself, he would have treated the same theme more profoundly. Elsewhere, she is not supposed to speak ("Taisez-vous, ignorante! âme toujours ravie!"), but at times the demon in her speaks, at times the phantom of the idol; in other words, to the woman herself, the poet prefers the image of her which he makes or unmakes at will.

Poet that he was, he sought two things in Madame Sabatier whom he treated as a work of art rather than as a real being. As early as 1853, in one of the first poems which he sends to her, he shows it ingenuously. First, her refreshing and salutary atmosphere, the contagion of health and cheerfulness which might impart tone and vigor to him. He does not wish to possess her; he wants rather, at times, to share in her robustness and her easy-going gaiety; he wants to believe in the contagion of physical good as the ancients did:

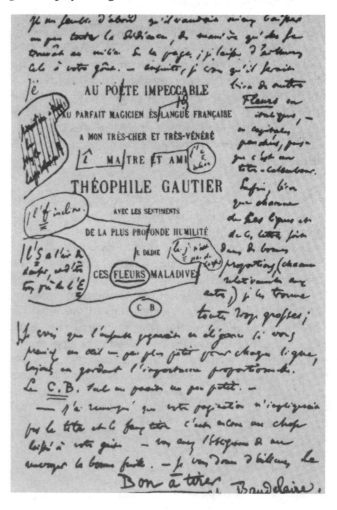

A proof of the dedicatory page of *Les fleurs du mal,* with Baudelaire's corrections.

David on his death bed would have implored health
From the emanations of your enchanted body. . . .

But chiefly he asks from her a continuous surprise, an ever-renewed opportunity for contrasts with himself. Obsessed with himself and his own problems, in her he finds his perfect opposite. It may be a chance to forget himself; more often still, an opportunity for comparing and opposing himself to her. That series of methodically developed contrasts is the theme of **"Reversibilité."** The beloved hardly appears; only her vaguest virtues are celebrated; she is the motionless wall against which the foam of her worshipper's contrary passions, the tide of his impure suffering, beats. The last stanza devotes three lines to her. There the real woman appears as if she were a sum of abstractions, a being of reason, an Angel, whose prayers the poet implores in concluding.

In most of the sonnets which come later, Baudelaire does not even ask the loved woman to participate in her own cult. She does not even need to understand herself, to wonder what kind of beauty she represents for the poet. Baudelaire celebrates her eyes; he has taken them as his guides; thanks to them, for a moment he ceases to be demoniacal or Christian. He allows himself to surrender to a love of simple and superficial gaiety, to admiration for the most natural and blossoming beauty. In a word, under a softer and more refined shape, with a suave quality which his elder and master did not have, he seems to profess the aesthetic and pagan religion of Théophile Gautier; he instills into it a mysticism without content, made solely of remote intentions and of purified images. Nothing designates the loved one in particular. These chants of adoration could be equally addressed to all women whose eyes are normal: for example . . .

They walk in front of me, those eyes filled with light

in **"Le Flambeau vivant,"** or the similar lines in **"L'Aube spirituelle."** According to the poet's own declaration, **"Harmonie du soir"** is a flower from the same bouquet of laudatory hymns: one may wonder whether it celebrates a living creature. A Spaniard, more accustomed than a Frenchman to a poetry of dolorous filial tenderness, might suppose that the poem is addressed to a mother rather than a mistress. The "Présidente" is more exactly depicted in **"Allégorie,"** if it is she who is designated in that poem, as evidence leads us to believe. There Baudelaire magnifies his model, but does not idealize it.

Upon receiving her copy of *Les Fleurs du mal* and rereading the poems which the poet had said were devoted to her, Mme. Sabatier never wondered why, in that volume of verse, she was more vague and indistinct, less real than Jeanne Duval. She apparently did not ask: "But have these pretty lines anything in common with me? Can I see and recognize myself there?"

She did not wonder, because she was one of those women who assume a modest air when the name of *beauty* is merely uttered in their presence. She did not understand that she served Baudelaire only as an embodiment of the ideal, and that, in such an ideal, the poet had put nothing of himself: he had only put the very opposite of himself. (pp. 170-77)

Jean Prévost, "Baudelairean Themes: Death, Evil, and Love," in *Baudelaire: A Collection of Critical Essays,* edited by Henri Peyre, Prentice-Hall., Inc. 1962, pp. 170-77.

F. W. HEMMINGS
(essay date 1982)

[Hemmings is an English biographer and critic who has written extensively on French literature and culture. In the following excerpt from his critical biography of Baudelaire, he discusses Baudelaire's prose poems.]

Over the last six years of Baudelaire's life, between 1861 and 1867, the Second Empire reached a zenith of prosperity and self-confidence. The Treaty of Villafranca (1859) had marked the conclusion of Napoleon III's successful campaign against Austria, in which France reasserted herself as the dominant military power in Europe, for the time being at any rate. There followed a period of peace on the Continent and of economic expansion inside France, powerfully assisted by a free trade treaty with Great Britain and by the completion of the internal railway network. The new era was symbolized by a surprising transformation of the external appearance of the capital, achieved within the space of a very few years thanks to the vision and energy of Baron Haussmann and the exertions of his hundreds of demolition and construction crews, working with pick, shovel, and wheelbarrow. Old slums disappeared, new squares and boulevards were laid out, and on all sides arose glittering restaurants, cafés, department stores and apartment houses, while below ground miles of sewers were tunnelled, helping to make the fearsome cholera outbreaks of earlier times nothing but a bad memory. All these extensive public works provided something like full employment in building and allied trades, which in that age were far more labour-intensive than today. The amusement industry—show-business—flourished too as never before; the old theatres of the Boulevard du Crime were pulled down and huge new ones, the Châtelet, the Vaudeville, the Gaîté, were erected in their place but in more convenient locations. This was the period when Offenbach popularized the *opéra-bouffe* and when the *café-concert* came into its own; while horse-racing, a sport imported from

England, attracted crowds of onlookers and punters to Longchamp, the Paris equivalent of Epsom Downs, on the edge of the Bois de Boulogne. Everywhere there was bustle, noise, activity and gaiety, as the well-sprung carriages swept down the streets and the gold napoleons chinked on marble counters.

Although the term had not yet been invented, it was already a consumer society ruled by the values appropriate to such a society. Baudelaire stood aloof from it, partly because he remained as poor as a churchmouse, partly because he judged these values to be immoral in any case or, as he would have put it, satanic; did they not depend on the exploitation of instincts rooted in at least four of the seven deadly sins: avarice, envy, lust and greed? If an eighth were to be added, it would be insensitivity, that amalgam of egoism and callousness which he saw as peculiar to his age and native country and which he denounced in a fable short enough to be quoted here in full.

The New Year had exploded in a chaos of snow and slush, everyone's carriage on the street, toys and confectionery glittering in the shops, greed and despair rampant everywhere; the licensed delirium to which the city had succumbed was of a kind to turn the brain of the most strong-minded solitary.

In the midst of this hubbub and hurly-burly, a donkey was trotting along briskly, harassed by a great brute armed with a whip.

As the donkey was rounding a corner near the footpath, a fine gentleman wearing gloves and patent leather shoes, his throat cruelly constricted in a tightly knotted cravat and his body squeezed into a suit of clothes straight from the tailor, swept off his hat and executed a courtly bow in front of the lowly animal, exclaiming as he did so: 'A happy and prosperous New Year to you!' Then he turned around to the rest of the party accompanying him, grinning fatuously as if to invite them to add their applause to his self-satisfaction.

The donkey, not seeing this elegant humorist, continued to trot zealously to where his duty called him.

As for me, I was left grinding my teeth in a towering rage against this witless exquisite, who seemed to me to embody the very quintessence of our sense of humour in France.

This text is one out of twenty similar pieces published in *La presse,* at that time edited by Arsène Houssaye, between August 26th and September 24th, 1862, under the general heading *Petits poèmes en prose.* The words designated the form rather than the content of this new kind of literature; at a later stage Baudelaire tried out an alternative title, *Le spleen de Paris,* using it for a collection of six prose poems published in *Le figaro* on February 7th, 1864. In the same issue of this newspaper Gustave Bourdin—the very man who had written the unfortunate review of *Les fleurs du mal* which had precipitated the prosecution of the book— offered an explanation of the title, an explanation almost certainly furnished by the author himself.

Le spleen de Paris is the title adopted by M. Charles Baudelaire for a book he is engaged on writing and which he hopes will prove a worthy complement to *Les fleurs du mal.* All the specificities of ordinary life which by their nature are impossible, or at least difficult, to express in verse have their place in a prose work in which the ideal and the trivial are fused in an inseparable amalgam.

As for the significance of the title, Bourdin goes on,

there are those who believe that Londoners alone enjoy the aristocratic privilege of suffering from spleen and that Paris, gay Paris, has never been subject to that grievous affliction. But it may be that, as the author claims, there exists a special kind of Parisian spleen, known, as he argues, to many people who will recognize what he is talking about.

The prose poem was to all intents and purposes a literary form of Baudelaire's own invention. He himself suggested he had a forerunner in the minor romantic Aloysius Bertrand, whose *Gaspard de la nuit* (published posthumously in 1842) can, however, at most have provided him with a starting-point. Bertrand's pseudo-medieval fantasies are poles apart from Baudelaire's rigorously modern and realistic street scenes; and his archaic vocabulary and contorted syntax have nothing in common with Baudelaire's limpid, contemporary style. He appreciated Bertrand's book, which is not without its special charm to which Debussy in his turn proved susceptible, but soon dismissed the idea of imitating him, if that idea ever really crossed his mind. At the most, *Gaspard de la nuit* may have suggested the title 'Poèmes nocturnes' under which the first specimens of his prose poetry appeared in the press in 1857.

This was only two months after the publication of the original edition of *Les fleurs du mal* and long before the appearance of the second edition with its numerous new poems. There was in fact a period of five years or so during which Baudelaire appeared to be hesitating between prose and poetry as his proper medium for creative writing in the future. Among the first prose poems to be published are several which are simply prose versions of what had previously been written as verse. Such doublets are sometimes even given identical titles; thus, we have two versions, the earlier in verse, the later in prose, of **'L'invitation au voyage'** and of **'La chevelure'**. It sometimes happens, however, that the same title was used for two compositions, one in verse and one in prose, of which the actual contents bear little resemblance to one another. Thus, **'Crépus-**

cule du soir' was the title used for an ode written towards the end of 1851 and included in the first edition of *Les fleurs du mal;* it was also the title given to a prose poem which exists in various versions, though the oldest certainly postdates the ode. In spite of the identical title, suggesting an identity of themes, the two works are very dissimilar in mood and content. The poem stresses the sinister aspects of the coming of dusk; under its cover the criminal will go about his business and the prostitute will steal forth to hunt for clients. The prose poem begins, it is true, in a similarly sombre tone by discussing how nightfall tends to darken still further the minds of those unfortunates who are subject to attacks of mania; but it finishes with a couple of paragraphs describing how very differently the crepuscular hour can affect a man of poetic disposition.

> Twilight, soft and gentle hour! The pale red streaks that glimmer still above the horizon like the day's death-wound delivered by night's victorious scimitar—the glow of street-lamps crimsoning dully against the ultimate incandescent glory of the sunset—the heavy hangings drawn from the abyssal east by an unseen hand—what are all these but a visible projection of the warring emotions in man's heart at the gravest hours of his life?

> Yet again the beholder will be put in mind of certain fantastic dresses worn by ballet-girls, whereon through a dark, transparent gauze shine the dimmed splendours of a skirt of brilliant colours, even as past joys shimmer through the sombre veil of the present; and the gold and silver spangles with which it is stitched, and which dance as the dancer moves, figure those lights of fantasy which never glint so brightly as under the funereal canopy of Night.

In the first section of this prose poem, to illustrate his contention that those whose minds are unhinged grow more frenzied as the night approaches, Baudelaire relates two brief but striking anecdotes. In *Les fleurs du mal,* narrative passages are rarely found, whereas in the prose poems they are a fairly constant feature, and it is indeed likely that Baudelaire, in switching to prose poetry, was at least partly impelled by the desire to appear in a new guise, as story-teller. Sometimes the story encapsulated in the prose poem is manifestly of his own invention, at other times it can be shown to have been borrowed from some earlier author, and occasionally it derives from an incident he witnessed or heard about. In this last category falls **'La corde'** ('The Rope'), one of the few prose poems which bears a dedication: 'To Edouard Manet'. In Antonin Proust's reminiscences of Manet one may read how 'while living in the Rue de la Victoire, he completed *The Child with the Cherries,* using as his model a little boy employed to wash his brushes and clean his palette. This poor lad, temperamentally very unstable, hanged himself; Manet was greatly upset by the tragic end of the little fellow to whom he was deeply attached.' The story, which Baudelaire must have had from Manet's own lips, is related in very much greater detail in **'La corde'.** We are told how the painter came to take the urchin under his roof, how his presence in the studio enlivened Manet's lonely and laborious life, and how he used him as the model for several pictures. We also learn how Manet gave him a severe scolding after discovering he had been raiding the larder—his great weakness being 'an unreasonable craving for sweetmeats and liqueurs'—and how, returning later in the day to the house, he found the boy had hanged himself from a nail driven into the same cupboard where Manet kept his provisions.

Up to this point the story sounds exactly as Manet might have told it to Baudelaire; but the sequel may as easily have been the poet's invention, though it gives point to what would otherwise be no more than a horrifying news-item. We are told how Manet had to cut down the corpse, face an embarrassing police inquiry, and finally break the news to the dead child's parents, who were poor, uneducated folk living in the neighbourhood. The mother appeared quite stunned and lost in thought; she asked only one thing of Manet, to be allowed into the studio, ostensibly to view the corpse; once admitted, she begged him with a kind of morbid insistence to let her carry away the rope with which her little son had hanged himself. The reason why she was so intent on gaining possession of this grisly relic became apparent the following day, when the bemused painter received a stack of letters from his neighbours on other floors of the house, all requesting a snippet of the fatal rope. It was only then that it dawned on him why the mother had been so intent on making off with it; he remembered the old superstition that a piece of the rope that has served a suicide brings good luck. She had lost her son, but had gained something she perhaps valued more: a highly marketable piece of merchandise.

As it stands, this gruesome little episode might have furnished Maupassant with the subject for one of his *contes;* it has everything that master of the short story required, even down to the 'whiplash ending'. But Maupassant would have been content to let the story stand for itself; not so Baudelaire, for whom the whole point of an anecdote was that it should serve as peg for some moral reflection, which sometimes frames it, sometimes concludes it, or else, as in **'La corde'**, precedes it. However, since Baudelaire's moral outlook was original to the point of perversity, the lessons he draws from the stories he tells in his prose poems are invariably unexpected and usually disconcerting. A more commonplace moralist might have used the tale of the rope as pretext for denouncing the prevalence of idle superstition among the lower classes. Baudelaire has something much more profound in mind. This is how he introduces his idea, in the first paragraph of **'La corde'**.

> 'It may well be,' my friend said to me, 'that illusion is present in all the dealings men have with one another or with the world of natural objects; and when the illusion ceases, that is, when we see the other person or fact as it exists objectively, we experience a strange feeling, compounded in equal measure of regret for the phantom that is no more, and pleasurable astonishment at the novelty, the reality. If there is one universal, unmistakable, and unchanging phenomenon, of a nature that can mislead no one, it is surely maternal love. It is as hard to imagine a mother without maternal love, as it is to imagine a source of light that is not also a source of heat; is it not therefore very understandable that we should attribute to maternal love everything a mother does, everything she says, where her child is concerned?'

After which the story is related, its unexpected purpose being to demonstrate how unwise we are to make any assumptions whatsoever about human nature, or perhaps to illustrate how events continually upset our preconceived view of reality.

(Of course, with the knowledge we now possess, but which was not available to his first readers, of Baudelaire's warped relations with his own mother, it would be perfectly possible to interpret **'La corde'** in terms of a private allegory in which he is obliquely denouncing Mme Aupick's scale of values where maternal affection took second place, in his judgement at least, to money and possessions.)

Dearly as Baudelaire would have liked to follow in Poe's footsteps and adopt the lucrative profession of short-story writer, he was never able to convince himself that an intelligent reader's interest could be sustained by nothing more than the dramatic tension generated by the narrative itself; the fiction had to point to some specific, if ambiguous, philosophical conclusion predetermined by the storyteller. This was never Poe's practice in the best of his works. What morals are implicit in 'The Black Cat' or 'The Pit and the Pendulum'? In the absence of any direction by the author, the reader could only reach some such banal conclusion as that 'murder must out' or that the instinct for self-preservation will survive everything. It is certainly not for such bits of humdrum wisdom that one reads the *Tales of Mystery and Imagination*.

Anecdotes play a part in perhaps thirty of the fifty prose poems that make up *Le spleen de Paris* as we have it. Not all of them are 'realistic' in the way **'The Rope'** is; a few are pure fables, like **'Which Is the True One?'**; others, like **'The Port'**, are non-narrative descriptive pieces, but still mingled with moralistic reflections. But a sufficient number are infused with the authentic flavour of contemporary life to demonstrate that, having by the 1860s reached some kind of re-

signed accommodation with his private predicaments, Baudelaire was ready to turn his vision outwards and interest himself in the humble dramas of ordinary life and in the sad, unassuming, sometimes pitiable lives of lowly folk. In **'Les fenêtres'** he describes himself looking out at night from his balcony into the uncurtained windows of other houses in the crowded, working-class district where he had his lodgings.

> Beyond a tossing sea of roofs I descry a woman advanced in years, her face already lined, poor, always bent over something, never leaving the room. Guided by what I can see of her face and her garb, by the movements of her hands, by the slightest hint or nothing at all, I have reconstructed this woman's history, or rather her legend, and now and again I weep to retell it to myself.
>
> Had it been a poor old man, I should have reconstructed his with as little trouble.
>
> And so I retire to bed, proud to have lived and suffered in others beside myself.
>
> You may ask: 'Are you sure this legend is the truth?' But what do I care for the facts, if this reality which is outside me has helped me to live, to know I exist, to understand the kind of man I am?

The subjective imagination still counts for more than fact-finding inquiry, and Baudelaire is still as much concerned with his own self as he always was and always would be; but the poetic gift is now allowed a wider sphere of operation.

Possibly De Quincey helped to point the way here, in those passages of his *Confessions* where he describes himself wandering, homeless and short of food, through the modern Babylon of broad streets and narrow passageways, splendid palaces and rat-infested hovels that made up the London of his youth. In his analysis of the book Baudelaire comments, concerning these chapters:

> Even if he had not naturally been, as the reader must have noticed, gentle, sensitive, and affectionate, one might readily suppose him to have learned, in the course of those long days spent wandering hither and thither and of the even longer nights passed in anguish of spirit, to love and pity the poor. The erstwhile scholar now desires to make fresh acquaintance with the lives of the humble; he wishes to plunge into the midst of the throng of the disinherited and, as the swimmer opens his arms to the sea and so embraces nature directly, so he too longs to bathe, as it were, in the multitudinous sea of men.

This last phrase (in the original, *prendre un bain de multitude*), is found textually repeated at the beginning of another of the pieces in *Le spleen de Paris,* entitled simply **'Les foules'** (**'Crowds'**). Baudelaire here speaks of the poet as a man peculiarly adapted to participate in the lives of others and thus, while retaining his singularity, to embrace thanks to his imaginative gift and powers of empathy, a plurality of existences.

The poet enjoys an incomparable privilege: he has the right, when he so desires, to be himself or someone other. Like those spirits that drift through the world seeking to be made flesh, he can enter into what soul he will. For him alone, there are no bolts nor bars; and if certain habitations seem closed to him, it is simply that in his eyes they are not worth his while to visit.

The solitary, pensive wanderer will derive a singular delight from this universal communion. He who finds no impediment in wedding the crowd makes himself familiar with such heady ecstasies as are for ever denied to the egoist padlocked like a strongbox, to the indolent loafer shut up like a shellfish. He adopts as his own all professions, and has his part in every joy and every sorrow that circumstance reveals to him.

What men call love is a pitifully mean, pinched, anaemic thing compared with this ineffable orgy, this temple prostitution of the soul which in poetic charity embraces whole-heartedly every unexpected appearance, every unknown passer-by.

(pp. 186-93)

F. W. J. Hemmings, in his *Baudelaire the Damned: A Biography,* Charles Scribner's Sons, 1982, 251 p.

SOURCES FOR FURTHER STUDY

Benjamin, Walter. *Charles Baudelaire: A Lyric Poet in the Era of High Capitalism.* Translated by Harry Zohn. London: NLB, 1973, 179 p.

> Examines in detail *The Flowers of Evil* in the context of a broad cultural analysis of France in the era of Baudelaire.

Bennett, Joseph D. *Baudelaire: A Criticism.* Princeton, N.J.: Princeton University Press, 1944, 165 p.

> Examines the influence of Baudelaire's dandyism and spirituality on his poetry. Bennett argues that "Baudelaire used the Christian concept of human nature and destiny as a touchstone to expose the falsity of the ideas of the nineteenth century."

Gilman, Margaret. *Baudelaire the Critic.* New York: Columbia University Press, 1943, 264 p.

> The foremost study of Baudelaire's critical writings. Gilman stresses the importance of his criticism to the creation of *The Flowers of Evil,* and analyzes the roots of his critical thinking.

Sartre, Jean-Paul. *Baudelaire.* Translated by Martin Turnell. Norfolk, Conn.: New Directions, 1950, 192 p.

> Discusses Baudelaire's life and works in relation to the social conditions and historical events of his time. Sartre contends that Baudelaire enjoyed sinning and that he only accepted ultimate good in order to violate it.

Starkie, Enid. *Baudelaire.* London: Faber and Faber, 1957, 622 p.

> The definitive biography in English. According to Starkie, Baudelaire's writing indicates his desire to rid himself of vice and to reflect "the beauty of God's creation."

Turnell, Martin. *Baudelaire: A Study of his Poetry.* Norfolk, Conn.: New Directions, 1953, 328 p.

> Examines the meaning and artistic value of *The Flowers of Evil,* particularly its prosody and syntax, and appraises Baudelaire's consequent impact on French poetry.

Simone de Beauvoir

1908-1986

(Full name Simone Lucie Ernestine Marie Bertrand de Beauvoir) French philosopher, novelist, autobiographer, nonfiction writer, essayist, short story writer, editor, and dramatist.

INTRODUCTION

*O*ne of the most prominent writers of her generation, Beauvoir was a member of the French left-wing intellectual circle associated with the existentialist philosopher Jean-Paul Sartre. She is known as both a chronicler of that milieu and as a literary explicator of existentialism. She was also a leading feminist theorist; her *Le deuxième sexe* (1949; *The Second Sex*) is a comprehensive study of the secondary status of women throughout history. Interest in her long-time relationship with Sartre and the controversies elicited by *The Second Sex* have often eclipsed recognition of Beauvoir's fiction. Yet she gained favorable attention for her first novel, *L'invitée* (1943; *She Came to Stay*), and her novel *Les mandarins* (1954; *The Mandarins*) received the prestigious Prix Goncourt.

Beauvoir was born in Paris and lived there most of her life. She was the elder of two daughters of a devoutly Roman Catholic mother and an agnostic father. Beauvoir entered the Cours Adeline Désir, a private Catholic school, in 1914. As family finances declined during World War I, she observed the uninspiring household chores that fell upon her mother and decided that she herself would never become a housewife or mother. In 1925 she began studying philosophy at the Sorbonne. Four years later she met Sartre, beginning an intimate personal and intellectual relationship that would continue until his death in 1980. Sartre and Beauvoir passed the *agrégation de philosophie* in 1929, placing first and second on the exam that provided their teaching credentials. From 1931 to 1943 Beauvoir taught philosophy at lycées in Marseilles, Rouen, and Paris. Her early short stories, written between 1935 and 1937, were originally rejected by publishers; they did not appear in print until 1979, in the collection *Quand le prime spirituel (When Things of the Spirit Come First)* in 1979. *She Came to Stay* was published in 1943. The following year, Beauvoir left her teaching position and devoted herself to writing.

Beauvoir's life and intellectual development may be traced in her four volumes of autobiographical writings. In *Mémoires d'une jeune fille rangée* (1958; *Memoirs of a Dutiful Daughter*), Beauvoir examined her early years and growing rebellion against bourgeois tradition. Valued for its insight into the development of the existentialist movement, *La force de l'âge* (1960; *The Prime of Life*) treats the continuing dialogue between Beauvoir and Sartre between 1929 and 1944. *La force des choses* (1963; *The Force of Circumstance*) focuses on the years following World War II and reflects the author's concerns with aging and death. In *Tout compte fait* (1972; *All Said and Done*), Beauvoir abandoned the chronological treatment of events employed in earlier volumes of her memoirs, speculating about how her life might have turned out if, for example, she had been born into a different family or had not met Sartre. Other writings include the nonfiction *L'Amérique au jour le jour* (1948; *America Day by Day*) and *La longue marche* (1957; *The Long March*), based respectively on Beauvoir's travels in America in 1947 and her tour of Communist China after the war.

Loosely based on an unconventional relationship between Sartre, Beauvoir, and one of her students, *She Came to Stay* examines Beauvoir's anguish over an intimate three-way sharing of lives. Her next novel, *Le sang des autres* (1944; *The Blood of Others*), is set in France during World War II and focuses on the issue of individual responsibility for one's actions. *The Mandarins* presents the euphoria of Liberation Day in Paris and the subsequent disillusionment of French intellectuals who found themselves gradually dividing into factions as the memory of Resistance companionship faded. Critical examinations of Beauvoir's novels often focus more on their autobiographical details and presentation of philosophical and social issues than on their literary merits.

In addition to documenting the persons and events of her generation, Beauvoir also sought to explain existentialist thought in her philosophical essays, including *Pyrrhus et Cinéas* (1944), *Pour une morale de l'ambiguité* (1947; *The Ethics of Ambiguity*), and *L'existentialisme et la sagesse des nations* (1948). In these works she probed the value of human activity, examining questions of freedom, communication, and the role of the other in the light of existentialist ideas presented in Sartre's *L'être et le néant: Essai d'ontologie phénoménologique* (1943; *Being and Nothingness: An Essay on Phenomenological Ontology*).

Beauvoir's international reputation rests primarily on *The Second Sex,* which examines the historical, biological, and social origins of the oppression of women. The opening statement of the section on childhood, "One is not born a woman, one becomes one," has become familiar throughout the world, and the book advises women to pursue meaningful careers and to avoid the status of "relative beings"—implied, in Beauvoir's view, by marriage and motherhood. Early reactions to *The Second Sex,* and especially to the sections discussing the female anatomy and homosexuality, were frequently hostile. Nevertheless, Beauvoir's work was widely translated and served as an important influence on feminists in the 1960s.

While Beauvoir's fiction has been recognized for its literary merits, most of the scholarly commentary has been directed at *The Second Sex.* Some critics have perceived a bias against women in Beauvoir's writings; conversely, others have argued that Beauvoir's depiction of women reveals anger at their circumstances, not their inherent inferiority. Regardless of this criticism, *The Second Sex* is esteemed as a pioneering feminist study of the secondary status of women, and Beauvoir is considered one of the most important and influential champions of women's rights.

(For further information about Beauvoir's life and works, see *Contemporary Authors,* Vols. 9-12, 118; *Contemporary Authors New Revision Series,* Vol. 28; *Contemporary Literary Criticism,* Vols. 1, 2, 4, 8, 14, 31, 44, 50; *Dictionary of Literary Biography,* Vol. 72: *French Novelists, 1930-1960;* and *Major 20th-Century Writers.* For related criticism, see the entry on Existentialism in *Twentieth-Century Literary Criticism,* Vol. 42.)

CRITICAL COMMENTARY

SIMONE DE BEAUVOIR WITH ALICE SCHWARZER
(interview date 1976)

[In the following interview, which took place in Paris in 1976, Beauvoir discusses her relationship with other feminists and comments on the oppression of women in society.]

[Schwarzer]: *Five years have passed since you first stated that you were a feminist. You, the writer who had been the greatest source of inspiration for the new feminism, had actually been an antifeminist until the new women's movement started, in the sense that you opposed an autonomous women's movement, and believed that the socialist revolution would automatically resolve the question of women's oppression. A great deal has happened since then. You are active in the women's movement yourself, and the women's struggle has entered public awareness. So-called International Women's Year seems symptomatic of that. What do you think?*

[Beauvoir]: We feminists have often said what we think of that. We have been made fools of and have been humiliated. The next thing will be an International Year of the Sea, then an International Year of the Horse, the Dog and so on . . . In other words, people think of women as objects that are not worth taking seriously for more than a year in this man's world. And yet we make up half of the human race. So it follows that it is absolutely grotesque to talk of *an* International Women's Year. Every year ought to be International Women's Year, in fact International People's Year . . .

But all the same, don't you think that—in complete contrast to the original intentions of those who initiated it—the open cynicism with which most men have celebrated International Women's Year has been an outrage to many women, and that the women's struggle has been strengthened as a result?

I do not think we have International Women's Year to thank for that; it was the efforts of the women's movement; i.e. women with no organised or official status. International Women's Year only came about because of the women's movement. And with the intention of taking over the women's movement, so to speak. To calm the waves. The Year itself has not brought us any further forward. Those women in Mexico were nothing more than puppets of male politics. That could be seen most clearly in the clash between the women representing Israel and those representing the Arab countries. They are both as patriarchal as each other, and Islam probably even more so than Judaism.

All the same, couldn't one say that International Women's Year was of some value, despite everything?

Of course. Basically, it has to be said that even quite miserable reforms always have some value but that they are dangerous as well. The best example is the new French Abortion Law. It is a completely inadequate measure which only came about in response to our struggle. That was M. Giscard d'Estaing's doing, in his desire to be modern, i.e. he does not attack actual privileges, but just scratches the surface of some things that are taboo. Fine. So it is a measure which in one sense does not signify any fundamental change. It is entirely consistent with a capitalist, patriarchal world (the best evidence of that is that there is also free abortion in the United States and Japan). But still one should not underestimate a reform of this kind. It makes many acute problems easier for women, and it is a beginning as well. Just like the Pill was. But like the Pill, which endangers women's health and which puts increasing pressure on women to take sole responsibility for contraception, free abortion could also easily rebound on us too. In a male dominated world, a male backlash is only to be expected. Men will use it as an additional means of applying pressure. They will say, 'Come on, there's no danger now, you can let me. You can always have an abortion . . .'

In 1971 you were one of the women who publicly admitted to having had an abortion. Since then you have taken part in various feminist initiatives and campaigns. What is your relationship with young feminists like today?

I have personal relations with individual women, not with groups or factions. I work with them on specific projects. For example, on *Les Temps Modernes* we do a regular page together on 'Everyday Sexism'. Apart from that, I am the president of the 'League for Women's Rights', and I support efforts to set up homes for battered women. So I'm not a militant in the strict sense—after all, I'm not thirty any more, I'm sixty-seven, an intellectual whose weapons are her words—but I follow the activities of the women's movement at very close hand, and I am at its disposal.

I consider this project for battered women to be of great importance, because, like the problem of abortion, the problem of violence affects nearly all women—regardless of their social class. It is not restricted to any one class. Women are beaten by husbands who are judges or presiding magistrates as well as by husbands who are labourers. So we have now

Principal Works

L'invitée (novel) 1943
  [She Came to Stay, 1949]
Pyrrhus et Cinéas (philosophy) 1944
Les bouches inutiles (drama) 1945
  [Who Shall Die? 1983]
Le sang des autres (novel) 1946
  [The Blood of Others, 1948]
Tous les hommes sont mortels (novel) 1946
  [All Men Are Mortal, 1955]
Pour une morale de l'ambiguité (philosophy) 1947
  [The Ethics of Ambiguity, 1948]
L'Amérique au jour le jour (nonfiction) 1948
  [America Day by Day, 1952]
L'existentialisme et la sagesse des nations (philosophy) 1948
*Le deuxième sexe. 2 vols. (nonfiction) 1949
  [The Second Sex, 1952]
Les mandarins (novel) 1954
  [The Mandarins, 1956]
Fait-il bruler Sade? (criticism) 1955
  [Must We Burn Sade?, 1963]
La longue marche: Essai sur la Chine (nonfiction) 1957
  [The Long March, 1958]
Mémoires d'une jeune fille rangée (autobiography) 1958
  [Memoirs of a Dutiful Daughter, 1959]

La force de l'âge (autobiography) 1960
  [The Prime of Life, 1962]
La force des choses (autobiography) 1963
  [Force of Circumstance, 1965]
Une mort très douce (reminiscences) 1963
  [A Very Easy Death, 1966]
Les belles images (novel) 1966
L'âge de discrétion (novel) 1967
La femme rompue (novellas) 1967
  [The Woman Destroyed, 1969]
La vieillesse (nonfiction) 1970
  [The Coming of Age, 1972; also published as Old Age, 1972]
Tout compte fait (autobiography) 1972
  [All Said and Done, 1974]
Quand prime le spirituel (short stories) 1979
  [When Things of the Spirit Come First: Five Early Tales, 1982]
La céremonie des adieux: Suivi de entretiens avec Jean-Paul Sartre (reminiscences) 1981
  [Adieux: A Farewell to Sartre, 1984]

*This work was published in two volumes under the same title. Vol. 1 was translated and published in England as A History of Sex in 1961 and Nature of the Second Sex in 1963.

founded an 'SOS Battered Women', and we are trying to get houses so that we can offer at least temporary shelter for a night or a few weeks to a woman—and her children—who risks being battered, sometimes to death.

You have taught the new feminists a great deal. Have they taught you anything?

Yes! A great deal! They have radicalised me in many of my views! Personally, I have got used to living in a world in which men are what they are, namely oppressors. Personally I have not really suffered from it all that much. I've escaped most of the usual kinds of female slave labour, I have never been a mother or a housewife.

Nowadays feminists refuse to be token women, like I was. And they're right! One must fight! The main thing they've taught me is vigilance, and not to let anything pass, not even the most trivial things like this ordinary sexism we've got so used to. It starts at the level of grammar, where the masculine always comes before the feminine.

Most men on the left have internalised their 'superiority complex' (as you yourself once called it) to such a degree that they go on treating feminists, who have always seen themselves as part of the left, as 'petites bourgeoises' or 'reactionary'. They see the sex war as a 'secondary contradiction' dividing the working class, the 'primary contradiction'.

The poor things. They can't help it. Even left-wingers are chauvinists. It's in their blood . . . this is another of those male mystifications. The contradiction between man and woman is just as primary and just as fundamental as any other. After all, it's one half of humanity against the other half. To me, it seems just as important as the class struggle. This is a very complicated matter, and the MLF [Mouvement de la Libération des Femmes] will have to find a link between the two.

And, in any case, nowadays, the idea that the class struggle takes priority is increasingly being called into question at various levels, even on the left, because one can see there are any number of struggles which go beyond the bounds of the class struggle. For example, the foreign workers' struggle, the struggle of French soldiers in barracks, and the struggle of young people . . . and especially the women's struggle, which is not specific to any one class.

Of course, the oppression of women takes on different forms, according to class. There are women who are victims on both fronts: working women who are themselves workers' wives. Others only suffer female oppression, in the sense that they are mothers and housewives. But even middle-class women, when their husbands abandon them, drop down to the proletariat very quickly. There they are—no jobs, no qualifications, no money of their own . . . to deny which is another male trick to confine things to the struggles between men. The most that women—these treasures—are asked to do is to lend a hand now and again. It's a bit like the relationship between blacks and whites.

The Second Sex, *still the bible of feminism, so to speak, with over a million copies sold in America alone, was originally a purely intellectual and theoretical work. What were reactions like when it came out in 1949?*

Very violent! Very, very hostile, to the book and to me.

From which quarter?

From all quarters. But perhaps we made a mistake in publishing the chapter on sexuality in *Les Temps Modernes* before the book actually came out. That was the beginning of the storm. And the vulgarity . . . Mauriac, for example, immediately wrote to one of our friends who was working with us at *Les Temps Modernes* at the time: 'Oh, I have just learned a lot about your employer's vagina . . .'

And Camus, who was still a friend then, bellowed, 'You have made a laughing-stock of the French male!' Some professors threw the book across their offices because they couldn't bear to read it.

And when I went into a restaurant, to La Coupole, say, dressed in a more feminine way, as is my style, people would stare and say, 'Ah, so that's her . . . I thought that . . . she must be both ways then . . .' Because at the time, I was generally reputed to be a lesbian. A woman who dares to say such things simply cannot be 'normal'.

Even the Communists tore me to shreds. They accused me of being a 'petite bourgeoise' and told me, 'You see, what you are saying really doesn't mean a thing to working-class women in Billancourt'—which is completely and utterly untrue. I had neither the right nor the left on my side.

Some even went as far as to say that Sartre had written your books, not you. And in any case, as far as male-dominated public opinion is concerned, you have always been the 'relative being' that you denounced in **The Second Sex,** *the woman who only exists in relation to a man, namely as 'Sartre's life companion'. Describing Sartre as 'de Beauvoir's life companion' would have been unthinkable!*

Exactly. In France particularly, their rage knew no bounds. Things were better abroad, because it's easier

to tolerate a foreigner. It's a long way away, and therefore less of a threat.

I know that for the last thirty years you have been getting letters every day from women the world over. Even before the new collective women's struggles came into existence, Simone, you were an idol for many of them, and you still embody our revolt. Without a doubt this results from your profound analysis of the position of women, and your autobiographical novels as well, because they have portrayed a woman with the courage to exist. Have you learned anything new from these letters?

I have come to understand the enormous extent of oppression! There are some women who are actually imprisoned! And it is by no means uncommon. They write to me in secret, before their husbands come home. The most interesting letters come from women between thirty-five and forty-five who are married and used to be very happy, but are now at a dead end . . . they ask me, 'What can I do? I have no professional training. I have nothing. I am nothing.'

At eighteen or twenty you get married for love, and at thirty it all hits you—and getting out of that situation is very, very difficult. It could have happened to me, which is why I feel particularly sensitive to it.

Giving advice is always a delicate matter, but if a woman does ask you . . .

I think a woman should be on her guard against the trap of motherhood and marriage. Even if she would dearly like to have children, she ought to think seriously about the conditions under which she would have to bring them up, because being a mother these days is real slavery. Fathers and society leave sole responsibility for the children to the mother. Women give up their jobs to look after small children. Women stay at home when the child has measles. And women are blamed if the child doesn't succeed.

If a woman still wants a child in spite of everything, it would be better to have one without getting married, because marriage is really the biggest trap of all.

But what if women are already married and already have children?

In the interview with you four years ago [published in *Simone de Beauvoir Today*], I said that a housewife of thirty-five or more really didn't stand much of a chance. Subsequently I had a lot of nice letters from women who said, 'But that's not true at all! We can still put up a very good fight!' So much the better. But whatever else, they should attempt to find a paid job so that they at least have some measure of independence and a chance to stand on their own two feet.

And housework? What about that? Should women refuse to do more housework and bringing up children than men do?

Yes, but that's not enough. We must find new ways of doing things for the future. Women should not be the only ones to do housework—everybody should. And, above all, it should not be done in such isolation!

I don't mean special groups to do the work, the way it used to be done in the Soviet Union at one time. That seems very dangerous to me, because it means there are people who spend their entire lives sweeping floors or ironing. That is not a solution.

What I do think is very good is what apparently happens in certain parts of China, where everybody—men, women, even children—get together on a particular day to make housework a public activity, which can also be a lot of fun. So they all get together to do the washing or the cleaning, or whatever.

There is no job which is degrading in itself. All jobs are of equal value. The degrading thing is working conditions. What's wrong with cleaning windows? It's just as useful as typing. What is degrading is the conditions under which the windows are cleaned.

Solitude, boredom, non-productivity, no integration into a collective. That is what's bad! As is the division of labour into private/public. Everything ought to be public, so to speak!

Some members of the women's movement—and indeed some people in the political parties—are calling for wages for housework . . .

I'm completely and utterly opposed to that! Of course! In the short term, maybe housewives who have no alternative would be glad of a wage. That is understandable. But in the long term, it would encourage women to believe that being a housewife was a job and an acceptable way of life. But being banished to the ghetto of domesticity and the division of labour along male/female, private/public lines is precisely what women should be rejecting if they want to realise their full value as human beings. So I am against wages for housework.

Some women argue that their demanding wages for housework would create an awareness of the value of housework.

I agree. But I don't think that is the right way to do it. The thing to change is the conditions of housework. Otherwise its value will continue to be associated with the isolation of women, which is something I think should be rejected. Men must be made to share the housework, and it should be done publicly. It must be integrated into the community and the collectives where everybody works together. That's the way it's done in some primitive societies, incidentally, where the family is not synonymous with isolation. The family ghetto must be destroyed!

You yourself, Simone, have solved the problem on an individual basis. You don't have any children and you and Sartre don't live together—in other words, you have never done any housework for a family or for a man. You have often been attacked for your

attitude to motherhood—by women as well as men. They accuse you of being against motherhood.

Oh no! I do not reject motherhood. I just think that these days motherhood is a very nasty trap for women. I wouldn't advise a woman to have children for that very reason. But I am not making a value judgement.

I'm not against mothers, but the ideology which expects every woman to have children, and I'm against the circumstances under which mothers have to have their children.

Then, too, there is a dreadful mystification of the mother-child relationship. I think the reason people place so much value on the family and children is because they generally live such lonely lives. They have no friends, no love, no affection. They are alone. So they have children for the sake of having someone. And that is terrible, for the child as well. It becomes a stop-gap to fill up this emptiness. And then as soon as the child is grown up, he leaves home anyway. A child is no guarantee against loneliness.

You have often been asked if you now regret not having had children?

Oh no! I congratulate myself every day on it. When I see grandmothers who have to look after small children—instead of finally having a bit of time to themselves—it's not always sheer pleasure for them.

What role do you think that sexuality, as it is understood today, plays in the oppression of women?

I think that sexuality can be a dreadful trap. Some women become frigid—but that is perhaps not the worst thing that can happen to them. The worst thing is for women to find sexuality so enjoyable that they become more or less slaves to men—which can be another link in the chain shackling women to men.

If I understand you correctly, you see frigidity, given the current state of malaise created by the power relationships between men and women, as a more cautious and more appropriate reaction, because it reflects this unease, and makes women less dependent on men?

Exactly.

There are women in the women's movement who refuse to continue to share their private lives with men in this male-dominated world, i.e. they do not have sexual or emotional relationships with men. In other words, women who have made a political strategy out of their female homosexuality. What do you think of that?

I have a lot of understanding for this political refusal to compromise, precisely for the reason I have just indicated. Love can be a trap which makes women put up with a great deal.

But this seems to me right only under present circumstances. In itself, female homosexuality is just as restricting as heterosexuality. The ideal thing would be to be able to love a woman just as well as a man, a human being pure and simple, without fear, without pressure, without obligations.

Your most famous statement is 'One is not born, but rather becomes, a woman.' Nowadays, it's possible to prove this 'shaping' of the sexes, and the result is that women and men are very different: they think differently, they have different emotions, they walk differently. They were not born like that, but they have become like that. It's the result of their education and their daily lives.

Almost everybody agrees that this difference exists. But this difference is not just a difference: it also implies the inferiority of women. In this context it is particularly remarkable that a renaissance of the eternal feminine, a general mystification of the feminine, is appearing at the same time as the new female revolt.

I think that today certain male failings are absent in women. For example, that grotesque masculine way of taking themselves seriously, their vanity, their self-importance. It's true that women who have a male career can easily acquire these failings too. But all the same, they do retain something of a sense of humour and tend to keep a healthy distance from hierarchies.

And then the habit of putting down all the competition—generally women don't do that. And patience—which can be a virtue up to a certain point, though after that it becomes a weakness—is also a female characteristic. And a sense of irony. And a straightforward manner, since women have their feet on the ground because of the role they play in daily life.

These 'feminine' qualities are a product of our oppression, but they ought to be retained after our liberation. And men would have to learn to acquire them. But we shouldn't go to the other extreme and say that a woman has a particular closeness with the earth, that she feels the rhythm of the moon, the ebb and flow of the tides . . . Or that she has more soul, or is less destructive by nature etc. No! If there is a grain of truth in that, it is not because of our nature, but is rather the result of our conditions of existence.

Those little girls who are so 'feminine' are made, not born, that way. Any number of studies have proved that. A woman has no particular value *a priori* simply because she is a woman. That would be the most sinister biological distortion, and in total contradiction to everything I think.

So what does this renaissance of the 'eternal feminine' really signify?

When men tell us, 'Just go on being a good little woman. Leave all the irksome things like power, honour, careers to us . . . Be glad that you are as you are, in tune with the earth, preoccupied with human concerns . . . ', it is really very dangerous. On the one hand, it's right that women no longer feel ashamed about their bodies, about pregnancy, about menstruation. I think it's excellent for women to get to know their own bodies.

But one should not make it a value in itself either; one should not believe that the female body gives one a new vision of the world. That would be ridiculous and absurd. That would mean turning it into a counterpenis. Women who believe that are descending to the level of the irrational, the mystical, the cosmic. They are playing the men's game, which allows men to oppress women all the more as a result, and keep them away from knowledge and power with more success.

The 'eternal feminine' is a lie because nature plays only a tiny part in the development of a human being; we are social beings. Furthermore, just as I do not believe that women are inferior to men by nature, nor do I believe that they are their natural superiors either. (pp. 67-79)

Simone de Beauvoir and Alice Schwarzer, in an interview in *Simone de Beauvoir Today: Conversations, 1972-1982,* translated by Marianne Howarth, Chatto & Windus/The Hogarth Press, 1984, 120 p.

MARY EVANS
(essay date 1980)

[An English sociologist and educator, Evans wrote *Simone de Beauvoir: A Feminist Mandarin* (1985), a critical study of Beauvoir's writings. In the following excerpt from an essay first published in 1980, she examines Beauvoir's views on men, women, and human relationships.]

Simone de Beauvoir occupies, and deservedly so, a central place in the history of feminism. *The Second Sex*, published in 1949, is a classic study of the status of women and the causes of their subordination in all aspects of social life. Her other works, which include novels, essays on existential philosophy, a four-volume autobiography and a lengthy study of old age, demonstrate a capacity for intellectual breadth (and, one must add a quite monumental talent for documentation) which is comparable to that of her life long companion, Jean-Paul Sartre. Yet whilst any essay on de Beauvoir must note her considerable intellectual power and range, it is also important to examine her work more critically than has generally been the case. Accolades, particularly from feminists, have been so generously heaped on her work that some of its shortcomings have been obscured. I would like to suggest here that whilst de Beauvoir claims that much of her work is concerned with the overall condition of women, she turns away from many of the issues which are central to women's lives and in particular accords very little place in her epistemology to areas of human experience which are not immediately amenable to rational understanding.

Thus in this paper I shall argue that a major weakness in de Beauvoir's work is a rejection of many of the problems which women (and indeed men) face and a failure to acknowledge that the actions of both sexes are often motivated by needs and desires which, although frequently explained and rationalized from the conscious mind, do not always derive from it. (p. 172)

De Beauvoir's personal history has, since 1929, been intimately linked with that of Jean-Paul Sartre. Their relationship has been one of the better documented aspects of French intellectual life in the twentieth century and although the couple's emotional equanimity has occasionally been upset by what de Beauvoir and Sartre describe as "contingent" love affairs, the association has clearly remained central to both their lives. Information about the history of the relationship has been provided for the public exclusively by de Beauvoir; Sartre has remained, at least in print, quite silent on the subject and the only emotional relationship of his life which he has exposed to the public view is that with his mother, which is discussed, albeit briefly, in *Les Mots.*

The relationship between de Beauvoir and Sartre was, from its outset guided by the principle of what might be described in another context as over-determination. They agreed not to marry and that both of them would be free to engage in affairs with others. "Sartre," de Beauvoir wrote [in *The Prime of Life*], "was not inclined to be monogamous by nature: he took pleasure in the company of women, finding them less comic than men. He had no intention, at the age of 23, of renouncing their tempting variety." Yet this decision, taken in the cold light of day and mutually agreed and accepted, was to provide numerous subsequent problems. For example, de Beauvoir was to admit in the second volume of her autobiography that her first novel (*She Came to Stay*) was written in an attempt to clarify and exorcise what she saw as a major crisis in her life with Sartre: the intrusion of a third party, a woman who threatened to replace her in Sartre's affections. This first (or at any rate the first fully documented) instance of the problems jealousy, emotional ties and constraints raised for the couple was to be repeated on subsequent occasions: de Beauvoir's own affair with the American writer Nelson Algren forced her to face the same problem, whilst Sartre's affair with a woman identified as "M." threatened once again the stability of her emotional world. In this last instance, the uncertainty of her own position eventually forced her to ask Sartre, in an uncharacteristically direct way, "Who means most to you, M. or me?" The answer is somewhat ambiguous, but eventually the situation was resolved by a quarrel, and the subsequent parting, between Sartre and M. After the difficulties encountered with Algren (and M.) neither de Beauvoir, nor Sartre, entered again into a relationship likely to threaten their own. De Beauvoir's friendship with Claude Lanzmann, and Sartre's with a woman named Michelle were in no sense challenging or disruptive.

The accounts given by de Beauvoir of these instances of personal anguish and misery reveal, I would argue, one of the central weaknesses in de Beauvoir's view of the world: the supposition that personal, and highly charged emotional relationships are always amenable to rational control and organization and that human beings are capable of the rigid compartmentalization of their emotional and intellectual worlds. When faced with situations which are rationally comprehensible, and quite predictable, yet deeply disturbing, de Beauvoir is clearly appalled at her failure to subject such experiences to her conscious will. Both de Beauvoir and Sartre show a marked reluctance to acknowledge, or come to terms with, anything outside their rational beings and nowhere is this more marked than in the attitude of each of them to their physical selves. Although de Beauvoir writes that she is critical of Sartre for his refusal to countenance the demands of the body, she herself is far from innocent of exactly the same attitude. She observes of Sartre [in *The Prime of Life*]: "I criticized Sartre for regarding his body as a mere bundle of strained muscles, and for having cut it out of his emotional world. If you gave way to tears or nerves or seasickness, he said, you were simply being weak. I, on the other hand, claimed that stomach and tear ducts, indeed the head itself, were all subject to irresistible forces on occasions." And it is clear that Sartre's views were practised as much as preached. On one occasion, de Beauvoir is overcome by terrible seasickness and unable to answer with any degree of coherence the questions about their itinerary that Sartre is asking. Unmoved by her pleas, Sartre remained persistent in his questioning and ascribed de Beauvoir's seasickness to "deliberate malice."

Whilst de Beauvoir denies that she shares Sartre's views on the possibility of the absolute subordination of the body to the mind, her autobiography reveals numerous occasions when she expresses an exactly similar position. The ills and sorrows which flesh is heir to are, in practice, no more an acceptable part of her view of the world than they are in the case of Sartre. Moreover, de Beauvoir is loathe to consider that there might be a link between the physical and the emotional self. For example, during her twenties she and Sartre were involved in a complex tripartite friendship with a younger woman. When relations between the three reached a particularly difficult stage, de Beauvoir fell dangerously ill. The possible psychosomatic origins of this illness are never mentioned or entertained—de Beauvoir admits that she might have become physically tired at the time but the possibility of a relationship between emotional stress and tension and physical illness is not canvassed.

The denial of the force, and in particular the incapacitating force, of physical needs and desires, is part of de Beauvoir's general dismissal of significant areas of human existence, and relations between men and women, as irrational and unworthy of serious attention. Thus we find, in her account of the early years of her relationship with Sartre, that de Beauvoir describes sexual passion as a "poisoned shirt" and a "shameful disease." She writes [in *The Prime of Life*]:

> I was forced to admit a truth that I had been doing my best to conceal ever since adolescence: my physical appetites were greater than I wanted them to be. . . . I said nothing (to Sartre). Now that I had embarked on our policy of absolute frankness, this reticence was, I felt, a kind of touchstone. If I dared not confess such things, it was because they were by definition unavowable. By driving me to such secrecy my body became a stumbling block rather than a bond of union between us, and I felt a burning resentment against it.

The reader is left with the distinct impression that the physical self, and particularly so in the case of women, is liable to lead only to uncontrollable, threatening passions and the destruction of all peace of mind. But no clues are provided as to how sexual relationships are to be conducted or physical affection is to be incorporated into personal life. Whilst we are told, quite explicitly, that Sartre and de Beauvoir were initially lovers, we are not told (although it is easy to make certain guesses on this point) why and when their relationship lost its sexual element and became an association in which the expression of physical affection no longer played a part. All we learn is that separation from Sartre (they took jobs hundreds of miles apart) allowed de Beauvoir, as she describes it, to "subdue my restless body." The transformation of the nature of the association is of interest which goes beyond biographical or voyeuristic concerns, namely that in it two problems are posed. In the first place one must ask how de Beauvoir both allows, and yet attempts to minimize, physical desire and secondly, how she conceptualizes relationships between the sexes.

In admitting the existence of physical desire, de Beauvoir also observed some of its problems and difficulties. She accepts, indeed condones, the physical expression of love, although she is critical of sexual promiscuity, especially in women. But she has no deeply ingrained fear of sexual activity *per se*, what is detectable is a concern, indeed almost a fear, of its possible results. For women, the integration of their sexuality into their personalities as a whole appears to be an impossible task. A constant threat seems to hang over all those women who, in either her novels or her nonfiction, indulge in the pleasures of the flesh: the threat of being hurtled down some slippery slope to moral and intellectual ruin. The majority of love affairs described

in her novels do not bring happiness ever after to all those concerned, on the contrary, they tend to bring, and particularly so to the women, destruction and humiliation. Portrayed with some considerable perception in de Beauvoir's novels are women who are fighting desperately to maintain relationships with men who are long tired of them. Women, in most cases, who have staked all on another human being and found that such complete dependence has left them with no alternative resources. One of the central characters in *The Mandarins,* a woman named Paule, goes almost mad with grief when her lover rejects her, *She Came to Stay* involves not just passion, but *crime passionel,* as a result of the conflict between old and new affections and *The Woman Destroyed* is a vivid account of a woman tortured by her husband's infidelity.

The path of true heterosexual love (homosexuality does not appear as a central theme in the fiction of either Sartre or de Beauvoir) clearly does not run smoothly in de Beauvoir's life or work. And it is difficult to see exactly where the path might run. One direction in which it does not lead is towards the establishment of domestic and family life. Both the characters in her novels and the friends and acquaintances she describes in her autobiography are nearly always both unmarried and childless. Women, in both de Beauvoir's fiction and non-fiction, do not express any desire for children, neither do they demonstrate any interest in their existence. The Parisian café society which de Beauvoir, and her created characters, inhabit is thus quite atypical of the world at large in that it is composed more or less entirely of adults, many of whom have no personal committments or responsibilities. From the volumes of her autobiography it is clear that de Beauvoir knew few families; when family life is mentioned it is generally in negative terms.

Sexual relations between men and women do not, therefore, in de Beauvoir's world lead to the establishment of family and domestic life. She quite rightly defends the right of women not to bear children and is deeply critical of the more repressive aspects of family life. Yet this attitude is hardly sufficient as an analysis of domestic and family life. Whilst the account, given in *The Second Sex,* of the social construction of false maternal desires is both relevant and laudable, there is also the possibility to consider—and in both its material and psychological aspects—that a desire to bear children does exist in women and is independent of all social and environmental pressures and expectations. The intellectual and social problems thus posed are considerable, in that it may be possible that the sexes have quite different, and perhaps irreconcilable, sexual needs and expectations.

But de Beauvoir is much concerned, as Margaret Walters has pointed out, to minimize the differences between the sexes and to show that feminine behaviour (and femininity) is a social construct. In short, she is sometimes very close to asking, Why can't a woman be more like a man? This is not to deny that de Beauvoir is absolutely correct to attack the more absurd and exaggerated notions of appropriate female demeanor but that her attack is sometimes so massive that the female baby is thrown out with the feminine bathwater. Both in *The Second Sex* and in the autobiographical works there are few positive statements about the female condition and many suggest that the physical world of women is in some sense beset with more problems and difficulties than that of men. In particular, she stresses that woman's physical nature makes her essentially and inevitably dependent. Thus in the section on "The Mother" in *The Second Sex* Simone de Beauvoir writes, of childbirth: "It is significant that woman . . . requires help in performing the function assigned to her by nature. . . . At just the time when woman attains the realization of her feminine destiny, she is still dependent. . . ." Women, it would seem, are naturally dependent and helpless creatures: the very essence of femininity is that of dependence, a state which above all others is to be avoided.

De Beauvoir, having argued that maternity is the basis of woman's dependence is much concerned to demonstrate that no "natural" desire for motherhood exists. If women would refuse to be duped by the social construction of false maternal instincts, they would no longer be mothers and hence no longer dependent. In short, they would be able to act in all respects as men act, free from social and sexual constraints and, in a quite literal sense, masters of their own fate. Yet such a possibility, and the argument on which it rests, takes for granted two premises which, I would argue, are incorrect. The first is that there is a rigid distinction to be made between a "natural" and a "social" instinct and secondly, that men's behaviour, and their attitude to sexuality and reproduction, is as homogeneous and free from constraint and dependence as de Beauvoir suggests.

As we have seen, and as is amply illustrated by *The Second Sex*, de Beauvoir distinguishes very sharply between behaviour which is "natural" and that which is "social." But she does not reject the possible existence of such a thing as "nature": in a quotation earlier in this paper we have seen that she speaks of Sartre as "not being monogamous by nature." And her work is littered with references to such attributes as "natural" grace and a "natural" liking and aptitude for philosophy. So it is admitted that people can be borne with certain characteristics, be they views on monogamy or intellectual ability. Yet throughout *The Second Sex* she attacks the very possibility of instinctive or "natural" predilections and desires. In making a perfectly justifiable attack on a society and a set of social conventions which regard women's sole role as that of wife and

mother she ignores, and dismisses out of hand, the very complex sets of social relationships which can either exaggerate or suppress "natural" behaviour. If she had dismissed altogether the idea that people are born with any innate characteristics, her argument would have been both more powerful, and a great deal more consistent. As it stands, she can be said to use "nature" in two contradictory ways: as a taken for granted concept, uncritically accepted and integrated into her main argument or as an impossibility, a concept with no real intellectual basis. It is not suggested here that "nature" has to be defended against its detractors, merely that it is perfectly viable to argue that innate abilities and characters do exist, be they differences in intelligence or inclinations towards maternity and that what constitutes the real issue for anyone interested in differences between the sexes is to try and determine the extent to which such differences are socially or naturally produced.

In *The Second Sex*, de Beauvoir argues with some insistance, that much of woman's psychological self is socially constructed. She illustrates her argument by referring to the passivity which is often encouraged by girls, by documenting the narcissism which is frequently regarded as a natural female trait and by showing how the education of girls, both moral and intellectual, is at best limited and constraining, rather than liberating. Very few critics would be able to question her attack on the socialization of girls: the argument has been too well substantiated for it to deserve or demand rational opposition. However, what is questionable in de Beauvoir's discussion is the way in which she sets the education of girls against the education of boys, and then suggests that men represent some sort of standard of self-hood and behaviour which women are prevented from emulating by the collusion of their fathers, mothers, and husbands.

Men emerge from *The Second Sex* as an extremely undifferentiated category. They constitute, in the existential terminology in which at least part of the book's argument is couched, the "other." Thus an opposition between the sexes is introduced in which few individual, let alone social, differences are allowed to emerge. Such an opposition—which must at least in part be derived from de Beauvoir—has become a characteristic of much feminist writing of recent years, two notable examples being Susan Brownmiller's *Against Our Will* (in which all women are constantly threatened by the superior physical force of men) and Germaine Greer's *The Female Eunuch* (in which women are exhorted to take on "male" psychological characteristics). But such an opposition is too simplistic for it to be analytically useful (whatever its rhetorical uses) since it obscures—most obviously—the differences between men, and—what is more complex—the way in which women's subordinate status is used by women as a weapon against men

Beauvoir and Jean-Paul Sartre during a weekly radio broadcast.

and is hence often fiercely defended by women themselves. It might be the case that the social elaboration of differentiation between the sexes, is the result not of a male conspiracy to suppress the interests of women but of the development by women of forms of social and sexual relationships which are best suited to allow the establishment of a female world which is independent of male interests. There is no doubt, of course, that such a world is a sub-world, or an under-world, but it is nevertheless a world which is able to manipulate certain processes in its own interests, precisely through those habits and patterns of behaviour which de Beauvoir regards, somewhat dismissively, and perhaps naively, as absurd and ridiculous. Just as Western feminists are appalled by some Islamic customs and conventions about women and fail to comprehend the totality of social relationships in which such practices are to be found, so de Beauvoir sees in the development of feminine characteristics behaviour which is, compared to that of men, merely childish and irrational.

The view of men which emerges from *The Second Sex* is that of human beings who are, compared with women, rational, independent and able to transcend

their sexuality in a way which is unknown to women. Men are able to integrate their sexuality into their lives with little ado, not for them the tortured concerns about the proper conduct of sexual relationships, or the inevitable horrors of guilt or frigidity which are pictured as accompanying the sexual life of women. Men's sexual life is apparently one of blissful enjoyment and the fulfillment of all erotic desires: the only stumbling block being that at some point such pleasures generally demand the presence of women. Unfortunately, as de Beauvoir points out, women cannot be relied upon to be sensible and rational about sexual relations. She writes: "Feminine sexual excitement can reach an intensity unknown to man. Male sex excitement is keen but localized and it leaves the man quite in possession of himself; woman, on the contrary, really loses her mind." Again, we are confronted with the idea that for women, sensual life, pleasure and activity is beset with the threat of the loss of her rational and conscious self. It is not so much that love constitutes woman's very existence, rather than physical affection, and its expression, threatens women by forcing them to lose all control over the direction of their lives.

In many ways, *The Second Sex* can be seen as a re-action against a highly particularistic set of social ex-pectations. The prohibitions and conventions that sur-rounded de Beauvoir in her childhood and adolescence were part of a bourgeois world whose outward appear-ance changed rapidly after the Second World War. But it would be incorrect simply to assume that the book is no longer relevant and that the contemporary world no longer forces the sexes into rigid and artificial ste-reotypes. In one important respect, however, the world has changed, in that women are now much better able than they were at the time when *The Second Sex* was written, to control their own fertility. The fears and tensions which de Beauvoir describes between the sexes have, perhaps, been much lessened by reliable methods of contraception and by a much greater public understanding of elementary physiology. Yet despite these changes, many feminists would argue that the in-herent differences between the sexes, and their needs and desires, are so great as to be insuperable by mere improvements in social organization or technology. Thus we are still confronted, nearly thirty years after the publication of *The Second Sex*, by arguments that suggest that men and women are irreconcilably differ-ent. They are no longer to be reconciled (*à la* de Beau-voir) by the assumption of more masculine behaviour by women; it is now supposed, often with a ferocity to match that of John Knox, that not only do men not know what women want, it is no business of either sex to inquire into the wishes and desires of the other. And it is invariably the existence of the possibility of sexual relations between men and women which is held ac-countable for the fundamental irreconcilability be-tween the sexes.

Such an argument, I would suggest, is implicitly contained in de Beauvoir's work, although never clear-ly stated and never allowed to question the ideal which she advances of rational, independent and freely cho-sen sexual relationships. The argument can be most clearly deduced from de Beauvoir's autobiographical works, in which she speaks with a ruthless, but some-what incomplete, honesty of her relations with others. Of those who inhabited her adult world by far the most significant is, of course, Sartre, and it is Sartre who is her most constant companion. At the beginning of their association he explained to her (the sex of the subject and the object of the sentence, is not, perhaps, without significance) that their relationship was one of "essen-tial" love. It was to be interrupted, as mentioned earlier, by contingent love affairs, but nothing was to be al-lowed to question or alter this fundamental love. The relationship did survive various interruptions and dif-ficulties but not without the growing realization by both the central characters that a primary commitment could not allow a secondary commitment of any real substance or importance. However, whilst it survived,

the relationship also changed, and in particular the sex-ual relationship between Sartre and de Beauvoir was abandoned. This fundamental change in the nature of the relationship clearly allowed de Beauvoir to develop a greater personal freedom and autonomy. What is being suggested therefore, is that whilst de Beauvoir does not reject heterosexual relationships she does, im-plicitly, argue that sexual relations in long standing re-lationship between men and women can only lead to the loss of the woman's happiness and independence. The happy and successful relationship between Sartre and de Beauvoir is mirrored in de Beauvoir's fiction in the marriage of the Dubreuilhs in *The Mandarins:* a re-lationship which seems to function very well and in which the two characters concerned live virtually sepa-rate lives.

Throughout de Beauvoir's fiction and volumes and autobiography relations between the sexes tend to fall into two categories: they are either relationships in which sexual relations have been abandoned (as in the case of Anne Dubreuilh and her husband or of Sartre and de Beauvoir herself) or they are relationships in which sexual attraction and passion are of fundamen-tal, if not single, importance. The conflict between the demands of the body, and the needs of the mind are ap-parently irreconcilable: sexual relations between men and women are admissable but they are, ideally, tran-scended. And it is to the advantage of women if this is the case, for they are much less able than men to main-tain some distance from their physical selves and are, as we have seen, likely to lose their heads in moments of passion or to become pregnant and hence finally, and irrevocably dependent.

The view of men, and women, in *The Second Sex* (and elsewhere in de Beauvoir's work) does not offer a great deal of hope to those who would advocate the in-tegration of the sexes nor to those who have any inter-est in the possible maintenance of social life and human society. A perceptive critic [Margaret Walters, in her essay in *The Rights and Wrongs of Women*, edited by A. Oakley and J. Mitchell] has pointed out that de Beau-voir's vision of the ideal woman is somewhat bleak, and writes: "de Beauvoir's emancipated woman sounds just like that familiar nineteenth century character, the self made man. . . . Early capitalist man, dominating and exploiting the natural world, living to produce, viewing his own life as a product shaped by will, and suppressing those elements in himself—irrationality, sexuality—that might reduce his moral and economic efficiency." And association with others, particularly in emotional relationships, is one of those situations that reduce most rapidly women's efficiency.

Explanations of de Beauvoir's view of the world, and in particular her view of sexual relations, must in-evitably involve some reference to her own childhood and to her parents. Whatever other significance is attached to the relations between parents and children, few would deny that parents are very powerful models for their children, although not always ones that are necessarily accepted. De Beauvoir's father seems to have been proud of his elder daughter's intelligence; it was an attribute which he valued and praised. He had much less praise for his daughter's appearance and particularly during her adolescence was ruthless in his criticism. But criticism, however pointed, must have been limited, since much of his time was spent in cafés and theatres and with little reference to his wife and daughters. The world of men was outside the home, full of fascinating, and quite forbidden, exploits and activities. The world of women was, at least as far as de Beauvoir knew it as a child entirely domestic. Her mother had no training for a job or a profession, but this was hardly exceptional at the time and neither did any of the female cousins and aunts whom de Beauvoir knew in her childhood. Bourgeois women did not work outside the home and were well employed managing their large households and supervising their children and servants.

So the association of women with the domestic world which de Beauvoir acquired from her childhood must have been very strong. And there was another association which was just as powerful, namely that between women and religion. De Beauvoir's father was an agnostic, but his wife was a convinced and practising Catholic who was determined that her daughters should remain within the influence of the Church and never be exposed to the rigours of secular education. To this end, both daughters were sent to an appalling (although utterly respectable and socially well regarded) Catholic school for girls, an institution whose shortcomings were made all too painfully clear as soon as Simone faced competition from those boys and girls who had been educated at the state *lycées*. Despite the pleadings and pleas of her mother, de Beauvoir's loyalty to the Catholic church was as shortlived as her confidence in its secondary education and she abandoned all religious faith at the age of 15. It produced a breach between mother and daughter which would seem never to have healed.

In reading de Beauvoir's account of her childhood and her adolescence in *Memoirs of a Dutiful Daughter* it is striking how strongly there emerges an association of women with all that is superstitious, petty, narrow minded, domestic, trivial, uneducated and ignorant. The concerns of de Beauvoir's mother and her other female relatives never extended much beyond their households. In contrast to this, the world of men must have seemed an alluring and exciting prospect, all the more so since the rigid demarcation between the worlds of the sexes inevitably enhanced the magic and glamour of the unknown, masculine world. The most positive character that emerges in *Memoirs of a Dutiful*

Daughter is de Beauvoir's cousin Jacques, by all accounts a very ordinary bourgeois youth and yet the first person to whom she was able to talk on subjects outside the supposed interests of young girls. Even de Beauvoir's much loved friend Zaza could not match Jacques in the scope and range of her interests. Moreover, Zaza was to remain utterly loyal to Catholicism and obedient to the demands which her mother made upon her. She, unlike Simone, did not question the endless succession of domestic tasks that were required of her or challenge the complete authority of her mother to organize and control every aspect of her social life. Zaza's eventual fate is tragic for, forbidden to see the man whom she wishes to marry, she develops meningitis and dies. Women, it would seem, cannot allow dissension in their children but neither can their female children oppose them without grave risks to themselves.

Psychoanalytic explanations of de Beauvoir's view of men and women would no doubt claim that in Sartre she found a man who fulfilled for her all the disappointed expectations which she had of her father and that her rejection of a traditional female role (and in particular of maternity) is derived from a hatred of all that her mother was and represented. Such an explanation is discounted by de Beauvoir herself, as indeed she rejects psychoanalysis in general. The work of Freud, and others, holds little interest for her since it relies upon the belief that an unconscious exists in the human mind and that it is not susceptible to conscious, rational control. The patterns of human relationships so dear to the heart of psychoanalysts are dismissed [in *The Prime of Life*] as "quasi-mechanical rationalizations" and although Freud is later accorded some more serious attention it remains limited.

Yet such a form of analysis might help to explain the intense grief that de Beauvoir describes in her book about the death of her mother, *A Very Easy Death*. Of all her books it is the most economical, the most terse and in some ways the most engaging. The relationship between mother and daughter had never been very close or sympathetic but they had managed to evolve some kind of *modus vivendi* since the time when Simone left home and established a way of life quite foreign to all her parents' wishes and expectations. But confronted by the possibility of her mother's death de Beauvoir is shattered and helpless with misery and despair. Despite the fact that she still finds her mother irritating and, on a conscious and rational level, someone with whom she has little in common, she is nevertheless, as she admits, virtually prostrated with grief at her death. It would seem that an imperfectly understood relationship has finally been revealed to her and that at last she has had to confront the ties, albeit unchosen and unwilling, that have united her with this particular dying woman. Precisely because de Beauvoir has always refused the possibility of maternity herself so perhaps the acknowledgement of her own relationship to her mother is the more surprising and disturbing to her. The conscious rejection that de Beauvoir had to make, at the age of 15, of her mother and all that she stood for, could always be seen as a conscious, rational design as long as the rejected figure remained alive. But as soon as the rejected figure dies, so the rejection becomes traumatic and much less easy to rationalize, since the threat of an emotional loss—and not just a conscious disagreement—now becomes present. There is no rational reason for de Beauvoir to mourn the loss of a woman whose opinions she finds childish and incoherent and yet mourn her she does, and with an intensity which she has not shown on the deaths of those who had been intellectually and politically much closer to her.

Simone de Beauvoir's work has provided, for many women, by far the most systematic and coherent account of the subordination of women. Yet precisely because of the influence that her work has had, it is necessary to consider the shortcomings and limitations of her understanding of the female, and to a certain extent, the male condition. Without wishing to elevate "nature" or the irrational to romantic levels of importance and explanation I would suggest that certain aspects of human life and experience, whilst entirely amenable to rational understanding and analysis, are not always derived from it. The real possibilities for the emancipation of women lie not in the denial of the "feminine" or the supposedly irrational needs and desires of women, but in their acceptance and integration within a totality of human experience. To deny women the possibility of bearing children and expressing maternal affection and commitment cannot be an aim of feminism. On the contrary, feminists should assert that women have the right to express all aspects of their creative potential and should not be asked to reject or suppress their emotional needs and desires for reasons of social and/or male convenience. Undeniably, the social construction and elaboration of motherhood and sexual relations between the sexes has often been to the disadvantage of women but the assumption by women of male patterns of behaviour can only increase, rather than lessen, the oppression of both sexes. The opposition suggested throughout de Beauvoir's work between the rational male and the irrational female reflects, all too uncritically, one of the more irrational elements in Western thought, and one which has long been used to distort the behaviour of both men and women. (pp. 173-83)

Mary Evans, "Views of Women and Men in the Work of Simone de Beauvoir," in *Critical Essays on Simone de Beauvoir*, edited by Elaine Marks, G. K. Hall & Co., 1987, pp. 172-84.

SOURCES FOR FURTHER STUDY

Bieber, Konrad. *Simone de Beauvoir*. Boston: Twayne Publishers, 1979, 198 p.

> Biographical and critical study of Beauvoir that includes sections discussing her autobiographical writings, essays, and fiction.

Cottrell, Robert D. *Simone de Beauvoir*. New York: Frederick Ungar Publishing Co., 1975, 168 p.

> Examines Beauvoir's writings and traces the development of her thought.

Francis, Claude, and Gontier, Fernande. *Simone de Beauvoir: A Life . . . A Love Story*. New York: St. Martin's Press, 1987, 412 p.

> Biographical study of Beauvoir.

Keefe, Terry. *Simone de Beauvoir: A Study of Her Writings*. Totowa, New Jersey: Barnes & Noble Books, 1983, 247 p.

> Examines Beauvoir's autobiographical writings, essays, and fiction.

Hatcher, Donald L. *Understanding "The Second Sex."* American University Studies, Series V, Vol. 8. New York: Peter Lang, 1984, 281 p.

> Critical study of *The Second Sex*. Hatcher comments: "This work is to a large extent the product of a number of years of teaching *The Second Sex* in philosophy courses which have dealt with ethical issues surrounding feminism."

Marks, Elaine, ed. *Critical Essays on Simone de Beauvoir*. Boston: G. K. Hall & Co., 1987, 263 p.

> Includes twenty-six reviews and essays by various critics and an interview with Jean-Paul Sartre.

Samuel Beckett

1906-1989

(Full name Samuel Barclay Beckett) Irish-born dramatist, novelist, short story writer, scriptwriter, poet, essayist, and translator.

INTRODUCTION

*O*ne of the most celebrated authors in twentieth-century literature, Beckett is especially recognized for his impact on contemporary drama. His play *En attendant Godot* (1953; *Waiting for Godot*), with its plotless scenario and seemingly senseless dialogue, helped advance the concept of "Theater of the Absurd" and has continued to be regarded as his masterpiece. Beckett's experimental novels, particularly the trilogy composed of *Molloy* (1951; *Molloy*), *Malone meurt* (1951; *Malone Dies*), and *L'Innommable* (1953; *The Unnamable*), have also been extremely influential as examples of his highly developed sense of alienation and his fragmented prose style. Beckett was awarded the 1969 Nobel Prize in Literature for contributing "a body of work that, in new forms of fiction and the theater, has transformed the destitution of modern man into his exultation."

Beckett was born to Anglo-Irish parents in the Stillorgan district of Dublin. As a youth, he preferred sports to academics, and consequently is the only Nobel prize recipient with a listing in *Wisden*, the cricket annual. Beckett's intellectual capabilities, according to biographers, were not stimulated until he enrolled in a course in French poetry during his third year at Trinity College, Dublin. After graduation, he spent the years 1928-1930 at the Ecole Normal Superiéure in Paris, where he became acquainted with James Joyce, an enormous influence on his art and thought; Beckett admired Joyce's ingenious linguistic games as well as his deep commitment to writing. After serving as Joyce's secretary during the writing of *Finnegan's Wake*, Beckett wrote "Dante . . . Bruno. Vico . . . Joyce" (1929), his first published essay.

Beckett's early literary career is marked by experiments in several genres, including *Whoroscope* (1930), a long poem about René Descartes written in one night; *Proust* (1931), a study of *Remembrance of Things Past; Dream of Fair to Middling Women,* an unpublished novel that was later broken down and published in the short story collection *More Pricks than Kicks* (1934); and Beckett's first published novel, a relatively traditional story called *Murphy* (1938). During World War II Beckett was active in the French Resistance and had to flee Paris in order to avoid capture by the Nazis. It is generally believed that Beckett reached the height of his artistic powers in the two decades following the war. Starting with the novel trilogy, he found that writing in the French language was more suitable to his purposes; he sometimes added or subtracted passages in his own translations of these works. *Molloy, Malone Dies,* and *The Unnamable* are enigmatically narrated by a succession of characters who might all be variations of a single individual. A. J. Leventhal has commented on the self-conscious style of the trilogy: "Again and again he challenges the value of his own verbal descriptions, impugning their accuracy, offering another verb, another noun, and finally dismissing them all as being as worthless as the thoughts whose messengers they are." At the end of *The Unnamable,* the narrator is only a mind and a mouth.

Regarded as one of the most controversial and seminal works of twentieth-century drama, *Waiting for Godot* is noted for its minimal approach to dramatic form, its powerful imagery, and its concise, fragmented dialogue. Whereas most traditional plays begin with some action or event that results in dramatic conflict, *Waiting for Godot* begins with no precipitative movement, only an abstract struggle involving the passage of time. Vladimir and Estragon, two vagrants known to one another by the nicknames Didi and Gogo, wait on a desolate plain by a gnarled tree to keep an appointment with someone called M. Godot. Although the play has elicited diverse interpretations, Beckett's portrayal of a world of insignificance and incomprehensibility has led many critics to identify *Waiting for Godot* with Existentialism, a post-World War II intellectual movement based upon the inadequacy of reason to explain human existence, as well as with the Theater of the Absurd, a post-World War II trend in drama characterized by experimental techniques and nihilism. Most concur with Eric Bentley's assessment: "[Beckett] has not only been able to define the 'existentialist' point of view more sharply than those who are more famously associated with it, he has also found for its expression a vehicle of a sort that people have been recommending without following their own recommendation."

Beckett's next play, *Fin de partie* (1957; *Endgame*), like *Godot,* focuses on a pair of characters faced with nothingness as they attempt to find meaning for their existence. Critics have noted that the characters of this play resemble chess pieces playing an "endgame" in which the outcome has already been determined. The black humor and pathetic circumstance of these players is grimmer and more intense than the plight of Vladimir and Estragon. In *Endgame* and subsequent plays, Beckett further developed his innovative theatrical techniques and metaphysical concerns. *Krapp's Last Tape* (1958) depicts a single character who, with the aid of a tape recorder, relives the past that has led to his present, alienated state. Winnie, the protagonist of *Oh, les beaux jours* (1961; *Happy Days*), continues to perform her daily rituals while sinking into the earth. The same year, Beckett published *Comment c'est* (*How It Is*), his first full-length prose work to appear since *The Unnamable.* In keeping with his experimentation with omitting the use of various grammatical elements, he abandoned almost all forms of punctuation in *How It Is.*

During the remainder of his career Beckett continued to produce experiments, two of the most noteworthy being *Film* (1967), a silent movie starring Buster Keaton, and *Breath* (1972), a thirty-five-second playerless drama. Critics who have perceived Beckett's career as a progression from language to silence often cite these works as reflections of the author's pessimistic vision. Although his works are indeed darkly comic, his characters often grotesque, and his themes usually absurdist, he is not generally considered a nihilist. In an obituary tribute, John Peter wrote: "Beckett is about as nihilistic as Aeschylus. That old Greek confirmed the immutability of divine justice; Beckett believed in the sad doggedness of human endurance. His art is a realisation and diagnosis of nihilism; he defies nothingness with the severe objectivity of his gaze and the purity of his observation."

(For further information about Beckett's life and works, see *Contemporary Authors,* Vol. 130; *Contemporary Authors New Revision Series,* Vol. 33; *Contemporary Literary Criticism,* Vols. 1, 2, 3, 4, 6, 9, 10, 11, 14, 18, 29, 57, 59; *Dictionary of Literary Biography,* Vols. 13, 15; and *Major 20th-Century Writers.* For related criticism, see the entry on Theater of the Absurd in *Twentieth-Century Literary Criticism,* Vol. 38.)

CRITICAL COMMENTARY

ALAIN ROBBE-GRILLET
(essay date 1963)

[A French novelist and critic, Robbe-Grillet is perhaps best known for proposing the nouveau roman
(New Novel), a concept that has gained a wide reference in describing the work of a group of French
novelists who wrote in the 1950s. In the following
excerpt from an essay first published in French in
1963, he discusses some of the moral and aesthetic
issues raised by *Waiting for Godot* and *Endgame*.]

The human condition, Heidegger says, is *to be there.*
Probably it is the theater, more than any other mode of
representing reality, which reproduces this situation
most naturally. The dramatic character *is on stage,* that
is his primary quality: he is *there.*

Samuel Beckett's encounter with this requirement afforded a priori, an exceptional interest: at last
we would see Beckett's man, we would see *Man.* For the
novelist, by carrying his explorations ever farther,
managed only to reduce more on every page our possibilities of apprehending him. (p. 111)

Thus all these creatures which have paraded past
us served only to deceive us; they occupied the sentences of the novel in place of the ineffable being who
still refuses to appear there, the man incapable of recu-
perating his own existence, the one who never manages
to be present.

But now we are in the theater. And the curtain
goes up. . . .

The set represents nothing, or just about. (p. 112)

This is called *Waiting for Godot.* The performance lasts nearly three hours.

From this point of view alone, there is something
surprising: during these three hours, the play *holds together,* without a hollow, though it consists of nothing
but emptiness, without a break, though it would seem
to have no reason to continue or to conclude. From beginning to end, the audience follows; it may lose countenance sometimes, but remains somehow compelled
by these two beings, who do nothing, who say virtually
nothing, who have no other quality than to be present.

From the very first performance, the virtually
unanimous critics have emphasized the *public* character
of the spectacle. As a matter of fact, the words "experimental theater" no longer apply here: what we have is
simply theater, which everyone can see, from which
everyone immediately derives his enjoyment.

Is this to say that no one misjudges it? Of course
not. *Godot* is misjudged in every way, just as everyone
misjudges his own misery. There is no lack of explanations, which are offered from every side, left and right,
each more futile than the next.

Godot is God. Don't you see that the word is the
diminutive of the root-word *God* which the author has
borrowed from his mother tongue? After all, why not?
Godot—why not, just as well?—is the earthly ideal of
a better social order. Do we not aspire to a better life,
better food, better clothes, as well as to the possibility
of no longer being beaten? And this Pozzo, who is precisely *not* Godot—is he not the man who keeps thought
enslaved? Or else Godot is death: tomorrow we will
hang ourselves, if it does not come all by itself. Godot
is silence; we must speak *while waiting for it:* in order to
have the right, ultimately, to keep still. Godot is that
inaccessible *self* Beckett pursues through his entire *oeuvre,* with this constant hope: "This time, perhaps, it will
be me, at last."

But these images, even the most ridiculous ones,
which thus try as best they can to limit the damages,
do not obliterate from anyone's mind the reality of the
drama itself, that part which is both the most profound
and quite superficial, about which there is nothing else
to say: Godot is that character for whom two tramps are
waiting at the edge of a road, and who does not come.

As for Gogo and Didi, they refuse even more
stubbornly any other signification than the most banal,
the most immediate one: they are men. And their situation is summed up in this simple observation, beyond
which it does not seem possible to advance: they are
there, they are on the stage.

Attempts doubtless already existed, for some
time, which rejected the stage movement of the bourgeois theater. *Godot,* however, marks in this realm a
kind of finality. Nowhere had the risk been so great, for
what is involved this time, without ambiguity, is what
is essential; nowhere, moreover, have the means employed been so *poor;* yet never, ultimately, has the margin of misunderstanding been so negligible. (pp. 114-
16)

What does *Waiting for Godot* offer us? It is hardly enough to say that nothing happens in it. That there
should be neither complications nor plot of any kind

*Principal Works

"Dante . . . Bruno. Vico . . .Joyce" (essay) 1929

Whoroscope (poem) 1930

Proust (essay) 1931

More Pricks than Kicks (short stories) 1934

Murphy (novel) 1938

Molloy (novel) 1951
  [Molloy, 1955]

Malone meurt (novel) 1951
  [Malone Dies, 1956]

En attendant Godot (drama) 1953
  [Waiting for Godot, 1954]

L'Innommable (novel) 1953
  [The Unnamable, 1958]

Watt (novel) 1953

Nouvelles et textes pour rien (short stories) 1955
  [Stories and Texts for Nothing, 1967]

All that Fall (drama) 1957

Fin de Partie, suivi Acte sans paroles [I] (dramas) 1957
  [Endgame, Followed by Act Without Words [I], 1958]

Krapp's Last Tape (drama) 1958

Comment c'est (novel) 1961
  [How It Is, 1964]

Happy Days (drama) 1961

Oh, les beaux jours! (drama) 1961

Comédie (drama) 1963
  [Play, 1964]

Imagination morte imaginez (drama) [first publication] 1965

[Imagination Dead Imagine, 1965]

†Eh Joe, and other Writings (dramas and screenplay) 1967

No's Knife: Collected Shorter Prose, 1945-1966 (dramas and short stories) 1967

Le dépeupleur (drama) 1970
  [The Lost Ones, 1972]

‡Mercier et Camier (novel) 1970
  [Mercier and Camier, 1974]

‡Premier amour (drama) [first publication] 1970
  [First Love, 1974]

Breath, and other Shorts (dramas) 1972

Ends and Odds (dramas and radio plays) 1976

That Time (drama) [first publication] 1976

Companie (novel) 1979
  [Company, 1980]

Rockaby, and other Short Pieces (dramas) 1981

Mal vu mal dit (prose poem) 1981
  [Ill seen Ill said, 1982]

Westward Ho (novel) 1983

Stirrings Still (novella) 1989

*Beckett himself translated or cotranslated from the French all of the translations listed.

†This work includes Film.

‡These works were originally written in 1945.

---

has already been the case on other stages. Here, it is *less than nothing*, we should say: as if we were watching a kind of regression *beyond* nothing. As always in Samuel Beckett, what little had been given to us at the start—and which seemed to be nothing—is soon corrupted before our eyes, degraded further, like Pozzo who returns deprived of sight, dragged on by Lucky deprived of speech—and like, too, that carrot which in the second act is no longer anything but a radish. . . .

"This is becoming really insignificant," one of the vagabonds says at this point. "Not enough," says the other. And a long silence punctuates his answer.

It will be evident, from these two lines, what distance we have come from the verbal delirium [found in theater before Beckett]. From start to finish, the dialogue of *Godot* is *moribund*, extenuated, constantly located at those frontiers of agony where all of Beckett's "heroes" move, concerning whom we often cannot even be certain that they are still on this side of their death. (pp. 116-17)

As for the argument, it is summarized in four words: "We're waiting for Godot"—which continually recur, like a refrain. But like a stupid and tiresome refrain, for such waiting interests no one; it does not possess, as waiting, the slightest stage value. It is neither a hope, nor an anguish, nor even a despair. It is barely an alibi.

In this general dilapidation, there is a kind of culminating point—that is to say, under the circumstances, the reverse of a culminating point: a nadir, an oubliette. . . . There is nothing left on stage but [a] wriggling, whining heap, in which we then observe Didi's face light up as he says, in a voice almost calm again, "We are men!" (pp. 117-18)

Thought, even subversive thought, always has something reassuring about it. Speech—beautiful language—is reassuring too. How many misunderstandings a noble and harmonious discourse has created, serving as a mask either for ideas or for their absence!

Here, no misunderstanding: in *Godot* there is no

more thought than there is beautiful language; neither one nor the other figures in the text except in the form of parody, of *inside out* once again, or of corpse. (p. 118)

Over seventy centuries of analysis and metaphysics have a tendency, instead of making us modest, to conceal from us the weakness of our resources when it comes to essentials. As a matter of fact, everything happens as if the real importance of a question was measured, precisely, by our incapacity to apply honest thinking to it, unless to make it retrogress.

It is this movement—this dangerously contagious retrogression—which all of Beckett's work suggests. (p. 120)

[Despite the disintegration around them, the] two tramps remain intact, unchanged. Hence we are certain, this time, that they are not mere marionettes whose role is confined to concealing the absence of the protagonist. It is not this Godot they are supposed to be waiting for *who has "to be,"* but they, Didi and Gogo.

We grasp at once, as we watch them, this major function of theatrical representation: to show of what the fact of *being there* consists. For it is this, precisely, which we had not yet seen on a stage, or in any case which we had not seen so clearly, with so few concessions. The dramatic character, in most cases, merely *plays a role,* like the people around us who evade their own existence. In Beckett's play, on the contrary, everything happens as if the two tramps were on stage *without having a role.*

They *are there;* they must explain themselves. But they do not seem to have a text prepared beforehand and scrupulously learned by heart, to support them. They must invent. They are free.

Of course, this freedom is without any use: just as they have nothing to recite, they have nothing to *invent* either; and their conversation, which no plot sustains, is reduced to ridiculous fragments. . . . The only thing they are not free to do is to leave, to cease *being there:* they must remain because they are waiting for Godot. . . . They will still be there the next day, the day after that, and so on . . . *tomorrow and tomorrow and tomorrow . . . from day to day . . .* alone on stage, standing there, futile, without past or future, irremediably present.

But then man himself, who is there before our eyes, ends by disintegrating in his turn. The curtain rises on a new play: *Endgame,* an "old endgame lost of old," specifies Hamm, the protagonist.

No more than his predecessors, Didi and Gogo, has Hamm the possibility of leaving to go elsewhere. But the reason for this has become tragically physical: he is paralyzed, sitting in an armchair in the middle of the stage, and he is blind. Around him nothing but high bare walls, without accessible windows. Clov, a kind of attendant, half-impotent himself, tends as well as he

can to the moribund Hamm: he manages to take him for a "turn," dragging the latter's chair on its casters around the edge of the stage, along the walls.

In relation to the two tramps, Hamm has therefore lost that ridiculous freedom they still possessed: it is no longer he who chooses *not to leave.* When he asks Clov to build a raft and to put him on it, in order to abandon his body to the ocean currents, it can this time only be a joke; as if Hamm, by immediately abandoning this project, were trying to give himself the illusion of a choice. As a matter of fact, he appears to us somehow imprisoned in his retreat; if he has no desire to emerge from it, he now does not have the means to do so either. This is a notable difference: the question for man is no longer one of affirming a position, but of suffering a fate.

And yet, within his prison, he still performs a parody of choice. . . . (pp. 120-22)

[Even in the] final image, we come back to the essential theme of *presence:* everything that is is here, offstage there is only nothingness, nonbeing. It is not enough that Clov, up on a ladder to get to the tiny windows that open onto the outside pseudo-world, informs us with a phrase as to the landscape: an empty gray sea on one side and a desert on the other. In reality this sea, this desert—invisible, moreover, to the spectator—are uninhabitable in the strictest sense of the word: as much as a back cloth would be, on which might be painted the water or the sand. (p. 123)

[Everything] is present in time as it is in space. To this ineluctable *here* corresponds an eternal *now:* "Yesterday! What does that mean? Yesterday!" Hamm exclaims several times. And the conjunction of space and time merely affords, with regard to a possible third character, this certitude: "If he exists he'll die there or he'll come here."

Without past, without place elsewhere, without any future but death, the universe thus defined is necessarily deprived of sense in the two acceptations of the term in French: it excludes any ideas of *direction* as well as any *signification.*

Hamm is suddenly struck by a doubt: "We're not beginning to . . . to . . . mean something?" he asks with feeling. Clov immediately reassures him: "Mean something! You and I, mean something! (*Brief laugh.*) Ah that's a good one!"

But this waiting for death, this physical misery which grows worse, these threats Hamm brandishes at Clov ("One day you'll be blind, like me. You'll be sitting there, a speck in the void, in the dark, for ever, like me. One day you'll say . . . I'm hungry, I'll get up and get something to eat. But you won't get up . . . "), all this gradual rot of the present constitutes, in spite of everything, a future.

Whence the fear of "meaning something" is perfectly justified: by this accepted consciousness of a tragic development, the world has thereby recovered its whole signification. (pp. 123-24)

And in parallel, before such a threat (this future simultaneously terrible and fatal), one can say that the present is no longer anything, that it disappears, conjured away in its turn, lost in the general collapse. (pp. 123-24)

[Finally] Hamm is driven to the acknowledgment of his failure: "I was never there. Clov! . . . I was never there . . . Absent, always. It all happened without me. . . ."

Once again the fatal trajectory has been made. Hamm and Clov, successors to Gogo and Didi, have again met with the common fate of all Beckett's characters: Pozzo, Lucky, Murphy, Molloy, Malone, Mahood, Worm, etc.

The stage, privileged site of *presence,* has not resisted the contagion for long. The progress of the disease has occurred at the same sure rate as in the narratives. After having believed for a moment that we had grasped the real man, we are then obliged to confess our mistake. Didi was only an illusion, that is doubtless what gave him that dancing gait, swaying from one leg to the other, that slightly clownlike costume. . . . He, too, was only the creature of a dream, temporary in any case, quickly falling back into the realm of dreams and fiction.

"I was never there," Hamm says, and in the face of this admission nothing else counts, for it is impossible to understand it other than in its most general form: *No one was ever there.* (pp. 124-25)

Alain Robbe-Grillet, "Samuel Beckett, or Presence on the Stage," in his *For a New Novel: Essays on Fiction,* translated by Richard Howard, Grove Press, Inc., 1966, pp. 111-25.

A. J. LEVENTHAL
(essay date 1963)

[Leventhal, an Irish-born French scholar and critic, was a close friend of Beckett. In the following excerpt from the text of a lecture delivered at Trinity College, Dublin, in 1963, he describes the typical protagonist in Beckett's works.]

One has to go back to Samuel Beckett's first published fictional work to find the image that is to figure almost continuously in the novels as well as in the plays, to find the character round which the Beckett world moved. The collection of short stories which make up the volume called *More Pricks than Kicks* relates the adventures of Belacqua. . . . Here is a stasis that was

to pursue (or should it be pin down) those creations that were to stand out in so markedly an individual manner.

Nor was it by chance that the hero in this book was named Belacqua. The Dante in the title of the first story ["**Dante and the Lobster**"] gives the clue. The name comes straight out of the *Purgatorio.* Little seems to be known about him in real life except that he was a lute maker in Florence, a friend of Dante and notorious for his indolence and apathy. He comes into the fourth canto of the *Purgatorio.* . . . [Dante's lines describing Belacqua] are reflected in the position taken up by Beckett's hero near the end of the story called "**A Wet Night**": "[he] disposed himself in the knee-and-elbow position on the pavement." . . . [Finally] he creeps with his poor trunk parallel to the horizon. Here we have the mode of locomotion that was to be repeated by characters in subsequent novels and in his . . . work *Comment c'est* where we are introduced to a painful cyclical crawl, symbolizing, perhaps, among other things, the slow progression of mankind. However, in "**A Wet Night**" Belacqua desists out of weariness from this method of self-propulsion and takes up the position I mentioned earlier, disposing himself in the knee-and-elbow position on the pavement.

It was thus that Botticelli depicted Belacqua in his drawing to illustrate this canto of the *Purgatorio.* I have seen it in a reproduction, showing him with his head between his clasped knees and with one eye fixed on Dante and Virgil, suggesting that he is even too weary to raise his head or to join his indolent companions in their mockery of the two poet visitors. (pp. 37-40)

When Beckett changes to writing his novels in French he leaves behind him much of the humor, grim as it was, in his previous work. He has less interest in making his characters indulge in games to pass the time as in *Waiting for Godot.* They are now concentrating on their *pénible* task of dying. In the opening passage of *Molloy,* the narrator says that what he wants to speak of are the things that are left, "say my goodbyes, finish dying." He remembers "in the tranquility of decomposition the long confused emotion that was my life." (May I point out the cynical echo of the well-known Wordsworth definition of poetry as "emotion recollected in tranquility"). . . . [There is little doubt] that there is an evolutionary process from Dante to the Belacqua of *More Pricks than Kicks* and through the various stages as manifested by the Murphys, Molloys, Morans, Watts, Estragons, Hamms, culminating in the Pims of *Comment c'est.*

Beckett has not given up the Belacqua picture. The embryo has haunted him to such an extent that in the final novel of his trilogy, the one called *L'Innommable,* he tries, in a frenzy of self-examination, to find out who these heroes of his are. He ranges over the characters he has created, Murphy,

Watt, Malone, Molloy, Mahood and picks on a new one whom he calls Worm. He wants to reduce them all to silence. He wants to reduce himself to silence and for a moment he finds solace in the thought of Worm. He would rather that Worm took over from the others with whom he frankly identifies himself. To be Worm means to be away from the world, away from all the other characters who have taken possession of him and at last to think nothing, to feel nothing. For this is himself, himself in embryo—literally in embryo. Many pages are given up to the description of womb life, that is life in the womb, if you can call it life. He would rather not call it by that name. There he cannot stir even though he suffers as a result. Indeed with bitter Beckettian irony he declares that "it would be to sign his life-warrant to stir from where he is." It is again Belacqua's weary phrase: *"L'andare in su che porta?"* What's the use in going up? Never in the history of literature (at least as I know it) has there been so poignant, so despairing a description of birth. Surely no one has ever dared to speak out of the womb as Beckett does here. Perhaps psychoanalysts may be able to send their recumbent patients sufficiently far back into their unconscious to imagine their unborn state but at the very most it could scarcely be much more than a blur—a clouded image based on knowledge acquired in life itself. Thus in the *L'Innommable* we are back to the foetal image of the unborn, the Botticelli drawing of Belacqua, Dante's Florentine friend, the lazy lute maker.

I referred earlier to the evolutionary process in the Beckett characters but the word "evolutionary" is hardly the right one in this connection, for it is normally associated with progression, with a series of biological changes, each improving on the previous condition. In Beckett's world the subject who has begun his fictional existence with his head on his knees ends in *Comment c'est* with his face in the mud. (pp. 42-3)

Stasis, or near stasis, is an outstanding characteristic of Beckett's creations. *"Cette inertie immortelle"* is how Beckett himself makes obeisance to human beings immobilized. Yet the febrile argumentation of his *personae* gives them a dynamic quality—a quality that sometimes borders on delirium. . . . They suffer, not gladly, but inevitably, accepting the ignominious situation, the insult, and turn more and more to the haven of their minds, finding their being as much in the mind's solace as in its *souillures*. (p. 43)

[In Beckett's plays] the very simplicity of the words is disarming and at first sight incompatible with the tragic import of the situations in which the characters find themselves. Soon however it becomes clear that the sparse, bare vocabulary is giving profundity to the statement. So that if, for example, there are many meanings read into *Waiting for Godot* there is none to say which is the inevitable one. The very fact that it lends itself to a religious interpretation that spells hope, the eternal expectation of a messiah, or its opposite, the futility of such an expectation, surely reflects the ambivalence of the human situation. Nothing is clear cut. Nothing can be known absolutely. (p. 46)

Never, in fiction, have so many words been used as by Beckett to underline the inefficiency of language and never, by his very language, has anyone disproved the point so brilliantly. In his French trilogy: *Molloy, Malone Meurt,* and *L'Innommable,* words, words, and more words pour themselves out in a cascade of affirmation and denial. It is an effort to stay the fleeting thought, to capture winging silences. Again and again he challenges the value of his own verbal descriptions, impugning their accuracy, offering another verb, another noun, and finally dismissing them all as being as worthless as the thoughts whose messengers they are. . . . (pp. 46-7)

The question of reality is to be found everywhere in the Beckett *oeuvre.* Beckett understands how Dante can condemn sinners to a limitless stagnation; to this, however, he adds the bewilderment of his *personae* when they become the victims of some luckless fate that brings other suffering. (p. 47)

Beckett seems to have carried with him something of the punning echoing system that he found in James Joyce. Everybody knows how the Joycean mind enjoyed the rather schoolboyish humor of what I might call the physical pun. Visitors to Joyce's flat in Paris were asked to admire a picture of the city of Cork—a picture which he had decided could be framed in only one substance—cork. Harmless enough as a joke—but it is possible to relate an idiosyncrasy of this kind to the complicated literary apparatus of *Finnegans Wake.*

In the same way there is a certain esoteric quality hidden skeletally in Beckett's work. It is not essential to the work itself but an awareness of its existence can be helpful. We know that a great number of his heroes have names that begin with M. There can be few authors or for that matter doctors who write a more illegible hand than does Sam Beckett. With most people signatures are difficult to read but knowing the identity of the writer one can make out the name Sam that concludes the communication. The S is so formed that it looks like an M standing on its side. And therefrom stem the dissyllables Murphy, Molloy, Malone, Mahood which echo the two syllabled "Beckett." There are monosyllable names like Pim, Pam, Bim, Bom which echo "Sam," while the name Sam itself, which may well refer to the author, occurs in *Watt.* Watt is not only another monosyllable echo but also throws light on his character. If one reads it as an interrogative, visually inserting an h and dropping a t, the quality of curiosity in the creation is pinpointed. In this connection I recall a conversation with the author who was at the time having difficulty in finding a publisher for his novel *Watt.* He cheered up considerably when he heard word from the literary agents to whom he had submitted the work that they were prepared to find a publisher. It was not so much because the agents were hopeful of placing the novel that Beckett was cheered but because *Watt* was to be handled by a firm called Watt and Watt. This comes near to Joyce's cork-framed Cork.

This is not meant to be a key to any symbolism that may run through the novels and plays. As I have probably said already the individual will read his particular reaction or that of a trusted critic into the significance of the text. I am just looking for clues to clearer understanding. And in the light of our familiarity so far with the fact that nomenclature plays a kind of secret part in fixing the sources of the characters it becomes possible to draw tentatively some elementary conclusions.

Let us look at the names of the characters in *Waiting for Godot:* Estragon, Vladimir, Pozzo, Lucky. Estragon is French, Vladimir, Russian, Pozzo, Italian, Lucky, English. . . . It occurs to me that if the names are not adventitious (and Beckett weighs all his words) it means that we are asked to think of this play, not as an isolated piece of inaction in a corner of France, or if you like Ireland, but as a cosmic state, a world condition in which all humanity is involved. (pp. 48-9)

The written word is not enough. His public (be it ever so small) must not be spared. He is bold enough to give physical form to his maimed characters. It is not enough that they be apprehended through the mind in the reading, they must be seen on the stage. The horror of Nagg and Nell immured (No, that's not the word) shall we say jack-boxed into dustbins! Never, since Swift, has there been what the French call *"humour noir"* in such cruel measure as in the dialogue between Hamm's parents. Their joking brings tears. Nor have I referred to his last play *Happy Days.* Photographs of his theatrical scene makes joyous copy for news editors. A woman buried up to the neck in a high mound in a barren landscape—even the Godot tree has vanished—can hold the attention of the student of the form of horses or of the vacillations on the stock market for a second or two, either to be puzzled or annoyed or extract a jocular remark. But the picture is that of Mother Earth tugging with Newtonian gravity to take her own to her bosom. How gaily our heroine carries on up to the end. As long as we have arms free (as in the first act) we can tinker with our handbag, color our lips, put a fine face on things, and chatter. Talk, talk, talk to anybody, to oneself, above all to one's self. Beckett's characters can only be silenced by death. But we rarely see them die. Only in *Comment c'est* do we meet executioner and victim; they are shown to us as undergoing what Mrs. Rooney in *All That Fall* calls a "lingering dissolution." (p. 50)

A. J. Leventhal, "The Beckett Hero," in *Samuel Beckett: A Collection of Critical Essays,* edited by Martin Esslin, Prentice-Hall, Inc., 1965, pp. 37-51.

━━━━━━━━━━━━

HUGH KENNER
(essay date 1968)

[Kenner is an American literary critic. In the following excerpt, he suggests that the novel trilogy composed of *Molloy, Malone Dies,* and *The Unnamable* contains forms and themes that recall the epic tradition.]

There is no literary parallel for [*Molloy, Malone Dies,* and *The Unnamable,*] the three books in which Samuel Beckett, releasing a certain violence of temperament evident in his earliest works and suppressed in *Murphy* and *Watt,* turned his face away from every accessible satisfaction, even from the familiar contours of his own language, and jettisoning the very matrices of fiction—narrator, setting, characters, theme, plot—devoted his scrutiny . . . to the very heart of novel writing: a man in a room writing things out of his head while every breath he draws brings death nearer.

From that everything flows, including the bedridden Malone's frequent proposal to enumerate his possessions, like a senescent Crusoe. Reminiscence, fantasy, description, reflection, all the paraphernalia of fiction pass through these books with the disarming obviousness of the unexpected. The narrator constantly shifts his focus of attention in order to keep himself interested. That is what the professional fictionist does too, though he would claim if pressed that he did it in order to keep the reader interested. Yet from no one is a reader more remote than from a novelist; the sheer labor of covering pages fills up his working days. (p. 62)

The trilogy is, among other things, a compendious abstract of all the novels that have ever been written, reduced to their most general terms.

And not only novels; for the trilogy also manages a sardonic counterpoint to the epic tradition of the West, which proved to be mortal, and indeed came to an end (unless we are going to take *Paradise Lost* for a new beginning) at about the time the novel was invented. That tradition started with Homer, who if he had been a twentieth-century Irishman living in Paris, might well have written the first half of *Molloy* instead of what he did write, if it was he who wrote it at all.

What Molloy is writing, sitting up in bed, is perhaps a faithful narrative, or perhaps he is making it up. At any rate, it purports to deal with his journey to that room. He set out, it seems, on a bicycle, intending to visit his mother (also bed-ridden); and he has executed a huge sweep, more or less circular, through the to him known world, in the course of which he has lost the bicycle, the use of his legs, the toes on one foot, everything indeed but his crutches and the will to proceed. There has been a Calypso, named Lousse, in whose house he stayed some months after an acquaintance founded on running his bicycle over her dog. There has been a Cyclopean police sergeant, who threatened him with a cylindrical ruler, and before whom our wanderer altered his fortunes by proclaiming his own name. ("My name is Molloy, I cried, all of a sudden, now I remember.") There have been ramparts, and seaboard privations. He had just reached the point when it was impractical to drag himself further on his stomach, and was considering rolling, when help mysteriously arrived.

The narrative is now assumed by a certain Moran. He also is writing, and his story follows Molloy's about as faithfully as Virgil's followed Homer's. Like Virgil, he also imparts a notably administrative tone, being (unlike Molloy, or Homer) a citizen of a substantial community. ("I have a huge bunch of keys, it weighs over a pound. Not a door, not a drawer in my house but the key to it goes with me, wherever I go.") He is writing the narrative of a journey, by bicycle and on foot, accompanied by his son, which was meant to be a search for Molloy, but which in fact brought him back to his own house, minus son and bicycle, crippled, stripped, discredited, and barely distinguishable from his quarry.

So much for the *Odyssey* and *Aeneid* of this new graph of civilization. We next encounter its *Divine Comedy,* which revolves about another man in bed. He is called Malone, at least that is what he is called now, though there are signs that he is a new phase of Molloy, or perhaps of Molloy and Moran together (unless a Molloy is simply what a Moran turns into when he goes looking for a Molloy). Malone too is writing, with a stub of a pencil in an exercise book. What he is writing is an account of his final weeks on earth, and also, by fits and starts, a piece of fiction, to distract himself from speculation about his mysterious surroundings. His narrative concerns a certain Sapo, who midway changes his name to Macmann, ends up in an institution not unlike that in which Malone appears to be confined, and expires at the same moment as his creator.

If The Unnamable, in turn, were Malone dead it would not be surprising. He is seated in a gray space, menaced by mysterious lights, and frantically writing, he is not clear how or with what. He can hardly be Malone, however, since Malone periodically executes an orbit about him. Indeed, he is convinced that all the previous characters are in this place with him, in fact that he invented them and the whole "ponderous

chronicle of moribunds in their courses, moving, clashing, writhing or fallen in short-lived swoons." (Were Molloy and Moran, for that matter, fictions of Malone's? Ulysses, it is true, appears in the *Divine Comedy,* and so do Virgil and Homer.) His problem, at the end of this counter-epic series, is to disappear, to cease from being and from troubling, a problem he will be powerless to resolve until he has given satisfactory evidence that he exists in the first place. This is difficult, since he is neither a kind of Virgil, nor of Homer, nor of Dante, but more or less a kind of Descartes (who Boileau asserted had cut the throat of poetry). Nevertheless he too tells sketchy stories, for instance about a certain Mahood who on one leg and crutches executed a world-wide spiraling Odyssey, and on another occasion was confined night and day outside a restaurant in a jar to which the menu was affixed, but despite his efforts to attract attention stayed apparently invisible to everyone but the proprietress. There is an important difference between these stories and Malone's, however, for it is not at all clear whether The Unnamable is inventing Mahood, or whether Mahood is partly responsible for inventing The Unnamable, having told the latter these stories about himself as part of the conspiracy to make him believe he exists. He is locked up with his fictions, at the mercy of an inchoate "they" who have supplied him with the very language he struggles with (yet which of us has made his own language?), and "they" are still perhaps fictions of his, or he of theirs.

Homer, Virgil, Dante, Descartes: these are not continents on a map Beckett has been following: Rorschach configurations, rather, which his groupings of tension and emphasis encourage us to see. They appear because his concentric narratives and serial narrators, each in turn more densely conscious of having had the experience of all the previous ones, succeed one another in the same manner as the major efforts of the Western imagination, each master in turn more burdened by responsibility for the preceding ones, as in Mr. Eliot's vision of The Mind of Europe. That is why outlines seem to grow clearer and purposes firmer as we work backward: Chaucer was not troubled by reading *Hamlet,* nor Homer by the cosmology of Mount Purgatory. It was the mind of Europe before the mind of Beckett that turned literature toward a more and more intricate self-consciousness, confronting a Joyce or a Proust with an intellectual landscape whose most mysterious feature is himself performing the act of writing. Beckett may be absolved of responsibility for turning even the novel in upon itself. Flaubert's first achieved fiction was a serious and powerful novel about a woman who has become what she is by reading novels.

The plays deal more openly with the past. *Waiting for Godot* reflects in its dusty but accurate mirror the Noh drama (tree, journey, concatenated rituals),

Greek theater (two actors, messengers, expectation of a *deus ex machina*), and *commedia dell'arte* (unflagging improvisation round a theme), while *Endgame* beats its bleak light on Shakespeare's stage, dominated by a prince of players named Hamm. Novels and plays alike recapitulate the past of their art, so sparely that if we stare at a parallel it vanishes, so casually that if we ask Beckett the meaning of all this incumbent tradition he can cry with Dan Rooney, "It is a thing I carry about with me!" Yet its presence contributes to the powerful sense—irradiating his inert material—that he has gotten at the form's central sources of energy, and looks into a long tradition with X-ray eyes.

So he propels the trilogy's extraordinary *reductio* for some 180,000 words, incorporating as he goes by the *roman policier*, the picaresque chronicle, the *Bildungsroman*, the universes of Proust and Defoe (these two superimposed), the fiction of self-interrogation. Our attention is held without a plot (a broom that sweeps everything in the same direction), without an undertow of ideas, with a minimum of incident, with no incubus of profundity. What holds us is in part the unquenchable lust to know what will happen in the next ten words, in part the hypnotic fascination of the nearly motionless (flies on a windowpane). Yet he has so distilled these appeals that they operate with uncomfortable immediacy; we are not allowed to suppose that we are reading "for the story," or for some improving purpose. His transparent syntax establishes a tone, a tone of genial resignation, within which the events of the trilogy declare themselves; and these events are small items become momentous, a minute shift of attention, the toot of a bicycle horn, the whereabouts of a boot. For Beckett, manipulating a form that has always indulged itself in copious triviality, has invented for it a convention that can accommodate any amount of detail while rendering nothing too trivial to be interesting. (pp. 63-8)

Hugh Kenner, in his *Samuel Beckett: A Critical Study,* revised edition, University of California Press, 1968, 226 p.

MARTIN ESSLIN

(essay date 1969)

[Esslin, a prominent and sometimes controversial critic of contemporary theater, is perhaps best known for coining the term "Theater of the Absurd." In the following excerpt, he discusses salvation and grace in *Waiting for Godot.*]

Beckett's real triumph . . . came when *Waiting for Godot,* which had appeared in book form in 1952, was first produced on 5 January 1953. . . . Roger Blin, always at the forefront of the avant-garde in the French theatre, directed, and himself played the part of Pozzo. And against all expectations, the strange tragic farce, in which nothing happens and which had been scorned as undramatic by a number of managements, became one of the greatest successes of the post-war theatre. . . . seen in the first five years after its original production in Paris by more than a million spectators—a truly astonishing reception for a play so enigmatic, so exasperating, so complex, and so uncompromising in its refusal to conform to any of the accepted ideas of dramatic construction.

This is not the place to trace in detail the strange history of *Waiting for Godot.* Suffice it to say that the play found the approval of accepted dramatists as diverse as Jean Anouilh . . . , Thornton Wilder, Tennessee Williams, and William Saroyan. . . . (pp. 20-1)

When Alan Schneider, who was to direct the first American production of *Waiting for Godot,* asked Beckett who or what was meant by Godot, he received the answer, 'If I knew, I would have said so in the play.'

This is a salutary warning to anyone who approaches Beckett's plays with the intention of discovering *the* key to their understanding, of demonstrating in exact and definite terms *what they mean.* Such an undertaking might perhaps be justified in tackling the works of an author who had started from a clear-cut philosophical or moral conception, and had then proceeded to translate it into concrete terms of plot and character. But even in such a case the chances are that the final product, if it turned out a genuine work of the creative imagination, would transcend the author's original intentions and present itself as far richer, more complex, and open to a multitude of additional interpretations. For, as Beckett himself has pointed out in his essay on Joyce's *Work in Progress,* the form, structure, and mood of an artistic statement cannot be separated from its meaning, its conceptual content; simply because the work of art as a whole *is* its meaning, *what* is said in it is indissolubly linked with the *manner* in which it is said, and cannot be said in any other way. Libraries have been filled with attempts to reduce the meaning of a play like *Hamlet* to a few short and simple lines, yet the play itself remains the clearest and most concise statement of its meaning and message, precisely because its uncertainties and irreducible ambiguities are an essential element of its total impact.

These considerations apply, in varying degrees, to all works of creative literature, but they apply with particular force to works that are essentially concerned with conveying their author's sense of mystery, bewilderment, and anxiety when confronted with the human condition, and his despair at being unable to find a meaning in existence. In *Waiting for Godot,* the feeling of uncertainty it produces, the ebb and flow of this uncertainty—from the hope of discovering the identity of Godot to its repeated disappointment—are themselves the essence of the play. (pp. 24-5)

Yet it is only natural that plays written in so unusual and baffling a convention should be felt to be in special need of an explanation that, as it were, would uncover their hidden meaning and translate it into everyday language. The source of this fallacy lies in the misconception that somehow these plays must be reducible to the conventions of the 'normal' theatre, with plots that can be summarized in the form of a narrative. If only one could discover some hidden clue, it is felt, these difficult plays could be forced to yield their secret and reveal the plot of the conventional play that is hidden within them. Such attempts are doomed to failure. Beckett's plays lack plot even more completely than other works of the Theatre of the Absurd. Instead of a linear development, they present their author's intuition of the human condition by a method that is essentially polyphonic; they confront their audience with an organized structure of statements and images that interpenetrate each other and that must be apprehended in their totality, rather like the different themes in a symphony, which gain meaning by their simultaneous interaction.

But if we have to be cautious in our approach to Beckett's plays, to avoid the pitfall of trying to provide an oversimplified explanation of their meaning, this does not imply that we cannot subject them to careful scrutiny by isolating sets of images and themes and by attempting to discern their structural groundwork. The results of such an examination should make it easier to follow the author's intention and to see, if not the *answers* to his questions, at least what the *questions* are that he is asking.

Waiting for Godot does not tell a story; it explores a static situation. [As Beckett states within the play], 'Nothing happens, nobody comes, nobody goes, it's awful.' On a country road, by a tree, two old tramps, Vladimir and Estragon, are waiting. That is the opening situation at the beginning of act I. At the end of act I they are informed that Mr Godot, with whom they believe they have an appointment, cannot come, but that he will surely come tomorrow. Act II repeats precisely the same pattern. The same boy arrives and delivers the same message. (pp. 25-6)

[Yet the] sequence of events and the dialogue in each act are different. Each time the two tramps encounter another pair of characters, Pozzo and Lucky, master and slave, under differing circumstances; in each act Vladimir and Estragon attempt suicide and fail, for differing reasons; but these variations merely serve to emphasize the essential sameness of the situation. . . .

Vladimir and Estragon—who call each other Didi and Gogo, although Vladimir is addressed by the boy

messenger as Mr Albert, and Estragon, when asked his name, replies without hesitation, Catullus—are clearly derived from the pairs of cross-talk comedians of music halls. Their dialogue has the peculiar repetitive quality of the cross-talk comedians' patter. (p. 26)

As the members of a cross-talk act, Vladimir and Estragon have complementary personalities. Vladimir is the more practical of the two, and Estragon claims to have been a poet. In eating his carrot, Estragon finds that the more he eats of it the less he likes it, while Vladimir reacts the opposite way—he likes things as he gets used to them. Estragon is volatile, Vladimir persistent. Estragon dreams, Vladimir cannot stand hearing about dreams. Vladimir has stinking breath, Estragon has stinking feet. Vladimir remembers past events, Estragon tends to forget them as soon as they have happened. Estragon likes telling funny stories, Vladimir is upset by them. It is mainly Vladimir who voices the hope that Godot will come and that his coming will change their situation, while Estragon remains sceptical throughout and at times even forgets the name of Godot. It is Vladimir who conducts the conversation with the boy who is Godot's messenger and to whom the boy's messages are addressed. Estragon is the weaker of the two; he is beaten up by mysterious strangers every night. Vladimir at times acts as his protector, sings him to sleep with a lullaby, and covers him with his coat. The opposition of their temperaments is the cause of endless bickering between them and often leads to the suggestion that they should part. Yet, being complementary natures, they also are dependent on each other and have to stay together.

Pozzo and Lucky are equally complementary in their natures, but their relationship is on a more primitive level: Pozzo is the sadistic master, Lucky the submissive slave. In the first act, Pozzo is rich, powerful, and certain of himself; he represents worldly man in all his facile and shortsighted optimism and illusory feeling of power and permanence. Lucky not only carries his heavy luggage, and even the whip with which Pozzo beats him, he also dances and thinks for him, or did so in his prime. In fact, Lucky taught Pozzo all the higher values of life: 'beauty, grace, truth of the first water'. Pozzo and Lucky represent the relationship between body and mind, the material and the spiritual sides of man, with the intellect subordinate to the appetites of the body. Now that Lucky's powers are failing, Pozzo complains that they cause him untold suffering. He wants to get rid of Lucky and sell him at the fair. But in the second act, when they appear again, they are still tied together. Pozzo has gone blind, Lucky has become dumb. While Pozzo drives Lucky on a journey without an apparent goal, Vladimir has prevailed upon Estragon to wait for Godot.

A good deal of ingenuity has been expended in trying to establish at least an etymology for Godot's

Beckett with Horst Bollmann and Stefan Wigger, in a rehearsal of *Waiting for Godot.*

name, which would point to Beckett's conscious or subconscious intention in making him the objective of Vladimir's and Estragon's quest. It has been suggested that Godot is a weakened form of the word 'God', a diminutive formed on the analogy of Pierre-Pierrot, Charles-Charlot, with the added association of the Charlie Chaplin character of the little man, who is called Charlot in France, and whose bowler hat is worn by all four main characters in the play. It has also been noted that the title *En Attendant Godot* seems to contain an allusion to Simone Weil's book *Attente de Dieu,* which would furnish a further indication that Godot stands for God. Yet the name Godot may also be an even more recondite literary allusion. As Eric Bentley has pointed out, there is a character in a play by Balzac, a character much talked about but never seen, and called Godeau. The play in question is Balzac's comedy *Le Faiseur,* better known as *Mercadet.* Mercadet is a Stock Exchange speculator who is in the habit of attributing his financial difficulties to his former partner Godeau, who, years before, absconded with their joint capital. . . . [The] hope of Godeau's eventual return and the repayment of the embezzled funds is constant-

ly dangled by Mercadet before the eyes of his numerous creditors. . . . The plot of *Mercadet* turns on a last, desperate speculation based on the appearance of a spurious Godeau. But the fraud is discovered. Mercadet seems ruined. At this moment the real Godeau is announced; he has returned from India with a huge fortune. (pp. 27-9)

The parallels are too striking to make it probable that this is a mere coincidence. In Beckett's play, as in Balzac's, the arrival of Godot is the eagerly awaited event that will miraculously save the situation; and Beckett is as fond as Joyce of subtle and recondite literary allusions.

Yet whether Godot is meant to suggest the intervention of a supernatural agency, or whether he stands for a mythical human being whose arrival is expected to change the situation, or both of these possibilities combined, his exact nature is of secondary importance. The subject of the play is not Godot but waiting, the act of waiting as an essential and characteristic aspect of the human condition. Throughout our lives we always wait for something, and Godot simply represents the objective of our waiting—an event, a thing, a person, death. Moreover, it is in the act of waiting that we experience the flow of *time* in its purest, most evident form. If we are active, we tend to forget the passage of time, we *pass* the time, but if we are merely passively waiting, we are confronted with the action of time itself. . . . The flow of time confronts us with the basic problem of being—the problem of the nature of the self, which, being subject to constant change in time, is in constant flux and therefore ever outside our grasp. . . . (pp. 29-30)

Being subject to this process of time flowing through us and changing us in doing so, we are, at no single moment in our lives, identical with ourselves. . . . If Godot is the object of Vladimir's and Estragon's desire, he seems naturally ever beyond their reach. It is significant that the boy who acts as go-between fails to recognize the pair from day to day. The French version explicitly states that the boy who appears in the second act is the same boy as the one in the first act, yet the boy denies that he has ever seen the two tramps before and insists that this is the first time he has acted as Godot's messenger. As the boy leaves, Vladimir tries to impress it upon him: 'You're sure you saw me, eh, you won't come and tell me tomorrow that you never saw me before?' The boy does not reply, and we know that he will again fail to recognize them. Can we ever be sure that the human beings we meet are the same today as they were yesterday? When Pozzo and Lucky first appear, neither Vladimir nor Estragon seems to recognize them; Estragon even takes Pozzo for Godot. But after they have gone, Vladimir comments that they have changed since their last appearance. Estragon insists that he didn't know them. (pp. 30-1)

In the second act, when Pozzo and Lucky reappear, cruelly deformed by the action of time, Vladimir and Estragon again have their doubts whether they are the same people they met on the previous day. Nor does Pozzo remember them: 'I don't remember having met anyone yesterday. But tomorrow I won't remember having met anyone today.'

Waiting is to experience the action of time, which is constant change. And yet, as nothing real ever happens, that change is in itself an illusion. The ceaseless activity of time is self-defeating, purposeless, and therefore null and void. The more things change, the more they are the same. That is the terrible stability of the world. . . . One day is like another, and when we die, we might never have existed. As Pozzo exclaims in his great final outburst:

'Have you not done tormenting me with your accursed time? . . . One day, is that not enough for you, one day like any other day he went dumb, one day I went blind, one day we'll go deaf, one day we were born, one day we'll die, the same day, the same second. . . . They give birth astride of a grave, the light gleams an instant, then it's night once more.'

And Vladimir, shortly afterwards, agrees: 'Astride of a grave and a difficult birth. Down in the hole, lingeringly, the gravedigger puts on the forceps.'

Still Vladimir and Estragon live in hope: they wait for Godot, whose coming will bring the flow of time to a stop. 'Tonight perhaps we shall sleep in his place, in the warmth, dry, our bellies full, on the straw. It is worth waiting for that, is it not?' This passage, omitted in the English version, clearly suggests the peace, the rest from waiting, the sense of having arrived in a haven, that Godot represents to the two tramps. They are hoping to be saved from the evanescence and instability of the illusion of time, and to find peace and permanence outside it. Then they will no longer be tramps, homeless wanderers, but will have arrived home. (pp. 31-2)

When Beckett is asked about the theme of *Waiting for Godot,* he sometimes refers to a passage in the writings of St Augustine: 'There is a wonderful sentence in Augustine. I wish I could remember the Latin. It is even finer in Latin than in English. "Do not despair: one of the thieves was saved. Do not presume: one of the thieves was damned."' And Beckett sometimes adds, 'I am interested in the shape of ideas even if I do not believe in them. . . . That sentence has a wonderful shape. It is the shape that matters.'

The theme of the two thieves on the cross, the theme of the uncertainty of the hope of salvation and the fortuitousness of the bestowal of grace, does indeed pervade the whole play. Vladimir states it right at the beginning: 'One of the thieves was saved. . . . It's a reasonable percentage.' Later he enlarges on the subject:

'Two thieves. . . . One is supposed to have been saved and the other . . . damned. . . . And yet how is it that of the four evangelists only one speaks of a thief being saved? The four of them were there or thereabouts, and only one speaks of a thief being saved. . . . Of the other three two don't mention any thieves at all and the third says that both of them abused him.'

There is a fifty-fifty chance, but as only one out of four witnesses reports it, the odds are considerably reduced. But, as Vladimir points out; it is a curious fact that everybody seems to believe that one witness: 'It is the only version they know.' Estragon, whose attitude has been one of scepticism throughout, merely comments, 'People are bloody ignorant apes.'

It is the shape of the idea that fascinated Beckett. Out of all the malefactors, out of all the millions and millions of criminals that have been executed in the course of history, two, only two, had the chance of receiving absolution in the hour of their death in so uniquely effective a manner. One happened to make a hostile remark; he was damned. One happened to contradict that hostile remark; he was saved. How easily could the roles have been reversed. These, after all, were not well-considered judgements, but chance exclamations uttered at a moment of supreme suffering and stress. As Pozzo says about Lucky, 'Remark that I might easily have been in his shoes and he in mine. If chance had not willed it otherwise. To each one his due.' And then our shoes might fit us one day and not the next: Estragon's boots torment him in the first act; in Act II they fit him miraculously.

Godot himself is unpredictable in bestowing kindness and punishment. The boy who is his messenger minds the goats, and Godot treats him well. But the boy's brother, who minds the sheep, is beaten by Godot. 'And why doesn't he beat you?' asks Vladimir. 'I don't know, sir.' . . . The parallel to Cain and Abel is evident: there too the Lord's grace fell on one rather than on the other without any rational explanation—only that Godot beats the minder of the sheep and cherishes the minder of the goats. Here Godot also acts contrary to the Son of Man at the Last Judgement: 'And he shall set the sheep on his right hand, but the goats on the left.' But if Godot's kindness is bestowed fortuitously, his coming is not a source of pure joy; it can also mean damnation. When Estragon, in the second act, believes Godot to be approaching, his first thought is, 'I'm accursed.' And as Vladimir triumphantly exclaims, 'It's Godot! At last! Let's go and meet him,' Estragon runs away, shouting. 'I'm in hell!'

The fortuitous bestowal of grace, which passes human understanding, divides mankind into those that will be saved and those that will be damned. When, in Act II Pozzo and Lucky return, and the two tramps try to identify them, Estragon calls out, 'Abel! Abel!' Pozzo immediately responds. But when Estragon calls out, 'Cain! Cain!' Pozzo responds again. 'He's all mankind,' concludes Estragon.

There is even a suggestion that Pozzo's activity is concerned with his frantic attempt to draw that fifty-fifty chance of salvation upon himself. In the first act, Pozzo is on his way to sell Lucky 'at the fair'. The French version, however, specifies that it is the *'marché de Saint-Sauveur'*—the Market of the Holy Saviour—to which he is taking Lucky. Is Pozzo trying to sell Lucky to redeem himself? Is he trying to divert the fifty-fifty chance of redemption from Lucky (in whose shoes he might easily have been himself) to Pozzo? He certainly complains that Lucky is causing him great pain, that he is killing him with his mere presence—perhaps because his mere presence reminds Pozzo that it might be Lucky who will be redeemed. When Lucky gives his famous demonstration of his thinking, what is the thin thread of sense that seems to underlie the opening passage of his wild, schizophrenic 'word salad'? Again, it seems to be concerned with the fortuitousness of salvation: 'Given the existence . . . of a personal God . . . outside

time without extension who from the heights of divine apathia divine athambia divine aphasia loves us dearly with some exceptions for reasons unknown . . . and suffers . . . with those who for reasons unknown are plunged in torment. . . .' Here again we have the personal God, with his divine apathy, his speechlessness (aphasia), and his lack of the capacity for terror or amazement (athambia), who loves us dearly—with some exceptions, who will be plunged into the torments of hell. In other words, God, who does not communicate with us, cannot feel for us, and condemns us for reasons unknown.

When Pozzo and Lucky reappear the next day, Pozzo blind and Lucky dumb, no more is heard of the fair. Pozzo has failed to sell Lucky; his blindness in thinking that he could thus influence the action of grace has been made evident in concrete physical form.

That *Waiting for Godot* is concerned with the hope of salvation through the workings of grace seems clearly established both from Beckett's own evidence and from the text itself. Does this, however, mean that it is a Christian, or even that it is a religious, play? There have been a number of very ingenious interpretations in this sense. Vladimir's and Estragon's waiting is explained as signifying their steadfast faith and hope, while Vladimir's kindness to his friend, and the two tramps' mutual interdependence, are seen as symbols of Christian charity. But these religious interpretations seem to overlook a number of essential features of the play—its constant stress on the uncertainty of the appointment with Godot, Godot's unreliability and irrationality, and the repeated demonstration of the futility of the hopes pinned on him. The act of waiting for Godot is shown as essentially *absurd*. (pp. 32-5)

There is one feature in the play that leads one to assume there is a better solution to the tramps' predicament, which they themselves both consider preferable to waiting for Godot—that is, suicide. . . . Suicide remains their favorite solution, unattainable owing to their own incompetence and their lack of the practical tools to achieve it. It is precisely their disappointment at their failure to succeed in their attempts at suicide that Vladimir and Estragon rationalize by waiting, or pretending to wait, for Godot. 'I'm curious to hear what he has to offer. Then we'll take it or leave it.' Estragon, far less convinced of Godot's promises than Vladimir, is anxious to reassure himself that they are not tied to Godot. (pp. 35-6)

When, later, Vladimir falls into some sort of complacency about their waiting—'We have kept our appointment . . . we are not saints—but we have kept our appointment. How many people can boast as much?' Estragon immediately punctures it by retorting, 'Billions.' And Vladimir is quite ready to admit that they are waiting only from irrational habit. (p. 36)

In support of the Christian interpretation, it might be argued that Vladimir and Estragon, who are waiting for Godot, are shown as clearly superior to Pozzo and Lucky, who have no appointment, no objective, and are wholly egocentric, wholly wrapped up in their sadomasochistic relationship. Is it not their faith that puts the two tramps on to a higher plane?

It is evident that, in fact, Pozzo is naïvely overconfident and self-centred. 'Do I look like a man that can be made to suffer?' he boasts. Even when he gives a soulful and melancholy description of the sunset and the sudden falling of the night, we know he does not believe the night will ever fall on him—he is merely giving a performance; he is not concerned with the meaning of what he recites, but only with its effect on the audience. Hence he is taken completely unawares when night does fall on him and he goes blind. Likewise Lucky, in accepting Pozzo as his master and in teaching him his ideas, seems to have been naïvely convinced of the power of reason, beauty, and truth. Estragon and Vladimir *are* clearly superior to both Pozzo and Lucky—not because they pin their faith on Godot but because they are less naïve. They do not believe in action, wealth, or reason. They are aware that all we do in this life is as nothing when seen against the senseless action of time, which is in itself an illusion. They are aware that suicide would be the best solution. They are thus superior to Pozzo and Lucky because they are less self-centred and have fewer illusions. (pp. 36-7)

For a brief moment, Vladimir is aware of the full horror of the human condition: 'The air is full of our cries. . . . But habit is a great deadener.' He looks at Estragon, who is asleep, and reflects, 'At me too someone is looking, of me too someone is saying, he is sleeping, he knows nothing, let him sleep on. . . . I can't go on!' The routine of waiting for Godot stands for habit, which prevents us from reaching the painful but fruitful awareness of the full reality of being.

[We] find Beckett's own commentary on this aspect of *Waiting for Godot* in his essay ["**Proust**" (1931)]:

Habit is the ballast that chains the dog to his vomit. Breathing is habit. Life is habit. Or rather life is a succession of habits, since the individual is a succession of individuals. . . . Habit then is the generic term for the countless treaties concluded between the countless subjects that constitute the individual and their countless correlative objects. The periods of transition that separate consecutive adaptations . . . represent the perilous zones in the life of the individual, dangerous, precarious, painful, mysterious, and fertile, when for a moment the *boredom of living* is replaced by the *suffering of being*.

(pp. 37-8)

Vladimir and Estragon talk incessantly. Why?

They hint at it in what is probably the most lyrical, the most perfectly phrased passage of the play:

VLADIMIR: You are right, we're inexhaustible.
ESTRAGON: It's so we won't think.
VLADIMIR: We have that excuse.
ESTRAGON: It's so we won't hear.
VLADIMIR: We have our reasons.
ESTRAGON: All the dead voices.
VLADIMIR: They make a noise like wings.
ESTRAGON: Like leaves.
VLADIMIR: Like sand.
ESTRAGON: Like leaves.
   [*Silence.*]
VLADIMIR: They all speak together.
ESTRAGON: Each one to itself.
   [*Silence.*]
VLADIMIR: Rather they whisper.
ESTRAGON: They rustle.
VLADIMIR: They murmur.
ESTRAGON: They rustle.
   [*Silence.*]

(pp. 38-9)

This passage, in which the cross-talk of Irish music-hall comedians is miraculously transmuted into poetry, contains the key to much of Beckett's work. Surely these rustling, murmuring voices of the past . . . are the voices that explore the mysteries of being and the self to the limits of anguish and suffering. Vladimir and Estragon are trying to escape hearing them. The long silence that follows their evocation is broken by Vladimir, *'in anguish',* with the cry 'Say anything at all!' after which the two relapse into their wait for Godot.

The hope of salvation may be merely an evasion of the suffering and anguish that spring from facing the reality of the human condition. There is here a truly astonishing parallel between the Existentialist philosophy of Jean-Paul Sartre and the creative intuition of Beckett, who has never consciously expressed Existentialist views. If, for Beckett as for Sartre, man has the duty of facing the human condition as a recognition that at the root of our being there is nothingness, liberty, and the need of constantly creating ourselves in a succession of choices, then Godot might well become an image of what Sartre calls 'bad faith'—'The first act of bad faith consists in evading what one cannot evade, in evading what one *is.'*

While these parallels may be illuminating, we must not go too far in trying to identify Beckett's vision with any school of philosophy. It is the peculiar richness of a play like *Waiting for Godot* that it opens vistas on so many different perspectives. It is open to philosophical, religious, and psychological interpretations, yet above all it is a poem on time, evanescence, and the mysteriousness of existence, the paradox of change and stability, necessity and absurdity. (pp. 39-40)

Martin Esslin, "Samuel Beckett: The Search for the Self," in his *The Theatre of the Absurd,* revised edition, 1969. Reprint by The Overlook Press, 1973, pp. 11-65.

████████

GEOFFREY STRICKLAND
(essay date 1986)

[In the following excerpt, Strickland evaluates *Waiting for Godot* as a "serious" work of art.]

Often when I read Beckett or watch one of his plays or films I feel as if my world were disintegrating; which is, of course, a tribute to his art. To take Beckett seriously can be a shattering experience and salutary if what is shattered in the process are illusions we are better without. But can one take Beckett seriously? For many the answer would appear to be no: fifty years of experiment with avant-garde writing have produced, according to this view, nothing which is not boring, bogus and merely lugubrious. For others it is at the very least paradoxical: that is to say, Beckett may be facetious to the point of nihilism (or vice-versa) but facetiousness or nihilism as witty and eloquent are more easily deplored than forgotten. He disturbs us if only because he leaves us seriously wondering what seriousness is. I think it would be a tribute to Beckett himself, as he enters his eighty-first year, a tribute certainly to the youthfulness of his intelligence, to assume that this more thoughtful view of the matter was one that corresponded to his own. It is a view which remains open to the possibility that what his most dismissive critics are saying could be true, even truer than they themselves realise. Art as original as this runs the risk of utter failure. . . . The questioning view of Beckett is not, however, one with which anyone, whether more or less favourably predisposed towards him, could remain content for very long; for it makes of him not a mystery (and he is, surely, for all his preoccupation with ultimate realities, among the least mysterious of writers) but an enigma. The more disturbing one finds him the more compelling the need to answer the question: should one take him seriously? Seriousness in art is not, we know, the same necessarily as bitterness or misery, even unrelieved misery like that of almost every new piece of writing by Beckett over the past thirty years. Misery, even sincere misery, can be found in art which is merely amateurish. Does enjoyment of the art entail contemplation of some inescapable truth? And what if those academics are right, who place him among the great classics of our literature? There is little uncontroversial one can say about the writers of the canon but we can usually agree that they give meaning in some way to human destiny, however terrible; whereas the glorious thing about Beckett's art, we are often told, is that it undermines the very means by which meaning is engendered; it shows us the delusive artificiality of all the stories we tell about one another, both false and ostensibly true. . . . If Beckett is in any way a serious artist, his art is, presumably, of the kind of which Eliot speaks in 'Tradition and the Individual Talent', the art which 'modifies' the 'ideal order' formed by the 'early monuments'.

The question is, of course, which work of Beckett's has this power? There is no obvious consensus among his admirers as to which is his *Macbeth* and which his *Titus Andronicus*. . . . The sardonic epigrams and the farcical or terrible moments which have this quality are scattered throughout his entire *oeuvre,* including his best known play *En attendant Godot,* the play that brought him international acclaim. If one wishes to raise the question of Beckett's ultimate seriousness there is perhaps then no better way of beginning than to ask in what sense *Godot* itself, whether it is performed or read in private, comes over to us as the work of a serious artist.

Whatever else we understand by this expression, I think we can assume that it means a work which holds our attention and concentrates it on what could conceivably matter to anyone, whether this is for tragic or comic effect. Anything, of course, might matter to anyone, depending on particular circumstances and needs. How or when one is going to get one's next drop of spirits can matter very much if one happens to find oneself in a certain dependent condition; even the question of how or whether one is going to get one's boot off one's foot. (pp. 13-15)

A play about an ordinary mortal seeing how he could buy or cadge a drink would not be a serious play; a play about an alcoholic to whom it seemed a matter of life or death might well be. . . . A play showing a man trying to get his boot off and realising he was too old and weak to do it on his own might also, in so far as it was about growing old, be serious. At the beginning of *Godot,* the struggle of Estragon with his boot is quite different. It's an effective piece of theatre, i.e. a gift for even the moderately accomplished actor, but it would be naïve to take it tragically. . . . There are critics, none the less, who find illumination in a literal understanding of the tramp's splendid *phrases.* The novelist Robbe-Grillet, for example, notes approvingly the remarks by Vladimir that there are 'worse things than thinking . . . '; though it is a compliment to Beckett's sophistication to assume that the tramps' sententiousness is part of the comedy and, as such, part of the play's overall effect. And it would be preposterous to argue that it's not serious because, to this extent, the play happens to be funny.

One of the main reasons for questioning the seriousness of *En attendant Godot* is the following. As we know (and this is, of course, in no way an objection to it) it is a play without the dénouement that traditionally comes in the third or fifth acts. Significantly, there are only two. It's a play that leaves us asking a great many questions and that drops what might seem like a number of hints as to their answer; especially during the questioning of the little boy who comes on to bring a message from the unseen Godot himself. It has in this respect a certain amount in common with the novel by Robbe-Grillet which inaugurated the age of *le nouveau roman, Les Gommes* which appeared in 1953, the year of the first performance of Godot. Many critics claim that it is a serious play because of the questions it leaves us asking; but I think the objection to this is that these are not questions about the human condition but simply about the meaning of the text. The most obvious question of all is, of course, not who is Godot? The word 'God' can stand for many different things. . . . The crucial unanswered question is what do the tramps themselves believe Godot to be? How does Vladimir, for instance, believe or imagine that Godot has communicated to him the instructions to wait by the tree? Do they see him, as certain believers see God, as the only being who can give meaning to their lives? Is he merely someone who they hope might fill their stomachs and let them sleep on his straw? Are they waiting above all because they have no particular reason for moving on? How much does it matter to them, in other words, whether or not Godot appears? To answer these questions, we would need to know more about Vladimir and Estragon than the text of the play reveals: far more about what it is like to be them. Beckett originally thought of calling the play just *En attendant* and brought in the notion of 'Godot' later. But a play which was just about 'waiting' could obviously not be serious or even interesting. . . . Bringing in 'Godot' makes it a lot less pointless . . . but it still leaves us wondering if it's about anything that matters very much, even to the two main characters.

Yet it is a play, we are often reminded by its critics and any competent director, in which we are acutely aware of the physical presence of the four main characters. The stage directions are both eloquent and precise. The bare décor and the intense lighting throw our attention on to the four oddly-dressed bodies; and at the same time, by depriving us of the means of answering the questions raised by the play, the play brings us back helplessly to the simple fact of their being *there*. (pp. 15-16)

It is doubtful, however, whether this argument can be taken very far either. Obviously, the comic choreography of the play is one of the most remarkable things about it and the sheer physicality not only of the action (if 'action' is the word) but of the dialogue as well: Vladimir's elaborate plans, for instance, of how they might hang themselves in order to achieve erec-

tion. However, in so far as this is true, Beckett is working at a disadvantage compared with artists whose performance depends on their own bodily presence, their own barely perceptible movements and the timing of what they do and say. The Vladimir and Estragon we recreate in imagination from the text or that an actor will try to impersonate are mere phantoms unless the actors happen to be actors of genius. . . . (pp. 16-17)

The theory that it is the presence, the sheer *Dasein* of Estragon and Vladimir that the play offers, in the final analysis, has the disadvantage too that the human body is never just a body and the eye of the spectator never a passive recorder like the film in a camera. One of the most obvious things we can say about Vladimir and Estragon is that though they are recognisably tramps, they are tramps such as we have never seen or heard of before; so that if, as spectators, we are fascinated by their physical presence, it is partly, if not entirely, because, in the very act of looking at them, we are asking ourselves what in the world they are.

Perhaps it is in this curiosity which the appearance of Beckett's two lugubrious clowns arouses and which almost everything they say arouses as well that we can find the play's *raison d'être* as well as the reason for its success. It is a play in which all the expectations we bring to the naturalistic theatre or the theatre of ideas are aroused only to be disappointed and yet in which the attention of whole audiences has been held from beginning to end. The means by which suspense is created are numerous and varied, including changes of idiom, register and mood: the build-up, for instance, of indignation and pity in the first of the Pozzo and Lucky interludes leading up to the moment when the play seems about to dissolve into recognisable humanitarian sentiment of the most deplorably reassuring kind; until suddenly, as Estragon goes to wipe away Lucky's tears, he receives his terrible kick on the shins. One's attention is held also by jokes which are unfinished and patent contrivances for filling the time, as well as a few wonderfully inventive gags of the Monty Python variety, such as the prevention of Lucky's voluble 'thinking' by the forcible removal of his hat. The activity of 'thinking', like the state of being 'human' are the subject of some of the best jokes in the play and give it that air of sardonic sophistication which discourages us or which, at least, ought to discourage us from looking within it for philosophical or human significance.

To the extent that it is often a good idea to laugh people *out* of being serious, *Godot* could perhaps be thought of, paradoxically, as, after all, a serious play and this despite, even because of, the volumes of serious learned commentary it has inspired. But to this extent only. It is, on this view of the play (which is the one I happen myself to find the most convincing), an impressive theatrical diversion, in which one of the main jokes is at the expense of the audience itself. The more knowing members of the audience, when I first saw it in 1956, could be heard laughing when Vladimir observed, after Lucky's and Pozzo's first exit, that their appearance had 'passed the time'; at the tramps' occasional fear that they may having nothing more to say to one another . . . and when the curtain went up for the second act and revealed the bare tree now covered with a few conspicuously artificial leaves. I can only assume that they were laughing at the sheer audacity of the actors and of all those responsible for the evening's entertainment. There must have been, of course, also those who were impressed by what they saw as a religious allegory, a modern Jansenist allegory perhaps in which Godot was not only hidden but conceivably non-existent or mortal and fallible. And those who, like my French companion on this occasion, were intrigued by being caught between both kinds of reaction, rather excitingly unsure. Whatever the reaction, in the kind of theatre represented by Beckett, the audience places itself willingly at the playwrights' and actors' mercy. It allows its emotions to be worked upon freely and its philosophical curiosity aroused. It allows itself to be exploited and hence to gain a common identity as a group. (pp. 17-18)

All theatrical audiences, of course, achieve a conscious collective identity of some kind but the kind of audience which fifty years ago, might have hissed *Godot* off the stage had defined and established its own identity before it went into the theatre, sometimes merely by putting on evening dress. The playwrights and actors were to a far greater extent at the mercy of the audience and complaint to the audience's view of what was decorous and reasonable and the result was naturalistic comedy and drama of a highly conventional kind. The success of *Godot* like the success of the plays of Ionesco and Pinter is an interesting cultural phenomenon in so far as it represents the evolution of the audience into a group finding its identity in the theatre rather than in the world outside. The members of the audience may be drawn mainly or exclusively from what it may still be possible to describe as the bourgeoisie, but it is not any more than the audience at a Rock Festival, collectively a bourgeois audience. A bourgeois audience would have been demanding a farce like the farces of Feydeau or Courteline or else a 'serious' play. (pp. 18-19)

Geoffrey Strickland, "The Seriousness of Samuel Beckett," in *The Cambridge Quarterly*, Vol. XV, No. 1, 1986, pp. 13-32.

SOURCES FOR FURTHER STUDY

Abbott, H. Porter. *The Fiction of Samuel Beckett: Form and Effect.* Berkeley: University of California Press, 1973, 167 p.

　　Explains the nature and purpose of Beckett's experimental fiction, focusing on works written between 1940 and 1959.

Cohn, Ruby. *Just Play: Beckett's Theater.* Princeton: Princeton University Press, 1980, 313 p.

　　Analysis of the formal and philosophical qualities of Beckett's dramatic works.

Esslin, Martin, ed. *Samuel Beckett: A Collection of Critical Essays.* Englewood Cliffs, N.J.: Prentice-Hall, 1965, 182 p.

　　Important collection of essays including pieces by Alain Robbe-Grillet and A. J. Leventhal (excerpted above) and "Three Dialogues," transcriptions of conversations between Beckett and George Duthuit in which Beckett discusses experimentation in art.

Federman, Raymond. *Journey to Chaos: Samuel Beckett's Early Fiction.* Berkeley: University of California Press, 1965, 243 p.

　　Examines Beckett's early fiction in order "to show both the gradual distintegration of form and content in Beckett's work."

Friedman, Melvin J., ed. *Samuel Beckett Now: Critical Approaches to His Novels, Poetry, and Plays.* Chicago: The University of Chicago Press, 275 p.

　　Collection of essays including "The Elusive Ego: Beckett's M's," by Frederick J. Hoffman and "Beckettian Paradox: Who Is Telling the Truth?" by Raymond Federman. The book ends with "Samuel Beckett: A Checklist of Criticism," compiled by Jackson R. Bryer.

Mercier, Vivian. *Beckett/Beckett.* New York: Oxford University Press, 1977, 254 p.

　　Conceives of Beckett's body of work as an illustration of the constant struggle between intellect and emotion.

Aphra Behn

1640?-1689

(Pseudonym of Aphra Johnson or Aphra Amis; also Aphara, Ayfara, and Afray; also wrote under pseudonyms Astrea and Astraea) English novelist, dramatist, poet, essayist, and translator.

INTRODUCTION

Behn is best remembered as the first English woman to earn her living solely by writing, and she is credited with influencing the development of the English novel toward realism. Attributing her success to her "ability to write like a man," she competed professionally with the prominent "wits" of Restoration England, including George Etherege, William Wycherley, John Dryden, and William Congreve. Behn's writings catered to the libertine tastes of King Charles II and his supporters. Her works, especially her dramas, are usually coarse, witty farces that focus on the amatory adventures of her characters. Occasionally they satirize the political and social events of the era. Behn's most enduring work is the novel *Oroonoko; or, The Royal Slave* (1688). This work is one of the earliest novels to use a realistic technique, and the title character is often regarded as the first portrait of the "noble savage" in English literature.

Behn's birthplace and date of birth, as well as the identity of her parents, have never been conclusively established. However, it is generally agreed that she and her family sailed to Surinam in South America, most likely in 1663, and that her father, who had been appointed lieutenant-general there, died en route. Living in Surinam for several months before the Dutch takeover and her return to England, Behn accumulated colorful impressions of the country, which she later recorded in *Oroonoko*. It is speculated that after returning to England in 1664 she married a man of Dutch descent. Behn seems to have been wealthy during this time: she was popular at the court of Charles II and admired for her charm and wit. However, her husband died shortly after their marriage and, for reasons unknown, she was left an impoverished widow. In 1666, Charles II employed Behn, a staunch royalist, to spy on a disaffected English group in Antwerp. Though the mission provided the crown with valuable information, Behn was not paid for her espionage efforts. She returned to England and spent a brief time in debtor's prison before deciding to, as she said, "write for bread." Behn's decision to join London's Grub Street hacks was unprecedented. Until this time a few women had been writers, but they were aristocrats who merely dabbled in the arts, and their works were not taken seriously. Behn's first play, *The Forced Marriage; or, The Jealous Bridegroom* (1670), demonstrates her familiarity with stage techniques, and the popularity of the work proved that a woman could write as bawdy a play as could a man. Behn's work was attacked as immoral by many of her contemporaries. Undaunted by the criticism, she continued to write and spent much of her time defending her works against charges of indecency—charges based primarily on the fact that the works were written by a woman. Behn lived an impecunious life as an author, and her material hardships contributed to a prolonged illness in her later years. She died in 1689 and was honored with burial in Westminster Abbey.

Most of Behn's early dramas mirror the romantic tragi-comedies popularized by Francis Beaumont and John Fletcher during the Jacobean period. Although her plots were hardly complicated or original—many were freely borrowed from both English and foreign authors, a common practice of the time—Behn wrote with wit, vitality, and a dramatic sense for creative staging. *The Forced Marriage* comically introduces Behn's first candid expressions regarding arranged marriages, while her second drama, *The Amorous Prince: or, The Curious Husband* (1671), portrays the difficulties of friendship between lovers. These works explicitly depict adulterous bedroom scenes and players appear in "night attire"—bold stage situations even for Restoration drama. Both of these works were popular successes and encouraged Behn to produce *The Dutch Lover* in 1673. This third play weaves together a comic and a serious plot, as several sets of lovers cavort through episodes of mistaken identities, masquerades, and love trysts. According to Frederick M. Link, "the number of plots [in *The Dutch Lover*] and their intricate fusing are clear signs of the influence of Spanish intrigue comedy" on Behn's literary work, and the complexity of such comedy "permitted full display of her superior craftsmanship." This play also contains some of Behn's most outspoken ideas on sexual freedom for men and women. In addition, the play's pastoral poem, "The Willing Mistress," freely discusses female sexual desire and has been read as a feminine counterpart to Andrew Marvell's poem "To His Coy Mistress." *The Dutch Lover* was not a popular success, and Behn was attacked by Puritan critics who found her work lewd and immoral. In a preface to the printed version of *The Dutch Lover,* Behn maintained that it was not the purpose of the stage to reform the audience's morals, but rather to entertain.

Behn's most productive and financially successful literary years were between 1676 and 1682. Her best-known work of this period is the drama *The Rover; or, The Banished Cavalier, Part I* (1677). Like *The Dutch Lover, The Rover* combines farce and intrigue with mistaken identities and masquerades. Allardyce Nicoll noted that *The Rover* is important as an expression of "the callousness of the age, a callousness that was more disastrous and soul-searching than the vilest libertinism." *The Roundheads; or, The Good Old Cause* (1681), Behn's first attempt to fuse comedy and politics, displays her Tory sympathies by portraying Whig politicians as purely comic figures. The play has been called a failure not because of Behn's blatant partisanship but because of the drama's clumsy construction. Behn's second attempt at political satire was much more successful. *The City Heiress; or, Sir Timothy Treat-all* (1682) was well-received by audiences, and critics regard it among her best comedies. As usual, *The City Heiress* utilizes several sets of lovers to convey Behn's innovative thoughts on marriage, love, and sexual freedom, but in this work her political satire is more artfully integrated into the framework of the drama. Behn's political commentaries were halted in 1682 when she was arrested for a written attack on the Duke of Monmouth, an English rebel and claimant to the throne. For the remainder of her life, she wrote only poetry and fiction to support herself.

Written during the last phase of Behn's literary career, *Oroonoko* is her most acclaimed work. According to Behn, the story of the Coramantien prince Oroonoko and his beautiful West Indian lover Imoinda is based on her own "true," "eyewitness" accounts of events in Surinam. The first-person narrative gives verisimilitude to the novel, as does the vividly described local color, and the theme of the natural goodness of the "noble savage" is skillfully exploited through juxtaposition with the barbarity of "civilized" English intruders. While some critics believe that *Oroonoko* is pure fabrication, others contend that most of Behn's narrative is true, though they admit that she may have used George Warren's travel book, *An Impartial Description of Surinam,* to embellish the novel with exotic details. Many commentators regard the work as an early attempt at realism in literature, and the novel has been seen as a precursor to the works of Daniel Defoe. *Oroonoko* also holds an important place in English literature as one of the first social statements against slavery. Although Behn was not truly an abolitionist but merely the author of a romantic tale, most credit her with antislavery sentiments and some commentators have compared *Oroonoko* to Harriet Beecher Stowe's nineteenth-century novel *Uncle Tom's Cabin,* which inspired widespread abolitionist feelings in the United States.

Behn was a controversial and vital figure during her lifetime. Disparagingly immortalized in Alexander Pope's couplet—"The stage how loosely does Astrea tread / Who fairly puts all characters to bed"—she dared to expose the hypocrisy of the era by advocating, through both her literary works and her manner of living, individual freedom for women in matters of love, marriage, and sexual expression. Although her works never equaled the polished, sophisticated writings of her more prominent contemporaries, such as Dryden or Congreve, they remain among the best surviving mirrors of their age—uniquely so for being the work of a woman.

(For further information about Behn's life and works, see *Dictionary of Literary Biography*, Vols. 39, 80 and *Literature Criticism from 1400 to 1800*, Vol. 1.)

CRITICAL COMMENTARY

ROSAMOND GILDER

(essay date 1931)

[An American drama critic, editor, and author, Gilder worked on the staff of *Theatre Arts Monthly* for over twenty-four years, first as the journal's drama critic and eventually as its editor in chief. She is the editor of several theater anthologies and author of *Enter the Actress: The First Woman in Theatre* (1931). In the following excerpt from that work, she argues that Behn is at her weakest when sentiment enters into her plays and at her strongest when she follows her natural talents at intrigue, wit, and farce.]

Aphra Behn was not only the first woman to succeed as a professional playwright, she was also in many ways the first modern—the first exponent of the revolutionary idea that men and women are created with an equal aptitude for life, liberty, and the pursuit of happiness. Finding herself 'forced to write for bread and not ashamed to own it,' Aphra Behn boldly entered the lists with the other playwrights of her day and carried off a not unworthy trophy. If she did not have the originality of Etherege, the force of Wycherley, and the incomparable refinement and polish of Congreve, her work will bear comparison with many writers of her period. She was one of the most popular and prolific of Restoration dramatists, and the charm of her personality, the vigour of her pen, and the honeyed sweetness of her verse are a delight to this day. (p. 174)

Mrs. Behn's earliest plays are of a romantic seriodramatic trend. *The Amorous Prince* . . . is of this school. The prologue describes it as

A damn'd intrigue of an unpracticed muse,
Not serious, nor yet comick, what is't then?
The imperfect issue of a lukewarm brain.

Which, to a modern reader, is not inapt as a description of this type of stilted romantic tale. *The Young King, or*

The Mistake, founded on an episode in La Calprenède's *Cléopâtre,* produced several years later, is of the same general description. It is supposed to be Mrs. Behn's first play, refused by the managers, and later rewritten and produced at the Duke's Theatre. In these three plays, as also in her one tragedy, *Abdelazer, or, The Moor's Revenge,* we see Aphra under the influence of her reading of the popular novels and tragedies of the day and in the mood, sentimental and grandiose, which was as distinctly a part of the Restoration atmosphere as the dissolute comedy for which it has become a synonym. *The Amorous Prince* is written in blank and rhymed verse as are also *The Forc'd Marriage, The Young King,* and *Abdelazer.* The first is touched with the romantic element we associate with *Twelfth Night* and moves with a decorousness that Aphra did not long maintain. There are Shakespearean reminiscences, too, in the scene where Cloris, 'in male attire,' woos her inconstant lover in words that echo Viola's—

Of her it was I learn'd to speak and sigh,
And look, as oft you say, I do on you.

But Mrs. Behn's individual talent was beginning to show itself. She is a master hand at 'the conduct of a plot,' and in these early plays her skill develops rapidly. With *The Dutch Lover,* produced in February, 1672, her mastery of the comedy of intrigue is plainly evident. (pp. 184-85)

In *The Rover* we have Mrs. Behn in her best vein of romantic intrigue, spiced with wit and sauced with buffoonery and displaying in the leading characters a high-spirited, rollicking adventurousness that has its own special charm. (p. 186)

In *The Town Fopp, or, Sir Timothy Tawdrey,* Mrs. Behn makes her first excursion into the type of comedy chiefly associated with the Restoration. The scene of her play is London, and the characters are akin to those

---

Principal Works

The Forced Marriage; or, The Jealous Bridegroom (drama) 1670

The Amorous Prince; or, The Curious Husband (drama) 1671

The Dutch Lover (drama) 1673

Abdelazer; or, The Moor's Revenge (drama) 1676

The Town Fop; or, Sir Timothy Tawdrey (drama) 1676

The Rover; or, The Banished Cavalier, Part I (drama) 1677

Sir Patient Fancy (drama) 1678

The Feigned Courtesans; or, A Night's Intrigue (drama) 1679

The Roundheads; or, The Good Old Cause (drama) 1681

The Second Part of the Rover (drama) 1681

The City Heiress; or, Sir Timothy Treat-all (drama) 1682

Love Letters between a Nobleman and His Sister (fictional letters) 1684

Poems upon Several Occasions, with a Voyage to the Island of Love (poetry) 1684

The Luckey Chance; or, An Alderman's Bargain (drama) 1686

The Emperor of the Moon (drama) 1687

The Fair Jilt; or, The History of Prince Tarquin and Miranda (novel) 1688

The History of the Nun; or, The Fair Vow-Breaker (novel) 1688

Oroonoko; or, The Royal Slave (novel) 1688

The Lucky Mistake (novel) 1689

The Histories and Novels of the Late Ingenious Mrs. Behn (dramas and novels) 1696

Love Letters to a Gentleman (letters) 1696

The Plays, Histories, and Novels of the Ingenious Mrs. Aphra Behn. 6 vols (dramas and novels) 1871

The Works of Aphra Behn. 6 vols. (dramas, poetry, and novels) 1915

Selected Writings of the Ingenious Mrs. Aphra Behn (novels, dramas, poetry, and essays) 1950

The Novels of Mrs. Aphra Behn (novels) 1969

---

first introduced to the stage by George Etherege and epitomised in his Sir Foppling Flutter who had taken the town by storm only the year before. The comedy of manners had just burst upon a delighted society, which saw in it, not what Charles Lamb so engagingly describes as a world apart, a Utopia of Gallantry where no cold moral reigns, but a vivid and speaking likeness of the times. (p. 188)

Mrs. Behn never achieved the ironic detachment, the crisp, elegant, indifference of the masters of the genre, but she aims many a pointed shaft at the follies of her day and her dialogue is fresh and vigorous. In Sir Timothy Tawdrey she draws one of the typical butts and laughing-stocks of the true wits of the age. He is the false variety, the sham gallant, the base imitation of an ideal of sophistication, who is 'fain to speak in the vulgar modish style of this damn'd Leud Town, and Railly Matrimony and the rest,' to the scorn and disgust of the real gentlemen of the play. There is a strong element of romantic intrigue still evident, however, and realistic scenes in a London brothel are incongruously mixed with blank verse despairs and heroic love-makings.

Sir Patient Fancy, given the following year, is a more uniform production and the best of her comedies of the 'manners' type. It is modelled largely on Molière, as are so many of the Restoration plays, but the plot is more intricate and the action more farcical. (pp. 188-89)

Mrs. Behn followed *Sir Patient* with a return to her favourite type of theatre—the comedy of romantic intrigue. The scene of *The Feign'd Curtizans, or, A Night's Intrigue,* is laid in Rome and the plot, entirely of Aphra's own devising, is one of those involved affairs that so much delighted her contemporaries. These complicated plots were evidently the cross-word puzzles of a day deprived of that form of intellectual stimulation, for it requires a lively attention and no little skill to unravel their intricacies. They are a direct descendant of the *commedia dell'arte* scenario, furbished up for the taste of the day. . . . *The Feign'd Curtizans* contains every ingredient the formula demands—several pairs of lovers, innumerable disguisings, girls dressed as men, sword-play, masques, music, mummery, love-making and slapstick, all combined in a quick-paced entertainment of which the text can give only the faintest echo. (p. 189)

Aphra Behn's wit has . . . barely succeeded in saving her writings from neglect and her fame from obloquy. Only in recent years has criticism shaken off the purely moralistic attitude and approached her writings with an open mind. Her latest biographers and editors have done much to rescue her from the Chamber of Horrors in which the Victorians had confined her, and set her once more in her proper place on the Restoration stage. That stage has disappeared from actuality, and with it Aphra Behn's plays which were so closely adapted to the needs and tastes of the theatre of the moment that they could not long survive its destruction. To-day we prefer a different order of bedroom farce. Mrs. Behn would undoubtedly be as horrified by some of the things she might see on our stage and in our moving pictures as Macaulay was by everything he read of hers. Nor should she be judged alone and without reference to the general tenor of her age. As Dryden pointed out, it was not only the Restoration stage that was licentious. The example of the Court and the life of the town was frankly pleasureseeking and disillusioned. The playwrights were preoccupied with the aesthetics of gallantry rather than the ethics of love. Aphra, for all her looseness of tread, was far from being the worst offender, as even her sharpest critics have been forced to acknowledge, but the fact that she was a woman and yet failed in the pretty prerogative of her sex, and, 'instead of raising man to woman's moral standards, sank woman to the level of man's coarseness,' could not be forgiven. (pp. 194-95)

Aphra Behn's plays taken as a whole are to-day chiefly interesting in that they present an illuminating cross-section of Restoration drama. She touched on almost every phase of dramatic expression, from the extremes of Love and Honour grandeurs to the wildest kind of theatrical horseplay. If she has not survived, as Dryden, Otway, Etherege, Wycherley, and Congreve have survived, it is because she was prone to mix her mediums. Highly sensitive to the tendency and point of view of her day, she reflected too many contradictory attitudes to produce a clear-cut result. Her poetic vein was not sufficiently sustained to carry her into the finer flights of tragedy, where her sincerity and passion might have found its natural outlet.

Her comedy, where it follows Etherege in a reflection of the manners and customs of those around her, slips again and again into a fine frenzy of feeling that shivers the brittle artificiality of this type of play. A scene such as that in *The City Heiress* in which Lady Gaillard, having been seduced in the usual airy manner by the typical gallant Wilding, returns to the stage with a sudden burst of Love and Honour emotions—'Undone, undone! Unhand me, false, forsworn!' is distressingly out of keeping with the tenor of the play. We feel like echoing Wilding's own protest when his mistress indulges in this sort of rant: 'Do you bring me into your chamber to preach virtue to me—what other business can I have but Love and Rapture and . . . ' Indeed, no one has any business in a thoroughgoing Restoration comedy unless he can be consistently gay and careless about sex. When Aphra allows sentiment to intervene, she spoils the picture. Her happiest creations are, in consequence, the pure comedies of intrigue, where the complexity of plot, the farcical treatment of underplot, and the complete artificiality of the situations evolved, preclude the possibility of taking the multitudinous couplings as anything but a merry jest. Willmore in *The Rover* is an excellent and completely successful exponent of the creed. (pp. 196-97)

[He announces it in] conversation with his friend Belville who asks his help in adventure:

BELV. Will you not assist me?
WILL. I know not what thou mean'st, but I'll make one at any Mischief where a Woman's concern'd—but she'll be grateful to us for the favour, will she not?
BELV. How mean you?
WILL. How should I mean? Thou know'st there's but one way for a Woman to oblige me.
BELV. Don't Prophane—the Maid is nicely virtuous.
WILL. Why, pox, then she's fit for nothing but a Husband!

Here in a sentence is the Restoration creed, the Restoration comedy attitude, the formula for almost every Restoration play, and no one knew better than Aphra Behn how to weave a complex adventure about this central theme. Her originality was less marked than her ingenuity, but the results were equally entertaining to her audiences. Perhaps her most distinguishing gift as a playwright was her power of vigorous and racy dialogue. She had a rich flow of verbal expression, a wealth and appositeness of phrase, that makes it possible to read her plays with pleasure to-day when theme and method have lost their interest. The cadence of Restoration prose lost nothing in her hands, though the speed and carelessness of her composition can often be detected. There is an exuberant vitality in her writing that shows a talent worthy, perhaps, of better uses than that to which it was dedicated.

Her poetry, too, indicates her latent power, even though it falls short of any transcendent achievement. In a day when every one wrote verse, Astraea's songs stand out as the product of a true poetic vein, neither exalted nor sustained, but genuinely lyric. Some of her songs are truly lovely in the patterned, artificial style of her choice. She had a delicate sense of the melody of words, an easy, flowing fancy, and, though her verse plays endlessly on the one theme of love and amorous dalliance, it yet achieves at times a true grace and a flowery perfection. Her poems, as well as her novels, were extraordinarily popular both in her own day and later.

She carried to the last extreme the sensuous, pastoral-passionate descriptions, so dear to the 'refined age' in which she lived. The same pen that could write the crude scenes of *The Luckey Chance* or of *Sir Patient Fancy* could pen the airy and sentimental trifles that fill *The Lovers Watch* and *Lycidus*. Her variations on her theme produced not a few lovely harmonies, which can well bear the test of time. In the midst of much artifice and conceit, we can hear again and again a true lyric note. . . . (pp. 197-98)

There is a gallant courage in her career, as in the high carriage of her head that cannot fail to provoke admiration. She was a woman not supremely gifted but supremely daring, one whose genius lay in an acceptance of the world as she found it rather than in any impulse toward its reformation or improvement. Thoroughly of her own day, she failed, perhaps, to transcend it, and, as has been the fate of many a better man, the evil that she did has lived after her. But whatever her shortcomings, literary and human, Aphra Behn remains a striking figure in the annals of stage history. The first woman to attempt a professional career as a playwright, she has had, among women, few rivals and no superior in what Molière termed the difficult undertaking of making gentlefolk laugh. 'I take it Comedy was never meant for a converting or conforming ordinance,' she wrote in one of her prefaces, 'and I think a play is the best divertissement that wise men have. This being my opinion, I studied only to make mine as entertaining as I could.' (pp. 200-01)

Rosamond Gilder, "Aphra Behn—England's First Professional Woman Playwright," in her *Enter the Actress: The First Woman in the Theatre,* 1931. Reprint by Theatre Arts Books, 1961, pp. 173-201.

GEORGE WOODCOCK
(essay date 1948)

[Woodcock's *The Incomparable Aphra* was one of the first full-length studies of Behn's life and works. In the following excerpt from that work, he discusses Behn's *Oroonoko* as an important precursor of the idea of the "noble savage" and a major influence on the use of realism in literature.]

In her age Mrs. Behn was regarded as a great dramatist and poetess. But in the perspective of social and literary history, it is her fiction and the almost adventitious fact of her struggle to live as a pioneer woman writer that contain her most influential achievements. These, indeed, were the aspects which to her contemporaries would have seemed of least importance. Her novels were regarded as mere ephemerae produced to satisfy an economic need, while her struggle for the recognition of woman's right to live by intellectual work stirred so little real attention that, outside her own writings, there is almost no reference to it in contemporary literature—certainly none that recognised its importance as the beginning of a great social revolution which would result in an entire change of feminine status. (p. 226)

It was [her] concern for man as an individual demanding room to grow freely that led her into those lines of thought and action which represent her historically important contributions.

Firstly, she soon realised the kind of institutions in society that make men the slaves they are, and, from the number of references in her works seems to have thought much about them. Some she thought could be attacked in topical satire, and thus she used her plays to lash these superficial evils of the age. But there were others that she felt must be endured, since they seemed to be inextricably bound up with the society in which she lived. They were such institutions as monarchy, religion, laws, means of interfering with the natural freedom of men which were evil in themselves but with which it would be hard to dispense.

Yet, while Aphra Behn was not revolutionary enough to envisage the early destruction of such institutions—and in this lagged behind some of her contemporaries, like Winstanley and, on the question of monarchy, Algernon Sidney and James Harrington—she envisaged a natural goodness in man which in ideal circumstances could dispense with them. It was this idea that man left to himself was not evil that some of the really revolutionary theorists of the next century turned into a basic idea in their radical and subversive doctrines. . . . [This] concern for the natural man finds its place here and there in Aphra's plays and poems, but it is set out most explicitly in *Oroonoko,* where she describes the lives and characters of the Carib Indians she encountered in Surinam. . . . (pp. 229-30)

Here we have already, in its simple form, the great conception of natural human goodness that served as the *mythos* of the Enlightenment, and inspired such revolutionary thinkers as the Encyclopaedists, Rousseau, Voltaire, Tom Paine and Godwin, the theoreticians of a century of revolutions. In *L'Ingenu,* Voltaire's Indian who criticises the faults of Western civilisation, we have a worthy follower of Mrs. Behn's savages who emphasised the faults of their white invaders, and there is a really amazing parallel between her comment on the Caribs and the opening passage of Rousseau's *Emile.* . . . (pp. 230-31)

The eighteenth-century thinkers planned in the dark, with no direct knowledge of primitive men. Mrs. Behn had actually seen them in their communal life, and, while there is not necessarily any reason to suppose that *Oroonoko* was read by the philosophers of the Enlightenment, it represents nevertheless a brilliant anticipation of the basic theory of Rousseau and his associates, and shows that in the seventeenth century a few minds had already perceived the ideas that would mould the succeeding age. Incidentally, it is an interesting fact that modern anthropologists and such sociologists as Peter Kropotkin in his *Mutual Aid* have in fact confirmed Aphra Behn's conclusions regarding the nature of life among primitive men.

If Aphra Behn acted as an indirect predecessor of Rousseau and the school of naturalist thinkers, she wielded a direct influence over the tradition of the "noble savage" as a subject for fiction, and Oroonoko was the ancestor of a whole succession of noble Indians and Negroes who emphasised by their virtue and courage the weaknesses of their civilised neighbours. Such varied writers as Voltaire and Fenimore Cooper, Chateaubriand and Maria Edgeworth, Bernardin de Saint Pierre, Herman Melville and Captain Marryat are among her successors in this vein, while an early and very obvious descendant of Aphra's *Oroonoko* was Defoe's Man Friday.

Another of the characteristics of the naturalist trend in eighteenth-century writing—and painting as well—was a discovery of the aesthetic possibilities of natural landscapes, and this tendency had its practical application in a deliberate planning of "natural" effects to replace the formal garden of the seventeenth century. This pleasant eighteenth-century preoccupation was also foreshadowed by Mrs. Behn in her descriptions of landscape in *Oroonoko*. . . . (pp. 231-32)

Undoubtedly it was the same concern with the dignity of the individual that led Aphra Behn to write the first novel to expose the horrors of slavery. Some critics have attempted to depreciate the importance of *Oroonoko* as an anti-slavery tract. Yet the fact remains that in writing such a novel Aphra Behn made a complete departure from the subject-matter of seventeenth-century fiction and, while the Negro prince himself retained many of the Amadis-like qualities of the traditional hero of romance, the conditions in which he was placed were wholly unlike those of any novel before Aphra Behn's time. To choose slavery for the theme of an unconventional novel shows a genuine concern with this question; evidently Aphra's own experiences in Surinam had left her with a vivid idea of the indignities to which human beings were submitted by such an institution.

Oroonoko, in fact, shows that individualism, which in the average Restoration wit was directed to a callous search after his own pleasure, turned into a concern for the well–being of other individuals, and the book breathes a deeply humane attitude which is only rarely to be found among Aphra Behn's contemporaries. (pp. 232-33)

For her pioneer work as an opponent of slavery and a precursor of the abolitionists, Aphra Behn undoubtedly deserves greater credit than has ever been accorded her. But it is doubtful whether she contributed more by this achievement than by her struggles for the emancipation of women from the professional, educational and intellectual fetters they had borne up to her time. (p. 235)

[Her struggle for personal liberation, for her own right to move as an equal among the male writers] was a solitary struggle, for until after her death she seems to have remained the only professional woman writer.

But she had opened a wide trail through the prejudices of English society, and by the time she died it was impossible to deny that a woman could write as well as a man, with both learning and style; there was no man, except Dryden, who could show greater versatility or a wider range of literary achievements. (pp. 235-36)

The last sphere where Mrs. Behn's influence has been important is in the development of the English novel . . . [She] began the tendency toward realism which proved the most fruitful tradition of English fiction. Her little romances of English life, her satirical stories like *The Court of the King of Bantam,* and especially *Oroonoko,* with its intense local colour, all had their influence on the development of this tradition, which can be seen very strongly in Defoe, who even adopted her technical devices for obtaining verisimilitude, and, less obviously, in Richardson and Fielding, whose picaresque novels followed much the same general pattern as those of Aphra Behn.

Not merely did she try to give realism to her stories by telling them as "true" narratives; she also attempted to build a rich background of detail and local colour against which her characters could act their parts. The background, indeed, is often more real than the actors. In *The Fair Jilt,* for instance, the blood-soaked sawdust for which the onlookers are ready to scramble gives a greater reality to the story than many of the improbable acts of the hero and heroine. *The Black Lady* is such a living story because it is related so closely to the details of London life, and *The Court of the King of Bantam* owes at least part of its quality to the fact that it is acted in those very streets where Aphra walked and jested. And *Oroonoko* is so unquestionably the first English realistic novel, not for the deeds or speeches of its characters, but for the rich and carefully constructed background of detail: the scenes of Surinam, the pleasures of Aphra's girlhood, the roguery of the colonial administration, the indignities to which the slaves were subjected, all of which give a conviction that carries the artificial figure of Oroonoko into the sunlight of reality. Yet Mrs. Behn was at times capable of considerable realism in character-drawing and psychological processes. There is a true and direct satire in such a figure as the unpleasant procuress in *The Unfortunate Happy Lady,* or the snobbish Mr. Prayfast in *The Wandering Beauty.* A deep psychological insight into the process of guilt and remorse is shown in Isabella's mental struggle in *The Fair Vow-Breaker,* while there is also acute perception in the final action of the heroine in *The Unfortunate Happy Lady,* where she not merely forgives her brother for his betrayals, but even helps to rehabilitate him in the world.

It is as a founder of the school of realistic novel-writing that Mrs. Behn is perhaps most important. Yet it should be remembered that such novels as *The Fair Jilt* and *The Lucky Mistake* also had their influence on the parallel romantic tendency which culminated in the great Gothic novelists of the late eighteenth century. . . . (pp. 237-38)

I have indicated the extent of Aphra Behn's contributions to the development of literature and social ideas since her own day. Yet, although in some respects she was enough in advance of her time to be able to express ideas more in keeping with the late eighteenth than the late seventeenth century, she was in other ways very much the child of her period, and even when she fought against its generally accepted standards, she was merely expressing a tendency towards innovation and intellectual revolution that was one of the strong currents of Restoration society. Above the turbulence of daily life, the intense political and religious conflict, the continual manoeuvring for power that resulted in a perpetual instability of authority, there emerged certain definite trends of social change, which became embodied in a few individuals more sensitive and original in personality and mind than their contemporaries. . . . Among this comparatively small group of individuals who almost symbolise the social awakening that began in this period, Aphra Behn holds a unique place. The pioneer of women's emancipation, the anticipator of abolitionism, the advocate of free marriage, the precursor of Rousseau, and the inventress of much that has become permanent in the English novel as it has been developed since her time, as well as the authoress of some of the best songs and plays in the English tongue, she holds a place second to none of her contemporaries as a historically important figure. (pp. 238-39)

George Woodcock, in his *The Incomparable Aphra*, T. V. Boardman and Company Limited, 1948, 248 p.

MARTINE WATSON BROWNLEY

(essay date 1977)

[In the following essay, Brownley examines the narrative voice in *Oroonoko*.]

In the past the narrator of *Oroonoko* has, with very few exceptions, been studied mainly in terms of the life and ideas of Aphra Behn. Since what little we know of Behn's life is just as exciting and romantic as any material in her writings, it is easy to see why the narrative *persona* of *Oroonoko* has taken second place to the woman who was traveler, spy, pioneer female author, and political intriguer. For the moment controversy over Behn's biography seems to have died down. Undoubtedly the lull is temporary, for many fascinating questions remain unanswered. Nevertheless, the pause

offers a useful chance to consider the role of the narrator within the context of the novel itself. *Oroonoko's* importance in early English prose fiction has long been established, and, as George Guffey points out, the "particularly well-defined narrator" [see Sources for Further Study] is one important element which distinguishes the work from other fiction of the time. Functioning as a strongly felt presence throughout *Oroonoko,* the narrator unifies the novel, enhances the tenuous realism of the basically heroic story, and offers a viable standard of judgment for the readers.

Since in general what the narrator says is more important than anything she actually does in the context of the story of *Oroonoko,* narrative control of language emerges as one of her most important functions. Other than the character of Oroonoko himself, the voice of the narrator is the major unifying element in the novel. Behn carefully develops a distinctive voice for her narrative *persona;* in *Oroonoko* the contrast of realism and romanticism in the narrator's expression gives the style its unique quality. This contrast in style, of course, reflects the uneasy alliance in *Oroonoko* of romantic elements from the heroic play and realistic elements later prominent in the novel. The synthesis is not entirely successful, but Behn's manipulation of the narrator's romantic and realistic styles to control point of view accounts for some of the success that she managed to achieve in *Oroonoko.*

The romantic element is apparent in the narrator's eloquent style, found particularly in the elaborate rhetorical speeches which reflect Behn's dramatic background. The overstatement and hackneyed imagery typical of the heroic play also occur, as one would expect, whenever narrator or characters speak of love. When Oroonoko faces separation from Imoinda by military duty, "every Day seem'd a tedious Year till he saw his *Imoinda*"; after their reunion in Surinam, the lovers agree that "even Fetters and Slavery were soft and easy, and would be supported with Joy and Pleasure; while they cou'd be so happy to possess each other." The narrator pulls out all the stops in her heroic description of Oroonoko's appearance, which abounds in superlatives. His shape is "the most exact that can be fancy'd"; his mouth is "the finest shaped that could be seen"; he has "the best Grace in the World." She combines the best of nature and of art to depict him: "The most famous Statuary cou'd not form the Figure of a Man more admirably turn'd from head to foot," while "bating his Colour, there could be Nothing in Nature more beautiful, agreeable, and handsome" than his face. Having exhausted superlatives in describing Oroonoko, she can only do justice to Imoinda's charms by calling her a fit consort for Oroonoko, "the beautiful Black *Venus* to our young *Mars.*" With one exception, the hyperbolic heroic style is always used in connection with Oroonoko and his activities. Only Oroonoko's execution, when he is finally destroyed by men who cannot tolerate what he represents, is described in realistic terms. In this passage the straightforward language heightens Oroonoko's heroic actions by the narrator's grimly effective contrast of style and content. Through the rest of the novel, the heroic style sets him apart within the narrative just as his ideal love, truth, and honor separate him from the ordinary standards of those around him.

Oroonoko is at least partially the story of these ordinary people and their reaction to the extraordinary. Neither these people nor the narrator herself could be appropriately delineated in heroic terms, and so realistic colloquial elements are a part of the narrative style. This informal oral style suggests Behn's contemporary reputation as a witty and enjoyable conversationalist. The narrative is filled with conversational insertions: "I had forgot to tell you"; "as I said before"; "I must say thus much." Using this style, the narrator adds realism by infusing her own personality into the narrative, enhancing the story with her own experiences—"I have seen 'em [the Blacks] so frequently blush, and look pale"—and her personal opinions—"For my part, I took 'em for Hobgoblins, or Fiends, rather than Men." To modern tastes, this realistic element is the most familiar and pleasing aspect of the style in *Oroonoko.* Unfortunately, though the oral style adds realism and is most effective at times, the colloquial narrative is too often difficult to follow. Poorly structured sentences, the mixing of verb tenses, and especially pronouns with ambiguous references hinder the reader's understanding of the action. The clumsiness can be defended, just as Defoe's similar carelessness has been, by suggesting that the author intended the grammatical mistakes to characterize the narrator's mind and outlook. In both cases any gain in characterization would seem to be more than offset by the reader's confusion. The speed at which Behn and Defoe were known to produce also seems to indicate that authorial carelessness rather than deliberate artistry in characterization caused the stylistic problems. That Behn managed in any way to fuse the realistic and the romantic styles in *Oroonoko* is an achievement of sorts. The effectiveness of the narrative voice unifies the disparate elements and appropriately focuses point of view. But style cannot finally account either for Behn's success in *Oroonoko,* or for her purposes in delineating the narrator.

Despite its inadequacy, the fact that the realistic style is present at all in *Oroonoko* leads us to the major function of the narrator. It is she who grounds the improbable romantic story in at least a semblance of reality. Very few of the other elements in the novel provide realism. The action, with its fantastic coincidences, noble posturings, and terrible catastrophes, is straight from the pure romance of heroic drama. Behn had chosen backgrounds which would arouse interest; Cora-

mentien provides the remote and glamorous setting typical of a heroic play, while Surinam combines similar exoticism with the topicality appealing to a public eager for information about the colonies in America. Horace Walpole, writing in the middle of the next century, indicates that because of the West Indian War, "I read nothing but American voyages, and histories of plantations and settlements," but even in times of peace Europeans enthusiastically devoured accounts of the new world. Although the African background is not portrayed realistically in any way, the descriptions of Surinam may well have seemed realistic enough to a public accustomed to paradisiacal accounts of the newly discovered hemisphere. Today, despite establishment of Behn's accuracy in describing parts of the background, the Edenic fantasy in too many of her descriptions makes the locale seem just as romantically unreal as the actions.

The characters of *Oroonoko* are in general no more realistic than the action and setting of the novel. Most of the characters in the story are described in exaggerated terms, emerging as excessively good or extraordinarily bad. Practically everyone in the novel is exceptional: Oroonoko and Imoinda are of course perfect; the Council "consisted of such notorious Villains as *Newgate* never transported"; Aboan is "not only one of the best Quality, but a man extremely well made and beautiful"; Banister is "a Fellow of Absolute Barbarity." Even the somewhat colorless Trefy is described as "a Man of Great Wit, and fine Learning," and "a Man of so excellent Wit and Parts." Only the narrator emerges as rather ordinary. Of her own characteristics, she heavily emphasizes only her credibility, obviously performing the standard obeisance to the anti-fictional bias of the age. She devotes the first two paragraphs of the story to establishing her reliability in the narrative role, assuring the reader of the literal truth of her tale and the trustworthiness of her sources. Astutely flattering her audience, she emphasizes her conscientiousness as a narrator; she is in complete control of her material and recognizes her obligations not to tell anything which "might prove tedious and heavy to my Reader, in a World where he finds Diversions for every Minute, new and strange." During the rest of the novel she establishes a pleasant enough narrative presence. Her most important trait is her fundamental decency and humanity, apparent in all of her actions and remarks. Critics note that she does try to emphasize her own importance whenever possible, but despite her insistence on her position, neither her remarks nor her actions establish her as an unusual person. No reader would characterize the narrator in the glowing terms she uses to describe the other characters in the story; she emerges as a character with whom the reader finds it easy enough to identify. Throughout the novel the narrator seems to be an ordinary woman in an extraordinary position, and she therefore adds a sense of realism lacking in the action, setting, and other characters in the story.

Thus in a strange and exotic world of romantic wonders, the narrator helps the reader to keep his bearings. She adds realism to the story, offering a standard of normalcy in an environment of extraordinary people and actions. As such, she can fulfill her other important narrative function, which is to provide an acceptable standard of judgment in ordinary terms for the events and characters in *Oroonoko.* Oroonoko himself of course provides the noblest example of human excellencies in the novel, but he is ideal rather than real. As Lore Metzger points out [in her introduction to a 1973 edition], Oroonoko's "heroic ideals cannot prevail in the real world." The novel requires standards in ordinary as well as ideal terms, and the narrator, a decent, average woman, can focus the scale of values in the realistic terms required. As a participant in the story she several times serves as a link between Oroonoko and the European world, and in the novel she interprets him to this world. It is her standards which finally emerge as most interesting to the reader, because of their possible applicability to his own experience.

The narrator provides standards of judgment at several levels for her audience. At the lowest level, she seeks to make the unusual comprehensible to her English audience by comparisons with things familiar to them. The Amazon is "almost as broad as the River of Thames"; the Indian stools are painted "in a sort of Japan-work"; the grove of trees near her house spreads "about half the length of the *Mall.*" But the narrator also has some advanced ideas to share with the audience. As Behn openly avowed, her main purpose in all of her writing was entertainment, but throughout *Oroonoko* she does not hesitate to include social, political, and moral observations in the narrator's commentary when opportunities arise. The narrator never interrupts the progress of the story by preaching; the remarks are brief, pithy, and usually pointed. Almost every commentator has pointed out that the ideas on civilization, religion, and morality expressed in *Oroonoko* presage those of the French thinkers of the Enlightenment. Although Oroonoko is clearly not a noble savage, Behn uses him in the way philosophers would later use the figure. As Haydn White points out, the myth was generally used not to gain better treatment for native people, but to attack "the concept of 'nobility' in Europe." Metzger, Guffey, and other critics have shown that claims for *Oroonoko* as an early anti-slavery novel are unjustified, and the narrator definitely does not finally indict the entire institution of slavery. She fails entirely to exploit the ironic potential in such situations as Oroonoko's inciting the men he himself enslaved to rebel against their masters. Nevertheless, the narrator exposes through Oroonoko the mis-

treatment of slaves, and his speeches are a powerful condemnation of the entire system. If he is not radical, she at least shows substantial humanitarian concern and sympathy. Always concerned with substance over form, her anger flashes against injustice and hypocrisy throughout the novel; her condemnation of certain practices in *"Christian* Countries, where they prefer the bare Name of Religion; and, without Vertue or Morality, think that sufficient" is typical.

Like all good stories, Behn's entertaining tale is an exploration of human nature, and in *Oroonoko* she knows what happens when the real confronts the ideal, with the narrator serving as a standard of judgment. Ostensibly the narrator is judging Oroonoko and the unprincipled inhabitants of Coramentien and Surinam, proving his unparalleled nobility and their irredeemable wickedness. In *Oroonoko* the weak are those who lack power as well as principles. The slaves in Surinam are of this class and their reaction to Oroonoko takes two extreme forms. They either worship him—he is, after all, described in divine metaphors throughout the novel—or they actively participate in destroying him. On the other side are those unprincipled men who wield power. More threatened than the weak by the confrontation with the ideal, they rely on deceit. They either play on Oroonoko's noble nature to save themselves (Coramantien's old king) or abuse his honor and trust to destroy him (the slave trader and the colonial administrators). Whether weak or strong, those lacking principles cannot live with the ideal in their midst. Such judgments are too obvious to be particularly interesting, but in the process of making them, the narrator also makes one more judgment. Guffey points out that in her hero Behn emphasizes the type rather than the individual, and the same is true for the other characters. Between the base who totally lack humanity and the heroic who live and die only for honor is a third group, in which the majority of people always fall. One of the most interesting judgments Behn finally makes through the narrator is on the narrator herself and on the ordinary, decent, principled people like her. The judgment is made implicitly through the narrator's actions at the end of the novel rather than explicitly in direct commentary.

The narrator's absence from the events at the end of her story is disturbing, and at first glance it seems to indicate sloppy craftsmanship. Her removal is presented somewhat awkwardly, and the excuses she gives for her flights seem weak for one who has previously presented herself as one of Oroonoko's strongest partisans. Yet her flights are realistic and valid in psychological terms. Despite her protestations of support for Oroonoko, the narrator has long before the end of the novel revealed a divided spirit. Her position is portrayed as ambiguous. She truly admires Oroonoko, but as a representative of western civilization her commitment to him shows a certain shakiness. Scattered remarks made in the first person plural show that she identifies with the Europeans in Surinam, although never with the colonial administrators. She is Oroonoko's supporter, but even though he has shown his devotion to honoring his commitments, she does not finally trust him. When he promises her to wait with patience for a little longer for the Lord Governor and his freedom, she does not think it "convenient to trust him much out of our view."

Her distrust of him emerges even more clearly during the rebellion. Oroonoko has previously vowed that he would never under any circumstances harm her and those around her: "As for my self, and those upon that Plantation where he was, he would sooner forfeit his eternal Liberty, and Life itself, than lift his Hand against his greatest Enemy on that place." Yet when the women hear of the revolt: "we were possess'd with extreme Fear, which no Persuasions could dissipate, that he would secure himself till night, and then, that he would come down and cut all our throats." She explains that this apprehension "made all the Females of us fly down the River, to be secured," and thus the narrator's first flight occurs. Her reactions perhaps suggest what social conditioning can do to the ordinary and decent individual; in a moment of fear, she falls back on stereotypical reactions, forgetting or distrusting all that she has learned of Oroonoko's honor and nobility. She finally is no more able than the wicked to live with the extraordinary and the ideal, because she cannot believe enough in the reality of Oroonoko's goodness to trust him fully.

This first flight to the river shows her divided spirit, her ultimate lack of commitment to the ideal under adverse circumstances. She returns, only to leave again when Oroonoko is dying, and her second flight reflects more than simply a last failure of belief in the extraordinary by the ordinary. Her excuse for leaving seems no more valid than the first one: "The Sight was ghastly: His Discourse was sad; and the earthy Smell about him so strong, that I was persuaded to leave the place for some time, (being myself but sickly, and very apt to fall into Fits of dangerous Illness upon any extraordinary Melancholy)." Similar incapacities have often enough been attributed to women under such conditions. As Johnson in his *Life of Pope* tries to account for Martha Blount's neglect of the sick poet in his last days, his first speculation is that Pope perhaps "considered her unwillingness to approach the chamber of sickness as female weakness. . . . " But the narrator has not previously shown any traits which would suggest weakness. For example, she was among three out of eighteen who went up to the Indian town when "the Hearts of some of our Company fail'd, and they would not venture on Shore." At the end of the novel, the reader gets the impression that the narrator can no lon-

ger cope with the situation and is so overwhelmed by what has happened that she can only disengage herself personally and allow events to sweep to their natural culmination in violence. It is difficult to avoid the feeling that the narrator could and should have done more. In fact, she herself directly contributes to that impression. After Oroonoko's whipping she says that had she not fled with the women, she could have prevented his mistreatment. In view of the final scene, this comment seems to be pure bravado, the last of the emphases on her personal importance inserted throughout the novel. At the end she says that even though her mother and sister were present during the terrible final mutilation and wanted to help Oroonoko, they were "not suffer'd to save him; so rude and wild were the Rabble, and so inhuman were the Justices who stood by to see the Execution. . . . " Since the narrator's position in the colony is derived from the importance of the post that her father was to have held, it would seem logical that all of his relatives would command the same kind of respect. Undoubtedly the narrator would have found herself as powerless to halt the execution as her mother and sister were.

At the end of the novel, all of the good people are ineffectual. The narrator has fled. Trefy, whose function as a foil to the wicked men who persecute Oroonoko has been pointed out by [Harrison Gray Platt, Jr., in "Astraea and Celadon: An Untouched Portrait of Aphra Behn," *PMLA*, 49 (1934), 544-59] has been lured away on false pretenses by Byam. The narrator's mother and sister can only watch ineffectually. In certain kinds of volatile situations, there is a point where the momentum of events becomes so great that any individual agents are powerless to stop the flow; a strange sense of inevitability takes over. The passions released are so violent and irrational that they seem to possess an inherent pattern, an inevitability all their own, and the culmination can only be atrocity, as it is in *Oroonoko*. It is at this point that normal standards cannot actively influence the course of events. These standards are useless because events have gone too far for normal, decent people to effectively assert their values. This sort of situation occurred on a giant scale in the French Revolution and recurs on a smaller scale in lynchings or other individual acts of mob violence. It happens whenever fanatics or evil men take control of a situation and are determined on destruction. Seen in this context, the narrator's flight emerges as realistic enough; at the end, whether or not her spirit was divided, she could not have done anything to stop the course of events.

Moreover, the narrator is no longer needed in the narrative to function as a standard of judgment for her readers. The final events are too terrible to require judgment by normal standards, just as they do not require heroic language for embellishment. Simply describing them accurately is condemnation enough, and editorial intrusions would be extraneous. The narrator's flight emphasizes that her standards cannot operate in the kind of world shown at the end of *Oroonoko.* The standards of ordinary, decent people become useless and paralyzed when madness assumes control.

Thus Behn uses her narrator in *Oroonoko* to unify and to add realism to the disparate elements of her novel. In addition, the narrator's words and actions also provide a standard of judgment for the honorable, for the wicked, and, most interestingly, for the average people she herself represents. The view of their potential for effective action in explosive situations is a bleak but starkly honest one. The ordinary man will do all that he can; after all, the people at Parham House try to aid Oroonoko, and Trefy resists with a brave ultimatum to Byam and his men. But as events assume a terrifying momentum of their own from those who intend evil, the good can only fly from the inevitable, as the narrator does, or stay to endure the pain of watching ineffectually, as her mother and sister do. The novel itself, however, indicates one further option for the ordinary people trapped in this kind of situation. They can remember, as the narrator has done in *Oroonoko,* and tell their stories again in regret, in remonstrance, and in warning. The standards of decent, average men fail in the world of *Oroonoko.* Nevertheless, the writing of this kind of novel is, indirectly, a retrospective assertion of the validity and importance of those standards, held securely within the context of an entertaining story. (pp. 174-80)

Martine Watson Brownley, "The Narrator in 'Oroonoko'," in *Essays in Literature,* Vol. 4, No. 2, Fall, 1977, pp. 174-81.

ANGELINE GOREAU

(essay date 1980)

[In the following excerpt from her *Reconstructing Aphra: A Social Biography of Aphra Behn,* Goreau examines Behn's literary achievement.]

The very act of publishing her writing would have been sufficient to destroy a lady's reputation in the seventeenth century; exposing oneself in print was a violation of feminine propriety. But Aphra offended the modesty of her sex still further by writing as her fellow playwrights did—bawdy. She obviously enjoyed it, but in any case she admitted that in order to succeed she had to write "to the taste of the age." Unfortunately, in the century that followed, the principle that what was not decent ought not to be read came to dominate. And Aphra, who had written about sex with the same

openness as her male contemporaries, was seen as infinitely more indecent, immoral, immodest, and unreadable because a woman. (p. 14)

Aphra, though she frankly rejected the appearance of modesty in her own life and in her writing created heroines who took for themselves the same swaggering sexual freedom that Restoration men in Cavalier circles enjoyed, bitterly resented being accused of immodesty by her detractors. She defended her feminine "reputation" by denying accusations—which, but for the exaggerations characteristic of slandering gossip, were more or less true. Her poems, however, like **"On Desire"** or **"The Willing Mistress"** or **"The Disappointment"** (on impotence), published her sexual stance for all who cared to see. Despite her rebellion and defiant remarks about the odious burden of feminine honor, Aphra did not seem to be able to fully rid herself of its domination. She still viewed it as an essential part of what makes a woman—particularly a young woman—attractive and desirable. In her adaptation of *The Lover's Watch,* a French etiquette book describing the contemporary stylized manner of making love, she referred to modesty as *"so commendable a virtue in the fair."* This virtue is exhibited in high degree in her heroine Cleonte (*The Dutch Lover*): when informed that she may marry the man she loves, she replies, "Sir, I must own a joy greater than is fit for a virgin to express." There is no hint of irony or distance from the character in the lines; Aphra seems to feel that this was a perfectly normal way for young women to talk. Women who talked otherwise were asking for trouble. The most striking illustration of Aphra Behn's attachment to modesty as a positive value, however, is in the description of the heroines who belong to the later period of her novels. Gracelove, the hero of *The Unfortunate Happy Lady,* falls in love with Philadelphia, partly because she steadfastly maintains her virtue in a situation where everything threatens it, her brother having imprisoned her in a brothel. (p. 39)

In the story *The Fair Jilt,* the heroine/villainess Miranda's attractions are enumerated in the following order: her physical beauty, her modesty, and last, her wit. The priority is characteristic of Aphra's fictional ladies. The two heroines of *The Lucky Mistake* are described similarly: their *"extreme beauty,"* innocence, modesty, and birth are duly noted. Finally, Aphra's most moving and sympathetic female protagonist, Imoinda, Oroonoko's bride, is hardly ever referred to without mention of her modesty. On her first appearance in the novel, the characteristics Aphra chooses to emphasize are the beauty of her *"face and person,"* her *"lovely modesty,"* and the *"softness in her look and sighs."*

Aphra Behn also created heroines of a very different sort, who rejected this image of passive femininity; but the fact that she could evoke two voices of such contrasting tenor is testimony to the ambivalent attitudes that she herself held toward the feminine behavior prescribed by her upbringing and her own instinct for freedom, which pressed toward the evolution of a new kind of heroine. (p. 40)

If Aphra Behn had courted immodesty on a symbolic level merely in the act of staging her plays or the publishing of her writing, she openly embraced it in what she wrote. She frankly addressed the question of sex and was not afraid to bring it onto the stage. Her second play, *The Amorous Prince* . . . opened on a seduction scene which had just been brought to fruition—the couple rising from their love-making. According to the stage directions, she is dressed in her "night attire" (probably a loose *robe de chambre*) and he is dressing himself; the setting is her bedroom. Not only has the act taken place outside the sanctity of marriage, but the gallant in question is not even the young lady's fiancé. By seventeenth-century definition, the scene was at least racy, and for a great many, it was out-and-out scandalous. Without a doubt, the English stage had never seen a scene like this from the pen of a woman. This was indeed a vast departure from the chaste friendships of Katherine Philips or the platonic gallantries of Mlle. de Scudéry. Aphra's version of the pastoral ideal did not portray shepherds and shepherdesses exchanging elevated vows without ever so much as touching each other; she believed that physical passion was an inseparable part of love and ought to be acknowledged as such. Women as well as men, she held, experience desire and are equally as capable of its intense expression. (p. 164)

Within the stiff form of pastoral convention, she was taking a position that was revolutionary for a woman writer of her time. Not only was such direct acknowledgment of her own desire considered unfeminine in a woman, but her equal activity in sexual advance—"and I returned the same"—must have been disconcerting even to the rakehell fops and seducers who pretended a disregard for female honor. Aphra's poem, called **"The Willing Mistress,"** was putting a period to the "Coy Mistress." She had taken a position for sexual freedom, for women as well as for men, that would make her name a scandal to be reckoned with for three centuries. Aphra's views were, of course, more complicated than a simple advocation of feminine sexual liberty: she was, first, very much aware of the practical difficulties of such a position, and second, too much subject to the conventional wisdom about women that was part of her education and upbringing to avoid equivocation. But the fact remains that she boldly ventured her stand, however much she might later attempt to elude the consequences. (p. 165)

Aphra, like the wits and libertines who were her friends, subscribed to an ideal of sexual freedom. Like them also, she regarded traditional feminine modesty as oppressive—though, as has been remarked earlier,

her attitude in the latter case was not altogether unambiguous; she had spoken of modesty elsewhere with a certain reverence, giving the impression that she regarded it a characteristic essential to femininity. Like Rochester and Wycherley and Etherege, she wrote poetry and plays considered scandalously sexy by the more conservative of their contemporaries. But there the similarity ended. Aphra's conception of the way affairs ought to be carried on between the sexes differed profoundly from that of her male friends and literary peers. Alone, she defended the feminine point of view; but the source of difference between Aphra and the wits was not merely a shift in perspective (male to female)—it had to do with her vision of love itself. Aphra detested the Restoration "game of love" and passionately desired sincerity. She had a reputation for "plain-dealing" and expected the same from men. (pp. 184-85)

For Aphra, sexual desire was naturally a part of love's expression, but if isolated from feeling, it atrophied into an endless repetition. Sexual freedom, without love, was no freedom at all, to her mind. (p. 186)

The vision of free love that Aphra opposed to the wits' libertinism was based on a philosophical system that underlies much of her writing: social convention, she held—whether the convention of modesty or that of liberated conformity—had denatured instinct. Aphra's moral system defined what was right as what came naturally. Society and its morality, based on false assumptions, were responsible for the corruption of relations between the sexes. (p. 187)

In writing plays and poetry, Aphra Behn was stepping into a tradition whose language, form, and metaphors had already been shaped. It was a literary heritage she could not have the same access to as the male writers of her generation who were educated in universities did. As poetry increasingly modeled itself on classical prototypes, Mrs. Behn's disadvantage in that field became more noticeable than it might have been otherwise. Even so, poetry presented at least a possibility of individual direction because of its private character; whereas the highly conventionalized theater had rules and imperatives that Aphra could not ignore. She had to imitate, though her special concerns nevertheless run through the works as a second, subversive voice that surfaces into statement from time to time, like an underground stream bubbling up.

The very novelty of the "novel," however, presented Aphra with an opportunity to define and construct her own literary universe. Though she drew on some of the formal characteristics of the historical romances her generation read with avidity, the principal architecture of her fictional world grew out of her own experience—which included the vicarious experience of gossip about people she knew or did not know. This association with oral rather than written tradition is quite clear in the opening lines of Aphra's story *The*

Wandering Beauty: "I was not above twelve years old, as near as I can remember, when a Lady of my acquaintance, who was particularly concerned in many of the passages, very pleasantly entertained me with the relation of the Lady Arabella's adventures, who was eldest daughter to Sir Francis Fairname, a gentleman of noble family, and of very large estate in the West of England."

This "I" was something new not only in literature but in history. It was a very early example of the growing selfconsciousness of the individual, which would, in the next century and a half, develop into a "given" in the way people thought about themselves. Aphra's focus on individual experience and self-expression was historically avant-garde. As historians of autobiography have recently demonstrated, that form of writing did not fully evolve into the personal history we now define it as until the late seventeenth century. Narcissus Luttrell's diary, written while Aphra Behn was alive, is still primarily a culling of his reading of newspapers rather than a record of his own thoughts and feelings. Samuel Pepys, writing only a short time before, was moving toward the new ethos of individualism. His diary, written in a mysterious cipher and unknown to his contemporaries, was, like most works of a "private" nature then, not published until much later. To have had the idea of bringing the private sphere of personal experience into the published domain of fiction was an original achievement—and one that set Aphra far ahead of most of her literary colleagues. (pp. 280-81)

What is particularly interesting about these revelations is that there was some truth to her claim to truth: she was not, like other writers, merely repeating a story-telling convention, but signaling a new kind of relation of writer to narrative.

The value and nature of Aphra Behn's contribution to the novel form has been the subject of much dispute among scholars. It is generally held that the first literary works in the English language that may properly be called novels were Daniel Defoe's *Robinson Crusoe* (1719) and Samuel Richardson's *Pamela* (1740). The first is so considered because of its unity of theme and its realistic recreation of the world through description, and the second because of its development of character in which inner reality is important. Aphra Behn began to write her "novels" thirty-six years before *Robinson Crusoe* and more than half a century before *Pamela;* and the innovative elements that each of these later novels is known for are unquestionably present in her work. (p. 282)

One qualifying factor must be noted in the debate over the extent to which Aphra's novels may be said to be "realistic." Realism, says one literary historian, depends on the "correspondence between the literary work and the reality which it imitates." It must be re-

membered that the world Aphra Behn was describing was only beginning to apply scientific criteria to the examination of evidence: the separation between the natural and supernatural, reality and magic, miracle and fact, had not yet entirely taken place, as it had by the time eighteenth-century novelists were writing. (p. 283)

If some of the events in Aphra Behn's novels which the twentieth century terms "improbable" or "romantic" in fact mirror this reality, then they must at least be considered realistic according to seventeenth-century lights. (p. 284)

Aphra's impassioned attack on the condition of slavery and defense of human rights in *Oroonoko* is perhaps the first important abolitionist statement in the history of English literature. There were a few other obscure voices raised in objection to the institution at the time, in the main marginal elements like religious dissenters (the Quaker George Fox for example). Certainly no other major literary figure producing work for a popular audience attempted such a subject until much later. *Oroonoko* was reprinted repeatedly in the eighteenth century and, along with the popular theatrical adaptation by Thomas Southerne, eventually became a rallying point for the abolitionist movement that grew into a political force more than a century after Aphra's death. (p. 289)

Aphra's *Oroonoko* also was the beginning of another important connection: the historical alliance of abolitionism and feminism. In the nineteenth century, during the years that led up to the Civil War in America, the feminists agitating for women's rights were closely tied to, and in fact worked within, the groups fighting for the abolition of slavery. The progression from one to the other is logical, and on reflection, it is not surprising that women—who had so few rights themselves, who were considered the "property" of their husbands by the legal system—should best understand and sympathize with the position of slaves. The language of "slavery" was applied to the case of women very early on by feminist writers who came on the heels of Aphra's pioneering. (pp. 289-90)

Angeline Goreau, in her *Reconstructing Aphra: A Social Biography of Aphra Behn,* The Dial Press, 1980, 339 p.

LENNARD J. DAVIS
(essay date 1983)

[In the following excerpt, Davis discusses Behn's *Oroonoko* as an example of "factual fiction."]

Aphra Behn was among the first novelists in England

to claim her work was true. Of course, ballads, news-books, and criminal tales had made such claims, so it does not seem unusual to have Behn make the same assertion. As early as 1688, when *Oroonoko* was written, Behn inaugurated, it would seem, the now familiar disclaimer:

> I do not pretend, in giving you the history of this royal slave, to entertain my reader with adventures of a feigned hero, whose life and fortunes Fancy may manage at the poet's pleasure; nor in relating the truth, design to adorn it with any accidents, but such as arrived in earnest to him: And it shall come simply into the world, recommended by its own proper merits, and natural intrigues; there being enough of reality to support it, and to render it diverting, without the addition of invention.

The tone one instantly perceives is a sort of general scorn for invention, entertainment, and feigned heroes. Works of imagination, which may be manipulated at the writer's discretion, are not really worth one's time. The hidden reference seems to be against the French romance's predeliction to add to history, to invent upon historical foundations. Behn has discarded Bishop Huet's justification of fiction by its elegance of style or by its moral instruction. She can do this because, according to the framing device she has established, she is not writing fiction. That there is "enough reality to support" the novel and that such facts as there are will divert the reader are sufficient justifications for the work.

Behn instinctively places herself in the news/novels discourse by inaugurating an inherently reflexive or double discourse based on contradictory assertions. For example, she places a sanction on the use of "accidents" and "intrigues." An "accident," as the word was used in the seventeenth century according to the *Oxford English Dictionary*, was "anything that happens without foresight or expectation, an unusual event, which proceeds from some unknown cause"; an intrigue was "a complicated state of affairs . . . plotting or scheming." In other words, Behn is saying that novelists should avoid coincidences, unexpected turns of event, plotting, scheming, reversals of plot—in short, a novel should avoid being a novel.

Behn is here practicing the essence of reflexive discourse—affirmation by denial. When she says her work is truth, she means that it must shun fictional devices such as coincidence. However, coincidence in a novel is a structuring device that aligns parallel plots, unites formally disparate elements, and allows metaphoric and moral meaning to be drawn from the work. Outside of the realm of literature, however, coincidence was seen during the seventeenth century as an act of Providence, the hand of God at work in the world. So if a novelist denied writing a fiction, thus attributing all coincidences to the hand of Providence,

then that novelist would put him or herself in the bad faith position of claiming to know how Providence *would have* acted in a particular situation. The author pretends, in effect, to be God—an action not generally smiled upon in religious circles.

Aphra Behn is very clear in claiming not to be writing a fiction: "I was myself an eye-witness to a great part of what you will find here set down; and what I could not be witness of I received from the mouth of the chief actor in this history, the hero himself, who gave us the whole transaction of his youth." This proof by physical contiguity is typical of the news/novels discourse. . . . In another work by Behn, *The Fair Jilt* . . . , the dedication is to one Henry Pain, Esq. However, we are not simply presented with a laudatory puff; Behn takes the occasion to ask Pain to authenticate the truthfulness of the text, a ploy which ballad writers had used as well. The work, writes Behn, is recommended by the fact that "it is truth: truth, which you so much admire. But 'tis a truth that entertains you with so many accidents diverting and moving, that they will need both a patron, and an assertor in this incredulous world." With a little help from her legal friend, Behn can claim to have backing for the assertion that her work is true. In this sense, patronage becomes attestation as well.

It seems fitting, in view of Behn's attitude toward fact and fiction that so much of *Oroonoko* should have to do with fabrications, deceit, and lying in one form or another. In Oroonoko's tribe, lies are unknown. Lying is seen by Behn as a natural consequence of civilization and does not exist in a natural state. She writes of Oroonoko's tribe that "these people represented to me an absolute idea of the first state of innocence, before man knew how to sin." The tribe is so oblivious to false statements that, for example, they begin to mourn an English governor who had sworn to come on a certain day and failed to show up or to send word that he could not come. The tribe believed that "when a man's word was past, nothing but death could or should prevent his keeping it." When the governor actually did arrive, ". . . they asked him what name they had for a man who promised a thing he did not do? The governor told them, such a man was a liar, which was a word of infamy to a gentleman. Then one of them replied *Governor, you are a liar, and guilty of that infamy.*" The joke here is that the black men are so innocent that they cannot even perceive that their response is an insult. This innocence constitutes an inability to perceive framings and fabrications—the tribe cannot make out the context, the series of frames, in which the "civilized" world is wrapped.

Aphra Behn's own narrative fares no better than the words of other whites. We doubt her from the opening "authentication" to the numerous lies and tall tales included in the exotica of the novel. She tells us, for example, that even the most severe wounds heal rapidly in the tropical zone—except, inexplicably, those sustained by the leg. Medical wonders are compounded by zoological anomalies such as the fact that a lion may live with several bullets in his heart—a fact which even the author has the good sense to note "will find no credit among men." Another wonder is the "numbeel" which will paralyze the fisherman who holds the rod at the moment the eel touches the bait. Aphra Behn's "truthful" account of Oroonoko's life ends with his execution during which he is castrated, has his nose and ears cut off, and his arms severed while he remains in an unlikely state of calm, continuing to smoke his pipe.

In the jungle, Behn even manages to meet Colonel Martin who, as it just happens, is to be the protagonist of a new play appearing in London called *The Younger Brother or the Amorous Jilt* surprisingly written by none other than Aphra Behn herself. Such a meeting is a shrewd bit of public relations work to encourage some financial success, but also intermixes fact and fiction a bit. One wonders if Behn is consciously testing the credulity of the reader as Oroonoko's own credulity had been tested.

From the prestructure, to the presentation, through the content and even the digressions of *Oroonoko*, fiction-making and lying are central to the work. Fabrications build up into frames within frames doubling back upon themselves until every turn reveals fact warped into fiction which turns back upon itself to become fact. This novel, as others, seems to be steeped in an insecurity resulting from bad faith, criminality, lying, and fabrication. (pp. 106-110)

Lennard J. Davis, "Theories of Fiction in Early English Novels," in his *Factual Fictions: The Origins of the English Novel,* Columbia University Press, 1983, pp. 102-22.

SOURCES FOR FURTHER STUDY

Cameron, William James. *New Light on Aphra Behn.* Auckland, New Zealand: University of Auckland, 1961, 106 p.

    Chronicles Behn's journey to Surinam in 1663 and her service as a spy in Flanders in 1666.

Duffy, Maureen. *The Passionate Shepherdess: Aphra Behn, 1640-89.* London: Jonathan Cape, 1977, 324 p.

    Provides new speculation on Behn's early life and attempts to correct the misconception that she was "a loose woman and a merely hack writer."

Gardiner, Judith Kegan. "Aphra Behn: Sexuality and Self-Respect." *Women's Studies* 7, Nos. 1 2 (1980): 67-78.

    Discussion of Behn's literary artistry and her candid expressions regarding female sexuality. Gardner argues that Behn should be respected for "maintaining the creative woman's ability to be at once sexually giving and intellectually active and independent."

Guffey, George. "Aphra Behn's *Oroonoko:* Occasion and Accomplishment." In *Two English Novelists: Aphra Behn and Anthony Trollope; Papers Read at a Clark Library Seminar, May 11, 1974,* by George Guffey and Andrew Wright, pp. 3-41. Los Angeles: William Andrews Clark Memorial Library, University of California, 1975.

    Views *Oroonoko* as a subtle political novel reflecting the turmoil of the monarchy in 1688.

Jerrold, Walter and Jerrold, Clare. *Five Queer Women.* New York: Brentano's Ltd., 1929, 356 p.

    Includes a chapter on Behn.

Sackville-West, V. *Aphra Behn: The Incomparable Astrea.* New York: Viking Press, 1928, 144 p.

    Survey of Behn's works.

Saul Bellow

1915-

Canadian-born American novelist, short story writer, dramatist, essayist, lecturer, editor, and translator.

INTRODUCTION

*T*he recipient of the 1976 Nobel Prize in Literature, Bellow is among the most celebrated authors of the twentieth century. In his works, he addresses the question of what it means to be human in an increasingly impersonal and mechanistic world. Writing in a humorous, anecdotal style that combines exalted meditation and modern vernacular, Bellow often depicts introspective individuals who suffer a conflict between Old World and New World values while trying to understand their personal anxieties and aspirations. In a period when many writers insist on the impossibility of human communication or heroism, Bellow has been commended for his humanistic celebration of sensitive individuals. He has received three National Book Awards and a Pulitzer Prize, and he is recognized as one of the most original stylists of the twentieth-century. According to Irving Howe, Bellow evolved "the first major new style in American prose fiction since those of Hemingway and Faulkner."

The son of Russian-born parents living in a slum in Lachine, Quebec, Bellow was confined to a hospital for a year during his childhood; he passed the time reading. At seventeen, he and friend Sydney J. Harris (later the noted newspaper columnist) ran away to New York to sell their first novels—without success. Eventually, Bellow enrolled at the University of Chicago. In 1937 he was graduated from Northwestern University, where he founded a socialists' club, with honors in sociology and anthropology. He found employment writing biographical sketches of midwestern writers. Later, he tried to join the Canadian Army, but he was turned down for medical reasons. This experience provided the germ for his first published novel, *Dangling Man* (1944). In 1943, he worked on Mortimer Adler's "Great Books" project for the Encyclopedia Britannica. He then returned to New York and did freelance work before taking a teaching job at the University of Minnesota in 1946. He published his second novel, *The Victim,* in 1947, and traveled to France in 1948. He has taught at various universities and traveled extensively ever since. In 1963, he accepted a permanent position on the Committee on Social Thought at the University of Chicago, where he continues to write and teach. He has married several times.

In their many books and essays on Bellow's works, critics often concentrate on two aspects of Bellow's fiction: his skillfully crafted protagonists, who collectively exemplify the "Bellow hero," and his expansive prose style. Bellow's typical protagonist, who is generally a male, urbanite Jewish intellectual, was described by the Nobel Committee as a man "who keeps trying to find a foothold during his wanderings in our tottering world, one who can never relinquish his faith that the value of life depends on its dignity, not its success." In developing his characters Bellow emphasizes dialogue and interior monologue, and his prose style features sudden flashes of wit and philosophical epigrams. As his protagonists speak to themselves and to others, the reader is drawn into their struggles with self and society. Bellow's earliest novels, *Dangling Man* and *The Victim,* are written in a disciplined, realistic style that he later rejected as constraining. In *Dangling Man,* a young man named Joseph anticipates being drafted into the United States Army. When his induction is delayed by bureaucratic bungling, Joseph attempts to decide how to structure his life. When he is finally inducted, he is relieved from the oppressive responsibility of choosing his own future. *The Victim* focuses on Ava Leventhal, an editor who attends a job interview arranged for him by an acquaintance, Kirby Allbee. When Leventhal insults the interviewer, Allbee loses his job and becomes increasingly unbalanced, demanding that Leventhal make restitution.

During the 1950s, Bellow developed a lively prose style that could accommodate comic misadventures and philosophical digression. He began to write picaresque narratives that employ larger-than-life protagonists and various rhetorical elements. *The Adventures of Augie March* (1953), for example, features an extroverted, exuberant character who believes that a "man's character is his fate." Disregarding his brother's materialistic values, Augie undertakes a personal odyssey and becomes involved in a variety of illegal ventures before learning to channel his energies toward positive ends. Bellow returned to his early formal style in his novella *Seize the Day* (1956), a highly successful work that focuses on Tommy Wilhelm, a middle-aged man who aspired to become rich and famous but who has failed in both business and human relationships. However, by coming to terms with his fear of mortality—a prominent theme in Bellow's fiction— Wilhelm gains a better understanding of himself and an

appreciation of others. In his next novel, *Henderson the Rain King* (1959), Bellow diverged from his usual subject matter to focus on an arrogant Anglo-Saxon millionaire who travels to Africa to confront his anomie and fear of death, a trip which some critics interpret as a journey into his subconscious. Originally seeking to assert his superiority over the natives, Henderson learns to surrender his excessive egoism in order to experience love.

With *Herzog* (1964), Bellow successfully fused the formal realism of his early works with the vitality of his picaresque novels of the 1950s. Like the typical Bellow hero, Herzog is an animated but tormented Jewish intellectual who has difficulty maintaining human relationships, especially with women. In response to his wife's decision to divorce him for his best friend, Herzog retreats from what he views as the corrupting influence of the urban environment. Although he initially becomes absorbed in pointless intellectual exercises, such as mentally composing letters to his wife and friend in which he justifies himself and denies any personal responsibility, Herzog is finally able to remain responsive to himself and to the world. *Herzog,* which garnered Bellow a wide popular and scholarly readership, won praise for its exploration of various Western intellectual traditions and for its evocation of poignant events and colorful minor characters.

Mr. Sammler's Planet (1970) has often been identified as Bellow's most pessimistic novel due to its protagonist's melancholy musings on the passing of Western culture. Mr. Sammler, an old man who has experienced the promises and horrors of twentieth-century life, offers an extensive critique of modern values and speculates on the future after observing a pickpocket on a bus. Although many critics disagreed as to whether Mr. Sammler succeeds as a perceptive commentator on contemporary existence, the character is often regarded as one of Bellow's most fully realized protagonists. *Humboldt's Gift* (1975), for which Bellow received the Pulitzer Prize, centers on the conflict between materialistic values and the claims of art and high culture. The protagonist, Charles Citrine, is a successful writer who questions the worth of artistic values in modern American society after enduring exhaustive encounters with divorce lawyers, criminals, artists, and other representative figures of contemporary urban life. He also recalls his friendship with the flamboyant artist Humboldt Fleischer, a composite of several American writers who despaired in their inability to reconcile their artistic ideals with the indifference and materialism of American society. Citrine finally concludes that he can maintain artistic order by dealing with the complexities of life through ironic comic detachment. Many critics have contended that Citrine's beliefs reflect those of Bellow himself and that Humboldt is modeled on Bellow's friend, poet Delmore Schwartz.

In *The Dean's December* (1982), Bellow more directly attacked negative social forces that challenge human dignity. Set in depressed areas of Chicago and Bucharest, Romania, this novel focuses on Albert Corde, a respected journalist who returns to academic life to revive his love of high culture. In the course of the book, Corde admonishes politicians, liberal intellectuals, journalists, and bureaucrats in both democratic and communist nations for failing to maintain humanistic values. Critics often disagree as to whether the novel's many autobiographical elements are as skillfully employed as in Bellow's previous fiction. *More Die of Heartbreak* (1987), set in a midwestern city reminiscent of Chicago, focuses on Benn Crader, a contemplative botanist engaged to the wealthy daughter of an avaricious surgeon who seeks to use Benn to undermine Benn's Uncle Vilitzer, a corrupt political boss. The novel is related by Benn's nephew, Kenneth Trachtenberg, a professor of Russian literature who draws parallels between the Russian revolution and the present state of America while ruminating on his own failed love relationships. Fearful of the possibility that "more die of heartbreak than of radiation," Benn finally deserts his bride-to-be. Although some critics found the novel overlong, disingenuous, or misogynistic, others concurred with Terrence Rafferty: "[Bellow] has always been a smart, likable trickster, even when, as in this new novel, he seems to take forever working his little surprises free of his sleeve. For better or worse, that's how he is."

Bellow has also written several works of short fiction. In the pieces collected in *Mosby's Memoirs and Other Stories* (1968) and *Him with His Foot in His Mouth and Other Stories* (1984), he depicted sensitive ordinary people and intellectuals who struggle to maintain personal dignity and to reaffirm humanistic faith.

Bellow's novella *A Theft* (1989) focuses on Clara Velde, a woman raised in a strict religious area of Indiana who has risen to become "the czarina of fashion writing" in the publishing industry of New York City. Intelligent yet vulnerable, Clara lives with her fourth husband while maintaining a relationship with Ithiel Regler, an erratic companion who once bought her an emerald ring as a symbol of their love. When Clara's ring is stolen, she finds her stability shattered. Most critics found the novella's development hasty and Clara's ultimate self-fulfillment willed rather than inherently realized. However, John Banville commented: "[*A Theft*] has the coherence and tension of a furled flower. It is packed with colour and wit, and a fervent gaiety." The unnamed narrator of a second novella, *The Bellarosa Connection* (1989), is a Russian Jew whose belief in the importance of memory in defining identity led him to found the Mnemosyne Institute of Philadelphia, where executives and politicians are trained in the art of total recall. The narrator relates the story of a Jewish man named Harry Fonstein, who was rescued from Hitler's Nazi regime during World War II by the "Bellarosa Society," a front for an entertainer named Billy Rose who wished to remain anonymous. Years later, Harry's wife attempts to blackmail Billy into seeing her dispirited husband and acknowledging his responsibility for her husband's present life.

(For further information about Bellow's life and works, see *Authors in the News,* Vol. 2; *Bestsellers 1989; Contemporary Literary Criticism,* Vols. 1, 2, 3, 6, 8, 10, 13, 15, 25, 33, 34, 63; *Contemporary Authors,* Vols. 5-8; *Contemporary Authors Bibliographical Series,* Vol. 1; *Dictionary of Literary Biography,* Vols. 2, 28; *Dictionary of Literary Biography Yearbook: 1982; Dictionary of Literary Biography Documentary Series,* Vol. 3; and *Concise Dictionary of American Literary Biography, 1941-1968.*)

CRITICAL COMMENTARY

EARL ROVIT
(essay date 1967)

[Rovit is an American novelist whose works are noted for their intricate structures and themes; he, according to critic Granville Hicks, "refuses to make the world he writes about simpler than that in which he lives." An important theme in his first novel, *The Player King* (1965), is the role of the Jew in American scholarship. In the following excerpt, he describes theme, style, and the typical protagonist in Bellow's works.]

The first of the American Jewish writers to capture a large reading audience without departing from an American Jewish idiom, [Saul] Bellow has been instrumental in preparing a way for other writers like Bernard Malamud, I. B. Singer, and Philip Roth. But his achievement has been impressive enough in its own right; he has developed a marvelously supple style of grotesque realism modulated by an ever-present sense

Principal Works

Dangling Man (novel) 1944

The Victim (novel) 1947

The Adventures of Augie March (novel) 1953

*Seize the Day 1956

Henderson the Rain King (novel) 1959

Great Jewish Short Stories [editor] (short stories) 1963

Recent American Fiction: A Lecture (lecture) 1963

Herzog (novel) 1964

The Last Analysis (drama) 1964

†Under the Weather 1966; also produced as The Bellow Plays, 1966

Mosby's Memoirs and Other Stories (short stories) 1968

Mr. Sammler's Planet (novel) 1970

The Portable Bellow (collection) 1974

Humboldt's Gift (novel) 1975

Nobel Lecture (lecture) 1976

To Jerusalem and Back: A Personal Account (memoirs) 1976

The Dean's December (novel) 1982

Him with His Foot In His Mouth and Other Stories (short stories) 1984

More Die of Heartbreak (novel) 1987

The Bellarosa Connection (novella) 1989

A Theft (novella) 1989

*Contains two short stories, a novella, and a one-act play, The Wrecker.

†Includes the one-act plays Out from Under, A Wen, and Orange Soufflé.

of irony. But the very success of his fictions may have drawn attention away from the intense moral seriousness of his concerns. (p. 5)

[The] creation of a recognizable character type, the Bellow hero, is Bellow's major accomplishment. The faces and individual circumstances of this hero have varied from fiction to fiction. He has been rich and poor, well- and ill-educated; he has grown from youth to middle age, gone to war, multiplied his wives and mistresses, narrowed and extended his field of operations with the world. But when we compare the personae of his earliest published sketches in 1941 ("Two Morning Monologues") with his latest, we realize that the alterations in the hero are surprisingly superficial. He postures to a Dostoevskian rhythm in *Dangling Man;* he is clumsy and vulnerable in *The Victim* and *Seize the Day;* as Augie March, he affects the free-wheeling manner of an unlikely reincarnation of Huck Finn; and . . . in the character of Moses Herzog, he absorbs all his previous roles in a comical apotheosis of

despair. The variations among the individual protagonists seem largely to be due to the expedients of their different dramatic settings. . . . In a strange way he is the introspective inversion of the Hemingway hero, his most immediate Chicago predecessor. Like him, he is fearfully alone and afraid; like him, he struggles incessantly to achieve dignity and to impose a moral dimension upon life. But unlike him, he is cursed or blessed with a pervasive sense of irony; he is mistrustful of action, skeptical of heroics, painfully aware of the limitations of reason as only an intellectual can be, but unwilling, at the same time, to surrender himself to the dangerous passions of unreason. (pp. 16-17)

Bellow differs . . . significantly from the contemporary "black" humorists and nihilistic practitioners of "the absurd." While their works tend to extract a dark humor from the very senselessness of the inhuman condition, concentrating on the stark outrageousness of their fictional situations for their comic effects, Bellow's concern is directed toward the articulated human response to that condition—the verbal phrases and kinetic metaphors with which suffering man escalates implacable defeats into comic impasses which are, at least, barely tolerable. For, with the contemporary hostility against language and logic—against words as a mechanism of submission and compromise—Bellow has nothing to do. For him, man becomes human because he uses words. And, more than that, *style* is the final resort for the victim—his means of transcendence out of slavishness into a kind of comic heroism. This, of course, does not mean that Bellow is advancing a rhetoric which besmears reality—which gives the grandiloquent lie to life. Rather, it is an employment of language to define more accurately the crosscurrents which roil the spirit between a will to live and an awareness of death. For Bellow, neither demonic rhetoric nor silence can define the human condition correctly. Rhetoric invites dishonesty and silence cuts both below and above the level of the human. Bellow's notion of man is far too dependent on the miracle of rationality—on man's internal dialogue with himself—for him to be hostile to words. And hence, it is in his style that the complexities of his humor and his moral concern with the human unite and most persuasively develop. (pp. 40-1)

Bellow's prose and the life style which his fictions have figured forth are, in a sense, an expansion and extension of that brooding voice—a rich fusion of sophisticated erudition and earthiness which brings the full current of man's coursing blood into the world of mind and spirit, and which is careful to retain the sensual as the root metaphor of all experience. It is Bellow's style, thus, which subsumes and encompasses the direction and shape of his achievement as a writer. Rational, honest, ironic, cognizant of human limitations but struggling not to be cowed by them, it gropes and grapples and learns to accept itself as a deliberate comic thrust against life. It is, at the end, its own justification, but one severely fought for, and one which holds its victories as cheap because it knows well the heavy price it has had to pay for them. It is in his style that one can see Bellow's weaknesses as a writer—the narrowness of his scope, the solipsistic closure, the forfeits which his imagination has had to surrender to irony, and to the realism of mortal flesh. But his style is triumphantly a record of his remarkable strengths as well—his success in establishing and making viable an image of the human in the face of the dual tides of mechanism and brute animality that threaten to obliterate the very concept of humanity in their sweep. And it is here, I believe, that his finest achievement ought to be read and reckoned. (pp. 42-3)

Earl Rovit, in his Saul Bellow, *University of Minnesota Press,* Minneapolis, 1967, 46 p.

SEYMOUR EPSTEIN

(essay date 1976)

[Epstein is an American novelist, short story writer, and critic. In the following excerpt, he examines the theme that unites *Seize the Day, Henderson the Rain King, Herzog, Mr. Sammler's Planet,* and *Humboldt's Gift.*]

The failures of Western civilization and the pleasures of it spin out the thematic thread that runs through the novels under discussion here. As a theme, it is as worthy as any being worked in contemporary fiction, and proof of this is in the unity and persuasiveness of Bellow's *oeuvre* as compared to any of his contemporaries who might be considered at the same level of seriousness. (p. 36)

Bellow's first three novels—*Dangling Man* (1944), *The Victim* (1947), and *The Adventures of Augie March* (1953)—are interesting, varied, but essentially diverse in theme. *Augie March,* that large, trumpeting announcement of Self, is in many ways a prototype of Bellow's subsequent use of character, and of those juxtapositions that make a novelist comfortable and fecund within the enclosure of his fictional world. In any event, the major theme, as perceived and discussed in this essay, does not yet make an unequivocal appearance. *Augie March* ends with the proclamation:

> Look at me, going everywhere! Why, I am a sort of Columbus of those near-at-hand and believe you can come to them in this immediate *terra incognita* that spreads out in every gaze. I may well be flop at this line of endeavor. Columbus too thought he was a

flop, probably, when they sent him back in chains. Which didn't prove there was no America.

But it is Bellow's named and occupied America that will be investigated here.

Dr. Tamkin, a Mephistophelean swinger, whose "bones were peculiarly formed, as though twisted twice where the ordinary human bone was turned only once" . . . , is one of Bellow's early "reality instructors". In *Seize the Day* . . . , Bellow has this charlatan play the role of one of man's legendary bedevilers. He is Puck, the Pied Piper, Loki, the Devil, and Baron Munchausen rolled into one. He is a swindler, a healer, and a mythomaniac. He is a creature who has mutated into his queer form in order to survive in a rapidly deteriorating culture. His client-victim, a Lumpen-Faust with as many names as failures (Tommy will do), is the single natural schlemiel in Bellow's entire cast of losers. (pp. 38-9)

The symbol of Tommy as a failure is in some respects crude, since he was so obviously doomed to fail; but his failure is instructive at least in its causes if not in its tragic implications. He is society's dupe. He is the quintessentially *modern* failure. The particular manner of his failure(s) would have been impossible for his historical counterpart fifty years previous, or indeed at any other previous time in human history. . . . Almost everything about him is synthetic. *Almost* everything. The only genuine thing in Tommy's life is his capacity to suffer—and this is what *Seize the Day* is about: the suffering of a totally alienated man. In all his subsequent novels, Bellow hasn't limned this much overdramatized and overpublicized condition as truly and poignantly as he did in this novella written in 1956. (pp. 39-40)

Almost to escape the realizations of *Seize the Day,* Bellow sends his next hero-failure off to Africa to see if some restorative mightn't be discovered by poking around in primitive origins.

Eugene Henderson of *Henderson the Rain King* is a large, lumbering man—a bigger, wiser, braver, gentile Tommy—but a man who also wears his suffering heart on his sleeve, whose desire to do good, to "burst the spirit's sleep", is no less than that of his pathetic, New York predecessor. Bellow suggests that Henderson has set out on his journey because he has been afflicted almost to destruction by the antilife forces present in technological America. Unlike Tommy, he is familiar with the Western world's art and philosophy, but this cranky millionaire's suffering takes the form of a huge hunger rather than a thwarted ambition. There is a voice in him that is always chanting, *"I want, I want, I want!"*

Among the Arnewi tribe, Henderson learns the expression *gruntu-molani*—man-wants-to-live—and this is precisely what he has come to Africa for: to learn how to live: to submit his volcanic energy to some natural imperative. His failure is neither personal nor small, but general and colossal. In attempting to rid the Arnewi watering place of a plague of frogs, he explodes both frogs and retaining wall, destroying the resource and the pollution in one blast. (p. 40)

Henderson's impulse was his society's impulse to subdue nature, and he brought this impulse to peoples whose religions and customs were all shaped around the accommodation and placation of nature rather than its conquest. Far from benefiting from his Rousseauian adventures, he has loused up the natural balance where it did exist, and confirmed his own hopeless addiction to Western civilization's drug of humanism.

Henderson was published in 1959, *Herzog* in 1964. Between those two dates (in November 1963, to be exact) there appeared in *Encounter* an article by Bellow entitled **"Some Notes on Recent American Fiction"**. In his comments on J. F. Powers's novel, *Morte d'Urban* (1962), Bellow finds deficiency in Powers's view of Self, because "there is curiously little talk of souls in this book about a priest. Spiritually, its quality is very thin." A look at the dates makes it clear that Bellow must have been working on *Herzog* at the time he wrote the article, and, of course, the views of a novelist-in-progress must be looked at with adjusted lens. Not every detraction need be a defense, but the two have more than a casual connection. Bellow goes on to say in his critique of *Morte d'Urban:*

A man might well be meek in his own interests, but furious at such abuses of the soul and eager to show what is positive and powerful in his faith. The lack of such power makes faith itself shadowy, more like obscure tenacity than spiritual conviction.

Whether or not Bellow personally holds any traditional theistic views is not to be determined from his novels, but that "spiritual conviction"—or the dread of its disappearance—is to become a growing part of his creative life is easily demonstrable. His advocacy of the individual, or the Self, as announced in his *Encounter* article, and reiterated with increasing thematic centrality in all subsequent works, is not a nineteenth-century, Romantic view of Self (Moses Herzog's studies in romanticism lay in a closet, "eight hundred pages of chaotic argument"), but rather a new individuality as conceived through social awareness and a deepening sense of responsibility. (pp. 40-1)

Most Bellow heroes are men in the middle—and no one is more in the middle than Moses Herzog. His middleness is his agony—or so Bellow would have us believe—but is it possible to believe in the agony of a man who has the wit and the locution to address himself to Presidents, philosophers, spiritual leaders, scientists, new frauds, and old lovers? A man who styles himself a "suffering joker"? A man who feels enormously sorry for himself but agrees with the saying, "Grief, sir, is a species of idleness"?

Herzog is an intellectual and a teacher. His major unfinished work, *Romanticism and Christianity,* stands as a sad analogue of his other sad defeats, particularly his marital defeats. In his book he had tried to trace those religious and political innovations that had aspired to bring man into a more advantageous relationship with himself and his fellow mortals; but it is critically, almost hysterically, apparent to Herzog that man is no better off now than he was a thousand years ago. The poison of historical hope has precipitated into the petty realization that he has been a bad husband and a bad father. People of Herzog's generation measure their failures not in terms of broken faith but in broken marriages. The Miltonic council of fallen angels takes place in the marriage counselor's office.

In *Herzog* it is sometimes difficult to know whether what one is hearing is a comic note in the despair or a desperate note in the comedy, but the fact that they are mingled in no way diminishes the sincerity of either. There is both desperation and comedy, and it is to be noted that the mixture is most pungent where the narration is most personal. *Herzog* is written in the first person. So is *Henderson*. And *Augie March*. And *Humboldt*. *Seize the Day* and *Mr. Sammler's Planet* are third-person novels, and in both instances the desperation far outweighs the comedy. Which would seem to indicate a greater degree of authorial self-consciousness working in the more personal form. That is not surprising, since the true fictional function of the first-person form is to give the creating mind the instantaneous freedom to turn on itself and reveal the mockery in every posture. (pp. 42-3)

Bellow's women are among the most misunderstood and castrating in all of literature. Not all his women, but those who do take on the bitch-role fairly sizzle in it. Madeleine is one of the angriest. She turns on Herzog with such hatred that one is prompted to go back and pick up the overlooked reasons for all that venom. There are a few hints that Herzog may have been sexually inconsiderate (or incompetent), and that he may have been equally inconsiderate in meeting Madeleine's intellectual needs, but these are rather inconclusive hints. What we are given to see most clearly is a picture of Herzog trotting devotedly after beautiful, blazing Madeleine, with her mixed religions and mixed ambitions.

There is a deliberate ironic comedy in the whole business of Madeleine's Catholic conversion, and in Herzog's being persuaded to try some religiosity himself in order to get better adjusted to Madeleine's nature. It serves to bring the failure of the last few centuries and the predicament of the modern intellectual, as personified in Herzog, into painful relief. The late twentieth-century's modality is not religious (even

Madeleine gave it up after a while), but the history of religion becomes one more item in the intellectual's inventory of ideas. The fact that traditional religions have lost their force has not obviated man's need to feel a passionate faith in some higher order, intelligence, or idea that will do as medium through which one can seek transcendence.

Herzog's search for such an absolute was conducted in places other than heaven. There was (in Herzog's historical time) the Marxist hope, and that, for many, failed. There was the hope that through self-understanding (the Freudian dispensation) man would come considerably closer to civilized behavior; and that, too, seems to have failed. These various failures have urged Herzog from idea to idea, as well as from woman to woman, and marriage to marriage. (pp. 43-4)

These personal mistakes are bad enough in themselves, but in Herzog's eyes they are also symptomatic of some kind of world disarrangement. Madeleine is not just another woman unhappy in her marriage, but an historical correction officer sent to teach him a lesson. Mind will not substitute for instinct, and the great thoughts of three centuries are not worth a damn in bed, or in the daily rub of domestic life. Beginning again over the wreckage of marriages, religions, and world systems is just too much for a man weighted down with daily responsibilities and a still-operative sex life. The young are fortunately free of the first, and the old are thankfully (or regretfully) free of the second, and what the young and old make of it is examined in Bellow's next novel, *Mr. Sammler's Planet.*

In *Mr. Sammler's Planet* (1970) we learn from the outset that Elya Gruner, Mr. Sammler's faulty but faithful nephew, has been hospitalized with a dangerous condition, a threatening aneurysm. This condition becomes the pervasive symbol of the novel. Civilization, too, is suffering a dangerous condition, but the difference between Elya Gruner and civilization is that Elya's death will be immediately ascertainable while civilization's death may be protracted and disguised through countless convulsions.

Bellow is here posing the imminent death of an attitude as well as a man. Elya is no saint. He has been corrupted by the times. He has connections with the underworld in his profession as gynecologist, performing illegal abortions for Mafia money. And he has spoiled his children to the point of imbecility, allowing his daughter too much money and license, and his son too much time and whimsy. (pp. 44-5)

The significant point about these two costly parasites is that their peculiar existences require very large subsidies. Centuries of scientific and artistic cultivation have produced such strange fruit. Removing all monetary and moral necessity from their lives, Elya Gruner has made his family a showcase of the final corruption of the Puritan ethic.

Artur Sammler himself is a survivor. He is from another country and another time. He is keenly aware of the anachronistic nature of his survival. He knows better than anyone else that his sense of values is rapidly disappearing from the world around him. More, he is that old and has been through so much that he has cast himself in the role of disinterested observer. He has absolutely no hope of changing anything, and the combination of his own experience and his living obsolescence gives him a special vantage point which has indissoluble links to the past and an apocalyptic view of the future. (p. 45)

Bellow places Mr. Sammler in New York City, where the stresses and contradictions of society are at their most severe. If there is something wrong with our civilization, it will find its most extravagant expression in this city; and what Mr. Sammler finds most seriously wrong is the almost total attrition of humanism. The people he comes into contact with seem to have lost all faith in the future. The incident of the princely Negro pickpocket who exhibits himself to Mr. Sammler in the lobby of an apartment house in Manhattan (one of the most vividly effective scenes in recent fiction) is illustrative of the condition Bellow is defining. The national sin of racial injustice has gone on for too long, and the victims of that injustice no longer have patience with the slow processes of history. (p. 46)

Civilization, Bellow would appear to be saying, maintains itself by a consensus of values and a desire to project those values into the future. Here is the principal area of breakdown. "The ideas of the last few centuries are used up." On one hand you have the pleasure-seekers like Angela; on the other hand you have cynics like Lionel Feffer, the young man who uses his brilliance and organizational abilities to practice every con game going in the intellectual and/or investment market. For Lionel, intellectuality is no longer tied to the ideal of improving mankind, but to mere cleverness and kicks. Idealism is not simply dead, it is ludicrous.

The novel ends with the death of Elya Gruner, and his death is indicative of Bellow's pessimism. (pp. 46-7)

The cry of all Bellow heroes: to do good. But they are all pleasure-seekers as well, striving, stumbling pleasure-seekers. Indeed, some of the most brilliant insights in Bellow's novels spring from the loss of love or money. Bellow characters declare their hunger for spiritual transcendence, and their author plays with as many means as past religions and philosophies can supply; but while there's a scintilla of pleasure to be wrung from the body, that's where the body is—in good restaurants, in expensive clothes, in the arms of dream-sexy lovers.

Having brought his theme of Western civilization's bankruptcy to near-ultimate definition in *Mr. Sammler's Planet,* Bellow has little choice other than reiteration or new ground. In *Humboldt's Gift* he went for reiteration, but a peculiar kind of reiteration. Enough has been said already about Von Humboldt Fleisher and Delmore Schwartz to avoid the point here, but it doesn't really matter whether the character of Humboldt was modeled on Delmore Schwartz or not. Another prototype could have been found who would have evoked the *Zeitgeist* equally as well. Bellow's shuffling between that bright beginning and the frayed present adds nothing to an understanding or appreciation of either. Charlie Citrine is an aging Augie March, still the Chicago boy sitting down to the feast of life; but now the exotic dishes are all familiar, and instead of the marvelous appetite that stimulated the early Bellow *fressers* there's a definite dyspepsia souring the many pages of *Humboldt's Gift.*

Perhaps a clue is to be taken from what Charlie has to say about the dead Humboldt:

> He blew his talent and his health and reached home, the grave, in a dusty slide. He plowed himself under. Okay. So did Edgar Allan Poe, picked out of the Baltimore gutter. And Hart Crane over the side of a ship. And Jarrell falling in front of a car. And poor John Berryman jumping from a bridge. For some reason this awfulness is peculiarly appreciated by business and technological America. The country is proud of its dead poets. It takes terrific satisfaction in the poets' testimony that the USA is too tough, too big, too much, too rugged, that American reality is overpowering.
>
> (p. 48)

The imperious, hot-eyed women are here, and the "reality instructors" who teach the hero the difference between idealism and reality, and the inventory of dead ideologies, and the onomastic fireworks (Proust and Charlus . . . Wheeler-Bennett, Chester Wilmot, Liddell Hart, Hitler's generals . . . Walter Winchell, Earl Wilson, General Rommel, John Donne, T. S. Eliot, and many more, all on a single page!), but somehow there is no plangency in the recitation of these names. They seem to be there for their own sake. The former wives and the present lovers are still as demanding and castrating as ever, but their connection to the hero doesn't seem as organic. It's as if Charlie Citrine and his retinue occupy separate stages where each works out separate disillusions and destinies. Indeed, the whole novel seems more a dramatic *theory* of a life than a dramatic presentation of one. The clownishness and cultural detritus has finally clogged the fictional pipeline, and it wouldn't be too unfair to assume that this has come about through a general debilitation of the theme's vitality. The push is no longer strong enough to wash it all through. (p. 49)

Bellow—or any novelist—owes us no answers. That's an old story. But the novelist who has raised important questions owes us the integrity not to trivialize those questions by repetitive improvisations on a theme, no matter how adroit. So adept is Bellow's hand that one can read *Humboldt's Gift* with almost all the pleasure that previous Bellow novels have given . . . but when the book is put away there is a curious lack of residue; there is the feeling that these ideas and these people can yield no more.

But what they have yielded is great. No contemporary American author has made his theme yield more. Historians must surely suffer from the plethora of means and materials at their disposal, and the very profusion must make a manageable perspective almost impossible to obtain. But if they would wish to know how it was in the hearts of men (and the discrimination is deliberate; Bellow is no feminist) in post-World War II America, there is no better single source than the novels of Saul Bellow. (p. 50)

Seymour Epstein, "Bellow's Gift," in *The Denver Quarterly,* Vol. 10, No. 4, Winter, 1976, pp. 35-50.

ALVIN H. ROSENFELD

(essay date 1977)

[An American educator and critic, Rosenfeld examined the effects of the Holocaust on post-World War II literature in his book *A Double Dying: Reflections on Holocaust Literature* (1980). In the following excerpt, he traces the evolution of ideas in Bellow's fiction.]

Bellow has been, right from the start, as much concerned with the invisible worlds opened up by thought and feeling, intuition and intimation, as he has been our busy chronicler of the mundane. . . .

The culture criticism is there sure enough, a spirited reading of the times for all of us to accept or quarrel with, but the fundamental engagement of thought is, in the first place, self-directed, and we, the readers, are let in on it only as it were afterwards. For while the novel of ideas, as Bellow has been developing it, exists to inform and entertain and communicate with us all, its primary aim is heuristic, designed as it is to enable the author to think himself through to clarity about certain preoccupying notions. . . .

As [Bellow's] career advances into more open explorations of the spiritual side of things, . . . [his] beliefs—or movements in the direction of belief—are becoming more pronounced, let out from under the cover of spoofing and ironic humor that have served to keep them somewhat disguised or restrained, and the author a bit too remote from his own metaphysical hunches. (p. 47)

Dangling Man (1944), Bellow's first novel, was, among other things, a meditation on the dilemmas of freedom and fate. "How should a good man live; what ought he to do?"—these are the questions that nag at Joseph, the book's central character, and complicate his life. (p. 48)

[One] does not read *Dangling Man* today with a great deal of pleasure or growing insight. That is not because the philosophical problems Bellow was pondering in the book are without interest but because he was unable to find the most appropriate fictional terms for them. The language of the novel is formal to the point of being wooden, a derivative code of sensibility that Bellow himself later came to acknowledge as unnatural to him and pretty much a failure for his purposes. Then, too, the novel carries much too heavy a burden of thought for its thin fictional frame: Joseph's introspection so outpaces his story as to turn the book into a kind of unanchored or disembodied monologue. Other problems arise from the journal form in which *Dangling Man* is written; this may have been right enough for the idle, house-bound side of Joseph but not for his more animated instincts, which could be kept alive only through contact with a wider world. Such contacts are not easily accommodated in the literary form Bellow employs in his first novel, however; almost of necessity the kinds of extended journal entries upon which *Dangling Man* is based are the product of a soul turned in upon itself, entrapped within a merely mental existence. . . . Joseph's monologues let in little company and less love, and, as a result, his sense of himself as a potentially good man is seriously frustrated, as is Bellow's initial attempt at defining and fictionalizing a virtuous life.

Some of these problems—problems of literary style and strategy but also of moral conception—begin to lift in *The Victim* (1947), Bellow's second novel and a more successful book. In telling the stories of Asa Leventhal and Kirby Allbee—and one dare not detach the one from the other: that is the major didactic point of the narrative—Bellow began to move out of the cramped cell of the interior life and into the more public spaces of social existence. He is concerned in *The Victim* with determining the crossing points of success and failure, with what it is that condemns one man to be a bum and allows another to win through to something that approximates a normal life. In particular, he is drawn to the most subtle movements of conflict and victimization that attach themselves to these themes, especially as they tend to play themselves out against the pressures of urban life, of family duties and devotions, and of the rough-and-tumble of the work world. . . . [The] novel not only presents but actually

begins to resolve some of these problems, even if not in a way that easily lends itself to a clearly defined moral philosophy. Such a task, Bellow, working at this stage of his career closer to naturalistic and psychological concerns than philosophic ones, could not take on. The victories over victimization that appear in this novel tend to be provisional ones, therefore, and arise more out of the moment's need than from more considered reflection. For that latter development, Bellow was still going to have to wait awhile. (pp. 48-9)

The first of [Bellow's] big books, *The Adventures of Augie March,* appeared in 1953 and signalled a breakthrough on several fronts. In his first two novels Bellow had been working within closed forms and nonrhetorical styles, which is to say, within the kinds of formal constraints that tended to pen in his characters and put checks on their ability to move out from under one kind of restriction or another. . . . With *The Adventures of Augie March* . . . he opened up the novel to new and far racier currents of feeling, wrote "catch-as-catch-can," and threw over determinism, both in its technical implications and as controlling theme. (pp. 49-50)

From its first sentence—"I am an American, Chicago-born, . . . and go at things as I have taught myself, free-style, and will make the record in my own way"—to its last, *The Adventures of Augie March* declared itself as Bellow's most *American* book to date. Its inspired blend of impulses sanctioned by Walt Whitman and Mark Twain, its democratic assertions of open-road advances and high-spirited adventure, of celebratory if comic selfhood—all these gave the novel an expansive, exuberant style that was something new not only for Bellow but for twentieth-century American fiction. Moreover, its easy way of incorporating aspects of Jewish street and family life into the narrative seemed exactly right for an urban novel and added a certain jauntiness it otherwise would not have had. *The Adventures of Augie March* was truly a new departure, a great improvisatory attempt to fasten on to "the surplus and super abundance of human material" and release it into an equally ample, naturally accommodating language. That language—a mix of high and low styles, of racy syntax and colloquial phrasing, of perky but probing intelligence—was Bellow's particular achievement in this novel. . . . (p. 50)

Seize the Day (1956), the author's fourth novel, has often been acclaimed his most "perfect" piece of fiction. That it may be, at least in formal terms, but in order to achieve this perfection, Bellow had to return his art to the reduced and comparatively restrained scale of his earliest work. *Seize the Day* followed *The Adventures of Augie March* by three years, but in terms of its more contracted fictional locus, its precise observance of the workings of time, its highly ordered, carefully narrated plot, and its more meticulous style, the novella links itself quite naturally to Bellow's first two books. Seen against these, though, and within the limitations it set for itself, *Seize the Day* must be regarded as a culminating and not a regressive work, for in this slim volume Bellow manages to combine and bring to a greater intensity of representation some of his major concerns in *Dangling Man* and *The Victim.* (p. 51)

Seize the Day is also linked to *The Adventures of Augie March* by its extension of the theme of anxiety over personal frustration into a full-blown, whimpering defeat. Not death, life's natural and inexorable limitation, but disappointment, the steady smothering of a man's best talents and efforts, is what Augie kicks against: "Not that life should end is so terrible in itself, but that it should end with so many disappointments in the essential. This is a fact." It is a fact that erodes the hope of Tommy Wilhelm's every day and brings him, at his story's end, to weep uncontrollably at the wasting away of a man's life—his own.

Bellow's major fiction after *Seize the Day* turns away from the spare, carefully managed forms of the early novels and the novella to the more open and expansive ways of *The Adventures of Augie March.* That is as it should be given the centrality of ideas that comes to characterize the author's work from this point on and, under its impact, brings his fiction—and, with it, the American novel—into a phase of maturity it had not previously known.

A significant foreshadowing of Bellow's turn to the novel of ideas can be gleaned, once more, from *The Adventures of Augie March.* "In the end, you can't save your soul and life by thought," Augie is told by Einhorn, the earliest and most important of his mentors, "but if you *think,* the least of the consolation prizes is the world." . . . Bellow expanded on this idea in his acceptance speech upon receiving the National Book Award for Fiction in 1965 (this time for *Herzog*):

> There is nothing left for us novelists to do but think. For unless we think, unless we make a clearer estimate of our condition, we will continue to write kid stuff, to fail in our function, we will lack serious interests and become truly irrelevant.

Following his own imperative to enliven fiction with a commanding intelligence, Bellow has given us in each of his last four novels a new kind of character, one so actively engaged by thought as to make thinking a large part of his business with the world and, in a heightened way, a restored part of the human definition. (p. 52)

The result has been invigorating and unusually lively, as one might expect from fiction refreshed by both imaginative and intellectual play. The stress here must remain on *fiction,* too, for while each of the four novels is in its way a substantial attempt to think through to some "clearer estimate of our condition,"

these are not severely analytic or abstractly philosophical books. . . . It is true that, for a novelist, Bellow is powerfully drawn to ideas and likes to go off on mental travel, but when he takes one of his characters out on a safari, as he does in *Henderson the Rain King,* the trek is through more than a mental landscape. The novelistic data—the smell of the night air, "the stars flaming like oranges," a sudden shower of frogs—remain sharp, too sharp, happily, for thought to ever dissolve them into abstractions. The *poet* in the novelist, we might say, insists on retaining a sense of life's concreteness and mystery, even as the *thinker* in the novelist tries to convert these into manageable ideas. Usually the poet wins out, for, as Bellow conceives of it, thought is a necessary but not a sufficient part of the human equation; it is complemented by strong surges of feeling, intuition, intimation—by all of those imaginative leaps of spirit that do not fit the categories of rationalism and that, indeed, tend to oppose them. . . . The result—the Bellovian novel of ideas—is philosophic in its emphases, then, but not in its methods of thought. The major work of truth-seeking and truth-telling, while dependent upon reason, neither begins nor ends with it.

Where *does* Bellow locate truth and how do his principal characters move towards it? In Henderson's case, "truth comes in blows"—through a knock on the nose, a wrestling match with a warrior-king, a face-to-face encounter with a lion. (pp. 52-3)

Herzog is a far more substantial intellectual than Henderson—as mental types the two are not really very comparable—but he is driven by much the same thing—"a striving for true wakefulness"; a felt obligation to "live," to "complete his assignment, whatever that was"; and, behind all of these and constantly empowering them, a resolve to face up to "the biggest problem of all, which was to encounter death." If there is an abiding philosophical task in *all* Bellow's fiction, in fact, it is the one put forth by Plato ages ago when he announced that philosophy is the study of death. Bellow's willingness to accept this Platonic challenge—the most difficult of all—and to try to find literary terms for it has added urgency to his fiction and, almost certainly, pointed it toward reflections on the soul. (p. 53)

Henderson the Rain King is a comic novel—perhaps Bellow's best. . . . [But] there is at the same time an unmistakable seriousness about these matters on Bellow's part that comes through all the spoofing clearly enough.

Herzog, written in a style that alternates between "philosophical piety" and a "clever goofiness," also aims to lighten its burden of speculative weight by comedy and, for the most part, it succeeds marvellously in doing so. (pp. 53-4)

The natural piety of Herzog's life—the confident

Saul Bellow (second from right) at the National Book Awards ceremony, 26 August 1954, with (l-r) Alistair Cooke, Cheryl Crawford, and Bruce Catton.

resolve "to be, to be just as it is willed, and for as long as I may remain in occupancy"—finds both its source and its sanction in [a] religious notion of "assignment," which carries through Bellow's fiction and, more than anything else, seems to indicate the author's most abiding sense of how we come into possession of truth. In an age of spiritual exhaustion, when "all the old dreams were dreamed out," the soul's deepest wisdom, as Herzog comes to learn, still finds its expression in the oldest and most permanent of Jewish dreams: "Evidently I continue to believe in God. Though never admitting it. But what else explains my conduct and my life? So I may as well acknowledge how things are, if only because otherwise I can't even be described." The seriousness of these ideas, at least when held by people of stable intellect, tends to deepen rather than to dissipate with age. It was entirely appropriate, then, that the hero of Saul Bellow's next novel, *Mr. Sammler's Planet,* should be an intellectual well into his seventies, beyond the claims of most kinds of worldly aspiration and given to the pleasures of the contemplative life. . . . (pp. 54-5)

Mr. Sammler's Planet, in its efforts to raise and answer [the question: "What is the true stature of a human being?"], extends Bellow's thinking—in its social, cultural, historical, moral and religious dimensions—beyond any points it had reached in his previous novels. . . . *Mr. Sammler's Planet* is a post-Holocaust novel—perhaps the most important of its kind written thus far by an American author—which means, among other things, that it is a study of Western culture *in extremis* and drives all of its considerations with severity and almost to exhaustion. . . .

[One] of these considerations we have already met in Bellow's earlier novels—it pertains to the death question. Given "the sexual madness [that] was overwhelming the Western world," "no one," as Mr. Sammler sees it and laments it, "was prepared to acknowledge death," to make "sober decent terms with death." That refusal—more than a childishness, it was a blasphemy, an impiety—not only condemns Western culture to unseriousness but to a kind of frenzied chaos. (p. 55)

[*Mr. Sammler's Planet* is] Saul Bellow's most

Jewish novel. *That* is an issue that is hardly to be debated, for while one can find prominent aspects of Jewishness in the earlier books—with the exception of Henderson, all of Bellow's major characters and many of his minor ones are Jews—no single novel before this one registers so completely the range of Jewish concerns and the tonalities of Jewish sensibility. Bellow began to open his prose to a recognizably Jewish idiom as far back as *The Adventures of Augie March;* he worked out something of the psychology of anti-Semitism in a still earlier book, *The Victim;* and *Herzog* unquestionably brought to its fullest flowering in American fiction the portrait of a certain kind of Jewish intellectual. When one adds as well his distinctively Jewish brand of humor, the strong emphases on fraternal ties and family feeling, and the centrality of ethical questions, it is clear that Bellow has been, all along and despite certain protestations to the contrary, an overtly Jewish writer. . . . *Mr. Sammler's Planet*, consummating work that it is, not only gathers these various elements into a heretofore unachieved unity but provides them with an historical context, an epistemology, and even the beginnings of a theology, the result being a novel so fundamentally rooted in Jewish consciousness as to bring one to wonder if perhaps a new day was about to arrive, not only for Bellow but for American culture. (pp. 56-7)

[In its intellectual concerns, *Humboldt's Gift*] takes off in so surprising a direction as to leave most of us behind. Charlie Citrine, the protagonist of *Humboldt's Gift,* is preoccupied by many of the same questions that absorbed Bellow's earlier heroes—the problem of "determining what a human being is"; "the question of death (the question of questions)"; whether intimations of "the existence of a soul [are] a tenacious illusion or else the truth deeply buried"; how "to do good"—but some of the teachers to whom Charlie looks for answers are of a kind the likes of which a Moses Herzog or an Artur Sammler could never take seriously. Chief among these is Rudolf Steiner, whose *Knowledge of the Higher Worlds and Its Attainment* Charlie is drawn to but can never get straight: "There were passages in Steiner that set my teeth on edge. I said to myself, this is lunacy. Then I said, this is poetry, a great vision." Which is it to be? The issue remains unresolved, badly so, and as a result the novel—despite its success in winning Bellow the Pulitzer Prize and helping to gain him the Nobel Prize—is, in crucial ways, at loose ends with itself. The high note on which *Humboldt's Gift* ends, in fact—"Now we must listen in secret to the sound of truth that God puts into us"—is a carry-over from *Mr. Sammler's Planet* more than an insight gained from any fresh thinking accomplished in this novel. Indeed, judged on the level of thought—which is to say, judged by Bellow's own standards for

literature—*Humboldt's Gift* is a diffuse and disappointing book.

Criticism can explain why this is so, but it cannot account for its causes or do more than speculate on what they might mean for the author's future work. (pp. 57-8)

This much, though, is clear: in pursuing his metaphysical hunches Bellow has been drawn all along in two somewhat diverse ways, each dictating its own mode of attaining truth. Following the first, he is moved to affirm both "an inordinate faith in the power of rationality" (his own definition of "Jewish transcendentalism") and the conviction that human life is rooted in and takes its directions from a received "bond." These ideas, never worked out systematically but given a recurring fictional life in the novels, are recognizably close to Jewish covenant thought; doubtless they arise from it. *Herzog* and *Mr. Sammler's Planet* derive clearly from such an orientation, which is to say, from a power of mind that seems to enable Bellow to accommodate the contingencies of his "local residence" with his longings for transcendent truth and to bring both under the governance of a critical, but humane and compassionate, intelligence.

There is also another side to Bellow, though, the "spell-prone" and "mediumistic" side, which encourages a kind of magical thinking, as seen from time to time in *Seize the Day* and *Henderson the Rain King.* Until *Humboldt's Gift,* though, this "thaumaturgical" or "mystical" cast of mind was usually tempered by Bellow's tough intelligence and not indulged lightly unless for comic effect. Yet while there is plenty of comedy in this last novel, it usually does not hang together with the anthroposophical speculations, which for the most part are presented as serious business, as an informing "light-in-the-being." So unexpected a leap from a reasonable, historically-grounded metaphysics to metempsychosis is both startling and troubling . . . it does not promise to bring Bellow any closer to his desired knowledge of the soul. To attain that and, as a thinker-in-fiction possibly even to keep from coming undone, he may have to wind back to points he touched in *Mr. Sammler's Planet* or else return (at least in imagination) to Jerusalem, as much a piety as a place and one that revealed to Bellow more about the origins of radiance than he is ever likely to get from the doctors of spiritualist philosophy. . . . (p. 58)

Alvin H. Rosenfeld, "Saul Bellow, on the Soul," in *Midstream,* Vol. XXIII, No. 10, December, 1977, pp. 47-59.

KEITH OPDAHL

(essay date 1979)

[In the following excerpt, Opdahl studies Bellow's handling of plot in his fiction.]

We can probably learn more about a writer from his difficulties than from his triumphs. His struggles reveal his intention and the obstacles that he must overcome to realize it. Most critics, I think, would agree that Saul Bellow's greatest difficulty lies in his plots. . . .

Bellow has two modes: intense, closely textured, moral; and light, energetic, open. *The Victim, Seize the Day,* and, yes, *Herzog* represent the former while *Augie March, Sammler,* and *Humboldt* represent the latter. . . . Bellow fears the dangers of constriction, of polishing the life out of a work. (p. 15)

[What] are the obstacles to plot that Bellow must face? What are the elements of style, theme, or vision that cause him difficulty? (p. 16)

Bellow's most obvious obstacle to plot lies in the fact that he is a realist—perhaps the reason that he wants a plot in the first place. . . . Plot in Bellow's work is hard won, wrested from a confusing density and multiplicity of people, ideas, events, and sensation. It's so hard won that we might well claim that the struggle *is* the plot, as all the protagonists seek to move from the overwhelming richness of experience to some kind of peace and clarity. . . .

Bellow loves energetic, driven characters who have a size and vitality that make them hard to control—so hard to control that the protagonist finds himself bullied by them, shoved about, as each tries to pull him *his* way.

And then the characters are inseparable from their ideas, which also fill Bellow's pages with a confusing abundance. Bellow often has sought a plot that would contain a number of ideologies and has imagined a quest that is mental, as he seeks to dramatize nothing less than the act of thinking. And yet there are too many thoughts finally for the plot line to be easy, since it is an *idea* after all which provides the shape of a novel. (p. 17)

[Another] obstacle associated with his realism [is] his commitment to ordinary life and the virtue of moderation. . . . In novel after novel, Bellow, like Henry James, portrays a special but ordinary phenomenon—a certain light or mood or psychology, the "sense" of a character such as Augie March, or the way a mediocre man in America tries desperately to "seize the day" or be outstanding. (p. 18)

When at his best, [Bellow is] . . . successful in achieving order within his chaotic imaginative world. It's fascinating to note that Bellow often describes the victory of his protagonist as a clearing away of the extraneous. He leaves his protagonist ready to begin—issues defined, emotions controlled, the oppressive diversity of the world somehow stilled. Bellow turns the obstacle on its head, in short, by making the confusing richness of his world the source and mainspring of his plot. . . .

Perhaps the best example of Bellow's success is *Herzog,* much maligned for its formlessness. . . . At the center of Herzog's experience is the contrast between a personal life and a civil one, the private man locked into his feelings and the citizen acting within the institutions of society. Herzog's unmailed letters, the most obvious device of the novel, crystallize this division, since the letters express emotions that can't find their way into action and, though unmailed, are the message of the private man to the "public" realm. In simple terms, Herzog moves from the mess of his private life—which he'd romantically hoped to make exemplary—to a faith in the public realm. (p. 19)

Bellow has found another obstacle to plot far less easy to resolve. As he struggles with the modesty of his subject, he must wrestle, too, with the ambition of his themes. In many ways, Bellow harkens back less to the realists of the nineteenth century than to the romantics, for his fiction attempts to see beyond society to the nature of reality itself. Bellow writes what we must call a novel of perception or revelation in which (as we might expect from a novelist who describes his plot as a coming to clarity) the protagonist desires more than anything else—more than getting the girl or the job or the whale—to see. One of Bellow's greatest tasks is to invent plots or situations that will permit this revelation, Joseph's diary [in *Dangling Man*], Leventhal's interviews [in *The Victim*], Augie's passive listening [in *Augie March*]; again and again Bellow presents the Jamesian conversation, two people groping to "see." Thus Henderson goes to Africa and Herzog reviews his experience. The Bellow protagonist is desperate for insight. (pp. 20-1)

[However] active the host of characters and memories, it is matter, the visible world, that fascinates the hero. If he's not on a couch or at a rooming house window, he's on a train or in a cab or on a plane, looking and looking and looking.

We can understand this staring if we remember that Bellow grew up in the naturalistic tradition which saw force or energy as a reality to be touched and felt, and controlling the intimate lives of man. . . . [*Augie March*] has a vision of a Darwinian world of pure force that is in theory simply indifferent or impersonal, but that becomes (as in the naturalistic novel) something malevolent, almost demonic. (p. 21)

Bellow's sense of this reality, which is clearly natural to his imagination, must have been reinforced by his interest in the experiments of Wilhelm Reich, who also saw the universe streaming with force capable of destruction. But Reich saw this energy as benevolent, too, and so did Bellow, who having portrayed the "white anger," asks a logical question: do our "spiritual qualities"—art, charity, love, generosity—have similar biological roots? Is there any way that love is built into the physical world in the way that struggle is built into the Darwinian one? (pp. 21-2)

Bellow has for the most part learned to be content, working his metaphysical bias into the texture of his work. Certainly the sense he conveys of something behind matter, pressing, a feeling that the physical world is permeated with something beyond our sense, enriches his style. At his best, Bellow conveys a sense of the transcendent within the physical world. The protagonist's painful awareness of the mystery of his being adds another dimension, a depth and richness to a simple scene. (p. 23)

In purely aesthetic terms, Bellow's belief in the transcendent is probably a draw—neither an overwhelming obstacle nor his greatest strength. . . . But many of Bellow's readers are put off by his transcendentalism. Like Augie, they have "resistance" in them, and it is true that a social or economic issue in the Bellow novel very quickly becomes a metaphysical or religious one, creating a certain confusion. (pp. 23-4)

Dimly aware of large forces within himself, [Bellow's] protagonist feels the urgency of a man driven by uncontrollable emotions. He talks to himself. He watches his actions with a horrible fascination. How many of the protagonists are out of control? Joseph in *Dangling Man* suffers his rages, and Leventhal his hypochondria. Tommy Wilhelm [in *Seize the Day*] must yield to his emotions while Henderson runs amuck. Herzog's letters dramatize how feelings may flow wildly and without recourse—the novel finds its center in his need for release.

In this sense the Bellow hero seeks to discover the health and strength that would permit him to act, making a traditional plot possible. On the other hand, Bellow finds a plot in the quest for therapy, in the question invariably asked by the protagonist: what is wrong with me? How may I rid myself of this burden?

The answer to this question, as well as the greatest obstacle to plotting in Bellow's work, is found in a pattern we can trace in all of the novels—a pattern based on the relationship of the protagonist to another male, often a father figure. (p. 24)

But what makes this pattern striking is its climax, which in almost every case involves an embrace and violence or death. . . . (p. 25)

What can we make of this pattern? Since it appears in every novel, and in some a couple of times, we're probably justified in calling it a compulsion. At the very least, it forms a pattern to which Bellow's imagination returns. Or is the encounter, similar to the childhood rape described in *Herzog,* a traumatic experience Bellow's fiction is designed to exorcise? While I suspect this to be true—Freud argued that all art serves to express and thus purge the artist's emotions—our concern here is Bellow's art and the use to which he puts such a pattern. Surely, since he repeatedly returns to it, the pattern creates an obstacle with which Bellow must wrestle and precisely the kind of formal requirement that challenges and channels the imagination.

Bellow has *had* to be ingenious in discovering stories and themes to accommodate this pattern. Allbee's suicide is a mark of his self-hatred, for example, and since he represents the physical world, the sweet gas he releases in the oven epitomizes his threat to Leventhal. Herzog on the other hand is masochistic, so that his threatened murder of Gersbach would destroy him, too. Bellow actually discovers a kind of logic in the pattern, for the father figure almost always represents the world, either as a cynic—the worldly instructor—or as a representative of matter. In the child's mind, of course, the father *is* the world, for the father's image is imposed indelibly on his mind, helping to shape his emotional life. Thus the father has much to do with the masochism the protagonist seems to share, and the desire to be free of an oppressive world becomes a desire to be free of the image of the father who is associated with that world and who does the protagonist harm.

It's not the father per se who creates difficulty in Bellow's plots, however, or even the violent encounter, though Bellow must surely have had to juggle a great deal to get it in. Rather Bellow has had to struggle with the emotional effect of the scene on his protagonist, for the protagonist tends to feel much better after the violence or death. (pp. 25-6)

I think the real story in a Bellow novel is one of catharsis, in an almost classically Freudian sense. The intense confrontation purges either an unconscious hostility, as the "father" dies, or a masochistic desire for pain as the protagonist himself almost "dies." Perhaps the point is that both emotions, which are related, are purged at once. . . . But my point is the way Bellow inverts such an obstacle, making what would be a limitation work for him. (p. 26)

Bellow is . . . successful in working with this experience in the book that has received the greatest praise, *Seize the Day.* Not a little of the power of that novella, I'd argue, derives from the fact that Bellow treats the climax as cathartic and so creates a plot in which the events and the emotions coincide. *Seize the Day* has the unity and solidity of a totally achieved fiction, the ease and grace of a work which makes a strength out of what might have been a limitation or obstacle. For what Tommy Wilhelm needs more than anything else is to break down, to cry, to purge himself of all sorts of pent-up emotions. . . . [When] he stumbles into the funeral parlor and sobs before the corpse of the stranger, his tears answer his need to cry. Bellow *uses* the need for catharsis. He uses the corpse, too, not just because it provides a stunning image with which to conclude the novel, but because it summarizes so many of the themes expressed. Standing before the dead man Tommy seems to feel *all* the pent-up emotions and to proclaim all the themes at once. . . .

In all of these climaxes, the distracting world is shut out and the energies of novel and protagonist sharply focused. In a way, since all of the novels move to such an experience, it is this climax which demands a plot. The confrontation with violence or death is so expressive of emotion, so *definitive,* that it requires a dramatic action that rises to a climax. (p. 27)

How many successful plots must a novelist invent? In a way, Bellow is a victim not only of our present distrust of any plot, but of our incredibly high demands for the ones we do accept. The New Critics have taught us to demand that a conclusion end a novel in a memorable way, summarizing all that went before and illuminating it, crystallizing the whole book in a single glowing image or scene. Never mind that such a scene near the end of a long traditional novel might well break the tone. We're perfectionists when we talk about structure and accept only an inspired unity. It's fitting, in view of such conflicts and inconsistencies, that Bellow forge his successful plots from the very obstacles that have plagued him. (p. 28)

Keith Opdahl, " 'Stillness in the Midst of Chaos': Plot in the Novels of Saul Bellow," in *Modern Fiction Studies,* Vol. 25, No. 1, Spring, 1979, pp. 15-28.

MALCOLM BRADBURY

(essay date 1982)

[An English scholar, Bradbury is best known as the author of such satiric novels as *Eating People Is Wrong* (1959) and *Stepping Westward* (1965). He has also written extensively on English and American literature. In the following excerpt, he contends that Bellow's work is distinct and commanding in its exploration of modern life.]

[Bellow's works] are intensely contemporary and are certainly firmly placed amid the directions, tendencies

and epistemologies that have shaped and then been amended in the novel of today. Bellow is an intellectual writer, and his sense of literary debts and derivations is serious and explicit: they are debts of great variousness. There is a clear debt to Emerson, Melville and the American Transcendentalists (Bellow refers to them often, either directly or by allusion, conspicuously, for example, in the ending of *Herzog*) and to the massed heritage of European Romanticism. There is another clear debt to Dreiser and the tradition of naturalism, deeply powerful in both its bleak and its optimistic forms in American fiction. Bellow often refers to this tradition, in both its ironizing and its vitalistic aspects (especially in *The Adventures of Augie March*), and has praised Dreiser, another Chicago novelist, for opening the American novel to the power of the unmediated, the open fact of American life, the commanding chaotic force of the American city. The debt also goes further, shaping Bellow's lasting struggle with the deterministic inheritance. His books show a deep sense of environmental intrusion, of the power of the conditioned, of life as competitive struggle chaotically releasing and suppressing energy. As a novelist he encounters an urban, mechanical, massed world—in which the self may be ironized, displaced or sapped by dominant processes and the laws of social placing, where victimization is real, and the assertion of self and the distillation of an act of will or a humanistic value is a lasting problem. Much of this naturalistic lore Bellow inherited from the 1930s, at the end of which he began to write. But what intersects with all this, and makes his work so convincing, is the deep penetration of his work by the classic stock of European modernism, especially that modernism in its more historically alert, postromantic and humanistically defeated forms.

Bellow is thus a novelist of a very different generation from that of Lewis, Faulkner, Hemingway, Steinbeck or James T. Farrell, all of whom might in different ways be associated with the centralizing of the American novel as a major twentieth-century form of expression. He is a novelist writing beyond the end of American pastoral; his works belong to a new order of American and world history. (pp. 24-5)

Politically active in the Depression, he none the less started to write in the mood of abeyance to dialectical politics that came with the Second World War. . . . His earliest fictional publication thus immediately precedes the Japanese attack on Pearl Harbor which plunged America into the Second World War, collapsed the thirties political spectrum and allied Americans with the bleakness and bloodiness of modern world history. It was a history that disoriented the liberal progressive expectations of the American left, challenged naturalism as a language of political attention, and raised the question of art's response to a totalitarian and genocidal world. Bellow's response was to write about an America newly exposed to history, affected by the desperations of existentialism and absurdism, war-pained, urban, materialist, angst-ridden, troubled with global responsibility, struggling to distil meaning and morality from the chaos of utopian and progressive thought.

All this was very apparent in *Dangling Man,* Bellow's first full-length novel, which appeared in 1944, as the war moved to an end—an extraordinary book which displays clear debts to a modern European writing of romantic disorientation and historical enclosure that comes from Dostoevsky, Conrad, Sartre and Camus. It is not hard to draw links between his and Dostoevsky's spiritually agonized heroes—caught in the fragmentations of a culture collapsing into urban strangeness, political disorder and waning faith which struggles with existential desire; nor between his world and Conrad's, where civilization is a thin veneer overlying anarchy, calling forth 'absurd' existential affirmations; nor between his imaginings and Kafka's, where the self moves solipsistically through an onerously powerful yet incomprehensible historical world. Yet it is as if this was a tradition which Bellow felt he had the power to qualify and amend, to recall toward humanism; and here his Jewish sources are deeply relevant, constituting another force that 'Europeanizes' his fiction.

Perhaps Isaac Bashevis Singer rather than Kafka—Bellow translated Singer's story 'Gimpel the Fool'—better suggests this origin, with his classic images of suffering and victimization irradiated with transcendental and mystical hopes; the recovering victim and the 'suffering joker' are part of the essential stuff of Bellow's writing, but so is that sense of human bonding which allows him to struggle toward a latter-day humanism and a new civility. Indeed it was that new civility, accommodating the experience of persecution and the path of survival, that made Bellow seem so central a figure in the post-war world, a world post-holocaust and post-atomic, urban and material, where progressive naturalism and innocent liberalism no longer spoke recognizably to experience.

Bellow thus went on to become a primary voice of a time when the Jewish-American writer, urban, historically alert, concerned to distil a morality and a possible humanism from a bland, material, encroaching reality in which all substantial meanings seemed hidden, moved to the centre of American writing. (pp. 25-7)

Bellow thus developed as a writer in a period when a distinct stylistic and aesthetic climate, which was also a political climate, was forming. It was a period of revived liberalism, invigorated by the reaction against totalitarianism that arose with the battle against and then the defeat of Nazism, and then with the new cold war struggle of the superpowers. The politics and aesthetics of liberalism were an important version of

recovered pluralism and democracy; yet at the same time the post-war social order, with its materialism, its pressure toward conformity, its move toward mass society, threatened the liberal self. (p. 28)

It was the Jewish writers, with their sense of traditional alienation and exile, their profoundly relevant witness to the recent holocaust, their awareness of the inadequacies of an older liberalism that could not cope with what Reinhold Niebuhr called 'the ultimately religious problem of the evil in man', who concentrated the spirit of the necessary imagination. Lionel Trilling would call this 'the liberal imagination', whose natural centre lies in the novel, the testing place where the ideal is perpetually forced to mediate with the contingent and the real, where ideology meets 'the hum and buzz of culture', where history and individual are compelled into encounter.

Bellow's fiction, as it developed from the tight form of *Dangling Man* (1944) and *The Victim* (1947) into the looser and more picaresque structures of *The Adventures of Augie March* (1953) and *Henderson the Rain King* (1959), thus seemed to gesture toward a revival of the liberal novel—a form that has had a strained history in our modern and modernist century. . . . Bellow's novels have certainly moved toward the salvaging of a liberal form. They are hero-centred to a degree unusual in modern fiction; the hero often gives his name to the novel. He is always a man and often a Jew, and often a writer or intellectual; he is anxious about 'self', concerned with exploring its inward claim, and about 'mind', which may be our salvation or the real source of our suffering. At the same time he is driven by an irritable desire to recognize his relation with others, with society as such, with the felt texture of common existence, with nature and the universe. Around such battles certain prime reminders occur: man is mortal, and death must be weighed; man is biologically in process, part of nature, and must find his measure in it; man is consciousness, and consciousness is indeed in history; man is real, but so is the world in its historical evolution, and the two substantialities evade understandable relation. So we are drawn toward thoughts of extreme alienation, urgent romantic selfhood, apocalyptic awareness, while at the same time we know ourselves to be in a post-romantic universe, Lenin's age of wars and revolutions, where our conditioning is inescapable. Social and historical existence may thus contend with mythical or metaphysical existence, but neither can finally outweigh the other, and the effort must be toward reconciliation—an end displayed in Bellow's own fictional endings, which frequently take the form of some complex contractual renewal between the self and the world, though, despite critical suspicion of them, these endings are less some rhetorical resolution than a suspended anxiety, often returned to in the next novel. (pp. 28-30)

As for the balance and nature of Bellow's work, that too changed. In the 1950s he had explored the expansive epic, testing out whether man can set himself free in history. By the 1960s that enquiry had tightened again, into the complex structural form of *Herzog* (1964), where historical presence becomes a form of madness, and the bleak irony of *Mr Sammler's Planet* (1970), which now looks less a bitter assault on the new radicalism than the beginning of a new kind of enquiry into the elements of evil secreted in our modern history, and in modern America, in an age marked by postcultural energy, a new rootless barbarism in which possibility and monstrosity contend for the soul. Bellow's books have grown not easier but harder to read. They have become in some ways more meditative, philosophical, transcendental. (pp. 31-2)

Bellow is not, in the fashionable sense of the term, a 'post-modern' or even an 'experimental' novelist. He does not question reflexively his own fictionality, or adopt the nihilist stoicism of black humour. His books still grant the dominant materiality of the outer world, which is process, system and power; and they continue to explore consciousness and mind in struggle with that power, as they hunt to find a significant human meaning, an inward presence and a sense of personal immediacy, and an outward awareness of the nature of the cosmic world. Consciousness and history still struggle at odds, but in an ever-compelled and ever-changing intimacy. His books have, indeed, largely changed by circling their own known subjects, intensifying the elements, deepening the enquiry. Bellow's perception of the nature, the substance and the pressure of the historical world has moved increasingly toward a definition of a new, post-cultural America, most clearly manifest in his own home city of Chicago, that 'cultureless city pervaded nonetheless by Mind', as its life has changed, accumulated and massed; as its old localities and ways of life fall under the hands of the new developers, as crime and terror haunt its inner city and the *inner* inner city of its inhabitants, as the doors are triple-locked and bourgeois life goes on under siege in some strange modern compact with a new barbarism, it becomes a central image of what the mind and the novel alike must come to terms with. His perception of the world of consciousness has also grown more intense and avid for right feeling, as it finds itself bereft yet busy, having nowhere else but history from which to draw versions of reality in its endless quest for awareness and fulfilment.

A novelist who registers the enormous pressure of modern life, and also the peculiar sense of existence, on a scale rare in fiction, Bellow has thus reacted with a considerable formal flexibility and variousness. Coming into being over four transforming decades of American life, his books have registered them with a vital historical *and* aesthetic attention, taking the novel form as *the* necessary mode of mediation between the world of process and the world of consciousness. A critic of apocalyptics, Bellow has grown more apocalyptic; a doubter of concepts, he has grown more conceptual and abstract, though searching always for those moments of immediacy and humanity when the soul feels its presence and its need to value existence. A voice of moral liberalism, he has grown more conservative, in a large sense, become a writer who explores the contrast between a culturally coherent past and a post-cultural present. A novelist who defends the novel's humanism, he has shown us, more than most novelists, the powers that point toward a post-humanist world, and hence challenge the novel's capacities to explore it. His books, especially his most recent, portraits of writers making the crucial attempt, show both the challenge and the indeterminacy of the solutions; in a sense, it is their indeterminacy that makes every new Bellow novel possible. Bellow not only has been, but remains, one of the most essential American writers of his age. . . . (pp. 32-4)

Bellow remains one of our most serious novelists, and our most commanding, because he is a great modern novelist of the attempt to reconciie mind, in all its resource and confusion, its fantastic fertility and unending anguish, with a life that is itself absurd, extravagant, pressing us not only with material forces but with ideas and forms of consciousness, information and concepts, boredoms and rewards. It is a world where the measure of man can hardly be taken, the right form of expression or idea never be found; but where our mind as a sense of felt existence insists that we take it. The resulting perception is indeed comedy in its seriousness: which is an observation of disparity, an awareness that we are, indeed, "suffering jokers", vital but absurd, and of a secret freedom, lying in our gift to know. History, environment, concept and the reality-instructors tell us much, and much of it makes us despair; but against that there is a self-presence, vivid and curious, and of it Bellow is surely one of the great modern metaphysical comedians. (pp. 103-04)

Malcolm Bradbury, in his *Saul Bellow,* Methuen, 1982, 110 p.

SOURCES FOR FURTHER STUDY

Cronin, Gloria L., and Goldman, L. H., eds. *Saul Bellow in the 1980's: A Collection of Critical Essays.* East Lansing: Michigan State University Press, 1989, 328 p.

> Contains original and reprinted essays on both general and specialized topics by such contributors as Daniel Fuchs, Ellen Pifer, and Matthew C. Roudané.

Cronin, Gloria L., and Hall, Blaine H. *Saul Bellow: An Annotated Bibliography.* 2d ed. New York: Garland Publishing, Inc., 1987, 312 p.

> Includes a chronology of Bellow's career, a primary bibliography, and a list of articles and books on the author up to 1986.

Fuchs, Daniel. *Saul Bellow: Vision and Revision.* Durham, N. C.: Duke University Press, 1984, 345 p.

> Attempts "to define the writer's literary and cultural milieus" and in separate chapters examines each of Bellow's major works, beginning with *The Adventures of Augie March* and concluding with *The Dean's December,* "from the point of view of how it was composed."

Kiernan, Robert F. *Saul Bellow.* New York: Continuum, 1989, 270 p.

> Detailed biographical and critical study of Bellow's life and works through *More Die of Heartbreak.*

Malin, Erving, ed. *Saul Bellow and the Critics.* New York: New York University Press, 1967, 227 p.

> Twelve essays of varying length, scope, and point of view by such critics as Tony Tanner, Keith Opdahl, and Earl Rovit.

Rovit, Earl, ed. *Saul Bellow: A Collection of Critical Essays.* Englewood Cliffs, N. J.: Prentice-Hall, Inc., 1975, 176 p.

> Twelve essays that "represent widely different critical perspectives, methodologies, and thematic interests" in an attempt to establish "the intellectual context within which [Bellow's] word will be heard."

Ambrose Bierce

1842-1914?

(Full name Ambrose Gwinett Bierce; also wrote under pseudonyms Dod Grile and William Herman) American short story writer, novelist, journalist, poet, essayist, and critic.

INTRODUCTION

Bierce's literary reputation is based primarily on his short stories about the Civil War and the supernatural—a body of work that makes up a relatively small part of his total output. Often compared to the tales of Edgar Allan Poe, these stories share an attraction to death in its more bizarre forms, featuring depictions of mental deterioration and uncanny, otherworldly manifestations and expressing the horror of existence in a meaningless universe. Like Poe, Bierce professed to be mainly concerned with the artistry of his work, yet critics find him more intent on conveying his misanthropy and pessimism. In his lifetime Bierce was famous as a California journalist dedicated to exposing the truth as he understood it, regardless of whose reputations were harmed by his attacks. For his sardonic wit and damning observations on the personalities and events of the day, he became known as "the wickedest man in San Francisco."

Bierce was born in Meigs County, Ohio. His parents were farmers and he was the tenth of thirteen children, all of whom were given names beginning with "A" at their father's insistence. The family moved to Indiana, where Bierce went to high school; he later attended the Kentucky Military Institute. At the outbreak of the Civil War, he enlisted in the Union army. In such units as the Ninth Indiana Infantry Regiment and Buell's Army of the Ohio, he fought bravely in numerous military engagements, including the battles of Shiloh and Chickamauga and in Sherman's March to the Sea. After the war Bierce traveled with a military expedition to San Francisco, where he left the army and prepared himself for a literary career.

Bierce's early poetry and prose appeared in the *Californian.* In 1868 he became the editor of *The News Letter,* for which he wrote his famous "Town Crier" column. Bierce became something of a noted figure in

California literary society, forming friendships with Mark Twain, Bret Harte, and Joaquin Miller. In 1872 Bierce and his wife moved to England, where during a three-year stay he wrote for *Fun* and *Figaro* magazines and acquired the nickname "Bitter Bierce." His first three books of sketches *Nuggets and Dust Panned Out in California* (1872), *The Fiend's Delight* (1873), and *Cobwebs from an Empty Skull* (1874)—were published during this period. When the English climate aggravated Bierce's asthma, he returned to San Francisco. In 1887 he began writing for William Randolph Hearst's *San Francisco Examiner*, continuing the "Prattler" column he had done for *The Argonaut* and *The Wasp*. This provided him with a regular outlet for his essays, epigrams, and short stories.

Bierce's major fiction was collected in *Tales of Soldiers and Civilians* (1891) and *Can Such Things Be?* (1893). Many of these stories are realistic depictions of the author's experiences in the Civil War. However, Bierce was not striving for realism, as critics have pointed out and as he himself admitted, for his narratives often fail to supply sufficient verisimilitude. His most striking fictional effects depend on an adept manipulation of the reader viewpoint: a bloody battlefield seen through the eyes of a deaf child in "Chickamauga," the deceptive escape dreamed by a man about to be hanged in "An Occurrence at Owl Creek Bridge," and the shifting perspectives of "The Death of Halpin Frayser." The classic Biercian narrative also includes a marked use of black humor, particularly in the ironic and hideous deaths his protagonists often suffer. The brutal satire Bierce employed in his journalism appears as plain brutality in his fiction, and critics have both condemned and praised his imagination, along with Poe's, as among the most vicious and morbid in American literature. Bierce's bare, economical style of supernatural horror is usually distinguished from the verbally lavish tales of Poe, and few critics rank Bierce as the equal of his predecessor.

Along with his tales of terror, Bierce's most acclaimed work is *The Devil's Dictionary* (1906), a lexicon of its author's wit and animosity. His definition —"the outward and visible sign of an inward fear"—clarifies his fundamentally psychological approach to the supernatural. In *The Devil's Dictionary* Bierce vented much of his contempt for politics, religion, society, and conventional human values. A committed opponent of hypocrisy, prejudice, and corruption, Bierce acquired the public persona of an admired but often hated genius, a man of contradiction and mystery. In 1914 he informed some of his correspondents that he intended to enter Mexico and join Pancho Villa's forces as an observer during that country's civil war. He was never heard from again, and the circumstances of his death are uncertain.

(For further information about Bierce's life and works, see *Concise Dictionary of American Literary Biography, 1865-1917; Contemporary Authors*, Vol. 104; *Dictionary of Literary Biography*, Vols. 11, 12, 23, 71, 74; and *Twentieth-Century Literary Criticism*, Vols. 1, 7.)

CRITICAL COMMENTARY

H. L. MENCKEN
(essay date 1927)

[From the era of World War I until the early years of the Great Depression, Mencken was one of the most influential figures in American letters. In the following excerpt, Mencken, having known Bierce personally, clarifies the relationship between Bierce's cynicism and his interest in war.]

Bierce, I believe, was the first writer of fiction ever to treat war realistically. He antedated even Zola. It is common to say that he came out of the Civil War with a deep and abiding loathing of slaughter—that he wrote his war stories in disillusion, and as a sort of pacifist. But this is certainly not believed by anyone who knew him, as I did in his last years. What he got out of his services in the field was not a sentimental horror of it, but a cynical delight in it. It appeared to him as a sort of magnificent *reductio ad absurdum* of all romance. The world viewed war as something heroic, glorious, idealistic. Very well, he would show how sordid and filthy it was—how stupid, savage and degrading. But to say this is not to say that he disapproved it. On the contrary, he vastly enjoyed the chance its discussion gave him to set forth dramatically what he was always talking about and gloating over: the infinite imbecility of man. There was nothing of the milk of human kindness in old Ambrose; he did not get the nickname of Bitter Bierce for nothing. What delighted him most in this life was the spectacle of human cowardice and folly. He put man, intellectually, somewhere between the sheep and the horned cattle, and as a hero somewhere below the rats. His war stories, even when they deal with the heroic, do not depict soldiers as heroes;

Principal Works

Nuggets and Dust Panned Out in California [as Dod Grile] (sketches) 1872

The Fiend's Delight [as Dod Grile] (sketches) 1873

Cobwebs from an Empty Skull [as Dod Grile] (sketches) 1874

The Dance of Death [with Thomas A. Harcourt under the joint pseudonym William Herman] (satire) 1877

Tales of Soldiers and Civilians (short stories) 1891; published in England as In the Midst of Life, 1892

Black Beetles in Amber (poetry) 1892

The Monk and the Hangman's Daughter [translator; with Gustav Adolph Danzinger] (novel) 1892

Can Such Things Be? (short stories) 1893

Fantastic Fables (satire) 1899

Shapes of Clay (poetry) 1903

The Cynic's Word Book (satire) 1906; also published as The Devil's Dictionary, 1911

The Shadow on the Dial, and Other Essays (essays) 1909

Write It Right (essay) 1909

The Collected Works of Ambrose Bierce. 12 vols. (short stories, sketches, poetry, essays, homilies, and satire) 1912

---

they depict them as bewildered fools, doing things without sense, submitting to torture and outrage without resistance, dying at last like hogs in Chicago, the former literary capital of the United States. So far in this life, indeed, I have encountered no more thorough-going cynic than Bierce was. His disbelief in man went even further than Mark Twain's; he was quite unable to imagine the heroic, in any ordinary sense. Nor, for that matter, the wise. Man to him, was the most stupid and ignoble of animals. But at the same time the most amusing. Out of the spectacle of life about him he got an unflagging and Gargantuan joy. The obscene farce of politics delighted him. He was an almost amorous connoisseur of theology and theologians. He howled with mirth whenever he thought of a professor, a doctor or a husband. His favorites among his contemporaries were such zanies as Bryan, Roosevelt and Hearst.

Another character that marked him, perhaps flowing out of this same cynicism, was his curious taste for the macabre. All of his stories show it. He delighted in hangings, autopsies, dissecting-rooms. Death to him was not something repulsive, but a sort of low comedy—the last act of a squalid and rib-rocking buffoonery. (pp. 260-62)

He liked mystification, and there are whole stretches of his long life that are unaccounted for. His end had mystery in it too. It is assumed that he was killed in Mexico, but no eye-witness has ever come forward, and so the fact, if it is a fact, remains hanging in the air. (pp. 263-64)

Unluckily, his stories seem destined to go the way of Poe's. Their influence upon the modern American short story, at least upon its higher levels, is almost nil. When they are imitated at all, it is by the lowly hacks who manufacture thrillers for the cheap magazines. Even his chief disciples, Sterling and Scheffauer, did not follow him. . . . Meanwhile, it remains astonishing that his wit is so little remembered. In *The Devil's Dictionary* are some of the most devastating epigrams ever written. "Ah, that we could fall into women's arms without falling into their hands": it is hard to find a match for that in Oscar himself. (p. 264)

His life was a long sequence of bitter ironies. I believe that he enjoyed it. (p. 265)

H. L. Mencken, "Ambrose Bierce," in his *Prejudices: Sixth Series,* Knopf, 1927, pp. 259-65.

CLIFTON FADIMAN
(essay date 1946)

[Fadiman is best known for the insightful and often caustic book reviews he wrote for the *Nation* and the *New Yorker* magazines during the 1930s. In the following excerpt from an essay first published in 1946 as the introduction to a collection of Bierce's writings, he maintains that Bierce is unsurpassed in his brute expression of misanthropy.]

The dominating tendency of American literature and social thought, from Benjamin Franklin to Sinclair Lewis, has been optimistic. It has believed in man, it has believed in American man. It has at times been satirical and even bitter—but not negative. It gave the world the positive statements of the Declaration, the Constitution, the Gettysburg Address, Emerson, Whitman, William James, Henry George, John Dewey. This has been the stronger current. But along with it there has coursed a narrower current, the shadowed stream of pessimism. Perhaps its obscure source lies in the southern philosophers of slavery or in the bleak hell-fire morality of early puritan divines. . . . It flows hesitantly in Hawthorne, with fury in *Moby Dick* and *Pierre,* with many a subtle meander in the dark symbolisms of Poe. It may appear in part of a writer (the Mark Twain of "The Mysterious Stranger" and "The Man That Corrupted Hadleyburg") and not in the whole of him. It runs through Stephen Crane. You may trace it in an out-of-the-main-stream philosopher such as Thorstein Veblen. You will find it in the thought of H. L. Mencken and the stories of Ring Lardner. And you will see it plain, naked, naive, and powerful, in the strange fables of Ambrose Bierce.

Bierce's nihilism is as brutal and simple as a blow, and by the same token not decisive. It has no base in philosophy and, being quite bare of shading or qualification, becomes, if taken in overdoses, tedious. Except for the skeleton grin that creeps over his face when he has devised in his fiction some peculiarly grotesque death, Bierce never deviates into cheerfulness. His rage is unselective. The great skeptics view human nature without admiration but also without ire. Bierce's misanthropy is too systematic. He is a pessimism-machine. He is a Swift minus intellectual power, Rochefoucauld with a bludgeon, Voltaire with stomach-ulcers.

Nevertheless he may appeal to a generation which all over the world is being carefully conditioned to believe in nothing but Force. His cynicism, phrased with really extraordinary concentration, appalled his contemporaries; but it may attract rather than appall us. His *Fantastic Fables* may strike us as neither fantastic nor fabulous. He seems quite a man of our time.

I do not wish to overstate the point, for much of Bierce is old-fashioned. His prose at its worst is flawed with the bad taste of his period; his weakness for melodrama occasionally makes us squirm; he frequently overdoes his effects. Yet it is difficult to forget, for instance, the best of the stories in *In the Midst of Life:* "An Occurrence at Owl Creek Bridge," less interesting as a trick than as a heart-freezing symbolical presentation of the depth of the passion for survival; "Chickamauga," which, by a device of brilliant originality, rams home the pure insanity of war; "One of the Missing," which, like so many of his tales, shows a completely modern interest in and understanding of abnormal states of consciousness. Bierce, despite his almost Spanish admiration for "honor," was one of the earliest American writers to dismiss the flapdoodle of war and hold up to our gaze something like its true countenance. It is not so much that he hated war; indeed these stories are marked by a sort of agony of joy over war's horrors. Perhaps Bierce took a cold pleasure in war as the perfect justification of his view of mankind. He may even have liked war—no true lover of war has ever been so weak-kneed or weak-stomached as to attempt to disguise its brutality. But, however complicated Bierce's attitude toward war may have been, what he writes has the bitter-aloes taste of truth. He helped blaze the trail for later and doubtless better realists.

It is pertinent that Bierce, who disliked human beings and scoffed at social relationships, should have written so much and on the whole so well about ghosts, apparitions, revenants, were-dogs, animated machines, extrasensory perception, and action at a distance. It is as though the man's inability to stomach the real world

forced him to try to establish citizenship in the country of the occult. He was so obsessed by the horror of real life that he had to call in the aid of another dimension in order to express it. . . . Bierce's morbidity is too controlled to have about it any touch of the insane; it merely expresses his fury at our placid healthiness. . . . It is this emotional drive behind his most calculated horrors that makes him much more than an American Monk Lewis. His Gothicism is no hothouse flower but a monstrous orchid.

Bierce's morbidity was exceptionally fertile—he made it produce humor as well as chills. I should say that in this extremely narrow field of the sardonic, of the ludicrous ghost story and the comical murder, he is unrivaled. He begins by somehow making you accept his basic premise: death is a joke. The rest is dead-pan elaboration, with the dead pan occasionally relieved by the rictus of a ghoul trying to laugh. Perhaps the two best examples are **"My Favorite Murder"** and **"Oil of Dog." "My Favorite Murder"** really creates a new shudder, a shudder in which laughter is grotesquely mingled. It is outrageous, it is frightening—it is funny. One finishes it in thorough agreement with the narrator that "in point of artistic atrocity" the murder of Uncle William has seldom been excelled. The humor of the unbelievable **"Oil of Dog"** depends on a careful, indeed beautiful use of ironical understatement, and the exhaustiveness of the technique whereby the macabre is pushed to such an extreme that it falls somehow into the gulf of laughter. (pp. 148-52)

The nuclear Bierce is to be found in the *Fantastic Fables.* One should not read more than a dozen of them at a time, just as one should not read more than a dozen jokes at a time. Their quality lies in their ferocious concentration of extra-double-distilled essential oil of misanthropy. They are so condensed they take your breath away.

The theme is always the same: mankind is a scoundrel. But the changes rung upon the theme demonstrate an almost abnormal inventiveness. They have no humor—they do not resemble at all, for instance, the fables of George Ade. They have wit but little fancy, they are undecorated, and they sting painfully. The brutal Bierce allows no exceptions. He aims to make mincemeat of all civilized humanity. . . . (p. 152)

Bierce is not, of course, a great writer. He has painful faults of vulgarity and cheapness of imagination. But at his best he is like no one else. He had, for example, a mastery of pared phrasing equaled in our time perhaps only by Wilde and Shaw. (pp. 152-53)

His style, for one thing, will preserve him, though for how long no one would care to say; and the purity of his misanthropy, too, will help to keep him alive. It is good that literature should be so catholic and wide-wayed that it affords scope to every emotion and attitude, even the unloveliest. It is fitting that someone should be born and live and die, dedicated to the expression of bitterness. For bitterness is a mood that comes to all intelligent men, though, as they are intelligent, only intermittently. It is proper that there should be at least one man able to give penetrating expression to that mood. Bierce is such a man—limited, wrongheaded, unbalanced, but, in his own constricted way, an artist. (p. 153)

Clifton Fadiman, "Portrait of a Misanthrope," in his *Party of One: The Selected Writings of Clifton Fadiman,* World Publishing Co., 1955, pp. 145-53.

EDMUND WILSON
(essay date 1962)

[Wilson is widely known as one of the foremost American literary critics of the twentieth century. In the following excerpt, he contends that Bierce was obsessed with death and examines the influence of this obsession on his life and works.]

It may very well be true [as some biographers claim] that the special ferocity and gusto with which Bierce played the Devil's advocate, as well as his readiness to castigate others as "wantons," liars and thieves—that is, blastingly, out of hand, from the point of view of old-fashioned morality—and the curious Puritanism that underlay his San Francisco rakishness, were due to a Calvinist background.

In any case, it is certainly true, not only that, as has been said by Clifton Fadiman, Death itself is Bierce's favorite character, but that, except in *The Monk and the Hangman's Daughter,* a rewriting of a story by someone else, Death may perhaps be said to be Ambrose Bierce's only real character. In all Bierce's fiction, there are no men or women who are interesting as men or women—that is, by reason of their passions, their aspirations or their personalities. They figure only as the helpless butts of sadistic practical jokes, and their higher faculties are so little involved that they might almost as well be trapped animals. But Bierce does succeed in making Death play an almost personal role. His accounts of battles he took part in are among the most attractive of his writings, because here he is able to combine a ceaseless looking Death in the face with a delight in the wonder of the world, as the young man from Elkhart, Indiana, finds himself in a land where "unfamiliar constellations burned in the southern midnights, and the mocking-bird poured out his heart in the moon-gilded magnolia." . . . [The] enchantment that Bierce's war memories had for him was partly cre-

ated by the charms of the South, so different from anything he had previously known. But eventually, in his horror stories, the obsession with death becomes tiresome. If we try to read these stories in bulk, they get to seem not merely disgusting but dull. The horror stories of Poe, with which they have been compared, have always a psychological interest in the sense that the images they summon are metaphors for hidden emotions. The horror stories of Bierce have only in a very few cases such psychological interest as may come from exploiting dramatically some abnormal phenomenon of consciousness. There is, otherwise, merely the Grand Guignol trick repeated again and again. The executioner Death comes to us from outside our human world and, capriciously, gratuitously, cruelly, slices away our lives. It is an unpleasant limitation of Bierce's treatment of violent death that it should seem to him never a tragedy, but merely a bitter jest. He seems rarely to have felt any pity for his dead comrades of the Civil War, and it is characteristic of him that he should write [of them] as if in derision. . . . (pp. 622-23)

Bierce's short stories are often distinguished from the hackwork of the shudder magazines only by the fact that the shudder is an emotion that for the author is genuine, and by the sharp-edged and flexible style, like the ribbon of a wound-up steel tape-measure. He has also a certain real knack for catching, in his stories about the West, the loneliness of solitary cabins, with their roofs partly fallen in and with a grave or two among the trees; of worked-out diggings in Nevada hills with a skeleton at the bottom of the shaft; of empty buildings in San Francisco of which nobody knows the owners but into which some unknown person creeps at night—all places where the visit of Death seems peculiarly blighting and final, where, in pinching out a tiny human spirit, it renders the great waste complete.

In most other departments of Bierce's work—his poetry, his commentary on public events, his satirical and humorous sketches—the reign of Death is only less absolute. He seems interested in denouncing political corruption mainly from the point of view of its giving him an opportunity to imagine macabre scenes in which the miscreants are received in Hell or left to survive alone in a universe divested of life. In his poetry, God and the angels and even the figure of Christ, as well as the Devil and his agents, are sometimes brought on to the scene, but these powers, celestial and infernal alike, act only to reject and to damn. (p. 624)

As for Bierce's opinions and principles, they were, as someone said of Voltaire, "a chaos of clear ideas." The dismay and the doubt which for such men as Bierce, in the era of big profits and abundant graft, came to cloud the success of the Union cause is given vehement expression in certain of his poems. And he detested the melodrama that the Northerners had made of the Civil War. . . . [At one time he wrote]: "They found a Confederate soldier the other day with his rifle alongside. I'm going over to beg his pardon."

There are moments when, like Justice Holmes, he is inclined to think that war itself is a purgative and bracing institution. . . . (pp. 625-26)

Ambrose Bierce, in the department of religion, was not a militant atheist as he might have been expected to be. Though he baited and made fun of the clergy, he had several clerical friends, and, according to the memoir of Walter Neale, he especially esteemed Jewish rabbis, for their "broad scholarship," their "devotion to the traditions of their religious order" and their "tolerance of other religions." He was respectful toward all the faiths, but conceived them to be all the creations of men. . . . [He] was haunted by visions of judgment, and he talks about God in a way which, even when he is being facetious, makes one feel that the conception is still real to him, that—remote above the power of Death—it still presides in Bierce's mind.

As for Bierce's political and social views, the disruption of the Republic by the Civil War, in shattering the integrity of the republican ideal, had shaken Bierce's faith in its purpose; yet, like Holmes, he was too much an old-fashioned American to feel himself really at home with the new ideals of social justice—with the socialists or with Henry George. The result was that, in commenting on current affairs in his San Francisco newspaper column, he was often quite inconsistent. . . . The degradation of public life that followed the Civil War and the activities of omnivorous Business which had worried Walt Whitman and others, were now causing younger men to conclude that if this was what democracy meant, there must be something wrong with democracy. The insistence of Ambrose Bierce on discipline, law and order, and on the need for the control of the disorderly mob by an enlightened and well-washed minority has today a familiar fascistic ring. Though Bierce sometimes jeered at the English, he was really—having lived for three years in England (1872-75)—quite distinctly an Anglophile, and he was sympathetic with British imperialism. He seems to have believed that monarchy was the most satisfactory form of government. (pp. 626-28)

[There is a] disconcerting contrast between the somewhat unpleasant impression that we are likely to get of Bierce when we read him or read about him at length, and the attraction which he evidently exercised on those with whom he came in contact. . . . And it is reported by several persons that Bierce seemed to exert a magnetic power over the animals he kept as pets, and that, by giving a "soft call" in the woods, "half a whisper and half a cry," he could bring the birds to perch on his shoulders and hop about on his uplifted hands; yet there is no love of life in his writings, and barely a flush of responsive warmth toward any other human being. Of the sunlight and flowers and fruit, of the gaiety and good wine and good eating, of the love affairs and friendships that Bierce enjoyed in and about San Francisco for something like thirty years, there is hardly a trace in his work.

Even the best of his fiction is monotonous and almost monomaniacal in its compulsive concentration on death, and the general run of his journalism would seem to have been equally sterile and even more disagreeable in its monotony of personal abuse. . . . [His] biographers cite many instances of his kindness and consideration. Yet the impression one gets from his journalism is that of a powerful impulse to denigrate for the lust of destroying. (pp. 628-30)

He abominated dialect literature and wanted to outlaw American colloquialisms. As Mencken says, "It never seems to have occurred to him that language, like literature, is a living thing, not a mere set of rules." It is the hand of death again. The best qualities of Bierce's prose are military—concision, severe order and unequivocal clearness. His diction is the result of training and seems sometimes rather artificial. The soldier commands one's respect, but the queer unsatisfactoriness of Bierce's writing is partly due to the fact that this marble correctitude is made to serve as a mask for a certain vulgarity of mind and feeling. . . . Bierce was aware of his crudeness, and it is plain from . . . books about him that he resolutely struggled against it. But there was something besides the crudeness that hobbled his exceptional talents—an impasse, a numbness, a void, as if some psychological short circuit had blown out an emotional fuse. The obsession with death is the image of this: it is the blank that blocks every vista; and the asthma from which Bierce suffered was evidently its physical aspect. . . . His writing—with its purged vocabulary, the brevity of the units in which it works and its cramped emotional range—is an art that can hardly breathe.

Ambrose Bierce lacks the tragic dimension; he was unable to surmount his frustration, his contempt for himself and mankind. . . . (pp. 631-32)

Edmund Wilson, "Ambrose Bierce on the Owl Creek Bridge," in his *Patriotic Gore: Studies in the Literature of the American Civil War*, Oxford University Press, Inc., 1962, pp. 617-34.

STUART C. WOODRUFF
(essay date 1964)

[In the following excerpt, Woodruff asserts that the conflict between the actual and the ideal dominated both Bierce's life and his fiction.]

If Bierce has proved a protean figure, his fiction, at least, has a curiously homogeneous quality which originates in his obsessive vision. Specifically, Bierce's fiction takes its form from a series of violent oscillations between art and life, idealism and cynicism, and a richly romantic imagination and a rational awareness of life as a diminished thing. It was the pressure of the warring impulses Bierce could never manage in his own life that determined the controlling conception of his short stories. The conception itself severely restricted the range of his ideas and finally destroyed him as a serious writer. But in a handful of his war tales, it also enabled him to do what time may judge to be his finest writing. (pp. 2-3)

As certain of his essays, and particularly his letters, make evident, behind all the raillery and bitter satire lay a romantic temperament and a frustrated idealism that left Bierce stranded when he could find no way to justify them through his experience. By his own admission and the testimony of friends, Bierce had once approached life filled with extravagant expectations and youthful dreams of achievement. Specifically, this time of promise was the period covered by Bierce's war service, which Bierce always regarded as the most exciting and significant experience of his life and looked back on with an almost incredible nostalgia. It became the focal point of his existence, against which he opposed the dreary civilian aftermath, a means of defining the gulf between former youthful hopes and dreams and a present experience that mocked all sanguine assumptions about life. Bierce talked about the war, thought about it, wrote about it, all his life, and paid repeated visits to the Civil War battlefields where he had fought. Emotionally, he never left the army at all, and as his disillusionment and frustration increased, his war days became increasingly a cherished memory. . . . It is difficult to understand Bierce as a writer without reference to his divided sensibility and to his contradictory responses to experience. Although the conflicts in Bierce are apparent to anyone reading his journalism and correspondence, . . . their relevance to his short stories has never been explored. . . . Bierce's inability to reconcile extremes in his temperament determines the very form and texture of his imaginative world. Too many critics have regarded his fiction either as mechanically contrived or as a fictional version of his cynicism and misanthropy. While this is true of his least successful stories, it misses the significance and symbolic complexity of his war fiction, which is highly idiosyncratic. . . .

In his imaginative literature Bierce instinctively turned away from the prosaic constricting world dissected in his journalism. He did so either by returning to the scenes of his war experience, with all their ambiguous associations or, less successfully, by working within the tradition of terror and the supernatural. This impulse to seek out the remote or unusual, part of his romantic theory of art and the imagination, explains why Bierce never dealt in his fiction with the world of everyday experience and why his stories fall within sharply defined limits. They are circumscribed by the fact that the impulse to withdraw into a world of imagination was invariably blocked by Bierce's pervasive sense of the futility and emptiness of life itself. A recurrent pattern in Bierce's fiction is one in which the imagination is denied or frustrated by rational knowledge and empirical experience. (pp. 12-14)

In his journalism and satiric verse, and especially in *The Devil's Dictionary,* Bierce is primarily concerned with castigating a flawed humanity. . . . In his short stories, on the other hand, Bierce's characteristic theme is the inscrutable universe itself, whose mechanisms checkmate man's every attempt to assert his will or live his dreams. If the universe is not actively hostile or malevolent, as in many of his tales of the supernatural, it is at best always indifferent to human need. . . . This dismal concept of the human situation is Bierce's central imaginative impulse in his short stories, the idea that gives shape to his fictional world. (p. 19)

As a scientific determinist, Bierce believed in evolution through natural selection, but to him it implied no march toward human perfection. Instead, he saw man caught in an eternal round of progress and disintegration. As a part of nature's principles of force and strife, man, innately selfish, engaged in an endless series of wars which destroyed the capable and strong while preserving the feeble and incompetent. Man's attempts at humanitarian and social reform, such as the rehabilitation of criminals, salvaged the very misfits and "incapables whom Nature is trying to 'weed out.'" (p. 21)

With the paradoxical irony some modern existentialists are so fond of, Bierce regarded self-destruction as a kind of creative act, a weird moral achievement in a universe virtually drained of moral purpose and meaning. It was as if the individual could only assert his will by relinquishing it altogether in a final destructive act. Suicide became a last salute to all those dark forces conspiring against man, a Pyrrhic victory that ushered in the "good, good darkness." (p. 31)

The fate that overtakes such characters as Jerome Searing, William Grayrock, and George Thurston, originates in what Bierce conceived of as the "pitiless perfection of the divine, eternal plan." Whether this fate manifests itself as some arbitrary pattern of external circumstance or as an inner "constitutional tendency" makes no difference. The result is the same: the annihilation of the protagonist or of his private dream. Sometimes death is preceded by a stupefying sense of disillusionment or horror; sometimes it comes so swiftly there is no time for reflection. In many of the war stories, Bierce creates a bitter contrast between the main character's hopes or youthful dreams and the harsh reality that reduces him to a meaningless cipher. . . . To Bierce, the ultimate horror of the "eternal plan" was that man could learn nothing from his ordeal except the lesson of his own futility and purposelessness. (pp. 37-8)

[The] sense of man's helplessness, of the terrible inevitability of his fate, is the most persistent theme running through Bierce's stories, especially those dealing with war. For Bierce, war was the ideal metaphor to define the human predicament, not simply because he had known war intimately, but because it was the clearest demonstration of how the instinctive and the accidental combined to thwart human endeavor. But war's most important function was to represent what Bierce regarded as the central fact of existence: one's physical annihilation. Believing that the "mind or spirit or soul of man was the product of his physical being, the result of chemical combinations," Bierce looked upon death as the "awful mystery," awful because of its irreducible finality, its negation of all of man's hopes and creative impulses. . . . Bierce's war stories are fables of life's essential movement toward disillusion, defeat, and death. They concentrate and accelerate the inexorable process of disintegration. (pp. 44-5)

In Bierce's most convincing stories we see little of that intemperate and sometimes hysterical assault on human folly that characterizes his expository writing; that is, his main characters are seldom the object of the narrator's scorn or abuse. Bierce is conscious of unmerited suffering and his despair is consequently centered not so much on man as on the destructive nature of his experience. This focus enabled him to manage tone more successfully in his war tales than in his other writings, and while it did not prevent his showing the human condition to be meaningless, it kept it from becoming merely absurd. (p. 46)

Because it was the reality of their suffering and frustration that Bierce responded to, his war figures make a serious claim upon our attention. Only in the war stories does Bierce achieve the sense of genuine concern for human frailty endlessly cheated and baffled by life. His characters are credible even when their dilemmas are not, because he believed in the agony of their ordeal, even if he believed in little else. (p. 53)

The essays are particularly useful as evidence of a strain of emotional fervor and romantic idealism which Bierce found increasingly untenable in the face of certain indigestible facts of his experience. (p. 57)

Bierce seems to have been bent on convincing himself that ideals had no real meaning, that there were no principles except those of expediency and, therefore, that they had no power to hurt or disappoint. They were the products of an idle fancy and emotional wishful thinking. As his writing clearly shows, he came

to feel that all painful emotions could be laughed and mocked out of existence. That such a strategy convinced some people is shown by the frequent charge of "inhumanity" leveled at Bierce's work. But Bierce was hardly inhuman, and his intellect never subverted his heart, although he prided himself on some sort of Olympian tragic vision, of looking down from "the dominating peaks austere and desolate" and "holding a prophecy of doom." (p. 78)

In going back to war's actions and images for the best fiction he ever wrote, Bierce was not simply drawing upon his own experiences. By the time Bierce began writing his tales, the war itself had crystallized into a symbol combining his youthful expectations of life and his postwar disillusionment. His perspective was one conscious of the distance between what once had *seemed* and what now *was*, between a sensuous involvement in experience and a detached contemplation of its limiting conditions. It is this perspective, in turn, which determines the symbolic action of Bierce's plots. The inward sense of impoverishment and frustration is externalized as some form of death or defeat which comes upon the protagonist through no fault of his own. He is carried along relentlessly by a whimsical destiny which propels him from illusions and false assumptions about life to a situation that points up the disparity between the knowledge and the dream. The success of the war tales generally lies in Bierce's ability to get outside himself sufficiently to objectify his own dilemma while at the same time his characters and their destructive experiences are close enough to be taken seriously and regarded with a measure of compassion. (p. 89)

Because Bierce saw nothing in life to look forward to, he spent much of it looking backward. His truest art is the result of his nostalgia, which he objectifies as some false assumption experience ruthlessly denies. Perhaps just because it had proved so insubstantial and unreliable in his own case, Bierce sometimes wrote about the imagination as if it were itself a "dream" he could never hold on to. Only in sleep and dreams did it have a valid existence, and so "the dreamer is your only true poet." . . . (p. 94)

In view of his emphasis upon the primacy of imagination, it is hardly surprising that next to poetry, Bierce regarded the romance as the noblest literary form. It was, in fact, the only type of fiction that Bierce would allow, the only kind that could be dignified with the name of "art." (pp. 94-5)

Unable to mediate between his head and his heart, between his rational self and his imaginative idealistic self, Bierce ended by exploiting the differences with a ruthless cynicism that reflected his frustration. As a writer he first distrusted, then tried to deny, his most creative impulses. He was always being pulled in opposite directions by his realistic satirical journalism and his romantic views on literature, by his antifactual imagination and his distrust of all that was not fact. (p. 103)

The polarity which Bierce was most conscious of, and which best summarizes all the others, was that between the true and permanent art he hungered for and the largely ephemeral journalism which took up his time and energy for almost forty years. It is not a question of Bierce's newspaper work leaving little opportunity for fiction—many writers with equal or greater demands upon their time have produced more imaginative literature than he did. The real significance of his journalism is that it defines, just as it intensified, the split between Bierce's imaginative and his empirical responses to life, between his desire to create an imaginary world of beauty, order, and permanence and an even stronger impulse to destroy a painfully real civilian world of windy oratory and business chicanery, of cheap patriotism and crass materialism. Both his short stories and his expository writing sprang from the common source of his postwar disillusionment which gave force and substance to his newspaper work while at the same time it undermined his attempts at serious fiction. (p. 104)

[A] good deal of Bierce's disillusionment stemmed from a gnawing sense of his own artistic limitations, as well as from his revulsion at a culturally starved and morally sick America. This is why Bierce always stressed an irreconcilable distinction between journalism and literature and why he actually despised the career which in his own day brought him considerable recognition. . . . What journalism lacked for Bierce was the quality of imaginative vision he prized so highly. It dealt only with prosaic facts and was, therefore, like the new realism he ridiculed, "mere reporting." (p. 106)

He never seems to have considered that true art also comes from close observation and experience of things as they are; he saw it instead as a mysterious realm far removed from real life. And that is why he idealized it, just as he idealized his war memories and the past in general. At the same time that he looked back nostalgically at the period of youthful ideals and enthusiasms, he distrusted his imagination for playing him false, so that his attitude wavers between sentimentality and bitter derision of all sentiment and untested assumptions. (p. 109)

Convinced of an impossible gulf between satirical personal journalism and imaginative literature, Bierce decided to make the most of his destined career. (p. 110)

Bierce's tales of terror and the supernatural derive from his love of the romance and from his belief that literature must treat themes and situations far removed from everyday life. Because he looked upon it as a distant dream and the most memorable period of his life,

the Civil War provided the desired diversion from a dreary world. When he had exhausted its possibilities in a few tales, he naturally looked for inspiration in what he calls in one of his stories "the realm of the unreal." . . . His interest in the supernatural is only another manifestation of a romantic temperament, as well as of a mind that habitually looked upon the dark side of life. (p. 124)

Although Bierce has frequently been praised for fertility of imagination, his imagination was actually restricted to a few conceptions which he repeats in story after story. . . . He could never seem to break out of the charmed circle circumscribed by his vision of futility and inevitable defeat. Bierce may have read Darwin and Spencer along with other pessimists of the age, but he knew determinism at first hand, in his own warring impulses and inadequacies and in an environment which, to say the least, violated "his keen sense of the beautiful." The knowledge served only to feed his frustration and his resentment. (p. 143)

Stuart C. Woodruff, in his *The Short Stories of Ambrose Bierce: A Study in Polarity,* University of Pittsburgh Press, 1964, 193 p.

EDWARD WAGENKNECHT
(essay date 1977)

[Wagenknecht has stated: "I have no theories about writing except that I think people should write what they care for." In the following excerpt, he provides a survey of Bierce's literary work.]

Late in 1866 [Bierce] . . . began writing for such publications as *The Californian, The Golden Era* and *The Alta California.* His reputation for stinging wit began with the publication of satirical paragraphs about local figures in the "Town Crier" department of *The News-Letter.*

On Christmas Day, 1871, he married Mollie Day; his father-in-law financed a trip to England, where Bierce remained until September 1875, becoming an habitué of the Fleet Street Bohemia and an intimate of lesser English literary lights and journalists. The piratical publisher John Camden Hotten, whom Mark Twain loathed, brought out his first, unimportant book, *The Fiend's Delight,* in 1872.

After his return to San Francisco, he wrote for *The Argonaut, The Call* and *The Wasp,* and in 1880 he was general agent for a mining company in Dakota. From 1887 until 1908 he wrote for the San Francisco *Examiner* and other publications controlled by William Randolph Hearst, who showed the patience of a saint in refusing to accept his numerous resignations when his copy had been tampered with and even failed to register resentment over the outrageous quatrain Bierce published after the assassination of the governor-elect of Kentucky, which gave Hearst's enemies the chance to accuse him of having inspired the killing of President McKinley:

The bullet that pierced Goebel's breast
Can not be found in all the West;
Good reason, it is speeding here
To stretch McKinley on his bier.

In the winter of 1895-96 Bierce had gone to Washington to represent the Hearst papers, campaigning against the Southern Pacific-inspired Funding Bill, and in 1905 he began writing **"The Passing Show"** for *Cosmopolitan.* (pp. xii-xiii)

Like Poe, Bierce believed that poems must be short, for otherwise the poetic quality cannot be sustained (a poem for him was essentially imagery), and that a novel was only "a short story padded." His style, even in his fiction, has something of the baldness and directness of journalism, but he combines this with a military or aristocratic formality and reserve. The eighteenth-century "serenity, fortitude and reasonableness" he professed to admire shows not in his subject matter, which is often highly sensational, but only in his passion for correctness and his emotional reserve; the last book published during his lifetime was a literary manual called *Write It Right* (1909). Like Aristotle and James Branch Cabell, he wanted a writer to "represent life, not as it is, but as it might be; character, not as he finds it, but as he wants it to be." In his own stories there is little character, as the psychological realists understand it, the whole emphasis being upon situation. He hated local color, and slang was for him "the grunt of the human hog," and he also hated realism, at least as it was practiced by "Miss Nancy Howells" and "Miss Nancy James, Jr." (p. xvii)

Bierce's sardonicism, often bitter, sometimes not unmixed with a grim kind of amusement, appears in its most undiluted form in *The Devil's Dictionary* . . . and in his fables (the principal collection of which, *Fantastic Fables,* was published in New York in 1899). . . . *The Monk and the Hangman's Daughter,* an interesting variation of the *Thaïs* situation, or the conflict between eros and agape (though the girl is certainly no courtesan), is something else again, for though it is in a sense our *pièce de résistance,* it can be called Bierce's work only in a somewhat Pickwickian sense, and it has often been warmly admired by those who do not care much for his more characteristic work. According to his preface to the story, Bierce substantially rewrote G. A. Danziger's attempted translation of a German tale. . . . In 1929 C. Hartley Grattan conjecturally credited Bierce not only with stylistic improvement but also with heightening the dramatic conflict and perceiving "the essentials of the sexual-psychological conflict" in the monk, and entered a high claim for the work as an American religious

novel, and as late as 1967 Richard O'Connor thought he discerned in the monk's feeling of exaltation upon his first sight of the mountains an echo of "Bierce's experience as a youthful soldier marching into the Appalachians of West Virginia" and in the treatment of "the role of sexuality in religious fervor" a reminiscence of his "unwilling attendance at backwoods revival meetings when a boy." (pp. xvii-xix)

The principal themes of the short stories upon which Bierce's claim as a writer must rest primarily are war, death, horror, madness, ghosts, and fear, and, as we might expect, his presentation of all of them is shot through with bitter irony. Thus **"One of the Missing"** is an almost sadistic study of a trapped, immobilized soldier, frightened to death by his own rifle pointed at his head—but the gun is not loaded; in **"One Officer, One Man,"** Captain Graffenreid falls upon his own sword when "the strain upon his nervous organism" grows "insupportable." Nor are such terrors confined to the battlefield; in **"The Man and the Snake,"** Harker Brayton, spending the night in a herpetologist's house, is frightened to death by a stuffed reptile in his bedroom.

In the "Parenticide" stories, Bierce treats death whimsically, but this seems even less "wholesome" to many of his readers than his reveling in its horrors. Historically he ranks with J. W. DeForest and Stephen Crane as having pioneered in the realistic portrayal of war in fiction. To him a soldier is an assassin for his country, a "hardened and impenitent man-killer." In his pages son kills father and troops fire on their own men and shell their own homes; in **"One Kind of Officer"** he offers a bleak picture of the mindlessness of military discipline. Yet he has none of the moral revulsion against war that characterized the war novels published after World War I; although he is free of "patriotics," one often finds it difficult to decide whether his emphasis upon war's horrors has been inspired by what he calls its "criminal insanity" or by his love of sensation. He himself carried the military temperament in some aspects into civil life, where he packed a gun, and he might well have stayed in the army had he received the commission he thought he deserved. Sometimes he gives the impression of preferring the horrors of war to the corruptions of peace, and he revisited Civil War battlefields (one fancies nostalgically) before disappearing into Mexico.

It has been objected to Bierce's stories of the supernatural that they lack atmosphere and that the entrance of the otherworldly element into the tale, being unprepared for, is therefore unimpressive and unconvincing. None of this is true, I think, except in such brief, bald tales as **"Present at a Hanging"** and **"The Difficulty of Crossing a Field,"** where the absence of atmosphere is very much the point of the yarn. These stories deal with just such inexplicable phenomena as have come without preparation into the experience of innumerable human beings from time to time, which seem to admit of no rational explanation, yet cannot be explained away, so that we are left helplessly ejaculating Bierce's question, "Can such things be?" But when atmosphere serves Bierce's purpose, he can supply it to burn, as in **"One Kind of Officer"**: "The gray fog, thickening every moment, closed in about him like a visible doom." The menacing setting in **"The Secret of Macarger's Gulch"** combines natural and supernatural threats, and **"An Inhabitant of Carcosa"** ("In all this there were a menace and a portent—a hint of evil, an intimation of doom") could hardly have been bettered by Poe himself.

Bierce's concentration upon particularities is perhaps seen most strikingly in his Civil War stories, which, so far from dealing with issues or large movements, generally present solitary soldiers facing individual dilemmas. The dull run-of-the-mill of day-by-day life in the military is not for this author; indeed, his preoccupation with the sensational and the unusual and his passion for smashing climaxes tempts the reader of contemporary short stories to regard his as artificially contrived or old-fashioned. Nevertheless, the best of his tales, both in this area and elsewhere, are much more varied in their technical expertise than some commentators have been willing to grant.

To be sure, such items as the **"Negligible Tales"** and the pieces in **"The Parenticide Club"** are essentially tall tales or burlesques, dedicated to achieving the broadest effects of what we now call "black humor." ("Having murdered my mother under circumstances of singular atrocity, I was arrested and put upon my trial"—**"My Favorite Murder."** "Early one June morning in 1872 I murdered my father—an act which made a deep impression on me at the time"—**"An Imperfect Conflagration."**) Some are ineffective. Those that succeed owe their success to a masterly use of incongruity or inversion of values, murderers being referred to as saints, et cetera. But Bierce's reputation does not rest upon such work as this.

Although he is best known for his ghost stories and Civil War tales, not all his work comes under these heads. The Western stories suggest a grim Bret Harte. **"Moxon's Master"** is science fiction, clearly allied to the Poe who wrote "Maelzel's Chess Player," and **"Haïta the Shepherd"** is straightforward allegory in the Cupid and Psyche tradition. But the variations and modifications of technique are more impressive than those that appear in subject matter. In one of the **"Negligible Tales,"** Bierce remarks parenthetically that "a story once begun should not suffer impedition." This is not in accord with his own practice, however, for he weaves forward and backward with great skill, a master of every device the narrator knows to enlist interest and build up suspense.

Look, for example, at **"A Horseman in the Sky,"** certainly one of the finest tales. It begins with an elaborate description of the setting. Then, in Section II, we get a long flashback, giving us the background of the leading character, so that we may understand the situation in which he finds himself. Next, the confrontation that is the essence of the tale is introduced, the father's own authority is invoked to sanction his killing, and the shot fired by Carter Druse at the end of the section is the only positive action in the story. In Section III the scene shifts to a Federal officer who sees the horseman fall. Section IV returns to the end of III and, at last, to Druse's specific admission that he knew the man he shot was his father.

In **"An Occurrence at Owl Creek Bridge,"** on the other hand, the situation in which Peyton Farquhar finds himself is set forth at the very beginning. There follows a precise description of scene and surroundings, creating suspense through a long paragraph, before we come back to "the man who was engaged in being hanged." Next comes further description of the setting and of the persons involved in the imminent action, some of it from the point of view of an omniscient narrator, some from Farquhar's own, and including such effective use of the irrelevant, faithful to the workings of the mind under stress, as his observation of the "piece of dancing driftwood" moving down the sluggish stream. His pondering how he might act if he could free his hands and throw off the noose is preparation; it misleads the reader into accepting what follows and makes the surprise ending more of a shock when it comes. The last sentence in Section I—"The sergeant

Caricature of Bierce in the *Wasp*, early 1890s.

stepped aside"—is really the end of the story, but we do not know that until we have read through two more sections. Section II gives us Farquhar's background and history, and Section III deals with what goes on in his mind before his fall at the end of the rope breaks his neck. This piece, which Howells chose for his anthology of great American stories, is probably Bierce's most brilliant achievement, but it is essentially a tour de force, much trickier than the "Horseman" and to that extent not quite so convincing.

Perhaps Bierce's most masterly use of the surprise ending is at the close of **"The Coup de Grâce,"** which is only an anecdote in itself but which requires every word of the elaborate build-up Bierce supplies for the full comprehension of its irony. Sometimes, as at the end of **"The Man and the Snake,"** Bierce carefully spells out what has happened, but sometimes he leaves the solution to the ingenuity of the reader: was Staley Fleming killed by the ghost of his victim's dog or by his own guilty fear? Both **"One Kind of Officer"** and **"The Coup de Grâce"** have an "open" ending; the climactic action comes after the story is over, but Bierce does not tell us what it was. As for "impedition," even the editorializing about euthanasia in **"The Coup de Grâce"** is necessary to the final effect: everybody recognizes the right of the hopelessly injured horse to be helped out of his misery, but Captain Madwell may well pay with his life for having been generous enough to grant the same to his friend. The revelation at the end of the terrible **"Chickamauga"** that the child is a deaf mute helps us to accept what we might have questioned before, for only complete incomprehension can justify complete indifference to suffering. **"Chickamauga"** has a disarmingly gentle beginning for so grim a tale, and the description of the horribly mangled soldiers approaches the bounds of the bearable, yet even the resemblance between the blood-bedaubed men and the make-up of the painted clowns the child has seen in the circus is at least partially true to the workings of the child mind. The turn of the screw comes, of course, with the realization that the pretty light that had so pleased him comes from his own burning house, where his mother lies horribly dead.

If **"The Death of Halpin Frayser"** seems more rambling and casual in its organization than these other tales, the numerous elements contained in it have still been fitted together with great ingenuity. **"John Bartine's Watch"** uses narrative within a narrative, and Ernest Hemingway could not have set down the expert notation of detail at the beginning of **"The Damned Thing"** any better. Both **"One of the Missing"** and **"Killed at Resaca"** make skillful use of an epilogue, but each in a different way. **"Resaca"** is a first-person narrative, but the narrator is not the principal character. There is a straightforward expositional introduction, which is followed by character analysis and generaliza-

tions about battle that run on for several pages before the action begins. This story is a character study, but the figure in the carpet does not emerge until the final epilogue records the narrator's visit to the dead hero's sinister sweetheart in San Francisco a year after the war, when we learn it was her taunt that inspired the foolhardiness which cost his life. Again the last sentence cracks the whip, and since the girl herself surely takes it literally, the irony is perfect and complete.

Benedetto Croce once remarked that in literature technique either did not exist at all or else it was synonymous with art itself. I have never been quite sure that this was not an overstatement, but there can be no question that, in the case of Ambrose Bierce at least, both subject matter and method were perfect mirrors of his own mind and soul. This is the measure of both his success and his failure, and it may well be that the same thing is quite as true of other writers. (pp. xix-xxiv)

Edward Wagenknecht, in an introduction to *The Stories and Fables of Ambrose Bierce,* edited by Edward Wagenknecht, Stemmer House, 1977, pp. xi-xxiv.

PHILIP M. RUBENS
(essay date 1978)

[In the following excerpt, Rubens investigates the gothic foundations of Bierce's fiction.]

Though there have been many attempts to place Ambrose Bierce's work into a variety of categories, one of the most persistent aspects of scholarship and criticism is its uniform insistence that he is somehow a gothic writer. . . .

In fact, it is possible to find many of the traditional gothic devices throughout his works that have a distinctive Biercian quality. [To] accomplish such an end, it will be necessary to isolate and describe those elements of Bierce's work that have a distinctive gothic quality. These elements include narrative technique, supernatural agents, setting and characterization, and the curse. . . .

Through his narrative style, Bierce extends the protagonist's quandary into the reader's mind. This style, like that of many other gothic works, at first seems loose and sprawling; in fact, it typically involves narratives within narratives. However, Bierce's abrupt transitions, discursive presentation of events, and reliance on psychological time typify three important methods he utilizes to achieve his objective of direct reader involvement. Bierce views the use of these techniques in terms of the "parted clew." . . . By offering evidence from several viewpoints and by altering time, he creates a conundrum saturated with clues the receptive reader can employ to unravel the *outré* events of the tale. In **"An Occurrence at Owl Creek Bridge,"** for instance, Bierce alters the times sequence from present to past to future to present to establish the confused nature of the protagonist's mind. He also uses Henri Bergson's ideas of durée to establish the psychic quality of this experience. That is, certain aspects of the phenomenal world force the protagonist into an interior world where he attempts to create a temporary order. This is evident in his observations on the physical environment immediately before his hanging and the relation of such observations to the hallucinations he has in the seconds before death.

The inability to separate the idealistic dreams of life from its harsh reality creates an impassable barrier for Bierce and prompts his interest in the world of dreams and imagination as a gothic medium. This concept allows him to produce landscapes where spectres do, in fact, exist: a fictional locale generated by repressed fears and guilts struggling into consciousness. It is the active nature of Bierce's ghosts that represents a marked departure from his predecessors. Most gothic spirits are characterized as pallid and helpless; they generally appear only to foretell a catastrophe, harass a guilty conscience, or request burial. Unlike Bierce's spectres, they are usually not so much characters as props and contribute little more to the gothic atmosphere than their general surroundings. In Bierce's tales, however, the ghost can often become the principal agent of retribution and actively, violently, and cruelly wreaks vengeance by physical means; such spectres strangle, shoot, and occasionally frighten their victims to death. His definition of ghosts as the "outward and visible sign of an inward fear" . . . aptly summarizes his interest in these phenomena. (p. 29)

Although Bierce's characters are trapped in a gothic world of horror and terror, their reactions are based upon the exaggeration of normal emotions. This response heightens the protagonists' sensibilities and makes them almost preternaturally observant. In keeping with the silence of the Biercian setting, these figures remain remarkably inarticulate; they expire without a whimper to forces elicited from their own subconscious, and their very silence comments on man's inability to understand such powers. Whether inextricably trapped in a collapsed building or bound by duty to face a dead man, the Biercian protagonist vacillates between hope and despair. Unable to comprehend his situation, he begins to examine his own emotions and abdicates to cowardice, fear, and finally death. Facing an unusual crisis and possessing an inordinate attitude toward courage, pride, or reason, he dies an ignoble death at the hands of his own imagination. In short, Bierce's characterization depends on the creation of solitary figures whose eminently rational nature forces them to ignore even the remotest possibility of a supernatural realm. . . .

Heredity is an extremely important as well as vexing topic for Bierce. He assiduously studied theories about heredity and wrote his own evaluations with great frequency. From such statements, it can be gathered that Bierce sees heredity in terms of a controlling influence; in fact, he writes of it as though it is deterministic or even worse, a manifestation of what one might call the gothic curse. For Bierce one thing is certain: the sins of the fathers *are* visited on their children. . . . From the storehouse of heredity, perhaps a collective unconscious would work just as well; Bierce's characters receive intimations of a hidden past that contains the possibility of the genuinely active supernatural in men's daily affairs. Yet, these characters cannot comprehend the import of such suggestions, or they simply and violently assert their incredulity about such phenomena. The complexity of Bierce's protagonist's response is always based on reason, but that intellectual basis continually is undercut by the emotional and imaginative. Bierce's characters refuse to admit that hereditary influences can have any effect on their lives; this stance forces them to undergo the rigors of a numinous experience. (p. 30)

The unique qualities of the Biercian gothic, then, are found first in his narrative technique. By the use of parted clues, by employing multiple narratives, and by the manipulation of time, Bierce attempts to actively and emotionally involve the reader in the terror his characters experience. His use of dreams and ghosts demonstrates both his preference for the "realm of the unreal" and an interest in a deeper psychology. Setting, regardless of its spatial nature, becomes a means of isolating man in order to expose him to supernatural intervention—real or imagined. Finally, Bierce's treatment of character is unique in that it clearly demonstrates his concern for the role of the past—psychological or phenomenal—on the lives of men. His ultimate concern—the fulfillment of his obligation as a writer by informing all men that the past, with its repressed fears and guilts, waits patiently to assail their reason and emotion—demonstrates an abiding interest in the psychological aspects of human nature, the proper domain of the Biercian gothic. (pp. 30-1)

Philip M. Rubens, "The Gothic Foundations of Ambrose Bierce's Fiction," in *Nyctalops*, Vol. 2, No. 7, 1978, pp. 29-31.

DONALD SIDNEY-FRYER

(essay date 1979)

[In the following excerpt, Sidney-Fryer discusses Bierce's poetry, arguing that the best of his verse deserves more attention than it has received.]

When we consider that [Bierce's] published verse must total somewhere around eight hundred pieces in all, and that this total represents around one fifth or one sixth of his over-all literary output (as assembled in his *Collected Works*), we have ample assurance that Bierce must have placed some value on his verse, whatever he may have said or written to the contrary. Today much of it seems little more than competent versifying, generally light in character and (more often than not) of a satirical nature, attacking the fads, foibles, and personalities of Bierce's day. His best poems lie embedded in a mass of typically Biercean satire in verse mainly apropos of persons who were once celebrities of the West Coast but who are now nonentities except to the specialist in Californian history and literature. Read infrequently and at the rate of a few pieces at a time, this satirical verse is apt and amusing; but read in a large quantity, it rapidly becomes tiresome, if not downright unbearable.

But a modicum remains of real poetry, compact, imaginative, and powerful; or—quite unexpectedly—tender with a tenderness not usually associated with one who has on occasion been called "The Devil's Lexicographer." (p. 10)

[On] the basis of his best poems Bierce clearly merits the attention of the discriminating lover and student of poetry.

In the tradition of Edgar Allan Poe, the American and now largely underground school of "pure poetry" has been peculiarly associated with Bierce, directly or indirectly. In form and in language he was a traditionalist, a purist of the most rigid kind; in this we may perhaps see something of an all-pervading life-attitude that he gained from his military experience during the Civil War. In his critical theories he was above all else a proponent of *la poésie pure.* And much of his taste and preference in verse may be gauged from the fact that he considered Coleridge's "Kubla Khan" the most nearly perfect poem in the English language. (p. 11)

It would be pleasant but scarcely accurate to claim for his best poetry a spectacular originality. While a good proportion of his output in verse—considered as poetry—may seem "negligible" and even "trivial" as some critics have maintained, yet his best is neither,

and well rewards sympathetic attention. At this best Bierce as a poet is, beneath a seemingly conventional exterior, very much his own man. (pp. 18-19)

Usually personal, Bierce's "sentimental" poems, evidently written during the apogée of late Victorian times, are singularly unsentimental, and refreshingly simple and direct statements of emotion. His love sonnets in particular may come as a surprise to the reader acquainted primarily with Bierce's pungent satire or with his unforgettable supernatural stories. His best serious poetry is largely to be found in *Shapes of Clay.* Apart from a handful of pieces, *Black Beetles in Amber* contains only satirical or humorous verse. The weary reader discovers the few serious poems in the latter collection almost with a sense of relief. However, even his satirical pieces considered collectively, too often like so many peas in a pod both in language and in substance, do not appear unfavorably against the background of late Victorian and of Edwardian poetry, but rather as agreeably nasty cast-iron thorns in the Victorian rose garden. (p. 19)

"Invocation" remains one of the best things of its kind, and far more than a mere *pièce d'occasion,* a mere piece of facile chauvinism made to order. Although not quite a hundred years have now passed since "Invocation" was first proclaimed, most of Bierce's thoughts on the good and evil possibilities inherent in liberty still hold true. The reader will note that the God that Bierce posits in his apostrophe (see particularly quatrains 10 through 25) is not the compassionate deity presented in the New Testament.

Moreover, the reader should not construe from these references to a conventional divinity (as well as from those in other poems) that Bierce was in any sense a strict religionist. Although highly moral—even puritanical—in his own lifestyle, he was of course very much of a freethinker. As he once wittily remarked in a letter to poet-pupil George Sterling, God ranked in the sphere of poetic reference as one of the most useful items (or "properties") from the poet's given repertoire of tropes. If God had not already existed as a reality, or merely as a figure of speech, then the poets would have been obliged to have invented Him out of sheer necessity.

Many critics have considered "Invocation" to be Bierce's greatest poem; actually it is not; such an honor should probably go to the tercet "Creation," that little masterpiece of boldness and compression. Nonetheless, "Invocation" does contain a number of magnificent and nominally great passages. (p. 20)

In the twenty-two tercets of "Basilica," Bierce relates and develops a comparatively simple story in terms of highly colored and often macabre imagery in the manner of Keats, Coleridge, or Poe. The poet or narrator is walking along the seashore and sees in the midst of some rocks what appears to be a radiant gem but which resolves itself into a weirdly shining cockatrice when the poet essays to grasp it. Thus, Nature or Life leads us ever onward with her external shows of beauty but when we try to plumb the mystery of loveliness we find only evil and corruption. The imagery is notable for its lurid imaginativeness: "The groaning sea, wind-smitten white" / "ocean's leprous agony" / "A glinting gem with lustrous sheen" / "An opal chalice brimming gold" / "dim with amber-tined air" / "Gem-tinct with gleams of prismic ice." The fulsome description of the basilisk is not without a certain effectiveness. . . . (pp. 22-3)

This type of vividly colored imagery descends in part from Poe and in part from the English Romantics and, before them and singularly influencing them, from Edmund Spenser and the concentrated, brilliantly hued, and highly symbolic imagery of "The Faerie Queene"; and it anticipates the characteristic, Late Romantic imagery of both [George] Sterling and [Clark] Ashton Smith. Not only is Bierce's imagery in **"Basilica"** concentrated but the poem itself is a concentration of such imagery developed on the foundation of a simple narrative. Since he considered imagery to be the heart, the soul, the essence of poetry—to him the imagery *was* the poetry—then in theory a poem successfully constructed along these lines would be the most poetic possible, that is, the most imaginative. (pp. 23-4)

In vision, in theory, and nominally in accomplishment, Bierce had prepared the way for both later poets through his essays and through his best poems.

As among his best and briefest poems we should consider the excellent and highly imaginative titles Bierce chose for his two volumes: *Shapes of Clay* and *Black Beetles in Amber.* Indeed, much of the best of his invention and mordant wit is to be found in his titles. For example, an early prose collection has the vivid and poetic title *Cobwebs from an Empty Skull.* For another example, **"To Dog,"** constructed on the analogy of "To Man" (Bierce apparently detested dogkind as much as he did mankind). For yet a further example, **"Oneiromancy"** which, in terms of the love poem it entitles, signifies not only divination through dreams but also "O Near Romance, See."

Exclusive perhaps of the two early pieces which are nonetheless effective, the poems in this selection reveal Bierce as an adroit and facile versifier. He is a master of the run-over line. His handling of rime, metre, consonance, assonance, etc., is assured and often ingenious. He is able to make his poetic statement move through difficult and demanding traditional forms with singular ease. He sometimes achieves some of his best effects—effects of power or of grim humor—simply through his punctuation: **"Creation"** in particular furnishes a good example of this. Although his diction may seem somewhat old-fashioned today, and perhaps

over-all somewhat conventional, it also possesses here and there subtle little touches of originality. He has a good ear for colloquial speech, and he has a good eye for the unexpected and homely detail, as well as a good instinct for the unexpected and homely resolution, usually presented at the end of a given poem in sharp contrast to what has preceded it. In many of his pieces both satirical and personal, he has anticipated the modern poetic temper at once ironical and colloquial. Although **"Invocation"** shows him as a master of the grand manner and the solemn "tense" or tone (a manner and a tone with which much of present-day taste appears to have little sympathy), in most of his poems he simply uses his own conversational style, anticipating the same in contemporary modes of poetic expression. Perhaps not in terms of versification, but at least in terms of "a vision of doom," Bierce is quite a modern poet. (pp. 25-6)

While there is less of the sardonic and often grimly playful sense of imagination in his verse over-all than what we find in his best and most characteristic prose fictions; yet many, if not most, of Bierce's best poems are unusually fantastic and macabre. Even those poems not overtly macabre Bierce seems to have written in the Valley of the Shadow of Death. The grim presence of Death stalks through most of his personal poems, even his love sonnets and other pieces. Bierce's verse at its best is austere, even angular, with an almost provincial sparseness; rather like a corpse whose bones have been clean-picked by some thoughtful scavenger. As always, there is something harsh and unyielding, and even cold, about Bierce and his best work; a quality well-summarized by the contemporary science-fiction author Fritz Leiber in his phrase "Bierce, the Man with the Phallus of Ice."

For all of Bierce's own personal preference for a rich Spenserian or Shakespearian imagery in the poems of other poets—for the overflowing purple and gold of *The Arabian Nights*—the reader will find little such in Bierce's own poetic works. Instead, he will discover something different, an unique savor not found quite anywhere else. While we must agree with H. P. Lovecraft, speaking of Bierce in the monumental essay *Supernatural Horror in Literature,* that "the bulk of his artistic reputation must rest upon his grim and savage short stories," his best verse clearly deserves more attention and appreciation than what it has received to date. (p. 28)

Donald Sidney-Fryer, "A Visionary of Doom (1979)," in *A Vision of Doom: Poems by Ambrose Bierce,* edited by Donald Sidney-Fryer, Donald M. Grant, 1980, pp. 9-32.

S. T. JOSHI

(essay date 1990)

[An American editor and critic, Joshi is an authority on the life and works of H. P. Lovecraft. In the following excerpt, he discusses Bierce's two most famous tales, "Death of Halpin Frayser" and "An Occurrence at Owl Creek Bridge."]

In the tales in *Can Such Things Be?* Bierce is just as careful in using the supernatural as he is in avoiding it in *Tales of Soldiers and Civilians.* . . . [The tales that approach science fiction] represent an extension of the boundaries of the natural world to encompass what, given our current state of scientific knowledge, appear to be supernatural events. Many other tales—perhaps the most effective is **"The Middle Toe of the Right Foot,"** although **"Staley Fleming's Hallucination," "The Night-Doings at 'Deadman's,' "** and **"Beyond the Wall"** all fit the pattern—are simply tales of revenge in which the supernatural is a scarcely veiled metaphor for the conscience of the guilty.

Perhaps Bierce's most remarkable supernatural tale is the much-discussed **"Death of Halpin Frayser."** Recently a controversy has arisen over what actually happens in this tale and whether the supernatural comes into play at all. In a brilliant and ingenious essay, Robert C. Maclean has argued that it is possible to explain all the events of the tale naturally, with the conclusion that the murderer of Halpin Frayser is his own father, disguised as the private detective Jaralson. Maclean's work is too involved to discuss in detail here, but both he and William Bysshe Stein, who discussed the problem earlier, reject the obvious supernatural "explanation" of the events of the tale—that Frayser is killed by his own deceased mother. But I sense that they and other critics do so because they are unwarrantedly embarrassed at the mere existence of the supernatural, which in any case does not preclude other (e.g., psychoanalytical) interpretations. Bierce leaves hardly any doubt of Frayser's incestuous love for his mother (a love that she reciprocates), and it appears—thus far Maclean is correct—that we are to understand that Frayser and his mother fled separately west and lived as man and wife. Frayser kills his wife/mother, but she comes back from the dead and murders her son as he lurks by her grave. Any other reconstruction of events will make the epigraph—a passage from the sage Hali—inexplicable: "Whereas in general the spirit that removed cometh back upon occasion, and is sometimes seen of those in flesh (appearing in the form of the body it bore) yet it hath happened that the veritable body without the spirit hath walked. And it is attested of those encountering who have lived to speak thereon that a lich so raised up hath no natural affection, nor remembrance thereof, but only hate." Frayser's mother is the "lich so raised up." The phrase "natural affection" is interesting; for the mother it suggests merely the blind destructiveness of the undead, but for Frayser it is meant to convey his profoundly unnatural love of his mother. At the end of the story the detective and a sheriff, standing over the murdered body of Halpin Frayser as it lies atop his mother's grave, hear "the sound of a laugh, a low, deliberate, *soulless* laugh . . . a laugh so *unnatural,* so *unhuman,* so devilish, that it filled those hardy man-hunters with a sense of dread unspeakable!" Now unless Bierce is deliberately trying to deceive us (something he never does in this precise way) or is suggesting that the two characters are victims of a collective hallucination, this can only be the laugh of the "body without the spirit" that is Halpin Frayser's mother. To say that this is merely a tale about "zombies" (as Mary Elizabeth Grenander does in dismissing the supernatural interpretation) is both to imply that there is something inherently subliterary about zombies (itself a questionable assertion) and to misconstrue the role of the supernatural here. What we have is a *double* irony: Halpin Frayser is killed by his own murder victim, not out of simple revenge (for his mother has no "remembrance" of the crime), but by sheer chance—the same sort of chance that trapped Cthulhu in the sinking R'lyeh in Lovecraft's "The Call of Cthulhu." It is the haplessness (and hopelessness) of human beings against the inexorable course of fate that is at the heart of this story.

The clarity and precision, both of diction and imagery, that are central to Bierce's actual methodology of writing—his scorn of slang and dialect is too well documented for citation—frequently augment and in some senses even create the sense of horror in his work. (pp. 160-62)

Clarity of expression is the key to [the] story, **"An Occurrence at Owl Creek Bridge."** This tale is a masterwork because of the almost mathematically exact way in which the style leads us to reverse the period of waking and dreaming in Peyton Farquhar. The first section of the tale is the "waking" part, with the grim preparations for an all too real execution; but Bierce presents it almost as if it were a dream (or nightmare) of Farquhar's: we are not told here the crime for which he is being executed; Farquhar's sensations seem both dulled ("A piece of dancing driftwood caught his attention and his eyes followed it down the current. How slowly it appeared to move! What a sluggish stream!") and preternaturally heightened (the ticking of his watch sounds like "the stroke of a blacksmith's hammer upon the anvil.") But in the brief second section we learn that Farquhar was convicted of passing on information to the enemy, and in the third section (Farquhar's delusion) every image is crystal clear: he feels a "sharp pain in his wrist" from the ropes; as he struggles in the water to free himself "his whole body was racked and wrenched with an insupportable anguish!" Freed, he finds himself

> now in full possession of his physical senses. They were, indeed, preternaturally keen and alert. Something in the awful disturbance of his organic system had so exalted and refined them that they made record of things never before perceived. He felt the ripples upon his face and heard their separate sounds as they struck. He looked at the forest on the bank of the stream, saw the individual trees, the leaves and the veining of each leaf—saw the very insects upon them: the locusts, the brilliant-bodied flies, the gray spiders stretching their webs from twig to twig. He noted the prismatic colors in all the dewdrops upon a million blades of grass. The humming of the gnats that danced above the eddies of the stream, the beating of the dragon-flies' wings, the strokes of the water-spiders' legs, like oars which had lifted their boat—all these made audible music. A fish slid along beneath his eyes and he heard the rush of its body parting the water.

And it goes on—in the split second before his death Farquhar's mind conjures up images far more lucid and precise than in the minutes before his execution. (pp. 163-64)

S. T. Joshi, "Ambrose Bierce: Horror as Satire," in his *The Weird Tale: Arthur Machen, Lord Dunsany, Algernon Blackwood, M. R. James, Ambrose Bierce, H. P. Lovecraft,* University of Texas Press, 1990, pp. 143-67.

SOURCES FOR FURTHER STUDY

Davidson, Cathy N. *Critical Essays on Ambrose Bierce.* Boston: G. K. Hall, 1982, 242 p.

> Selections presenting "an overview of the contemporaneous and the current assessments of Bierce as well as a representative sampling of the best Bierce criticism to date."

Fatout, Paul. *Ambrose Bierce: The Devil's Lexicographer.* Norman: University of Oklahoma Press, 1951, 349 p.

> Comprehensive biography.

Grenander, M. E. *Ambrose Bierce.* New York: Twayne Publishers, 1971, 193 p.

> Surveys Bierce's life and literary works.

McWilliams, Carey. *Ambrose Bierce: A Biography.* New York: Albert & Charles Boni, 1929, 358 p.

> Early biography with a chapter devoted to criticism of the short stories.

O'Connor, Richard. *Ambrose Bierce: A Biography.* Boston, Toronto: Little, Brown and Co., 1967, 333 p.

> Popular biography that perpetuates some misinformation concerning Bierce's personal life and literary career.

Woodruff, Stuart C. *The Short Stories of Ambrose Bierce: A Study in Polarity.* Pittsburgh: University of Pittsburgh Press, 1964, 193 p.

> Examines a few representative tales in an effort "to define Bierce's controlling conceptions, to describe his characteristic fictional devices and technique, and to show significant parallels of theme, action, and symbolic imagery."

William Blake

1757-1827

English poet and artist.

INTRODUCTION

A visionary poet and artist, Blake was often ridiculed during his lifetime but has since been recognized as one of the major poets of English literature. His work is distinguished by the creation and illustration of a complex mythological system. Imagination is of paramount importance in Blake's system, serving as the vehicle of humanity's communion with the spiritual essence of reality. By bringing his unconventional perspective to bear on such subjects as religion, morality, art, and politics, Blake is recognized as both a social rebel and as a "hero of the imagination" who played a key role in advancing the Romantic revolt against rationalism. These thematic concerns inform the lyrics in Blake's best-known publication, *Songs of Innocence and of Experience: Shewing the Two Contrary States of the Human Soul* (1794).

Blake was the second of five children born to James Blake, a London hosier, and his wife, Catherine. He exhibited visionary tendencies as a child, claiming to see God at his window and a tree adorned with angels, and was artistically precocious as well. Following several years' study at Henry Pars's Drawing School, he was apprenticed in 1772 to the master engraver James Basire, who helped stimulate Blake's interest in the Gothic style by assigning him to make drawings of the monuments in Westminster Abbey. Blake took up studies at The Royal Academy of Arts in 1779, but he openly disagreed with his instructors' artistic theories and soon focused his energies on engraving. This work brought him into contact with the radical bookseller Joseph Johnson and with such fellow artists as Thomas Stothard, John Flaxman, and Henry Fuseli. It was through Flaxman's efforts in particular that Blake obtained many of the engraving and drawing commissions that were the principal source of his meager income. In 1782 Blake married Catherine Boucher, the illiterate daughter of a Battersea market-gardener. Catherine was devoted to Blake, and under his instruction she learned to read, write, and help illuminate his books. Although commentators detect signs of conjugal stress in Blake's works, they generally agree that the couple enjoyed a loving union that benefited the poet greatly.

Blake first attracted literary notice in the salon of the Reverend and Mrs. A. S. Mathew, where he read his poems and occasionally sang them to his original musical compositions. In 1783, Flaxman and the Reverend Mathew funded the printing of *Poetical Sketches* (1783), Blake's first collection of verse. Blake opened a short-lived print business in 1784, the year to which bibliographers tentatively assign the manuscript of his satire, *An Island in the Moon*. Three years later, he suffered the loss of his younger brother Robert, with whose spirit he later claimed to communicate in the "regions of . . . Imagination." At about the same time, he developed his technique of illuminated printing. Blake first employed this method in about 1788 while producing two treatises entitled *There Is No Natural Religion* and *All Religions Are One,* which urge the claims of imagination over rationalist philosophy. Two more illuminated works, *Songs of Innocence* and *The Book of Thel,* were printed in 1789. Inasmuch as Blake painstakingly engraved the plates for his illuminated works, printed them personally, and colored each copy by hand, his books are as rare as they are beautiful. This restricted circulation limited Blake's income and prevented his reputation and works from spreading beyond a fairly closed society of friends and connoisseurs.

The outbreak of the French Revolution in 1789 found Blake in the company of Joseph Johnson's radical coterie, which included such prominent activists as Joseph Priestley, Thomas Paine, and Mary Wollstonecraft. In their society he evidently discussed the democratic revolutions in America and France and the political and social turmoil they engendered at home, topics that also became major focuses of his poetry: *The French Revolution* (1791), for example, covers events in France during May to mid-July, 1789, emphasizing the oppressive authoritarianism of the old regime, while *America: A Prophecy* (1793) predicts the spread of the American experiment to Europe. Blake's sympathy with political and civil liberties put him at odds with the notoriously repressive government of William Pitt, and thus some critics have speculated that Blake obscured his ideas behind the veil of mysticism to circumvent government censure.

In 1790, Blake and his wife moved to Lambeth, where he completed *The French Revolution* and *America.* In addition to these works, he produced *The Marriage of Heaven and Hell* (1790-93?). In this paradoxical work, Blake exposes the evils inhering in the ortho-

dox conception of virtue and the virtues inhering in the orthodox conception of evil. Characteristically, Blake identifies religion with laws that focus on restrictions and divisions rather than on spiritual harmony. A series of minor symbolic books also belongs to the Lambeth period: in *Visions of the Daughters of Albion: The Eye Sees More than the Heart Knows* (1793), *America, The First Book of Urizen* (1794), *Europe: A Prophecy* (1794), *The Song of Los* (1795), *The Book of Ahania* (1795), and *The Book of Los* (1795), Blake developed the symbolic mythology that he first introduced in *Tiriel* (1789?), and *The Book of Thel* (1789), setting in motion what Mark Schorer describes as "a system of ever-widening metaphorical amplification" through which Blake attempted "to explain his story, the story of his England, the history of the world, prehistory, and the nature of all eternity." Scholars generally agree that Blake's mythology reaches its fullest expression in *The Four Zoas: The Torments of Love & Jealousy in the Death and Judgement of Albion the Ancient Man* (composed 1796-1807?), which he probably began to compose during the Lambeth years, and in *Jerusalem: The Emanation of the Giant Albion* (1804-20?), a prophetic work of later origin. *Songs of Innocence and of Experience,* regarded by many critics as the lyrical counterpart of the symbolic books, is also a product of the Lambeth period.

From 1800 to 1803, Blake and his wife lived at the seaside village of Felpham under the patronage of the minor poet William Hayley, whose mundaneness soon became a source of vexation to the visionary Blake. Scholars speculate that Blake revised *The Four Zoas* during his unhappy stay there and that he began to draft *Milton,* a reworking of *Paradise Lost,* at this time also. Both poems have been interpreted in light of his statement that he had "fought thro' a Hell of terrors & horror . . . in a Divided Existence" during these years. The Blakes returned to London in 1803, but their homecoming was marred by accusations that he had uttered seditious sentiments while expelling a soldier named Scofield from his garden at Felpham. He was tried for sedition and acquitted in 1804. Blake's next significant publication, his series of illustrations of an 1808 edition of Robert Blair's *The Grave,* attracted more notice than all of his poetical works combined. However, reviewers castigated his corporeal representation of spiritual phenomena as a piece of imaginative and theological impertinence, and the book also embroiled Blake in a dispute with the publisher, R. H. Cromek. These and other frustrations came to the fore in 1809, when he mounted a private exhibition of his paintings that he hoped would publicize his work and help to vindicate his visionary aesthetic. This it failed to do: not only was the exhibition poorly attended, but the descriptive catalogue that he wrote to accompany it largely inspired ridicule among its few readers.

Blake's later years were distinguished by his completion of *Jerusalem* (1804-20?), his last and longest prophetic book, and by his creation of a series of engraved illustrations for the Book of Job that is now widely regarded as his greatest artistic achievement. The latter work was commissioned in the early 1820s by John Linnell, one of a group of young artists known as the "Ancients" who gathered around Blake and helped support him in his old age.

Blake once defended his art by remarking, "What is Grand is necessarily obscure to Weak men. That which can be made Explicit to the Idiot is not worth my care." He thus characterized his work as a combination of grandness and obscurity that he was not particularly eager to elucidate. Fortunately, his aesthetic philosophy emerges clearly in his writings, forming a firm basis for critical insight into his perplexing oeuvre. Blake held the radical view that "Nature is Imagination itself "; by extension, he also maintained that exercise of the imagination leads to wisdom and insight (synonymous with vision) and, according to Jerome J. McGann, that poetry, painting, and other imaginative pursuits serve as "vehicles for vision." Given this perception, the world of imagination took precedence for Blake over the world of matter, and rational philosophical systems, based as they are in the material world, gave way to the "Divine Arts of Imagination." Moreover, Blake considered it his personal mission both to express and embody this philosophy in his art, thus giving a prophetic quality to his work.

Blake's passion for originality and imagination informs his creation of a private cosmology that embraces both his lyric and prophetic poetry. Stated in the most general terms, his system posits a universe whose most sweeping movements and minutest particulars reflect ever-fluctuating relationships between reason, love, poetry, energy, and other vital forces. While these forces appear most prominently in the symbolic mythology of the prophetic books, taking the guise of such titanic characters as Urizen, Luvah, Los, and Orc, critics generally maintain that they are integral to the symbolism of the lyric poems as well. Hazard Adams, for example, states that "the whole of Blake's great symbolic system" is assimilated in the symbolic structure of the lyric "The Tyger," while Joseph Wicksteed sees Blake's ideas concerning matter and the flesh reflected in such symbols as dew and grass in the "Introduction" to *Songs of Experience*. Great as this symbolic system might be, however, it has also been described as "notoriously private" and "hieroglyphic," pointing to a difficulty in interpreting Blake's symbols that led early critics to question the lucidity and even the sanity of Blake's prophetic books.

By virtue of its versification, *Jerusalem* is considered by many as the culmination of a lifetime of experimentation befitting a poet who despised restriction in all its forms: "Poetry Fetter'd, Fetters the Human Race!" Blake declared in the preface to *Jerusalem,* proclaiming his liberation from the "monotony" and "bondage" of metered verse. As early as *Poetical Sketches,* he explored the elimination of end rhyme, substituting rhythmical devices such as word repetition that he subsequently used to great advantage in *Songs of Innocence and of Experience.* The poems in the latter work are also celebrated for their compression and economy, yet Blake appears to have deemphasized these qualities in selecting the lengthy septenary line for *The Four Zoas, Milton* (1804-08?) and *Jerusalem.* Even here, however, he deviated from his standard line at will, leading to Alicia Ostriker's observation that "Blake, even in his metrics, deliberately breaks every rule he makes, refuses to impose order in art where there is no order in his visions, . . . [insisting on] keeping beauty afar until he is ready for her." Ostriker and other commentators generally agree that Blake's greatest stylistic triumph occurs in "Night IX" of *The Four Zoas,* in which the poet triumphantly orchestrates his varied measures in announcing the restoration of universal harmony at the Last Judgment.

Ironically, Blake was better known among his contemporaries for his engravings and designs than for his poetry. The scarcity of his books and his reputation for madness contributed to the lack of attention from his peers, although Samuel Taylor Coleridge privately recognized Blake as a "man of Genius" and Charles Lamb conceded that he was "one of the most extraordinary persons of the age." Blake's critical fortunes did not improve until 1863 with the publication of Alexander Gilchrist's sympathetic biography, which sparked a revival of interest in the poet that was sustained by the editorial and critical commentary of such nineteenth-century luminaries as Dante Gabriel Rossetti and Charles Algernon Swinburne. This impetus has continued unabated into the twentieth century as well, with Northrop Frye and other critics providing explications of Blake's symbolic system that have abetted an ever-widening array of studies.

Blake once wrote, "One Law for the Lion and the Ox is oppression." A kindred appreciation of the claims of individualism may well inform the willingness of modern scholars to elevate this most individual of writers to the front ranks of English poetry. At the same time, however, enthusiasts stress that he transcends the merely personal in his works. In the words of George Saintsbury, Blake set forth an aesthetic in which, in place of the "battered gods of the classical or neo-classical Philistia, are set up Imagination for Reason, Enthusiasm for Good Sense, the Result for the Rule; the execution for the mere conception or even the mere selection of subject; impression for calculation; the heart and the eyes and the pulses and the fancy for the stop-watch and the boxwood measure and the table of specifications." In establishing a system based on these objectives, Blake anticipated many of the dominant artistic impulses of the modern era.

(For further information on Blake's life and works, see *Dictionary of Literary Biography*, Vol. 93: *British Romantic Poets, 1789-1832; Nineteenth-Century Literature Criticism*, Vol. 13; and *Something About the Author*, Vol. 30. For related criticism, see the entry on English Romantic Poetry in *Nineteenth-Century Literature Criticism*, Vol. 28.)

CRITICAL COMMENTARY

WILLIAM BLAKE

(letter date 1802)

[In the following excerpt from a letter to Thomas Butts, Blake describes conflicts he has experienced as an artist and visionary.]

I find on all hands great objections to my doing any thing but the meer drudgery of business, & intimations that if I do not confine myself to this, I shall not live; this has always pursu'd me. You will understand by this the source of all my uneasiness. This from Johnson & Fuseli brought me down here, & this from Mr H. will bring me back again; for that I cannot live without doing my duty to lay up treasures in heaven is Certain & Determined, & to this I have long made up my mind, & why this should be made an objection to Me, while Drunkenness, Lewdness, Gluttony & even Idleness itself, does not hurt other men, let Satan himself Explain. The Thing I have most at Heart—more than life, or all that seems to make life comfortable without—Is the Interest of True Religion & Science, & whenever any thing appears to affect that Interest (Especially if I myself omit any duty to my . . . Station as a Soldier of Christ), It gives me the greatest of torments. I am not ashamed, afraid, or averse to tell you what Ought to be Told: That I am under the direction of Messengers from Heaven, Daily & Nightly; but the nature of such things is not, as some suppose, without trouble or care. Temptations are on the right hand & left; behind, the sea of time & space roars & follows swiftly; he who keeps not right onward is lost, & if our footsteps slide in clay, how can we do otherwise than fear & tremble? . . . But if we fear to do the dictates of our Angels, & tremble at the Tasks set before us; if we refuse to do Spiritual Acts because of Natural Fears of Natural Desires! Who can describe the dismal torments of such a state!—I too well remember the Threats I heard!—If you, who are organised by Divine Providence for Spiritual commu-

nion, Refuse, & bury your Talent in the Earth, even tho' you should want Natural Bread, Sorrow & Desperation pursues you thro' life, & after death shame & confusion of face to eternity. Every one in Eternity will leave you, aghast at the Man who was crown'd with glory & honour by his brethren, & betray'd their cause to their enemies. You will be call'd the base Judas who betray'd his Friend!—Such words would make any stout man tremble, & how then could I be at ease? But I am now no longer in That State, & now go on again with my Task, Fearless, and tho' my path is difficult, I have no fear of stumbling while I keep it. (pp. 69-71)

William Blake, in a letter to Thomas Butts on January 10, 1802, in his *The Letters of William Blake,* edited by Geoffrey Keynes, The Macmillan Company, 1956, pp. 68-71.

HENRY CRABB ROBINSON

(essay date 1811)

[A journalist and later a barrister, Robinson cultivated friendships with Blake, William Wordsworth, and other writers and recorded his impressions in diaries and correspondence. He published the following commentary on Blake in the German periodical *Vaterländisches Museum* in 1811—nearly a decade and a half before he first met the poet personally. Here, Robinson surveys Blake's criticism and poetry.]

Of all the conditions which arouse the interest of the psychologist, none assuredly is more attractive than the union of genius and madness in single remarkable minds, which, while on the one hand they compel our admiration by their great mental powers, yet on the other move our pity by their claims to supernatural

*Principal Works

Poetical Sketches (poetry and drama) 1783

An Island in the Moon [MS] (satire) 1784

All Religions Are One (treatise) 1788?

There Is No Natural Religion (treatise) 1788?

The Book of Thel (poetry) 1789

Songs of Innocence (poetry) 1789

Tiriel [MS] (poetry) 1789?

The Marriage of Heaven and Hell (prose, proverbs, and poetry) 1790-93?

The French Revolution (poetry) 1791

America: A Prophecy (poetry) 1793

Visions of the Daughters of Albion: The Eye Sees More than the Heart Knows (poetry) 1793

Europe: A Prophecy (poetry) 1794

The First Book of Urizen (poetry) 1794

Songs of Innocence and of Experience: Shewing the Two Contrary States of the Human Soul (poetry) 1794

The Book of Ahania (poetry) 1795

The Book of Los (poetry) 1795

The Song of Los (poetry) 1795

The Four Zoas: The Torments of Love & Jealousy in the Death and Judgement of Albion the Ancient Man [MS] (poetry) 1796-1807?; published as Vala in The Works of William Blake, Poetic, Symbolic, and Critical. 3 vols. 1893

Milton (poetry) 1804-08?

Jerusalem: The Emanation of the Giant Albion (poetry) 1804-20?

The Pickering Manuscript [MS] (poetry and proverbs) 1807?

A Descriptive Catalogue (catalogue) 1809

The Poetical Works of William Blake, Lyrical and Miscellaneous (poetry and drama) 1874

The Works of William Blake, Poetic, Symbolic, and Critical. 3 vols. (poetry) 1893

† The Note-Book of William Blake (notebook) 1935

The Poetry and Prose of William Blake (poetry, prose, drama, marginalia, and letters) 1965

The Complete Writings of William Blake (poetry, prose, drama, marginalia, and letters) 1966

The Letters of William Blake (letters) 1968

*Dating the original publication of Blake's works is difficult, for he alternately printed and revised some of his individual writings over a long period of time and left few plates and copies of books for bibliographers to examine as evidence. The dates in this list of principal works, reflecting the speculative nature of Blake bibliography, are taken mainly from Blake Books by G. E. Bentley, Jr. [see Sources for Further Study]. The designation [MS] following a title indicates that Blake left the work in manuscript form.

†Blake's notebook is also referred to as the "Rossetti Manuscript."

---

gifts. Of such is the whole race of ecstatics, mystics, seers of visions and dreamers of dreams, and to their list we have now to add another name, that of William Blake.

This extraordinary man, who is at this moment living in London, although more than fifty years of age, is only now beginning to emerge from the obscurity in which the singular bent of his talents and the eccentricity of his personal character have confined him. (p. 236)

One attempt at introducing him to the great British public has indeed succeeded, his illustrations to Blair's 'Grave.' . . . (p. 238)

Only last year he opened an exhibition of his frescoes, proclaiming that he had rediscovered the lost art of fresco. He demanded of those who had considered his works the slovenly daubs of a madman, destitute alike of technical skill and harmony of proportion, to examine them now with greater attention. . . . At the same time he published a *Descriptive Catalogue* of these fresco pictures, out of which we propose to give only a few unconnected passages. The original consists of a veritable folio of fragmentary utterances on art and religion, without plan or arrangement, and the artist's idiosyncracies will in this way be most clearly shown. The vehemence with which, throughout the book, he declaims against oil painting and the artists of the Venetian and Flemish schools is part of the fixed ideas of the author. . . . [His preface begins with the following words:] 'The eye which prefers the colouring of Rubens and Titian to that of Raphael and Michael Angelo should be modest and mistrust its own judgement,' but as he proceeds with his descriptions his wrath against false schools of painting waxes, and in holy zeal he proclaims that the hated artists are evil spirits, and later art the offspring of hell. Chiaroscuro he plainly calls 'an infernal machine in the hand of Venetian and Flemish demons.' . . . Correggio he calls 'a soft, effeminate, and consequently most cruel demon.' Rubens is 'a most outrageous demon.' . . . [The] following passage, while it reveals the artist's views on the technique of his art, contains a truth which cannot be denied, and which underlies his whole doctrine. 'The great and golden rule of art, as well as of life, is this: That the more distinct, sharp and wiry the bounding line, the more perfect the work of art.' . . . In the same spirit he proclaims the guilt of the recent distinction between a painting and a drawing. 'If losing and obliterating the outline constitutes a picture, Mr. B. will never be so foolish as to do one. . . . There is no difference between Raphael's Cartoons and his Frescoes or Pictures, except that the Frescos or Pictures are more highly finished.' (pp. 240-42)

[Blake's] greatest enjoyment consists in giving bodily form to spiritual beings. Thus in the 'Grave' he has represented the reunion of soul and body, and to both he has given equal clearness of form and outline. . . .

In his Catalogue we find . . . vindication of the reproaches brought against his earlier work. 'Shall painting be confined to the sordid drudgery of facsimile representations of merely mortal and perishing substances, and not be, as poetry and music are, elevated into its own proper sphere of invention and visionary conception?' He then alleges that the statues of the Greek gods are so many bodily representations of spiritual beings. 'A Spirit and a Vision are not, as the modern philosophy asserts, a cloudy vapour or a nothing; they are organised and minutely articulated beyond all that the mortal and perishing nature can produce. Spirits are organised men.' (p. 243)

Elsewhere [in the *Descriptive Catalogue*] he says that Adam and Noah were Druids, and that he himself is an inhabitant of Eden. Blake's religious convictions appear to be those of an orthodox Christian; nevertheless, passages concerning earlier mythologies occur which might cast a doubt on it. . . . [His] system remains more allied to the stoical endurance of Antiquity than to the essential austerity of Christianity. (pp. 246-47)

[Blake's] poems breathe the same spirit and are distinguished by the same peculiarities as his drawings and prose criticisms. As early as 1783 a little volume was printed with the title of *Poetical Sketches, by W. B.* No printer's name is given on the title-page, and in the preface it states that the poems were composed between his thirteenth and twentieth years. They are of very unequal merit. The metre is usually so loose and careless as to betray a total ignorance of the art, whereby the larger part of the poems are rendered singularly rough and unattractive. On the other hand, there is a wildness and loftiness of imagination in certain dramatic fragments which testifies to genuine poetical feeling. (pp. 249-50)

A still more remarkable little book of poems by our author exists, which is only to be met with in the hands of collectors. It is a duodecimo entitled *Songs of Innocence and Experience, shewing the two contrary states of the human soul. The Author and printer W.*

Blake. . . . It is not easy to form a comprehensive opinon of the text, since the poems deserve the highest praise and the gravest censure. Some are childlike songs of great beauty and simplicity; these are the *Songs of Innocence,* many of which, nevertheless, are excessively childish.

The *Songs of Experience,* on the other hand, are metaphysical riddles and mystical allegories. Among them are poetic pictures of the highest beauty and sublimity; and again there are poetical fancies which can scarcely be understood even by the initiated. (pp. 250-51)

Besides these songs two other works of Blake's Poetry and Painting have come under our notice, of which, however, we must confess our inability to give a sufficient account. These are two quarto volumes which appeared in 1794, printed and adorned like the *Songs,* under the titles of *Europe, a Prophecy,* and *America, a Prophecy.*

The very 'Prophecies of Bakis' are not obscurer. *America* appears in part to give a poetical account of the Revolution, since it contains the names of several party leaders. The actors in it are a species of guardian angels. We give only a short example, nor can we decide whether it is intended to be in prose or verse.

On these vast shady hills between America's and Albion's shore,
Now barred out by the Atlantic Sea: called Atlantean hills,
Because from their bright summits you may pass to the golden world,
An ancient palace, archetype of mighty empires,
Rears its immortal summit, built in the forests of God,
By Ariston the King of Heaven for his stolen bride.

The obscurity of these lines in such a poem by such a man will be willingly overlooked.

Europe is a similar mysterious and incomprehensible rhapsody, which probably contains the artist's political visions of the future, but is wholly inexplicable. (pp. 254-55)

We have now an account of all the works of this extraordinary man that have come under our notice. We have been lengthy, but our object is to draw the attention of Germany to a man in whom all the elements of greatness are unquestionably to be found, even though those elements are disproportionately mingled. Closer research than was permitted us would perhaps shew that as an artist Blake will never produce consummate and immortal work, as a poet flawless poems; but this assuredly cannot lessen the interest which all men, Germans in a higher degree even than Englishmen, must take in the contemplation of such a character. We will only recall the phrase of a thoughtful writer, that those faces are the most attractive in which nature has set something of greatness which she has yet left unfinished; the same may hold good of the soul. (pp. 255-56)

Henry Crabb Robinson, "An Early Appreciation of William Blake," translated by K. A. Esdaile, in *The Library,* n.s. Vol. V, No. 19, July, 1914, pp. 229-56.

W. B. YEATS
(essay date 1897)

[The leading figure of the Irish Renaissance and a major twentieth-century poet, Yeats was also an active critic. He judged the works of others on their sincerity, passion, and vital imagination—standards that were largely inspired by his admiration for Blake. In the following excerpt from an essay that first appeared in the *Academy* in 1897, he portrays Blake as a poet blessed with the mission of introducing the "religion of art" to the world but cursed with the burden of inventing his own mythology.]

There have been men who loved the future like a mistress, and the future mixed her breath into their breath and shook her hair about them, and hid them from the understanding of their times. William Blake was one of these men, and if he spoke confusedly and obscurely it was because he spoke things for whose speaking he could find no models in the world about him. He announced the religion of art, of which no man dreamed in the world about him; and he understood it more perfectly than the thousands of subtle spirits who have received its baptism in the world about us, because, in the beginning of important things—in the beginning of love, in the beginning of the day, in the beginning of any work, there is a moment when we understand more perfectly than we understand again until all is finished. . . . We [now] write of great writers, even of writers whose beauty would once have seemed an unholy beauty, with rapt sentences like those our fathers kept for the beatitudes and mysteries of the Church; and no matter what we believe with our lips, we believe with our hearts that beautiful things, as Browning said in his one prose essay that was not in verse, have 'lain burningly on the Divine hand,' and that when time has begun to wither, the Divine hand will fall heavily on bad taste and vulgarity. When no man believed these things William Blake believed them, and began that preaching against the Philistine, which is as the preaching of the Middle Ages against the Saracen.

He had learned from Jacob Boehme and from old alchemist writers that imagination was the first emanation of divinity, 'the body of God,' 'the Divine members,' and he drew the deduction, which they did not draw, that the imaginative arts were therefore the greatest of Divine revelations, and that the sympathy with all living things, sinful and righteous alike, which the imaginative arts awaken, is that forgiveness of sins commanded by Christ. The reason, and by the reason he meant deductions from the observations of the senses, binds us to mortality because it binds us to the senses, and divides us from each other by showing us our clashing interests; but imagination divides us from mortality by the immortality of beauty, and binds us to each other by opening the secret doors of all hearts. He cried again and again that every thing that lives is holy, and that nothing is unholy except things that do not live—lethargies, and cruelties, and timidities, and that denial of imagination which is the root they grew from in old times. Passions, because most living, are most holy—and this was a scandalous paradox in his time—and man shall enter eternity borne upon their wings. (pp. 168-71)

This philosophy kept him more simply a poet than any poet of this time, for it made him content to express every beautiful feeling that came into his head without troubling about its utility or chaining it to any utility. Sometimes one feels, even when one is reading poets of a better time—Tennyson or Wordsworth, let us say—that they have troubled the energy and simplicity of their imaginative passions by asking whether they were for the helping or for the hindrance of the world, instead of believing that all beautiful things have 'lain burningly on the Divine hand.' But when one reads Blake, it is as though the spray of an inexhaustible fountain of beauty was blown into our faces, and not merely when one reads the *Songs of Innocence,* or the lyrics he wished to call 'The Ideas of Good and Evil,' but when one reads those 'Prophetic Works' in which he spoke confusedly and obscurely because he spoke of things for whose speaking he could find no models in the world about him. He was a symbolist who had to invent his symbols; and his counties of England, with their correspondence to tribes of Israel, and his mountains and rivers, with their correspondence to parts of a man's body, are arbitrary as some of the symbolism in the *Axël* of the symbolist Villiers De L'Isle Adam is arbitrary, while they mix incongruous things as *Axël* does not. He was a man crying out for a mythology, and trying to make one because he could not find one to his hand. Had he been a Catholic of Dante's time he would have been well content with Mary and the angels; or had he been a scholar of our time he would have taken his symbols where Wagner took his, from Norse mythology; or have followed, with the help of Prof. Rhys, that pathway into Welsh mythology which he found in *Jerusalem;* or have gone to Ireland—and he was probably an Irishman—and chosen for his symbols the sacred mountains, along whose sides the peasant still sees enchanted fires, and the divinities which have not faded from the belief . . . and have been less obscure because a traditional mythology stood on the threshold of his meaning and on the margin of his sacred darkness. If 'Enitharmon' had been named Freia, or Gwydeon, or Danu, and made live in Ancient Norway, or Ancient Wales, or Ancient Ireland, we would have forgotten that her maker was a mystic; and the hymn of her harping, that is in *Vala*, would but have reminded us of many ancient hymns. (pp. 172-75)

W. B. Yeats, "William Blake and the Imagination," in his *Ideas of Good and Evil*, A. H. Bullen, 1903, pp. 168-75.

MARK SCHORER
(essay date 1946)

[In the following excerpt from his *William Blake: The Politics of Vision*, Schorer examines Blake's commitment to the revolutionary ideals of liberty, equality, and fraternity.]

That the content of Blake's poetry is primarily social and that his criticism of society is radical, commentary on Blake does not readily concede even now. Not many years ago Stephen Spender wrote: "The error of poetry was surely the romantic movement. . . . If Blake had not been so unique a figure, if he had been a greater poet and perhaps less of a genius, he might have been the leader of a reaction from the late eighteenth century, which would have been a 'criticism of life'—that is, of the Industrial Revolution.

> But most through midnight streets I hear
> How the youthful harlot's curse
> Blasts the new-born infant's tear,
> And blights with plagues the marriage hearse,

is poetry that is a function of life, as distinct from poetry that is an escape into dreams." Mr. Spender meant that in Blake, as in his contemporaries, in spite of the flickering promise of genuine perception into the actual, the "escape into dreams" triumphed over the "criticism of life."

This is the conventional view of Blake's development, but it is a view that declines to read closely. If a radical is a thinker who challenges and repudiates the assumptions of the dominant class in his society on the basis of revolutionary assumptions of his own, and if a radical poet is one whose utterance, in image and structure as well as in matter, is informed by the challenge and the repudiation—then Blake was and always remained a radical poet. The radical content of his poetry came out of well-known revolutionary discussion concentrated in the thought of that "remarkable coterie" associated with the London printer Joseph Johnson at the end of the eighteenth century. Yet the influence on Blake of republicans like Price and Paine and Priestley, of anarchists like Holcroft and Godwin, of the feminist Mary Wollstonecraft, of industrial and social developments toward which these persons held attitudes, is a focus for Blake rather than a "source," an atmosphere of opinion in which he found a direction rather than a set of fixed ideas. They provided a point at which his own revolutionary concepts were freed and from which they more or less evolved. (pp. 151-52)

Blake criticism has not always denied the influence of these theorists, but it has decreed a sharp separation—dating the year, of course, as 1792, and the month as September—between Blake the heedless young radical and Blake the sagely retreating mystic. His biography and his casual utterances show that this separation is not real, that he maintained his connections with other radicals while they were available, and sustained his interest in their ideas after they were not. (p. 153)

The fact that ideas as used in poetry are subject to the imagination sometimes makes them difficult to recognize, and with a poet like Blake, who seized at ideas from so many diverse directions and who was almost always so different in one way or another from their source, the opportunity of overlooking his debt is great. Face Blake with Godwin in fancy—one could hardly produce a temperamental clash more harsh. And of course Blake's sharp opposition to some of the most basic assumptions of current revolutionary dogma makes this debt particularly obscure. Yet ideas mesh and are pushed into movement not so much through gentle elisions as through partial antagonisms, and this is the relation between revolutionary theory and Blake's intellectual development. He sharpened his borrowings by his rejections; and by his very rejection of certain elements in that theory he refreshed it, and at precisely the point in history when it seemed to be expiring.

Blake's intellectual and poetic stature was greater than Shelley's precisely to the extent that he attempted a restatement of the assumptions of revolutionary doctrine. Whitehead has said: "The literary exposition of freedom deals mainly with the frills. The Greek myth was more to the point. Prometheus did not bring to mankind freedom of the press. He procured fire." One would despair of reading a poem on the freedom of the press, to be sure, and Prometheus brought mankind more than fire. Yet Shelley's Prometheus brought less than either, the unconverted theory, and even those poems of his over which we murmur names of real events like Peterloo are nearly as abstract as the doctrine of his mentors. The rejection of the doctrine of necessity was not enough; for poetry, a *recasting* was the required act. In two important ways Blake avoided the defect of Shelley. He fought against the abstraction of revolutionary theory by criticizing, and not abstractly, that element in the theory itself; and he countered it further by building the most intimate portion of his poetry, its imagery, not on the frills of freedom but on the facts of contemporary life.

In his extremely personal way Blake measures up to the very definition of poetry by which Mr. Spender finds him wanting. "The task of the poet of the future," the latter said, "is to win back the ground that has been lost by the romantic movement: that is to say he has to apply himself minutely to observe the life of people round him, and he has also to understand and to feel in himself the development of recent history. Poetry is at once a description of the conditions of living and an affirmation of the permanent in life, of real values. . . . I do not mean that poets must write exclusively, or even of necessity at all, of machines and towns. . . . What is required of the poet is not up-to-date-ness but an awareness of the extent to which the external conditions of today, towns, machinery, etc., have, like an acid, eaten into conscious and subconscious humanity."

Blake's poetry is of an elaborately concentric order. He is the most difficult of English poets because he was the most ambitious. He wished, in a system of ever-widening metaphorical amplification, to explain his story, the story of his England, the history of the world, prehistory, and the nature of all eternity. Almost unanimously, critics have attended to the eternal elements, to what they have called the "mysticism," or at least to the religion, or simply to an exposition of the system itself. Or they have elucidated in very general terms what Spender calls the "real values" at the expense of "the conditions of living," and in separating the two, they have altered the meaning of the first. In Blake's scheme, "eternity" is the cause, but man, and most specifically man in Blake's day, is the tragic or the triumphant effect, and "eternity" itself is a solid, even a somewhat lumpish, affair. "All things Begin & End," in his narratives, "in Albion's Ancient Druid Rocky Shore," and Ephesians 6:12 served as the epigraph to [*The Four Zoas,*] one of his longest and perhaps his central poem: "For our contention is not with the blood and the flesh, but with dominion, with authority, with the blind world-rulers of this life, with the spirit of evil in things heavenly."

This was Shelley's implicit epigraph, but the two dramatized it differently. Several of Blake's poems, like some of Shelley's, take historical events as their subject matter, but in Shelley the "conditions of living" vanish in moonlight and high sound; in Blake, even as the poetry grows more bewildering, the "conditions of living" more and more insistently force themselves into the imagery, the fabric of the poems. In Shelley, the Rights of Man remains the defective historical generalization that it was in eighteenth-century liberal theory. In Blake, it is converted into its psychological actuality, which, as a political axiom, remains undisputed even though varieties of interest have interpreted it in varieties of ways. The slogan The Rights of Man Blake avoided, as he avoided most slogans. But the abiding theme of all his poems is the integrity of the individual, and the imperative right of the personality to expression and fulfillment.

When Blake said, "I in Six Thousand Years walk up and down," he was laying claim to a vaster knowledge of the developments of history than any man can support, and he was placing on poetry a greater burden that it can endure apart from religious ritual. He did so because he was convinced that his function, in spite of his inadequate theology, was religious, that under the multiple and shifting historical tides he perceived the enduring psychological facts. These, as he envisaged them, he could not have perceived except at the end of his century, in a generation of political upheaval and in the time of a terrorized reaction, and even then, he could not conceivably have expressed them if his eyes had indeed been only on the elusive "real values" and never on the mere, brutal, corrosive, outrageous fact. Walking up and down in six thousand years meant that Blake, like Shelley, was

. . . as a nerve o'er which do creep
The else unfelt oppressions of this earth;

but much more, too. (pp. 153-56)

"Each Identity is Eternal" and "All Things Common"—the intellectual struggle to which Blake gave his life was to bring these two together. In French Revolutionary doctrine, their names were Liberty and Fraternity, but the French Revolution failed to unite them. In Blake's lifetime and (with the possible exception of such ambiguous social experiments as Robert Owen's), at least until the formulations of Marx, liberty alone found defenders. Isolated from its triad, it developed on the one hand into the dreary shopkeeper's philosophy of Bentham, and on the other into the aggressive power philosophy of Carlyle, where liberty was the monopoly of the exceptional, and most men were intended to lapse gratefully into the slavery they deserved. Blake's correction of eighteenth-century liberalism from which he certainly derived, prevents his falling into some poetic approximation either of the drab Benthamite liberalism, with its uninspired approval of the bourgeoisie, or of the glittering negations of Carlyle and Nietzsche, with their exaltation of the most frightening aristocracy of all. For Blake, exalting neither man's reason nor, in the usual sense, his virtue, yet *loved* men, individual men. To Bentham the mass of individuals were colorless atoms; to Carlyle and Nietzsche they were scum in a quagmire. Blake's concern was with the individual man within the mass of individual men.

Individualism was his main value, as it was the main value of all liberals of whatever color in the first half of the nineteenth century; but he detected the ambiguities and the contrasts that inhabit this term, and he struggled in his poetry to express them, and to assert one set of meanings against another. His long poems are dramatic parables about the conflicts between these forms of individualism. Urizen, the mistaken spirit, represents individualism, after all, as much as does Orc, or Los, or any good spirit. When is the impulse mistaken, and when is it good? It is mistaken when, like Urizen, it separates itself from its members to exalt itself, when it is in competition with its members, when it destroys order. It is good when, like Orc or Los, it attempts to force or weld the original whole together again and establish a harmony of parts. Individualism is evil when it is a will to power, good when it is a will to order. The quarrel is between competition, a reckless laissez-faire, and co-operation. The way to achieve the good is through the only social virtue that Blake recognized, love, or forgiveness, or brotherhood, which as often as not he called imagination.

"Each Identity is Eternal" and "All Things Common." This is to ask for complete individuality within the widest universality. The paradox here between individualism and harmony is the great paradox of democracy itself: the right of the personality to develop, and the evil of any personality's "developing" at the expense of any other. The second "developing" is crucial, and it resolves the paradox; for preventing another means reducing, not expanding, the self and thereafter the society. This concept Blake labored ceaselessly, in every way, to express; in the lyric imagery of nature—

> Each outcry of the hunted Hare
> A fibre from the Brain does tear.
> A Skylark wounded in the wing,
> A Cherubim does cease to sing—

and in moralistic verse—

> The iron hand crush'd the Tyrant's head
> And became a Tyrant in his stead—

and in straightforward prose: "All Those who, having no Passions of their own because No Intellect, Have spent their lives in Curbing & Governing other People's by the Various arts"; [and] "Poverty is the Fool's Rod, which at last is turn'd on his own back." . . . (pp. 182-84)

But the difficulty of stating a perception that had not yet been formulated in history was great. . . . Chiefly, he had to rely on his mythical representations, in which the unity of opposites could be embodied, and this paradox resolved. The figure of Albion, who "falls" into sleep and sickness when a part (which now degenerates, too) rebels, and awakens to a glorious day when the part is reassimilated (and finds itself well

again)—this figure may be taken as the symbol of a great composite democratic individual, the archetype for a society whose members live co-operatively, and for the individual whose self-expression is then complete and who is then in perfect health. Blake's treatment of the sexes represents a parallel unity of opposites. They are separate, with separate impulses, and only when the impulses of each are given free expression *in love* is the separateness broken down. The androgynous figure of Blake's eternity is the symbol of this attainment.

Blake could sometimes only perilously maintain his concept of variety in unity ("the MOST UNITED VARIETY"). Often enough he rejects his ideal of individuality within the whole for that other individualism which pits the single *against* the whole, man *against* the universe, and the poet *against* society; when he seems to say that his concern, like that of the mystics, is the development of his individuality alone, the achievement of his own spiritual life, of a private salvation—all of which is laissez-faire, too. But these occasions are found in his discouraged, fragmentary utterances, not in his poems. He wrote no palinodes. In his poetry he repeatedly sought to state what we recognize now as the greatest modern social pardox. He did not think this pardox through as a political or an economic problem, but he struggled with it valiantly and constantly as a psychological problem, and he knew how current politics and economics taxed it. He was the first to know. When others fought for liberty alone, he insisted on equality and fraternity also; and he saw that you cannot gain the first if you sacrifice the second or the third. Toward the adjustment of these three our civilization still strives. (pp. 184-85)

Mark Schorer, in his *William Blake: The Politics of Vision,* Henry Holt and Company, 1946, 524 p.

NORTHROP FRYE

(essay date 1947)

[In the following excerpt from his *Fearful Symmetry: A Study of William Blake*, Frye examines Blake's conception of the poet.]

The Bible is the world's greatest work of art and therefore has primary claim to the title of God's World. It takes in, in one immense sweep, the entire world of experience from the creation to the final vision of the City of God, embracing heroic saga, prophetic vision, legend, symbolism, the Gospel of Jesus, poetry and oratory on the way. It bridges the gap between a lost Golden Age and the time that the World became flesh and dwelt among us, and it alone gives us the vision of the life of Jesus in this world. For some reason or other the Jews managed to preserve an imaginative tradition which the Greeks and others lost sight of, and possessed only in disguised and allegorical forms. The Classical poets, says Blake:

> Assert that Jupiter usurped the Throne of his Father, Saturn, & brought on an Iron Age & Begat on Mnemosyne, or Memory, The Greek Muses, which are not Inspiration as the Bible is. Reality was Forgot, & the Vanities of Time & Space only Remember'd & call'd Reality. Such is the Mighty difference between Allegoric Fable & Spiritual Mystery. Let it here be Noted that the Greek Fables originated in Spiritual Mystery & Real Visions, which are lost & clouded in Fable & Allegory, while the Hebrew Bible & the Greek Gospel are Genuine, Preserv'd by the Saviour's Mercy. The Nature of my Work is Visionary or Imaginative; it is an Endeavour to Restore what the Ancients call'd the Golden Age.

We shall come to this distinction between allegory and vision in a moment. There are two obvious inferences from the passage: first, that Blake's poetry is all related to a central myth; and secondly, that the primary basis of this myth is the Bible, so that if we know how Blake read the Bible "in its infernal or diabolical sense" we shall have little difficulty with his symbolism. (pp. 108-09)

The Bible is therefore the archetype of Western culture, and the Bible, with its derivatives, provides the basis for most of our major art: for Dante, Milton, Michelangelo, Raphael, Bach, the great cathedrals, and so on. The most complete form of art is a cyclic vision, which, like the Bible, sees the world between the two poles of fall and redemption. In Western art this is most clearly represented in the miracle-play sequences and encyclopedic symbolism of the Gothic cathedrals, which often cover the entire imaginative field from creation to the Last Judgment, and always fit integrally into some important aspect of it.

However, while "The Old & New Testaments are the Great Code of Art," to regard them as forming a peculiar and exclusive Word of God is a sectarian error. . . . There are many great visions outside the range of the Bible, such as the Icelandic Eddas and the *Bhagavadgita,* almost equally faithful to the central form of the Word of God, and the Bible no less than Classical legends comes from older and more authentic sources. . . . [Blake hints] at older Scriptures still from which the Bible itself has been derived:

> The antiquities of every Nation under Heaven, is no less sacred than that of the Jews. . . . How other antiquities came to be neglected and disbelieved, while those of the Jews are collected and arranged, is an enquiry worthy both of the Antiquarian and the Divine.

This feeling that the Bible does not exhaust the Word of God accounts for the phenomenon of what we may call contrapuntal symbolism, that is, the use of un-Christian mythology, usually Classical, to supplement and round out a Christian poem. (pp. 109-10)

The meaning of history, like the meaning of art, is to be found in its relation to the same great archetype of human existence. The inner form of history is not the same thing as the progress of time: a linear chronicle is a wild fairy tale in which the fate of an empire hangs on the shape of a beauty's nose, or the murder of a noble moron touches off a world war. And no poet concerned with human beings ever bothers to draw an individual as such: he is concerned with selecting the significant aspects of him. Significant in relation to what? In relation to the unity of his conception. But what makes that conception worth conceiving in the first place? Its relation, Blake would say, to the primary Word of God. We say that there is something universal in Quixote, Falstaff, Hamlet, Milton's Satan. But "something universal" is rather vague: just what is universal about them? As soon as we attempt to answer

"The Tyger," as it appears in *Songs of Innocence and Experience.*

this, we begin in spite of ourselves to elaborate our own versions of the archetypal myth. (p. 111)

[The] primary activity of all communication with the poet is to establish the unity of his poem in our minds. . . . [Blake maintained] that every poem is necessarily a perfect unity. This unity has two aspects: a unity of words and a unity of images. (p. 113)

To the poet the word is a storm-center of meanings, sounds and associations, radiating out indefinitely like the ripples of a pool. It is precisely because of this indefiniteness that he writes poems. The poem is a unity of words in which these radiations have become the links of imaginative cohesion. In a poem the sounds and rhythms of words are revealed more clearly than in ordinary speech, and similarly their meanings have an intensity in poetry that a dictionary can give no hint of.

This respect for the imaginative integrity of poetry is the reason for Blake's distrust of set patterns of meter and rhyme. Only lyrics, and not many of them, can be in a strict stanzaic form: longer works must have much greater fluency if the sound, sense and subject are to make a complete correspondence at all times. (pp. 114-15)

[According to Blake:]

Fable or Allegory are a totally distinct & inferior kind of Poetry. Vision or Imagination is a Representation of what Eternally Exists, Really & Unchangeably. Fable or Allegory is Form'd by the daughters of Memory. . . . Fable is allegory, but what Critics call The Fable, is Vision itself. The Hebrew Bible & the Gospel of Jesus are not Allegory, but External Vision or Imagination of All that Exists. Note here that Fable or Allegory is seldom without some Vision. Pilgrim's Progress is full of it, the Greek Poets the same; but Allegory & Vision ought to be known as Two Distinct Things. . . .

"Allegory" in the above sense is closely related to the kind of symbolism which is founded on the simile. To say that a hero is *like* a lion is a reference to something else on the same imaginative plane. Subject and object, as in Lockian philosophy, are considered to be only accidentally related. Even an epic simile enriches the symbolism only at the price of digressing from the narrative. The artist, contemplating the hero, searches in his memory for something that reminds him of the hero's courage, and drags out a lion. But here we no longer have two real things: we have a correspondence of abstractions. The hero's courage, not the hero himself, is what the lion symbolizes. And a lion which symbolizes an abstract quality is not a real but a heraldic lion. Some lions are cowardly; some are old and sick; some are cubs; some are female. And it is no use to say that a mature courageous male healthy lion is an "ideal" one: we should need an old and sick lion for an

old and sick hero. Whenever we take our eye off the image we slip into abstractions, into regarding qualities, moral or intellectual, as more real than living things. So Blake opposes to "Similitude" the "Identity," the latter being the metaphor which unites the theme and the illustration of it. (pp. 116-17)

All symbolism that deals with qualities has too many bad qualities of its own to be of any use to art. Hence we must not expect to find in Blake any kind of personification, or attempt to give life to an abstraction. When we read in *The Four Zoas* that Los attempts to embrace Enitharmon but that she is jealous and goes over to the embraces of Urizen, it is neither very helpful nor very interesting to translate that as: "Time or Prophecy attempts to overcome Space but Space falls under the domination of Reason." The continuous translation of poetic images into a series of moral and philosophical concepts is what usually passes for the explanation of an allegory. Now a reconstruction of a poem in abstract nouns is not necessarily a false interpretation of part of its meaning. But it is a translation, which means that it assumes the reader's ignorance of the original language. (p. 117)

[Thus] we see that art is neither inferior nor equal to morality and truth, but the synthesis of civilized life in which alone their general laws have any real meaning. Art is neither good nor bad, but a clairvoyant vision of the nature of both, and any attempt to align it with morality, otherwise called bowdlerizing, is intolerably vulgar. "Is not every Vice possible to Man," asked Blake, "described in the Bible openly?" Art is neither true nor false, but a clairvoyant vision of the nature of both, and any attempt to estimate its merits by the accuracy with which it reproduces the data of history or science is foolish. A subtler problem, once again, is presented by religion, which claims to be the synthesis of morality and truth we have said that art is, and hence to be superior to it. (pp. 117-18)

[Let us look at] the eleventh plate of *The Marriage of Heaven and Hell* . . . :

The ancient Poets animated all sensible objects with Gods or Geniuses, calling them by the names and adorning them with the properties of woods, rivers, mountains, lakes, cities, nations, and whatever their enlarged & numerous senses could perceive. . . .

Till a system was formed, which some took advantage of, & enslav'd the vulgar by attempting to realize or abstract the mental deities from their objects: thus began Priesthood;

Choosing forms of worship from poetic tales.

And at length they pronounc'd that the Gods had order'd such things.

Thus men forgot that All deities reside in the human breast.

Now just as the poet is brought up to speak and write one particular language, so he is brought up in the traditions of one particular religion. And his function as a poet is to concentrate on the myths of that religion, and to recreate the original imaginative life of those myths by transforming them into unique works of art. The essential truth of a religion can be presented only in its essential form, which is that of imaginative vision. "Every thing possible to be believ'd is an image of truth"; in which case everything possible to be believed by the ordinary man is actually to be seen by the visionary. The human imagination knows that man fell: the Biblical story of Adam and Eve is a vision of that fact which has frozen into a myth. Milton's reason told him that that story was "true"; his imagination told him that it was an image of truth, and stimulated him to recreate it in that form.

The artist *qua* artist neither doubts nor believes his religion: he sees what it means, and he knows how to illustrate it. His religion performs two great services for him. It provides him with a generally understood body of symbols, and it puts into his hands the visionary masterpieces on which it is founded: the Bible particularly, in the case of Christian poets. Many of these latter have petrified into sacred Scriptures supposed now to impart exclusive formulas of salvation rather than vision. It is the business of a poet, however, to see them as poems, and base his own poetry on them as such.

To do this he must bring out more sharply and accurately what the human mind was trying to do when it first created the beings we now call gods. Jupiter is a sky-god: he is a product of the imaginative tendency to see the sky as an old man . . . and not as an abstraction called Heaven. Originally he was conceived as a tyrannical old bully because he represented the imaginative feeling of a hostile mystery in the sky-world. Venus became a beautiful harlot because the imagination sees "nature" as a woman and finds her lovely but treacherous. As the original "organized men," or "Giant forms" dwindle into gods, the clarity of their relationship to the archetypal myth becomes blurred, and irrelevant stories and attributes cluster around them. They become increasingly vague and general until, in their final stages, they are mere personifications. . . . (pp. 118-19)

This is why we meet so many new names in Blake and find ourselves reading about Vala and Urizen instead of Venus and Zeus. It may be thought that the more familiar names would make the Prophecies easier, but actually it would make them more difficult. To Venus and Zeus we bring memories and associations rather than a concentrated response, and are thus continually impelled to search outside the poem being read for its meaning. And as no two poets can possibly mean the same thing by "Venus," we should have to go through a long process of discarding misleading associations which the use of a new name prevents at once. Those who think that a greater writer would be less exacting are under an illusion. Some poets, including Homer, Chaucer and Shakespeare, present a smooth readable surface for the lazy reader to slide over: others, including Dante, Spenser and Blake, make it impossible for any reader to overlook the fact that they contain deeper meanings. The wails of protest which the latter group arouses show only that the real profundity of the former group has not been touched. Blake has tried to show us, in his essay on Chaucer, how inadequate it is to bring preconceived notions of medieval monks and friars and merry widows to the *General Prologue*. It follows, of course, that the familiar names we do find in Blake, such as Reuben, Satan and Merlin, do not depend for their meaning on one's memory of Genesis, Milton or Malory. (pp. 119-20)

The Bible is in a very special category compared with other works of art, but it too yields precedence to the imagination. . . . The central form of Christianity is its vision of the humanity of God and the divinity of risen Man, and this, in varying ways, is what all great Christian artists have attempted to recreate. Insofar as they regard the divinity worshipped by Christians as other than human, they produce cloudy and inaccurate visions. Milton's Satan comes off more clearly than his God because he has attempted to equate the latter with abstract goodness and perfection. There is nothing for such a God to do except recite the creed and rationalize the miserable agony of fallen man into a defense of his own virtue. Satan is human and real, a mixture of good and evil, imagination and Selfhood, and therefore has a place in a work of art.

Poetry cannot be made, either of morality and personifications, or of mythology and gods, as long as the artist considers himself to be an illustrator or a transcriber. Spenser . . . had a tendency to personification and Milton to theology, and it is instructive to see in their work how their interest in them is always in inverse proportion to the quality of the writing. Shakespeare and Chaucer follow a sounder poetic policy. They avert their eyes from both gods and abstract nouns, and concentrate on living men and real things, on the particular rather than the general. (pp. 120-21)

This universal perception of the particular applies to natural objects as well as human forms. Ordinarily, our perception of the world is haphazard; it is often unrelated to our simultaneous mental processes, and hence when we use a real thing to "symbolize" a state of mind it seems to us only a fancied or arbitrary resemblance. At most, a natural object may symbolize a mental event because it "corresponds" to something in the mind. Here we still have Lockian dualism and its simile.

But when we speak of the desire of the Selfhood or ego to restrict activity in others, it is rather inadequate to say that a prison is a "symbol" of the Selfhood. Prisons exist because Selfhoods do: they are the real things the Selfhood produces, and symbols of it only in that sense. To say that in Blake the sea is a symbol of chaos is incorrect if it assumes that "chaos" has any existence except in a number of real things which includes the sea. The sea is the image of chaos. "Image" and "form" being the same word in Blake, the sea is the form of chaos. As even chaos is only an abstract idea unless it is a perceived form, the sea is the reality of chaos.

And when we realize that everything exists in the form it does because man is fallen God, it becomes evident that all things are the realities of fall and regeneration. Art could not possess its infinite variety if archetypal visions could be represented only by a group of special symbols. In his poem called **"Auguries of Innocence"** Blake says:

> He who the Ox to wrath has mov'd
> Shall never be by Woman lov'd.

This is obviously not true of the state of experience: the title of the poem shows that Blake is talking about a Paradise or Beulah into which men who abuse oxen cannot enter. This "augury of innocence" is of the same order of thought as Jesus': "Blessed are the meek, for they shall inherit the earth." This is simple enough, but another couplet from the same poem is more complicated:

> The Bat that flits at close of Eve
> Has left the Brain that won't Believe.

The bat is black and prefers darkness to light. For this reason a superstitious man would see it as something ominous, and a Lockian poet would see it as a symbol of doubt. But to Blake it is neither of these things. Blake means precisely what he says. In human society everything from the Sistine ceiling to thumbscrews owes its form to man's mind and character in one of its various aspects. Similarly the character of everything in nature expresses an aspect of the human mind. We say that a snowflake has a symmetrical design, not because the snowflake has consciously produced it, but because we can see the design. We see that the snowflake has achieved something of which we alone can see the form, and the form of the snowflake is therefore a human form. It is the function of art to illuminate the human form of nature, to present the ferocity of the weasel, the docility of the sheep, the drooping delicacy of the willow, the grim barrenness of the precipice, so that we can see the character of the weasel, the sheep, the willow and the precipice. This vision of character, or total form, is something of course much more inclusive than the words given, which express only aspects of that character, can suggest.

"The man was like a lion" is a Lockian simile, an attempt to express a human character in natural terms. "The man was a lion" is a much more dramatic and effective figure, and more suggestive of their real relationship; but still it is essentially a simile with the word "like" omitted. But if we say "the lion is like a man" we are getting somewhere, and beginning to achieve the concentrated focus of the artist's vision on the lion which reveals his form to the human eye. As we proceed in our vision, everything positive and real about the lion becomes an aspect of our perception of him, and we can take the next step and say that the lion is entirely a human form, a human creature. All art interprets nature in human terms in this way, so vividly that we hardly dare admit what art tells us about the relation between tears and tempests, joy and sunshine, love and the moon, death and winter, resurrection and spring. The real bat, therefore, is that aspect of the human imagination which prefers darkness to light; and this bat is the exact opposite of the bat which is a symbol of doubt. The famous "Ghost of the Flea" similarly shows the human form of that insect.

The painted lion is not alive; the natural lion has not been emancipated into a human order. The painter's task is not a hopelessly quixotic attempt to capture his model's life, but to show its relationship to a universal human order, a Paradise in which lions owe their generation as well as their form to human minds. The most concentrated vision of the lion sees this archetypal human creature in the ferocious wildcat of nature, as Blake's poem on the tiger does. (pp. 121-24)

Those who do not love living things do not love God or Man, as the Ancient Mariner found to his cost. But because some Greek poet loved the nightingale, he created from her the human figure of Philomela, and by doing so passed from love into vision, from a sensitive reaction to nature into the intelligent form of civilized human life, or Pararadise. The story of Philomela is not a fantasy suggested by the nightingale, but a vision of the fall of the original human nightingale into its present natural shape. Blake says:

> Think of a white cloud as being holy, you cannot love it; but think of a holy man within the cloud, love springs up in your thoughts, for to think of holiness distinct from man is impossible to the affections.

But if the poet can see the world in a grain of sand, it is because he already has that archetypal vision of "All that Exists," of which everything he sees is a form or image. All Blake's poetry is related to his particular view of this vision, that "Central Form composed of all other Forms" which he concedes to Reynolds. Within the huge framework of this central form, certain states of the human mind that created it inevitably appear and take on human lineaments, just as a pantheon crystallizes from a religious vision. Blake's characters are the "Giant forms" that religions worship as gods and artists visualize as "organized men." (p. 124)

[Blake held] that in a perfectly imaginative state all individuals are integral units of a race, species or class, related to it as tissues and cells are to a body. This larger unit is not an abstraction or aggregate, but a larger human body or human being. . . . The most inclusive vision possible, then, is to see the universe as One Man, who to a Christian is Jesus. On nearer view Jesus is seen as a "Council of God" or group of "Eternals" or Patriarchs, seen by ancient prophets as dwelling in a Golden Age of peace and happiness. On still nearer view these patriarchs, the memory of whom survives in the Bible under the accounts of Abraham, Isaac and Jacob, resolve themselves into vast numbers of individual men.

One of these Eternals, named Albion, has fallen. Albion includes, presumably, all the humanity that we know in the world of time and space, though visualized as a single Titan or giant. The history of the world from its creation, which was part of his fall, to the Last Judgment is his sleep. The yet unfallen part of God made seven attempts to awaken him, and in the seventh Jesus himself descended into the world of Generation and began his final redemption.

This myth of a primeval giant whose fall was the creation of the present universe is not in the Bible itself, but has been preserved by the Cabbala in its conception of Adam Kadmon, the universal man who contained within his limbs all heaven and earth, to whom Blake refers. A somewhat more accessible form of the same myth is in the Prose Edda, a cyclic work systematizing the fragmentary apocalyptic poems of the Elder Edda, which to Blake contained traditions as antique and authentic as those of the Old Testament itself. In the sleep of the giant Ymir, the Edda tells us, the earth was made of his flesh, the mountains of his bones, the heavens from his skull, the sea from his blood, the clouds from his brains—this last has a particularly Blakean touch.

The Greeks have also kept a dim memory of a Golden Age before the Fall in their legend of a lost island of Atlantis and of a giant who contained the world in the figure of Atlas, the Titan who bears the world on his back, a perfect image of the fallen Albion with nature outside him and pressing upon him, and of the etymology of that curious word "understanding." Atlantis, according to Plato's *Critias,* was settled by the god Poseidon (possibly Blake's "Ariston"), whose eldest son was Atlas: this correspondes to the English tradition, preserved in Spenser, that Albion, the eponymous ancestor of England, was the son of Neptune. . . . (pp. 125-26)

Northrop Frye, in his *Fearful Symmetry: A Study of William Blake,* Princeton University Press, 1947, 462 p.

LEOPOLD DAMROSCH, JR.

(essay date 1980)

[In the following excerpt, Damrosch argues that Blake's greatest achievement is not his imaginative vision but his moral passion.]

Blake believed that his symbols, although compromised by participation in a fallen world, were ultimately guaranteed by being "comprehended" in the divine body of Jesus. If we do not share that faith, how shall we respond to the symbols? It is one thing for Blake to assert that they afford a privileged insight into truth, and another for us to agree that they do. (p. 364)

The preeminent exponent of Blake's desire-fulfilling symbols is Northrop Frye [see excerpt above], who asserts with truly Blakean logic, "Imagination creates reality, and as desire is a part of imagination, the world we desire is more real than the world we passively accept." This claim, as in Frye's later criticism where it is generalized to accommodate all symbolic writing, is offered in support of a rejection of science that is just as bitter and unfair as Blake's: "As long as science means knowledge organized by a commonplace mind it will be part of the penalty man pays for being stupid." And since men who are not stupid understand that desire creates reality, it follows that "the work of art is the product of this creative perception, hence it is not an escape from reality but a systematic training in comprehending it." Such an approach does a disservice to Blake, exaggerating the achieved security of his visions of desire and minimizing the great theme of man's struggle against the internal obstacles that thwart desire. Blake's imaginative vision is admirable because it wrestles so honestly with the intractable facts of fallen experience. Moreover, the symbolist approach depends upon what Murray Krieger has called "the mythification of art," whereas Blake is expressly concerned to define the limits of both myth and art.

It would be more just to Blake to say that he is profoundly aware of the anguish of experience, but wants to believe that experience is finally an illusion. If we deny the conclusion we can still appreciate the brilliance of the diagnosis. The *Songs of Experience* are widely admired because they analyze the facts of experience so tellingly and protest against them with so noble a passion. And our admiration need not be any the less if we cannot follow Blake into a philosophical system that locates Experience near the bottom of a hierarchy of levels and dismisses most of it as mere "error."

> For he saw that life liv'd upon death
> The Ox in the slaughter house moans
> The Dog at the wintry door
> And he wept, & he called it Pity
> And his tears flowed down on the winds.

The speaker is Urizen, and his pity is futile if not downright hypocritical, but Blake's myth is large enough to do justice to the depth of feeling here even as he criticizes Urizen's response. Enion, Emanation of Tharmas the parent power, also speaks of the dog at the wintry door and the ox in the slaughterhouse; her words haunt us because Blake means them to be haunting.

> What is the price of Experience do men buy it for a song
> Or wisdom for a dance in the street? No it is bought with the price
> Of all that a man hath his house his wife his children
> Wisdom is sold in the desolate market where none come to buy
> And in the witherd field where the farmer plows for bread in vain. . . .

Perhaps a clarified vision should sweep these images away as delusions of Satan and Vala, but they come from Blake's most bitter experience, and we respond to them truly even if we cannot accept his hopeful call for their abolition. What one carries away most of all from the prophecies is man's desperate need for reintegration, not the ease with which he can hope to gain it.

Where the poems are most disappointing, by the same token, is in their frequent refusal to be true to the experience from which they were born. Just as suffering is finally translated into other terms, so also death is so far from being real that what we call life is Blake's "Eternal Death." Of course one may say that death is omnipresent in the myth by the very urgency with which Blake denies it. Imagination itself, according to Bergson, is "a defensive reaction of nature against the representation by intelligence of the inevitability of death." Blake's art is a fight to the death against death. But any Christian poet denies the ultimate reality of death. What is harder to accept is Blake's concomitant rejection of life, which is dismissed as entrapment in materiality except in those epiphanic moments when it breaks free of life as we ordinarily live it. There can be no Wordsworthian solitary reaper in Blake, with her mournful song that fills the heart of the wayfarer, and no Michael with the tragedy of his family and land. Hegel exalts tragedy because it mediates the destructive fury of warring "truths"; Blake, like Plato, despises it because it encourages an emotional acceptance of destruction as a necessary consequence of the nature of things. "Drinking & eating, & pitying & weeping, as at

a trajic scene / The soul drinks murder & revenge, & applauds its own holiness." . . . It is not that nothing is destroyed in Blake, but that what is destroyed is not *real.* "You cannot go to Eternal Death in that which can never Die." . . . No wonder Blake draws so little upon the greatest of English poets; Shakespeare is the repudiated master in the descent of the spirit from poet to poet that culminates in Blake.

It is not only tragedy that we miss in Blake; it is much of human life. The notebook lyrics of love or anti-love are fascinating because they deal with themes that are usually submerged or allegorized out of recognition in the prophecies. It is inconceivable that Blake could have written the lines,

> Then, while time serves, and we are but decaying,
> Come, my Corinna, come, let's go a-Maying.

For that is merely [of the world of Beulah]. . . . And because it is only Beulah, Blake will make no compromise with it. Herrick's speaker addresses a real woman, not an idea ("O Rose thou art sick"), he accepts mortality and the consequent attitude to pleasure, and his slow and thoughtful verse is remote from Blake's declarative (often declamatory) style. Such a mood is not incompatible with religious faith:

> It is the blight man was born for,
> It is Margaret you mourn for.
>   [Gerard Manley Hopkins, "Spring and Fall."]

But it must be a faith like Hopkins' that accepts both the reality and the significance of mortal life. In the end, for all his awareness of the weight of experience, Blake cannot come to terms with

> . . . the very world which is the world
> Of all of us,—the place in which, in the end,
> We find our happiness, or not at all.
>   [William Wordsworth, *The Prelude*]

"A roller & two harrows lie before my window," Blake wrote to Butts on reaching Felpham. "I met a plow on my first going out at my gate the first morning after my arrival & the Plowboy said to the Plowman, 'Father The Gate is Open'." . . . The plow and harrows get into *The Four Zoas* and *Milton;* the plowboy and his father do not.

If Blake deliberately cuts himself off from the phenomenology of lived experience, and if the modern reader cannot join him in that exclusion, why should one read him? Among other reasons two seem particularly compelling: his exploration of the possibilities and limits of the symbol, and his passionate demand for moral commitment. Let us consider symbols first. (pp. 365-68)

[I argue] against the assumptions that symbols offer a privileged view of reality (unless artistic symbols be accepted as having the same status as all other symbolic forms) and that they should be welcomed for their tendency to construct reality in accordance with heart's desire. I hold rather . . . that although all thought is symbolic, this represents a problem rather than a victory, and that mythical thinking needs to be criticized as well as admired for its tendency to reshape the world in conformity with desire. But I would argue also that Blake understands this very point and wants to make us understand it. For if the fallen world is the only world we have, then its symbols are the only symbols; and in that case Blake's deconstruction of symbols can be immensely valuable. At the same time, by clinging to symbols in spite of their flaws, Blake exemplifies the all but universal refusal to imagine a truly empty universe. The imagination must people it with symbols of vitality. . . . [Blake] insists that the entire universe participates in the agony of the divided mind. In this sense Hume is a modern and Blake a late inheritor of Plotinus and Valentinus. But as the modern yearning for myths—even the most home-built and rickety—has proved, the desire for humanized symbols is irresistible. And here again Blake can help us to regard them critically, just because he himself aspires to transcend them and therefore regards them with suspicion.

Shelley suggests that symbols may represent the only reality there is and may protect us from the abyss of unmeaning that lies beyond. For as he says in the *Defense,* "All things exist as they are perceived; at least in relation to the percipient. . . . But poetry defeats the curse which binds us to be subjected to the accident of surrounding impressions. And whether it spreads its own figured curtain, or withdraws life's dark veil from before the scene of things, it equally creates for us a being within our being. It makes us the inhabitants of a world to which the familiar world is a chaos." Blake, by the very force of his belief, compels us to recognize the provisional and wish-fulfilling nature of such a manifesto. If reality only exists as it is perceived "in relation to the percipient," then there is no guarantee that it exists at all except as subjective construction. And if poetry spreads a figured curtain rather than drawing the veil aside, then it is only a mask to hide the chaos of the world, and we would do well to know it. In his absolutism Blake encourages us to recognize—even if we continue to need—the groping and imperfect nature of the achievements available to the imagination.

Finally, we come to Blake for the exhilaration of contact with a prophetic spirit that never relents in the quest for truth.

> I will not cease from Mental Fight,
> Nor shall my Sword sleep in my hand:
> Till we have built Jerusalem,
> In Englands green & pleasant Land. . . .

To read Blake at all is to enter, however provisionally, into the quest, for as Auerbach says of biblical narrative, "Without believing in Abraham's sacrifice, it is impossible to put the narrative of it to the use for which it was written." And if in the end we cannot believe it, if we must put it to other uses, we are then forced to confront the meaning of our disbelief, to see plainly the empty universe which no religion of art can fill again with split meaning. It may be that aesthetic disinterestedness is the right response to art, but if so, it is all the more salutary to immerse oneself for a time in an art like Blake's that violently repudiates it. (pp. 368-70)

We read Blake's myth to know what it would be like to believe in man's spiritual power while fully recognizing the self-deluding tendencies of the imagination and its symbols. In Blake there is no reliance on received faith, as in the later Wordsworth, or on natural piety as a mode of transposed faith, as in the earlier Wordsworth. On the contrary, he provides a searching analysis of the basis of *all* faiths, and of their inevitable corruption, in the human imagination. His extraordinary exploration of the psyche is framed in a myth that offers imaginative answers to the fact of alienation. If we cannot share Blake's faith and accept his answers, we must admire the honesty and insight with which he strives to reconcile the direst aspects of human experience with our profound longing for harmony and meaning.

Within the category of moral and religious writing—as contrasted with tragedy or elegy or the other modes that Blake dismisses—his poems retain the power of their conception in spite of all obstacles of execution, and in spite of the gaping philosophical rifts that no amount of revision could ever close. In contrast with an extinct document such as, for instance, Pope's *Essay on Man,* Blake's epics survive because their religious passion overwhelms mere ethical earnestness. . . . Blake's vision of truth, in its violence of commitment, is exciting to many a reader who has only the sketchiest idea of what he is actually talking about. (pp. 370-71)

[My comments have] been directed toward elucidating Blake's meanings, but I want to close by affirming that all of this would have a merely antiquarian function if Blake did not possess the power of religious vision. His meanings command our imaginative as well as scholarly respect because they are forged and reforged in the furnace of that vision; Blake does not force us to accept his answers, but he demands that we enter into his mental strife and make it ours. And if we inhabit a world that no longer believes in its symbols— if we can neither trust the products of our symbol-making imagination nor bear to live without them— then Blake speaks to us with a special poignancy. His Eden is forever closed to us by the Cherub with the flaming sword, but we are all too well acquainted with Los weeping at the silent forge, struggling to make the accusing Spectre of despair join again in creative labor. Rather than rhapsodizing about Blake's apocalyptic breakthrough as if it were easily attained, we might dwell instead on the bitter honesty with which he has dramatized the pre-apocalyptic condition, which may be the only condition we can ever know. And in that case what continues to move us in Blake's myth is not its answers but its questions, which are posted with a prophetic urgency that remains alive and life-giving. (p. 371)

Leopold Damrosch, Jr., in his *Symbol and Truth in Blake's Myth*, Princeton University Press, 1980, 395 p.

SOURCES FOR FURTHER STUDY

Bentley, G. E., Jr. *Blake Books*. Oxford: Clarendon Press, 1969, 678 p.

> The leading reference guide to Blake's works and to Blake criticism.

Damon, S. Foster. *A Blake Dictionary: The Ideas and Symbols of William Blake.* Brown University Bicentennial Publications: Studies in the Fields of General Scholarship. Providence, R.I.: Brown University Press, 1965, 460 p.

> Highly regarded reference work providing definitions of terms from "Abarim" to "Zoa."

Frye, Northrop, ed. *Blake: A Collection of Critical Essays.* Twentieth Century Views, edited by Maynard Mack. Englewood Cliffs, N.J.: Prentice-Hall, 1966, 183 p.

> Contains essays by leading Blake scholars on a variety of works, including "The Chimney Sweeper," "Ah! Sun-Flower," "The Crystal Cabinet," and "The Golden Net."

Paley, Morton D., and Phillips, Michael, eds. *William Blake: Essays in Honour of Sir Geoffrey Keynes.* Oxford: Clarendon Press, 1983, 330 p.

> Presents commentary on a wide variety of Blake-related topics, including his poetic language, early reputation, and relation to Samuel Taylor Coleridge and William Wordsworth.

Pinto, Vivian de Sola, ed. *The Divine Vision: Studies in the Poetry and Art of William Blake.* London: Victor Gollancz, 1957, 216 p.

> Collection of essays by Blake scholars, commemorating the bicentenary of Blake's birth.

Plowman, Max. *An Introduction to the Study of Blake.* New York: E. P. Dutton, 1927, 183 p.

> Highly regarded general study, indicating approaches to Blake's poetry.

Heinrich Böll

1917-1985

(Full name Heinrich Theodor Böll; also transliterated as Boell) German novelist, short story writer, translator, and essayist.

INTRODUCTION

*O*ne of Germany's most popular and prolific authors, Böll gained international fame—winning the Nobel Prize in 1972—as a chronicler of the Federal German Republic (1949-1990). Critics have generally emphasized his strong ethical stance, which stemmed from his personal philosophy of Christian humanism and sympathy for the downtrodden. As Theodor Ziolkowski has observed, Boll's writings constitute a true oeuvre, "if we take oeuvre to mean a unified fictional view informed by a consistent moral vision."

Born in Cologne and raised by devout but liberal Roman Catholic parents, Böll embraced humanistic ideals early in life. As a schoolboy he stood up to peer pressure and refused to join the Hitler Youth. In 1939, however, he was drafted into the German infantry, serving throughout the war and suffering several wounds. Returning to Cologne after the war, he published his first short story in 1947. Critical and popular acclaim followed quickly, enabling Böll to devote his life to literature.

Böll's early works focus on the impact of Nazi rule on ordinary people, particularly soldiers like himself, affected by events beyond their control. In *Der Zug war pünktlich* (1949; *The Train Was on Time*), a haunting story of a soldier who foresees his own death while waiting to be transported to the eastern front, and *Wo warst du, Adam?* (1951; *Adam, Where Art Thou?*), he describes the horror and absurdity of war. As a writer, Böll reacted to the war with anger and condemnation. While revealing the complicity of respectable institutions, such as the Catholic church, in Hitler's political success in Germany, Böll points to the catastrophic consequences of Nazi policies. According to Wilhelm Johannes Schwarz, Böll's "predominant attitude to the war is disgust and vexation. . . . He tells only of its boredom, of filth and vermin, senselessness, and futile waste of time."

Postwar Germany is the setting of Böll's novels of the 1950s. *Und sagte kein einziges Wort* (1953; *And Never Said a Word*) relates a family man's difficulties in adjusting to civilian life. This novel received much critical attention and helped establish Böll's reputation as a master storyteller. *Haus ohne Hüter* (1954; *The Unguarded House*) is about the struggle for daily survival in a warn-torn city as experienced by two fatherless boys.

Böll's novels written in the 1950s and 1960s examine Germany's efforts to forge a new identity while exorcising the demons of its Nazi past. As in his earlier work, he approaches his subject from an individual's point of view. Always a perceptive and ironic oberver, Böll mercilessly uncovers the moral blindness, historical amnesia, rapacity, vulgar consumerism, and indifference to human values of a production-oriented society that adopts materialism as a means of forgetting its infernal past. In *Ansichten eines Clowns* (1963; *The Clown*), a frustrated performer exposes the hypocrisy of prosperous Germans, including his own family, who subordinate ethical principles to opportunistic concerns. *Gruppenbild mit Dame* (1971; *Group Portrait with Lady*), an ambitious work that received a mixed response from critics, is structured as a biography based on accounts by the protagonist's friends and acquaintances. Late works, such as *Fürsorgliche Belagerung* (1979; *The Safety Net*) and *Frauen vor FluBlandschaft* (1985; *Women in a River Landscape*), treat the complex political reality of the last decade of the Federal German Republic.

Critics have praised Boll for his ability to convey his feelings and ideas in simple, concise, and effective prose. Furthermore, some commentators view Böll's style as a conscious protest against the formal complexity of classical German literature, comparing his work to that of Ernest Hemingway, whom Böll himself cited as an influence. The directness and accessibility of Böll's prose especially comes to the fore in his witty portrayal of the absurdity of everyday life, as exemplified by his two short story collections, *Wanderer, kommst du nach Spa* (1950; *Traveler, If You Come to the Spa*) and *18 Stories* (1966).

Although aware of his importance, critics have hesitated to bestow unqualified praise on Böll. As Robert C. Conard concluded: "Böll has never received universal critical acceptance, not even from those who find his stories some of the best written in the middle decades of the century. That sentimentalism and idealism dominate his work and that he cannot always adequately execute his intentions are the charges most often heard. Minor weaknesses in Böll's work, however, seem not to affect his popularity with a discriminating public. Already he stands in the company of two of his favorite writers: Dostoyevsky and Tolstoy. Like them, he has produced eminently readable work imbued with moral power.

(For further information about Böll's life and works, see *Contemporary Authors*, Vols. 21-24, 116; *Contemporary Authors New Revisions Series*, Vol. 24; *Contemporary Literary Criticism*, Vols. 2, 3, 6, 9, 11, 15, 27, 39; and *Dictionary of Literary Biography*, Vols. 69, 85.)

CRITICAL COMMENTARY

W. E. YUILL

(essay date 1966)

[In the following excerpt, Yuill describes Böll as an author who utilizes his remarkable narrative skills to address important social, ethical, and religious issues.]

Heinrich Böll was born in the last year of the Kaiser's reign and the first of the Russian revolution. Almost all of his stories have the local and topical affinities that this suggests: they are mostly set in the city of his birth and deal with the tumultuous era of European history that coincides with his life. Like a character whom he describes in one of his short stories he is "as old as the hunger and the filth in Europe, and the war".

The local associations of Böll's work go beyond mere setting and local colour, for, as a writer, he displays many of the attributes of his fellow-citizens: traditional Catholic faith, unquestioned but not unquestioning, level-headedness and practicality, humour and a drastic wit. He has the disrespect for authority and the sound political sense that prompted the Cologne crowds to greet Hitler not with flowers but with flower-pots; he has, too, the introspective and faintly melancholy temperament that characterizes what he calls "the gin-drinker's Rhine"—the part of the river that extends from Bonn to the mists of the North Sea. For Böll, however, Cologne is not simply an urban landscape: the dimensions of space merge for him into that of time, for he is constantly aware of the past that liter-

Principal Works

Der Zug war pünktlich (novella) 1949
  [The Train Was on Time, 1956; also published in Adam and the Train: Two Novels, 1970]
Wanderer, kommst du nach Spa (short stories) 1950
  [Traveler, If You Come to Spa, 1956]
Wo warst du, Adam? (novel) 1951
  [Adam, Where Art Thou?, 1955; also published in Adam and the Train: Two Novels, 1970; and as And Where Were You, Adam?, 1974]
Und sagte kein einziges Wort (novel) 1953
  [Acquainted with the Night, 1954; also published as And Never Said a Word, 1979]
Haus ohne Hüter (novel) 1954
  [Tomorrow and Yesterday, 1957; also published as The Unguarded House, 1957]
Das Brot der frühen Jahre (novel) 1955
  [The Bread of Our Early Years, 1957; also published as The Bread of Those Early Years, 1976]
Irisches Tagebuch (travel essays) 1957
  [Irish Journal, 1967]
Doktor Murkes gesammeltes Schweigen, und andere Satiren (satires) 1958
Billard um Halbzehn (novel) 1959
  [Billiards at Half Past Nine, 1961]
Ein Schluck Erde (drama) 1962

Ansichten eines Clowns (novel) 1963
  [The Clown, 1965]
Entfernung von der Truppe (novella) 1964
  [Absent without Leave published in Absent without Leave: Two Novellas, 1965; also published in Absent without Leave, and Other Stories, 1967]
18 Stories (short stories) 1966
Ende einer Dienstfahrt (novel) 1966
  [End of a Mission, 1967; also published as The End of a Mission, 1968]
Gruppenbild mit Dame (novel) 1971
  [Group Portrait with Lady, 1973]
Die verlorene Ehre von Katharina Blum oder: Wie Gewalt entstehen und wohin sie führen kann (novel) 1974
  [The Lost Honor of Katharina Blum; or, How Violence Develops and Where It Can Lead, 1975]
Fürsorgliche Belagerung (novel) 1979
  [The Safety Net, 1982]
Was soll aus dem Jungen bloss werden? Oder: Irgendwas mit Büchern (memoirs) 1981
  [What's to Become of the Boy? or, Something to Do with Books, 1984]
Frauen vor FluBlandschaft (novel) 1985
  [Women in a River Landscape, 1988]

ally and metaphorically lies buried beneath the present—not only the past of his own experience but the remote past of Roman settlers. The past is not thought of in terms of a "cultural heritage" but rather as a continuity of human experience linking the Roman colonist with the modern artisan or clerk. Certainly Böll's fascination by the past is not of the kind that one would expect to issue in the form of historical novels or stories that are quaintly local; it is an aspect rather of his imaginative insight into basic human situations—and perhaps also of his belief in the ultimate timelessness of human existence.

Böll has always been more than a local writer: he is concerned with the fate and experience of a whole generation of Germans and of the individual in the great materialistic urban societies of the modern world. It was as the spokesman of his own generation that Böll first came into prominence; he subsequently developed into a mentor and critic of all those who seemed to forget too easily the sufferings of that generation and the causes of that suffering. . . . The tone of Böll's early war stories is certainly not nostalgic or romantic, but neither is it as hysterical as that of Borchert's play

Draussen vor der Tür: the writer's reaction is one of sober, sombre, seemingly dispassionate disgust. . . . It is only in . . . *Entfernung von der Truppe,* that Böll, looking back over twenty years, can see his experience of war in a satirical and at times scurrilously comic light. In the early stories, when memories were still painfully fresh, there was no room for humour. In an age of conscription and mechanization war had lost whatever glamour it might formerly have had, and was unmitigated by heroism. There is certainly nothing romantic or heroic about the soldiers in *Der Zug war pünktlich* and *Wo warst du, Adam?* They are cannon-fodder. The railway station, which in Böll's stories so often epitomizes the impersonality, restlessness and rootlessness of modern life, becomes in war-time the ante-chamber of fate. Men are driven by "the grey authoritarian scourge" of loudspeakers into trains which, as symbols of destiny, carry them unresisting to a punctual death. Scarcely one figure in these early stories eludes death. Feinhals, in *Wo warst du, Adam?,* escapes until the last moment, only to be blown to pieces—by a random German shell—on the threshold of his own home. The stories are not designed, however, as hair-raising accounts of the horrors of battle, for the writer is concerned with deeper issues than physical ordeal and destruction. . . . It is the demoralization and degradation, the spiritual maiming and blinding that are emphasized. The killing of men's bodies is not the worst; their souls are enthralled or crushed by mindless discipline. (pp. 141-43)

Böll's stories are full of war-wounded and convalescents in the figurative sense, people for whom the war can never be "over"—not only the physically handicapped or the manifestly neurotic, but also those who are simply demoralized. The returning soldier and his attempts to adjust himself to life in post-war Germany naturally figure prominently in the stories. These "Heimkehrer" are not burdened like Beckmann, the hero of *Draussen vor der Tür,* with a sense of guilt, they do not succumb to hysterical despair. They suffer, rather, from an inarticulate malaise, a paralysis of will and feeling. (p. 143)

[The characters from Böll's early novels] are moody and uncommunicative. It is symptomatic of their alienation that they prefer to speak on the telephone rather than face to face. They turn their backs on the reviving world around them and, young as they are, live in their memories. Reminiscence is the characteristic dimension of Böll's writing. He is fascinated by the counterpoint of time and place and by the changes worked through time and circumstance. (p. 144)

It is not unnatural that the drastic disruption of their lives by the war made the whole of Böll's generation obsessively conscious of a pattern of change and continuity. For characters like Albert and Nella in *Haus ohne Hüter* time is out of joint in a special sense. For them the past is the time before the war, the present is the time since, and between past and present lies a limbo, a gulf that has swallowed what might have been. Besides the actual past and present there is in their minds a potential time, "le temps perdu", "the third level", as Böll calls it. He is continually seeking metaphors to express all this: in *Haus ohne Hüter,* three "times" are visualized as discs superimposed upon one another and revolving eccentrically. . . .

Many of Böll's introspective characters, like the young widow Nella, cannot shake off the nostalgia for what might have been. They are haunted by the memory of a turning point in their lives. For these people time is essentially private and cannot be divorced from inner experience. (p. 145)

Hypnotized by the notion of time, [Böll's characters] often see in habit a means of arresting its flow. In the sacramental form of ritual, habit is a legitimate escape from time, an access to eternity, the rituals of his Church playing a large part in Böll's stories. In a secular context, however, habit can be a baleful force. The attempt to resurrect the past by repetition may have harrowing effects: Hans Schnier in *Ansichten eines Clowns*

describes his abortive experiments in this respect and confesses that moments cannot be repeated. Habit can be an aid to survival, but it may also be an inert weight that crushes individuality and impoverishes life. In the story entitled **"Über die Brücke"**, the narrator, passing years later over a railway bridge he regularly used to cross, observes with mingled relief and dismay that the windows of a house are being cleaned in exactly the same sequence as before the war: the daughter, having taken over from her mother, the hypnotic routine of the "Putzplan" is becoming the same kind of household drudge. It may be that Böll has here put his finger on a particular weakness of his nation—the fondness for ceremony and regulated routine. (pp. 146-47)

The part played by time, memory and habit in Böll's works points to a concentration on emotion and inner sensation rather than on action. Only the satirical short stories tend to have definable plots: many others simply trace the changes of emotional climate in a character or the evolution of attitudes from a germ of experience. Even in the novels the external action—as distinct from reminiscence—rarely occupies more than a few hours. There is little of what one might call epic objectivity: frequently the author identifies himself with the protagonist, while the more complex works are built up from a series of private views.

The tone of the first person narrative so common in Böll is generally subdued, resigned, melancholy, often with a hint of the morbid. . . . To the ideal of frantic activity for which his countrymen are renowned Böll opposes the ascetic motto of *memento mori.* Too few of his compatriots, he asserts, are capable of melancholy—the mark of humility and hence of true humanity. . . .

Although often struck, this muted note is by no means the only one in the register of Böll's work. In many of his stories, particularly since about 1952 when symptoms of over-indulgence began to appear in German society, Böll looks round him with a critical eye, and the tone becomes ironical, sometimes hilariously satirical. (p. 148)

Böll tends to dwell in the minds of his characters, to convey his own view in their reflections and utterances. But it is not only their minds that he inhabits but their bodies as well. He sees with their eyes—it is perhaps significant that, when he describes the appearance of his protagonists, he often does so through the reflection in a mirror. Even more characteristically, he feels with them in the physical as well as the emotional sense: he feels the itch of stiff new uniforms, registers the peptic climate of his characters, is aware of their defective teeth. Above all, particularly in the later works, he seems to be sharply conscious of everyday smells. . . . (p. 149)

Few German writers have evoked so effectively

the familiar texture and repetitive patterns of ordinary urban life. His meticulous descriptions have a certain aura of professional craftsmanship about them. . . . His technique might in a specific sense be called "realistic", but his realism is not simply objective, does not consist only in accumulation of detail. It is largely subjective: physical reality is nearly always apprehended through the senses and minds of characters in the stories. Nearly always it is restricted to features within the purview of one individual; we do not often find extensive description of landscape, setting or background. The author identifies himself with figures moving in urban surrounds—often precisely named real localities—so familiar or so restricted that the wider background is taken for granted. He operates, as it were, with a very short focal length, sometimes creating an effect that is almost obsessive or claustrophobic. One might perhaps detect in Böll an absorption in familiar things and in particular a leaning towards the drab and sordid that almost constitutes a kind of inverted romanticism with which readers of Graham Greene will be acquainted.

Böll's realism might be described as poetic as well as subjective. A poetic quality is manifested on two levels. In the first place, Böll imparts to the perceptions of the people in his stories the awareness of an urban poet, a sense of the intrinsic strangeness of familiar things. Secondly, as author, he invests objects with symbolic significance and employs them in thematic patterns. The sharp contours of everyday objects in the stories often give the impression that these items of reality have been torn from their context by the prehensile mind of the observer—it is not the natural coherence or proportions of things in themselves that matters but their emotional or emblematic associations. Familiar actions—the making of a telephone call, for instance—may be seen in close-up or slow motion, as it were, because the moment is fraught with emotional significance. Trivial objects acquire meaning as the evidence of fateful events: Bruno Schneider in **"Die Postkarte"** pores over the scrap of paper that changed the course of his life—the registration slip from his calling-up papers. . . . The relationship, at once spiritual and physical, between a man and a woman, between Schnier and Marie Züpfner, is commemorated in a mosaic of trivial objects and gestures. One of the charges that Schnier levels at Catholics is precisely that they "have no sense of detail". It is in keeping with Schnier's character that the obsession with what the song-writer calls "these foolish things" descends into near-maudlin sentimentality; for Böll, as a writer a concern with the details of ordinary living is linked with his awareness that man is a psychosomatic entity, that the soul inhabits a body and must express itself in a world that is physically real. Mundane things and actions can readily acquire a sacramental significance: the sensuous pleasure of

eating fresh bread so exactly described in *Das Brot der frühen Jahre* has sacramental implications. (pp. 149-51)

This kind of symbolism is one of the features that give Böll's stories depth and make them much more than evocations of mood and setting. Many are mounted on a framework of parable: singly and together marking out a moral universe which has the objective coherence that the physical world they describe seems to lack. Behind the topicality is a timeless reality. In the grouping of characters and in typical experiences they undergo one may detect a kind of theology: figures superficially somewhat diverse fall into opposing categories that have the unambiguity of those in a morality play. (p. 151)

The division of characters into opposite moral types is not in itself an artistic weakness. However, the difference of approach to the two fundamental types, a consequence of Böll's theological view, might be considered an aesthetic drawback. It possibly deprives the stories of balance and involves a danger of oversimplification. The reluctance to fathom the "evil" character, or even to see him as problematic, and the habit of seeing him through the eyes of his anti-type suggest a certain limitation in the writer's imaginative range. The sympathetic characters, although superficially diverse, tend to share a resigned and inhibited temperament. Nevertheless, Böll's later works, particularly *Entfernung von der Truppe*, do suggest that he is acquiring more insight into bitterly rebellious or sardonic characters. (p. 152)

Böll's criticism of the political aspect of Roman Catholicism may be less specific than the much-publicized attack launched by Hochhuth in *The Representative;* it is hardly less outspoken and all the more impressive in that it is based on the personal experience of a sincere and thoughtful Catholic. *Brief an einen jungen Katholiken* embodies the first direct attack on the political attitude of the Church. Böll notes that the Vatican was the first foreign state to seek an understanding with Hitler and recalls the religious instruction which he himself received as a conscript. This instruction was concerned almost solely with sexual morality never referring to the real moral dangers threatening young men pressed into the service of an evil totalitarian system; the concept of conscience hardly entered into it. In post-war Germany Böll sees the Church again in danger of becoming too closely identified with the Establishment, of ceasing to be a theological and moral power and becoming instead a political pressure group.

In the novels and stories true faith is seldom linked with efficiency, success and prosperity, and is not found in the loveless organizational religion of Frau Franke and her like. Faith is most authentic in failure, in squalid surroundings or where it verges on despair—a paradoxical truth familiar to readers of Graham Greene. (pp. 153-54)

It is in keeping with the theological implications of Böll's works that many of his central characters have a strong impression that their lives are pre-ordained, that they are in some cases subject to supernatural guidance. . . .

Andreas in *Der Zug war pünktlich* has a premonition of his death, a premonition that is punctually fulfilled, but in most of the stories it is love which strikes the hero with the force of revelation. . . . The kind of love shown in these encounters is not narrow and selfish; it initiates a reconciliation with mankind at large. Love emancipates the individual from isolation and imagined self-sufficiency, [and] breaks down a psychic blockage. . . . (p. 154)

Love, in Böll's view, even in its basest manifestations is never totally devoid of a sacramental element. Its true culmination, however, is in marriage and family life. Marriage is not simply a social institution; it is a sacrament as distinct from a ceremony, a communion of souls ordained in heaven and independent of—even on occasion in contravention of—social sanction. The harmony of souls in marriage is a facet of the divine cosmic order. (p. 155)

Among the writers of post-war Germany Heinrich Böll has earned a prominent place as a literary artist and moralist. His works appeal not only as authentic renderings of atmosphere, setting and mood, but also because they clearly embody emblematic characters and situations demonstrating moral problems and truths. They deal with ideas and experiences that are none the less profound because they can be understood by the great majority of people. In this, as in more obvious senses, Böll is a democrat. Unlike many German writers he is not hampered by philosophical systems or fettered by a pretentious "literary" tradition. It is hardly a compliment to a writer to say that his language is "simple", but Böll's idiom is at any rate not obscure or difficult: "workmanlike" might be the best word to describe it. Clear it certainly is and always to the point. That he is capable, however, of considerable sophistication is evident from the stories written in a parodistic style and also from the complex structure of works like *Billard um halbzehn* and *Entfernung von der Truppe*. Although his themes and settings may not be very diverse, the range of Böll's technique is in fact much wider than it might appear at first sight. The form in which Böll is most obviously at home is the short story, and even the novels, with their brief span of "real" time and their episodic structure, have the economy of short stories. Nevertheless, within the novels and in individual short stories there is a considerable variety of idiom, ranging from laconic description of incident, through impressionistic evocation of atmosphere to the regular structure of *Novellen* like *Die Waage der Baleks* or *Wir Besenbinder*, forming altogether a body of work remarkable for humour and perceptiveness.

As a Christian moralist Böll tries to apply the values of a traditional faith to the problems of modern man, isolated as he often is in an over-populated environment where economic considerations are paramount. The moral issues of the urban lower and middle classes with which Böll principally deals are not sensational. Men are corrupted in a banal fashion, "as in second-rate films". (pp. 155-56)

Böll wishes men to cleanse themselves of the grimy sediment that is deposited in an atmosphere of mere "respectability", he wishes to lead them back to a positive faith, to the humanistic nucleus of Christianity, to charity. Where he satirizes the social provisions of our industrial society it is because he fears their dehumanizing influence. Where he criticizes his Church it is because he fears that it is falling into dogmatism, working for sectional interests, becoming modish rather than modern. The motive behind much that Böll writes is compassion. In this compassion there is an element of sentimentality that has led one critic to speak of "allegorical confectionery", but nearly everywhere—and particularly in his latest works—the sweetness is neutralized by the acid of satire. It is the critical vein in Böll's writing as well as his technical skill that has kept him in the *avant-garde* of German writing and given him an appeal and authority far beyond the membership of his Church. (pp. 156-57)

W. E. Yuill, "Heinrich Boll," in *Essays on Contemporary German Literature: German Men of Letters, Vol. IV*, edited by Brian-Keith Smith, Oswald Wolff, 1966, 141-58.

WALTER HERBERT SOKEL
(essay date 1967)

[Sokel is an Austrian-born scholar whose writings include *The Writer in Extremis* (1959), *Franz Kafka: Tragik und Ironie* (1964), and *Franz Kafka* (1966). In the excerpt below, he analyzes the thematic and symbolic background of Boll's best-known works, concentrating on the author's characteristic irony and pessimism.]

Events in Böll's novels are presented from the perspective of alienated characters through whose minds and eyes we view the German scene. Böll undoubtedly learned from the American successors of Joyce and of Gertrude Stein. Hemingway, Thomas Wolfe, and Faulkner are influences, direct and indirect, on the form of his narratives. Böll eliminates the omniscient comment of the authorial voice and presents all situations and events through the sense impressions, memory, and reflections of his characters. At times he approaches the stream of consciousness.

Böll's earliest novels dealing with postwar Germany—*Und sagte kein einziges Wort* (1953) and *Haus ohne Hüter* (1954)—present a world in which the determining force of events seems to be material and economic. In naturalistic fashion, environment and circumstances seem to determine human actions and fate. In specific terms, the material and social consequences of the lost war apparently mould human life in Böll's postwar Germany. . . .

The structure of *Haus ohne Hüter* seems to reinforce the naturalistic view of human destiny as determined by socioeconomic circumstances. The novel consists largely of five alternating perspectives on a postwar German city. Two war widows and the only child of each provide four of these perspectives. . . . Each must come to grips with life deprived of its center, life without help, comfort, and completeness. This parallelism of perspectives of human deprivation in two widely different economic strata makes us suspect that the naturalistic interpretation may be less than adequate.

In one passage of the novel Böll makes the socioeconomic interpretation of the novel's events give way to a moral evaluation. The shift takes place literally and explicitly before the reader's eyes. Young Heinrich Briesach considers his mother's love life and the succession of "uncles" it imposes upon him. Why doesn't she get married, he wonders. (p. 11)

Haus ohne Hüter shows that the victimization of postwar Germans by historical circumstances—the war and its aftereffects—is much more than that. It is a victimization by evil, by human wickedness and folly. Nella becomes a war widow because her husband, Rai, was deliberately sacrificed to the offended vanity of his wartime commanding officer, Lieutenant Gäseler. Rai, Nella, and their child are victims, not of impersonal historical forces or social determinants, but of a villain's chicanery. Böll thus clearly presents a morally determined chain of cause and effect.

The unmasking of apparently social and economic causes as moral, psychic, and spiritual problems is essential to Böll's early novels. (In the later novels it is unnecessary, since the moral and spiritual basis of human behavior is explicitly shown from the beginning.) In *Und sagte* the marriage of the two persons through whose perspectives we experience early postwar Germany is apparently destroyed by the strains and stresses of overcrowded living conditions. On a deeper level, however, it is not the external situation that determines the fate of the marriage, but the husband's inner conflict between the drive for selfish freedom and the restrictive obligations that monogamous love and fatherhood impose. Self-indulgent *eros* and self-curtailing *agape* struggle in him for the possession of his soul. Essentially we witness not a social, but a Christian problem clothed in social and economic guise. The subtle interaction between the disguise and the underlying psychic and moral truth informs this novel with an inner tension that makes *Und sagte,* after *Wo warst du, Adam?,* Böll's artistically most successful work.

The conclusion of *Wo warst du, Adam?* (1951), the earliest of Böll's novels, takes place in the concluding stages of the Second World War. It can be taken as an apt point of departure for a closer consideration of the perspectives on postwar Germany given in Böll's three longest and latest novels, *Haus ohne Hüter, Billard um halbzehn* (1959), and *Ansichten eines Clowns* (1963).

At the end of *Wo warst du, Adam?* two perspectives converge upon a German town as the war is drawing to a close. The town lies in a no man's land between the American troops, who are not yet ready to enter, and the German army that, obedient to Hitler's command, refuses to give an inch. From the windows of the town's houses fly white flags of surrender.

One perspective is that of the German deserter Feinhals. The town is his home and he has decided that as far as he is concerned the war is over. Before descending, he gazes down upon his native place from an adjacent hill. Feinhals is a decent chap; he despises the Nazis and has always been defeatist about the war. He fell in love with a Jewish girl, Ilona (who, without his knowledge, has meanwhile been murdered in a concentration camp), and he looks forward to his homecoming and a modest career. Above all he plans to savor the joy of being alive.

The other perspective is that of the German army post located on another hill above the town. The post has orders to observe the town and bombard it in case of suspicious activity. There is "suspicious activity," since an American vehicle drives over from the American-occupied area and parks for a while in front of a certain house. The vehicle actually brings an American officer to his German sweetheart. The officer formerly in command of the observation post, knowing that the war was senseless and over in any case, but yet attempting to obey commands, spares the town and lets some shots fall in a swampy marsh nearby. Schniewind, however, new commander of the post, an ambitious and insecure careerist whose war decorations are of very recent date, resents the "traitorous" white flags and decides to punish the town. He shoots into it. One of the grenades kills Feinhals as he is about to enter his parental home.

This conclusion of Böll's war novel adumbrates his subsequent novels about postwar Germany in a number of ways. The opposition between Feinhals and Schniewind as representative characters of Germany anticipates the structural basis of the three novels: *Haus ohne Hüter, Billard um halbzehn,* and *Ansichten eines Clowns.* In these novels the descendants of Feinhals and Schniewind face each other as victims and victimizers both during and after the Nazi period. The Feinhals group of characters are decent, kind, and gentle. These characters are lovers of life, opponents of war, and haters of Nazism. Both during and after the Nazi era they are destined to be victims of the Schniewind type.

The Schniewind characters are vain, ambitious careerists, profoundly insecure, and obsessed with the need to collect worldly honors—the craving for war decorations characterizes them. They are fanatics and bullies, petty, mean, and contemptible. Naturally, they are or were ardent supporters of Nazism and the war. Feinhals' descendants are simple, humble, and self-assured. Life and love are self-evident values for them. Schniewind's descendants are those who fear and hate life, twisted egotists in constant need of being reassured. The slightest opposition unnerves and infuriates them. In the display of love and friendship they see provocations to be punished. It is symptomatic and symbolic that the "suspicious activity" observed by the German post is a love tryst between two recent enemies, and that what particularly annoys Schniewind is the display of the white flags of peace.

Apart from the general dualism represented by the two camps (so reminiscent of Dostoevsky, whom Böll . . . [has] named as one of the most important influences on his development), particular details of structure link Böll's novels of postwar Germany (the exception of *Und sagte* always understood) to the pattern established by the end of *Wo warst du, Adam?* In all three novels the bloodstained inheritance of Nazism and war overshadows the postwar period. In that past, Nazis or militaristic supporters of the war committed the direct or indirect murder of good, innocent persons. In each case the murderers are inferior, vain, narrow, pretentious, obviously insecure, and thus easily provoked to anger like Schniewind in *Wo warst du, Adam?* Their victims are infinitely superior to them. They are cut off in the flower of their youth, and because of their innocence and capacity for enjoying life and love their death appears all the more horribly and tragically senseless, a wasteful sacrifice without meaning, a destruction of human values never to be recouped.

In all these cases there is a surviving witness to the murders, as the orderly, Bechtels, in *Wo warst du, Adam?,* who witnesses Schniewind's decision to bombard the town. In the later novels this witness-figure is at the same time a victim who managed to survive. . . . In postwar Germany, Böll's witness-figure lives in self-chosen seclusion and will have nothing to do with the accepted mores, fashions, and powers of the Bonn Republic. An inward petrifaction, an absence of all ambition and worldly interest, characterizes him. Most perspectives of Böll's novels are the perspectives of such

shocked and hurt witness-figures, who carry the deep wound of what they saw into the postwar era. (pp. 11-16)

These witnesses and victims, surviving in postwar Germany, live curiously detached lives. They are so deeply hurt that they are not able to recover and overcome their traumatic loss. They have renounced all desire to participate in life. They keep, often outwardly and always inwardly, aloof from society and resemble relics from a bygone era. The tragedy of postwar Germany, as seen through Böll's perspectives, is this non-participation of her best children, who are too bruised to be of use. Nella, in *Haus ohne Hüter,* refuses to remarry and instead drifts in and out of meaningless affairs because she is resolved never again to offer the reassuring sight of a happy wife and mother to the country that murdered her husband. The appearance of domestic bliss would be an advertisement of forgiveness and forgetfulness to which she will not lend herself. (pp. 16-17)

Robert Fähmel, in *Billard um halbzehn,* leads a life of inhuman formality and rigid routine. To his young secretary, who cannot comprehend a life so lifeless and devoid of human spontaneity and warmth, he presents a disquieting enigma. He who has the talent to be a first-rate architect does not take up architecture after the war. He is content to serve as a humble consultant in statics. What he has witnessed under the Nazis has killed all creative ambition in him. His life now is only a shadow of what it might have been and a memory of the hurt received long ago. Like Nella, Robert Fähmel denies himself the act of re-creating. Nella will have no part in the re-creation of a happy family, and Robert Fähmel will not contribute his talent to the recreation of the ruined German cities. . . .

Schrella, in his London exile, has similarly withdrawn into the routine of teaching German grammar in an English school. He refuses to find renewed attachment to his native city, and to life itself, when he pays a visit to the scenes of his past. . . . Like Nella and Fähmel, Schrella declines to make the gesture of reconciliation with normalcy, which, in his case, would be to return from exile. The remembrance of that which they witnessed remains the basic truth of these lives—a truth they will not change, cover up, and, least of all, forget.

An extreme form of exile from normal life is the insane asylum to which Robert Fähmel's mother was retired after she witnessed the deportation of the Jews and where she still finds herself sixteen years later. There cannot be a more telling detachment from the bustling and forgetful new normalcy of postwar Germany than life among the extreme deviants from normality. (p. 17)

In *Wo warst du, Adam?* the life of the victimized

witness to Hitler's war is snuffed out physically on the threshold of the postwar world. The lives of Böll's subsequent witness-figures are cut off emotionally, arrested and frozen inwardly, before they enter the postwar era. It is their destiny to be permanently estranged from the life of their country.

The complementary side of this victimization of the best is the continuing triumph of the worst. Nothing has basically changed since the Nazi period. The confrontation of anti-Nazi victim with Nazi victimizer persists in the postwar years in essentially the same constellation as during the Nazi era. . . . It is symptomatic that Feinhals suffers his fate almost under the noses of the Americans. This spatial arrangement shows that the military victory of the Allies and the occupation of Germany will neither dislodge the Nazis from their positions of power in German society, nor aid and protect their victims. . . . In *Haus ohne Hüter* former Nazis, under old and new Christian labels, are the shapers of the cultural scene, and go on speaking of "elites." (pp. 18-19)

There are ironic touches: In *Haus ohne Hüter* Gäseler plans to publish the poems of the man he murdered. In *Billard* Schrella owes his release from the prison of the Federal Republic to his one-time Nazi torturer, Nettlinger, which does not prove the ex-Nazi's kindness, but rather shows his power and influence in the Bonn Republic. (p. 19)

This pessimistic view derives from the essentially Christian dualism underlying the structure of Böll's novels. In them, the anti-Nazis resemble the persecuted and despised followers of the Lord, martyrs and confessors of the truth. A small band of the forlorn few, they face the huge army of the wicked, who rule the world for Satan. Nazi Germany had waged the ancient war of evil against innocence with brutal frankness. Postwar Germany continues it subtly and hypocritically.

The opposition of the two camps reaches, in Böll's novels, far beyond Nazism and anti-Nazism. It is ultimately not a political, but a moral, spiritual, and religious dualism, which is founded on Christianity but has a Manichaean element in it. The Nazis' persecution of their victims is seen as a variant of the age-old battle between good and evil, light and darkness, holy grace and unholy power. (p. 20)

Böll's dualism receives its most explicit, allegorical formulation in *Billard um halbzehn*. In this novel Germany (and mankind) is divided into two groups: One group consists of those who have consumed the sacrament of the buffalo, which is the sacrament of violence, and they form the vast majority. The other group, a tiny minority, consists of those who follow the sacrament of the lamb of peace. The latter refuse to partake of the sacrament of violence and are, therefore,

destined to be the victims of violence. They will, in each generation, be singled out for persecution by the followers of the buffalo. Nazism is a phase in the buffalo's timeless orgy of oppression. In the 1930's the Nazi bully Nettlinger led the other boys in terrorizing Schrella, who was of the lamb's brotherhood. In the 1950's the bellboy Hugo suffers the same kind of juvenile persecution, but no no Nazis are among the tormentors. Hugo, gifted with marvelous charm and grace, is by his very grace and gentleness fated to be in his generation what Schrella was in the last—the lamb that forever arouses the buffalo's urge to persecute and violate. We are reminded of Abel, who, favored with the grace of the Lord, aroused the murderous envy of Cain. The symbolism of lamb and shepherd used by Böll establishes immediate associations not only with Abel, the shepherd slain like a lamb, but also with Christ, who is lamb and shepherd, sacrifice and judge, in one. As we shall see, in Böll the lamb sometimes becomes shepherd; the victim may turn judge. In that ancient battle between buffalo and lamb, Cain and Abel, world and Christ, labels and watchwords change, but the essence remains the same. In this struggle the lambs, who are not of this world, must go under, while the buffalo wins and reinherits, again and again, the power and glory of this world. In the framework of Böll's dualism, the Nazi type, therefore, cannot be truly defeated, but after each apparent defeat continues to hold power and victimize the good.

As stated before, Böll produces the image of Germany through perspectives, through literal as well as figurative views. The physical or mental act of viewing a place, a scene, a person, has decisive structural and symbolic significance in Böll's works. The world of his novels is a focal area of converging perspectives. (pp. 21-2)

The act of seeing is structurally and symbolically decisive at the end of *Und sagte.* Having separated from his wife, the husband sees a woman in the street who moves and fascinates him with a strange intensity. Tense with excitement, he watches the stranger, follows her with his glances, and discovers that she is his wife. Seeing through the perspective of estrangement teaches him that the woman who touches his life's nerve, the woman destined for him, is his wife. He sees her now as if for the first time, and this view restores in him the sacredness of his marriage, against which he had rebelled. From a distractedness of the heart, which used poverty as a pretext, he had degraded marriage to the imitation of an illicit love affair conducted in hotel rooms. The visionary recognition of his wife shows him the sacrament as his inner truth. The husband's last words, "nach Hause" (homewards), with which the novel closes, point to a spiritual significance contained in the physical homecoming to wife and children.

The importance of view and vision in Böll's work

becomes clear to us when we recall the thematic and structural significance of the witness-figure. A witness, we must remember, is one who sees and on the basis of his vision testifies to the truth. Böll's novels are told from the point of view of victims and witnesses. The view of victim and witness tends to become, in his later novels, the view of accuser and judge.

The view of the avenging judge forms the nucleus around which *Billard um halbzehn* is structured. Robert Fähmel executes Hitler's scorched-earth strategy literally with a vengeance. Ostensibly an instrument of the buffalo, he avenges the martyred lamb. He becomes a demolition expert in order to blow up prized buildings and monuments of his buffalo-worshipping nation. In the enemy's service, he explodes the enemy's pride.

Robert Fähmel's judgment on the objects of German national pride—monuments and precious buildings—is literally based upon the act of viewing. Perspective and action merge in this novel. Taking the view of the object and determining the *Schussfeld* is the condition for executing the moral judgment and verdict of condemnation. The accusing witness and judge's view carries the plot both literally and figuratively.

With each act of viewing Robert Fähmel delivers a judgment. As he gazes out on the lobby of the fashionable Hotel Prinz Heinrich his vision transforms the hotel guests into damned souls in hell; his look pronounces the Last Judgment. (pp. 22-3)

In *Haus ohne Hüter* we view Rai's murderer, Gäseler, through the witness, Albert, who relates the murder, and through Rai's widow, Nella, who is eager to avenge her husband. These two viewings of Gäseler form two bridge posts, as it were—one in the recollected past, the other in the immediate present—that connect two major strands of the plot like a bridge across time. Planning her revenge, Nella literally views Gäseler, as she sits next to him in his car. The man she sees now, however, is too trivial to serve as the objective of something so great and meaningful as vengeance. (pp. 23-4)

Robert Fähmel's mother yearned for an opportunity to kill those Nazi officials of her city who were responsible for so much suffering. Yet when the occasion does come and she views, with loaded pistol, the former Nazis preparing for their parade, she sees them as a group of aging, pathetic, and ridiculous philistines—museum pieces not worth a bullet.

These insights into the futility of vengeance, which occur near the end of Böll's novels, are never signs of Christian forgiveness. Böll, with his nearly Manichaean separation of good and evil characters, never presents contrition and regeneration in the villains, nor do his characters refrain from retribution because they feel that judgment belongs to God

alone. . . . The Nazi villains turn out to be banal philistines and petty snobs who lack all access to the daemonic. They are merely bores, and boredom makes vengeance irrelevant. These Nazi murders are not in the least diabolical. They are small and laughable men who do not have the slightest inkling of the scope and the meaning of their actions. (p. 24)

In Böll's novels, however, a sharp distinction is made between vengeance on individuals and the struggle against Nazism or, more broadly speaking, the attitudes of which Nazism formed the most vicious manifestation. Viewing the personal enemy makes vengeance seem fatuous; viewing the scene of the enemy's actions or the works of his pride confirms the resolve to battle against him. (p. 25)

Robert Fähmel, as we have seen, dedicates his whole life to vengeance; but it is not a vengeance against individuals. He punishes human pride by leveling its objects. In Böll the deadly sin of pride appears in its specific modern form as snobbery. It is the bread of the unholy sacrament of violence. Snobbery invests the architectural monuments and landmarks of one's country with an aura of national superiority. Snobbery ranges in Böll from gluttonous ostentation to arrogant intellectualism. In all its varieties, however, it contains two principles: hierarchy and exclusiveness. The soldier's mania for collecting war medals and decorations—a *leitmotiv* in the stories and novels of Böll; the officer's insistence on having his rank respected and obeyed; the Nazi's racial arrogance; the gourmand's gorging himself while others have to starve; the gourmet's connoisseurship; the clique member's contempt of the uninitiated; and the intellectual's sneer at those educated in other ways than himself: all these are the variants of snobbery in Böll's work.

In Böll's perspectives snobbery always embraces cruelty. There is cruelty in the gloating emphasis with which Martin's grandmother, in *Haus ohne Hüter*, seated in an expensive restaurant, tears apart and devours her portion of lamb. She and all other diners in that plush restaurant consume their food as though proclaiming their triumphant power in the universe. The view of this frightens the boy Martin and sickens him. . . . Martin identifies with the lamb and, therefore, cannot eat it. Like the followers of the sacrament of the lamb in the later novel, Martin excludes himself from the sacrament of violence into which his anxiety-inspired vision transforms the restaurant. These bourgeois diners seem to be performing a cannibalistic ritual. Viewed by the outside, they have become a savage society which bestows status upon those who can kill, lacerate, and consume the greatest number of victims. The novel makes an implicit connection between the smug voracity of these gourmands and the murderous cruelty by which the Nazis realized their idea of social exclusiveness and superiority. In Böll the ultimate form of snobbery is murder. Murder drives exclusiveness, on which all snobbery is founded, to its logical conclusion.

A subtle form of snobbery is found to be the decisive flaw in Heinrich Fähmel's life, as he reviews it. He had possessed grace. He was talented, worked without effort, was distinguished by suppleness of body and mind. Frail of build, a spiritual type, he resembled a young rabbi. Heinrich Fähmel's Jewish appearance confirmed the impression that he was one of the chosen. For in Böll's works Jews are always among the elect, endowed with grace, but victimized and slain by the envious descendants of Cain. The racially Jewish girl, Ilona, in *Wo warst du, Adam?*, whose marvelous singing in the extermination camp affirms the Creator in the midst of hell, and Absalom Billig, in *Haus ohne Hüter*, whose brilliant caricatures of the Nazis earned him their special hatred and destined him to be the first Jewish victim in his city, both exemplify the role of the Jews as vanguard in the ranks of Abel. (pp. 25-7)

Heinrich Fähmel, however, had strayed from his nature. He compromised with the world. He betrayed himself by adopting the appearance of snobbery, which is the mark of Cain, the sign of the buffalo's sacrament. Heinrich Fähmel's snobbery was based upon his decision to get on in the world and adapt himself outwardly to the violent buffalo. . . . Taking his daily breakfast in the Café Kroner bestowed that aura of distinction upon Heinrich Fähmel. The Café Kroner routine symbolized his surrender to the world. . . . Heinrich Fähmel attempted to live in both worlds. His heart remained with the lambs; but his façade was established among the worshippers of the buffalo. He was ready to serve the powers that were and gave his share to his country's war effort. The formula worked. He succeeded famously among the respectable and violent. The first, and most gratifying, token of his success was his victory in the competition for building the new abbey of St. Anton's. He obtained the order to build it, and the abbey became one of those architectural landmarks of which educated Germans were proud.

The conflict, however, between his true nature, represented by his marriage and home life, and his social role, symbolized by the Café Kroner, was reflected in the radically opposed characters of his sons. Otto, adopting his father's outward adjustment as his own inner conviction, became a Nazi; faithful to his father's original nature, Robert joined the persecuted lambs as their "shepherd" and helper, and lived to annul his father's work.

In the end, Heinrich Fähmel comes, independently of Robert's judgment, to the same conclusion. Because it had been divided between personal truth and public falsehood, he judges his life as wanting, and condemns the public façade and the monument it has become as worth being defaced and spat upon. When he learns that it was his own son who had blown up the monument of his fame, the abbey of St. Anton's, he approves with relief. What his son had destroyed was a false idol, a monument to his and his country's disastrous egotism. As he brings his wife home from the insane asylum to which he had allowed the Nazis to consign her, he discontinues his breakfast ritual at the Café Kroner. His last act in the novel is to repeat symbolically the execution of his pride which his son had performed actually; he cuts into the birthday cake which had been presented to him in the shape of his famous abbey and joyfully proceeds to demolish it.

The Catholic author Böll chooses a Catholic monument to represent false values. Destroying his father's abbey, Robert Fähmel executes judgment over the self-betrayal of Catholicism. This is, indeed, a major theme of Böll's more recent novels. A significant shift in the role played by Catholicism, and Christianity in general, occurs in his work.

In the early *Wo warst du, Adam?* Catholicism plays an entirely positive role. It shames and inwardly overcomes the concentration camp commander. His victim, distinguished by grace, is Jewish by race but Catholic by faith, a combination that infuriates him. Upon his command, she sings Catholic hymns with an artless perfection that proclaims the grace within her and testifies to God and life eternal. The message reaches him as it refutes him, his ideology, and his whole way of life. Killing her and ordering all Jews massacred immediately, he admits his defeat and confirms her victory; for his rash action thwarts all his plans and shows that he has lost all control of himself. He has his pet project and possession, his choir of Jewish inmates, wiped out with the rest of the camp. That strange choir, art literally imprisoned, had served the gratification of the commander's snobbery. As owner of such an oddity in an extermination camp, he appeared as a connoisseur, a capricious and refined Nazi, one possessing the power to indulge strange whims. Issuing forth from the voice of the Jewish girl, Catholicism proves its triumph by driving him to destroy the object of his special pride.

Und sagte also presents Catholicism positively. The husband's final recognition of his monogamous love, his wish to return to his family and home, are consonant with the Catholic view of the sacredness and the sacramental character of marriage. Organized Christianity begins to play a negative role in *Haus ohne Hüter*. Although most of the good characters are churchgoing and genuinely pious, the villains in the novel are militant Christians. The leader of their circle, Schurbigel, attempted to infuse Christianity into Nazism and advocated joining the Storm Troopers in order to Christianize them from within. Here we come upon one reason why Christianity is connected with negative characters. These "Christians" opt for compromise with worldly ambition. They wish to join the violence of the world with one half of themselves, while keeping the other in the camp of Christ. Thereby they commit the kind of self-betrayal by which Heinrich Fähmel jeopardizes his grace.

The guilt of the militant Christians in *Haus ohne Hüter,* however, is even more fundamental. After the war and the defeat of Nazism, they use the prestige of Christian views to rehabilitate themselves and rise to dominant positions in the postwar world. They make of Christian culture and politics the fashionable cult of a clique, to which they can tie their careers. They sin against the Christian spirit of humility and nondiscrimination. Although calling themselves Christians, they exercise the arrogant exclusiveness that was the essence of Nazism.

In this novel one may even detect a subtle parable of the relationship between fallible churchmen and Christ. The poet Rai, bearer of true grace, is slain. Afterwards he is idolized by the churchlike coterie of intellectuals that is of one spirit with the force that slew him. Indeed, his murderer has become a part of the group. They abuse his name by exploiting it for the reputation it gets them. Promoting the poetry of an anti-Nazi, they can prove how anti-Nazi they themselves had been, whereas it was they—one of theirs—who slew him. (pp. 27-30)

The role of Catholicism in *Billard* is the reverse of what it was in Böll's earlier work. What we see of it now is not even ambiguous, as Christianity was in *Haus ohne Hüter;* it is entirely negative. In *Billard* Catholicism is clearly allied with the buffalo and condones the persecution of the lambs, in whom we must see symbolic representatives of the true Church. Yet even though the perspective and the plot of *Billard* do mete out severe judgment on the representatives of the Catholic Church, Catholics are as yet merely subsidiary fellow travelers of evil, and not its prime embodiment. In Böll's latest novel, *Ansichten eines Clowns,* however, militant and proselytizing spokesmen of intellectual Catholicism are the primary antagonists and persecutors of the hero-narrator of the novel. Catholicism has suffered a complete reversal of its original function in Böll's work; it has become the villain.

The only positive character in *Ansichten eines Clowns,* the clown-narrator himself, is an agnostic. But he, the nonbeliever, is a good man, while the proselytizing Catholics, his opponents, are hypocrites and snobs. (pp. 30-1)

The clown's Nazi mother and the Catholic intellectuals of postwar Germany represent and enact the same attitude. In the name of ideology, they destroy human life. Their ideological dedication is the means by which they are able to exercise their power and indulge their hostility toward the innocent, natural joy of life. The clown's mother is not only a Nazi fanatic, but an avaricious Spartan as well. She kept her children on a lean and joyless diet, and from principle denied them everything that might brighten and cheer their lives. Similarly, Böll's Catholics despise the unpretentious joy afforded by the clown's natural art, and resent the simple happiness of his relationship with Marie. Because they cannot bear the sight of such ingenuous and pure fulfillment, they are set upon destroying it. Cain's envy of Abel's grace remains for Böll, in this latest work, the archetypal model of persecution and murder, as it was in his previous works. (pp. 31-2)

It is the irony of this novel that the agnostic clown is, in a fundamental sense, more truly Catholic than the Catholic ideologues who despise him. For he, the infidel, holds the Catholic idea of the indissolubility of marriage, whereas they not only persuade his wife to desert him, but also ask him to acquiesce to her new marriage to another man. As in *Und sagte,* monogamous love is, this time explicitly, the symbol of true Catholic Christianity. It is a token and a representation of eternity in earthly life. The clown's relationship to Marie is not consecrated by the Church; officially it is not a marriage. However, in the clown's heart his love for Marie is his marriage to her and there cannot ever

Dust jacket by Werner Labbé for Böll's 1958 collection of satires.

be any other woman for him. His physical and emotional union with her has the force of a sacrament. Böll seems to adopt the view of his clown in *Brief an einen jungen Katholiken,* where he says: "It is impossible for me to despise that which is erroneously called physical love; such love is the substance of a sacrament, and I pay to it the reverence that I give to unconsecrated bread because it is the substance of a sacrament." In deserting the clown and marrying one of the Catholic leaders, Marie transgresses against the Catholic idea, as interpreted by Böll. Canonical law, by sanctioning Marie's new marriage, contradicts the law of the heart. It consecreates a union that is betrayal of an existing love and therefore, according to the law of the heart, adultery. With this juxtaposition of religious essence and ritualistic legalism, of the true faith of the individual soul and the meretricious formality of the Church, Böll's clown approaches a position that is almost Protestant and is certainly romantic. The clown's position constitutes the extreme point of a development noticeable in Böll's work from its beginnings.

Böll cites the Protestant Kleist as his earliest and most profound literary experience. There is indeed something of Kleist's ideal of the marionette-figure, an ultimately romantic and Rousseauistic ideal, in Böll's heroes—especially in those who, like Ilona, Rai, Absalom Billig, Robert Fähmel, and the clown, are artists or have something artistic in them. They resemble the marionette-type characters of Kleist—Alkmene, the Marquise of O—, Käthchen, and Michael Kohlhaas (Robert Fähmel, the implacable avenger, bears a profound resemblance to the latter). Like these Kleist characters, they possess the unshakable self-assurance and inner certainty that is the mark of innocence. As in Kleist, the primary conflict in Böll's work is that between innocence and worldly crookedness, between the purity of the simple, natural soul and the envious arrogance of the twisted careerist. But, whereas in Kleist innocence and justice win the battle in the end and force the world to acknowledge them, the contemporary author makes a distinction between the obvious physical victory that goes to the wicked and false, and an intangible, ill-definable, spiritual or moral victory that the just obtain for themselves.

Even in *Ansichten eines Clowns*—in a way, Böll's most pessimistic novel—a kind of victory is wrested from bleak defeat. For the clown is able to resist, and will continue to judge and to accuse. He will not be unfaithful to the memory of his sister's senseless sacrifice and he will not forgive her Nazi murderers; he refuses to betray the sacrament of love; and he will not surrender the art that is his nature. His triple loyalty makes him the figure who remembers in a world that wants only to forget. It also makes him a beggar, because the world will not support so uncomfortable a reminder. It is precisely as a beggar, however, that the clown fulfills

his role, which is to be the fool in the traditional sense of the term—the jesting conscience of his society, the living contradiction of its pretended wisdom, the living refutation of its pretended happiness. (pp. 33-4)

Walter Herbert Sokel, "Perspective Dualism in the Novels of Böll," in *The Contemporary Novel in German: A Symposium,* edited by Robert R. Heitner, University of Texas Press, 1967, pp. 9-35.

THEODORE ZIOLKOWSKI

(essay date 1973)

[Ziolkowski is an American scholar whose writings include *Hermann Broch* (1964) and *Hermann Hesse* (1966). In the following excerpt, he provides a concise overview of Böll's principal works, with particular emphasis on their moral and intellectual content.]

Böll is one of the very few postwar German novelists who have created what can properly be called an oeuvre, if we take oeuvre to mean a unified fictional world informed by a consistent moral vision. Faulkner's chronicles of Yoknapatawpha County, no less than Alexander Solzhenitsyn's accounts of the labyrinthine mazes of Soviet prison camps and cancer wards, constitute an oeuvre in this sense, while the novels of many other writers, who may be equally or more prolific, never amount to more than a series of individual works. Böll has not only added to the literary map of Germany a province that is unmistakably his own; he has also established himself as the leading fictional historian of Germany at mid-century. To this extent his oeuvre provides a fitting complement, both spatially and temporally, to that of the two earlier German-language novelists who won the Nobel Prize, Thomas Mann and Hermann Hesse. . . .

Böll's fictional era, beginning roughly where *Steppenwolf* and *Doctor Faustus* end, extends down to the present. Like Thomas Mann in *Buddenbrooks,* Böll has made one significant excursion into an earlier period: *Billiards at Half-Past Nine (Billard um halb zehn,* 1959) traces the roots of present-day Germany back to the turn of the century. Otherwise his fictional world embraces the Germany of the Hitler years, the postwar depression, and the subsequent *Wirtschaftswunder.* . . .

Böll has marked off for his fictional realm that industrialized wasteland of the lower Rhine beyond the Main River that an appalled Bavarian in Böll's latest novel calls "Northmainia"—a geography of the soul that extends no further north, south or west of Cologne than you can travel in forty minutes by train and where Böll's *Kölsch* is readily understood. . . .

It is this humane society that Böll has set out to render in the oeuvre he has been creating for over twenty-five years in some forty volumes of novels, stories, plays and essays. This is not the occasion for detailed analyses of Böll's individual works. So let me simply suggest that the nature of his fictional world, this "Northmainian" society at mid-century, can best be characterized in its totality as "pastoral." . . .

Böll's figures do not, of course, flee into the backwoods like their American counterparts. There are few forests in the bleak terrains of Northmainia, and in any case nature descriptions are conspicuously absent from Böll's narratives. In fact, Böll has written only one work that has the conventional form of the pastoral—his *Irish Journal* (*Irisches Tagebuch*, 1957), in which the journey to a simpler society provides the author with contrasts that harshly illuminate the social situation back in Germany. Yet it can be argued that all his works, despite their generally urban settings, are pastorals. For in all of them Böll and his figures are searching for a way out of the alienation of contemporary Germany back into a realm where true human community is possible, where people are still united by common values of decency and by the bonds of solidarity.

In his **"Frankfurt Lectures"** Böll called his attempts to depict a binding human society "an aesthetics of the humane." Symptomatically, his oeuvre focuses on men and women united by the simple and "humane" things of life—love, religion, even food. It is no accident, for instance, that the sharing of bread occurs so frequently, assuming an almost sacramental meaning—from the early story *The Bread of the Early Years* (*Das Brot der frühen Jahre*, 1955), whose young hero can never get enough fresh bread to satisfy his hunger, right down to Böll's latest novel, whose heroine ritually consumes two crisp rolls for breakfast every morning. Characteristically, Böll finds the pastoral solidarity that he admires primarily among the little people whom he called the "lambs" of this world. Their very defenselessness compels them to unite in opposition to the powers of church, government, and industry—those faceless powers referred to simply as "they"—that threaten to corrupt them.

Few writers today have written as well as Böll about women and children. If the children in his stories and novels are the figures who bear most directly the burden of society's crimes—war, poverty, benign neglect—it is the women who must often preserve the humane values that are disappearing from a prosperous and increasingly superficial society. Love between men and women—not sex—lies at the heart of virtually all of Böll's works, beginning with the earliest stories, the novella *The Train Was on Time* (*Der Zug war pünktlich*, 1949) and the novel *Adam, Where Art Thou?* (*Wo warst du, Adam?,* 1951). . . .

If Böll's women are the custodians of humane values, his men are usually quixotic outsiders who have the integrity to stand up against the anonymous power of "them." One of Böll's earliest stories was called **"The Black Sheep"** (**"Die schwarzen Schafe,"** 1951), a title that heralds the outsider in his works—from Hans Schnier in *The Clown* (*Ansichten eines Clowns,* 1963), who earns his living by criticizing society in his pantomime acts, to the hero of *Absent without Leave* (*Entfernung von der Truppe,* 1964), who concludes his autobiographical report by encouraging all his readers to "desert"—that is, to drop out of conventional society. A parallel theme is announced in the early tale in which a young veteran, whose job it is to count the traffic across a certain bridge, refuses to include his sweetheart in what he considers this dehumanization by statistics. Increasingly, Böll's works have emphasized resistance to established authority. . . .

Even though Böll needs "very little reality," he cannot do without telephones. The innumerable and often seemingly endless phone conversations that punctuate his works often convey the most important information. . . .

The high point is reached in *The Clown,* where the entire story is told in the course of several phone calls the hero makes one evening from his apartment in Bonn. It has often been noted that the telephone in Böll's world is a symbol of alienation. We can accept that and suggest, at the same time, that the telephone also embodies the preeminence of the human world as the essential mode of social communication. For the telephone, excluding facial expression and gesture and making no appeal to the written document, reduces communication to the pure spoken word.

Böll's reliance on spoken discourse, of which the inner monologue, the first person narrator and the telephone are symptoms, has another implication for his fiction. It enables him to express the extent to which the past is contained in the present. Because of his reliance on the spoken word Böll rarely tells a story in smooth chronological sequence from start to finish. . . . Böll shares Kierkegaard's conviction that "It is not worth remembering that past which cannot become a present." . . .

At a time when [Böll] has been increasingly criticized in Germany for the content of his works, he is no doubt doubly pleased to have the international confirmation of the Nobel Prize. At the same time, the reputation of the Prize as a *literary* award is enhanced by the selection of a writer whose oeuvre displays such reverence as Böll's for the word as the repository of humane values and the foundation of all true human community.

Theodore Ziolkowski, "The Inner Veracity of Form," in *Books Abroad,* Vol. 47, No. 1, Winter, 1973, pp. 17-24.

V. S. PRITCHETT

(essay date 1973)

[Pritchett is a highly esteemed English novelist, short story writer, and critic. In the following excerpt, he comments on the formal and thematic character-istics of *Group Portrait with Lady*, praising Böll as a perceptive and inventive novelist.]

The novel as interrogation has turned out to be more than experiment; it is as natural a product of war, the fixed trial, as it is of personal guilt and self-defence. Psychoanalysis, sociology, case-histories and the huge bureaucracy of files and records train the novelist for the techniques of inquisition and tempt him away from the private graces on which we contrive, as best we can, to live. Not only are we now watched by Big Brother in what Heinrich Böll (in his new novel for which he will get the Nobel Prize this year) calls 'the achieve-ment-oriented society': this society has produced innu-merable Little Brothers who have us taped as well. This is awkward news for novelists who cling to their old omniscience: but Böll has seen a satirical and romantic compromise in interrogating the interrogators. [*Group Portrait with Lady*] is an exhaustive series of plain in-terviews with the groups of people who knew Leni, his 'heroine' or, rather, 'subject' at discernible stages of her life—which still goes on. With a half-bow to the com-puting of social, medical and other sciences he poses as a fact-fetishist and calls himself the Au (rather than Author) throughout; and to the objection that emo-tional states are not easily computed he reduces them to those that produce 'l' and W, L and B (tears and weeping, laughter and bliss). Suffering and pain will also occur to Leni and others, but the encyclopaedia settles that neatly: 'S or P is felt by a person with a se-verity proportionate to his quality of life and to the sensitivity of his nature.' (p. 694)

But *Group Portrait with Lady* is not straight sat-ire. Herr Böll's interrogation enables him to cut deeply where he chooses into German lives of many kinds from the Thirties, the rise of Nazism, the war, the dev-astation and the boom, without lecturing us on history. And he has done this as a revaluer. We see all kinds of Germans shifting their ground and their fates as success or disaster catches them. The interrogation method, carried on with tact, irony, impartiality touched by in-dulgence, stirs each man and woman to a self-justifying account of the desperate moments of their lives. One gets an intimate picture of the war as it demoralises ev-eryday life. It is brilliant that we see Leni's wartime life as a worker in a place, close to a cemetery, where she

is making wreaths for the growing population of the killed; and that the daylight raids in the last year give her a chance to get away from supervision into the fields with her lover for an hour or two. Herr Böll's sharp eye for everything that is human in folly, chica-nery or the tragic anarchy of defeat that followed, en-ables him to escape the lumbering quality of panoramic writing. That eye is always on the accident of being human. He is never stuck in set descriptions, but is fol-lowing his own mind. The Au is not a tape-recorder; he disarmingly elicits the detail he wants to know; if he is inclined to enjoy his own dilatory manner and to lose us in some of his family histories, he does show us peo-ple confronting or dodging the awkward facts. His vir-tue lies in his silences and his humanity; his only seri-ous fault is occasional jauntiness.

Herr Böll's method succeeds completely with the groups and particularly with the women who have been close to Leni; but the portrait of Leni herself suf-fers from a vital defect. The more we hear about her, the less we see of her. A little more is lost with every new piece of hearsay. She is so thoroughly known fac-tually that she is static. And she is romanticised, if not sentimentalised. It is astonishing to know so much about her and yet not to *see* her except now and then. (One reason for this is that we do not hear her speak: the omniscient novelist would have given her a voice or would have made her silences expressive. Indeed, he would have obeyed his rule of self-effacement, where-as Herr Böll who adores her, overwhelms her with every kind of tentative speculation.) We are also under the strain of seeing her as both symbol and a woman with her own oddities. She has a strong sensual appe-tite for food, a scatological curiosity—she has picked up near-mystical notions about excrement from a half-Jewish nun hidden in her convent. She has shy but de-termined notions about sex in the heather; she thinks of love as 'the laying on of hands'; is a bit of a pianist; has a passion for enlarged scientific drawings of all or-gans of the human body. These convince neighbours that she must be a prostitute. She has given years to a large and still uncompleted drawing of the cross-section of one layer of the retina, to be called 'Part of the Retina of the Left Eye of the Virgin Mary alias Rahel'. Rahel was the Jewish-Celtic nun for whom Leni had had a probably erotic passion as a girl.

Yet at school the robust Leni was voted 'the most German girl of the year'. . . . In the end we see her liv-ing with a Turkish worker who is a Mohammedan and already has a wife and children, and vilified by her neighbours, who have the local German hatred of im-ported foreign labour. She is perfectly happy even though her son is a drop-out who refuses to be any-thing but a dedicated garbage-collector. According to the psychiatrist's report the youth is suffering from a state called d.u.a. (deliberate under-achievement), though he can speak and write Russian and has read widely. From the achievement society's point of view he is one more victim of 'moral antiprocess'; he has been in prison for forging cheques, but that was a personal aggression against his cousins who had adroitly got hold of the property of his mother's family. Not that she cared at all. She is the shadow of Herr Böll's message. Herr Böll's strong convictions are not concealed by his mocking and hearty Rhenish manner. This sometimes runs toa coarse morbidity which is dangerously close to hospital jokeyness. I would do without Klementina, the wavering intellectual nun who at the end of the novel abandons the habit and goes to live with Au and consoles him, after he had corrupted her with a packet of Virginia cigarettes and a kiss. And the episode in which roses are made to bloom miraculously in the wrong season in a convent garden and allegedly from the ashes of Rahel—an unsuspected hot water spring is the cause—is like one of those naughty miracle jokes so often spun out by knowing Irish priests. But these incidents are the errors of a grave writer who is usually sound in farce and comedy. . . . Böll's comedy depends on a gift for turning points of accurate observation into critical fantasy. And he has one quality indispensable to the interrogatory novelist; the ear for the clichés in which ordinary people hide their secrets and the rulers and moneymakers their policies. He is listening to people turning excuses into articles of faith. No doubt Leni is the heroine because she says so little. The Au makes a list of her few known phrases. What did she say to her son when he forged the cheque? What to her young, absurdly formal Turkish lover? How did she escape the unmeaning phrase? Not quite the Virgin Mary, not remorseful enough to be a Magdalene, brighter than Martha—what is she? We shall never be quite sure. (pp. 694-95)

V. S. Pritchett, "Grand Inquisitor," in *New Statesman*, Vol. 85, No. 2199, May 11, 1973, pp. 694-95.

D. J. ENRIGHT

(essay date 1985)

[Enright is an English poet, novelist, and critic whose poetry and fiction are noted for their empathy, expressed in a direct style, for the victims of betrayal. In the following excerpt, he pays tribute to Böll, commenting on the role that the writer played as the conscience of post-Nazi Germany.]

Since Günter Grass soon showed himself rather too fantastical for the part, it was Heinrich Böll who by natural process became the conscience of post-war Germany, attacking complacent amnesia concerning the past and complacent pride concerning the present.

Yet, while Germany provided the local habitation and the name, in its gently ironic way his best writing is universally and timelessly pertinent. A fine story, **"Murke's Collected Silences,"** tells of a radio talks editor who is so sickened by the high-flown guff he deals with that he cuts out the bits of tape where the speaker has paused for a rare moment, splices them together, and preserves his sanity by playing back the tape at home in the evenings.

The "clown" in the moving and trenchant novel of that name is a mime who could make a rich living in Leipzig with his "Board Meeting" act and in Bonn with his "Party Conference Elects its Presidium"— except that he sees no point in this, and wants to perform the first in Bonn and the second in Leipzig.

And in *Group Portrait with Lady*, Böll's most sustained and complex novel, the all-important question is raised: "What has happened to justice?" For some women are rewarded with villas and cars and large sums of money for providing the same service which brings other women merely a cup of coffee and a cigarette. One woman lies in hospital with venereal disease, caught from a foreign statesman whom, on official instructions, she won round to a "treaty mood," an act which benefited the society which despises her. She dies, not of the disease, but of blushing; she was a modest woman.

Böll's passionate sympathy—at times a little too overt perhaps, but often conveyed in deceptively comic guise—is for the underdog, the victim of bureaucracy, of ideologies political, social or religious, of those big words that Stephen Dedalus feared. The heroine of *The Lost Honour of Katharina Blum* is punished for shooting an obnoxious and lecherous reporter by having her reputation and, worse, her privacy torn to shreds by the media: the killing of a reporter is in a different category from that of a bank manager or shopkeeper; it is virtually a ritual murder. Friends who describe Katharina as "cool and level-headed" find their words transmogrified into "ice-cold and calculating." The quality papers are more restrained, but—she comments ruefully—the people she knows all read the other ones.

We may have faint doubts even about the charming Katharina, and we may suspect that even exposing the sins of capitalism in a capitalist theatre can be a little too easy, or *de rigueur*. There is a price to pay for being—and being conscious of being—a national conscience, on top of Nobel laureate and president of International PEN. So many good causes to espouse, so many big words to speak, such anxiety to be always and scrupulously fair (having searched the faces of the Soviet troops in Prague in 1968, Böll reported that they "did not seem imperialistic"). . . .

It was ironical, yet inevitable, that the loving champion of the private person should have become himself a public figure. Yet the writer remained firmly private, and his fiction will surely live and last by virtue of its unique blend of qualities not unique in themselves: tenderness, anger, humour, shrewdness, pathos and cheerfulness, an earthy humanism and a persistent strain of religious feeling, plus the ability to tell a good story while enlightening and instructing.

There is no post-war European novelist who could seriously be considered his equal as a writer about and for the so-called "common man," that ill-done-by but resilient creature.

D. J. Enright, "Heinrich Böll," in *The Observer,* July 21, 1985, p. 21.

SOURCES FOR FURTHER STUDY

Bazarov, Konstantin. "Heinrich Böll: Enemy of Materialism." *Books and Bookmen* (October 1973): 42-5.

Identifies religious humanism as the source of Böll's opposition to the predominant materialism of industrial societies.

Cunliffe, W. G. "Heinrich Böll's Eccentric Rebels." *Modern Fiction Studies* (Autumn 1975): 473-79.

Analyzes the role of the rebel in Böll's writing, concluding that in "moving from the passive hero to the eccentric rebel who is no longer satisfied with the virtues of the lamb, Böll has reflected an important change in German attitudes since the war."

Maddocks, Melvin. "Heinrich Böll's Song of Innocence." *The Atlantic Monthly* (July 1973): 95-7

Discusses Böll's literary accomplishments, praising *Group Portrait With Lady* as "the completest statement of what he believes."

Murdoch, Brian. "Point of View in the Early Satires of Heinrich Böll." *Modern Languages* LIV, No. 3 (September 1973): 125-31.

Comments on Böll's innovative approach to satirical narrative.

Reid, J. H. *Heinrich Böll, a German for His Time.* Oxford: Berg, 1988, 245 p.

An overview of Böll's life and literary career.

Schwarz, Wilhelm Johannes. *Heinrich Böll, Teller of Tales: A Study of His Works and Characters.* New York: Ungar, 1929, 123 p.

Focuses on the characteristic features of Böll's narrative art.

Jorge Luis Borges

1899-1986

(Also wrote with Adolfo Bioy Casares under joint pseudonyms B. Lynch Davis, H[onorio] Bustos Domecq, and B. Suarez Lynch) Argentinian short story writer, essayist, poet, translator, critic, biographer, travel writer, novelist, and scriptwriter.

INTRODUCTION

Among the foremost literary figures to have written in Spanish, Borges is best known for his erudite short stories in which he blended fantasy and realism to address complex philosophical problems. Involving such thematic motifs as time, infinity, identity, and memory, Borges's stories combine elements of fiction and personal essay in hybrid forms that resist classification. His prose works were commended by André Maurois for "their wonderful intelligence, their wealth of invention, and their tight, almost mathematical, style." Making minimal use of plot and characterization, Borges employed paradox and oxymoron to combine such seemingly contradictory concepts as universality and particularity, illusion and reality. Occasionally faulted by critics for his refusal to address social and political issues, Borges maintained: "I have no message. I am neither a thinker nor a moralist, but simply a man of letters who turns his own perplexities and that respected system of perplexities we call philosophy into the forms of literature."

Borges was born in Buenos Aires, where he lived for most of his childhood. His father, Jorge Guillermo Borges, was a respected lawyer, author, and educator; Borges once commented: "If I were asked to name the chief event in my life, I should say my father's library." From an early age Borges absorbed a wide range of world literature. He learned to read English before Spanish due to the influence of his English grandmother, and when he was seven years old he translated Oscar Wilde's parable "The Happy Prince." Borges's first original story, "El rey de la selva," was published when he was thirteen. While his family was stranded in Switzerland following the outbreak of World War I, Borges enrolled at the Collége de Génève, where he studied French and German and familiarized himself with such European philosophers as Arthur Schopenhauer and George Berkeley. Upon graduating in 1918, Borges traveled to Spain. There he published reviews, essays, and poetry and associated with the Ultraístas, an avant-garde literary group whose fiction combined elements of Dadaism, Imagism, and German Expressionism. Striving in their poetry to transcend boundaries of time and space, the Ultraístas championed metaphor as the ultimate form of expression; their influence permeates much of Borges's early work, particularly *Fervor de Buenos Aires* (1923), his first poetry collection.

Borges returned to Buenos Aires in 1921. He helped develop several small Argentinian publications, including the literary magazine *Prisma* and the journal *Proa,* and became reacquainted with Macedonio Fernandez, a writer and colleague of his father. Encouraged by Fernandez to develop his interest in metaphysics and the complexities of language, Borges began publishing essays on these topics. In 1938 he developed septicemia, a form of blood poisoning, from a head wound he suffered in a fall down a staircase. Concerned that the condition had impaired his writing ability, Borges published a short story as his first work after the accident, intending to attribute its possible failure to inexperience in the genre rather than a loss of literary skill. The tale, "Pierre Menard, autor del Quijote" ("Pierre Menard, Author of Don Quixote"), unexpectedly garnered positive reactions, and Borges's ensuing short fiction earned increasingly widespread critical recognition in Argentina.

In 1943, after signing a manifesto denouncing Argentinian military dictator Juan Perón, Borges was demoted from his government post as an assistant librarian to poultry inspector, a position he refused, however, in favor of becoming an itinerant lecturer and teacher. Following the ouster of Perón in 1955, Borges was named director of the prestigious National Library of Argentina and later awarded the Premio Nacional de Literatura, the country's highest literary honor. Yet Borges remained largely unknown outside Latin America. In 1961 Borges and Irish dramatist Samuel Beckett shared the Prix Formentor, an international prize established in 1960 by six avant-garde publishers to recognize authors whose work they deemed would "have a lasting influence on the development of modern literature." This achievement closely coincided with the publication of his short fiction collection *Ficciones* and helped establish his reputation throughout the world. Beginning in the late 1950s, Borges's eyesight started to fail; although his increasing blindness slowed his literary output, he continued to publish volumes of stories, poetry, and essays. During this period, Borges's mother increased her role as his secretary, a position she had occupied throughout his career, taking dictation of his work and reading to him in Spanish, English, and French. In 1985 Borges was diagnosed with liver cancer, and he left Buenos Aires for Geneva, Switzer-

land, where he married his companion and former student, María Kodama. Three weeks later, at age eighty-seven, Borges died.

Although he became best known for his imaginative short fiction, in the early years of his career Borges wrote poetry and criticism almost exclusively. In his first collection of poetry, *Fervor de Buenos Aires* (1923; revised, 1969), Borges utilized Ultraíst concepts to portray colorful individuals and events in Buenos Aires. His next volume, *Luna de enfrente* (1925), contains confessional and love poetry as well as pieces that anticipate his later concern with such topics as time and memory. *Cuaderno San Martín* (1929) consists chiefly of tributes to deceased poets, among them Francisco López Merino, Borges's friend and associate, who committed suicide. Borges's best-regarded volumes of early essays include *Inquisiciónes* (1925), *El tamaño de mi esperanza* (1927), and *El idioma de los argentinos* (1928). Borges won praise for "The Language of the Argentines," the title essay of the third collection, in which he urged writers to reject the artificial stylization common to Latin American letters at the turn of the century. *Discusión* (1932), a collection of film reviews and articles on metaphysical and aesthetic topics, includes the noted essay "Narrative Art and Magic," in which Borges defended the capacity of fantasy literature to address realistic concerns. *Historia de la eternidad* (1936), a volume exploring humanity's concepts of eternity from ancient times to the present, includes "The Approach to al-Mu'tasim," Borges's review of an imaginary detective novel. By critiquing a nonexistent work, Borges proposed that content exists in the reader's imagination and, according to John Sturrock, "that the 'real' aspect of books, their physical presence, does not matter."

Borges's early short stories derive in style and subject from his essays and are often interpreted as parables illustrating the potentialities and limitations of creative art. "Pierre Menard, Author of the Quixote" depicts a modern writer who independently composes portions of a text corresponding precisely to Miguel de Cervantes's *Don Quixote.* According to Katherine Singer Kovács, Menard has created "a new and more profound work, one of particular relevance to his own historical period and life." Borges's first short story collection, *Historia universal de la infamia* (1935; *A Universal History of Infamy*), purports to present a fictional felon's encyclopedia of criminals drawn from history. The translated edition includes "The South," a semiautobiographical story in which a troubled librarian, desiring the chivalric life of the Argentinian gaucho, becomes involved in a fatal knife fight that may exist only in his imagination. The title piece of *El jardín de senderos que se bifurcan* (1941; *The Garden of Forking Paths*), which Borges described as "a detective story," links two apparently unrelated crimes, one committed in the present, the other in the past. Max Byrd observed that "both crimes blend in a single moment; the solution of one simultaneously resolves the other." This collection also includes Borges's acclaimed story "The Library of Babel," in which a symmetrically arranged library, representing humanity's rational view of the universe, is revealed to contain illegible books.

Ficciones (1944) is generally regarded as Borges's most significant work. In this story collection, which is primarily concerned with conflicts between reality and imagination, Borges utilized what he considered to be the four fundamental aspects of fantasy. James E. Irby described these aspects in his introduction to Borges's 1962 collection *Labyrinths:* "the work within the work, the contamination of reality by dream, the voyage in time, and the double." In "Tlön, Uqbar, Orbis Tertius," one of his most frequently analyzed stories, Borges combined fiction with such elements of the essay as footnotes and a postscript to describe the attempts of a secret philosophical society to create an invented world free of linear space and time. As their ideas cohere, objects from their imagined realm surface in reality. Frances Wyers Weber commented: "The story develops the contrasts not only between the cohesiveness of Tlön and the incomprehensible, unstable realities of the experienced world, but also the inevitable mutilation that order imposes. The utopian world of unlimited capricious speculation becomes a carefully wrought complex that eliminates all alternatives and bewitches humanity with its utter intelligibility."

The enlarged English edition of *El aleph* (1949), entitled *The Aleph and Other Stories, 1933-1969* (1970), consists of stories and essays from various periods in Borges's career. This work is the first of several acclaimed collaborations between Borges and translator Norman Thomas di Giovanni aimed at producing creative translations that read as though the original pieces were written in English. The "aleph" of the title story is a stone representing the equivalent of all visual images of the universe, containing all points of space, and indicative of humanity's limitless but not entirely lucid perspectives and possibilities. The aleph's opposite, described in "The Zahir," is a magical coin universally representative of every particular coin, real or imagined. According to Diana Armas Wilson, the zahir differs from the universal aleph in that it signifies "a local and particular perspective that a man uses to order reality—any belief, scheme, or dogma that saves him from chaos."

For several years after his vision began to fail, Borges limited his literary work to lectures, translations, and poetry. Keith Botsford deemed these later poems "among the most skillful and immaculate in Spanish. Strict in their rules and sober in their imagery, gentle in tone, recollected in tranquility, they are elegiac, formal,

symmetrical." *El hacedor* (1960; *Dreamtigers*), a collection of brief poems, quotations, and parables, uses the tiger as an ambivalent symbol of unnatural evil and natural change. In the title poem of *Elogio de la sombra* (1969; *In Praise of Darkness*), Borges proposed the paradoxical notion that old age and blindness may signify deep happiness because of the imminence of death. Dualities involving physical blindness and spiritual sight also pervade *El oro de los tigres* (1972; *The Gold of the Tigers: Selected Later Poems*).

Borges returned to writing fiction in the 1970s, preferring a straightforward, realistic approach to the elaborate fantasies and literary games of his earliest work. Edward G. Warner described the stories in *El informe de Brodie* (1970; *Doctor Brodie's Report*) as "mostly plain, unadorned tales—some harsh, some tender—of love, hate, and the inevitability of death." *El libro de arena* (1975; *The Book of Sand*), although similar in style, returns to the fantastical themes of Borges's early fiction. This volume includes "The Congress," a long story in which a world congress attempts to incorporate all of humanity's views and ideologies by securing thousands of books. Realizing the arbitrary and conjectural nature of their task, the congress eventually recognizes the need to reject limited, predominating world views and destroys the books, concluding that "every few centuries, the library of Alexandria must be burned down."

Although critics have praised the formal precision and mellifluous tone of Borges's poetry and the stylistic originality of his essays, it is for his short fiction that Borges is recognized as one of the most influential and innovative Latin American authors of the twentieth century. His experiments with the intermingling of fantasy and realistic detail presaged the magical realist style of writing practiced by such major Latin American authors as Gabriel García Marquez and Julio Cortázar; the latter writer referred to Borges as "the leading figure of our fantastic literature." His insights into the nature of learning, literature, and the fictive process, exemplified in such works as "The Circular Ruins," have established him as one of modern literature's most philosophically accomplished authors. While some critics have criticized Borges's writings as esoteric, intellectually rarified games, most consider the author's work particularly relevant to his time, when, as Borges himself remarked in an essay, traditional fictional treatments of character and emotion were too greatly exhausted to illuminate further the human condition. By exploring intellectual and philological issues, they contend, Borges also addressed humankind's deepest concerns about the nature of mind and existence. As critic Carter Wheelock commented: "[Borges] plays only one instrument—the intellectual, the epistemological—but the strumming of his cerebral guitar sets into vibration all the strings of emotion, intuition, and esthetic longing that are common to sentient humanity."

(For further information about Borges's life and works, see *Contemporary Authors*, Vols. 21-22; *Contemporary Author New Revision Series*, Vol. 19; *Contemporary Literary Criticism*, Vols. 1, 2, 3, 4, 6, 8, 9, 10, 13, 19, 44, 48; *Dictionary of Literary Biography Yearbook: 1986;* and *Short Story Criticism*, Vol. 4.)

CRITICAL COMMENTARY

JAIME ALAZRAKI
(essay date 1971)

[Alazraki is an Argentine-born American educator and critic who has written and edited several scholarly works on Latin American authors, including Borges, Julio Cortázar, and Pablo Neruda. In the following excerpt, he examines the philosophical and theological themes of Borges's fiction.]

The themes of [Borges'] stories are inspired by the metaphysical hypotheses accumulated through many centuries of the history of philosophy, and by theological systems that are the scaffoldings of several religions. Borges, skeptical of the veracity of the former and of the revelations of the latter, strips them of their claims of absolute truth and pretended divinity and makes them instead raw material for his inventions. In this way, he returns to them the character of aesthetic creation and wonder for which they are valued and justified.

In his stories we find echoes of these doctrines. At times he makes them function as the frame on which the fiction is woven. Having read any one of his narratives, we sense beneath the design the presence of a metaphysics or the reverberation of a certain theology, which in some way explains the story and at the same time confers on it a transcendental flavor which all his stories have, although Borges denies this and laughs at such transcendentalisms. In his stories, the particular is intertwined with the general, but they are also confounded within each other and integrated into a unity where it is difficult to distinguish one from the other. We perceive a meaning that goes beyond the events of the story and which projects the fable of the narrative to a level of generic or symbolic values. . . . Borges' stories can be read as a direct narration of fictional actions, but we know that other values throb beneath these actions. In **"Deutsches Requiem"** the protagonist will be shot for being a torturer and murderer, but he also represents the destiny of Nazi Germany, in the same way that the perplexities of Averroës with regard to the Greek words "comedy" and "tragedy," in the story **"Averroës' Search,"** are a symbol of the perplexities of Islam with respect to Greek culture.

Thus, Borges projects the individual in a broader context and the singular is explained in the generic as much as the generic in the singular. . . . It is not difficult to see that in many of his stories, or perhaps in all of them, Borges attributes to the concrete a generic value. The concrete realities of his stories are what the concrete world is for the mystics: a system of symbols. Borges enlightens the concrete with the perspective of the generic and in this way confers upon it an intensity that it does not have as an individual entity.

Confounding the limits of the individual and the generic, of the relative of a singular reality with the absolute of an abstraction, Borges widens the scope of his stories, giving them an elasticity, a simultaneity, that if at first makes them seem fantastic, "unreal," in the end saves them from becoming a very gross simplification of reality. It is true that, for Borges, the doctrines that form the backdrop of his stories are very far from being essential truths. It is true that he judges them to be literature, to be inventions of the imagination that at best have value as marvels, but the metaphysical systems which he handles constitute the synthesis of the human mind in its attempt to penetrate the arcana of the universe, and the theologies which he uses as literary ingredients for his stories are, to this day and throughout centuries of history, the theoretic foundation of religions whose followers number in the millions. The fact that these metaphysics and theologies appear in his stories as the solutions to the puzzle posed by the narration, in his essays as an interpretation of cultural phenomena, and in his poems as an expression of the inexorable condition of human destiny, not only does not contradict the value of a marvel that Borges confers on them, but is a way of underlining the character of invention of all literature. . . . [The stories, essays, and poems of Borges] suggest that, in man's pow-

Principal Works

Fervor de Buenos Aires (poetry) 1923; revised edition, 1969

Luna de enfrente (poetry) 1925

Inquisiciones (essays) 1925

El tamaño de mi esperanza (essays) 1927

El idioma de los Argentinos (essay) 1928

Cuaderno San Martín (poetry) 1929

Evaristo Carriego (essay) 1930

Discusión (essays and criticism) 1932

Historia universal de la infamia (short stories) 1935
    [A Universal History of Infamy, 1972]

Historia de la eternidad (essays) 1936

El jardín de senderos que se bifurcan (short stories) 1941

Poemas, 1922-1943 (poetry) 1943

Ficciones, 1935-1944 (short stories) 1944
    [Ficciones, 1962; also published as Fictions, 1965]

El aleph (short stories) 1949
    [The Aleph and Other Stories, 1933-1969 (revised edition), 1970]

Otras inquisiciónes, 1937-1952 (essays) 1952
    [Other Inquisitions, 1937-1952, 1964]

Obras completas. 10 vols. (essays, short stories, and poetry) 1953-67

Manual de zoología fantastica [with Margarita Guerrero] (prose) 1957; also published as El libro de los seres imaginarios [revised edition], 1967
    [The Imaginary Zoo, 1969; also published as The Book of Imaginary Beings (revised edition), 1969]

Poemas, 1923-1958 (poetry) 1958

Antología personal (poetry and prose) 1961
    [A Personal Anthology, 1967]

El hacedor (prose and poetry) 1961
    [Dreamtigers, 1964]

Labyrinths (short stories and essays) 1962

Obra poetica, 1923-1967 (poetry) 1967
    [Selected Poems, 1923-1967, 1972]

Nueva antología personal (poetry and prose) 1968

Elogio de la sombra (poetry and prose) 1969
    [In Praise of Darkness, 1974]

El informe de Brodie (short stories) 1970
    [Doctor Brodie's Report, 1972]

*El oro de los tigres (poetry) 1972

Borges on Writing (interviews) 1973

El libro de arena (short stories) 1975
    [The Book of Sand, 1977]

*La rosa profunda (poetry) 1975

Historia de la noche (poetry) 1977

Obras completas (poetry and prose) 1977

Obras completas en colaboración [with Adolfo Bioy Casares, Betina Edelberg, Margarita Guerrero, Alicia Jurado, Maria Kodama, Maria Esther Vázquez] (short stories, essays, and criticism) 1979

Prosa completa. 2 vols. (prose) 1980

Siete noches (lectures) 1980
    [Seven Nights, 1984]

Antología poética, 1923-1977 (poetry) 1981

Atlas [with Maria Kodama] (prose) 1984
    [Atlas, 1985]

*These works were translated and published as The Gold of the Tigers: Selected Later Poems in 1977.

erlessness to perceive the laws that govern the world, he has invented his own reality, ordered according to human laws which he can know. (pp. 4-8)

[One] can say that in Borges' short stories his metaphysical and theological motivations and his literary inventions are resolved in symbols and allegories. . . . In Borges we . . . find a system of myths but in it Borges has mythicized the "findings" of philosophy and the "revelations" of theology. In this operation (one must remember that the first tries to replace myth with reason, and the second, exorcism with doctrine, in order to understand the hugeness of the irony) Borges reduces these ideas to creations of the imagination, to intuitions that now are not fundamentally different from any other mythical form. Hence, these "myths of the intelligence" would be returned to the only reality to which they correspond: not to the world created by gods, but to the one invented by men. . . . [The] sym-

bols coined by Borges always find their precise context in theories and doctrines created by human intelligence. . . . No less vigorous is his devotion to theology. . . . (pp. 8-9)

The *chaos* of the world and the *order* created by man could be considered the abscissa and the ordinate of his narrative world. . . . Doubly motivated by Gnostic theories and by the Argentine's concept of the world, Borges arrives in his stories at the view of the universe as a chaos. (p. 10)

"The Babylon Lottery" is . . . a variation of the theme of **"The Library of Babel"** (one need not be reminded that the connotation of Babel or Babylonia is that of disorder and confusion). The library is the symbol of the chaos of the universe; the lottery shows this chaos translated into chance which rules human life. In both cases the possibility of a divine order is presented, of a labyrinth ordered according to laws which are incomprehensible to human intelligence and which are, consequently, undecipherable. (p. 12)

From the chaotic view of the universe emerges that favorite image of Borges, the labyrinth. The labyrinth expresses both sides of the coin: it has an irreversible order if one knows the solution (the gods, God) and it can be at the same time a chaotic maze if the solution constitutes an unattainable secret (men). The labyrinth represents to a greater or lesser degree the vehicle through which Borges carries his world view to almost all his stories. (p. 15)

[The] doctrine of the world as a dream of Someone or of No One becomes another of the main themes in Borges' writings. . . . The existence of two dreamers [in the story **"The Circular Ruins"**] implies the possibility of an infinite series of dreamers. . . . **"The Circular Ruins"** gives expression to the Buddhist idea of the world as a dream, or to the hallucinatory character of the world as the idealist philosophers postulate. . . . [By opening the story with] a quotation from Lewis Carroll's [*Through the Looking Glass*], Borges transfers the Buddhist doctrine to a line extracted from that fantastic story. With finesse, with subtlety, Buddhist doctrine is reduced to a marvel of the enchanted world behind the looking-glass.

The idea of the universe as the book of God appears in several of his essays. . . . In his story **"The Dead Man,"** Borges capitalizes on this idea. (pp. 16-18)

[The] tragic contrast between a man who believes himself to be the master and the maker of his fate and a text or divine plan in which his fortune has already been written parallels the problem of man with respect to the universe: the world is impenetrable, but the human mind never ceases to propose schemes. Man's ambition to resolve the enigma of the universe is as vain as Otálora's endeavor: Otálora wants to map out his destiny according to a human geometry, alien to the design which Someone has already drawn and which he does not know about. In this book (i.e., the universe), God or Someone has already written out our fate. For us this text is illegible because, explains Borges, quoting Bloy, "there is no human being on earth who is capable of declaring who he is. No one knows what he has come to this world to do, to what his acts, feelings, and ideas correspond, or what his real *name* is." (p. 19)

The dreamer of **"The Circular Ruins"** [and] the wild divinity of **"The Dead Man"** . . . are projections of an inexorable will that has dreamed or written the world. (p. 20)

In these stories we recognize the condition of man's fate reduced to a fragile and contingent manifestation of an unappealable Will. . . . This will that dreams or writes us, and of which we are imperfect simulacra (as in the poem **"The Golem"**) or pieces in an infinite game (as in the poem **"The Game of Chess"**), is God. Behind God, however, Borges suggests the possibility of a second god who repeats the dream, the text, or the game, and so on *ad infinitum,* as in the case of the dreamers of **"The Circular Ruins."** This insistence on the infinite character of the dream is not fortuitous. Besides being a recurrent motif which in greater or lesser degree appears in almost all his stories, the infinite is translated on the stylistic level as an insistent adjective whose repetition permits us to define it as a "linguistic tic." . . . This adjective and a few others which are repeated with almost obsessive frequency . . . express certain key attributes of Borges' world view and are indicative of his preference for certain ideas. The infinite is the only dimension which suits a world conceived as an insoluble labyrinth. Its function is clear: the spatial and temporal infinity of the universe accentuates its chaotic nature and reinforces its impenetrable condition.

The theme of the world as a dream of God is related to the pantheistic notion that "everything is everywhere and any one thing is all things." . . . The idea that anything is all things may be the solution not only to the enigmas of history but also to the riddles posed in his stories. (pp. 20-2)

The pantheistic notion that one man is all men implies the negation of individual identity, or more exactly, the reduction of all individuals to a general and supreme identity which contains all and at the same time makes all contained in each one. In the stories **"The Shape of the Sword"** and **"Abenjacán the Bojarí, Dead in His Labyrinth,"** this notion functions as a narrative technique. (p. 24)

A derivation of pantheism is the idea that "God is the primordial nothingness." . . . The idea . . . appears with reference to George Bernard Shaw, who wrote in a letter: "I understand everything and everyone, and am nobody and nothing," and it undoubtedly constitutes the axis of the story **"The Immortal."** The incongruencies and anachronisms that at the beginning of the tale confuse the reader so much are cleared up at the end, and the story recovers an essential coherence which in all of Borges' stories binds the most contradictory details into an unquestionable unity. . . . There is [in the story] an apparent contradiction which can only be explained with the aid of the pantheistic doctrine: God, Shakespeare, Homer, are immortal because they live in everyone, and they have died because to be everyone they have had to renounce their identity, which is a form of nonbeing, of dying. . . . The theme of **"The Immortal"** is the pantheistic idea that a man is nothing and no one in order to be all men. The structure of the tale re-creates, in part, the implications of the theme. (pp. 26-9, 30)

For Borges, time is the central problem of metaphysics, and so it is only natural that time becomes one of the main themes of his work. Of all the temporal schemes, the one Borges prefers and the most frequent in his work is cyclical or circular time. . . . Of all the versions of the eternal return, Borges seems to enjoy most the one that considers the cycles which repeat themselves infinitely not as identical, but as similar. Such a conception of time promises an interpretation of reality with fertile consequences, and Borges applies it ingeniously in his essays, poems, and stories. In the story **"Theme of the Traitor and the Hero,"** . . . we witness an assassination that is a replica of that of Julius Caesar. . . . When we are about to believe that we are seeing in Fergus Kilpatrick's death (hero of an Irish rebellion) a cyclical repetition of the assassination of the Roman hero, Borges reveals the artifice to us: there is no such repetition of cycles; the plan of Kilpatrick's assassination has been copied from Shakespeare's tragedy. This story is another typical exponent of the incessant exchange between fiction and reality where Borges delights in confounding one with the other. . . . [The] whole story describes a constant pendulum movement which oscillates between the real and the fictitious, between the historical and the imaginary, which in braiding confound themselves. (pp. 35-7)

Borges proposes a task on the level of art, of fantastic literature, that idealist metaphysics undertakes on the level of reality: if the world exists only as my idea of it, myself, a part of this world, is just an idea in the mind that perceives me or projects me as its perception. To achieve this task Borges creates fictious characters who acquire historical validity (although within the frame of fiction). When we think of them as real, he returns them to the level of fiction. Conversely, Borges renders historic and real beings fictitious characters. When, finally, the narrator of the story explains the incoherencies of these identities in constant movement, Borges converts the narrator—like Scheherazade in *A Thousand and One Nights*—into a character of his own narration. (p. 38)

In [Borges'] stories, reality is seen *sub specie aeternitatis,* which is to say, not as ordinary everyday occurrences but as generic ones, not through individual beings but through archetypes. Such a view of reality should perforce be organized into a system. Borges uses the systems already outlined by philosophy and theology. If representing reality means transporting the sillinesses and trivialities which Borges associates with the psychological novel—or at least with one type of psychological novel—to literature, systematizing it is more interesting, more creative, and more imaginative: not this or that fortuitous gaucho, but Martín Fierro, who is the archetype of the gaucho; not puzzling chaos, but reality arranged into cycles and symmetries; not time in its ironbound flow, but in circles, spirals, and infinite webs. Subjected to "a system of symmetries, coincidences, and contrasts," the narrative of Borges is orga-

nized into symbols which achieve on the level of fiction that which is denied to philosophy on the level of reality: the knowledge of the ultimate ends of things, the revelation of the essences and of the laws which govern the world.

Another of the philosophical ideas which has insistently occupied the attention of Borges is the law of causality. Borges applies it with fruitful results in his "inquisitions," in the territory of his stories, and in some lines of his poetry. (pp. 39-40)

[In the stories **"Deutsches Requiem"** and **"Averroës' Search"**] Borges delights in the possibility of a world intelligently ordered by men's restless imaginations. With the idea that "the world is an interminable chain of causes, and every cause is an effect" Borges weaves these two narratives. But zur Linde's Germany and Borges' Averroës are inventions of the human mind which have very little to do with the Germany of history and the Averroës of Islam. In both cases, Borges has constructed the destiny of a country and the destiny of a man, with an impeccable logic which he himself proceeds to destroy with an irony that returns the reader to a reality whose most intrinsic condition is its impenetrability. . . . Borges knows that the world perceived by the human mind is an invention or a dream which has very little to do with the real world, with

Borges (right, front) with his sister Norah (left, rear) at their family home in Geneva, 1916.

that other dream dreamed by a god. His stories, which first propound a reality only to tell us later that this reality is a design of symmetrical geometry totally unrelated to the world which it intends to describe, are a form of expressing the agony of man faced with the enigma of the universe. Borges' essential skepticism and his feeling of defeat overwhelmed by an order of divine laws—which for man is chaos—make possible, nevertheless, a new understanding of man's confrontation with the world. This defeat is then a triumph. Borges suggests that since man can never find the solution to the gods' labyrinth, he has constructed his own labyrinths; since the reality of the gods is impenetrable, man has created his own reality. He thus lives in a world which is the product of his fallible architecture. He knows that there is another world which constantly besieges him and forces him to feel the enormousness of its presence, and between these two worlds, between these two dreams (a Borges who lets himself go on living and likes the taste of coffee and the Borges who weaves laborious books of fantastic literature), between these two stories (one imagined by God and another invented by man) flows the agonizing history of humanity. Borges deflects these agonies into art, humor, irony, and at times into intense poetry. . . . (pp. 43-5)

The common denominator of all his fiction can be defined as a relativity which governs all things and which, by being the result of a confrontation of opposites, takes on the appearance of a paradox and, at times, of an oxymoron. . . . This relativity compels us to see reality in perpetual movement and incites us to transcend it beyond its daily occurrences in order to discover new dimensions in it. Borges' stories, which trite criticism insists on seeing as an evasion of reality, bring us in fact much closer to reality—not to the reality of loud and flashy newspapers which bewilders us, but to an essential reality which reduces us to a fortuitous number in a gigantic lottery and at the same time links us with everything that was and is to be, to a reality which transforms us into a cycle which already has occurred and yet teaches us that a minute can be the receptacle of eternity, to a reality which effaces our identity and yet converts us into depositories of a supreme Identity—in short, an improbable, contradictory, ambiguous, and even absurd reality. . . . The multiple vision of reality which Borges suggests to us is an attempt to grasp the contradictory elements that compose it. Although "A" may exclude "B," Borges presents them together, co-existing, to show that exclusion is deceitful because, while they reject and oppose each other, they also complement and need each other. This fictitious world, where the measure of all things is a relativism which grants validity to the improbable and to the absurd, is not an evasion of reality; it is more precisely its return, but with a flower which, like Coleridge's,

proves that it exists and that it is also a dream. (pp. 45-6)

Jaime Alazraki, in his *Jorge Luis Borges,* Columbia University Press, 1971, 48 p.

JOHN UPDIKE
(essay date 1975)

[A perceptive observer of the human condition and an accomplished literary stylist, Updike is one of America's most distinguished men of letters. In the following excerpt, he discusses stylistic elements of Borges's criticism, poetry, and fiction.]

[Borges'] driest paragraph is somehow compelling. His fables are written from a height of intelligence less rare in philosophy and physics than in fiction. Furthermore, he is, at least for anyone whose taste runs to puzzles or pure speculation, delightfully entertaining. The question is, I think, whether or not Borges' lifework, arriving in a lump now (he was born in 1899 and since his youth has been an active and honored figure in Argentine literature), can serve, in its gravely considered oddity, as any kind of clue to the way out of the dead-end narcissism and downright trashiness of present American fiction.

Borges' narrative innovations spring from a clear sense of technical crisis. For all his modesty and reasonableness of tone, he proposes some sort of essential revision in literature itself. The concision of his style and the comprehensiveness of his career . . . produce a strangely terminal impression: he seems to be the man for whom literature has no future. . . .

A constant bookishness gives Borges' varied production an unusual consistency. His stories have the close texture of argument; his critical articles have the suspense and tension of fiction. The criticism collected in *Other Inquisitions, 1937-1952* almost all takes the form of detection, of uncovering what was secret. He looks for, and locates, the hidden pivots of history: the moment (in Iceland in 1225) when a chronicler first pays tribute to an enemy the very line (in Chaucer in 1382) when allegory yields to naturalism. His interest gravitates toward the obscure, the forgotten: John Wilkins, the 17th-century inventor *ab nihilo* of an analytical language; J. W. Dunne, the 20th-century proponent of a grotesque theory of time; Layamon, the 13th-century poet isolated between the death of Saxon culture and the birth of the English language. Where an arcane quality does not already exist, Borges injects it. (pp. 170-71)

Implacably, Borges reduces everything to a condition of mystery. His gnomic style and encyclopedic supply of allusions generate a kind of inverse illumination, a Gothic atmosphere in which the most lucid and famous authors loom somewhat menacingly. (p. 171)

The tracing of hidden resemblances, of philosophical genealogies, is Borges' favorite mental exercise. Out of his vast reading he distills a few related images, whose parallelism, tersely presented, has the force of a fresh thought. "Perhaps universal history is the history of a few metaphors. I should like to sketch one chapter of that history," he writes in **"Pascal's Sphere,"** and goes on to compile, in less than four pages, twenty-odd instances of the image of a sphere "whose center is everywhere and whose circumference nowhere." These references are arranged like a plot, beginning with Xenophanes, who joyously substituted for the anthropomorphic gods of Greece a divine and eternal Sphere, and ending with Pascal, who, in describing nature as "an infinite sphere" had first written and then rejected the word *"effroyable"*—"a frightful sphere." Many of Borges' genealogies trace a degeneration: he detects a similar "magnification to nothingness" in the evolutions of theology and of Shakespeare's reputation; he watches an Indian legend succumb, through its successive versions, to the bloating of unreality. He follows in the works of Léon Bloy the increasingly desperate interpretations of a single phrase in St. Paul—*"per speculum in aenigmate"* ("through a glass darkly"). (p. 172)

Borges is not an antiseptic pathologist of the irrational; he is himself susceptible to infection. His connoisseurship has in it a touch of madness. In his **"Kafka and His Precursors,"** he discovers, in certain parables and anecdotes by Zeno, Han Yü, Kierkegaard, Browning, Bloy, and Lord Dunsany, a prefiguration of Kafka's tone. He concludes that each writer creates his own precursors. . . .

As a literary critic, Borges demonstrates much sensitivity and sense. The American reader of [*Other Inquisitions, 1937-1952*] will be gratified by the generous amount of space devoted to writers of the English language. Borges, from within the Spanish literary tradition of "dictionaries and rhetoric," is attracted by the oneiric and hallucinatory quality he finds in North American, German, and English writing. He values Hawthorne and Whitman for their intense unreality, and bestows special fondness upon the English writers he read in his boyhood. The *fin-de-siècle* and Edwardian giants, whose reputations are generally etiolated, excite Borges afresh each time he rereads them. . . . (p. 173)

[Of] this generation none is dearer to Borges than Chesterton, in whom he finds, beneath the surface of dogmatic optimism, a disposition like Kafka's. . . . Much in Borges' fiction that suggests Kafka in fact derives from Chesterton. As critic and artist both, Borges

mediates between the post-modern present and the colorful, prolific, and neglected pre-moderns.

Of the moderns themselves, of Yeats, Eliot, and Rilke, of Proust and Joyce, he has, at least in *Other Inquisitions,* little to say. Pound and Eliot, he asserts in passing, practice "the deliberate manipulation of Anachronisms to produce an appearance of eternity" (which seems, if true at all, rather incidentally so), and he admires Valéry less for his work than for his personality, "the symbol of a man who is infinitely sensitive to every fact." The essays abound in insights delivered parenthetically—"God must not theologize"; "to fall in love is to create a religion that has a fallible god"—but their texts as a whole do not open outward into enlightenment. Whereas, say, Eliot's relatively tentative considerations offer to renew a continuing tradition of literary criticism. Borges' tight arrangements seem a bizarre specialization of the tradition. His essays have a quality I can only call *sealed.* They are structured like mazes and, like mirrors, they reflect back and forth on one another. There is frequent repetition of the adjectives and phrases that denote Borges' favorite notions of mystery, of secrecy, of "intimate ignorance." From his immense reading he has distilled a fervent narrowness. The same parables, the same quotations recur; one lengthy passage from Chesterton is reproduced three times. (pp. 174-75)

Turning from Borges' criticism to his fiction, one senses the liberation he must have felt upon entering "the paradise of the tale." For there is something disturbing as well as fascinating, something distorted and strained about his literary essays. His ideas border on delusions; the dark hints—of a cult of books, of a cabalistic unity hidden in history—that he so studiously develops are special to the corrupt light of libraries and might vanish outdoors. It is uncertain how seriously he intends his textual diagrams, which seem ciphers for concealed emotions. Borges crowds into the margins of others' books passion enough to fill blank pages; his essays all tend to open inward, disclosing an obsessed imagination and a proud, Stoic, almost cruelly masculine personality.

Dreamtigers, a collection of paragraphs, sketches, poems, and apocryphal quotations titled in Spanish *El Hacedor* (*The Maker*), succeeds in time the creative period of narrative fiction his essays foreshadow. It is frankly the miscellany of an aging man. (pp. 175-76)

One feels in *Dreamtigers* a calm, an intimation of truce, a tranquil fragility. Like so many last or near-last works—like *The Tempest, The Millionairess,* or "Investigations of a Dog"—*Dreamtigers* preserves the author's life-long concerns, but drained of urgency; horror has yielded to a resigned humorousness. These sketches can be read for their grace and wit but scarcely for narrative excitement; the most exciting of them, **"Ragnarök,"** embodies Borges' most terrible vision, of an imbecilic God or body of gods. But it occurs within a dream, and ends easily: "We drew our heavy revolvers—all at once there were revolvers in the dream—and joyously put the Gods to death."

The second half of this slim volume consists of poems, late and early. Poetry was where Borges' ramifying literary career originally took root. The translations, by Harold Morland, into roughly four-beat and intermittently rhymed lines, seem sturdy and clear, and occasional stanzas must approximate very closely the felicity of the original. . . . (p. 178)

Together, the prose and poetry of *Dreamtigers* afford some glimpses into Borges' major obscurities—his religious concerns and his affective life. Physical love, when it appears at all in his work, figures as something remote, like an ancient religion. . . . Though *Dreamtigers* contains two fine poems addressed to women—Susana Soca and Elvira de Alvear—they are eulogies couched in a tone of heroic affection not different from the affection with which he writes elsewhere of male friends like Alfonso Reyes and Macedonio Fernández. This is at the opposite pole from homosexuality; femaleness, far from being identified with, is felt as a local estrangement that blends with man's cosmic estrangement. There are two prose sketches that, by another writer, might have shown some erotic warmth, some surrender to femininity. In one, he writes of Julia, a "sombre girl" with "an unbending body," in whom he sensed "an intensity that was altogether foreign to the erotic." In their walks together, he must have talked about mirrors, for now (in 1931) he has learned that she is insane and has draped her mirrors because she imagines that his reflection has replaced her own. In the other, he writes of Delia Elena San Marco, from whom he parted one day beside "a river of vehicles and people." They did not meet again, and in a year she was dead. From the casualness of their unwitting farewell, he concludes, tentatively, that we are immortal. "For if souls do not die, it is right that we should not make much of saying goodbye."

It would be wrong to think that Borges dogmatically writes as an atheist. God is often invoked by him, not always in an ironical or pantheistic way. . . . While Christianity is not dead in Borges, it *sleeps* in him, and its dreams are fitful. His ethical allegiance is to pre-Christian heroism, to Stoicism, to "the doctrines of Zeno's Porch and . . . the sagas," to the harsh gaucho ethos celebrated in the Argentine folk poem of Martín Fierro. Borges is a pre-Christian whom the memory of Christianity suffuses with premonitions and dread. He is European in everything except the detachment with which he views European civilization, as something intrinsically strange—a heap of relics, a universe of books without a central clue. (pp. 180-81)

Perhaps Latin America, which has already given us the absolute skepticism of Machado de Assis, is destined to reënact the intellectual patterns of ancient Greece. Borges' voracious and vaguely idle learning, his ecumenic and problematical and unconsoling theology, his willingness to reconsider the most primitive philosophical questions, his tolerance of superstition in both himself and others, his gingerly and regretful acknowledgment of women and his disinterest in the psychological and social worlds that women dominate, his almost Oriental modesty, his final solitude, his serene pride—this constellation of Stoic attributes, mirrored in the southern hemisphere, appears inverted and frightful. (p. 182)

The great achievement of his art is his short stories. (p. 183)

"The Library of Babel," which appears in *Ficciones,* is wholly fantastic, yet refers to the librarian's experience of books. Anyone who has been in the stacks of a great library will recognize the emotional aura, the wearying impression of an inexhaustible and mechanically ordered chaos, that suffuses Borges' mythical universe, "composed of an indefinite, perhaps an infinite, number of hexagonal galleries, with enormous ventilation shafts in the middle, encircled by very low railings." Each hexagon contains twenty shelves, each shelf thirty-two books, each book four hundred and ten pages, each page forty lines, each line eighty letters. The arrangement of these letters is almost uniformly chaotic and formless. The nameless narrator of "The Library of Babel" sets forward, pedantically, the history of philosophical speculation by the human beings who inhabit this inflexible and inscrutable cosmos, which is equipped, apparently for their convenience, with spiral stairs, mirrors, toilets, and lamps ("The light they emit is insufficient, incessant").

This monstrous and comic model of the universe contains a full range of philosophical schools—idealism, mysticism, nihilism. . . . (p. 185)

Though the Library appears to be eternal, the men within it are not, and they have a history punctuated by certain discoveries and certain deductions now considered axiomatic. Five hundred years ago, in an upper hexagon, two pages of homogeneous lines were discovered that within a century were identified as "a Samoyed-Lithuanian dialect of Guaraní, with classical Arabic inflections" and translated. The contents of these two pages—"notions of combinational analysis"—led to the deduction that the Library is total; that is, its shelves contain all possible combinations of the orthographic symbols. . . . (p. 186)

The Library of Babel . . . has an adamant solidity. Built of mathematics and science, it will certainly survive the weary voice describing it, and outlast all its librarians, already decimated, we learn in a footnote, by "suicide and pulmonary diseases." We move, with Borges, beyond psychology, beyond the human, and confront, in his work, the world atomized and vacant. Perhaps not since Lucretius has a poet so definitely felt men as incidents in space.

What are we to make of him? The economy of his prose, the tact of his imagery, the courage of his thought are there to be admired and emulated. In resounding the note of the marvellous last struck in English by Wells and Chesterton, in permitting infinity to enter and distort his imagination, he has lifted fiction away from the flat earth where most of our novels and short stories still take place. Yet discouragingly large areas of truth seem excluded from his vision. Though the population of the Library somehow replenishes itself, and "fecal necessities" are provided for, neither food nor fornication is mentioned—and in truth they are not generally seen in libraries. I feel in Borges a curious implication: the unrealities of physical science and the senseless repetitions of history have made the world outside the library an uninhabitable vacuum. Literature—that European empire augmented with translations from remote kingdoms—is now the only world capable of housing and sustaining new literature. Is this too curious? Did not Eliot recommend forty years ago, in reviewing *Ulysses,* that new novels be retellings of old myths? Is not the greatest of modern novels, *Remembrance of Things Past,* about its own inspiration? Have not many books already been written from within Homer and the Bible? Did not Cervantes write from within Ariosto and Shakespeare from within Holinshed? Borges, by predilection and by program, carries these inklings toward a logical extreme: the view of books as, in sum, an alternate creation, vast, accessible, highly colored, rich in arcana, possibly sacred. Just as physical man, in his cities, has manufactured an environment whose scope and challenge and hostility eclipse that of the natural world, so literate man has heaped up a counterfeit universe capable of supporting life. Certainly the traditional novel as a transparent imitation of human circumstance has "a distracted or tired air." Ironic and blasphemous as Borges' hidden message may seem, the texture and method of his creations, though strictly inimitable, answer to a deep need in contemporary fiction—the need to confess the fact of artifice. (pp. 187-88)

John Updike, "The Author as Librarian," in his *Picked-Up Pieces,* Alfred A. Knopf, 1975, pp. 169-88.

JULIO CORTÁZAR
(essay date 1976)

[An Argentine novelist, short story writer, poet, essayist, and critic, Cortázar is considered a seminal figure of "The Boom," a surge of talented and innovative writers in Latin America during the 1950s and 1960s. Like Gabriel García Marquez and Borges, he often combined the fantastic with the realistic in his fiction. In the following excerpt, he examines Borges as a leading figure of twentieth-century Latin American letters.]

Suddenly, and without logical and convincing reasons, a culture produces in a few years a series of creators who spiritually fertilize each other, who emulate and challenge and surpass each other until, also suddenly, there enters a period of drying up or of mere prolongation through imitators and inferior successors.

That chance seems to have manifested itself in modest but clearly perceptible proportions in the cultural zone of the River Plate in a period that runs approximately from 1920 to the present. There, without too many premonitory signs, the dimension of the fantastic bursts forth in the principal works of Jorge Luis Borges. It erupts in Borges with a force so compelling that, seen from outside of the River Plate, it appears to concentrate itself almost exclusively in his works. We in Argentina, however, situate Borges's narrative within a context which contains important precursorial and contemporary figures. . . ; even before Borges the fantastic was already a familiar and important genre in our midst. (pp. 527-28)

In Jorge Luis Borges, the leading figure of our fantastic literature, misunderstandings accumulate, usually to his great delight. I will limit myself here to pointing out that what some literary critics admire above all in Borges is a genius of geometrical invention, a maker of literary crystals whose condensation responds to exact mathematical laws of logic. Borges has been the first to insist on that rigorous construction of things which tend to appear, on the surface, as absurd and aleatory. The fantastic, as it appears in Borges's stories, makes one think of a relentless geometrical theorem—a theorem perfectly capable of demonstrating that the sum of the square of the angles of a triangle equals the execution of Madame DuBarry. Stories such as **"The Circular Ruins," "The Garden of Forking Paths"** and **"The Library of Babel"** reflect this type of theorem construction, which would seem to hide a secret dread not only of what Lugones called strange forces, but also of the imagination's own powers, powers which in Borges are subjected immediately to a rigorous intellectual conditioning.

Nonetheless, others of us feel that despite this rational rejection of the fantastic in its most irreducible and incoherent manifestations, Borges's intuition and sensitivity attest to its presence in a good portion of his stories, where the intellectual superstructure does not manage to, nor does it probably want to, deny that presence. When Borges entitles a collection of stories *Ficciones* or *Artifices,* he is misleading us at the same time that he winks a conspiratorial eye at us; he is playing with that old ideal of every writer, the ideal of having at least some readers capable of suspecting a second version of each text. I will limit myself, of necessity, to one example which hits close to home. In his story **"The Secret Miracle"** Borges plays with the idea that in certain circumstances a man can enter into another dimension of time and live a year or a century during what other men live as a second or an hour. There is already a story based on this idea in a medieval Spanish text, *El Conde Lucanor,* and Borges himself uses as an epigraph to his story a fragment from the Koran which reflects the same concept. The theme is also dealt with in the psychology of oneiric life, which shows that certain dreams encompass multiple episodes that would demand considerable time to be carried out consecutively, and that, nonetheless, the complex plot of such dreams can end, for example, with a shot from a gun which abruptly awakens us and makes us realize that someone just knocked at the door. It is clear that the dream has been integrally constructed in order to lead to that supposed shot from a revolver, a fact which obliges one to admit that the dream's fulfillment has been almost instantaneous while the fact of dreaming it seemed to transpire over a long period of time. In other words, one could say that on certain occasions we slip into a different time, and those occasions can be, as is always the case with the fantastic, trivial and even absurd.

But Borges does not want things to be trivial and absurd, at least not in his stories, and **"The Secret Miracle"** is based once again on the rational and erudite crystallization of something which others grasp only in its unrefined state. The story relates that Jaromir Hladik, a Jewish writer condemned to death by the Nazis, awaits with anguish the day of his execution by firing squad. This man has written philosophical texts in which the notion of time is examined and discussed, and he has begun a play whose ending suggests that the work is circular, that it repeats itself interminably. On the eve of his execution Hladik asks God to grant him one more year of life in order to finish this play, which will justify his existence and assure his immortality. During the night he dreams that the time has been given to him, but the next morning he realizes that it was only a dream, since the soldiers come and take him to the firing squad. In the moment that the rifles take

aim at his chest Hladik continues to think about one of the characters in his play; and in that same moment the physical universe becomes immobile, the soldiers do not shoot, and the smoke of Hladik's last cigarette forms a small petrified cloud in the air. Only Hladik can know that the miracle has been fulfilled and that, without moving from his place, thinking it instead of writing it, he has been granted the year he had asked for to complete his play. During the course of this year Hladik creates and re-creates scenes, he changes the characters, he eliminates and adds on. Finally, he needs to find only one word, an epithet. He finds it, and the soldiers shoot. For them only an instant has passed.

This theme, which we also find in Ambrose Bierce's admirable story "An Occurrence at Owl Creek," is not, as Borges's story might pretend, simply a literary artifice. I have already noted the frequent presence of this theme in literature and in dreams, and I have even included it in a passage of my own story, "The Pursuer"; in my case, however, I have no reason to obscure the authenticity of my personal experience and to create of it an ingenious superstructure of fiction. In my story what happens is exactly the same as what has happened to me various times in analogous circumstances. (pp. 528-30)

I think that at this point you have an idea of our way of living and writing the fantastic in the River Plate area. . . . (p. 530)

Julio Cortázar, "The Present State of Fiction in Latin America," translated by Margery A. Safir, in *Books Abroad,* Vol. 50, No. 3, Summer, 1976, pp. 533-40.

JORGE LUIS BORGES WITH AMELIA BARILI

(interview date 1985)

[In the following excerpt from a November 1985 interview conducted by Amelia Barili, book review editor of the Buenos Aires newspaper *La Prensa,* Borges discusses the philosophical aspects of his fiction.]

I met Jorge Luis Borges in 1981, when I returned to Buenos Aires from a job at the BBC in London and began working for *La Prensa.* He received me very kindly, remembering that during the 1920's, when he was not well known, *La Prensa* had been the first newspaper to publish him. Later I returned to see him frequently. Sometimes he would dictate a poem that he had been composing during a long night of insomnia. After typing it, I would put it in his desk near his collection of Icelandic sagas, a precious gift from his father.

Sometimes we would walk to a nearby restaurant, where he would eat something very simple. Or we would go to a bookstore, searching for yet another book by Kipling or Conrad in an English edition for friends to read to him. People would stop to greet him, and he would jokingly tell me they must have mistaken him for someone else. His fame as a writer seemed to burden him, and he often regretted that he had to go on living so that Borges the writer could weave his literary fantasies.

One morning shortly before he left Argentina in November, we spoke about his recent work, his beliefs, his doubts. I did not know it would be our last conversation before his death in Geneva. We started by discussing one of his latest books, *Los Conjurados (The Conspirators)*, in which he calls Geneva "one of my homelands."

[Barili]: *Where does your love for Geneva come from?*

[Borges]: In a certain manner, I am Swiss; I spent my adolescence in Geneva. We went to Europe in 1914. We were so ignorant that we did not know that was the year of the First World War. We were trapped in Geneva. The rest of Europe was at war. From my Genevan adolescence I still have a very good friend, Dr. Simon Ishvinski. The Swiss are very reserved people. I had three friends: Simon Ishvinski, Slatkin, and Maurice Abramowicz, a poet who is now dead.

You remember him in **Los Conjurados.**

Yes. It was a beautiful night. Maria Kodama (Borges's secretary, traveling companion and, during his final weeks, wife), Maurice Abramowicz's widow and I were at a Greek tavern in Paris, listening to Greek music, which is so full of courage. I remembered the lyrics: "While this music lasts, we will deserve Helen of Troy's love. While the music lasts, we will know that Ulysses will come back to Ithaca." And I felt that Maurice was not dead, that he was there with us, that nobody really dies, for they all project their shadow.

In **Los Conjurados** *you also speak about one of your nightmares. Do some repeat themselves?*

Yes. I dream of a mirror. I see myself with a mask, or I see in the mirror somebody who is me but whom I do not recognize as myself. I arrive at a place, and I have the sense of being lost and that all is horrible. The place itself is like any other. It is a room, with furniture, and its appearance is not horrible. What is atrocious is the feeling, not the images. Another frequent nightmare is of being attacked by beings who are children; there are many of them, very little but strong. I try to defend myself, but the blows I give are weak.

In **Los Conjurados,** *as in all your work, there is a permanent search for meaning. What is the sense of life?*

If life's meaning were explained to us, we probably wouldn't understand it. To think that a man can

find it is absurd. We can live without understanding what the world is or who we are. The important things are the ethical instinct and the intellectual instinct, are they not? The intellectual instinct is the one that makes us search while knowing that we are never going to find the answer. I think Lessing said that if God were to declare that in His right hand He had the truth and in his left hand He had the investigation of the truth, Lessing would ask God to open His left hand—he would want God to give him the investigation of the truth, not the truth itself. Of course he would want that, because the investigation permits infinite hypotheses, and the truth is only one, and that does not suit the intellect, because the intellect needs curiosity. In the past, I tried to believe in a personal God, but I do not think I try anymore. I remember in that respect an admirable expression of Bernard Shaw: "God is in the making."

Even though you present yourself as a nonbeliever, there are in your works some references to mystical experiences that have always puzzled me. In the story **"The God's Script"** *you say: "From the tireless labyrinth of dreams I returned as if to my home, to the harsh prison. I blessed its dampness, I blessed its tiger, I blessed the crevice of light, I blessed my old, suffering body, I blessed the darkness and the stone. Then there occurred what I cannot forget nor communicate. There occurred the union with the divinity, with the universe." It seems that when you accept your circumstances and you bless them, then you come back to your center, and clarity dawns upon you. In the story* **"El Aleph"** *too, only when you accept your circumstances do you get to see the point where every act in the whole history of the cosmos comes together.*

This is true. It is the same idea. Since I do not think often about what I have written, I had not realized that. Nevertheless, it is better that it should be instinctive and not intellectual, don't you think? The instinctive is what counts in a story. What the writer wants to say is the least important thing; the most important is said through him or in spite of him.

Another idea that appears in many of your stories is that of the union of all creatures. In **"The God's Script"** *the pagan priest realizes that he is one of the threads of the whole fabric and that Pedro de Alvarado, who tortured him, is another one. In* **"The Theologians,"** *Aureliano and Juan de Panonia, his rival, are the same, and in* **"The End"** *Martin Fierro and El Negro have one and the same destiny.*

That is true. But I do not think about what I have already written; I think about what I am going to write—which is usually what I have already written, lightly disguised. Let's see. These days I am writing a short story about Segismund, one of the characters of *La Vida Es Sueño.* We will see how it turns out. I am going to read *La Vida Es Sueño* again, before writing the story. I thought of it some nights ago. I woke up; it was about 4 o'clock and I could not get back to sleep. I thought, let's use this sleeplessness. And suddenly I remembered that tragedy by Calderón, which I must have read 50 years ago, and I told myself, "There is a story here." It should resemble (but not too much) *La Vida Es Sueño*. To make that clear, it is going to be titled **"Monologue of Segismund."** Of course, it will be quite a different soliloquy than the one in that play. I think it is going to be a good story. I told it to Maria Kodama and she approved of it. It has been some time since I wrote a story. But that is the source of this one.

What is the source of "The God's Script"? When the priest says the fact that a prison surrounded him was not an obstacle to his finding the clue to the hidden language, I thought that was similar to what happened with you and your blindness.

I lost my sight some years later. But in a certain way there is a purification in the blindness. It purifies one of visual circumstances. Circumstances are lost, and the external world, which is always trying to grab us, becomes fainter. But **"The God's Script"** is autobiographical in another sense. I united there two experiences. Looking at the jaguar in the zoo, I thought the spots on the jaguar's skin seemed to be a writing; that is not true of the leopard's spots or the tiger's stripes. The other experience was the one I had when, after an operation, I was forced to lie on my back. I could only move my head to the right or left. Then I put together the idea that occurred to me, that the jaguar's spots suggest a secret writing, and the fact that I was virtually imprisoned. It would have been more appropriate to the story for the main character not to have been a priest from a barbarian religion but a Hindu or a Jew. However, the jaguar had to be placed in Latin America. That impelled me toward the pyramid and the Aztecs. The jaguar could not appear in other scenery. Although Victor Hugo describes the Roman circus and says that among the animals there are *"jaguars enlacés,"* that is impossible in Rome. Maybe he mistook leopards for jaguars, or maybe he did not mind that sort of mistake, just as Shakespeare didn't.

Like the kabbalists, you try to find in that story the sense of God's writing. You consider that the whole cosmos could be present in one word. How do you personally conceive the beginning of the universe?

I am naturally idealistic. Almost everyone, thinking about reality, thinks of space, and their cosmogonies start with space. I think about time. I think everything happens in time. I feel we could easily do without space but not without time. I have a poem called **"Cosmogony"** in which I say it is absurd to think the universe began with astronomical space, which presupposes, for example, sight, which came much later. It is more natural to think that in the beginning there was an emotion. Well, it is the same as saying, "In the beginning was the Word." It is a variation on the same theme.

Can we find a relationship among the various conceptions

about the origin of the universe among the Greeks, the Pythagoreans, the Jews?

Strangely enough, they all start with astronomical space. There is also the idea of the Spirit; that would come prior to space, of course. But in general they think of space. The Hebrews believe that the world was created from a word of God. But then that word should exist prior to the world. Saint Augustine gave the solution to that problem. Let's see, my Latin is poor, but I remember that phrase: *"non in tempore sed cum tempore Deus creavit . . . I* do not know what *. . . ordinem mundi."* That means, "Not in time but with time God created the world." To create the world is to create time. If not, people would ask, what did God do before creating the world? But with this explanation they are told that there was a first instant without a before. This is inconceivable, of course, because if I think of an instant I think of the time before that instant. But they tell us that, and we rest content with the inconceivable. An infinite time? A time with a beginning? Both ideas are impossible. To think that time began is impossible. And to think that it doesn't have a start, which means that we are going, in Shakespeare's words, to "the dark backward and abysm of time," is also not possible.

I would like to come back to the idea of the word as origin of the world. For example, in the Hebrew tradition there is a search through cryptographic and hermeneutic methods for that exact word.

Yes, that is the kabbala.

Not long ago Haaretz, a newspaper in Israel, reported that computer experiments on the Bible had discovered in Genesis a secret clue that had remained hidden up to then and that is too complicated to have been thought of by human beings. The letters that form the word "Torah" appear all through Genesis, one by one, in strict order, at regular intervals of 49 letters, perfectly integrated into the words that compose the text.

How strange that the computer would be applied to the kabbala! I did not know that they were making those experiments. It is beautiful, all that.

Is it necessary to prove that the Scriptures are the revealed word of God in order to believe in the existence of God, or is that something that is felt regardless of proofs?

I cannot believe in the existence of God, despite all the statistics in the world.

But you said you believed some time ago.

No, not in a personal God. To search for the truth, yes; but to think that there is somebody or something we call God, no. It is better that He should not exist; if He did he would be responsible for everything. And this world is often atrocious, besides being splendid. I feel more happy now than when I was young. I am looking forward. Even I don't know what forward is left, because at 86 years of age, there will be, no doubt, more past than future.

When you say you are looking forward, do you mean looking forward to continuing to create as a writer?

Yes. What else is left for me? Well, no. Friendship remains. Somehow, love remains—and the most precious gift, doubt.

If we did not think of God as a personal God but as concepts of truth and ethics, would you accept Him?

Yes, as ethics. There is a book by (Robert Louis) Stevenson in which we find the idea that a moral law exists even if we don't believe in God. I feel that we all know when we act well or badly. I feel ethics is beyond discussion. For example, I have acted badly many times, but when I do it, I know that it is wrong. It is not because of the consequences. In the long run, consequences even up, don't you think? It is the fact itself of doing good or doing bad. Stevenson said that in the same way a ruffian knows there are things he should not do, so a tiger or an ant knows there are things they should not do. The moral law pervades everything. Again the idea is "God is in the making."

What about truth?

I don't know. It would be very strange for us to be able to understand it. In one of my short stories I speak about that. I was rereading *The Divine Comedy*, and, as you will remember, in the first canto, Dante has two or three animals, and one of them is a leopard. The editor points out that a leopard was brought to Florence in Dante's time and that Dante, like any citizen of Flor-

ence, must have seen that leopard, and so he put a leopard into the first canto of the *Inferno*. In my story, **"Inferno, I, 32,"** I imagine that in a dream the leopard is told it has been created so Dante can see it and use it in his poem. The leopard understands that in the dream, but when he awakens, naturally, how could he understand that he exists only so a man could write a poem and use him in it? And I said that if the reason he wrote *The Divine Comedy* had been revealed to Dante, he could have understood it in a dream but not when he awoke. That reason would be as complex for Dante as the other one was for the leopard.

In "The Mirror of Enigmas," you say, quoting Thomas De Quincey, that everything is a secret mirror of something else. That idea of the search for a hidden sense is in all your work.

Yes, I think so. It is a very common human ambition—is it not?—to suppose everything has an explanation and to think we could understand it. Let's take as an example the various conceptions about the origin of the world, of which we spoke a while ago. I cannot imagine an infinite time, nor a beginning of time, so any reasoning about that is barren, since I can't conceive of it. I haven't arrived at anything. I am just a man of letters. I am not sure I have thought anything in my life. I am a weaver of dreams. (pp. 1, 27-9)

Jorge Luis Borges and Amelia Barili, in an interview in *The New York Times Book Review*, July 13, 1986, pp. 1, 27-9.

SOURCES FOR FURTHER STUDY

Barrenechea, Ana Maria. *Borges, the Labyrinth Maker.* Edited and translated by Robert Lima. New York: New York University Press, 1965, 175 p.

Examines the themes of chaos and entropy in Borges's work, focusing on his symbolic treatment of the universe as a labyrinth.

Bell-Villada, Gene. *Borges and His Fiction: A Guide to His Mind and Art.* Chapel Hill: University of North Carolina Press, 1981, 292 p.

Comprehensive study of Borges's work. The critic traces various themes, including those of violence and dreams, throughout Borges's collections of fiction.

Monegal, Emir Rodriguez. *Jorges Luis Borges: A Literary Biography.* New York: E. P. Dutton, 1978, 502 p.

Critical biography of Borges.

Sturrock, John. *Paper Tigers: The Ideal Fictions of Jorge Luis Borges.* Oxford: Clarendon Press, 1977, 227 p.

Analysis of the philosophical content and fantastical nature of Borges's stories. Sturrock argues that Borges's fiction is important because it stands apart from the "psychological" concerns of traditional character-oriented fiction.

Triquarterly 25: Prose for Borges (Fall 1972): 1-467.

Special issue dedicated to Borges. Includes an anthology of Borges's poetry and essays, critical essays by Borges scholars, a transcription of a Borges lecture, and a list of Borges's principal works.

Wheelock, Carter. *The Mythmaker: A Study of Motif and Symbol in the Short Stories of Jorge Luis Borges.* Austin: University of Texas Press, 1969, 190 p.

Critical analysis of symbolism in Borges's short fiction.

James Boswell

1740-1795

Scottish biographer, diarist, essayist, poet, and critic.

INTRODUCTION

*O*ne of the most colorful and widely read figures in eighteenth-century English literature, Boswell is esteemed for his inimitable conversational style and pictorial documentation of life in such nonfiction works as *Journal of a Tour to the Hebrides* (1785), *London Journal* (1950), and the masterpiece for which he has been labelled the greatest of English biographers: *The Life of Samuel Johnson* (1791). In this immensely readable and memorable work, Boswell firmly established biography as a leading literary form through a conscious, pioneering attempt to recreate his subject by combining life history with anecdote, observation, dialogue, theme, and plot. Its multifariousness reflects Boswell's several distinctive characteristics, which included an acute grasp of social setting and human nature, a rigid attention to realistic depiction, a hypochondriac's sensibility, and a compulsive need for public self-analysis and self-exposure. In addition to the *Life,* Boswell's staggering production of journals and letters, many undiscovered until recent years, heighten his reputation as an engagingly introspective writer, unique in vision and authorial voice.

Boswell was born into a prominent Edinburgh lawyer's family. His father eventually attained a position both on the bench of Scotland's highest court and in the peerage; taking the title Lord Auchinleck, he assumed the lordship of a large estate. This privileged social environment greatly aided Boswell's own progression to literary and social prominence. Following a brief, early education in a private school, Boswell was trained in classical literature through a personal tutor who introduced him to Joseph Addison's and Richard Steele's *Spectator* essays, the elevated prose style, moralistic bent, and Augustan wit of which markedly influenced the tenor and style of Boswell's mature writings. In 1753 Boswell enrolled in the general curriculum at the University of Edinburgh. By the end of his four years there he entertained thoughts of becoming a man of letters, his hopes fueled by advice from several eminent Scots, including philosopher David Hume. However, Boswell's father wished him to continue studies in preparation for a legal career; for a while, Boswell complied, matriculating at the University of Glasgow for nearly a year. By this time, despite being sickly and introverted as a child, Boswell had begun a significant physical and emotional self-transformation, in a short time attaining the characteristics by which he is popularly remembered: a plump, sanguine, and confident man of unflagging wit and charm. Along with this rapid transformation came a mounting antagonism between father and son, compounded by Boswell's intention to convert to the Roman Catholic Church (and thereby relinquish his right to hold professional office). Eventually, Boswell sought refuge with sympathetic Catholics in London in the spring of 1760. A London acquaintance of Lord Auchinleck learned of Boswell's presence and helped dissuade Boswell from the monastic life he was leaning toward.

The spirited Boswell, whose religious leanings were at this time still tenuous (and vacillated throughout his life), took to the gallant, rakish existence that the city of London fostered, consorting with numerous prostitutes to the frequent damage of his health. Mingling in both low and high circles and making the acquaintance of such literary celebrities as Laurence Sterne and David Garrick, Boswell became infatuated with his new life and surroundings. He subsequently asked his father if he could remain in London and seek a commission with the Foot Guards, a privileged military patrol. Determined to see his son through law training, Auchinleck left for London and returned to Scotland with Boswell, planning to reestablish the direction of his son's behavior, which he feared, if left unchecked, would severely disgrace the family name. For more than a year, Boswell remained in Scotland, spending much of his time completing law training under his father's tuition. Yet, unwilling to submit wholeheartedly to this involuntary isolation from London society and literary activity, Boswell attended dramatic performances in Edinburgh, kept a journal, and published his first works: pamphlets of dramatic criticism, poetry, and light satire. Recognized as ephemeral, generally tedious imitations of Sternian humor, the pamphlets drew little attention.

Appeasing his father, Boswell passed the Civil Law examination in 1762 and was allowed to return to London and pursue his ambition to join the Foot Guards. Yet, despite considerable inquiry, enlistment of support, and repeated requests of several high contacts, Boswell never obtained the post. This was undoubtedly due to the fact that substantial monies, which Auchinleck was unwilling to provide, were requi-

site for preferment. However, while pursuing this ambition, Boswell also popularized himself as a bright new man on the literary scene, making numerous social calls and acquiring several influential acquaintances. In 1763 he published his first work under his own name, *Letters between the Honourable Andrew Erskine, and James Boswell, Esq.,* a collection of actual correspondence between Boswell and a friend, both of whom hoped to impress the literati by dint of the extensive literary discussions found in the letters. This work, for its alternating insouciance and pertinent commentary on life and literature, received favorable reviews and sales.

From this point on, Boswell's aims became decidedly literary. For some time he had been endeavoring to meet one of his greatest idols, Samuel Johnson, who enjoyed august standing at the time as the author of *The Vanity of Human Wishes* (1749) and *A Dictionary of the English Language* (1755). After several failed attempts, Boswell met the aging scholar by accident in a bookseller's shop. Although their initial conversation was brief, and marred both by Johnson's gruff manner and by some inappropriate and ludicrous remarks from Boswell, the two soon became close and lasting friends. While set on a literary career, Boswell had reconsidered law as a field which would afford him added respectability. He took his leave of Johnson later that year to study civil law in Utrecht, Holland. There, while maintaining a rigorous schedule of study for several months, Boswell refined his journal-keeping techniques and produced a staggering amount of material. Unhappy and restless with his isolated situation, Boswell left Utrecht in 1764 and embarked on a two-year tour of Europe, corresponding with his London and Edinburgh acquaintances while recording in a journal his experiences, changing surroundings, and successful efforts to meet and intellectually engage such luminaries as Jean-Jacques Rousseau, Voltaire, and Pasquale Paoli, revolutionary leader of the Corsicans in their fight against the Genoese and the French for independence. During this tour it is believed that Boswell first realized the potential of one of his most unique talents, that of intimately identifying with others whom he met, regardless of their disparate personalities. After his stay with Voltaire he wrote: "I can tune myself so to the tune of any bearable man I am with that he is as much at freedom as with another self, and, till I am gone, cannot imagine me a stranger." Boswell brought to each relationship an intuitive sense of the other, including his or her habits, mannerisms, speech, and thoughts.

Returning to Edinburgh in 1766, Boswell gained admission to the Scottish bar and began a law practice. For the remainder of his life he often traveled on extended visits from Edinburgh to London, spending much of his time there in the company of Johnson and his literary coterie, The Club. Boswell's habit of recording Johnson's conversations on the spot became well known, as did his relentless, occasionally annoying, efforts to extract from Johnson opinions on virtually every imaginable topic. Boswell had become obsessed with accurately recording for posterity the Johnson he came to know so well; and Johnson, greatly valuing Boswell's friendship and vivacity, and also greatly aware of his own abilities as a conversationalist, allowed the unusual arrangement to continue. In 1768 Boswell's first major work appeared, *An Account of Corsica, The Journal of a Tour to that Island; and the Memoirs of Pascal Paoli.* Well received throughout Britain, it won especial praise from Johnson, who advised Boswell to continue exercising his talents in writing such works, for memoirs and biography, Johnson believed, were fields in which Boswell could excel. Boswell, in turn, concerned himself with Johnson's literary career, fearing that the often indolent older writer might grow infirm before publishing all that he was capable of. Partly for this reason, he planned a tour with Johnson in 1773 to the western islands of Scotland, the Hebrides, hoping that Johnson might publish an account of his trip there. This Johnson did, and it was Boswell's misfortune that his own account, in order not to compete with Johnson's, remained unpublished for over a decade. This greatly hampered the growth of his literary reputation since most of his published works, from the time of his admittance to the bar until Johnson's death, consisted of politically or legally oriented essays of little interest to the literary-minded public. The two major exceptions were *An Account of Corsica* and *The Hypochondriack,* the latter being a series of seventy monthly articles written in the *London Magazine* from 1777 to 1783 on a wide variety of subjects.

With the death of Johnson in 1784, Boswell's life grow dooidodly dicmal. Saddened and depressed by the loss of this friend who had grown to be a father-figure to him, and plagued by recurrent, agonizing bouts with gonorrhea, Boswell came to a single resolve: to complete *The Life of Samuel Johnson* before his death. Although his chief competitors, Hester Thrale and Sir John Hawkins, preceded him by several years in publishing their accounts, Boswell's completed *Life,* over which he labored with the aid of editor Edmond Malone, immediately superseded all such accounts in scope and compelling narration when it appeared in 1791. A corrected and expanded edition of the *Life,* overseen by Boswell and Malone, was published in 1793. Boswell died of acute urinary tract infection two years later.

In his preface to the *Life* Boswell wrote that his biography was intended to be an expansion of the procedure employed by William Mason in his 1775 "Memoirs" of Thomas Gray. In this work, Mason narrated his subject's life largely through quotation from Gray's letters. Improving upon this, Boswell employed, in addition, liberal use of first-hand accounts by Johnson's friends and of Johnson's own conversation, along with an introspective narrative voice and a fictionlike structure consisting of vivid scenes linked by such universal concerns as love, fear, morality, and contemplation of the afterlife. Perceived as scrupulously accurate in detail and comprehensiveness, and considered incomparably lively in portaiture, style, and narration, the *Life* was hailed as the highest achievement in English biography. Not until Thomas Babington Macaulay's reappraisal of the work in 1831 did Boswell's artistic abilities seriously come under question. Although Macaulay conceded the work's merit, he belittled Boswell, labelling him a "fool" and charging that his *Life* was far more a bizarre accident than an intelligently executed masterpiece. Most nineteenth- and twentieth-century scholars have refuted Macaulay's charges, but though they have come to consider the *Life* of great literary merit, many are still uncertain of how best to categorize and examine it; it has been studied not only as biography but as drama, tragiromantic narrative, and psychological autobiography. In addition, some have questioned the authenticity of several passages in the *Life,* particularly the numerous lengthy speeches uttered by Johnson; for it is known that as often as Boswell dictated Johnson's words verbatim he also wrote brief jottings which he would, perhaps days or weeks later, expand into fullscale dialogue and scene. Furthermore, it has been noted that Boswell himself occupies such an extensive portion of the *Life* that the work appears as much autobiography as biography. Indeed, some critics, notably Percy Fitzgerald, have asserted that Boswell's achievement cannot be praised since his motivations were supremely egocentric, his practices underhanded, and the outcome responsible for a gross misrepresentation of Johnson. Although a final consensus on this issue has not been reached, it is generally believed that the portrait of Johnson is largely accurate and, more importantly, is one that endures for its brilliant evocation of the man and his time.

The world's foremost Boswellian scholar, Frederick A. Pottle, has written of Boswell: "All his significant books—*The Journal of A Tour to Corsica, The Journal of a Tour to the Hebrides,* and the *Life of Johnson*—were quarried out of his journal. Though the *Life* will probably always be considered his greatest artistic achievement, critics and historians will come to see that his central, his unique performance lies in the private record of which he published only samples. It is a rare kind of journal in that it is consistently dramatic." Through twentieth-century discoveries of these papers at Malahide Castle, Ireland, and Fettercairne House, Scotland, and gradual publication thereof, Boswell's reputation as a journal writer continues to rise. In these private papers Boswell's complex personality—idol seeking, spiritually searching, hypersexual, hypochondriac, exuberant—fully emerges, captivating the reader, according to critics, through its self-analyses and almost incredible life story, narrated with a sure conception of scene, character, and motive.

(For further information about Boswell's life and works, see *Dictionary of Literary Biography*, Vol. 104: *British Prose Writers, 1660-1800* and *Literature Criticism from 1400 to 1800*, Vol. 4)

CRITICAL COMMENTARY

THOMAS BABINGTON MACAULAY

(essay date 1831)

[Macaulay was a distinguished English historian, essayist, and politician. In the following excerpt from an 1831 essay that sparked defiant rebuttals for more than a century, he praises *The Life of Samuel Johnson* but disparages Boswell's literary talents and personal traits.]

The *Life of Johnson* is assuredly a great, a very great work. Homer is not more decidely the first of heroic poets. Shakespeare is not more decidely the first of dramatists, Demosthenes is not more decidely the first of orators, than Boswell is the first of biographers. He has no second. He has distanced all his competitors so decidely that it is not worth while to place them. Eclipse is first, and the rest nowhere.

We are not sure that there is in the whole history of the human intellect so strange a phenomenon as this book. Many of the greatest men that ever lived have written biography. Boswell was one of the smallest men that ever lived, and he has beaten them all. He was, if we are to give any credit to his own account or to the untied testimony of all who knew, him, a man of the meanest and feeblest intellect. Johnson described him as a fellow who had missed his only chance of immortality by not having been alive when the *Dunciad* was written. Beauclerk used his name as a proverbial expression for a bore. He was the laughing-stock of the whole of that brilliant society which has owed to him the greater part of its fame. He was always laying himself at the feet of some eminent man, and begging to be spit upon and trampled upon. . . . All the caprices of his temper, all the illusions of his vanity, all his hypochondriac whimsies, all his castles in the air, he displayed with a cool self-complacency, a perfect unconsciousness that he was making a fool of himself, to which it is impossible to find a parallel in the whole history of mankind. He has used many people ill; but assuredly he has used nobody so ill as himself.

That such a man should have written one of the best books in the world is strange enough. But this is not all. Many persons who have conducted themselves foolishly in active life, and whose conversation has indicated no superior powers of mind, have left us valuable works. Goldsmith was very justly described by one of his contemporaries as an inspired idiot, and by another as a being

Who wrote like an angel, and talked like poor Poll.

La Fontaine was in society a mere simpleton. His blunders would not come in amiss among the stories of Hierocles. But these men attained literary eminence in spite of their weaknesses. Boswell attained it by reason of his weaknesses. If he had not been a great fool, he would never have been a great writer. Without all the qualities which made him the jest and the torment of those among whom he lived, without the officiousness, the inquisitiveness, the effrontery, the toad-eating, the insensibility to all reproof, he never could have produced so excellent a book. He was a slave, proud of his servitude, a Paul Pry, convinced that his own curiosity and garrulity were virtues, an unsafe companion who never scrupled to repay the most liberal hospitality by the basest violation of confidence, a man without delicacy, without shame, without sense enough to know when he was hurting the feelings of others or when he was exposing himself to derision; and because he was all this, he has, in an important department of literature, immeasurably surpassed such writers as Tacitus, Clarendon, Alfieri, and his own idol Johnson.

Of the talents which ordinarily raise men to eminence as writers, Boswell had absolutely none. There is not in all his books a single remark of his own on literature, politics, religion, or society, which is not either commonplace or absurd. His dissertations on heredi-

Principal Works

Observations, Good or Bad, Stupid or Clever, Serious or Jocund on Squire Foote's Dramatic Entertainment, entitled, The Minor. By a Genius. (criticism) 1760

A View of the Edinburgh Theatre during the Summer Season, 1759, by a Society of Gentleman (criticism) 1760

Letters between The Honourable Andrew Erskine, and James Boswell, Esq. (letters) 1763

Dorando, A Spanish Tale (prose allegory) 1767

An Account of Corsica, The Journal of a Tour to that Island; and the Memoirs of Pascal Paoli (journal and biography) 1768

Journal of a Tour to the Hebrides with Samuel Johnson, LL.D. (journal) 1785

The Life of Samuel Johnson, LL.D. Comprehending an Account of His Studies and Numerous Works in Chronological Order . . . the Whole Exhibiting a View of Literature and Literary Men in Great Britain for Near Half a Century during Which He Flourished. 2 vols. (journal and biography) 1791; also published as Boswell's Life of Johnson, 1848 [Boswell's Johnson (abridged edition), 1903]

No Abolition of Slavery; or, The Universal Empire of Love (poetry) 1791

Letters of James Boswell. 2 vols. (letters) 1924

The Hypochondriack. 2 vols. (essays) 1928

*The Yale Editions of the Private Papers of James Boswell (journals) 1950-

Boswell's Book of Bad Verse (A Verse Self-Portrait); or, "Love Poems and Other Verses by James Boswell" (poetry) 1974

*This is an ongoing, multivolume series. Boswell's London Journal, 1762-1763 is the first and most critically prominent volume.

---

tary gentility, on the slave-trade, and on the entailing of landed estates, may serve as examples. To say that these passages are sophistical would be to pay them an extravagant compliment. They have no pretence to argument, or even to meaning. He has reported innumerable observations made by himself in the course of conversation. Of those observations we do not remember one which is above the intellectual capacity of a boy of fifteen. He has printed many of his own letters, and in these letters he is always ranting or twaddling. Logic, eloquence, wit, taste, all those things which are generally considered as making a book valuable, were utterly wanting to him. He had, indeed, a quick observation and a retentive memory. These qualities, if he had been a man of sense and virtue, would scarcely of themselves have sufficed to make him conspicuous; but because he was a dunce, a parasite, and a coxcomb, they have made him immortal.

Those parts of his book which, considered abstractedly, are most utterly worthless, are delightful when we read them as illustrations of the character of the writer. Bad in themselves, they are good dramatically, like the nonsense of Justice Shallow, the clipped English of Dr. Caius, or the misplaced consonants of Fluellen. Of all confessors, Boswell is the most candid. Other men who have pretended to lay open their own hearts, Rousseau, for example, and Lord Byron, have evidently written with a constant view to effect, and are to be then most distrusted when they seem to be most sincere. There is scarcely any man who would not rather accuse himself of great crimes and of dark and tempestuous passions than proclaim all his little vanities and wild fancies. It would be easier to find a person who would avow actions like those of Caesar Borgia or Danton, than one who would publish a day dream like those of Alnaschar and Malvolio. Those weaknesses which most men keep covered up in the most secret places of the mind, not to be disclosed to the eye of friendship or of love, were precisely the weaknesses which Boswell paraded before all the world. He was perfectly frank, because the weakness of his understanding and the tumult of his spirits prevented him from knowing when he made himself ridiculous. His book resembles nothing so much as the conversation of the inmates of the Palace of Truth.

His fame is great; and it will, we have no doubt be lasting; but it is fame of a peculiar kind, and indeed marvellously resembles infamy. We remember no other case in which the world has made so great a distinction between a book and its author. In general, the book and the author are considered as one. To admire the book is to admire the author. The case of Boswell is an exception, we think the only exception, to this rule. His work is universally allowed to be interesting, instructive, eminently original: yet it has brought him nothing but contempt. All the world reads it, all the world delights in it: yet we do not remember ever to have read or ever to have heard any expression of respect and admiration for the man to whom we owe so much instruction and amusement. (pp. 284-89)

An ill-natured man Boswell certainly was not. Yet the malignity of the most malignant satirist could scarcely cut deeper than his thoughtless loquacity. Having himself no sensibility to derision and contempt, he took it for granted that all others were equally callous. He was not ashamed to exhibit himself to the whole world as a common spy, a common tattler, a humble companion without the excuse of poverty, and to tell a hundred stories of his own pertness and folly, and of the insults which his pertness and folly brought upon him. . . . The best proof that Johnson was really an extraordinary man is that his character, instead of being degraded, has, on the whole, been decidedly raised by a work in which all his vices and weaknesses are exposed more unsparingly than they ever were exposed by Churchill or by Kenrick. (pp. 289-90)

Thomas Babington Macaulay, "Boswell's 'Life of Johnson'," in *A Selection from the Best English Essays Illustrative of the History of English Prose Style,* edited by Sherwin Cody, A. C. McClurg & Company, 1903, pp. 284-321.

CHAUNCEY BREWSTER TINKER
(essay date 1922)

[A distinguished American scholar, Tinker helped build Yale University's superlative collection of material by and concerning Boswell and Samuel Johnson. He is particularly remembered for his collected *Letters of James Boswell* (1924) and for his popular biography *Young Boswell* (1922). In the following excerpt from the latter work, he praises *Tour to the Hebrides* as Boswell's highest accomplishment.]

[Boswell] knew his journals as a musician knows his score, or a lover his mistress. When he was engaged in reading the proof-sheets of the [*Life of Johnson*], he altered a statement that he had set down about the conversation of Edmund Burke. In the proofs Johnson is quoted as remarking, "His vigour of mind is incessant"; but Boswell has corrected this to read, "His stream of mind is perpetual"; and adds (as an explanation to the proof-reader): "I restore. I find the exact words as to Burke." What happened is, I think, clear. Boswell had lost the original record, and had reconstructed the remark about Burke from memory, using such words as he imagined Johnson to have employed; but, in the course of his labours on the proofs, he discovered the original entry in some one of his numerous note-books.

In view of this meticulous carefulness, it is not surprising that he boasted of the "scrupulous fidelity" of his journal. He knew the value of what he was doing. He knew that his journals were, even in their undeveloped form, very near to the level of literature. In his Commonplace Book he records, *à propos* of nothing, the following sentence: "My journal is ready; it is in the larder, only to be sent to the kitchen, or perhaps trussed and larded a little." He had no intention of wasting the contents of his larder. He had proved the value of his wares, while still a young man, with his *Account of Corsica.* The portion of the book which had been praised by everyone was the journal of his personal ex-

periences and conversations with Paoli, the part which is commonly referred to by the separate title of the *Tour to Corsica.* He had found his vein of genius. It ran in the direction of personal reminiscence, not in the direction of history. He had kept records of all his experiences on the Continent, and had planned some time or other to publish them, including the conversations which he had held there with the Great.

This plan was never realised; but a more remarkable experience than any which had befallen him upon the Continent awaited him in his own country. In August, 1773, his long-cherished plan of visiting the Highlands and the Hebrides in company with Dr. Johnson was carried out. They left Edinburgh on the eighteenth of the month, consumed almost two months and a half in travel, and arrived at Auchinleck, on their return, on the second day of November. Throughout this trip Boswell employed all his ingenuity and brought into play all the varied influence which the son of Lord Auchinleck could exert in Scotland, in order to give the Great Lexicographer a good time. Their journey was a royal progress, save that they were spared that boredom which royalty must endure. Their trip was thorough and complete, and they returned without any vain regrets. They had seen everything worth seeing, and had met everybody worth meeting. They had had a great deal of pure fun, and acquired a store of information. And Johnson owed all this to Boswell. Perhaps no man ever exerted himself more continuously or ingeniously to pleasure a friend on his travels. Boswell's hope was that Johnson would write a book about it. Of course, he himself kept a journal of everything they had seen and everything Johnson had said. (pp. 204-07)

When it was known that Johnson was to visit Scotland, his friends were convulsed with mirth. It was as if an anti-Semite were to propose to go and disport himself in Jewry. There was no doubt that the public would buy and read any book on Scotland which he might publish. Boswell knew both his country and his friend too well to fear that any real injustice would be done to a great and good people. His apprehension was of a quite different kind. He feared that Johnson might never bring himself to write the book. (pp. 207-08)

When the book [*Journey to the Western Islands of Scotland*] appeared, Boswell at once wrote to Johnson in its praise: "The more I read your *Journey,* the more satisfaction I receive. . . . I can hardly conceive how, in so short a time, you acquired the knowledge of so many particulars." And yet that knowledge was not perfect. A native Scot, with a keen eye and a well-stored journal of his own, could detect in the book a multitude of minor errors, and, what was more important, a number of lost opportunities to entertain the general reader. He, therefore, with a *naïveté* characteristic of him, as if the mere truth were the only matter to be considered, sat down and wrote out a series of "Remarks on the Journey to the Western Islands of Scotland," in which he not only pointed out errors, but made suggestions here and there respecting the improvement of the fiction. (pp. 210-11)

Of the reception of this document by the Sage we have no account, but it may safely be left to the reader's imagination. Boswell ultimately went so far as to propose to publish a sort of supplement to the *Journey;* but, after his trip to London in the spring of 1775, this amazing plan was, happily, dropped. In May he wrote to Temple:—

I have not written out another line of my "Remarks on the Hebrides." I found it impossible to do it in London. Besides, Dr. Johnson does not seem very desirous that I should publish any supplement. Between ourselves, he is not apt to encourage one to *share* reputation with himself. But don't you think I may write out my remarks in Scotland, and send them to be revised by you, and then they may be published freely?

Such was the origin of the *Journal of a Tour to the Hebrides with Samuel Johnson, LL.D.,* perhaps the sprightliest book of travels in the language. A decade was to elapse, and Johnson to pass away, ere the publication of the book; but Boswell had his reward for fulfilling the Horatian principle of delay. The lapse of time enabled him to publish, not a supplement to Johnson's book, but an independent volume, in which he was not to "share" Johnson's fame as a writer of travels, but totally to eclipse it. Moreover, the death of his eminent companion enabled him to cast all restraint aside and to print, as literally as he chose to do, the diary which he had kept during the tour. Of this diary and of the *Tour to the Hebrides* he speaks in identical terms. Once only (under date of September 4) does he speak of suppressing material in the diary.

This diary had, as it were, the approval—though by no means the *imprimatur*—of Samuel Johnson. He was well acquainted with Boswell's journal-keeping habits, and had often seen him at work upon it. After reading it, he made the remark that it was a very exact picture of a portion of his life. We have Boswell's word for it that Johnson was also aware of his intention to produce a biography of him. And yet to assert all this is not to say that Johnson ever conceived of the possibility of Boswell's printing the journal as it stood. Print the journal! He would as soon have permitted Reynolds to paint him in a state of nature.

When, in 1785, the *Tour* appeared, Johnson had been in his grave nearly a twelvemonth; but though he was not alive, to protest in person, his friends protested for him. Nothing like it had ever been read. It became at once a standard of indiscretion. To compare it with the autobiographical revelations made, in our own day, by the wife of a former Prime Minister of Great Britain

would be to adduce but a feeble parallel. Boswell calmly recorded Johnson's casual remarks about everybody he had met. (pp. 212-14)

One page, in particular, roused the dismay of everyone who had known Johnson. This was the sheet of advertisement at the end, in which Boswell announced to the public that he was at work upon a biography of Johnson, that he had been collecting materials for twenty years, and that the book would include "several curious particulars," as well as "the most authentick accounts that can be obtained from those who knew him best."

Johnson's acquaintances were seized with alarm. What would be their fate in the new book? If Boswell had created so great a disturbance in Scotland by his account of three months in Johnson's life, what would be the result in England when he published a history of the whole seventy-five years of it? (pp. 216-17)

One of his best friends, Sir William Forbes, who was later to be appointed one of his literary executors, took umbrage at the fact that Boswell had quoted his approval of the journal, before it was in print, and took the liberty of "strongly enjoining him" to be more careful about personalities in the later work.

But Boswell was not dismayed. He had the solid satisfaction of seeing two large editions of the *Tour* devoured by the eager public. He might, indeed, have gone too far in certain instances. He answered his critics, in the second edition, by charging them with a failure to understand the true motive of his recording anecdotes which were sometimes to his own disadvantage, the objections to which he saw as clearly as did they. "But it would be an endless task," he continued, "for an authour to point out upon every occasion the precise object he has in view. Contenting himself with the approbation of readers of discernment and taste, he ought not to complain that some are found who cannot or will not understand him."

It may be doubted whether such attacks as Boswell suffered ever really injure a book. The indiscretions which shocked the nerves of the eighteenth century have lost something of their tang in the passage of the years; but the naïve charm of the book remains. More than any work of Boswell's it preserves the freshness and authenticity of his journals. If one of the objects of literature be to mirror human association and companionship when at their fullest and most zestful, then this book must ever be accorded a very high rank. It has a unity and an intimacy denied even to the great *Life of Johnson;* for the geographical isolation of the Hebrides, and the limitation of the account to a single period in the life of the man recorded, render it, if possible, a more vivid book than the biography, which is, inevitably, more diffuse. Moreover, it has the advantage of depicting Johnson in an unusual environment, likely to stimulate his powers of observation and lend point and colour to his remarks. It tells the story of a long holiday; and it has, therefore, the mirth and abandon of spirit characteristic of two friends whose chief aim, at the moment, is to have a good time. All that is most likable in Boswell appears, and all that is depressing—his melancholy, for instance—takes flight from its cheerful pages. It is the happiest of books, and it has lost none of its original power of rendering its readers happy, too. (pp. 217-19)

Chauncey Brewster Tinker, in his *Young Boswell,* The Atlantic Monthly Press, 1922, 266 p.

FREDERICK A. POTTLE
(essay date 1966)

[Pottle is recognized as one of the foremost authorities on Boswell's life and literary career. In the following excerpt, he surveys the author's early writings.]

If one is to get a proper conception of Boswell, it is necessary to have some idea of the bulk and variety of [his] early writing and of the gestures which accompanied the publication of that portion of it that got into print. He was not (as is too often assumed) a man who turned author at the age of fifty and wrote a single book, *The Life of Samuel Johnson.* On the contrary, he commenced author in his teens, and was an old hand at publishing before he ever met Johnson. Like most authors, he began with verse. His juvenile poems (still largely unpublished) are voluminous and of considerable interest to his biographer and the editors of his papers, but they contain no pieces worthy of salvaging as wholes for intrinsic poetic merit; indeed, one can pick few happy phrases or fine single lines out of them. Since Boswell obviously had a literary gift, and, first and last, wrote a great deal in metre, the almost complete lack of distinction in his verse must seem puzzling. He had a fine ear in music (perhaps not the same thing as a fine ear in verse) and a good sense of rhythm, and when he wrote without self-consciousness—that is, in familiar prose—he constantly displayed a power of original, apt, and striking metaphor. It was he, for example, who said that Christopher Smart had "shivers of genius here and there." But except for lively songs, which he sometimes turned quite neatly, and the scurrilous **"Ode by Dr. Samuel Johnson to Mrs. Thrale upon their supposed approaching Nuptials,"** his accomplishment in verse is simply nil. The things that were really his own, the things he really wanted to say, could not be said effectively in any of the contemporary modes of verse, or, for that matter, in verse at all.

The easiness of expression which he correctly asserted to be in his power was a conversational ease that could not survive the artificialities of rhyme and metre. When he attempted verse, he had to affect a manner, and it made him artificial all the way through. He parroted, he was content with clichés. His announced preference in metaphor was for the gaudy, the overblown, the over-explicit. His poems are mere husks, coarse and empty.

One can go even farther. He was not merely limited to prose; even within prose he was limited in the ways in which he could give his talent expression fully and with integrity. He was poles removed from, let us say, Oliver Goldsmith, who could write with distinction in any of the favoured contemporary modes: poetry, the drama, the essay, the novel. Goldsmith cribbed shamelessly from other authors and made a good deal of use of autobiography. But he reshaped imaginatively what he stole and he turned autobiography into fiction. Boswell was tied to matter of fact. He could never have written a good serious poem, nor a good play, nor a good novel. He had not yet found out what it was that he *could* write. But, being possessed of literary genius, he had to write; and as poetry was the most esteemed of literary modes, he wrote poems.

It was so far a good sign that his taste in verse was up-to-date and his models contemporary. He had read with deep enjoyment most of Shakespeare and Milton and Dryden and Pope, and could quote many lines from all four, but the poets he imitated in serious verse were Thomson and Young and Shenstone and Gray and Mason. . . . The first of his extended efforts, **"October, a Poem,"** is a close and avowed imitation of Thomson. The first of his pieces to be printed, so far as any one knows, was composed in May 1758, when he was still five months short of attaining his eighteenth birthday, and was published in *The Scots Magazine* for August of that year. It is unsigned, runs to about fifty lines, is a meditation on a text from Shakespeare, and is in the style of Young's *Night Thoughts.* The title is **"An Evening Walk in the Abbey-Church of Holyroodhouse."** The opening lines may be taken as a better-than-average example of Boswell's serious verse:

Now let imagination form a time
    When creeping murmur and the poring dark
    Fills the wide vessel of the universe.

SHAKESPEARE

Such is the present time, now sober Eve
    Has drawn her sable curtain o'er the earth
    And hush'd the busy world to soft repose.
    Come then, my soul, compose each faculty,
    And bid thy restless passions be at peace.
                                    (pp. 58-60)

His first separate publications were in prose. The earliest that has been traced was . . . *A View of the Edinburgh Theatre during the Summer Season,*

1759. . . . Although a trifle, it is no disgraceful trifle for a boy of nineteen to have written. Apart from an obvious and amusing partiality for Mrs. Cowper, it seems to give just and intelligent critiques of the various performances. The literary judgements expressed are respectable and show a considerable range of reading, not only in the drama itself, but also in books of dramatic theory. What is most interesting, the author shows that he has thought seriously about the problem of dramatic impersonation.

The verse that he wrote in London in 1760 was, as one would have expected, of a frivolous and libertine cast. One of these pieces, *The Cub at Newmarket,* has hitherto been accorded an unduly prominent place in the story of his early years because it has always been known to be his, whereas much of his other early work remained unrecognized or unstudied until fairly recently. Actually a much less interesting piece than the unpublished epistle to Sterne, the *Cub* is an extreme example of his lifelong strategy of lying down of his own accord to avoid being thrown down. (p. 61)

The willingness of publishers to take the risk of Boswell's juvenile pamphlets is testimony to a considerable journalistic knack on his part, as his next separate publication illustrates. Shortly after he returned to Edinburgh, Samuel Foote opened his season at the Little Theatre in the Haymarket, London, with his own comedy, *The Minor,* a boisterous satire on the Methodists and especially on George Whitefield. The piece made a great stir, ran thirty-five nights, and got talked and written about more than any work that appeared that year except *Tristram Shandy.* Boswell had not seen *The Minor* presented and in his heart disapproved of the tendency of the work, but he could not resist an opportunity to float something on the tides of controversy. *Observations, Good or Bad, Stupid or Clever, Serious or Jocular, on Squire Foote's Dramatic Entertainment intitled "The Minor," by a Genius,* a pamphlet which he later called "an idle performance, and written inconsiderately," appeared in Edinburgh in November 1760, and had enough success to induce Wilkie, a London publisher, to order a reprint. The *Observations,* though judicious, are in no way remarkable, but the pseudonym and the envelope of bantering conversation which surrounds them are of interest to a biographer. In the pseudonym "A Genius" Boswell first displays to the public the façade of impudence and self-conscious vanity with which he will henceforth screen the uncompleted structure of his breeding. The enveloping conversation illustrates the abjectness of his addiction at this time to Shandyism and reveals a fact of prime importance about Boswell himself:

Bless my soul!—are you a mimic, *Mr. Genius?*—Am I a mimic? ay, and a good one too, let me tell you.—I never was with a man in my life, who had got any-

thing odd about him, but I could take him off in a trice.

This is Boswell's first reference to mimicry, an art which he was now practising assiduously and with enormous gusto. He was indeed a remarkable mimic; and there can be no doubt that the famous ability to reconstruct conversations from memory which he was now beginning to demonstrate was partly due to his skill in taking people off. He could stimulate the recall of words he had heard spoken by assuming the facial expression, gestures, and tone of voice of the speakers; and he could verify his reconstructions by trying them out on his muscles and viscera as well as in his brain. Foote (whom he had certainly seen in Edinburgh) probably incited him to mimicry, but he could not have learned from Foote how to express in words what the mimic gives directly by gesture. He must, I think, have been roused by Richardson, whose pervasive attention to minutely described gesture was something new in English fiction, but he no doubt learned more from Sterne, whose brilliant use of the isolated characteristic gesture, described with unparalleled verbal economy, makes Richardson seem over-emphatic and stagy. From the biographical point of view, *Observations on "The Minor"* might well have been entitled *Homage to Two Masters.* (pp. 62-4)

Early in August [of 1761] there appeared with Alexander Donaldson's imprint a pamphlet containing two short poems: **"An Elegy on the Death of an Amiable Young Lady"** and **"An Epistle from Lycidas to Menalcas."** The book is a queer affair altogether. The greater part of it—fourteen pages out of a total of twenty-four—is taken up by three "critical recommendatory letters" signed G. D., A. E., and J. B. We learn from an Advertisement that the poems had been submitted to Donaldson for inclusion in the forthcoming second volume of his miscellany, but had been found by G. D., A. E., and J. B. to be of such remarkable excellence that the author had been prevailed upon to publish them separately—accompanied by the letters. Actually, the letters are burlesques of the broadest sort, ridiculing by extravagant and ironic praise the style, diction, and even the spelling of the hapless poems. J. B.'s recommendatory letter is just as quizzing and ironic as the other two. But following J. B.'s recommendatory letter is another, a letter from the author of the poems submitting them to Donaldson. It is brief, completely serious, and is signed J. B.

Both poems were undoubtedly written with no thought of burlesque. The **"Elegy"** is a feeble piece on a trite subject and shocked Birkbeck Hill by recurring lapses into Scots grammar ("thou lies" instead of "thou liest"), but it was not meant to be funny. Nor was the **"Epistle,"** though a modern reader is bound to grin when he finds Boswell in it apostrophizing a visioned fair one by the name of Ammonia. (In 1761 Ammonia was merely a classical female name; the chemical term was not invented until twenty years later.) Boswell, in short, in the device of the commendatory letters is giving another instance of his willingness to anticipate hostile criticism by writing himself down. He is not sure whether he prefers to be known as a serious poet or as a heedless rattling fellow who might say or do every ridiculous thing, so he aims at both. If any one likes the poems, good; the letters are merely a gesture of modesty; if any one calls the poems execrable, he can point out that he has laughed at them himself. He is willing to copy any style that is popular, no matter how meretricious, and to call attention to his works by any device, no matter how undignified. (Shelley, whom I have already advanced as a parallel, did much the same thing with his *Posthumous Fragments of Margaret Nicholson.*) (pp. 65-6)

Early in December 1761, another pamphlet with Donaldson's imprint made its appearance: an *Ode to Tragedy,* by a Gentleman of Scotland, *dedicated* to James Boswell, Esq. The dedication is a more elaborate version of the gimmick used in **"An Elegy on the Death of an Amiable Young Lady."** With those who merely read the advertisements of the piece in the newspapers, or who saw the book lying about but did not read it, he would at least get the reputation of being a patron of literature. The careless and uninitiated could even read the dedication and be taken in by it. Those with any degree of literary sophistication would realize at once that he was dedicating to himself. Critics of this last group who thought the *Ode* execrable might still concede that the author was quite a card.

The *Ode to Tragedy,* the most ambitious effort in verse that Boswell ever published, consists of sixteen regular ten-line stanzas. . . . It provides a more ecstatic statement than any to be found in Boswell's prose of the delight he took in serious plays, and is of some slight interest to the historian of drama as a document in an acrimonious literary controversy then going on between "regular" poets like Mason and the spectacular newcomer Charles Churchill. As verse, however, it is quite dead and had better be left unquoted. (p. 68)

All through the autumn of 1761 the second volume of Donaldson's [anthology *A Collection of Original Poems by Scotch Gentlemen*] had been going forward; Boswell and [Andrew] Erskine wrote new pieces for it and furbished old ones. When Erskine was called back to his regiment, Boswell took over the task of correcting the proofs—a task which Erskine said he bungled. Donaldson ran out of copy before the volume was as thick as he thought it should be, and Boswell provided two hundred lines more on short notice. When the book appeared in February 1762, it contained far more pieces by Boswell and Erskine than by any of the other contributors.

Boswell's thirty poems in the *Collection* may be roughly grouped into five categories: graveyard poems, war poems, theatrical poems, poems addressed to Kitty Colquhoun, and (the largest group of all) what may be called Soaping-Club verse. I shall quote two stanzas from one of the poems in the last-named group as the best description extant of the mask which Boswell wore to make himself easy. It was no less a mask because it reproduced to some extent his natural features. The title is **"B——, a Song"**; the air (one of those used by Gay in *The Beggar's Opera*), "To Old Sir Simon the King." I fancy as Boswell sang it it may have been quite entertaining.

> B—— is pleasant and gay;
>   For frolic by nature design'd,
> He heedlessly rattles away
>   When the company is to his mind.
> This maxim he says you may see,
>   We can never have corn without chaff;
> So not a bent sixpence cares he
>   Whether *with* him or *at* him you laugh.

> B—— does women adore
>   And never once means to deceive;
> He's in love with at least half a score;
>   If they're serious, he smiles in his sleeve.
> He has all the bright fancy of youth
>   With the judgement of forty-and-five;
> In short, to declare the plain truth,
>   There is no better fellow alive.

(pp. 70-1)

The collection as a whole received no very high commendation, but it was found [by the *Critical Review*] to afford "some sparks of genius, which may one day kindle into a brighter flame." The sparks? The Hon. Andrew Erskine and James Boswell, Esq. Two of Erskine's odes were praised and one printed entire. "In the collection," continued the reviewer (who may have been Tobias Smollett himself—Boswell reported to Erskine that he had been buttering Smollett up and had got a gracious letter in reply), "we find some agreeable light pieces by J. B. Esq., such as the following song, which we take to be a good-humoured joke upon himself." There follows the entire text of **"B——, a Song."** Boswell professed himself delighted. "Had they said more, I should have thought it a burlesque." The volume contained pieces by John Home and William Julius Mickle. James Beattie had a signed poem in it, and so had James Macpherson, already famous as the "translator" of Ossian. The reviewer praised and quoted Home, but mentioned none of the others; furthermore, that same number of the *Critical* that treated Boswell so generously gave only balanced and regretful praise to the *Crazy Tales* of Sterne's friend, the ingenious Mr. Hall-Stevenson, and the *Resignation* of the aged and honoured author of *Night Thoughts.* For his continual meddling with rhyme Boswell at least had the excuse that his early poems had been praised by one of the most influential reviews of the day.

He had always intended to bring out *The Cub at Newmarket* with a dedication to the Duke of York, but had not been able to find a publisher who would take the risk of it, and did not dare himself to underwrite the cost of printing it in as handsome a style as he thought the dedication demanded. Rendered confident by the appearance of Donaldson's *Collection,* he instructed an unidentified London printer to get the copy from the Dodsleys in Pall Mall, who had had it for some time, and to print it at once. He would guarantee costs himself. "Let no expense be spared to make it genteel. Let it be done on large quarto, and a good type. Price, one shilling." The *Cub,* in a format far more elegant than it deserved, was published anonymously on 4 March 1762. Except for the fact that it sold enough copies to pay costs, it was a disappointment all round. Boswell had added a Shandyan preface and people were getting sick of Shandyan imitations. The reviewers found the humour of the piece esoteric. Worst of all, the dedication backfired. One does not dedicate to a royal duke without asking permission, but Boswell, still wandering in his day-dream of simple Ned, had done just that. The Duke was very angry, his anger brought Eglinton into a sad scrape, Eglinton was in a passion. The whole Guards scheme was threatened.

Soon after the *Collection* came out, Boswell drew up a table of contents for an entire volume of poems "to be published for me by Becket and Dehondt" (Sterne's publishers), and started making fair copy for the printer. He calculated the number of lines, and thought that "counting the blank spaces" he had enough copy to make one hundred and fifty printed pages—"a neat pocket volume." The nature of the unpublished pieces may be indicated by a selection from the titles: **"Ode to Ambition," "Ode to the Elves," "Ode on Whistling," "Ode on the Death of a Lamb"**; epistles to Erskine. Lady Mackintosh, Miss Home (Lord Kames's daughter), Temple; paraphrases from Holy Scripture; prologues for *Macbeth, Love Makes a Man, The Coquettes;* songs and epigrams galore. The unpublished verse is seldom worse than the published, and is perhaps occasionally better.

For six years or so of his youth, then, Boswell regarded himself as a poet and had some encouragement in the belief. It is the usual beginning of men with literary gifts, and is not to be written off as insignificant when it proves to be a dead-end street. Writing verse nourished his conviction of literary genius, as prose writing at that age could not have done. It gave him opportunities for more frequent and more extensive publication than he could have had if he had stuck to prose; and few men who wish to be authors will ever realize their ambition unless they are encouraged by early and frequent publication. I do not know that Boswell could

have avoided his destiny if he had never turned a verse, but I think it certain that his voluminous early scribblings brought him more quickly to the discovery of his true gift and made him more confident in the exercise of it.

But if that were the whole story, the proper course for a biographer would be merely to say so and to excuse himself from particularization. It is not the whole story. The most rewarding focus for a biography of Boswell is not that which makes him a neurotic or a buffoon; it is that which faces up to the central facts and presents him as an author. In the biographies of most literary men, the juvenilia can be written off cursorily as largely irrelevant: all the really characteristic writings come later. In the case of Boswell the juvenilia remain characteristic. *No Abolition of Slavery*, published when he was past fifty, is as silly as *The Cub at Newmarket. A Letter to the People of Scotland* (1785) is as extravagant and indiscreet as **"An Original Letter from a Gentleman of Scotland to the Earl of * * * in London"** (1761). Boswell discovered, not long after the period we are now considering, the kind of writing he was uniquely fitted for, and as time went on he developed a conscience about it. But as he acquired literary honesty and sobriety, he did not simultaneously abandon the postures he had found so delightful as a young man. To the end of his days he wrote and printed banal and doggerel verse, he puffed himself and his writings in the newspapers, he wrote letters to himself and he answered them. An account of his writing and publication during 1756-1762 is in some sort an epitome of his entire literary career. (pp. 71-3)

Frederick A. Pottle, in his *James Boswell: The Earlier Years, 1740-1769*, McGraw-Hill Book Company, 1966, 606 p.

FRANK BRADY

(essay date 1984)

[Brady is best known as coeditor, with Frederick A. Pottle, of the Boswell papers. In the following excerpt from his *James Boswell: The Later Years, 1769-1795*, he recounts the publication of *Tour to the Hebrides* and *The Life of Samuel Johnson*, analyzing each work's characteristics and style.]

Like most great writers, Boswell had a good deal of confidence in his talent, but his Hebridean journal was an impromptu private performance that would need extensive revision before it was turned outwards to appear as a public memoir of Johnson. In particular, he worried about his phrasing: was it slovenly? did he use Scotticisms? On their tour, Boswell had said he wished Johnson would turn the journal into good English, and

Johnson told him, "Sir, it is very good English." But [editor Edmund] Malone was confident he could improve it. If he knew anything, he knew how to put together a literary work, in English acceptable to a cultivated audience.

Their first decision concerned linked questions of format and copy. Boswell had started to sink his material under topographical heads (St. Andrews, Laurencekirk) as Johnson had done in the *Journey to the Western Islands,* but after preparing a specimen along these lines, Reynolds, Sir Joseph Banks, and others unnamed (certainly including Malone), persuaded him to revert to his original day-by-day notation. This was a vital decision for it committed Boswell to the immediacy of journal presentation. And Malone must have initiated him into the labyrinthine method of preparing copy which Boswell used here and in the *Life of Johnson.* The prime rule was never to transcribe one word more than was necessary. When revisions, additions, deletions, and transpositions made the original journal pages impossible to follow, they were supplemented by loose leaves, called "papers apart," which were cued to the main body of the manuscript by a series of signposts. A modern printer would reject this wondrous tangle at sight, but Baldwin's compositors deciphered it with remarkable accuracy.

Malone's guidance and hand appear everywhere in the manuscript, revising this phrase, clarifying that reference or sequence of ideas, smoothing out Boswell's simple paratactic sentence structure. Typically, "agreeable schemes of curiosity" turns into "occasional excursions," and "might push the bottle about" is dignified as "urged drinking." In the journal, Johnson's sermon, "in a boat upon the sea" between Raasay and Skye, takes place "upon a fine, calm Sunday morning"; Malone elevates this to "in a boat upon the sea, which was perfectly calm, on a day appropriated to religious worship." The text gains in precision and "elegance," while it loses in directness and force. Boswell, however, must have been responsible for recasting indirect speech ("he said that") in dramatic form ("JOHNSON")

More important than verbal alterations were the heavy substantive changes Boswell and Malone made as they focused the *Hebrides* on Johnson—actions, reactions, pronouncements on men and manners, effect on the natives. Many of Boswell's own hopes, fears, and acts of piety became irrelevant, as did a good deal of patient description and measurement. This last was no loss; as Boswell himself admitted, "I find I can do nothing in the way of description of any visible object whatever." A mechanical factor came into play: Boswell had chosen an octavo format with a large typeface and wide margins so that, midway, he realized he must throw out material by the handful if the book was not to become unpleasantly thick and expensive.

The need to cut detail and maintain decorum accounted for other large chunks of discarded journal. Boswell's ample reports of meals disappeared—"Shall the dinner *stet?*" is his wistful marginal query at one point. When Boswell complained, amidst the hospitality of Raasay, about the lack of privies in Scotland, "Mr. Johnson laughed heartily and said, 'You take very good care of one end of a man, but not of the other.'" This remark went. Even plain field-notes could be too outspoken for the contemporary audience. Boswell says,

> I observed tonight a remarkable instance of the simplicity of manners or want of delicacy among the people in Skye. After I was in bed, the minister came up to go to his. The maid stood by and took his clothes and laid them carefully on a chair, piece by piece, not excepting his breeches, before throwing off which he made water, while she was just at his back.

Johnson's dignity also had to be preserved. Even in the heat of argument, he could not be permitted to recall the Rev. Kenneth Macaulay as "the most ignorant booby and the grossest bastard." It might have damaged his reputation to include his remark that for five years of his life he made a bowl of punch for himself every night. But perhaps lack of space rather than a suspicion of triviality deleted mention of his fishing for cuddies at Ullinish. Boswell, elsewhere, hangs on to that kind of detail.

The nature of the collaboration between Boswell and Malone appears most clearly in their give-and-take about changes in the second edition. As soon as the first edition was published at the end of September 1785, Boswell left for Auchinleck; when a second edition was immediately called for, Malone was put in charge of the proofs, and discussed alterations with Boswell in voluminous correspondence. Both discovered obvious ways to improve the book, but some basic stylistic disagreements emerged. The charge that he had committed a Scotticism always brought Boswell to his knees; otherwise he could be highly resistant to suggestion. When Malone wanted to substitute "It gave me pleasure to behold" for "I loved," in "I loved to behold Dr. Samuel Johnson rolling about in this old magazine of antiquities," Boswell responded "I think 'I loved' a good warm expression." (Though Malone seldom made a change without Boswell's approval, he felt strongly enough about this phrase to substitute "I was pleased to behold.") His preference for conventional diction shows itself when he says of one phrase, "It is too colloquial, not book language, and nothing got by it." A related objection arose to another passage in which Johnson was discussing free will:

> But stay! (said he, with one of his satiric laughs). Ha! ha! ha! I shall suppose Scotchmen made necessarily, and Englishmen by choice.

"I wish the 'ha! ha! ha!' were omitted," Malone

wrote. "It is only fit for the drama. What can a reader do with it? It adds nothing." Boswell replied, "I resign the 'ha! ha! ha!' to your deleting pen." But when Malone wanted to cut out the emphatic "myself" in the phrase, "I myself," Boswell argued, "I like the passage as it stands. I like *myself.—Moi.* It is more *avowed.* So let it remain." (pp. 285-87)

Malone pressed on in the pursuit of correctness until Boswell, his spirits drooping at Auchinleck, rebelled: "Are you not too desirous of perfection? We must make *some* allowance for the book being a *journal.*" Still, he was properly appreciative: "Your kind attention to my book is wonderful." And again, "You have certainly the art of book-making and book-dressing in the utmost perfection."

Boswell's own revisions tended to be brief, though occasionally he recalls a detail omitted at the time or adds a comment about later events. One revision, however, gives a striking example of his need to bring a scene into line with his mental image of it. Johnson had burst into one of his mysterious paroxysms of laughter at The Club, and only Garrick reacted, saying, according to the journal, "Mighty pleasant, Sir; mighty pleasant, Sir!" But this didn't come close enough to suit Boswell and, after experimenting further in the manuscript, he came up with a new version in the first edition of the **Hebrides:** "Only Garrick in his significant smart manner, darting his eyes around, exclaimed, '*Very* jocose, to be sure!'" What is remarkable is that Boswell had not even witnessed the scene himself; Langton had told him about it. But he could see that the repetition of the original phrase was clumsy, and he *knew* Garrick's characteristic speech and manner.

Such changes, both wholesale and minute, demonstrate how professionally self-critical a writer Boswell was, but they may also seem to cast doubt on Boswell's repeated assertions of authenticity in the *Hebrides.* To the entry for 18 August, very near to the work's beginning, he appended a footnote: "My journal, from this day inclusive, was read by Dr. Johnson." A few days later, in recounting the conversation between Johnson and Monboddo, Boswell advances his most extreme claim:

> My note of this is much too short. "Brevis esse laboro, obscurus fio." Yet as I have resolved that *the very journal which Dr. Johnson read* shall be presented to the public, I will not expand the text in any considerable degree, though I may occasionally supply a word to complete the sense, as I fill up the blanks of abbreviation in the writing; neither of which can be said to change the genuine journal.

Not only does Boswell continue to remind the reader several times that Johnson had read the journal, he includes Johnson's comment that it "might be printed, where the subject fit for printing." Finally, in a footnote to 26 October, Boswell writes:

> Having mentioned more than once that my journal was perused by Dr. Johnson, I think it proper to inform my readers that this is the last paragraph which he read.

Also Johnson had authenticated the journal as a whole by calling it "a very exact picture of a portion of his life," and showed his satisfaction with Boswell's report by approving Boswell's intention to write his biography.

But Boswell didn't direct his claims only to the public; he told Malone, who knew the truth, "*authenticity* is my chief boast." To make sense of his assertion it has to be taken in its contemporary context. No one in the eighteenth century hesitated to revise letters, memoirs, or journals for publication, and justifiably if the point of publication was to edify: effect was more important than authenticity.

> Lives of great men all remind us
> We can make our lives sublime.

Longfellow reduces the point to doggerel, but it still holds: who is going to be inspired by learning that his hero was vain or stingy or cowardly or mean to his children? Yet all such contemporary publications claimed, at least implicitly, to be authentic.

Boswell's assertion of authenticity might seem to us more warranted if he had restricted it to Johnson's own words. No one could think, then or now, that every word of Johnson's Boswell reported was exact. But Boswell did write down, as nearly as possible, Johnson's key words, and he was very reluctant to alter them, though occasionally he softened some of Johnson's harsher comments or provided him with rather more elevated language than he had used. (After 22

Boswell and Samuel Johnson experience Edinburgh by night.

October when his journal fails, Boswell attributes far less direct discourse to Johnson.) And once printed, Johnson's language acquired the status of Sacred Writ. "I am determined," Boswell told Malone in revising for the second edition, "not to alter *now* in *any* degree *any* saying of Dr. Johnson's." Boswell shows no qualms otherwise about rewriting his journal; he had provided its material himself, and that he can recast either for stylistic reasons or to bring it closer to memory. Deletions hardly counted. What is authentic is Boswell's memory as proved genuine by the record of the journal, and that is what he is proud of. (pp. 289-90)

The *Hebrides* was an instant success, widely reviewed and excerpted. The first edition of 1,500 copies sold out almost at once, and two more editions were called for during the next year. But it was a work that fitted customary genres and expectations awkwardly, and the critics, conscious they upheld standards of taste and judgement in an ever-collapsing world, were more hesitant than the public. Everyone, of course, had to admit that the book was continuously entertaining, but was it also instructive? Indeed, was the entertainment itself seemly? Even John Nichols, who wrote a very favourable review of it for the *Gentleman's Magazine*, failed to see or at least to remark that it had taken unusual skill to put together what he called a "plain and simple narrative of the ordinary business and manner" of Johnson's life. And most critics had strong reservations—of one or more of three kinds.

First, what should biography include? A few years later, Vicesimus Knox, who could be relied on to impart sonority to any cliché, declared apropos of Boswell:

> Biography is every day descending from its dignity. Instead of an instructive recital it is becoming an instrument to the mere gratification of an impertinent, not to say a malignant, curiosity.

Biography should conceal blemishes; it needs a vein of panegyric to arouse "ardour of imitation." Johnson himself, in the *Lives of the Poets*, had been unusually blunt about the failings of his subjects, but that did not disarm Boswell's critics. The *English Review* put the point:

> But allowing to Dr. Johnson all the merit which his warmest admirers ascribe to him, was it meritorious, was it right or justifiable in Mr. Boswell to record and to publish his prejudices, his follies and whims, his weaknesses, his vices? . . . It was counteracting, we should imagine, his design, which, if we mistake not, was to hold up Dr. Johnson in the most respectable light.

Second, and a closely connected point, was Boswell's inclusion of so much minutiae. Detail was associated with low forms like the novel or comedy or sat-

ire; it had no place in an elevated or instructive work. In the *Account of Corsica* Boswell adhered to conventional practice: his Plutarchian depiction of Paoli could not accommodate unedifying detail.

In the *Hebrides* Boswell's approach was guided by intuition rather than theory: what he chose to do, without wholly grasping his own method or its implications, was to present Johnson through a mosaic of widely varied and apparently unselected detail, from which his unique character would enable him to stand forth triumphantly. But, of course, Boswell's mind composed each scene. (pp. 296-97)

With a critical vocabulary restricted to "instruction," "entertainment," and "decorum," the reviewers were too limited in technique to be able to explain, or even to suspect the need of explaining, why the *Hebrides* was so wonderfully readable. Without trying to make that appeal fully explicit, some reasons for it can be suggested. It is unified by a constant cross-play among topics: some immediate (Ossian, emigration), some personal or contemporary (Burke, subordination), some perennial (evil, the variety of human nature)—as they recur in varying contexts and are perceived from varying viewpoints. But the *Hebrides* also has an inherent structure: it moves from the civilized (Edinburgh and the Lowlands) through the primitive (the Highlands and Hebrides) back to the civilized (the Lowlands and Edinburgh), with all the shadings and ironies that the travellers' experiences of "civilization" and "nature" provide. The savage-shopkeeper debate, which opens the work's central issue, is settled when near the end of their tour Johnson and Boswell laugh heartily "at the ravings of those absurd visionaries who have attempted to persuade us of the superior advantages of a *state of nature*." (This is one literary work where art is accounted superior to nature.)

Further, the sustained tension in the Johnson-Boswell-Scots triangle supplies each new situation with the potential for almost any reaction—comic, explosive, or harmonious—while the inner play between Johnson and Boswell strengthens the narrative line. Tension is heightened by contrast between Johnson and whomever or whatever—a Highland guide, an old Presbyterian minister, a small pony. Boswell builds on a fundamental incongruity; as he wrote to Garrick from Inverness:

> Indeed, as I have always been accustomed to view [Johnson] as a permanent London object, it would not be much more wonderful to me to see St. Paul's Church moving along where we now are.

The underlying suspense of the *Hebrides*— how will the situation work out?—is resolved by Johnson's reaction to Iona, the grail of their pilgrimage. And this reaction has been foreshadowed by reversal when

Johnson assumed the accoutrements of an ancient Caledonian bard.

All these factors are equally characteristic of well-made novels; one important factor that differentiates the *Hebrides* from them is Boswell's carefully cultivated sense of authenticity, the sense that the scene we are reading about actually occurred. The ordered selectivity of the imagination seems to give way to the rich randomness of experience. The sense of familiarity reinforces the effect, taken to the point today where the devotee authenticates the narrative by travelling over the same route. Authenticity in itself is never enough, of course; there are plenty of dull authentic narratives. Rather, authenticity provides the foundation for Boswell's vision of existence. (pp. 299-300)

A satisfactory theory of biography depends on the assumption that a biography is a work of fact and not fiction. Fact and fiction evoke fundamentally different mental sets, and faced with a written work a reader is profoundly uneasy until he knows which set is appropriate. Tell a six-year-old a story, and the first question he will ask is whether it is real or pretend. For adults, the question of whether the Bible is a work of fact or of fiction, even if fiction of the greatest significance, arouses argument so passionate that until a few centuries ago it could cost a man his life, and can still cost him his job. Authenticity, Boswell's proudest claim for [his final biographical work, the *Life,*] as for his other biographical works, meant above all to him truth to fact.

The differences in response to fiction and fact are far easier to suggest than to define. Fiction widens into potentiality, while fact offers the pleasing resistance of the actual. Fiction may move us more deeply, but we trust fact. Fictional characters can be developed to any degree of complexity, but who can say where the resonance of real persons like Garrick and Burke dies out? Fictional narrative can please with wonderful invention, but factual narrative invites increased alertness: if this happened to someone else, it could happen to me.

The mental set of fiction derives from imagination, and of fact from memory. Of course the two must overlap: imagination becomes unintelligible if it loses touch with what we already know, while memory involves imaginative reconstruction. But there are essential distinctions between "imaginative" modes, like drama or the novel, and "memorial" modes, like biography and history.

Imaginative works are closed forms, while memorial works are open ones. *Don Quixote* is a self-limiting novel; nothing more can be learned about its hero because he was not a real person. But the *Life of Johnson* is permeable, so to speak; the adequacy of its Johnson can be checked by information from other sources, just as we impart to Boswell's depiction certain characteris-

tics drawn from other works about him. A character in a novel has only to be plausible, but the subject of a biography must be credible. At most, novels can be compared; biographies can be corrected. Usually a biography is too full of the unresolved dissonances typical of our own lives to attain the satisfying conclusion of a novel.

The eighteenth century thought much more highly of factual literature than of fiction; today the opposite is true. This shift in prestige to the imagined or imaginatively reconstituted is partly responsible for obscuring the biographical traditions on which Boswell drew. Virtually all serious biography before Boswell's time was ethical; its model in purpose was Plutarch's *Lives,* and its aim to instruct and to judge. This noble tradition now seems pompous because of our distaste for the explicitly didactic, but Johnson justifies it when he asserts, "We are perpetually moralists, but we are geometricians only by chance." Johnson is not suggesting that we adopt a high moral tone or spy on our neighbours. He is merely emphasizing that the most important decisions we make every day are ethical decisions. Basically, we are ethical beings; our intellectual knowledge of the world is, by comparison, unimportant. And biography has the advantage over history, its rival among memorial genres, of offering individual rather than general models of thought and behaviour. "I esteem biography," Johnson told Lord Monboddo, "as giving us what comes near to ourselves, what we can turn to use."

But the kernel and origin of biography is the anecdote, nothing more than the story one person tells to a second about a third; and the tradition of anecdotal biography is also long, going back at least to Xenophon's *Memorabilia* of Socrates. One basic distinction between the two types is that in ethical biography incident serves the humble function of illustrating moral points, while in anecdotal biography incident comes to the fore and the ethical is apt to be left to fend for itself. In the eighteenth century, though anecdotal biography had strong admirers, including Johnson himself, it was open to the charge that it pandered to idle curiosity—a frequent criticism, as mentioned, of the *Hebrides*—and lacked redeeming moral value.

Johnson's two important pre-Boswellian biographers neatly illustrate the extremes of ethical and anecdotal types. Hawkin's *Life of Johnson* plucks out the moral *exempla* to be derived from Johnson's career, but Johnson himself peers through only at intervals. In contrast, his character—often in its most unpleasant moods—emerges vividly in the brief, disjointed stories that make up Mrs. Piozzi's *Anecdotes,* which is a classic of moral confusion.

Boswell made the necessary connection: his *Life of Johnson* embodies a crucial moment in the history of biography because in it he unifies the ethical and anecdotal traditions. (In the same period, Gibbon similarly unified the traditions of philosophical and antiquarian history.) And Boswell extended a third biographical element, the role of psychological analysis. For this he had Johnson's example in the *Lives of the Poets* to go on. But he also had his own journal-practice as background, as well as models of introspection ranging from confessions and autobiographies by splendid saints and sinners, like Augustine and Rousseau, to those of spiritual and temporal journalists whom a contemporary unkindly referred to as "a thousand . . . old women and fanatic writers." (pp. 423-25)

The sheer quantity of Boswell's material, beginning with his massive journal, put fullness and exactness within reach. But quantity also helped to force a new biographical approach on him. In his **"Memoirs of Pascal Paoli,"** where his notes were somewhat sparse and he wanted to disguise the fact that his visit to Paoli had lasted only a week, Boswell suppressed dates and filled out his account by interspersing what Paoli said and did with general comment on the Corsicans. A contrasting problem emerged in the *Hebrides,* where he worried that his narrative would be choked with detail; there he experimented by abridging it under topographical headings (St. Andrews, Laurencekirk), until he reverted with great success to the day-by-day entries of his original journal.

But the method that served for a three-month narrative like the *Hebrides* would not do for a far more comprehensive portrait and, as early as 1780, Boswell had determined to write the *Life of Johnson* "in scenes," that is, to centre his presentation on conversations which would approximate scenes in a play. This was a key decision and it meant that Johnson, whom Boswell praises in the opening sentence of the *Life* as the greatest of biographers, could not provide an appropriate model. Though Johnson included dialogue and anecdote, the principal interest of his *Lives of the Poets* lay in his unrelenting judgemental commentary. This suited neither Boswell's aim nor his material.

Instead, early in the *Life* Boswell announces, "I have resolved to adopt and enlarge upon the excellent plan of Mr. Mason, in his *Memoirs of [Thomas] Gray."* Well known at the time, William Mason's *Gray* was un-

usual in being made up of a long series of the subject's letters—which Mason, we now know, rephrased, bowdlerized, truncated, spliced together, and misdated—linked by a trickle of mealymouthed explanation. But even in these butchered versions Gray's letters, as Boswell remarked to Temple, "show us the *man*." They present Gray so directly, they reveal so much about him, that Mason the memoirist is forgotten and Gray stands before us plain. Self-presentation and self-revelation by his subject to the greatest extent possible: this too was part of Boswell's plan. Of course he had been born knowing how to set figures directly before an audience, as he had shown in his earlier studies of Paoli and Johnson. But Mason's example may have crystallized his decision about how to present Johnson in the *Life,* and at the least it offered a convenient precedent.

To the union of the ethical and anecdotal on an epic scale, Boswell joined, then, one more innovation of the greatest significance to biography: mimesis, the setting of a subject immediately before the reader. "Presentness" was the decisive effect Boswell wanted to achieve: to get Johnson to present himself, to reveal himself, first in conversation, but also in all those documents Boswell quotes or summarizes: letters, prayers and meditations, essays and biographies with working notes and discarded readings, political pamphlets, definitions, parodies, fables and allegories, decisions on literary disputes, an appeal for votes, poems, legal opinions, a novel, and even the minor forms of eulogy—dedication, obituary, and epitaph. Johnson appears further in what was said about him in various forms, from diplomas to memorable opinions: Garrick's "Johnson gives you a forcible hug and shakes laughter out of you, whether you will or no"; Goldsmith's "he has nothing of the bear but his skin"; Dr. John Boswell's "a robust genius born to grapple with whole libraries." Presentness is the brightest of Boswell's talents. He became the first mimetic biographer and he remains without equal.

If the glory of art is to conceal art, then the *Life of Johnson* belongs in the first rank. (pp. 427-28)

Frank Brady, in his *James Boswell: The Later Years, 1769-1795,* McGraw-Hill Book Company, 1984, 609 p.

SOURCES FOR FURTHER STUDY

Brooks, A. Russell. *James Boswell.* New York: Twayne Publishers, 1971, 181 p.

Critical study of Boswell's literary career which emphasizes "the unique coalescence of his personal experiences with his artistic outlook."

Clifford, James L., ed. *Twentieth-Century Interpretations of Boswell's "Life of Johnson."* Englewood Cliffs, N.J.: Prentice-Hall, 1970, 123 p.

Collection of critical essays on *The Life of Johnson.*

Collins, P. A. W. *James Boswell.* London: Longmans, Green & Co., 1956, 48 p.

Highly favorable critical biography.

Daiches, David. *James Boswell and His World.* New York: Charles Scribner's Sons, 1976, 128 p.

Heavily illustrated, general treatment of Boswell's life.

Pearson, Hesketh. *Johnson and Boswell: The Story of Their Lives.* New York: Harper & Brothers, 1958, 390 p.

Double biography of Johnson and Boswell which examines the influence of each upon the other.

Quennell, Peter. "James Boswell." In his *Four Portraits: Studies of the Eighteenth Century,* pp. 15-78. Hamden, Conn.: Archon Books, 1965.

Biographical and psychological treatment of Boswell's literary career.

Ray Bradbury

1920-

(Full name Raymond Douglas Bradbury; has also written under pseudonyms Douglas Spaulding and Leonard Spaulding) American short story writer, novelist, scriptwriter, poet, dramatist, nonfiction writer, editor, and author of children's books.

INTRODUCTION

*A*n important figure in the development of science fiction, even though he does not write primarily in that genre, Bradbury was among the first authors to combine the concepts of science fiction with a sophisticated prose style. Often described as economical yet poetic, Bradbury's fiction conveys a vivid sense of place in which everyday events are transformed into unusual, sometimes sinister situations. In a career that has spanned more than forty years, Bradbury has written fantasies, crime and mystery stories, supernatural tales, and mainstream literature as well as science fiction. In all of his work, he emphasizes basic human values and cautions against unthinking acceptance of technological progress. His persistent optimism, evident even in his darkest work, has led some critics to label him sentimental or naive. Bradbury, however, perceives life, even at its most mundane, with a childlike wonder and awe that charges his work with a fervent affirmation of humanity.

Bradbury began his career during the 1940s as a writer for such pulp magazines as *Black Mask, Amazing Stories*, and *Weird Tales*. The last-named magazine served to showcase the works of such fantasy writers as H. P. Lovecraft, Clark Ashton Smith, and August Derleth. Derleth, who founded Arkham House, a publishing company specializing in fantasy literature, accepted one of Bradbury's stories for *Who Knocks?*, an anthology published by his firm. Derleth subsequently suggested that Bradbury compile a volume of his own stories; the resulting book, *Dark Carnival* (1947), collects Bradbury's early fantasy tales. Although Bradbury rarely published pure fantasy later in his career, such themes of his future work as the need to retain humanistic values and the importance of the imagination are displayed in the stories of this collection. Many of these pieces were republished with new material in *The October Country* (1955).

The publication of *The Martian Chronicles* (1950) established Bradbury's reputation as an author of sophisticated science fiction. This collection of stories is connected by the framing device of the settling of Mars by human beings and is dominated by tales of space travel and environmental adaptation. Bradbury's themes, however, reflect many of the important issues of the post-World War II era—racism, censorship, technology, and nuclear war—and the stories delineate the implications of these themes through authorial commentary. Clifton Fadiman described *The Martian Chronicles* as being "as grave and troubling as one of Hawthorne's allegories." Another significant collection of short stories, *The Illustrated Man* (1951), also uses a framing device, basing the stories on the tattoos of the title character.

Bradbury's later short story collections are generally considered to be less significant than *The Martian Chronicles* and *The Illustrated Man*. Bradbury shifted his focus in these volumes from outer space to more familiar earthbound settings. *Dandelion Wine* (1957), for example, has as its main subject the midwestern youth of Bradbury's semiautobiographical protagonist, Douglas Spaulding. Although Bradbury used many of the same techniques in these stories as in his science fiction and fantasy publications, *Dandelion Wine* was not as well received as his earlier work. Other later collections, including *A Medicine for Melancholy* (1959), *The Machineries of Joy* (1964), *I Sing the Body Electric!* (1969), and *Long after Midnight* (1976), contain stories set in Bradbury's familiar outer space or midwestern settings and explore his typical themes. Many of Bradbury's stories have been anthologized or filmed for such television programs as "The Twilight Zone," "Alfred Hitchcock Presents," and "Ray Bradbury Theater."

In addition to his short fiction, Bradbury has written three adult novels. The first of these, *Fahrenheit 451* (1953), originally published as a short story and later expanded into novel form, concerns a future society in which books are burned because they are perceived as threats to societal conformity. In *Something Wicked This Way Comes* (1962) a father attempts to save his son and a friend from the sinister forces of a mysterious traveling carnival. Both of these novels have been adapted for film. *Death Is a Lonely Business* (1985) is a detective story featuring Douglas Spaulding, the protagonist of *Dandelion Wine*, as a struggling writer for pulp magazines. Bradbury has also written poetry and drama; critics have faulted his efforts in these genres as lacking the impact of his fiction.

While Bradbury's popularity is acknowledged even by his detractors, many critics find the reasons for his success difficult to pinpoint. Some believe that the tension Bradbury creates between fantasy and reality is central to his ability to convey his visions and interests to his readers. Peter Stoler asserted that Bradbury's reputation rests on his "chillingly understated stories about a familiar world where it is always a few minutes before midnight on Halloween, and where the unspeakable and unthinkable become commonplace." Mary Ross proposed that "Perhaps the special quality of [Bradbury's] fantasy lies in the fact that people to whom amazing things happen are often so simply, often touchingly, like ourselves." In a genre in which futurism and the fantastic are usually synonymous, Bradbury stands out for his celebration of the future in realistic terms and his exploration of conventional values and ideas. As one of the first science fiction writers to convey his themes through a refined prose style replete with subtlety and humanistic analogies, Bradbury has helped make science fiction a more respected literary genre and is widely admired by the literary establishment.

(For further information about Bradbury's life and works, see *Authors in the News*, Vols. 1-2; *Concise Dictionary of American Literary Biography, 1968-1988*; *Contemporary Authors*, Vols. 1-4; *Contemporary Authors New Revision Series*, Vols. 2, 30; *Contemporary Literary Criticism*, Vols. 1, 3, 10, 15, 42; *Dictionary of Literary Biography*, Vols. 2, 8; *Major 20th-Century Writers*; and *Something about the Author*, Vol. 11.)

CRITICAL COMMENTARY

RUSSELL KIRK
(essay date 1969)

[Kirk is an American historian, political theorist, novelist, journalist, and lecturer. In the following excerpt, he contends that Bradbury's science fiction is concerned with man's soul and moral imagination, not with "gadgets of conquest."]

Ray Bradbury has drawn the sword against the dreary and corrupting materialism of this century; against society as producer-and-consumer equation, against the hideousness in modern life, against mindless power, against sexual obsession, against sham intellectuality, against the perversion of right reason into the mentality of the television-viewer. His Martians, spectres, and witches are not diverting entertainment only: they become, in their eerie manner, the defenders of truth and beauty. (p. 117)

[Bradbury] thinks it . . . probable that man may spoil everything, in this planet and in others, by the misapplication of science to avaricious ends—the Baconian and Hobbesian employment of science as power. And Bradbury's interior world is fertile, illuminated by love for the permanent things, warm with generous impulse. . . .

Bradbury knows of modern technology, in the phrase of Henry Adams, that we are "monkeys monkeying with a loaded shell." He is interested not in the precise mechanism of rockets, but in the mentality and the morals of fallible human beings who make and use rockets. He is a man of fable and parable. (p. 118)

Bradbury is not writing about the gadgets of conquest; his real concerns are the soul and the moral imagination. When the boy-hero of *Dandelion Wine,* in an abrupt mystical experience, is seized almost bodily by the glowing consciousness that he is really *alive,* we glimpse that mystery the soul. When, in *Something Wicked This Way Comes,* the lightning-rod salesman is reduced magically to an idiot dwarf because all his life he had fled from perilous responsibility, we know the moral imagination.

"Soul," a word much out of fashion nowadays, signifies a man's animating entity. That flaming spark the soul is the real space-traveller of Bradbury's stories. "I'm alive!"—that exclamation is heard from Waukegan to Mars and beyond, in Bradbury's fables. Life is its own end—if one has a soul to tell him so. (pp. 118-19)

[The] moral imagination, which shows us what we ought to be, primarily is what distinguishes Bradbury's tales from the futurism of Wells' fancy. For Bradbury, the meaning of life is here and now, in our every action; we live amidst immortality; it is here, not in some future domination like that of Wells' *The Sleeper Awakens,* that we must find our happiness. (p. 119)

What gives [*The Martian Chronicles*] their cunning is their realism set in the fantastic: that is, their portrayal of human nature, in all its baseness and all its promise, against an exquisite stage-set. We are shown normality, the permanent things in human nature, by the light of another world; and what we forget about ourselves in the ordinariness of our routine of existence suddenly bursts upon us as fresh revelation. (p. 120)

In Bradbury's fables of Mars and of the carnival [in *Something Wicked This Way Comes*], fantasy has become what it was in the beginning: the enlightening moral imagination, transcending simple rationality. (p. 123)

The trappings of science-fiction may have attracted young people to Bradbury, but he has led them on to something much older and better: mythopoeic literature, normative truth acquired through wonder. Bradbury's stories are not an escape from reality; they are windows looking upon enduring reality. (p. 124)

Russell Kirk, "The World of Ray Bradbury" and "Depravity and Courage in Modern Fable," in his *Enemies of the Permanent Things: Observations of Abnormality in Literature and Politics,* Arlington House, 1969, pp. 116-20, 120-24.

ANITA T. SULLIVAN
(essay date 1972)

[In the excerpt below, Sullivan traces the progression of themes in Bradbury's works.]

Elements of what may be called "fantasy" were present in Ray Bradbury's works from the beginning of his writing career. His own recent remark distinguishing science fiction from fantasy in literature is that "science fiction could happen." This implies, of course, that fantasy could not happen. But in today's world, where change occurs at such rapid rate, nobody would ven-

Principal Works

Dark Carnival (short stories) 1947

The Martian Chronicles (novel) 1950; also published as The Silver Locusts [revised edition], 1951

The Illustrated Man (short stories) 1951; revised edition, 1952

Timeless Stories for Today and Tomorrow (short stories) 1952

* Fahrenheit 451 (novel and short stories) 1953

The Golden Apples of the Sun (short stories) 1953; revised edition, 1953

The October Country (short stories) 1955

Switch on the Night (juvenile fiction) 1955

Dandelion Wine (short stories) 1957

A Medicine for Melancholy (short stories) 1959; also published as The Day It Rained Forever [revised edition], 1959

The Ghoul Keepers (short stories) 1961

The Small Assassin (short stories) 1962

Something Wicked This Way Comes (novel) 1962

R Is for Rocket (short stories) 1962

The Machineries of Joy (short stories) 1964

The Autumn People (short stories) 1965

The Vintage Bradbury (short stories) 1965

S Is for Space (short stories) 1966

Tomorrow Midnight (short stories) 1966

† Twice Twenty-Two (short stories) 1966

I Sing the Body Electric! (short stories) 1969

Old Ahab's Friend, and Friend to Noah, Speaks His Piece: A Celebration (poetry) 1971

The Halloween Tree (juvenile fiction) 1972

The Wonderful Ice-Cream Suit and Other Plays (drama) 1972; also published as The Wonderful Ice-Cream Suit

and Other Plays for Today, Tomorrow, and Beyond Tomorrow, 1973

When Elephants Last in the Dooryard Bloomed: Celebrations for Almost Any Day in the Year (poetry) 1973

Zen and the Art of Writing (essay) 1973

Ray Bradbury (short stories) 1975

The Best of Bradbury (short stories) 1976

Long after Midnight (short stories) 1976

To Sing Strange Songs (short stories) 1976

Where Robot Mice and Robot Men Run Round in Robot Towns (poetry) 1977

The Ghosts of Forever (poetry, short story, essay) 1980

The Stories of Ray Bradbury (short stories) 1980

The Haunted Computer and the Android Pope (poetry) 1981

‡ The Complete Poems of Ray Bradbury (poetry) 1982

Dinosaur Tales (short stories) 1983

Forever and the Earth (poetry) 1984

A Memory of Murder (short stories) 1984

Death Is a Lonely Business (novel) 1985

Death Has Lost Its Charm for Me (poetry) 1987

The Toynbee Convector (short stories) 1988

A Graveyard for Lunatics (novel) 1990

*This collection contains the novel Fahrenheit 451.

†This work contains The Golden Apples of the Sun and A Medicine for Melancholy.

‡This work contains When Elephants Last in the Dooryard Bloomed, Where Robot Mice and Robot Men Run Round in Robot Towns, and The Haunted Computer and the Android Pope.

ture to state dogmatically that any idea is incapable of realization. Therefore, whether or not a work of literature is fantasy becomes more a matter of the author's intention rather than a matter measurable by objective criteria. This is especially true of an author such as Bradbury, who by his own admission writes both science fiction and fantasy.

Bradbury's own brand of fantasy apparently came to birth in the world of the carnival. His imagination was nurtured with carnival imagery. . . . Whenever a travelling circus or carnival came through Waukegan in the 1920s and early 1930s, Bradbury and his younger brother were always present. . . . (p. 1309)

[The] carnival became for him a sort of subconscious touchstone for a whole system of moods and images which emerged later in his writings. As a result, the carnival world can be thought of as a clearinghouse

for Bradbury's imagination—the place where he goes for his symbols when he is writing a tale of horror, nostalgia, fantasy, or some combination of the three. (pp. 1309-10)

But of Bradbury's tales [during the 1940s] more were horror than fantasy. Perhaps he would regard an attempt to distinguish between horror and fantasy in his works as mere semantic quibbling. The difference, it seems to me, can almost be described as a matter of levity. In the horror tales, he was completely serious and trying his best to achieve a shock effect upon his readers. In the best of these, he probably succeeded because he also achieved, in the writing process, a shock effect upon himself. He was trying to exorcise something in himself as he wrote. Thus his horror tales were not written to enable his readers to escape, but rather to cause them to suffer so that they might be cleansed. . . . The fantasy stories, on the other hand, allow the readers' spirits to expand rather than to contract, as is the effect in the horror tales. The thrust of his effort seems to lie in the creation of a mood, and, lost in this mood, the readers can escape to a Secondary World. (p. 1310)

The theme running through [*Something Wicked This Way Comes*] is that Evil is a shadow: Good is a reality. Evil cannot exist except in the vacuum left when people let their Good become not an active form, not a pumping in their veins, but just a memory, an intention. As Bradbury has indicated in other stories and articles, he feels that the potential for evil exists like cancer germs, dormant in all of us, and unless we keep our Good in fit condition by actively using it, it will lose its power to fight off the poisons in our system. (p. 1313)

Love is the best humanizing force man possesses, Bradbury seems to be saying. . . .

The idea of the healing powers of love is perhaps most beautifully expressed in the story **"A Medicine for Melancholy"** (1959). The story is almost a parable. A young girl in eighteenth-century London is slowly fading away before the eyes of her concerned parents. No doctor is able to diagnose her illness, and finally in desperation they take her, bed and all, and put her outside the front door so that the passersby can try their hand at identifying what is wrong with her. A young Dustman looks into her eyes and knows what is wrong—she needs love. He suggests that she be left out all night beneath the moon, and during the night he visits her and effects a cure. In the morning the roses have returned to her cheeks and she and her family dance in celebration. . . .

[This] idea, or moral, if that is a better word, . . . seems to be at least implicit in the majority of Bradbury's stories from the late 1950s until the present. He did not cease to be a teacher when he stopped writing science fiction, but he did place a moratorium upon the more evangelistic kind of moralizing which he was practicing in the late 1940s and early 1950s. Now, at last, his own sense of values seems to have become completely at one with his art. (p. 1314)

Anita T. Sullivan, "Ray Bradbury and Fantasy," in *English Journal,* Vol. 61, No. 9, December, 1972, pp. 1309-14.

WILLIS E. McNELLY
(essay date 1976)

[McNelly has written widely on science fiction. In the excerpt below, he examines Bradbury's use of metaphor and irony in *Fahrenheit 451* and selected short stories.]

If Bradbury's ladders lead to Mars, whose chronicler he has become, or to the apocalyptic future of *Fahrenheit 451,* the change is simply one of direction, not of intensity. He is a visionary who writes not of the impediments of science, but of its effects upon man. *Fahrenheit 451,* after all, is not a novel about the technology of the future, and is only secondarily concerned with censorship or book-burning. In actuality it is the story of Bradbury, disguised as Montag, and his lifelong love affair with books. (p. 169)

"Metaphor" is an important word to Bradbury. He uses it generically to describe a method of comprehending one reality and then expressing that same reality so that the reader will see it with the intensity of the writer. His use of the term, in fact, strongly resembles T. S. Eliot's view of the objective correlative. Bradbury's metaphor in *Fahrenheit 451* is the burning of books; in **"The Illustrated Man,"** a moving tattoo; and pervading all of his work, the metaphor becomes a generalized nostalgia that can best be described as a nostalgia for the future.

Another overwhelming metaphor in his writing is one derived from Jules Verne and Herman Melville—the cylindrical shape of the submarine, the whale, or the space ship. It becomes a mandala, a graphic symbol of Bradbury's view of the universe, a space-phallus. Bradbury achieved his first "mainstream" fame with his adaptation of Melville's novel for the screen, after Verne had aroused his interest in science fiction. (pp. 169-70)

Essentially a romantic, Bradbury belongs to the great frontier tradition. He is an exemplar of the Turner thesis, and the blunt opposition between a tradition-bound Eastern establishment and Western vitality finds itself mirrored in his writing. The metaphors may change, but the conflict in Bradbury is ultimately between human vitality and the machine, between the expanding individual and the confining group, between the capacity for wonder and the stultification of conformity. These tensions are a continual source for him, whether the collection is named *The Golden Apples of the Sun, Dandelion Wine,* or *The Martian Chronicles.* Thus, to use his own terminology, nostalgia for either the past or future is a basic metaphor utilized to express these tensions. Science fiction is the vehicle.

Ironic detachment combined with emotional involvement—these are the recurring tones in Bradbury's work, and they find their expression in the metaphor of "wilderness." To Bradbury, America is a wilderness country and hers a wilderness people. (p. 170)

For Bradbury the final, inexhaustible wilderness is the wilderness of space. In that wilderness, man will find himself, renew himself. There, in space, as atoms of God, mankind will live forever. Ultimately, then, the conquest of space becomes a religious quest. The religious theme in his writing is sounded directly only on occasion, in such stories as **"The Fire Balloons,"** where two priests try to decide if some blue fire-balls on Mars have souls, or **"The Man,"** where Christ leaves a far planet the day before an Earth rocket lands. Ultimately the religious theme is the end product of Bradbury's vision of man; the theme is implicit in man's nature.

Bradbury's own view of his writing shows a critical self-awareness. He describes himself essentially as a short story writer, not a novelist, whose stories seize him, shake him, and emerge after a two or three hour tussle. It is an emotional experience, not an intellectual one; the intellectualization comes later when he edits. To be sure, Bradbury does not lack the artistic vision for large conception or creation. The novel form is simply not his normal medium. Rather he aims to objectify or universalize the particular. He pivots upon an individual, a specific object, or particular act, and then shows it from a different perspective or a new viewpoint. The result can become a striking insight into the ordinary, sometimes an ironic comment on our limited vision.

An early short story, **"The Highway,"** illustrates this awareness of irony. A Mexican peasant wonders at the frantic, hurtling stream of traffic flowing north. He is told by an American who stops for water that the end of the world has come with the outbreak of the atom war. Untouched in his demi-Eden, Hernando calls out to his burro as he plows the rain-fresh land below the green jungle, above the deep river. "What do they mean 'the world?' " he asks himself, and continues plowing.

Debate over whether or not Bradbury is, in the end, a science fiction writer, is fruitless when one considers this story or dozens like it. The only "science" in the story is the "atom war" somewhere far to the north, away from the ribbon of concrete. All other artifacts of man in the story—the automobile, a hubcap, a tire—provide successive ironies to the notion that while civilization may corrupt, it does not do so absolutely. A blownout tire may have brought death to the driver of a car, but it now provides Hernando with sandals; a shattered hubcap becomes a cooking pan. Hernando and his wife and child live in a pre-lapsarian world utilizing the gifts of the machine in primitive simplicity. These people recall the Noble Savage myth; they form a primary group possessing the idyllic oneness of true community. The strength of Hernando, then, is derived from the myth of the frontier; the quality and vigor of life derive from, indeed are dependent upon, the existence of the frontier.

Yet irony piles on irony: the highway—any highway—leads in two directions. The Americans in this fable form a seemingly endless flowing stream of men and vehicles. They ride northward toward cold destruction, leaving the tropical warmth of the new Eden behind them. Can we recreate the past, as Gatsby wondered. Perhaps, suggests Bradbury, if we re-incarnate the dreams of our youth and reaffirm the social ethic of passionate involvement. And nowhere does he make this moral quite as clear as in *Fahrenheit 451*. (pp. 171-72)

Fahrenheit 451 illustrates his major themes: the freedom of the mind; the evocation of the past; the desire for Eden; the integrity of the individual; the allurements and traps of the future. At the end of the novel, Montag's mind has been purified, refined by fire, and phoenix-like, Montag—hence mankind—rises from the ashes of the destructive, self-destroying civilization. " 'Never liked cities,' said the man who was Plato," as Bradbury hammers home his message at the end of the novel. " 'Always felt that cities owned men, that was all, and used men to keep themselves going, to keep the machines oiled and dusted.' " . . . (p. 173)

[The] vision of the future which Bradbury provides at the end of *Fahrenheit 451* shows his essentially optimistic character. In fact, Bradbury seized upon the hatreds abroad in 1953 when the book was written, and shows that hatred, war, desecration of the individual are all self-destructive. Bradbury's 1953 vision of hatred becomes extrapolated to a fire which consumes minds, spirits, men, ideas, books. (pp. 173-74)

Bradbury has proved that quality writing is possible in [a] much-maligned genre. Bradbury is obviously a careful craftsman, an ardent wordsmith whose attention to the niceties of language and its poetic cadences would have marked him as significant even if he had never written a word about Mars.

His themes, however, place him squarely in the middle of the mainstream of American life and tradition. His eyes are set firmly on the horizon-Frontier where dream fathers mission and action mirrors illusion. And if Bradbury's eyes lift from the horizon to the stars, the act is merely an extension of the vision all Americans share. His voice is that of the poet raised against the mechanization of mankind. (p. 174)

Willis E. McNelly, "Ray Bradbury: Past, Present, and Future," in *Voices for the Future: Essays on Major Science Fiction Writers, Vol. 1*, edited by Thomas D. Clareson, Bowling Green University Popular Press, 1976, pp. 167-75.

A. JAMES STUPPLE
(essay date 1976)

[Stupple is an American educator who specializes in science fiction. In the following excerpt, he explores the meeting of past and future in *The Martian Chronicles* and *Dandelion Wine*, concluding that ". . . the past is not one-dimensional. It is at once creative and destructive. It can give comfort, and it can unsettle and threaten."]

[Of] all the writers of science fiction who have dealt with [the] meeting of the past and the future, it is Ray Bradbury whose treatment has been the deepest and most sophisticated. What has made Bradbury's handling of this theme distinctive is that his attitudes and interpretations have changed as he came to discover the complexities and the ambiguities inherent in it. (p. 175)

Bradbury's point [in *The Martian Chronicles*] here is clear: [the Earthmen] met their deaths because of their inability to forget, or at least resist, the past. Thus, the story of this Third Expedition acts as a metaphor for the book as a whole. Again and again the Earthmen make the fatal mistake of trying to recreate an Earth-like past rather than accept the fact that this is Mars—a different, unique new land in which they must be ready to make personal adjustments. Hauling Oregon lumber through space, then, merely to provide houses for nostalgic colonists exceeds folly; it is only one manifestation of a psychosis which leads to the destruction not only of Earth, but, with the exception of a few families, of Mars as well. (p. 177)

[Despite] the fact that it cannot be called science fiction, *Dandelion Wine* closely resembles *The Martian Chronicles* and much of Bradbury's other writing in that it is essentially concerned with the same issue— the dilemma created by the dual attractions of the past and the future, of stasis and change.

In *Dandelion Wine* Bradbury uses the experiences of his adolescent protagonist during one summer to dramatize this set of philosophical and psychological conflicts. At twelve, Douglas Spaulding finds himself on the rim of adolescence. On one side of him lies the secure, uncomplicated world of childhood, while on the other is the fascinating yet frightening world of "growing up." (p. 178)

[In *Dandelion Wine*] Bradbury seems to be reiterating what he has said in *The Martian Chronicles*—that the past, or stasis, or both, is enticing but deadly, and that Douglas, like the colonists, must forsake the past and give himself up to change and progress. But it is not so simple and clearcut. . . . [What brings Douglas] out of his coma is a swallow of a liquid . . . concocted out of pieces of the past (such as Arctic air from the year 1900). With this development, Bradbury's thesis seems to fall to pieces, for Douglas is saved for the future by the past. He is liberated from a static condition by bottled stasis. The ambiguous nature of his recovery is further compounded by the strange, anti-climactic nature of the last chapters of the novel in which Bradbury indulges in a nostalgic celebration of old-fashioned family life. This conclusion so detracts from the story of Doug and his rebirth that one can only conclude that the author was confused, or more probably ambivalent, about these past-future, stasis-change dichotomies.

It is evident, then, that in *Dandelion Wine,* Bradbury began to become aware of the complexity of his subject. Where in *The Martian Chronicles* he seemed confident in his belief that a meaningful future could only be realized by rejecting the past, in this later novel he appears far less certain about the relative values of the past and stasis. Perhaps in this regard Bradbury can be seen as representative of a whole generation of middle class Americans who have found themselves alternately attracted to the security of an idealized, timeless, and static past (as the current nostalgia vogue illustrates) and the exciting, yet threatening and disruptive future world of progress and change, especially technological change. (p. 181)

[This] stasis-change conflict, besides being a function of Bradbury's own history and personality, also seems to be built into the art form itself. What distinguishes Bradbury and gives his works their depth is that he seems to be aware that a denial of the past demands a denial of that part of the self which is the past. . . . [He] has not been able to come to any lasting conclusion. Instead, he has come to recognize the ambiguity, the complexity, and the irony within this theme. (p. 182)

Bradbury had discovered through his years of working with this theme, the past is not one-dimensional. It is at once creative and destructive. It can give comfort, and it can unsettle and threaten. (p. 184)

A. James Stupple, "The Past, the Future, and Ray Bradbury," in *Voices for the Future: Essays on Major Science Fiction Writers, Vol. 1,* edited by Thomas D. Clareson, Bowling Green University Popular Press, 1976, pp. 175-84.

RAY BRADBURY

(essay date 1979)

[In the following excerpt from an interview with Jeffrey M. Elliot, Bradbury offers his views about science fiction, predicting that the effort to "explain ourselves to ourselves. . . . will dominate our thinking in the next forty years."]

[The difference between the genres of science fiction and fantasy is that science] fiction is the art of the possible. There's never anything fantastic about science fiction. It's always based on the laws of physics; on those things that can absolutely come to pass. Fantasy, on the other hand, is always the art of the impossible. It goes against all the laws of physics. When you write about invisible men, or walking through walls, or magic carpets, you're dealing with the impossible. (p. 21)

I don't give a damn about the critics. I'm not interested in what they have to say. Really, I don't care about other people's opinions. If I did, I wouldn't have any career at all. I've been warned time and time again not to write science fiction by my friends, my teachers, and all the great intellectuals of our time. That's what's wrong with our culture. Too many people listen to what other people have to say. Who cares? Don't look to others for guidance. Look to yourself ! That's what's great about science fiction. Every writer in the science fiction world is a different kind of writer. We all have different views of the world. (p. 23)

I'm an idea writer. Everything of mine is permeated with my love of ideas—both big and small. It doesn't matter what it is as long as it grabs me, and holds me, and fascinates me. And then I'll run out and do something about it. My poetry, all of it, is idea poetry. (p. 26)

[Writing science fiction is] more exciting today. A lot of my poetry is science fiction poetry. My new play, *The Martian Chronicles,* has been extremely satisfying. I'm older now, my enthusiasm is high, and I'm trying to find new ways of understanding my younger self. And so, my new plays, my science fiction plays, represent a new level of consciousness. . . .

I suspect [science fiction will] move more into philosophy, more into theology, at least I think so. The further we go into space, the more we're going to be awed and terrified by our lonely position in the universe. That means we'll need to do a lot of thinking about the future, which is what I'm trying to do with my poetry. I want to help us to explain ourselves to ourselves. That has always been a constant in science fiction, but I think it will dominate our thinking in the next forty years. (p. 27)

The same attributes that characterize fiction writing in any field are equally true for science fiction— namely, observation and truth. . . . *The Martian Chronicles* is a metaphor for a way of viewing the universe, of viewing our planet and the other planets. It works because it rings a bell of truth. It looks like a fantasy, but it isn't. It will only work if you, the reader, feel that the writer has an honest way of looking at the world. (pp. 27-8)

Ray Bradbury, "Ray Bradbury: Poet of Fantastic Fiction," in an interview with Jeffrey M. Elliot, in *Science Fiction Voices #2,* The Borgo Press, 1979, pp. 20-9.

EDWARD J. GALLAGHER

(essay date 1980)

[In the following excerpt, Gallagher studies the chronological and thematic unity of *The Martian Chronicles*.]

The Martian Chronicles (1950) is one of those acknowledged science fiction masterpieces which has never received detailed scholarly study as a whole. Its overall theme is well known. Clifton Fadiman says that Bradbury is telling us we are gripped by a technology-mania, that "the place for space travel is in a book, that human beings are still mental and moral children who cannot be trusted with the terrifying toys they have by some tragic accident invented." Richard Donovan says that Bradbury's fear is that "man's mechanical aptitudes, his incredible ability to pry into the secrets of the physical universe, may be his fatal flaw." And from "we Earth Men have a talent for ruining big, beautiful things" to "science ran too far ahead of us too quickly, and the people got lost in a mechanical wilderness . . . emphasizing machines instead of how to run machines," *The Martian Chronicles* itself provides an ample supply of clear thematic statements.

The structural unity of the novel's twenty-six stories, however, is usually overlooked or ignored. Six of the stories were published before Bradbury submitted an outline for *The Martian Chronicles* to Doubleday in June 1949. Thus, while individual stories have been praised, discussed, and anthologized out of context, it has been widely assumed that the collection, though certainly not random, has only a vague chronological and thematic unity. (p. 55)

The Martian Chronicles may not be a novel, but it is certainly more than just a collection of self-contained stories. Bradbury, for instance, revised **"The Third Expedition"** for collection in the *Chronicles,* adding material about the first two expeditions and drastically changing the ending. *The Martian Chronicles* has the coherence of, say, Hemingway's *In Our Time.* The ordering of stories has a significance that goes beyond chronology and which creates a feeling of unity and coherence; thus it almost demands to be read and treated as though it were a novel. (p. 56)

To facilitate discussion, the twenty-six stories in *The Martian Chronicles* may be divided into three sections. The seven stories in the first section, from **"Rocket Summer"** to **"And the Moon Be Still as Bright,"** deal with the initial four attempts to successfully establish a footing on Mars. The fifteen stories in the second section, from **"The Settlers"** to **"The Watchers,"** span the rise and fall of the Mars colony; and the four stories in the final section, from **"The Silent Towns"** to **"The Million-Year Picnic,"** linger on the possible regeneration of the human race after the devastating atomic war.

Bradbury's purpose in this first group of stories is to belittle man's technological achievement, to show us that supermachines do not make supermen. The terse power of **"Rocket Summer"** is filtered through three humiliating defeats before man is allowed to celebrate a victory. In fact, "celebration," the goal men seek as much as physical settlement, is the main motif in this section. Bradbury uses it to emphasize the pernicious quality of human pride. The stories build toward the blatant thematic statement of **"And the Moon Be Still as Bright"**; but this story is artistically poor, since the section does not depend on it, either for meaning or for effect. Next to a sense of delayed anticipation, the strength of the section stems from a sense of motion; the stories of the three defeats are not repetitive of one another. Bradbury varies both style and tone in **"Ylla,"** **"The Earth Men,"** and **"The Third Expedition,"** increasing the intensity from the mellow and the comic to the savage. In this way, **"And the Moon Be Still as Bright"** serves a cohesive function as the climax of and clarification of views which we have already felt. Another significant motif in this section comes from the phantasmagoric atmosphere that Bradbury associates with Mars. This trapping, this "accident" of his fantasy, produces clashes of dream and reality, sanity and insanity, which serve functionally to underscore Bradbury's desire for us to view technology from a different perspective. (pp. 56-7)

The second section of *The Martian Chronicles,* the fifteen stories from **"The Settlers"** to **"The Watchers,"** spans the rise and fall of the Mars colony. Because of the large span of events, this section seems less taut, less focused and more discursive than the first section. Whereas the very short stories in the first section (**"Rocket Summer,"** **"The Summer Night,"** **"The Taxpayer"**) were stories in their own right, as well as introductions to the main stories about the three expeditions, here the nine very short stories seem burdened with the "history" of the settlement. As a result, the flow is a bit choppy. The most important stories in the section are **"Night Meeting"** and **"The Martian,"** and the purpose of the section is to point to mankind's hostility toward difference—toward otherness, another manifestation of human pride—as the factor which determines the quality of colonization. (p. 65)

The four stories [of the third section]—**"The Silent Towns,"** **"The Long Years,"** **"There Will Come Soft Rains,"** and **"The Million-Year Picnic"**—linger on the possible regeneration of the human race after a devastating atomic war and the consequent evacuation of Mars. Bradbury does not allow hope to come easy, and when it does, it comes almost grudgingly. Just as Bradbury filters the power of **"Rocket Summer"** through three unsuccessful expeditions, he squeezes optimism about a second beginning on Mars—a really new life—through three resounding defeats. **"The Silent Towns"** is a parody of the familiar new-Adam-and-Eve motif in science fiction, which comically thwarts notions of a new race of humans. **"The Long Years"** and **"There Will Come Soft Rains"** focus on the machines, the sons of men, which inherit the Earth. Both stories end with meaningless mechanical rituals which mock the sentience that gave them life. *The Martian Chronicles* does not turn upward until the last story, **"The Million-Year Picnic."** Only in the complete destruction of Earth, Earth history, and Earth values, plus the complete acceptance of a new identity, can hope be entertained. "It is good to renew one's wonder," says Bradbury's philosopher in the epigraph, "space travel has again made children of us all." In the context of game, vacation, and picnic, this last story entrusts the possibility of new life to a small band of transformed Earth children. (pp. 76-7)

Unless we pay close attention to the sermons of Spender [Bradbury's mouthpiece in **"And the Moon Be Still as Bright"**] and the symbolism of **"The Million-Year Picnic,"** it is easy to feel that in *The Martian Chronicles,* Bradbury is against space travel per se. Nothing could be further from the truth. Over and over again in his personal statements, Bradbury has stressed that space is our destiny. Speaking as Jules Verne in an imaginary interview, Bradbury says that the function of the writer is to push the wilderness back. "We do not like this wilderness, this material universe with its own unfathomable laws which ignore our twitchings. Man will only breathe easily when he has climbed the tallest Everest of all: Space. Not because it is there, no, no, but because he must survive and survival means man's populating all the worlds of all the suns." There is only one thing that can stop this journey—the wilderness in man himself. . . . (pp. 81-2)

The threat of atomic war, kept in the background and off stage in *The Martian Chronicles,* is more on Bradbury's mind than it might appear. "Today we stand on the rim of Space," he says; "man, in his immense tidal motion is about to flow out toward far new worlds, but man must conquer the seed of his own self-destruction. Man is half-idealist, half-destroyer, and the real and terrible thing is that he can still destroy himself before reaching the stars." Perhaps, he suggests, a book for his time would be one "about man's ability to be quicker than his wars." "Sometimes there is no solution, save flight, from annihilation. When reason turns murderously unreasonable, Man has always run. . . . If but one Adam and Eve reach Mars while the entire stagecraft of Earth burns to a fine cinder, history will have been justified, Mind will be preserved, Life continued."

Bradbury, then, comes not "to celebrate the defeat of man by matter, but to proclaim his high destiny and urge him on to it." The rocket is the conqueror of Death, the "shatterer of the scythe." The proper study of God is space. Bradbury—like Jonathan Edwards, for example—is truly a moralist. Edwards said that if you believe in the certainty of a hell, it makes good sense to scare people away from it. *The Martian Chronicles* is Bradbury's hellfire-and-brimstone sermon. (p. 82)

Edward J. Gallagher, "The Thematic Structure of 'The Martian Chronicles'," in *Ray Bradbury,* edited by Martin Harry Greenberg and Joseph D. Olander, Taplinger Publishing Company, 1980, pp. 55-82.

SARAH-WARNER J. PELL
(essay date 1980)

[In the excerpt below, Pell examines the use of metaphor and simile in *S Is for Space, The Martian Chronicles*, and *I Sing the Body Electric!*]

Imagery is not a new literary device. Aristotle lauded it as the most potent way to find similarities in dissimilar things. Bradbury is especially adept with imagery. His writing style brings galactic fantasy and an incredible imagination within the grasp of the reader, especially through the use of simile and metaphor. Unfortunately for readers of science fiction, not all authors are as able as Bradbury in using either the "tied" or the "free" image. (By this bit of technicality, I mean that the tied image has a meaning or associative value that is the same or nearly the same for all of us, while the free image has various values and meanings for different people.) (pp. 187-88)

If imagery is an index to able craftsmanship, of

beauty and poetry of style, Bradbury qualifies as a master. In examining three works—*S Is for Space, The Martian Chronicles,* and *I Sing the Body Electric!*—all similes and metaphors used were extracted. Since the reading and revealing of these Bradbury classics continues to be a source of wonder and delight, there is no guarantee that a simile or metaphor will not have escaped, like the evanescent Martians. We are left with well over three hundred graphically original figures of speech. This imagery is marked by originality and imagination. Typically, it is tied, in that the metaphors and similes relate to common experiences of mankind. This is not to say that Bradbury will not make up his own original verb forms from existing nonverbs or simply from sound combinations suggesting his meaning.

How do we classify such a body of material? What can we say definitively about Bradbury? (p. 188)

Middletown, dreamtown America, untouched by violence, pestilence, famine, world wars, prejudice; the idyllic small-town American boyhood, never far from nature; an American boyhood of sounds, tastes, sights, feelings of birth, life, death, seasons—this is Bradbury's touchstone for the largest portion of his imagery.

As imaginary Martians with only our chronicles and two other slim volumes, let us look at Bradbury's Hometown, U.S.A. Could it be a small Midwestern town with "candy-cheeked boys with blue agate eyes" . . . ? We consistently find the denizens of this galactic hometown populating space. There is the fantasy trolley, "epaulets of shimmery brass cover it, and pipings of gold. . . . Within, its seats prickle with cool green moss." . . . There are Civil War statues, wooden Indians, trains and twelve-year-old boys. There are seasons, "summer swoons," a "marble-cream moon," autumn leaves crackling and winter: " . . . panes blind with frost, icicles fringing every roof . . . housewives lumbering like great black bears in their furs." . . . (pp. 188-89)

Long metaphoric passages in the three novels populate Hometown, U.S.A. and its inhabitants, mainly through the eyes of youth. . . . How can we describe colonists to another planet? "They would come like a scatter of jackstones on the marble flats beside the canals" . . . , or: "small children, small seeds . . . to be sown in all the Martian climes."

What about machinery, computers, and rocket ships? Again, Bradbury metaphorically bonds science not only to the familiar hometown childhood but to nature as well. The beauty of nature abounds in Bradbury's imagery. Computers?—"a school of computers that chatter in maniac chorus . . . a cloud of paper confetti from one titan machine, holes punched out to perhaps record his passing, fell upon him in a whispered snow." . . . "Machines that trim your soul in silhouette like a vast pair of beautiful shears, snipping away the rude brambles, the dire horns and hooves to leave a finer profile." . . . In addition to the skillful manipulation of simile and metaphor, these examples illustrate the connection to Earth's nature and times.

Rockets? Rockets can be either "flowers of heat and color" or pummeling objects. The following passage from *The Martian Chronicles* shows the Earthling and Martian picture series we used earlier for images tied to nature and small towns:

> The rockets came like drums, beating in the night. The rockets came like locusts, swarming and settling in blooms of rosy smoke . . . men with hammers in their hands to beat the strange world into a shape that was familiar to the eye, to bludgeon away all the strangeness, their mouths fringed with nails so they resembled steel-toothed carnivores, spitting them into their swift hands. . . .

So closely does Bradbury weave galactic travel and interplanetary settlement to experiences on Earth that the extracted metaphor does not seem to come from science-fiction literature. (p. 189)

Somehow, as we wander through space and future time with Bradbury, we remain tethered to the town and to nature. Twelve-year-old boys empty their pockets of treasures; this metaphor is used to describe alien machinery. Baseball is an important metaphorical vehicle: "He stared at the baseball in his trembling hand, as if it were his life, an interminable ball of years strung around and around and around, but always leading back to his twelfth birthday." . . . Bradbury frequently uses boyhood games in his imagery, for instance, "the entire planet Earth became a muddy baseball tossed away." . . .

As common as childhood games for Bradbury is the mirror: "Heat snapped mirrors like the brittle winter ice" . . . or "In his bureau mirror he saw a face made of June dandelions and July apples and warm summer-morning milk" . . . and, importantly: "The sand whispered and stirred like an image in a vast, melting mirror." . . . This combination of the melting mirror brings us to another important image for Bradbury—melting: "The waves broke on the shore, silent mirrors, heaps of melting, whispering glass." . . . Bradbury uses the simile of bones melting like gold, knees melting, a girl melting like a crystal figurine, melting like lime sherbet, people melting like metal, deserts melting to yellow wax, and spacemen, drained of rocket fever, melting through the floor. (p. 190)

People, star travelers—what are they like? How do they feel? "The world swarms with people, each one drowning, but each swimming a different stroke to the far shore," Bradbury tells us. . . . In imagery, Bradbury describes humans as great ships of men, red-shagged hounds, a chemist's scale, litmus paper, as an

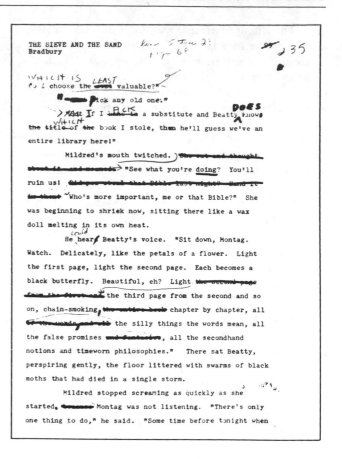

Bradbury's revision of a manuscript page of *Fahrenheit 451.*

insect, a beetle, metallic and sharp, a hawk, "finished and stropped like a razor by the swift life he had lived" . . . , a tobacco-smoking bear. He is remarkably gentle with the elderly, describing one man as a "blind old sheepherder-saint" . . . and an old lady who "gestured her cane, like an ancient goddess." . . . Withering apples in a bin and the hammer blows of the years shattering faces into a million wrinkles, describe the aging process as faces toll away the years. An old lady is viewed as "skittering quick as a gingham lizard." There are dry and crackling people and dried-apricot people. Remember the library, appearing in imagery several times. You know the librarian, Bradbury suggests:

> a woman you often heard talking to herself off in the dark dust-stacks with a whisper like turned pages, a woman who glided as if on hidden wheels.

> She came carrying her soft lamp of face, lighting her way with her glance. (*Sing*. . .)

Maids or live-in sitters or teachers don't fare as well; they are characterized with this metaphor: ". . . a crosscut saw grabbing against the grain. Handaxes and hurricanes best described them. Or, conversely, they were all fallen trifle, damp soufflé." . . . And, *some* people in groups . . . "with everything well on its way to Safety, the Spoil-Funs, the people with mercurochrome for blood and iodine-colored eyes, come now to set up their Moral Climates and dole out goodness to everyone." . . . More hopefully for the human condition, however, "good friends trade hairballs all the time, give gifts of mutual dismays and so are rid of them." . . .

In describing human emotion and thought, Bradbury again draws on nature. Adventure and excitement become dancing fire; rage is sour water in the mouth. Fear is a cold rock, a winter chill. Joy is a white blossom or a downpour of soft summer rain. Pain is a great impacted wisdom tooth. (p. 191)

Not knowing Bradbury at all, our Martian observer could detect an interest in photography, the theater, and, most certainly, science—simply through his use of imagery in these categories. As the famous author from Tau Ceti reveals his interest in geology through this startling metaphor, translated into Intergalactic—"The zxboric captain's thought weighed as the pstoralic cliffs with as many zenotropic caves of mystery"—so Bradbury centers similes around science; circuits; lubricating oil; eyes like small, blue electric bulbs; thoughts like gusts of pure oxygen; bitterness like black-green acid, as well as references to astronomy.

We can identify Shakespeare's influence in this image: "they kept glancing over their shoulders . . . as if at any moment, Chaos herself might unleash her dogs from there." . . . Greek classics are evident in similes using the Fates, the Arcadian silo, Apollo's chariot, and the Delphic caves. We find similes whose vehicle is *Moby-Dick*. . . . [Other passages] reveal how the Hometown Library served to enrich the imagery. . . . (p. 192)

A last major category of metaphor and simile in the three novels we are discussing is Biblical or religious in nature. In general, the religious references are vengeful, negative ones. "Oh, oh. Here he comes, Moses crossing a Black Sea of bile." . . . Helicopters and bus fares are likened to manna. Old Testament characters such as Delilah and Baal appear in simile. Metaphorically we find, "One God of the machines to say, you Lazarus-elevator, rise up! You hovercraft, be reborn! And anoint them with leviathan oils, tap them with magical wrench and send them forth to almost eternal lives." . . . (p. 193)

Whether Martian or Earthling, science fiction fan or not, one comes away enriched by the creative language and style of Bradbury. He is a master of imagery, the implied analogy. In metaphorical use he most often compares both the qualities and the emotions evoked in humans by an ideal hometown and nature. He finds compelling similarities in dissimilar objects and events.

He is a master of the simile, which is usually tied to earthly associations and is described concretely. As with the metaphor, hometown and nature are the most common vehicles employed in his construction of simile.

There is no doubt that, like it or not, after examining Bradbury's use of simile and metaphor in conducting us on our galactic tours, other science-fiction writing seems anemic and one-dimensional. Not only can we, the readers, tell a good bit about Bradbury—his childhood, hometown, relationship to nature and such disparate experiences and interests as theater, photography, science and religion—but Bradbury, using these stylistic forms of imagery, makes other worlds and far-flung reaches of space seem as understandable as our own back yards.

The adroit use of images seems to show that the author, with consummate skill and originality, makes his science fiction reach far beyond the banal, pedestrian "pulp," beyond the stereotype "blast-'em-up" future fiction. Bradbury brought respectability to science fiction. Beyond this, his fertile imagination, as evidenced in his use of simile and metaphor, creates vivid images. To continue the juxtaposition of Martian and Earthling, the Martian grasps Hometown, U.S.A.—its sights, smells, sounds, tastes, and feelings—while the Earthling feels at home among the stars.

Two metaphors of Bradbury's seem to sum up the man and his style: " . . . I leapt high and dove deep down into the vast ocean of Space." . . . But " . . . I was tethered to heaven by the longest, I repeat, longest kite string in the entire history of the world!" (pp. 193-94)

Sarah-Warner J. Pell, "Style Is the Man: Imagery in Bradbury's Fiction," in *Ray Bradbury*, edited by Martin Harry Greenberg and Joseph D. Olander, Taplinger Publishing Company, 1980, pp. 186-94.

DONALD WATT

(essay date 1980)

[Watt has written extensively on science fiction authors Aldous Huxley, Isaac Asimov, and Bradbury. In the excerpt below, he praises Bradbury's "evocative, lyrical style," focusing on his use of symbolism in *Fahrenheit 451*.]

"It was a pleasure to burn," begins Bradbury's *Fahrenheit 451*. "It was a special pleasure to see things eaten, to see things blackened and *changed*." In the decade following Nagasaki and Hiroshima, Bradbury's eye-catching opening for his dystopian novel assumes particular significance. America's nuclear climax to World War II signalled the start of a new age in which the awesome powers of technology, with its alarming dangers, would provoke fresh inquiries into the dimensions of man's potentiality and the scope of his brutality. . . . The opening paragraph of Bradbury's novel immediately evokes the consequences of unharnessed technology and contemporary man's contented refusal to acknowledge these consequences.

In short, *Fahrenheit 451* (1953) raises the question posed by a number of contemporary anti-utopian novels. In one way or another, Huxley's *Ape and Essence* (1948), Orwell's *Nineteen Eighty-Four* (1948), Vonnegut's *Player Piano* (1952), Miller's *A Canticle for Leibowitz* (1959), Hartley's *Facial Justice* (1960), and Burgess's *A Clockwork Orange* (1962) all address themselves to the issue of technology's impact on the destiny of man. In this sense, Mark R. Hillegas is right in labeling *Fahrenheit 451* "almost the archetypal anti-utopia of the new era in which we live." Whether, what, and how to burn in Bradbury's book are the issues—as implicit to a grasp of our age as electricity—which occupy the center of the contemporary mind.

What is distinctive about *Fahrenheit 451* as a work of literature, then, is not what Bradbury says but how he says it. With Arthur C. Clarke, Bradbury is among the most poetic of science fiction writers. Bradbury's evocative, lyrical style charges *Fahrenheit 451* with a sense of mystery and connotative depth that go beyond the normal boundaries of dystopian fiction. Less charming, perhaps, than *The Martian Chronicles, Fahrenheit 451* is also less brittle. More to the point, in *Fahrenheit 451* Bradbury has created a pattern of symbols that richly convey the intricacy of his central theme. Involved in Bradbury's burning is the overwhelming problem of modern science: as man's shining inventive intellect sheds more and more light on the truths of the universe, the increased knowledge he thereby acquires, if abused, can ever more easily fry his planet to a cinder. Burning as constructive energy, and burning as apocalyptic catastrophe, are the symbolic poles of Bradbury's novel. Ultimately, the book probes in symbolic terms the puzzling, divisive nature of man as a creative/destructive creature. *Fahrenheit 451* thus becomes a book which injects originality into a literary subgenre that can grow worn and hackneyed. It is the only major symbolic dystopia of our time.

The plot of *Fahrenheit 451* is simple enough. In Bradbury's future, Guy Montag is a fireman whose job it is to burn books and, accordingly, discourage the citizenry from thinking about anything except four-wall television. He meets a young woman whose curiosity and love of natural life stir dissatisfaction with his role in society. He begins to read books and to rebel against the facade of diversions used to seal the masses away from the realities of personal insecurity, officially con-

doned violence, and periodic nuclear war. He turns against the authorities in a rash and unpremeditated act of murder, flees their lethal hunting party, and escapes to the country. At the end of the book he joins a group of self-exiled book-lovers who hope to preserve the great works of the world despite the opposition of the masses and a nuclear war against an unspecified enemy.

In such bare detail, the novel seems unexciting, even a trifle inane. But Bradbury gives his story impact and imaginative focus by means of symbolic fire. Appropriately, fire is Montag's world, his reality. Bradbury's narrative portrays events as Montag sees them, and it is natural to Montag's way of seeing to regard his experiences in terms of fire. This is a happy and fruitful arrangement by Bradbury, for he is thereby able to fuse character development, setting, and theme into a whole. Bradbury's symbolic fire gives unity, as well as stimulating depth, to *Fahrenheit 451.*

Bradbury dramatizes Montag's development by showing the interactions between his hero and other characters in the book; the way Bradbury plays with reflections of fire in these encounters constantly sheds light on key events. Clarisse, Mildred, the old woman, Beatty, Faber, and Granger are the major influences on Montag as he struggles to understand his world. The figure of Clarisse is, of course, catalytic; she is dominant in Montag's growth to awareness. The three sections into which Bradbury divides the novel are, however, most clearly organized around the leading male characters—Beatty in Part One, Faber in Part Two, and Montag himself (with Granger) in Part Three. Beatty and Faber—the one representing the annihilating function of fire, the other representing the quiet, nourishing flame of the independent creative imagination—are the poles between which Montag must find his identity, with Mildred and Clarisse reflecting the same polar opposition on another level. The men are the intellectual and didactic forces at work on Montag, while the women are the intuitive and experiential forces. Beatty articulates the system's point of view, but Mildred lives it. Faber articulates the opposition's point of view, but Clarisse lives it. Fire, color, light, darkness, and variations thereof suffuse Bradbury's account of the interplay among his characters, suggesting more subtly than straight dialogue or description the full meaning of *Fahrenheit 451.* (pp. 195-97)

From its opening portrait of Montag as a singed salamander, to its concluding allusion to the Bible's promise of undying light for man, *Fahrenheit 451* uses a rich body of symbols emanating from fire to shed a variety of illuminations on future and contemporary man.

To be sure, the novel has its vulnerable spots. For one thing, Montag's opposition is not very formidable. Beatty is an articulate spokesman for the authorities, but he has little of the power to invoke terror that Orwell's O'Brien has. The Mechanical Hound is a striking and sinister gadget; but for all its silent stalking, it conveys considerably less real alarm than a pack of aroused bloodhounds. What is genuinely frightening is the specter of that witless mass of humanity in the background who feed on manhunts televised live and a gamey version of highway hit-and-run. For another thing, the reader may be unsettled by the vagueness with which Bradbury defines the conditions leading to the nuclear war. Admittedly, his point is that such a lemming-like society, by its very irresponsibility, will ultimately end in destruction. But the reader is justifiably irritated by the absence of any account of the country's political situation or of the international power structure. The firemen are merely enforcers of noninvolvement, not national policymakers. The reader would like to know something more about the actual controllers of Beatty's occupation. Who, we wonder, is guarding the guardians?

Probably a greater problem than either of these is what some readers may view as a certain evasiveness on Bradbury's part. Presumably, the controversies and conflicts brought on by reading books have led to the system of mass ignorance promulgated by Beatty. Even with this system, though, man drifts into nuclear ruin. Bradbury glosses over the grim question raised by other dystopian novelists of his age: if man's individuality and knowledge bring him repeatedly to catastrophe, should not the one be circumscribed and the other forbidden? Such novels as *A Canticle for Leibowitz*, *A Clockwork Orange*, and *Facial Justice* deal more realistically with this problem than does *Fahrenheit 451*. Although the religious light shining through Montag from the Bible is a fitting climax to the book's use of symbolism, Bradbury's novel does risk lapsing at the very close into a vague optimism.

Yet *Fahrenheit 451* remains a notable achievement in postwar dystopian fiction. . . . The book's weaknesses derive in part from that very symbolism in which its strength and originality are to be found. If *Fahrenheit 451* is vague in political detail, it is accordingly less topical and therefore more broadly applicable to the dilemmas of the twentieth century as a whole. Like the nineteenth-century French symbolists, Bradbury's purpose is to evoke a mood, not to name particulars. His connotative language is far more subtle, his novel far more of one piece, than Huxley's rambling nightmare, *Ape and Essence*. Though the novel lacks the great impact of *Nineteen Eighty-Four*, Kingsley Amis is right when he says that *Fahrenheit 451* is "superior in conciseness and objectivity" to Orwell's anti-utopian novel. If *Fahrenheit 451* poses no genuinely satisfying answers to the plight of postindustrial man, neither is the flight to the stars at the end of *A Canticle for Leibowitz* much of a solution. We can hardly escape from ourselves. By comparison with Bradbury's novel, *Facial Jus-*

tice is tepid and *A Clockwork Orange* overdone. On the whole, *Fahrenheit 451* comes out as a distinctive contribution to the speculative literature of our times, because in its multiple variations on its fundamental symbol, it demonstrates that dystopian fiction need not exclude the subtlety of poetry. (pp. 212-13)

Donald Watt, "Burning Bright: 'Fahrenheit 451' as Symbolic Dystopia," in *Ray Bradbury*, edited by Martin Harry Greenberg and Joseph D. Olander, Taplinger Publishing Company, 1980, pp. 195-213.

WILLIAM F. TOUPONCE
(essay date 1984)

[In the following excerpt, Touponce examines surrealist elements in Bradbury's works.]

Ray Bradbury is known primarily as a writer of science fiction, fantasy, and children's literature, and he is especially noted for two books which he wrote during the 1950s, *Fahrenheit 451* and *The Martian Chronicles*. When critics today discuss his work, it is usually in the context of genre theory. Not surprisingly, in view of certain aspects of surrealism in his writings that it is my purpose in this paper to present, Bradbury does not fare very well at the hands of these critics. He is often accused of narrative inconsistencies and poor knowledge of science (if not protofascist revulsion towards progress and technology). For example, the Marxist-structuralist critic Darko Suvin consigns Bradbury's writings to a monstrous and misshapen subgenre of real science fiction, "science-fantasy," which according to him does not use scientific logic for a validation of the story's premises, but only as an excuse or rationalization that is later abandoned at the author's whim. Actually, and as I have demonstrated elsewhere, this is only the apparent truth about Bradbury's work. And it is at least ironic (especially when one considers that Suvin's poetics of science fiction claims to study *metamorphoses* of science fiction) that his generic logic of antinomies never allows him to consider the possibility that Bradbury's "whims" may be intended to direct the reader towards surrealist imaginings—or even surrational imaginings—to use a phrase coined by Gaston Bachelard that André Breton employed when he discussed surrealism's relationship to scientific knowledge.

In my opinion, Bradbury's work should be studied first for its rich imaginative vision, and secondarily for the way in which it links up with the larger literary movements of the twentieth century, surrealism and existentialism. While it is certainly relevant to take a generic approach to individual stories or novels, I would rate this approach last in terms of real value, for too often we find a critic using a text by Bradbury to exemplify a notion of what science fiction is, whereas another critic with a different set of conceptual schemata will cite the same text as an example of what science fiction is not. In short, at the current state of our knowledge of this genre and how it demands to be read, everyone is his own Aristotle. On the other hand, it has been obvious for some time now to writers of surrealist inspiration that such themes as telepathy (Bradbury's use of which in *The Martian Chronicles* still baffles theorists who are bent on creating a generic logic) and paranoia are a shared common interest with writers of science fiction.

Yet if the foreshadowing of an individual future and telepathic communication are themes essential to both surrealism and science fiction, the surrealist imagination surpasses the limits of any generic logic. Its basic structures of consciousness, and I would argue that they are delusion, dream and reverie, are expressed in many different literary forms. So if the concept of genre is going to be of use to us in discussing Bradbury's work, it must be modified to allow the claims of surrealism to overcome antinomies to be considered. I cannot give a precise account here of how this might be done, nor do I wish to. My simple aim is to measure the degree to which Bradbury approaches the central concerns of surrealism. In short, I believe we can achieve a more balanced view of Bradbury's work by arguing that he is a surrealist in science fiction and not vice versa. (pp. 228-29)

From the presentation in [Michel] Carrouges' book [*André Breton and the Basic Concepts of Surrealism*] it would seem that there was ample precedent for the acceptance of at least some science fiction writing as embodying authentic surrealist goals at the time when Bradbury's work was first translated in French. No French critic of the 1950s ever asserted that there was any influence of surrealism on Bradbury's work, however. Rather, he seems to have discovered surrealist territory entirely on his own and spontaneously, manifesting a kind of native American surrealism. Nor should this be surprising, since the surrealists have always said that the desires they speak of are eternal, and that every man has access to them. (p. 230)

The Martian Chronicles, which depicts the colonization and destruction of the nearly mystical and telepathic Martian civilization by successive waves of Earthmen, is not to be understood as a simple reflection of social and economic conditions. Yet it is nevertheless haunted by social upheavals which permit the reader's consciousness to have a glimpse of sudden fissures that accompany them. Cannily observing that many works of science fiction ostensibly about the future seem to offer us a retrospective glance as well, Carrouges explains that Bradbury's *Martian Chronicles* (and other works of science fiction; Carrouges here extends his argument to include the entire genre) expresses the guilt of the twentieth century's destruction of exotic and primitive civilizations. The ruins of Bradbury's Mars are a haunted domain, a dark mirror where the reader projects that which haunts him in his deepest secrets. . . . (pp. 230-31)

Carrouges' argument is cogent, if at times narrowly skirting a reductive stance, because it reveals that Bradbury's Mars is intended to haunt the reader in a surrealist fashion, speaking to him of his deepest desires and consequently liberating him from his deepest repressions. Bradbury's Martians thus represent our own lost oneiric being, the dreaming pole of our minds, which is normally suppressed by rationality. But outside of a short discussion of the relationship of telepathy and point of view, Carrouges does not discuss the novel's poetics. As interesting as this kind of analysis would be in terms of the central concerns of surrealism, for reasons of space I cannot offer it here. Let me simply draw on some observations made by another reviewer of Bradbury, Michel Deutsch, whose attempt to characterize Bradbury's imagination in a grouping of six of his works complements that of Carrouges' generic approach to one work. . . . His science fiction is . . . , according to Deutsch, characterized by . . . openness, which combines in a highly original alliance the ambiguities of the dream and the scientific hypothesis. But Bradbury is a surrealist for Deutsch primarily because of the situation of the object in his poetics, i.e., how Bradbury transforms those technological gadgets that populate his imaginary worlds. The future for Bradbury is essentially a poetic object, and his narratives unfold around them in an inspired surrealist vision. . . . (p. 231)

[Electric fireflies] begin a long list of objects gleaned by Deutsch from the writings of Bradbury and which seem to him to evince a marked turning away of the object from its functional use, liberating it and lending it a sort of sublimated quality which reaches an absolute stage in *The Martian Chronicles* (where golden fruit grows from crystal walls of houses that turn, like sunflowers, to follow the sun). But although Deutsch points out that they offer an oneiric support for the reader's own surrealist imaginings, he does not analyze them in a narrative context. . . . [Here] again we have an instance of a critic writing in a different literary milieu who strongly affirms Bradbury's affinity with surrealism. The contradictions manifestly committed by the author in his descriptions of Mars pose no problem, therefore, to Deutsch's understanding; it is not a question of astronomy, of pure scientific logic, but of the landscape of a dream. (p. 232)

Bradbury's own statements about the creative ambiance of his work approach surrealist notions of automatic writing and the waking dream. In giving his advice to other writers, like the surrealists he insists that all men have direct access to the marvelous if they will just try to make contact with the subconscious. Quoting Coleridge about the flow of the writing process and the streamy nature of association which thinking curbs and rudders, he declares a "Middle Way" which resolves for him the antinomies of writing "literary" as opposed to "commercial" fiction. He advises the aspiring writer to relax and concentrate on the unconscious message. This way of writing shorts out the mind's critical and categorizing activities, allowing the subconscious to speak. Then, he says, the writer will begin to see himself in his work in a kind of dreamlike state: "At night the very phosphorescence of his insides will throw long shadows on the wall." This oneiric atmosphere described by Bradbury is reminiscent of certain remarks made by Breton concerning the state of receptivity required of the surrealist writer. Bradbury describes his writing of science fiction as plunging into a wild meadow, if not a dizzying descent into the self. For Bradbury, writing is human desire let run, and the writer's sole task (although he allows for some revisions later) is first of all to enable self and world to interact in a state of "dynamic relaxation" and lucid reverie. He regards this way of writing, finally, as the only guarantee of authenticity:

What do you think of the world? You, the prism, measure the light of the world; it burns through your mind to throw a different spectroscopic reading onto white paper than anyone else anywhere can throw.

Let the world burn through you. Throw the prism light, white hot, on paper. Make your own individual spectroscopic reading.

Then you, a new Element, are discovered, charted, named!

Prominent in this passage with its visual metaphor of the prism is the sense of surrealist discovery, suggesting, indeed, a parallel with scientific discovery: a new element is discovered, but not predicted beforehand. Self and world together make a new Element. At first glance, though, we may think that Bradbury is recommending that the writer become involved with visual images that he should try to transcribe—and this goes counter to Breton's strong rejection of the seeking of immediate enjoyment in one's images produced during the writing process. Breton feared that these images would block the flow of automatism, and he was convinced that Rimbaud and Lautréamont had no prior enjoyment of what they had still to describe. They did not understand the sibylline voices they listened to any better than we do when we first read them. In surrealism, Breton says, illumination comes afterwards.

But actually, the element most active in Brad-

bury's text is fire, and elsewhere in the same volume he expresses his idea more forcefully. During writing itself one must "explode—fly apart—disintegrate," just as in surrealism, a total disintegration of the mind is required to enter the avenues and dazzling zones of the marvelous. Even more revealing of Bradbury's surrealist desires, if one thinks of all the prestige that Breton gave to childhood and the manner in which children invest words and objects with a magical love, are these remarks concerning the writing of his semiautobiographical novel of childhood in an American small town, *Dandelion Wine:*

. . . in my early twenties I floundered into a word-association process in which I simply got out of bed each morning, walked to my desk, and put down any word or series of words that happened along in my head.

(pp. 232-33)

Written during the 1950s also, *Dandelion Wine* is arguably the purest surrealist text Bradbury has produced (in the same sense that it is free of any admixture of science fiction, gothic horror, etc.). Clearly, Bradbury's remarks in the passage describe the receiving of a linguistic message from the subconscious which is then later piloted and elaborated by the conscious mind in active cooperation with it. In short, the need to observe and to try to discern the play of dreamlike elements and the very subtle reintroduction of consciousness into the heart of automatism—just the very kind of intelligent surrealism advocated by Breton himself— lie at the heart of Bradbury's poetic practice. . . . *Dandelion Wine* is a text of pure reveries, organized by oneiric scenes of dandelion winemaking. This beneficial elixer becomes the substance of archetypal childhood which attracts the reader's own happy imagination. . . . [But] *Dandelion Wine* is not a work of science fiction. If it embodies surrealist structures of consciousness in their unadulterated form (no pun intended), that is because Bradbury is a surrealist in nearly everything he writes. . . . **"The Rocket Man"** (1951) . . . is one of Bradbury's earliest science fiction stories in which we can detect an interior world of magical preoccupations. Indeed, it deals—"innocently," to be sure—with several desires and central themes of surrealism. There is first of all the desire to fuse conscious and unconscious in a new concrete synthesis that leads to the possession of a world of marvels. But also, as in any attempt by surrealism to recover lost powers of imagination, there is the danger that the sun of rational awareness will destroy reverie. The mind must allow itself to be so strongly attracted, so rapidly borne along by the flow of automatism that it will dash after it in breathless pursuit with no desire to go back. (pp. 234-35)

The focus of the narrator's reverie towards childhood is his father's uniform, no utilitarian object to him, but one charged with the antinomies of light and dark. In his imagination it seems a dark nebula with little faint stars glowing through it. It is this object which is transformed in the story and which forms the pivot around which the narrative turns, for it lies directly on the axis of desire that organizes the characters and their roles. . . . The fabric of the cloth, its textuality as it were, organizes and constellates all the metaphors, those points of light along the boy's itinerary. It also functions phenomenologically as an unconscious complex, an organizer of psychic energy, for the nebula is mostly black, unconscious, although it bears within it points of light which offer the promise of conscious transformation if developed surrealistically into the worlds in themselves.

In this story the narrator tells how he wanted to become a rocket man like his father who travels among the distant stars and dangerous planets and who was seldom home on Earth. A basic Freudian question in the story revolves around whether or not the boy's desire will be defined by the mother, who wants to keep the father at home, or by the father through the mechanism of identification. But although this mechanism is set up in the story, the boy comes to define, through reverie, his own desire. The uniform is obviously involved in this play of desire because it is an object never displayed at home and which the boy wants to see. However, the boy's mother and father are both anxious that the boy not take up this life of sometimes intense loneliness and danger, but the boy, full of the allure of space travel and rockets, can only think of those faraway places his father visits.

At times the boy feels deprived and rejected because the father never brings him any gifts from these miraculous places. . . . At any rate, the Earthbound boy has to trade the ordinary objects he likes with other boys in order to get these surreal ones. One night, when the father has just returned from a tour of duty in the solar system and both parents are asleep in bed, the boy steals his father's travel case which contains his uniform, still smelling of metal and space, fire and time. He examines it in his own private world, apart from the parents. . . . (pp. 235-36)

If we examine this movement of reverie-consciousness a bit more closely, we discover that as the boy begins to knead the fabric of his dreams, the "dark stuff " in his warm hands, he smells traces of several worlds: Venus, Mars, Mercury—and we can assume here also the presence of the archetypal elements giving rise to many a surrealist cosmology; I mean, of course, fire, earth, and water. As olfactory images they bring about a released spontaneity of the imaginary in the boy's mind, the traces in the black fabric serving to generate an aspiration toward other worlds, function-

ing as passive syntheses of experiences the father has lived through and in which the boy desires to participate actively.

Once the boy touches matter imaginatively, he begins to materialize his desire. . . . The boy in our story has found that malleable matter which Bachelard says offers to the imagination a marvellous dynamic equilibrium between accepting forces and refusing forces. Through reverie, he has abolished the distance between himself and the objects of his desire, transforming self and world at the same time. A dynamic joy touches matter, kneads it, makes it lighter. The boy travels from microcosm to macrocosm, penetrating those magical crystals he has sublimated into "worlds themselves." A truly successful reverie, I might add, always develops this sense of cosmic participation both in Bachelard and Bradbury.

Since later on in the story the father's rocket falls into the sun, killing him, and the sun becomes a gaze almost impossible for the mother and son to avoid, we might be tempted to think that this story concludes with a defeat of the imagination. But on the contrary, Bradbury shows us their continuing desire to live in a world created and ordered by imagination: they have breakfast at midnight, go to all-night shows and go to bed at sunrise. Thus the sun of rationality (i.e., death) does not defeat man's desires. They transform a hostile world into a habitable one by their acts of imagination.

There are, of course, surrealist objects in the story of the sort Michel Deutsch mentions. But they are all asleep, significantly, along with the parents, in the passage I have chosen for analysis. One further, perhaps most important thing, argues for this story as an embodiment of surrealist imagination. Carrouges writes that if it were possible to come up with an objective standard for fidelity to surrealist concerns, he would be tempted to find it in the image of the *clair-obscur* (literally, clear-dark), the sense that there has to be a real and authentic encounter of the night and the day in the mind, between awareness and subconsciousness. And if it is this reciprocal presence of the dark worlds appearing in the clarity of the words or the layers of immanent brightness in the dark verbal fields which must be the authentic value of the surrealist image, then we have such an image in Bradbury's "black nebula," which bears luminous motes that are signs of the highest cooperation in them of the conscious and the subconscious. I would say that in almost all of Bradbury's writings this encounter takes place, but most certainly the story I have analyzed here. (pp. 236-38)

William F. Touponce, "Some Aspects of Surrealism in the Work of Ray Bradbury," in *Extrapolation,* Vol. 25, No. 3, Fall, 1984, pp. 228-38.

SOURCES FOR FURTHER STUDY

Bleiler, E. F., ed. *Science Fiction Writers: Critical Studies of the Major Authors from the Early Nineteenth Century to the Present Day.* New York: Charles Scribner's Sons, 1982, 623 p.

> Collection of 76 essays—one of which focuses on Bradbury—examining the lives and works of authors important to the development of science fiction.

Greenberg, Martin Harry, and Olander, Joseph D., eds. *Ray Bradbury.* New York: Taplinger, 1980, 248 p.

> Collection of critical essays on such issues as Bradbury's attitude toward science and technology and the relationship between the past and the future.

Johnson, Wayne L. *Ray Bradbury.* New York: Ungar, 1980, 173 p.

> Overview of Bradbury's works that "places [him] within science fiction but relates him to such broader traditions as fantasy and *Winesburg*-like studies of Americana."

Linkfield, Thomas P. "The Fiction of Ray Bradbury: Universal Themes in Midwestern Settings." *Midwestern Miscellany* 8 (1980): 44-101.

> Examines Bradbury's development of such themes as stasis versus change and fear of darkness and dying in *The Halloween Man, Something Wicked This Way Comes,* and *Dandelion Wine.*

Nolan, William F. *The Ray Bradbury Companion: A Life and Career History, Photolog, and Comprehensive Checklist of Writings with Facsimiles from Ray Bradbury's Unpublished and Uncollected Work in all Media.* Detroit: Gale Research, 1975, 339 p.

> Extensive biographical and bibliographical treatment of Bradbury's life and career.

Slusser, George Edgar. *The Bradbury Chronicles.* San Bernardino, Calif.: Borgo Press, 1977, 63 p.

> Studies Bradbury's fiction, giving brief synopses of several stories.

Bertolt Brecht

1898-1956

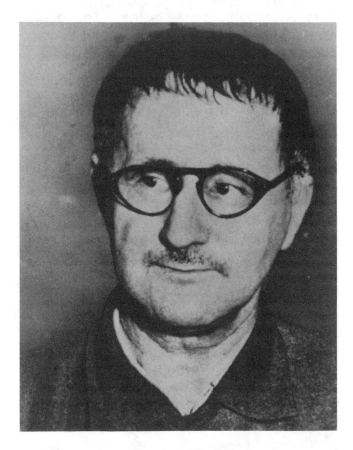

(Full name Eugen Bertolt Friedrich Brecht; also wrote under pseudonym Berthold Eugen) German dramatist, poet, critic, novelist, and short story writer.

INTRODUCTION

*B*recht's imagination, artistic genius, and profound grasp of the nature of drama establish him as a chief innovator of modern theatrical techniques. The concept of "epic theater" and use of "alienation effects" are the best known features of his dramatic theory. Brecht effectively exploited an exquisite stage-sense to promote his political and humanistic concerns, using theater to arouse the social conscience of his audience. The "epic" style of drama is, according to Brecht, intended to appeal "less to the feelings than to the spectator's reason." This is achieved through various "alienation effects" that undermine the lifelike illusion of traditional theater and demand that the audience consider the intellectual, not merely the emotional, issues presented by the play. For example, an actor may comment on the play itself, creating viewer detachment from artificial character roles. The resulting estrangement should cause the spectator to apprehend hackneyed ideas and situations in a new way.

Brecht was born in the Bavarian town of Augsburg, where his family lived the middle-class existence he came to reject in favor of the Marxist ideal of a proletarian society. He studied medicine at the Ludwig Maximillian University in Munich and served in a military hospital toward the end of the First World War. His first play, *Baal*, was written at this time, though not produced until 1923. Like Brecht's other early plays and poetry, *Baal* displays the influence of German expressionism. *Trommeln in der Nacht* (*Drums in the Night*), his first play to be produced, in 1922, and the 1923 *Im Dickicht der Städte* (*In the Jungle of Cities*) also exemplify the sordid themes and mood of this literary movement. *Drums in the Night* earned Brecht the Kleist Prize and gained him national recognition.

After his expressionist period, Brecht wrote his first work of "epic theater," the 1926 play *Mann ist*

Mann (*A Man's a Man*). This is also one of a series of "didactic plays," works in which Brecht expressed his newfound committment to the philosophy of communism. Less overtly dogmatic, and one of the playwright's most popular productions, is the 1928 *Die Dreigroschenoper* (*The Threepenny Opera*), which also formed the basis of Brecht's only novel. One of several collaborations with composer Kurt Weill, *The Threepenny Opera* is an extravaganza of humor, bitterness, and social statement. Brecht based this drama on John Gay's *The Beggar's Opera.* Throughout his career, Brecht adapted the works of other authors, transforming them with modern and highly original interpretations. His literary erudition allowed him to combine a wide range of influences in his work, including Spanish, Oriental, and Elizabethan drama, popular songs, folk literature, and films. This remarkable variety of sources creates in Brecht's plays a lively conglomeration of styles and moods, from the farcical and grotesque to the sternly antitragic.

In 1933 Brecht's Marxist politics forced him to leave fascist Germany and go into self-imposed exile in Scandinavia and the United States. Later, the Nazi government annulled the playwright's citizenship. While in exile Brecht became an anti-Nazi propagandist, writing for a German-language periodical published in Moscow and composing the 1938 drama *Furcht und Elend des dritten Reiches* (*Fear and Misery of the Third Reich*). During this time Brecht also wrote what are critically regarded as his greatest works.

Brecht's genius for artistic invention and his desire to motivate social concerns in the playgoer combine in his mature dramas to form a rich and varied view of existence. Through the crisis of its scientist hero, *Leben des Galilei* (1943; *Galileo*) reexamines Brecht's recurrent theme of the obstacles to social progress. Yet despite its focus on philosophical issues, critics find in this play a strong main character who, along with the protagonist of *Mutter Courage und ihre Kinder* (1949; *Mother Courage and Her Children*), enlists the spectator's feelings as well as reason. In his mature works Brecht transcended the single-minded message of his earlier didactic pieces and achieved a more complex viewpoint than that permitted by the official policies and doctrines of communism. About the 1943 *Der gute Mensch von Sezuan* (*The Good Woman of Setzuan*), critic Raymond Williams remarked: "Brecht is as far as possible, in this play, from the method of special pleading which insists on the spectator or reader seeing the world through the actions and tensions of a single mind."

Brecht's ability to express his political and philosophical views in fresh and formally ingenious ways is also observable in his poetry, which he produced throughout his career. In both poetry and drama he attained one of the most controlled and completely realized aesthetic visions in literature. During the last part of his life, Brecht returned to Berlin and formed his own company, the Berliner Ensemble, enabling him to implement his dramatic theories and gaining him the admiration of devotees of dramatic art.

(For further information about Brecht's life and works, see *Contemporary Authors,* Vol. 104; *Dictionary of Literary Biography,* Vol. 56: *German Fiction Writers, 1914-1945;* and *Twentieth-Century Literary Criticism,* Vols. 1, 6, 13, 35.)

CRITICAL COMMENTARY

JOHN GASSNER

(essay date 1954)

[Gassner, a Hungarian-born American scholar, was a great promoter of American theater, particularly the work of Tennessee Williams and Arthur Miller. He edited numerous collections of modern drama and wrote two important dramatic surveys, *Masters of the Drama* (1940) and *The Theatre in Our Times* (1954). In the following excerpt from the latter work, he examines Brecht's style of theater.]

Brecht has viewed the past and present with a twentieth-century mind. His political outlook has always been far left of center, although his left-wing orthodoxy has been questionable even when he has spoken dogmatically. He is essentially an extreme individualist, if not indeed a bohemian artist-intellectual, weaving his way through mazes of collectivist ideals and policies as a poet rather than as a politician. Like others of his time, he has ridden the two horses of idealism and materialism, or of romanticism and Marxism, without any particular sense of discomfort or incongruity. He has also been a moralist of contemporary caliber for better or worse, pondering ethical problems in relation to political realities and expedients until ethics and strategy become indistinguishable in his thought—a dangerous way of thinking mitigated in his case by an

Principal Works

Trommeln in der Nacht (drama) 1922
[Drums in the Night, 1966]
Baal (drama) 1923
[Baal, 1964]
Im Dickicht der Städte (drama) 1923
[In the Jungle of Cities, 1957]
Das Leben Eduards des Zweiten von England (drama) 1924
[Edward II, 1966]
Mann ist Mann (drama) 1926
[A Man's a Man, 1957]
Die Hauspostille (poetry) 1927
[A Manual of Piety, 1966]
Die Dreigroschenoper (drama) 1928
[The Threepenny Opera, 1949]
Aufstieg und Fall der Stadt Mahagonny (drama) 1930
[The Rise and Fall of the Town of Mahagonny, 1960]
Der Jasager (drama) 1930
[He Who Said Yes/He Who Said No, 1946]
Die Massnahme (drama) 1930
[The Measures Taken, 1956]
Die heilige Johanna der Schlachthöfe (drama) 1932
[St. Joan of the Stockyards, 1956]
Die Mutter (drama) 1932
[The Mother, 1956]
Dreigroschenroman (novel) 1933
[A Penny for the Poor, 1937; also published as Three-penny Novel, 1956]

Fünf Schwierigkeiten beim Schreiben der Wahrheit (essays) 1934
[Writing the Truth: Five Difficulties, 1948]
Lieder, Gedichte, Chöre (poetry) 1934
Furcht und Elend des dritten Reiches (drama) 1938
[Fear and Misery of the Third Reich, 1942]
Der gute Mensch von Sezuan (drama) 1943
[The Good Woman of Setzuan, 1941]
Leben des Galilei (drama) 1943
[Galileo, 1947]
Die Ausnahme und die Regel (drama) 1947
[The Exception and the Rule, 1954]
Herr Puntila und sein Knecht Matti (drama) 1948
[Puntila, 1954]
Kalendergeschichten (short stories and poetry) 1948
[Tales from the Calendar, 1961]
Der Kaukasische Kreidekreis (drama) 1948
[The Caucasian Chalk Circle, 1948]
Kleines Organon für das Theatre (essays) 1949
[Little Organ for the Theatre, 1951]
Mutter Courage und ihre Kinder (drama) 1949
[Mother Courage and Her Children, 1949]
Der aufhaltsame Aifstieg des Arturo Ui (drama) 1958
[The Rise of Arture Ui, 1957]
Poems (poetry) 1976

essential humanism apparent in his passion for justice and his sympathy for the underdog. For Brecht does not quite succeed in suppressing the human sympathy that he would theoretically banish from the stage, if his theories are construed rigorously. He has endeavored to make drama out of themes and material usually excluded from a theatre dedicated to private emotion. In ways that recall the efforts of Koestler, Malraux, and other contemporary novelists, Brecht has certainly tried to make political reality the center of his art and the springboard of his inquiry into private and public conduct. Even when his main characters themselves have only a hazy awareness of politics, they exemplify the political nature of human existence, and the "human condition" with which Brecht has concerned himself has always been intrinsically a political condition. How Brecht's outlook has determined his form is, however, the paramount question; for his uniqueness as an artist lies not in his content or politics, common enough these days, but in the manner in which he has translated a

bias into drama, production style, and dramatic theory. (pp. 83-4)

Galileo . . . is not merely a biographical drama such as we are accustomed to, but a cool analysis of the problems and state of mind of a man who stands between two worlds and compromises between intellectual integrity and personal safety. . . . It was written with the intention of exposing a situation rather than emotionally involving the spectators; we are not made to sympathize with Galileo but to understand his problem . . . a historical situation which may repeat itself and therefore must be comprehended. . . . Brecht's intentionally cold dramaturgy, whether we like it or not, has a special place in modern theatrical art, if due attention is given to the expansion of radio, television, and motion picture documentary or semi-documentary drama. His objective method does seem the most appropriate one for treating historical events. Sidney Howard's *Yellowjack,* which employed the documentary style, would actually be more effective in my opinion if the dramaturgy and style were "colder"; the audience would be less disappointed then because the play isn't "warmer," in the sense of being closer to conventional affective drama. At the same time, Howard's play would have been more lyrical, too, if Brecht had been the author. It is an error to make lyricism invariably synonymous with "feeling"; Brecht, like Aristophanes, John Gay, and W. S. Gilbert, has the talent to achieve "non-emotional" and ironical lyricism. (p. 87)

The Caucasian Circle of Chalk, . . . [though somewhat] unwieldy, . . . is, nevertheless, a good example of the manner in which Brecht deliberately turns even an intrinsically emotional situation into an exposition of attitudes and values. He is the anti-sentimentalist *par excellence* even when his subject is sentiment. The other parable, *The Good Woman of Setzuan,* is, in my opinion, a masterpiece, although it is difficult to produce with sufficient verisimilitude, considering the prevailing taste of our theatre, because the same actress must play both a woman and a man—that is, the heroine's cousin. Brecht, however, has little use for verisimilitude, and would be pleased rather than disturbed if the production violated illusion. He is opposed to illusion-mongering and actually wants his audience to know that it is witnessing theatre rather than life; just as the public watching a demonstration knows that reality is not being photographed but being arranged for the purposes of an analysis. Actions in his type of drama are not intended to represent reality but to explain it and to challenge the critical intelligence of the observer.

Here, as in other plays, Brecht avails himself freely of Chinese theatrical style in which verisimilitude is of no consequence. Although he wrote *The Good Woman of Setzuan* with great charm and resorted to fantasy in bringing several little Chinese deities down to earth parable-wise in order to see how the human race is behaving, his object was to demonstrate a far-reaching point rather than to create illusion. . . . There is a sort of sophrosyne in this demonstration of how goodness must be practical and strong but not so "practical" as to take advantage of human helplessness and play the dictator. The sophrosyne at the core of this presentation of the problem of good and evil in social action determines the style and tone of the work. Here, too, Brecht effects a "cooling off" of the drama by means of a quizzical tone, lyric interruptions of the plot, and an "angle of vision" that tilts the picture of life with sardonic emphasis. Brecht, who can be a master of eloquence, knows that "coolness," too, can be a sort of rhetoric—if not an Aristotelian rhetoric of *persuasion,* then a rhetoric of inquiry or analysis. The method is Socratic or, more accurately, Silenic. . . .

Brecht is in all respects a rebel against Aristotelian and post-Aristotelian esthetics. Although Aristotle was the son of a physician and himself a biologist, he relied on illusion and emotion when he considered dramatic art. Brecht, who was a medical student, is consistently the surgeon; and this not only in his plays but in his ballads, that often vary eloquence with a sudden flatness, with a lapse into caustic colloquialism, and with an eighteenth-century rationalistic sharpness. He is given to pouring cold water on his work whenever it threatens to become overheated. His "epic" theory of drama and stagecraft is a protest against the priority of feeling and the principle of identification in drama. He does not allow feeling to preempt the field of observation, nor does he want us to get into other people's skin, lest we fail to observe them, assess them, and draw objective conclusions.

Brecht is the most anti-tragic of modern artists, not excluding Bernard Shaw; and for the same reason that Shaw was anti-tragic except in *Saint Joan*—that is, because Brecht has unlimited faith in the perfectability of man, the effectiveness of rational inquiry, and the power of men to improve the "human condition" by concerted action. It may be interesting to observe, in fact, that the great ages of high tragedy are not notable for any strong conviction that mankind is committed to progress and capable of it, that improvement is a social rather than individual problem, and that it can be effected by materialistic rather than spiritual means. Tragic art is neither "liberal" nor "radical," in the Western sense of either term since the Renaissance or, at least, since the ultra-optimistic eighteenth-century Enlightenment that promulgated the belief in unlimited progress of mankind on earth. The tragic sense includes a hard truth, harder than anything the tough-fibered Brecht accepts—namely, a sense of "life's impossibilities."

Brecht also abides by the principle of naturalistic objectivity in spite of his rejection of naturalistic technique. One might describe him as a lyric Henry Becque, if we waive the fact that Brecht has favored epic expansion of the drama whereas Becque sought dramatic compression. Brecht, one should add, exercises great economy in building scenes and writing dialogue and lyrics; the expansiveness he requires is of the Elizabethan variety—that is, free-flowing, multifarious, and multi-scened action.

Brecht favors a type of dramatic composition that projects the various facets of man's life in society without accepting an obligation to abide by any strict unity of time, place, action, mood, and style. . . . [Episodes] combined with narrative and lyrical passages, and augmented with pantomime, dance, projected slogans, signs or placards, slides, and even motion-picture sequences, if necessary, all following one another in rapid succession, may form one big tumultuous play somewhat in the manner of the "multiplicity novels" of John Dos Passos.

The result of this horizontal dramaturgy is "epic drama," according to Brecht. Since he also takes an analytical view of reality and institutes an inquiry or demonstrates his argument with every conceivable device, his epic style serves the purpose of social realism, and the most accurate term for his type of drama is "epic realism." Foregoing the esthetic advantages of a complete synthesis by tone or mood (the ideal since the nineteenth century of both the conventional realists and the art-for-art's-sake symbolists), Brecht concentrates on the diversity of a problem or situation, because the interrelationship of many facts and forces comprises its social reality. (pp. 88-90)

No one . . . has gone as far as Brecht in banishing Aristotelian pity, terror, catharsis, unity, and illusion as paramount dramatic values. He prides himself upon reflecting the scientific and analytical spirit of modern society, as well as the specially materialistic dialectic of Marxism. . . .

Nothing, indeed, is more remarkable in Brecht's career than that he should have been able to satisfy two contemporary needs at the same time—to extend realism and invigorate it, on the one hand, and to promote a theatre of imagination and poetry on the other hand. Imaginative drama and realistic drama are supposed to be the opposite poles of theatrical art. Brecht has resolved the major dichotomy of the modern stage in his own work and has proved that it need not exist. (p. 92)

John Gassner, "Drama and Detachment: A View of Brecht's Style of Theatre," in his *The Theatre in Our Times: A Survey of the Men, Materials and Movements in the Modern Theatre,* Crown Publishers, 1954, pp. 82-96.

MARTIN ESSLIN

(essay date 1969)

[Esslin, a prominent and sometimes controversial critic of contemporary theater, is perhaps best known for coining the term "theater of the absurd." His *The Theater of the Absurd* (1961) is a major study of the avant-garde drama of the 1950s and early 1960s, including the works of Samuel Beckett, Eugène Ionesco, and Jean Genet. In the following excerpt, Esslin evaluates Brecht's career.]

It may indeed sound heretical today, but may well be true nevertheless, that posterity might attribute greater importance to Brecht's poems and some of his short stories than to his work as a dramatist; or that of his twenty-one full-length and sixteen shorter plays, and six major adaptations, perhaps no more than half a dozen might stand the test of time. As to his theoretical writings, they have played an important part in creat-

ing Brecht's world-wide fame, for they have stimulated discussion about his plays among actors, directors, and critics and have made the study of his work particularly attractive in academic circles. They might, however, also prove the most vulnerable element in Brecht's posthumous reputation, resting, as they do, on the fairly shaky foundations of Brecht's own peculiar view of Marxism, a very questionable conception of the psychological basis of the audience's experience in the theatre, and on many passing fashions of the political and aesthetic climate of his times. (pp. 3-4)

Brecht's career . . . shows a clear pattern of development and its own dialectic: anarchic exuberance (1918-*ca.* 1927) abruptly turning to the opposite extreme, austere self-discipline (*ca.* 1927-1934); a brief interlude of openly propagandist, almost journalistic, work, undertaken to help the good cause of anti-Fascism (1934-38); then, as a synthesis of emotional exuberance, severe Marxist rationalism, and some elements of political special pleading, the great works of the mature phase (1938-47); and, finally, to crown the whole, the period from Brecht's return to Europe to his death (1947-56) when in the theatre he fulfilled his theories by his practice as a great director, while, as a lyrical poet, he reached sublime heights of detached self-knowledge and melancholic self-irony. It is a pattern which bears the marks of the great career of a great man. (p. 8)

The recognition that rebellion to accomplish freedom can only succeed if the rebel's own freedom is ruthlessly suppressed in the discipline of party forms the ironical, yet tragic, *leitmotiv* of Brecht's *oeuvre.* This ambivalence—which must also be seen as a highly characteristic German quality—explains the fascination which the Hegelian dialectic held for Brecht; it is also the basis of his genius as a dramatist. (p. 9)

In their famous essay *On Epic and Dramatic Poetry* (1797) Goethe and Schiller asserted that the "great, essential difference" between the two kinds of literature "lies in the fact that the epic poet presents the event as totally past, while the dramatic poet presents it as totally present." (pp. 11-12)

There can be little doubt that Brecht's entire theory of a truly Marxist theatre springs from his angry reaction against [this] very essay by Goethe and Schiller. . . . In Brecht's theatre the action must *not* take place in a total present, but in a strictly defined historical past—hence the streamers with precise dates for each scene in plays like *Mother Courage;* in Brecht's theatre the spectators must *not* be allowed to identify with the actors on stage to the extent of forgetting their own personalities—hence Brecht's striving for a multitude of *Verfremdungseffekte,* i.e., devices which would prevent identification to the point of annihilating the suspension of disbelief (e.g., the actors stepping out of their parts, or grotesque masks that clearly reveal them to be puppets, etc.). And, finally, the spectator in Brecht's theatre *must be made* to rise to thoughtful contemplation, must be led to detached critical reflection on the play and its meaning. For only a detached spectator could appreciate the *distance* between the historical characters, determined by the social relations of their time on the one hand and contemporary man on the other. . . .

Brecht's theory of "epic—i.e., nondramatic—drama" can thus be seen both as an earnest endeavor to find a Marxist aesthetic of the theatre and as an angry rejection of the official, classical aesthetic codified by those twin deities of the German cultural establishment, Goethe and Schiller. (pp. 13-14)

[Brecht] not only rejected the "classics" and their reactionary aesthetics, he ridiculed them by making them the target of a stream of overt and covert *parody*. And he went for inspiration and example to the alternative sources of a German dramatic tradition: to Baroque dramatists like Gryphius; the Austro-Bavarian folk theatre, whose last living exponent, the great beerhall comedian Karl Valentin, became Brecht's mentor and friend; and above all to Büchner, a dramatist whose genius is today generally acknowledged to have been at least equal, if not superior, to that of Goethe or Schiller. (p. 15)

Brecht's very first completed play [*Baal*] already contains that characteristic tension that will dominate his entire *oeuvre:* the tension between a desire to drift in the glorious, passive stream of life, on the one hand, and, on the other, a yearning for rationality which rejects that oceanic feeling with its passivity and amoral yielding to sensual impulse. (p. 16)

In the first, anarchic phase of Brecht's career, it is the sensuous, emotional, uncontrolled, passive attitude, the yielding to impulse, which dominates, while the rational, disciplined, activist attitude merely appears in the undertone of satire, mockery, ridicule with which the impulsive demeanor of the main character is portrayed. . . .

Emotion/Reason—Selfishness/Discipline—Chaos/Order, these three polarities sum up the dialectic of Brecht's life and work. (p. 17)

The change from the anarchic to the didactic phase of Brecht's development is clearly marked in the evolution of his language. The Büchneresque exuberance of daring metaphors strung together in chains of image-laden main clauses yields to laconic severity and sparseness of expression. . . . (p. 18)

In the great plays of his years of exile Brecht's style has lost the austerity of his didactic phase; and his characters, who had been reduced to the bare essentials (reminiscent of the highly stylized characters of French classical tragedy, who also lack all individual little human touches), again acquired a rich texture of personal idiosyncrasies. Nevertheless, these plays remain *didactic* in the sense that they are conceived as *parables,* models of human situations, cited, like the parables in the New Testament, not for their own intrinsic interest, but because of their general applicability to *other* human situations and problems. Galilei stands for all scientists who have submitted to the dictates of political authority (and for the atomic scientists of our time in particular); Mother Courage for all little people who do not realize that, deriving their small profit from war or the preparation of war, they are themselves guilty of causing the death of their children and the destruction of their country (as the little people of Hitler's Germany did); Puntila—evil when sober, human when drunk—is an emblem and exemplar of the irreconcilability between capitalistic attitudes and genuine humanity; while Shen Te, the good woman of Setzuan, demonstrates the impossibility of goodness in a world where survival depends on commercial success. The greatest of these plays, *The Caucasian Chalk Circle,* quite openly uses the parable form; it illustrates the solution of a problem which is posed in the prologue: who has the better right to a tract of land in a socialist country—a fairly mythically drawn Soviet Union—the legal owners or those who cultivate the land to the best purpose? . . .

Brecht's use of the parable form expresses another aspect of his revolt against the state of German culture and the German theatre in his youth: as much as he rejected the grandiloquent classicism of the followers of Goethe and Schiller (and, to a lesser extent, of the masters themselves), he also detested the naturalistic theatre which had become dominant in Germany at the turn of the century. All of Brecht's dramatic work can be seen as a refutation of naturalism, the use of the stage to reproduce photographically accurate slices of life. (pp. 19-20)

The quotability of gestures is a key concept in Brecht's aesthetics: for Brecht the essence of art, of poetry, is, indeed, the fact that through its perfection of form, through its concentration of thought, poetry enables truth to become transmittable, accessible to the mass of people. But a merely *verbal* quotation merely transmits an abstract version of the truth. The importance of drama lies, precisely, in its concreteness, in its ability to embody actual models of *human behavior*. Instead of merely hearing people quote the noble words from some play by Shakespeare or Schiller, Brecht wanted them to repeat wholesome, rational, and noble *actions* they might have seen on the stage. Hence his desire to create *quotable gestures,* in his narrative prose as well as in his plays. (p. 23)

Much of German poetry—and therefore also of the poetic language of drama—revels in grand philosophical abstractions and flowery, nebulous concepts. Brecht not only rejected these bombastic abstractions, he also set himself against the subjectivity, the sentimental self-involvement, of the lyrical tradition. (p. 26)

Brecht's *Hauspostille* is typical of his first exuberant, anarchic phase. The ballads it contains celebrate a kind of wild acceptance of nature and its processes of growth and decay. . . . There is no introspection in these poems; even the few which deal with Brecht's personal life treat of him objectively, in the third person almost; there are no elaborate similes: the images are put before the reader directly, starkly, and stand by and for themselves. Formally there is still a good deal of artifice and elaboration: ballad metres, even sonnets, abound. (p. 27)

Brecht's later poetry is more cerebral, severe, and economical. . . . [His] best late poems are short, almost epigrammatic: they speak of the tribulations of exile, the sorrows of the poet's return to his ravaged homeland, aging, and death. They are among the finest poems in the German language. They reveal the real Brecht behind the façade of cheerful support for the East German regime; a wistful, disillusioned man, dreaming of the landscape of his childhood in Augsburg, praising the humble pleasures of homely food, cheese, bread, and cool beer. There even creeps into this private, late poetry a note of wry rejection of the hollow claims of the totalitarian state to which he had committed his fortunes. (p. 28)

Poetry thus holds a central position in any consideration of Brecht as a dramatist as well as a prose-writer. (p. 29)

Brecht's endeavors to create a truly Marxist aesthetic of theatre are brilliant and stimulating and have given rise to endless misunderstandings. Above all, it must be kept in mind that these writings do not present a unitary, finished theory but are, themselves, the documentation of a constant process of changing and developing thought. (p. 33)

[It] is Brecht's unique achievement that he has reconciled two traditions in German literature which had been kept in different compartments before him, a state of affairs which had had most unfortunate effects on the cultural life of Germany. In Brecht the rough, plebeian, popular tradition and the sophisticated, academic, refined, respectable tradition have come together. Thanks to Brecht's achievement the work of the Austro-Bavarian folk comedians and the plays of the *poètes maudits* of the eighteenth and early nineteenth centuries appear in a new light and have assumed a new importance. And what is more: by introducing his new rough, popular, almost dialect tone, Brecht succeeded in forging a new German stage idiom, which is neither the highly refined, but unnatural *Bühnendeutsch* (stage German) of the one nor the broad vernacular regional speech of the other tradition. This is an achievement which has greatly eased the difficulties of the genera-

tion of young postwar dramatists and poets in Germany. (p. 45)

Martin Esslin, in his *Bertolt Brecht,* Columbia University Press, 1969, 48 p.

ROBERT W. CORRIGAN
(essay date 1973)

[An American critic and educator, Corrigan has written and edited numerous works on drama, especially modern world drama. In the following excerpt, he discusses an underlying theme in Brecht's work.]

A Man's a Man marks the beginning of a course of development which Brecht [followed] for the remainder of his career as a playwright. Although one will still find, like an almost invisible watermark, the haunting despair of spiritual isolation, Brecht's dominant concern [in and after this play was] to create a theatrical form capable of expressing the conflicts of social personalities as they live within a collective society. His ultimate achievement [was] *Mother Courage.* For Mother Courage is the perfect embodiment of the social personality; she is a woman whose very stature is the result of her being able to sacrifice her individual humanity to the collective system of which she is a part and which she affirms to the end. *Mother Courage* is articulate testimony that to destroy the humanist concept of the individual does not necessarily mean a loss of stature in the theatre, nor the disappearance of dramatic conflict. Rather there is a new kind of character and new kinds of conflict, and Brecht's theatre [provides] the forms and language to express them.

The subject of Brecht's Marxism always seems to create problems. I can think of very few critics who agree. . . . I do not believe that Brecht's temperament was political in any activist way, nor do I believe that he was spiritually attuned to the methods and practices of the Communist party. On the other hand, I am convinced that Marxism did fulfill Brecht's "overpowering impulse to construct a system which will enable him to feel that he does not stand alone but is intimately associated with some force or group infinitely more powerful and significant than himself." I see Brecht's embrace of Marxism as a strategy of despair and while the strategy may have worked successfully, it was nonetheless an act of will imposed by the intellect upon the sadness, the loneliness, the sense of emptiness which were the ground of Brecht's being. (pp. 216-17)

Now while Marx certainly played a major role in the nineteenth-century "re-evaluation of values" which brought about the modernist revolution in the theatre, the modernist view of the irrational is completely incompatible with Marxist thought. (p. 217)

For Brecht, the idea that there are in nature (including human nature) hidden and uncontrollable forces which can dominate the mind has no objective reality whatsoever. Indeed, such forces have no real existence. For him . . . "apparent chaos exists only because our head is not a perfect one and therefore that which remains outside it we call the irrational." Since we cannot know it rationally, it *seems* chaotic; but this "remainder is irrational only in respect to the capacity of our mind for knowing." Thus, while Brecht does not believe in the perfectibility of man (Marx believed that only the powers of reason can master the natural world), he does believe that the mind's range can be stretched. This distinction is crucial because all Brecht's theatrical theories are based upon it.

For example, it is the basis of his anti-empathic theories of production and explains his controversial Alienation-effect. Here Brecht, although he was passionately antipsychological, got his clue from Freud. Just as psychiatric therapy—and I think it is very significant that psychiatrists were first known as "alienists"—seeks to detach us from ourselves so we can begin to see ourselves in a more objective way (almost as an object), so Brecht believed that if the theatre was "to stretch the mind's range" it must not encourage the spectator to identify with the action but must show it so the audience can come to know itself better. . . . So throughout his plays, Brecht is trying to isolate the inconspicuous moral drama, to estrange it, to set it in a sharp light, so that it is not taken for granted before it falls, dragged down by the weight of society. (pp. 218-19)

Seen in this light, *Mother Courage* is not a pacifist tract, nor is Brecht the playwright a polemicist. His most daring achievement in this play is his use of war as an all-encompassing metaphor for the modern world, and his presentation of Mother Courage, who lives off the war and continues to exist because of it, as the symbol of the ordinary human condition. However, the play is not an attack on war, but an attempt to show all aspects of that war which is the central fact of the contemporary human condition. From the ironical speech of the Top Sergeant on the "horrors" of peace in the first scene, it is very clear that Brecht is very much aware of the negative and destructive aspects of our warring condition, but other parts of the play make it equally clear that war does make money, which we hold dear; war does create courage, which we admire; war does support the established institutions of society, which we want to maintain; and war does promote a sense of love and brotherhood, which we find valuable. As the play ends, Mother Courage is seen trudging after another regiment. In her (our) circum-

stances she cannot do otherwise. The tragedy of the situation, indeed, if it is a tragedy, is that her perception of what is wrong cannot alter her situation as it traditionally does in tragedy. In *Mother Courage* the situation completely dominates the individual. Brecht was in all likelihood not very happy about this, but he has been one of the few playwrights in our time who was capable of facing up to the realities of life in an industrialized collective society without having to abdicate his responsibility as an artist. (pp. 219-20)

Brecht sees that man is changed by the forces of the world outside him. And it follows that he must reject the characteristics of the traditional inner-directed drama in the Aristotelian mode. (p. 220)

Brecht's epic form . . . is his way of expressing the complexity, multiplicity, variety, and even the contradictions of a collective world while still maintaining that unity of form which is essential for art. He uses its episodic structure as a kind of counterpoint of estrangement for the purpose of stretching the limits of the audience's mind. Finally, it is a form that seeks to achieve the capacity of the novel (the literary mode which emerged out of the industrial revolution and is probably best suited to express our times) in dealing with the central issues of the modern world, without sacrificing the immediacy and force of the actor on a stage. (p. 223)

When viewed in the context of an industrialized collective society, Brecht believed the actions of . . . "old-fashioned" heroes tend to be little more than the empty posturings of the foolish, the headstrong, or the selfish. Genuine goodness, such as Kattrin's in *Mother Courage*, is equally irrelevant. While her behavior in the play seems to have a mute nobility about it, Brecht makes it very clear that her dramatic function in the play is to reveal the futility of the instinct to goodness and the impossibility of its surviving in a world in which the evergrowing cult of the celebrity, with its tendency to value charm without character, showmanship without real ability, bodies without minds, and information without wisdom, celebrates the triumph of ordinariness. . . . Thus, beginning with *A Man's a Man*, the idea that the assertion of individuality in the name of virtue is the chief cause of human failure in a collective society is a recurring and dominant theme in almost all of Brecht's plays. However, it should be pointed out that the Marxist playwright Brecht never completely represses the lonely poet Brecht. . . . For while it is true that he sees [some] characters as . . . failures because they give in to their human feelings and good instincts, paradoxically, he also believes that to be overwhelmed by the gratuitous impulse to do a good act is the beginning of freedom. (pp. 224-25)

As a poet he put his trust in words. He believed in the power of verse to deal with the contradictions of reality. He knew that by virtue of elision, concentration, and obliqueness, poetry can create an image of life which is far denser and more complex than that of prose. And, finally, he was aware that his new vision of reality as dialectical had to be expressed in poetry, for only poetry can advance discordant persuasions simultaneously and still retain that gestural quality which is essential to the theatre. Thus it may very well turn out that Brecht's greatest contribution as a poet in the theatre was to create a poetry of the collective. (pp. 228-29)

His life and his work were always in a state of dialectical tension. He rejected nature and emotional feelings overtly expressed and yet the most moving and powerful scenes in his plays are pervaded by the sense of them. He once told Max Frisch that he liked the large picture window in his home which looked out onto the Alps only because it gave lots of light; nonetheless, he chose to live in a house that had a magnificent view. Brecht in his last years was the high priest of collectivist drama, but he never genuflected to communism and as long as he lived he never allowed his theatre to become a shrine. His spiritual makeup always had enough heresy in it to permit the poet in him to work against the grain of orthodoxy. There is no doubt that he embraced the realities of a collective society and sought to find the language, forms, and characters that would best express such a world; but everything he wrote reveals a profound kind of rebellion against such acceptance. (p. 229)

Robert W. Corrigan, "Bertolt Brecht: Poet of the Collective," in his *The Theatre in Search of a Fix,* Delacorte Press, 1973, pp. 210-29.

RONALD D. GRAY

(essay date 1976)

[Gray is an English educator and critic who specializes in German literature. In the following excerpt, he surveys Brecht's plays.]

Brecht's first plays were written in the chaos of postwar Germany. When he returned to civilian life in 1919, after serving briefly in a military hospital, two literary movements seemed to the *avant-garde* to matter most, Expressionism and Dadaism, and he responded to them at the same time as he rejected them. (p. 16)

[Brecht's *Baal*] is not Expressionistic either in style or purport. It has no staccato rhythms, stabbing spotlights, crazily angular sets, no 'telegraphese', which was the name given to the short, sharp mode of speech some Expressionists favoured, and it is not unintentionally comic, or melodramatic. It does share with the

Expressionists, though not in their mood, a concern with a new kind of individual. Baal, not so very aptly named after the heathen god who devoured small children, is at once a lyric poet, a practical joker, a homosexual, every man's dream of a potent lover, a helper of elderly women, and the only really outspoken character in the play. He is also, conveniently for him, without conscience or self-awareness. He might be called a Dionysus. He might be said to express 'a passionate acceptance of the world in all its sordid grandeur'. In fact, that is what he does not do. It was the Expressionists who used that kind of language. *Baal* has more subtlety. (p. 17)

Brecht establishes his play by the way he uses words, more than by any other means. Any dramatist who could write as he did ought to have won attention by that fact alone. There are lyrical passages, for instance, in which he gropes for words at a level where the sound carries as much of his meaning as the literal sense, and this poetic concern, not always so much in evidence later on, occasionally overrides everything else. . . . (p. 18)

In structure, *Baal* is episodic, like the later plays. The scenes are loosely strung together, in no compelling sequence. (p. 19)

The common theme that does unite the scenes up to a point is that a complete realisation of his personality is essential for Baal, and must involve evil as well as good actions—a post-Nietzschean idea. (p. 20)

Of the other early plays which rapidly followed, all take some cognisance of society, whether to accept or reject its claims. *Drums in the Night* is mainly concerned with the reactions of a returned prisoner of war to the abortive left-wing uprisings of late 1918 and early 1919, and is surprisingly different from *Baal,* in taking so much notice of contemporary events. Yet it takes notice only to reject any responsibility for them, or so it appears. (p. 22)

There is a presage of later developments in the insistence that what the audience is seeing is a play. When Kragler rejects Spartacus he knocks down the moon, which is really a Chinese lantern, and the moon 'falls into the river, which has no water in it'. There is a rough reminder here, that the events on stage are not the revolution anyway. (p. 23)

Closer to the later 'alienation' for which Brecht became known is the scene in which a heated argument in a restaurant is interrupted by a waiter, who then retells the whole thing over again for the benefit of a new arrival. By this means, Brecht introduces a pause which can be reflective, as he did later in a variety of ways. Events seen a second time, or narrated as though they had happened before, take on a different look. There is something ironical in the mere fact of the repetition, and absurdities show up which might otherwise not have been apparent. Whether they lead, as the 'alienation' theory later maintained, to any further thought by the audience, let alone to Marxist solutions, is another question. For the moment, all that matters is Brecht's presumably intuitive use of this device, at a time when he can scarcely have thought out its implications.

The New Man and Revolution were the themes of the first two plays. For the third, *In the Cities' Jungle,* Brecht echoed yet another contemporary theme, Dada, or the vogue for nonsense with serious implications. Though the play has none of the special hallmarks of Dadaism—'bruitisme', or the cultivation of noise, 'simultaneity', or the coincidence of incongruities and dissonances as in real life—it has the same rejection of logic, psychology and verisimilitude as not only Dadaists but Futurists, Vorticists and the French followers of Apollinaire and Jarry cultivated. It is grotesque, and incomprehensible, giving a fantastic caricature of American capitalism, and making no attempt to interest the spectator. (pp. 23-4)

If there was little political matter in these plays, it was largely because Brecht was still questioning himself, still trying to understand himself, and experimenting with all the new ideas in vogue. For the most part they were Romantic in implication: surprisingly often Brecht comes to an uncommitted standpoint, closer to Buddhism than to Marxism, though expressed in his usual laconic way, rather than ecstatically. He drifts, changes like a cloud. . . . (p. 26)

Homosexual themes are prominent not only in *Baal* and *In the Cities' Jungle,* but also in his next play, *The Life of Edward II, King of England,* adapted from Marlowe, and largely concerned with the downfall of a ruthless king on account of his sexual fascination for a worthless favourite, Piers Gaveston. . . . All through these early plays, Brecht is partly dramatising a personal sense that femininity is lax and despicable, that hardness and even harshness is demanded of a man, and possibly some sexual attraction to men might account for the sudden predilections for violence shown by his characters, as in *The Good Woman of Setzuan* where the heroine feels obliged to adopt the mask of a man in order to exercise the harshness she believes to be necessary. Certainly, homosexuality and violence are prominent themes of *Edward II,* though here Brecht's personal concerns are also reflected in Mortimer—a single character instead of the two in Marlowe's play—here presented as an intellectual revolutionary whose chief care is the welfare of working people. (p. 28)

[Brecht was] engaged on a dual path. In one sense he was aiming at complete self-realisation, even if this involved what had till that time been accounted inhumanity. In another he was beginning to experiment with the belief that social change requires such inhumanity. The exploration of what humanity means was the theme of his next play. (p. 30)

[*A Man's a Man*] is the fantastic account of an extremely adaptable character, Galy Gay, who is beguiled by three British soldiers (inspired by Kipling's *Soldiers Three*) into taking the place of a comrade in the Indian Army. Step by step, he is transformed from a peaceable citizen into a ferocious warrior, armed to the teeth and thirsting for blood. The play presents a case of brainwashing, achieved by means of a subtle undermining of the sense of personal identity, with the difference that it is carried out not by trained interrogators but by the hirelings of imperialism, and that the mood of the whole is one of prolonged extravaganza and farce. Bitter farce: as the title indicates, men are men, a man is a man, and any one man can be turned into another and still remain 'man'; once the full potentialities of 'man' are realised, they can be channelled in any direction. Shaw attempted with great success a more lighthearted treatment of a similar theme in *Pygmalion.* Brecht was unwittingly foreshadowing transformations that were to change all Germany within a few years. (pp. 30-1)

Brecht's concern with the condition of the poor appears only dimly in the earlier plays. In the *Threepenny Opera* it found an opportunity to express itself more vigorously, for one of the main themes of Gay's *Beggar's Opera,* from which it was adapted, was poverty. Yet here also, the cynical mood of the day did not allow of a direct appeal to charitable sentiments. Brecht took over the eighteenth-century text, modified it considerably, was helped considerably by Kurt Weill's music, but aimed at his audience's heads rather than at their hearts. The opera was conceived in terms of parody: it went with the current in so far as it appeared to give the public what it wanted, but it did so in such outrageous fashion as to make it deliberately unpalatable. Brecht, in the usual forthright mood of exaggeration which made him paint the faces of soldiers in *Edward II* chalkwhite, to represent fear as their only emotion, went the whole hog with the conventions in this work also. It was one more instance, and for the time being almost the last, of the violent caricature which was meant to force the audience into demanding a contrary. (pp. 33-4)

On the other hand, there is a note of compassion running through the opera which contrasts with all that has been said of it and of Brecht's work so far. (p. 35)

The brief glimpse of what human nature might be, in contrast to what it is, that appeared in *A Man's a Man,* becomes a longer look. It still does not, however, provide insight into the theme of the opera as a whole, which retains a dual aspect, partly amoral, partly charitable. . . . (p. 37)

Not merely is it difficult to relate his characters to the prototypes they are meant to satirise; Brecht's still 'all-embracing' attitude allows him to move at will from one standpoint to another completely contradictory one: at one moment he seems to aim at arousing a general compassion for the condition of all men, at another he allows his characters to advocate extreme brutality, and the oscillation from one to the other renders every reaction uncertain. It is not surprising that his audiences, for whom he had meant to write a 'report' on the kind of entertainment they liked to see, seized on those aspects which took their fancy and ignored the rest. There was grist in the text for everybody's mill. (pp. 37-8)

The didactic plays [including *The Measures Taken, St. Joan of the Stockyards,* and *The Mother*] contribute less than the plays of the 1920s to Brecht's reputation. (p. 64)

[Brecht's] portrayal of social conditions, even in those plays where social criticism is intended, is wildly exaggerated: the America of *Mahagonny* and *St. Joan of the Stockyards* and the England of *The Threepenny Opera* are unrecognisable, and it is only in *Drums in the Night* (and later *Fear and Misery of the Third Reich*) that Brecht gives anything like a picture of conditions in Germany. For the most part, the early plays contain no scenes where human beings enter into any relationship with one another, except in such a parodistic form as the friendship between Macheath and Tiger Brown. The audience is often invited to draw conclusions from what it sees before it, while what it sees is presented in such a form that conclusions are either undrawable or contrary to those pronounced on stage. And when Brecht deliberately turns to the advocacy of reason in his plays, he shows little regard for rationality.

It is a strange mixture, this unadorned forthrightness and lack of sentiment on the one hand, this frankness and originality, receptivity and unshrinking penetration, and on the other hand this seemingly wilful blindness, unwillingness to reason, prejudice, occasional hysteria, and preference for parody and adaptation. Brecht's openness, his 'all-embracing' attitude, was critical only on the impulse of the moment, and his dramatic unities were the largely fortuitous assemblies of these impulses, able to exist side-by-side because they left out of account the continuum of the outside world. Yet the early plays do show also the ability to observe and take account of the rest of humanity. The language of the working men in *Baal,* unlike that in *The Mother* and *St. Joan,* is full of idiomatic turns of phrase. The note of concern about the direction to be taken by human nature enters in *A Man's a Man,* and grows louder in *The Threepenny Opera,* for all that it takes so abrupt a modification into inhumanity in the propagandist plays. . . . Moreover, Brecht had shown repeatedly his ability to make use of the theatre: he was no armchair dramatist but one who constantly envisaged effects in terms of theatrical performance. In *Seño-*

ra Carrar's Rifles, a priest raises his hands above his head in a reverent gesture of resignation: he is held in the act by a word, and sits there, a dramatic image of a man 'surrendering'. In *The Measures Taken,* the young agitator removes his mask to declare his true identity, and the physical revelation of his human personality comes as a shock which almost in itself undoes the inhuman doctrine of the play. These, with many other devices reveal Brecht as the man of the theatre he was: a brilliant innovator, a fertile mind, an iconoclast, a man with innumerable facets, but still a dramatist more capable of momentary effects than integrated wholes. (pp. 65-6)

From early days, Brecht was evolving not only plays, but theories of what he was doing and the effect he expected to produce. . . . The 'V-Effekt', or 'alienation technique'—'V' standing for 'Verfremdung'—is at its simplest a means of making the events on the stage seem strange, unfamiliar. (p. 67)

The action was commented upon or announced by intervening or accompanying projections, a practice which Brecht continued in all his productions, although it has been felt at times to be an affectation. He also used a low curtain masking only half the height of the stage, behind which the movements of actors and stage-hands could easily be seen. In *Puntila* a mountain is made out of chairs. In [*The Horatians and the Curiatians*] the sun is represented by a spotlight carried across the rear of the stage by a technician. . . . [On the whole] the later productions forwent many of the more surprising features of the earlier practice. In the twenties, Brecht was still concerned to avoid anything beautiful, lyrical, or directly moving. He denied emotion, as he denied beauty, as an indulgence that could not be afforded while suffering still existed. Only rational thought would serve to change the human situation as he saw it.

The 'V effect' was not, however, merely a matter of production technique. The style of acting also required a radical change. . . . Brecht required his actors to maintain the same distance from the characters they were protraying as the audience was expected to adopt. . . . The basic function of the actor is thus to 'show', just as a person in conversation may break off in order to demonstrate in pantomime a part of his story. (pp. 67-8)

Brecht frequently abandons the complexities of exposition. Characters do not sustain the Ibsen-like illusion that they are unaware of the audience's presence and must reveal themselves and their relationships by carefully dropped hints which must still preserve the appearance of being natural ingredients of their conversation. In *The Mother,* Pelagea Wlassowa begins the play by directly addressing the audience, explaining who she is, and what her problems are. The same simple opening is found in *The Threepenny Opera* and *The*

Good Woman of Setzuan. Alternatively, the audience is placed in possession of the necessary facts of the situation by a narrator who sits at one side of the stage throughout, as in *The Caucasian Chalk Circle,* or the story of the next scene is written on hanging boards. And in most of the plays the action is interrupted by songs which summarise, comment on, or predict the action. In all these ways it becomes inevitable that whatever method of acting or production is used, some element of alienation will make itself felt. (pp. 70-1)

The kind of theatre which these devices would produce was called by Brecht 'epic' theatre, in contrast to the earlier, 'bourgeois' theatre, which was 'dramatic'. The word 'epic' here, translating the German 'episch', is unfortunate. 'Episch' has, in this context, none of the associations with heroism and greatness that 'epic' often has, as in 'an epic tale'; it is merely a literary category, and in German this category includes not only narrative poetry, but also novels, and is often used to distinguish these from the lyric and the drama. In speaking of an 'epic' theatre, Brecht meant to imply a theatre which would not be exciting, 'dramatic', full of tensions and conflicts, but slower-paced, reflective, giving time to reflect and compare. (pp. 71-2)

None of the specifically anti-Nazi plays represents [Brecht's] best work. Yet since they bulk largest in the whole of the anti-Nazi theatre of the period, they are worth attention. *Round Heads and Pointed Heads* . . . is the least satisfying. Like *St. Joan of the Stockyards,* it uses a rough-and-ready blank verse, of a quasi-Shakespearean kind, in order to mock the pretensions of the speakers. But there is more than imitation of Shakespearean forms. On this occasion Brecht took over the main outline of a Shakespeare play, and adapted it to a political purpose, his principal idea being, perhaps, to show that what for Shakespeare was a moral problem was in Brecht's day and age an economic one. (p. 93)

[*The Resistible Rise of Arturo Ui*] is without any doubt the most striking and effective of his explicitly anti-Nazi plays. . . . The deflating of Hitler's pretensions to greatness—and of any tendency in Germany to go on speaking of him as a great man—by linking his career in detailed parallels with the life of a Chicago gangster was a genial idea. Its biggest success is in the scene where the murder by Hitler of Ernst Röhm and his associates is parodied by a mass-slaughter in a garage in front of the headlights of a Ford saloon, an incident that seems to come straight out of a life of Al Capone. Equally telling in an opposite spirit is the scene, based also on Hitler's life, in which Ui receives instruction from a Shakespearean actor on how to make political speeches. (pp. 96-7)

While propagandist and anti-Nazi works were among the first fruits of Brecht's exile, he turned after a while to writing the plays which did most to establish his reputation abroad, *The Life of Galileo, Mother Courage, The Good Woman of Setzuan, Herr Puntila and his Man Matti. (The Caucasian Chalk Circle,* belonging with these in style, was written later. . . .) These were works of a quite different kind. It is possible, though not logically necessary, to read out of them the corollary that only Communism can cure the ills they represent. Their general sphere of interest and concern is not, however, directly political, but rather one of general humanity. They are plays in which the spectator is implicitly invited to consider the behaviour of human beings, to understand, sometimes to sympathise, sometimes to be revolted, and always to ask himself how he might have acted in similar circumstances. There are no incomprehensible farragos or flippant shocks for shock's sake such as occur from time to time in the plays of the twenties, nor are there any choruses ramming home the 'message', as there are in the plays of the early thirties. No one is counselled to do evil so that good may come. Instead, there is an in many ways humane theatre, tolerant, offering comprehension rather than persuasion; though still rigging the balances at times, ranging in mood from tender lyricism to agony of mind, from admiration for the most insignificant details of ordinary living to a buffooning zest in wine, women, and song, from sharp compassion with the miseries of the poor to a not wholly unsympathetic portrayal of the pleasures of the rich. It is the 'human comedy' that Brecht seems most of all bent on showing in these works, and the Communist implications are at most a side-issue. (p. 109)

Galileo's dilemma has been seen, its causes traced, and sympathy for him aroused. But, as Brecht knew, . . . the ability to adapt to circumstances has been far too prevalent in Central European countries for centuries past. The issue of Galileo's cowardice thus takes on a sharp contemporary edge: Galileo, the play affirms, stands at the threshold of a new age, as we seem to do ourselves since 1945. If he recants, the cause of science will suffer a setback, for science depends on a relentless honesty, and cannot be associated with hypocrisy. . . . Brecht sought to stress individual rather than vicarious responsibility. In his habitually exaggerating fashion Brecht does imply . . . that a whole epoch of European history turns on one man's failure.

The confrontation of these two attitudes makes good dramatic material, despite the fundamental intellectual weakness of the play, and it provides notable moments of conflict and tension. (pp. 112-13)

[One] weakness, however, does not appear remediable. In his last long speech Galileo reviews the position of science as he now leaves it, crippled for centuries by his recantation. His own failure, he declares, has been that he sought to accumulate knowledge for the sake of knowledge, without regard to the primary aim of science, the easing of human existence. (p. 113)

But this failure is asserted in a long and intricate monologue which relies entirely on verbal argument, amounting to a lecture from the stage lasting for several minutes. This is bad drama, by any criterion, and it is made to look worse by the irrationality of Galileo's case. He argues, against the historical evidence, that his single failure will reduce scientists from his time on to a race of dwarfs, subservient to the wishes of monarchs and governments. Considering that the first dwarf to appear after Galileo was Newton, born in the year Galileo died, and that even Italian science, which might have been thought most likely to suffer under Papal obdurateness, went on to produce Malpighi, Volta, and Galvani within the next hundred years, it is clear that one defection cannot halt so widespread a human activity. (p. 114)

Thus, as in much of Brecht's work, the theatricality is largely vitiated by the lack of any realistically thought-out content. (p. 115)

Yet *Galileo* remains one of the riper plays. It is riper in one sense, as many East Europeans know, in that it shows with great imagination the alternating self-condemnations and self-reassertions of all who live deviously under a stifling regime. . . . But it is riper in other ways. The fairness with which Galileo's opponents, the cardinals, are treated (not the Aristotelian scientists, who are grotesquely caricatured), and the hearing which is given to the unanswered arguments of the little monk, who asks what simple Christian believers are to make of their harsh lives if they are deprived of the rich comforts of religion, are signs of the complexity which raises *Galileo* above the purely propagandist works. The effect of the play is incalculable—while it is possible to come out of the theatre feeling that an intense demand for heroic courage has been made, it is also possible to see what is gained by taking an adaptive course. The new unwillingness to impose or suggest single answers was the essential mark of the Brecht who emerged in the late 1930s. (pp. 115-16)

Mother Courage is decidedly one of the best things Brecht wrote, and it is significant of it, as an example of 'epic' or 'narrative' theatre, that it is not the story or the political implications, not a connected theme, which remains most strongly in the memory, but a series of isolated moments. (p. 121)

The character of Mother Courage herself is one of the most attractive features. She is adept at turning every situation to her own advantage, conforming with and adapting herself to it in a way that recalls . . . Galileo. She has the vitality of Puntila without his drunkenness or lapses into sobriety, and at the same time she contributes a laconic cynicism of her own, a cunning and ingenuity which are essential for her sheer existence. As a rule she knows exactly how far she can go and how far she can let others go. When the recruiting sergeant threatens to take away her son, she pulls a knife on him, but it is clear that she means the threat as a move in the game, which will not be countered: there is shrewdness in her attitude, not heroism. . . .

Yet when the structure of the play as a whole is considered, it becomes apparent that these qualities do little to bind it together. In its total effect, it is oddly without impact, a series of moments and *coups de théâtre* without coherence. (p. 126)

The impelling power in the play is the sense of waste—not of tragedy. . . . Brecht did not want a sense of tragedy; he was angry with the first-night audience who wept in traditional mood over the bereaved mother, and he included a sardonic chorus offstage, chanting a raucous injunction to her to look alive, as she humped the empty wagon round the stage in the final scene. The mood is akin to the mood in which he had Kattrin beat her drum—a ferocious insistence on the idiocy of the destruction, spoken by a Thersites in the wings, biting in its almost cynical desperation, which is only not cynical, in the last resort, because it is desperate.

But there is no cure offered. All that Brecht gives—as in all the maturer plays—is the intolerable awareness of how things are, not a Marxist or any other solution. He may have thought, it is true, that he had shown sufficient of the causes of war to justify him in maintaining he had written something other than a tragedy. If, on the other hand, we find his analysis too flimsy, we are left with an irremediable awareness of a tragic situation. The difference between this kind of tragic situation and those of earlier centuries is that . . . it does not provide us with a cheap seat in the gods, but kicks us in the shins. That is the peculiarly twentieth-century quality of it, and a reason why it attracts audiences unattuned to its political philosophy. (pp. 135-36)

[*Puntila*] is more of an 'epic' play in its structure than almost any other of Brecht's works, a possible exception being *Mother Courage*. There is no argument, no problem, but rather a loose sequence of scenes, and almost no plot; at one point all thought of 'dramatic' interest, in the traditional sense, is abandoned while four women sit by the roadside to exchange stories and reminiscences. . . .

Not having the wartime background of *Mother Courage*, *Puntila* relies on comic incidents to sustain interest. . . . It is boisterous humour, unintellectual—there is no religious satire . . . or any political point to any of Puntila's larking, but it establishes the relaxed mood of the whole work, and its prime aim of entertaining. (p. 137)

Brecht's political influence in the world at large probably consists more in the general idea that his plays convey a Marxist message, rather than in the actual conveying of one. (p. 163)

[Like] almost all modern dramatists of revolt, Brecht does not, in [Robert] Brustein's phrase 'offer any substitute ideas or ideals'. Clearly, he intends a transformation of the world, in which poverty and exploitation no longer exist, but there is no more clarity about it than that. (p. 170)

Ronald D. Gray, in his *Brecht the Dramatist*, Cambridge University Press, 1976, 232 p.

TERRENCE DES PRES
(essay date 1980)

[In the following excerpt, Des Pres discusses Brecht's poetry.]

To most of us Brecht's poetry is new. We know him by his plays, and if we come to the poetry from Brechtian theater we shall be, if not misled, then surprised. The two careers ran broadly parallel, but in view of the poems the famous cynicism of the plays looks less savage, less brazenly hard. The whole of Brecht's enormous output, thanks to the poetry now available, needs reading in a different light, not only of genius politically inspired, but of an art directed always to care for how people live. (p. 5)

Graceful and charming Brecht's poetry is not. He detested decorum and polish, any sort of evident refinement, preferring instead the rough vigor of the street and lowbrow forms like the ballad, the popular song, or just "straight-talk." This turn toward the rude and lowly, as Brecht said of his early poetry, was less "a protest against the smoothness and harmony of conventional poetry" than "an attempt to show human dealings as contradictory, fiercely fought over, full of violence." Such poetry, given its sinewy flex and spring, might possibly be called supple. . . .

His poetry does not charm, invite, or tease out of thought. It would be heard, not overheard, and does not bank on its status as Art. Its import is in its occasion and it does not, therefore, claim to be transcendent or self-contained, but rather insists upon its place in history, its provisional nature as utterance *in situ*. Most modern poetry posits *a* world, whereas Brecht's responds to *the* world, in particular to events and conditions which determine—to the benefit of some and the harm of many—people's lives. His position is therefore political. In relation to poetry the term "political" may simply refer to poems which bear witness or, going a step further, to poems which confront and defend or, going all the way, to poems which directly speak for and against. The last kind disturbs us most, and that is the kind Brecht principally wrote. He therefore stands as the extreme example of an art which we in America prefer to believe cannot exist in superior form: political poetry, verse openly didactic, aesthetic energy taking a stand. (p. 6)

[There] is no denying that Brecht wrote some great poetry, and no denying its political bent. Brecht disliked poets who write solely of inner experience. He did not value poetic vision which cultivates itself only, nor did he think that the poet's main job is to feel and perceive in rarefied ways. Poets ought to *say* something, and what they say should be worth hearing even in a world where global politics—the threat of nuclear wipeout, the terrorist who strikes anyone anywhere—increasingly penetrates private life. History is too much with us, and if we would believe Max Frisch, looking upon the ruins of Europe after the Second World War, Brecht's poetry is of the kind we need: the kind that "can stand up against the world in which it is spoken."

By that standard, almost all poetry being written in America fails, or embarrasses, or leaves us lamenting that nobody takes poetry seriously anymore. Times change, so do we, and the poetry of self—the Emersonian mandate—has lost its authority. Our times are not as dark as Brecht's, but they are far from happy and no one, I presume, would predict improvement. Brecht's Marxist vision and his didactic attitude may not be ours but his example still instructs and is potentially liberating, especially if we admit that our lives are more and more knocked about by political forces and that poems worth having are those which can "stand up against" the prevailing climate of violence. (p. 7)

In **"Place of Refuge"** the time is 1937, the place is a fisherman's cottage outside the Danish city of Svendborg. Soon Hitler would invade Denmark, forcing Brecht to use one of the "four doors to escape by." (From there he would go to Sweden, then Finland, then across Russia to the Pacific, and finally to the United States where he would stay until the end of the war.) Much of Brecht's early poetry invents its imagery, in the manner of Rimbaud. But midway his imagery begins to come from the actual situation of which the poem itself is a part. No doubt a paint-peeled oar lay on the picturesque roof. But oar-on-thatch is an image of disorder, of things out of place, and we understand that destructive winds might come. The mail also comes, so do the boats, and in the poem's context these images of things approaching take on sinister tones. The children may play, but not safely. Mail will cause as much pain as gladness. And business as usual—ferries crossing the water—is not to be trusted.

Like many of Brecht's poems, this one is based on personal circumstances, but like his poetry in general, it is not really personal. Of his work he once said: "maybe the poems in question describe me, but that was not what they were written for. It's not a matter of 'getting acquainted with the poet' but of getting ac-

A 1965 production of *Mother Courage and her Children*.

quainted with the world, and with the people in whose company he is trying to enjoy it and change it." To become acquainted with the world, in this case, is to discover that no place is safe, no refuge secure. Political forces drive us into an exile which, like the poet's retreat, cannot be counted on, neither in life nor in art. (pp. 8-9)

Parody of liturgical forms is one of Brecht's favorite devices; implemented by the ironies of cliché and doggerel, the result is clawlike indeed. Brecht's ["**Spring 1938**"] . . . would be a sentimental rerun of the theme of rebirth, were it not for the political references. But now rebirth cannot be counted on; our defenses, like our stock of traditional themes, are pathetically inadequate. Yet there are only the old themes. Brecht gives them new life by allowing politics to intrude; and in consequence, a mythical experience, punctured by history, loses *and* gains in primitive force. Anyone with children, reading the papers, listening for signals of war, knows how poignant that silence is, when with nothing but a miserable sack, a son and father try to save a dying tree. Slight in itself, the poem is like a stone around the neck. It stood up against the time in which it was written, it stands up now. (p. 10)

Brecht declared himself a Marxist in 1929, and critics often speak of his "conversion" as if there were two Brechts, the rampaging satirist and then the somber ideologue. Over-simple at best, the distinction is misleading and in the end serves no purpose. Over time, of course, the poetry shows change: it turns less often to rhyme and fixed forms; expansiveness gives way to concentration; more poems are rooted in fact, and Brecht's splendid didactic mode moves from ironic depiction to straight-forward statement as its central vehicle. But what never changes is Brecht's bedrock loyalty to victims—to losers, outcasts, whole strata of society who from birth were doomed to wretchedness. The disposition, not the system, came first. Many early poems take a plural point of view or address collective experience. Images of mass death occur with upsetting frequency. And Brecht's dominant early form, the narrative, is handled with the dedication and authority proper to a poet whose concern would always be with action, with the ways men and women determine, or have forced upon them, basic conditions of life. Which is to say that Brecht's relation to the world was political from the start. (p. 11)

[For Brecht] might the aesthetic point of view be used against itself ? And at what cost?

One solution, for Brecht, was satire as savage as history itself. Another was reliance on didactic forms, which draw their strength from the conviction that life can be changed. A third strategy was to avoid metaphor, especially insofar as metaphor creates the illusion of transcendence—of being "above" X by seeing it in terms of Y. Of his *Svendborg Poems* Brecht said: "From the bourgeois point of view there has been a staggering impoverishment. Isn't it all a great deal more one-sided, less 'organic,' cooler, more self-conscious (in a bad sense)?" One-sided like an ax, cool like metal at night, and thus a poetry which sometimes seems disrespectful of the reader's sensibilities, at other times insisting on a distance between reader and poem, a sort of aesthetic estrangement. Brecht's famous concept of *Verfremdungseffekt* or "alienation effect" applies not only to his theory of theater, but to the central grain of his poetry as well. He will not grant emotional solace, nor catharsis either. The appeal, here, is more to the mind than the heart. We are not to indulge but to see, and to see we must not feel too much at home. (pp. 17-18)

The didactic element is constant in Brecht. He thought of himself as a teacher, and the point of his work, as he often said, was to make people see. There have of course been great didactic poets, Virgil and Lucretius among them, but for sheer formal inventiveness and for aesthetic effects as powerful as any "pure" poet might hope to create, Brecht's poetry seems to me the supreme example of successful didactic art. The didactic mode served as Brecht's most durable device for bringing poetry and politics into fruitful union, and if, as Walter Benjamin has argued, the important artist not only uses a mode but also transforms and extends it, then Brecht's importance is obvious. Satire is inherently didactic, but the lyric is not, and that Brecht could be didactic *and* lyrical enlarges our idea of poetry in general. And finally, Brecht used the didactic stance to solve perhaps his biggest problem: in radical contrast to the Soviet brand of Marxism, which pretends to speak *for* oppressed peoples, Brecht would go no further than to speak *to* them, propounding no authorities or programs but only insisting that victims everywhere should see themselves in the full sadness of their plight and see also that if politics is part of the human condition, very much of the human condition is a matter of politics.

And yet there is something else, subtler, more delicate, about Brecht's use of didactic forms. They allow him to remain impersonal, they rule out small-talk and self-pity, and where deep emotion arises the didactic stance becomes a technique for restraint, for expression of feeling about world events without splashing the event or the feeling all over the page. (pp. 21-2)

Brecht's poetry embraces a political vision, beautiful in its ideals, which did not survive its totalitarian perversion. The historical failure of Marxism has had enormous consequences for all of us, but for people directly involved the outcome was shattering. Recurring anti-Soviet sentiment and outbreaks of bitterness in Brecht's late poetry reveal the suffering of a man coming to see—as a generation of decent men and women came painfully to see—that the great moment had passed, that the magnificent dream of human liberation would go unrealized. But if political defeat is the end in actual politics, in poetry the case is strangely otherwise. Brecht's vision was betrayed by history but his poetry does not therefore suffer forfeit or become irrelevant. On the contrary, it gains in retroactive depth, taking on dignity and an import which did not exist when the poems were written but which exists now because of the way events turned out.

Political poetry—at least the kind committed to a cause—possesses a destiny, and when destiny ends in defeat, the result is not failure but tragedy. For this reason Brecht's poetry, as we read it now, bears within it a tragic sense of life which the poet himself could not detect. (pp. 24-5)

Terrence Des Pres, "Poetry in Dark Times," in *Parnassus: Poetry in Review,* Vol. 8, No. 2, 1980, pp. 5-28.

SOURCES FOR FURTHER STUDY

Bentley, Eric. *The Brecht Commentaries: 1943-1980.* New York: Grove Press, 1981, 320 p.

   Collection of Bentley's critical essays, covering a span of almost twenty years, on Brecht's dramas and his epic theater.

Demetz, Peter, ed. *Brecht: A Collection of Critical Essays.* Englewood Cliffs, N.J.: Prentice-Hall, 1962, 186 p.

   Includes important commentaries by Eric Bentley, Walter H. Sokel, Hanna Arendt, and Martin Esslin, among others.

Esslin, Martin. *Brecht: The Man and His Work.* Rev. ed. Garden City, N.Y.: Anchor Books, 1971, 379 p.

   Major biographical and critical study of Brecht.

Ewen, Frederic. *Bertolt Brecht: His Life, His Art, and His Times.* New York: Citadel Press, 1967, 573 p.

Major critical biography in English.

Fuegi, John. *The Essential Brecht.* Los Angeles: Hennessey & Ingalls, 1972, 343 p.

Important critical work, focusing on Brecht's major dramas within the context of his own productions of them. Fuegi's work also includes photos and illustrations of Brecht's plays during their various productions.

Mews, Siegfried, and Knust, Herbert, eds. *Essays on Brecht: Theater and Politics.* Chapel Hill: University of North Carolina Press, 1974, 238 p.

Collection of critical essays on Brecht's theory of drama and his political ideology. Includes essays by Siegfried Mews, Darko Suvin, Grace M. Allen, and John Fuegi.

Charlotte Brontë

1816-1855

(Also wrote under pseudonym Currer Bell) English novelist and poet.

INTRODUCTION

*T*he author of vivid, skillfully constructed novels, Brontë broke the traditional nineteenth-century fictional stereotype of a woman as submissive, dependent, beautiful, but ignorant. Her highly-acclaimed *Jane Eyre; An Autobiography* (1847) best demonstrates this change in attitude: its heroine is a plain woman who possesses intelligence, self-confidence, a will of her own, and moral righteousness. For her originality in form and content, Brontë is hailed as a precursor of feminist novelists and regarded as an author whose talents were highly superior to those of many of her contemporaries.

The oldest surviving daughter in a family of six, Brontë helped raise her brother, Branwell, and two sisters, Emily and Anne. Their father, a strict clergyman, believed in self-education and limited his family's opportunities to socialize with other children. Intellectual growth was encouraged by Mr. Brontë, however, and he introduced his family to the Bible and to the works of William Shakespeare, William Wordsworth, and Sir Walter Scott. Though the Brontë children were intellectually precocious, their cloistered upbringing created a sense of isolation that made social interaction outside the family difficult.

In 1824, Mr. Brontë sent Charlotte, Emily, Anne, and his two oldest daughters, Maria and Elizabeth, to Cowan Bridge, a school for the daughters of poor clergymen. Undoubtedly he selected the school for its low tuition, but the living conditions were intolerable and the discipline overly rigid; Charlotte later based Lowood School in *Jane Eyre* on her experiences there. Several months after their arrival at Cowan Bridge, Maria and Elizabeth, weakened by a poor diet, lack of sleep, and chilly, damp living quarters, returned home, where they died of tuberculosis. Maria's death was especially traumatic for Charlotte; biographers believe that she was the inspiration for the character of Helen Burns, Jane's stoic friend at Lowood.

After the deaths of their sisters, Charlotte, Emily, and Anne returned home. It was during this period that the Brontë siblings created the imaginary kingdoms of Angria and Gondal, which they chronicled in poems, stories, and plays. In these youthful writings, Charlotte and Branwell's Angria provides the settings for wars, romance, and intrigue. Although the literary value of the Angrian chronicles is slight, they indicate the genesis of Charlotte's creative talents. During this period, Charlotte taught her sisters at home and worked briefly as a governess, an experience she described in *Jane Eyre.* However, Brontë disliked her position and left in 1842 to study French in Belgium. There, she developed a passionate attachment to Constantin Héger, her married instructor. Héger provided Charlotte with a strong literary background and helped her develop confidence to write. Though their relationship was ill-fated, many scholars believe that Héger inspired the character of Jane Eyre's employer, Fairfax Rochester.

Upon her return from Belgium, Charlotte discovered that Emily and Anne shared her interest in writing poetry, and the three published, at their own expense, *Poems by Currer, Ellis, and Acton Bell* (1846). The sisters assumed male pseudonyms both to preserve secrecy and to avoid the patronizing treatment they believed critics accorded women. Nevertheless, the book received few reviews and sold only two copies. Undeterred by the poor response, Charlotte continued to write. In 1847 she finished her first novel, *The Professor,* but could not sell it to a publisher until ten years later. When one publishing house agreed instead to consider a lengthier, more exciting novel, Charlotte immediately completed *Jane Eyre,* which she had begun several months earlier. The novel, which Brontë presented as an autobiography edited by Currer Bell, met with immediate popular acclaim. Its appeal, both in the nineteenth century and the present, derives from Brontë's insightful depiction of a sensitive, intellectually aware woman who seeks love but is able to suppress her emotions for the sake of her moral convictions.

While *Jane Eyre* was popularly well-received, the initial critical reception of the novel varied. Several commentators admired the power and freshness of Brontë's prose; others, however, termed the novel superficial and vulgar. Perhaps the best known early review, by Elizabeth Rigby, flatly condemned *Jane Eyre* as "an anti-Christian composition." Still other critics questioned the authorship of the novel. Some doubted that a woman was capable of writing such a work, while a critic in the *North American Review* contended that a man and a woman were its coauthors. In another early assessment, George Eliot expressed her admiration for the novel but complained that Brontë's charac-

ters spoke like "the heroes and heroines of police reports."

Critical interpretations during the twentieth century have tended to be more specific in their approach. The characters of Jane, Rochester, and Bertha are the subjects of detailed analyses, and the nature and import of Rochester's disability is also debated. Critics frequently discuss the novel's structure, its symbolism, and its autobiographical elements.

Although most critics have praised Brontë's narrative technique, some have argued that the story of *Jane Eyre* is unrealistic. Many commentators have lauded the novel's powerful language and have explored the work's unity, which they attribute to the use of the heroine as narrator as well as to Jane's process of spiritual growth.

Symbolism, too, figures prominently in critical treatments of *Jane Eyre.* Several critics have discussed the symbolic overtones of the paintings that Jane brings to Thornfield. To some commentators, these works reveal both Jane and the author's personalities. Other critics have proposed that the paintings chart Jane's emotional maturation and indicate various points of plot development. One critic, Kathleen Tillotson, discussed the pattern of recurring characters in the novel, concluding that the cruel Mr. Brocklehurst is reincarnated as St. John Rivers, and Jane's aunt, Mrs. Reed, reemerges as the snobbish Lady Ingram. In the late twentieth century, Brontë's novel has notably inspired critical writing from a feminist perspective.

Much attention has been devoted to determining the central theme of *Jane Eyre.* While interpretations still vary, most scholars agree that in the novel Brontë wished to stress the possibility of equality in marriage. Other suggestions include that Brontë attempted to depict the neuroses of women in society; that she intended to detail the power of human love while simultaneously indicating the role Providence plays in the characters' lives; and that the spiritual overtones of *Jane Eyre* present Brontë's message that a divine being governs our lives. More recently, some critics have maintained that Brontë sought to depict a woman's triumph over society's strictures.

While *Jane Eyre* undoubtedly reflects aspects of Brontë's own life, scholars have disputed whether its merits result chiefly from autobiographical elements or from Brontë's creative vision. Some have argued that Brontë relied too heavily on her own life for the plot and thus reduced the novel's dramatic impact, but most concur that such immediacy of experience enriched the novel. Perhaps the most concise assessment of Brontë's personal impact on the plot of *Jane Eyre* came from G. K. Chesterton, who termed the novel "the truest book that was ever written."

(For further information about Brontë's life and

works, see *Dictionary of Literary Biography*, Vol. 21: *Victorian Novelists before 1885* and *Nineteenth-Century Literature Criticism*, Vols. 3, 8).

CRITICAL COMMENTARY

GEORGE SAINTSBURY

(essay date 1896)

[Saintsbury was an English literary historian and critic. In the following excerpt, he examines Brontë's place in English literature.]

Perhaps the most interesting way of looking at Charlotte Brontë, who . . . has been violently attacked, and who has also been extravagantly praised (though not so extravagantly as her sister Emily), is to look at her in the light of a precursor or transition-novelist, representing the time when the followers of Scott had wearied the public with second-rate romances, when Thackeray had not arisen, or had only just arisen, and when the modern domestic novel in its various kinds, from the religious to the problematic, was for the most part in embryo, or in very early stages. [The novel *Shirley*] she in fact anticipated in many of its kinds, and partly to the fact of this anticipation, partly to the vividness which her representation of personal experiences gave to her work, may the popularity which it at first had, and such of it as has survived, be assigned. In this latter point, however, lay danger as well as safety. It seems very improbable that if Charlotte Brontë had lived, and if she had continued to write, her stock of experiences would have sufficed her; and it would not appear that she had much else. She is indeed credited with inventing the "ugly hero" in the Mr. Rochester of *Jane Eyre,* but in the long-run ugliness palls almost as much as beauty, perhaps sooner. Except in touches probably due to suggestions from Emily, the "weirdness" of the younger sister was not exhibited by the elder. The more melodramatic parts of the book would not have borne repetition, and its main appeal now lies in the Lowood scenes and the character of Jane herself, which are both admittedly autobiographical. So also Shirley is her sister Emily . . . , and *Villette* is little more than an embroidered version of the Brussels sojourn. How successful an appeal of this kind is, the experience of Byron and many others has shown; how dangerous it is, could not be better shown than by the same experience. It was Charlotte Brontë's good fortune that she died before she had utterly exhausted her vein, though those who fail to regard Paul Emanuel with the affection which he seems to inspire in some, may think that

she went perilously near it. But fate was kind to her: some interesting biographies and brilliant essays at different periods have revived and championed her fame: and her books—at least *Jane Eyre* almost as a whole and parts of the others—will always be simply interesting to the novel-reader, and interesting in a more indirect fashion to the critic. For this last will perceive that, thin and crude as they are, they are original, they belong to their own present and future, not to their past, and that so they hold in the history of literature a greater place than many books of greater accomplishment which are simply worked on already projected and accepted lines. (pp. 319-20)

George Saintsbury, "The Novel Since 1850," in his *A History of Nineteenth Century Literature (1780-1895),* Macmillan and Co., 1896, pp. 317-41.

DAVID CECIL

(lecture date 1931-32)

[Cecil has been highly acclaimed for his work on the Victorian era. In the following excerpt from a lecture delivered at Oxford University in 1931 or 1932, he evaluates the strengths and weaknesses of Brontë's fiction.]

Charlotte Brontë, in one of the formidable compliments which she paid to the few among her contemporaries who managed to win her esteem, once congratulated Thackeray on his power of revealing the painful realities that underlie the pleasing exterior of human society. He deserved such praise. But it was odd that she should have thought so. For to judge by their books no two writers had more different ideas of reality. The Victorian novelists are individualists, in nothing more alike than in their unlikeness to one another; and this is never more noticeable than when we shut up *Pendennis* and open *Jane Eyre.* Gone is the busy prosaic urban world with its complicated structure and its trivial motives, silenced the accents of everyday chatter, vanished are newspapers, fashions, business houses, duchesses, footmen and snobs. Instead the gale rages under

Principal Works

Poems by Currer, Ellis and Acton Bell [as Currer Bell, with Ellis and Acton Bell (pseudonyms of Emily and Anne Brontë)] (poems) 1846

Jane Eyre; An Autobiography [as Currer Bell] (novel) 1847

Shirley [as Currer Bell] (novel) 1849

Villette [as Currer Bell] (novel) 1853

The Professor [as Currer Bell] (novel) 1857

Emma (unfinished novel) 1860; published in periodical Cornhill

*The Brontës' Life and Letters (letters) 1908

Legends of Angria (juvenilia) 1933

Five Novelettes: Passing Events, Julia, Mina Laury, Henry Hastings, Caroline Vernon (novellas) 1971

*This work includes letters written by Charlotte, Emily, and Anne Brontë.

the elemental sky, while indoors, their faces rugged in the fierce firelight, austere figures of no clearly defined class or period declare eternal love and hate to one another in phrases of stilted eloquence and staggering candour. (p. 119)

[With Charlotte Brontë] we return to the characteristic type of Victorian novelist, untutored, unequal, inspired. . . . Of course, she is not so great a novelist as Dickens; apart from anything else she had a narrower range. For—and in this she is not a typical Victorian—not only do her books cover nothing of the religious, the intellectual, and the purely animal sides of life; they also cover none of that vast area of everyday life which was the subject of Dickens and Thackeray and Trollope. Like them she does not write about prophets or prostitutes; but unlike them she does not write about Mr. and Mrs. Smith in the next street either. Her range is confined to the inner life, the private passions. Her books are before all things the record of a personal vision. So, of course, in a sense are all great novels; if they were not they would not be great novels at all. But the personality of Charlotte Brontë's predecessors appears in their books implicitly. (p. 120)

With [Charlotte Brontë] the hero or more frequently the heroine for the first time steps forward and takes a dominating position on the stage; and the story is presented, not through the eyes of impersonal truth, but openly through her own. Except in *Shirley*, she actually tells it herself: and even in *Shirley* the principal characters tell a great deal of the story for themselves in journals. Charlotte Brontë's imagination is stimulated to create by certain aspects of man's inner life as that of Dickens or Thackeray by certain aspects of his external life. As Thackeray was the first English writer

to make the novel the vehicle of a conscious criticism of life, so she is the first to make it the vehicle of personal revelation. She is our first subjective novelist, the ancestor of Proust and Mr. James Joyce and all the rest of the historians of the private consciousness. And like theirs her range is limited to those aspects of experience which stimulate to significance and activity the private consciousness of their various heroes and heroines. (p. 121)

[Charlotte Brontë's] heroines do not try to disentangle the chaos of their consciousness, they do not analyse their emotions or motives. Indeed, they do not analyse anything. They only feel very strongly about everything. And the sole purpose of their torrential autobiographies is to express their feelings. *Jane Eyre, Villette, The Professor,* the best parts of *Shirley,* are not exercises of the mind, but cries of the heart; not a deliberate self-diagnosis, but an involuntary self-revelation.

Further, they are all revelations of the same self. It might be thought that since they are about different people her books had different imaginative ranges. But they have not; and inevitably. You can learn about the external life of many different sorts of people by observation: but no amount of observation can teach you about the inner life of anyone but yourself. All subjective novelists write about themselves. Nor was Charlotte Brontë an exception. Fundamentally, her principal characters are all the same person; and that is Charlotte Brontë. Her range is confined, not only to a direct expression of an individual's emotions and impressions, but to a direct expression of Charlotte Brontë's emotions and impressions. In this, her final limitation, we come indeed to the distinguishing fact of her character as a novelist. The world she creates is the world of her own inner life; she is her own subject.

This does not mean, of course, that she never writes about anything but her own character. She is a storyteller, and a story shows character in action, character, that is, as it appears in contact with the world of external event and personality. Only the relation of Charlotte Brontë's imagination to this world is different from that of most novelists. Theirs, inspired as it is by some aspect of human life outside their own, works, as it were, objectively. . . . Charlotte Brontë's picture of the external world is a picture of her own reactions to the external world. . . . And similarly her secondary characters are presented only as they appear to Jane Eyre or Lucy Snowe. We see as much of them as they saw of them: and what we do see is coloured by the intervening painted glass of Lucy Snowe's or Jane Eyre's temperament. At the best they are the barest sketches compared with the elaborately-finished portrait of the character through whose eyes we look at them. (pp. 121-23)

Charlotte Brontë is very far from being a consistent artist. She has all the Victorian inequality. She is even more startlingly unequal than Dickens. Her faults may not be worse faults—in point of fact she is never, as he is, vulgar—but she had less art to conceal them. She was a very naïve writer, her faults have the naked crudeness of a child's faults; and in consequence we pass with a sharper jolt from her good passages to her bad. For example, like Dickens', her books are badly constructed. But this does not mean, as it does with him, that the structure is conventional, that the emphasis of the interest falls in a different place from the emphasis of the plot. There is not enough structure in her books to be conventional; their plots are too indeterminate to have an emphasis. Her books—and this is true of no other English novelist of comparable merit—are, but for the continued presence of certain figures, incoherent. Nor is this because they are like *Pickwick*, a succession of adventures only connected by a hero. No, each is a drama: but not one drama. Charlotte Brontë will embark on a dramatic action and then, when it is half finished, without warning abandon it for another, equally dramatic, but without bearing on what has come before or will follow after. . . . However, *Jane Eyre* does maintain a continuous interest in one central figure. *Villette* and *Shirley* do not even possess this frail principle of unity. . . . In *Shirley* Charlotte Brontë does attempt a more regular scheme. But the result of her effort is only to show her disastrous inability to sustain it. Not only is the story cumbered up with a number of minor characters like the Yorke family and Mrs. Pryor, who have no contribution to make to the main action; but that action is itself split into two independent parts. . . . Once fully launched on her surging flood of self-revelation, Charlotte Brontë is far above pausing to attend to so paltry a consideration as artistic unity.

She does not pause to consider probability either. Charlotte Brontë's incapacity to make a book coherent as a whole is only equalled by her incapacity to construct a plausible machinery of action for its component parts. Her plots are not dull; but they have every other defect that a plot could have; they are at once conventional, confusing and unlikely. *The Professor*, indeed, save in the affair of Mr. Vandenhuten, palpably introduced to establish Crimsworth in the comfortable circumstances necessary to give the book a happy ending, is credible enough; while *Shirley*, though its plot is mildly unconvincing all through, is marred only by one gross improbability, the conduct of Mrs. Pryor. But the stories of her masterpieces, *Jane Eyre* and *Villette*, are, if regarded in a rational aspect, unbelievable from start to finish.

Jane Eyre, and here too Charlotte Brontë shows herself like Dickens, is a roaring melodrama. But the melodrama of *Bleak House* itself seems sober compared with that of *Jane Eyre.* Not one of the main incidents on which its action turns but is incredible. (pp. 124-26)

Villette has not a melodramatic plot. But by a majestic feat of literary perversity Charlotte Brontë manages to make this quiet chronicle of a school teacher as bristling with improbability as *Jane Eyre.* She stretches the long arm of coincidence till it becomes positively dislocated. (p. 127)

Nor are her faults of form her only faults. Her imagination did not know the meaning of the word restraint. This does not appear so much in her narrative, for there imagination is confined to its proper function of creating atmosphere and suggesting the stress of passion. But now and again she allows herself an interval in which to give it free rein: Caroline has a dream, Jane Eyre is inspired to paint a symbolic picture, Shirley Keeldar indulges in a flight of visionary meditation. And then across the page surges a seething cataract of Gothic romanticism and personification, spectres, demons, bleeding swords, angelic countenances, made noisy with all the ejaculation, reiteration, and apostrophe that a turgid rhetoric can supply. Even if such passages were good in themselves they put the rest of the book out of focus. . . . (p. 128)

[Charlotte Brontë] can be ridiculous. And this brings us to another of her defects—her lack of humour. Not that she is wholly without it. Like all the great Victorian novelists, she has a real and delightful vein of her own. But she does not strike this vein often: and when she does not she shows herself as little humorous as it is possible to be. . . . Charlotte Brontë was about as well-equipped to be a satirist as she was to be a ballet-dancer. Satire demands acute observation and a light touch. Charlotte Brontë, indifferent to the outside world and generally in a state of tension, observes little, and never speaks lightly of anything. In consequence her satirical darts fall wide of the mark and as ponderous as lead. Painstakingly she tunes her throbbing accents to a facetious tone, conscientiously she contorts her austere countenance to a humorous grimace. (pp. 128-29)

But though her lack of humour prevents her amusing us when she means to, it often amuses us very much when she does not. Her crudeness, her lack of restraint, and the extreme seriousness with which she envisages life, combine to deprive her of any sense of ironic proportion. (p. 129)

[However], unconscious humour is not her worst fault; if it is a fault at all. It springs from the very nature of her work, from the fact that she presents life from an individual point of view: to remove the absurdity would be to remove the individuality at the same time. Moreover, it is possible to describe a scene vividly without seeing its funny side. . . . The play in *Villette*, Rochester's proposal, are among the most memorable scenes in Charlotte Brontë's books; and we enjoy them whole-heartedly. Only, our enjoyment is enriched by an ironic amusement which it could hardly have been her intention to stimulate.

But her chief defect cannot be so lightly dismissed. Charlotte Brontë fails, and fails often, over the most important part of a novelist's work—over character. Even at her best she is not among the greatest drawers of character. Her secondary figures do not move before us with the solid reality of Jane Austen's: seen as they are through the narrow lens of her heroines' temperament, it is impossible that they should. And the heroines themselves are presented too subjectively for us to see them in the round as we see Maggie Tulliver or Emma Bovary. Nor is her failure solely due to the limitations imposed by her angle of approach. Since she feels rather than understands, she cannot penetrate to the inner structure of a character to discover its basic elements. Most of her characters are only presented fragmentarily as they happen to catch the eye of her heroine; but in the one book, *Shirley,* in which she does try to present them objectively, they are equally fragmentary. And sometimes they are not only fragmentary, they are lifeless. Her satirical, realistic figures, of course, are especially lifeless. The curates in *Shirley,* the house-party in *Jane Eyre,* these are as garishly unreal as the cardboard puppets in a toy theatre. . . . Lady Ingram is not original: she is extremely conventional, the conventional silly grande dame of third-rate farce. Charlotte Brontë, unacquainted with such a character herself, has just copied it from the crude type which she found in the commonplace fiction of the time. And her lack of technical skill has made her copy even cruder than its model.

She can fail over serious character too; particularly male character. Serious male characters are always a problem for a woman novelist. And for Charlotte Brontë, exclusively concentrated as she was on the reactions of her highly feminine temperament, they were especially a problem. Nor did she solve it. She does not usually err by making them too feminine; her heroes are not all sisters under their skins. . . . [As] a rule Charlotte Brontë errs in the other extreme. Ignorant what men are like, but convinced that at any rate they must be unlike women, she endows them only with those characteristics she looks on as particularly male: and accentuates these to such a degree that they cease to be human at all. . . . Charlotte Brontë's more orthodox heroes . . . have not even got imaginative life; they are mere tedious aggregations of good qualities, painted figureheads of virtue like the heroes of Scott. Only in Paul Emanuel has Charlotte Brontë drawn a hero who is also a living man. And he is deliberately presented on unheroic lines. (pp. 131-34)

Charlotte Brontë's hand does not only falter over her heroes. In Caroline and Shirley, her two objectively conceived heroines, it is equally uncertain. Both are departures from her usual type. Caroline is described as gentle, sweet and charming, Shirley as charming, brilliant and high-spirited. In company they sustain their rôles convincingly enough. But the moment they are alone they change, they become like each other and unlike either of the characters in which they first appear. . . . (pp. 134-35)

Formless, improbable, humourless, exaggerated, uncertain in their handling of character—there is assuredly a great deal to be said against Charlotte Brontë's novels. So much, indeed, that one may well wonder if she is a good novelist at all. All the same she is; she is even great. Her books are as living today as those of Dickens; and for the same reason. They have creative imagination; and creative imagination of the most powerful kind, able to assimilate to its purpose the strongest feelings, the most momentous experiences. Nor is it intermittent in its action. Charlotte Brontë, and here again she is like Dickens, is, even at her worst, imaginative. . . . Every page of Charlotte Brontë's novels burns and breathes with vitality. Out of her improbabilities and her absurdities, she constructed an original vision of life; from the scattered, distorted fragments of experience which managed to penetrate her huge self-absorption, she created a world.

But her limitations make it very unlike the life of any other novelists' world. For, unhelped as she is by any great power of observation and analysis, her world is almost exclusively an imaginary world. Its character and energy derive nothing important from the character and energy of the world she purports to describe; they are the character and energy of her own personality. (pp. 135-36)

Charlotte Brontë could express love and passion and despair, she could also express guilt and moral aspiration. Her pages throb with an unquenchable zest for life; only it is life conceived, not as a garden of pleasure, but as a tense and sublime battle.

Finally, her ingenuousness is an ingredient in her unique flavour. For one thing, it disinfects her imagination; blows away the smoke and sulphur which its ardent heat might be expected to generate, so that its flame burns pure and clear. Further, it breathes round it an atmosphere, not usually associated with its other outstanding characteristics, an atmosphere of artless freshness, a candid virginal charm. Nor does this diminish its force. The fact that we feel Charlotte Brontë's imagination to be in some degree the imagination of a child, with a child's hopeful credulity, a child's eager, unselfconscious responsiveness, so far from weakening its intensity, rather invests it with a sincerity irresistibly touching and winning.

Her imagination illuminates the whole of Charlotte Brontë's achievement. But there are certain aspects in which it shines especially bright. The characters, first of all: it is true that some of them, like Miss Ingram, are so preposterously conceived that no imagination could make them convincing; it is also true that we never see Charlotte Brontë's characters in the round as we see Tolstoy's or Jane Austen's, but only as they happen to cross her line of vision. Still, it is possible to see a man vividly in one line of vision; and, if it is Lucy Snowe's or Jane Eyre's, very vividly indeed. Not Henry James himself can convey the impact of a personality more forcibly than Charlotte Brontë at her best. . . . Charlotte Brontë is always at her best in describing children; and best of all when she is describing them from the inside, when, in the person of little Jane Eyre or fifteen-year-old Lucy Snowe, she is speaking as a child herself. Indeed her vision of life, like that of Dickens, appears most convincing from the eye of a child. For, like his, it has a child's intensity, a child's crudeness; the first quarter of *Jane Eyre,* with the first quarter of *David Copperfield,* is the most profoundly-studied portrait of childhood in English.

Her imagination shows itself in her settings as much as in her characters. . . . Nor are her interiors less memorable. (pp. 143-45)

[The] power of creating a scene associates itself with Charlotte Brontë's power of suggesting the eerie. She never actually brings in the supernatural. Indeed her lack of imaginative restraint would probably have made her fail if she had. . . . Charlotte Brontë's plots are full of sinister secrets and inexplicable happenings. And the lurid light of her vision does invest these with a weirdness beyond that of ordinary mundane horror. (p. 145)

Love, indeed, is the central theme of her stories: for it was inevitably the main preoccupation of so passionate a temperament. Her power to describe it is, of course, conditioned by the nature of her genius. She cannot dissect the workings of passion, nor can she illuminate its effect on character. What she can do is to convey its actual present throb. And this she does as it had never been done before in English fiction. Naturally she was too much of a Victorian and too much of a Puritan to do more than hint at its animal side. But her hints are quite enough to prevent the emotion seeming disembodied and unreal. . . . Hers is a frustrated love.

And writing as she does of the emotions of her own unsatisfied heart, Charlotte Brontë is most characteristically concerned to describe frustrated love: Jane Eyre's love for Rochester, so hopelessly, as it would seem, out of her reach; Lucy Snowe's for Dr. John, absorbed already in Ginevra Fanshawe. But the fact that it is frustrated does not make the love of Charlotte Brontë's heroines less intense. Indeed it makes it more of an obsession. Moreover, Charlotte Brontë can describe happy love equally well, if her story gives her a chance. As a matter of fact love is the occasion of her

few successful flights of humour. Jane Eyre teasing Rochester, Lucy Snowe sparring with Paul Emanuel—in these she achieves real comedy. It is a little stiff and shy; it is also enchantingly demure and delicate; a sort of Puritan comedy of the sexes, unlike anything else in English literature. And she can rise higher.

In addition to love's gaieties she can describe love's ecstasy. Like most of the other novelists of her school, she is a poet; and her poetry is the pure lyrical poetry of passion. It connects itself with her sensibility to landscape. The special emotion of her love-scenes swells to assimilate to itself the emotional quality of the scenery amid which they take place. (pp. 146-47)

Even more characteristic are Charlotte Brontë's moments of *solitary* emotion, the gusts of inexplicable anguish, yearning, exultation, which sweep across the spirit, unprovoked by any actively dramatic incident. And they are most vivid when some abnormal physical circumstance has heated them to a morbid intensity; the agony of the starving Jane Eyre, lost a whole burning July day on the Yorkshire moors; Caroline Helstone's delirious broodings that mingle tumultuously with raging wind and brilliant winter moonlight, as she tosses on her sick bed; Lucy Snowe's tormented loneliness rising to hallucination, during her three months' sojourn in the deserted school; the strange exaltation induced by drugs that compels her from her sickbed to wander through festal Villette. These scenes, indeed, are the peak of Charlotte Brontë's achievement; for in them, as in no others, her imagination finds the perfect field for its expression. Her pictures of love and character, though they reveal her powers, reveal also her defects. But solitary obsession, while it offers equal scope to her intensity and more to her imaginative strangeness, makes no demands on her she cannot satisfy. No power of psychological penetration or accurate observation is needed to communicate the impressions of the senses in an abnormal nervous state; while to be dream-like and unrestrained is characteristic of such impressions. For once Charlotte Brontë is true not only to imagination, but to fact.

Her technical ability is akin to the rest of her genius. In certain ways she is hardly a craftsman at all. As we have seen, she cannot construct a plausible or even a coherent plot; the fabric of her books is woven with irrelevancies, frayed with loose threads. But she was a born story-teller: continuously from her first sentence to her last she engages our interest. It is partly due to the fire of her personality; like the Ancient Mariner she holds us with her glittering eye. It is also due to an exceptional mastery of the art of awaking suspense. (pp. 147-49)

Her style is similarly unequal, similarly inspired; indeed it is the mirror and microcosm of her achievement. It is an odd style, with its mixture of grandeur and provinciality, of slovenly colloquial grammar and

An 1854 portrait of Brontë's husband, Arthur Bell Nicholls.

place and absurdity, some evocative image, some haunting, throbbing cadence. . . . [At] every turn of its furious course Charlotte Brontë's imagination throws off some such glinting spark of phrase. And now and again the sparks blaze up into a sustained passage of De Quinceyish prose poetry. (pp. 149-50)

She was a genius. She had, that is, that creative imagination which is the distinguishing quality of the artist, in the very highest intensity. No writer has ever been able to infuse his material with a stronger and a more individual vitality. No writer's work is more obviously of the stuff of which great art is made. But imagination, though it can make an artist, cannot make a craftsman. This needs other qualifications, and of these, except her turn for telling a story. Charlotte Brontë had none at all. No other English novelist of her power sat down to his task so glaringly deficient in some of the essential qualities which it required. She had no gift of form, no restraint, little power of observation, no power of analysis. And her novels suffer from it. They are badly constructed, they are improbable, they are often ridiculous. Moreover, her lack of critical capacity meant that, like those of Dickens, her books often involved themes and characters outside her imaginative range, the range of her personal impressions. The result of all this is that in spite of her genius she never wrote a wholly satisfying book. *Shirley* is her greatest failure, for there she set out to tell the story of two normal girls in the first place, and in the second to give a picture of the industrial revolution in Northern England. *Jane Eyre* is more personal and therefore better. Indeed, its first quarter is the most sustained expression of her genius. But it is marred by a grotesque plot and two full-length male portraits. *Villette*, with little regular plot, and concerned only with personal life, is her most consistently successful book. But it, too, is disfigured by unnecessary and improbable incidents; and it is nearly incoherent.

This makes her achievement almost impossible finally to estimate. . . . She cannot be placed with the great painters of human character, the Shakespeares, the Scotts, the Jane Austens; her faults are too glaring, her inspiration too eccentric. But equally she cannot be dismissed to a minor rank, to the Fanny Burneys, the Charles Reades; for unlike them she rises at times to the greatest heights. She is predestined to hover restlessly and for ever, now at the head now at the foot of the procession of letters, among the unplaceable anomalies, the freak geniuses; along with Ford and Tourneur and Herman Melville and D. H. Lawrence. Such writers never achieve a universally accepted reputation. The considerable body of people who set a paramount importance on craftsmanship and verisimilitude will never admire them. But their strange flame, lit as it is at the central white hot fire of creative inspiration, will in every age find them followers. And on these they ex-

stilted archaic phraseology, of abrupt paragraphs and rolling sentences. And in some ways it is a very bad style. Even at its best it flows turbid and irregular. It never exhibits the exact translucency of the true stylist, that sensibility to the quality and capacity of language which marks the writing of Thackeray, for instance. It is deformed by all Charlotte Brontë's customary clumsiness, all her customary lack of restraint. The words tend perpetually to get in the way of the meaning. For not only is she incapable of expressing herself briefly and smoothly, she further disfigures her plainest piece of narrative by plastering it with rhetoric; a rhetoric, too, which, undisciplined as it is by an educated taste, is as often as not extremely bad, bedizened with imagery, spasmodic with ejaculation, a compound of the commonplace and the grotesque.

All the same, Charlotte Brontë's writing is a powerful agent in her effect. For she manages to infuse her personality into it. Cliché, rhetoric and bad grammar alike are pulsing with her intensity, fresh with her charm. Moreover, her strange imagination expresses itself in her actual choice of words. There is hardly a page where we do not meet, sandwiched between common-

ercise a unique, a thrilling, a perennial fascination. (pp. 152-54)

David Cecil, "Charlotte Brontë," in his *Early Victorian Novelists: Essays in Revaluation,* 1934. Reprint by The Bobbs-Merrill Company, Inc., 1935, pp. 119-54.

M. H. SCARGILL

(essay date 1950)

[In the excerpt below, Scargill examines *Jane Eyre*'s unique contributions to the tradition of the English novel.]

From the day of its first appearance *Jane Eyre* has been credited with adding something new to the tradition of the English novel, though just what this is, and whether it is desirable, continues to puzzle the critics. To some the new quality is the voice of a woman who speaks with perfect frankness about herself; to others it is "passion," though the nature of this "passion" is left undefined. To all, *Jane Eyre* is remarkable for its intensity, and this intensity is usually taken as sufficient to counteract what critics regard as a sensational and poorly constructed plot. The cause of this intensity remains uncertain. Some have suggested that it is love; some even go so far as to suggest that it is the memory of a real love which Charlotte Brontë herself had experienced, that is that the novel is some kind of autobiography and, if we take this view to its logical conclusion, not a novel at all. (p. 120)

With the publication of *Jane Eyre,* the English novel, which had already absorbed elements from the essay, the "character," and the drama, turned away from the external towards the expression of an experience exclusively personal. This experience is not necessarily factual, but it is none the less real, and it is important, as much poetry is important, for the intensity of its feeling and the adequacy of its expression. It is intensity of feeling which has attracted readers to *Jane Eyre;* it is the origin and nature of this feeling and its means of expression, adequate or inadequate, that have puzzled them.

To many readers passion is synonymous with love, and to these it is as a love story that *Jane Eyre* appeals, a love story told with great frankness by a woman who, as [W. L. Cross] would put it, is "a realist of the feelings." To others passion is an admirable but indescribable feeling, which appeals simply because it is a feeling—by no means a foolish value to attract one to a book and infinitely superior to that which leads to admiration of *Jane Eyre* as a kind of real "confession." Intensity of feeling *Jane Eyre* has, but it is not centred

exclusively upon love; in fact, in the total impact of *Jane Eyre* religious ecstasy plays a part as important as love for a person.

The greatness of a work of art is commensurate with the greatness of its inspiration and the adequacy of its means of communication. Now, the story of a woman in love would be interesting but not necessarily great; the story of a woman's fight to express her own personality in love would be even more interesting but yet not necessarily great. *Jane Eyre* is great because it is these things and also something more. It is a love story; it is a fight for the free expression of personality in love; but it is also a record of the eternal conflict between the flesh and the spirit, a conflict which is solved satisfactorily when all passion is spent. *Jane Eyre* may speak for many women, but it speaks also for all humanity, and it speaks in unmistakable terms. *Jane Eyre* is the record of an intense spiritual experience, as powerful in its way as King Lear's ordeal of purgation, and it ends nobly on a note of calm.

The expression of such an experience in terms of the novel creates considerable difficulty. The poet, for an identical purpose, takes the means of communication which is to hand, the language of his day, and has permission to put new life into it. The closer he can fashion it to his purpose, the more he is admired. . . . (p. 121)

We make no demands of probability on the poet. All we ask is that he shall symbolize his experience, recreate it for us, by whatever means he thinks best. But of the novelist we seem inclined to demand probability, a reproduction of life, regardless of the novelist's purpose. Charlotte Brontë had experienced an emotion which one would expect her to express through the medium of poetry. But she used the conventional elements of the novel, the medium she understood best. It seems logical to suppose that such a use, conscious or unconscious, of the elements of fiction would produce a new type of novel. And this is precisely the case with *Jane Eyre.* The conventions have become symbols: the fictional lover has become The Lover; the mad woman of the Gothic novel has been put to an allegorical use. *Jane Eyre* contains the elements of fiction used as a poet employs language and imagery—to impose belief, even though it be by irrational means. (p. 122)

[*Jane Eyre,* as it appears to me, is] a new contribution to English fiction, a novel which must not be criticized in the spirit in which we criticize *Vanity Fair* or *Tom Jones.* . . .

If *Jane Eyre* is to be blamed, because it doesn't do what *Tom Jones* and *Vanity Fair* do, then literary criticism is at fault. We must be willing to accept *Jane Eyre* as a profound, spiritual experience, expressed in the most adequate symbolism, a symbolism which, if divorced from its emotion, is as improbable as all poetic symbols.

That way lies a truer appreciation of *Jane Eyre*. We have felt its greatness: we have often excused its means of expression. Let us now admit that in *Jane Eyre* fiction has become poetry, and let us enlarge our idea of fiction accordingly. (p. 125)

M. H. Scargill, " 'All Passion Spent': A Revaluation of 'Jane Eyre'," in *University of Toronto Quarterly*, Vol. XIX, No. 2, January, 1950, pp. 120-25.

ROBERT B. HEILMAN
(essay date 1958)

[In the following excerpt from an essay first published in 1958 in *From Jane Austen to Joseph Conrad: Essays Collected in Memory of James T. Steinmann, Jr.*, Heilman explores the nature and function of Gothic elements in Brontë's novels.]

[Charlotte Brontë's *The Professor*] is conventional; formally she is for "reason" and "real life"; but her characters keep escaping to glorify "feeling" and "Imagination." Feeling is there in the story—evading repression, in author or in character; ranging from nervous excitement to emotional absorption; often tense and peremptory; sexuality, hate, irrational impulse, grasped, given life, not merely named and pigeonholed. This is Charlotte's version of Gothic: in her later novels an extraordinary thing. . . . [The] vital feeling moves toward an intensity, a freedom, and even an abandon virtually nonexistent in historical Gothic and rarely approached in Richardson. From Angria on, Charlotte's women vibrate with passions that the fictional conventions only partly constrict or gloss over—in the center an almost violent devotedness that has in it at once a fire of independence, a spiritual energy, a vivid sexual responsiveness, and, along with this, self-righteousness, a sense of power, sometimes self-pity and envious competitiveness. To an extent the heroines are "unheroined," unsweetened. Into them there has come a new sense of the dark side of feeling and personality.

The Professor ventures a little into the psychic darkness on which *Villette* draws heavily. . . . Charlotte draws on sex images that recall the note of sexuality subtly present in other episodes: " . . . I had entertained her at bed and board . . . she lay with me, . . . taking me entirely to her death-cold bosom, and holding me with arms of bone." The climax is: "I repulsed her as one would a dreaded and ghastly concubine coming to embitter a husband's heart toward his young bride. . . . " This is Gothic, yet there is an integrity of feeling that greatly deepens the convention. (pp. 97-8)

In both *Villette* and *Jane Eyre* Gothic is used but characteristically is undercut.

Jane Eyre hears a "tragic . . . preternatural . . . laugh," but this is at "high noon" and there is "no circumstance of ghostliness"; Grace Poole, the supposed laughter, is a plain person, than whom no "apparition less romantic or less ghostly could . . . be conceived"; Charlotte apologizes ironically to the "romantic reader" for telling "the plain truth" that Grace generally bears a "pot of porter." Charlotte almost habitually revises "old Gothic," the relatively crude mechanisms of fear, with an infusion of the anti-Gothic. When Mrs. Rochester first tried to destroy Rochester by fire, Jane "baptized" Rochester's bed and heard Rochester "fulminating strange anathemas at finding himself lying in a pool of water." The introduction of comedy as a palliative of straight Gothic occurs on a large scale when almost seventy-five pages are given to the visit of the Ingram-Eshton party to mysterious Thornfield; here Charlotte, as often in her novels, falls into the manner of the Jane Austen whom she despised. When Mrs. Rochester breaks loose again and attacks Mason, the presence of guests lets Charlotte play the nocturnal alarum for at least a touch of comedy: Rochester orders the frantic women not to "pull me down or strangle me"; and "the two dowagers, in vast white wrappers, were bearing down on him like ships in full sail."

The symbolic also modifies the Gothic, for it demands of the reader a more mature and complicated response than the relatively simple thrill or momentary intensity of feeling sought by primitive Gothic. (p. 98)

[In] various ways Charlotte manages to make the patently Gothic more than a stereotype. But more important is that she instinctively finds new ways to achieve the ends served by old Gothic—the discovery and release of new patterns of feeling, the intensification of feeling. . . . Charlotte leads away from standardized characterization toward new levels of human reality, and hence from stock responses toward a new kind of passionate engagement.

Charlotte moves toward depth in various ways that have an immediate impact like that of Gothic. Jane's strange, fearful symbolic dreams are not mere thrillers but reflect the tensions of the engagement period, the stress of the wedding-day debate with Rochester, and the longing for Rochester after she has left him. The final Thornfield dream, with its vivid image of a hand coming through a cloud in place of the expected moon, is in the surrealistic vein that appears most sharply in the extraordinary pictures that Jane draws at Thornfield: here Charlotte is plumbing the psyche, not inventing a weird *décor*. . . . In her flair for the surreal, in her plunging into feeling that is without status in the ordinary world of the novel, Charlotte discovers a new dimension of Gothic.

She does this most thoroughly in her portrayal of characters and of the relations between them. If in Rochester we see only an Angrian-Byronic hero and a Charlotte wish-fulfillment figure (the two identifications which to some readers seem entirely to place him), we miss what is more significant, the exploration of personality that opens up new areas of feeling in intersexual relationships. Beyond the "grim," the "harsh," the eccentric, the almost histrionically cynical that superficially distinguish Rochester from conventional heroes, there is something almost Lawrentian: Rochester is "neither tall nor graceful"; his eyes can be "dark, irate, and piercing"; his strong features "took my feelings from my own power and fettered them in his." Without using the vocabulary common to us, Charlotte is presenting maleness and physicality, to which Jane responds directly. (pp. 99-100)

Aside from partial sterilization of banal Gothic by dry factuality and humor, Charlotte goes on to make a much more important—indeed, a radical—revision of the mode: in *Jane Eyre* and in the other novels . . . that discovery of passion, that rehabilitation of the extra-rational, which is the historical office of Gothic, is no longer oriented in marvelous circumstance but moves deeply into the lesser known realities of human life. This change I describe as the change from "old Gothic" to "new Gothic." The kind of appeal is the same; the fictional method is utterly different.

When Charlotte went on from *Jane Eyre* to *Shirley,* she produced a book that for the student of the Gothic theme is interesting precisely because on the face of things it would be expected to be a barren field. It is the result of Charlotte's one deliberate venture from private intensities into public extensities: Orders in Council, the Luddites, technological unemployment in 1811 and 1812, a social portraiture which develops Charlotte's largest cast of characters. Yet Charlotte cannot keep it a social novel. Unlike Warren, who in the somewhat similar *Night Rider* chose to reflect the historical economic crisis in the private crisis of the hero, Miss Brontë loses interest in the public and slides over into the private.

The formal irregularities of *Shirley*—the stop-and-start, zig-zag movement, plunging periodically into different perspectives—light up the divergent impulses in Charlotte herself: the desire to make a story from observed outer life, and the inability to escape from inner urgencies that with centrifugal force unwind outward into story almost autonomously. Passion alters plan: the story of industrial crisis is repeatedly swarmed over by the love stories. But the ultimate complication is that Charlotte's duality of impulse is reflected not only in the narrative material but in two different ways of telling each part of the story. On the one hand she tells a rather conventional, open, predictable tale; on the other she lets go with a highly charged

private sentiency that may subvert the former or at least surround it with an atmosphere of unfamiliarity or positive strangeness: the Gothic impulse.

For Charlotte it is typically the "pattern" versus the "strange." She describes "two pattern young ladies, in pattern attire, with pattern deportment"—a "respectable society" in which "Shirley had the air of a black swan, or a white crow. . . . " When, in singing, Shirley "poured round the passion, force," the young ladies thought this "strange" and concluded: "What was *strange* must be *wrong*. . . . " True, Charlotte's characters live within the established "patterns" of life; but their impulse is to vitalize forms with unpatterned feeling, and Charlotte's to give play to unpatterned feeling in all its forms. (pp. 101-02)

True to convention, the love stories end happily. But special feelings, a new pathos of love, come through. . . . There is that peculiarly tense vivacity of talk between lovers (the Jane-Rochester style), who discover a heightened, at times stagey, yet highly communicative rhetoric, drawing now on fantasy, now on moral conviction, verging now on titillating revelation, now on battle; a crafty game of love, flirting with an undefined risk, betraying a withheld avowal, savoring the approach to consummation, as if the erotic energy which in another social order might find a physical outlet were forcing itself into an electric language that is decorous but intimately exploratory. (p. 103)

Though *Shirley* is not pulled together formally as well as *Jane Eyre* or even the more sprawling *Villette,* and though the characters are as wholes less fully realized, still it accommodates the widest ranging of an extraordinarily free sensibility. Constantly, in many different directions, it is in flight from the ordinary rational surface of things against which old Gothic was the first rebel in fiction; it abundantly contains and evokes, to adapt Charlotte's own metaphor, "unpatterned feeling." It turns up unexpected elements in personality: resentfulness, malice, love of power; precocities and perversities of response; the multiple tensions of love between highly individualized lovers; psychic disturbances. And in accepting a dark magnetic energy as a central virtue in personality, Charlotte simply reverses the status of men who were the villains in the sentimental and old Gothic modes.

Of the four novels, *Villette* is most heavily saturated with Gothic—with certain of its traditional manifestations (old Gothic), with the undercutting of these that is for Charlotte no less instinctive than the use of them (anti-Gothic), and with an original, intense exploration of feeling that increases the range and depth of fiction (new Gothic). (pp. 104-05)

In *The Professor* the tensions in the author's contemplation of her own experience come into play; in *Shirley* various undercurrents of personality push up into the social surfaces of life; in *Jane Eyre* moral feeling is subjected to the remolding pressures of a newly vivid consciousness of the diverse impulses of sexuality; and in *Villette* the feeling responses to existence are pursued into sufferings that edge over into disorder. The psychology of rejection and alienation, first applied to Polly, becomes the key to Lucy, who, finding no catharsis for a sense of desolation, generates a serious inner turmoil. (p. 106)

These strains prepare us for the high point in Charlotte's new Gothic—the study of Lucy's emotional collapse and near breakdown when vacation comes and she is left alone at the school with "a poor deformed and imbecile pupil." "My heart almost died within me; . . . My spirits had long been gradually sinking; now that the prop of employment was withdrawn, they went down fast." . . .

From now on, overtly or implicitly, hypochondria and anxiety keep coming into the story—the enemies from whose grip Lucy must gradually free herself. (p. 107)

There is not room to trace Lucy's recovery, especially in the important phase, the love affair with Paul which is related to our theme by compelling, as do the Jane-Rochester and Louis Moore-Shirley relationships in quite different ways, a radical revision of the feelings exacted by stereotyped romance. What is finally noteworthy is that Charlotte, having chosen in Lucy a heroine with the least durable emotional equipment, with the most conspicuous neurotic element in her temperament, goes on through the history of Lucy's emotional maturing to surmount the need for romantic fulfillment and to develop the aesthetic courage for a final disaster—the only one in her four novels.

Some years ago Edmund Wilson complained of writers of Gothic who "fail to lay hold on the terrors that lie deep in the human soul and that cause man to fear himself " and proposed an anthology of horror stories that probe "psychological caverns" and find "disquieting obsessions." This is precisely the direction in which Charlotte Brontë moved, especially in Lucy Snowe and somewhat also in Caroline Helstone and Shirley Keeldar; this was one aspect of her following human emotions where they took her, into many depths and intensities that as yet hardly had a place in the novel. This was the finest achievement of Gothic. (pp. 107-08)

The first Gothic writers took the easy way: the excitement of mysterious scene and happening, which I call old Gothic. Of this Charlotte Brontë made some direct use, while at the same time tending toward humorous modifications (anti-Gothic); but what really counts is its indirect usefulness to her: it released her from the patterns of the novel of society and therefore permitted the flowering of her real talent—the talent

for finding and giving dramatic form to impulses and feelings which, because of their depth or mysteriousness or intensity or ambiguity, or of their ignoring or transcending everyday norms of propriety or reason, increase wonderfully the sense of reality in the novel. To note the emergence of this "new Gothic" in Charlotte Brontë is not, I think, to pursue an old mode into dusty corners but rather to identify historically the distinguishing, and distinguished, element in her work. (pp. 108-09)

Robert B. Heilman, "Charlotte Brontë's 'New' Gothic," in *The Brontës: A Collection of Critical Essays,* edited by Ian Gregor, Prentice-Hall, Inc., 1970, pp. 96-109.

ROBERT A. COLBY
(essay date 1960)

[In the excerpt below, Colby provides an overview of *Villette*, focusing on its function in English literary history.]

In the last century *Villette* was something of a fashionable shocker. . . . The reputation of the book seems for the most part to have been preserved by Miss Brontë's sister novelists of various generations—Mrs. Gaskell, George Eliot, Mrs. Ward, May Sinclair, Virginia Woolf—so that the pressed flower fragrance of the "woman's novel" has tended to cling to it. . . .

In our time, as it was in Charlotte Brontë's, *Villette* is thought of mainly as "by the author of *Jane Eyre*." to be sure, there are good reasons why *Jane Eyre* should have edged out its successor in popularity. By comparison with the steady excitement of *Jane Eyre, Villette* may seem to some readers loosely woven and desultory in pace, not so carefully plotted. There is no mysterious manor house here, nor any hidden mad wife. The romance around which *Villette* principally turns is between two outwardly rather unattractive people, and nothing much (practically speaking) comes of it. Yet it may still be argued that in many ways Miss Brontë's last novel was her most profound accomplishment. To read *Villette* as carefully as it deserves to be read is to follow the curve of Charlotte Brontë's literary development to its completion—and at the same time to follow the direction of the nineteenth-century novel. . . .

Villette is most fruitfully approached as Charlotte Brontë's literary, not her literal, autobiography. Lucy Snowe's turbulent emotional experiences may be taken as an analogue of Charlotte Brontë's creative life, in that her achievement of mastery over her morbidly introverted imagination parallels Miss Brontë's own emancipation from the dream world she had envisaged in the Angrian legends of her youth. (p. 410)

The Professor will always be of interest to readers of Villette since Miss Brontë undertook the writing of her last novel after another unsuccessful attempt to publish the first. However, the relationship between the two novels is elusive. The Professor is not really an underdone Villette as it is sometimes said to be. The germ of Villette is contained not in what Miss Brontë tried and failed to do in The Professor, but in what she deliberately tried not to do there. (pp. 410-11)

[The] superiority of Villette over The Professor does not lie merely in its greater power. What Miss Brontë tried to repress in The Professor re-asserts itself in Villette, it is true, but with a sense of proportion. While throughout the novel passion and rationality, art and nature, romance and reality continuously exert their rival claims on Lucy's imagination, in the end these tensions are resolved. Greater richness is produced also by the contrast between the tragedy of Lucy Snowe and the happier fates of the lesser heroines Polly Home and Ginevra Fanshawe.

Many readers may feel that of the three stories developed in Villette, the only one that is really "done," as Henry James might have put it, is the romance between Lucy Snowe and Monsieur Paul. Had Miss Brontë succeeded in penetrating the other two romances with equal insight perhaps she would have produced a masterpiece on the order and scale of, say, Middlemarch, instead of the erratic and uneven masterpiece that Villette admittedly is. However, the superficial treatment of the secondary characters actually serves a purpose in the scheme of the novel. . . .

The characters are contrasted not only by their sensibilities. Significant differences in the descriptions of the three pairs of lovers indicate something also of the Brontëan scale of values with respect to nature and art. . . .

[The] subtle interpenetration of nature and art really informs the entire novel, binding together the loosely woven first two-thirds of the story with the more taut and tense latter portion. A good part of Villette, particularly its early sections, is taken up with literature and the other arts, both explicitly and by allusion. In this novel, on the whole, the arts are associated with passivity and escapism, nature with the active mind and reality. (p. 412)

[In] the very framework of Villette and in the point of view from which it is told, there is embedded that circularity of life and literature, romance and reality that envelops its incidents, characters, and thought. "I used to think what a delight it would be for one who loved him better than he loved himself to gather and store up those handfuls of gold dust, so recklessly flung to heaven's reckless winds," Lucy recalls in connection with one of the sylvan story hours. So she writes a book about a man who didn't write books. Villette then is one of those special novels that we have become more used to in our century which have a novelist writing a novel at their center. Lucy is really observing herself in the process of composing, creating characters and re-creating herself, and one understands therefore why she is so preoccupied with the workings of the mind and the imagination.

In this respect Villette can be contrasted with Jane Eyre. Where Lucy's impulse is to take up the pen, Jane's is to reach for the crayon. Jane feels that she has 'pinned down' a character when she has managed to sketch his lineaments at the drawing board. Lucy, on the other hand, is every minute the writer. . . . Jane characteristically is interested in the features of the people she meets, to the extent that they reveal character. That is to say, Jane is an amateur phrenologist, as are other Brontë characters. Lucy, it is true, makes some use also of "Gall's Science" but on the whole phrenology plays a lesser part in the characterization of the personages of Villette than in that of the other three novels of Charlotte Brontë. (p. 415)

Much went into the moulding of *Villette;* more, undoubtedly, than we can hope to trace. Coming as it does in mid-century, Miss Brontë's final novel, more than is generally realized, is a meeting place of the streams of early nineteenth-century fiction. As an *éducation sentimentale* it links the continent with England, the sensibility of Romanticism with mid-Victorian realism. One wishes he knew more exactly just what French novels Miss Brontë steeped herself in during the 1830's and 1840's. We know she admired Balzac's *Modeste Mignon* and *Illusions perdues* for their "analysis of motives" and "subtle perception of the most obscure and secret workings of the mind." The early chapters of *Consuelo,* her favorite novel of George Sand, anticipate the master-pupil relationship of *Villette.* (p. 417)

If a certain phase of Miss Brontë's imagination moves back to the late eighteenth century, another is lodged in a period more within her actual recall. Woven through the fabric of *Villette* are threads of various modes of fiction that flourished during her youth—here given a new twist. . . .

[Charlotte Brontë] deflates the glamorous and rationalizes the ghostly, thereby integrating the "wild, wonder and thrilling" with the "plain and homely." Her treatment of terror in particular reminds us that readers in the early nineteenth century were beset on one hand by a spate of Gothic novels and on the other by the plethora of fictions that proclaimed "A Tale Founded on Facts" on the title pages. In her wry way Miss Brontë seems to be giving us something of both worlds. We know already the good use to which she put the tale of the concealed wife in a castle, which has its origin in Mrs. Radcliffe's *A Sicilian Romance.* She may well have been recalling at this time a later romance of Mrs. Radcliffe's called *The Italian; or, The Confessional of the Black Penitents,* for in the schemes of the Marchesa Vivaldi and her confessor Schedoni, we suspect, lies the germ of the situation towards the end of *Villette* where Mme. Beck and her confessor Père Silas also plot to separate two lovers. However, this is as far as Miss Brontë permits herself to carry the situation. The pair who momentarily appear to Lucy as "a secret junta" plan no assassination, as they would if they were Radcliffean characters, but merely send Paul off to the West Indies to claim some real estate. Thus they achieve their dire ends by quite ordinary means. (p. 418)

With the nun, as with other characters in *Villette,* Charlotte Brontë distorted outmoded literary conventions in a pointedly perverse way. Making the source of the ghost stem from the comic side of the novel—in a prank played by Ginevra's foppish lover de Hamal—is surely the author's way of mocking the tradition that once had teased her own fevered fancy. This, her last word on the Gothic novel, is a laugh at it—and a laugh that liberates. Lucy Snowe, destroying the empty vest-ments of the nun, is the heroine of the "new" realistic novel sloughing off the trappings of the shadowy heroine of the "old" romantic novel. As Lucy Snowe clears her mind of the phantoms from the past that have haunted it, so Charlotte Brontë exorcises the Gothic novel that once fired her imagination, even as Miss Austen had exorcised it earlier in the century. . . .

One likes to think that the genius that first found itself in *Jane Eyre* ultimately fulfilled itself in *Villette.* In the history of the novel *Villette* may be said to look simultaneously backwards and forwards. It is at once a retrospect and a prospect. Certainly Miss Brontë has here anticipated some of our present-day literary techniques: the probing into the sub-conscious and the unconscious mind, even if with an archaic faculty psychology rather than with the benefit of Freudian apparatus; the exposing of instinctual passion, though imaged in poetical symbolism, rather than set forth in the blunter language to which we have grown accustomed; and, through the burning, prismatic sensibility of Lucy Snowe, the venturing into the "stream of consciousness," though Lucy calls it simply the "flow of time." Through this melange of diary, memoir, and devoir, wrung from the anguished heart of Lucy Snowe, reverberates much that in the English novel was past, and passing, and to come. (p. 419)

Robert A. Colby, " 'Villette' and the Life of the Mind," in *PMLA,* Vol. LXXV, No. 4, September, 1960, pp. 410-19.

CAROL A. BOCK

(essay date 1988)

[In the following excerpt, Bock examines "[the degree to which Brontë's] decision to abandon poetry and become a novelist [was] influenced by the fact that she was a woman."]

In considering the role that gender may have played in leading Brontë to this decision, it is important to ask first whether this development in her career was peculiar to her as a woman writer and whether it can, in fact, be attributed primarily to the issue of gender. Those familiar with the history of Victorian poetics will surely recognize significant parallels between the difficulties of Brontë's poetic life and the aesthetic concerns that complicated the careers of Tennyson, Browning, and Arnold. Like Brontë, all three were troubled by the essentially subjective nature of poetry writing. They, too, feared that the imaginative act might be solipsistic, that the poet was, of necessity, either completely isolated from the human community or wracked by a divided allegiance to private vision and public duty. Indeed, these are the central issues of early Victorian poetics—professional dilemmas inherited from the Romantics, who first made the poetic imagination an object of veneration and intense scrutiny.

It is important to understand Brontë's anxieties in this regard as fears that were experienced by her male contemporaries as well. As we seek to establish the parameters of the traditions in women's writing, we must not lose sight of the ways in which those traditions intersect or parallel the dominant tradition of primarily male writers. Failing to do so in Brontë's case has resulted, I believe, in a distorted and condescending view of her aesthetic life. It has not only drawn disproportionate attention to her artistic insecurities—a critical path already well worn by numerous biographical and psychoanalytic scholars—but it also has emphasized her "anxiety of authorship" as more peculiarly feminine than it actually was. Any Victorian poet, whether male or female, was likely to have experienced such anxiety. To fail to acknowledge this is to minimize Brontë's accomplishments and obscure her importance as a representative figure in the history of Victorian literature. Even worse, it presents Brontë—and by implication other Victorian women writers as well—as comparatively "weaker vessels" than they really were.

Those male writers who have been represented as the major Victorian poets underwent experiences that were similarly debilitating. Hurt by devastating reviews of his first collection of poems, Tennyson published nothing for ten years and appeared to have given up his career as a poet. Likewise, Browning's response to John Stuart Mill's stinging criticism of *Pauline*—"The writer seems to me possessed with a more intense and morbid self-consciousness than I ever knew in any sane human being"—was to give up poetry altogether. Only after ten years of rather unsuccessful play writing could Browning return to his career as a poet, this time armed with aesthetic techniques for fusing the confessional and the dramatic into ironic monologues. Arnold was more immediately successful as a poet but chose to write only essays later in his career because the poetic genre insistently evoked in him a romantic despair that was antithetical to his intellectual and humanistic commitments. For all three writers, the creation of poetry was fraught with difficulties since it appeared to necessitate a subjective self-concern that neither they nor their Victorian audience could approve. The effect of this dilemma on each poet's life and work was profound. It nearly ended and, in fact, interrupted the careers of Tennyson and Browning for a decade as they groped toward new poetic forms like the dramatic monologue. It forced Arnold to redefine himself as a prose essayist. Viewed in this context, Brontë's anxieties about poetry writing seem less peculiar to her as an individual or as a woman. They seem, in fact, representative of a dilemma shared by most Victorian poets.

If the conflicting demands of reason and public duty on the one hand and imagination and private experience on the other are a common inheritance of the Victorian writer, and if the anxiety that Brontë experienced with regard to these issues was shared by her male counterparts, then what role *did* gender play in the shaping of her literary career? Tennyson, Browning, and Arnold all established themselves as reputable poets. Brontë did not. To what degree was her decision to abandon poetry and become a novelist influenced by the fact that she was a woman?

It is certainly reasonable to point out that, as a woman, Brontë experienced greater pressure than her male counterparts to dedicate herself to work that could not be considered self-centered: that the demand to eschew the world of poetry and private vision was necessarily more imperative for Victorian women than for Victorian men. Quite clearly, certain individuals who influenced Brontë—most notably the poet laureate Robert Southey—considered it inappropriate for a woman to follow literary pursuits. His response to her request that he evaluate the poems she had sent him has become infamous:

> Literature cannot be the business of a woman's life, and it ought not to be. The more she is engaged in her proper duties, the less leisure she will have for it, even as an accomplishment and a recreation. To those duties you have not yet been called, and when you are you will be less eager for celebrity. You will not seek in imagination for excitement, of which the vicissitudes of this life, and the anxieties from which you must not hope to be exempted, be your state what it may, will bring with them but too much.

Such evidence suggests that the anxiety that Brontë shared with her male contemporaries about the dangers of the private imagination was likely to have been exacerbated by social expectations that were particularly intense for women. Indeed, Brontë's response to Southey has often been cited as a troubled submission to his male authority on this matter. But her letter is complexly ironic and has been, I would argue, somewhat misunderstood. Choosing her words carefully, she concedes that Southey's comments are just, then remarks that he does not forbid her to write but only to make certain that her imaginative pursuits do not interfere with her familial duties. On a first reading, this advice was most disappointing, Brontë admits, but having "read it again and again, the prospect seemed to clear." Indeed, since Southey does not expressly urge her to stop writing, Brontë is able to interpret his advice so that it reinforces the personal and professional task she had inherited from the Romantics: to write subjective, imaginative poetry without neglecting objective reality and social duty. As such, his letter can be saved and labeled "Southey's advice to be kept forever." The apparent humility of Brontë's letter can surely be explained as the assumption of a modesty that she would have considered decorous for a young woman corresponding with one of England's most famous poets. The humble tone tells us relatively little, I would argue, about Brontë's poetic identity and self-assessment, as the disingenuous comments of Lucy Snowe should warn us. Moreover, while Southey's letter may have had an impact on Brontë, it did not cause her to stop writing poetry. In fact, his discouraging comments were received in the middle of Brontë's second, most prolific period of poetic composition and had no apparent effect on her output. As others have remarked, she may have kept his advice, but she was not following it. These facts suggest a resiliency and resistance that Brontë is usually not credited with and should encourage us to modify the notion that her literary career is best described as a painful struggle to free herself from male dominance. Brontë's strategy in this case may also shed light on her later decision to abandon poetry for a career of novel writing.

In order to understand the ways in which gender influenced the course of Brontë's literary career, it is necessary to examine the manner in which the conditions of her life intersected with the values of the poetic tradition she had inherited. After a childhood of enthusiastic imaginative engagement in the cultural affairs of the day, Brontë slowly awoke to the realities of her life as the daughter of a poor clergyman in a patriarchal society. Those realities were stark and uncompromising: she needed to work to support herself, but employment opportunities for women of her class were appallingly limited. Thus, at the age of eighteen, she was forced into the only career open to her, teaching. Temperamentally unsuited to this position, she further resented her duties because they left her little time for writing and separated her from the home environment that had helped to sustain her emotional and artistic well-being. Unlike her brother, Charlotte was not given the opportunity to turn her talents to professional ends; conse-

quently, she could not think of writing as gainful employment or a responsible use of her time. Instead, it became an escape from the "wretched bondage" of a job she hated but was compelled to maintain. In these circumstances, writing could no longer be considered an honorable profession to be practiced openly among colleagues. Of necessity, it became a private and selfish activity that emphasized her difference from others and intensified the emotional isolation that was already so painful to her.

Given this description of Brontë's early career, one may wonder why she continued writing at all. The fact that she did so can be attributed, I believe, to her resourcefulness and to her knowledge of the issues of early nineteenth-century English poetry. As her response to Southey illustrates, Brontë possessed a remarkable talent for creating strategies that were self-preserving. Faced with a situation threatening to end her work as a literary artist, she neither submitted passively nor resisted outright, but instead adopted a view of the situation that nurtured her writing and gave direction to her career. Confronted with her own conviction that, given her circumstances, writing could only be considered a private, isolating, and even selfish experience, Brontë drew upon the anti-romantic elements of the poetic tradition she knew and exploited them in a way that freed her of the anxieties threatening her career. Specifically, she transferred to the genre of poetry all of the debilitating associations that the pursuit of writing had accumulated in her early adulthood. In this way, poetry in particular rather than writing in general could be thought of as a form of self-indulgent escapism and solipsistic withdrawal. Then, by abandoning poetry, she could redefine herself as a writer of realistic fiction and thereby continue her literary career. (pp. 59-63)

Carol A. Bock, "Gender and Poetic Tradition: The Shaping of Charlotte Brontë's Literary Career," in *Tulsa Studies in Women's Literature*, Vol. 7, No. 1, Spring, 1988, pp. 49-67.

SOURCES FOR FURTHER STUDY

Fraser, Rebecca. *The Brontës: Charlotte Brontë and Her Family.* New York: Crown Publishers, 1988, 543 p.

> Biography focusing on "[showing] Charlotte Brontë as she appeared to her era, . . . [and revealing] what a phenomenon she was considered."

Gaskell, E. C. *The Life of Charlotte Brontë.* London: E. P. Dutton & Co., 1908, 411 p.

> Biographical novel. In the introduction to this book, May Sinclair states that *The Life of Charlotte Brontë* is

"a classic in its kind" and praises the book as "the finest, tenderest portrait of a woman that a woman ever drew."

Hardy, Barbara. *"Jane Eyre" (Charlotte Brontë).* Notes on English Literature, edited by John Harvey. Oxford: Basil Blackwell, 1964, 95 p.

> A detailed classroom guide to *Jane Eyre.* Hardy includes a list of questions designed to aid the student at the end of each chapter.

Kinkead-Weekes, Mark. "The Place of Love in *Jane Eyre* and *Wuthering Heights*." In *The Brontës: A Collection of Critical Essays,* edited by Ian Gregor, pp. 76-95. Englewood Cliffs, N.J.: Prentice-Hall, Inc., 1970.

Discusses Brontë's metaphorical treatment of love in *Jane Eyre,* focusing on how she portrayed the "life of the heart" through characters, scenes, and actions. This essay compares Charlotte to her contemporaries, particularly her sister Emily.

Martin, Robert Bernard. *"Jane Eyre."* In his *The Accents of Persuasion: Charlotte Brontë's Novels,* pp. 57-108. London: Faber & Faber, 1966.

An interpretation of *Jane Eyre* as a novel that seeks a balance between reason and passion.

Williams, Judith. *Perception and Expression in the Novels of Charlotte Brontë.* Ann Arbor, Mich.: UMI Research Press, 1988, 175 p.

Analyzes the imagery of *The Professor, Jane Eyre, Shirley,* and *Villette* in great detail.

Emily Brontë

1818-1848

(Full name Emily Jane Brontë; also wrote under pseudonym Ellis Bell) English novelist and poet.

INTRODUCTION

Brontë is considered one of the most important yet elusive figures in nineteenth-century English literature. Although she led a brief and circumscribed life, spent in relative isolation in a parsonage on the Yorkshire moors, she left behind a literary legacy that includes some of the most passionate and inspired writing in Victorian literature. Today, Brontë's poems are well regarded by critics, but they receive little attention, and her overall reputation rests primarily on her only novel, *Wuthering Heights* (1847). A story of superhuman love and revenge enacted on the English moors, the novel has attracted generations of readers and critics alike, and has been elevated to the status of a literary classic. At the same time, Brontë's writings have raised many questions about their author's intent. Unable to reach a consensus concerning the ultimate meaning of her works and reluctant to assign them a definite place in the English literary tradition, critics continue to regard Brontë as a fascinating enigma in English letters.

Although Brontë's life was outwardly uneventful, the unusual circumstances of her upbringing have prompted considerable scrutiny. One of six children born to Maria Branwell Brontë and the Reverend Patrick Brontë, she was raised in the parsonage at Haworth by her father and maternal aunt following her mother's death in 1821. In 1825, she was sent to the Clergy Daughters' School at Cowan Bridge, but she returned to Haworth when her sisters Maria and Elizabeth became ill at the institution and died. A significant event in Brontë's creative life occurred in 1826 when Patrick Brontë bought a set of wooden toy soldiers for his children. The toys opened up a rich fantasy world for Emily and her siblings Charlotte, Branwell, and Anne: Charlotte and Branwell created an imaginary African land called Angria, for which they invented characters, scenes, stories, and poems, and Emily and Anne later conceived a romantic legend centered upon the imaginary Pacific Ocean island of Gondal. The realm of Gondal became a lifelong interest for Brontë and, according to many scholars, a major imaginative source for her writings. In addition to composing prose works concerning the history of Gondal that are now lost, she wrote numerous poems that were evidently directly inspired by Gondal-related themes, characters, and situations.

While Brontë was intellectually precocious and began writing poetry at an early age, she failed to establish social contacts aside from her family. She briefly attended a school in East Yorkshire in 1835 and worked as an assistant teacher at the Law Hill School near Halifax in about 1838, but these excursions from home were unsuccessful, ending in Brontë's early return to Haworth. She stayed at the parsonage, continuing to write poetry and attending to household duties until 1842, when she and Charlotte, hoping to acquire the language skills needed to establish a school of their own, took positions at a school in Brussels. Her aunt's death later that year, however, forced Brontë to return to Haworth, where she resided for the rest of her life.

In 1845, Charlotte discovered one of Emily's private poetry notebooks. At Charlotte's urging Emily reluctantly agreed to publish some of her poems in a volume that also included writings by her sisters. *Poems by Currer, Ellis, and Acton Bell,* reflecting the pseudonyms adopted by Charlotte, Emily, and Anne, was published in May 1846. While only two copies of the book were sold, at least one commentator, Sydney Dobell, praised Emily's poems, singling her out in the *Athenaeum* as a promising writer and the best poet among the "Bell" family. Meanwhile, Brontë had been working on *Wuthering Heights,* which was published in an edition that also included Anne's first novel, *Agnes Grey.* Ironically, Brontë's masterpiece was poorly received by contemporary critics who, repelled by the vivid portrayal of malice and brutality in the book, objected to the "degrading" nature of her subject. Brontë worked on revising her poetry after publishing *Wuthering Heights,* but her efforts were soon interrupted. Branwell Brontë died in September 1848 and Emily's health began to decline shortly afterwards. In accordance with what Charlotte described as her sister's strong-willed and inflexible nature, Brontë apparently refused medical attention and died of tuberculosis in December 1848.

Even though Brontë is more distinguished as a novelist than as a poet, scholars regard her poetry as a significant part of her oeuvre. In particular, lacking firsthand information concerning her life and opinions, commentators have looked to the poems as a source of insight into Brontë's personality, philosophy, and imagination. Critics have attempted to reconstruct a

coherent Gondal "epic" from Brontë's poems and journal entries. In addition to identifying Gondal's queen, commonly referred to as Augusta Geraldine Almeda, and her lover Julius Brenzaida as key characters in the Gondal story, scholars have underscored the presence of wars, assassination, treachery, and infanticide in Brontë's fantasy realm. Critics have consequently noted many similarities between the passionate characters and violent motifs of Gondal and *Wuthering Heights,* and today a generous body of criticism exists supporting the contention that the Gondal poems served as a creative forerunner of the novel.

In *Wuthering Heights,* Brontë chronicles the attachment between Heathcliff, a rough orphan taken in by the Earnshaw family of Wuthering Heights, and the family's daughter, Catherine. The two characters are joined by a spiritual bond of preternatural strength, yet Catherine elects to marry her more refined neighbor, Edgar Linton of Thrushcross Grange; ultimately, this decision leads to Catherine's madness and death and prompts Heathcliff to take revenge upon both the Lintons and the Earnshaws. Heathcliff eventually dies, consoled by the thought of uniting with Catherine's spirit, and the novel ends with the suggestion that Hareton Earnshaw, the last descendant of the Earnshaw family, will marry Catherine's daughter, Catherine Linton, and abandon Wuthering Heights for Thrushcross Grange. Commentators observe that Brontë heightened her story with fierce animal imagery, scenes of raw violence, and supernatural overtones. Dream motifs figure prominently in *Wuthering Heights* as well, and critics also stress the importance of windows as symbolic vehicles for spiritual entrance and escape in the novel. The structure of Brontë's book is noted for two prominent attributes: a highly schematized order that is reflected in the symmetry of the family pedigrees, and an involved narrative method featuring dual narrators and a "Chinese box" arrangement of narratives within narratives.

While scholars recognize the importance of these and other facets of Brontë's craftsmanship in *Wuthering Heights,* they especially acknowledge the special power and significance of her characterization of Heathcliff and Catherine Earnshaw. Both characters are vividly realized in their own right—George Henry Lewes described Heathcliff as a "devil . . . drawn with a sort of dusky splendour which fascinates," and Q. D. Leavis hailed Catherine as a "dazzling original character"—and they seem to suggest larger meanings as well. In fact, critics commonly regard them as figures in a dialectic pitting the civilized and refined values of Thrushcross Grange against the natural and primitive values of Wuthering Heights. Thus, Heathcliff is often interpreted as a representative of natural man or pure passion whose ideological foil in the story is Edgar Linton; by choosing Edgar over Heathcliff, then, Catherine is frequently understood to be embracing civilized values and rejecting natural ideals. There have also been readings featuring the opposition between spiritual and material standards, as well as between a number of economic and social systems, creating a variety of interpretations that underscore both the profundity and the thematic ambiguity of Brontë's work. Some commentators attribute the ambiguous quality of *Wuthering Heights* to Brontë's own ambivalence toward her materials, maintaining, for example, that it is not possible to ascertain whether the novel's conclusion is meant to affirm the standards associated with Wuthering Heights or those linked with Thrushcross Grange.

Initially, critics failed to appreciate Brontë's literary significance. While commentators acknowledged the emotional power of *Wuthering Heights*, they also rejected the malignant and coarse side of life that it depicted. Charlotte Brontë responded to this latter objection in 1850, defending the rough language and manners in her sister's novel as realistic. At the same time, however, she apologized for the dark vision of life in the book, which she attributed to Emily's reclusive habits. This focus on Brontë's aloofness, combined with the mystical aspects of her poetry and the supernatural overtones of *Wuthering Heights*, fostered an image of the writer as a reclusive mystic that dominated Brontë criticism into the twentieth century. Charles Percy Sanger's 1926 monograph, *The Structure of "Wuthering Heights"*, was one of the first modern studies to bring Brontë's craftsmanship to light. Subsequently, recognition of her artistry increased dramatically as scholars discovered the sophistication and complexity of her images, characterizations, themes, and techniques in *Wuthering Heights*. Interest in her poetry has also grown, primarily due to investigations into its Gondal background, so that today Brontë is the focus of considerable scholarly attention as both a novelist and poet. However, Brontë has eluded categorization in both of these genres: although critics have discerned Gothic and Romantic elements in her works, no consensus has emerged concerning her relationship to the English literary tradition, confirming Mary A. Ward's observation that Brontë occupies "a place apart in English letters."

(For further information about Brontë's life and works, see *Dictionary of Literary Biography*, Vols. 21, 32; and *Nineteenth-Century Literature Criticism*, Vols. 16, 35.)

CRITICAL COMMENTARY

CURRER BELL [PSEUDONYM OF CHARLOTTE BRONTË]

(essay date 1850)

[In the following excerpt from her preface to the 1850 edition of *Wuthering Heights*, Charlotte Brontë discusses her sister's treatment of language, setting, and characterization in the novel.]

I have just read over *Wuthering Heights,* and, for the first time, have obtained a clear glimpse of what are termed (and, perhaps, really are) its faults; have gained a definite notion of how it appears to other people—to strangers who knew nothing of the author; who are unacquainted with the locality where the scenes of the story are laid; to whom the inhabitants, the customs, the natural characteristics of the outlying hills and hamlets in the West Riding of Yorkshire are things alien and unfamiliar.

To all such *Wuthering Heights* must appear a rude and strange production. The wild moors of the North of England can for them have no interest: the language, the manners, the very dwellings and household customs of the scattered inhabitants of those districts must be to such readers in a great measure unintelligible, and—where intelligible—repulsive. Men and women who, perhaps, naturally very calm, and with feelings moderate in degree, and little marked in kind, have been trained from their cradle to observe the utmost evenness of manner and guardedness of language, will hardly know what to make of the rough, strong utterance, the harshly manifested passions, the unbridled aversions, and headlong partialities of unlettered moorland hinds and rugged moorland squires, who have grown up untaught and unchecked, except by Mentors as harsh as themselves. A large class of readers, likewise, will suffer greatly from the introduction into the pages of this work of words printed with all their letters, which it has become the custom to represent by the initial and final letter only—a blank line filling the interval. I may as well say at once that, for this circumstance, it is out of my power to apologise; deeming it, myself, a rational plan to write words at full length. The practice of hinting by single letters those expletives with which profane and violent persons are wont to garnish their discourse, strikes me as a pro-

---

Principal Works

*Poems by Currer, Ellis, and Acton Bell [as Ellis Bell] (poetry) 1846

†Wuthering Heights [as Ellis Bell] (novel) 1847

*Life and Works of the Sisters Brontë. 7 vols. (novels and poetry) 1899-1903

*The Shakespeare Head Brontë. 19 vols. (novels, poetry, and letters) 1931-38

Gondal Poems (poetry) 1938

The Complete Poems of Emily Jane Brontë (poetry) 1941

*These collections include works written by other members of the Brontë family.

†This edition of Wuthering Heights also includes the novel Agnes Grey, written by Anne Brontë.

---

ceeding which, however well meant, is weak and futile. I cannot tell what good it does—what feeling it spares—what horror it conceals.

With regard to the rusticity of *Wuthering Heights,* I admit the charge, for I feel the quality. It is rustic all through. It is moorish, and wild, and knotty as a root of heath. Nor was it natural that it should be otherwise; the author being herself a native and nursling of the moors. Doubtless, had her lot been cast in a town, her writings, if she had written at all, would have possessed another character. Even had chance or taste led her to choose a similar subject, she would have treated it otherwise. Had Ellis Bell been a lady or a gentleman accustomed to what is called 'the world,' her view of a remote and unreclaimed region, as well as of the dwellers therein, would have differed greatly from that actually taken by the home-bred country girl. Doubtless it would have been wider—more comprehensive: whether it would have been more original or more truthful is not so certain. As far as the scenery and locality are concerned, it could scarcely have been so sympathetic: Ellis Bell did not describe as one whose eye and taste alone found pleasure in the prospect; her native hills were far more to her than a spectacle; they were what she lived in, and by, as much as the wild birds, their tenants, or as the heather, their produce. Her descriptions, then, of natural scenery are what they should be, and all they should be.

Where delineation of human character is concerned, the case is different. I am bound to avow that she had scarcely more practical knowledge of the peasantry amongst whom she lived, than a nun has of the country people who sometimes pass her convent gates. My sister's disposition was not naturally gregarious; circumstances favoured and fostered her tendency to seclusion; except to go to church or take a walk on the hills, she rarely crossed the threshold of home. Though her feeling for the people round was benevolent, intercourse with them she never sought; nor, with very few exceptions, ever experienced. And yet she knew them: knew their ways, their language, their family histories; she could hear of them with interest, and talk of them with detail, minute, graphic, and accurate; but *with* them, she rarely exchanged a word. Hence it ensued that what her mind had gathered of the real concerning them, was too exclusively confined to those tragic and terrible traits of which, in listening to the secret annals of every rude vicinage, the memory is sometimes compelled to receive the impress. Her imagination, which was a spirit more sombre than sunny, more powerful than sportive, found in such traits material whence it wrought creations like Heathcliff, like Earnshaw, like Catherine. Having formed these beings, she did not know what she had done. If the auditor of her work, when read in manuscript, shuddered under the grinding influence of natures so relentless and implacable, of spirits so lost and fallen; if it was complained that the mere hearing of certain vivid and fearful scenes banished sleep by night, and disturbed mental peace by day, Ellis Bell would wonder what was meant, and suspect the complainant of affectation. Had she but lived, her mind would of itself have grown like a strong tree, loftier, straighter, wider-spreading, and its matured fruits would have attained a mellower ripeness and sunnier bloom; but on that mind time and experience alone could work: to the influence of other intellects it was not amenable.

Having avowed that over much of *Wuthering Heights* there broods 'a horror of great darkness'; that, in its storm-heated and electrical atmosphere, we seem at times to breathe lightning: let me point to those spots where clouded daylight and the eclipsed sun still attest their existence. For a specimen of true benevolence and homely fidelity, look at the character of Nelly Dean; for an example of constancy and tenderness, remark that of Edgar Linton. . . . There is a dry saturnine humour in the delineation of old Joseph, and some glimpses of grace and gaiety animate the younger Catherine. Nor is even the first heroine of the name destitute of a certain strange beauty in her fierceness, or of honesty in the midst of perverted passion and passionate perversity.

Heathcliff, indeed, stands unredeemed; never once swerving in his arrow-straight course to perdition, from the time when 'the little black-haired swarthy thing, as dark as if it came from the Devil,' was first unrolled out of the bundle and set on its feet in the farmhouse kitchen, to the hour when Nelly Dean found the grim, stalwart corpse laid on its back in the panel-enclosed bed, with wide-gazing eyes that seemed 'to sneer at her attempt to close them, and parted lips and sharp white teeth that sneered too.'

Heathcliff betrays one solitary human feeling, and that is *not* his love for Catherine; which is a sentiment fierce and inhuman: a passion such as might boil and glow in the bad essence of some evil genius; a fire that might form the tormented centre—the ever-suffering soul of a magnate of the infernal world: and by its quenchless and ceaseless ravage effect the execution of the decree which dooms him to carry Hell with him wherever he wanders. No; the single link that connects Heathcliff with humanity is his rudely-confessed regard for Hareton Earnshaw—the young man whom he has ruined; and then his half-implied esteem for Nelly Dean. These solitary traits omitted, we should say he was child neither of Lascar nor gipsy, but a man's shape animated by demon life—a Ghoul—an Afreet.

Whether it is right or advisable to create beings like Heathcliff, I do not know: I scarcely think it is. But this I know: the writer who possesses the creative gift owns something of which he is not always master—something that, at times, strangely wills and works for itself. He may lay down rules and devise principles, and to rules and principles it will perhaps for years lie in subjection; and then, haply without any warning of revolt, there comes a time when it will no longer consent to 'harrow the valleys, or be bound with a band in the furrow'—when it 'laughs at the multitude of the city, and regards not the crying of the driver'—when, refusing absolutely to make ropes out of sea-sand any longer, it sets to work on statue-hewing, and you have a Pluto or a Jove, a Tisiphone or a Psyche, a Mermaid or a Madonna, as Fate or Inspiration direct. Be the work grim or glorious, dread or divine, you have little choice left but quiescent adoption. (pp. liii-lviii)

Wuthering Heights was hewn in a wild workshop, with simple tools, out of homely materials. The statuary found a granite block on a solitary moor; gazing thereon, he saw how from the crag might be elicited a head, savage, swart, sinister; a form moulded with at least one element of grandeur—power. He wrought with a rude chisel, and from no model but the vision of his meditations. With time and labour, the crag took human shape; and there it stands colossal, dark, and frowning, half statue, half rock: in the former sense, terrible and goblin-like; in the latter, almost beautiful, for its colouring is of mellow grey, and moorland moss clothes it; and heath, with its blooming bells and balmy fragrance, grows faithfully close to the giant's foot. (p. lviii)

Currer Bell [pseudonym of Charlotte Brontë], in a preface to "Wuthering Heights," in *Life and Works of the Sisters Brontë: "Wuthering Heights" by Emily Brontë and "Agnes Grey" by Anne Brontë, Vol. V,* 1903. Reprint by AMS Press, Inc., 1973, pp. liii-lviii.

MARY A. WARD
(essay date 1903)

[Ward was an English novelist and social activist whose interest in social and intellectual concerns is reflected in her most famous work, the novel *Robert Elsmere*. Here, she discusses *Wuthering Heights*, comparing the novel with works by the author's sister Charlotte.]

'Stronger than a man, simpler than a child:'—these words [taken from Charlotte Brontë's "Biographical Notice of Ellis and Acton Bell"] are Emily Brontë's true epitaph, both as an artist and as a human being. Her strength of will and imagination struck those who knew her and those who read her as often inhuman or terrible; and with this was combined a simplicity partly of genius partly of a strange innocence and spirituality, which gives her a place apart in English letters. It is important to realise that of the three books written simultaneously by the three sisters, Emily's alone shows genius already matured and master of its tools. Charlotte had a steady development before her, especially in matters of method and style, the comparative dulness of *The Professor,* and the crudities of *Jane Eyre* made way for the accomplished variety and brilliance of *Villette.* But though Emily, had she lived, might have chosen many happier subjects, treated with a more flowing unity than she achieved in *Wuthering Heights,* the full competence of genius is already present in her book. The common, hasty, didactic note that Charlotte often strikes is never heard in *Wuthering Heights.* The artist remains hidden and self-contained; the work, however morbid and violent may be the scenes and creatures it presents, has always that distinction which belongs to high talent working solely for its own joy and satisfaction, with no thought of a spectator, or any aim but that of an ideal and imaginative whole. Charlotte stops to think of objectors, to teach and argue, to avenge her own personal grievances, or cheat her own personal longings. . . . But Emily is pure mind and passion; no one, from the pages of *Wuthering Heights* can guess at the small likes and dislikes, the religious or critical antipathies, the personal weaknesses of the artist who wrote it. She has that highest power—which was typically Shakespeare's power, and which in our day is typically the power of such an artist as Turgueniev—the power which gives life, intensest life, to the creatures of imagination, and, in doing so, endows them with an independence behind which the maker is forgotten. The puppet show is everything; and, till it is over, the manager—nothing. And it is his delight and triumph to have it so.

Yet, at the same time, *Wuthering Heights* is a book of the later Romantic movement, betraying the influences of German Romantic imagination, as Charlotte's work betrays the influences of Victor Hugo and George Sand. The Romantic tendency to invent and delight in monsters, the *exaltation du moi*, which has been said to be the secret of the whole Romantic revolt against classical models and restraints; the love of violence in speech and action, the preference for the hideous in character and the abnormal in situation—of all these there are abundant examples in *Wuthering Heights.* The dream of Mr. Lockwood in Catherine's box bed, when in the terror of nightmare he pulled the wrist of the little wailing ghost outside on to the broken glass of the window, 'and rubbed it to and fro till the blood ran down and soaked the bed-clothes'—one of the most gruesome fancies of literature!—Heathcliff 's long and fiendish revenge on Hindley Earnshaw; the ghastly quarrel between Linton and Heathcliff in Catherine's presence after Heathcliff 's return; Catherine's three days' fast, and her delirium when she 'tore the pillow with her teeth' . . . —all these things would not have been written precisely as they were written, but for the 'Germanism' of the thirties and forties, but for the translations of [German writings in] *Blackwood* and *Fraser,* and but for those German tales, whether of Hoffmann or others, which there is evidence that Emily Brontë read both at Brussels and after her return.

As to the 'exaltation of the Self,' its claims, sensibilities and passions, in defiance of all social law and duty, there is no more vivid expression of it throughout Romantic literature than is contained in the conversation between the elder Catherine and Nelly Dean before Catherine marries Edgar Linton. And the violent, clashing egotisms of Heathcliff and Catherine in the last scene of passion before Catherine's death, are as it were an epitome of a whole *genre* in literature, and a whole phase of European feeling.

Nevertheless, horror and extravagance are not really the characteristic mark and quality of *Wuthering Heights.* If they were, it would have no more claim upon us than a hundred other forgotten books—Lady Caroline Lamb's *Glenarvon* amongst them—which represent the dregs and refuse of a great literary movement. As in the case of Charlotte Brontë, the peculiar force of Emily's work lies in the fact that it represents the grafting of a European tradition upon a mind already richly stored with English and local reality, possessing at command a style at once strong and simple, capable both of homeliness and magnificence. . . . [Emily] is master of herself at the most rushing moments of feeling or narrative; her style is simple, sensuous, adequate and varied from first to last; she has fewer purple patches than Charlotte, but at its best, her insight no less than her power of phrase, is of a diviner and more exquisite quality.

Wuthering Heights then is the product of romantic imagination, working probably under influences from German literature, and marvellously fused with local knowledge and a realistic power which, within its own range, has seldom been surpassed. Its few great faults are soon enumerated. The tendency to extravagance and monstrosity may, as we have seen, be taken to some extent as belonging more to a literary fashion than to the artist. Tieck and Hoffmann are full of raving and lunatic beings who sob, shout, tear out their hair by the roots, and live in a perpetual state of personal violence both towards themselves and their neighbours. Emily Brontë probably received from them an additional impulse towards a certain wildness of manner and conception which was already natural to her Irish blood, to a woman brought up amid the solitudes of the moors and the ruggedness of Yorkshire life fifty years ago, and natural also, alas! to the sister of the opium-eater and drunkard Branwell Brontë.

To this let us add a certain awkwardness and confusion of structure; a strain of ruthless exaggeration in the character of Heathcliff; and some absurdities and contradictions in the character of Nelly Dean. The latter criticism indeed is bound up with the first. Nelly Dean is presented as the faithful and affectionate nurse, the only good angel both of the elder and the younger Catherine. But Nelly Dean does the most treacherous, cruel, and indefensible things, simply that the story may move. She becomes the go-between for Catherine and Heathcliff; she knowingly allows her charge Catherine, on the eve of her confinement, to fast in solitude and delirium for three days and nights, without saying a word to Edgar Linton, Catherine's affectionate husband, and her master, who was in the house all the time. It is her breach of trust which brings about Catherine's dying scene with Heathcliff, just as it is her disobedience and unfaith which really betray Catherine's child into the hands of her enemies. Without these lapses and indiscretions indeed the story could not maintain itself; but the clumsiness or carelessness of them is hardly to be denied. In the case of Heathcliff, the blemish lies rather in a certain deliberate and passionate defiance of the reader's sense of humanity and possibility; partly also in the innocence of the writer, who, in a world of sex and passion, has invented a situation charged with the full forces of both, without any true realisation of what she has done. Heathcliff 's murderous language to Catherine about the husband whom she loves with an affection only second to that which she cherishes for his hateful self; his sordid and incredible courtship of Isabella under Catherine's eyes; the long horror of his pursuit and capture of the younger Catherine, his dead love's child; the total incompatibility between his passion for the mother and his mean ruffianism towards the daughter; the utter absence of any touch of kindness even in his love for Catherine, whom he scolds and rates on the very threshold of death; the mingling in him of high passion with the vilest arts of the sharper and the thief:—these things o'erleap themselves, so that again and again the sense of tragedy is lost in mere violence and excess, and what might have been a man becomes a monster. There are speeches and actions of Catherine's, moreover, contained in these central pages which have no relation to any life of men and women that the true world knows. It may be said indeed that the writer's very ignorance of certain facts and relations of life, combined with the force of imaginative passion which she throws into her conceptions, produces a special poetic effect—a strange and bodiless tragedy—unique in literature. And there is much truth in this; but not enough to vindicate these scenes of the book, from radical weakness and falsity, nor to preserve in the reader that illusion, that inner consent, which is the final test of all imaginative effort.

Nevertheless there are whole sections of the story during which the character of Heathcliff is presented to us with a marvellous and essential truth. The scenes of childhood and youth; the up-growing of the two desolate children, drawn to each other by some strange primal sympathy, Heathcliff 'the little black thing, harboured by a good man to his bane,' Catherine who 'was never so happy as when we were all scolding her at once, and she defying us with her bold saucy look, and her ready words;' the gradual development of the natural distance between them, he the ill-mannered ruffianly no-man's-child, she the young lady of the house; his pride and jealous pain; her young fondness for Edgar Linton, as inevitable as a girl's yearning for pretty finery, and a new frock with the spring; Heathcliff 's boyish vow of vengeance on the brutal Hindley and his race; Cathy's passionate discrimination, in the scene with Nelly Dean which ends as it were the first act of the play, between her affection for Linton and her identity with Heathcliff 's life and being:—for the mingling of daring poetry with the easiest and most masterly command of local truth, for sharpness and felicity of phrase, for exuberance of creative force, for invention and freshness of detail, there are few things in English fiction to match it. One might almost say that the first volume of *Adam Bede* is false and mannered beside it,—the first volumes of *Waverley* or *Guy Mannering* flat and diffuse. Certainly, the first volume of *Jane Eyre,* admirable as it is, can hardly be set on the same level with the careless ease and effortless power of these first nine chapters. (pp. xxiii-xxxi)

And as far as the lesser elements of style, the mere technique of writing are concerned, one may notice the short elastic vigour of the sentences, the rightness of epithet and detail, the absence of any care for effect,

and the flashes of beauty which suddenly emerge like the cistus upon the rock. (pp. xxxi-xxxii)

The inferior central scenes of the book, after Catherine's marriage, for all their teasing faults, have passages of extraordinary poetry. Take the detail of Catherine's fevered dream after she shuts herself into her room, at the close of the frightful scene between her husband and Heathcliff, or the weird realism of her half-delirious talk with Nelly Dean. In her 'feverish bewilderment' she tears her pillow, and then finds

childish diversion in pulling the feathers from the rents she had just made, and ranging them on the sheet according to their different species: her mind had strayed to other associations.

'That's a turkey's,' she murmured to herself: 'and this is a wild duck's; and this is a pigeon's. Ah, they put pigeons' feathers in the pillows—no wonder I couldn't die! Let me take care to throw it on the floor when I lie down. And here is a moor-cock's; and this—I should know it among a thousand—it's a lapwing's. Bonny bird; wheeling over our heads in the middle of the moor. It wanted to get to its nest, for the clouds had touched the swells, and it felt rain coming. This feather was picked up from the heath, the bird was not shot: we saw its nest in the winter, full of little skeletons. Heathcliff set a trap over it, and the old ones dared not come. I made him promise he'd never shoot a lapwing after that, and he didn't. Yes, here are more! Did he shoot my lapwings, Nelly? Are they red, any of them? Let me look.'

'Give over with that baby-work!' I interrupted, dragging the pillow away, and turning the holes towards the mattress, for she was removing its contents by handfuls. 'Lie down, and shut your eyes: you're wandering. There's a mess! The down is flying about like snow.'

I went here and there collecting it.

(pp. xxxiii-xxxiv)

Of what we may call the third and last act of *Wuthering Heights,* which extends from the childhood of the younger Catherine to the death of Heathcliff, much might be said. It is no less masterly than the first section of the book and much more complex in plan. The key to it lies in two earlier passages—in Heathcliff 's boyish vow of vengence on Hindley Earnshaw, and in his fierce appeal to his lost love to haunt him, rather than leave him 'in this abyss where I cannot find her.' The conduct of the whole 'act' is intricate and difficult; the initial awkwardness implied in Nelly Dean's function as narrator is felt now and then; but as a whole, the strength of the intention is no less clear than the deliberate and triumphant power with which the artist achieves it. These chapters are not always easy to read, but they repay the closest attention. Not an incident,

---

Major Media Adaptations: Motion Pictures

Wuthering Heights, 1939. Samuel Goldwyn. Director: William Wyler. Cast: Laurence Olivier, Merle Oberon, David Niven, Hugh Williams, Flora Robson, Geraldine Fitzgerald, Donald Crisp, Leo G. Carroll, Cecil Kellaway, Miles Mander.

Wuthering Heights, 1970. AIP. Director: Robert Fuest. Cast: Anna Calder-Marshall, Timothy Dalton, Harry Andrews, Pamela Brown, Judy Cornwell, James Cossins, Rosalie Crutchley, Julian Glover, Hugh Griffith, Ian Ogilvy, Aubrey Woods.

---

not a fragment of conversation is thrown away, and in the end the effect is complete. It is gained by that fusion of terror and beauty, of ugliness and a flying magic—'settling unawares'—which is the characteristic note of the Brontës, and of all that is best in Romantic literature. Never for a moment do you lose hold upon the Yorkshire landscape and the Yorkshire folk—look at the picture of Isabella's wasteful porridge-making and of Joseph's grumbling rage, amid her gruesome experience as a bride; never are you allowed to forget a single sordid element in Heathcliff's ruffianism; and yet through it all the inevitable end developes, the double end which only a master could have conceived. Life and love rebel and reassert themselves in the wild slight love-story of Hareton and Cathy, which breaks the final darkness like a gleam of dawn upon the moors; and death tames and silences for ever all that remains of Heathcliff's futile cruelties and wasted fury.

But what a death! Heathcliff has tormented and oppressed Catherine's daughter; and it is Catherine's shadow that lures him to his doom, through every stage and degree of haunting feverish ecstasy, of reunion promised and delayed, of joy for ever offered and for ever withdrawn. And yet how simple the method, how true the 'vision' to the end! Around Heathcliff's last hours the farm-life flows on as usual. There is no hurry in the sentences; no blurring of the scene. Catherine's haunting presence closes upon the man who murdered her happiness and youth, interposes between him and all bodily needs, deprives him of food and drink and sleep, till the madman is dead of his 'strange happiness,' straining after the phantom that slays him, dying of the love whereby alone he remains human, through which fate strikes at last—and strikes home.

'Is he a ghoul or vampire?' I mused. 'I had read of such hideous incarnate demons.' So says Nelly Dean just before Heathcliff's death. The remark is not hers in truth, but Emily Brontë's, and where it stands it is of great significance. It points to the world of German horror and romance, to which we know that she had access. That world was congenial to her, as it was congenial to Southey, Scott, and Coleridge; and it has left

some ugly and disfiguring traces upon the detail of *Wuthering Heights.* But *essentially* her imagination escaped from it and mastered it. As the haunting of Heathcliff is to the coarser horrors of Tieck and Hoffmann, so is her place to theirs. For all her crudity and inexperience, she is in the end with Goethe, rather than with Hoffmann, and thereby with all that is sane, strong, and living in literature. 'A great work requires many-sidedness, and on this rock the young author splits,' said Goethe to Eckermann, praising at the same time the art which starts from the simplest realities and the subject nearest at hand, to reach at last by a natural expansion the loftiest heights of poetry. But this was the art of Emily Brontë. It started from her own heart and life; it was nourished by the sights and sounds of a lonely yet sheltering nature; it was responsive to the art of others, yet always independent; and in the rich and tangled truth of *Wuthering Heights* it showed promise at least of a many-sidedness to which only the greatest attain. (pp. xxxv-xxxviii)

Mary A. Ward, in an introduction to *Life and Works of the Sisters Brontë: "Wuthering Heights" by Emily Brontë and "Agnes Grey" by Anne Brontë, Vol. V,* 1903. Reprint by AMS Press Inc., 1973, pp. xi-xl.

DAVID CECIL
(lecture date 1933?)

[Cecil, an important modern English literary critic, is highly acclaimed for his work on the Victorian era. Among Brontë scholars, he is well known for the following commentary, in which he introduced the influential theory that calm and storm are key concepts in the author's thought and works. Cecil first made his comments in a lecture delivered in approximately 1933.]

[Emily Brontë was] a mystic. She had on certain occasions in her life known moments of vision—far and away the most profound of her experiences—in which her eyes seemed opened to behold a transcendental reality usually hidden from mortal sight. And it is in the light of these moments of vision that she envisages the world of mortal things; they endow it with a new significance; they are the foundation of the philosophy on which her picture of life rests. What precisely this philosophy was she never tells us in explicit terms. She was an artist, not a professor. Moreover, founded as it was on sporadic flashes of vision, she seems never to have made it wholly clear even to herself. And any attempt to state it explicitly reveals it as full of dark places and baffling inconsistencies of detail. However, its main features are clear enough.

The first is that the whole created cosmos, animate and inanimate, mental and physical alike, is the expression of certain living spiritual principles—on the one hand what may be called the principle of storm—of the harsh, the ruthless, the wild, the dynamic; and on the other the principle of calm—of the gentle, the merciful, the passive and the tame.

Secondly, in spite of their apparent opposition these principles are not conflicting. Either—Emily Brontë does not make clear which she thinks—each is the expression of a different aspect of a single pervading spirit; or they are the component parts of a harmony. They may not seem so to us. The world of our experience is, on the face of it, full of discord. But that is only because in the cramped condition of their earthly incarnation these principles are diverted from following the course that their nature dictates, and get in each other's way. They are changed from positive into negative forces; the calm becomes a source of weakness, not of harmony, in the natural scheme, the storm a source not of fruitful vigor, but of disturbance. But when they are free from fleshly bonds they flow unimpeded and unconflicting; and even in this world their discords are transitory. The single principle that ultimately directs them sooner or later imposes an equilibrium.

Such convictions inevitably set Emily Brontë's view of human life in a perspective fundamentally different from that presented to us by other English novelists. For they do away with those antitheses which are the basis of these novelists' conceptions. The antithesis between man and nature to begin with: Emily Brontë does not see animate man revealed against inanimate nature, as Mrs. Gaskell does. She does not even see suffering, pitiful, individual man in conflict with unfeeling, impersonal, ruthless natural forces, like Hardy. Men and nature to her are equally living and in the same way. To her an angry man and an angry sky are not just metaphorically alike, they are actually alike in kind; different manifestations of a single spiritual reality.

"One time, however,"—it is Catherine Linton speaking of Linton Heathcliff—

"we were near quarrelling. He said the pleasantest manner of spending a hot July day was lying from morning till evening on a bank of heath in the middle of the moors, with the bees humming dreamily about among the bloom, and the larks singing high up overhead, and the blue sky and bright sun shining steadily and cloudlessly. That was his most perfect idea of heaven's happiness: mine was rocking in a rustling green tree, with a west wind blowing, and bright white clouds flitting rapidly above; and not only larks, but throstles, and blackbirds, and linnets, and cuckoos pouring music on every side and the moors seen at a distance, broken into cool dusky dells; but close by great swells of long grass undulat-

ing in waves to the breeze; and woods and sounding water, and the whole world awake and wild with joy. He wanted all to lie in an ecstasy of peace; I wanted all to sparkle and dance in a glorious jubilee. I said his heaven would be only half alive; and he said mine would be drunk; I said I should fall asleep in his; and he said he could not breathe in mine."

In this passage Linton's and Catherine's choices represent no chance preference, but the fundamental bias of their different natures. Each is expressing his or her instinctively felt kinship with that aspect of nature of which he or she is the human counterpart. When Linton says that he could not "breathe" in Catherine's heaven he is stating a profound truth. He draws the breath of his life from a different spiritual principle.

Again, and more important, Emily Brontë's vision of life does away with the ordinary antithesis between good and evil. To call some aspects of life good and some evil is to accept some experiences and to reject others. But it is an essential trait of Emily Brontë's attitude that it accepts all experience. Not that she is an optimist who believes that the pleasant parts of life are its only real aspects. The storm is as much part of her universe as the calm. Indeed, she is peculiarly aware of the storm; she makes out the harsh elements of life to be as harsh as they can be. Her characters set no bridle on their destructive passions; nor do they repent of their destructive deeds. But since these deeds and passions do not spring from essentially destructive impulses, but impulses only destructive because they are diverted from pursuing their natural course, they are not "bad." Further, their fierceness and ruthlessness have, when confined to their true sphere, a necessary part to play in the cosmic scheme, and as such are to be accepted. Emily Brontë's outlook is not immoral, but it is premoral. It concerns itself not with moral standards, but with those conditioning forces of life on which the naïve erections of the human mind that we call moral standards are built up. (pp. 161-65)

The conflict in her books is not between right and wrong, but between like and unlike. No doubt she herself did find some characters more sympathetic than others. But this did not lead her to think them "better," in the strict sense of the word. Sympathetic and unsympathetic alike, they act only according to the dictates of the principle of which they are the manifestation; and are not, therefore, to be blamed or praised. Even when one of her characters undergoes a change of heart, she never represents this as a moral process. Catherine Linton is first cruel to Hareton, and then kind: but she shows no remorse for her cruelty; nor does her creator give any sign that she thinks she ought to have.

Emily Brontë's attitude to human emotion is . . . different from that of her contemporaries. Her characters have extremely intense emotions, the most intense in English fiction. They are implacable and irresistible as the elemental forces they resemble; unchanging as the hills, fierce as the lightning; beside them, even Mr. Rochester's passions seem tame and tea-party affairs. But they are not awakened by the same causes as the emotions in other Victorian novels. Emily Brontë's heroes and heroines do not love each other because they find each other's personalities pleasant, or because they admire each other's characters. They may be superficially attracted for such reasons, as Catherine Earnshaw is attracted to Edgar Linton. But their deeper feelings are only roused for someone for whom they feel a sense of affinity, that comes from the fact that they are both expressions of the same spiritual principle. Catherine does not "like" Heathcliff, but she loves him with all the strength of her being. For he, like her, is a child of the storm; and this makes a bond between them, which interweaves itself with the very nature of their existence. In a sublime passage she tells Nelly Dean that she loves him—

> "not because he's handsome, Nelly, but because he's more myself than I am. Whatever our souls are made of, his and mine are the same, and Linton's is as different as a moonbeam from lightning, or frost from fire. . . . My great miseries in this world have been Heathcliff 's miseries, and I watched and felt each from the beginning: my great thought in living is himself. If all else perished, and *he* remained, *I* should still continue to be; and if all else remained, and he were annihilated, the universe would turn to a mighty stranger: I should not seem a part of it. My love for Linton is like the foliage in the woods: time will change it, I'm well aware, as winter changes the trees. My love for Heathcliff resembles the eternal rocks beneath: a source of little visible delight, but necessary. Nelly, I *am* Heathcliff ! He's always, always in my mind; not as a pleasure, any more than I am always a pleasure to myself, but as my own being."

The quality of these emotions is as remote from that of the ordinary lover's passion as its origin. For all its intensity, Catherine's love is sexless; as devoid of sensuality as the attraction that draws the tide to the moon, the steel to the magnet; and it is as little tender as if it were hate itself. Catherine does not care whether her death will make Heathcliff unhappy or not. She fears only lest it may break the bond between them. If inconsolable anguish will keep him faithful to her, she is glad of it. (pp. 165-67)

Finally, Emily Brontë does away with the most universally accepted of all antitheses—the antithesis between life and death. She believes in the immortality of the soul. If the individual life be the expression of a spiritual principle, it is clear that the mere dissolution of its fleshly integument will not destroy it. But she does more than believe in the immortality of the soul in the orthodox Christian sense. She believes in the immortality of the soul *in this world.* The spiritual principle of which the soul is a manifestation is active in this life; therefore, the disembodied soul continues to be active in this life. Its ruling preoccupations remain the same after death as before. Here she is different from other Victorian novelists, and, as far as I know, from any novelists of any time. Emily Brontë does not see human conflict as ending with death. Catherine Earnshaw dreams that she goes to heaven, but is miserable there because she is homesick for Wuthering Heights, the native country of her spirit. Nor is this a parable: it is a sort of prophecy. For when in fact she comes to die, her spirit does take up its abode at Wuthering Heights. And not just as an ineffective ghost: as much as in life she exerts an active influence over Heathcliff, besieges him with her passion.

Thus the supernatural plays a different part in *Wuthering Heights* from that which it does in other novels. Most novelists, intent on trying to give a picture of life as they know it, do not bring in the supernatural at all. Those who do, either use it as a symbol, not to be believed literally, like Nathaniel Hawthorne—or like Scott, as an extraneous anomaly at variance with the laws of nature. With Emily Brontë it is an expression of those laws. It is, in truth, misleading to call it supernatural: it is a natural feature of the world as she sees it.

Her characters hold this view of death as much as she does. They may regret dying, but it is only because death means a temporary separation from those with whom they feel an affinity. For themselves they welcome it as a gateway to a condition in which at last their natures will be able to flow out unhampered and at peace; a peace not of annihilation, but of fulfillment.

"And," cries the dying Catherine,

> "the thing that irks me most is this shattered prison, after all. I'm tired of being enclosed here. I'm wearying to escape into that glorious world, and to be always there: not seeing it dimly through tears, and yearning for it through the walls of an aching heart: but really with it, and in it. Nelly, you think you are better and more fortunate than I; in full health and strength: you are sorry for me—very soon that will be altered. I shall be sorry for *you.* I shall be incomparably beyond and above you all."

And Nelly, gazing on her dead body, has the same thought.

> "I see a repose that neither earth nor hell can break, and I feel an assurance of the endless and shadowless hereafter—the Eternity they have entered— where life is boundless in its duration, and love in its sympathy, and joy in its fulness."

(pp. 168-70)

David Cecil, "Emily Brontë and 'Wuthering Heights'," in his

Early Victorian Novelists: Essays in Revaluation, 1934. Reprint by The Bobbs-Merrill Company, Inc., 1935, pp. 157-203.

DOROTHY VAN GHENT

(essay date 1952)

[The following commentary is taken from Van Ghent's critically acclaimed analysis of the window and two-children motifs in *Wuthering Heights*.]

Wuthering Heights exists for the mind as a tension between two kinds of reality, a restrictive reality of civilized manners and codes, and the anonymous unregenerate reality of natural energies. The poetic structure which, in Emily Brontë's novel, associates these two kinds of reality is a structure of variations on the possibility of a break-through from one mode of being into the other. The present paper considers certain metamorphic patterns by which the break-through and conversion are suggested.

Our first contact with the Catherine-Heathcliff drama is established through Lockwood's dream of the ghost child at the window. Lockwood, you will remember, is a vacationer from the city, who has no prime connection with the events but who serves as narrator. He has been forced by a storm to spend the night at Wuthering Heights, and has fallen asleep while reading the dead Catherine's youthful diary. During his sleep a tempest-blown branch is scratching on the window-pane, and he hears it as the scratching of a child's hand. But why should Lockwood, the well-mannered urbanite, dream of giving *this* treatment to the ghost child? He says, "I pulled its wrist on to the broken pane, and rubbed it to and fro till the blood ran down and soaked the bed-clothes." The image is probably the most cruel one in the book. The novel is full of inflicted and suffered violence, but except in this instance the violent act has always a set of emotionally motivating circumstances—revengefulness, or hysterical frustration, of the savagery of despair. The peculiar cruelty of Lockwood's dream lies not only in the idea of bloody hurt wrought on a child, but more especially in the dreamer's lack of emotional motivation for dreaming it: the cruelty is in the gratuitousness of the dreamed act. The bed in which Lockwood lies in an old-fashioned closet bed with a window set in it; its paneled sides he has

Top Withens, near Haworth, believed to be the model for Wuthering Heights.

pulled together before going to sleep. The bed is like a coffin; at the end of the book, Heathcliff dies in it, behind its closed panels; it had been Catherine's bed, and the movable panels themselves suggest the coffin in which she is laid, whose "panels" Heathcliff has bribed the sexton to remove at one side. Psychologically, Lockwood's dream has only the most perfunctory determinations, and nothing at all of result for the dreamer except to put him uncomfortably out of bed. But poetically the dream has its reasons, compacted into the image of the daemonic child scratching at the pane, trying to get from the "outside" "in," and of the dreamer in a bed like a coffin, released by that deathly privacy to indiscriminate violence. The coffin-like bed shuts off any interference with the wild deterioration of the psyche. Had the dream used any other agent than the effete, almost epicene Lockwood, it would have lost this symbolic force; for Lockwood, more successfully than anyone else in the book, has shut out the powers of darkness (the pun in his name is obvious in this context); and his lack of any dramatically thorough motivation for dreaming the cruel dream suggests those powers as existing autonomously, not only in the "outsideness" of external nature, beyond the physical windowpane, but also within, even in the soul least prone to passionate excursion.

The windowpane is the medium, treacherously transparent, separating the "inside" from the "outside," the "human" from the alien and terrible "other." Immediately after the incident of the dream, the time of the narrative is displaced into the childhood of Heathcliff and Catherine, and we see the two children looking through the drawing room window of the neighboring Lintons. Heathcliff relates their adventure to the nurse, Nellie, thus:

"Both of us were able to look in by standing on the basement, and clinging to the ledge, and we saw—ah! it was beautiful—a splendid place carpeted with crimson, and crimson-covered chairs and tables, and a pure white ceiling bordered by gold, a shower of glass-drops hanging in silver chains from the centre, and shimmering with little soft tapers. Old Mr. and Mrs. Linton were not there; Edgar and his sister had it entirely to themselves. Shouldn't they have been happy? We should have thought ourselves in heaven!"

Here the two unregenerate waifs look *in* from the night on the heavenly vision of the refinements and securities of the most privileged human estate. But Heathcliff rejects the vision: seeing the Linton children blubbering and bored there (*they* cannot get *out!*), he senses the menace of its limitations; while Catherine is fatally tempted. She is taken in by the Lintons, and now it is Heathcliff alone outside looking through the window:

"The curtains [he says] were still looped up at one corner, and I resumed my station as a spy; because, if Catherine had wished to return, I intended shattering their great glass panes to a million of fragments, unless they let her out. She sat on the sofa quietly . . . the woman-servant brought a basin of warm water, and washed her feet; and Mr. Linton mixed a tumbler of negus, and Isabella emptied a plateful of cakes into her lap. . . . Afterwards, they dried and combed her beautiful hair. . . ."

Thus the first snare is laid by which Catherine will be held for a civilized destiny—her feet washed, cakes and wine for her delectation, her beautiful hair combed. The motifs are limpid as those of fairy tale, where the changeling in the otherworld is held there mysteriously by bathing and by the strange new food he is given.

Through her marriage to Edgar Linton, Catherine yields to that destiny, but her yielding is uneasy, her resistance tormented, and she finds her way out of it by death. Literally she "catches her death" by throwing open the window. During a feverish illness, she cries to Nellie, "Open the window again wide: fasten it open! Quick, why don't you move?" "Because I won't give you your death of cold," Nellie answers. "You won't give me a chance of life, you mean," Catherine says; and in her delirium she opens the window, leans out into the winter wind, and calls across the moors to Heathcliff. . . . On the night after her burial, unable to follow her into death . . . , he returns to the Heights *through the window*—for the door has been barred against him—to wreak on the living the fury of his frustration. It is years later that Lockwood arrives at the Heights and spends his uncomfortable night there, dreaming of the dead child scratching on the pane. Lockwood's outcry in his dream brings Heathcliff to the window, Heathcliff who has been caught ineluctably in the human to grapple with its interdictions long after Catherine has broken through them. The treachery of the window is that Catherine, lost now alone in the "otherness," can look through the transparent membrane that separates her from humanity, can scratch on the pane, but cannot get "in," while Heathcliff, though he forces the window open and howls into the night, cannot get "out." When he dies, Nellie Dean discovers the window swinging open, the window of that old-fashioned coffin-like bed where Lockwood had had the dream. Rain has been pouring in during the night, drenching the dead man. Nellie says: " 'I hasped the window; I combed his black long hair from his forehead; I tried to close his eyes: to extinguish, if possible, that frightful, life-like gaze of exultation before any one else beheld it. They would not shut. . . . ' " Earlier, Heathcliff 's eyes have been spoken of as "the clouded windows of hell" from which a "fiend" looks. The refusal of his lids to shut (the "fiend" has not got "out," leaving the window open) elucidates with simplicity the meaning of the "window" as a separation between the daemonic depths of the soul and the lucidities of consciousness, a separation between the soul's "otherness" and its humanness.

The imagery of the window is metamorphic, suggesting a total change of mode of being by the breaking-through of a separating medium. The boldest and most radiant figuration that Emily Brontë has given to her subject is the two-children figure, also a metamorphic figure of break-through and transsubstantiation. Here the separating medium is the body and personality of another. The type or classic form of this figure is a girl with golden hair and a boy with dark hair and shadowed brow, bound in kindship and in a relationship of charity and passion; the dark boy is to be brightened, made angelic and happy, by the beautiful golden girl. But the dynamics of the change are not perfectly trustworthy. In one of Emily Brontë's poems, describing a child who might be the child Heathcliff, the ambivalent dark boy will apparently sink further into darkness:

> I love thee, boy; for all divine
> All full of God they features shine . . .
> Too heavenly now, but doomed to be
> Hell-like in heart and misery.

Under the title of **"The Two Children"** two companion pieces appear, in the first of which the dark boy is still unchanged:—

> Frowning on the infant,
> Shadowing childhood's joy,
> Guardian angel knows not
> That melancholy boy . . .

In the second of these pieces, the golden child—a "Child of Delight! with sunbright hair"—appears, and through her the change in the dark one is promised. Asked of her origin, she says that she is "not from heaven descended," but that she has seen and pitied "that mournful boy":

> And I swore to take his gloomy sadness
> And give to him my beamy joy . . .

Here, with the change in the dark child, the golden one will be changed also, for she will take his "gloomy sadness." In another set of verses, the light-dark contrast is turned around bewilderingly:

> And only *he* had locks of light,
> And *she* had raven hair;
> While now, his curls are dark as night,
> And hers as morning fair.

What really seems to be implied by all these shifts is not a mere exchange of characteristics between the two children, but a radical identification, so that each can appear under the aspect of the other, the bright one in the mode of darkness and the dark one in the mode of light.

In still another of the poems that dramatize affairs in the kingdom of Gondal, a brooding phantom figure haunts the moonlit grounds of a castle. Apparently the cause of his death was adoration of another man's wife, and it is for this reason that his spirit is "shut from heaven—an outcast for eternity." The woman for whom he died is represented as an "infant fair," looking from a golden frame in a portrait gallery.

> And just like his its ringlets bright,
> Its large dark eye of shadowy light,
> Its cheeks' pure hue, its forehead white,
> And like its noble name.

A deliberate confusion of the planes of reality—a shifting into the life inside the picture frame (like the shafts through the window in *Wuthering Heights*), and with it a shifting from despairing adulthood into childhood—is suggested with the following questions:

> And did he never smile to see
> Himself restored to infancy?

> Never part back that golden flow
> Of curls, and kiss that pearly brow,
> And feel no other earthly bliss
> Was equal to that parent's kiss?

The suggestions are those of metamorphic changes, but all under the aspect of frustration. The despairing lover cannot get through the picture frame where the child is. Kinship is implied between him and the child in the picture ("And just like his its ringlets bright . . . And like its noble name"), and one is left to imagine that the queen whom he loved was his sister, wherefore the frustration of their love. The last stanza remarks ambiguously on the parental feeling involved in the relationship: is it not the infant who is the "parent" here? The fact that *both* have golden hair seems, in this elusive fantasy, to be a mark of perversion of the metamorphic sequence, at least of its having gone awry.

In the relationship of Catherine and Heathcliff, the fantasy has its typical form. She is golden, he is dark. His daemonic origin is always kept open, by reiterations of the likelihood that he is really a ghoul, a fiend, an offspring of hell, and not merely so in behavior. And Catherine also, like the guardian child in the **"Two Children"** poems, is "not from heaven descended": she has furious tantrums, she lies, she bites, her chosen toy is a whip. They are raised as brother and sister; there are three references to their sleeping in the same bed as infants. She scolds and orders and cherishes and mothers him. The notions of somatic change and discovery of noble birth, as in fairy tale, are deliberately played with, as, when Catherine returns from her first sojourn at the Lintons's and Heathcliff asks Nellie to "make him decent," he says, comparing himself with

Edgar: " 'I wish I had light hair and a fair skin, and was dressed and behaved as well, and had a chance of being as rich as he will be!' " and Nellie answers: " 'You're fit for a prince in disguise. . . . Were I in your place, I would frame high notions of my birth. . . . ' " Some alluring and astonishing destiny seems possible. *What* that phenomenon might be or mean, we cannot know, for it is frustrated by Catherine's marriage to Edgar. Catherine's decision dooms her as well as Heathcliff, for she is of the same daemonic substance as he, and a civilized marriage and domesticity are not sympathetic to the daemonic quality. With the second generation, the two-children figure is distorted and parodied in the relationship of Catherine's daughter and Heathcliff 's son. Young Cathy, another "child of delight, with sun-bright hair," has still some of the original daemonic energy, but the subject of her compassion is a *pale-haired* and pallid little boy whose only talents are for sucking sugar candy and torturing cats. Her passionate charity finally finds her "married" to his corpse in a locked bedroom. With young Cathy and Hareton Earnshaw, her cousin on her mother's side, the "two children" are again in their right relation of golden and dark, and now the pathos of the dark child cures the daemon out of the golden one, and the maternal care of the golden child raises the dark one to civilized humanity and makes of him a proper husband.

In these several pairs, the relation of kinship has various resonances. Between Catherine and Heathcliff, identity of "kind" is greatest, although they are foster brother and sister only. Catherine says she *is* Heathcliff; and when she dies, Heathcliff howls that he cannot live without his "life," he cannot live without his "soul." But one does not "mate" with oneself, with one's own life, with one's own soul. Catherine and Heathcliff are unthinkable in adult domestication as lovers. . . . The foster kinship between these two provides an imaginative reason for the unnaturalness and impossibility of their mating. In Emily Brontë's use of the symbolism of the incestual motive, it appears as an attempt to make what is "outside" oneself identical with what is "inside" oneself, a performance that can be construed in physical and human terms only by destruction of personality bounds, by rending of flesh, and at last by death. With Catherine's daughter and young Linton, who are cousins, the implicit incestuousness of the two-children figure is suggested morbidly by Linton's disease and by his finally becoming a husband only as a corpse. With young Cathy and Hareton Earnshaw, who are also cousins, Victorian meliorism finds a way to sanction the relationship by symbolic emasculation; Cathy literally teaches the devil out of Hareton, and "esteem" between the two takes the place of the old passion for identification. With this successful mating, the daemonic quality has been completely suppressed, and though humanity and civilization have been secured for the "two children," one feels that some magnificent bounty is now irrecoverable.

We are led to speculate on what the bounty might have been, had the windowpane not stood between the original pair, had the golden child and the dark child not been secularized by a spelling book. In the two patterns we have spoken of, there is a double movement always, not only a movement to get "outside"—that is, to break through the limitations of civilized life and of personal consciousness—but also a movement to get "inside"—a movement toward passionate fulfillment of consciousness by deeper ingress into the matrix of its own and all energy. Together, the two movements represent an attempt to identify in a unity the "outside" and the "inside," the dark world of unknown powers with the bright world of the known, in such a way that they could freely assume each other's modes of revelation. Perhaps, had the ideal and impossible eventuality taken place, the universe of animals and elements—of wild moor and barren rock, of fierce wind and attacking beast, that is the strongest palpability in *Wuthering Heights*—would have offered itself completely to human understanding and creative intercourse. Perhaps the dark powers that exist within the soul, as well as in the outer world, would have assumed the language of consciousness, or consciousness would have bravely entered into companionship with those dark powers and transliterated their language into its own. Emily Brontë's book has been said to be non-philosophical—it is certainly nonethical; but all philosophy is not ethics, and the book seizes, at the point where the soul feels itself cleft within and in cleavage from the universe, the first germs of philosophic thought, the thought of the duality of human and non-human existence, and the thought of the cognate duality of the psyche. (pp. 189-97)

Dorothy Van Ghent, "The Window Figure and the Two-Children Figure in 'Wuthering Heights'," in *Nineteenth-Century Fiction*, Vol. VII, No. 3, December, 1952, pp. 189-97.

FELICIA GORDON
(essay date 1989)

[In the excerpt below, Gordon explores the themes of imagination, death, and religion in Brontë's poetry.]

In May 1846 under the pseudonyms Ellis, Acton and Currer Bell, the Brontës published a book of poems at their own expense. Charlotte paid the publishers, Aylott and Jones, £37. This venture was a luxury permitted by a small legacy from their Aunt Branwell. Of the one thousand copies printed, only two were sold. The collection included sixty-one poems; nineteen by Charlotte and twenty-one each by Emily and Anne. Subsequent scholarship has discovered further poems. . . . Whereas from a biographical point of view the poems of all three sisters have interest, it is chiefly Emily's poetry which lays a claim to literary merit.

One can suggest various perspectives from which to approach Emily's poems. The most tempting, but perhaps the least rewarding, is that of a personal confession. Because most of the poems figured in the Gondal saga, they remain largely resistant to biographical interpretation. Emily evidently revelled in imagining extremes of emotion; towering rages, brutal revenge, endless woe and so on. She must have drawn on her own feelings, but in an essentially impersonal mode. Her poetry might be said to illustrate Keats's theory of 'negative capability', the capacity to project oneself imaginatively in another's mind. 'The poet', said Keats, 'has no identity.' Emily's identity cannot be said to emerge from her poetry any more than it emerges from *Wuthering Heights.*

One area of personal revelation that has been extensively canvassed involves the poems reputed to concern Branwell, as, for example, the verse beginning:

Well, some may hate, and some may scorn,
And some may quite forget thy name,
But my sad heart must ever mourn
Thy ruined hopes, thy blighted fame.

(14 Nov. 1839)

The date alone makes clear that the poem antedated Branwell's death by nine years. Emily was unlikely to have foreseen his dramatic decay quite so clearly, though she may have feared it. The Brontë biographer, Winifred Gérin, suggests that the themes of guilt and disappointment showed a marked increase in her poetry from the time of Branwell's unsuccessful London trip in the summer of 1835 and her own return to Haworth after her short period at Roe Head.

Similarly, **'The Wanderer from the Fold'**, with its Romantic evocation of early promise, is dated 11 March 1844, before Branwell's catastrophe at Thorp Green. It is addressed to A.G.A. (Augusta Geraldine Almeda, Queen of Gondal) from E. W. (Lord Eldred W., Captain of the Queen's Guard) and forms part of a lament for Augusta's tragic end:

Sometimes I seem to see thee rise,
A glorious child again—
All virtues beaming from thine eyes
That ever honoured men—

The identification of Emily's poems with Branwell is not entirely sustainable, although as in Charlotte's juvenilia (we note the figure of the brother and cad, Hastings) the theme of disappointment and waste makes a plausible link with Branwell. Branwell, had, of course, become a family disappointment long before he became a disaster. From as early as 1835, when he failed to enter the Royal Academy, he must have been a worrying preoccupation for them all. But in addition, the idea of the promise of childhood, contrasted with the limitations of adult life, is a peculiarly Romantic theme, which would have appealed to Emily. One recalls Wordsworth's lament in the 'Immortality Ode': 'shades of the prison house begin to close around the growing boy.' Precocious children, the Brontës often found the constraints of adult life unbearable. 'Liberty', said Charlotte of Emily, 'was the breath of her nostrils.' Branwell's decay dramatized in real terms what they had all experienced: 'but my sad heart must ever mourn, Thy ruined hopes, thy blighted fame.' To have imagined oneself a genius, in charge of kingdoms, and to become a governess or a railway clerk must have seemed a bitter decline.

From dating and internal evidence, the majority of Emily's poems can be read as commemorating stages in the career of Augusta Geraldine Almeda (also confusingly called Rosina Alcona) and of her consort, Julius Brenzaida. A. G. A.'s life, as we know, was tempestuous. She took, as lovers, Alexander, Lord of Elbe, then Lord Alfred of Aspin Castle. Lord Alfred, after marrying Augusta, killed himself, presumably a commentary on the conjugal life they enjoyed. She then married Julius Brenzaida, King of Almedore in Gaaldine. With Gerald of Exina, Julius invaded Gondal and took the throne. He was subsequently assassinated. A. G. A. fled, but after a period of exile, eventually regained the throne of Gondal. Following further political intrigues and love affairs, Augusta was finally slain in her turn.

Even this brief and incomplete summary throws up certain key Gondal themes; among them, love, ambition, power, liberty, revenge and death. The characters pursue their own passions, living in an almost entirely amoral universe. Particularly striking are the range and extent of A. G. A.'s love affairs and her ruthless quest for power. She is an untrammelled egotist, a female Byronic 'hero'. Augusta, never subject to the constraints of realist fiction, projects an almost Nietzschean version of the will to power.

The thematic links with *Wuthering Heights* are of great interest. Egotism, revenge, passion and especially the desire for death echo through the poems and prefigure the more concretely realized world of the novel. But although such thematic links can be drawn, differences are equally significant. Emily's novel forswears the self-indulgent Byronism of much of the poetry or projects it upon individual characters, towards whom we take an external viewpoint. Because no Gondal prose manuscripts survive, we cannot judge their quality, but they, like Charlotte's Angrian tales, were probably conceived as pure fantasy.

Two poems of especial interest in this regard deal with the imagination and its role in the poet's life. . . . (pp. 182-84)

'To Imagination' is characteristic of Emily's work on several levels. The tone is intense, announced by the exclamation 'Oh my true friend', the vocabulary generalized but spare. It sometimes borders on bathos ('pain', 'despair', 'lone'). Abstract qualities are personified ('Danger', 'Nature', 'Truth', 'Fancy') and there is some recourse to cliché ('The flowers of Fancy newly born'). Nevertheless the poem achieves a powerful tension in the ambiguous feelings aroused by Imagination. The poet's relationship with her equivalent of the Muse is problematic. Imagination is simultaneously a solace, a strange visitant and an integral part of herself ('Thou and I and Liberty'). Against the realm of freedom in the mind, the poet unfavourably contrasts the world, distinguished by 'guile', 'hate', 'doubt', 'cold suspicion', 'danger', 'guilt' and 'darkness'. Yet Truth and Reason testify against 'the bright untroubled day' created by the Imagination. The pull between opposite poles operates strongly in the last two verses. On the one hand, 'but thou art ever there to bring the hovering vision back' and, on the other, 'I trust not to thy phantom bliss'. Belief and scepticism are finely balanced. An overriding despair in the real world is the poem's other dominant theme, 'So hopeless is the world without'. The temptation merely to retreat from reality is resisted, however; the claims of Truth and Nature are acknowledged.

The second poem on the same theme is simply entitled **'Stanzas'**:

Often rebuked, yet always back returning
To those first feelings that were born with me,
And leaving busy chase of wealth and learning
For idle dreams of things which cannot be:

Today, I will seek not the shadowy region:
Its unsustaining vastness waxes drear;
And visions rising, legion after legion,
Bring the unreal world too strangely near.

I'll walk, but not in old heroic traces,
And not in paths of high morality,
And not among the half-distinguished faces,
The clouded forms of long-past history.

I'll walk where my own nature would be leading:
It vexes me to choose another guide:
Where the grey flocks in ferny glens are feeding;
Where the wild wind blows on the mountain side.

What have those lonely mountains worth revealing?
More glory and more grief than I can tell:
The earth that wakes *one* human heart to feeling

Can centre both the worlds of Heaven and Hell.

The first verse raises the problem of the poet's failure to adapt to the world. In the realm of the imagination, she makes a distinction, not apparent in the previous poem, between what Coleridge termed the primary and secondary imaginations. 'Those first feelings born in me' suggest an authentic self which has been dominated by the 'clouded forms of long-past history', presumably the kingdom of Gondal. The poet goes on to affirm the primacy of imagination grounded in nature and to offer a foretaste of the achievement of *Wuthering Heights:* 'I'll walk where my own nature would be leading'. This world is explicitly that of Emily's Haworth surroundings 'where the grey flocks in ferny glens are feeding'. The final verse encapsulates the feeling of paradoxes locked in strife that pervades *Wuthering Heights;* glory opposed to grief, Heaven to Hell. Both aspects are envisaged as necessary to the whole, both centred on the earth ('what have those lonely mountains worth revealing?'). It is evident that for the poet, all meaning is to be found in the natural world. The poem expresses powerfully what is often referred to as Emily Brontë's pantheism. Also significant here is the extent to which she abandons the world of Fancy. Like Charlotte, she seems to have felt the need to repudiate her adolescent fantasies. Yet, as Charlotte put it, 'when I depart from these [her Angrian characters] I feel almost as if I stood on the threshold of a home and were bidding farewell to its inmates. . . . Still, I long to quit for awhile that burning clime where we have sojourned too long' ('Farewell to Angria', 1839). **'Often Rebuked'** affirms the creative power of the imagination linked to nature, while evoking with nostalgia the world of Gondal.

Death is perhaps the most pervasive theme running through Emily's poetry. In this she shows herself a child of the Romantic movement with its sometimes obsessive delight in contemplating mortality and decay. Even poems which begin by celebrating the natural world do so in order to contrast the transience of life with the permanence of death:

The linnet in the rocky dells,
The moor lark in the air,
The bee among the heather-bells
That hide my lady fair.

This lyric records a lament for Augusta Almeda over her grave. The song birds, the linnet and the moor lark, contrast with the silent dead. Undying desire endlessly survives the death of the individual loved, prefiguring Heathcliff's obsession with the dead Cathy. Separation of lovers also emerges in Augusta's mourning for her lost love, Julius. In addition, death of the beloved is portrayed as a kind of betrayal, recalling Heathcliff's anger with Cathy when she dies. Emily understands the egotistical element in the composition of grief, as in **'The Appeal'** (18 May 1840):

> If grief for grief can touch thee,
> If answering woe for woe,
> If any ruth can melt thee,
> Come to me now!
>
> I cannot be more lonely,
> More drear I cannot be!
> My worn heart throbs so wildly,
> T'will break for thee.
>
> And when the world despises,
> When heaven repels my prayer,
> Will not mine angel comfort?
> Mine idol hear?
>
> Yes, by the tears I've poured thee,
> By all my hours of pain,
> O I shall surely win thee,
> Beloved, again!

The insistent repetitions ('if ', 'if ', 'if '; 'grief for grief '; 'woe for woe'; 'more and more') convey the obsessive nature of Augusta's passion. The economy of the short lines and the shortened fourth line suggest a catch at the heart, the physical pain of heartbreak. In spite of some banal phrases ('drear', 'my heart throbs so wildly') the poem speaks convincingly of painful longing. As in many of the poems of mourning, the final object of desire becomes death itself. Heaven 're-pels' the poet's prayer; the angel invoked is not a heavenly angel.

The attraction of death is also the theme of Rosina Alcona's lament to Julius Brenzaida (3 March 1845). Here the grave is seen as the place of reunion; the world is empty since the loved object who gave it meaning has vanished. Heathcliff 's declaration, 'The entire world is a dreadful collection of memoranda that she did exist, and that I have lost her' (Ch. 33) suggests a similar sense that the death of the beloved cancels life's significance and leaves the world a void:

> Cold in the earth—and the deep snow piled above thee!
> Far, far removed, cold in the dreary grave!
> Have I forgot, my Only Love, to love thee,
> Severed at last by Time's all-severing wave?

The last verse reads:

> And even yet, I dare not let it languish,
> Dare not indulge in Memory's rapturous pain;
> Once drinking deep of that divinest anguish,
> How could I seek the empty world again?

In the poetry as a whole, the natural world is understood as a spectacle of conflicting forces, where the end product of conflict is annihilation. Emily's dramatic rendering of a summer storm in her earliest known poem (13 Dec. 1836) expresses in its rhythms and language this sense of a destructive but exhilarating process:

> High waving heather, 'neath stormy blasts bending,
> Midnight and moonlight and bright shining stars;
> Darkness and glory rejoicingly blending,
> Earth rising to heaven and heaven descending,
> Man's spirit away from its drear dongeon sending,
> Bursting the fetters and breaking the bars.

The apocalyptic tone and galloping rhythms suggest biblical parallels in the *Book of Revelation,* or a verbal rendition of a John Martin landscape.

Emily's last known poem, published posthumously by Charlotte, is remarkable for forging, beyond the sometimes facile Romantic identification with death, a statement of individual religious belief:

"No Coward Soul Is Mine"

> No coward soul is mine
> No trembler in the world's storm-troubled sphere
> I see Heaven's glories shine
> And Faith shines equal arming me from Fear.
>
> O God within my breast
> Almighty ever present Deity
> Life, that in me has rest
> As I Undying Life, have power in Thee.
>
> Vain are the thousand creeds
> That move men's hearts, unutterably vain,
> Worthless as withered weeds
> Or idlest froth amid the boundless main
>
> To waken doubt in one
> Holding so fast by thy infinity
> So surely anchored on
> The steadfast rock of Immortality.
>
> With wide-embracing love
> Thy spirit animates eternal years
> Pervades and broods above,
> Changes, sustains, dissolves, creates, and rears.
>
> Though Earth and moon were gone
> And suns and universes ceased to be
> And thou wert left alone
> Every Existence would exist in thee.
>
> There is not room for Death
> Nor atom that his might could render void
> Since thou art Being and Breath
> And what thou art may never be destroyed.

'No Coward Soul is Mine' expresses with a proud stoicism the scorn Emily felt for doctrinal debates. Her religious beliefs, from the evidence of this poem, bore little resemblance to orthodox Christianity. There is no mention of Redemption through Christ, rather an affirmation of God's presence in all aspects of his created universe. Anne Brontë, as we have seen, conveyed a similar universalism in *The Tenant of Wildfell Hall,* invoking the 'God who hateth nothing that He hath made' (Ch. 49). Emily creates a vision of time within eternity; the meditation on change and permanence is brilliantly evocative: 'Thy spirit animates eternal years / Pervades and broods above, / Changes, sustains, dissolves, creates, and rears.'

In its affirmation of faith as an essentially creative principle, this poem renounces the death obsession of much of the earlier poetry: 'There is not room for Death'. The universe is conceived as a plenitude of life. Even process, change and struggle partake of the 'Almighty ever present Deity'. God is understood as part of the poet's being, but also separate, a rôle similar to that of Imagination in **'Often Rebuked'**. Here, the Romantic ego is simultaneously preserved and overcome.

If Emily had not written *Wuthering Heights* her poetry might have gone largely unremarked. Though tightly controlled and with a musical sensitivity to language, it remained tied to the private world of Gondal. Neither she nor her sisters experimented widely in poetic form and the imprint of Scott and Byron is frequently too apparent. Her poems are, nevertheless, a remarkable legacy and remind us that *Wuthering Heights* did not arise from nothing. Heathcliff 's lament for Cathy was already written years before the novel:

> O come again; what chains withhold
> The steps that used so fleet to be?
> Come, leave thy dwelling dank and cold
> Once more to visit me.

(pp. 185-90)

Felicia Gordon, in her *A Preface to the Brontës,* Longman, 1989, 225 p.

SOURCES FOR FURTHER STUDY

Craik, W. A. *"Wuthering Heights."* In her *The Brontë Novels,* pp. 5-47. London: Methuen and Co., 1968.

> An objective assessment of *Wuthering Heights.* Craik aims "to discover what are Emily Brontë's purposes in writing, how she goes to work, what effects she brings about, how original, and, finally, how great is her achievement."

Everitt, Alastair, ed. *"Wuthering Heights": An Anthology of Criticism.* London: Frank Cass & Co., 1967, 208 p.

> Presents a variety of interpretations of *Wuthering Heights.*

Gregor, Ian, ed. *The Brontës: A Collection of Critical Essays.* Twentieth Century Views, edited by Maynard Mack. Englewood Cliffs, N.J.: Prentice-Hall, 1970, 179 p.

> Includes commentary on the control of sympathy in *Wuthering Heights,* the place of love in the novel, and other aspects of Brontë's work.

Sanger, Charles Percy. "The Structure of *Wuthering Heights.*" In *Critics on Charlotte and Emily Brontë,* edited by Judith O'Neill, pp. 49-113. Miami, Fla.: University of Miami Press, 1968.

> A landmark study that examines Brontë's close attention to detail.

Smith, Anne, ed. *The Art of Emily Brontë.* London: Vision, 1976, 246 p.

> A collection of critical essays on Brontë's poems and *Wuthering Heights.*

Winnifrith, Tom. *"Wuthering Heights."* In his *The Brontës,* pp. 46-65. Masters of World Literature Series, edited by Louis Kronenberger. New York: Macmillan Publishing Co., 1977.

> A wide-ranging discussion of *Wuthering Heights.* Winnifrith addresses some of the major issues surrounding the interpretation of the novel, including the effectiveness of Brontë's narrators, the significance of the opposition between Thrushcross Grange and Wuthering Heights, and the ambiguity of the novel's conclusion.

Rupert Brooke

1887-1915

English poet, critic, dramatist, essayist, and journalist.

INTRODUCTION

Considered England's foremost young poet at the time of his death in 1915, Brooke is best known today for his war poetry and for his personal mystique as the embodiment of idealized youth. Of the war sonnets in *1914, and Other Poems* (1915), Brooke's "The Soldier," celebrating a life gladly given in England's service, is world-renowned—hailed for its noble sentiments by many, and scorned for its naiveté by others.

One of three brothers, each of whom died before reaching age thirty, Brooke was born in Rugby, England, where his father served as a schoolmaster at Rugby School. An athletically and intellectually talented youth, Brooke attended Rugby from 1901 to 1905, writing of this period: "I am so joyful that I fear lest the Greek idea may be true, and Nemesis fall bleakly and suddenly." Brooke composed two prize poems while at Rugby and entered King's College, Cambridge, in 1906. While there, his extraordinary good looks (William Butler Yeats called him "the handsomest man in England") and personal charm drew an admiring circle of literary friends, notable among them Henry James, Edward Marsh, Walter de la Mare, and Virginia Woolf. Marsh, Brooke's patron, encouraged him to publish *Poems* in 1911; this early collection reveals Brooke's evolving poetic style at a time when his interests shifted from an early fascination with the fin-de-siècle writings of Charles Baudelaire and Oscar Wilde to an admiration of John Donne and Robert Browning. *Poems*—the only volume of Brooke's poetry published in his lifetime—was regarded even by its detractors as a herald of major talent.

Brooke suffered an emotional breakdown in 1912, following a selfthwarted love affair with Ka Cox, a female student at nearby Newnham College. Brooke's love for Cox inspired some of his best Donne-

432

like sonnets, but it left him frustrated by an ingrained disapproval of pre-marital sex and guilt-ridden over earlier homoerotic encounters; biographers attribute Brooke's apparent sexual ambivalence to his domineering, puritanical mother. During a period of recovery in Berlin, Brooke completed one of his finest poems, "The Old Vicarage, Grantchester," a whimsical, sentimental revelation of his homesickness. Upon his return to England, Brooke joined Marsh in collecting the poems that comprise the anthology *Georgian Poetry, 1911-12,* which includes contributions from forty poets and featured Brooke's own "Grantchester". The collection, entitled with reference to the reign of George V (1910-1936), was succeeded by four more anthologies during the ensuing decade; taken together, these volumes, according to their editor Marsh, reflect a belief that English poetry was "once again putting on new strength and beauty" and beginning a new "Georgian" period.

Largely a forum for publication and recognition of the works of a diverse body of English poets—John Masefield, D. H. Lawrence, Walter de la Mare, and John Drinkwater prominent among them—these collections were a popular success. Modern critics, however, cite the diversity of styles, themes, and subject matter in the volumes as proof that this so-called "Georgian movement" was little more than a successful commercial venture.

Brooke embarked on a year-long trip to North America and the South Pacific in 1913, recording his experiences and impressions in a series of articles and letters published in the *Westminster Gazette* and collected in his *Letters From America* (1916). Brooke was a competent and often highly entertaining journalist and correspondent: he embellished his enthuisiastic and witty observations with the descriptive skills of an adept lyricist. He continued to compose poetry during this time, completing "Tiare Tahiti" early in 1914; considered one of his best sonnets, "Tahiti" was inspired by his love for one of the natives he met while visiting the South-sea island. World War I began shortly after Brooke's return to England and, though he never saw the horror of battle, was the greatest influence on the poetry for which he is remembered today. Commissioned an officer in the Royal Naval Division, he completed his famed "1914" sonnets during the early stages of the war, demonstrating in them a romantic, crusading vision typical of the English civilian spirit at that time. Brooke gained national attention when "The Soldier" was read aloud in St. Paul's Cathedral on Easter Sunday, 1915. Shortly thereafter, while preparing for the assault on Gallipoli, Turkey, Brooke died of blood poisoning aboard ship in the Aegean Sea. He was buried in an olive grove on the island of Scyros.

The idolatrous praise heaped upon Brooke following his death attracted a tremendous readership to his poetry. Often nostalgic and sentimental, his verse fueled the tragic "young Apollo" image against which critics have struggled to assess his literary achievement. Shortly after World War I, Brooke's poetry was rejected by critics who viewed his work as little more than the idealistic musings of a pampered darling, objecting most emphatically to his war sonnets for their glorification of war and of the soldier's martyrdom. Present-day commentators, however, while acknowledging Brooke's excesses, have drawn favorable attention to his skill as a sonneteer, his gift for language, and the romantic intensity of his best verse, focusing a renewed appreciation on Brooke's stylistic accomplishments. More importantly, however, Brooke has come to be viewed, in recognition of both the qualities and the defects of his poetry and character, as the embodiment of his age, closely reflecting the thoughts and sentiments of his pre-War generation. As such, he remains an important figure in the history of English literature.

(For further information about Brooke's life and works, see *Contemporary Authors,* Vol. 104; *Dictionary of Literary Biography,* Vol. 19: *British Poets, 1880-1914*; and *Twentieth–Century Literary Criticism,* Vols. 2, 7.)

CRITICAL COMMENTARY

JOHN DRINKWATER

(essay date 1916)

[Drinkwater was an English dramatist, poet, biographer, and critic. In the following excerpt from a 1916 essay, he praises Brooke's poetic technique.]

The development of Rupert Brooke's poetic power was, it seems to me, unlike that of most poets. The early verse of men who afterwards prove their authenticity generally shows a great emotional force with little intellectual power of arrangement, and a weakly imitative craftsmanship. . . . But in Rupert Brooke's beginnings there is none of this. The volume of *Poems* . . . , which contains work written as early as

Principal Works

Poems (poetry) 1911

The Collected Poems of Rupert Brooke (poetry) 1915

Lithuania (drama) 1915

1914, and Other Poems (poetry) 1915

John Webster and the Elizabethan Drama (essay) 1916

Letters from America (travel essays) 1916

The Poetical Works of Rupert Brooke (poetry) 1946

The Prose of Rupert Brooke (essays and criticism) 1956

1905, when he was eighteen, shows an art curiously personal, skilful, deliberate. It shows, too, an intellectual deftness altogether unexpected in so young a poet, and it shows finally, not always but often, an indifference to the normal material upon which poets good and bad are apt to work from the outset, and in the shaping of which ultimately comes all poetry that is memorable. Nearly every page is interesting on account of its art and intellectual deftness, qualities that we should not expect to be marked. But there are many pages where we do not get the real glow of poetry, and this because the content, it seems to me, often fails to satisfy the demands of poetry. It is true enough to say that it does not matter what subject the poet may contemplate, but there is an implied provision that the subject shall be one that grips his emotions, one, that is to say, that he perceives poetically. It so happens that this capacity in subject-matter for stirring the emotion to poetic intensity is nearly always coincident with a sympathy with the common experience of the world. A poet may write in praise of his mistress as freshly to-day as if none had written before him, but, although we say that he may choose what theme he will, we could not respond to him if he told us in his song that, while he loved his lady and her beauty and his wooing was in all ways prosperous, the thing that he most desired was never to see her again. We should at once know that the attitude was a piece of cold intellectuality, that it was against poetry in substance.

In Rupert Brooke's earliest work there is a strain of this intellectual coldness. . . . The most common note that we find in his first book in illustration of my meaning is the presence at love's moment of the knowledge that women grow old and beauty fades. The reflection is true in fact, but is not poetically true, and so, in its present shape, it is false. That is to say, we know that, although women do grow old, the lover in the delight of his mistress does not realise this, and that the assertion that he does is not emotional passion of conviction but intellectual deliberation. Rupert Brooke

goes one step further into danger; not only does he assert that the lover feels something that we know he does not feel, but—it is perhaps an equitable penalty for the first false step—he makes the realisation of a fact that we know is not realised in the circumstances, a source of revulsion, when we know that if the lover felt at all about his mistress's old age it would certainly be with peace and surety. (pp. 180-84)

We find, then, in a great many pages of this first book, an instrument that on so young lips is efficient and enchanting against almost all example, yet playing a tune that does not come wholly from the heart. Never, I think, has technique reached so great a perfection without corresponding authenticity of impulse. Only half a dozen times in the book do we get such phrases as "rife with magic and movement," or "whirling, blinding moil," and even in the poems where most we feel the lack of emotional truth, there is a beauty of words that made the book full of the most exciting promise. Already, too, there was in certain poems assurance against the danger that this intellectual constraint might degenerate into virtuosity. In the song beginning:

"Oh! Love!" they said, "is King of kings,"

the intellectual mood, even in the love traffic in which it has been most shy, is adjusting itself finely to the clear and common impulses of mankind, while in **"Dust," "The Fish," "The Hill," "The Jolly Company," "Ambarvalia," "Dining-Room Tea,"** and the lovely opening sonnet . . . there is a movement, a perfect visualisation of image and a clarity of individual thought, that mark him as being of the great tradition, and endowed with the spontaneity that fellowship in that tradition implies.

In the volume published after his death, Rupert Brooke seems to me to have passed into full and rich communion with the great normal life of the world. There are three poems: **"All suddenly the Wind comes soft," "The way that Lovers use is this,"** and **"Mary and Gabriel,"** that are just a little formal perhaps, by no means valueless, but touched with some literary memory at a moment when the poetic faculty was not as alert as usual. There are two poems: **"There's Wisdom in Women,"** and **"Love,"** where the old detached and ironic mood that was once unreal returns not quite happily, and another, **"The Chilterns,"** in which it has been transmuted into a gracious and acceptable humour. Also there is a sonnet, **"Unfortunate,"** in which there is a reminiscence of the old mood, but it is now treated very reverently and with superb psychological insight. For the rest we have thrilling and adventurous beauty from beginning to end. There is no more tender landscape in English poetry than **"Grantchester,"** suffused as it is with a mood that never changes and yet passes between the wittiest laughter and the profoundest emotion with perfect naturalness. The subject-matter throughout the book no longer forces us to dissent or question. It has become wholly merged in the corporate art, and we accept it unhesitatingly as we accept the content of all splendid work. As in all really fine achievement in poetry, there is in his choice of form a glad acceptance and development of the traditions that have been slowly evolved through generations, and a perfect subjection of those forms to his own personality, until a sonnet becomes as definitely his own as if he had invented the external structure. We find, too, that the early constraint, even though it led to a touch of falsity at the time, has not been without its uses. The common emotions of the world he has, after jealous waiting, truly discovered and won for himself, unstaled of the world's usage. His passion is extraordinarily clean, burning among all simple things, clear, untroubled, ecstatic. Except in the two of three pages of which I have spoken, we find everywhere an almost fierce renunciation of anything that would not stir the plain knitters in the sun, with an unwearying determination to translate all this common simple life into the most exact and stirring beauty. It is true that in one or two cases, notably **"Heaven,"** the image that he creates of this simplicity of passion is such as not to relate itself easily at first glance to the clear normal thought that is nevertheless its basis if for a moment we consider its significance. When the poet elects to make brief intellectual holiday, so long as he does so in the terms of his own personality, we should do nothing but make holiday gladly with him. And we may well do so at intervals in a book that moves in the high consciousness of rare but natural poetic achievement, alert with the freshness and daring of splendid youth, grave in that profoundest knowledge which is imagination; a book that, will surely pass to vigorous immortality. (pp. 184-88)

John Drinkwater, "Rupert Brooke," in his *Prose Papers*, Elkin Mathews, 1918, pp. 174-92.

EDWARD A. McCOURT
(essay date 1944)

[McCourt is an Irish-born Canadian educator and critic. In the following excerpt, he surveys Brooke's poetry, finding his war sonnets most representative of his personal philosophy.]

Brooke's popularity has suffered a marked decline, particularly during the past decade. Part of the decline is due to the inevitable reaction which always follows excessive praise; but in addition Brooke, more than most poets, has been the victim of that sincere but some-times fatal form of flattery—imitation. As a rule, widespread imitation ultimately creates antagonism towards the thing imitated, and at least two of Brooke's poems, **"Grantchester"** and **"The Great Lover,"** have suffered an undeserved fate. Since the appearance of Brooke's collected poems, prefaced by Edward Marsh's sensitive memoir, in 1918, a thousand earnest versifiers, mostly female, have proclaimed in halting iambics their passionate devotion to assorted tastes, smells, feels, articles of household furniture and kitchen crockery, until **"The Great Lover"** has come to be judged not on the basis of its own very considerable merits, but on those of the unspeakable brood of whimsies to which it has given rise. To a lesser degree **"Grantchester"** has been similarly damned.

But the main reason for the decline of Brooke's popularity is to be found in the lack of spiritual identity between him and his successors. The faith in the ultimate triumph of Justice, the conviction that one can do no better than to die for one's country, implicit in at least three of the five sonnets of the *1914* sequence, find no echo in the work of those who came after. For the disillusioned poets of the 20's, whose prophet was T. S. Eliot and whose testament *The Wasteland,* life was without meaning. . . . To men like Eliot, Sassoon and their fellows, the faith of Rupert Brooke must have seemed like the naivete of a child brought up on William Ernest Henley and the laureate poems of Alfred Lord Tennyson.

Nor is there any more in common between Brooke and the militant revolutionists of the 30's. It is true that while at Cambridge he had been a member—ultimately President—of the Fabian Society, but his radicalism was evidence not so much of a social conscience as of a boyish desire to shock his conservative friends. In the early 1900's most of the Cambridge undergraduate intellectuals joined the Fabian Society as a matter of course, but in Brooke's time at least their interest in social and political reform was rather superficial. Brooke was at heart essentially conservative, and after leaving Cambridge does not seem to have bothered his head very much about the state of society. An occasional doctrinaire cliché—"In strikes the men are always right"—adorns his correspondence, but his interest clearly lay in other directions. For this and other reasons, most of the poets of the 30's, profoundly agitated by the class struggle, and by the seeming need of evolving new techniques through which to communicate their ideas, have found little in Brooke to admire.

More than a quarter of a century has passed since he died, so that it should now be in a measure possible to separate the reality from the myth and pass impartial judgment upon the nature of his achievement. On the one hand . . . we are far enough removed from Brooke in time to be unaffected by considerations of personality; on the other hand, we are still sufficiently aware of the spiritual trends of the last two decades to see how far Brooke's loss of reputation has been the consequence of a critical attitude not primarily concerned with aesthetic values.

A re-reading of Brooke is likely to confirm the impression that for some years following his death he was absurdly overpraised. . . . It is true that Brooke usually exhibits the technical competence which is one of the distinguishing attributes of Georgian verse, and the authentic poetic note is frequently present. But much of his early work is marred by imitativeness, not merely of phrasing—a characteristic fault in young writers—but of actual substance. Too often he seems to record the emotional and imaginative experiences of someone other than himself. He had read widely, and his mind sometimes gave back what it had received before the process of transmutation was complete. The verses of a hundred poets echo in his own,—John Donne in such a passage as:

> . . . we love, and gape,
> Fantastic shape to mazed fantastic shape,
> Straggling, irregular, perplexed, embossed,
> Grotesquely twined, extravagantly lost
> By crescive paths and strange protuberant ways
> From sanity and from wholeness and from grace—

Alice Meynell, in the delicate opening lines of **"Day That I Have Loved"**:

> Tenderly, day that I have loved, I close your eyes,
> And smooth your quiet brow, and fold your thin
>   dead hands—

and Ernest Dowson in the sensuous sentimental melancholy of **"The Wayfarers"**:

> Oh, I'll remember, but . . . each crawling day
> Will pale a little your scarlet lips, each mile
> Dull the dear pain of your remembered face.

Too much, however, has been made of Brooke's indebtedness to Keats. Such a poem as **"The Great Lover"** undoubtedly shows the poet rejoicing in the bands that bind him to the earth,—but this, after all, is a joy common to many men. Lines such as:

> . . . the cold
> Graveness of iron; moist black earthen mould;
> Sleep; and high places; footprints in the dew;
> And oaks; and brown horse-chestnuts, glossy-new;
> And new-peeled sticks; and shining pools on
>   grass;—

have the unadorned concreteness of portraiture. In them there is none of the sensuous music of:

> The coming musk-rose, full of dewy wine,
> The murmurous haunt of flies on summer eves,

or

> . . . magic casements opening on the foam
> Of perilous seas, in fairy lands forlorn.

In his own time Brooke enjoyed some reputation as a rather daring realist, and at least two of his poems, **"Lust"** and **"A Channel Passage,"** aroused a good deal of criticism on the grounds that the first was indecent, the second disgusting. Edward Marsh, after reading **"A Channel Passage,"** "expressed an apologetic preference for poems that [he] could read at meals," and Brooke was moved to defend himself.

> There are common and sordid things—situations and details—that may suddenly bring all tragedy, or at least the brutality of actual emotions, to you. I rather grasp relievedly at them, after I've beaten vain hands in the rosy mists of poets' experiences. Lear's button, and Hilda Lessways turning the gas suddenly on, and—but you know more of them than I. Shakespeare's not unsympathetic—'My mistress's eyes are nothing like the sun.' And the emotions of a sea-sick lover seem to me at least as poignant as those of the hero who has 'brain-fever' . . . .

Both **"Lust"** and **"A Channel Crossing"** are likely to strike coldly on the reader to-day. **"Lust"** is a self-conscious attempt, on the part of an emotionally immature poet, to shock his elders:

> . . . I starved for you;
> My throat was dry and my eyes hot to see.
> Your mouth so lying was most heaven in view,
> And your remembered smell most agony.

It is not likely that even Brooke himself intended such lines to be taken as a serious record of intense physical experience. **"Lust"** smacks of an academic exercise in which the poet sets himself the task of creating a certain pre-conceived effect and doesn't quite succeed. The same is true of **"A Channel Passage."** The poem might revolt the reader, if its strict attention to physical detail was not so patently designed to achieve precisely that end.

The fact is that when Brooke attempted to write in realistic vein he went against the grain of his own temperament. For he was not primarily a realist at all, as he himself would have us believe, but an out-and-out romanticist. But a boyish love of sensation, of being reputedly worldly and cynical, is responsible for a spiritual dichotomy apparent in much of his early verse, and most obviously in such a poem as **"Menelaus and Helen,"** where the true romanticist and the cynical pursuer are exhibited side by side:

> Hot through Troy's ruin Menelaus broke
> To Priam's palace, sword in hand, to sate
> On that adulterous whore a ten years' hate
> And a king's honour. Through red death, and
>   smoke,
> And cries, and then by quieter ways he strode,
> Till the still innermost chamber fronted him.
> He swung his sword, and crashed into the dim
> Luxurious bower, flaming like a god.

High sat white Helen, lonely and serene.
He had not remembered that she was so fair,
And that her neck curved down in such a way;
And he felt tired. He flung the sword away,
And kissed her feet, and knelt before her there,
The perfect Knight before the perfect Queen.

This is an admirable example of poetry in a traditional romantic vein. The sonnet is complete in itself, but it is necessary to shock the reader, and so a second part is added, showing Menelaus and Helen in old age:

> . . . Menelaus bold
> Waxed garrulous, and sacked a hundred Troys
> 'Twixt noon and supper. And her golden voice
> Got shrill as he grew deafer. And both were old.
>
> Often he wonders why on earth he went
> Troyward, or why poor Paris ever came.
> Oft she weeps, gummy-eyed and impotent;
> Her dry shanks twitch at Paris' mumbled name.
> So Menelaus nagged; and Helen cried;
> And Paris slept on by Scamander side.

In the first sonnet the real Brooke speaks; in the second, the poseur. Happily, towards the end of his life, when he was profoundly stirred by the great emotional experience of participation in war, he had wisdom enough to speak only the truth.

"Grantchester" and "The Great Lover," both belonging to the years immediately preceding the first World War, are fundamentally romantic. There is a good deal of artificially engendered sentiment in "Grantchester," but there can be no questioning the sincerity of "The Great Lover." In the expression of joy in the common things of life—in the passionate yearning for immortality which breaks through in the line, "O never a doubt that somewhere I shall wake!"— "The Great Lover" is the spiritual antithesis of those poems in which Brooke struggled to achieve stark reality and seldom got beyond adolescent affectation.

Of the remaining poems which precede the *1914* sequence several seem worth remembering; in particular, "Heaven," a brilliantly conceived little satire on the anthropomorphism of popular theology, and the fine sonnet, "The Hill," in which Brooke for once succeeds in striking a true realistic note. "The Hill" is an artful and moving expression of the poet's awareness that the things he cherishes most in life are not enduring, and of his wistful regret at the passing of the fine and lovely dreams that transfigure youth:

> "We are earth's best, that learnt her lesson here.
> Life is our cry. We have kept the faith" we said;
> "We shall go down with unreluctant tread
> Rose-crowned into the darkness" . . . Proud we
>   were,
> And laughed, that had such brave true things to say.
> And then you suddenly cried, and turned away.

Otherwise there does not seem to be a great deal in the early Brooke that is likely to survive, although even his most commonplace poems are frequently illuminated by fine individual lines, like

> And evening hush, broken by homing wings—

and

> One face, with lips than autumn-lilies tenderer,
> And voice more sweet than the far plaint of viols is,
> Or the soft moan of any grey-eyed lute-player.

It is in the *1914* sequence that Brooke for the first time speaks with the assurance that is born of faith. Hitherto all had been uncertainty and doubt, but Britain's entry into war and the tragic slaughter that so quickly ensued inspired Brooke to moving and passionate utterance. What he had to say he said with a conviction, an intense moral earnestness, that commanded immediate attention. And never was his control over his medium more flawless, never his choice of words more subtle. As technical achievements, the five sonnets which make up the sequence are beyond praise.

But technique is not enough in itself to win either passing popularity or enduring reputation. The popularity of the *1914* sequence is accounted for by the fact that through it Brooke expressed perfectly the mood of the moment. He was the mouthpiece of the generation who, in Mr. Churchill's words, were moving "blithely and resolutely" forward into battle. He said what the young men of 1914 wanted to say, and what their elders wanted to hear. To those who doubted that the youth of England were prepared to pay the full price which freedom demanded, the second sonnet, "Safety," offered ready assurance:

> We have built a house that is not for Time's throwing.
> We have gained a peace unshaken by pain for ever.
> War knows no power. Safe shall be my going,
> Secretly armed against all death's endeavour;
> Safe though all safety's lost; safe where men fall;
> And if these poor limbs die, safest of all.

To those who mourned, the third sonnet, with its majestic and thrilling note of pride in the achievement of the dead, offered courage and consolation:

> Blow, bugles blow! They brought us, for our dearth,
> Holiness, lacked so long, and Love, and Pain.
> Honour has come back, as a king, to earth,
> And paid his subjects with a royal wage;
> And Nobleness walks in our ways again;
> And we have come into our heritage.

But the great poet is more than the voice of his generation; he is a prophet as well. Indeed, many of the greatest poets have been in revolt against their time, as witness Milton in his last years, Burns, Wordsworth, Shelley, Browning, Tennyson before he assumed the Laureateship. But Rupert Brooke is not a prophet. The faith he proclaims is the simple nationalistic faith of his own day, perfectly expressed in the opening lines of the concluding sonnet of the sequence:

> If I should die, think only this of me;
> That there's some corner of a foreign field
> That is forever England.

But traditional patriotism has largely ceased to be an inspirational force. Hence it is that the reader of today, acutely conscious of the fact that the forces of good and evil are not separated by international boundaries, and haunted by the dream of that universal brotherhood or at least understanding which alone can ensure lasting peace, finds little in Brooke that is of importance to the present generation.

But it is not fair to suggest that none of the sonnets of the sequence has meaning beyond its own time. The fourth sonnet, "The Dead," has little relation to any particular time or place. It makes clear that the poet of "The Great Lover," who yearned for the things of earth and lamented their passing, has developed spiritually to the point where he is able to accept without regret the fact of death, and to find in it a beauty surpassing anything that he has found in life. There is no other poem in Brooke which quite matches "The Dead" in its spirit of austere, passionless serenity, and there are few in English poetry:

> These hearts were woven of human joys and cares,
> Washed marvellously with sorrow, swift to mirth.
> The years had given them kindness. Dawn was theirs,
> And sunset, and the colours of the earth.
> These had seen movement, and heard music; known
> Slumber and waking; loved; gone proudly friended;
> Felt the quick stir of wonder; sat alone;
> Touched flowers and furs and cheeks. All this is ended.
>
> There are waters blown by changing winds to laughter
> And lit by the rich skies, all day. And after,
> Frost, with a gesture, stays the waves that dance
> And wandering loveliness. He leaves a white
> Unbroken glory, a gathered radiance,
> A width, a shining peace, under the night.

(pp. 149-56)

Edward A. McCourt, "Rupert Brooke: A Re-Appraisal," in *The Dalhousie Review,* Vol. 24, No. 2, July, 1944, pp. 148-56.

CHRISTOPHER HASSALL
(essay date 1956)

[Hassall was an English poet, playwright, biographer, and librettist. In the following excerpt, he traces the development of Brooke's artistry.]

[Brooke's] earliest published poems were written in 1903 when he was sixteen. Until April 1909 (when he composed the sonnet **'Oh death shall find me'** and **'The Voice'**) he wrote nothing of much value except, perhaps, **'Seaside'** . . . , and yet this period, when he was at first luxuriating in, and then trying to throw off, the influence of the 'nineties, constitutes a third of his whole output. Nothing much more of note was done until a year later when he wrote **'Dust'** and **'Dining-room Tea.'** The latter deserves rather special notice. One imagines a young man who has been reading Donne's *The Ecstasy* in a room upstairs (the poem records an actual experience he had among his friends at Limpsfield) being summoned by a decorous bell to join the family for a meal. He goes down to the dining-room with one of the great love poems of the world still murmuring in the back of his head, enters the Edwardian social scene (one visualizes it like the second act of a play by Pinero) and walks straight into an imaginative experience which makes a deep impression upon him. . . . It may seem invidious to speak of such a masterpiece in the same breath with Brooke's light-weight poem, but he was clearly aiming at nothing more profound than what he precisely and, for the first time, with delicate artistry accomplished. It was a distinct stage in his development. There is no evidence, of course, for what he was actually reading during that week-end. . . . His copy [of Donne's poetry] is underscored in pencil at the lines 'All day the same our postures were, And we said nothing all the day.' In Brooke's case, this time in a social setting, in circumstances far less intense, and only for a moment, the indoor light seemed to be falling 'on stiller flesh, and body breathless'. This is not to suggest that the one poem is derived from the other. The discovery of a master has often led the young poet, not so much to the writing of pastiche, as to the discovery of *himself.* An instant of revelation while reading a poem is enough to show at once a new aspect of life and a way of communicating it. Although it was not Donne whom Brooke resembled when his individual character was fully apparent, as we shall see, he never quite abandoned the master who had rescued him from the late-Victorian 'decadence'. In the second and best of his war sonnets . . . there is a direct and conscious quotation from *The Anniversarie* on which the whole poem, again one of his most successful, is built as a variation.

After 'Dining-room Tea' another year elapsed before we notice a change. This time (in 'Thoughts on the Shape of the Human Body,' for instance) it is hardly to be wondered at that there should be signs of Jacobean rhetoric, since much of the past year had been spent among the texts of the old dramatists. Then in 1912 . . . came 'The Old Vicarage, Grantchester,' another lightweight poem, again successful, but this time on a more expansive scale and at last, most splendidly, a masterpiece of his own.

The difference between the new manner and the old can best be measured by comparing two poems in the same metre and almost identical in theme, 'The Fish' (March 1911) and 'Heaven' (December 1913), both good poems, but the latter in an altogether superior category. 'The Fish' will only be read because it is by the author of 'Heaven.' This applies to almost all his poetry before 1912—which is more than three-quarters of the whole. (pp. xxxviii-xl)

After that short burst in the spring of 1912, practically nothing more that is worthwhile was written until he was at Mataiea in the Pacific a year and a half later. Probably the first to come were the fine sonnets, 'Clouds' and 'Psychical Research.' He had been constantly badgered by [Edward] Marsh to write more verse now that he was free of the *Westminster* letters. 'You have achieved your instrument,' Marsh wrote to him in Tahiti, 'and I expect a time will come when you will want to play on it again. . . . By the way, when I made my impertinent remark about your running Love to death, or whatever I said, I didn't mean love as a subject, but Love with a capital L as an abstraction, it seemed to be becoming a mannerism of style.' Such was the gentle hint from London, but already, determined to oblige his friend by avoiding abstractions at least for once, Brooke had written 'The Great Lover,' almost in a spirit of defiance, a poem which is little more than a list of concrete images, and a curiously successful list it is, in that the items are so managed as to add up to a unit of poetry. 'Retrospect' and 'Tiare Tahiti' also came of this same Tahiti vintage. By comparison, the five war sonnets of December in the same year, which suddenly made his reputation, are slightly retrogressive. The heroic theme which circumstances had thrust upon him could not have been treated in the serio-comic manner which had become peculiarly his.

Since May 1912, having learned what he could from Donne, he had brought to his verse something of his own nature, a quality light-in-hand and, so to speak, playful, which brought him into the neighbourhood of Marvell. And there, with Marvell, helped a little to shine rather than overshadowed by his poetical ancestor, he belongs. Although the last lines of the 'Psychical Research' sonnet are a close parallel of a passage in Marvell's *Dialogue between Soul and Body*, I suspect that this was a coincidence. Granted the discovery of Donne, I think it was in Brooke's nature to develop in this direction. The intellectual parlour-game he played with the Platonic Ideas in 'Tiare Tahiti,' for instance, would have been just to the taste of Marvell complaining 'by the tide of Humber'. And as to 'tone of voice', if a young player in a literary guessing game were to be confronted with 'Annihilating all that's made To a green thought in a green shade' and were to guess 'Brooke' he would lose a mark, and perhaps the game, but he would be no fool.

Within less than three months of finishing the war sonnets (January 1915) he was entering on a new stage of progress, or so I believe, although there are only a few fragments to go by. . . . [Knowing] that a hazardous campaign was imminent, he had begun, I suspect, to anticipate not his own death so much as the loss of his friends. His theme was love of country, in a far broader sense than was implied in the war sonnets ('In Avons of the heart her rivers run'), and sacrificial death. Only one short poem in blank verse (itself a new departure for him) and a few disconnected sentences exist to hint at this, but any scrupulous follower of his development, who pays Brooke the compliment of taking him a little more seriously than at first glance he may seem to warrant, will detect these beginnings of a change. . . . One can only judge a man by what he has actually done to his satisfaction, and so, in considering Brooke, one must go back to what might have been called his early Marvell period (1912-1914) in order to assess his contribution to poetry. It is distinctive and delightful, but a little more of life and another poem might have made it look by comparison rather small. (pp. xli-xliv)

The quality peculiar to Brooke is a combination of wit and emotional feeling, not alternating, as in Byron, but inextricably at one, so that the conception of the poem, as well as each of its details, is a witticism. The quality is of course what we have come to know as 'metaphysical'. In 'Tiare Tahiti' or 'The Old Vicarage' the gravity makes fun of itself, the levity takes itself seriously. Is he sincere? one asks. Does he *really* want so much to go back to Grantchester? Does he *honestly* want to know what there is for tea? Or is the whole thing just a decorative verbal gesture? And while we are wondering, the poem has quietly come and gone, not wanting to stay for question, like the ghost in *Hamlet*. It was a delicate, slight thing, with a life and a will of its own, and saw no good reason why it should hang about while we made these plodding, cerebral enquiries. What we did manage to catch was an undertone of simple, carefully measured music. (pp. li-lii)

Perhaps it would be easier for Brooke if he were not *quite* so engaging. One feels the Georgian self-consciousness in the presence of an audience, and that the poem was posted when the ink was hardly dry and forthwith delivered on a salver in the drawing-room, or is it the dining-room where, contrary to usual custom, tea is laid? At any rate it is a world of gracious living, too recent in time to be regarded objectively as 'historical', too remote—almost incredibly remote—in spirit to be thoroughly understood. It is in fact (as are the poems) 'old-fashioned'. The grace, the amplitude, the air of sumptuous living, the rooted hopefulness, all are gone. And Brooke realized their transience. There is a passage in one of his letters in which he seems almost to see himself and his world with our latter-day eyes and to be anticipating our slightly critical (and perhaps envious) remarks about his conscious charm, so proper to an age of gracious literary manners, his unaustere view of things, his radiant . . . optimism. (pp. lii-liii)

> With such superb work to do, and with the wild adventure of it all, and with the other minutes (too many of them) given to the enchantment of being even for a moment alive in a world of real matter (not that imitation gilt stuff one gets in Heaven) and actual people—I have no time now to be a pessimist.

It is that gone world of 'real matter' which he evokes in his prose writings, more in the manner of the telling, than in what he tells. It may remind those who have too readily accepted the symbolic Soldier figure as the beginning and end of the matter that Brooke was a man-about-town in a time of peace, Cambridge scholar-poet and traveller about a globe where men had the wits, and the world still had the time, for leisurely and lighthearted discussions on the Beautiful and the Good. (pp. liii-liv)

Christopher Hassall, in his introduction to *The Prose of Rupert Brooke* by Rupert Brooke, edited by Christopher Hassall, Sidgwick and Jackson, 1956, pp. ix-liv.

BERNARD BERGONZI

(essay date 1965)

[An English novelist, scholar, and essayist, Bergonzi has written extensively on the works of H. G. Wells, T. S. Eliot, and other major figures of twentieth-century literature. In the following excerpt, he examines Brooke's war poetry, objecting to its inclusion of personal elements amid those Bergonzi considers more representative of "popular feeling".]

[Of] all the myths which dominated the English consciousness during the Great War the greatest, and the most enduring, is that which enshrines the name and memory of Rupert Brooke: in which three separate elements—Brooke's personality, his death, and his poetry (or some of it)—are fused into a single image. Brooke was the first of the 'war poets'; a quintessential young Englishman; one of the fairest of the nation's sons; a ritual sacrifice offered as evidence of the justice of the cause for which England fought. His sonnet, **'The Soldier'**, is among the most famous short poems in the language. If the Tolstoyan theory of art had any validity it would be one of the greatest—as, indeed, it is considered to be by the numerous readers for whom the excellence of poetry lies in the acceptability of its sentiments rather than in the quality of its language. (p. 36)

To extricate Brooke's poetry from the personal legend in which it played a merely contributory role is not at all easy, but the critic and literary historian must make the attempt. In the first place, the poetry can best be understood by placing it in its proper context in the Georgian movement. . . . [No] matter how remote and old-fashioned the Georgians may seem now, at the time they regarded themselves, and were regarded, as somewhat revolutionary. Their comparative bluntness of language, and liking for 'ordinary', unpretentious subjects, was not to everyone's taste; and Brooke found himself in a good deal of trouble over one of his early poems, **'A Channel Passage'**, which deals with love and sea-sickness in a self-consciously brutal fashion. . . . (pp. 37-8)

In one of Brooke's most famous poems, **'The Old Vicarage, Grantchester'**, we have a lucid instance of the Georgian concentration on rural England; this poem was written in Berlin, and Christopher Hassall observes that Brooke originally intended to call it 'The Sentimental Exile', and suggests that the public might in that case have read it less solemnly. This is possibly true, and such a reading may have been closer to Brooke's intention; the fact remains that the whole poem displays a kind of switchback irregularity of tone, alternatively satirizing the Cambridge landscape (and by implication the poet) and idealizing it. Such uncertainty is a perhaps inevitable concomitant of Georgian Little Englandism: it is difficult for the retreat to a rural fastness, no matter how delectable, to be entirely wholehearted. At the same time as he wrote **'The Old Vicarage'** Brooke was concerned about the possible advent of a European war.

What we think of as the characteristic 'war poetry' of 1914-18 was, in fact, a continuation of the Georgian movement by poets who, volunteering in defence of the England they had written about so lovingly, found themselves thrust into the melting pot which Forster had envisaged at the conclusion of *Howards End*. . . . In a prose piece [Brooke] indicates the state of mind of innumerable young men like himself at the start of the war: **'An Unusual Young Man'**, published in the *New Statesman* on 29th August 1914, supposedly describes the state of mind of a friend on the outbreak of war, though this figure is clearly a vehicle for Brooke's own opinions. He thinks about Germany, a country he knows and likes, and is incredulous at the idea of an armed conflict between England and Germany. . . . Brooke continues the essay with a rhapsodic description of the Southern English landscape in a passage recalling the similar descriptions in *Howards End*. This passage has been subjected to a withering analysis by Cyril Connolly in *Enemies of Promise;* Connolly describes it in this way: ' "England had declared war," he says to himself, "what had Rupert Brooke better feel about it?" His equipment is not equal to the strain and his language betrays the fact . . . ' As a critical judgment this is undoubtedly penetrating. And yet it is not the most interesting thing that one can say about this piece of writing: Brooke was having to fake up an emotional attitude precisely because the experience of England being involved in a major war was so alien and ungraspable. There was, too, a curious interplay between the literary cult of rural England fostered by the Georgians, and the degree of patriotism that it is traditionally proper to feel when one's country goes to war: Brooke's feelings are very literary indeed in their mode of expression, but are not thereby prevented from being genuine. As Connolly says, Brooke's equipment was unequal to the strain: but so was that of every other writer in those days. (pp. 40-1)

[Brooke's *1914* sonnets] are not very amenable to critical discussion. They are works of very great mythic power, since they formed a unique focus for what the English felt, or wanted to feel, in 1914-15: they crystallize the powerful archetype of Brooke, the young Apollo, in his sacrificial role of the hero-as-victim. Considered, too, as historical documents, they are of interest as an index to the popular state of mind in the early months of the war. But considered more narrowly and exactly as poems, their inadequacy is very patent. Such a judgment needs qualification. It is, for instance, a commonplace to compare Brooke's sonnets with the work of later war poets, notably Wilfred Owen. This seems to me to prove very little, except, in a purely descriptive way, that poets' attitudes changed profoundly as they learned more about the war. Beyond this one might as well attempt to compare the year 1914 and the year 1918. A more useful comparison is with Brooke's own earlier poetry, and with contemporary works that express a broadly similar state of mind. Brooke's poetic gifts were never robust, and he was very far from being the most talented of the Georgian group, but at his best he had a certain saving irony and detachment of mind, which, very naturally, were absent from the 1914 sonnets. At the same time, the negative aspects of his poetry, a dangerous facility of language and feeling, are embarrassingly in evidence. To compare like with like, the sonnets seem to me inferior to Kipling's 'For All We

Have and Are' and to Julian Grenfell's 'Into Battle', both products of the opening phase of the war.

One very pressing difficulty in reading these sonnets is that elements that can be called representative, expressing currents of popular feeling, are closely interwoven with others which are purely personal to Brooke himself. Thus, to take the octet of the first sonnet, **'Peace'**:

> Now, God be thanked Who has matched us with His
>   hour,
> And caught our youth, and wakened us from sleep-
>   ing,
> With hand made sure, clear eye, and sharpened
>   power,
> To turn, as swimmers into cleanness leaping,
> Glad from a world grown old and cold and weary,
> Leave the sick hearts that honour could not move,
> And half-men, and their dirty songs and dreary,
> And all the little emptiness of love!

I do not think I am alone in finding these lines disagreeably lax in movement, and excessively facile in much of their detail; in a phrase like 'old and cold and weary' the words seem to be thrusting ahead of the sense. Yet there can be no doubt that they expressed quite closely a dominant state of mind . . . : a turning aside from the stately familiar, and an eager acceptance of new and unknown experience. . . . Brooke was also expressing certain wholly personal preoccupations, whose nature is apparent from Hassall's biography. Professor D. J. Enright, in a sharp comment on these poems, has asked, referring to the line 'the little emptiness of love', 'whose love?' On the level of intention, at least, the love in question seems to be Brooke's long and gruelling affair with 'Ka'.

This self-regarding element is very much in evidence in the poems, cutting across their apparent glad transcendence of the merely personal; the result can be called theatrical, and it is this, rather than Brooke's blank ignorance of things that no one else at that time knew much about either, that makes the sonnets hard to accept as poems. In the most famous of them, **'The Soldier'**, Brooke uses the Georgian concentration on rural England as a focus for a meditation on his own possible death. He identifies his own body and the soil of England in an almost mystical fashion. . . . The oratorical tone . . . seems to be part of the poem's essential intention: not for nothing has it become a set-piece for recitation at school prize-giving days and similar public occasions. Yet though the poem aims at oratorical impersonality, it is also an insistently self-regarding performance. There is an unresolved conflict between a subjective lyric impulse, not at all sure of its language, and the assumed decorum of patriotic utterance. As Mr. Enright has observed: 'The reiteration of "England" and "English" is all very well; but an odd uncertainty as to whether the poet is praising England or himself—

"a richer dust"—remains despite that reiteration.' (pp. 41-4)

Bernard Bergonzi, "Poets I: Brooke, Grenfell, Sorley," in his *Heroes' Twilight: A Study of the Literature of the Great War,* Constable and Company Ltd., 1965, pp. 32-59.

JOHN LEHMANN
(essay date 1980)

[Lehmann is a noted English biographer, poet, editor, and critic. In the following excerpt, he assesses the merits of Brooke's travel writings as well as his war poetry.]

On 22 May 1913 Rupert left on his travels to America and further west. (p. 79)

Just before he left, Naomi Royde Smith, still literary editor of the *Westminster Gazette,* to which he had contributed so often over so many years, persuaded the editor-in-chief, J. A. Spender, to commission a series of articles from him about his travels. This made a vital difference to his finances for the trip, as his own funds were low. Indeed it is doubtful whether he could have travelled anything like as far or as long as he did if it had not been for this providential assignment.

The thirteen articles he wrote duly appeared in the *Westminster,* and were republished after his death [as **Letters from America**] . . . , with two other articles he sent to the *New Statesman.* (p. 82)

The *Westminster* articles reveal a new side to Rupert's talents, as an accomplished travel-writer. They are written with a restrained and graceful skill; the general tone is sophisticated and urbane, with a continual undertone of irony and humour. His descriptions of people he met, and above all places he visited, are witty and imaginative; and some of the bravura pieces, for instance the pictures of Niagara Falls and of Lake Louise, are fresh and poetic and exact. They undoubtedly strengthen the view of some of his contemporaries that his eventual literary career could have been even more as a prose writer than as a poet.

Landing in New York, his first impressions of America were overwhelming. He was struck above all by the way men dressed and walked along the streets.

The American by race [he wrote in his second article] walks better than us; more freely, with a taking swing, and almost with grace. How much of this is due to living in a democracy, and how much to wearing no braces, it is very difficult to determine. But certainly it is the land of belts, and therefore of more loosely moving bodies. This, and the padded shoulder of the coats, and the loosely cut trousers, make a figure more presentable, at a distance, than most urban civilizations turn out. Also, Americans take off their coats, which is sensible; and they can do it the more beautifully because they are belted, and not braced. They take their coats off anywhere and anywhen, and somehow it strikes the visitor as the most symbolic thing about them. They have not yet thought of discarding collars; but they are unashamedly shirt-sleeved. Any sculptor, seeking to figure their Republic in stone, must carve, in future, a young man in shirtsleeves, open-faced, and rather vulgar, straw hat on the back of his head, his trousers full and sloppy, his coat over his arm. The motto written beneath will be, of course, "This is some country".

The other aspect of America that struck him at once was the commercialism, the supremacy of Business, and therefore of advertising. 'Business,' he wrote, 'has developed insensibly into a Religion, in more than the light, metaphorical sense of the word. It has its ritual and theology, its high places and its jargon, as well as its priests and martyrs. America has a childlike faith in advertising. They advertise here, there, everywhere, and in all ways. Nothing is untouched.' (pp. 83-4)

Rupert's impressions of the United States are so fresh and alive that one is inclined to regret that he didn't explore further in New England, though on his return from the South Seas he visited Washington and Chicago, when his mind was full of island impressions; but he seemed determined to get away to Canada, perhaps longing for wider open spaces. . . . (p. 87)

It was the war sonnets that changed [Brooke] into the almost sacred, supreme poet-figure of his generation, the mellifluous mouthpiece of the sentiments that had before been half incoherently felt by all those English people who were struggling to make sense of the war into which they had so suddenly been plunged, and who clung to the hope that the trials and sufferings, still only mistily revealed, that lay before them could be considered as part of a crusade of right against wrong, as a testing ground of courage and belief in their own country and its cause.

At the same time it is possible that with a subsequent generation who saw the noble sentiments as glib idealism and unrealistic day-dreaming, his name might not have fallen into the disrepute that has lasted until today; a generation whose fathers and elder brothers had lived through the senseless horrors of the Flanders trenches, and who found in the poetry of Siegfried Sassoon, Wilfred Owen and Isaac Rosenberg the true response to modern warfare at its most futile and morally degrading. No thoughtful and sensitive young man could imaginably have gone into the fighting of the Second World War with the lines of Brooke's sonnets **'The Dead'** and **'Peace'** echoing in his mind to inspire his vision and steel his purpose. If, however, those son-

Rupert Brooke

nets had not been written, such young men might still have delighted in the lyrical freshness of **'Tiare Tahiti'**, the light-hearted nostalgia of **'Grantchester'**, and the debunking wit and technical skill of his remodelled fish poem, **'Heaven'**, and a number of others where the sentiment is not forced and the language keeps rhetoric under a more caustic intellectual control. That he had seen how important such discipline was is shown by his whole-hearted admiration for the poetry of John Donne. (pp. 132-33)

The chief weakness of [Brooke's] poetry—and it is a weakness markedly in contrast to the mastery in this particular sphere shown by Donne and by his almost equally admired Webster—was a preference for vague grandiloquence and high-sounding generalities in preference to the concrete word and the freshly illuminating image, the poetical cliché instead of the original imaginative discovery. It may be partly due to a lingering fondness for the affected romanticism of the nineties he had felt in his youthful phase; it continued to slip into his more mature poetry all too often when his mind was not working at top pressure.

Phrases such as 'in wise majestic melancholy train', 'some low sweet alley between wind and wind', 'dark scents whisper', 'the grey tumult of these after-years', 'song's nobility and wisdom holy', 'the heart of bravery swift and clean', which have a fine exalted ring

but when examined mean nothing precise at all, from time to time pad out his verses throughout his adult career and not merely his beginnings when he was searching for a style; in fact they become his style as soon as he forgets his wit and light-heartedness and abandons those realistic touches that so shocked the critics of his first book. With what relief, then, one comes across the precise and vivid images with which in **'The Great Lover'** he enumerates the concrete things that evoke his love in recollection: 'wet roofs, beneath the lamplight', 'the rough male kiss of blankets', 'the good smell of old clothes', 'brown horse-chestnuts, glossy new'; though even in this attractive and original, though imperfect, poem he cannot resist the glib poetical rhetoric of phrases such as 'the inenarrable godhead of delight' and 'out on the wind of Time, shining and streaming'.

The weakness of the war sonnets lies not merely in their even more fulsome use of such insubstantial rhetoric, but in the fundamental shallowness and inadequacy of the sentiments expressed in relation to the grimness of the challenge which faced the young men on the German as well as the British side. Two years after Rupert Brooke's death the nature of the beast was fully apparent to the armies engaged in the fighting, if not to the civilians in the comparative safety of Britain; but one should after all remember that before he left on the Dardanelles expedition Rupert had had a glimpse, which shocked and deeply affected his outlook, of the reality of modern mechanized slaughter and destruction.

The vague high-sounding generalities appear so profusely in the sonnets that it would be tedious to list them all. Worst of all, perhaps, in this respect is the second sonnet, **'Safety'.** The poet, addressing his beloved, enumerates the phenomena, 'all things undying', which make them feel 'safe':

The winds, and morning, tears of men and mirth
The deep night, and birds singing, and clouds flying,
And sleep, and freedom, and the autumnal earth.

Every image in these lines is obvious and of the most general kind, and contributes nothing concrete to the idea, or makes any imaginative discovery that can be called in any way original: it is little more than a lulling incantation of clichés. The same process is almost disastrously at work in the fourth sonnet, called **'The Dead'** like the third, in which we are bidden to lament the death of the young soldiers because their hearts were

Washed marvellously with sorrow, swift to mirth.
The years had given them kindness. Dawn was theirs,
And sunset, and the colours of the earth.
These had seen movement, and heard music. . . .

And when in their death they are compared with

the effect of frost on 'waves that dance / And wandering loveliness' (whatever that last phrase may mean), we are told that they leave 'a white

> Unbroken glory, a gathered radiance,
> A width, a shining peace, under the night',

one can only register astonishment that Brooke, who could be so precise when he liked, can crowd so many nouns denoting vaguely emotive general concepts, 'unbroken glory', 'gathered radiance', 'shining peace' into two lines.

The two most quoted and probably most popular sonnets—certainly most popular at the time—are the first, **'Peace'**, and the fifth, **'The Soldier'**. The first, **'Peace'**, is the sonnet that most successors of a younger generation, and probably most soldiers who saw more of the war than Rupert ever saw, have jibbed at as shallowy sentimental and unrealistic. What soldier, who had experienced the meaningless horror and foulness of the Western Front stalemate in 1916 and 1917, could think of it as a place to greet 'as swimmers into cleanness leaping' or as a welcome relief 'from a world grown old and cold and weary'? These are the sentiments of one who at least had had no opportunity to face the reality of twentieth-century warfare—killing and maiming and being killed and maimed in the most appalling ways by the most devilish devices of terror. To say that is not to deny admiration for those, in both wars, who were aware of what they were facing and chose it out of determination to defend what they believed was worth defending—and Rupert Brooke might well have been one of those if he had lived and been active as a soldier in 1917; nor to deny that such an attitude as finds expression in **'Peace'** was common to many poets, on both sides of the frontiers, in the curious excitement and hysteria that the outbreak of war in 1914 aroused.

What is peculiarly disturbing about **'Peace'** is that it gives sudden and violent expression to Rupert's always latent puritanism. The soldiers are awakened 'from sleeping' and are leaping 'into cleanness' in getting away from their everyday pursuits (though **'The Dead'** seems to express an entirely opposite point of view); fighting redeems a world 'grown old and cold and weary' even though it involves killing and destruction and waste; the whole of Rupert's past life is characterized as

> The sick hearts that honour could not move,
> And half-men, and their dirty songs and dreary,
> And all the little emptiness of love.

Who are these 'half-men' and 'sick hearts' unmoved by honour? What poet was singing 'dirty songs and dreary'? Were his passionate and unhappy involvements with Ka Cox and his new, joyful love for Cathleen Nesbitt to be brushed aside as 'all the little emptiness of love'? Or was he thinking again, obsessively, of the

emotional shocks he endured at Lulworth in the New Year of 1912, with Lytton Strachey and other denizens of Bloomsbury as the 'sick hearts' and 'half-men' who wounded him so mysteriously? And if so, why did they now become symbols of all that had made up civilian existence before the war, as if civilized peaceful living itself was only worth throwing away *in toto*?

'The Soldier' is as eloquent and skilful a piece of verse-making as anything Rupert ever produced, with its repeated plangent harping on the word 'England' and all the historic and patriotic overtones it evoked. The movement of the argument and the tone are both flawless, and one can easily see how in the anxious, emotional mood of the early months of the war it could bring tears to any sensitive eye. And yet, looked at dispassionately today, it is difficult not to feel that it is riddled with sentimentality and narcissistic fantasy, whatever he may have meant in imagining himself 'a pulse in the eternal mind' purified of all unworthy thought and feeling. Even at the time, while the guns were still thundering, there were not a few, and among them his intellectual peers, who questioned his attitudinizing. One of these, his fellow poet Charles Sorley, eight years younger, wrote to a friend when he heard of Rupert's death that he found the sonnet sequence over-praised:

> He is far too obsessed with his own sacrifice, regarding the going to war of himself (and others) as a highly intense, remarkable and sacrificial exploit, whereas it is merely the conduct demanded of him (and others) by the turn of circumstances, where non-compliance with this demand would have made life intolerable. It was not that "they" gave up anything of that list in one sonnet: but that the essence of these things had been endangered by circumstances over which he had no control, and he must fight to recapture them. He has clothed his attitude in fine words: but he has taken the sentimental attitude.

> (pp. 134-38)

John Lehmann, in his *Rupert Brooke: His Life and His Legend*, Weidenfeld & Nicolson, 1980, 178 p.

DALLAS PRATT
(essay date 1987)

[In the following excerpt, Pratt offers a favorable assessment of Brooke's verse while discussing the legends surrounding Brooke's life and character.]

Sub-lieutenant [Rupert] Brooke, when his life was cut short, was eagerly looking forward, in spite of a warning of heavy casualties, to the imminent invasion of

Turkey. Its purpose was to force a passage through the Dardanelles, destroy Gallipoli, and open the Black Sea to beleaguered Russia. As he wrote to his friend Violet Asquith, the Prime Minister's daughter, "I've never been quite so happy in my life, I think. Not quite so *pervasively* happy, like a stream flowing entirely to one end."

In just over twelve months, the poet's life had been dramatically transformed. A year before, he was saying farewell to Tahiti, after eight months in the South Sea islands, leaving behind "those lovely places and lovely people . . . going far away from gentleness and beauty and kindliness and the smell of the lagoons and the thrill of that dancing and the scarlet of the *flamboyants* and the white and gold of other flowers. . . ."

More tangible than these soon-to-fade memories were the manuscripts of poems he had brought home with him, or had already sent back, including **"Tiare Tahiti," "The Great Lover,"** and **"Heaven."** The last is a gentle satire on orthodox religion, in which the fish put forth their idea of Heaven. An excerpt is worth quoting to show how the poet, who was shortly to write the magnificent elegies of 1914, was also a master of seriocomic verse:

. . . Somewhere, beyond Space and Time,
Is wetter water, slimier slime!
But there (they trust) there swimmeth One
Who swam ere rivers were begun,
Immense, of fishy form and mind,
Squamous, omnipotent, and kind;
And under that Almighty Fin,
The littlest fish may enter in.
Oh! never fly conceals a hook,
Fish say, in the Eternal Brook,
And more than mundane weeds are there,
And mud, celestially fair;
Fat caterpillars drift around,
And paradisial grubs are found;
Unfading moths, immortal flies,
And the worm that never dies.
And in that Heaven of all their wish,
There shall be no more land, say fish.

Brooke arrived back in England on June 6, 1914. Six pleasant weeks passed seeing old friends and meeting new ones. The simple joys of Tahiti were exchanged for the sophisticated pleasures of lunch with Henry James and a memorable dinner with G. B. Shaw, J. M. Barrie, Yeats, Chesterton, and Mrs. Patrick Campbell. There was also a dinner, two days after Austria had declared war on Serbia, at 10 Downing Street. Brooke sat between Prime Minister Asquith and the latter's daughter Violet, and opposite Winston Churchill, First Lord of the Admiralty. Further contacts with Churchill and the discreet assistance of his close friend Edward Marsh, Private Secretary to the First Lord, resulted in Brooke's receiving a commission as sublieutenant in the Second Naval Brigade. In less than a week, on October 4, the Brigade sailed for Dunkirk in an effort to save Antwerp from the advancing Germans. They were too late: surrounded by thousands of refugees fleeing from the stricken city, the British retreated and were back in Dover just five days after leaving that port.

The declaration of war, the casualty lists which now included the names of many of his school friends, either killed or missing, and the tragedy he had witnessed in Belgium, fired Brooke with a new moral purpose. As Christopher Hassall writes in his admirable biography of the poet [*Rupert Brooke: A Biography,* 1972], "Everything he was once so passionately concerned about had dwindled in significance. . . . It was a sensation as of 'swimmers into cleanness leaping'; the forlorn tangle of his private existence, his obsessive disgust, the sense of futility and failure, were all resolved in the realization of one purpose." His discovery of this filled him with exultation; as he wrote to his friend in New York, Russell Loines, "Apart from the tragedy, I've never felt happier or better in my life than in those days in Belgium. And now I've the feeling of anger at a seen wrong—Belgium—to make me happier and more resolved in my work. I know that whatever happens I'll be doing some good, fighting to prevent *that.*"

But he was not destined to fight. Instead, in the last four months of 1914, he wrote five sonnets which rank among the most moving elegiac poems in the English language. Although they are about death, and death in a very poignant form, that of young men in war, still, grief for the agony, the broken body, the pouring out of "the red sweet wine of youth" is always tempered by an image of peace or of ultimate victory. So the poet writes of honor "come back, as a king, to earth," of "the laughing heart's long peace," of "safety with all things undying," and, again, of the heart, which

. . . all evil shed away,
A pulse in the eternal mind, no less
Gives somewhere back the thoughts by England
given.

In Sonnet IV, Death is symbolized as frost, staying "the waves that dance," but leaving

. . . a white
Unbroken glory, a gathered radiance,
A width, a shining peace, under the night.

"A gathered radiance": in this phrase the poet unconsciously summed up the effect he produced on many of his contemporaries. People were dazzled by his brilliance of mind and poetical gifts, his legendary life and death, and, inseparable from these, his charm of manner and physical beauty. H. W. Garrod said that "no one ever met him without being sensible that he belonged to the company of the gods." In Homer, disguised gods often revealed their divinity by a burst of radiance at the moment of departure for Olympus; so Rupert Brooke "gathered radiance" by the nature of his death and the classical appropriateness of his burial place, as if he too were passing into the company of the immortals. (pp. 14-18)

In the last chapter of his biography, Hassall has written very perceptively of the transformation of "man into marble" which occurred after Brooke's death. Just as the war had changed the romantic "young Apollo" and passionate rebel into a poet-soldier willing to die, as Winston Churchill put it, "for the dear England whose beauty and majesty he knew," so his death and the publication a few months later of *1914 and Other Poems* produced a second metamorphosis: that of Brooke into a heroic figure. Many of his friends and a minority of critics deplored the blurring of his "human" attributes, but the radiant myth appealed to a nation groping through the dark years of war. In the first decade after Brooke's death, the popularity of his poems challenged the records set in the previous century by Byron and Tennyson. Sales, not counting those in America, amounted to something like 300,000 copies.

Inevitably, a reaction set in as the memories of the war dimmed. In the edition of *Twentieth-Century Writing,* published in 1969 and edited by Kenneth Richardson, David L. Parkes writes:

> As a war poet Brooke is limited by the fact that he died in 1915 and did not succeed to the disillusioned realism of Owen and Rosenberg. He left behind a group of sonnets titled *1914* which upon his death gained immense popularity from a combination of almost jingoistic patriotism and a sense of the sentimental in the eclipse of youth. . . .

Indeed, Brooke's "war" poetry might appear thus to the youth of the 1960s, whose ingenuity was not directed, as Brooke's was, to getting accepted for military service, but more often to avoiding it. Today a more discerning reader will find not only the 1914 sonnets but also much of the earlier work vigorous and interesting. In addition to the poems already mentioned, a touch of genius is in **"Clouds," "The Fish,"** and **"Dining-Room Tea,"** to name just a few. (pp. 18-19)

[Much] of Rupert Brooke's poetry, as well as his letters and the vivid story of his life, wait to be rediscovered by a new generation of readers in this centennial year of his birth. It is true that some of his poems speak of death, and for the dead, but equally they speak of love and of the joy of living; of war, and of peace. He combines these opposites with a rich subtlety rarely surpassed in English literature, perhaps never better than in the sonnet entitled **"Safety"**:

> Dear! of all happy in the hour, most blest
> He who has found our hid security,
> Assured in the dark tides of the world at rest,
> And heard our word, "Who is so safe as we?"
> We have found safety with all things undying,
> The winds, and morning, tears of men and mirth,
> The deep night, birds singing, and clouds flying,
> And sleep, and freedom, and the autumnal earth.
> We have built a house which is not for Time's
>   throwing.
> We have gained a peace unshaken by pain forever.
> War knows no power. Safe shall be my going,
> Secretly armed against all death's endeavor;
> Safe though all safety's lost; safe where men fall;
> And if these poor limbs die, safest of all.

> (pp. 19-20)

Dallas Pratt, "Rupert Brooke's 'Gathered Radiance'," in *Columbia Library Columns,* Vol. 37, No. 1, November, 1987, pp. 12-20.

SOURCES FOR FURTHER STUDY

Cornford, Frances. "Rupert Brooke." *Time and Tide* 28, No. 1 (4 January 1947): 17-18, 20.

> Evaluation of Brooke's life and poetic achievement, occasioned by the publication of *The Poetical Works of Rupert Brooke* (edited by Geoffrey Keynes). Cornford highlights "the inevitable tragicness of love" as a prominent theme in Brooke's writings.

Delany, Paul. *The Neo-Pagans: Rupert Brooke and the Ordeal of Youth.* New York: The Free Press, 1987, 270 p.

> Biography examining Brooke "in the context of 'Neopaganism' " in order to "restore him to the true company he kept, and in which he can best be judged."

Hassall, Christopher. *Rupert Brooke: A Biography.* London: Faber and Faber, 1964, 556 p.

> Seminal critical biography.

Hastings, Michael. *The Handsomest Young Man in England: Rupert Brooke.* London: Michael Joseph, 1967, 240 p.

> Leisurely discussion of Brooke's life and works.

Pearsall, Robert Brainard. *Rupert Brooke: The Man and the Poet.* Amsterdam: Rodopi, 1974, 174 p.

> Traces chronologically the influences on and development of Brooke's thought and artistry.

Rogers, Timothy. *Rupert Brooke: A Reappraisal and Selection.* New York: Barnes & Noble, 1971, 231 p.

Seeks to "bring together the best of [Brooke's] writing, both in verse and prose, and to suggest (chiefly by doing so) a fairer basis for his appraisal."

Gwendolyn Brooks

1917-

American poet, novelist, editor, autobiographer, and author of children's books.

INTRODUCTION

A major contemporary poet and the first black American writer to win a Pulitzer Prize, Brooks is best known for her sensitive portraits of urban blacks who encounter racism and poverty in their daily lives. In her early work, Brooks avoided overt statements about the plight of many blacks in America, prompting critics to define the appeal of her poetry as "universal." During the late 1960s, however, her writing underwent a radical change in style and subject matter. Inspired by the black power movement and the militancy of such poets as Amiri Baraka (LeRoi Jones) and Haki R. Madhubuti (Don L. Lee), Brooks began to explore the marginality of black life through vivid imagery and forceful language and to recognize rage and despair among black people as her own.

Brooks was raised in Chicago, the eldest child of Keziah Wims Brooks, a schoolteacher, and David Anderson Brooks, a janitor who, because he lacked the funds to finish school, did not achieve his dream of becoming a doctor. According to George Kent, as a child Brooks "was spurned by members of her own race because she lacked social or athletic abilities, a light skin, and good grade hair." Brooks was hurt by such rejection, and she found solace in her writing. Impressed by her early poems, her mother predicted she would become "the lady Paul Laurence Dunbar." Brooks received compliments on her poems and encouragement from James Weldon Johnson and Langston Hughes, prominent writers with whom she initiated correspondence and whose readings she attended in Chicago. By the age of sixteen, Brooks had compiled a substantial portfolio, including about seventy-five published poems. After graduating from Wilson Junior College in 1936, she worked briefly as a cleaning woman and then as a secretary to a "spiritual advisor" who sold potions and charms to residents of the Mecca, a

Chicago tenement building. During this time she participated in poetry workshops at Chicago's South Side Community Art Center, producing verse that would appear in her first published volume, *A Street in Bronzeville* (1945).

At the request of publishers, Brooks focused on her experiences as a black American in *A Street in Bronzeville*. The work chronicles the aspirations and disappointments of citizens living in Bronzeville, a black district in Chicago that serves as the setting for many of her poems. The first part of *A Street in Bronzeville* provides a realistic depiction of the neighborhood; the second section, a sequence of twelve sonnets entitled "Gay Chaps at the Bar," explores the unfair treatment of blacks in the Armed Forces during World War II. This work introduced thematic issues that would feature prominently in Brooks's works during the next two decades: family life, war, the quest for contentment and honor, and the hardships caused by racism and poverty. Her second collection of poetry, *Annie Allen* (1949), for which she received the Pulitzer Prize, is similar in structure to a prose narrative. The poems in *Annie Allen* focus on the growth of the title character from childhood to adulthood in an environment replete with indigence and discrimination. Critics generally praised Brooks for her subtle humor and irony, her skillful handling of conventional stanzaic forms, and her invention of the sonnet-ballad, a verse structure integrating colloquial speech and formal diction. Brooks's next major collection of poetry, *The Bean Eaters* (1960), details the attempts of ghetto inhabitants to escape feelings of hopelessness. The verse in *Selected Poems* (1963) evidences Brooks's growing interest in social issues and the influence of the early years of the civil rights movement.

Brooks experienced a change in political consciousness and artistic direction after witnessing the combative spirit of several young black authors at the Second Black Writers' Conference at Fisk University in 1967. She later explained her revelations in her autobiography, *Report from Part One* (1972): "I—who have 'gone the gamut' from an almost angry rejection of my dark skin by some of my brainwashed brothers and sisters to a surprised queenhood in the new Black sun—am qualified to enter at least the kindergarten of new consciousness now. . . . I have hopes for myself." With *In the Mecca* (1968), which most critics regard as her transitional volume, Brooks abandoned traditional poetic forms in favor of free verse and increased her use of vernacular to make her works more accessible to black readers. Based on Brooks's experiences working in the Mecca, the poems chronicle Mrs. Sallie's search for her missing daughter, Pepita, whom she later discovers has been murdered by a fellow resident of the Mecca.

In *Riot* (1969) and *Family Pictures* (1970), Brooks evoked the revolutionary legacy of such slain black activists as Medgar Evers, Malcolm X, and Martin Luther King, Jr., and examined the social upheavals of the late 1960s with objectivity and compassion. While her concern for the black nationalist movement and racial solidarity continued to dominate her verse in the early 1970s, the energy and optimism of *Riot* and *Family Pictures* were replaced with disenchantment resulting from the divisiveness of the civil rights and black power movements. In *Beckonings* (1975) and *To Disembark* (1981), Brooks urged blacks to break free from the repression of white American society, advocating violence and anarchy as acceptable means. The literary quality of her later poetry has been debated by critics. Some commentators have faulted her for sacrificing formal complexity and subtlety for political polemic. According to D. H. Melhem, however, Brooks "enriches both black and white cultures by revealing essential life, its universal identities, and the challenge it poses to a society beset with corruption and decay."

Having received over forty honorary doctorates and served as Consultant in Poetry to the Library of Congress from 1985-86, Brooks continues to read her works throughout the United States. She established and continues to support the Poet Laureate Awards competition for young writers in Illinois in an effort to bring poetry to a larger audience of young black people. As she revealed in a 1974 interview, she wishes to "develop a style that will appeal to black people in taverns, black people in gutters, schools, offices, factories, prisons, the consulate; . . . to reach black people in pulpits, black people in mines, on farms, on thrones."

(For further information about Brooks's life and works, see *Authors in the News*, Vol. 1; *Black Writers*; *Concise Dictionary of American Literary Biography, 1941-1968*; *Contemporary Authors*, Vol. 1; *Contemporary Authors New Revision Series*, Vols. 1, 27; *Contemporary Literary Criticism*, Vols. 1, 2, 4, 5, 15, 49; *Dictionary of Literary Biography*, Vols. 5, 76; and *Something About the Author*, Vol. 6.)

CRITICAL COMMENTARY

HOUSTON A. BAKER, JR.
(essay date 1972)

[Baker, a poet and critic, examined a "vernacular" theory of black American cultural expression in his critical work *Blues, Ideology, and Afro-American Literature* (1984). In the following essay, originally published in *CLA Journal* in 1972, he argues that Brooks's poetry is an example of "white style and black content."]

Gwendolyn Brooks, like W. E. B. Du Bois, seems caught between two worlds. And both she and Du Bois manifest the duality of their lives in their literary works; Du Bois wrote in a beautiful, impressionistic style set off by quotations from the world's literary masters. Brooks writes tense, complex, rhythmic verse that contains the metaphysical complexities of John Donne and the word magic of Appollinaire, Eliot, and Pound. The high style of both authors, however, is often used to explicate the condition of black Americans trapped behind a veil that separates them from the white world. What one seems to have is white style and black content—two warring ideals in one dark body.

This apparent dichotomy has produced a confusing situation for Gwendolyn Brooks. The world of white arts and letters has pointed to her with pride; it has bestowed kudos and a Pulitzer Prize. The world of black arts and letters has looked on with mixed emotion, and pride has been only one part of the mixture. There have also been troubling questions about the poet's essential "blackness," her dedication to the melioration of the black American's social conditions. The real duality appears when we realize that Gwendolyn Brooks—although praised and awarded—does not appear on the syllabi of most American literature courses, and her name seldom appears in the annual scholarly bibliographies of the academic world. It would seem she is a black writer after all, *not* an American writer. Yet when one listens to the voice of today's black-revolutionary consciousness, one often hears that Brooks's early poetry fits the white, middle-class patterns that Imamu Baraka has seen as characteristic of "Negro literature."

When one turns to her canon, one finds that she has abided the questions of both camps. Etheridge Knight has perfectly captured her enduring quality in the following lines:

O courier on Pegasus, O Daughter of Parnassus

O Splendid woman of the purple stitch.
When beaten and blue, despairingly we sink
Within obfuscating mire,
O, cradle in your bosom us, hum your lullabies
And soothe our souls with kisses of verse
That stir us on to search for light.
O Mother of the world. Effulgent lover of the Sun!
For ever speak the truth.

She has the Parnassian inspiration and the earth-mother characteristics noted by the poet; her strength has come from a dedication to truth. The truth that concerns her does not amount to a facile realism or a heavy naturalism, although "realism" is the word that comes to mind when one reads a number of poems in *A Street in Bronzeville* (1945).

Poems, or segments, such as "kitchenette building," "a song in the front yard," and "the vacant lot," all support the view that the writer was intent on a realistic, even a naturalistic, portrayal of the life of lower-echelon urban dwellers:

We are things of dry hours and the involuntary plan,
Grayed in, and gray. "Dream" makes a giddy sound,
    not strong
Like "rent," "feeding a wife," "satisfying a man."

My mother, she tells me that Johnnie Mae
Will grow up to be a bad woman.
That George'll be taken to Jail soon or late
(On account of last winter he sold our back gate.)

And with seeing the squat fat daughter
Letting in the men
When majesty has gone for the day—
And letting them out again.

These passages reinforce the designation of Brooks as a realist, and poems such as **"The Sundays of Satin-Legs Smith," "We Real Cool," "A Lovely Love,"** and the volume *Annie Allen* can be added to the list. If she had insisted on a strict realism and nothing more, she could perhaps be written off as a limited poet. But she is no mere chronicler of the condition of the black American poor. Even her most vividly descriptive verses contain an element that removes them from the realm of a cramped realism. All of her characters have both ratiocinative and imaginative capabilities; they have the ability to reason, dream, muse, and remember. This ability distinguishes them from the naturalistic literary victim caught in an environmental maze. From the realm of "raw and unadorned life," Satin-Legs

---

Principal Works

A Street in Bronzeville (poetry) 1945

Annie Allen (poetry) 1949

Maud Martha (novel) 1953

The Bean Eaters (poetry) 1960

Selected Poems (poetry) 1963

In the Mecca (poetry) 1968

Riot (poetry) 1969

Family Pictures (poetry) 1970

Report from Part One (autobiography) 1972

The Tiger Who Wore White Gloves; or, What You Are You Are (poetry) 1974

Beckonings (poetry) 1975

Primer for Blacks (poetry) 1980

To Disembark (poetry) 1981

The Near-Johannesburg Boy, and Other Poems (poetry) 1986

Blacks (poetry and novel) 1987

Gottschalk and the Grande Tarantelle (poetry) 1988

Winnie (poetry) 1988

Smith creates his own world of bright colors, splendid attire, and soft loves in the midst of a cheap hotel's odor and decay. The heroine of **"The Anniad"** conjures up a dream world, covers it in silver plate, populates it with an imaginary prince, and shores up magnificent fragments against the ruins of war. And Jessie Mitchell's mother seeks refuge from envy and death in a golden past:

> She revived for the moment settled and dried-up triumphs,
> Forced perfume into old petals, pulled up the droop,
> Refueled
> Triumphant long-exhaled breaths.
> Her exquisite yellow youth. . . .

Gwendolyn Brooks's characters, in short, are infinitely human because at the core of their existence is the imaginative intellect.

Given the vision of such characters, it is impossible to agree with David Littlejohn, who wishes to view them as simplistic mouthpieces for the poet's sensibility; moreover, it is not surprising that the characters' concerns transcend the ghetto life of many black Americans. They reflect the joy of childhood, the burdens and contentment of motherhood, the distortions of the war-torn psyche, the horror of blood-guiltiness, and the pains of the anti-hero confronted with a heroic ideal. Brooks's protagonists, personae, and speakers, in short, capture all of life's complexities, particularly the complexity of an industrialized age characterized by swift change, depersonalization, and war.

In **"Gay Chaps at the Bar,"** the poet shows her concern for a theme that has had a great influence on twentieth-century British and American art. In one section, "my dreams, my works, must wait till after hell," she employs the food metaphors characteristic of her writing to express the incompleteness that accompanies war:

> I hold my honey and I store my bread
> In little jars and cabinets of my will.
> I label clearly, and each latch and lid
> I bid, Be firm till I return from hell.
> I am very hungry. I am incomplete.

In another section, "piano after war," she captures the mental anguish occasioned by war. The rejuvenation the speaker has felt in the "golden rose" music feeding his "old hungers" suddenly ends:

> But suddenly, across my climbing fever
> Of proud delight—a multiplying cry.
> A cry of bitter dead men who will never
> Attend a gentle maker of musical joy.
> Then my thawed eye will go again to ice.
> And stone will shove the softness from my face.

In **"The Anniad"** and the **"Appendix to the Anniad,"** the poet deals once again with the chaos of arms: War destroys marriage, stifles fertility, and turns men to creatures of "untranslatable ice." Her work, therefore, joins the mainstream of twentieth-century poetry in its treatment of the terrors of war, and her message comes to us through, as I have mentioned, the imaginative intellect of characters who evoke sympathy and identification.

War, however, is not the only theme that allies Gwendolyn Brooks with the mainstream. One finds telling and ironical speculation in "the preacher; ruminates behind the sermon":

> Perhaps—who knows?—He tires of looking down.
> Those eyes are never lifted. Never straight.
> Perhaps sometimes He tires of being great
> In solitude. Without a hand to hold.

In **"Strong Men, Riding Horses,"** we have a Prufrockian portrait of the anti-hero. After his confrontation with the ideals of a Western film, the persona comments:

> I am not like that. I pay rent, am addled
> By illegible landlords, run, if robbers call.
>
> What mannerisms I present, employ,
> Are camouflage, and what my mouths remark
> To word-wall off that broadness of the dark
> Is pitiful.
> I am not brave at all.

In **"Mrs. Small,"** one has a picture of the "Mr. Zeros" (or Willie Lomans) of a complex century, and in **"A Bronzeville Mother Loiters in Mississippi. Mean-**

while a Mississippi Mother Burns Bacon," we have an evocation of the blood-guiltiness of the white psyche in an age of dying colonialism. Brooks presents these themes with skill because she has the ability to endow each figure with a unique, individualizing vision of the world.

If they were considered in isolation, however, the characters and concerns of the verse would not mark the poet as an outstanding writer. Great poetry demands word magic, a sense of the infinite possibilities of language. In this technical realm Brooks is superb. Her ability to dislocate and mold language into complex patterns of meaning can be observed in her earliest poems and in her latest volumes—*In The Mecca* (1968), *Riot* (1969), and *Family Pictures* (1970). The first lines of **"The Sundays of Satin-Legs Smith"** are illustrative:

> INAMORATAS, with an approbation,
> Bestowed his title. Blessed his inclination.
>
> He wakes, unwinds, elaborately: a cat
> Tawny, reluctant, royal. He is fat
> And fine this morning. Definite. Reimbursed.

The handling of polysyllabics is not in the least strained, and the movement is so graceful that one scarcely notices the rhymed couplets. Time and again this word magic is at work, and the poet's varying rhyme schemes lend a subtle resonance that is not found in the same abundance in the works of other acknowledged American writers. It is important to qualify this judgment, however, for while Brooks employs polysyllabics and forces words into striking combinations, she preserves colloquial rhythms. Repeatedly one is confronted by a realistic voice—not unlike that in Robert Frost's poetry—that carries one along the dim corridors of the human psyche or down the rancid halls of a decaying tenement. Brooks's colloquial narrative voice, however, is more prone to complex juxtapositions than Frost's, as a stanza from **"The Anniad"** illustrates:

> Doomer, though, crescendo-comes
> Prophesying hecatombs.
> Surrealist and cynical.
> Garrulous and guttural.
> Spits upon the silver leaves.
> Denigrates the dainty eves
> Dear dexterity achieves.

This surely differs from Frost's stanzas, and the difference resides in the poet's obvious joy in words. She fuses the most elaborate words into contexts that allow them to speak naturally or to sing beautifully her meaning.

Brooks is not indebted to Frost alone for technical influences; she also acknowledges her admiration for Langston Hughes. Although a number of her themes and techniques set her work in the twentieth-century mainstream, there are those that place it firmly in the black American literary tradition. One of her most effective techniques is a sharp, black, comic irony that is closely akin to the scorn Hughes directed at the ways of white folks throughout his life. When added to her other skills, this irony proves formidable. **"The Lovers of the Poor"** is unsparing in its portrayal of ineffectual, middle-age, elitist philanthropy:

> Their guild is giving money to the poor.
> The worthy poor. The very very worthy
> And beautiful poor. Perhaps just not too swarthy?
> Perhaps just not too dirty nor too dim
> Nor—passionate. In truth, what they could wish
> Is—something less than derelict or dull.
> Not staunch enough to stab, though, gaze for gaze!
> God shield them sharply from the beggar-bold!

Hughes could not have hoped for better. And the same vitriol is directed at whites who seek the bizarre and exotic by "slumming" among blacks in **"I love those little booths at Benvenuti's"**;

> But how shall they tell people they have been
> Out Bronzeville way? For all the nickels in
> Have not bought savagery or defined a "folk."
> The colored people will not "clown."
>
> The colored people arrive, sit firmly down,
> Eat their Express Spaghetti, their T-bone steak,
> Handling their steel and crockery with no clatter,
> Laugh punily, rise, go firmly out of the door.

The poet's chiding, however, is not always in the derisive mode. She often turns an irony of loving kindness on black Americans. **"We Real Cool"** would fit easily into the canon of Hughes or Sterling Brown:

> We real cool. We
> Left School. We
>
> Lurk late. We
> Strike straight. We
>
> Sing sin. We
> Thin gin. We
>
> Jazz June. We
> Die soon.

The irony is patent, but the poet's sympathy and admiration for the folk are no less obvious (the bold relief of "We," for example). A sympathetic irony in dealing with the folk has characterized some of the most outstanding works in the black American literary tradition, from Paul Laurence Dunbar's "Jimsella" and the novels of Claude McKay to Ralph Ellison's *Invisible Man* and the work of recent writers such as George Cain and Louise Meriwether. All manifest a concern with the black man living in the "promised land" of the American city, and Brooks's *A Street in Bronzeville, Annie Allen*, **"The Bean Eaters,"** and **"Bronzeville Woman**

in a Red Hat" likewise reveal the employment of kindly laughter to veil the tears of a desperate situation. In her autobiography, *Report from Part One,* she attests to having been in the situation and to having felt its deeper pulsations: "I lived on 63rd Street [in Chicago] . . . and there was a good deal of life in the raw all about me. You might feel that this would be disturbing, but it was not. It contributed to my writing progress. I wrote about what I saw and heard in the street."

Finally, there are the poems of protest. A segregated military establishment comes under attack in both **"The Negro Hero"** and "the white troops had their orders but the Negroes looked like men." The ignominies of lynching are exposed in **"A Bronzeville Mother Loiters in Mississippi. Meanwhile, a Mississippi Mother Burns Bacon."** And in poems like **"Riders to the Blood-red Wrath"** and **"The Second Sermon on the Warpland,"** Brooks expresses the philosophy of militant resistance that has characterized the black American literary tradition from the day a black slave first sang of Pharaoh's army. The poet, in short, has spoken forcefully against the indignities suffered by black Americans in a racialistic society. Having undertaken a somewhat thorough revaluation of her role as a black poet in an era of transition, she has stated and proved her loyalty to the task of creating a new consciousness in her culture. Her shift from a major white publishing firm to an independent black one (Broadside Press) for her autobiography is an indication of her commitment to the cause of black institution-building that has been championed by a number of today's black artists. One might, however, take issue with her recent statement that she was "ignorant" until enlightened by the black activities and concerns of the 1960s. Although she is currently serving as one of the most engaged artistic guides for a culture, she is more justly described as a herald than as an uninformed convert. She has mediated the dichotomy that left Paul Laurence Dunbar (whose *Complete Poems* she read at an early age) a torn and agonized man. Of course, she had the example of Dunbar, the Harlem Renaissance writers, and others to build upon, but at times even superior talents have been incapable of employing the accomplishments of the past for their own ends. Unlike the turn-of-the-century poet and a number of Renaissance writers, Brooks has often excelled the surrounding white framework, and she has been able to see clearly beyond it to the strengths and beauties of her own unique cultural tradition.

Gwendolyn Brooks represents a singular achievement. Beset by a double consciousness, she has kept herself from being torn asunder by crafting poems that equal the best in the black and white American literary traditions. Her characters are believable, her themes manifold, and her technique superb. The critic (whether black or white) who comes to her work seeking only support for his ideology will be disappointed for, as Etheridge Knight pointed out, she has ever spoken the truth. And truth, one likes to feel, always lies beyond the boundaries of any one ideology. Perhaps Brooks's most significant achievement is her endorsement of this point of view. From her hand and fertile imagination have come volumes that transcend the dogma on either side of the American veil. In their transcendence, they are fitting representatives of an "Effulgent lover of the Sun!" (pp. 21-8)

Houston A. Baker, Jr., "The Achievement of Gwendolyn Brooks," in *A Life Distilled: Gwendolyn Brooks, Her Poetry and Fiction,* edited by Maria K. Mootry and Gary Smith, University of Illinois Press, 1987, pp. 21-9.

GEORGE KENT
(essay date 1982?)

[Kent was one of the foremost authorities on Brooks's life and works. In the following essay, written sometime before his death in 1982, he explores the development of Brooks's syntax and language in her poetry.]

The consciousness producing *A Street in Bronzeville* (1945) was one making its first compassionate outreach to the broad range of humanity. On the one hand, it represented the mastered past: [Brooks'] old neighborhood and youth. On the other hand, it represented an intense getting acquainted with the present which was pressurized by the raw currents of Chicago's racial practices, and by World War II. Optimism prevailed, however, since the war situation had produced both threatening violence and some evidence that a broadened democracy would be born from it. In the poet's early work, one result is a deceptively simple surface. Syntax is most often either in close correlation with the usual subject plus verb plus object or complement pattern of a familiar prose sentence or within calling distance. Wielding this syntax is a friendly observer giving one a tour of the neighborhood or quick views of situations. Thus abrupt beginnings sound pretty much the way they do in our communications with friends with whom we share clarifying reference points. The observer [in **"The Old-Marrieds"**] begins: "But in the crowding darkness not a word did they say." Joining the group in "kitchenette building," the observer-narrator pitches at us a long question but one so well ordered that it is painless: "But could a dream send up through onion fumes / Its white and violet, fight with fried potatoes / And yesterday's garbage ripening in the hall, / Flutter, or sing an aria down these rooms . . . ?" At the end of three more lines we complete the question, and are then given quick relief through a series of short declarative statements whose brevity drives home the drama and the pathos of the situation.

There are poems with much simpler syntax within this group and one sonnet with a far more complex syntax. The simplest derive from closeness to conversational patterns, from reproduction of speech tones, and from the already mentioned patterning upon simple prose statements. A form such as the ballad also has conventions which allow for great simplicity of syntactical structure. The more complex structure which probably puzzles on a first reading actually derives . . . from exploitation of one of the more complex rhetorical but conventional structures—the periodic sentence. (pp. 89-90)

In terms of the relationship to conversational language and actual speech tones one will find in the style a range running from "folk" speech (the Hattie Scott poems) to that which is more self-consciously literate and affected by formal traditions (**"The Sundays of Satin Legs Smith"** and the sonnets, for example). Brooks is also alert to the richness provided by bringing contrasting traditions into strategic conjunctions or, by movement, into a very formal eloquence; again, examples of both may be seen in **"Satin Legs Smith."** And finally there is the colloquial and hip level provided by such a poem as **"Patent Leather":** "That cool chick down on Calumet / Has got herself a brand new cat. . . . "

For the most part imagery goes beyond the simple functions of representing an object or pictorializing, activities characteristic of the most simple poems, and manages to do so quietly. "Pretty patent leather hair" obviously has its total effect in the literal picture it creates and the comment it makes upon the judgment of the cool chick. But Brooks expanded the range and function of the realistic image in several ways: attaching to it a striking descriptive term ("crowding darkness"), combining it with a figurative gesture ("could a dream send up through onion fumes / Its white and violet"), contrasting realistic and symbolic functions (crooked and straight in **"Hunchback Girl . . . "**), presenting expressionistic description of a condition ("Mabbie on Mabbie with hush in the heart"), and emphasizing the figurative role of a basically realistic or pictorial expression ("wear the brave stockings of night-black lace," and "temperate holiness arranged / Ably on asking faces").

Perhaps the foregoing elements may be allowed to stand for other devices making up the total struggle with language meant by the word *style.* I have tried to suggest that the central trait of most of the language devices is that they convey the impression of actual simplicity and thus offer the appearance of easy-going

accessibility. It is certainly not a total accessibility, in several cases. On one level people and their life stories appear in sharply outlined plots presenting easily recognized issues from the daily round of existence, and move to definite decisive conclusions. However, recognizing certain devices or reading at the tempo required not only by the story but by imagery and language changes will, at times, take us to another level. **"Southeast corner,"** for example, seems interested in the artistry, as well as the vanity, of the deceased madam of the school of beauty, an interpretation suggested by the vivid image of shot silk shining over her tan "impassivity." **"Satin Legs"** has meanings which reveal themselves in the imagery, language shifts, and mixture of narrative attitudes, which go beyond the basic story, and so on.

But there is no question that in *A Street in Bronzeville* (and in individual poems over the body of her work) there is a general simplicity which seems easily to contain specific complexities. The fact makes Brooks a poet speaking still, not merely to critics and other poets, but to people.

It is probable that nearly all the stylistic developments of Brooks' subsequent works are embryonically present in *A Street in Bronzeville,* since, with its publication, she was emerging from a very long and earnest apprenticeship. Some clear foreshadowing of more complex stylistic developments is in the sonnets, and in **"The Sundays of Satin Legs Smith."** Whereas, for example, the full capacity of the narrator of the Hattie Scott poems may be shaded in the background, the sophistication and perception of the narrator of the sonnets and the life of Smith are clearly those of the narrator of *Annie Allen.* Yet it is understandable that people found the stylistic developments in this second work startling and complex.

If the opening poem of *A Street* makes things seem easy by providing a friendly narrator using language in seemingly customary ways, the opening poem of *Annie Allen,* **"the birth in a narrow room,"** makes the reader feel that the narrator's assumption is that he is to the poetic manner born. The poem demands the reader's absolute commitment, an acceptance of the role of a tougher elliptical syntax, and a comprehension of imagery which functions both realistically and mythically. Actually, the syntax is difficult largely because for several lines the infant remains the *unnamed* subject of the poem. The sources for imagery are the fairy and timeless world and the "real" objects of the "real" world, both of which function to sustain temporarily complete freedom for the young child in an Edenic world. Thus the first poem warns the reader to expect to participate in complex struggles with language.

The style of *Annie Allen* emerges not only from the fact that the poet of the highly promising first book naturally expects to present greater mastery of craft in the second but also from a changed focus in consciousness. In her first book Brooks' emphasis had been upon community consciousness. In [*Annie Allen*] her emphasis is upon self-consciousness—an attempt to give artistic structure to tensions arising from the artist's experience in moving from the Edenic environment of her parents' home into the fallen world of Chicago tenement life in the roles of young wife, mother, and artist. Her efforts, however, were not an attempt to be confessional but an attempt to take advantage of the poetic form to move experiences immediately into symbols broader than the person serving as subject. A thoroughgoing search of the territory and the aspiration for still greater mastery of craft called for a struggle with language, a fact which would require the reader to make also a creative struggle.

One device is to play conventional and unconventional structures against each other, and, sometimes, to work apparently conventional structures for very special effects. In **"the parents: people like our marriage, Maxie and Andrew,"** the reader abruptly confronts the synecdochial opening lines: "Clogged and soft and sloppy eyes / Have list the light that bites or terrifies." Afterward the poem gradually settles into the more conventional approach, though it demands that the reader absorb its realities from simple symbols instead of editorial statements. In such poems the reader's creative participation is sustained by other devices: unusual conjunctions of words, shifts in pace and rhythm, reproductions of speech tones at the point of the colloquial and at varying distances from it, figurative language, challenging twists in the diction, and others. (pp. 90-2)

The long poem on young womanhood entitled **"The Anniad"** has the task of taking Annie into maturity by carrying her from the epic dreams of maidenhood into the prosaic and disillusioning realities provided by the married life. More concretely, having inherited the romance and love lore of Euro-Americans and disabilities imposed upon Black identity, she is, at once, the would-be heroine of song and story and the Black woman whom "the higher gods" forgot and the lower ones berate. The combination of the realistic and romantic portrays the flesh and blood person and the dreamer. (p. 94)

To express the climax of accumulated problems, storms, and confusions of Annie's young life, Brooks turns completely to expressionistic imagery:

In the indignant dark there ride
Roughnesses and spiny things
On infallible hundred heels.
And a bodiless bee stings.
Cyclone concentration reels.
Harried sods dilate, divide,
Suck her sorrowfully inside.

The last stanzas return to the language of the realistic scale, although the language itself is not simply mimetic or pictorial. Annie is described as salvaging something of the more usual day-to-day fruits from her experiences: "Stroking swallows from the sweat. / Fingering faint violet. / Hugging gold and Sunday sun. / Kissing in her kitchenette / The minuets of memory." (p. 95)

On the level of telling the Annie Allen story, Brooks was thus able to experiment extensively with stylistic devices and license herself to move beyond realistic imagery. She did so by retaining realism as the base of conception and the norm for the behavior patterns the personalities must ultimately adopt. Thus the form includes devices for humor and pathos which register, in the world of the possible, Annie's excess of idealism, dreaminess, or self-absorption: intense pictures of imbalance, rhythms suggesting frenetic behavior, and a vocabulary suggesting the occupation of worlds which must prove incompatible. In short, the kindly satiric pat appears to halt unrealism, though the unrealism if it could be transformed into "reality" might make a richer world.

Annie Allen represents Brooks' most energetic reach for simply a great command of the devices of poetic style. Having developed this command, she could now wield the devices at will and make them relate more efficiently to form and intention. With this mastery of numerous devices came also the power to achieve originality by making variations in the contexts in which they were used and in the relationships one device makes with another. Then, too, a device which in the earlier stages of the artist's career could be completely summed up in the term *conventional* or *traditional* could, at times, now be put into innovative roles. In such a poem as **"Beverly Hills, Chicago,"** for example, the very precision of a syntax based upon the simple declarative sentence drives home the tension of the rest of the structures: "It is only natural, however, that it should occur to us / How much more fortunate they [the rich] are than we are." (pp. 95-6)

In *The Bean Eaters* (1960) and certain of the new poems of *Selected Poems* (1963), developments in style, for the most part, are responses to experimentations with loosened forms and the milage one can gain from very simple statements. In *Annie Allen* Brooks had loosened up the form of the sonnet in **"The Rites for Cousin Vit,"** with the use of elliptical syntax, the pressures of colloquial speech, and the cumulative capacity of all the poetic devices to create the impact of hyperbole. Cousin Vit was simply too vital to have died; thus Brooks interjects into the language of the sonnet the idiomatic swing and sensuality of the street: that Vit continued to do "the snake-hips with a hiss. . . . " In *The Bean Eaters* she again loosened up sonnet form in **"A Lovely Love"** by adapting the Petrarchan rhyme scheme to the situation of the tenement lovers, intermingling short and long complete statements with elliptical ones, and managing a nervous rhythm which imposes the illusion of being a one-to-one imitation of the behavior of the lovers. The diction of the poem is a mixture of the romantic ("hyacinth darkness"), the realistic ("Let it be stairways, and a splintery box"), and the mythically religious ("birthright of our lovely love / In swaddling clothes. Not like that Other one"). Although the elliptical structures are more numerous and informal in **"Cousin Vit,"** the rhythm of **"A Lovely Love"** seems to make that poem the more complex achievement.

Another technical development is the poet's bolder movement into a free verse appropriate to the situation which she sometimes dots with rhyme. The technique will be more noticeable and surer in its achievement in the next volume, *In the Mecca*. But the poem **"A Bronzeville Mother Loiters in Mississippi. Meanwhile, A Mississippi Mother Burns Bacon"** gives the technique full rein, except for the rhyming. The lines frequently move in the rhythms of easygoing conversation or in the loose patterns of stream of consciousness, as the poet portrays the movement from romantic notions to reality in the consciousness of the young white woman over whom a young Black boy (reminiscent of the slain Emmett Till), has been lynched by her husband and his friend. The dramatic situation determines the length of lines, and the statements vary in form; short declarative sentences, simple sentences, phrase units understandable from their ties to preceding sentences, and long, complex structures. Additional sources of rhythm are repetition, parallel structures, and alliteration.

One of the more interesting techniques of the poem is that of playing romantic diction against the realistic. Thus a stanza containing such terms as "milk-white maid," "Dark Villain," "Fine Prince," and "Happiness-Ever-After" precedes one containing the following lines:

Her bacon burned. She
Hastened to hide it in the step-on can, and
Drew more strips from the meat case. The eggs and
    sour-milk biscuits
Did well.

Two new poems in *Selected Poems*, **"To Be in Love"** and **"Big Bessie Throws Her Son into the Street,"** have lines and a use of rhyme closer to the method of the poems in *In the Mecca* in their tautness. **"To Be in Love,"** a portrait of that state of being, leans as close as possible to direct statement. "To be in love / Is to touch things with a lighter hand." The next one-line stanza: "In yourself you stretch, you are well." Rhymes then dot several areas of the poem and, near the end, combine with more complex diction to provide the emotional climax. **"Big Bessie,"** a portrait of a

mother encouraging her son to seize his independence, has similar strategies, although it is less realistic and moves toward the impressionistic. (pp. 96-7)

In the Mecca is comprised of the poem **"In the Mecca"** and several under the heading **"After Mecca."** The long poem **"In the Mecca"** has for setting a famous Chicago apartment building, half a block long, located between State and Dearborn streets, one block north of Thirty-fourth Street. The title poem in the company of the others marks Brooks' turn from Christianity and the hope of integration to that of nationalism. Obviously the situation means that motives different from those of the preceding works will place at the foreground the necessity for new stylistic developments. The language must emphasize Blacks developing common bonds with each other instead of the traditional "people are people" bonding. For a poet who has so intensively devoted herself to language, the situation means a turn to ways of touching deeply an audience not greatly initiated into the complexity of modern poetry and yet retaining a highly disciplined use of language. The challenge would seem all the greater since to acquire such brilliant command over so wide a range of poetic devices as Brooks had done over the years was also to build a set of reflexes in consciousness which, one would think, would weight the balance toward complex rendering. (pp. 97-8)

[*In the Mecca*] represents, on the one hand, the poet at the very height of her command and utilization of complex renderings. On the other, it represents change of concern and expansion of the use of free verse. Actually, the poem **"In the Mecca"** required complex resources and rendering. Its unifying story line is simple. Mrs. Sallie, a domestic worker, returns from work to find that she has lost her courageous battle to support and rear nine "fatherless" children. Her missing child Pepita, who seemed, at first, astray in the slum-blasted building, turns out to have been murdered and hidden under the bed of the mentally twisted murderer. However, the total story is complex: the rendering of the Mecca universe and what is happening to the holiness of the souls of nearly thirty people, if one counts only those characterized either by extended treatment or by the single incisive line or phrase. Obviously, all the resources the poet had accumulated over the years were needed.

The older stylistic resources seem, at times, to have received further growth. Mrs. Sallie leaves the repressive environment of her employer: "Infirm booms / and suns that have not spoken die behind this / low-brown butterball." The imagery, strategic repetitions, ritualized and moralizing lines—some of which are rhymed for special emphasis—give further revelation of Mrs. Sallie's strength, complex responses, and dogged determination. Imagery and unusual conjunctions of words make each child memorable and his or her situation haunting. Yvonne of "bald innocence and gentle fright," the "undaunted," once "pushed her thumbs into the eyes of a thief." Though given a touch of irony, her love story has something of the direct style of the poem **"To Be in Love."** (pp. 98-9)

The language usage extends from the realistic to the expressionistic, from actual speech tones to formal eloquence. It is a language which must extend itself to engage the balked struggle and melancholy defeat of Mrs. Sallie; the embattled but tough innocence of the children; the vanities, frustrations, insanity, futility, and ruthlessness of certain characters—and the pathos of others; and, finally, the desperation, philosophies, and intellectual reaches of the young hero intellectuals seeking a way out. It also is a language which unites the disinherited of the Mecca Building with the disinherited across the universe. (p. 99)

[The] wide range of achievement in free verse is further tested by the varied functions it was required to serve in the remaining poems of the book. The function of **"In the Mecca"** was to continue deep definition, to lay bare, and to foreshadow. Though it contains rage, its central emotion is compassion, and Mrs. Sallie is bound within a traditional mode of responding and does not undergo a change of consciousness. Except for **"To a Winter Squirrel,"** the succeeding poems are largely about new consciousness and the raw materials of the Black community. **"The Chicago Picasso"** is technically outside such a conclusion judged in its own right, but it is also present to highlight the communal celebration represented by **"The Wall,"** since it represents individualism and conventional universalism.

The two sermons on the warpland represent the high point in the poet's struggle to move to the center of the Black struggle, with the first urging the building of solid bases for unity and communion and the second urging Blacks to bear up under the pains of the struggle and to "Live! / and have your blooming in the noise of the whirlwind." Parts I, III, and IV seem the more effective, since their style better combines the abstract and the concrete and their language moves more easily between the areas of formal eloquence and the colloquial. Effective poems addressing the communal concerns of Blacks are also in the pamphlet *Riot* (1969). . . . [The directness of **"Riot"**] and, above all, its satire regarding the privileged John Cabot are effective when read to a Black audience. The satiric approach was both an older device of Brooks' and a feature of the new movement. The last poem, **"An Aspect of Love, Alive in the Ice and Fire,"** reproduces the directness and simplicity of the earlier **"To Be in Love."**

Gwendolyn Brooks' subsequent poetry has seen the observer of the poems evidence more easily and casually membership in the group. As part of her mission to help inspire the bonding of Blacks to each other, she wished to write poetry which could be appreciated by

Front cover of *Riot,* published in 1969.

the person in the tavern who ordinarily did not read poetry. This ambition required some additional emphasis upon simplicity. She had already had the experience of writing prose of poetic intensity in her novel *Maud Martha* (1953) and in the short story **"The Life of Lincoln West."** . . . Making minor revisions she was able to rearrange **"The Life of Lincoln West"** in verse lines, and it became the lead-off poem in *Family Pictures* (1970), whose title signified the intimate relationship between the observer-writer and the community. It is the story of a little boy who is disliked because of his pronounced African features and who becomes reconciled to his situation when he learns that he "is the real thing." In style it creates an imagery, a syntax, and a diction which do not press greatly for meanings beyond the requirements of its narrative line and development. It moves close to what the poet would shortly be calling verse journalism in referring to her piece **"In Montgomery,"** in which she evoked the current situation and mood of the survivors and descendants of the Montgomery Bus Boycott. (pp. 100-01)

In the long poem **"In Montgomery,"** . . . [Brooks employs] realism but also ranges, extending from direct, prosy statement to a heightening produced by some of the older but simple approaches to diction in poetry. . . . The poet also clearly evidences the fact that she is visiting Montgomery as a concerned relative, a definite part of the family. In the opening passages she continuously announces her presence.

My work: to cite in semi-song the
meaning of Confederacy's Cradle.
Well, it means to be rocking gently, rocking gently!
In Montgomery is no Race Problem.
There is the white decision, the white and pleasant
    vow
that the white foot shall not release the black neck.

In phrases which serve as structuring devices in parallel form, she continues to present the evidence of her presence, kinship, and role in the historical continuum. . . . (pp. 101-02)

Such poems as those devoted to Lincoln West and to Montgomery display many qualities of post-*In the Mecca* style, and they should be added to from other poems in *Family Pictures, Beckonings,* and *Primer for Blacks* and from new poems as they arrive. Some stylistic qualities can be listed: use of various types of repetition, alliteration, neologisms (crit, creeple, makiteer), abstract terms gaining depth of meaning from reference to the group's shared experiences, epithets ("whipstopper," "Treeplanting Man"), variations in expressional patterns usually associated with the simple ballad, ritualistic echoing of childhood-game rhythms and rhyme, gestural words, and simple words forced to yield new meanings from dramatic context. To these one might add the creation of sharp contrasts, and become inclusive by stating that the repertoire involves all the traditional resources provided for simplicity by free verse.

But such a list does not say as much as it seems to, since many of the above devices were already used in the more complex style, and the true distinguishing point is the new combination made of many of them in the later poetry. Under the caption Young Heroes in *Family Pictures* is a poem devoted to a young African poet, **"To Keorapetse Kgositsile (Willie),"** which illustrates the new simplicity and some carry-over of older devices in a somewhat simpler pattern. . . . The poem is an introduction to Kgositsile's book *My Name is Afrika!,* and concludes simply, " 'MY NAME IS AFRIKA / Well, every fella's a Foreign Country. / This Foreign Country speaks to You.' " Certainly, the use of capitals and lower-case expressions, unusual word conjunctions ("pellmelling loneliness," "lenient dignity"), and repetition can be found in the more complex style, but here, for the most part, the usage adapts to the creative capacity of an audience not drilled in poetic conventions.

In the same work, **"To Don at Salaam"** retains simplicity throughout and creates a warm portrait suggestive of disciplined intensity. The first stanza creates

a symbolic picture of a person who poises himself easily amid forces that are usually overwhelming, and is notable for depending almost entirely upon monosyllabic words. . . . The third stanza notes his affectionateness, the fourth registers his definiteness in an indefinite world, the fifth brief stanza points to his harmoniousness and capable action, and the sixth, a one-line stanza, ends simply but dramatically: "I like to see you living in the world." Part of the style is the structuring of stanzas according to function and place in the dramatic whole.

Poems dealing with persons or fraternal situations within the family of Blacks tend to be the more successful, especially those dealing with specific persons. But the sermons and lectures contain effective passages and, frequently, longer and more complex movements. In *Beckonings,* **"Boys, Black"** admonishes the boys to develop health, proper Blackness, and sanity, in their approach to existence, and urges heroic struggle. The dramatic opening gives a sense of the positive direction suggested by the poem, and is noteworthy for drawing images and figures made simple by having been first validated by traditional usage. . . . The poem also gives an example of a distinctive use of repetition in the first line, and, in the first and second lines, the creative use of alliteration. As it proceeds, it accumulates an in-group set of references. Aside from such expressions as the opening one and the second address ("boys, young brothers, young brothers"), there is the stanza offering caution:

Beware
the easy griefs
It is too easy to cry "ATTICA"
and shock thy street,
and purse thy mouth,
and go home to "Gunsmoke." Boys,
black boys,
beware the easy griefs
that fool and fuel nothing.

The ending is one of love and faith and admonition: "Make of my Faith an engine / Make of my Faith / a Black Star. I am Beckoning." Much revised and addressed to Blacks in general, **"Boys, Black"** appears in a new collection of poems entitled *To Disembark.* . . . (pp. 102-04)

With the publishing of *To Disembark* it is apparent that Gwendolyn Brooks' change in outlook and consciousness has crystallized in an altered and distinctive style that offers the virtues of its own personality without denying its kinship with an earlier one. Most dramatic are the speaker's position in the center of her kinship group and the warmth and urgency of her speech. As indicated, the tendency of the language is toward a new simplicity. It can be seen in poems which, on the surface, remain very close to a traditional style of poetic realism but always evidence the fact that they proceed from an artist who is choosing from a wide range of resources. It can be seen in poems which will still, in particular passages, place language under great strain. Such patterns create also a recognizably new voice in the poetry. Thus the always-journeying poet sets the example of doing what she asks of others in the new poem **"To the Diaspora."**

> Here is some sun. Some.
> Now off into the places rough to reach.
> Though dry, though drowsy, all unwillingly a-
>   wobble,
> into the dissonant and dangerous crescendo.
> Your work, that was done, to be done to be done to
>   be done.
>
> (pp. 104-05)

George Kent, "Gwendolyn Brooks' Poetic Realism: A Developmental Survey," in *Black Women Writers (1950-1980): A Critical Evaluation,* edited by Mari Evans, Anchor Books, 1984, pp. 88-105.

GARY SMITH
(essay date 1983)

[In the following excerpt, Smith examines Brooks's first collection of poetry, *A Street in Bronzeville*.]

The critical reception of *A Street in Bronzeville* contained, in embryo, many of the central issues in the scholarly debate that continues to engage Brooks's poetry. As in the following quotation from *The New York Times Book Review,* most reviewers were able to recognize Brooks's versatility and craft as a poet:

> If the idiom is colloquial, the language is universal. Brooks commands both the colloquial and more austere rhythms. She can vary manner and tone. In form, she demonstrates a wide range: quatrains, free verse, ballads, and sonnets—all appropriately controlled. The longer line suits her better than the short, but she is not verbose. In some of the sonnets, she uses an abruptness of address that is highly individual.

Yet, while noting her stylistic successes, not many critics fully understood her achievement in her first book. This difficulty was not only characteristic of critics who examined the formal aspects of prosody in her work, but also of critics who addressed themselves to the social realism in her poetry. Moreover, what Brooks gained at the hands of critics who focused on her technique, she lost to critics who chose to emphasize the exotic, Negro features of the book. . . .

The poems in *A Street in Bronzeville* actually served notice that Brooks had learned her craft well

enough to combine successfully themes and styles from both the Harlem Renaissance and Modernist poetry. She even achieves some of her more interesting effects in the book by parodying the two traditions. She juggles the pessimism of Modernist poetry with the general optimism of the Harlem Renaissance. (p. 35)

Because of the affinities *A Street in Bronzeville* shares with Modernist poetry and the Harlem Renaissance, Brooks was initiated not only into the vanguard of American literature, but also into what had been the inner circle of Harlem writers. Two of the Renaissance's leading poets, Claude McKay and Countee Cullen, addressed letters to her to mark the publication of *A Street in Bronzeville.* McKay welcomed her into a dubious but potentially rewarding career:

> I want to congratulate you again on the publication of *A Street in Bronzeville* and welcome you among the band of hard working poets who do have something to say. It is a pretty rough road we have to travel, but I suppose much compensation is derived from the joy of being able to sing. Yours sincerely, Claude McKay. (October 10, 1945.)

Cullen pinpointed her dual place in American literature:

> I have just finished reading *A Street in Bronzeville* and want you to know that I enjoyed it thoroughly. There can be no doubt that you are a poet, a good one, with every indication of becoming a better. I am glad to be able to say 'welcome' to you to that too small group of Negro poets, and to the larger group of American ones. No one can deny you your place there. (August 24, 1945.)

The immediate interest in these letters is how both poets touch upon the nerve ends of the critical debate that surrounded *A Street in Bronzeville.* For McKay, while Brooks has "something to say," she can also "sing"; and for Cullen, she belongs not only to the minority of Negro poets, but also to the majority of American ones. Nonetheless, the critical question for both poets might well have been Brooks's relationship to the Harlem Renaissance. What had she absorbed of the important tenets of the Black aesthetic as expressed during the New Negro Movement? And how had she addressed herself, as a poet, to the literary movement's assertion of the folk and African culture, and its promotion of the arts as the agent to define racial integrity and to fuse racial harmony?

Aside from its historical importance, the Harlem Renaissance—as a literary movement—is rather difficult to define. . . . Likewise, the general description of the movement as a Harlem Renaissance is often questioned, since most of the major writers, with the notable exceptions of Hughes and Cullen, actually did not live and work in Harlem. Finally, many of the themes and literary conventions defy definition in terms of what was and what was not a New Negro poet. Nonetheless, there was a common ground of purpose and meaning in the works of the individual writers that permits a broad definition of the spirit and intent of the Harlem Renaissance. Indeed, the New Negro poets expressed a deep pride in being Black; they found reasons for this pride in ethnic identity and heritage; and they shared a common faith in the fine arts as a means of defining and reinforcing racial pride. But in the literal expression of these artistic impulses, the poets were either romantics or realists and, quite often within a single poem, both. The realistic impulse, as defined best in the poems of McKay's *Harlem Shadows,* was a sober reflection upon Blacks as second class citizens, segregated from the mainstream of American socio-economic life, and largely unable to realize the wealth and opportunity that America promised. The romantic impulse, on the other hand, as defined in the poems of Sterling Browns's *Southern Road* (1932), often found these unrealized dreams in the collective strength and will of the folk masses. In comparing the poems in *A Street in Bronzeville* with various poems from the Renaissance, it becomes apparent that Brooks agrees, for the most part, with their prescriptions for the New Negro. Yet the unique contributions she brings to bear upon this tradition are extensive: 1) the biting ironies of intraracial discrimination, 2) the devaluation of love in heterosexual relationships between Blacks, and 3) the primacy of suffering in the lives of poor Black women.

The first clue that *A Street in Bronzeville* was, at the time of its publication, unlike any other book of poems by a Black American is its insistent emphasis on demystifying romantic love between Black men and women. The **"old marrieds"**, the first couple encountered on the walking tour of Bronzeville, are nothing like the youthful archetype that the Renaissance poets often portrayed:

> But in the crowding darkness not a word did they say.
> Though the pretty-coated birds had piped so lightly
>   all the day.
> And he had seen the lovers in the little side-streets.
> And she had heard the morning stories clogged with
>   sweets.
> It was quite a time for loving. It was midnight. It was
>   May.
> But in the crowding darkness not a word did they
>   say.

In this short, introductory poem, Brooks, in a manner reminiscent of Eliot's alienated *Waste Land* characters, looks not toward a glorified African past or limitless future, but rather at a stifled present. Her old lovers ponder not an image of their racial past or some symbolized possibility of self-renewal, but rather the overwhelming question of what to do in the here-and-now. Moreover, their world, circumscribed by the incantatory line that opens and closes the poem, "But in

the crowding darkness not a word did they say," is one that is distinctly at odds with their lives. They move timidly through the crowded darkness of their neighborhood largely ignorant of the season, "May," the lateness of the hour, "midnight," and a particular *raison d' etre,* "a time for loving." Their attention, we infer, centers upon the implicit need to escape any peril that might consume what remains of their lives. The tempered optimism in the poem, as the title indicates, is the fact that they are "old-marrieds": a social designation that suggests the longevity of their lives and the solidity of their marital bond in what is, otherwise, an ephemeral world of change. Indeed, as the prefatory poem in *A Street in Bronzeville,* the **"old marrieds,"** on the whole, debunks one of the prevalent motifs of Harlem Renaissance poetry: its general optimism about the future.

As much as the Harlem Renaissance was noted for its optimism, an important corollary motif was that of ethnic or racial pride. This pride—often thought a reaction to the minstrel stereotypes in the Dunbar tradition—usually focused with romantic idealization upon the Black woman. (pp. 36-8)

In *A Street in Bronzeville,* this romantic impulse for idealizing the Black woman runs headlong into the biting ironies of intraracial discrimination. In poem after poem in *A Street in Bronzeville,* within the well-observed caste lines of skin color, the consequences of dark pigmentation are revealed in drastic terms. One of the more popular of these poems, **"The Ballad of Chocolate Mabbie,"** explores the tragic ordeal of Mabbie, the Black female heroine, who is victimized by her dark skin and her "saucily bold" lover, Willie Boone. . . . Mabbie's life, of course, is one of unrelieved monotony; her social contacts are limited to those who, like her, are dark skinned, rather than "lemon-hued" or light skinned. But as Brooks makes clear, the larger tragedy of Mabbie's life is the human potential that is squandered:

> Oh, warm is the waiting for joys, my dears!
> And it cannot be too long.
> O, pity the little poor chocolate lips
> That carry the bubble of song!

But if Mabbie is Brooks's parodic victim of romantic love, her counterpart in **"Ballad of Pearl May Lee"** realizes a measure of sweet revenge. In outline, Brooks's poem is reminiscent of Cullen's *The Ballad of the Brown Girl* (1927). There are, however, several important differences. The first is the poem's narrative structure: Pearl May Lee is betrayed in her love for a Black man who "couldn't abide dark meat," who subsequently makes love to a white girl and is lynched for his crime of passion, whereas Cullen's "Brown Girl" is betrayed in her love for a white man, Lord Thomas, who violated explicit social taboo by marrying her rather than Fair London, a white girl. Moreover, Cullen's poem, "a ballad retold," is traditional in its approach to the ballad form. . . . Brooks's ballad, on the other hand, dispenses with the rhetorical invocation of the traditional ballad and begins *in medias res:*

> Then off they took you, off to the jail,
> A hundred hooting after.
> And you should have heard me at my house.
> I cut my lungs with my laughter,
> Laughter,
> Laughter.
> I cut my lungs with my laughter.

This mocking tone is sustained throughout the poem, even as Sammy, Pearl May Lee's lover, is lynched:

> You paid for your dinner, Sammy boy,
> And you didn't pay with money.
> You paid with your hide and my heart, Sammy boy,
> For your taste of pink and white honey,
> Honey,
> Honey,
> For your taste of pink and white honey.

Here, one possible motif in the poem is the price that Pearl May Lee pays for her measure of sweet revenge: the diminution of her own capacity to express love and compassion for another—however ill-fated—human being. But the element of realism that Brooks injects into her ballad by showing Pearl May Lee's mocking detachment from her lover's fate is a conscious effort to devalue the romantic idealization of Black love. Furthermore, Pearl May Lee's macabre humor undermines the racial pride and harmony that was an important tenet in the Renaissance prescription for the New Negro. And, lastly, Pearl May Lee's predicament belies the social myth of the Black woman as *objective correlative* of the Renaissance's romanticism. (pp. 39-41)

For Brooks, unlike the Renaissance poets, the victimization of poor Black women becomes not simply a minor chord but a predominant theme of *A Street in Bronzeville.* Few, if any, of her female characters are able to free themselves from the web of poverty and racism that threatens to strangle their lives. The Black heroine in **"obituary for a living lady"** was "decently wild / As a child," but as a victim of society's hypocritical, puritan standards, she "fell in love with a man who didn't know / That even if she wouldn't let him touch her breasts she / was still worth his hours." In another example of the complex life-choices confronting Brooks's women, the two sisters of **"Sadie and Maude"** must choose between death-in-life and life-in-death. Maude, who went to college, becomes a "think brown mouse," presumably resigned to spinsterhood, "living all alone / In this old house," while Sadie who "scraped life / With a fine-tooth comb" bears two illegitimate children and dies, leaving as a heritage for her children her "fine-tooth comb." What is noticeable in the lives of these Black women is a mu-

tual identity that is inextricably linked with race and poverty. (pp. 43-4)

Brooks's relationship with the Harlem Renaissance poets, as *A Street in Bronzeville* ably demonstrates, was hardly imitative. As one of the important links with the Black poetic tradition of the 1920s and 1930s, she enlarged the element of realism that was an important part of the Renaissance world-view. Although her poetry is often conditioned by the optimism that was also a legacy of the period, Brooks rejects outright their romantic prescriptions for the lives of Black women. And in this regard, she serves as a vital link with the Black Arts Movement of the 1960s that, while it witnessed the flowering of Black women as poets and social activists as well as the rise of Black feminist aesthetics in the 1970s, brought about a curious revival of romanticism in the Renaissance mode.

However, since the publication of *A Street in Bronzeville,* Brooks has not eschewed the traditional roles and values of Black women in American society; on the contrary, in her subsequent works, *Annie Allen* (1949), *The Bean Eaters* (1960), and *The Mecca* (1968), she has been remarkably consistent in identifying the root cause of intraracial problems within the Black community as white racism and its pervasive socioeconomic effects. Furthermore, as one of the chief voices of the Black Arts Movement, she has developed a social vision, in such works as *Riot* (1969), *Family Pictures* (1970), and *Beckonings* (1975), that describes Black women and men as equally integral parts of the struggle for social and economic justice. (p. 45)

Gary Smith, "Gwendolyn Brooks's 'A Street in Bronzeville', the Harlem Renaissance and the Mythologies of Black Women," in *MELUS,* Vol. 10, No. 3, Fall, 1983, pp. 33-46.

NORRIS B. CLARK

(essay date 1987)

[In the following excerpt, Clark explores Brooks's later poems, including the collections *Aloneness, Beckonings, Family Pictures,* and *Riot.*]

In essence, Gwendolyn Brooks's thematic concerns, the tense and complex dimensions of living through the paths of petty destinies, have changed but have not eliminated an acceptance of those who choose to live and to love differently. Unlike the more radical black aesthetic poets, she does not condemn the "Intellectual Audience" as Nikki Giovanni has done, or equate Negroes with repulsive beasts as does Welton Smith in "The Nigga Section," or curse white people, as in Carolyn Rodgers's "The Last M. F." Brooks's later works,

Riot, Aloneness, Family Pictures, and *Beckonings,* instead, emphasize a need for black unity by using "the exile rhythms of a Black people still seeking to establish at-homeness in America," but not to the exclusion of universal themes and subjects such as "brotherly love," literary critics, heroes, music, love between man and woman, false ideals, friendship, beautiful black blues. Nor like the more radical or political black poets of the sixties and early seventies such as Imamu Baraka, Sonia Sanchez, the "radical" phase of Nikki Giovanni, Welton Smith, or other black aesthetic advocates does Brooks create racist, propagandistic, and taciturn poems that advocate violence as therapeutic (Fanon's dictum), exhort whites to bring about equality, castigate or demean others. Instead, she depicts black realities without brutally frank language via her black voice, a voice that emanates a conscious humanistic concern for others. Similar to "great masters," Brooks's poetry does not tell us that there is evil, corruption, oppression, futility, or racism; rather, she shows us the tragedy and its relationship to individuals in hopes that we may learn a moral insight from the juxtaposition of beauty and horror, death in life as in **"The Life of Lincoln West."**

Brooks's unique voice in her latest poetry is one that not only ideologically varies from a narrowly defined black aesthetic, but also thematically deviates from its total reliance on obscure African references or Africa as a source of inspiration or upon a doctrine of how to live, as in Ron Karenga's Kawaida Doctrine, or a pro-Muslim religious orientation as some black aestheticians advocate:

> Blackness
> is a going to essences and to unifyings.
> "MY NAME IS AFRIKA!"
> Well, every fella's a Foreign Country.
> This Foreign Country speaks to you.

Not surprisingly, Brooks's voice which contrasts the American ideals and practices—W. E. B. Du Bois's "Veil Metaphor"—especially the insensitivity and ignorance of whites toward blacks, as in *Riot,* is not filled with private symbolism or biting satire. Rather, self-identity in Brooks's poems leads to group-identity. She does not, as Baraka has done, only focus on a black nationalist, black Muslim, black power, or blacker-than-black perspective. Rather, her voice is one that recreates the feelings and thoughts of the unheard, as riots do, rather than merely languish in a black aesthetic of polemics devoid of lyricism. Even though Brooks's poetry calls for a black dignity and a black pride, erstwhile symbolized by Africa, she acknowledges that blacks "know so little of that long leap languid land [Africa]" and suggests that enacting "our inward law"—unity (community, family) among black Americans—is more important than any external reliances upon a leader, a

god or God(s) or the heat of "easy griefs that fool and fuel nothing." Her attempt to create black unity is not to establish a bond among third-world peoples but to establish a bond between those oppressed black Americans who "are defining their own Roof. . . . " Consequently, her content is not only specifically American but is, more so than many writers of a black aesthetic persuasion, also reflective of the attitudes, aspirations, and concerns of black Americans as they *historically* have been confronted with the denial of American ideals, racism, and pathos of human choice.

Unlike the black writers of polemics and propaganda or the rhetoricians of hate and violence, Brooks doesn't attempt to impose her personal philosophy upon others; she does not demean or denigrate blacks whose psychological mechanism to survive leads them to be "Toms" or race traitors. (In fact, some critics have questioned her attitudes or personal voice as not being strong enough on issues such as abortion.) Brooks's poetry remains one of love and affirmation, one that accepts some hate and perhaps some violence as necessary without condemning or castigating those who have been pawns to interracial and intraracial forces. Adequately reflecting the hopes and aspirations of the black community, Brooks displays a love for her brothers and sisters regardless of psychosocial or socioeconomic position. In doing so, she clearly embraces "blackness" and the values of liberation, and thus the values of all humanity. That quality, despite an emphasis on embracing blacks first, is one that is universal in literature of self-affirmation and self-identity; the universal is revealed through the particular. As her sensitivity to the spirit of social revolution emanates from her sense of "love," Brooks advocates a sense of self-love and compassion while reflecting the tensions of her time period, a tension due to racial oppression: "On the street we smile. / We go / in different directions / down the imperturbable street."

Thematically and imagistically, Brooks's poetry after *In the Mecca* reflects a social sensibility that incorporates, as her earlier work has done, especially war poems, the expressive and mimetic aspects of a black experience rather than an arbitrary, political black aesthetic. An art form that has aesthetic qualities related to the black experience should, by definition, incorporate a sense of what it is like to face life's multitude of complexities as a person affected by racial values (Afrocentric and Eurocentric) pertaining to the black communities. Regardless of the ideological or social position the writer has, the genre should render that representation in a manner that is most particular, although not necessarily unique, to an existence as a person confronted with the issues of "blackness." This is not meant to imply that the central theme must be about blackness; rather it is to suggest that the world view that the art conveys, in theme as well as in image and structure, should provide a sense of what it is like to see historically, culturally, and psychologically through the eyes of a black person. The tensions of living as a black person—whether in blackness or whiteness—should be illustrated and discernible. To that end, Brooks's poetry extends. If one considers her multidimensional themes combined with her conscious attempt to fuse the traditional with the colloquial or common, it is evident that Brooks's later poetry is not thematically "more black" than her earlier poetry. Her poetry, despite her diminished reliance upon formal diction, continues to be an expression of her craftsmanship as well as an expression of her black voice as expressed in 1950. "Every Negro poet has 'something to say.' Simply because he is a Negro he cannot escape having important things to say."

The technical proficiency with which Brooks creates those meaningful lives, whether heroic, mock heroic, or parody, is what poetry is about. It is to that specific end, exposing the truth of human existence in forms meaningful to the black community, that Brooks's poetry leads. Despite the extension of Gwendolyn Brooks's poetry to a new black consciousness of the late 1960s and 1970s, her formal devices remain as alive in her later poetry as they are in her earlier poetry. She does continue to pay attention to craft, to the neat turn of phrase: "Now the way of the Mecca was on this wise," "as her underfed haunches jerk jazz," or "In the precincts of a nightmare all contrary. . . . " She "blackens English": "That Song it sing the sweetness / like a good Song can, . . . ", "Unhalt hands," or uses extensive alliteration: "These merely peer and purr / and pass the passion over." She continues to infuse the traditional standard American English not only with her intuitional phrasing and coinage of words, but also with the "common folk phrasing" as exhibited in songs and folk sermons. In doing so, Brooks's poetry is more reflective of aesthetic relativism while maintaining some elements of traditional "white" culture as in "Que tu es grossier!" or "death in the afternoon." That relativism related to the black experience can be observed in her use of black folk heroes, or in **"The Wall,"** a poem in which art for art's sake is not a valid concept whereas the wall allows celebration and commitment (i.e., it is communal and functional as "Negritude" advocates). Specific references are made to black literary heroes as in **"Five Men Against the Theme, 'My Name is Red Hot. Yo Name ain Doodley Squat,' "** or musical heroes as in **"Steam Song"**, (Al Green) or **"The Young Men Run"** (Melvin Van Peebles). Combined with the sounds and sense of sermons, jazz, blues, and double entendre, these references help to bring ghetto life alive and to enhance the significance of an idea and its "metaphysical function" as in **"Elegy in a Rainbow."** In addition, Brooks continues to exhibit irony, a complex sense of reality, a sensitivity

to traditional line and beats, metered as well as in free verse. She juxtaposes lines that appear to move rapidly with those that tend to slow the reader down, as in **"The Boy Died in My Alley."** Furthermore, she uses sudden contrasts or repetition to make each word bear the full measure of weight and suggestion. "I don't want to stop a concern with words doing good jobs. . . . " Whether extravagant overstatement or understatement as in **"A Poem to Peanut,"** all of those elements not only exist in black literature, but have always been a part of Brooks's concept of polishing her technique. (pp. 90-4)

Although the forms of Gwendolyn Brooks's poetry contribute to and enhance an understanding of the content—move it from the simple, mundane, and colloquial to a complex, eternal, and universal—her recent poetry does achieve aesthetic beauty and historical truth. It fails functionally in her terms only. Her latest objective: "I want to write poetry that will appeal to many, many blacks, not just the blacks who go to college but also those who have their customary habitat in taverns and the street. . . . " is not, as she acknowledges, achieved because it doesn't reach those "taverneers." Brooks acknowledges her failure of *Riot*—"It's too meditative"—and *Beckonings* has a dual impulse (a self-analytic commentary on the nature of her own poetry). She also states that only two love poems (songs), **"When you've forgotten Sunday"** and **"Steam Song,"** can be well received in tavern readings. Similar to some of the "Broadside poets," as well as other black writers who desire to write for the black masses—as Walt Whitman and Ralph Waldo Emerson had also advocated—Gwendolyn Brooks falsely assumes that her task is to create art for those who don't appreciate formal art. As with most poetry, even that which infuses informal folk elements with formal literary elements, undereducated or subeducated persons—those to whom the fourth-to-sixth-grade reading level of newspapers appeals—cannot or choose not to be subjected to it. Rarely do they appreciate the subtlety and interrelationships of finely turned phrases or understand, reflectively or meditatively, the appeal of formal alliteration and repetition to a complex meaning or abstract idea. The unsophisticated generally expresses an emotional understanding or appreciation of rhythm or meter by nodding or tapping his or her foot; the sophisticated generally searches, from an objective distance, for rhetorical and metrical relationships or correlations to history, psychology, religion, or culture. Ironically, it is precisely because Brooks's poetry fails to appeal to the black masses that it appeals aesthetically to the "blacks who go to college" as well as those *littérateurs* who can and will reflect upon the "sound and sense" of a poetic artifact. (p. 95)

The aesthetic success of Gwendolyn Brooks's later poetry, and her sense of its failure, reflects the historical literary dilemma of cognitively and emotively appreciating the truth and beauty of a black experience and art per se. To create art reductively, only for one group, limits the art; to create art without letting it organically or ontologically exist limits the number of persons who have the faculties with which to appreciate it. Formal art can never be truly functional; folk art is always functional. To infuse, as Gwendolyn Brooks has, the informal with the formal, in a medium designed to be formal, subsumes the informal component, especially when it evolves from a self-conscious literary formalism. Thus attempting to reach those in taverns, the origins of some folk traditions, alters and negates the ontological component of art. It necessarily extends it beyond the folk to the formal by making it solely functional in a "literary" sense. What Brooks does with words, forms, and content—not consciously imitating anyone—is the essence of the aesthetic imagination unifying disparate elements into a coherent whole—structurally, semantically, and phonetically. As a spokesperson of the black masses, Brooks is literally different from those for whom she writes; consequently, she is the "seer and the sayer," the Emersonian poet, who articulates the needs, ideas, and aspirations of others. In doing so, she can only create, to make clear in terms she knows and understands, her perception of the raw material. Her quest, then, is to create works of an aesthetic nature and of a "black origin"—whether critics appreciate it or not. To do so, as she has, is not "to be content with offering raw materials. The Negro poet's most urgent duty, at present, is to polish his technique, his way of presenting his truths and beauties, that those may be more insinuating, and therefore, more overwhelming." (p. 96)

Norris B. Clark, "Gwendolyn Brooks and a Black Aesthetic," in *A Life Distilled: Gwendolyn Brooks, Her Poetry and Fiction,* edited by Maria K. Mootry and Gary Smith, University of Illinois Press, 1987, pp. 81-99.

SOURCES FOR FURTHER STUDY

Dawson, Emma Waters. "Vanishing Point: The Rejected Black Woman in the Poetry of Gwendolyn Brooks." *Obsidian II* 4, No. 1 (Spring 1989): 1-11.

> Traces the development of Brooks's depiction in her poetry of the black woman's attitude toward her physical appearance.

Kent, George E. *A Life of Gwendolyn Brooks.* Lexington: University Press of Kentucky, 1990, 287 p.

> Definitive biography completed by Kent, a leading Brooks scholar, prior to his death in 1982. An afterword by D. H. Melham provides material on Brooks's life and career since 1978.

Mootry, Maria K., and Smith, Gary, eds. *A Life Distilled: Gwendolyn Brooks, Her Poetry and Fiction.* Urbana: University of Illinois Press, 1987, 286 p.

> Collection of essays exploring Brooks's career and analyzing her works.

Ryan, William F. "Blackening the Language." *American Visions* 3, No. 6 (December 1988): 32-7.

> Interview with Brooks and overview of her career.

Satz, Martha. "Honest Reporting: An Interview with Gwendolyn Brooks." *Southwest Review* 74, No. 1 (Winter 1989): 25-35.

> Brooks discusses her poetry and her perceptions of herself as a black woman and a poet.

Whitaker, Charles. "Gwendolyn Brooks: A Poet for All Ages." *Ebony* XLII, No. 8 (June 1987): 154 ff.

> Profile of Brooks's life and career, occasioned by her seventieth birthday.

Elizabeth Barrett Browning

1806-1861

English poet and translator.

INTRODUCTION

Browning is remembered for her masterful *Sonnets from the Portuguese* (1850), one of the most beautiful love cycles in English literature. Written to celebrate the courtship of Elizabeth and her husband, the poet Robert Browning, this collection is an intimate depiction of the intricacies of romantic love. Although her poetry has been criticized for technical carelessness, recent critics have contended that her unconventional rhymes and loose diction were neither negligent nor haphazard, but deliberate experiments by a conscientious student of prosody. Nevertheless, critics concur that Browning's poetry is damaged by her emphasis on passionate emotion over clear expression, and most agree that she achieved her highest poetic expression in the sonnet, whose formal structure restrained her effusiveness.

Elizabeth Barrett was the eldest of eleven children of a wealthy and domineering father who, while forbidding his daughters to marry, nevertheless encouraged their scholarly pursuits. He was so proud of Elizabeth's extraordinary proficiency in classical studies that he privately published her juvenile epic, *The Battle of Marathon,* when she was fourteen. Around this time, she injured her spine in a riding accident and seemed doomed to a life of infirmity and confinement. The drowning death several years later of her favorite brother sent her into a depression that made her condition worse. Elizabeth continued to study and write, however, publishing *An Essay on Mind, with Other Poems* in 1826, followed by a translation of Aeschylus's *Prometheus Bound* in 1833, both of which appeared anonymously. These efforts, along with *The Seraphim, and Other Poems* (1838), her first signed volume, attracted much favorable attention, and almost immediately she was regarded as a serious and talented poet. From her sickroom in the family home on

Wimpole Street in London, Barrett dedicated herself to the literary life, receiving select guests, notably Mary Russell Mitford, and corresponding frequently with various literati, among them Edgar Allan Poe, James Russell Lowell, and Thomas Carlyle, all of whom sent flattering appraisals of her poetry. When asked for a description of her life at this time, she said: "A bird in a cage could have as good a story. Most of my events and nearly all my intense pleasures have passed in my thoughts."

But the poet's life was to undergo dramatic change. Elizabeth Barrett admired *Bells and Pomegranates,* the work of a little-known poet six years her junior, and expressed her appreciation in "Lady Geraldine's Courtship": "Or from Browning some 'Pomegranate' which, if cut deep down in the middle, / Shows a heart within, Blood-tinctured, of a veined humanity." Deeply moved by this tribute from a recognized poet, Robert Browning responded in a letter, "I love your verses with all my heart, dear Miss Barrett," and a few lines later, "I love you, too." Robert Browning became a frequent visitor to Wimpole Street. In 1846, ignoring her poor health and the disapprobation of Mr. Barrett, the poets eloped to Italy and settled briefly in Pisa before relocating to Florence in 1848. Elizabeth's triumphant emergence from the sick room, in addition to her son's birth in 1849 and the stimulating presence of her husband, inspired in her a creative energy that did not flag until her death at age fifty-five.

Sonnets from the Portuguese records the growth of love between Elizabeth Barrett and Robert Browning. The volume includes Sonnet XLIII, which commences, "How do I love thee? Let me count the ways," Barrett's most inspired poem and the work most closely identified with her name. Although Elizabeth began the sonnets early in their courtship, she refrained from showing them to her husband, for she had once heard him object to writing about one's loves. It was not until 1849 that she showed Robert the forty-four poems. Overwhelmed, he convinced her to include them in her *Poems* of 1850, yet because of the intensely personal quality of the verse, neither wanted to acknowledge its autobiographical nature. The title, *Sonnets from the Portuguese,* was thus selected to present the poems as translations instead of original compositions.

Browning expressed her political passion for Italian liberal causes in *Casa Guidi Windows* (1851) and *Poems before Congress* (1860). Critics generally dismiss this fervent verse as reckless and overly emotional. Although these volumes originally generated great controversy, they are now little read. A gentler statement is found in *Aurora Leigh* (1856), an ambitious novel in blank verse. While praising the power of many passages in the work, critics have found fault with the somewhat colorless didacticism of the social criticism.

Nevertheless, the poem was widely read and admired in its day. More recently, Browning's unorthodox rhyme and diction, once scorned, have been cited as daring experiments that prefigure the techniques of George Meredith and Gerard Manley Hopkins. *Aurora Leigh* remains one of Browning's most characteristic creations, embodying both her strengths and weaknesses as a writer.

When *Sonnets from the Portuguese* was published, most critics completely overlooked the work. It was not until a few years later, when the autobiographical nature of the sonnets' composition became known, that they received widespread critical recognition. Response to the poems was glowingly favorable. Early commentators praised their sincerity and intensity; most concurred that no woman had ever written in such openly passionate tones. In addition, it was argued that the emotion of Browning's verse was effectively balanced by the strict technical restraints of the sonnet form. Several critics compared the adept technique utilized in the sonnets to that of John Milton and Shakespeare. Typical comments include those of Richard Henry Stoddard, who termed the sonnets "the noblest ever written . . . by anybody," and William T. Herridge, who stated that they were "an exquisite revelation of a woman's heart."

By the turn of the century, critics were more cautious in their praise of the sonnets. Some of the topics discussed at this time were Browning's lyricism, rhyme schemes, and, as before, the affective content of her verse. Browning's emotionality was reevaluated in later years; what had been earlier defined as impassioned honesty was now deemed overbearing and, according to Marjory A. Bald, acutely self-conscious sentimentalism. Some critics, however, have stressed such technical merits of the sonnets as their versification and imagery and have expressed unqualified admiration for the cycle in its entirety.

In the lavish eulogies that appeared at the time of her death, Elizabeth Barrett Browning was called Britain's greatest woman poet. While her reputation has faltered, she is revered not simply as a sonneteer but as a literary heroine. It has been suggested, in fact, that the overpowering Browning legend—the brilliant invalid fleeing from tyrannical father to poet-lover—has distracted critics from the merits of her work. Both as a revealing chronicle of a famous love story and as a technically skilled rendering of poetry's most demanding form, *Sonnets from the Portuguese* endures as a testimony to Browning's poetic powers.

(For further information about Browning's life and works, see *Dictionary of Literary Biography,* Vols. 21, 32; and *Nineteenth-Century Literature Criticism,* Vols. 1, 16)

CRITICAL COMMENTARY

THE SATURDAY REVIEW
(essay date 1856)

[In the excerpt below from an unsigned review, the critic finds fault with *Aurora Leigh*'s "three component parts, of fable, manners, and diction" but praises its "abundant store of poetical thought, of musical language, and of deep and true reflection."]

Aurora Leigh is wholly and obviously a fiction. The characters are few and unreal—the incidents, though scanty, are almost inconceivable—and the heroine and autobiographer, as a professed poetess, has tastes and occupations which are, beyond all others, incapable of poetical treatment. With all nature and life at its command, Art is only precluded from selecting its own mechanism as its subject. But, of late, the poet's eye, instead of glancing from earth to heaven, seems, by some strange inversion, to be exclusively fixed on the process of writing verses. The details of authorship probably possess a professional interest for those whom they concern; but life at a college, in a hospital, or in a special pleader's chambers, would furnish more interesting pictures to the world at large. . . .

Imagination and passion naturally express themselves, from time to time, in figurative terms, when they overleap or outrun the capabilities of ordinary language; but an unbroken series of far-fetched metaphors indicates a deliberate exercise of ingenuity which is in itself essentially prosaic, and all dramatic illusion disappears when two persons pitch their dialogue in the same artificial key. . . . [The heroine of this poem,] poetess Aurora, in controversy with her philanthropic cousin and lover, may perhaps be allowed to vindicate Art as opposed to utilitarian practice, in long strings of allusive phrases; but [the hero] Romney Leigh is equally incapable of calling a spade, in plain language, a spade; and when one of the disputants starts a metaphor, the other almost invariably hunts it down. (p. 776)

Mrs. Browning's poem is open to criticism in all its three component parts, of fable, manners, and diction. The story is fantastical, the conduct of the personages in the narrative is whimsically absurd, and their language is as euphuistic as that of Don Armado or of Sir Piercie Shafton. . . .

[However,] after eliminating the story, the eccentricities of the actors, and a great part of the dialogue, there will remain an abundant store of poetical thought, of musical language, and of deep and true reflection. The book will best display its real merits on a second reading, when the paradoxes in action, language, and thought which encumber the composition are tacitly set aside. Mrs. Browning has a fine ear, and an observant mind. Her partial failure is far less attributable to a want of poetical instinct than to the erroneous theory that art is the proper subject for itself. When Aurora forgets that she is a poetess—or, still better, when she is herself forgotten—the troublesome machinery which had been interposed between the writer and reality is effectually removed. If Mrs. Browning would trust her first thoughts, and condescend to be simple, she would be almost always picturesque and forcible. (p. 777)

With all her imperfections, most of which are voluntary, Mrs. Browning may claim at least an equal rank with any poetess who has appeared in England. (p. 778)

A review of "Aurora Leigh," in *The Saturday Review, London,* Vol. 2, No. 61, December 27, 1856, pp. 776-78.

COVENTRY PATMORE
(essay date 1857)

[Patmore occupies a minor but conspicuous place in Victorian literature as the poet of both married and mystical love. Here, he describes Browning's weaknesses and strengths as a sonneteer.]

Mrs. Browning shines nowhere to greater advantage than in the sonnet. Her lyrical verse is seldom good. In proportion as poetry aims at lyrical character, it becomes necessary that it should possess that absolute perfection of verbal expression, which is given by vivid lyrical feeling—that rarest of all poetical qualities. To write a good sonnet demands power of a high order. It requires that some grave and novel thought should be expressed in high and pure language, and in an extremely elaborate form, the limits of which are fixed. Mrs. Browning brings to her task the industry, the thoughtfulness, and the power of language which are requisite; and accordingly she has written several sonnets which will bear comparison with the best in the language. It must be confessed, however, that Mrs. Browning gives us specimens of sonnets presenting

Principal Works

An Essay on Mind, with Other Poems (poetry) 1826

Prometheus Bound, Translated from the Greek of Aeschylus And Miscellaneous Poems by the Translator [translator] (poetry) 1833

The Seraphim, and Other Poems (poetry) 1838

*Poems (poetry) 1844; also published as A Drama of Exile and Other Poems, 1844; revised edition, 1850

Casa Guidi Windows (poetry) 1851

Aurora Leigh (poetry) 1856

Poems before Congress (poetry) 1860

Last Poems (poetry) 1862

*The 1850 revision of this work contains Sonnets from the Portuguese.

---

very marked defects. It is quite wonderful into what mistakes this lady sometimes falls, particularly when she is under the impression that she is doing something remarkably good. Perhaps the most absurd line that was ever written by so good a poet is the following, concluding the sonnet to **"Hiram Powers' Greek Slave,"** and adjuring her to

> Strike and shame the strong,
> *By thunders of white silence overthrown.*

Mrs. Browning's worst fault is her almost constant endeavour to be "striking." This tendency has deformed her volumes with scores of passages scarcely less offensive to true taste than the above. Such passages are not only bad in themselves, but, being as it were, the hypocrisy of art, they cast suspicion and discredit upon their context wherever they occur. They are proof positive of absence of true feeling—of the tone of mind that "voluntary moves harmonious numbers"—at the time of writing; and the only poem of Mrs. Browning's from which they are almost entirely absent, is the series of *Sonnets from the Portuguese,* for the originals of which we fancy that we must seek in vain, unless we detect them in the personal feelings of the writer. In this series of sonnets we have unquestionably one of Mrs. Browning's most beautiful and worthy productions. In style they are openly—indeed by the title avowedly—an imitation of the fourteenth and fifteenth century love-poetry; but to imitate this is so nearly equivalent to imitating nature of the simplest and loftiest kind, that it is scarcely to be spoken of as a defect of originality. The forty-four sonnets constitute consecutive stanzas of what is properly speaking one poem. They are lofty, simple, and passionate—not at all the less passionate for being highly intellectual and even metaphysical. (pp. 446-47)

Coventry Patmore, in an originally unsigned essay titled, "Mrs. Browning's 'Poems'," in *The North British Review,* Vol. XXVI, No. LII, February, 1857, pp. 443-62.

EDMUND CLARENCE STEDMAN
(essay date 1875)

[In the excerpt below, Stedman offers a mixed appraisal of Browning's poetry.]

[Elizabeth Barrett Browning's] first venture of significance was in the field of translation. *Prometheus Bound, and Miscellaneous Poems,* was published in her twenty-fourth year. The poems were equally noticeable for faults and excellences, of which we have yet to speak. The translation was at that time a unique effort for a young lady, and good practice; but abounded in grotesque peculiarities, and in fidelity did not approach the modern standard. In riper years she freed it from her early mannerism, and recast it in the shape now left to us, "in expiation," she said, "of a sin of my youth, with the sincerest application of my mature mind." This later version of a most sublime tragedy is more poetical than any other of equal correctness, and has the fire and vigor of a master-hand. No one has succeeded better than its author in capturing with rhymed measures the wilful rushing melody of the tragic chorus. Her other translations were executed for her own pleasure, and it rarely was her pleasure to be exactly faithful to her text. She was honest enough to call them what they are; and we must own that her "Paraphrases on" Theocritus, Homer, Apuleius, etc., are enjoyable poems in themselves, preserving the spirit of their originals, yet graceful with that freedom of which Shelley's "Hymn to Mercury" is the most winsome English exemplar since Chapman's time. (pp. 121-22)

The disadvantages, no less than the advantages, of [Miss Barrett's] education, were apparent at the outset. She could not fail to be affected by various masterminds, and when she had outgrown one influence was drawn within another, and so tossed about from world to world. **"The Seraphim,"** a diffuse, mystical passion-play, was an echo of the Aeschylean drama. Its meaning was scarcely clear even to the author; the rhythm is wild and discordant; neither music nor meaning is thoroughly beaten out. . . . Miss Barrett's early verse was strangely combined of . . . semi-musical delirium and obscurity, with an attempt at the Greek dramatic form. Her ballads, on the other hand, were a reflection of her English studies; and, as being more English and human, were a vast poetic advance upon **"The Seraphim."** Evidently, in these varied experiments, she was conscious of power, and strove to exercise it, yet with no direct purpose, and half doubtful of her themes, when, therefore, as in certain of these lyrics, she got hold of a rare story or suggestion, she made an artistic poem; all are stamped with her sign-manual, and one or two are as lovely as anything on which her fame will rest. (pp. 124-25)

The effect of Miss Barrett's secluded life was visible in her diction, which was acquired from books rather than by intercourse with the living world; and from books of all periods, so that she seemed unconscious that certain words were obsolete, or repellent even to cultured and tasteful people. . . . The difficulty with her obsolete words was that they were introduced unnaturally, and produced a grotesque effect instead of an attractive quaintness. Moreover, her slovenly elisions, indiscriminate mixture of old and new verbal inflections, eccentric rhymes, forced accents, wearisome repetition of favored words to a degree that almost implied poverty of thought,—such matters justly were held to be an outrage upon the beauty and dignity of metrical art. An occasional discord has its use and charm, but harshness in her verse was the rule rather than the exception. When she had a felicitous refrain—a peculiar grace of her lyrics—she frequently would mar the effect and give a shock to her readers by the introduction of some whimsical or repulsive image. Her passion was spasmodic; her sensuousness lacked substance; as for simplicity, it was at one time questionable whether she was not to be classed among those who, with a turbulent desire for utterance, really have nothing definite to say. (pp. 126-27)

In **"A Drama of Exile,"** where she had a more definite object, these faults are less apparent, and her genius shines through the clouds; so that we catch glimpses of the brightness which eventually lighted her to a station in the Valhalla of renown. . . . [In "A Drama of Exile"] she aimed at the highest, and failed; but such failures are impossible to smaller poets. It contains wonderfully fine passages; is a chaotic mass, from which dazzling lustres break out. . . . (pp. 127-28)

None of her later or earlier compositions were equal to [*Casa Guidi Windows, Sonnets from the Portuguese,* and *Aurora Leigh*] in scope, method, and true poetical value.

[A] surprising advance was evident in the rhythm, language, and all other constituents of her metrical work. The Saxon English, which she hitherto had quarried for the basis of her verse, now became conspicuous throughout the whole structure. Her technical gain was partly due to the stronger themes which now bore up her wing,—and partly, I have no doubt, to the companionship of Robert Browning. Even if he did not directly revise her works, neither could fail to profit by the other's genius and experience. . . . (p. 136)

I am disposed to consider the *Sonnets from the Portuguese* as, if not the finest, a portion of the finest subjective poetry in our literature. Their form reminds us of an English prototype, and it is no sacrilege to say that their music is showered from a higher and purer atmosphere than that of the Swan of Avon. . . . Here, indeed, the singer rose to her height. Here she is absorbed in rapturous utterance, radiant and triumphant with her own joy. The mists have risen and her sight is clear. Her mouthing and affectation are forgotten, her lips cease to stammer, the lyrical spirit has full control. The sonnet, artificial in weaker hands, becomes swift with feeling, red with a "veined humanity," the chosen vehicle of a royal woman's vows. (p. 137)

If Mrs. Browning's vitality had failed her before the production of *Aurora Leigh,* . . . her generation certainly would have lost one of its representative and original creations; representative in a versatile, kaleidoscopic presentment of modern life and issues; original, because the most idiosyncratic of its author's poems. An audacious, speculative freedom pervades it, which smacks of the New World rather than the Old. Tennyson, while examining the social and intellectual phases of his era, maintains a judicial impassiveness; Mrs. Browning, with finer dramatic insight,—the result of intense human sympathy, enters into the spirit of each experiment, and for the moment puts herself in its advocate's position. *Aurora Leigh* is a mirror of contemporary life, while its learned and beautiful illustrations make it, almost, a handbook of literature and the arts. As a poem, merely, it is a failure, if it be fair to judge it by accepted standards. One may say of it, as of Byron's *Don Juan* (though loath to couple the two works in any comparison), that, although a most uneven production, full of ups and downs, of capricious or prosaic episodes, it nevertheless contains poetry as fine as its author has given us elsewhere, and enough spare inspiration to set up a dozen smaller poets. The flexible verse is noticeably her own, and often handled with as much spirit as freedom; it is terser than her husband's, and, although his influence now began to grow upon her, is not in the least obscure to any cultured reader. The plan of the work is a metrical concession to the fashion of a time which has substituted the novel for the dramatic poem. Considered as a "novel in verse," it is a failure by lack of either constructive talent or experience on the author's part. . . . Mrs. Browning essayed to invent her whole story, and the result was an incongruous framework, covered with her thronging, suggestive ideas, her flashing poetry and metaphor, and confronting you by whichever gateway you enter with the instant presence of her very self. But either as poem or novel, how superior the whole, in beauty and intellectual power, to contemporary structures upon a similar model, which found favor with the admirers of parlor romance or the lamb's-wool sentiment of orderly British life! As a social treatise it is also a failure, since nothing definite is arrived at. Yet the poet's sense of existing wrongs is clear and exalted, and if her exposition of them is chaotic, so was the transition period in which she found herself involved. Upon the whole, I think that the chief value and interest of *Aurora Leigh* appertain to its marvellous illustrations of the development, from childhood on, of an aesthetical, imaginative nature. Nowhere in literature is the process of culture by means of study and passional experience so graphically depicted. (pp. 140-42)

Her metres came by chance, and this often to her detriment; she rarely had the patience to discover those best adapted to her needs, but gave voice to the first strain which occurred to her. Hence she had a spontaneity which is absent from the Laureate's work. This charming element has its drawbacks: she found herself hampered by difficulties which a little forethought would have avoided, and her song, though as fresh, was too often as purposeless, as that of a forestbird. There is great music in her voice, but one wishes that it were better trained. (p. 145)

Her spontaneous and exhaustless command of words gave her a large and free style, but likewise a dangerous facility, and it was only in rare instances, like the one just cited, that she attained to the strength and sweetness of repose. Her intense earnestness spared her no leisure for humor, a feature curiously absent from her writings: she almost lacked the sense of the ludicrous, as may be deduced from some of her two-word rhymes, and from various absurdities solemnly indulged in. But of wit and satire she has more than enough, and lashes all kinds of tyranny and hypocrisy with supernal scorn. It is perhaps due to her years of indoor life that the influence of landscape-scenery is not more visible in her poetry. . . . [She] uses by preference the works of man rather than those of Nature: architecture, furniture, pictures, books above all, rather than water, sky, and forest. Men and women were the chief objects of her regard,—her genius was more dramatic than idyllic, and lyric first of all.

The instinct of worship and the religion of humanity were pervading constituents of Mrs. Browning's nature, and demand no less attention than the love which dictated her most fervent poems. A spiritual trinity, of zeal, love, and worship, presided over her work. If in her outcry against wrong she had nothing decisive to suggest, she at least sounded a clarion note for the incitement of her comrades and successors. . . . (pp. 146-47)

Edmund Clarence Stedman, "Elizabeth Barrett Browning," in his *Victorian Poets,* revised edition, Houghton Mifflin Company, 1875, pp. 114-49.

VIRGINIA WOOLF
(essay date 1931)

[Woolf was an English novelist, essayist, and short story writer. In the excerpt below from an essay first published in 1931 in *The Times Literary Supplement*, she praises the spirit of *Aurora Leigh*, stating that "we laugh, we protest, we complain of a thousand absurdities, but . . . we read to the end enthralled."]

[We] cannot read the first twenty pages of *Aurora Leigh* without becoming aware that the Ancient Mariner who lingers, for unknown reasons, at the porch of one book and not of another has us by the hand, and makes us listen like a three years child while Mrs. Browning pours out in nine volumes of blank verse the story of Aurora Leigh. Speed and energy, forthrightness and complete self-confidence—these are the qualities that hold us enthralled. (p. 220)

[*Aurora Leigh*] is a masterpiece in embryo; a work whose genius floats diffused and fluctuating in some pre-natal stage waiting the final stroke of creative power to bring it into being. Stimulating and boring, ungainly and eloquent, monstrous and exquisite all by turns, it overwhelms and bewilders; but, nevertheless, it still commands our interest and inspires respect. For it becomes clear as we read that, whatever Mrs. Browning's faults, she was one of those rare writers who risk themselves adventurously and disinterestedly in an imaginative life which is independent of their private lives and demands to be considered apart from personalities. Her "intention" survives; the interest of her theory redeems much that is faulty in her practice. Abridged and simplified from Aurora's argument in the fifth book, that theory runs something like this. The sole work of poets, she said, is to present their own age, not Charlemagne's. More passion takes place in drawing-rooms than at Roncesvalles with Roland and his knights. . . .

It was true that the old form in which poetry had dealt with life—the drama—was obsolete; but was there none other that could take its place? Mrs. Browning, convinced of the divinity of poetry, pondered, seized as much as she could of actual experience, and then at last threw down her challenge to the Brontës and the Thackerays in the nine books of blank verse. It was in blank verse that she sang of Shoreditch and Kensington; of my aunt and the vicar, of Romney Leigh and Vincent Carrington, of Marian Erle and Lord Howe, of fashionable weddings and drab suburban streets, and bonnets and whiskers and railway trains.

The poets can treat of these things, she exclaimed, as well as of knights and dames, moats and drawbridges and castle courts. But can they? Let us see what happens to a poet when he poaches upon a novelist's preserves. . . .

In the first place there is the story; a tale has to be told, and the poet must somehow convey to us the necessary information that his hero has been asked out to dinner. This is a statement that a novelist would convey as quietly and prosaically as possible; for example, "While I kissed her glove in my sadness, a note was brought saying that her father sent his regards and asked me to dine with them next day." That is harmless. But the poet has to write:—

> While thus I grieved, and kissed her glove,
>   My man brought in her note to say,
> Papa had bid her send his love,
>   And would I dine with them next day.

Which is absurd. The simple words have been made to strut and posture and take on an emphasis which makes them ridiculous. Then again, what will the poet do with dialogue? . . . [Poetry] when it tries to follow the words on people's lips is terribly impeded. Listen to Romney in a moment of high emotion talking to his old love Marian about the baby she has born to another man;—

> May God so father me, as I do him,
> And so forsake me, as I let him feel
> He's orphaned haply. Here I take the child
> To share my cup, to slumber on my knee,
> To play his loudest gambol at my foot,
> To hold my finger in the public ways . . .

and so on. Romney, in short, rants and reels like any of those Elizabethan heroes whom Mrs. Browning had warned so imperiously out of her modern living room. Blank verse has proved itself the most remorseless enemy of living speech. . . . Forced by the nature of her medium she ignores the slighter, the subtler, the more hidden shades of emotion by which a novelist builds up touch by touch a character in prose. Change and development, the effect of one character upon another—all this is abandoned. The poem becomes one long soliloquy and the only character that is known to us and the only story that is told us are the character and story of Aurora Leigh herself.

Thus, if Mrs. Browning meant by a novel-poem a book in which character is closely and subtly revealed, the relations of many hearts laid bare, and a story unfalteringly unfolded, she failed completely. But if she meant rather to give us a sense of life in general of people who are unmistakably Victorian, wrestling with the problems of their own time, all brightened, intensified, and compacted by the fire of poetry, she succeeded. . . . The broader aspects of what it felt like to be a Victorian are seized as surely and stamped as vividly upon us as in any novel by Trollope or Mrs. Gaskell.

And indeed if we compare the prose novel and the novel-poem the triumphs are by no means all to the credit of prose. As we rush through page after page of narrative in which a dozen scenes that the novelist would smooth out separately are pressed into one in which pages of deliberate description are fused into a single line, we cannot help feeling that the poet has outpaced the prose writer. Her page is packed twice as full as his. Characters, too, if they are not shown in conflict but snipped off and summed up with something of the exaggeration of a caricaturist, have a heightened and symbolical significance which prose with its gradual approach cannot rival. The general aspects of things, markets, sunsets, scenes in church, owing to the compressions and elisions of poetry have a brilliance and a continuity which mock the prose writer and his slow accumulations of careful detail. For these reasons *Aurora Leigh* remains, with all its imperfections, a book that still lives and breathes and has its being. . . . [We] may suspect that Elizabeth Barrett was inspired by a flash of true genius when she rushed into the drawing-room and said that here, where we live and work, is the true place for the poet. At any rate, her courage was justified in her own case. Her bad taste, her tortured ingenuity, her floundering, scrambling and confused impetuosity have space to spend themselves here without inflicting a deadly wound, while her ardour and abundance, her brilliant descriptive powers, her shrewd and caustic humour infect us with her own enthusiasm. We laugh, we protest, we complain of a thousand absurdities, but—and this, after all, is a great tribute to a writer—we read to the end enthralled. (pp. 225-31)

Virginia Woolf, "Aurora Leigh," in her *The Common Reader, first and second series,* Harcourt, Brace and Company, 1948, pp. 218-31.

CORA KAPLAN
(essay date 1978)

[In the following excerpt, Kaplan examines the role and position of women in Victorian literature as revealed in *Aurora Leigh*.]

[*Aurora Leigh*] produces the fullest and most violent exposition of the 'woman question' in mid-Victorian literature. . . . [It] is a collage of Romantic and Victorian texts reworked from a woman's perspective. Gender difference, class warfare, the relation of art to politics: these three subjects as they were argued by the English and Continental intelligentsia are all engaged as intersecting issues in the poem. The longest poem of the decade, it is, to use another 'woman's figure', a vast quilt, made up of other garments, the pattern dazzling because, not in spite, of its irregularities. (p. 5)

Aurora Leigh comes between two very explicitly political books: *Casa Guidi Windows* . . . and *Poems Before Congress* . . . , verse which deals much more directly than *Aurora Leigh* with the revolutionary issues of 1848 and after. Elizabeth Barrett was a lyric poet with an interest in political and social questions; Elizabeth Barrett Browning was primarily a political poet whose subjects were slavery, suppressed nationality (Italy), the plight of the poor and the position of women.

Aurora Leigh is Barrett Browning's fullest exploration of this last subject. . . . *Aurora Leigh's* . . . more modern preoccupation is whether marriage itself is a good thing, especially for women with a vocation. (p. 6)

In the opening of Book V of *Aurora Leigh* there is a long discursive section on the poet's vocation where the author dismisses the lyric mode—ballad, pastoral and Barrett Browning's own favourite, the sonnet—as static forms. . . . The move into epic poetry chipped at her reputation in establishment circles, but enhanced her popularity. It was a venture into a male stronghold; epic and dramatic verse are associated with the Classicists and with Shakespeare, Milton, Shelley and Tennyson, and later, Browning. (p. 8)

The taboo, it is stronger than prejudice, against women's entry into public discourse as speakers or writers, was in grave danger of being definitely broken in the mid-nineteenth century as more and more educated, literate women entered the arena as imaginative writers, social critics and reformers. . . . Patriarchal dominance involved the suppression of women's speech outside the home and a rigorous censorship of what she could read or write. All the major women writers were both vulnerable to and sensitive about charges of 'coarseness'. The Brontë sisters, Sand and Barrett Browning were labelled coarse by their critics, and occasionally, by other women. Sexual impurity, even in thought, was *the* unforgivable sin, the social lever through which Victorian culture controlled its females, and kept them from an alliance with their looser lived working-class sisters. (p. 9)

Public writing and public speech, closely allied, were both real and symbolic acts of self-determination for women. Barrett Browning uses the phrase 'I write' four times in the first two stanzas of Book I, emphasising the connection between the first person narrative and the 'act' of women's speech; between the expression of woman's feelings and thoughts and the legitimate professional exercise of that expression. . . . *Au-*

rora Leigh enters, however tentatively, into debates on *all* the forbidden subjects. In the first person epic voice of a major poet, it breaks a very specific silence, almost a gentlemen's agreement between women authors and the arbiters of high culture in Victorian England, that allowed women to write if only they would shut up about it.

Barrett Browning makes the condition of the poem's very existence the fact that its protagonist is a woman and a poet. Aurora's biography is a detailed account both of the socialisation of women and the making of a poet. . . . The female voice, simultaneously the author's and Aurora's, speaks with authority on just those questions about politics and high culture from which women were generally excluded. *Aurora Leigh's* other subject, the relationship between art and political change, is reformulated by the fact that, in the poem, the poet is female and the political reformer male. The poetic and all it stands for in *Aurora Leigh*—inspiration, Christian love, individual expression—becomes feminised as a consequence. The mechanical dogmas of utopian socialism, Romney's 'formulas', are straw theories with little chance against this warm wind. Abstract political discourse yields, at the end of the work, to poetry. (pp. 10-11)

In spite of [*Aurora Leigh's*] conventional happy ending it is possible to see it as contributing to a feminist theory of art which argues that women's language, precisely because it has been suppressed by patriarchal societies, re-enters discourse with a shattering revolutionary force, speaking all that is repressed and forbidden in human experience. . . .

The strains in *Aurora Leigh* which prefigure modern radical feminism are not only the heroine's relation to art, but also the way in which Barrett Browning manipulates her working-class figure, Marian Erle. Marian is given the most brutal early history of any figure in the poem—drunken ignorant parents, a mother who 'sells' her to the first male buyer—but she enters the world of our genteel protagonists literate and unsullied. . . . When Aurora finds and rescues her in Book VII, a genuine alliance of female sympathy is formed between women of different classes who have the added complication of loving the same man. (p. 11)

Aurora Leigh is more than a single text. It is different as it is read and understood at each separate point in history, as it is inserted into historically particular ideological structures. There is a danger in either blaming the poem for its political incoherence by relegating those debates to history or in praising it only for the euphoria with which it ruptures and transforms female language. Works of art should not be attacked because they do not conform to notions of political correctness, but they must be understood in relation to the seductive ideologies and political possibilities both of the times in which they were written and the times in which they are read. Otherwise Barrett Browning's belief that the 'artist's part is both to do and to be' stands in place of, not on behalf of, political transformation. (p. 12)

Aurora Leigh is a dense and complex text. Deliberately discursive and philosophical, the reflective sections of the poem state very clearly Barrett Browning's position on women's relation to self-determination, art, love, politics. The self-conscious didacticism of the poem includes some of its best 'poetic' passages: Aurora's description of her aunt; her bitter diatribe on female education; her definition of modern poetry. But these sections are complemented by a less visible polemic built into the poem's structure and narrative. . . . The narrative, often criticised for its lack of realism or simple credibility, is an elaborate collage of typical themes and motifs of the novels and long poems of the 1840s and 1850s. (p. 14)

Victorian readers already familiar with Tennyson, Clough, Kingsley, the Brontës, Gaskell and Sand would have caught echoes that we are too far away to hear. Barrett Browning played very self-consciously too on earlier, romantic sources. The growth of the poet in Books I and II takes us very naturally back to Wordsworth, and large parts of the poem play with themes and characters from a novel that every literate lady of Elizabeth Barrett's generation loved. Mme de Staël's *Corinne, or Italy* (1807). The narrative of *Aurora Leigh* is a critical revaluation of its multiple sources in which didactic asides are interleaved with the story, much as de Staël leavened her romance with long sections on Italian manners, culture and art.

Crucially, the seemingly fragmented, discursive poem . . . is tightened and held by a rope of female imagery. . . . Approved and taboo subjects are slyly intertwined so that menstruation, childbirth, suckling, child-rearing, rape and prostitution, are all braided together in the metaphorical language. (p. 15)

Aurora Leigh should be read as an overlapping sequence of dialogues with other texts, other writers. None of these debates are finished, some pursue contradictory arguments. The poem tries to make an overarching ideological statement by enlarging the personal to encompass the political, but the individual history interior to the poem—its 'novel'—cannot answer the questions which the work as as a whole puts to discourses outside it. What is true of *Aurora Leigh* is, of course, true of all writing. The pauses and awkward jumps in the text, the sense that the speaker has turned abruptly from one discussion to another, has omitted some vital point or has clammed up just as the argument gets interesting—those moments should claim our attention as powerfully as the seeming integration of structure and symbol. The text's unity is that adult voice that does not permit interruption as it tells us how things should be: its unintegrated remarks and

A portrait of Robert Browning, husband of Elizabeth Barrett Browning.

pointed silences remind us that the 'knowledge' of any one age is constantly open to rupture and revision. (pp. 16-17)

In her celebration of 'sexual passion' and woman's right to feel it, Barrett Browning is clearly on the side of Sand and the Brontës, 'coarse' to the bone. While the Brontës emphasize society's demand that women suppress their expression of passion, Sand and Barrett Browning insist that women could and should have passion and vocation. (p. 23)

Corinne and the romantic feminism it represents provided the palette from which Elizabeth Barrett Browning worked in creating *Aurora Leigh*. The composition, the style and the subject are altered, but the colours are unmistakable. George Sand and Barrett Browning herself are superimposed on each other and the composite portrait placed on the faded outlines of Corinne to produce Aurora. Its deliberate double exposure reflects the identification of the English poet with the French novelist. Yet the subject of *Aurora Leigh* is larger than the mere recreation of a poet-heroine. (pp. 25-6)

[Arthur Gordon Clough's *The Bothie of Tober-Na-Vuoliche,*] and its callow philosophy of modern marriage, in one of the targets in *Aurora Leigh.* The cross-class marriage is parodied in Romney's determination to wed Marian. There is cruel and direct send-up of Clough's sensual obsession with women at work in Book V. . . . These lines stand out in the poem as the only ones where corrupt sensuality is vividly evoked as a by-product of utopian socialism. Clough's voyeurism and chauvinism are unmasked along with his phony politics.

Barrett Browning's critique of Tennyson and Clough reflects her refusal to accept male versions of female experience and the co-option by liberal men of the women's issue. But the male writer who engaged her critical attention most completely during the writing of *Aurora Leigh* was Charles Kingsley, the utopian socialist to whose novel *Alton Locke, Tailor and Poet* (1850), *Aurora Leigh* is a sort of counter-text. (p. 29)

Kingsley was the richest contemporary resource for Barrett Browning because his reformist programme included attention to the woman question, explicitly treated in *Yeast* and dealt with marginally but seriously in *Alton Locke, Tailor and Poet.* The latter book forms the ideal foil for *Aurora Leigh.* The problems of social identity and self-determination for both working-class men and middle-class women were temptingly parallel. (pp. 30-1)

Barrett Browning also uses *Alton Locke* for her description of the riot at Leigh Hall. . . . It is a reactionary running together of two very different episodes in Kingsley's novel in order to drive home the point that utopian socialism cannot alter the natural depravity of the lower orders. (p. 32)

Also taken up and argued in *Aurora Leigh* are the role of the poet and the proper vocation for intelligent women. Kingsley was committed to the idea that Locke should remain loyal to his class as a 'People's Poet' rather than enter the bourgeoisie. . . .

Kingsley rejects class mobility for Locke—and Barrett Browning's Aurora reject androgyny as a masque or aspiration for women writers. She refuses all current definitions of women's roles and rejects the notion that there is a creative limitation on women as artists. . . . This argument appears at various points in the poem and has a particular relation to Kingsley's view of the liberated woman represented by Eleanor. . . . Proud of her intellect [Eleanor] delves into Bentham, Malthus, Fourier and Proudhon and helps her husband with his social experiments. When Lynedale died the 'blow came. My idol— . . . To please him I had begun—To please myself in pleasing him I was trying to become great . . . '. . . . Here, in brief, is Corine converted into a female reformer. (p. 33)

Elizabeth Barrett Browning saw the representation of her age of steam as a kind of duty to the future. Her sense of the 'age' is both wider and narrower than that of the contemporary social novel. *Aurora Leigh* combines the pleasures of the Victorian novel with those of the Victorian poem. Our obsession is with the Victorian and Edwardian worlds themselves. They are our middle-ages. There, in fancy dress, the still-present hierarchies of class and gender are displayed without shame, unsuppressed by the rhetoric of equality which glosses our own situation. Class conflict and the inequality between sexes were the spoken subjects of much of that literature and sexual transactions across class lines the erotic subtext of many popular works. In modern fiction sexuality is the spoken subject, power relations the subtext which must wear a fig leaf. Consequently our literary appetite for the Victorians is easily explained. They give us two kinds of coarseness: a coarse drama of class against class and men against women, picked out in strong colours, and even coarser interpretations of these conflicts. They offer solutions which swing between the compassionate and cowardly, the needle often poised at silly. They are our fairy-tales; the Brontës, Mrs. Gaskell, George Eliot, Christina Rosetti, Emily Dickinson, Elizabeth Barrett Browning our sisters Grimm. (p. 36)

Cora Kaplan, in an introduction to *Aurora Leigh, and Other Poems,* by Elizabeth Barrett Browning, The Women's Press Limited, 1978, pp. 5-36.

DOROTHY MERMIN

(essay date 1981)

[In the following excerpt, Mermin explores the intensely personal side of *Sonnets from the Portuguese.*]

[*Sonnets from the Portuguese*] deserves much more attention from literary historians [than is often offered] . . . , both because of Barrett Browning's influence on later women poets and because it is the first of the semi-autobiographical, amatory, lyrical or partly lyrical sequences in modern settings that comprise one of the major innovations of Victorian literature. The poetry is much more subtle, rich, and varied than one would guess from "How do I love thee"—the only one of the sonnets that most of us know. The poem's enormous popularity with unliterary (presumably female) readers, along with the even more popular legend of the fair poetess, the dashing poet-lover, and the mad tyrant of Wimpole Street partly account for the repugnance—often expressed as ridicule—that *Sonnets from the Portuguese* is apt to inspire. But the real problem is that the female speaker produces painful dislocations in the conventions of amatory poetry and thus in the response of the sophisticated twentieth-century reader, whose first overwhelming though inaccurate impression of the poems is that they are awkward, mawkish, and indecently personal—in short, embarrassing.

The speaker fills roles that earlier love poetry had kept separate and opposite: speaker and listener, subject and object of desire, male and female. While this produces a rich poetic complexity, it also produces embarrassment, which . . . can arise from the clashing of apparently incompatible roles. Traditionally in English love poetry the man loves and speaks, the woman is beloved and silent. In *Sonnets from the Portuguese,* however, the speaker casts herself not only as the poet who loves, speaks, and is traditionally male, but also as the silent, traditionally female beloved. Insofar as we perceive her as the lover, we are made uneasy both by seeing a woman in that role and by the implications about the beloved: the man seems to be put in the woman's place, and—especially if we recall the origins of the female lyric tradition in Sappho—we may seem to hear overtones of sexual inversion. Insofar as the speaker presents herself as the beloved, however, she transfers the verbal self-assertion and many of the attributes which in poems traditionally belong to the subject of desire, to desire's normally silent and mysterious object. The result is a devaluation of the erotic object that casts the whole amorous and poetical enterprise in doubt. For the object is both the speaker and the text, an identity like that which Browning asserted in his first letter to Elizabeth Barrett: "I do, as I say, love these books with all my heart—and I love you too." The identification troubled her, though she could not entirely disavow it: "There is nothing to see in me," she told him; "my poetry . . . is the flower of me . . . the rest of me is nothing but a root, fit for the ground & the dark." She assumed at first that his love was "a mere poet's fancy . . . a confusion between the woman and the poetry." Many of the sonnets say, in effect: *"Look at me, and you will cease to desire me."* So solicited, many readers turn away.

They turn from a sight that violates both literary and social decorum: a distinctly nineteenth-century woman in the humble posture of a courtly lover. This blurring of sexual roles is established in the third sonnet, which imagines the beloved as a glorious court musician "looking from the lattice-lights" at the speaker, who is just a "poor, tired, wandering singer, singing through / The dark, and leaning up a cypress tree." Later the speaker compares her bewilderment after seeing her lover to that of a rather Keatsian "acolyte" who "fall[s] flat, with pale insensate brow, / On the altar-stair." . . . The traditional poet-wooer, insofar as he describes himself at all, is pale, wan, and weary from unsatisfied desire. In *Sonnets from the Portuguese,* pallor and weariness belong to the woman both as signs of passion, as in the images of minstrel and acolyte,

and—more disturbingly still—as the self-portraiture of an aging woman.

The self-portrait, furthermore, is detailed, unflattering, and accurate. In one of the poem's most vivid scenes from a recognizably nineteenth-century courtship, the speaker gives her lover a lock of hair and reminds him that her hair is no longer dressed with rose or myrtle like a girl's:

> it only may
> Now shade on two pale cheeks the mark of tears,
> Taught drooping from the head that hangs aside
> Through sorrow's trick. . . .

She has "trembling knees" . . . , "tremulous hands" . . . , and "languid ringlets." . . . This is a literally faithful picture of the poet (whereas Shakespeare's description of himself in the *Sonnets* as marked by extreme old age presumably is not). The unfashionable ringlets and the characteristic droop of the head can be seen in her pictures. Elizabeth Barrett was forty years old when she married (Browning was six years younger) and had been an invalid, grieving and blaming herself for the death of her favorite brother, addicted to opium, and mostly shut up in one dark airless room, for years. The extraordinary biographical accuracy with which the poem depicts its female speaker violates the decorum of the sonnet sequence almost as much as the sex of the speaker does.

As is usual in love poetry, there is much less physical description of the man than of the woman. And his appearance, in significant contrast to her own, is always imaginatively transformed when it is described at all. *Her* hair is just "brown" . . . , but *his* seems fit for verse: "As purply-black, as erst to Pindar's eyes / The dim purpureal tresses gloomed athwart / The nine white Muse brows." . . . We can usually accept her exaltation of her beloved—who is characteristically described as royal, whose color is purple, whose merit knows no bounds—because the terms and images are familiarly literary. She gives no sketch of him to match her cruel self-portrait and apologizes for her ineptitude in portraying him:

> As if a shipwrecked Pagan, safe in port,
> His guardian sea-god to commemorate,
> Should set a sculptured porpoise, gills a-snort
> And vibrant tail, within the temple-gate. . . .

No apology is really necessary, however, for this flattering comparison of the lover to a sexy sea-god or for the disarmingly erotic porpoise.

Sometimes she is herself transformed by her own imagination, but into an object unworthy of desire. Her house is desolate and broken. . . . She praises him at her own expense: she is "an out-of-tune / Worn viol," but "perfect strains may flat / 'Neath master-hands, from instruments defaced." . . . His imagination, that is, might be able to transform her even if her own cannot. Earlier she had offered herself as the object of his poems (rather than the subject of her own):

> How, Dearest, wilt thou have me for most use?
> A hope, to sing by gladly? or a fine
> Sad memory, with thy songs to interfuse?
> A shade, in which to sing of palm or pine?
> A grave, on which to rest from singing?
> Choose. . . .

This extreme self-abnegation is also an incisive commentary on male love poems, however, since the alternatives require not only the woman's passivity and silence but her absence and finally her death. . . . But the speaker in *Sonnets from the Portuguese* initiates and writes her own poems. She does not choose merely to respond to her lover's words, to be silent, to be abandoned, or to die.

And so the sequence works out terms of reciprocity between two lovers who are both poets. His love calls forth her poems, but she writes them. He is the prince whose magic kiss restores her beauty, which in turn increases her poetical power (in love poems as in fairy tales, women draw power from their beauty). (pp. 351-55)

Finally, of course, we know that the story the *Sonnets* tells is true. Elizabeth Barrett was a legendary public figure even before her marriage, by virtue of her poems, her learning, her seclusion, and her sex, and for most readers the personal element has been inseparable from the sonnets since their first publication. We know the story of her courtship, which was largely epistolary and has been available in print since 1899, and the many parallels between the letters and the poems tempt us to assume that the poems were spontaneously produced at the moments they appear to describe.

It is worth noting, however, that the letters themselves don't embarrass us; only the poems do. We are more disturbed by the incongruity we feel between the sentiments and the genre than by the sentiments themselves. Little scenes from Victorian life and characteristically Victorian modes of feeling and turns of phrase give a strange context to the sonnets' erotic intensities and traditional form. They seem to belong in prose fiction instead. (pp. 357-58)

Insofar as the *Sonnets* are autobiographical (and not just spontaneous), however, they inaugurated a new Victorian convention to which almost every significant poet except Robert Browning contributed: the use of autobiographical material in long poems that play specifically "modern" experience against some of the traditions of amatory poetry. Arnold's *Switzerland,* Patmore's *The Angel in the House,* Tennyson's *Maud,* and Clough's *Amours de Voyage* were published in the 1850's, Meredith's *Modern Love* in 1862. Of all of these, only *Sonnets from the Portuguese* does not, so far as we can tell, fictionalize the story or attempt to disguise the personal references. The male poets presented their own experiences and feelings as exemplifying those of modern man, or at any rate the modern sensitive intellectual or poet, but the modern woman's personal experience could not easily be made to carry so heavy a contextual burden. There were no ancestral female voices to validate her own and define by contrast its particular quality. Nor, as Barrett Browning knew, were readers disposed to hear women as speaking for anything more than themselves. (pp. 359-60)

The unusual situation of a female poet in love with a male one was not easy to show as representative, but Barrett Browning worked in many ways to generalize and distance her experience. The use of the sonnet sequence, first of all, seems an obvious choice now, but in fact *Sonnets from the Portuguese* inaugurated the Victorian use of the old genre. Although she noted the absence of female Elizabethan poets—"I look everywhere for grandmothers and see none"—the sonnet sequence offered a way to subsume her own experience into a wider tradition. Within the sonnet form itself she curbed the liberties with rhyme and meter for which she was notorious, although she did not keep to the usual structure of the Petrarchan sonnet, allowed herself great variety of tone, and broke up lines in fresh and surprising ways. She reminds us, too, that she is writing poems, not love letters, when a poem represents what she does not say to the lover . . . or suppresses words of his letters that are too private to repeat. . . . (p. 360)

She generalizes her situation most clearly and deliberately through literary allusions, particularly in the first two sonnets, which draw on Theocritus, Homer, Milton, and Shakespeare. *Sonnets from the Portuguese* begins: "I thought once how Theocritus had sung / Of the sweet years. . . . " This refers to the song in the fifteenth idyll which anticipates Adonis' return from death to the arms of Aphrodite and is proleptic both of the speaker's movement from death to love and of the coming of her lover. The speaker "mused" Theocritus' story "in his antique tongue," she says, thus establishing her credentials as a reader of Greek, a serious, educated person. And as she mused: "a mystic Shape did move / Behind me, and drew me backward by the hair"—a typically female image of passivity, no doubt, but taken from the episode in *The Iliad* when Achilles in his wrath is similarly pulled back by Athena. The allusions are deft and easy, the voice that of one who lives familiarly with Greek texts. The second sonnet draws with the same casual confidence on Milton and Shakespeare. Only she, her lover, and God, she says, heard the word "Love"—and God "laid the curse / So darkly on my eyelids, as to amerce / My sight from seeing thee"—a more "absolute exclusion" than death itself. . . . The rebirth of Adonis, Achilles' injured love and pride, Satan's exclusion from heaven, Shakespeare's celebration of human love—these and not the stuffy room in Wimpole Street are the context in which *Sonnets from the Portuguese* initially establishes itself.

The poem does seem increasingly to take place within a particular domestic interior, but the space it occupies is symbolical and highly schematic. It is sharply constricted on the horizontal plane but open to heaven above and the grave below. At worst, the speaker is like "a bee shut in a crystalline" . . . , in a "close room." . . . In her childhood she ran from one place to another . . . , but the movements she imagines for the future are almost always vertical. Typical repeated words are *down, fall, deep, rise, beneath,* and especially *drop,* used eleven times in the forty-four poems, and *up,* used twelve times. Even marriage, leaving one home for another, means that her eyes would "drop on a new range / Of walls and floors." . . . The reader may feel a bit claustrophobic, but the speaker usually imagines enclosure as protection rather than imprisonment. (pp. 360-61)

For the space, which becomes at the end a garden of art, belongs like the story enacted within it as much to Victorian artistic convention as to the setting of Elizabeth Barrett's life. . . . [The] woman in the *Sonnets* finds her lover more passionate and alive than she is herself. He is not imprisoned; he draws her back to life. (In fact, Browning drew Elizabeth Barrett into marriage, motherhood, society, travel, political engagement—the ordinary social, human world that women often represent to their lovers in Victorian poems: but the poem is less proleptically literary than life was and does not anticipate this outcome.) The speaker has the qualities, then, both of the male Victorian poet as introverted self-doubting lover and of the female figures in which Tennyson embodies passive, withdrawn, and isolated aspects of the poetic character.

The unspecified sufferings and griefs that have marked the speaker's face and almost killed her are also signs not only of Petrarchan love, feminine weakness, and biographical fact (Barrett Browning's long illness and her brother's death) but of the poetical character too, as many Romantic and Victorian poets conceived it. (pp. 361-62)

Another major point of intersection between conventional and personal, male and female, poet and beloved, occurs in the general area in which *Sonnets from the Portuguese* anticipates the Pre-Raphaelites. Here as elsewhere, Barrett Browning is the precursor, though we are likely to read her through expectations formed by those who followed. Sometimes her accents have a Meredithian wit, quickness, cleverness, and variety, as in the tenth sonnet, "Yet love, mere love." Sometimes the poems resemble Dante Rossetti's *House of Life* in their personifications, marmoreal cadences, archaisms, and heated slow simplicities. . . . But if she speaks like a

Pre-Raphaelite poet, she also resembles such poets' favorite subject, the fatal woman: enclosed, passive, pale, deathly. Like Morris' Guenevere or Rossetti's Lilith, she often seems to be looking at herself in a mirror. . . . From the lover's point of view, she is silent and unresponsive in the earlier sonnets, hiding her feelings from him and speaking to be heard only by the reader. But she lacks the fatal woman's guile, mystery, and beauty. As speaker she must let the reader hear her, while her bent for self-analysis and formal commitment to lyric self-expression preclude duplicity.

Such persistent doubling of roles accounts for most of the disconcerting strangeness of *Sonnets from the Portuguese.* The speaker is cast as both halves of a balanced but asymmetrical pair, speaking with two voices in a dialogue where we are accustomed to hearing only one. Obviously there are rich possibilities for irony here, but Barrett Browning does not take them—does not appear even to notice them. Nor does she call our attention to the persistent anomalies and contradictions even without irony. This above all distinguishes her from her male contemporaries. The juxtaposition of traditional amatory poetry and the Victorian idea that love should be fulfilled in marriage, combined with the desire of almost every important Victorian poet to write within the context of contemporary social life, inevitably opened up the disjunction between the passionate certainties of literature, and the flawed complexities of life, between the amatory intensity of poetic lovers and the confusion and distractedness of modern ones. (pp. 363-64)

Barrett Browning does not want to show up disparities: she wants to find a place within the tradition for modern poems, and especially for female poets—not to mark how far outside it she is. Nor can she mock the sonnet tradition from within as Shakespeare and Sidney could, since she wants to assert her right to use it at all. *Sonnets from the Portuguese* is organized around the double discovery that love's seeming illusions are realities, still accessible, and that one can be both subject and object of love, both poet and poet's beloved. Because she does not use irony to mark the points at which the old and the new come together—she wants to create fusion, not show disjunction—she runs the risk of leaving us disoriented and uneasy instead of releasing us . . . into the ironical recognition of a familiar failure. And since success for the poet in this poem involves a happy ending for the lovers, or at least not an unhappy one, there is no release such as Tennyson and Arnold would give us into the lyrical pain of loss.

Barrett Browning knew that embarrassment always threatens to engulf the woman poet, particularly in an amatory context. (pp. 364-65)

The extreme paucity of good lyric poetry by Victorian women, which is in such striking contrast to their success in narrative, is largely due to the felt pressure of forms, convention, and above all readers' responses that could not accommodate female utterance without distorting it. This is a problem of the female speaker, not just of the woman writer. . . . One reason that *Aurora Leigh* seems to many readers fresher and more alive than *Sonnets from the Portuguese* is that the

novelistic form of the later poem enabled the poet to speak freely, and without arousing significant conflict in the reader, in her own distinctive, distinctively female voice. (pp. 365-66)

Dorothy Mermin, "The Female Poet and the Embarrassed Reader: Elizabeth Barrett Browning's 'Sonnets from the Portuguese'," in *ELH*, Vol. 48, No. 2, Summer, 1981, pp. 351-67.

SOURCES FOR FURTHER STUDY

Cooper, Helen. *Elizabeth Barrett Browning, Woman and Artist*. Chapel Hill: University of North Carolina Press, 1988, 219 p.

Tightly constructed feminist treatment of Browning's works.

Forster, Margaret. *Elizabeth Barrett Browning: A Biography*. New York: Doubleday, 1989, 400 p.

General biography, with selected bibliography.

Hayter, Alethea. *Mrs. Browning*. London: Faber and Faber, 1962, 261 p.

Combines critical, biographical, and historical information to assess and illuminate specific works or specific aspects of Browning's works.

Leighton, Angela. *Elizabeth Barrett Browning*. Brighton: Harvester, 1986, 179 p.

Interprets Browning's poetry from a feminist perspective, focusing on *Aurora Leigh*.

Mermin, Dorothy. *Elizabeth Barrett Browning: The Origins of a New Poetry*. Chicago: University of Chicago Press, 1989, 310 p.

Biographical work containing astute critical readings of both Robert's and Elizabeth's poetry.

Taplin, Gardner B. *The Life of Elizabeth Barrett Browning*. New Haven: Yale University Press, 1957, 482 p.

A careful account of Browning's life, including information on the composition and critical reception of each of her books and an epilogue summarizing critical views of Browning in the years since her death.

John Bunyan

1628-1688

English allegorist, autobiographer, prose writer, homilist, and poet.

INTRODUCTION

*B*unyan is recognized as a master of allegorical prose, and his art is often compared in conception and technique to that of John Milton and Edmund Spenser. Although he wrote nearly fifty works, he is chiefly remembered for *The Pilgrim's Progress from This World to That Which Is to Come* (1678), which, translated into numerous foreign languages and dialects, has long endured as a classic in world literature. While structured from a particular religious point of view, *The Pilgrim's Progress* has drawn both ecclesiastical and secular audiences of all ages and has enjoyed a worldwide exposure and popularity second only to the Bible.

Bunyan was born in Elstow, a town in rural Bedfordshire. He was taught to read and write at a local parish school and apprenticed to a tinker. Although details of his early life are sparse, it is believed that Bunyan's rigid Puritan upbringing aggravated his inherently sensitive nature; exposed from childhood to graphic depictions of eternal damnation, Bunyan was inwardly tormented throughout his youth by fearful dreams and visions of hell. Outwardly, however, he engaged in the customary pastimes of other youths, and for a time he successfully mollified his obsessive fears. At the age of seventeen Bunyan joined the Parliamentary army, from which he was discharged after two years, shortly before his marriage in 1648 to a woman whose piety reawakened his own religious conscience. For a brief period, the Anglican ceremonials in Elstow satisfied Bunyan's spiritual hunger, although his basic convictions and daily life remained unchanged. Several personal experiences, including becoming conscience-stricken while swearing and sporting on the Sabbath, precipitated Bunyan's conversion to the Baptist faith in 1653. His reformation was arduous and not without numerous setbacks and conflicts. He was tortured relentlessly by the question of his own salvation. Verses of Scripture, to which he turned for solace and direction, would reverberate in his mind until they were rendered meaningless or, worse, assumed the aspect of a personal knell of doom. Bunyan's confusion in the face of complex theological questions and biblical ambiguity—understandable even in a more educated and less excitable man—verged on despair when confronted with the Calvinist doctrine of predetermined election to salvation. The enlightened counsel of John Gifford, pastor of neighboring Bedford, allayed some of Bunyan's fears, but new ones arose to replace them. When he became convinced that he might rely on scriptural support to counteract whatever trials awaited him, Bunyan committed himself to serving the Baptist community of Bedford, where he took up residence in 1655.

Bunyan quickly assumed an active ministerial role in Bedford. He spoke boldly at meetings and was vigorously combative in print, as illustrated by his first published work, *Some Gospel-Truths Opened according to the Scriptures* (1656), a doctrinal controversy with the Quakers. He began preaching both in Bedford and with his brethren on their appointed circuits, adopting the frenzied fire-and-brimstone speaking style characterized in his successful *A Few Sighs from Hell,* published in 1658. About this time Bunyan's wife died, leaving him with four small children, but he married again after a short interval. With the Restoration in 1660, Charles II assumed the throne, ministers of the Church of England and church liturgy were restored, and immediately sects without official sanction risked prosecution. Bunyan was arrested and, having declined to desist from further preaching, was subsequently tried, convicted, and jailed for three months in 1661. Offered the opportunity for release if he agreed to abstain from attending and ministering to the private meetings now prohibited by law, Bunyan refused to compromise his faith, and he was held prisoner for twelve years.

Bunyan was initially permitted a great deal of freedom by the jailer. Allowed to leave confinement periodically, he resumed his preaching, exhorting his congregation to remain steadfast in its beliefs. Although he was eventually forbidden to preach, he reached an even larger audience through discourse written and published throughout his imprisonment. If still fervent in treating certain incontrovertible issues, Bunyan less frequently invoked sheer dread of damnation and, relying on scriptural edict and human example, became expostulatory. He infused his works with a sense of authority; he no longer prefaced them with apologies for his limitations, and he began to address his readers more in fatherly than brotherly fashion, as is clearly evidenced in his autobiography, *Grace Abounding to the Chief of Sinners* (1666).

Although freed briefly in 1666, Bunyan resumed his now largely nominal imprisonment in the same year,

with much of his previous liberty restored, including permission to preach and to expedite church matters. In 1672, after the issue of Charles II's Declaration of Indulgence, Bunyan petitioned for and received his release and was formally licensed to preach by the Bedford church authorities. The first years of Bunyan's pastorate were not tranquil. He was obliged to rebuke and punish the transgressions of growing numbers of Bedford's congregation, many of whom had been more tractable under the influence he had exerted while confined. These difficulties were compounded by vague rumors about Bunyan, including one involving him in a scandal with a young woman parishioner who openly but innocently admired him and whose father, who did not admire the pastor, died under sudden, unexplained circumstances. As his ministry was not confined to Bedford, however, Bunyan's spirited preaching of the gospel in outlying counties and in London secured scores of enthusiastic followers, which, with the continued success of his publications, greatly consoled him.

In 1675 the Declaration of Indulgence was withdrawn and persecution of religious dissenters resumed. While Bunyan, now forty-eight, was again imprisoned for about six months, he began writing *The Pilgrim's Progress,* at first with no greater intention than to divert his mind. At its completion, he had it printed, and the immediate acclaim accorded it precipitated a second edition. While Bunyan had been doubtful of his ability to extend and intensify symbolic representation throughout a lengthy piece, enthusiastic reception of *The Pilgrim's Progress* encouraged him to write a contrasting study of sinful pursuit, *The Life and Death of Mr. Badman* (1680). Bunyan had, by now, effectively integrated much of his former impassioned style with the orderly progression of ideas. He followed the dialogue relating Badman's history with an allegorical chronicle of the soul's struggles, *The Holy War* (1682), succeeded by the second part of *The Pilgrim's Progress* (1684). After the death of Charles II in 1685, Bunyan, now able to preach more openly, renewed his vocation with vigor and published several more works. Active until the last year of his life, when he was appointed chaplain to the Lord Mayor of London, Bunyan died of an illness resulting from exposure to inclement weather while performing his pastoral duty.

The Pilgrim's Progress records in allegorical form the author's spiritual awakening and growth. The idea of human life as a pilgrimage was not new in Bunyan's time; its literary antecedents predated even such adventurous journeys as the *Odyssey,* and its popularity further intensified with the chivalric romances of the Middle Ages. For generations, the virtues and vices had been formulaically personified; those peopling the Christian's difficult road to spiritual salvation—many who assist him when he is beset by obstacles and others who are the obstacles themselves—were hardly strangers to Bunyan's first readers. Specific incidents in *The Pilgrim's Progress* were borrowed directly from the Scriptures as well as from numerous secular and less edifying works available to Bunyan. But generations of critics have testified to Bunyan's own comprehensive scope, rich characterization, and genuine spiritual torment and joy drawn from personal experience. Charles Doe, one of Bunyan's contemporaries, remarked: "What hath the devil, or his agents, gotten by putting our great gospel minister Bunyan, in prison? For in prison he wrote many excellent books, that have published to the world his great grace, and great truth, and great judgment, and great ingenuity; and to instance in one, the *Pilgrim's Progress,* he hath suited to the life of a traveller so exactly and pleasantly, and to the life of a Christian, that this very book, besides the rest, hath done the superstitious sort of men more good than if he had been let alone at his meeting at Bedford, to preach the gospel to his own auditory."

The Life and Death of Mr. Badman and *The Holy War,* while not as celebrated as Bunyan's renowned allegory, are works equally representative of the author's spiritual concerns, albeit from different perspectives. The first is a dialogue between Mr. Wiseman, Bunyan's fictional counterpart, and his faithful disciple, Attentive, who discuss the progressive degeneracy of Mr. Badman from youthful vices to profligate adulthood. The catalog of Badman's sins includes profanity, drunkenness, fornication, and fraud. Badman, although provided with numerous opportunities to reform, is wicked and unrepentant to the end. Mr. Wiseman and Attentive act as spokesmen for Bunyan's digressional discourses on wrongdoing, many of which were intended for unnamed residents of Bedford. Yet Badman himself is no caricature of evil but a distinct individual fully and richly portrayed, the better to render his sins reprehensible and his consequent need for and rejection of redemption horrifying. *The Holy War,* like *The Pilgrim's*

Progress, is an allegorical depiction of spiritual struggle but, rather than employing the metaphor of quest or journey, it makes the human soul itself a bastion besieged by evil forces. In *The Holy War,* the righteous Prince Emmanuel's army must defend the city of Mansoul against Diabolus and his troops, who wish to take over the fortress, constructed by Emmanuel's father, King Shaddai. Mansoul, threatened continually, is occupied twice by Diabolus but is finally purged of its enemies when the prince returns to power. *The Holy War* chronicles the original fall of humanity, the personal acceptance of salvation through Christ, the falling away after conversion, and ultimate restitution; on a more personal level, it also stresses the lifelong vigilance against sin that each person must wage.

Although individual critical interpretations and appraisals of his writings have varied over time, the popularity and relevance of Bunyan's work, most notably of *The Pilgrim's Progress,* remain undiminished today. . . . James Anthony Froude affirmed: "It has been the fashion to dwell on the disadvantages of his education, and to regret the carelessness of nature which brought into existence a man of genius in a tinker's hut at Elstow. . . . Circumstances, I should say, qualified Bunyan perfectly well for the work which he had to do. . . . He was born to be the Poet-apostle of the English middle classes, imperfectly educated like himself; and, being one of themselves, he had the key of their thoughts and feelings in his own heart. . . . [His] mental furniture was gathered at first hand from his conscience, his life, and his occupations. Thus, every idea which he received falling into a soil naturally fertile, sprouted up fresh, vigorous, and original."

(For further information about Bunyan's life and works, see *Literature Criticism from 1400 to 1800,* Vol. 4 and *Dictionary of Literary Biography,* Vol. 39: *British Novelists, 1660-1800.*)

CRITICAL COMMENTARY

EDWARD DOWDEN

(essay date 1900)

[Dowden, an Anglo-Irish poet, scholar, and critic, is best remembered for studies of Shakespeare. In the following excerpt, he considers the individual merits of several of Bunyan's works.]

The *Pilgrim's Progress* is a gallery of portraits, admirably discriminated, and as convincing in their self-verification as those of Holbein. [Its] personages live for

us as few figures outside the drama of Shakespeare live. They are not, like the humourists of Ben Jonson's plays, constructed by heaping a load of observations on a series of ethical abstractions; they are of a reasonable soul and human flesh subsisting. We are on terms of intimate acquaintance with each of them; with Talkative, the son of one Say-well, who dwelt in Prating-row,— wherever the notional apprehension of things is taken for the real apprehension, there is that discoursing wit to-day; with By-ends, always zealous when a good

---

Principal Works

Some Gospel-Truths Opened according to the Scriptures (prose) 1656

A Few Sighs from Hell; or, The Groans of a Damned Soul (sermon) 1658

Grace Abounding to the Chief of Sinners; or, A Brief and Faithful Relation of the Exceeding Mercy of God in Christ to His Poor Servant John Bunyan (autobiography) 1666

The Pilgrim's Progress from This World to That Which Is to Come, Delivered under the Similitude of a Dream Wherein Is Discovered, the Manner of His Setting Out, His Dangerous Journey, and Safe Arrival at the Desired Country (allegory) 1678

The Life and Death of Mr. Badman Presented to the World in a Familiar Dialogue between Mr. Wiseman, and Mr. Attentive (dialogue) 1680

The Holy War Made by Shaddai upon Diabolus for the Regaining of the Metropolis of the World; or, The Losing and Taking Again of the Town of Mansoul (allegory) 1682

The Pilgrim's Progress from This World to That Which Is to Come: The Second Part, Delivered under the Similitude of a Dream Wherein Is Set Forth the Manner of the Setting Out of Christian's Wife and Children, Their Dangerous Journey and Safe Arrival at the Desired Country (allegory) 1684

The Advocateship of Jesus Christ Clearly Explained and Largely Improved (sermon) 1688; also published as *The Work of Jesus Christ as an Advocate,* 1688

The Entire Works of John Bunyan. 4 vols. (allegories, meditations, tracts, sermons, dialogues, autobiography, and poetry) 1859-60

The Miscellaneous Works of John Bunyan. 11 vols. (allegories, meditations, tracts, sermons, dialogues, autobiography, and poetry) 1979-

---

cause goes in silver slippers, a gentleman of excellent quality, though his grandfather was but a waterman, looking one way and rowing another; with that brisk lad Ignorance, who came into the path by a little crooked lane leading from the country of Conceit; there is a narrow gate in science and in art as well as in religion, which the kinsfolk of Bunyan's Ignorance decline to enter; with Mrs Lightmind, who yesterday at Madam Wanton's was as merry as the maids—surely she is cousin to the brothers Jolly and Griggish, who came to an ill fate at the hands of my Lord Willbewill, and so ended their ticking and toying with my Lord's daughters; with Mr Brisk, who, since Mercy was of a fair countenance and therefore the more alluring, offered her his love, but was dashed when she explained that her needlework was meant to clothe the naked, and decided on reconsideration that she was indeed a pretty lass, but troubled with ill conditions; with that old pilgrim Father Honest, a cock of the right kind, for he had said the truth; with Mr Fearing, one of the most troublesome of pilgrims, a chicken-hearted man, yet having the root of the matter in him, and who at last almost dryshod crossed the river, when it was at its lowest ebb; with Mr Feeble-mind, who must needs be carried up the Hill Difficulty by one of the Interpreter's servants, yet bravely resolved to run when he could, to go when he could not run, and to creep when he could not go; with Mr Ready-to-halt, who, despite the crutch, footed it well in view of the dead giant's head, hand in hand with Despondency's daughter Much-afraid, both answering the music handsomely; with Madam Bubble, that tall comely dame, somewhat swarthy of complexion, speaking very smoothly, and giving you a smile at the end of a sentence, while still she kept fingering her money as if it were her heart's delight; with Mr Valiant-for-truth, Mr Standfast, who crossing the river in a great calm, like the saintly John Wesley, when he was half-way in, stood for a while and talked to his companions; with the dozen enlightened jurymen of Vanity Fair, and many another. Yet these are but examples from the drawings of the Holbein of spiritual England.

One book of Bunyan's is, indeed, a detailed study of English middle-class life and of its vulgar vices. Recent criticism has assigned to *The Life and Death of Mr Badman* a higher place in literature than it deserves; but it presents one side of its author's mind more fully than any other of his writings. Having published the first part of the *Pilgrim's Progress,* and enjoyed the surprise of its extraordinary success, Bunyan seems to have thought of presenting a counterpart in the story of one who had travelled another road than that of Christian, the road leading not to the Celestial City, but to the gates of hell. The book is not a vision or a dream; it lacks the beautiful ideality of the *Pilgrim's Progress,* which has made that allegory of universal interest. It has, on the other hand, something of Hogarth's naturalism and something of Hogarth's enforcement of morality by means of the tomahawk; it is the tale of an Idle Apprentice; it is a bourgeois Rake's Progress. The narrative, thrown into the form of dialogue, is interrupted by discourses on the several species of sin practised by that rascally provincial tradesman, the hero, with many examples drawn from real life of God's judgments against sinners.

The book had its origin not in Bunyan's personal experiences, idealised and purified by the imagination, but in his observations of the evil that lay around him. Even as a child Badman was a highly promising pupil of the destroyer—addicted to lying, a pilferer, abandoned (like young Richard Baxter) to the joy of robbing orchards, a blackmouthed wretch who cursed and swore, a boy who could not endure the Lord's Day, swarming, indeed, with sins as a beggar is with vermin. When his good father would rebuke him, what would young Badman do but stand gloating, hanging down his head in a sullen pouching manner, while he secretly wished for the old man's death? As an apprentice he read beastly romances and books full of ribaldry, slept in church, or stared at pretty faces and whispered and giggled during sermon, being thus grown to a prodigious height of wickedness. His knavish fingers found their way to his master's cash-box, and soon his first apprenticeship closed disgracefully in flight. After a second apprenticeship, during which a base-born child was laid to his charge, Badman set up in business, but through dissipation, high-living, idleness, and evil company quickly came to the end of the money obtained from his over-indulgent father. To retrieve his fortunes he sought out a maid who had a good portion, and as she was godly, he made religion his stalking-horse; but after marriage he hanged his religion upon the hedge, oppressed his unhappy wife, squandered her coin upon his drabs, and towards morning would come home as drunk as a swine. He reached a yet lower depth of degradation, when he turned informer, obtaining a wretched hire by betrayal to the authorities of the non-conformist religious assemblies. Running up credit and paying five shillings in the pound—the neatest way of thieving—Badman in time gained hatfuls of money. He knew all tricks of the trade—the art of deceitful weights and measures, that of mingling commodities so that what was bad might go off, and he was skilled in misreckoning men in their accounts. So he goes, with hardly an interruption, from bad to worse. During a dangerous fit of sickness, indeed, consequent on the breaking of his leg in a drunken bout, he thought of death and hell-fire, and altered his carriage to his wife, who was now his duck and dear; but his repentance was worth no more than the howling of a dog. The broken-hearted wife dies, and Badman is tricked into marriage with a woman as wicked as himself. At last dropsy and consumption seize their victim; he lies upon his bed given up to hardness and stupidity of spirit. "Pray how was he," asks Attentive, "at his death? was death strong upon him? or did he die with ease, quietly?" The last and severest earthly judgment of God is not an agony of remorse; it is apathy. He died "as quietly as a lamb." And with this terrible word Bunyan's book concludes.

Such a narrative as this could not connect itself with work of an order so different as the *Pilgrim's Progress*. The two inventions move on different planes.

The *Pilgrim's Progress* is the poetry of Bunyan's soul; the *Life and Death of Mr Badman* is the prose of his moral observation of the world. Successive generations may in general be trusted to preserve the heirlooms of literature. *Mr Badman* is not one of these; but it deserves the attention of a student of Bunyan, and the attention of a student of Bunyan's age.

The great allegories of human life commonly make choice between two modes of representation; they describe life as a journey or they describe life as a warfare. The *Divine Comedy* is a journey through the realms of eternal life and death; the *Vision of Piers Plowman* is a pilgrimage in search of the highest good; the *Faerie Queene* is a series of knightly crusades against the powers of evil. In his two allegories Bunyan has presented both conceptions; the *Pilgrim's Progress* is a journey from the City of Destruction to the Celestial City; the *Holy War* tells of the assault upon the town of Mansoul by Diabolus, his conquest by fraud and force, the recapture of the town for Shaddai, its lawful possessor, by Prince Emmanuel, its invasion and partial ruin by the enemy, and the final victory of righteousness.

In one respect, and in that alone, can Bunyan's later allegory the *Holy War* be said to surpass the *Pilgrim's Progress*—it is more ingenious in the adaptation of its details. The design was not fortunate; there is no central personage having the parts and passions of a man; the town, with its walls, and gates, and citadel, is an inanimate abstraction—a generalisation of humanity, not a living and breathing human creature. The multitude of its inhabitants, the multitude of their foes and of their friends, parcel out the powers of good and evil in the soul into fragments and atoms. No single figure interests us supremely; not one lives in the popular memory. We hardly feel on closer terms of familiarity with Captain Credence, or Captain Goodhope, or Captain Patience, than with the five points of Calvinistic controversy. In the *Pilgrim's Progress* womanhood is presented side by side with manhood; even in the first Part gracious female forms appear; in the *Holy War* counsellors and warriors leave no place for women; half of our human society is unrepresented. The pilgrimage of Christian is an individual experience idealised in art; it is the *Wahrheit und Dichtung* ["truth and literature"] of Bunyan's spiritual life; the allegory of Mansoul is a piece of universal history; it is the work of Bunyan the preacher, who, having taken his side in the warfare of good and evil, was interested in a great cause. But the epic of a cause requires as its representative a champion exposed to the vicissitudes of fortune and in the end falling or triumphant. Bunyan's Emmanuel is too much of a *deus ex machina;* his beleaguered city is an abstraction of humanity; the epic is one without a hero. Bunyan's ingenuity in detail astonishes and fatigues the reader; poetry is replaced by wit in the form of allegory. One episode, indeed, rises to the height of Bunyan's nobler work, but it is difficult to find a second of equal merit. The town of Mansoul has been conquered by Emmanuel, who has not yet made his entrance and remains in the fields. The guilty inhabitants, freed from the tyranny of their oppressors, are still uncertain of the temper of their deliverer. The prisoners, with ropes about their necks, go forth to stand before the Prince; trembling and amazed they hear his doom of mercy; "the grace, the benefit, the pardon, was sudden, glorious, and so big that they were not able, without staggering, to stand up under it." The joy of Bunyan's own heart, when he could have spoken of God's love and mercy to the very crows sitting on the furrows, returned upon him: "They went down to the camp in black, but they came back to the town in white; they went down to the camp in ropes, they came back in chains of gold; they went down to the camp in fetters, but came back with their steps enlarged under them; they went also to the camp looking for death, but they came back from thence with assurance of life; they went down to the camp with heavy hearts, but came back again with pipe and tabor playing before them. So, as soon as they were come to Eye-gate, the poor and tottering town of Mansoul adventured to give a shout; and they gave such a shout as made the captains in the Prince's army leap at the sound thereof."

The *Holy War* is a construction, not a vision. The *Pilgrim's Progress* came to Bunyan unsought. His imagination seemed to be the subject of its own involuntary creations. He tells us in *Grace Abounding* how, in the days of his spiritual distress, the blessed state of the poor and pious folk of Bedford was imaged before his inner eye. He saw them set upon the sunny side of a high mountain, refreshing themselves with the pleasant beams of the sun, while he was shivering and shrinking in the cold, afflicted with frost, snow, and dark clouds. A wall compassed the mountain, through which his soul greatly desired to pass; by and by he perceived a narrow gap, like a little doorway, in the wall, through which he attempted, but in vain, to enter: "at last with great striving methought I at first did get in my head, and, after that, by a sidling striving, my shoulders and my whole body. Then was I exceeding glad, and went, and sat down in the midst of them, and so was comforted with the light and heat of their sun." This parable was no deliberate shaping of Bunyan's intellect or imagination; it came to him and announced itself. And in like manner arose his dream of the pilgrim, uncalled for and with no laboured research, as if it were the courteous revelation of some ministering spirit. (pp. 253-61)

The second part [of the *Pilgrim's Progress*]—the pilgrimage of Christiana—was written several years later. Another Christian on the same journey could only have repeated in essentials the adventures of the first with artificial variations, and the book must have been a feebler version of the original narrative. But women and children desire the Celestial City as well as men. It has been suggested that in Christiana we have an idealised portrait of Bunyan's second wife, Elizabeth, who in the Swan Chamber pleaded his cause before Sir Matthew Hale, while Mercy may perhaps have been created from memories of the wife of his youth. The second part is doubtless inferior to the first in its intensity and directness; it was less a record of Bunyan's personal experiences. The terrors of the way are softened; its consolations, if not more exquisite, are more freely distributed—"and one smiled, and another smiled, and they all smiled for joy that Christiana was become a pilgrim." There is no moment in the women's pilgrimage so dreadful as that when Christian in the Valley of the Shadow of Death took the voice of the wicked one, suggesting many grievous blasphemies, for his own utterance. Roaring giants armed with clubs are less appalling than the soft-footed and whispering fiend; and Great-heart is at hand, conveying his weak ones, a conductor sufficiently skilled in the art of decapitating giants or piercing them under the fifth rib.

Yet we could ill spare the second part of the *Pilgrim's Progress.* Mr Froude was surely in error when he called it a feeble reverberation of the first; on the contrary, it is the best of all after-pieces. And the manly tenderness of Bunyan's heart finds expression here as it does nowhere else. He honours Christiana for her courage; he leans lovingly over Mercy—a little tripping maid who followed God. Beelzebub shoots no arrows at the women as they stand knocking at the gates; it is bad enough that a dog (and a great one too) should make a heavy barking against them; while they knock the Master gives them a wonderful innocent smile. If the two ill-favoured ones cause them alarm, the Reliever is presently at hand. The Interpreter, with a "sweetheart" and a "dear-heart" to encourage Mercy, shows them things easy to understand, His garden where was great variety of flowers, the robin with a spider in his mouth, the hen walking in a fourfold method towards her chickens—a simplified text of an Evangelical Aesop's fables. When arrayed in fine linen, white and clean, the women, fair as the moon, had more than joy in their beautiful garments; they seemed to be a terror one to the other, for in their marvellous humility "they could not see that glory each on herself which they could see in each other." They are comforted in departing with a bottle of wine, some parched corn, together with a couple of pomegranates—delightful fare for pilgrims. Before descending to the Valley of Humiliation they hear the birds singing their curious melodious notes, which had been learnt, as might happen with pious birds, from Sternhold's version of the Psalms. The valley, beautified with lilies, was for them as fruitful a place as any the crow flies over, and there it was that they espied the fresh-favoured shepherd-boy feeding his father's sheep, who sang of the blessedness of a lowly spirit, and wore more of that herb called heart's-ease in his bosom than he that is clad in silk and velvet. Even in going through the Valley of the Shadow they had daylight. They heard the celebration of their sex from the lips of the good Gaius; they had a medical adviser as well as a beloved spiritual conductor; they had the happiness of being interested in several weddings; and instead of lying in the dungeon, nasty and stinking, of Despair, they enjoyed a pious dance around the giant's head; the shepherds decorated them with such bracelets and earrings as Delectable Mountains afford; and it was the men of Bunyan's earlier pilgrimage—so courteous is he—not the adorned women, of the later, who were taken in the flatterer's net. The token sent to Christiana that she should make haste to cross the river was an arrow with a point sharpened with love; and even Despondency's daughter, Much-afraid, went through the waters singing—singing of some incomprehensible consolation, for none on the hither side could comprehend what she said. (pp. 263-65)

[The *Pilgrim's Progress* is a] dream of terrors, but also of consolations, hope, and joy; more than a dream, the veritable history of a human soul, lifted into a higher reality by the power of imagination. Bunyan's material was given to him by a series of agonising personal experiences, which seemed at times to border on insanity, and by a great deliverance wrought in his own heart. Nothing is more remarkable than the mastery with which his imagination controls and pacifies and purifies his memories of pain and rapture; the humblest realities coalesce with spiritual passions that belong to eternity as much as to time. Every thing verifies itself as actual, yet the total effect is ideal. And thus the book acquired an universal import, and may serve as a manual of the inner life even for persons whom Bunyan, with his Puritan theology, would have classed among heathen men and infidels. All his powers co-operated harmoniously in creating this book—his religious ardour, his human tenderness, his sense of beauty, nourished by the Scriptures, his strong common sense, even his gift of humour. Through his deep seriousness play the lighter faculties. The whole man presses into this small volume. The purport of what he writes in its most general significance is no other than that exhortation of all great spiritual teachers—to live for what is best and highest and most real, and to live for these with the loins girt and the lamp lit—"Viriliter age, exspectans Dominum" *quit ye like men.* (pp. 268-69)

Edward Dowden, "John Bunyan," in his *Puritan and Anglican: Studies in Literature*, Kegan Paul, Trench, Trübner & Co., Ltd., 1900, pp. 232-78.

WILLIAM YORK TINDALL
(essay date 1934)

[In the following excerpt, Tindall examines Bunyan's art within the tradition of seventeenth-century lay preaching.]

For the success of the holy war Bunyan relied upon the work of the enthusiastic lay preachers, whose sermons and prayers turned the obstinacy of the profane into a wearied acquiescence and charmed the susceptible into the way of truth. The spiritual descent of Jesus to assume the crown, which, in His physical absence, the ministry could be relied upon to support over the throne at a suitable elevation, depended upon ministerial propaganda and awaited the triumph of the preacher, who controlled by divine assistance the sword of the word. (p. 165)

The sword of the word is a very pretty instrument, which can annoy the wicked without wounding the tenderest sentiments of a saint; and when it is bent conveniently into a hook, it is useful for angling. Since engine and bait were metaphorical and the fish were men, the pious were much attracted to the sport and assiduously practiced it, less for entertainment, however, than for use, under the impression that the cause of their Saviour was at stake. To fish for men by words, to lure them into an agreeable captivity for the advancement of heaven on earth, was the principal occupation and delight of the lay preachers. These virtuous men had reduced their piscatory pursuits to a conscious and elaborate art, of which they were able to speak with great authority. John Bunyan devoted considerable attention to the capture of fishes, and by the more knowing of his admirers he was said to be adept at this elegant accomplishment.

The popular style of preaching and writing, to which Bunyan and many of his fellows looked for the establishment of Christ's earthly kingdom, was simple, colloquial, redundant, and conspicuously metaphorical. From the friars of the Middle Ages, who had availed themselves of *exemplum* and anecdote for the greater conviction of the poor, this variety of ministerial blandishment had descended by the obscure channels of apostolic succession to the humble preachers of the seventeenth century. These successful propagandists also addressed the "mean and poorer sort of men" in language and imagery which their hearers understood, and they adopted every traditional device of vulgar rhetoric to achieve the color, simplicity, and vehemence by which laborers and farmers were pleased.

Sometimes from necessity but more often by design the lay preachers employed the idiom of their social class; they avoided, even when they were capable of, the scholarly allusions, the Ciceronian schemes and tropes, and the witty conceits of the clergy; they drew their metaphors and analogies from the Bible and from the common life about them; and some of them, like Bunyan, cultivated a racy colloquialism with full awareness of its effect. The popular style had been developed in the early years of the Civil Wars by radicals who found in the rhetoric of Martin Marprelate and ultimately of the friars a means of disconcerting the Presbyterians and of stealing their audience. The careful perfection of this popular mode accounts for the great difference between the sermons of lay preachers and those of the clergy, who declined to abate their gentility by stooping to the methods of the demagogue. It is not surprising that the vulgar preferred the attractive rhetoric of barn and hedge to the chill and academic cadences of the established pulpit. The loose and inviting style of the lay preachers was so inimical to the reputations and prejudicial to the interests of the clergy that it could not but be considered a menace to respectability and the state. (pp. 166-67)

The sermon was the engine of Bunyan's conventional angling, but when the capture of more difficult fish demanded the almost incredible method of tickling, Bunyan abandoned himself without hesitation to this unorthodox pursuit and produced *Pilgrim's Progress.* This work and the others for which Bunyan is now remembered were "tracts," as Bunyan's contemporaries correctly described them, both in that they were composed with the purpose of his sermons, and in that they were logical extensions of the art of familiar preaching. By the promotion of the similitudes and the other popular devices which he had developed in his sermons from an incidental to an essential function Bunyan sought to catch the fancy and effect the salvation of a wider audience. Those who were immune from the occasional embellishment of the obvious tract might succumb to a more generous bait, a gilded engine, and a seductive manipulation.

Though Bunyan wanted the inclination and the accomplishments of the theologian, he possessed those of the popularizer. By the arts of metaphor, allegory, and colloquial speech and by the ingratiating disguise of verse or fiction, he adorned Calvin, yet made him familiar, concealed him without impropriety, yet introduced him to the curiosity and the favor of the public. As Charles Doe observed of that ingenious enhancement of Calvinism, *Pilgrim's Progress,* "it wins . . . smoothly upon their affections, and so insensibly distills the Gospel into them." For over two hundred years this useful work has been the favorite resort of missionary and Sunday-school superintendent alike in

their delicate task of enlightening without antagonizing the untutored mind.

The invocation of the Muses for the enlargement of piety was the almost inevitable consequence, as it was the extension, of Bunyan's art of popular preaching; but his interest in poetry and fiction may also be traced to a literary tradition then current among the Baptists and other dissenters, whose pleasing tracts inspired his emulation. In the early years of the century the Puritan Arthur Dent, whose popular manner Baxter attempted in vain to imitate, had employed the graces of dialogue "for the better understanding of the simple" and for the instruction of "the meaner capacity." Dent's *Plaine Mans Pathway to Heaven,* which Bunyan had thoughtfully perused, was an effort to popularize the fundamentals, as were his familiar dialogues on predestination for the use of the young. The example of Dent and that of Richard Bernard, who had used allegory for the same purpose, were influential. Among the Baptists to follow this practice were Benjamin Keach, Thomas Sherman, and William Balmford, who had published virtuous dramas and allegorical verses before Bunyan turned his serious attention to the lighter evangelism. Though Bunyan had found encouragement in the example of his predecessors, he succeeded more conspicuously than they; and the popularity of his works not only occasioned in turn the imitation of others, among whom were both Keach and Sherman, but served to establish the propriety of the familiar method. (pp. 179-81)

For each of his more popular books Bunyan composed a preface wherein he declared and defended his literary and evangelistic principles. More elaborate than the incidental criticism, which we have noticed, these formal commentaries upon his aim, method, and scriptural precedent also testify to his thorough consciousness of the arts which he employed, and by their apologetic tone indicate the conservative hostility of some readers to the use of those popular devices by which alone others were to be taken. Though it is probable that these introductions were occasioned rather by the necessity of defense than by an impulse toward analysis, they are, nevertheless, Bunyan's essays in criticism, which differ from Dryden's less in kind than in magnitude and importance, and which reveal both deliberation of method and awareness of effect.

The first of these prefaces is to be found in *Profitable Meditations,* 1661, a small volume of verse, written for the most part in the ancient tradition of the poetical debate, and devoted to the harmonious advancement of truth. Bunyan had been moved to venture from the ways of prosaic evangelism into the gracious purlieus of poetry by the conviction that rhyme had power to seduce the obstinate and to confirm the pliable:

Men's heart is apt in Meeter to delight,
Also in that to bear away the more:
This is the cause I hear in Verses write,
Therefore affect this Book, and read it o're.
When Doctors give their Physick to the Sick,
They make it pleasing with some other thing:
Truth also by this means is very quick,
When men by Faith it in their hearts do sing.

The variety of metaphors at Bunyan's command permitted this surprising deviation from the imagery of fishing to that of physic, which was, however, of equal merit for the discovery of his intention. His poetical preface was not limited to the subtleties of practical medicine but also embraced the more specious province of propriety. The generous influence of nature, and possibly of grace, had reconciled Bunyan to the assistance of the carnal arts; but no influence had power to abate the scrupulous antipathy of many Baptists to this almost idolatrous employment of the Muses. Before the stern tribunal of the pious, whose disinclination to countenance the questionable delights of poetry was as great an impediment to popular evangelism as to the singing of hymns, Bunyan was constrained by necessity and hope to plead his justification by an ingenious apology:

Take none offence, Friend, at my method here,
Cause thou in Verses simple Truth dost see:
But to them soberly incline thine ear,
And with the Truth it self affected be.
'Tis not the Method, but the Truth alone
Should please a Saint, and mollifie his heart:
Truth in our out of Meeter is but one;
And this thou knowst, if thou a Christian art.

In the need for extreme methods to attract the immature and the aesthetic and in the illiberal displeasure of the conservative lay the dilemma of the Baptist poet. But undismayed by the misunderstanding of his excellent purpose, Bunyan continued the melodious celebration of sublimity and truth by suitable numbers, and eventually by works of fiction, for which he also provided prefaces of explanation and defense. The apologetic evangelist enjoyed the gratifications of art and the consciousness of virtue.

Bunyan devoted the Preface to the first part of *Pilgrim's Progress* to an apology for fiction, allegory, and the popular method. He had offered his manuscript to the judgment of the godly, some of whom said, "John, Print it; others said, not so"; but the encouragement of the former had more effect with the liberal author than the obduracy of the latter, with whom he took this prefatory occasion to expostulate:

May I not write in such a style as this?
In such a Method too, and yet not miss
My end, thy good? why may it not be done?

For the enlightenment of those who maintained that his book was obscure, insubstantial, and giddy,

Bunyan called attention to the example and implication of the Scriptures, whose irreproachable protagonists, the prophets, the apostles, and the Saviour had known and practiced the arts of metaphor, allegory, and obscurity. Inspired and justified by the parables, types, and shadows of his heavenly model, Bunyan had piously adopted the metaphorical craft, to which he had also been attracted by the consideration that "Truth within a Fable" was more memorable and more solacious than doctrine unadorned. . . . The objection which Bunyan encountered was occasioned not only by his use of allegory, to which many of his readers were accustomed, but by his familiarity, his homeliness, and his want of proper dignity. If Bunyan had presented his similitudes with the sobriety of Keach or Patrick, he would have escaped the condemnation of the solemn; but he had introduced to fiction the agreeable familiarity of his preaching, and what had been and continued to be the cause of his success was now the occasion of reproach. . . . The extravagant acclamation of the public encouraged the hesitant author and vindicated in his own eyes the employment in fiction of the homeliness of his tracts. The second part of the *Progress* is racier than the first; and his subsequent writings increasingly abounded in that familiarity whose virtue his triumph had proved.

The confident Preface to the second part of *Pilgrim's Progress* is not an apology. To those who objected he could now say that their dislike of his method was an unfortunate peculiarity of the sort which keeps some from the wholesome enjoyment of cheese, fish, or swine. Though the Prefaces of *Mr. Badman* and *The Holy War* contain less of a critical nature, they advance the claim of realism, repeat the theory of instruction through amusement, and justify the author's use of dialogue by his own convenience and the pleasure of the reader. It was Bunyan's growing assurance which enabled him to say in *Mr. Badman:* "Why I have handled the matter in this method, is best known to my self."

Before we investigate the last and most extraordinary example of Bunyan's popular manner, we must pause to inquire into the natures and the prefaces of those less ingratiating works which Bunyan intended for men of riper parts. As we have observed, Bunyan had two styles: the popular for the immature; and the simple and direct for the knowing. His serious propaganda, he implied, was meat for the strong, and his familiar verses and allegories milk for the feeble. Accordingly Bunyan advised those readers who were desirous of milk and incapable of meat to avoid *The Holy City* in which he had treated without frivolity a subject worthy of the interest of men. The Preface, which contains this advice, expresses some apprehension lest the learned and the exacting should despise his plain and homely manner, but the emphasis is upon the plain, and the homeliness is not that of his familiar tracts.

Throughout this Preface he professed an intentional simplicity and indicated his avoidance of "high swelling words of vanity" in favor of "pure and naked truth" as appropriate to his noble purpose and serious audience. Simplicity had also recommended itself to Bunyan as suitable for those readers whose profundity was superior to entertainment and whose spiritual maturity was more apparent than their wit or learning. . . . The Preface to *Grace Abounding* also states the virtue of plainness and simplicity for solemn purposes. . . . By simplicity Bunyan referred to that plain and relatively unmetaphorical style which he preferred for exhortation and for addressing those who required no adornment. His recognition of the need for two methods was founded upon the practice of the Saviour, who, he said, had used parables to reach the emotions of the people, but had appealed by directness and simplicity to the understandings of the disciples.

The last conspicuous example of Bunyan's familiar style is *A Book for Boys and Girls,* 1686, a collection of unpretentious verses, by which the author hoped to enlarge the bounds of holiness by folly. To avoid misunderstanding of his intention, Bunyan devoted his Preface to the ironic praise of frivolity, that subtle means of awakening the immature and the obstinate, and to securing himself from the imputation of childishness. He had designed this book of crude and homely emblems to appeal directly to children and to shame those adults whom the despair and effort of the ministry had failed to disturb. Since both children and childish adults were addicted to the sports of immaturity, Bunyan had supplied them with appropriate toys:

Wherefore good Reader, that I save them may,
I now with them, the very Dottril play.

The abandonment of gravity had an illustrious precedent; for

Paul seem'd to play the Fool, that he might gain
Those that were Fools, indeed. . . .

This extraordinary and almost impious statement, which is, however, an ingenious explanation of the perplexing character of Paul, served to establish the necessary precedent. . . . Bunyan's "Homely Rhimes" on pigs, frogs, and flyspecks are drawn from barnyard, home, and countryside, and couched in an inelegant idiom. The refined editors, who preserved the seemliness of the eighteenth century by the omission or the correction of these imperfect verses, revealed both their ignorance of the popular method and their contempt for the Saviour, to whose example, in his thirty-first emblem, Bunyan had devoutly attributed the familiar quality of his eloquence.

Two years before the publication of this book for the young and the foolish, whose capture he had planned by means of homeliness and irony, Bunyan had cast his net for women and children in the second part of *Pilgrim's Progress.* For their enticement he had introduced the agreeable machinery of connubial, domestic, and infantile deportment, such as the nuptials of Mercy, the gratifying increase of the faithful by her industrious parturition, and the indigestion and relief of Matthew. But this tender audience was equally fascinated by Bunyan's riddles, proverbs, catechisms for the young, and emblems of instructive beasts. The "book of the creatures" had been opened by the diligent iconographer of Bedford, who looked with devotion upon stone and fish, pondered the symbolic inclination of the Deity, and wisely concluded that there was nothing on earth but had "some spiritual mystery in it." "It is the wisdom of God," he said, "to speak to us, ofttimes by trees, gold, silver, stones, beasts, fowls, fishes, spiders, ants, frogs, lice, dust, etc." Upon this celestial mystery and the habit of the Creator, Bunyan based the ministerial conduct of his Interpreter, who instructed the travelers of *Pilgrim's Progress* by emblems of dust, raindrops, and unobjectionable animals. The Interpreter had enlightened Christian, not by abstractions of doctrine, but by symbols; and for the inferior capacities of the women and children, this skillful minister displayed emblematic objects of a more homely variety, the muckraker, the spider, the comfortable hen, and the robin. "I chose, my Darlings," said he, "to lead you into the Room where such things are, because you are Women, and they are easie for you." The popular and familiar method of the Interpreter was that of his creator, who had devised this gifted character, as he had his critical prefaces, in commentary upon his art.

Though ignorant of the advice of Horace, Bunyan gained the world as he dedicated his later years to the mixture of the useful and the sweet. He also knew, however, the power of the useful without the admixture of the sweet. Upon these two methods, which served in turn to present the same subject in *The Holy City* and *The Holy War,* Bunyan relied for the expansion of the theocratic church by the valuable increment of men, children, women, and fools. Bunyan's two-handed engine was the sword of the word, but in the light of his preference and later practice, better had it been called the hook. (pp. 181-89)

William York Tindall, in his *John Bunyan: Mechanick Preacher,* Columbia University Press, 1934, 309 p.

C. S. LEWIS
(broadcast date 1962)

[Lewis is considered one of the foremost mythopoeic authors of the twentieth century. In the following excerpt from the text of a 1962 radio broadcast, he comments on *The Pilgrim's Progress*, assessing Bunyan's style and the competence of his allegory.]

There are books which, while didactic in intention, are read with delight by people who do not want their teaching and may not believe that they have anything to teach—works like Lucretius' *De Rerum Natura* or Burton's *Anatomy*. This is the class to which *The Pilgrim's Progress* belongs. Most of it has been read and re-read by those who were indifferent or hostile to its theology, and even by children who perhaps were hardly aware of it. I say, most of it, for there are some long dialogues where we get bogged down in sheer doctrine, and doctrine, too, of a sort that I find somewhat repellent. The long conversation, near the end of Part I, which Christian and Hopeful conduct *"to prevent drowsiness in this place"*—they are entering the Enchanted Ground—will not prevent drowsiness on the part of many readers. Worse still is the dialogue with Mr Talkative.

Bunyan—and, from his own point of view, rightly—would not care twopence for the criticism that he here loses the interest of irreligious readers. But such passages are faulty in another way too. In them, the speakers step out of the allegorical story altogether. They talk literally and directly about the spiritual life. The great image of the Road disappears. They are in the pulpit. If this is going to happen, why have a story at all? Allegory frustrates itself the moment the author starts doing what could equally well be done in a straight sermon or treatise. It is a valid form only so long as it is doing what could not be done at all, or done so well, in any other way.

But this fault is rare in Bunyan—far rarer than in *Piers Plowman*. If such dead wood were removed from *The Pilgrim's Progress* the book would not be very much shorter than it is. The greater part of it is enthralling narrative or genuinely dramatic dialogue. Bunyan stands with Malory and Trollope as a master of perfect naturalness in the mimesis of ordinary conversation.

To ask how a great book came into existence is, I believe, often futile. But in this case Bunyan has told us the answer, so far as such things can be told. It comes in the very pedestrian verses prefixed to Part I. He says that while he was at work on quite a different book he *"Fell suddenly into an Allegory."* He means, I take it, a little allegory, an extended metaphor that would have filled a single paragraph. He set down *"more than twenty things."* And, this done, *"I twenty more had in my Crown."* The *"things"* began *"to multiply"* like sparks flying out of a fire. They threatened, he says, to *"eat out"* the book he was working on. They insisted on splitting off from it and becoming a separate organism. He let them have their head. Then come the words which describe, better than any others I know, the golden moments of unimpeded composition:

For having now my Method by the end;

Still as I pull'd, it came.

It came. I doubt if we shall ever know more of the process called "inspiration" than those two monosyllables tell us.

Perhaps we may hazard a guess as to why it came at just that moment. My own guess is that the scheme of a journey with adventures suddenly reunited two things in Bunyan's mind which had hitherto lain far apart. One was his present and lifelong preoccupation with the spiritual life. The other, far further away and longer ago, left behind (he had supposed) in childhood, was his delight in old wives' tales and such last remnants of chivalric romance as he had found in chapbooks. The one fitted the other like a glove. Now, as never before, the whole man was engaged.

The vehicle he had chosen—or, more accurately, the vehicle that had chosen him—involved a sort of descent. His high theme had to be brought down and incarnated on the level of an adventure story of the most unsophisticated type—a quest story, with lions, goblins, giants, dungeons and enchantments. But then there is a further descent. This adventure story itself is not left in the world of high romance. Whether by choice or by the fortunate limits of Bunyan's imagination—probably a bit of both—it is all visualized in terms of the contemporary life that Bunyan knew. The garrulous neighbours; Mr Worldly-Wiseman who was so clearly (as Christian said) "a Gentleman," the bullying, foul-mouthed Justice; the field-path, seductive to footsore walkers; the sound of a dog barking as you stand knocking at a door; the fruit hanging over a wall which the children insist on eating though their mother admonishes them "that Fruit is none of ours"—these are all characteristic. No one lives further from Wardour Street than Bunyan. The light is sharp: it never comes through stained glass.

And this homely immediacy is not confined to externals. The very motives and thoughts of the pilgrims are similarly brought down to earth. Christian undertakes his journey because he believes his hometown is going to be destroyed by fire. When Mathew sickens after eating the forbidden fruit, his mother's anxiety is entirely medical; they send for the doctor. When Mr. Brisk's suit to Mercy grows cold, Mercy is allowed to speak and feel as a good many young women would in her situation:

I might a had Husbands afore now, tho' I spake not of it to any; but they were such as did not like my Conditions, though never did any of them find fault with my Person.

When Christian keeps on his way and faces Apollyon, he is not inspired by any martial ardour. He goes on because he remembers that he has armour for his chest but not for his back, so that turning tail would be the most dangerous thing he could do.

A page later comes the supreme example. You remember how the text "the wages of sin is death" is transformed? Asked by Apollyon why he is deserting him, Christian replies: "Your wages [were] such as a man could not live on." You would hardly believe it, but I have read a critic who objected to that. He thought the motive attributed to Christian was too low. But that is to misunderstand the very nature of all allegory or parable or even metaphor. The lowness is the whole point. Allegory gives you one thing in terms of another. All depends on respecting the rights of the vehicle, in refusing to allow the least confusion between the vehicle and its freight. The Foolish Virgins, within the parable, do not miss beatitude; they miss a wedding party. The Prodigal Son, when he comes home, is not given spiritual consolations; he is given new clothes and the best dinner his father can put up. It is extraordinary how often this principle is disregarded. The imbecile, wisely anonymous, who illustrated my old nursery copy of *The Pilgrim's Progress* makes a similar blunder at the end of Part II. Bunyan has been telling how a post came for Christiana to say that she was to cross the river and appear in the City within ten days. She made her farewells to all her friends and "entered the *River* with a *Beck'n*" (that is a wave) "of Fare well, to those that followed her to the River side." The artist has seen fit to illustrate this with a picture of an old lady on her death-bed, surrounded by weeping relatives in the approved Victorian manner. But if Bunyan had wanted a literal death-bed scene he would have written one.

This stupidity perhaps comes from the pernicious habit of reading allegory as if it were a cryptogram to be translated; as if, having grasped what an image (as we say) "means," we threw the image away and thought of the ingredient in real life which it represents. But that method leads you continually out of the book back into the conception you started from and would have had without reading it. The right process is the exact reverse. We ought not to be thinking "This green valley, where the shepherd boy is singing, represents humility"; we ought to be discovering, as we read, that humility is like that green valley. That way, moving always into the book, not out of it, from the concept to the image, enriches the concept. And that is what allegory is for.

There are two things we must not say about the style of *Pilgrim's Progress*. In the first place we must not say that it is derived from the Authorised Version. That is based on confusion. Because his whole outlook is biblical, and because direct or embedded quotations from Scripture are so frequent, readers carry away the impression that his own sentences are like those of the

English Bible. But you need only look at them to see that they are not:

> Come *Wet*, come *Dry*, I long to be gone; for however the Weather is in my Journey, I shall have time enough when I come there to sit down and rest me, and dry me.

Who in the Old or New Testament ever talked like that?

> Mr. *Great-heart* was delighted in him (for he loved one greatly that he found to be a man of his Hands).

Is that like Scripture?

The other thing we must not say is that Bunyan wrote well because he was a sincere, forthright man who had no literary affectations and simply said what he meant. I do not doubt that is the account of the matter that Bunyan would have given himself. But it will not do. If it were the real explanation, then every sincere, forthright, unaffected man could write as well. But most people of my age learned from censoring the letters of the troops, when we were subalterns in the first war, that unliterary people, however sincere and forthright in their talk, no sooner take a pen in hand than cliché and platitude flow from it. The shocking truth is that, while insincerity may be fatal to good writing, sincerity, of itself, never taught anyone to write well. It is a moral virtue, not a literary talent. We may hope it is rewarded in a better world: it is not rewarded on Parnassus.

We must attribute Bunyan's style to a perfect natural ear, a great sensibility for the idiom and cadence of popular speech, a long experience in addressing unlettered audiences, and a freedom from bad models. I do not add "to an intense imagination," for that also can shipwreck if a man does not find the right words. (pp. 146-50)

Part of the unpleasant side of *The Pilgrim's Progress* lies in the extreme narrowness and exclusiveness of Bunyan's religious outlook. The faith is limited "to one small sect and all are damned beside." But I suppose that all who read old books have learned somehow or other to make historical allowances for that sort of thing. Our ancestors all wrote and thought like that. The insolence and self-righteousness which now flourish most noticeably in literary circles then found their chief expression in theology, and this is no doubt a change for the better. And one must remember that Bunyan was a persecuted and slandered man.

For some readers the "unpleasant side" of *The Pilgrim's Progress* will lie not so much in its sectarianism as in the intolerable terror which is never far away. Indeed *unpleasant* is here a ludicrous understatement. The dark doctrine has never been more horrifyingly stated than in the words that conclude Part I:

Then I saw that there was a way to Hell, even from the Gates of Heaven, as well as from the City of *Destruction.*

In my opinion the book would be immeasurably weakened as a work of art if the flames of Hell were not always flickering on the horizon. I do not mean merely that if they were not it would cease to be true to Bunyan's own vision and would therefore suffer all the effects which a voluntary distortion or expurgation of experience might be expected to produce. I mean also that the image of this is necessary to us while we read. The urgency, the harsh woodcut energy, the continual sense of momentousness, depend on it.

We might even say that, just as Bunyan's religious theme demanded for its vehicle this kind of story, so the telling of such a story would have required on merely artistic grounds to be thus loaded with a further significance, a significance which is believed by only some, but can be felt (while they read) by all, to be of immeasurable importance. These adventures, these ogres, monsters, shining helpers, false friends, delectable mountains, and green or ghastly valleys, are not thereby twisted from their nature. They are restored to the weight they had for the savage or dreaming mind which produced them. They come to us, if we are sensitive to them at all, clothed in its ecstasies and terrors. Bunyan is not lending them an alien gravity. He is supplying, in terms of his own fundamental beliefs, grounds for taking them as seriously as we are, by the nature of our imagination, disposed to do. Unless we are very hidebound we can re-interpret these grounds in terms of our own, perhaps very different, outlook. Many do not believe that either the trumpets "with melodious noise" or the infernal den await us where the road ends. But most, I fancy, have discovered that to be born is to be exposed to delights and miseries greater than imagination could have anticipated; that the choice of ways at any cross-road may be more important than we think; and that short cuts may lead to very nasty places. (pp. 152-53)

C. S. Lewis, "The Vision of John Bunyan," in his *Selected Literary Essays,* edited by Walter Hooper, Cambridge at the University Press, 1969, pp. 146-53.

ELIZABETH W. BRUSS

(essay date 1976)

[In the following excerpt, Bruss examines the autobiographical content of *The Pilgrim's Progress* and *Grace Abounding to the Chief of Sinners.*]

One can see easily enough how much Bunyan's autobi-

ography has in common with his more famous allegorical novel, not only in source material and imagery but even in didactic goals. Yet Bunyan continued to reissue *Grace Abounding* long after the great success of his novel [*Pilgrim's Progress*]. Thus, for him and for his reading public, the earlier work achieved something that his fiction could not. The distinction between these two works, written in such close succession and with so many ties of theme and figure between them, exposes the heart of the autobiographical act as conceived by Bunyan and allows us to see the meaning and the purposes that made it unique in his eyes. Both works make use of actual events from the life of their author and both are religious teachings, but only the autobiography changes the value of that life and instructs to prove as much as to memorialize the touch of grace upon his life, and he himself is the party most interested in the sufficiency of his evidence and the validity of his conclusion. (pp. 37-8)

As a proof, therefore, *Grace Abounding* must be an argument rather than merely an attractive rhetorical display; artful persuasion will not suffice to convince when the goal is to convince the artist himself. The more seductive effects of narrative are often foregone for the sake of minute analysis and logical inference. The stern and unflinching character of Bunyan's sobriety, his refusal to "play" with stylistic adornments or to mitigate in any way his plain dealing, is a reflection of how serious are the consequences of his autobiographical act. Even if one could indulge in fancy when recalling the most deadly afflictions of one's life, there can be no playfulness when the act of writing is itself under judgment and will contribute to the ultimate salvation or perdition of one's own soul. This is the case when Bunyan is writing *in propria persona,* ["in his own person"], something he does not do in his novel. As autobiographer, Bunyan must suppress the sinful vanities of his own nature and overcome his carnal imagination; for, according to Calvin, "the mind of man is so entirely alienated from the righteousness of God that he cannot conceive, desire, or design anything but what is wicked, distorted, foul, impure, and iniquitous."

Thus *Grace Abounding,* unlike *Pilgrim's Progress,* is a work of the letter as well as the spirit, and its literal quality, its numberings and citations, its scrupulous or even obsessive attention to the naked Word of the scriptures, is possibly its most prominent feature. It is also a work which stresses its empirical foundations, and Bunyan's sobriety is intimately linked with his need to quash anything that could distort his vision or distract his attention. He must strive to remain in a state of receptive watchfulness—empty, earnest, expectant. The mimetic probability of fiction, internal consistency and necessity, is not enough; he must have the actual, the externally verifiable fact. Bunyan stresses, even in his subtitle, that his is a "faithful" account and interrupts his narrative at several points to stress it again. "In these things, I protest *before God,* I lye not, neither do I feign this sort of speech: these were really, strongly, and with all my heart, my desires." . . .

How different is this strident insistence from the casual and inviting tone Bunyan adopts in the preface to *Pilgrim's Progress.* (p. 38)

Grace Abounding is the story of Bunyan's increasing capacity for discerning God's order and bringing it to light in appropriate manner. Each stage of his spiritual development features a paragraph or more which illustrates his hermeneutic skill, the kind of analysis reflecting the degree of sophistication the aspiring convert has achieved. We can therefore see Bunyan growing toward the exegetical skill he will need when he finally becomes the itinerant preacher who addresses us from the preface of the autobiography. There are definite levels of interpretive method along the way, as definite as the steps of a Calvinist conversion. (p. 47)

External and internal, active and contemplative aspects of his life are here reduced to a single plane,

personal sensations and private anxieties becoming a newer testament from which Bunyan extracts the message for his autobiographical sermon. Using his life as text, Bunyan earns the right to make typological comparisons between himself and figures such as Samson and Moses, comparisons which might otherwise seem narcissistic or even sinful in their pride. It is proper, given the tendency of his autobiography as a whole, that Bunyan's last chapter should concern his imprisonment, whatever the chronological distortion. As a prisoner for the sake of his religion, Bunyan's entire existence takes on the status of an exemplum: "Indeed, I did often say in my heart before the Lord, 'That if to be hanged up presently before their eyes, would be a means to awaken them, and confirm them in the truth, I gladly should be contented'." . . .

In prison, his sphere of action is identical with his sphere of contemplation; he is physically constrained to the passive activities of observation, expectation, and memory—the very activities which go into the autobiographical act itself. His greatest triumph in prison is his discovery that he can cling to his faith through will alone, when no further visitations of Grace come upon him, when he is empty of images and even emotion. "I will leap off the Ladder even blindfold into Eternitie, sink or swim, come heaven, come hell; Lord Jesus, if thou wilt catch me, do; if not, I will venture for thy Name." . . . The autobiography concludes at that point at which Bunyan's life seems to have achieved some coherent purpose as a lesson for himself and for others. In the paragraphs that immediately follow this triumphant declaration, the lesson is rendered in a form free from all corporeal accidents and carnal imagery, a form that will impress itself upon the memory of those to whom it is addressed. And the chief of these is the autobiographer himself, who must struggle constantly with his own tendency to distraction, despair, and forgetfulness. . . . (p. 49)

The strain of effort is visible throughout *Grace Abounding,* down to the very modal verbs Bunyan uses. His capacity and his intense consciousness of obligation, what he "can" and "cannot" express, what he "must" do, is always on display, nor is this inartistic or irrelevant to the purposes of his autobiography. His novel, however, is quite another matter; there a strained or willful narration would intrude between reader and representation. The allegory allows Bunyan to restructure mundane time and space so that it is no longer necessary to impose an extrinsic, spiritual order upon his material. The road upon which the pilgrims travel provides an absolute standard, and the significance of any place or event can immediately be measured with respect to it. There is no need for topical headings or numbered paragraphs, no need to interrupt the narrative to propound the meaning of an event; the religious implications of any action or state of being are evident from the distance one must travel off the road to encounter them or the fate of the characters that represent them. Formalist, Hypocrisy, and By-Ends, for example, are never "seen again in the way" after going over to Lucre Hill. Bunyan can allow far more autonomy to the characters he creates than to the characters he remembers, since they are environed so clearly by the Celestial Journey. As a result, there is far more direct discourse in *Pilgrim's Progress* than in his autobiography. Indeed, during the later stages of their journey, Christian and Hopeful take over the task of narrating the book, telling tales within the larger tale, as they attempt to keep alert crossing the Enchanted Ground. Characters can act out their attributes through the texture and the content of their own directly reported words. . . . (pp. 49-50)

The identity between author, narrator, and protagonist which is a necessary part of Bunyan's autobiography is unwoven in *Pilgrim's Progress;* the adventures of Christian and his fellow pilgrims are observed and interpreted by the marginal notes. Bunyan himself transcends the text, replaced by these mediaries. It is

Frontispiece for *The Pilgrim's Progress,* showing Bunyan asleep in his cell and dreaming the events of the tale.

because of this that he can indulge his carnal imagination, since the fanciful imagery belongs to another voice, one for which Bunyan is not directly responsible. Images are also sanctioned because the marginal notes assure their appropriate interpretation. No ambiguity, no polysemy is involved; the novel simultaneously describes and expounds. In *Grace Abounding,* however, Bunyan must take great care with figures of speech. . . . (p. 51)

At the close of *Grace Abounding,* it is impossible to distinguish between the self who writes and the self who is written about; the narrator who "finds to this day seven abominations in my heart" has become one with the content of the book. The autobiographer embraces his task and his destiny, almost joyously reaffirming his imprisonment: "I have seen that here, that I am persuaded I shall never, while in this world be able to express. . . . I never knew what it was for God to stand by me at all turns, and at every offer of Satan to afflict me, etc., as I have found him since I came hither." . . . (p. 54)

The world is contracted to this prison cell, and all movement measured according to it. It is an intensely private world, moreover, a personal space which Bunyan shares with no other man. Even his converts and followers are denied admission. "The Milk and Honey is beyond this Wilderness: God be merciful to you, and grant that you be not slothful to go in and possess the Land." . . . Resigned and sublimely alone, Bunyan remains behind, gazing on from his own Mount Pisgah as his children pass over into the Promised Land.

The world which the characters of *Pilgrim's Progress* inhabit is just the reverse of this private one. The Way they follow is necessarily open; their success or failure in seeking it out and persisting in it is precisely what marks their spiritual capacity. There can be no question of anchoring the novel's space or time to any one character or even the dreamer—the Way exists before them all, and remains even after the hero has been assumed into heaven and the narrator awakes from his dream. Aside from their mutual journey, in fact, there is no other point where the experience of character and narrator coalesce. And it is a Way equally open to the readers of the novel. The dreamer may naively speak in the past tense, as though of an elapsed event, but the marginal notes make it clear that the rewards and the hazards of this journey are timeless. It is the function of the dreamer's tale to arouse others to the desire for a better world which he himself experienced at seeing the Celestial City; thus the progress of spiritual development must be something that begins afresh whenever the book is read. (pp. 54-5)

The novel has ample room for its readers and makes ample narrative concessions to their interests. Since it is not an act of direct self-expression, the novel frees Bunyan from a dominant textual concern for the evidence for and against his own salvation. *Pilgrim's Progress* can give greater scope in its scheme of election and greater universality to its treatment of religious experience. More than one valid mode of conversion is possible. Hopeful, though no pioneering spirit, is as true a convert as any, and there are differences even in the awakenings of the patriarchs, Christian and Faithful. Each man experiences his own form of trial in the Valley of Humiliation, according to his individual vulnerabilities. The distinction between these heroes and the narrator of the novel means that there is a bridge between those who successfully complete the journey and those hopeful believers in the audience who are just beginning the pilgrimage or struggling to continue it. The dreamer is escaped alone to tell us, and to prepare and inspire us for what we shall meet. (p. 55)

The narrator of *Grace Abounding* cannot be anonymous . . . nor does Bunyan seem to make any attempt at reducing the distance between himself and his audience. It is his identity, his uniqueness, after all, which is the principal warrant for writing an autobiography. His text is full of references to himself; it is subordinate to self. While the author's Apology to *Pilgrim's Progress* turns attention away from Bunyan and toward "this book," in *Grace Abounding* the focus of attention is always upon "me" and "my discourse." Nor is his identity only that of a narrator and spectator. He is "the chief of sinners," he is minister, martyr, and "God's servant"—any name, in fact, which applies to the religious occupations and roles he has publicly established for himself. (p. 56)

Bunyan cannot achieve here the perfect, transcendental resolution of his fiction, in which the dreamer can actually witness "just men made perfect." Christian is able to leave all carnal inclinations on the far side of the River of Death, but the autobiographer-hero must continue to encounter and abhor these elements in himself. "I can do none of those things which God commands me, but my corruptions will thrust in themselves; When I would do good, evil is present with me." . . .

Yet there is resolution in *Grace Abounding,* even if it is in the form of a paradox. For prison frees Bunyan by confining those carnal corruptions which frustrate his will to be pure and without spiritual division. Bunyan's punishment is his reward, for it proves his capacity to sacrifice himself and removes forever what he calls the worst of all his temptations, "to question the being of God, and the truth of his Gospel." . . . Here at last he discovers that his faith is sufficient, that he requires no further proof of either God or himself: "How now . . . is this the sign of an upright Soul, to desire to serve God for nothing rather then give out?" (p. 60)

Elizabeth W. Bruss, "John Bunyan: The Patriarch and the Way," in her *Autobiographical Acts: The Changing Situation of a Literary Genre,* The Johns Hopkins University Press, 1976, pp. 33-60.

SOURCES FOR FURTHER STUDY

Batson, E. Beatrice. *John Bunyan: Allegory and Imagination.* Totowa, N.J.: Barnes & Noble Books, 1984, 157 p.

>Important study of Bunyan's thought and artistry.

Brittain, Vera. *In the Steps of John Bunyan: An Excursion into Puritan England.* London: Rich and Cowan, 1950, 440 p.

>Detailed biography of Bunyan, focusing on his seventeenth-century milieu.

Keeble, N. H., ed. *John Bunyan, Conventicle and Parnassus: Tercentenary Essays.* Oxford: Clarendon Press, 1988, 278 p.

>Contains twelve original essays by prominent literary and religious scholars. Keeble notes that each essay examines various features of "Bunyan's Christian faith and his imagination" so that "the book as a whole might . . . offer a comprehensive summary of the present state of Bunyan scholarship and criticism."

Knott, John R., Jr. "John Bunyan and the Experience of the Word." In his *The Sword of the Spirit: Puritan Responses to the Bible,* pp. 131-63. Chicago: University of Chicago Press, 1980.

>Illustrates Bunyan's artistic approach to scriptural authority.

Sharrock, Roger. *John Bunyan.* London: Hutchinson's University Library, 1954, 167 p.

>Biography providing critical commentary on Bunyan's major works.

Talon, Henri. *John Bunyan: The Man and His Works,* translated by Barbara Wall. London: Rockliff, 1951, 340 p.

>Comprehensive study that includes discussion of Bunyan's sermons and minor works.

Edmund Burke

1729-1797

Irish-born English essayist, political writer, and philosopher.

INTRODUCTION

Widely recognized as the founder of modern Anglo-American conservatism, Burke is considered by many the most important and influential English statesman and political writer of the eighteenth century. In his speeches and essays he addressed major issues of his time, including the precepts of the American and French revolutions, the two-party political system, principles of economic reform, and the rights of government versus the rights of the individual. To each issue Burke brought the dramatic eloquence of a professional orator, the cool rationalism of a classical logician, the confident prescience of a social prophet, and the moral fervor of a Christian polemicist. Despite his lack—indeed, rejection—of any systematized theory to answer the political problems he faced, his writings continue to shape responses to major contemporary dilemmas. Such works as *Speech on Moving His Resolutions for Conciliation with the Colonies* (1775), *Reflections on the Revolution in France* (1790), and *A Letter from the Right Honourable Edmund Burke to a Noble Lord* (1796) stand as testaments to one of the most remarkably original and powerful voices in the history of political thought.

Born in Dublin to middle-class parents of different faiths—his father an Anglican attorney and his mother a staunch Roman Catholic—Burke was a sickly child who spent much of his boyhood reading and studying. Although raised in his father's faith, he developed an early appreciation for the plight of oppressed Irish Catholics. In his teens he attended a Quaker boarding school in County Kildare before entering Trinity College in Dublin in 1744. During his years at Trinity, Burke demonstrated a proclivity for poetry, history, mathematics, and logic. He vigorously participated in literary coffeehouse gatherings and eventually formed a debating society, in which he honed his rhetorical skills.

He also launched and edited a literary review/social issues weekly titled the *Reformer,* which went through thirteen numbers before folding. After receiving his bachelor of arts degree in 1748, Burke remained at Trinity for some time to continue work on an independent study of human responses to aesthetics, a field that had interested him since his first reading of the anonymous first-century Greek treatise *On the Sublime.* Revised and expanded several years later and published as *A Philosophical Enquiry into the Origin of Our Ideas of the Sublime and Beautiful* (1757), Burke's study anticipated the nineteenth-century Romantic interest in the Gothic.

Satisfying both his own inclination to move to London and his father's desire that he become a barrister, Burke began law studies at the Middle Temple in 1750. To augment his study there, he attended meetings of various debating clubs as well as a school of elocution. However, Burke gradually began neglecting his studies, to his father's bitter disappointment, and entered a six-year period of relative withdrawal from society. During this time, biographers believe, he was frequently ill, directionless, and intensely self-searching. He arose from this inertia in 1756 and anonymously published *A Vindication of Natural Society.* Labeled by Carl B. Cone "the opening blast in his long campaign against the enemies of the traditional order of things in western Europe," this work cleverly imitates the style of recently deceased Tory leader Henry St. John Bolingbroke, attacks Jean-Jacques Rousseau's *Discours sur l'origine et les fondements de l'inégalité parmi les hommes* (1755), and satirizes Bolingbroke's promotion of a natural society ruled by instinct and individual judgment rather than tradition, religious institutions, and ingrained cultural mores. The work was much admired in conservative intellectual circles, but several reviewers and the public at large failed to recognize Burke's satiric intent, and some even mistook the work for another of Bolingbroke's posthumous writings. As a result, Burke added an explanatory preface to his *Vindication* the following year.

With the publication of his aesthetic treatise in 1757, Burke's intellectual and literary abilities were quickly made apparent to London literary circles. By the end of the decade he was closely acquainted with several of the leading figures of the time, including David Garrick, Oliver Goldsmith, Elizabeth Montagu, Samuel Johnson, and David Hume. By the time he launched the weekly conversational society The Club in 1764 with Johnson and Joshua Reynolds, Burke was being commended by Johnson as "the first man everywhere," and his intimates believed him capable of succeeding brilliantly at anything he chose to do. Having no intention of resuming his legal training, Burke sought to support himself and his wife, whom he married in 1757, by applying his literary and scholarly tal-

ents. Contracting with publisher Robert Dodsley in 1758, he agreed to compile a yearly review of world affairs and noteworthy publications entitled the *Annual Register,* which he edited for 31 years. It is very probable that Burke wrote the entire journal through the year 1765. The historical articles he contributed remain primary sources for the study of mid- to late-eighteenth-century English life. Burke also contracted with Dodsley to write a survey of English history, but he abandoned this project by 1760 after having written some 90,000 words.

By this time, though still desirous of a literary career, Burke had turned to politics as a means of insuring financial security and public advancement. Following a failed attempt to obtain a foreign consulship, he secured employment with William Hamilton, serving as his private secretary and adviser from 1759 to 1764. In 1761 Burke accompanied Hamilton, then named Chief Secretary of Ireland, to Dublin, where Burke's indignation over the oppression of Irish Catholics peaked. The difficulty of effecting reform in Ireland, and the machinations of legislators in general, disgusted Burke and led him to confide in a friend that he hoped to remain aloof from "crooked politicks." No longer in Hamilton's service and having twice failed to obtain official agentries, Burke aligned with the second Marquis of Rockingham, who had marshaled the largest and most powerful Whig faction in England—the faction that was, at the time, the least threatening in its conservative ideology and practices to the viability of the Crown. (Although the English Tory party is commonly understood as emblematically conservative, the Whig establishment of Burke's time more closely embodied the principles of modern-day conservatism than did the authoritarian opposition. It was not until the early nineteenth century that the Tory party began evolving, through considerable absorption of "New" Whig principles, into its present form.) In 1765, Rockingham and his supporters received cautious royal favor and established a new government; as Rockingham's private secretary, Burke had at last attained a position of power. Although Rockingham's administration was short-lived, Burke remained among the most prominent framers of Whig theory and legislation throughout the rest of his career. Shortly after his secretarial appointment, Burke was elected to the House of Commons. He immediately made a mark as a forcible, accomplished speaker. Yet, for his loyalty to Rockingham (whose political career remained stormy until his death in 1782), Catholic leanings, and common, Irish heritage, Burke was forced to battle almost continual opposition. He therefore accumulated comparatively little power, no wealth, only minor offices, and few political victories. Although he desperately yearned to devote himself fully to literary endeavors, he never achieved this goal; as Russell Kirk has written, it was "not until he had become hotly entangled in the struggles over American and Indian affairs, and in domestic reform" that he found, "with Cicero, that the career of the statesman may provide occasions and themes for the moral imagination and the literary genius."

Burke's first major political work, the 1770 essay *Thoughts on the Cause of the Present Discontents,* was inspired by mounting tension between the Whigs and George III, who sought to restore a measure of autonomy to the Crown and to fortify his own Tory party, both of which had been checked severely since the Glorious Revolution of 1688 and the passage of the Bill of Rights the following year. During the mid-1770s Burke turned his attention to another issue: growing tensions in colonial America regarding the issue of taxation without representation. Burke set out to alleviate the conflict while protecting both the rights of Americans and the interests and integrity of the British Empire. In *Speech on American Taxation* (1775), *Speech on Moving His Resolutions for Conciliation with the Colonies,* and *Letter . . . to the Sheriffs of Bristol* (1777), Burke displayed what scholars deem an enviable command of colonial history and a prudent sympathy for American grievances, as well as a notable willingness to advocate governmental reform to heal the British-American rift. Although his speeches and writings directly stimulated American revolutionary leaders to urge a public call to arms (and, in addition, his political principles significantly shaped the constitutional theories espoused by James Madison, John Jay, and Alexander Hamilton in *The Federalist* (1787-88) a decade later), Burke abhorred violent, radical change and was disillusioned by the onset of the American Revolution.

Burke's most significant appointment to office came when Rockingham was made paymaster general in 1782. Burke urged serious economic reform within the English government to quell abuses of the system as well as to control a mounting national deficit. A version of Burke's economic bill passed into law the same year and became, according to many, his chief legislative success. As a member of a committee appointed to investigate imperial impropriety in India, Burke entered into perhaps his most ardent and sustained battle for the rights of British subjects. In 1787 he served as the principal force behind the impeachment of Warren Hastings, India's governor general, which led to a highly publicized eight-year trial ending in Hastings's acquittal. Although his failure to implicate Hastings in administrative abuses devastated Burke, his efforts have been recognized as some of the most imaginative, powerful, and self-revelatory—if highly emotional—oratory of his career. Following the outbreak of the French Revolution in 1789, Burke took upon himself the security and defense of the tradition, government, and constitution of Britain in his most praised and en-

during work, *Reflections on the Revolution in France.* This work, like later ones on the same subject, produced an irreparable division between Burke and several of his Whig colleagues, especially his longtime friend and then-Whig leader, Charles James Fox. *Reflections,* which eventually proved a prophetic vision of France's future, won wide European support but also engendered serious counterattacks, among them Mary Wollstonecraft's *A Vindication of the Rights of Men in a Letter to the Right Honourable Edmund Burke; Occasioned by His "Reflections on the Revolution in France"* (1790) and Thomas Paine's *The Rights of Man: Being an Answer to Mr. Burke's Attack on the French Revolution* (1791-92). Burke retired from Parliament in 1794, after having labored intensely for a variety of unpopular, unsuccessful causes; perhaps his greatest disappointment was his largely ineffectual, though long-standing, attempt to promote greater toleration of Catholics throughout Great Britain. He continued to write on such topics as Irish rights, economic reform, and the disintegration of French society for the rest of his life. In 1797 he died at Beaconsfield, Buckinghamshire, and is buried there in an unknown, unmarked grave.

"If there is one recurrent theme in Burke's letters, speeches, and writings," claims Harvey C. Mansfield, Jr., "it is his emphasis on the moral and political evils that follow upon the intrusion of theory into political practice." Burke, indeed, despised all abstract thought when applied to political situations. He believed that to solve specific problems, well-reasoned, historically founded solutions, applied with prudence, were required. Thus Burke considered Rousseau, for his love of abstraction and reverence for theoretical human rights, an "insane Socrates"; likewise, he esteemed Charles Louis de Secondat, Baron de La Brède et de Montesquieu for his conservative view of tradition and deep respect for the British Constitution, calling him "the greatest genius, which has enlightened this age." Burke has been credited with two major contributions to politics: his exposition, in *Thoughts on the Cause of the Present Discontents* (1770), of the structure and function of political parties, and his well-defined blueprint—apparent throughout his works, but found particularly in his *Reflections*—of the fundamental principles of political conservatism. Burke conceived of party as a vehicle by which, above all, constitutional integrity could be maintained in the legislative process; parties represented the necessary link between king and Parliament, serving as a check to misguided power and as a means toward sound governing. Regarding his conservative principles, custom, convention, continuity, presumptive virtue (a trust in the capability of the aristocracy to rule, albeit policed by the good judgment of the common classes), and the tenets of the British Constitution dominated and directed all his thought.

Still, Burke remained amenable to gradual change and always sympathetic to the rights and needs of the people. His system succeeds, according to Woodrow Wilson, because: "There is no element of speculation in it. It keeps always to the slow pace of inevitable change, and invents nothing, content to point out the accepted ways and to use the old light of day to walk by."

A major charge levied against Burke is that he was inconsistent in the moral and political values he espoused. Several commentators have claimed that Burke, while once an ardent defender of the individual rights of the Irish, Americans, and Indians, abandoned his praiseworthy efforts during the French Revolution to defend the royalty, the aristocracy, and the grand French tradition instead. Henry Thomas Buckle, for example, asserted that with the furor of the time, Burke's emotional nature overstepped the bounds of reason, the harsh inveighing of the *Reflections* proving that Burke had suffered a profound deterioration of mind and worldview. Other critics, however, have objected to this view, vindicating Burke for his consistent approach toward governmental reform. According to these writers, Burke believed that what occurred in America, Ireland, and India was simply the assertion of the legitimate rights held by British subjects against the depredations of a burgeoning, increasingly repressive government that sought to deny those rights it was bound to defend. On the other hand, Burke held that the French Revolution saw the accession of rootless and ruthless ideology, and that custom, convention, and continuity, along with their religious underpinnings, were eradicated so that the mob, guided only by speculation and abstract reason, might rule. The tenets of the French National Assembly to which Burke reacted so vehemently were those that unequivocally renounced all the institutions and customs upon which ordered European society had relied for centuries. For Burke, as for his mentor Cicero, reform was advisable only when favored by the majority, and then only provided such reform could be executed through careful refinement, not endangerment, of existing social structures. Perhaps the most telling indictment of this philosophic position was written by John MacCunn: "As a gospel for his age, or for any age, it has the fatal defect that, in its rooted distrust of theories and theorists, it finds hardly any place for political ideals as serious attempts

to forefigure the destinies of a people as not less Divinely willed than its eventful past history or present achievement. And, by consequence, it fails to touch the future with the reformer's hope and conviction of better days to come." Despite this charge, Burke's theories are among the most prevalent that modern-day politicians, conservative and liberal, have used to guide their legislative decisions.

Apart from political and philosophical evaluations of his work, Burke has received encomiums for the sheer ascendancy of his oratory and the inimitable style of his prose. His writings on America are models of rhetorical eloquence: his *A Letter from the Right Honourable Edmund Burke to a Noble Lord,* according to W. Somerset Maugham, is "the finest piece of invective in the English language," and his *Reflections* is one of the most impassioned and inspired documents in the history of the English essay. Although Burke has been faulted for an excessive emotionalism that hindered his philosophic purposes, his supporters suggest that he habitually combined beautifully metaphorical language with resounding moral statement to express his inmost philosophic convictions. Consequently, he is regarded not only as a vastly influential political philosopher but as an equally influential orator and prose writer.

What, finally, was Burke's contribution to English letters? Many critics see it as an astonishingly broad and enduring one, affirming that he addressed the major issues of his day not only in a lofty, imaginative prose unparalleled in the latter eighteenth century, but by means of explicitly stated concepts that have remained valid to a host of succeeding writers and politicians. As Kirk has written, "He enlivened political philosophy by the moral imagination; he shored up Christian doctrine; he stimulated the higher understanding of history; he enriched English literature by a mastery of prose that makes him the Cicero of his language and nation. And to the modern civil social order, he contributed those principles of ordered freedom, preservation through reform, and justice restraining arbitrary power, which transcend the particular political struggles of his age."

(For further information about Burke's life and works, see *Literature Criticism from 1400 to 1800,* Vol. 7.)

CRITICAL COMMENTARY

WOODROW WILSON

(essay date 1896)

[A political scientist and president of Princeton University before becoming the twenty-eighth president of the United States, Wilson published studies on American history and political theory. In the following excerpt, he examines Burke's approach to four key political issues and comments on the statesman's literary abilities.]

Four questions absorbed the energies of Burke's life and must always be associated with his fame. These were, the American war for independence; administrative reform in the English home government; reform in the government of India; and the profound political agitations which attended the French Revolution. Other questions he studied, deeply pondered, and greatly illuminated, but upon these four he expended the full strength of his magnificent powers. There is in his treatment of these subjects a singular consistency, a very admirable simplicity of standard. It has been said, and it is true, that Burke had no system of political philosophy. He was afraid of abstract system in political thought, for he perceived that questions of government are moral questions, and that questions of morals cannot always be squared with the rules of logic, but run through as many ranges of variety as the circumstances of life itself. "Man acts from adequate motives relative to his interest," he said, "and not on metaphysical speculations. Aristotle, the great master of reasoning, cautions us, and with great weight and propriety, against this species of delusive geometrical accuracy in moral arguments, as the most fallacious of all sophistry." And yet Burke unquestionably had a very definite and determinable system of thought, which was none the less a system for being based upon concrete, and not upon abstract premises. It is said by some writers (even by so eminent a writer as [Henry Thomas] Buckle that in his later years Burke's mind lost its balance and that he reasoned as if he were insane; and the proof assigned is, that he, a man who loved liberty, violently condemned, not the terrors only,—that of course,—but the very principles of the French Revolution. But to reason thus is to convict one's self of an utter lack of comprehension of Burke's mind and motives: as a very brief examination of his course upon the four great questions I have mentioned will show.

From first to last Burke's thought is conservative. Let his attitude with regard to America serve as an example. He took his stand, as everybody knows, with the colonies, against the mother country; but his object was not revolutionary. He did not deny the legal right of England to tax the colonies (*we* no longer deny it ourselves), but he wished to preserve the empire, and he saw that to insist upon the right of taxation would be irrevocably to break up the empire, when dealing with such a people as the Americans. He pointed out the strong and increasing numbers of the colonists, their high spirit in enterprise, their jealous love of liberty, and the indulgence England had hitherto accorded them in the matter of self-government, permitting them in effect to become an independent people in respect of all their internal affairs; and he declared the result matter for just pride. (pp. 141-43)

The question with me is, not whether you have a right to render your people miserable, but whether it is not your interest to make them happy. It is not what a lawyer tells me I *may* do, but what humanity, reason, and justice tell me I *ought* to do. . . . Such is steadfastly my opinion of the absolute necessity of keeping up the concord of this empire by a unity of spirit, though in a diversity of operations, that, if I were sure that the colonists had, at their leaving this country, sealed a regular compact of servitude, that they had solemnly abjured all the rights of citizens, that they had made a vow to renounce all ideas of liberty for them and their posterity to all generations, yet I should hold myself obliged to conform to the temper I found universally prevalent in my own day, and to govern two million of men, impatient of servitude, on the principles of freedom. I am not determining a point of law; I am restoring tranquillity: and the general character and situation of a people must determine what sort of government is fitted for them. That point nothing else can or ought to determine.

(pp. 147-48)

Here you have the whole spirit of the man, and in part a view of his eminently practical system of thought. The view is completed when you advance with him to other subjects of policy. He pressed with all his energy for radical reforms in administration, but he earnestly opposed every change that might touch the structure of the constitution itself. He sought to secure the integrity of Parliament, not by changing the system of representation, but by cutting out all roots of corruption. He pressed forward with the most ardent in all plans of just reform, but he held back with the

Principal Works

A Vindication of Natural Society; or, A View of the Miseries and Evils Arising to Mankind from Every Species of Artificial Society (essay) 1756

A Philosophical Enquiry into the Origin of Our Ideas of the Sublime and Beautiful (essay) 1757

*The Annual Register (journal) 1759-65

An Essay towards an Abridgement of the English History (unfinished history) 1760

Thoughts on the Cause of the Present Discontents (essay) 1770

Speech on American Taxation, April 19, 1774 (essay) 1775

Speech on Moving His Resolutions for Conciliation with the Colonies (essay) 1775

A Letter from Edmund Burke, Esq., One of the Representatives in Parliament for the City of Bristol, to John Farr and John Harris, Esqrs., Sheriffs of That City, on the Affairs of America (essay) 1777

Speech . . . on Presenting, on the 11th of February 1780—a Plan for the Better Security of the Independence of Parliament and the Economical Reformation of the Civil and Other Establishments (essay) 1780

Mr. Burke's Speech, on the 1st December 1783, upon the Question for the Speaker's Leaving the Chair, in Order for the House to Resolve Itself into a Committee on Mr. Fox's East Indian Bill (essay) 1784

Articles Exhibited by the Knights, Citizens, and Burgesses in Parliament Assembled, in the Name of Themselves, and of All the Commons of Great Britain, against Warren Hastings . . . in Maintenance of Their Impeachment against Him for High Crimes and Misdemeanors [with others] (essays) 1787

Reflections on the Revolution in France and on the Proceedings in Certain Societies in London Relative to That Event (essay) 1790

An Appeal from the New, to the Old Whigs, in Consequence of Some Late Discussions in Parliament, Relative to the Reflections on the French Revolution (essay) 1791

A Letter from Mr. Burke, to a Member of the National Assembly: In Answer to Some Objections to His Book on French Affairs (essay) 1791

A Letter from the Right Honourable Edmund Burke to a Noble Lord, on the Attacks Made Upon Him and His Pension, in the House of Lords, by the Duke of Bedford and the Earl of Lauderdale, Early in the Present Sessions of Parliament (essay) 1796

Two Letters . . . on the Proposals for Peace, with the Regicide Directory of France (essays) 1796

†Thoughts and Details on Scarcity Originally Presented to the Right Hon. William Pitt in the Month of November, 1795 (essay) 1800

Works of the Right Honourable Edmund Burke, 16 vols. (essays and letters) 1803-27

The Correspondence of Edmund Burke, 10 vols. (letters) 1958-78

‡The Writings and Speeches of Edmund Burke (essays and letters) 1981-

Selected Letters of Edmund Burke (letters) 1984

*This journal was edited by Burke through 1789 and may have been written entirely by him through 1765.

†This work was written in 1795.

‡This is an ongoing, multi-volume series published by Oxford University Press.

---

most conservative from all propositions of radical change. (pp. 148-49)

Time is required to produce that union of minds which alone can produce all the good we aim at. Our patience will achieve more than our force. If I might venture to appeal to what is so much out of fashion in Paris,—I mean to experience,—I should tell you that in my course I have known, and, according to my measure, have coöperated with great men; and I have never yet seen any plan which has not been mended by the observations of those who were much inferior in understanding to the person who took the lead in the business. By a slow, but well sustained progress, the effect of each step is watched; the good or ill success of the first gives light to us in the second; and so, from light to light, we are conducted with safety, through the whole series. . . . We are enabled to unite into a consistent whole the various anomalies and contending principles that are found in the minds and affairs of men. From hence arises, not an excellence in simplicity, but one far superior, an excellence in composition. Where the great interests of mankind are concerned through a long succession of generations, that succession ought to be admitted into some share in the counsels which are so deeply to affect them.

It is not possible to escape deep conviction of the wisdom of these reflections. They penetrate to the heart of all practicable methods of reform. Burke was doubtless too timid, and in practical judgment often mistaken. Measures which in reality would operate only as salutary and needed reformations he feared because of the element of change that was in them. He erred when he supposed that progress can in all its stages be made without changes which seem to go even to the substance. But, right or wrong, his philosophy did not come to him of a sudden and only at the end of his life, when he found France desolated and England threatened with madness for love of revolutionary principles of change. It is the key to his thought everywhere, and through all his life.

It is the key (which many of his critics have never found) to his position with regard to the revolution in France. He was roused to that fierce energy of opposition in which so many have thought that they detected madness, not so much because of his deep disgust to see brutal and ignorant men madly despoil an ancient and honorable monarchy, as because he saw the spirit of these men cross the Channel and find lodgment in England, even among statesmen like Fox, who had been his own close friends and companions in thought and policy; not so much because he loved France as because he feared for England. . . . He hated the French revolutionary philosophy and deemed it unfit for free men. And that philosophy is in fact radically evil and corrupting. No state can ever be conducted on its principles. For it holds that government is a matter of contract and deliberate arrangement, whereas in fact it is an institute of habit, bound together by innumerable threads of association, scarcely one of which has been deliberately placed. It holds that the object of government is liberty, whereas the true object of government is justice; not the advantage of one class, even though that class constitute the majority, but right equity in the adjustment of the interests of all classes. It assumes that government can be made over at will, but assumes it without the slightest historical foundation. For governments have never been successfully and permanently changed except by slow modification operating from generation to generation. It contradicted every principle that had been so laboriously brought to light in the slow stages of the growth of liberty in the only land in which liberty had then grown to great proportions. The history of England is a continuous thesis against revolution; and Burke would have been no true Englishman, had he not roused himself, even fanatically, if there were need, to keep such puerile doctrine out.

If you think his fierceness was madness, look how he conducted the trial against Warren Hastings during those same years: with what patience, with what steadiness in business, with what temper, with what sane and balanced attention to detail, with what statesmanlike purpose! Note, likewise that his thesis is the same in the one undertaking as in the other. He was applying the same principles to the case of France and to the case of India that he had applied to the case of the colonies. He meant to save the empire, not by changing its constitution, as was the method in France, and so shaking every foundation in order to dislodge an abuse, but by administering it uprightly and in a liberal spirit. . . . Good government, like all virtue, he deemed to be a practical habit of conduct, and not a matter of constitutional structure. It is a great ideal, a thoroughly English ideal; and it constitutes the leading thought of all Burke's career.

In short . . . , this man, an Irishman, speaks the best English thought upon the essential questions of politics. He is thoroughly, characteristically, and to the bottom English in all his thinking. He is more liberal than Englishmen in his treatment of Irish questions, of course; for he understands them, as no Englishman of his generation did. But for all that he remains the chief spokesman for England in the utterance of the fundamental ideals which have governed the action of Englishmen in politics. (pp. 152-58)

A man of sensitive imagination and elevated moral sense, of a wide knowledge and capacity for affairs, he stood in the midst of the English nation speaking its moral judgments upon affairs, its character in political action, its purposes of freedom, equity, wide and equal progress. It is the immortal charm of his speech and manner that gives permanence to his works. Though his life was devoted to affairs with a constant and unalterable passion, the radical features of Burke's mind were literary. He was a man of books, without being under the dominance of what others had written. He got knowledge out of books and the abundance of matter his mind craved to work its constructive and imaginative effects upon. It is singular how devoid of all direct references to books his writings are. The materials of his thought never reappear in the same form in which he obtained them. They have been smelted and recoined. They have come under the drill and inspiration of a great constructive mind, have caught life and taken structure from it. Burke is not literary because he takes from books, but because he makes books, transmuting what he writes upon into literature. It is this inevitable literary quality, this sure mastery of style, that mark the man, as much as his thought itself. Every sentence, too, is steeped in the colors of an extraordinary imagination. The movement takes your breath and quickens your pulses. The glow and power of the matter rejuvenate your faculties.

And yet the thought, too, is quite as imperishable as its incomparable vehicle. (pp. 159-60)

Woodrow Wilson, "The Interpreter of English Liberty," in his *Mere Literature, and Other Essays,* Houghton Mifflin Company, 1896, pp. 104-60.

W. SOMERSET MAUGHAM

(essay date 1950-51)

[Maugham was an English dramatist, short story writer, and novelist. In the following excerpt from an essay originally published in the *Cornhill Magazine*, he admiringly explores the literary texture, technique, and antecedents of Burke's prose.]

I think there are few writers who write well by nature. Burke was a man of prodigious industry and it is certain that he took pains not only over the matter of his discourse, but over the manner. . . . A glance at the *Origin of Our Ideas of the Sublime and Beautiful* is enough to show that Burke's style was the result of labour. Though this work, praised by Johnson, turned to account by Lessing and esteemed by Kant, cannot now be read with great profit it may still afford entertainment. In arguing that perfection is not the cause of beauty, he asserts:

> Women are very sensible of this; for which reason they learn to lisp, to totter in their walk, to counterfeit weakness, and even sickness. In all this they are guided by nature. Beauty in distress is much the most affecting beauty. Blushing has little less power; and modesty in general, which is a tacit allowance of imperfection, is itself considered as an amiable quality, and certainly heightens every other that is so. I know it is in everybody's mouth, that we ought to love perfection. This is to me a sufficient proof that it is not the proper object of love.

Here is another quotation:

> When we have before us such objects as excite love and complacency, the body is affected so far as I could observe, much in the following manner: The head reclines something on one side, the eyelids are more closed than usual, and the eyes roll gently with an inclination to the object; the mouth is a little opened, and the breath drawn slowly, with now and then a long sigh; the whole body is composed, and the hands fall idly to the sides.

This book is supposed to have been first written when Burke was nineteen and it was published when he was twenty-six. I have given these quotations to show the style in which he wrote before he submitted to the influence which enabled him to become one of the masters of English prose. It is the general manner of the middle of the eighteenth century and I doubt whether anyone who read these passages would know who was the author. It is correct, easy and flowing; it shows that Burke had by nature a good ear. . . . He was not a melodious writer as Jeremy Taylor was in the seventeenth century or Newman in the nineteenth; his prose has force, vitality and speed rather than beauty; but notwithstanding the intricate complication of many of his sentences they remain easy to say and good to hear. I have no doubt that at times Burke wrote a string of words that was neither and in the tumult of his passion broke the simple rules of euphony which I have indicated. An author has the right to be judged by his best.

I have read somewhere that Burke learnt to write by studying Spenser and it appears that many of his gorgeous sentences and poetical allusions can be traced to the poet. He himself said that: 'Whoever relishes and reads Spenser as he ought to be read, will have a strong hold of the English language.' I do not see what he can have acquired from that mellifluous but (to my mind) tedious bard other than that sense of splendid sound of which I have just been speaking. He was certainly never influenced by the excessive use of alliteration which (again to my mind) makes the *Faerie Queene* cloying and sometimes even absurd. It has been said, among others by Charles James Fox, who should have known, that Burke founded his style on Milton's. I cannot believe it. It is true that he often quoted him and it would be strange indeed if with his appreciation of fine language Burke had failed to be impressed by the magnificence of vocabulary and grandeur of phrase in *Paradise Lost;* but the *Letters on a Regicide Peace,* on which, such as it is, the evidence for the statement rests, were written in old age: it seems improbable that if Burke had really studied Milton's prose for the purpose of forming his own its influence should not have been apparent till he had one foot in the grave. Nor can I believe, as the *Dictionary of National Biography* asserts, that he founded it on Dryden's. I see in Burke's deliberate, ordered and resonant prose no trace of Dryden's charming grace and happy-go-lucky facility. There is all the difference that there is between a French garden of trim walks and ordered parterres and a Thames-side park with its coppices and its green meadows. For my part I think it more likely that the special character of Burke's settled manner must be ascribed to the robust and irresistible example of Dr. Johnson. I think it was from him that Burke learnt the value of a long intricate sentence, the potent force of polysyllabic words, the rhetorical effect of balance and the epigrammatic elegance of antithesis. He avoided Johnson's faults (small faults to those who like myself have a peculiar fondness for Johnson's style) by virtue of his affluent and impetuous fancy and his practice of public speaking. (pp. 128-32)

His style, it must be obvious, is solidly based on balance. Hazlitt stated that it was Dryden who first used balance in the formation of his sentences. That seems an odd thing to say since one would have thought that balance came naturally to anyone who added two sentences together by a copulative: there is balance of a sort when you say: 'He went out for a walk and came home wet through'. Dr. Johnson on the other hand, speaking of Dryden's prose, said: 'The clauses are never balanced, nor the periods modelled: every word seems to drop by chance, though it falls in its proper place.' Thus do authorities disagree. Burke was much addicted to what for want of a better word I will call the triad; by this I mean the juxtaposition of three nouns, three adjectives, three clauses to reinforce a point. Here are some examples: 'Never was cause supported with more constancy, more activity, more spirit.'—'Shall there be no reserve power in the Empire, to supply a deficiency which may weaken, divide or dissipate the whole?'—'Their wishes ought to have great weight with him: their opinion, high respect; their business, unremitted attention.'—'I really think that for wise men this is not judicious; for sober men, not decent; for minds tinctured with humanity, not mild or merciful.' Burke had recourse to this pattern so often that in the end it falls somewhat monotonously on the ear. It has another disadvantage, more noticeable perhaps when read than when heard, that one member of the triad may be so nearly synonymous with another that you cannot but realise that it has been introduced for its sound rather than for its sense.

Burke made frequent use of the antithesis, which of course is merely a variety of balance. Hazlitt says it is first found in *The Tatler.* I have discovered no marked proof of this in an examination which I admit was cursory; there are traces of it, maybe, but adumbrations rather than definite instances. You can find more striking examples in the *Book of Proverbs.* (pp. 142-43)

The antithetical style is vastly effective, and if it has gone out of common use it is doubtless for a reason that Johnson himself suggested. Its purpose is by the balance of words to accentuate the balance of thought, and when it serves merely to tickle the ear it is tiresome. (p. 143)

Now, the vogue of the antithesis had a marked effect on sentence structure, as anyone can see for himself by comparing the prose of Dryden, for example, with that of Burke. It brought into prominence the value of the period. I may remind the reader that a period is a sentence in which the sense is held up until the end: when a clause is added after a natural close the sentence is described as loose. The English language does not allow of the inversions which make it possible to suspend the meaning, and so the loose sentence is common. To this is largely due the diffusiveness of our prose. When once the unity of a sentence is abandoned there is little to prevent the writer from adding clause to clause. The antithetical structure was advantageous to the cultivation of the classical period, for it is obvious that its verbal merit depends on its compact and rounded form. I will quote a sentence of Burke's.

Indeed, when I consider the face of the kingdom of France; the multitude and opulence of her cities; the useful magnificence of her spacious high roads and bridges; the opportunity of her artificial canals and navigations opening the conveniences of maritime communication through a solid continent of so immense an extent; when I turn my eyes to the stupendous works of her ports and harbours, and to her whole naval apparatus, whether for war or trade;

when I bring before my view the number of her fortifications, constructed with so bold and masterly a skill, and made and maintained at so prodigious a charge, presenting an armed front and impenetrable barrier to her enemies upon every side; when I recollect how very small a part of that extensive region is without cultivation, and to what complete perfection the culture of many of the best productions of the earth have been brought in France; when I reflect on the excellence of her manufactures and fabrics, second to none but ours, and in some particulars not second; when I contemplate the grand foundations of charity public and private; when I survey the state of all the arts that beautify and polish life; when I reckon the men she has bred for extending her fame in war, her able statesmen, the multitude of her profound lawyers and theologians, her philosophers, her critics, her historians and antiquaries, her poets and her orators, sacred and profane; I behold in all this something which awes and commands the imagination, which checks the mind on the brink of precipitate and indiscriminate censure, and which demands that we should very seriously examine, what and how great are the latent vices that could authorise us at once to level so spacious a fabric with the ground.

The paragraph ends with three short sentences.

I should like to point out with what skill Burke has given a 'loose' structure to his string of subordinate clauses, thus further suspending the meaning till he brings his period to a close. Johnson, as we know, was apt to make periods of his subordinate clauses, writing what, I think, the grammarians call an extended complex, and so lost the flowing urgency which is characteristic of Burke. I should like to point out also what a happy effect Burke has secured in this compound sentence by forming his different clauses on the same plan and yet by varying cadence and arrangement avoiding monotony. He used the method of starting successive clauses with the same word, in this case with the word *when,* frequently and with effectiveness. It is of course a rhetorical device, which when delivered in a speech must have had a cumulative force, and shows once more how much his style was influenced by the practice of public speaking. I do not know that there is anyone in England who is capable now of writing such a sentence; perhaps there is no one who wants to; for, perhaps from an instinctive desire to avoid the 'loose' sentences which the idiosyncrasy of the language renders so inviting, it is the fashion these days to write short sentences. Indeed not long ago I read that the editor of an important newspaper had insisted that none of his contributors should write a sentence of more than fourteen words. Yet the long sentence has advantages. It gives you room to develop your meaning, opportunity to constitute your cadence and material to achieve your climax. Its disadvantages are that it may be diffuse, flaccid, crabbed or inapprehensible. The stylists of the seventeenth century wrote sentences of great length and did not always escape these defects. Burke seldom failed, however long his sentence, however elaborate its clauses and opulent his 'tropes', to make its fundamental structure so solid that you seem to be led to the safety of the full stop by a guide who knows his business and will permit you neither to take a side-turning nor to loiter by the way. Burke was careful to vary the length of his sentences. He does not tire you with a succession of long ones, nor, unless with a definitely rhetorical intention, does he exasperate you with a long string of short ones.

He has a lively sense of rhythm. His prose has the eighteenth-century tune, like any symphony of Haydn's, though with a truly English accent, and you hear the drums and fifes in it, but an individual note rings through it. It is a virile prose and I can think of no one who wrote with so much force combined with so much elegance. If it seems now a trifle formal, I think that is due to the fact that, like most of the eighteenth-century writers, he used general and abstract terms when we are now more inclined to use special and concrete ones. This gives a greater vividness to modern writing, though at the cost perhaps of concision. (pp. 145-48)

Dr. Johnson has told us that in his day nobody talked much of style, since everybody wrote pretty well. 'There is an elegance of style universally diffused,' he said. Burke was outstanding. His contemporaries were impressed, as well they might be, by his command of words, his brilliant similes, his hyperboles and fertile imagination, but did not invariably approve. Hazlitt relates a conversation between Fox and Lord Holland on the subject of his style. It appears that this

> Noble Person objected to it as too gaudy and meretricious, and said that it was more profuse of flowers than fruit. On which Mr. Fox observed, that though this was a common objection, it appeared to him altogether an unfounded one; that on the contrary the flowers often concealed the fruit beneath them; and the ornaments of style were rather a hindrance than an advantage to the sentiments they were meant to set off. In confirmation of this remark, he offered to take down the book and translate a page anywhere into his own plain, natural style; and by his doing so, Lord Holland was convinced that he had often missed the thought from having his attention drawn off to the dazzling imagery.

It is instructive to learn that Noble Persons and Eminent Politicians were interested in such questions in those bygone days and with such amiable exercises beguiled their leisure. But of course if his lordship's attention was really drawn off the matter of Burke's discourse by the brillancy of the manner, it is a reflection on his style. For the purpose of imagery is not to divert the reader, but to make the meaning clearer to him; the purpose of simile and metaphor is to impress it on his mind and by engaging his fancy make it more acceptable. An illustration is otiose unless it illustrates. Burke had a romantic and a poetic mind such as no other of the eighteenth-century masters of prose possessed, and it is this that gives his prose its variegated colour; but his aim was to convince rather than to please, to overpower rather than to persuade, and by all the resources of his imagination not only to make his point more obvious, but by an appeal to sentiment or passion to compel acquiescence. I don't know when Mr. Fox held his conversation with the Noble Lord, but if the *Reflections on the French Revolution* had then appeared he might well have pointed to it to refute his lordship's contention. For in that work the decoration so interpenetrates the texture of the writing that it becomes part and parcel of the argument. Here imagery, metaphor and simile fulfil their function. The one passage that leaves me doubtful is the most celebrated of all, that in which Burke tells how he saw Marie Antoinette at Versailles: 'and surely never lighted on this orb, which she hardly seemed to touch, a more delightful vision.' It is to be found in anthologies, so I will not quote it, but it is somewhat high flown to my taste. But if it is not perfect prose it is magnificent rhetoric; magnificent even when it is slightly absurd: 'I thought ten thousand swords must have leapt from their scabbards to avenge even a look that threatened her with insult'; and the cadence with which the paragraph ends is lovely:

> The unbought grace of life, the cheap defence of nations, the nurse of manly sentiment and heroic enterprise is gone! It is gone, that sensibility of principle, that chastity of honour, which felt a stain like a wound, which inspired courage whilst it mitigated ferocity, which ennobled whatever it touched, and under which vice itself lost half its evil, by losing all its grossness.

(pp. 150-52)

As the quotations I have given plainly show, Burke made abundant use of metaphor. It is interwoven in the substance of his prose as the weavers of Lyons thread one colour with another to give a fabric the shimmer of shot silk. Of course like every other writer he uses what Fowler calls the natural metaphor, for common speech is largely composed of them, but he uses freely what Fowler calls the artificial metaphor. It gave concrete substance to his generalisations. He used it to enforce a statement by means of a physical image; but unlike some modern writers, who will pursue the implications of a metaphor like a spider scurrying along every filament of its web, he took care never to run it to death. (pp. 152-53)

On the other hand Burke used the simile somewhat sparingly. Modern writers might well follow his example. For of late a dreadful epidemic has broken out. Similes are clustered on the pages of our young authors as thickly as pimples on a young man's face, and they are as unsightly. A simile has use. By reminding you of a familiar thing it enables you to see the subject of the comparison more clearly or by mentioning an unfamiliar one it focuses your attention on it. It is dangerous to use it merely as an ornament; it is detestable to use it to display your cleverness; it is preposterous to use it when it neither decorates nor impresses. (Example: 'The moon like a huge blanc-mange wobbled over the tree-tops.') When Burke used a simile it was generally, as might be expected, with elaboration. (p. 153)

I have harped upon the fact that Burke's style owed many of its merits to his practice of speaking in public; to this it owed also such defects as a carping critic might find in it. There is more than one passage in the famous speech on the Nabob of Arcot's Debts when he asks a long series of rhetorical questions. It may have been effective in the House of Commons, but on the printed page it is restless and fatiguing. To this may be ascribed his too frequent recourse to the exclamatory sentence. 'Happy if they had all continued to know their indissoluble union, and their proper place! Happy if learning, not debauched by ambition, had been satisfied to continue the instructor, and not aspired to be the master.' Something of an old-fashioned air he has by his frequent use of an inverted construction, a mode now seldom met with; he employs it to vary the monotony of the simple order—subject, verb, object—and also to emphasise the significant member of the sentence by placing it first; but such a phrase as 'Personal offence I have given them none' needs the emphasis of the living voice to appear natural. On the other hand it is to his public speaking, I think, that Burke owed his skill in giving to a series of quite short sentences as musical a cadence and as noble a ring as when he set himself to compose an elaborate period with its pompous train of subordinate clauses; and this is shown nowhere to greater advantage than in the *Letter to a Noble Lord.* Here a true instinct made him see that when he was appealing for compassion on account of his age and infirmities and by reminding his readers of the death of his beloved and only son, he must aim at simplicity. The passage is deeply moving:

> The storm has gone over me; and I lie like one of those old oaks which the late hurricane has scattered about me. I am stripped of all my honours, I am torn up by the roots, and lie prostrate on the earth . . . I am alone. I have none to meet my enemies in the gate. Indeed, my lord, I greatly deceive myself, if in this hard season I would give a peck of refuse wheat for all that is called fame and honour in the world. This is the appetite but of a few. It is a luxury, it is a privilege, it is an indulgence for those who are at

their ease. But we are all of us made to shun disgrace, as we are made to shrink from pain, and poverty, and disease. It is an instinct; and under the direction of reason, instinct is always in the right. I live in an inverted order. They who ought to have succeeded me have gone before me. They who should have been to me as posterity are in the place of ancestors. I owe to the dearest relation (which ever must subsist in memory) that act of piety, which he would have performed to me; I owe it to him to show that he was not descended, as the Duke of Bedford would have it, from an unworthy parent.

Here the best words are indeed put in the best places. This piece owes little to picturesque imagery, nothing to romantic metaphor, and proves with what justification Hazlitt described him as, with the exception of Jeremy Taylor, the most poetical of prose-writers. I hope it will not be considered a literary conceit (a trifling, tedious business) when I suggest that in the tender melody of these cadences, in this exquisite choice of simple words, there is a foretaste of Wordsworth at his admirable best. If these pages should persuade anyone to see for himself how great a writer Burke was I cannot do better than advise him to read this *Letter to a Noble Lord.* It is the finest piece of invective in the English language and so short that it can be read in an hour. It offers in its brief compass a survey of all Burke's dazzling gifts, his formal as well as his conversational style, his gift for epigram and for irony, his wisdom, his sense, his pathos, his indignation and his nobility. (pp. 154-57)

W. Somerset Maugham, "After Reading Burke," in his *The Vagrant Mood: Six Essays,* William Heinemann Ltd., 1952, pp. 123-57.

HARVEY C. MANSFIELD, JR.

(essay date 1984)

[Mansfield was an American educator and political scientist. In the following excerpt, he outlines prominent features of Burke's political philosophy.]

Burke is known today as the philosopher of "conservatism." But he has not yet shared much in the revival of American conservatism in the 1980s. Of the two schools of thought that have been identified in that revival, traditionalism and libertarianism, Burke is very much with the former. Although he favored the freeing of commerce whenever possible, contributed his *Thoughts and Details on Scarcity* . . . to the new school of political economy, and was an admiring friend of Adam Smith, he so opposed unhampered individual freedom, theoretical systems of self-interest, and the influence of new property that he surrounded and enveloped the abstract free economy of political economists with the traditions of the British constitution. But of course these traditions—"establishments," Burke called them—are far from the provisions of the American constitution, and even farther . . . from the planned character of the American constitution. Such are the obstacles to Burke's influence in American politics today. (p. 3)

If there is one recurrent theme in Burke's letters, speeches, and writings, it is his emphasis on the moral and political evils that follow upon the intrusion of theory into political practice. It is theory as such that he rejects; his emphasis on the evils of intrusive theory is not balanced by a compensating reliance on sound theory that men would need as a guide to their politics. Sound theory, to him, would seem to be self-denying theory. Although Burke may occasionally refer to "the pretended philosophers of the hour," thus implying the existence of another sort, he is usually content to denounce philosophers, metaphysicians, and speculators as such without making a point of what might seem to be the vital distinction among them. In a famous passage in *A Letter to a Member of the National Assembly* . . . , he attacks Rousseau—"the philosopher of vanity," "a lover of his kind but a hater of his kindred"—in terms no philosopher had flung publicly at another, until a decline of decorum in this matter occurred in the nineteenth century. In that place Burke distinguishes "modern philosophers," which expresses "everything that is ignoble, savage and hard-hearted," from "the writers of sound antiquity" whom Englishmen continue to read more generally, he believes, than is now done "on the continent." But Burke does not propose that ancient authors be adopted, even remotely, as guides to show the way out of the crisis into which modern philosophers have brought all mankind. Reading them is not so much the cause as the effect of English good taste, something that is sadly lacking "on the continent." Considering Burke's hostility to the intrusion of philosophy in politics, yet recalling too that Burke does not merely despair at the growing influence of philosophy, the problem of his political philosophy would seem to be to design a theory that never intrudes into practice. Our question in assessing it is: can theory serve solely as a watchdog against theory and never be needed as a guide?

The harms done by theory to sound practice had been under Burke's eye from the first. His first publication, *A Vindication of Natural Society* . . . , was a satire showing the absurd political consequences of Bolingbroke's theory, and in the early pamphlets on party, *Observations on a Late Publication Intituled "The Present State of the Nation"* . . . and *Thoughts on the Cause of the Present Discontents* . . . , he argued against the factious effects of a theoretical preference for "men of ability and virtue" over parties composed of gentlemen acting together publicly in mutual trust. In his speeches opposing British policy in America, he attacked the government's insistence on the rights of taxation and sovereignty without regard to consequence or circumstance as a speculative, legalistic reliance on "the virtue of paper government." For lawyers with their concern for rights and forms do not have regard to the actual exercise of formalities, substitute legal correctness for prudent policy, and seek to generalize in the manner of law—which is also that of theory. In a speech given in 1785, Burke was already denouncing "the speculatists of our speculating age." But it was in the French Revolution that the evils of speculation in politics became visible in their full extent and as a whole. Burke was surprised by the outbreak of that revolution, but he had been prepared by every major concern of his previous career in politics to identify it as a philosophical revolution, the first *"complete"* revolution," a "revolution in sentiments, manners and moral opinions" that reached "even to the constitution of the human mind." The French Revolution displayed and summed up all the evils of speculative politics. (pp. 4-5)

[Burke] does not offer a theoretical clarification and reconstruction which would meet the revolutionaries on their own ground. Instead, he attempts to stand on the ground and stay within the realm of political practice, insofar as possible. His writings proposing action are much richer in political wisdom—hence seemingly more "theoretical"—than those of ordinary statesmen even when reminiscing, yet they are also much more circumscribed and circumstantial than treatises which are intended to interest theorists: thus, fullsome for historians, meager for philosophers. He once said: "The operation of dangerous and delusive first principles obliges us to have recourse to the true ones"—thereby admitting the necessity of such recourse, by contrast to ordinary statesmen, and declaring his reluctance, against the habit of theorists.

Yet the first principles to which Burke has recourse do not appear to be first principles. Instead of providing theoretical clarification, he asserts that direction of human affairs belongs to prudence; and instead of establishing what might be the best or legitimate state, he celebrates the genius of the British constitution. Burke's political philosophy emerges from the elaboration of these two things, prudence and the British constitution. They may not be the first, grounding principles, but they are surely the principles Burke puts forward to claim our attention before all others.

Prudence, Burke says, is "the god of this lower world," since it has "the entire dominion over every exercise of power committed into its hands." Prudence is "the first of all the virtues, as well as the supreme director of them all." This means, in particular, that "practical wisdom" justly supersedes "theoretic science" whenever the two come into contention. The reason for the sovereignty of prudence is in the power of circumstances to alter every regularity and principle. "Circumstances (which with some gentlemen pass for nothing) give in reality to every political principle its distinguishing color and discriminating effect." Burke emphasizes that the prudence he speaks of is a "moral prudence" or a "public and enlarged prudence" as opposed to selfish prudence, not to mention cleverness or cunning. But he does not say how to be sure of the morality of prudence. If prudence is supreme, it must reign over morality; but if prudence can be either moral or selfish, it would seem to require the tutelage of morality. Aristotle, when facing this problem, was led to understand prudence as the comprehensive legislative art, and then to subordinate that to theory. Burke makes a different disposition. Instead of pursuing an inquiry into the first principles or ends of prudence, which necessarily leads beyond prudence, he distinguishes within prudence between "rules of prudence" available to ordinary statesmen and "prudence of a higher order." Rules of prudence are not mathematical, universal, or ideal; but they are nonetheless rules, Burke says grandly, "formed upon the known march of the ordinary providence of God," that is, visible in human experience. But as these rules are sovereign over all theoretical rights or metaphysical first principles, so higher prudence, the prudence of prudence, can suspend the rules of prudence when necessary.

This distinction within prudence, by which Burke attempts to secure the morality of prudence without subverting its sovereignty, corresponds to a distinction he draws between presumptive virtue and actual virtue: "There is no qualification for government but virtue and wisdom, actual or presumptive." Presumptive virtue and wisdom are the lesser, probable virtue that can be presumed in well-bred gentlemen of prominent families born into situations of eminence where they are habituated to self-respect; to the "censorial inspection of the public eye"; to taking a "large view of the wide-spread and infinitely diversified combinations of men and affairs in a large society"; to having leisure to reflect; to meeting the wise and learned as well as rich traders; to military command; to the caution of an instructor of one's fellow citizens thus acting as a "reconciler between God and man"; and to being employed as an administrator of law and justice. Actual virtue, such as Burke's own perhaps, is higher but more dubious; it must intervene when the rules of prudence fail, but it must not rule ordinarily lest society fall victim to the instability of men of ability. The idea of presumptive virtue presumes ability, not the highest but ordinarily sufficient, in men of property; at the same time it presumes at least instability, and sometimes immorality, in those who have nothing but ability, and rather than being born and bred in an elevated condition they

must rise to eminence by means that may not be moral and should not be exemplary. No country can reject the service of those with actual virtue, but "the road to eminence and power, from obscure condition, ought not to be made too easy." When that road is made too easy, too many follow it, and men of actual virtue are encouraged to display their ability rather than their virtue, and are crowded out by new men who have cleverness and little property, as happened in the French Revolution. Actual virtue therefore must be kept subordinate ordinarily to presumptive virtue, while being allowed, after due probation, the right of intervention in an emergency, such as the French Revolution, when men of presumptive virtue are confronted with an event so astonishing that they do not know how to react.

Thus Burke solves the problem of prudence within prudence: he keeps moral prudence distinct from mere cleverness, yet maintains its sovereignty over clever theorists except for occasional interventions by higher prudence. (pp. 8-10)

It is the ruling characteristic of Burke's political philosophy as well as the guiding theme of his politics to avoid the ground on which theory and practice converge. Founding, which prior to Burke had been considered by all political thinkers to be the essential political act, is for him a nonevent. The making of a constitution can never be "the effect of a single instantaneous regulation." It cannot happen, and it is wrong to try to make it happen.

In complete disagreement with Tocqueville, Burke does not consider that democracy is a possible regime. The people cannot rule; they are the passive element in contrast to the "active men in the state." Though the people may be led by a vicious oligarchy of some kind, it should be led by a "true natural aristocracy," by ministers who "are not only our natural rulers, but our natural guides." Thus, for Burke, one cannot choose between democracy and aristocracy, nor can there be a democratic or an aristocratic age, as for Tocqueville; nature has made the many incapable of governing themselves. "A perfect democracy is . . . the most shameless thing in the world," because each person's share of responsibility is so small that he does not feel it, and because public opinion which should restrain government is in the case of democracy nothing but the people's self-approbation. Responsible government is capable of shame, perhaps more than anything else; it is defending what one has had to do rather than taking credit for what one has chosen to do. No aristocracy, any more than a democracy, can rule long or well without the sense of a power above it; the lack of this sense is what makes democracy impossible as well as shameless. Only in an attenuated sense, therefore, is any human government, even a true natural aristocracy, a kind of self-government. Government is so far from a matter of choice, of choosing a form of rule, that it is a "power out of ourselves."

Fundamentally, government is not ruling; it is changing, reforming, balancing, or adjusting. Government is not nourished, as Aristotle thought, by claims to rule asserted by democrats and oligarchs in defense (and exaggeration) of their equality and inequality to others. The people do not claim to rule of their own accord; only when inflamed by a few do they believe they want to rule. And aristocrats, however natural, are bred to their eminence, which they accept rather than demand.

As far as Burke is from the Aristotelian sense of rule—government by human choice, art, and political science—he does not rush into theocracy and grasp at divine right in order to keep governments under control by shame. To make it certain that government has a human origin, Burke adopts the language of contract from modern theorists. But since government by contract might seem calculated, if not chosen, for convenience—in effect, a matter of arbitrary will or pleasure, not of judgment—he stresses the great differences between ordinary contracts "taken up for a little temporary interest" and the social contract that establishes the state. The latter contract is a "partnership in all science; a partnership in all art; a partnership in every virtue, and in all perfection." And it is a contract made between the living, the dead, and those to be born—that is, a contract not in the power of the present generation but in trust for the past and the future. (pp. 11-13)

Natural rights, which Burke deprecatingly calls "metaphysic rights," do not come to us directly, but "like rays of light which pierce into a dense medium, are, by the laws of nature, refracted from their straight line." Taking a cue from this famous remark, we might say that for Burke laws of nature are laws of refraction. They are laws describing the ways in which men, making their own conventions, constitutions, or property, imitate or follow nature as nature conducts itself without reference to humans. For example . . . , men making constitutions imitate nature in finding harmony through the struggle of its discordant powers and permanence through the rise and fall of its transitory parts. "Art is man's nature," Burke says, in reproach of the modern philosophers who place the "state of nature" outside civil society. Art (not choice) is nature's special gift to humans, but the gift is not used in a manner to preserve human specialness. All society is artificial, yet all artifice is according to natural law; the gift of art must be given back to nature. One wonders whether prudence is after all sovereign for Burke, if it must operate "under that discipline of nature."

The sovereign rule of prudence is also a rule *for* prudence. It is prescription, "this great fundamental part of natural law," which describes the manner of growth of property and constitutions and lays down the method of inheritance. Strange to say, prescription before Burke was never considered to be unequivocally part of natural law, for it was not thought to be applicable in public law. Burke borrowed the concept from Roman law, in which prescription gives title to property without a deed by long-continued use or takes it away despite a deed after long-continued disuse. This rule of private law was transformed by Burke into a rule of public law applicable to constitutions (not merely to the law of nations). Thus, a rule of private property becomes *the* rule for government, "the most solid of all titles, not only to property, but, which is to secure that property, to government"; "a title which is not the creature, but the master, of positive law," "the sacred rules of prescription." If the problem of theory's intrusion into practice is the theme of Burke's political philosophy, prescription is his special discovery—one must say, since he could not abide the word "innovation," his grand reform. It was merely a description of the working of the British constitution, he claimed; but as theory it was certainly new. Indeed, Burke had, he said, "a very full share" in the passage of the Nullum Tempus Act of 1769, by which he attempted to establish prescription as public law in Britain. Burke made this claim proudly in his splendid self-defense against the Duke of Bedford, *A Letter to a Noble Lord,* but he did not similarly advertise the theoretical reform which justified the legal novelty (which went against the authority of Blackstone). Nor did he remark that prescription became public law in 1769 not through prescription but by statute. That not merely *a* title, but the *most solid* title to property comes from long use rather than a deed implies that government, which issues deeds, is bound by long-continued practices rather than by principles. Property by prescription implies government without a founding or a theory; the best claim to rule comes not from establishing one's own claim as best but by securing the abandonment of rival claims. Yet it required a theory to show this, and even if Burke had tread softly to introduce it, even if his theory had fit neatly the shape of fact, it cannot be denied that his theory intrudes upon the prudence of statesmen. (pp. 19-20)

[For Burke], prescription is a "great fundamental part of natural law." He does not quite say it is *the* fundamental part, and he does not specify the full content of natural law in the manner of more theoretical theorists such as Aquinas or Hobbes. He is satisfied that natural law be understood as a law beyond and above human legislation; he does not require that human law be seen as application of natural law. In the debate between Cicero and Hobbes as to whether "men have a right to make what laws they please," Burke is on the side of Cicero in denying this. He then says that "all human laws are, properly speaking, only declaratory; they may alter the mode and application, but have no power over the substance of original justice." But since Burke has imported prescription into natural law itself, and has said little to establish the substance of original justice, it seems in effect that the mode and application, more than the substance, of natural law is to guide practice. Natural law is more means than ends because prescription, in order to exclude violent, comprehensive change, prevents the ends of politics from appearing in politics unrefracted by materials and circumstances. Prescription is prudence crystallized in theory. As such it is censor to the rest of natural law, so that natural law can speak in its own voice only "the principle of a superior law." Human liberty is so far from opposed to the principle of a superior will that it cannot survive without one. Although society is the product of a contract among men, men cannot live freely if they are free to make a new contract in every generation. Each generation must regard its liberties as an "entailed inheritance," as its property precisely because those liberties were not created by it. One may venture to conclude that at the center of Burke's political philosophy is the British constitution, not natural law. Natural law is the ground, but only because a constitution, made by accidents, needs a ground. However admirable it may be, the British constitution is not, for Burke, the rational state. But the ground of the constitution must be unseen and unfelt lest it upset the constitution that rests on it.

Here one might object that we are forgetting the "laws of commerce," which Burke, in a passage in his *Thoughts and Details on Scarcity* . . . , once equated, to the disgust of Karl Marx, with the "laws of nature, and consequently the laws of God." The laws of commerce, it would seem, promote too much novel enterprise to be held accountable to the principle of prescription. That is so, except insofar as prescription welcomes and justifies private enterprise without deeds or charters from the government. But the mobile property of merchants, together with the active abilities that create it, could be held in check and kept in balance, Burke believed, by the establishment of landed property and by the rule of gentlemen. With some basis in English experience, and some degree of hope, he joined together the supremacy of the landed interest, which he rightly said was recommended by "the practical politics of antiquity" (particularly Aristotle and Cicero), with a statement that could not be found, except as satire or disapproval, in ancient writers: "The love of lucre, though sometimes carried to a ridiculous, sometimes to a vicious, excess, is the grand cause of prosperity to all states." (pp. 21-2)

Burke, the champion of gentlemanly prudence, spent his political life beyond the limits of gentlemanly prudence, looking ahead to what his party could not see, urging it on to unaccustomed activity on uncongenial ground. One should say also that he devoted himself to securing and improving the boundaries of gentlemanly prudence, to keeping out subversive speculators and refashioning constitutional practices, such as party and impeachment, that would facilitate the rule of gentlemen. Having helped to found his party—by giving it a doctrine and a soul rather than by directing it—he abandoned it after the French Revolution and then attacked it. His colleagues could not see the difference between the American Revolution and the French; they did not appreciate the uniqueness of the latter event, the most complete revolution ever known. Burke's political philosophy centers on the defense of an actual constitution rather than the construction of an imaginary one. His theme is the sufficiency—rather, the perfection—of gentlemanly prudence. But his defense of his beloved gentlemen reveals their limitations, perhaps better than any revolutionary attack. For the revolutionaries found no suitable replacement for gentlemen; nor indeed have we, though we have sought among bureaucrats, technocrats, and democrats. One could almost define "gentlemen" by adding up everything that is lacking in bureaucrats, technocrats, and democrats. Burke's admiring view of them is clearer than that of their critics; the defects of gentlemen are to be seen in the need for his own contribution to their defense. That contribution went well beyond warning them of perils they were too dull to sense and arousing them with fine phrases. Using what he once called "the seasonable energy of a single man," Burke tried to fortify the rule of gentlemen so as to make them less liable to subversion and attack. The result in the nineteenth century was both to fix them in place, immobile in their newly philosophical prejudice (the conservatives), and to loosen their attachments, trusting in the promise that reform would be the means of their conservation (the liberals). Somewhat unwillingly, Burke bears testimony to the necessary imperfection of politics in the very midst of his inspiring speeches and noble deeds. (pp. 26-7)

Harvey C. Mansfield, Jr., in an introduction to *Selected Letters of Edmund Burke,* edited by Harvey C. Mansfield, Jr., The University of of Chicago Press, 1984, pp. 1-27.

PETER J. STANLIS
(essay date 1991)

[Stanlis is considered one of the world's foremost Burke scholars. In the following excerpt, he emphasizes the consistency of Burke's political thought, responding to what he considers some "very dubious or simply false" conclusions about Burke drawn by Conor Cruise O'Brien in his essay "A Vindication of Edmund Burke" (see Sources for Further Study).]

Mr. Conor Cruise O'Brien's "A Vindication of Edmund Burke," (*National Review,* December 17, 1990), contains many long established truths about Burke's politics—his consistency in principle, his remarkable insights and powers of prophesy, his strong critique of revolutionary ideology, and so forth. But amidst these trite truisms, which vindicate O'Brien's subject only to the uninitiated, he asserts some claims about the Enlightenment and Burke's religion and politics that are very dubious or simply false.

In 1975 the British historian John Lough warned against the loose use of "Enlightenment" as an abstract, all-inclusive category: "It is surely obvious that the greater the diversity of ideas which the term *Enlightenment* is stretched to cover, the less use it has as a scholarly tool. By the time the lowest common denominator can be discovered for ideas produced under such vastly different conditions, *Enlightenment* and *Lumières* become empty words." O'Brien would have done well to heed Lough's warning. Unless one equates the Enlightenment with the entire 18th century, it is meaningless rhetoric to call Burke "a child of the Enlightenment." O'Brien's indiscriminate inclusion of him under that term raises grave doubts that he understands either Burke or the enormously complex nature of that elusive category, and its vast range of interpretations.

O'Brien segments the Enlightenment arbitrarily, and identifies Burke with what he calls "the early, English or English-inspired phase of the Enlightenment. This was the Enlightenment of Locke . . . an Enlightenment that was compatible with a tolerant version of Christianity. This was Burke's Enlightenment." This is a colossal error. Burke always defended what he called the Christian commonwealth of Europe from its "enlightened" enemies—the materialists, atheists, deists, freethinkers, and epicureans who made their private "natural reason" the sole criterion for truth. In 1790 he charged that the primary objective of the French Revolution, which was based upon atheism, was to destroy the religious, legal, moral, and political social order and civilization of Europe that Christianity had built up over many centuries. Moreover, during the last seven years of his life Burke expressly denied that his era was any more "enlightened" than past ages.

Even when dealing with persons, O'Brien is a victim of his abstract categories. He knows that Locke and Burke were both members of the Church of England, both approved of the Revolution of 1688, and both are universally classified as Whigs. On this basis he concludes that Burke is a disciple of Locke. But in every one of these religious and political areas there is overwhelming historical evidence that Burke differed profoundly from his predecessor.

Burke was a philosophical dualist, for example, and believed in the reality of both matter and spirit, whereas Locke was a materialist and monist. Those who believe Burke was a follower of Locke's politics ignore their great differences in such matters as the following: their conceptions of the nature of man; the nature and proper relationship of Church and State; the role of history in society and politics; their understanding of the English constitution and meaning of political sovereignty; the distinctions between innovation, reform, and revolution; the meaning of the term "the people"; the fitness of a form of government to a given society; the relation of law or normative reason to will or power.

This inventory is by no means exhaustive. They also digressed in their use of language, in the meanings they each ascribed to such key terms as "natural law" and "natural rights," or "reason" and "rational," "liberty," "equality," etc. What is perhaps equally important, Burke's character, temperament, and personality are a world apart from Locke, as is very evident in the complex prose styles of Burke, which appeal aesthetically to the whole nature of man, in contrast to Locke's plain, flat, abstract, discursive, and utilitarian prose.

When O'Brien unites Burke and Locke as defenders of Christianity, as opposed to Voltaire, its declared enemy, he is betrayed into error once more by his wholly unhistorical and loose-jointed use of categories. Burke despised Voltaire's deism and attacks on Christianity. But despite his membership in the Church of England, Locke in his religious beliefs is practically indistinguishable from Voltaire. Sterling P. Lamprecht, a noted Locke scholar, has said: "He stood so close to the deists that he has sometimes been classified as one of their number." Locke's pupil, the Third Earl of Shaftesbury, so classified his tutor. (pp. 51-2)

In *The Reasonableness of Christianity,* Locke's most radical and polemical work, he wrote as a "minimalist" and pleaded in good conscience as a believing Christian, a rational defender of revelation, and a loyal Anglican that the Church of England should reform itself in order to attract members from the Dissenters. How? Locke advocated that it should reject its hierarchical structure and the authority of its bishops, abandon its canon law and theology, its creed and sacraments, its liturgy, all belief in mysteries and miracles, all external discipline, the Thirty-Nine Articles and Book of Common Prayer, all its religious customs and traditions—in short, its entire historical inheritance—as so many superstitions and "prejudices," in favor of one requirement for membership and salvation—to acknowledge that Christ is the Messiah. In the last section of his *Essay,* Locke stated the central principle of deism: "Reason must be our last judge and guide in everything." (p. 52)

Unlike Locke, Burke accepted the Church of England just as it was, with all of its virtues and weaknesses. He adhered to the Church out of personal convictions and real affection. Moreover, he regarded the Church with piety, as an important branch of Christianity, and a vital part of "the chain that connects the ages of a nation" with "the great mysterious incorporation of the human race," because religion was "one of the bonds of human society," and "its object [was] the supreme good, the ultimate end and object of man himself."

Burke was certainly aware of the great gap between himself and Locke in religious toleration. Burke's belief that "toleration was good for all, or it was good for none," made him both preach and practice universal religious toleration. In 1781, for example, when he learned that some Hindu Brahmins in London could not find the proper means of practicing the rituals of their faith, and had become the objects of derision of some rationalist freethinkers and wits, Burke placed his home at their disposal.

Burke knew that what passed for creedal toleration was often merely indifference to religion. His **"Speech on the Acts of Uniformity"** (1772) was his response to two Church of England clergymen, "minimalists" like Locke, who on grounds of reason and conscience had petitioned Parliament to be relieved from subscribing to the doctrines of their Church. His political rebuttal to their petition turns upon his important distinction between "the original rights of nature" for individuals and the civil and legal rights of institutions created by positive law and conventions, a basic principle in his political philosophy. Since the disaffected clergymen were free to follow their conscience outside the Church, Burke's religious rebuttal was that "the matter . . . does not concern toleration, but establishment."

Unlike Locke, Burke believed that membership in the Church was a moral duty, not a voluntary relationship to be determined arbitrarily and whimsically by each individual. In his rebuttal to the two clergymen, he cleverly used Locke against his two disciples:

> If the Church be, as Mr. Locke defines it, *a voluntary society*, etc., then it is essential to this voluntary society to exclude from her voluntary society any member she thinks fit, or to oppose the entrance of any upon such conditions as she thinks proper. For, otherwise, it would be a voluntary society acting contrary to her will, which is a contradiction in terms. And this is Mr. Locke's opinion, the advocate for the largest scheme of ecclesiastical and civil toleration to Protestants (for to Papists he allows no toleration at all).

Burke was well aware that Locke's famous and much admired theory of religious toleration, in *A Letter Concerning Toleration* (1689), was wholly sectarian, but on the broad all-inclusive basis of a generalized Protes-

tantism. This did not distinguish it in principle from the more narrow, bigoted antipopery of the Levellers and Puritan sects of the Commonwealth. Burke also knew that in his lifetime, when religion and politics were closely intertwined, Locke's total lack of toleration for Roman Catholics was what gave sanction to such systems of persecution as the Penal Laws against Catholics in Ireland, and the rule of the Protestant Ascendency.

Not only in religion, but also in their politics regarding the Revolution of 1688 and the Whig tradition, Burke and Locke are in entirely different camps. Burke approved of the Revolution of 1688 on constitutional grounds—that it was morally necessary, legally legitimate, and politically prudent to prevent James II from establishing absolute monarchy, and to return England to its traditional form of constitutional limited monarchy, with power divided and balanced by Parliamentary rule. Burke never considered the king's Catholicism as a legitimate factor in his constitutional reasons for opposing his rule. To him, 1688 was "a revolution not made but prevented," because the king was in revolution to the constitution, and 1688 completed the Restoration that was made in 1660.

Locke approved of the Revolution of 1688 not on constitutional grounds, but out of religious bigotry against Catholics. He was eager to replace James with William, not in order to restore constitutional limited monarchy, since his real convictions did not include such a regime as a legitimate form of government. He preferred William because he believed that no Catholic had a legitimate claim to the Crown. Locke's antipapist revolutionary activities were clearly evident during the decade before James became king, in his intimate association with his patron, Lord Ashley, later First Earl of Shaftesbury, whose hatred of Catholicism was pathological. Shaftesbury was involved or was the leader of a series of movements to prevent James from becoming king, including the infamous "Popish Plot," an unsuccessful attempt to place the Duke of Monmouth, Charles II's illegitimate son, on the throne, and the Exclusionist efforts in Parliament. For his revolutionary activities Shaftesbury was charged with high treason and imprisoned in the Tower of London, and Locke found it prudent to go into exile in Holland.

The year after his return to England in 1689, Locke published his *Two Treatises of Government*, with a preface that was intended to create the impression that these works were written to justify the Revolution of 1688. Locke's motive was to obscure his former revolutionary activities, to disguise his radical Commonwealth antimonarchical political philosophy, which the Whig aristocracy of 1689 strongly opposed, and to thus win the favor of the Whigs by convincing them he was in harmony with their political views. The myth his preface created was highly successful, and he confirmed it by his conservative behavior, which entailed refraining from any revolutionary activity between 1689 and his death in 1704. Thus throughout the entire 18th century there was a widespread conviction that Locke was a good Whig in the tradition of the Revolution of 1688.

This popular Whig myth endured for 266 years, until Peter Laslett shattered it in 1956 in his superb edition of Locke's two treatises. He proved that Locke wrote his two treatises between 1678 and 1681, not to justify the future revolution, but in support of Shaftesbury's anti-Catholic policy. Moreover, Laslett showed the Locke's politics were rooted in "the Good Old Cause" of the Commonwealth Levellers, not in the Whig politics of the aristocracy in 1688.

For O'Brien to admit that Locke's politics is rooted in the radical theories of the Commonwealth Levellers would compel him to abandon his claim that Burke is in the political tradition of Locke. If the Whig tradition begins with the Levellers of the Commonwealth, then Locke, not Burke, is the archetypal true Whig. But if it derives from the Revolution of 1688, then Locke's claim to the Whig tradition is illegitimate, and Burke is its true voice. In 1790, since the conflict was over whether the French Revolution was an extension of 1688, Burke was perfectly right to deny that Price and his colleagues in the Revolution Society could claim 1688 as their justification of the French Revolution. When Burke noted of Price and his colleagues that "in all their reasonings on the Revolution of 1688" they have in mind "a revolution which happened in England about forty years before," he identified Price with the Commonwealth radicals and thus connected him with Locke's politics.

Richard Ashcraft has recently shown that Locke's ties with the Levellers makes his politics far more radical than historians have supposed, and makes it wholly unfeasible to connect Burke with Locke. To Burke, the revolutionary theories of the Commonwealth radicals were outside of the Whig political tradition. It is remarkable indeed that O'Brien's "child of the Enlightenment" should have provoked over four hundred replies to his *Reflections* and other writings on the French Revolution, from the true children of the Enlightenment, those who followed Locke. I have read more than a hundred of these "replies" to Burke written between 1790 and 1797, and Locke is cited either by name, or by quoting him, or by referring to his doctrines, particularly to "natural rights," "equality," and "the sovereignty of the people."

O'Brien's frayed use of categories leaves him wondering about how much Burke understood his political differences with the "New Whigs." In the introduction to his edition of Burke's *Reflections*, O'Brien writes: "It is probable that Burke had never fully realized—until the events in France provided the critical test—how profoundly he was at odds with much that was fundamental in the philosophy of Englishmen with whom he had allied himself: Englishmen who cherished the principles of the Glorious Revolution and of the Enlightenment, and felt these principles to be essentially the same." Burke was too well read in British history and politics, and too perceptive, not to know how and where he differed from any of his fellow Whigs who were deceived by the myth Locke had created about his political orthodoxy. In discussing the Revolution of 1688 Burke heaps praise on many of its defenders, but he never mentions Locke. This is no careless oversight. Toward Locke Burke practices what he called "the precedence of reserve and decorum," which "dictates silence in some circumstances."

All that I have said against O'Brien's claim that Burke is in the religious and political tradition of Locke's Enlightenment has great bearing upon the conviction of many Americans today that Burke is the founder of modern political conservatism. For if O'Brien is right, then the liberals, not the conservatives, have the better claim to Burke. This claim should surprise no one who has read O'Brien's essay, "A New Yorker Critic," in the *New Statesman* (June 1963), where he agrees with Tom Paine, who pictures Burke as a "gifted liberal" who "kisses the aristocratic hand that hath purloined him from himself." O'Brien agrees with the left critics of Burke that he was a potential revolutionary, an Irish outsider and alienated man, who hypocritically served the English Whig aristocracy against his true political convictions.

In the introduction to his 1968 edition of Burke's *Reflections,* O'Brien severely castigates Ross Hoffman, Russell Kirk, and me for claiming that Burke was a political conservative. His criticism assumes that conservatism consists of a mindless defense of any established political authority, regardless of the beliefs or actions of those in power. Since Burke was a severe critic of King George III's ministers during the American War of Independence and attacked the established Protestant Ascendency in Ireland and Governor Warren Hastings' misrule in India, by O'Brien's reasoning he was not a conservative, but a liberal.

This line of reasoning totally ignores that conservatism includes a body of normative moral, legal, and constitutional principles by which to judge those who use or abuse political power. Since, as I showed in *Edmund Burke and the Natural Law,* Burke adhered strictly in his politics to the norms of moral natural law and constitutional law in holding rulers accountable for their uses of power, he was never more conservative than when he condemned those in power who violated these norms.

O'Brien attacked Ross Hoffman and Russell Kirk for making an analogy between Burke's account of the French Jacobins and contemporary Communists. He even quoted with approval Alfred Cobban's glib comment that "Burke has escaped from the more foolish jibes of the Left in Britain only to fall victim to the uncritical adulation of the Right in America." But ironically, in 1990, in "A Vindication of Edmund Burke," O'Brien himself greatly extends the very same analogy made by Hoffman and Kirk, but he does it in the name of liberalism. Apparently it was all wrong in 1968 for Hoffman and Kirk to "make the equation Jacobin equals Communist," and to "derive from Burke's later writings a repertory of maxims and incitements in support" of a conservative foreign policy, but if Burke can be claimed as a liberal, then O'Brien is justified in using the analogy.

It is to be regretted that the conservative claim to Burke should be attacked in *National Review*, by a man who in 1965 identified himself as a socialist and the type of liberal who is not "a false friend" to the revolutionary aspirations of "Africa, Asia and Latin America." In his article "The Perjured Saint," in the *New York Review of Books* (November 1964), O'Brien defended Alger Hiss through a sustained attack on the moral integrity of his accuser, Whittaker Chambers, a longtime *NR* contributor, whom he pictured as a chronic liar.

O'Brien's "A Vindication of Edmund Burke" is an attempt to destroy the thesis of Russell Kirk in *The Conservative Mind* by claiming that Burke is not the founder of modern political conservatism, but a liberal like John Locke and O'Brien himself. Fortunately, the case for Burke as a moral natural law and constitutional political philosopher is too well-established. (pp. 52-4)

Peter J. Stanlis, "A True Vindication of Edmund Burke," in *Chronicles: A Magazine of American Culture,* Vol. 15, No. 5, May, 1991, pp. 51-4.

SOURCES FOR FURTHER STUDY

Cone, Carl B. *Burke and the Nature of Politics.* 2 vols. Lexington: University of Kentucky Press, 1957-64.
> Highly regarded political biography.

Kirk, Russell. *Edmund Burke: A Genius Reconsidered.* New York: Arlington House, 1967, 255 p.
> Underscores the influence and preeminence of Burke's political conservatism.

O'Brien, Conor Cruise. "A Vindication of Edmund Burke." *National Review* XLII, No. 24 (17 December 1990): 28-35.
> Examines Burke's *Reflections on the Revolution in France,* highlighting the seemingly "prophetic" power of his insight and indicating modern applications of his warnings.

Reid, Christopher. *Edmund Burke and the Practice of Political Writing.* New York: St. Martin's Press, 1985, 238 p.
> Examines the relationship between the development of literary technique in Burke's writings and the political circumstances that prompted them.

Stanlis, Peter J. *Edmund Burke and the Natural Law.* Ann Arbor: University of Michigan Press, 1958, 311 p.
> Seminal study that, according to scholar Russell Kirk, "does more than any other . . . to define Burke's position as a philosopher, relating the convictions of Burke to the great traditions of Christian and classical civilization."

————, ed. *Edmund Burke: The Enlightenment and the Modern World.* Detroit: University of Detroit Press, 1967, 129 p.
> Seven symposium essays treating various aspects of Burke's career and thought.

Robert Burns

1759-1796

(Born Robert Burnes) Scottish poet and lyricist.

INTRODUCTION

*C*alled the national poet of Scotland, Burns has attained an almost mythical stature not only in his native land but around the world. He is revered as the poet of the "common man," the "heaven-taught ploughman" who expressed the soul of his people and sang of universal humanity. His work made acceptable for the first time the use of Scots dialect in "serious" poetry, and his depiction of rural Scottish life and manners marked a radical departure from the stateliness and decorum of eighteenth-century verse. Burns is admired for his naturalness, his compassion, his humor, and his fervent championship of the innate freedom and dignity of humanity.

Born in Alloway, Ayrshire, to impoverished tenant farmers, Burns received little formal schooling, although his father, William Burnes (whose famous son later altered the spelling of the family name), sought to provide his sons with as much education as possible. He managed to employ a tutor for Robert and his brother Gilbert, and this, together with Burns's extensive reading, furnished the poet with an adequate grounding in English education. Burns's family moved from one rented farm to another during his childhood, enduring hard work and financial difficulties. As the family was too poor to afford modern farming implements, their hardships progressively worsened. All his efforts notwithstanding, William Burnes was forced to declare bankruptcy in 1783; his death followed soon afterwards. Many biographers believe that watching his father slowly succumb to the ravages of incessant work and despair was a factor in Burns's later condemnation of social injustice.

While a young man, Burns acquired a reputation for charm and wit and began to indulge in romance. He once attributed the impetus of his poetry to his sensuality: "There is certainly some connection between Love

514

and Music and Poetry. . . . I never had the least thought or inclination of turning poet till I once got heartily in love, and then rhyme and song were, in a manner, the spontaneous language of my heart." Outspoken in matters ecclesiastical as well as sexual, Burns was frequently involved in scrapes with the church, both for his relationships with women and for his criticism of church doctrine. Throughout his life, Burns was fervently opposed to the strict Calvinism that prevailed in the Scottish kirk. The doctrine of the "Auld Licht" Calvinists included a rigid conception of predestination and a belief in an arbitrarily chosen religious elite who were to attain salvation regardless of moral behavior. But although Burns was repelled by this, as well as by the Calvinist notion of humankind as innately and inevitably sinful, he was not irreligious; his theology has been summed up as a vague humanitarian deism.

In 1786, Burns proposed to Jean Armour, who was pregnant with his child. Her parents forbade the match but demanded financial restitution from Burns. Angry at this rejection by the Armours and hurt by what he deemed the too-ready capitulation of their daughter to their demands, Burns resolved to sail to Jamaica to start a new life. The plan never materialized, however, for during that year his *Poems, Chiefly in the Scottish Dialect* was published in Kilmarnock. The volume catapulted Burns to sudden remarkable, but short-lived, fame; upon its success he went to Edinburgh, where he was much admired by the literati, though he afterward remained in relative obscurity for the rest of his life. In the meantime, he was still involved with Jean Armour, who again became pregnant and whom he was finally able to marry in 1788. Burns carried on his dual professions of poet and tenant farmer until the next year when he obtained a post in the excise service. Most of Burns's major poems, with the notable exception of "Tam o' Shanter," had been written by this point in his life; the latter part of his creative career was devoted to collecting and revising the vast body of existing Scottish folk songs. In 1796, at the age of 37, Burns died from rheumatic heart disease, apparently caused by excessive physical exertion and frequent undernourishment as a child.

Through his treatment of such themes as the importance of freedom to the human spirit, the beauties of love and friendship, and the pleasures of the simple life, Burns achieved a universality that commentators believe is the single most important element in his work. Although his poetry is firmly set within the context of Scottish rural life, most critics agree that Burns transcended provincial boundaries. Edwin Muir commented: "His poetry embodied the obvious in its universal form, the obvious in its essence and truth." This quality makes his work vulnerable to one charge often leveled against it—lack of imaginative subtlety. Some critics contend that Burns's passionate directness renders him insensible to a more delicate expression of imagination; they find his poetry too accessible, too easily penetrated. A related objection is that Burns's philosophical themes are platitudinous and trite, coming dangerously close to the sentimental and naive. Iain Crichton Smith carried the argument further, stating that Burns's very universality weakens his stature as an individual poet: as Burns has no voice or philosophy that is uniquely his own, his poetry is "artless" in the negative sense of that word. The majority of critics, however, hold that Burns's simplicity of theme is true to life—that his philosophy, while not profound, is true to itself and to human nature. It is widely admitted that Burns's message is not primarily an intellectual one; rather, he expresses the familiar emotions and experiences of humanity. Critics agree that this talent rendered Burns particularly fit for his role as a lyricist. His deep interest in Scotland's poetic heritage and folkloric tradition resulted in his amending or composing over 300 songs, for which he refused payment, maintaining that this labor was rendered in service to Scotland. Each written to an existing tune, the songs are mainly simple yet affecting lyrics of the common concerns of love and life. A great part of Burns's continuing fame rests on such songs as "Green Grow the Rashes O" and, particularly, "Auld Lang Syne."

The topic of freedom—political, religious, personal, and sexual—dominates Burns's poetry and songs. The poem beginning "Is there, for honest poverty," generally referred to by its refrain, "A man's a man for a' that," is an implicitly political assertion of Burns's beliefs in equality and freedom. His outrage over what he considered the false and restricting doctrine of the Scottish kirk is clear in such satirical poems as "Holy Willie's Prayer" and "The Holy Fair." The former concerns a self-professed member of the elect who through his own narration inadvertently exposes his hypocrisy and ethical deficiencies. "The Holy Fair," a lively, highly descriptive account of a religious gathering, contrasts the dour, threatening view of life espoused by the Calvinist preachers with the reality of life as it is actually lived. The simple celebrants, after dutifully and respectfully attending to the sermons, continue their pleasurable everyday pursuits—the enjoyment of conviviality, drink, and romance, which are ever present in Burns's work. "Scotch Drink," a rousing drinking song, celebrates the joys of love and friendship. The title of "The Jolly Beggars" indicates Burns's attitude toward the main characters of this cantata. Poor and disreputable as these jolly beggars are, they have found their personal freedom and happiness in living outside the mainstream of society. Burns's innumerable love poems and songs are acknowledged to be touching expressions of the human experience of love in all its phases: the sexual love of "The Fornicator"; the emotion of "My Luve is Like a Red, Red Rose"; the happiness of a couple grown old together in "John Anderson, My Jo." Another frequently cited aspect of Burns's poetry is its vitality. Whatever his subject, critics find in his verses a riotous celebration of life, an irrepressible joy in the fact of living; Bonamy Dobrée has said that Burns "sang of life because he possessed so unusual, so shining a quantity of it." This vitality is often expressed through the humor prevalent in Burns's work, from the bawdy humor of "The Jolly Beggars" and the broad farce of "Tam o' Shanter" to the irreverent mockery of "The Twa Dogs" and the sharp satire of "Holy Willie's Prayer." Burns's subjects and characters are invariably humble, their stories told against the background of the Scottish rural countryside. Although natural surroundings figure prominently in his work, Burns differed from Romantic poets in that he had little interest in nature itself, which in his poetry serves but to set the scene for human activity and emotion.

Although initial publication of Burns's poems in 1786 was attended by immense popular acclaim, eighteenth-century critics responded with more reserve. They eagerly embraced the romantic image of Burns as a rustic, untaught bard of natural genius—an image which Burns himself shrewdly fostered—but some critics, particularly English, were somewhat patronizing. The Scots dialect they found quaint to a point, but ultimately intrusive and distracting. Sentimental poems such as "The Cottar's [or 'Cotter's'] Saturday Night" and "To a Mountain Daisy" received the most favorable attention; Burns's earthier pieces, when not actually repressed, were tactfully ignored. "The Jolly Beggars," for example, now considered one of his best poems, was rejected for years on the grounds that it was coarse and contained low subject matter. Although these assessments held sway until well into the nineteenth century, more recent critics have taken an opposing view. "The Cottar's Saturday Night," an idealized portrait of a poor but happy family, is today regarded as affectedly emotional and tritely moralizing. "To a Mountain Daisy," ostensibly occasioned by the poet's inadvertent destruction of a daisy with his plow, is now considered one of Burns's weakest poems. Like "The Cottar's Saturday Night," it is sentimental and contains language and images which contemporary critics find bathetic and false. "To a Mountain Daisy" is often compared with "To a Mouse," as the situations described in the poems are similar; the latter is the poet's address to a mouse he has disturbed with his plow. Most critics today believe that "To a Mouse" expresses a genuine emotion that the other poem lacks, and does so in more engaging language. Interestingly, "To a Mountain Daisy" was written primarily in standard English, while "To a Mouse" is predominantly in Scots; critical reaction to these two poems neatly encapsulates the debate over whether Burns's best work is in English or Scots. The issue remains unresolved, but on the whole, earlier critics preferred Burns's English works, while recent critics have favored his Scots. Eighteenth-century commentators viewed Burns's use of dialect as a regrettable idiosyncrasy, but modern critics contend that his English poems tend to degenerate into stilted neoclassical diction and overstated emotion.

It has long been asserted as a general tenet that for Burns, English was the language of thought and Scots the language of emotion. Adherents of this belief argue that Burns's characteristic passion and liveliness are expressed almost invariably in Scots, whereas his more thoughtful, philosophical ideas are couched in English. David Daiches, among others, has found this assessment of Burns's poetic bilingualism too simplistic. He maintains that Burns was quite aware of the effects of his use of language; Daiches cites the sole exclusively English passage of "Tam o' Shanter" as an example of Burns's deliberate use of formality to heighten the ironic effect of the poem. Few of Burns's poems are entirely in English or in Scots; the pieces most commentators acknowledge as his best are those in which he judiciously mingled the two languages. Burns's letters, however, were generally written in English. Burns was a prolific letter writer whose theory of successful correspondence was to suit each letter to the taste of the intended recipient; his letters, therefore, vary in style and tone.

In contrast, the apparent artlessness of Burns's poetry, the natural expression of common experience and simple emotion, has appealed to critics from the eighteenth century to the twentieth. For many years it was generally accepted that Burns was as he presented himself: a simple plowman possessed of little art save "ae spark o' Nature's fire"; a completely natural poet whose verse was but the inevitable outpouring of a sensitive soul. In the closer inspection of twentieth-century criticism, Burns's technical achievement alone has been found to invalidate this romantic perception of his talent. Critics contend that Burns experimented with a variety of verse forms and exhibited mastery over most of them, including the octosyllabic couplet of "Tam o' Shanter," the Spenserian stanza of "The Cottar's Saturday Night," the nine-line stanza of "The Holy Fair," and the standard Habbie of "To a Mouse," this last the verse form most closely associated with Burns. Modern scholarship has also revealed his use of the song rhythms of Scottish folk tradition and his masterful integration of intricate internal rhymes. The idea that Burns's poetry is simply personal expression has likewise been repudiated in recent criticism. Modern commentators have stated that among Burns's poetic techniques is a talent for dramatic monologue comparable to Robert Browning's. They cite "Holy Willie's Prayer" as an example of a narrative poem which gains an added dramatic dimension through its use of a narrator-persona. It has also been said that the effectiveness of the satire in this poem presupposes not only the poet's thorough understanding of the mind of such a one as Willie, but an implicit pity for him as well, evidencing Burns's ability to sympathetically create realistic characters. A more subtle example of the dramatic narrator-persona is found in "Tam o' Shanter," a recital by an anonymous narrator of Tam's narrow escape from a coven of witches after a convivial evening at the pub. Critics have remarked that the narrator emerges as a character in his own right, as his way of telling the story shapes our perception both of the tale and of him.

The vitality and sincerity which critics and the public alike have found in Burns's work strike a chord which seems to translate the national poet of Scotland into a universal poet claimed by all. Although many of Burns's concerns are ostensibly local ones, and the setting and circumstances of his poetry are unmistakably Scottish, the themes he sounds are those which transcend particulars to achieve universality.

(For further information about Burns's life and works, see *Literature Criticism from 1400 to 1800*, Vol. 3.)

CRITICAL COMMENTARY

WILLIAM WALLACE

(essay date 1896)

[In the following excerpt, Wallace compares Burns with other prominent literary artists, assessing his achievement.]

How to classify Burns, what position to assign him in the great Pantheon of genius, is a task that must be attempted, but also one not easily accomplished. (p. 461)

[William] Dunbar's powers of humour, satire, and graphic representation were of a very high order, barely second, if at all, say his admirers, to Chaucer's, whose literary disciple he avowed himself to be. His command of language, also, and the easy flow of his versification are admirable, and worthy of all the praise bestowed upon them by Sir David Lyndsay of The Mount. But in all these respects Burns at least equalled, and in some far excelled him, while he had poetics qualities of the most exquisite character which are not to be found in Dunbar. The tenderness, the sympathy, the music, the passion by which Burns touched the finest chords in the human heart, and which make his immense laughter a joy as well as a judgment, are absent from Dunbar's genius. Dunbar's derision, which is probably his strongest point, is of a bitter and biting character, and leads him not seldom into false positions, where a true poet should not be found. . . . In this comical diversion at the expense of the unfortunate there is an element of cruelty which was alien to the nature of Burns. There is a pervading humour in the **'Twa Dogs,' 'The Brigs of Ayr,' 'Mailie's Dying Words and Elegy,' 'The Mouse,' 'The crawlin' ferlie'** on Miss's bonnet, the **'Address to the Deil,' 'Tam o' Shanter,'** the **'Haggis,' 'Captain Grose,' 'Meeting with**

Lord Daer,' 'Guid Mornin' to your Majesty,' 'Duncan Gray,' 'Last May a braw Wooer,' 'Tam Glen,' and many another; but it is a genial and sympathetic humour which we may fully enjoy without the sense of having been accessory to an act of inhumanity.

Burns, of course, when he chose, could raise a sufficiently scathing laughter against the object of his aggressive humour; but, as a rule, he did so only when he believed that object deserved it. In that case, his power of ridicule became a scourge wielded by his moral indignation. **'Holy Willie,' 'The Holy Fair,' 'The Ordination,' 'The Kirk's Alarm,'** and others have been and will continue to be the vehicles of a gigantic laughter that is perfectly Olympian in its overwhelming power. (pp. 462-63)

It was the reverse side of his love of truth and honesty. Hence he threw the whole of his highest soul into the attack, his passion enlisting in its service the vivid directness, the bounding movement, the picturesque and mirth-moving facility, and all the qualities of a style almost unmatched in its varied power; with the result of producing a form of high-pitched satire unsurpassed, if even equalled, in any literature. (p. 463)

Dunbar's *Golden Targe* is justly admired for the ingenuity of its construction, and the art with which, in a complicated strophe, it is ornamented with imagery felicitously adapted from external nature. But it is inferior in power of conception and execution, in relevancy to fact, in moral elevation, in rapidity of word-painting, to **'The Vision'** of Burns, the one production of his with which it can be compared. . . . The whole plot [of the *Golden Targe*] is an allegory of the impotence of reason—which can resist the attacks of all other tempting

---

Principal Works

Poems, Chiefly in the Scottish Dialect (poetry) 1786; also published as Poems, Chiefly in the Scottish Dialect [enlarged edition], 1787

"Tam o' Shanter" (poetry) 1791; published in The Antiquities of Scotland

Poems Ascribed to Robert Burns, the Ayrshire Bard (poetry) 1801

Reliques of Robert Burns, Consisting Chiefly of Original Letters, Poems, and Critical Observations on Scottish Songs (letters, poetry, criticism) 1808

The Poetry of Robert Burns. 4 vols. (poetry, songs) 1896-97

The Letters of Robert Burns. 2 vols. (letters) 1931

---

influence—in the presence of beauty. . . . There is certainly nothing like this in Burns. Half his work consists in describing the victories of love over the whole nature of man; but it did not occur to him to employ the allegory, or the rebus, or the puzzle, to help him out with his account of matters. It may be doubted if any one of these devices would have proved successful if inserted into **'A' the airts,'** or **'Mary Morison,'** or **'The Lass of Balloch myle,'** or **'My Nanie O,'** or the **'Rigs o' Barley,'** or **'My ain kind Dearie,'** or **'Green grow the Rashes,'** or fifty others that might be quoted. Dunbar certainly had graphic power. But so had Burns—in the highest degree. He was not a mere man of books, though he knew not a few books thoroughly. His eye had rested often and keenly on nature, on human character and action, and on the specialisms of many occupations; and his work is full of rapid touches derived from this close practical observation, which book-knowledge of itself must inevitably miss. It is no disparagement to the genius and performances of Dunbar to say that in nothing except monkish scholarship, and what it may bring, is he the superior of Burns, while in the broader and higher endowments and achievements of a great poet he falls distinctly behind.

What of [Sir Walter] Scott? . . . Was Scott a greater poet than Burns? If this were to be decided by the comparative quality of their best rhymed work, there could not be much hesitation about the answer. Scott could not have written **'The Jolly Beggars,'** or **'The Holy Fair,'** or **'The Epistles'** to Smith, Davie, and Lapraik, or **'Holy Willie's Prayer,'** or **'Highland Mary,'** or **'Tam o' Shanter,'** or **'Mary in Heaven,'** or **'Scots wha hae,'** probably not **'The Cotter's Saturday Night,'** and he certainly would not have written **'A Man's a Man for a' that'** even if he could.

It may be said, Neither could Burns have written the 'Lay of the Last Minstrel' or 'Marmion.' That is

probable enough; but mainly because he would not have thought it worth his pains to try. (pp. 465-67)

Burns had more soul in him than Scott, with all his admitted amiabilities. Scott dealt more with the outside of things; Burns penetrated to the core. His spirit was deeper, his view wider, his emotion intenser, his sympathy more catholic, his sensibility more tender, his affection more glowing, and he could rise to heights of passionate and picturesque utterance which Scott could never reach. Thus, as regards the materials of a lofty poetry, Burns was by much the more fully furnished in resource. As regards its form, Scott is undoubtedly musical—with breaks—within his range; but, with not less facility, Burns has a richer melody, a swifter, more varied, and flashing movement, a fuller moral suggestiveness. (pp. 468-69)

Take as illustration:

Opening of 'Lady of the Lake.'

The stag at eve had drunk his fill,
Where danced the moon on Monan's rill,
And deep his midnight lair had made
In lone Glenartney's hazel shade;
But, when the sun his beacon red
Had kindled on Ben Voirlich's head, &c.

Opening of 'Tam o' Shanter.'

When chapman billies leave the street,
And drouthy neibours neibours meet,
As market-days are wearing late,
An' folk begin to tak' the gate;
While we sit bousing at the nappy,
An' getting fou and unco happy, &c.

In the Scott quotation there is only one line that is not thrown out of arrangement by inversion, in Burns there is only one that is. Hence, whatever may be thought of the contrasted pictures, there is a sense of effort in the one case and of ease in the other—and ease is characteristic of most of Burns's best writing, making the music of his verse perfect. (p. 470)

If we must thus set Burns above Dunbar and Scott, it is scarcely worth saying that we must put him very much higher than any other Scottish poet of note—Semple of Beltrees, Hamilton of Gilbertfield, Allan Ramsay, Fergusson, Hogg, Tannahill, Motherwell. Burns, of course, owed much to his predecessors. (p. 471)

[But] wherever Burns has borrowed he has improved on what he has taken, or rather he has transfigured it altogether, and raised it from mediocrity or failure to the rank of participation in a great poetic triumph. Compare Ramsay's 'Nanie,' or 'Lang Syne,' or 'Corn Rigs,' or 'Vision,' with Burns's; or compare Fergusson's 'Hallowfair,' or 'Leith Races'—better work than Ramsay's—with Burns's **'Hallowe'en'** and **'Holy Fair;'** take scores of the old songs transformed by Burns into things of beauty, humour, or tenderness, and compare them as they were before and after passing through his hands; it will be seen that the difference is well-nigh that between abortion and Apollo. (p. 478)

And it is not merely that power has replaced feebleness of execution; poetry is enabled to discharge its mission of conveying passion, sympathy, or moral impressiveness. Fergusson's 'Hallow-fair' deals merely with the external, with the oddities and amusing features of popular activity as displayed in the scene it pictures. In 'Hallowe'en' Burns deals with the heart of the people and the weird beliefs still lingering in the darker recesses of their minds; and the impression left is not that of mere condescending amusement, but of sympathy with the side of human nature to which we are introduced. In 'Leith Races,' again, Fergusson merely dishes up the eccentricities and drolleries of the actors and spectators, 'Mirth' being avowedly the sole companion he seeks in the demonstration. But in the 'Holy Fair' Burns has an eye for the two additional figures of 'Superstition' and 'Hypocrisy' as well as 'Fun,' and so the poem, instead of resting merely on the plane of the ludicrous, soars into a powerful and picturesque satire upon the falsehood in religious thought and action that insults reason and corrupts conduct. And here it is that we find a vital difference between Burns and the Scottish school generally. Burns never forgets the reverence due to humanity. The key struck in the 'Twa Dogs' is never changed. On the other hand, 'Peebles to the Play' and 'Christ's Kirk on the Green,' with the imitations of them by Ramsay and by Fergusson deriving through Ramsay, are content to extract diversion out of the people, to make game of them for the amusement of their 'betters,' and are to that extent contemptuous of the mass of humanity. But that is not the lesson of the 'Twa Dogs' or 'Hallowe'en,' and above all it is not the lesson of 'The Jolly Beggars.'

Here is a picture entirely in the realistic spirit and on the traditional lines of the Scottish school, in a sense an imitation of 'Peebles' and 'Christ's Kirk' and Ramsay's and Fergusson's sketches of popular life, only executed with a power that dwarfs every other artist into insignificance. But it has not been painted for the amusement of the onlooker. Indeed, the average dweller amid the conventionalities and the respectabilities shrinks from it as a revolting spectacle. But persons of more heart and larger calibre can see in it something that attracts, something that appeals to their deepest and best human instincts. The poet forces us to feel a certain respect for those lawless ragamuffins who have the courage—call it a sinister courage if you will—to assert themselves against the world. . . . The whole effect, indeed, is a triumph of poetic power of the highest and finest order, constraining, as it does amidst seemingly insurmountable difficulties, every mind of adequate discernment and sensibility to realise that

nothing that is human, however distasteful to the ordinary and average type of nature, is alien to that catholic sympathy which, whether moved by love or pity, breaks through every artificial limitation that it may clasp the race in its comprehensive embrace. It was this power of everywhere seeing the universal in the particular that placed Burns on a higher and special eminence of his own. He entered the Scottish school like a great sculptor entering his studio, where pupils or apprentices or understudies have been blocking out work with a view to his coming. Their results are not without merit, especially the merit of preparation, yet they do not satisfy the ideal. With half an hour of his chisel the master transmutes the well-aimed or half-successful attempts into perfect achievement. And such was Burns in his relation to his predecessors. They were his auxiliaries and foreworkers, but not his artistic equals. He stands by himself, supreme, without a peer.

The considerations that lead to the recognition of Burns as the greatest poet and one of the greatest men of his country go far to determine also his position among the great poets of the world. Here it has been rather the fashion in certain quarters to do what can be done to keep Burns out of the front and even the second row. The well-spring of his genius, it is said, though its yield is pure and sparkling, is but 'a little Valclusa fountain' after all. He may be unsurpassed as a song-writer, but he must not be named beside Homer and Dante, Shakespeare and Milton, Molière and Goethe. He wants their majesty. Neither must he be ranked with Chaucer, Wordsworth, Byron, Shelley, Keats, Browning, Tennyson, and the like, because he lacks the philosophic subtlety of one moiety of them, and the ornate beauty of the other. To ask a place for him in the loftiest rank, within the poetic Pantheon, might at first raise a smile. . . . The trombone and the big drum can drown the violin and the flute; but the latter in the hands of a master can give out the more exquisite music when they get a chance of being heard. It was with those finer instruments that Burns worked, and he has done things with them, isolated perhaps and not large to look at, but which some of the Masters could not have done at all, and none of them could have done better. (pp. 478–81)

The strength of Burns was that his work was 'inevitable.' (p. 481)

In this respect Burns had an enormous advantage over even the greatest poets. His work was not concocted. It was inspired. His own nature forced it on him. A call came to him higher than his own will, and he was merely nature's editor, happy in this, that his own laborious study and practice had equipped him with a facile and felicitous mastery of language which formed a ready vehicle for the fiery message fresh born within his spirit. Many of the greater poets, however, must have done much of their greatest work quite wilfully.

Dante's highest merit is not spontaneity. Goethe must have set about the construction of *Faust* very deliberately; and accordingly it is not surprising to find a critic, who is certainly not backward in Goethe's praise, saying of Burns's 'Jolly Beggars,' an effort inspired by the occasion, that 'it has a breadth, truth, and power which make the famous scene in Auerbach's cellar, of Goethe's *Faust,* seem artificial and tame beside it, and which are only matched by Shakespeare and Aristophanes.' Milton clearly went to work of set purpose. He cannot have felt a genuine call to 'justify the ways of God to men,' at all events in the particular case to which he addressed himself, otherwise he could scarcely have failed so completely of his object and won the world's everlasting sympathy for Satan as his real hero. Nay, Shakespeare himself must often have written less at the call of nature than of the manager of the Globe Theatre, although his fancy seems to have fallen in with his task in equal readiness and fertility. But even among those Titans of song Burns has a uniqueness of attitude that commands attention. He is the creation of nature, the instantaneous embodiment of the immediate afflatus. His message is straight from the deepest source of truth and beauty, and therefore original. Moreover, he speaks to us, not at us through dramatic or allegorical machinery, and of realities that have an intense interest for us, and not of invented circumstances and artificial sentiments. (pp. 481-82)

That Burns did not propound schemes of philosophy or theology after the manner of Wordsworth and Browning is true enough; but possibly it was a correct instinct that led him to feel that rhymed sermonising or metaphysics in blank verse was not poetry, whose function surely lies in the concrete. Had there not been something else and better in Wordsworth and Browning than homiletic versifying, their names would already have been forgotten. That it was not for want of speculative power that Burns deals little in abstract thinking is sufficiently evidenced by his ecclesiastical satires and the ethical element in his Epistles to Sillar, Lapraik, Smith, and others, to say nothing of his Letters. But he knows the limits which his art prescribes to this vein of thinking, and admits no more than is useful for enriching a poem by apt allusion, without turning it into an essay in either Ontology or Deontology. When he is compared with Chaucer, a more formidable rival is cited. Chaucer, it is said, deals with a wider and a lovelier world, and exhibits a greater wealth of characters in a diction not less easy and picturesque. But Burns's characters are more striking, his force and fire and tenderness are greater, and he can rise to heights of passionate utterance inaccessible to the father of English poetry. (pp. 483-84)

When poets of the ornate order, like Keats, Shelley, or Tennyson, come in question, an entirely new point arises. The marvellous beauty of Keats— marvellous not only for his years but in itself—is not in Burns, nor is the peculiar music and rich decoration of Tennyson, or the dogmatic and brilliant Pantheism and transcendental metaphysics of Shelley, continually losing himself among the stars and the universe at large. But neither are they in Homer nor any of the great poets of classic antiquity, nor in Shakespeare in those highest passages that have placed him on the throne of poetry. The manner of those great singers is that of a severe simplicity, using no more descriptive touches than are needed to make the object of the delineation speak for itself and reveal its own beauty, power, or pathetic impressiveness. The manner of the ornamental school is to crowd the canvas with highly-coloured and shining accessories, dazzling the eye and distracting the mind in search of the central figure. The contrast between the classic and the decorative school is like that between a Greek statue, perfectly chiselled but colourless and nude, and a wax figure carefully tinted, dressed out in the most fashionable glories of Regent Street, and diamonded with all the resources of Hatton Garden. (pp. 484-85)

The truth is, to compare such a poet as Burns with Keats, or Shelley, or Tennyson is to do injustice on both sides. You might almost as fairly compare him with Titian, or Phidias, or Beethoven. They are different types of artists, and it is about as futile to compare them as it would be to compare a snuff-box with a policeman. The only question that can be asked as between the simple and classic school on the one hand and the ornate and luscious school on the other is, Whether do the classics or the decorators represent the higher and truer form of the poetic art? It is a question for an intellectual jury. . . . Burns happened to belong to the classic school, and in that school stood high, in certain respects the highest. Moreover, he had qualities which most of his fellow-classics lack. Like Shakespeare he saw keenly the humorous side of life, and knew how to hit it off in light and instantaneous strokes. . . . Then he could not only command the admiration of his peers, but had the secret of making himself appreciated by the mass of mankind. His charm touches at once the highest and the lowest capacity. By unerring instinct he seized a subject of universal interest, or rather the subject seized him. He presented it in a manner of his own not only infinitely attractive but absolutely perspicuous, and distinguished by that brevity which is not only the soul of wit but the token of mastery. So that, while Milton at last becomes wearisome, and even Shakespeare looks a serious undertaking, and the rest are left to the leisured and curious few, Burns is universally welcome, universally intelligible, universally instructive or delightful. Probably no poet of the first rank has ever been more popular, and in the best sense of popularity. (pp. 486-87)

William Wallace, "The Character and Genius of Burns," in *The Life and Works of Robert Burns, Vol. IV*, by Robert Burns, edited by Robert Chambers and William Wallace, Longmans, Green, and Co., 1896, pp. 413-504.

DAVID DAICHES

(essay date 1950)

[Daiches, an English scholar and critic, has written extensively on modern English literature and is a widely recognized authority on Scottish literature. In the following excerpt, he provides a detailed explication of the tone and technique of *"Tam o' Shanter,"* which is considered one of Burns's finest works.]

"Tam o' Shanter" is Burns's most sustained single poetic effort, as well as the only example among his poems of this kind of narrative poetry. . . . [It] showed him a master of verse narrative as no Scots poet had been since the fifteenth century. The speed and verve of the narration, the fine, flexible use of the octosyllabic couplet, the effective handling of the verse paragraph demonstrate a degree of craftsmanship that few other users of this verse form have achieved. Matthew Prior, who also used octosyllabic couplets for narrative poetry, had something of this ease and fluency, but Prior's verse tales have a city swagger about them, a deliberate air of a man about town displaying his humor and familiarity, as well as a looseness of structure and little concern for the verse paragraph, which put them far below **"Tam o' Shanter"** in literary quality.

The opening of the poem marks the characteristically Scottish contrast between the wild weather outside and the snug fireside within. This introductory section, describing Tam drinking happily at the inn, has a structure of its own, and moves to a climax at the end of the seventh verse paragraph. The first twelve lines give us first a brief but vivid impression of market day at a country town, with the evening closing in, and then an equally vivid picture of the farmer's wife waiting suspiciously at home for his return. . . . (pp. 282-83)

There is a pause here, before Burns proceeds to nail the general description down by applying it to Tam o' Shanter, in four sturdy lines:

This truth fand honest Tam o' Shanter,
As he frae Ayr ae night did canter,
(Auld Ayr, wham ne'er a town surpasses,
For honest men and bonny lasses).

The parenthetical remark about "auld Ayr" and its inhabitant adds just the note of familiarity, of personal knowledge, that the mood of the poem requires.

This is an anecdote told by someone who knows the hero and his environment; Tam becomes one of us, and the casual note of compliment to Ayr puts the reader, as it were, up at the bar, having a drink with the narrator.

The perspective shifts a little in the lines that follow. After another pause (and it should be noted how effectively Burns places his pauses and varies his tempo) the narrator takes the reader by the arm and moves with him to the rear of the pub, from which they look at the back of the unconscious Tam as he drinks at the bar with his cronies, and remind themselves of his faults and of his waiting wife. . . . And as the narrator lets himself go in depicting Tam's wife's view of Tam (which becomes as it proceeds also our view of him), he breaks out with a somewhat beery generalization:

Ah, gentle dames! it gars me greet,
To think how mony counsels sweet,
How mony lengthen'd sage advices,
The husband frae the wife despises!

The narrator is lost for a moment in contemplation of the stupidity of men (of other men, that is). And all the time Tam, growing more and more unconscious of the demands of domesticity, morality, or even self-preservation, is drinking happily at the bar with his cronies. . . . Here there is another pause, and then the narrator again describes how the hour is growing later and the night wilder. . . . (pp. 283-84)

And then we come to the climax of this interior and to the end of the first section of the poem. . . . The picture of the jovial interior is expanded, in a blaze of happy sympathy, into a celebration of Tam's mood. The double rhymes ("happy" and "nappy"; "treasure" and "pleasure") help to give the impression of a grand, carefree, snap of the fingers, while the final rhyming of "glorious" with "victorious" sounds a slightly drunken organ note which swells the climax of this account of Tam's state of mind.

There is a long pause now, and the echoes of that "glorious" and "victorious" die away in the reader's ears. Then, in a most interesting transitional passage, the tone is suddenly changed, and the narrator, using standard English and talking with deliberate sententiousness, brings the cold world of reality into this warm atmosphere. First, we have a series of deliberately poetic generalizations about the transitory nature of human pleasures, and the application is then punched home with a proverbial statement in simple, direct language and a return to Scots diction and to Tam. . . . Mr. Edwin Muir cites the eight lines in standard English as proof of his thesis that ever since the end of the Middle Ages the Scot, because of the peculiar linguistic and cultural situation in which he found himself, has had to feel in Scots and think in English. But it would have been easy for Burns to have found a number of Scots proverbial lines which would have expressed the thought conveyed by the lines about the poppies and the borealis. The point here is not, surely, that the poet is introducing *thought* and must therefore employ standard English, but that he is being deliberate, cold, and formal, in order to contrast the unwelcome truth about pleasure with Tam's cosy feeling about it. The English in these lines is a deliberately "fancy" English, piling up simile after simile as though to draw attention to the literary quality of the utterance. . . . Burns is seeking a form of expression which will set the sternness of objective fact against the warm, cosy, and self-deluding view of the half-intoxicated Tam, and he wants to do this with just a touch of irony. What more effective device than to employ a deliberate neoclassic English poetic diction in these lines?

The next verse paragraph builds up the storm scene until it reaches the point where the name of the Devil can be introduced. (pp. 285-87)

We return to Tam and follow him as he rides "thro' dub and mire," crooning to himself to keep his courage up. . . . We now move, after a pause, to another paragraph, in which Kirk-Alloway is introduced as a climax of a series of horrors. . . . Tam hears the sound of "mirth and dancing" coming from the kirk, and at this point Burns pauses, and breaks into an exclamation of wonder at the boldness which whisky can inspire. This interruption effectively keeps the reader in suspense and gives him an excuse to dismiss, if he so wishes, all that Tam saw as the product of the man's drunken imagination. (It is to be noted that Burns nearly always provided this "out" in his supernatural scenes: yet before the poem is over we find that he has made all details *but one* (Maggie's loss of her tail) capable of rational explanation. This set the formula used ever since in tales of the supernatural.)

Inspiring bold John Barleycorn!
What dangers thou canst make us scorn!

Thus inspired, Tam presses forward, in spite of the reluctance of Maggie his mare:

And, wow! Tam saw an unco sight!

This sharp, sudden, exclamatory line is very different in movement from the slower exclamation about the effects of whisky. . . . In the later line he is not halting the narrative to make a generalization but pressing forward into his tale in a mood of sudden excitement and astonishment. There follows immediately the eerie catalogue of what Tam saw. . . . (pp. 287-88)

The note of superstitious terror is exaggerated here almost to the point of absurdity, and certainly to the point where some kind of humorous effect is achieved. Here is the devil of folklore, Auld Nick, surrounded by all his traditional properties. The objects described are so monstrously horrible that they are not quite real, like the setting of an eighteenth-century Gothic novel, and so a note of comic mockery emerges, as though Burns is gently laughing at people who could believe in such things. Yet this note does not lessen the suspense. Tam all this while has remained motionless on his mare, watching the incredible scene, and the longer the description the more interested we become in finding out how Tam has reacted. But Burns deftly increases our suspense with another exclamation, one of a series planted effectively at intervals throughout the poem. . . . (p. 289)

We return to Tam, whose discerning eye has picked out one of the witches as a "winsome wench and wawlie," though Burns makes clear in a parenthetical description of her that once she grew to her full witch status she would do serious damage in the countryside. For a moment, however, the picture of Nannie dancing is human and strangely touching. . . . The suggestion of a fall from an earlier happy, human state gives a momentary flash of pathos to the narrative; but it is modified by humor and not sustained long enough to threaten the mood of the poem as a whole.

The next verse paragraph describes Nannie's furious dancing, the verse getting faster and faster, carrying the reader along with a rush, until he becomes identified with Tam as he shouts applause. And with that shout the scene changes abruptly:

Till first ae caper, syne anither,
Tam tint his reason a' thegither,
And roars out, "Weel done, Cutty-sark!"
And in an instant all was dark:
And scarcely had he Maggie rallied,
When out the hellish legion sallied.

It is interesting that the change is described without taking a new paragraph: to begin a new paragraph after Tam's shout would be to suggest a pause between the shout and the resulting change, whereas the effect of sudden alteration is desired. So Burns describes the beginning of the witches' attack without taking breath and only after he has got the attack going does he pause. The next paragraph continues and elaborates the description of the pursuing witches and the fleeing Maggie. . . . (pp. 290-91)

At this moment of suspense Burns deliberately tantalizes the reader again by holding up the narrative while he wags his finger and shakes his head at Tam. The poet's mock-sympathetic confidence in his hero's doom has comic implications, which are reinforced by the imagery:

Ah, Tam! Ah, Tam! thou'll get thy fairin!
In hell they'll roast thee like a herrin!

Maggie pushes on; the verse—after that sudden slowing down—gains speed again, until Tam and his mare gain the bridge, and safety, for witches cannot cross running water. But Nannie, pressing close behind, had removed poor Maggie's tail. . . . (p. 291)

There is an abrupt pause at this point. The story is now told, but the poet's tone indicates that something more is to come. And, after the expectant pause, it does come—a mock moral, a deliberately absurd oversimplification of the meaning of the tale to make it a warning against drinking and wenching. . . . And on that note of "Remember!"—like the speech of the ghost in *Hamlet*—the poem comes to an end.

Among the many qualities of **"Tam o' Shanter"** which show Burns's technical skill in handling this kind of verse narrative—the effective use of the octosyllabic couplet, the variations in tempo, the use of the verse paragraph, and the placing of the pauses— perhaps the most remarkable is his handling of the *tone* of the poem. The tone is at once comic and full of suspense, shrewd yet irresponsible, mocking yet sympathetic; there is a fine balance here between mere supernatural anecdote and the precisely etched realistic picture, and it is maintained throughout the poem. **"Tam o' Shanter"** is the work of a virtuoso. (p. 292)

David Daiches, in his *Robert Burns,* Rinehart & Company, 1950, 376 p.

JOHN C. WESTON
(essay date 1982)

[In the following excerpt, Weston examines Burns's satirical technique.]

There has long been a belief that Burns's satire is essentially comic, that there is really no bite to it, that it proceeds from a person of gentle good humour, whose veins flow with the milk of human kindness. . . . It is easy to take the edge from Burns's poems because of his obvious charm, *joie de vivre,* and sentimental benevolence. And one is tempted to do so in order to make Burns a cheery companion generally pleased with his world. But one must not do so, because his edges were formed by the harsh world in which he struggled and to which his satire responds.

Burns certainly does not have a misanthropic view like Swift's, nor does he effect his satiric purpose, as Juvenal does, by disgusting us with loathsome descriptions of physical detail reflecting moral depravity. If we were to divide all satire into Horatian (comic) and Juvenalian (tragic), Burns's satires, with the single exception of **'Address of Beelzebub'**, would be on the Horatian side of the line, although unlike Robert Fergusson, whose satires are all strikingly like Horace's, only **'To a Louse'**, if indeed it is a satire at all, and per-

haps **'Address to the De'il'**, are strictly Horatian. But that Burns's satires are not tragic, black, visceral does not mean that they are merely gently bantering and wittily amusing. Their power derives from the fierceness of Burns's hatreds and his intention to wound his adversary. The splenetic and the friendly temperament can exist together. . . . (pp. 36-7)

[Class] conflicts and economic insecurities make his satire complex and full of felt emotions. His kirk satires attack the Evangelical faction on the parish level and thus social control and by implied extension the state church, Whigs, and Hanoverianism; but they nevertheless attack a popular tradition and side by implication with the Moderates and Deists, the upper hierarchy of the kirk and the controlling class supporting it through patronage. However, in several kirk satires the warmth, fun, and colourful humanity of the popular religion shows through the ridicule of Calvinism and in at least one (**'Holy Fair'**) the Moderates get their lumps for being boring, English, and sycophantic. The political satires consistently attack the possessing class and the state: landlords, reactionary politicians, monarchy. But with the exception of one poem, **'Address of Beelzebub'**, the attack is softened, modulated by indirection (dialogue, dramatic voice, humour). (pp. 43-4)

Critics have conceived of Burns as a friendly, comic satirist not only because of the obvious warm humanity of his character and their desire to mystify his radicalism but because of his almost invariable satiric practice of using an ironic voice, what he called 'ironic satire, sidelins sklented'. The speaker of the poem represents the group attacked, the ostensible view of the poem is the very view attacked in it. In the kirk satires, the speaker is sympathetic to the Evangelicals; in the political satires, to the Whigs, the Hanoverians, and repressive landlords, and anti-Jacobins. We take direct expressions of hostility as more sincerely felt. Artfulness and cunning indirections seem to soften the force of the enmity. Further, the imaginative projection of self necessary to speak from the position of one's enemy, indicates a humane understanding, and even at times produces a somewhat sympathetic villain, like Holy Willie, whose very high spirit of pretence and gall we are awed by. (p. 48)

If the satirist uses the voice of his enemy, he can degrade him by putting low words and figures in his mouth. Thus the satiric device of what David Craig calls 'subjugation' is with Burns a product and ancillary of his characteristic method of the opponent's voice. . . . **'Holy Willie's Prayer'** and **'A New Psalm'** . . . expose the speaker's religion by the crudeness of his terminology and his provincialism by giving his Deity a completely local orientation. Holy Willie uses the pulpit diction of a country High-flyer to portray his primitive God, who seeks pleasure and glory by whimsically choosing a few and letting the rest of

His creation suffer in Hell-fire and brimstone, and who is called upon to blast the basket, store, kail and potatoes of Willie's village enemies and to reward Willie himself with 'temporal mercies'. He exposes his moral insensibility by the gutter-talk of his confession and his craven excuses.

The psalmist in his hymn treats British politics in the same terms as the members of a kirk session would speak of parish affairs. A provincial Calvinist dialectic is imposed upon matters of high state. This is a kind of satirical levelling: by calling down the same anathema upon both the enemies of George III and a local Moderate minister, the Scots-Whig kirkman exposes his own provincial inability to discriminate. He is shown to see the whole world through the small lenses of his local vision.

Both **'Twa Herds'** and **'The Ordination'** employ the traditional figure of the minister as a shepherd protecting his congregation as a flock of sheep against such heretical dangers as weasels, badgers, foxes, and poisoned water. The first of this pair uses the metaphor centrally, as the title suggests, to determine the whole poem. The expanded metaphor creates an allegorical beast fable. Both degrade the affairs of the Evangelical party by the speaker's expressing those affairs in their own barnyard images and figures. In both, the speakers show their unfeeling enthusiasms by the bloody terms of their appeal for floggings, hangings, and transporting of personified qualities of the Moderate faction.

'The Dean of the Faculty' uses subjugation less extensively than those we have been considering, but it is clearly there. Burns has his speaker degrade himself by his ludicrous Biblical allusions, his partisan assumption that God is on his side, his vulgarity ('Which shews that Heaven can boil the pot / Though the devil piss in the fire'), and in general his tendency, like the New Psalmist, to interpret politics from a Calvinistic viewpoint: like the Calvinist God, the Faculty chose Dundas not for merit (parallel to works) but to demonstrate their own 'gratis grace and goodness'.

One need not explain the more straightforward choice of **'Address of Beelzebub'**: the devil speaks in character and thus condemns his own position, which is equated with that of the rackrenting peers. Burns is saying, in effect, that the rapacious Highland landlords are of the devil's party. The devil speaks to them in language they can understand, their own. There is no trace here, of course, of Burns's more common treatment of the devil (from *Paradise Lost*) as hero (as in **'Address to the De'il'**) and (from Scots folklore and sermons) as comedian (in **'Tam o' Shanter'** and in **'The De'il's awa wi' th' Exciseman'**). . . . (pp. 51-2)

The speaker of **'The Holy Fair'** is an Evangelical only ambiguously, unlike the unfaltering zealous spokesmen of **'Twa Herds'** and **'Ordination'**; and only by understanding the difference can one understand **'The Holy Fair'**. If Burns had merely wanted in **'The Holy Fair'** to attack Calvinism generally for petty puritanism and tyranny, as in the other two poems, his speaker in this would have upheld those values. He would have accompanied to the fair those allegorical personages introduced at the beginning of the poem, Hypocrisy and Superstition, and he would have attacked Fun. But Burns wanted to attack Calvinism for something more particular, its blind inability to cope with the human spirit, its incapacity to relate meaningfully to human desire, in other words, its unreality, its inappropriateness to people. Thus Burns chose a speaker who is generally on the side of life and enjoyment without thinking about it much, so that he reports on pleasures with innocent, wide-eyed admiration, but who admires the pulpit oratory of Evangelical preachers and condemns the cold sermon of one Moderate and the favour-seeking sermon of the other. . . . He implies his rejection of Hypocrisy and Superstition as companions to the fair, but applauds both in the auldlicht sermons. The auld-licht bias of the speaker is not only historically accurate, because the Evangelicals were the popular party, but emphasizes the ironic anomaly of the parishioners' views. The speaker does not much like the 'greedy glowr' of the elder who takes the admission fee, nor the 'screw'd-up, grace-proud faces' of a group of saints, but he admires the frenzied preaching of Moodie and condemns the 'cauld harangues, / On practice and on morals' of the new-licht Smith. He defends alcoholic drink at length but is very affected by Black Russell's rant. The whole poem is determined by ironic contrasts between social pleasure and religious fear, between the body and the soul, between erotic and divine love; and the division in the speaker between his allegiance to the High-flyer preachers and to social pleasures is just another one of these ironic contrasts that serve to indict Calvinism for unreality, for being, in spite of its pride in a rigorously logical theology, a religion full of the wildest contradictions because its message, if not its manner, is not adjusted to warm humanity.

The speaker of **'The Kirk's Alarm'** has the same general views as those in the other kirk satires, but they do not function strongly. He calls for support for orthodoxy in united opposition to M'Gill's dangerous book, but he insults the auld-licht ministers at the same time he calls them forward to do their duty. There is consistent subjugation, by the use of low diction and imagery. There is obvious amusement in having one enemy, unconscious of the effect he is producing, insulting more enemies, but, unlike all the others, there is no exploitation of the ironic voice to achieve consistent effects, Burns being in a too rousingly disrespectful mood in this boisterous song to be very fastidious about singleness of viewpoint.

In **'Address to the Deil'**, Burns uses an interesting variation of his favourite satiric technique. Instead of causing the dramatic voice to express the sentiments of his opponent unalloyed, he makes a mixture. He wanted to ridicule certain Scots attitudes towards the devil: the superstition, love of folk lore, the intimacy, the scapegoating. Therefore he causes the person who makes the address to demonstrate these attitudes. But Burns also wanted to contrast a warm humanity to the kirk's hostility to the devil. Therefore he caused the speaker to have, besides those traditional Scots attitudes to the devil just mentioned, a sentimental heart, one appropriate to a man of feeling, capable of pitying the devil . . . and incapable of understanding how even a devil could take pleasure in the pain of others. . . . Thus for a complicated satire, he created a comic, mixed voice, part ridiculed, part exemplary. (pp. 52-4)

['A Dream' and 'The Twa Dogs'] are departures from Burns's usual technique in satire. His gentle ridicule of the royal family in **'A Dream'** is done by assuming the pose of a naïve, downright, frank country person, a moderately loyal Hanoverian, who innocently runs on, with occasional sarcasms, in the royal presence. Burns in his ordinary manner would allow us to hear how a wild Whig, a rabid royalist, anti-Jacobite celebrates the king's birthday. **'The Twa Dogs'** is of course a dialogue poem, and the voices, therefore, after the opening narrative, are those of a workingclass dog and an aristocratic dog. The attack on the cruelty, moral indifference, triviality, and psychosis of the aristocracy is not accomplished by a single ironic voice, as in his other satires, but by both voices, more particularly by the two naïve misunderstandings made by Luath: (1) that the aristocrats have to be absent from their estates to serve Britain; (2) that they are happy. Both of these errors provide Caesar with an occasion for damning descriptions. Luath is a kind of straight man in a comic routine. And his simplicity calls into question his idealized description of the generally happy life of the poor, in spite of the injustices they suffer, which heightens by ironic contrast the self-inflicted miseries of the gentry.

Because Burns spoke his satires in the dramatic voice of his Scots adversaries, most are in vernacular Scots, a few in Scots-English. Thus he avoided in his satires the genteel pose of Henry Mackenzie's Anglicized man of feeling, which is a dreadful poison in much of his poetry, one of his serious deficiencies. Tied to colloquial expression by his chosen satiric manner, he wrote a body of serious poetry in Scots, contrary to his usual practice of writing in English when he felt very solemnly serious about something. . . . He was able to express his most serious class resentments in Scots vernacular satire, turning to his advantage, by the device of the enemy's voice, the severely truncated native language and literary tradition he inherited, which has been said, with too little discrimination, to be too exclusively rural to communicate serious, contemporary ideas. Burns's adversaries had deficiencies Burns wanted to expose. Part of those deficiencies was a rural language of relatively narrow reference and restricted purview. Burns used that very language to attack them and in so doing he wrote some satires which rank very high in eighteenth-century European literature. (pp. 54-5)

John C. Weston, "Robert Burns's Satire," in *The Art of Robert Burns,* edited by R. D. S. Jack and Andrew Noble, Barnes & Noble, 1982, pp. 36-58.

DAVID SAMPSON
(essay date 1985)

[In the following excerpt, Sampson discusses major themes of Burns's work, assigning the poet a unique position in the literary and moral traditions of both England and Scotland.]

Burns confronted the English literary milieu as the representative of an essentially foreign culture, Scottish, rural, and 'low', although he did so with the authority of poetic excellence. If his authority was his own, his originality was that of his culture. (p. 16)

The one poem most responsible for popularizing the exemplary image of the Scottish poor, the poem to which nearly every commentator on the subject referred, was Burns's **'The Cotter's Saturday Night'**. (p. 19)

Rarely in poetry has the good will of the reader been so assiduously solicited and his expectations so fully satisfied as in **'The Cotter's Saturday Night'**. Burns's stated purpose at the outset of the poem is to demonstrate the moral superiority of cottage life in such a way that the cultivated reader, represented in the poem by Robert Aiken, a solicitor and an early patron of Burns, would be willing to emulate the cotter. To this end Burns is anxious to establish his credentials before a polite audience, whether Scots or English, that relied for its standards of excellence on English literature. The poem is sprinkled liberally with references to Pope, Gray, and Goldsmith and, at its most solemn (when, for instance, Burns is directly addressing Aiken or summarizing biblical themes), its style is wholly English. The poem's characters are defined by those qualities which formed the themes of much of the poetry of Cowper, Burns's contemporary: the cotter is characterized by his industry and piety, his wife by her thrift and devotion, their children by their modesty and obedience. . . . Burns, as his influence suggests, was concerned to advertise his subject, and this attitude informs the most mundane details of the poem; he describes supper, for example, as 'the healsome *Porritch*, chief of SCOTTIA's food'. . . . Fergusson, by contrast, in the poem which was Burns's immediate model ['The Farmer's Ingle'], establishes the wholesomeness of his farmer's food by implicit rather than assertive recommendation, describing it within the context of a busy steaming kitchen:

> Wi' butter'd *bannocks* now the *girdle* reeks,
> I' the far nook the *bowie* briskly reams;
> The readied *kail* stand by the chimley cheeks,
> And had the riggin het wi' welcome steams. . . .

Whereas Burns's porridge is merely nutritious, Fergusson's supper seems almost active with the vitality of robust health. Burns could not afford this kind of detail because of the risk of offending an audience to whom the association of food with kitchens was more remote. He carefully precludes offence by qualifying every description: the family prepares for the reading ['wi' serious face, the cotter opens the Bible 'with patriarchal grace,' laying aside 'his bonnet rev'rently' and reading 'with judicious care' and 'solemn air'.] . . . By this profusion of adjectives and adverbs Burns determines the reading of the poem, continually intervening to emphasize the proper response: 'They tune their hearts, by far the noblest aim'. . . . (pp. 20-1)

Burns's emphasis in the poem on the 'heart' as the source of the moral sense belongs to the cult of sensibility and explains the appearance of the villainous seducer . . . , a stock figure in sentimental literature whose very inhumanity serves to confirm the fundamental benevolence of ordinary folk. One of Burns's favourite books ('a book', he wrote, 'I prize next to the Bible') was Henry Mackenzie's popular novel *The Man of Feeling* (1771). One of the first and most influential reviews of Burns's poems was written by Mackenzie. . . . In describing Burns as a 'Heaven-taught ploughman', a kind of animated 'natural object', Mackenzie was responding to the way in which poems such as **'The Cotter's Saturday Night'** repress any traces of individuality that might hinder the satisfaction of the reader's emotional expectations.

But if **'The Cotter's Saturday Night'** generally flatters the reader in the sentimental manner, Burns allowed himself at one point to be more aggressively 'democratic', equating the aristocrat with the seducer as the villain of melodrama:

> What is a lordling's pomp? a cumbrous load,
> Disguising oft the *wretch* of human kind,
> Studied in arts of Hell, in wickedness refin'd! . . .

Significantly it is this passage alone that attracted criticism. . . . [John] Wilson's objection to these lines alone suggests that he was otherwise content to be 'laid asleep', in his own revealing words, by Burns's accommodating manner. His criticism does not merely compare the falsity of this passage with the truth of the rest of the poem; he also rebels against the poet's intentions becoming too intrusively obvious and blunt. It is Burns's animus, a reminder of an individual author with which the reader must attempt to come to terms, that upsets Wilson.

'Saint' or 'ranter' were alternative images of the poet common to Scots verse. One of Burns's contemporaries, John Learmont, a journeyman gardener, published an answer ['Answer to the Devil's Reply to Mr. Burns'] to a poem which was itself a hostile reply to Burns's **'Address to the De'il'**. It includes the following advice:

> Flee straught to Lon'on, or St. Peter's place,
> An' for my blessin' learn some better grace:
> For gif ye stay ye'll whiggish rites embrace,
> An' roar an' rant,
> Syne turn the biggest rascal i' the place,
> Or Psuedo [*sic*] Saint. . . .

In many ways Burns also felt able to choose between the stances of ranter or 'Psuedo Saint', as though he were less concerned with the moral principles they represented than with the dramatic possibilities they opened up. He sometimes looked to London for his imprimatur; sometimes he was defiantly coarse. Burns's temperamental idiosyncrasies responded to ambivalences inherent in eighteenth-century Scots vernacular poetry. (pp. 21-2)

The image of Burns conveyed by his poetry is not so much that of the uneducated peasant participating in polite culture by means of inspiration as that of the articulate representative of an alternative culture. At the same time, blurring this distinction and to some extent accounting for the differing interpretations, the poetry is disjointed, its tone ranging inconsistently from defiance through irony and humour to sentimental appeal.

'The Twa Dogs' is an example of the way in which a potentially offensive poem is muted by a difficult tone. Burns draws the conventional contrast between the imaginary suffering of the wealthy and the real hardship of the poor. The qualities he admires are identical to those by which Crabbe and Cowper define the virtuous poor: industry, contentment, familial care, and duty. Burns draws no distinction, however, between approved qualities and what he calls 'social Mirth' . . . : drinking, talking politics, 'caressan' . . . , precisely the activities that conventionally characterized the idle poor. The difference between 'social Mirth' and the 'deep debauches' of the gentry . . . refers not to an ideal of self-restraint but to a sense of community, of fellow-feeling, evoked by the phrase 'common recreation'. . . . The only point of contact

A manuscript page of "Tam o'Shanter," in Burns's handwriting.

between the two groups is the despised 'factor' and the only relationship prefigured is one of commercial exploitation. At the same time Burns implies that pity is an inappropriate response to the humiliation of the poor. The high-born Caesar exclaims: 'I see how folk live that hae riches, / But surely poor-folk maun be *wretches!*' . . . But Luath, the 'ploughman's collie' . . . , replies: 'They're no sae wretched's ane wad think' . . . and introduces the description of the common pastimes of the poor. In other words, the world of the poor is not simply a more humble version of the gentry's but is distinct, with its own customs and centres of interest. The poor fulminate against the church and the government, and gossip about Londoners with amused wonder at an alien and slightly silly way of life; they 'ferlie at the folk in LON'ON' . . . ('ferlie' means 'to marvel' but it is also a term of contempt).

To conclude our reading here would be to present the poem as more straightforward than it actually is, for the opening description of the two dogs provides a context which resonates with contrasts and parallels. The companionship of the dogs, for example, measures by contrast the hostility of the two social groups. At the same time their relationship dramatizes the fellow-

feeling of the poor; they sit down to discuss 'the lords o' the creation' . . . just as 'the bodies' . . . discuss politics over their ale. The first image of a cotter is reminiscent of the description of the dogs: 'A *Cotter* howckan in a sheugh'. . . . The dialogue form of the poem works to expose the dogs' mutual ignorance, emphasizing the separation of the two social groups rather than expressing two contrasting viewpoints. Caesar, however, represents not the gentry so much as the average reader, uninformed but curious and concerned, more closely associated with the gentry than with the poor but nevertheless distinct from both.

Burns's sympathies are never in doubt; he appears in the poem as Luath's owner. Like Luath, Burns is the representative of the poor and asks from the reader the kind of response that Caesar freely gives in spite of his social remoteness. The form of this appeal is as unorthodox as that of **'The Cotter's Saturday Night'** is conventional. Burns's real achievement is to establish the characters' dogginess ('Whyles scour'd awa in lang excursion' . . .) and at the same time to convey real voices, thus enlivening the descriptions of the 'social Mirth' of the poor by means of the dogs' convincing *camaraderie*. Burns expects, but does not plead for, approval:

Hech man! dear sirs! is that the gate,
They waste sae mony a braw estate!
Are we sae foughten an' harass'd
For gear to gang that gate at last! . . .

The passage brilliantly realizes a sense of exasperation quickening into anger, the stress falling dismissively on 'gear', the hard consonants spat out at the end. Even the juxtaposition of exclamations, the outright 'Hech man!' with the satirically effete 'dear sirs!', is social comment; an assertion of equality between dog and dog, based on shared 'manhood', is coupled with a sneering reference to a form of address which insists on a more deferential relationship determined by status. Nevertheless, the fact that this voice has a dog's body gives it an air of arch effrontery which, while apparently reinforcing the poem's sympathy with the lower classes, actually undercuts the seriousness of the commentary. The poem is, after all, only 'a lang digression' . . . from the more genial business of hunting mice and moles; its occasional bitterness is merely shrugged off at the end: 'up they gat, an' shook their lugs, Rejoic'd they were na *men* but *dogs*'. . . . (pp. 29-30)

The humour of **'The Twa Dogs'** emasculates the social criticism. It is not therefore perhaps surprising that the poem's early readers responded only to its conventional themes without apparently noticing the transformations which Burns's animus had effected. Burns introduces the traditional imagery of contentment, not, it seems to me, as an ideal for the poor to imitate, but in order to berate the gentry for so often destroying the degree of well-being that the poor manage to retain. The contentment of the poor in the poem does not extend to their position in the social hierarchy: 'They'll talk o' *patronage* an' *priests*, Wi' kindling fury i' their breasts'. . . . Nor does it comprise reconciliation to labour. Burns never portrays agricultural labour as anything but demeaning and oppressive. . . . In fact, the contentment described in **'The Twa Dogs'** is equivalent to 'social Mirth' and has little to do with the conventional virtues. (p. 30)

'The Holy Fair' similarly proposes gregarious communality as a moral standard by which the religion of the preachers is found wanting. Warnings of sin and retribution are uttered in the midst of drunkenness and love-making. The carefree nature of the gathering implicitly questions the thundered terrors of the sermons; hell becomes a neighbour's snores. . . . Compared with the Fun of the crowd the religious orthodoxy is Superstition and Hypocrisy. Burns is less concerned to establish the falsity of the sermons, however, than to emphasize their unintelligible foreignness. One preacher has an 'English Style' . . . , his speech is 'barren' . . . , another offends against common sense, personified as a fleeing member of the crowd. . . . The religion of the preachers is embodied by the 'chosen swatch, / Wi' screw'd up, grace-proud faces'. . . . Their individuality is lost within the conformity of the Elect. Vain of their distinction, they nevertheless disapprove of difference in others. Burns's debunking description, 'swatch', implies that their election has less than divine sanction. The word recalls an earlier group, 'a batch o' *Wabster lads*' . . . ; their company represents the shared interests of youth and locality rather than the repressive anonymity of adherence to principle. The most important conversions that occur at the meeting are, in parody of the intended progression, from stone to flesh, that is, from the sterile fixity of the 'chosen swatch' to the amorous vitality of the *'Wabster lads'*:

How monie hearts this day converts,
O' Sinners and o' Lasses!
Their hearts o' stane, gin night are gane
As soft as only flesh is. . . .

Dr Hugh Blair objected to the poem's irreverence, criticizing in particular the lines '[Moodie] speels the holy door, / Wi' tidings o' s-lv-t-n'. . . . Burns in response altered 's-lv-t-n' to 'd-mn-t-n' in the Edinburgh edition. It has been suggested that this is a great improvement. It seems to me to be, on the contrary, false to the poem. The audience are simply not conscious of the need for salvation, and hence Moodie's preaching is to them irrelevant nonsense; they look forward not to heaven but to the assignations with which the meeting and the poem conclude. Burns's emendation tames the poem by narrowing its focus; the satire is no longer directed in this passage at a repressive religion which seeks to regiment the heterogeneous communality of

the crowd, but at a ranting clergyman. Yet the true religious values inhere not in the barren religion of the sermons but in the fecund geniality of the crowd:

Wi' *faith* an' *hope*, an' *love* an' *drink*,
They're a' in famous tune
For crack that day. . . .

To 'charity', with its contemporary implications of superiority, Burns preferred 'love', a word that is more democratic and perhaps more faithful to the original. In any case, it is a word that has less in common with vainglory than with the companionability of drinking. (pp. 31-2)

It was clearly the drama rather than the moral quality of human relationships that fascinated Burns. Those who seek to regulate their behaviour by an immutable morality act according to a view of humankind which, he thought, could be easily exposed: 'There's some are fou o' *love divine*; / here's some are fou o' brandy'. . . . Spiritual ecstasy is as superficial and transient as the effects of brandy. In **'The Jolly Beggars'** . . . , the promiscuity of the women and the rough bullying of the men are presented as humanity without its self-conscious pretensions. . . . Burns is nevertheless not denying the existence of qualities beyond an anarchic hedonism. Transcending this, in **'The Jolly Beggars'**, is the honest courage and selfless dedication of the soldier, the indignant loyalty of the woman to her executed Highlandman. What matters to the soldier is not the justice of his wars but the fact that someone relies on him; what concerns the woman is not the legality of her lover's death but the fact that he was killed. If their courage and anger are occasional only, and inspired partly by whisky, this in itself does not make Burns's irony satirical. The precise extent of Burns's irony in the poem, which has been the major concern of recent criticism, becomes significant, it seems to me, only if the poem is read primarily as a social critique. The fact that the poem has been interpreted both as a satire, in which 'the victims of [Burns's] irony . . . are not his moral readers, but the beggars themselves', and as a portrayal of heroism in the face of oppression has led Karl Miller to argue that the poem is flawed by a compromising ambivalence which 'allows healthy and wealthy readers to play at outlaws, while consoling them with the thought that love and liberty must be paid for in rags and sores and stumps'.

Just as the poem's pervasive irony prevents the inference of any certain social attitude, however, so it also precludes any final judgement by the reader, and makes the sense of play which Miller identifies potentially disconcerting rather than consoling. . . . What the poem invites us to accept is that questions of honour and love are, when men and women come together, tested on the pulse; law and morality are, finally, abstractions, inventions for the sake of social convenience: 'Courts for Cowards were erected, / Churches built to please the Priest'. . . . Even these statements of principle, however, are presented with a spirit of bravado that implies its own criticism. (pp. 32-3)

Burns's poems tend to be relatively unstructured; they casually open and close with little development. As with **'The Twa Dogs'**, they often seem a digression within a larger context of activity. It is as if the contingencies of the situation dictate the thoughts and emotions presented so as to emphasize their dramatic, fleeting, open-ended quality. Yet the effect of this is not, I think, to reduce the poetry to a succession of shallow sensations. At his best Burns dramatizes living and changing individuals who give voice to their feelings idiomatically, tangentially, casually, incoherently, as real people do. 'Conviviality' implies the ability to live together; in Burns's poetry it is prior to, but does not exclude, 'higher qualities'. At its best Burns's humour is neither evasive, as in **'The Twa Dogs'**, nor cynical. In **'The Holy Fair'** and **'The Jolly Beggars'**, for example, it is sceptical, questioning not the existence of 'higher qualities' but their permanence and universality and, above all, resisting their elevation to fixed standards of judgement. (p. 33)

The belief in 'natural man', whose universal nature is obscured by adventitious distinctions of status and wealth, a belief made popular by Rousseau, coincided to some extent with the emphasis of moral philosophers on a common human nature. Part of the 'lesson of contentment' which James Currie read in **'The Twa Dogs'**, for example, was that 'human nature is essentially the same in the high and the low'. Indeed, Luath and Caesar are identical in speech and manner; all that separates them are an accident of birth and Caesar's brass collar. This is equally open, however, to the interpretation that social distinctions are unjustifiable, an interpretation which, it seems to me, the poem as a whole favours. Belief in the artificiality of social distinctions seems to have been stronger in the Scots than in the English literary tradition. Perhaps the central theme of [Ramsay's] *The Gentle Shepherd* is that the 'Poor and Rich but differ in the Name' . . . , a formulation of the argument significantly different from [James] Currie's. Currie characterizes the social distinctions as a natural division ('the high', 'the low'), while attempting to prevent possible antagonism by stressing a common humanity; Ramsay, on the other hand, suggests that social distinctions are merely adventitious classifications.

Moral-sense theory might be thought to have had some influence on this dichotomy, for, popularly interpreted, it meant that virtue depended for its definition not on rational principles or social orthodoxies but on a natural law recognized by the individual heart. . . . [The] moral sense was often justified by an appeal to the natural law traditionally held to sanction the social order. Burns, however, by advocating in his best poems a relativity which was both moral and social, and so challenging the notion of hierarchically arranged 'spheres o' being', emphasized the individualist aspect of the theory to an extent that was more unacceptable to the body of reviewers. The latter tended to assert a view of society at once sufficiently hierarchical to ensure their own centrality, and sufficiently homogeneous to be regulated by a universal code of behaviour which [Francis] Jeffrey defined as 'prudence, decency and regularity'. . . . In his first commonplace book Burns wrote that

no man can say in what degree any person besides himself can be, with strict justice, called wicked. Let any of the strictest character for regularity of conduct among us examine impartially how many of his virtues are owing to constitution and education; how many vices he has never been guilty of, not from any care or vigilance, but from want of opportunity, or some accidental circumstance intervening.

These sentiments, which inform poems such as **'The Jolly Beggars'**, represent a challenge to Jeffrey's triad. It was a challenge met in part by a strict division of Burns's poetry into pathos, which required serious attention, and comedy, which, as Scott wrote of **'The Jolly Beggars'**, deserved 'indulgence for a few light strokes of broad humour'. As the popularity of **'The Jolly Beggars'** indicates, standards of decorum were relaxed for comic poems. (pp. 35-7)

[Burns's politics] extended from Jacobinism to Jacobitism; both were opposed to English authority and both appealed to his image of himself as a social rebel. For the same reason he adopted Milton's Satan as a literary hero. As in his poetry, these professions of belief were the temporary poses of a shifting personality. Scottish and English reviewers alike attempted to accommodate Burns's poetry to the standards of English literary culture in which the principles of 'prudence, decency and regularity' were paramount. Jeffrey's nationalism took the form of asserting that the Scots could beat the English at their own game. Because of this the distinctiveness of Burns's poetry was either overlooked or assumed to be Jacobinical. But an essential aspect of Burns's rebelliousness was his opposition to the very concept of principles as immutable ideals. When Burns 'startled' the reader, the reader was to some extent expected to be aware of a game. . . . Burns's declarations of allegiance are always disconcertingly liable to go 'pop'. At the same time it would be unjustifiable to conclude that Burns's sense of humour reveals his social dissatisfaction to have been nugatory. The effect of poems such as **'The Holy Fair'**, **'Tam o'Shanter'**, and **'The Jolly Beggars'**, if the reader consents to them, is to render less earnest the reader's commitment to the principles questioned. Burns was concerned not to replace one set of principles with another but to ensure that whatever beliefs were invoked by those in authority would be made to respect human vitality and individuality. (pp. 37-8)

Burns's scepticism ensured that the weapon which his poetry provided for the armoury of Scottish nationalism had to be handled gingerly. Scottish literati, accustomed to the condescension of their English counterparts, seized the opportunity given by Burns's excellence to claim for Scotland an indigenous literary culture of a quality comparable to England's. In doing so, however, they did not abandon what they had come to accept as the measure of quality, namely, Anglicized gentility; Burns's own wavering between polite and vernacular idioms mirrors this ambivalence. They were forced to be selective in their championing of Burns and as a result missed the chance to encourage what was truly distinctive in his poetry: the challenges it posed to the genteel, predominantly English tradition of poetry by emphasizing the 'low' and anarchic aspects of the Scottish vernacular tradition. (p. 38)

David Sampson, "Robert Burns: The Revival of Scottish Literature?" in *The Modern Language Review,* Vol. 80, Part I, January, 1985, pp. 16-38.

SOURCES FOR FURTHER STUDY

Angus-Butterworth, L. M. *Robert Burns and the 18th-Century Revival of Scottish Vernacular Poetry.* Aberdeen: Aberdeen University Press, 1969, 309 p.

> Study of Burns's position in the context of Scottish literary history. The book includes biographical information and relates it to the composition of Burns's poetry.

Brown, Hilton. *There Was a Lad: An Essay on Robert Burns.* London: Hamish Hamilton, 1949, 260 p.

> Critical overview.

Carswell, Catherine. *The Life of Robert Burns.* London: Chatto & Windus, 1930, 467 p.

> Sympathetic biography of Burns, long considered a standard.

Daiches, David. *Robert Burns and His World.* London: Thames and Hudson, 1971, 128 p.

> Biography augmented by relevant information of Scottish life and conditions in Burns's time. The book includes copious photographs and illustrations.

Fitzhugh, Robert T. *Robert Burns, the Man and the Poet: A Round, Unvarnished Account.* Boston: Houghton Mifflin Co., 1970, 508 p.

> Biography of Burns's life and discussion of his works. Fitzhugh states that he proceeds from the premise that Burns himself is the highest authority for a Burns biography, and thus the text is interspersed with numerous quotes from Burns's poetry and correspondence.

Jack, R. D. S., and Noble, Andrew, eds. *The Art of Robert Burns.* London: Vision Press, 1982, 240 p.

> Collection of several essays on Burns.

William S. Burroughs

1914-

(Full name William Seward Burroughs; has also written under pseudonyms William Lee and Willy Lee) American novelist, short story writer, nonfiction writer, essayist, scriptwriter, and editor.

INTRODUCTION

*A*n innovative and controversial author of experimental fiction, Burroughs is best known for *Naked Lunch* (1959), a surreal account of his fourteen-year addiction to morphine and other drugs. Intended, according to Burroughs, to be "necessarily brutal, obscene and disgusting," the novel was first published in Europe and aroused heated critical debate in the United States even before its American publication, which followed three years of court trials for obscenity. Although some reviewers denounced the book on moral grounds, condemning its graphic descriptions of drug injections, casual murders, and sadomasochistic homosexual acts, such writers as Mary McCarthy, Allen Ginsberg, and Norman Mailer lauded it as an experimental masterpiece notable for its radical break with traditional language and narrative. In *Naked Lunch* and his subsequent fiction, Burroughs uses addiction as a metaphor for the human condition, postulating a cosmic vision in which all human consciousness is addicted to some form of illusory gratification. As Burroughs stated, his major concern throughout his work has been "with addiction itself (whether to drugs, or sex, or money, or power) as a model of control, and with the ultimate decadence of humanity's biological potentials."

Burroughs is the grandson of the industrialist who modernized the adding machine and the son of a woman who claimed descent from Civil War General Robert E. Lee. In 1936, he received his bachelor's degree in English from Harvard University. In 1944, he began using morphine. During the 1950s, Burroughs, together with Allen Ginsberg and Jack Kerouac, helped found the Beat movement. The writers who became part of this group produced works that attacked moral and artistic conventions. Burroughs's addiction to increasingly harder substances, his unsuccessful search for cures, and his travels to Mexico to elude legal authorities are recounted in his first novel, *Junkie: The Confessions of an Unredeemed Drug Addict* (1953; republished as *Junky*). Written in the confessional style of pulp magazines under the pseudonym William Lee, the novel received little critical notice. In 1957, Burroughs traveled to London to undergo a controversial drug treatment known as apomorphine. Following two relapses, he was successfully cured of his addiction.

Ostensibly the story of junkie William Lee, *Naked Lunch* features no consistent narrative or point of view. The novel has been variously interpreted as a condemnation of the addict's lifestyle, as an allegory satirizing the repressiveness of American society, and as an experiment in form, exemplified by its attacks upon language as a narrow, symbolic tool of normative control. Consisting of elements from diverse genres, including the detective novel and science fiction, *Naked Lunch* depicts a blackly humorous, sinister world dominated by homosexual madness, physical metamorphoses, and cartoon-like characters, including Dr. Benway, who utilizes grotesque surgical and chemical alterations to cure his patients. Escape from the imprisoning concepts of time and space are dominant themes in this work and in Burroughs's later fiction, reflecting the addict's absolute need for drugs and his dependency on what Burroughs termed "junk time." Burroughs explained the book's title as "the frozen moment when everyone sees what is on the end of every fork."

Burroughs's unused writings from *Naked Lunch* make up the bulk of its sequels, *The Soft Machine* (1961), *The Ticket That Exploded* (1962), and *Nova Express* (1964). During the process of writing these works, Burroughs, influenced by artist Brion Gysin, developed his "cut-up" and "fold-in" techniques, experiments similar in effect to collage painting. Collecting manuscript pages of his narrative episodes, or "routines," in random order, Burroughs folds some pages vertically, juxtaposing these with other passages to form new pages. This material, sometimes drawn from the works of other authors, is edited and rearranged to evoke new associations and break with traditional narrative patterns. In the surrealistic, quasi-science fiction sequels to *Naked Lunch,* Burroughs likens addiction to the infestation of a malignant alien virus, which preys upon the deep-seated fears of human beings and threatens to destroy the earth through parasitic possession of its inhabitants. The title of *The Soft Machine,* a novel emphasizing sexuality and drugs as a means of normative control throughout history, indicates the innate biological device which allows the virus entry into the human body. Mind control through word and image is the subject of *The Ticket That Exploded.* In this novel and in *Nova Express,* Burroughs suggests a number of remedies to the viral infestation. Although he expresses a cautious optimism, the crisis remains unresolved, and humanity's fate is uncertain at the saga's end.

In 1970, Burroughs announced his intention to write a second "mythology for the space age." Although his recent novels have generally received less acclaim than *Naked Lunch* and its sequels, critics have discerned a remarkably straightforward approach to these works, which rely less on cut-up strategies and horrific elements and more on complex, interrelated plots and positive solutions to escaping societal constraints. As Jennie Skerl noted: "In Burroughs's recent fiction, pleasure and freedom through fantasy balance the experience of repression, bondage, and death that the earlier works had emphasized." The universe of *The Wild Boys: A Book of the Dead* (1971) is similar to that of Burroughs's earlier books but is epic in proportion, encompassing galactic history and the whole of humanity in its scope. In this work, which again involves a destructive virus, a near-future Western society is fragmented into large totalitarian cities and vast unsettled regions. The cities are challenged by "the wild boys," a libertarian, homosexual society of nomadic gunfighters engaged in guerrilla warfare with the forces of control. The wild boys are led by Audrey Carsons, one of Burroughs's alter egos. Carsons also appears in two interrelated works, *Exterminator!* (1973) and *Port of Saints* (1975), which feature a similar blend of science fiction, juvenile novel, Western novel, and fairy tale. Time and space travel figure prominently in *Cities of the Red Night: A Boys' Book* (1981), in which detective Clem Snide traces the source of the alien virus to an ancient dystopian society. *The Place of Dead Roads* (1984) transfers the conflict to near-future South America, where descendents of the wild boys ally themselves with Venusian rebels in an escalating battle for galactic liberation.

Burroughs's recently published novel, *Queer* (1985), was one of his first literary attempts and is considered a companion piece to *Junkie.* According to Burroughs, the book was "motivated and formulated" by the accidental death of his wife in Mexico in 1951, for which Burroughs was held accountable. The novel centers once again on William Lee, chronicling a month of withdrawal in South America and his bitter, unrealized pursuit of a young American male expatriate. Harry Marten stated that the book functions as "neither a love story nor a tale of seduction but a revelation of rituals of communication which substitute for contact in a hostile or indifferent environment."

Burroughs is also well known for his nonfiction works. *The Yage Letters* (1963) contains his mid-1950s correspondence with Allen Ginsberg concerning his pursuit in Colombia of the legendary hallucinogen *yage.* Further correspondence is collected in *Letters to Allen Ginsberg, 1953-1957* (1982). During the mid-1960s, Burroughs became an outspoken proponent of the apomorphine treatment, claiming that its illegal status in the United States was the result of a conspiracy between the Food and Drug Administration, police, and legal authorities. His arguments are presented in *Health Bulletin, APO 33: A Report on the Synthesis of the Apomorphine Formula* (1965) and *APO 33, a Metabolic Regulator* (1966). Burroughs's observations on literary, political, and esoteric topics appear in a collaborative venture with Daniel Odier, *Entretiens avec William Burroughs* (1969; revised and translated as *The Job: Interviews with William Burroughs*), and in his recent collection, *The Adding Machine: Collected Essays* (1985). *The Third Mind* (1979), written in collaboration with Brion Gysin, is a theoretical manifesto of their early "cut-up" experiments. Burroughs has also written a screenplay, *The Last Words of Dutch Schultz* (1970).

Burroughs's controversial novels have provoked extreme critical reactions, ranging from claims of genius to allegations that he is little more than a pornographer. While his work is generally offensive to those with bourgeois values, it has elicited much serious criticism, and Burroughs is regarded by many scholars as an innovative, even visionary, writer. Critics credit Burroughs's hallucinatory prose and antiestablishment views with inspiring the Beat movement and such counterculture groups as hippies and punks. Among other accomplishments, Burroughs has, perhaps more effectively than any other author, rendered the nightmarish, paranoid mind-set of the drug addict. Harry Marten observed that Burroughs "has been mixing the satirist's impulse toward invective with the cartoonist's relish for exaggerated gesture, the collage artist's penchant for radical juxtapositions with the slam-bang pace of the carnival barker. In the process, he has mapped a grotesque modern landscape of disintegration whose violence and vulgarity is laced with manic humor."

(For further information about Burroughs's life and works, see *Contemporary Authors*, Vols. 9-12; *Contemporary Authors New Revision Series*, Vol. 20; *Contemporary Literary Criticism*, Vols. 1, 2, 5, 15, 22, 42; *Dictionary of Literary Biography*, Vols. 2, 8, 16; *Dictionary of Literary Biography Yearbook: 1981;* and *Major 20th-Century Writers.*)

CRITICAL COMMENTARY

ALVIN J. SELTZER

(essay date 1974)

[An American educator and critic, Seltzer is the author of *Chaos in the Novel: The Novel in Chaos* (1974). In the following excerpt from this work, he assesses the struggle between chaos and control in Burroughs's novels.]

Burroughs' novels are so chaotic that life itself seems calm and ordered by comparison. Structure and plot simply do not exist; characters are flat, interchangeable, and strangely unimportant; the narrative thrashes about with no apparent direction or coherence, and words scatter like so many jig-saw-puzzle pieces thrown into the air. Each book is a montage of startling images, fragmented episodes, scraps of dialogue, patches of exposition, and cultural echoes ranging from Renaissance drama to modern poetry, from Christian and Eastern myth to Madison Avenue jargon. The language itself is a pastiche from the media of journalism, film, literature, Holy Scriptures, textbooks. Burroughs seems to have cast the novel out like a net to catch whatever debris it can drag in from the outside world, and the result is a circus of confusion: laughs, thrills, horrors— you name it, it's all there. Images zoom by, explode, writhe, choke, puke themselves up into new combinations. Subtle satire merges with outrageous burlesque; low comedy mixes with the most sordid reality; the worlds of business, science, and entertainment become indistinguishable. Everything gushes together in a dizzying experience that revolts, amuses, shocks, and confuses the disoriented reader. Even familiar images, adjectives, styles, and references cannot be worked with in a conventional manner, since the random juxtaposition which places them in strange contexts somehow distorts their reality into a grotesque reflection of the sort that greets us in funhouse mirrors, nightmares, and drug fantasies. The reader, in short, can never feel comfortable, and his insecurity works for the author, who forces him into a position of openness to new ways of viewing which lead to experiencing new layers of feeling. (p. 339)

[Burroughs] forces his novels to spill out of any frames—even their own—which might confine them to a single system. Material from one novel is likely to appear intact in another novel—and such material ranges from phrases to whole chapters. Interestingly enough, though, the novels do seem to vary in quality and impact, and this suggests that an examination of Burroughs' four most important novels may help to deter-

Principal Works

Junkie: Confessions of an Unredeemed Drug Addict (novel) 1953; republished as Junky, 1977

Naked Lunch (novel) 1959

The Soft Machine (novel) 1961

The Ticket That Exploded (novel) 1962

Nova Express (novel) 1964

The Last Words of Dutch Schultz: A Fiction in the Form of a Film Script (screenplay) 1970

The Wild Boys: A Book of the Dead (novel) 1971

Exterminator! (short stories) 1973

Port of Saints (novel) 1975

The Third Mind (nonfiction; with Brion Gysin) 1978

Cities of the Red Night: A Boy's Book (novel) 1981

The Place of Dead Roads (novel) 1984

The Adding Machine: Collected Essays (essays) 1985

The Western Lands (novel) 1987

mine where and why his techniques are most successful. While some of his effects seem to enlarge the novel's capacity to communicate multilevel experience, others seem only to bore and desensitize the reader, thus closing off more possibilities than are opened. By allowing himself maximum freedom, Burroughs opens the doors to chaos so widely that he invites at the same time admiration for artistic courage and condemnation for artistic irresponsibility. (pp. 339-40)

[In *Naked Lunch*] all structure is discarded: one can pick up the novel and start his reading anywhere, then go forward, backward or jump around at will—it makes no difference where you get on or where you get off. . . . [The book] offers free license to the imagination. It is not a question of stopping when one has made his point, for there is really no point to be made; the novel is set up to break down any rational approach to it, any logical system which attempts to reduce a multilevel experience directed toward our central nervous systems . . . to a one-dimensional experience aimed at the intellect. There is no logical beginning or end to a book drifting in chaos. (p. 341)

Like any prescription for mysticism, however, what provides the source of revelation for one man may remain sheer nonsense to another. Random techniques such as the cutup can sometimes provide astonishing effects, and occasionally even produce a revelation. That in itself, though, is really no more than what poets have been doing for quite some time. . . . By leaving the context to chance, however, Burroughs hopes to surprise himself as well as the reader, for he is seeking to break through traditional modes of perception. From his interviews, we can assume that he

has included within the novels themselves only those experiments which he felt to be successful. . . . But all these experiments have in my own experience provided interest and amusement only at isolated moments amid long stretches of boredom. Although I think *Naked Lunch* does sustain interest through most of its parts, the obvious danger for Burroughs is the tendency of random techniques to sacrifice cumulative effect for the impact of an instant. (pp. 343-44)

[Burroughs *does* have a vision] to impose on his material, even though he has denied it. And the subtlety of his method here can hardly be a result of accidental juxtaposition. . . . What seemed at first a series of incoherent, unrelated, and chaotic passages turns out to be a highly unified sequence, projecting different facets and manifestations of the same idea. In this way, the writer throws his thoughts to us on many levels at once, thereby breaking through the usual one-dimensional response of our intellects. The mental idea is embodied emotionally . . . so that it will jar us not just in our minds, but deep down in our central nervous system as well. One may of course argue that great art has always done this—and that is true—but to do Burroughs justice, he would probably say that modern life has dulled us emotionally to the point where very few traditional artistic experiences can have much impact. Shock treatments are necessary to awaken us from our numbed existences, and the deeper the shock penetrates, the more of ourselves will spring back to responsive life.

In *Miracle of the Rose,* Genet uses prison life as a powerful metaphor for an existence of pure despair, and Burroughs sees the life of a junky as a suitable metaphor for a political system that dominates and degrades the individual. Again, while sex and sordidness are used to communicate vision, they are not themselves the real subject of either novel. *Naked Lunch* is no more an exposé of the junkies' world than *Miracle of the Rose* is an exposé of criminal or prison life. It is, rather, an exposé of all modern life, but patterned on the junk scene as a recurring image of such devastating emotional impact that the reader will be repulsed by what is ultimately his own "normal" life. Abstractions will not work: we need to be shocked into awareness of what our own lives in this society have become, and Burroughs has found the metaphor to break through our apathy.

Like Genet, Burroughs also uses *his* world (that of the addict) as a metaphor for Hell, the lowest level of human abjection and degradation. . . . The junky's life is painful, unproductive, uneventful; yet even the horror of it is lost on the victim himself, who is oblivious of his surroundings and conscious of nothing but his physical need to ease the pain of his body. As his mind decays and his body rots, the junky becomes so much carrion to be devoured by the buzzards streaming out of the sewers of the contaminated city. (pp. 347-48)

Burroughs has said that his fiction is deliberately addressed to the area of dreams, and this is no doubt why surrealistic effects run rampant throughout the book. In almost every case that I can think of, the surrealistic detail adds horror and hideousness to what is already seamy material; as a result, our repugnance is heightened to such an extreme that we either recoil or laugh. In short, we are forced to *react,* and strongly, to release the emotion created by intense shock. . . . The alert reader of *Naked Lunch* is indeed treated to a surrealistic feast, but the effect is rather like that of Thyestes' learning of the contents of his meal. Our gorges rise right along with our intellects and emotions.

At other times, however, the distasteful description evokes laughter rather than revulsion, probably because the exaggeration of reality is so incredible that we simply cannot take it seriously enough to feel threatened by it. The talking asshole is a case in point, but the book abounds with great comic passages based on the same kind of shock effect that typified the repugnant ones. The difference between black horror and black humor is difficult to pin down, but some of the funniest episodes here involve an uncharacteristically bland acceptance of the most outrageous and chaotic situations. (pp. 349-51)

[We] may hate ourselves for laughing, because the events here are completely degrading and inconsistent with any notion we may have of the dignity of human life. But the validity of the satire finally does justify Burroughs' savage treatment of the human species. Like Swift's, his contempt results from idealism, and finds expression in the most debased aspects of life. . . . Death, disease, blood, shit, urine, and the like lurk on every page of *Naked Lunch* because they are finally what matter most in the process of living and dying. (p. 352)

[What] *does* the reader experience through *Naked Lunch?* Above all, a dizzying trip through time and space in the form of random images and episodes which explode all around him, juxtaposing in new combinations aspects of his life and society that he must see as intolerable. In the guise of a gigantic carnival, modern civilization is out on display, and Burroughs takes us on all the rides: the spiritual dimension of modern life is so much hocus-pocus; political systems are all parasitic, inefficient, and inhumane; social and personal relationships are sadistic, manipulative, and exploitive. In each case, Burroughs uses metaphor, analogy, and allegory to attack a decadent system. (p. 354)

To an extent, *Naked Lunch* certainly succeeds in breaking down traditional associative patterns, yet the ironic (though perhaps predictable) result is that we eventually adapt to the new pattern and are just as restricted to it as we were to all the others. After all the farts have faded, after the scatology has lost its shock value, after the sexual perversions have lost their punch, etc., we ultimately settle down to a vicious but hardly unprecedented satire of American life. . . . Certainly such material is not accidental, nor does its creator seem to be a revolutionary novelist—Faulkner's novels are filled with similar passages of broad satire. Ironically, the most brilliant effects in *Naked Lunch* are not usually those that smash our traditional word-image associations, but those that communicate *through* them.

Still, no matter how many conventional techniques it contains, *Naked Lunch* is unique in its encompassing so many diverse effects in a single work. Time and space are opened up in a way that enables the novel to breathe more freely; lurching through chaos, the novel no longer stops to organize what it sees into a consistent, unified vision but is instead content to consider the diversity of experience and pour it through the reader's senses with a barrage of images so striking that they stick in his mind and filter down through his nervous system. (pp. 356-58)

Burroughs pushes the reader through a cyclone of images and events, and as reality and dream become indistinguishable, as the novel embodies elements of other media, and as language begins to transmit new associative signals, we feel the literary form expanding to the dimensions of life itself. If the experience is inconclusive, if the novel seems inseparable from the chaos caught within it, then we might console ourselves with the thought that art has always sought new directions from which to approach reality, and perhaps it was inevitable that it would eventually try them all at once. (pp. 358-59)

Burroughs' increasing disrespect for his reader, his form, and the language which creates and communicates becomes more apparent with each novel, and the novels themselves become duller, more private, more indulgent, and less impressive. What seemed shocking in *Naked Lunch* becomes repetitious in *The Soft Machine,* and alternately annoying and uninteresting in *Nova Express* and *The Ticket That Exploded.* What was innovative and exciting in *Naked Lunch* becomes stale and tiresome in the succeeding novels. And finally, while the creator of *Naked Lunch* seems original and challenging in his refusal to orient the reader to his chaotic work, the creator of the other novels seem simply self-indulgent and irresponsible. As his earlier preoccupations settle into propaganda, his experiments into formulas, and his intensity into petulance, Burroughs has less and less to offer both the reader and the novel. As his theories become more explicit, they become less powerful; as his methods become more obvious, they become less effective; and as his books become more chaotic, they become, also, more parochial.

What has gone wrong here? For one thing, Burroughs has used up his reader's patience by repeating concepts, effects, and even whole sections that he had already delivered in *Naked Lunch.* For another, he has estranged himself from the reader by permitting his novels to be overridden by the theories behind them; he has fallen into the very trap against which he cautioned us—that of sending the message rather than creating the experience. Finally, as an artist of chaos, he has surrendered so much of his control over his material that the reader, faced with real rather than apparent chaos, simply cannot function, and so has no alternative but to shrug off the whole confrontation as an unnecessary and unproductive experience. This is not to say that Burroughs' later books are devoid of many stunning effects, but only that they seem to me increasingly isolated. Certainly, none of these novels has the richness or power of *Naked Lunch,* and none impresses as a whole.

The Soft Machine, like *Naked Lunch,* contains a good many startling images, but here they are quite obviously the result of cutup methods. By using a limited number of control words and phrases, and juxtaposing them arbitrarily until a variety of combinations has been accumulated, Burroughs puts into the novel itself those techniques which he had implied in interviews were primarily for his own revelation, and preceded the actual act of creation. Now he is either unwilling or unable to select from all the alternatives the one he considers most interesting and valuable; instead, he throws them all in. . . . Burroughs has given us a do-it-yourself novel: here are the pieces; you put it together. The artist of the cutup has become a cutup artist. First cut up, then fold in, splice together, and just follow the simple directions. . . . (pp. 359-61)

What *is* a reader to do with . . . a jig-saw-puzzle passage? If we attempt ingeniously to read coherence into it, we are simply resorting to traditional control systems, which is just the habit Burroughs wants to break us of. So finally, we give up all attempts to *read* the novel and simply gaze at the words. For a writer who has promised to expand our awareness, Burroughs seems much more successful at turning us into retarded readers, staring dumbly at blocks of print while—except for a few striking combinations which amuse, evoke, or disgust—nothing at all is happening in our minds or emotions. The reader is put into a trance.

One wants to be fair to Burroughs, and certainly the reader who works hard may find some scattered rewards which he feels justifies the chaos. But if the author is intent on keeping his own mind out of the goings-on here, then *we* might as well make up our *own* list of images and play with *them.* . . . By abdicating his role of leader, Burroughs may be asserting humility or arrogance; it is hard to tell which. At any rate, the result is not a novel, but the raw materials for one that the

reader may put together for himself. This means, of course, that the novel must be a personal and different experience for every reader, a fact which renders critical evaluation meaningless. Whereas the novel traditionally has tried to universalize experience, Burroughs seems intent on personalizing it. That is, in fact, his message for the reader: resist all control systems and storm the reality studio where your life is being programmed by the parasitic exploiters (in this case, the media) who, by sending images through the soft machine inside your head, are controlling your mental associative patterns, and ultimately your body, your soul, your life. (p. 362)

While Burroughs' random techniques seem quite legitimate as a means for the novelist to make new connections, their appearance in the novel itself can be justified only so far as the reader can be expected to share in the revelation. Men have never lacked the means to blow up existing institutions; few things are as easy as finding explosive devices. But rubble and debris are no compensation for an outmoded system; the artist must accept the responsibility of rebuilding new structures to provide new insights. Destruction is always exciting—and *The Soft Machine* does generate some startling effects—but creation is infinitely more valuable. Burroughs has succeeded in his mission to storm the reality studio, but he has failed to make that mission seem worthwhile.

The Ticket That Exploded, is another thesis novel . . . which includes its own book of exercises for the reader to help himself break out of the control system which lives his life for him. . . . Again, Burroughs' motives seem noble, while the novel itself seems unenlightening and tedious. Again he promises to promote awareness while the novel itself only dulls it. A new raid on the reality studio has yielded approximately the same results: the theory remains more exciting than the work it has engendered. (p. 364)

[*The Ticket That Exploded*] offers us a way out of words that seems more practical than the attempts of Beckett and Robbe-Grillet, yet less successful artistically. . . . [Many passages] from the book are didactic, direct addresses to the reader—hardly fictional embodiments of Burroughs' ideas just because they appear in a "fictional" work. The author now seems to have turned into a hard-core, hard-sell huckster, always hawking the same idea and trying to hammer it into our heads by sheer force rather than by the subtleties of artistic propaganda, which can at least make its appeal on a deep level. As author, Burroughs is failing more and more to present his readers with a valid artistic experience. As pauses for ideological messages (even ones professing anti-ideological sentiments) become increasingly frequent, the show itself seems thinner and weaker for the intrusions. (p. 366)

Still, if Burroughs fails to pull the reader beneath

words to a deeper, more conscious level of awareness (and this, of course, is a matter of opinion), he does prescribe some remarkably ingenious exercises to help get us there on our own. . . . Is Burroughs serious? Probably not—and yet why not? His examples are extreme and amusing, but the basic idea behind them is valid and important: a desensitized society must be reawakened to life; cells must once again become *living* tissue, and man's acts of love must become acts of intense, spontaneous feeling rather than word-induced gestures, image-controlled responses, etc. When communication finally becomes total and conscious, then words will no longer be necessary and can drop off into extinction. (pp. 366-67)

[Words] have become for Burroughs the chief villains of our lives, feeding off our cells like tapeworms until all substance has been eaten away and we are left as empty as ghosts. The struggle against control systems, which seemed little more than a science-fiction plot in *The Soft Machine,* here becomes *the* significant theme for the modern writer. Burroughs has now justified his chaos as a vital liberating force by which the novelist can lead humanity out of its Hell and into the world of the living. His experiments thus become crucial channels through which the reader can escape an existence that belongs in the grave. (p. 368)

Nova Express includes much of the material from Burroughs' other novels, and by now the junk and virus metaphors have become as stale as our old associations of "naked" with "bodies." Burroughs here is still trying to explode familiar connotations of words in order to create new life; he is still trying to dissociate words from images as a means toward reaching silence; and he still spends most of his time explaining his approach rather than making it work for us. . . . [In] Burroughs' novels, the language of instruction is actually used for purposes of instruction, and the result seems increasingly to resemble a tract much more than a novel. . . . Burroughs insists on throwing theory and practice together with the result that his novels have no life of their own but seem to contain by chance whatever is found between the covers.

"The enemy exists where no life is," says Burroughs, and so *Nova Express* becomes another attempt to expose the enemy for us—the word, the image, the junk, the virus which eats away at our tissues and sends us into a state of mental stupor where we are blinded to the possibilities of our lives. . . . Clearly, we must take a cure for the junk habit that is restricting our sense of reality, and Burroughs continues to find hope in the equivalent of apomorphine—the resistant drug that enabled him to break his own junk habit. . . . There does come a time when the reader himself would indeed enjoy a bit of silence, but Burroughs' constant banter seems only to intrude on our senses, keeping the quiet away. Finally, we come to the conclusion that

great—and conscious—fiction may itself induce the highest, purest, most appropriate form of silence. The work of art that arrests us seems to freeze our own thoughts and keep us suspended in a timeless, spaceless world where our minds are quiet and watchful as our senses take in new experience. Burroughs' novels *rant*—they *will* not keep quiet. . . . The novelist that doth protest too much stands at the door of his creation, keeping us out. There is no room for *us* at the still center of the novel's world.

Burroughs' theories are fascinating, and his experiments often exciting, but there is such a rush of sensations, such a conglomeration of diverse effects that we are distracted, rather than liberated, in his later novels. Only *Naked Lunch* seems somehow to remain vivid in the memory as an experience that has engrossed us sufficiently to cut out the outside noise of the world which confuses us. True, it contains as much chaos as life itself, but it also creates, ultimately, its own system which justifies and compensates for the confusion it forces us to submit to. Ironically, too, it is most effective because its effects have been most controlled by the artist. Theories and techniques may be interesting, but they can never count for much until they are embodied as vital experience; and it is the novel which has so often given life to ideas by using the art of fiction to humanize, formalize, or intensify them into emotional realities. Burroughs finally fails the reader not because his experiments are too radical for us to adjust to, but because most of his novels do not offer us *enough* to adjust to. Life slips in and out of his works, but is rarely held there long enough for the novel to begin breathing its own life. And for the reader, that is all that ever really matters. (pp. 373-74)

Alvin J. Seltzer, " 'Confusion Hath Fuck His Masterpiece': The Random Art of William S. Burroughs," in his *Chaos in the Novel: The Novel in Chaos,* Schocken Books, 1974, pp. 330-74.

WILLIAM S. BURROUGHS WITH DANIEL ODIER
(interview date 1974)

[Odier is a Swiss novelist, critic, and poet who has written popular thrillers under the pseudonym Delacorta. In the following excerpt from his *The Job: Interviews with William S. Burroughs* (1974), he and Burroughs discuss Burroughs's novels, the cut-up technique, Burroughs's relationship to the Beat movement, and the role of politics in works of literature.]

[Odier]: *Your books, since* **The Ticket That Exploded** *especially, are no longer "novels"; a breaking up of novelistic form is* *noticeable in* **Naked Lunch.** *Toward what end or goal is this break-up heading?*

[Burroughs]: That's very difficult to say. I think that the novelistic form is probably outmoded and that we may look forward perhaps to a future in which people do not read at all or read only illustrated books and magazines or some abbreviated form of reading matter. To compete with television and photo magazines writers will have to develop more precise techniques producing the same effect on the reader as a lurid action photo.

What separates **Naked Lunch** *from* **Nova Express?** *What is the most important evolution between these two books?*

I would say that the introduction of the cut-up and fold-in method which occurred between *Naked Lunch* and *Nova Express* is undoubtedly the most important evolution between these books. In *Nova Express* I think I get further from the conventional novel form than I did in *Naked Lunch*. I don't feel that *Nova Express* is in any sense a wholly successful book.

You wrote: "Writing is fifty years behind painting." How can the gap be closed?

I did not write that. Mr Brion Gysin who is both painter and writer wrote "writing is fifty years behind painting." Why this gap? Because the painter can touch and handle his medium and the writer cannot. The writer does not yet know what words are. He deals only with abstractions from the source point of words. The painter's ability to touch and handle his medium led to montage techniques sixty years ago. It is to be hoped that the extension of cut-up techniques will lead to more precise verbal experiments closing this gap and giving a whole new dimension to writing. These techniques can show the writer what words are and put him in tactile communication with his medium. This in turn could lead to a precise science of words and show how certain word combinations produce certain effects on the human nervous system.

Did you use the techniques of fold-up and cut-up for a long time before moving on to the use of the tape recorder? What were your most interesting experiences with the earlier technique?

The first extension of the cut-up method occurred through the use of tape recorders and this extension was introduced by Mr Brion Gysin. The simplest tape recorder cut-up is made by recording some material and then cutting in passages at random—of course the words are wiped off the tape where these cut-ins occur—and you get very interesting juxtapositions. Some of them are useful from a literary point of view and some are not. I would say that my most interesting experience with the earlier techniques was the realization that when you make cut-ups you do not get simply random juxtapositions of words, that they do mean something, and often that these meanings refer to some future event. I've made many cut-ups and then later recognized that the cut-up referred to something that I read later in a newspaper or in a book, or something that happened. To give a very simple example, I made a cut-up of something Mr. Getty had written, I believe for *Time and Tide*. The following phrase emerged: "It's a bad thing to sue your own father." About three years later his son sued him. Perhaps events are pre-written and pre-recorded and when you cut word lines the future leaks out. I have seen enough examples to convince me that the cut-ups are a basic key to the nature and function of words.

For you the tape recorder is a device for breaking down the barriers which surround consciousness. How did you come to use tape recorders? What is the advantage of that technique over the fold-in cut-up technique?

Well, I think that was largely the influence of Mr Brion Gysin who pointed out that the cut-up method could be carried much further on tape recorders. Of course you can do all sorts of things on tape recorders which can't be done anywhere else—effects of simultaneity, echoes, speed-ups, slow-downs, playing three tracks at once, and so forth. There are all sorts of things you can do on a tape recorder that cannot possibly be indicated on a printed page. The concept of simultaneity cannot be indicated on a printed page except very crudely through the use of columns and even so the reader must follow one column down. We're used to reading from left to right and then back, and this conditioning is not easy to break down.

When you have arrived at a mix or montage, do you follow the channels opened by the text or do you adapt what you want to say to the mix?

I would say I follow the channels opened by the rearrangement of the text. This is the most important function of the cut-up. I may take a page, cut it up, and get a whole new idea for straight narrative, and not use any of the cut-up material at all, or I may use a sentence or two out of the actual cut-up.

It's not unconscious at all, it's a very definite operation . . . the simplest way is to take a page, cut it down the middle and across the middle, and then rearrange the four sections. Now that's a very simple form of cut-up if you want to get some idea of one rearrangement of the words on that page. It's quite conscious, there's nothing of automatic writing or unconscious procedure involved here.

You don't know what you're going to get simply because of the limitations of the human mind any more than the average person can plan five moves ahead in chess. Presumably it would be possible for someone with a photographic memory to look at a page and cut it up in his mind, that is, put these words up here and those up there . . . I've recently written a film script on the life of Dutch Schultz, now this is perfectly straight writing. Nonetheless I cut up every page and suddenly

Burroughs in Paris, 1962.

got a lot of new ideas that were then incorporated into the structure of the narrative. This is a perfectly straight film treatment, quite intelligible to the average reader, in no sense experimental writing. (pp. 27-30)

In making up a text out of various materials, what is the importance of points of intersection? Starting with this material, how do the "sequences" and "rhythms" organize themselves?

The points of intersection are very important certainly. In cutting up you will get a point of intersection where the new material that you have intersects with what is there already in some very precise way, and then you start from there. As to the sequences and rhythms organizing themselves, well, they don't. The cut-ups will give you new material but they won't tell you what to do with it. (p. 32)

Do you think that the prejudice that exists against the cut-up method and its extension can be attributed to the fear of really penetrating into time and space?

Very definitely. The word of course is one of the most powerful instruments of control as exercised by the newspaper and images as well, there are both words and images in newspapers . . . Now if you start cutting these up and rearranging them you are breaking down the control system. Fear and prejudice are always dictated by the control system just as the church built up prejudice against heretics; it wasn't inherent in the population, it was dictated by the church which was in

control at that time. This is something that threatens the position of the establishment of any establishment, and therefore they will oppose it, will condition people to fear and reject or ridicule it. (pp. 33-4)

Your books are rarely obscure or hard to understand, and you have mentioned to me in conversation a desire to become even more clear. Is the concern for clarity consistent with a still vaster exploration of the infinite possibilities offered by your literary methods?

When people speak of clarity in writing they generally mean plot, continuity, beginning middle and end, adherence to a "logical" sequence. But things don't happen in logical sequence and people don't think in logical sequence. Any writer who hopes to approximate what actually occurs in the mind and body of his characters cannot confine himself to such an arbitrary structure as "logical" sequence. [James] Joyce was accused of being unintelligible and he was presenting only one level of cerebral events: conscious sub-vocal speech. I think it is possible to create multilevel events and characters that a reader could comprehend with his entire organic being. (p. 35)

Your characters are engulfed in a whirlwind of infernal happenings. They are bogged in the substance of the book. Is there a possible way to salvation for them?

I object to the word salvation as having a messianic Christian connotation, of final resolution . . . I don't feel that my characters, or the books in which they appear, are reflecting a mood of despair. Actually, in many ways they're in the tradition of the picaresque novel. It's a question of your interpretation of "infernal happenings," some people have much more tolerance for unusual happenings than others. People in small towns are absolutely appalled by some very slight change, whereas people in large cities are very much less upset by change, and if riots go on and on and on people are going to take them as a matter of course; they're already doing it.

Do free men exist in your books?

Free men don't exist in anyone's books, because they are the author's creations. I would say that free men don't exist on this planet at this time, because they don't exist in human bodies, by the mere fact of being in a human body you're controlled by all sorts of biologic and environmental necessities. (p. 37)

You write: "I am a recorder . . . I do not pretend to impose 'story,' plot, or continuity." Is it possible?

I can only answer that question by saying that when I said that I was perhaps going a bit far. One tries not to impose story plot or continuity artificially but you do have to compose the materials, you can't just dump down a jumble of notes and thoughts and considerations and expect people to read it.

"Words—at least as we use them—tend to hide non-physical experience from us." Once one has removed the barriers

which Aristotle, Descartes and Co. put in the way, is this "non-physical experience" parallel to (i.e., interrelated with) physical experience? Is every physical experience therefore undergone on various levels?

Yes, very definitely. For example, so-called psychic experiences are experienced insofar as one experiences them at all through the physical senses. People see or hear ghosts, feel various emanations, presences, etc.

Do you think that classical philosophical thought has had a damaging effect on human life?

Well, it's completely outmoded, as Korzybski, the man who developed general semantics, has pointed out, the Aristotelian "either-or"—something is either this or that—is one of the great errors of Western thinking, because it's no longer true at all. That sort of thinking does not even correspond to what we now know about the physical universe. (pp. 48-9)

Where does humor fit into the scheme of your work?

Well, I think of my work as being, I won't say largely humorous, but certainly having a considerable element of humor.

The hell which you describe, and the accusations which you make, imply their opposites and their expiations; so they might be taken as offering man a way out. It has been said that you are a great moralist; what do you think?

Yes, I would say perhaps too much so. There are any number of things that could be done in the present situation. The point is that they are not being done, none of them are being done. And, I don't know whether there's any possibility of their being done, given the extent of stupidity and bad intentions on the part of the people in power. You're running up against a wall to even point this out; but all sorts of things can be done that would alleviate the present situation. Perfectly simple things in terms of present techniques. What it amounts to is breaking down three basic formulas: one is the formula of a nation. You draw a line around a piece of ground and say this is a nation. Then you have to have police, customs control, armies, and eventually trouble with the people on the other side of the line. That is one formula; and any variation of that formula is going to come to the same thing. The UN is going to get nowhere. What are they doing? They're creating more of these bloody nations all the time. That's one formula. The next formula is of course the family. And nations are simply an extension of the family. And (possibly this is a matter for future techniques) the whole present method of birth and reproduction. Those are basic formulas that need to be broken down. (pp. 50-1)

You set yourself apart from the postwar American novel which does not really know what imagination means. American writers suppose that the public is interested only in real facts, in the most material sense of the word. Your books are widely read in the

United States; perhaps they describe a universe which is at the same time imaginary and real.

Well, yes, I think so. So many novels now really come under the head of journalism, they try accurately to describe just what people actually do. It's rather journalism and anthropology than writing. It seems to me that a novel should rework that, not just dump a lot of purely factual observations on the reader. (pp. 51-2)

What is your relation to the Beat movement, with which you associate yourself? What is the literary importance of this movement?

I don't associate myself with it at all, and never have, either with their objectives or their literary style. I have some close personal friends among the Beat movement: Jack Kerouac and Allen Ginsberg and Gregory Corso are all close personal friends of many years standing, but were not doing at all the same thing, either in writing or in outlook. You couldn't really find four writers more different, more distinctive. It's simply a matter of juxtaposition rather than any actual association of literary styles or overall objectives. The literary importance of this movement? I would say that the literary importance of the Beatnik movement is perhaps not as obvious as its sociological importance . . . it really has transformed the world and populated the world with Beatniks. It has broken down all sorts of social barriers and become a worldwide phenomenon of terrific importance. The Beatniks will go to someplace like North Africa, and they contact the Arabs on a level that seems to me to be more fundamental than the old Arab-speaking settlers, who are still thinking in T. E. Lawrence terms. It's an important sociological phenomenon, and, as I say, worldwide. (pp. 52-3)

[James Joyce's] Finnegans Wake *is generally regarded as a magnificent literary dead end. What is your opinion?*

I think *Finnegans Wake* rather represents a trap into which experimental writing can fall when it becomes purely experimental. I would go so far with any given experiment and then come back; that is, I am coming back now to write purely conventional straightforward narrative. But applying what I have learned from the cut-up and the other techniques to the problem of conventional writing. It's simply if you go too far in one direction, you can never get back, and you're out there in complete isolation. . . . (p. 55)

What is your impression of the commitments of writers who hope to achieve, by political activity, a remedy or an improvement for our civilization? Do you think that this kind of activity tends to limit one's creative capacity, or perhaps reveals its limits?

Well, I think overcommitment to political objectives definitely does limit one's creative capacity; you tend to become a polemicist rather than a writer. Being very dubious of politics myself, and against the whole concept of a nation, which politics presupposes, it does seem to me something of a dead end, at least for myself. I suppose that there are writers who really derive their inspiration from political commitments and who sometimes achieve good results: Malraux is an example. In his early work, like *Man's Fate,* which definitely grew out of his political commitments, and yet was a very fine novel.

The literary techniques to Raymond Roussel attempt to enmesh the writer in a system; yours tend on the other hand to free him. What might be the importance of a technique to a writer?

Well, those can be interesting experiments, some of them will work and some of them won't. Some of these, you can say he's done a very interesting experiment, and it's quite unreadable. I know I've done a lot of that myself. I've done writing that I thought was interesting, experimentally, but simply not readable.

Do you need the reader?

A novelist is essentially engaged in creating character. He needs the reader in that he hopes that some of his readers will turn into his characters. He needs them as vessels, on which he writes. The question frequently asked of a writer is: "Would you write if you were on a desert island and no one would ever read it?"

I would say certainly, yes, I would write, in order to create characters. My characters are quite as real to me as so-called real people; which is one reason why I'm not subject to what is known as loneliness. I have plenty of company. (pp. 55-6)

William S. Burroughs and Daniel Odier, in an interview in *The Job: Interviews with William S. Burroughs* by Daniel Odier, revised edition, Grove Press, Inc., 1974, pp. 27-56.

FREDERICK R. KARL
(essay date 1983)

[An American educator and critic, Karl has written critical studies on English and American literature, including *American Fictions, 1940/1980: A Comprehensive History and Critical Evaluation* (1983). In the excerpt below from that work, he favorably appraises Burroughs's career from *Naked Lunch* through *Exterminator!*]

Well before he met the artist Brion Gysin, whose ideas of collages and cut-ups directly influenced the preparation of *Exterminator!* (written 1966-73, published 1973), William Burroughs had conceived of fiction as a plastic art. Burroughs is perhaps our best example of the writer borrowing from other art forms, the amalgamator of the arts by way of their infusion into the word. Like the action painters of the 1950s, Burroughs conceived of the field (canvas, page) as a series of clashes and conflicts; like the innovators in electronic music or John Cage, he found sounds more significant than traditional communication; like those shaping modern dance, he saw that movement existed for its own sake as much as for its continuity with other movements. Burroughs tried to discover a "montage language." What he found, however we respond to the particulars of his vision, has permanently entered our literature, not only as a reflection of our culture but as an avatar of what we are becoming. Burroughs has positioned himself as no less than an American prophet, a doom-filled Emerson, a no less lyrical Whitman.

Although *Naked Lunch* (published in Paris in 1959, in the United States in 1966) appears avant-garde, even postmodernist, as some critics would have it, the title has a traditional ring to it, recalling works from Dante's *Convivio* to Carlyle's *Sartor Resartus.* Common to each is a metaphor which strives to achieve the real. Despite obvious differences, Burroughs and Carlyle share common characteristics of anger, intensity, and desire to get beneath the "outer garment." Burroughs says that the title was suggested by Kerouac, and that it was unclear to him until his recent recovery from addiction. It means: "NAKED Lunch—a frozen moment when everyone sees what is on the end of every fork."

The metaphor of food recalls not only Dante's banquet but Swift's "Modest Proposal" for the disposition of Irish babies. For Burroughs, a "modest proposal" would be the elimination of all restraints. If we are to comprehend what we are, where we have gone, we must eat a "naked lunch." Since people, he says, favor capital punishment, then let them really rub their noses in "what they actually eat and drink. Let them see what is on the end of that long newspaper spoon." Burroughs's revilement of human practices, all heightened to cross both pleasure and pain, is aimed at liberation of the self, a Sadean measurement of self against others.

In such a probe, degradation is never distant from revelation. The overriding consideration is the self martyring itself in order to approach a form of joy otherwise unattainable. Everything must be experienced on the edge. To gain the junkie's paradise, one must sink to the junkie's hell; they are indistinguishable. Burroughs's work in the 1950s is significant for its adversariness—it was banned in this country and became an underground book—and for its foreshadowing of that explosion of self which characterized the 1960s and 1970s. Through his fictions, we can observe the decades in change; the more the change, the closer the continuity to his racing imagination. (p. 205)

Burroughs moves rapidly into that consummate expression of self, the junkie's self-indulgent paradise, a circuitry of pleasure which drugs can convey and which nothing else—neither sex, nor police, nor personal danger—can enter. Burroughs cites the ultimate

---

John Vernon on fragmentation in Burroughs's novels:

[The] bombardment of objects in Burroughs' novels is the visible manifestation of a world fragmenting itself . . . to the degree that it becomes total administration, and hence total clutter. Burroughs' world is one in which everything is on the verge of achieving complete separation and complete autonomy, it is a world in the state of explosion. "Explosion" is finally (and paradoxically) the most uniform quality of Burroughs' novels, the polarity toward which his world most consistently gravitates. Even administrative control and map-space cannot finally help objects to cohere, since administration and maps have their own separate space. This is why "context" and "landscape" in Burroughs always exist in pure states; they are the ground out of which objects fly and explode, but they are motionless and ideal, sealed-off from those objects. There is the landscape of the City, a mechanical labyrinth, and the landscape of "Nature," the Garden of Delights, a swamp, or a mud flat; and these are not so much environments in which actions occur, as pure spaces for themselves. Actions and incidents that have any continuity usually occur in ill-defined rooms or on an ill-defined plain. Between these, which become less frequent with each novel, the wanderings of consciousness describe objects in a constant state of permutation and explosion, objects deprived of their context, and hence each one in the context of itself, in its own exclusive space. . . . Burroughs' solution to the repressive control that the image of reality imposes is to fragment it and mix it together, to erase all lines between things. If reality is a film, then you loosen its grip by submitting it to a state of explosion, by cutting it up and splicing all spaces and times randomly in together. . . .

John Vernon, in his 1972 *Iowa Review* essay "William S. Burroughs."

---

trip as not that furious activity posited by Kerouac and Cassady, but the passivity of the junkie's inner journey. The junkie is never bored, he says, because he can focus on his shoe for eight hours; only the effectiveness of the drug alters his perception. That absorption in self was the line of liberation for Burroughs. What he is presenting is something very dangerous, and we can see that while he was banned here for his views on drugs and his sexual explicitness, he is really far more threatening in other areas.

Burroughs is Raskolnikov without restraints. For him, the supreme experience is the moment when life and death meet, as in hanging. For then, as is well known, the male ejaculates as the tension of spine and penis are broken. The bursting, explosive, flowing semen is for Burroughs a life force, stilled only by the drug trip. But just as the drug trip brings the individual down to the line between life and death, so does hanging. Burroughs must constantly seek encounters in which life and death meet on the edge. His role is demonic.

The method is to achieve the "ultimate moment" in the ultimate verbal montage, what he strove for more defiantly after he met Brion Gysin. That verbal montage is the linguistic equivalent of the drug-induced fantasies that make up most of his fictions. Almost arbitrarily divided into segments called novels or narratives, the fictions are really one. They are marked by a potentially endless sequence of fantasies, any number of which can be snipped off and combined into a book, called *Naked Lunch, The Soft Machine, The Ticket That Exploded, The Wild Boys,* or *Exterminator!* The center of this exploding universe of montage-ordered images is always William Burroughs or William Lee. Every narrative is also a journey, that journey into fantasy worlds where Burroughs seeks the real, the actual. Interconnected with this journey is the making of art, for the drug-induced fantasies are associated with those experiments with drugs, sex, and synesthetic experiences which characterized much nineteenth-century French poetry. Burroughs is our modern Rimbaud, only wilder, less artistically disciplined.

To gain balance, Burroughs plays off the fantasies in *Naked Lunch* against areas of fact: the Appendix (concerned with addiction), the Introduction (Burroughs's autobiographical "Deposition"), and excerpts from the book's obscenity trial in Massachusetts. Structurally, his so-called novel is also a montage of fact/fiction, long sections of fictional narrative interspersed with large bodies of factual material. In the latter, Burroughs is analytical, even clinical; whereas in the fictional parts, he develops what will be his characteristic style of verbal shorthand. (p. 206)

The key to Burroughs's prose is condensation, a foreshortened voice, as it were. He drops off articles, both definite and indefinite; he leaves off the *s* in the third person singular verb—to achieve a mix of illiterate and literate; he often cuts out subjects for his verbs, or verbs for his subjects—to gain a notational effect. He treads a line between conventional narrative and free association; and although he does not dissolve words, as Joyce did in *Finnegans Wake,* he does dissolve passages by way of rapid movement, montage (long before the "cut-up" method of Gysin), and spinoffs, reeling in his line and then suddenly letting it out. The overall sense is one of great nervousness, great movement and vitality. Burroughs's legacy for the future, I think, will not be his narratives as such, nor his sexual vision of rectums and hard cocks; but his fluid prose style, which conveys vitality in ways Kerouac never achieved despite years of intense experimentation.

Burroughs's description of the "buyer"—the man who sets up a seller for the police but is not himself a user—does not include the full run of his prose strategies, but it does support his sense of irony and negative force: energy expended on doing one thing, while the opposite is shaping up. (pp. 206-07)

The ultimate mechanical man, the buyer is the one for whom the "soft machine" was designed, the man who refuses to see the "naked lunch" at the end of his fork. He joins with Dr. Benway and all those other counterfeit creatures who make restrictive institutions possible, for he achieves his success by negating others' experiences. Burroughs here is moving along the line of pure anarchy, supporting the self that has the right to indulge itself and destroy itself as it sees fit, mounting an assault on all those elements—buyer, Benway, others—who place obstacles in their way. Burroughs's sense of individual freedom recapitulates de Sade's argument, that one achieves such freedom at the expense of others, regardless of consequences, with ruthlessness, cruelty, etc. Burroughs's narratives, then, are meaningful only as drug-induced fantasies, or as pure idea. For in the world outside fantasy or dream, they would be fascistic impulses; or impulses which literature (fiction or otherwise) cannot explain.

As a writer of fantasies, with drugs as the catalyst, Burroughs can enjoy the same broad swings as the allegorist or parodist. He can be as outrageous as Swift in "A Modest Proposal" or the Laputa section of *Gulliver's Travels,* or de Sade in *120 Days of Sodom and Gomorrah.* His hallucinatory version of "on the road" can infuse energy into areas Kerouac retreated from as too wild. The United States, as can be expected, is itself hallucinatory. . . . (p. 207)

The literary advantage of Burroughs's world of hanging boys, endless sex (mainly anal), crumbling cities, continuous movement is that it highlights an America that lacks coherence, a real place which in its confusions equals the fantasy world. Dr. Benway, called in "as advisor to the Freedland Republic," is the organizing genius behind Kafka-land. Benway is an expert in "T.D.," Total Demoralization. In Annexia, he had abolished concentration camps and mass arrests, except under special circumstances, and substituted for brutality what he calls "prolonged mistreatment." The latter, when applied skillfully, gives rise to "anxiety and a feeling of special guilt." The subject does not, of course, recognize he is being mistreated; he must be "made to feel that he deserves *any* treatment he receives because there is something (never specified) horribly wrong with him. The naked need of the control addicts must be decently covered by an arbitrary and intricate bureaucracy so that the subject cannot contact his enemy direct." In Freedland, confusing documents,

missing park benches, ringing bells, police interference are all part of a disarray that allows the individual no opportunity to define himself, subject and object hopelessly jumbled. Burroughs describes a dystopia, pastoral not only gone sour but turned into hell.

Here, Burroughs can place his characters: the Vigilante, the Rube, Lee [Burroughs], the Agent, A. J., Clem and Jody, the Ergot Twins, Hassan O'Leary the After Birth Tycoon, the Sailor, the Exterminator, Andrew Keif, "Fats" Terminal, Doc Benway, "Fingers" Schafer—no longer literary or novelistic characters, but men (never women) who people a middle region of the imagination. Pynchon would pick up this ragtag bunch for his "Whole Sick Crew" in *V.* In common, they are figures of disorder, a crowd that breaks down rather than builds. Energy here is destructive, which is for Burroughs good energy, since it defuses the distorted satisfactions of the real world. Self-induced distortions are preferable to those imposed upon us.

Naked Lunch, then, is a blueprint, a how-to manual: "How-To extend levels of experience by opening the door at the end of a long hall. . . . Doors that only open in *Silence.*" We enter Bluebeard's castle. *Naked Lunch* demands silence from the reader; that is, he must approach it as holy text, its contents as sacred experience. Everything outside it is secular, waste matter. It is the Word. (pp. 207-08)

Burroughs is so continuous with himself that his work of the 1950s leads directly into the experiments of the next two decades. Once he discovered a prose style and a method of collage/montage, he cut himself adrift from contemporary sources, conceiving of himself as Lazarus returned from the dead to tell us what he has seen. The succeeding fictions become wilder and more intense efforts at liberation, and Burroughs's own embracing of Hubbard's Scientology movement is his way of negating the "Reactive Mind," which includes the practical world as well as history, Freud's unconscious and Jung's archetypes. Burroughs is moving toward Nietzsche's superman, but without Nietzsche's ironic morality.

Like Blake, he has a vast vision, each segment of which has personal significance for him. He must only find suitable words, words being his vehicle and also his curse. He says he wrote *Naked Lunch* under the influence of cannabis, but now that he has discontinued using it, he can achieve "the same results by non-chemical means: flicker and music through headphones, cut-ups and fold-ins of my texts, and especially by training myself to think in association blocks instead of in words." To be tied in to orthodox forms of language is to be part of the "switchboard" in *Naked Lunch,* a device for conditioning people. . . .

Consistent throughout is the need to escape from words by finding an alternative aural culture, thus achieving the defamiliarization of the ordinary. Gaddis in *JR* was confronted by the same problems: how to use words, yet escape words, how to plug into an aural culture, oral as well. Words are for Burroughs a virus, part of the conditioning associated with the Reactive Mind. Words transformed by splicing, cut-outs, fold-ins, taping, are less manipulative, are in fact evocative. Once again we note how Burroughs was moving toward the literary equivalent of Cage in music, Pollock in painting, free or expressive form in dance. (p. 208)

The Soft Machine (1961) is a series of montage images in which the machine is gutted. The ultimate enemy is Trak: "The Trak Reservation so-called includes almost all areas in and about the United Republics of Freelandt and, since the Trak Police process all matters occurring in Trak Reservation and no one knows what is and is not Reservation cases, civil and criminal are summarily removed from civilian courts with the single word TRAK to unknown sanctions." Dr. Benway, from *Naked Lunch,* is deeply involved in Trak activities. Trak serves here as cartels the way I. G. Farben does in Pynchon's *Gravity's Rainbow,* the cartel or organization (the soft machine) as an "invisible city" which controls all aspects of our experience, draining free will even as we try to exert it.

By use of the "soft machine" as his central metaphor for the way of the (American) world, Burroughs has a common image for the "sell-out": something accessible and yet mechanical. The softness of the machine suggests its accommodation, which is another way of stressing its seductive powers and, thus, its increased destructiveness. In the section called "Gongs of Violence," the succession of images indicates Burroughs's prose as well as his vision. The context is a planet war brought on by the struggle between the sexes.

> Spectators scream through the track—The electronic brain shivers in blue and pink and chlorophyll orgasms spitting out money printed on rolls of toilet paper, condoms full of ice cream, Kotex hamburgers—Police files of the world spurt out in a blast of bone meal, garden tools and barbecue sets whistle through the air, skewer the spectators—crumpled cloth bodies through dead nitrous streets of an old film set—grey luminous flakes falling softly on Ewyork, Onolulu, Aris, Ome, Oston—From siren towers the twanging tones of fear—Pan God of Panic piping blue notes through empty streets as the berserk time machine twisted a tornado of years and centuries.

The listing is the obverse of Rabelaisian, not life force but death energy. The question arises whether or not we can cite "energy," even "prose style," for something so pathologically nihilistic. The omission of the first letter from cities suggests they lack a vital part, Burroughs dehumanizing them as they have their citizens. But what is left if death is the obsession? If all imagery and energy are consecrated to nihilism (well beyond anarchism), what role can Burroughs play in our literary imagination?

The question is a profound one that strikes at much in (post)modernist fiction. It arose fifty years ago with Kafka (especially) and Eliot, and is not distant from the contemporary sensibility. It became even more immediately apparent in the work of Céline, where death orientation, nihilism, and fascistic ideology combined to make him a pariah from the Western humanistic tradition. Yet if we reject Céline as a realist, view him as a prophet, or fantasist, read his books as "bibles" or holy texts, we can understand if not accept him.

The pairing of Céline with Burroughs, even more than Kafka, is not an idle one. Once we move past obvious differences—Burroughs's stress on homosexual sex, acts of sexual martyrdom, sadistic and masochistic impulses in all social activity—we can perceive common characteristics. Burroughs's intense sexual manipulation is part of his view of sex as power, and power is for him, as it is for Céline, the motivating element. Both bring great bursts of energy, a vibrating prose, a language that leaps from the page to nihilistic and anarchistic views. Both move close to the apocalypse; *The Soft Machine,* in fact, ends with an apocalyptic scene, as observed from a penny arcade. Burroughs's drug-induced fantasies are such visions, of nuclear devices dropped into the imagination, which then reacts with vistas of destruction, doom, final things. Céline is, along with Kafka, our prophet of Western doom, our incarnation of Nazi nihilism and the destruction of the Second World War. In his way, more fantasist than historian, Burroughs is our guide to the new apocalypse, the new wars of the world. (p. 209)

Coming back to the point of Burroughs's significance—or marginality, for some—I think we must locate him as a "lyricist of nihilism." If one writer has brought himself down near death, flirted with it, examined it, tried to find the flimsy boundary between life and death, between personal death and death of a world, then Burroughs is that writer, and we must view him in those terms. His imagination is the film strip of our postwar world, an endless reel of images, scenes, characters, all of which are playbacks of himself. This goes beyond narcissism, however, since it involves indecent exposure. Burroughs has placed himself in a nuclear plant's core, so that radioactive waste can bathe him. He takes on all cancers, all illnesses, all spin-offs from the "soft machine," and if he survives, it is to return from the near-dead to tell us what he, Lazarus, has observed. The heir to the hard machinery of computers and other business hardware observes that not only toughness but "soft machines" destroy. Whatever accommodates us ends us.

Burroughs's remaining fiction of the last two decades becomes even wilder, more dire and threatening. His release from drugs, his association with Brion Gysin have intensified, not lessened, the horror. Often, as in *Nova Express,* he borrows heavily from science fiction to achieve another level of fantasy or nightmare. Communities and societies give way to universal struggles; the planet's survival rests in the balance. Burroughs, more demonic than ever, orchestrates our demise, each work a foray into *Götterdämmerung.* (p. 210)

Nova Express (1964) presents a war between two elements for the survival of the universe. It is, like the medieval morality plays, a conflict between the forces of good and evil; and the outcome depends on moral force. There has been a strain of morality in Burroughs, a Puritan ethic of sorts, which is not usually cited: the desire to find the right way, despite the horrors piled on horrors. Like Kurtz, he hovers between nightmare and moral fervor.

The first words of the book, in fact, are a Jonathan Edwards sermon about the horrors of hell: "Listen to my last words anywhere. Listen to my last words any world. Listen all you boards syndicates and governments of the earth. And you powers behind what filthy deals consummated in what lavoratory to take what is not yours. To sell the ground from unborn feet forever—" Nova criminals have poisoned the world. Burroughs see his role as something of a filmmaker, to present before our eyes the fact that the "Garden of Delights is a terminal sewer." The pastoral vision has been turned into an urban nightmare; but more, our expectations of happiness have been transformed into sequences of destruction. The Nova criminals plan "Orgasm Death" and "Nova Ovens," which Burroughs warned about in *Naked Lunch* and *The Soft Machine.* He sees his writing of those books as martyrdom, to demonstrate to us what will happen if we do not arrest the Nova criminals. . . .

Writing in the 1960s—for him a decade continuous with the 1950s—Burroughs saw the basic disorder of our time as forms of control by the "nova mechanism." "Always create as many insoluble conflicts as possible and always aggravate existing conflicts—This is done by dumping life forms with incompatible conditions of existence on the same planet." The "Nova Mob" exists to make certain the conflicts continue, to lead "to the explosion of a planet that is to nova." Like Pynchon with the Tristero System, he visualizes the "Nova Mob" as part of a continuous conspiracy: " . . . recording devices fix the nature of absolute need and dictate the use of total weapons." In the aural attack, feedback of recorded sounds, thrust into every situation, will create chaos, a playback of "nuclear war and nova." (p. 212)

The Wild Boys: A Book of the Dead (finished 1969, published 1971) and *Exterminator!* are very much outgrowths of Burroughs's sense of American culture in the sixties. The first—really a number of sequential episodes, a narrative—is presented as a film script. Cameraman, reels, angles of observation, characters who perform: all these are structural elements of the narrative. "The camera eye [Burroughs begins] is the eye of a cruising vulture flying over an area of scrub, rubble and unfinished buildings on the outskirts of a Mexican city." The first line has many of the images that will inform the book. The outskirts of the Mexican city are marginal areas of life which Burroughs draws together to become his "symbolic city." The "camera eye"—which structures "peep hole" chapters—becomes the observation post of the author as he charts the "wild boys," but it is also part of the sexual imagery, the target of all sexual activity, the anal hole, which is described as an eye, a target, a tube. The vulture prefigures the "book of the dead," a reference on one hand to the Buddhist document and on the other to its American counterpart: death without transfiguration.

Kaleidoscopic scenes of pleasures and pains, usually climaxed by wild and obsessive anal intercourse, are foreshadowings of the book's motif: the wild boy, dedicated to death without transfiguration. Burroughs's wild boys are not simply the generation of young in revolt sweeping the earth for victims, not only a sense of the sixties; but the young who have turned into vicious, merciless killers, intent only on their own group. They have moved outside civilization. Their culture is not a counterculture; it is a return to a primitive state of eat, screw, kill. The wild boys are "an overflow from North African cities that started in 1969," and they continue for the next two decades, which Burroughs foresees as the era of wild boys.

Burroughs himself, as controller of the narrator, is only one step from the wild boys. For he enters into the pain they cause, and he enjoys the pain they convey buggering each other. He borrows from Genet the miracle of the rose, which becomes the "rose of flesh," the areola around the rectum. All that degradation is part of the burden Burroughs must assume in order to "normalize" his observations. Since he is so close to the wild boys in their philosophy, even while reeling them in, he is able to convey their facelessness, their denial of alternative forms of life, their primitive desire for blood. They mutilate their victims, they eat flesh, they burn and slash and gouge. . . . The wild boy *is* the new culture, not just urban but international.

The wild boys sweep through jungles, villages, and vast territories, bringing their form of death. They are, in semihuman shape, like the napalm used in Vietnam, which not only brings individual death, but kills an entire area for generations to come. Beyond their qualities as death-givers, the wild boys are feral images of sexual abandon. Their prime satisfaction after the kill is the mutilation of their victims, and often they cannibalize the flesh and boil the bones for soup. Their destruction of every taboo and form of civilization is complete. Their form of communication is not words, not language, not any form of civilized achievement. The "wild boys" are nothing less than a vision.

Burroughs structured *Exterminator!* directly on Brion Gysin's fold-in method, with each episode a "short story" or narrative prose element of differing material. The presentation is like that of a film. . . . Like so many other Burroughs pieces, it concerns conspiracies, not politically but personally motivated. The conspirators are his usual collection (an "embittered homosexual," a Chinese cameraman, a lesbian, a "Negro castrated in his cradle by rat bites"), funded by an eccentric billionaire "perturbed by overpopulation, air and water pollution, and the destruction of wild life."

Like Kosinski's *Steps,* which employs a similar structuring of episodes, *Exterminator!* moves rapidly, the film technique creating fold-in, wraparound montage. Burroughs is also concerned with transformation. At one time, he considers himself as a "middle-aged Tiresias moving from place to place with his unpopular thesis." He plays numerous roles in the book, from exterminator in the opening sequence, to bartender, to someone who changes his very face by draining another person of his life's elements. The transformational qualities of *Frankenstein* and *The Island of Dr. Moreau* are never distant.

Even when film is not mentioned, the scene is still a "set," a scenario, a working out of a property. The world has become all theater. Late in the book, Burroughs describes episodes from the 1968 Chicago convention riots; and his presentation is of the city as a vast amphitheater, with the good actors (the rioters) and the bad actors (the police, the politicians behind them). The arena is like that of a morality play, in which violence, rioting, and planned brutality by Daley's police are filmed or staged. Like junk, the film goes on and on: "The more you use the more you need." The final episode, a prose poem, "Cold Lost Marbles," is a symbolic world of marmoreal deadness, where the "film is finished" and "City night fences dead fingers you in your own body." Comparably, Burroughs has played exterminator and other roles which allow him access to deadness, killing, sudden violence.

He flits from role to role, but essentially all roles are similar, part of the incoherent life which identifies our planet. In the episode in which he is a bartender,

he serves commuters, all of whom have been psychoanalyzed and therefore have no fight left in them; while he saves his tips for a spaceship he is building on his Missouri farm. The confusion of roles, the sudden shifts, the lack of center, the black hole for a plot recall the Dada movement, in itself an adversary response to social/political intrusion into individual lives. Burroughs follows Kurt Schwitters in this movement, and his use of the fold-in method in his later work parallels some of Schwitters's ideas. The latter's collages were created out of rubbish and refuse: gigantic arrangements of diverse material in tribute to trash. A garbage society, for Schwitters, with memories of the First World War, is best manifested in a trash art.

Like Schwitters and his random compositions, Burroughs has attempted to find in the artwork itself some principle of incoherence which can be caught in words without loss of its essential irregularity. Burroughs fears order; and his drug-induced fantasies earlier were paradigms of his world. He presented such fantasies as cautionary tales—as part of the evil of drugs—but he also achieved literary coherence by way of these fantasies. Even as he attacked the drugs, they were essential to his powers of expression.

By working along paradoxes and contradictions, Burroughs is quintessentially American. Whatever he scorns, he ends up indulging as a form of imagination. Frontiers, distances, castles on earth and in the sky, even spaceships, are never far from his vision; but they are chimeras or illusions and, therefore, the greater reality. Fantasies and dreams, with their side effects of theater, film, reels, reeling, Dada manifestations, are really *the* thing: the way in which America can be captured in words. When Burroughs rages against those fantasies as punishment for drug hallucinations, then he rages, paradoxically, against what makes his art possible, what allows him his manifestation of America.

It would be a great mistake to read Burroughs as a "novelist," for he is, more broadly, a maker of visions, which are episodes in a vast history of his developing imagination. He is, also, a writer of epics, like Dos Passos in *U.S.A.,* wherein his U.S.A. is an internal journey and all roles are his. His body of short fictions is a remarkable achievement; for he became not only the greatest of the Beats, not only their finest poet, but a unique voice of America in the fifties. (pp. 213-14)

Frederick R. Karl, "The Counterfeit Decade," in his *American Fictions, 1940/1980: A Comprehensive History and Critical Evaluation,* Harper & Row, Publishers, 1983, pp. 176-253.

SOURCES FOR FURTHER STUDY

McCarthy, Mary. "Burroughs' *Naked Lunch*." In her *The Writing on the Wall and Other Literary Essays,* pp. 42-53. New York: Harcourt, 1970.

> Important essay on Burroughs's masterwork. McCarthy calls *Naked Lunch* a "new kind of novel, based on statelessness. . . . Like a classical satirist, Burroughs is dead serious—a reformer."

Mottram, Eric. *William Burroughs: The Algebra of Need.* London: Marion Boyars, 1977, 282 p.

> Scholarly study of Burroughs's work. Examines his use of science fiction and black humor to delineate society's myriad addictions.

Review of Contemporary Fiction 4, No. 1 (Spring 1984): 4-144.

> Special Burroughs number featuring criticism on his novels, personal reminiscences by fellow writers, an interview with the author, and fiction and essays by Burroughs.

Skerl, Jennie. *William Burroughs.* Boston: Twayne, 1985, 127 p.

> Basic introduction to the novels through *Cities of the Red Night.*

Tanner, Tony. "Rub Out the Word." In his *City of Words: American Fiction, 1950-1970,* pp. 109-40. New York: Harper & Row, 1971.

> Highly regarded analysis of Burroughs's themes and techniques. Tanner states that "Burroughs has developed a whole mythology dramatizing all those malign pressures which seem bent on absorbing or exploiting the unique identity of the distinctively human individual."

Tytell, John. "The Black Beauty of William Burroughs." In his *Naked Angels: The Lives and Literature of the Beat Generation,* pp. 111-39. New York: McGraw Hill, 1976.

> Insightful survey of Burroughs's fiction through *Exterminator!* Tytell concludes: "The cumulative message of these novels is a warning of throttling controls on freedom and a world ruled by robot forces."

Samuel Butler

1835-1902

English novelist, essayist, and critic.

INTRODUCTION

*B*utler is one of the most renowned English authors of the late-Victorian period. A notorious iconoclast, he presented a scathing portrait of Victorian family life in the autobiographical novel *The Way of All Flesh* (1903), created pungent satires of English society in his *Erewhon; or, Over the Range* (1872) and *Erewhon Revisited Twenty Years Later* (1901), and opposed dominant literary, religious, and scientific ideas of his day in numerous essays. Butler's perceptive criticisms of Victorian England, influential during his lifetime, exerted even greater impact on subsequent generations of writers and thinkers. As a result, he is often cited as one of the primary progenitors of the early twentieth-century reaction against Victorian attitudes.

Butler was born in a small village in Nottinghamshire, the son of an Anglican clergyman and the grandson of a bishop. Educated at a boarding school near his home, he later attended the prestigious Shrewsbury School, where the curriculum emphasized classical studies. Butler continued his education at Cambridge, and, after graduating in 1858, he followed family tradition by preparing to enter the clergy. However, during his clerical training he developed doubts about his vocation, and the next year he announced to his father that he did not wish to be ordained. After much debate, during which alternate careers in medicine, art, and diplomacy were proposed, it was decided that Butler would be allowed to emigrate to New Zealand with a small financial endowment and there attempt to establish himself as a rancher. He left England soon afterward, arriving in the Canterbury region of New Zealand in January of 1860.

Butler remained in New Zealand for nearly five years, running a highly successful sheep ranch and eventually doubling the value of his original investment. As owner of the ranch his duties were light, and he was able to read a great deal during this period. In 1861 Butler read Charles Darwin's *Origin of Species* (1859), a book that strongly influenced him; he later commented that, for him, the theory of evolution had replaced Christianity. He subsequently submitted a series of articles to the *Canterbury Press* in 1862, defending and extrapolating from Darwin's theory. Butler's writings attracted much attention throughout New Zealand, and in 1863 Darwin himself wrote to the *Press,* praising Butler's clear comprehension of his work. That year Butler's father compiled a collection of his son's letters and had them published as *A First Year in Canterbury Settlement* (1863). Soon afterward Butler sold his ranch to become a full-time contributor to the *Canterbury Press.*

Returning to England late in 1864, Butler settled in London, and, aspiring to a career as a painter, enrolled at Heatherley's School of Art. However, after several years of determined effort, he came to feel that his artistic talents were limited, and in 1870 he began writing his first major satire, *Erewhon; or, Over the Range.* Published anonymously in 1872, *Erewhon* was an immediate success; when Butler let it be known that he was the author of the work, he was thrust into the limelight. His renown was soon augmented by the publication of *The Fair Haven* (1873), a satirical denunciation of Christian doctrines which was misinterpreted by some clergymen as a brilliant defense of those beliefs. Butler next began work on the novel *The Way of All Flesh,* but soon realized that its intensely negative portrait of his family would gravely offend those members still living, and in 1878 he set the uncompleted work aside.

Throughout the next decade Butler focused on topics that he had pursued early in 1878 with the publication of *Life and Habit,* in which he addressed the issue of biological evolution. After long consideration of Darwin's theory, Butler had come to believe that Darwin had failed to accurately identify the mechanism by which evolutionary adaptations were passed on from one generation to the next. Butler developed in *Life and Habit* and in three subsequent volumes the theory that biological traits are inherited through an unconscious memory of adaptations made by an organism's progenitors in response to some specific need or desire, suggesting that this memory was incorporated into the physical structure of an embryo at the time of conception. Butler's concern with Darwin's work led to a celebrated conflict between the two men, produced not by the differences in their theories, but by a misunderstanding. In 1879 Darwin wrote a preface for the English translation of Ernst Krause's essay on Darwin's grandfather, who had also written about evolution. To the translation of his essay Krause added negative remarks concerning Butler's theory, and Butler, who had read the original German version, erroneously attributed these revisions to Darwin. Embittered by what he considered unfair and unprofessional attacks on his ideas, Butler harbored resentment toward Darwin for the rest of his life, and Butler's subsequent volumes of scientific writings contain numerous acerbic references to Darwin's work.

During the last two decades of his life, Butler continued to oppose dominant ideas of his time by publishing two controversial philological essays, contending in one that the *Odyssey* had been written by a woman and in the other that Shakespeare had written his sonnets for a homosexual lover, who, although socially inferior to the playwright, had treated him in a cavalier fashion. He also published English translations of the *Iliad* and the *Odyssey,* collaborated with his friend Henry Festing Jones on a number of musical compositions, and intermittently worked on the manuscript of *The Way of All Flesh.* Before his death in 1902 Butler left instructions that this last work should not be published until after the deaths of his two sisters, but his literary executor, R. A. Streatfeild, ignored those instructions and published *The Way of All Flesh* in 1903.

Critics regard *The Way of All Flesh* as Butler's most important work, significant both as a perceptive autobiography and as a brilliant criticism of the attitudes and institutions of Victorian England. Through the central character of the novel, Ernest Pontifex, Butler portrayed his own childhood in a pious household, his early attempts to transcend his intellectually stifling social milieu, and his ultimate rejection of the ideals and mores of his family. The plot of the second half of the novel diverges drastically from the facts of Butler's life, with Pontifex spending time in prison for attempting to solicit the sexual favors of a woman he mistakes for a prostitute, marrying a servant, and receiving a large inheritance. The primary targets of *The Way of All Flesh* are the fiercely patriarchal Victorian family and the Christian church. Remembering his own feelings of frustration at his father's absolutism and frequent use of corporal punishment, Butler portrayed Ernest Pontifex's childhood as a period of emotional and physical agony. As a clergyman, Pontifex's father, Theobald, embodies Butler's view of the Anglican church as not only ossified and morally impotent but as perverse in its stubborn adherence to practices antithetical to such Christian ideals as charity and tolerance. While critics praise the satiric wit and keen intelligence displayed in these criticisms, many suggest that Butler's bitterness led him to subordinate such literary elements as plot and characterization to invective, resulting in a powerful but nevertheless flawed work of literature. Others, however, have defended the depth and subtlety of Butler's characterizations, noting that the only unsuccessful character in the novel is Ernest Pontifex, who appears to have been imbued with Butler's great intelligence but with limited emotional depth.

Butler further satirized Victorian England in *Erewhon* and *Erewhon Revisited*. In the former, Butler created a fictional nation, Erewhon ("Nowhere" reversed), by skewing and in some cases inverting features of his own society. Thus, the Anglican church is represented in *Erewhon* by "Musical Banks," which dispense currency that is monetarily worthless yet important as a mark of status, and the courts treat crime as an illness and doctors treat illness as a crime. Butler also incorporated elements of his evolutionary theories into the futuristic society depicted in *Erewhon*, most notably in the section entitled "The Book of the Machines," wherein he suggested that machines represent humanity's attempt to transcend its physical limitations and are therefore another step in human evolution.

Aside from his two philological studies, *The Authoress of the "Odyssey"* (1897) and *Shakespeare's Sonnets Reconsidered* (1899), the bulk of Butler's discursive writings deal with his theory of evolution. Of these, critics regard *Life and Habit* as by far the best, suggesting that *Evolution, Old and New* (1879) is essentially a restatement of the ideas set forth in the earlier book, and that Butler's later essays were inspired largely by his resentment of Darwin. Butler also wrote a number of essays describing his annual trips to Italy, and some critics contend that these writings are among Butler's best, displaying humor and eloquence while avoiding the acrimonious didacticism that occasionally mars his other works.

During his lifetime, Butler's critical reputation was based on the success of *Erewhon*. His scientific writings were viewed with interest but were generally dismissed as inferior to those of Darwin, whom critics deemed more qualified to discuss questions of biological evolution. Nevertheless, a number of commentators have noted that Darwin himself failed to adequately describe the mechanisms of natural selection and maintain that Butler's approach was, although incorrect, a well-wrought extrapolation of the teleological evolutionary theories of eighteenth-century scholars Georges-Louis Buffon, Jean-Baptiste Lamarck, and William Paley. After 1903 the widely read and much-discussed *Way of All Flesh* overshadowed all of Butler's previous writings; appearing during one of the first waves of anti–Victorian reaction, the novel was hailed by critics as a brilliant exposé and praised for its satiric wit. *The Way of All Flesh* was admired in particular by Bloomsbury critics Virginia and Leonard Woolf, Desmond MacCarthy, and E. M. Forster, who, while admitting that the novel was flawed, nevertheless found in it the embodiment of their own ideals. During the 1920s and 1930s, however, Butler's reputation suffered a decline, with many politically and socially radical critics viewing his iconoclasm as limited and entirely conventional. In a renowned, caustic biography of Butler, Malcolm Muggeridge suggested that despite his outward posture of dissent Butler in fact failed to free himself from the most essential preconceptions of Victorian society, concluding that he was "not so much the anti–Victorian, as the ultimate Victorian."

Several recent studies have focused on these charges and others pertaining to elements of Victorianism in Butler's thought; most contemporary critics suggest that while his radicalism was limited, his criticisms of Victorian society were deeply felt, intellectually profound, and undeniably influential in formulating modern attitudes toward that era. Butler's writings and ideas have been cited as sources of inspiration for a number of major twentieth-century authors, including Forster, Virginia Woolf, Bernard Shaw, and James Joyce, and *The Way of All Flesh* and *Erewhon* are acknowledged as literary classics in their own right.

(For further information about Butler's life and works, see *Contemporary Authors,* Vol. 104; *Dictionary of Literary Biography,* Vols. 18, 57; and *Twentieth-Century Literary Criticism,* Vols. 1, 33. For related criticism, see the entry on Darwinism and Literature in *Nineteenth-Century Literature Criticism,* Vol. 32.)

CRITICAL COMMENTARY

PAUL ELMER MORE

(essay date 1921)

[More was an American critic who, along with Irving Babbitt, formulated the doctrines of New Humanism in early twentieth-century American thought. In the following excerpt, he discusses Butler's iconoclastic approach to science and literature.]

In a moment of candour [Butler declared] that he had "never written on any subject unless [he] believed that the authorities on it were hopelessly wrong"; and the authorities happen to have included the philologians entrenched in the universities, the most eminent names in science, and in religion both the orthodox theologians of the Church and the sceptics of the higher criticism. It is not wonderful that he should have exclaimed

Principal Works

A First Year in Canterbury Settlement (essays) 1863

The Evidence for the Resurrection of Jesus Christ, as Given by the Four Evangelists (essay) 1865

Erewhon; or, Over the Range (novel) 1872

The Fair Haven: A Work in Defence of the Miraculous Element in Our Lord's Ministry upon Earth, both as against Rationalistic Impugners and Certain Orthodox Defenders, by the Late J. P. Owen, Edited by W. B. Owen, with a Memoir by the Author (fictional biography) 1873

Life and Habit: An Essay after a Completer View of Evolution (essay) 1878

Evolution, Old and New; or, The Theories of Buffon, Dr. Erasmus Darwin, and Lamarck, as Compared with That of Mr. Charles Darwin (essay) 1879

Unconscious Memory: A Comparison between the Theory of Dr. Ewald Hering, Professor of Physiology at Prague, and the Philosophy of the Unconscious of Dr. Edward von Hartmann; with Translations from These Authors (essay) 1880

Alps and Sanctuaries of Piedmont and the Canton Ticino (travel essays) 1882

Luck or Cunning as the Main Means of Organic Modification? (essay) 1886

The Authoress of the "Odyssey": Where and When She Wrote, Who She Was, the Use She Made of the "Iliad," and How the Poem Grew under Her Hands (criticism) 1897

Shakespeare's Sonnets Reconsidered, and in Part Rearranged; with Introductory Chapters, Notes, and a Reprint of the Original 1609 Edition (criticism) 1899

Erewhon Revisited Twenty Years Later, both by the Original Discoverer of the Country and by His Son (novel) 1901

The Way of All Flesh (novel) 1903; also published as Ernest Pontifex; or, The Way of All Flesh [revised edition], 1964

The Note-Books of Samuel Butler (notebooks) 1907

The Shrewsbury Edition of the Works of Samuel Butler. 20 vols. (essays, novels, fictional biography, criticism, notebooks, and letters) 1923-26

Further Extracts from the Note-Books of Samuel Butler (notebooks) 1934

---

with a sad pride: "In that I write at all I am among the damned."

His bout with the philologians took place in the lists of Homeric and Shakespearian criticism. To supplant the "nightmares of Homeric extravagance," as he calls them, rightly enough, "which German professors have evolved out of their inner consciousness," he evolved for his part a delicious fancy that the *Odyssey* was composed by a young woman, and that the palace of Odysseus was set by her in her own home in the Sicilian Trapani. I have never met a Greek scholar who would confess that he had even read Butler's work on *The Authoress of the "Odyssey"*; they prefer the Butlerian canon of condemning without reading. Well, I have perused the book, but I shall neither accept nor condemn. It is uncommonly clever, and the part at least which deals with the question of authorship is amusingly plausible; but the argument, of course, is all based on inference, and does not amount to much more than a *jeu d'esprit*. His other contention in philology, in which he rearranges the order of Shakespeare's Sonnets and builds up a new story of the events underlying them, should, I feel, be taken rather more seriously. I would not say that, in my judgment, he has made out his case; for here again the evidence is too inferential, too evasive, to be thoroughly conclusive. But I do think that he has demolished the flimsy theories of Sidney Lee and certain other so-called authorities, and that his own constructive criticism is worthy of attention.

But these tilts with the entrenched philology of the universities were mere skirmishes, so to speak; the real battle was with the authorities in science and theology. These were the gentlemen, "hopelessly wrong," whom Butler undertook to set right by the genial art of "heaving bricks." In science the great enemy was none other than Darwin himself, with all those who swore by the name of Darwin. The dispute did not touch the fact of evolution itself, for Butler to the end was a staunch evolutionist; nor did it concern the Darwinian theory of the survival of the fit, for here again Butler was thoroughly orthodox. The question at issue was the cause of those variations out of which the more fit were selected for survival—and this, I take it, is still the *casus belli* which renders the resounding warfare of the biologists so amusing a spectacle to one who has set his feet in the serene temples of scepticism. . . . (pp. 182-84)

On the one side stood in array the host of Darwinians—or ultra-Darwinians, for Darwin himself was provokingly muddled and inconsistent in his statements—who held that the *via vitae* was a path of incalculable hazard, to whom life was pure mechanism and evolution meant a transference to biology of the mathematical law of probability. On the other side, in which for some time Butler was almost the sole champion in

England, stood those who believed that the significant variations arose from the purposeful striving of individual creatures to adapt themselves to their surroundings, and that the selective power of fitness was part of a grand design working itself out consciously in the evolution of life.

Now it is not my business to pronounce judgment in so learned a dispute; the non-scientific critic who should presume to come between such quarrelsome kinsfolk would probably fare like the proverbial peacemaker between man and wife. I can only say that to Butler the dignity of science and the very issues of life seemed to be involved in the debate: "To state this doctrine [of the Darwinians]," he declares, "is to arouse instinctive loathing; it is my fortunate task to maintain that such a nightmare of waste and death is as baseless as it is repulsive." Butler's particular contribution to the Lamarckian side was what he called "unconscious memory," the theory, that is, that the acquired experience of the parent was passed on to the embryo and carried by the offspring into life as an instinctive propensity. Later he learned that the same theory had been propounded by an Austrian biologist named Hering, and thereafter he was careful to ascribe full credit to his predecessor. (pp. 184-86)

But I hasten to descend from the aërial heights of pure science to a region where the critic of letters may feel that he is walking with his feet on the ground. The notable fact is that Butler's whole literary career took its start from his interest, at first merely amateurish, in the Darwinian theory of evolution. Readers of *Erewhon* will remember the three chapters of that Utopian romance entitled "The Book of the Machines." These chapters stand out as the most brilliant section of the romance; they are furthermore the germ out of which the whole narrative grew, and in a way strike the keynote of much of his later writing. No one, I think, can read this "Book of the Machines" without feeling that it is the work of a powerful and original intellect, but one is likely also to lay it down with a sense of bewilderment. There is insight here, the insight of a mind brooding on the course of human history and speaking with apparent sincerity of a terrible danger to be avoided. Yet there is withal a note of biting irony; and what precisely the object of this irony may be, or how this irony is to be reconciled with the tone of sincerity, the book itself gives one no clue to determine.

Nor do the author's direct allusions to his purpose give us much ease. In a letter to Darwin accompanying a present of the first edition of *Erewhon,* in 1872, Butler disclaims any intention of being "disrespectful" to the *Origin of Species,* and avows that the chapters on Machines, written primarily as a bit of pure fun, were rewritten and inserted in *Erewhon* as a satire on the pseudoscientific method of Bishop Butler's *Analogy.* Again, in the preface to the second edition of the book pub-

lished a few months after the first, he expresses his "regret that reviewers have in some cases been inclined to treat the chapters on Machines as an attempt to reduce Mr. Darwin's theory to an absurdity." He is surprised that the specious misuse of analogy really aimed at should not have occurred to any reviewer. Evidently he is alluding again to Bishop Butler, yet if one turns to . . . the narrative itself, one sees that Paley's famous analogy of the watch, and not Bishop Butler at all, was in the author's mind when he wrote the book. This is already a little confusing, but confusion is worse confounded by the statement in a letter written shortly before our Erewhonian's death. Now, looking back at the matter through the bitterness engendered by what he regarded as a long persecution, he says: "With *Erewhon* Charles Darwin smelt danger from afar. I knew him personally; he was one of my grandfather's pupils. He knew very well that the machine chapters in *Erewhon* would not end there, and the Darwin circle was then the most important literary power in England."

Here is a beautiful case for genetic criticism—if the word "genetic" has any meaning outside of the dictionary and the laboratory—and by following the development of Butler's ideas one may learn perhaps how the baffling mixture of irony and sincerity got into the famous chapters on Machines and became a kind of fixed habit with him. Darwin's *Origin of Species* reached Butler in New Zealand soon after its publication, and evidently quite carried him off his feet. Under the first spell of admiration he composed a little essay on **"Darwin among the Machines,"** which was printed in the *Press* of Canterbury, New Zealand, in 1863. Years later, commenting in one of his scientific books on this article, he admits that he had taken Darwin at his face value without much reflection; "there was one evolution" for him then, and "Darwin was its prophet." And the article itself fully bears out this statement. Caught by the plausible simplicity of evolution as an extension of purely inorganic law into the organic world, Butler carried the mechanical analogy a step further and undertook to show what would happen when machines had progressed to the stage of independent racial existence and had surpassed man, just as the animal kingdom had been evolved out of the vegetable, and the vegetable from the mineral. His conclusion is "that war to the death should be instantly proclaimed against them. Every machine of every sort should be destroyed by the well-wisher of his species. . . . Let us at once go back to the primeval condition of the race."

It must be remembered that Butler wrote this essay while living in the free primitive uplands of New Zealand, during the happiest period of his life, and that the note of primitivism in his peroration is probably in large measure sincere. At the same time there is a word in his later comment which points to another trait in his intellectual make-up which was active from the beginning. He started, he says, with the hypothesis of man as a mechanism, because that was the easiest strand to pick up, and because "there was plenty of amusement" to be got out of it. Now one may amuse one's self with a theory which one holds in all sincerity; but fun of that sort has a way of running into irony or sarcasm, and so one may detect in this first essay the germ of Butler's later manner. He was ever prone to make fun, and sometimes a very strange sort of fun, when he was most in earnest.

It is clear that Butler was both attracted and teased by Darwin's great work, and that he did not rest with his first impression. Two years later, having meanwhile returned to England, he sent another letter to the Canterbury *Press*, which he entitled **"Lucubratio Ebria"** and signed with a different name. "It is a mistake, then," he says in this second letter, "to take the view adopted by a previous correspondent of this paper." His thesis now is that machines are really an extension, so to speak, of a man's limbs, of the tools, that is to say, which the mind invents in its progress towards a higher organization; as such the development of machinery is the measure of an inner growth and need not be feared.

As yet, apparently, the fun of the thing was still uppermost in Butler's mind. He put the two essays together as "The Book of the Machines" and wrote his Utopian romance about them without feeling any serious discordance in the points of view, and could even send the volume to Darwin with an assurance of his loyalty. But the rift was already there. As he continued to reflect on the matter, the significance of the second point of view took on more importance and he began to see its scientific implications. Out of these reflections grew his book on *Life and Habit*, in which he first, frankly and definitely, announced himself as a champion of the teleological theory of evolution against the mechanistic principles of the ultra-Darwinians.

But our concern now is with the fact that in the latest, revised edition of *Erewhon* the two essays on machines, though much enriched and enlarged in the process of revision, still lie side by side, with no word to tell the reader which of the two represents the author's real views. The result is piquant to say the least. In one chapter the dread of machines, as they have been developed to a state of almost independent consciousness, is expressed with a depth of conviction that can leave no doubt of the author's sincerity. Here he speaks as a Darwinian *à outrance,* but as a Darwinian filled with loathing for the spectres conjured up by his own science. Yet turn a few pages, and you will find machines glorified "as a part of man's own physical nature," the instruments by which alone he advances in "all those habits of mind which most elevate [him] above the lower animals":

Thus civilization and mechanical progress advanced hand in hand, each developing and being developed by the other, the earliest accidental use of the stick having set the ball rolling, and the prospect of advantage keeping it in motion. In fact, machines ought to be regarded as the mode of development by which human organism is now especially advancing, every past invention being an addition to the resources of the human body.

What is one to make of this flagrant contradiction? I might answer by asking what one is to make of the contradictions of life. It is true that the progress of civilization seems to be coincident with mechanical invention. We believe that; and yet can any one look at the state of the world today, at the monotony of lives that have been enslaved to machinery, at the distaste for work and the unrest of the worker that have arisen partly as a consequence of this subservience, can any one seriously contemplate the growing materialism of modern life, its dependence for pleasure on the whirl of wheels and the dance of images, with its physical distraction and its lessening care for the quiet and ideal delights of the intellect—can any one see these things and not feel a stirring of something like terror in the soul at the tyranny of the creatures we have evoked from the soulless forces of nature? Life is a dilemma, and only the fool thinks it is simple. In "The Book of the Machines" one of its enigmas is presented with a keenness of observation and a cogency of style that must give the author a high place among the philosophical writers of the age.

However Butler may have been disposed towards the evolution of machines, the Erewhonians themselves chose to see in them a menace to humanity, and decreed that they should be ruthlessly destroyed. *Erewhon* is thus the story of a people who are living backwards, so to speak, of a country seen through the looking-glass and conceived in the spirit of irony. There is no doubt of this intention, you will feel it on every page of the romance; only, and this is the tantalizing spell of the book, it is not always easy to guess against whom the irony is directed. We know from Butler's statement elsewhere, not from the book itself, that the account of the Erewhonian treatment of crime as a disease to be cured in hospitals and of disease as a crime to be punished in prisons was meant to be taken *au pied de la lettre* and that the law of *Erewhon* was commended by way of satirizing the law of England. But no sooner has the reader adjusted his mind to this form of attack than he finds himself engaged in that terrible arraignment of the Church as working through the so-called Musical Banks, where the Erewhonians themselves become the object of irony. And so the satire sways this way and that from chapter to chapter. It is all good fun, but it is mighty bewildering unless one comes to the book with a knowledge of Butler's ideas derived from other sources; and even then one does not always know on which side of the mouth to laugh—though of the laughter there is never any doubt. The fact is that irony had become a habit with Butler, and of its application he little recked. He could even believe he was ironical when in truth he was perfectly sincere; which is still more delightfully puzzling than his ambiguous application of irony.

This trait comes out in his treatment of Christianity. He had early become interested in the problem of the Resurrection of Christ as the corner-stone of the whole dogmatic edifice, his own sober conclusion apparently being that Christ did not die on the Cross, but was buried while in a trance, and afterwards appeared actually in the flesh to the disciples. His first thoughts on the question were published in a pamphlet, now quite forgotten; and late in life he wrote his *Erewhon Revisited,* which is nothing less than an elaborate and vicious satire, in rather bad taste, on the miraculous birth and the Ascension. But between these two publications comes *The Fair Haven,* as enigmatical a work as ever was penned. Here the problem of the Resurrection is discussed by a priest, who, having fallen into scepticism, finds for himself at last a haven of peace in the solution of every doubt. Now, for all that one can learn from Butler's life, the solution offered by his fictitious hero was intended to be taken ironically, and the whole treatise should be regarded as a diatribe against Christian dogma. To his friend, Miss Savage, it is "sanglant satire," and so apparently it appeared to Mr. Jones. Very well; but what really happened? The book was reviewed in several of the Evangelical periodicals of the day as perfectly orthodox, and so alert a critic as Canon Ainger sent it to a friend whom he wished to convert. And to-day a candid reader, even with full knowledge of Butler's avowed intention, is likely to close the book with an impression that, despite a note of irony that breaks through the language here and there, the argument as a whole forms a singularly powerful and convincing plea for Christianity. The hallucination theory of the Resurrection propounded by Strauss is analysed and refuted with remorseless logic. Even the trance theory, which Butler himself was inclined to accept, is answered, briefly indeed, but plausibly. On the other side Dean Alford's half-hearted attempt to reconcile the discordant Gospel narratives of the Resurrection undergoes the same deadly analysis. But the truth of the Resurrection, Butler then argues, is dependent on no such reconciliation of the records; in fact a divine revelation, he maintains, designed for the needs of all sorts and conditions of men, ought, in the nature of the case, to present the truth in a variety of manners. Here at last one begins to feel that the satire of Christianity itself is coming out into the open, and in [Henry Festing Jones's *Samuel Butler* (see Sources for Further Study)] a bit of conversation is recorded which would seem to confirm such a view. Butler is talking with the Rev. Edwin A. Abbott:

> He said to me: "And did you really mean none of that part seriously?"
>
> I said: "Certainly not; I intended it as an example of the kind of rubbish which would go down with the *Spectator.*"
>
> Abbott said: "Well, I can only say you would have found a great many to sympathize with you, if you had meant it seriously."
>
> I said, rather drily: "That, I think, is exceedingly probable," meaning that there was no lack of silly insincere gushers.

That has a categorical ring; yet in an article published in the *Universal Review* four years after the date of this conversation, where there can be no possible suspicion of irony, Butler is repeating as his own this same argument for the adaptibility of revelation and of the Christ-Ideal.

What can we make of all this? The key to the difficulty may be found, I think, in a sentence of his preface to *The Fair Haven:* "I was justified," he says, "in calling the book a defence—both as against impugners and defenders," i.e., of Christianity. Butler held it his mission to "heave bricks" at two groups of eminent men: he was himself deeply immersed in science, but he nursed a magnificent grudge against the professional scientists of his day both for their bigotry and for personal reasons; and in like manner he was interested in religion and indeed always called himself a churchman of a sort, but he hated any one else who assumed that name. And so in *The Fair Haven* he was having his fun—and powerful good fun it is—with Strauss and the scientific impugners on the one side, and with Dean Alford and his tribe of puzzled defenders on the other; he enjoyed the sport so much that he persuaded his friend and almost made himself believe that he was having fun also with the object impugned and defended by them. But besides the faculty of irony Butler possessed in equal measure the faculty of hard logic. And so it happened that when he came to present the case in support of Christianity any lurking intention of irony was soon swallowed up in the pure delight of building up a constructive argument such as the professional champions of the Church, in his opinion, had quite failed to offer. He was helped in this by his firm belief that of the two the professors of science were a more bigoted and dangerous class than the professors of religion.

In this union of logic with irony Butler belongs with Huxley and Matthew Arnold, as he is their peer in the mastery of a superbly clear and idiomatic English style. He differs from them in that he possessed also a certain gnome-like impudence of fancy which led him into strange ambiguities and throws a veil of seeming irresponsibility over much, not all, of his writing. Readers who are not made uneasy by this remarkable combination of qualities, and who have no fear for their own heads where brickbats are flying, will find in him one of the most fascinating authors of the Victorian age. Only, perhaps, a word of caution should be uttered in regard to Butler's one regular novel, *The Way of All Flesh.* There is no irony here, but the bludgeoning of a direct and brutal sarcasm; he is no longer our Victorian Swift of *A Tale of a Tub* or of *Laputa,* but a voyager to the land of the Yahoos. It is a powerful book, even a great book in a way; but it is bitter, malignant, base, dishonourable, and dishonest. Unfortunately, to the smudged and smeared minds of a Bernard Shaw and a Gilbert Cannan it appeals as Butler's masterpiece, and much of his fame, so far as he is known to the general public, derives from Shaw's eulogy of this one work. That is a pity, in my judgment; for the true Butler, perhaps I should say the finer Butler, is not there, but in the books where irony plays waywardly backwards and forwards through a network of subtle logic. (pp. 187-99)

Paul Elmer More, "Samuel Butler of Erewhon," in his *A New England Group and Others: Shelburne Essays,* eleventh series, 1921. Reprinted by Phaeton Press, 1967, pp. 167-200.

LEONARD WOOLF

(essay date 1927)

[Woolf is best known as one of the leaders of the Bloomsbury group of artists and thinkers, a circle that included Woolf's wife, the novelist Virginia Woolf, as well as Clive and Vanessa Bell, John Maynard Keynes, Lytton Strachey, Desmond MacCarthy, and several others. In the following excerpt, he assesses Butler's importance as a writer and thinker.]

Butler is not, nor will he ever become, a popular writer. When time has had the last word with him and has given him his final and fossilized place in the strata of literature, he will be less popular and in a lower stratum than he is to-day. This judgement is not the result of prejudice or of some lack of sympathy with Butler. In my own private hierarchy of letters he occupies an extremely high place. His peculiar humour, his dialectic, his precise eccentricities, a certain dryness of mind which seems able to convert so many things to a pinch of fine dust—all these qualities happen to appeal very strongly to me personally. But the critic ought sometimes to allow his mind to work undisturbed by his personal likes and dislikes.

To read through Butler's early miscellaneous writings . . . , and then to go on from them to his later and latest works, gives one a solid basis for criticism. At first sight, it is extraordinary how little of the characteristic Butler of *Erewhon, The Way of All Flesh,* and *The Note-Books* there appears to be in the early writings. Only very rarely does one catch a glimpse of the original and satirical mind which later made its temporary home in Clifford's Inn and the British Museum. And yet closer inspection reveals the fact that the foundation upon which the later books were built had already been laid in the Cambridge essays and *Canterbury Settlement.* Here is a mind which thinks, not other people's thoughts, but its own—honest, clear, argumentative, singularly unemotional; and here is a style which never sinks below or attempts to rise above a certain level. In *Erewhon,* Butler found both a subject and himself. The elaborate satire on English life and society in the nineteenth century gives scope for the qualities mentioned above, and also for his eccentricities, originalities, and humour. Yet it remains in many ways the queerest satire that has ever been written. It is extraordinarily unemotional. With Swift or Cyrano de Bergerac or any other of the writers who have created these inverted Utopias somewhere on the other side of the moon or the mountains, one always feels that they are animated by some human emotion towards the customs or institutions which they are satirizing. They feel anger or indignation or pity or mere amusement at the antics of mankind which they show us through the telescope or microscope of satire. But when Butler describes the Musical Banks or the attitude of the Erewhonians towards disease, it is impossible to detect the least flicker of emotion either towards us and our ways or the Erewhonians and their ways. This makes *Erewhon* a very queer book, for what can be more strange and disquieting than a humorist who is apparently never amused? It appeals to me personally, I repeat; I happen to have a particular liking for cranks, and the explanation of much which is puzzling in Butler should be looked for in crankiness. But this kind of queerness, crankiness, and unemotional frigidity is bound to narrow the circle of an author's readers. I will not enter upon the question whether it also precludes the book from greatness, whether, in fact, a great book, as some of our modern critics declare, must have something in it capable of appealing to all men. I rather suspect these vague generalizations about greatness and goodness. But in Butler's case, I think, the qualities which prevent him from being widely popular also prevent him from being a great writer. *Erewhon* and *The Way of All Flesh,* despite their originality of thought and humour, are not great books, and the reason is that the thought is always twisted a little, and kept from soaring by a twinge of crankiness, while thought, humour, satire, and language, owing to the absence of emotion, lack the warmth or glow which seems inseparable from great literature.

Erewhon, The Way of All Flesh, and the *Note-Books* contain the best things which Butler wrote, but *The Fair Haven* in some ways reveals more nakedly than any of Butler's other works the peculiar way in which his mind operated. It is an attack upon Christianity, and it is designed to show that the evidence for the Resurrection which we find in the New Testament cannot be accepted. The form of the book is elaborately ironical. It is supposed to be written by an imaginary person, the late John Pickard Owen, whose imaginary brother, William Bickersteth Owen, writes a prefatory memoir. The imaginary author is represented as having lost and then recovered his faith in Christianity, and the object of his posthumous book is to put his own experiences at the service of the infidel and the atheist, and so to convert them. His theory is that the kernel of Christianity is to be found in the story of the Resurrection, and that, while much of the New Testament must be rejected as unhistorical, if the central fact of the Resurrection can be established, everything else which really matters will remain. On the surface, the book professes to prove conclusively that Christ died on the cross, was buried, and rose again on the third day.

Butler's irony consists in making John Pickard Owen unconsciously disprove the very thing which he thinks that he is proving. So far there is nothing extraordinary in the scheme and form of the book; there are many precedents, particularly in English literature, for this kind of irony, which solemnly and elaborately disproves what on the surface you are solemnly and elaborately professing to prove. But the great ironists have never left the reader in any doubt as to what the real meaning is behind the façade of irony. One would have to be a very stupid person to misunderstand Swift when, in *A Modest Proposal to the Publick,* he writes:

I have been assured by a very knowing *American* of my acquaintance in *London,* that a young healthy child, well nursed, is at a year old a most delicious, nourishing, and wholesome food, whether *stewed, roasted, baked,* or *boiled;* and I make no doubt that it will equally serve in a *fricassée,* or a *ragoust.* I do therefore humbly offer it to the *publick consideration,* that of the hundred and twenty thousand children already computed, twenty thousand may be reserved for breed, whereof only one-fourth part to be males. . . . That the remaining hundred thousand may, at a year old, be offered in sale to the persons of *quality* and *fortune* through the kingdom; always advising the mother to let them suck plentifully in the last month, so as to render them plump, and fat for a good table. A child will make two dishes at an entertainment for friends; and when the family dines alone, the fore or hind quarter will make a reasonable dish, and seasoned with a little pepper or salt, will be very good boiled on the fourth day, especially in *winter.*

All Butler's paraphernalia is in this passage of Swift's; the extraordinarily detailed, reasonable, quiet, serious argument which the reader is not intended to "take seriously." The remarkable thing about Butler is that nearly all his readers did take him seriously. The façade of irony is so delicate, the argument is so detailed and intricate, the real meaning below the surface so elusory, that, even though his book appeared in 1873, when the Resurrection was still a burning question of controversy, very few people saw what was its real meaning. Most reviewers and religious papers accepted Owen as a real person and the book as a defence of Christianity and orthodoxy, and Canon Ainger "sent it to a friend whom he wished to convert." So wide was the misunderstanding that Butler decided to bring out a second edition immediately, under his own name and with a preface in which he made it clear that the book was intended to be ironical.

I read *The Fair Haven* for the first time over twenty years ago, and I remember being astonished that its real meaning had not been understood. On re-reading it more carefully I am inclined to revise that original judgement. Of course, if one reads the book knowing its history, knowing that it is by Samuel Butler, the author of *Erewhon,* it is easy enough to detect the irony, though I believe that a large number of people who profess to understand the book would not be able to state clearly the exact way in which Butler makes Owen's proof of the Resurrection disprove it. But I am convinced that in 1873 it would have been the easiest thing in the world to fail in detecting that the book was ironical. There is nothing obviously ridiculous anywhere in the book. The irony is most marked in the prefatory memoir, in the incident of the lady saying her prayers, and in a sentence such as: "He therefore, to my mother's inexpressible grief, joined the Baptists, and was immersed in a pond near Dorking." The argument of the book and the hinge of irony upon which it turns are so elaborately contrived that, as I have said, very few even of those readers who know that the book is an attack on Christianity could explain exactly how the hinge is supposed to work. If I ever had to set an examination paper in English Literature for advanced students, one of the questions would be: "Summarize as briefly as possible John Pickard Owen's defence of the Resurrection in *The Fair Haven.*"

Whether it has to be reckoned as a failure on the part of the satirist and ironist if, for some reason, the vast majority of his readers mistake his meaning and intentions is an interesting question. In the case of Butler the failure was not due to any bungling or want of skill on his part, but to the very odd, individual conformation of his mind. His squib misfired, not because it was badly made, but because it was made to go on fizzling, fizzling, fizzling ironically, and never to explode. It is not everyone who can appreciate a squib which does not go off, or a rocket which never bursts into coloured stars. But for those who do, for those who can acquire a taste for caviare, or for the products of queer and "cranky" minds, *The Fair Haven* is a fascinating book. None of Butler's other books are more characteristic of his method of approaching and handling a subject or of his curious sense of humour. It has, however, upon me a strange psychological effect which I cannot explain, but which, to a much less degree, some of his other books also have: I enjoy reading it immensely; the elaborate argument and irony give me great intellectual pleasure; I am never at all bored by it; and yet from time to time I put the book down and say to myself: "Really, it is almost inconceivable that any human being ever had the patience to *write* this book."

The Fair Haven will always remain a literary curiosity, and Butler's fame will probably always rest on *Erewhon, The Way of All Flesh,* and *The Note-Books.* In some ways, however, he is at his best in *Alps and Sanctuaries,* a charming book which is the model of all modern books of ruminating, philosophical, cultured travellers. Those who knew Butler say that you can hear him talking in it, and what higher praise could there be than that? It flows on easily like good talk, giving infinite opportunities for that curious humour, irony, and gently twisted thought of its author. It is not a great book, though an extremely good one, and I can see in it no trace of a little man's mind. But if you turn to Butler's scientific works on evolution you see him at his worst, for he shows unexpectedly an exasperating littleness of mind. There can be no question of the cleverness and ability displayed in them. And though much of the controversy is dead, one can still read them with interest and with pleasure. No books on scientific subjects have ever been better written, and the flicker of Butler's irony gives them a strange, twinkling light of their own which is very attractive. And yet there is a littleness of mind displayed in them which is extremely irritating. It comes out partly in the personal hostility of Butler towards those with whom he disagrees. No doubt, Butler had much to complain about in his treatment by the scientists. They looked upon him with the jealous eye which professionalism and trade unionism always turn upon the amateur interloper. In fact, they ignored him. This may explain, but, to my mind, it does not excuse, Butler's tone of personal rancour and pique. It is the tone of a small-minded man nursing a grudge and unable to give his undivided attention to anything because he must always stop to see how he may "get his own back" on someone. Butler's charges against Darwin in *Unconscious Memory* are certainly not substantiated, and Darwin was quite justified in refusing to be drawn into a long, personal, acrimonious, and useless controversy. The continual girding at Darwin, which had already begun in *Evolution, Old and New,* becomes in the two later books intolerably irritating. And when exactly the same note begins to be struck in *Luck or Cunning?* against Herbert Spencer, Romanes, Huxley, and when one notices that in most cases the point about which Butler is arguing is his own claim to be this or to have done that, the gusts of one's irritation become more violent and more prolonged.

It is becoming fashionable to make exaggerated claims for Butler as a scientific thinker. Thus, in a little book by Mr. Joad, [see Sources for Further Study] the whole point of which is that it should be informative, if not educative, one is told that Butler made "an original contribution to the theory of Creative Evolution on the biological side, the inspired audacity of which places him second to none, not even to Darwin himself, among the pioneers of the nineteenth century." The statement is absurd. Butler was a man of great cleverness and intelligence, with a mind of considerable, but curiously limited, originality. When, in his prime, he applied his mind to the problem of evolution—at the moment when Darwinism was carrying all before it—he achieved two things. He subjected the Darwinian theory, particularly with regard to natural selection, to a very salutary criticism. He struck out for himself a highly ingenious theory that the offspring is one in personality with its parents, that instinctive and habitual actions are performed through unconscious memory of what we did in past generations when we were in the persons of our ancestors, and that evolution is due to variations which have been caused by the wants and endeavours of the living forms in which they appear. Both these achievements were of considerable interest, but it is fantastic to apply Mr. Joad's words to them. In both cases Butler stopped short long before he had produced anything of first-class importance. He stopped his constructive criticism to go off into interminable sterile personal controversy as to whether Darwin had committed a scientific felony or Herbert Spencer given him (Butler) the credit due to him. He left his own theory in the air, one of those clever improvisations which obviously contain much which is not true, but which may contain a vague adumbration of subsequently discovered truths. That may be inspired audacity, but it does not entitle Butler to the first place among scientific pioneers of the nineteenth century.

Butler's place in literature is really not very different from his place in science. *The Way of All Flesh* is the nearest he came to writing a great book, but it misses greatness. Its cleverness and originality are very great; the drabness of its irony is tremendous; it is solid and its characters are solid. It ought to have been either one of the great satires or of the great novels, but it is neither; it falls in between, into the place reserved for the "queer" books which one can always re-read and

Butler at Cambridge during the mid-1850s.

which always slightly disappoint one. The kink of crankiness in Butler's mind gives a kink to the book which only passion could have straightened out. But Butler was without passion. The temperature of his writing is, in fact, too low; it is cold to the touch, like something that is dead or nearly dead. Or to put it in another way, the atmosphere of his writing is like the atmosphere of the reading-room in the British Museum.

Though Butler cannot be numbered among the greatest writers, his books will probably be read by a small number of people long after many greater names are only remembered in histories of literature. In the history of English society he himself ought to have an honoured place. For he was a great iconoclast. The end of the nineteenth century was a time of breaking up, the breaking up of images and bonds and creeds and superstitions. In that salutary process of destruction Samuel Butler was one of the earliest and most efficient of the pioneers. (pp. 46-56)

Leonard Woolf, "Samuel Butler," in his *Essays on Literature, History, Politics, Etc.,* L. and Virginia Woolf, 1927, pp. 44-56.

G. D. H. COLE
(essay date 1961)

[Cole, an English economist and novelist, wrote widely on socialism and Marxism and was a prolific author of detective fiction. In the following excerpt, he discusses major themes of Butler's works and assesses the author's achievements.]

While Butler lived, *Erewhon* was by far his best-known book. Indeed, no other had reached at all a wide public. Even *Erewhon* was never a "best-seller," and brought its author little enough in money. For the rest, Butler paid for the printing and publication of his own books, and usually lost on them. He was incapable of writing anything that he did not really want to write, apart from getting money by it; and the books he wanted to publish were not such, apart from *Erewhon,* as any large numbers of his contemporaries wanted to read. But with *Erewhon*—and of course posthumously with *The Way of All Flesh*—he did catch the taste of a substantial public. *Erewhon Revisited,* written nearly thirty years later, had no corresponding success, although it is in a number of respects a better book than its predecessor. It has some attempt at characterization—whereas *Erewhon* has none; it is much more of a story, and much better constructed; and its satire is not less pointed or effective. To some extent these very merits tell against it. Satire does not go well with delineation of character, especially of characters the author likes. The story does not allow the digressions which make up some of the best of *Erewhon.* The satire is more concentrated on a single theme, and that theme—the growth of the Sun-Child legend—is of a sort to antagonize a good many readers. But the thing that matters most is that *Erewhon Revisited,* as a sequel, could not possibly make its impact with the same freshness and surprise as *Erewhon.* The reader knew what manner of satire to expect, though not the direction in which it would be launched; and that took some of the gilding off the gingerbread.

In *Erewhon,* from title to subject-matter and from matter to style of writing, Butler first showed his remarkable talent for turning familiar things the wrong way round. Nothing pleased him . . . better than to invert a proverb or a quotation in such a way as to present a startling thought—a verbal paradox that was much more than a play on words. His *Note-Books,* and his correspondence with Miss Savage, are full of such inversions; and he loved, having made one, to keep on juggling with it for his own—and posthumously for his readers'—delight. In *Erewhon* he juggled in public, but not so much with phrases as with observances and familiar habits which most people had taken for granted. One example is the Erewhonian treatment, not merely of crime as illness, but of illness as crime—a most pleasant conceit, with enough of underlying truth in it to enable the paradox to bear a large burden of elaboration. Another example, no less evocative, is that of the "Musical Banks," which proceeds from the paradox of a currency of high moral prestige that lacks all purchasing power to the still more entertaining notion of the Church as a Bank for laying up treasure in heaven by fair pretensions. This is excellent satire on the worldly church-goer, who was much more in the social ascendant then than now. Admirable fun, too, is the goddess Ydgrun (Mrs. Grundy the wrong way round), to whom the Erewhonian ladies gave their real worship. Moreover, "The Book of the Machines" was finely pointed paradox at a time when Darwinism was new, and the controversy between mechanistic and spiritual interpretations of the world raging in every articulate section of society, under the first full impact of science on the popular mind. *Erewhon* was too shocking to become a best-seller, and also too intellectual to be read except by intellectuals. But among intellectuals it was read quite widely, with a sense of novelty and of a number of caps fitted very neatly to the correct heads.

Erewhon had its serious side. Butler meant what he said about the Musical Banks. But for the most part it was a putting out of the tongue at his contemporaries, with no attempt at persuading them. In *Erewhon Revisited*, on the other hand, Butler presented his readers, in the form of a tale, with a development of his theory about the Resurrection, which he had expounded previously in his early pamphlet, and, in a different satirical form, in *The Fair Haven*. The ascent of the Sun-Child into heaven and the subsequent growth of the legend of his divinity are an open and direct satire on the entire supernatural element in the Christian religion, an attempt to show, logically, how the beliefs embodied in it could have developed without any real foundation, and how vested interests could have grown up round them, committed to uphold their influence by all means. This, however well done, could not be quite such fun as the sheer irresponsibility of the paradoxes of the earlier book; and it was bound, being more open, to give even greater offence in many quarters. Last but not least, by the time *Erewhon Revisited* appeared, the Higher Criticism had come to be regarded as *vieux jeu* by many of the intellectuals who were Butler's public. God, and Anti-God, were both rather out of fashion in 1901: indeed, Butler's *Note-Books* make it plain that he thought so himself. "God," he informed an imaginary lexicographer, "is simply the word that comes next to 'go-cart,' and nothing more."

Nevertheless, Butler could not stop thinking about God, and making notes about him. God had been

so dinned into him in childhood, and so closely identified with Canon Butler, that the son could never get either of them out of his mind. Towards both, when he had escaped from them, he achieved a degree of tolerance in retrospect; but essentially he continued to dislike them both, as wielders of irrational and repressive power. This comes out in many passages in the *Note-Books;* and *Erewhon Revisited* shows that, even if he had become milder about God, he had not changed his attitude to clergymen or to Churches.

The second main theme developed in *Erewhon Revisited* is largely a repetition of the chapters in *Erewhon* about the "Colleges of Unreason." Professors Hanky and Panky and Professor Gargoyle are legitimate successors to Mr. Thims and the Professor of Worldly Wisdom. What is new in the later book is the attempt to paint—say, rather, the success in painting—portraits of pleasant people, such as Mrs. Humdrum and the Sun-Child's son by Yram, George.

George, in *Erewhon Revisited,* Towneley, in *The Way of All Flesh,* these are the people Butler most admired, and would most have wished to be like. They are happy, healthy, good-looking, and well-to-do. They understand the world, not from having learnt about it, but by instinct. They have no money troubles, no uncertainties about themselves. They are amiable without cost, because nothing thwarts them. They get what they want without meanness and without trampling upon others. They are kind, because they are kindly by nature; but they do not vex themselves about other people's troubles unless they are obtruded upon them. They do good works when the doing comes their way; but "good works," done of set moral purpose, they have no use for. Take this, from the *Note-Books,* as an epitome. "To love God is to have good health, good looks, good sense, experience, a kindly nature and a fair balance of cash in hand." Or this, from the same source: "Heaven is the work of the best and kindest men and women. Hell is the work of prigs, pedants, and professional truth-tellers. The world is an attempt to make the best of both."

I know a number of people who do not like Butler's *Note-Books.* They find his paradoxical inversions irritating, and many of his preoccupations out of date. It is quite possible to be as allergic to Butlerisms as some people are to puns, and to dismiss his wisecracks as no more than verbal displays. For my part, I enjoy his verbal juggling and the uses he puts it to. I too have lived in Arcadia—or near enough to it to have a lively sense of the absurdities and crampings of that Victorian world. I have encountered, though not in my own upbringing, the Victorian father and his wife: I have come across will-shaking disinheritors, and the shams of pseudo-religious respectability. I have dined, cheek by jowl, with Professors of Unreason: I have met plenty of aggravating dogmatists of science, as well as of religion.

These enemies of the spirit of man are fewer than they were, and have to walk more warily; and now devils a great deal worse have arisen in their place. But, though it would be better to be off with the old devils before we are on with the new, that is not how these things happen. There are enough of the old still left to give Butler's satire continuing point. Its point is, nevertheless, I agree, less penetrating than it was; and the new devils are well-armoured against it. *The Way of All Flesh,* much more than *Erewhon,* is becoming a period-piece, because the changes in family life have gone further than those in many other fields. The growth of democracy and of the Welfare State has eclipsed the patriarchal father and taxed away the Towneley's incomes so that they can no longer lord it as they could. "Three per cents, paid quarterly" are no longer what they were, after two wars and the inflations they have brought with them. "Good works" have given place to social justice, and "social workers" have lost their awfulness in the process. It is now possible to be both possessed of a social conscience, and reasonably human and sinful to a moderate degree.

These changes would have perplexed Butler, who was fully as much a child as a critic of his own time. Intellectually, he made daring sallies against his contemporaries; but he remained tied on a string to many of their conventions. He envied the Towneleys, who could be gentlemen without effort and could carry all before them with hardly a thought; but he knew that such a way of living was not for him. He was too timid in action, except with a pen; too much a worrier; and too self-conscious. He wanted to be respectable, as well as a prodigal: a gentleman, as well as a *gamin.* Above all, once bit by speculation, he wanted to be secure, and at the same time to go his own way, flouting the world's opinion, and yet deferring to it. (pp. 38-42)

His achievement as a writer I know not how to sum up. I regard *The Way of All Flesh* as a great novel, despite its falling off in its later chapters—of which Miss Savage was well aware. I regard both *Erewhon* and *Erewhon Revisited* as excellent satires, and the John Pickard Owen memoir in *The Fair Haven* as a little masterpiece in the same genre. I believe Butler had something real and important to say about evolution, especially human evolution, though I do not think he said it quite right, largely because he could never disentangle his doctrine of unconscious memory from his quarrel with the Darwinians about Natural Selection. I delight in *Alps and Sanctuaries,* enjoy his Homeric translations, and feel sure he was mainly in the right about Shakespeare's *Sonnets.* I can always quarry happily in the *Note-Books:* I like declaiming *A Psalm of Montreal;* and I am astonished at the excellence of two or three of his few sonnets. But I do not believe that a young woman composed *The Odyssey,* and I doubt if it was composed in Sicily. I am quite unconvinced that either the scientists or the literary critics were in a conspiracy to befoul Butler's name; and I am not prepared to accept his version of his father's character as more than three-parts of the truth, or quite to forgive him some of the ungenerous things he wrote about Miss Savage when his bad mood was on him. In short, I have a strong, but not an uncritical, liking for his books, but, at bottom, no great liking for the man who wrote them. That, however, from the standpoint of his artistic achievement, is neither here nor there. Butler has what he asked for, and rather more—a narrow, but not precarious, niche in the temple of literary fame. (pp. 43-4)

G. D. H. Cole, in his *Samuel Butler,* revised edition, Longmans, Green & Co., 1961, 52 p.

GOVIND NARAIN SHARMA
(essay date 1980)

[Sharma is an Indian-born Canadian critic and scholar. In the following excerpt, he examines Butler's use of Darwin's theories in *Erewhon.*]

"In his youthful essays on evolution and the machine, as well as in the first (1872) edition of *Erewhon,*" says Herbert Sussman, "Butler approaches mechanistic biology with nearly perfect intellectual ambivalence, with an ironic detachment that only seeks to play with the paradoxes of philosophical mechanism rather than resolve them. Only after *Erewhon* did Butler change from satirist to scientist as he sought to develop a vitalistic theory that could supplant the mechanistic system of Darwin." And he concludes his discussion of Butler with the statement: "Butler never linked his intellectual objection to mechanistic thought with social or moral criticism. In *Erewhon,* the "Book of Machines" is a separate text set off from the main narrative; Butler in no way dramatizes the relation between the absence of machinery and the quality of Erewhonian life." It will be my contention in this essay that though Butler had not made up his mind on the Darwinian theory when he published the first edition of *Erewhon,* the direction of his thought was distinctly towards a teleological view, the position being the same as with *Life and Habit* in which, though he was not aware of it at the time of writing it, "the spirit of the book was throughout teleological." Also the "Book of Machines," far from being "a separate text," is central to the artistic and moral economy of *Erewhon,* to the projection of Butler's satiric as well as his utopian vision.

There has been a great deal of controversy about Butler's purpose in writing the machine chapters and his own contribution has been to increase rather than diminish the confusion. In the preface to the second edition he repudiated the suggestion that they were an attempt to reduce Darwin's theory to an absurdity and wrote to Darwin himself disavowing any such intention. But he has also said that he wrote the preface to "stroke him [Darwin] down," suspecting that the machine chapters were the "peccant matter" offending him. Whichever of these statements we accept, they leave little doubt that Butler did see a connection between his view of the machines and the Darwinian theory of evolution, the reflections on machines being a direct consequence of his acquaintance with the theory of evolution as set forth by Charles Darwin. Commenting on the latter's observation in the preface to his last edition of the *Origin of Species* that Lamarck was partly led to his conclusions by the analogy of domestic productions, Butler says in *Life and Habit*:

> . . . If they imply that Lamarck drew inspirations from the gradual development of the mechanical inventions of man, and from the progress of man's ideas, I would say that of all sources this would seem to be the safest and most fertile from which to draw. Plants and animals under domestication are indeed a suggestive field for study, but machines are the manner in which man is varying at this moment.

Thus the study of machines has a direct bearing on the study of human evolution and hence of all organic life. Since the latter study is for Butler never confined to the biological aspect alone, it is reasonable to assume that his reflections on machines have relevance to man's social and moral problems.

But what exactly is the nature of this relevance, the link between Butler's objection to mechanistic thought as represented by the Darwinian view of evolution and his social and moral outlook? Dwight Culler is one of the few critics who have tried to explore this link in a most forthright way by examining Darwin's influence on *Erewhon*. The influence, according to him, "lies somewhere not in the substance but in the total feeling and structure of the book," more particularly in Butler's satiric technique, in the embodiment of the upside-down view of England through a device which he calls the Darwinian reversal. *Erewhon,* however, appears to be Darwinian even more in substance than in form. Erewhonian morality seems to be "natural," evolution being the basis of the ethics: "a physical excellence is considered in Erewhon as a set-off against any other disqualification," and disease is regarded as a crime. "Moreover, they [the Erewhonians] hold their deities to be quite regardless of motives. With them it is the thing done which is everything, and the motive goes for nothing." There is the example of the air-god who will kill a man if he stays without air for more than a few minutes, whatever be his motives. In their social norms too Darwinism is a powerful determinant. They respect wealth and success, and in their eyes earning money is synonymous with "doing good" to society, the true philanthropy.

> So strongly are the Erewhonians impressed with this, that if a man has made a fortune of over £20,000 a year they exempt him from all taxation, considering him as a work of art, and too precious to be meddled with; . . . so magnificent an *organization* overawes them; they regard it as a thing dropped from heaven.

This attitude of the Erewhonians may appear irreverent to those who would prize moral virtue more highly than worldly success, but it is not so; it is based on a "spirit of the most utter reverence for those things . . . which are, which mould us and fashion us, be they what they may; for our masters therefore." Obviously, for the Erewhonians there is no distinction between "is" and "ought": the "is" dictates the "ought."

The Erewhonian attitude to machines is also Darwinian. In a ruthless struggle for survival a living being's first duty is to look after his own survival. The machines, evolving at a terrific pace and acquiring a greater degree of sophistication every day, hold the possibility of supplanting man and reducing him to a state of servitude. Evidently, if he is to ensure his own survival, he has to stop the proliferation and development of machines. But this very way of looking at things, of looking at the machine as a competitor and an adversary, betrays a deeper concern than could be explained in terms of "mere fun" or "gigantic bluffs," and the writer's attitude could scarcely be described as that of "perfect intellectual ambivalence."

I would suggest that the machine is the key symbol in *Erewhon*, embodying the antithesis between mechanism and life, which, according to Basil Willey, is the central problem of Butler's thought. This antithesis forms the basis of his utopian and satiric vision and projects itself into the leading ideas which are worked out in *Erewhon:* for example, on crime and disease, Hebraism and Hellenism, reason and faith, logic and common sense, duty and pleasure. It helps us in understanding the relationship between man and his laws, customs and institutions. The latter, like machines, are good friends and allies but bad masters. Insofar as they contribute to human development and happiness, they are good; when they stand in the way of these they are undesirable. When the machine tends to become machinery in Arnold's sense of the word, and when it leads men to erect impressive and elaborate structures of thought in the realm of religion, morals, philosophy or science, it becomes positively dangerous. It is then a symbol of rigidity and dogmatism, whereas it is moderation, flexibility and compromise which are man's prime needs in life. But men cannot do without the machine entirely: he needs the prop of customs, laws and institutions to function till he reaches "the true millennium," "the unconscious state of equilibrium which we observe in the structures and instincts of bees and ants, and an approach to which may be found among some savage nations." If these customs, laws and institutions are flexible, can move with the spirit of the times, they can be of immense value to man. In fact, to mould them in this manner, to modify and perfect them to suit his needs, is a challenge to him. His success in doing so would be a mark of his intelligence and cunning, just as the invention of superior machines has been, and would ensure the victory of life over mechanism.

The antithesis can first be seen in the projection of the author's satiric outlook. It is characteristic of what Northrop Frye calls "the second or quixotic phase of satire." The central theme in this phase of satire is the setting of ideas and generalizations and theories and dogmas over against the life they are supposed to explain. Butler's preferences are clear. He emphasizes the superiority of life over ideas—of faith and instinct over reason, of the unconscious over the conscious. It is an important feature of Butler's philosophical strategy in *Erewhon* to bring out the dichotomy between the Erewhonians' unconscious and conscious life, the essential rightness of the former and the intriguing hypocrisy of the latter. It is mainly the latter which finds expression in their articulated doctrines and beliefs—their banishment of machinery, their penal code, double coinage and Birth Formulae; and in the institutions which are supposed to uphold them—the Colleges of Unreason, the law courts, the Musical Banks. Whenever they try to be logical and consistent—in other words, set ideas above life—they end up in absurdities and self-deceiving clichés. But this should not tempt us to laugh them out of court; they have a native common sense, an instinctive mother-wit which guides them and in their practical conduct makes them steer clear of a slavish subservience to their dogmas and theories. They recognize the supreme value of the principle of compromise and make it the lodestar of their lives. In the instinctive recognition of this value lies the superiority of the high Ydgrunites, who exemplify best the maxim that "perfect ignorance and perfect knowledge are alike unselfconscious." They are "nice, sensible, unintrospective people" in whom right living has become an instinct which "does not betray signs of self-consciousness as to its own knowledge. It has dismissed reference to first principles, and is no longer under the law but under the grace of a settled conviction." The rest of the Erewhonians have not attained to this perfection of unconscious knowledge; they are still dominated by machinery in the form of the abstract systems which advocate prescribed modes of thought and behaviour like beliefs in the objective personalities of hope, justice and love, ritualistic worship at the Musical Banks and assiduous pursuit of the hypothetical language. They can be imposed upon by any prophet who can make a show of learning and wisdom, thus sacrificing common sense at the shrine of logic. The high Ydgrunites, on the contrary, though they are faithful believers in "conformity until absolutely intolerable," the law of Ydgrun ("Grundy" in the first edition), and would never run counter to her dictates, yet when there is ample reason for doing so and necessity arises, they are capable of overriding her with due self-reliance without being punished by the goddess, "for they are brave, and Ydgrun is not." Thus "they have no real belief in the objective existence of beings [like justice, love and hope] which so readily explain themselves as abstractions, and whose personality demands a quasi-materialism which it baffles the imagination to realise." They have no sense of a hereafter, and their only religion is that of self-respect and consideration for other people. Though they have studied the hypothetical language, it did not have much hand in making them what they are; rather the fact of their being generally possessed of its rudiments is one reason for the reverence paid to the hypothetical language itself.

Butler's chief device to put forward his own point of view is his invention of the naive hero, later in *Erewhon Revisited* given the name Higgs. Higgs is in some respects Butler himself, or what he would have liked to be—a handsome, personable young man with blue eyes and light hair, having much to glory in the flesh. These attractions appear, however, to be partly marred by his priggish Anglicanism and his religious zeal which makes him continually harp on his favourite tune of earning religious merit by converting to Christianity the Erewhonians whom he takes to be the descendants of the lost ten tribes of Israel. But in actual fact, these obsessions do not put us off very much: the angularity of his character turns out to be a comic trait which proves endearing, like the patriotism of Gulliver or the optimism of Candide. Like the hero of the low mimetic mode, of most comedy and realistic fiction, he is superior neither to other men nor to his environment but one of us, and we respond to a sense of his common humanity. He has also some of the characteristics of the hero of the ironic mode, the awkwardness of his personality giving us a sense of superiority to him and thus flattering our vanity and sustaining our interest in his thoughts and deeds. But he is not as simple as he appears. Far from being silly, obtuse and self-deceived, he has the *eiron's* sense of his own shortcomings, occasionally deprecates himself, as opposed to the *alazon,* who pretends or tries to be something more than he is. There can be no doubt of his shrewd intellegence, even his essential decency and good sense. This, according to A. E. Dyson, is a trump-card that Butler keeps up his sleeve in case readers become overconfident. His decency is strong enough to keep him in the right direction, even when his reasoning seems to be going wildly astray. As in the case of the Erewhonians, his instincts and settled convictions—the promptings of his unconscious—are sound; his doctrines and theories—the dictates of his conscious—are defective.

His very first encounter while entering Erewhon is significant. The Ten Statues creating a frightful cacophony scare him, but these represent nothing else than the decrees of his conscious self, his superego, the injunctions of the Mosaic code which have been a part of his moral drill since childhood. If he wishes to enter Erewhon he must free himself of this "thou-shalt-not" morality. Those like Chowbok (Kahabuka) who are unable to do so shall not enter the utopian land of Erewhon. It is clear that the Erewhonians reject the morality of the categorical imperative. The moral point of view according to them is not that of impartial legislators like Moses, as Kant supposed, but rather the point of view of the man with certain interests, specifically in human happiness and welfare. Such a man will believe in compromise and moderation. Unlike many other utopians, Butler's utopian outlook is free from any doctrinaire bias, and the symbol of the machine is highly relevant here. His conception of society is rather functional than ideological, the principle of function being the secret of the good community. Happiness would be achieved not by creating new customs, laws and institutions but by trying to observe and work the existing ones in the proper spirit. Erewhon, though not an ideal world, is certainly an attractive one in which people live more "naturally" and happily than in our own. If their lives are more "natural" it is not because they follow the evolutionary morality based on Darwinism, either in the personal or social sphere, for instance, by treating disease as a crime and giving the greatest respect to the most successful men. The "naturalness" of their lives lies in their disregard of reason and logic and in the instinctive adherence to modes of behaviour whose soundness has been demonstrated through long usage. They are happy and "ideal" not because they have freed themselves from the anomalies and hypocrisies which riddle our world but because they have accepted their existence. In his role of a literal-minded Evangelical the narrator finds them "really a very difficult people to understand" because

the most glaring anomalies seemed to afford them no intellectual inconvenience; neither, provided they did not actually see the money dropping out of their pockets, nor suffer immediate physical pain, would they listen to any arguments as to the waste of money and happiness which their folly caused them.

The narrator is, however, shrewd enough to note the desirable consequences of this inconsistency and evasiveness;

But this had an effect of which I have little reason to complain, for I was allowed almost to call them life-long self-deceivers to their faces, and they said it was quite true, but that it did not matter.

What Butler seeks to emphasize is that the happiness of the Erewhonians has been purchased at the price of an unlimited number of compromises, from permitting the use of machinery which was more than 271 years old to acceptance of the Musical Bank coinage as the more valuable one in theory. The Erewhonian Birth Formulae, for instance, require every child to sign a confession that he had been a free agent in coming into the world. This the Erewhonians make him do at an age when "neither they nor the law will for many a year allow any one else to bind him to the smallest obligation." Professors generally are not a very pleasant breed, being doctrinaire, rigid and dogmatic, and the Erewhonian ones were no different from their peers elsewhere in this respect. But the Professor with whom Higgs talked was a delightful person and his defense of this practice was most disarming: the world is full of compromises and there is hardly any affirmation which would bear being interpreted literally; the boy would have to begin compromising sooner or later, and this was part of his education in the art. In simple words, the sooner he learnt to disregard the constraints imposed by machinery the better it would be for his health and happiness in life.

Erewhon has been called a utopia and is undoubtedly so in many respects. But if the utopian impulse can be identified as idealistic and visionary, dominated by reason and logic and in love with order and perfection, then *Erewhon* is as much of a satire on utopias as a utopia. Paradoxical as it may appear—nothing unusual in the case of a writer like Butler—the Erewhonian world is utopian only insofar as it repudiates the utopian impulse and embraces the spirit of realism and compromise, accepting the validity of experience in preference to theory, of unreason in preference to reason, of unconscious instinctive wisdom in preference to the conscious. Where it sets out to be consciously utopian, it betrays life and becomes a slave to the machine. (pp. 3-10)

Govind Narain Sharma, "Butler's 'Erewhon': The Machine as Object and Symbol," in *The Samuel Butler Newsletter,* Vol. III, No. 1, Summer, 1980, pp. 3-12.

SOURCES FOR FURTHER STUDY

Blackmur, R. P. "Samuel Butler." In his *The Double Agent: Essays in Craft and Elucidation,* pp. 226-33. 1935. Reprint. Gloucester, Mass.: Peter Smith, 1962.

> Surveys Butler's literary career, asserting that "in no aspect did he approach perfection except in that for which he cared for perfection least—that of the humorous essayist or lecturer."

Holt, Lee E. *Samuel Butler.* New York: Twayne, 1964, 183 p.

> Study of Butler's works, outlining the development of his literary career.

Jeffers, Thomas L. *Samuel Butler Revalued.* University Park: Pennsylvania State University Press, 1981, 146 p.

> Asserts that Butler has erroneously been viewed as "a lonely seer, a studious eccentric who exhumed and galvanized the ideas of forgotten theorists," when in fact his thought clearly evidences "the pre-Victorian tradition of libertarianism in education, hedonism in ethics, and a sort of reverent agnosticism in natural theology."

Joad, C. E. M. *Samuel Butler (1835-1902).* London: Leonard Parsons, 1924, 195 p.

> Early biographical and critical study.

Jones, Henry Festing. *Samuel Butler: Author of "Erewhon."* 2 vols. London: Macmillan, 1910.

> Sympathetic biography written by Butler's friend and literary collaborator.

Muggeridge, Malcolm. *A Study of Samuel Butler: The Earnest Atheist.* London: G. P. Putnam's Sons, 1937, 230 p.

> Highly acerbic biography written to counter what Muggeridge considers the unwarranted adulation of Butler's works. Muggeridge instead maintains that Butler was essentially a shallow thinker.

Lord Byron

1788-1824

(Full name George Gordon Noel Byron) English poet, dramatist, and satirist.

INTRODUCTION

Although many contemporary critics considered his work immoral and inferior, Byron is now recognized as one of the most important poets of the nineteenth century. His literary reputation has varied more from one era to another than that of any other major English poet. Enormously popular during his lifetime, Byron was almost forgotten in the latter half of his century. Since then, however, critical acclaim for his work has been restored.

Born to "Mad Jack" Byron, a dissipated nobleman from an old and revered English family, and to Catherine Gordon, a hot-tempered descendant of a Scottish noble family, Byron soon displayed the unconventional traits of his heritage. He was notoriously proud of his lineage and was often accused of pretension. However, a club foot was an embarrassment to him throughout his life. Unable to tolerate criticism, he was quick to anger and often used his rage as a source of inspiration.

Byron's first publication was a collection of juvenilia, *Hours of Idleness* (1807), which drew a scathing attack in the *Edinburgh Review*. He replied with a vicious satire in *English Bards and Scotch Reviewers* (1809), which lashes out at authors and critics alike, saving an especially vitriolic section for Francis Jeffrey, to whom Byron had mistakenly attributed the review of *Hours of Idleness*. Although the satire in *English Bards* is often unfair, it earned Byron the respect, or at least the fear, of his critics. However, he felt a career in writing to be below his rank and decided to try politics. After taking a seat in the House of Lords and making several stirring speeches in the cause of reform, he journeyed to Europe and the Near East. When he returned, he casually handed the first two cantos of *Childe Harold's Pilgrimage* (1812), to a friend, thinking it not worthy of publication. Yet, when the poetry appeared in print, it became an enormous success.

For the next few years, Byron wrote verse tales, all of which sold well, though critics disagree about their quality. The great turning point in his life came, after a prolonged affair with the vivacious "little volcano," Lady Caroline Lamb, when Byron married Annabella Milbanke. Though their marriage seems to have gone well for a time, Annabella left Byron in 1816. Rumor and allegation of incest between Byron and his half-sister, Augusta, may have caused the rift, but clear evidence of the matter has never been presented. Many critics cite Byron's relationship with Augusta as the inspiration for his later verse drama, *Manfred* (1817).

When the scandal surrounding his marital separation spread through England, Byron was vilified by press and public alike, and he left the country. During his travels throughout Europe, he met Percy Bysshe Shelley, with whom he stayed in Italy. Shelley, Byron, and Leigh Hunt launched an ill-fated magazine, *The Liberal,* which published Byron's *The Vision of Judgment* (1822), a satire on Robert Southey's poem of the same name. While in Europe, Byron also began what is generally regarded as his masterpiece, *Don Juan* (1819-24). Variously described as a satire, epic satire, mock epic, and novel in verse, the unfinished work eludes critical categorization despite the consensus that it contains some of the finest satire in the English language. Writing in an animated and virtually unclassifiable style, Byron utilized a variety of narrative perspectives to comment on a wide range of human concerns—from the nature of the universe to the common physical sensations of everyday existence. The poet's ironic observations and brutally candid portrayal of human strengths and weaknesses earned the widespread condemnation of his contemporaries, who subjected *Don Juan* and its author to an unforgiving and almost relentless campaign of personal slander and critical abuse. Today, however, critics regard Byron's complex, profoundly skeptical, and ruthlessly realistic work as a remarkable anticipation of the mood and thematic preoccupations of modern literature. *Don Juan* is now considered one of the most important (if least characteristic) works of the Romantic era.

Because of the satiric nature of much of his work, Byron is difficult to place within the Romantic movement. He had a decided distaste for poetic theory and ridiculed the critical work of William Wordsworth and Samuel Taylor Coleridge. And though he was a friend to Shelley, Byron was not a part of the mystic tradition of Romanticism. His most notable contribution to Romanticism is the Byronic hero: a melancholy man, often with a dark past, who, eschewing societal and religious strictures, seeks truth and happiness in an apparently meaningless universe.

Still drawn to politics, Byron left Italy for Greece in 1823 to join a group of insurgents fighting for independence from the Turks. He died of a fever at Missolonghi. The England that had scorned him only eight years before now mourned him as a national hero. Despite his enormous influence in Europe—both Johann Wolfgang von Goethe and Aleksander Pushkin saw him as a master poet—his own country did not give its complete critical approval to Byron's work until almost a century after his death. While the literary quality of Byron's poetry deserves merit, continued interest in his work is also rooted in Byron's legendary personality and exploits. As Northrop Frye has written, "Byron is, strictly, neither a great poet nor a great man who wrote poetry, but something in between: a tremendous cultural force that was life and literature at once."

(For further information about Byron's life and works see *Dictionary of Literary Biography,* Vol. 96: *British Romantic Poets, 1789-1832,* Second Series and *Nineteenth-Century Literature Criticism,* Vols. 2, 12. For related criticism, see the entry on English Romantic Poetry in *Nineteenth-Century Literature Criticism,* Vol. 28.)

CRITICAL COMMENTARY

LORD BYRON

(letter date 1819)

[The following excerpt from a letter to John Murray contains many of Byron's most famous remarks on *Don Juan,* including his extended defense of the poem's rapid juxtaposition of levity and seriousness, a discussion of his lack of concrete plans for continuing the work, and the often-quoted statement "do you suppose I could have any intention but to giggle and make giggle?"]

You are right—Gifford is right—Crabbe is right—Hobhouse is right—you are all right—and I am all wrong—but do pray let me have that pleasure.—Cut

Principal Works

Hours of Idleness (poetry) 1807

English Bards and Scotch Reviewers (satire) 1809

Childe Harold's Pilgrimage: A Romaunt (poetry) 1812

The Bride of Abydos: A Turkish Tale (poetry) 1813

The Giaour: A Fragment of a Turkish Tale (poetry) 1813

Waltz: An Apostrophic Hymn (poetry) 1813

The Corsair (poetry) 1814

Lara (poetry) 1814

Ode to Napoleon Buonaparte (poetry) 1814

Hebrew Melodies (poetry) 1815

Childe Harold's Pilgrimage: Canto the Third (poetry) 1816

Parisina (poetry) 1816

The Prisoner of Chillon, and Other Poems (poetry) 1816

The Siege of Corinth (poetry) 1816

The Lament of Tasso (poetry) 1817

Manfred (dramatic poetry) 1817

Beppo: A Venetian Story (poetry) 1818

Childe Harold's Pilgrimage: Canto the Fourth (poetry) 1818

Mazeppa (poetry) 1819

Don Juan, Cantos I-XVI. 6 vols. (poetry) 1819-1824

Cain (drama) 1821

Marino Faliero, Doge of Venice (drama) 1821

Sardanapalus (drama) 1821

The Two Foscari (drama) 1821

The Vision of Judgment (poetry) 1822

Heaven and Earth (poetry) 1823

The Island; or, Christian and His Comrades (poetry) 1823

Werner (drama) 1823

The Deformed Transformed (drama) 1824

Letters and Journals. 11 vols. (letters and journals) 1975-1981

---

me up root and branch—quarter me in the "Quarterly"—send round my "disjecti membra poetae" like those of the Levite's Concubine—make—if you will—a spectacle to men and angels—but don't ask me to alter for I can't—I am obstinate and lazy—and there's the truth.—But nevertheless—I will answer your friend [Francis Cohen] who objects to the quick succession of fun and gravity—as if in that case the gravity did not (in intention at least) heighten the fun.—His metaphor is that "we are never scorched and drenched at the same time!"—Blessings on his experience!—Ask him these questions about "scorching and drenching."—Did he never play at Cricket or walk a mile in hot weather?—did he never spill a dish of tea over his testicles in handing the cup to his charmer to the great shame of his nankeen breeches?—did he never swim in the sea at Noonday with the Sun in his eyes and on his head—which all the foam of ocean could not cool? did he never draw his foot out of a tub of too hot water damning his eyes & his valet's? did he never inject for a Gonorrhea?—or make water through an ulcerated Urethra?—was he ever in a Turkish bath—that marble paradise of sherbet and sodomy?—was he ever in a cauldron of boiling oil like St. John?—or in the sulphureous waves of hell? (where he ought to be for his "scorching and drenching at the same time") did he never tumble into a river or lake fishing—and sit in his wet cloathes in the boat—or on the bank afterwards "scorched and drenched" like a true sportsman?——"Oh for breath to utter"—but make him my compliments—he is a clever fellow for all that—a very clever fellow.——You ask me for the plan of *Donny Johnny*—I *have* no plan—I *had*

no plan—but I had or have materials—though if like Tony Lumpkin—I am "to be snubbed so when I am in spirits" the poem will be naught—and the poet turn serious again.—If it don't take I will leave it off where it is with all due respect to the Public—but if continued it must be in my own way—you might as well make Hamlet (or Diggory) "act mad" in a strait waistcoat—as trammel my buffoonery—if I am to be a buffoon—their gestures and my thoughts would only be pitiably absurd—and ludicrously constrained.—Why Man the Soul of such writing is it's licence?—at least the *liberty* of that *licence* if one likes—*not* that one should abuse it—it is like trial by Jury and Peerage—and the Habeas Corpus—a very fine thing—but chiefly in the *reversion*—because no one wishes to be tried for the mere pleasure of proving his possession of the privilege.——But a truce with these reflections;—you are too earnest and eager about a work never intended to be serious;—do you suppose that I could have any intention but to giggle and make giggle?—a playful satire with as little poetry as could be helped—was what I meant—and as to the indecency—do pray read in Boswell—what *Johnson* the sullen moralist—says of *Prior* and Paulo Purgante. . . . (pp. 206-08)

Lord Byron, in a letter to John Murray on August 12, 1819, in his *"The Flesh is Frail": Byron's Letters and Journals, 1818-1819, Vol. 6,* edited by Leslie A. Marchand, Cambridge, Mass.: Belknap Press of Harvard University Press, 1976, pp. 206-10.

ALGERNON CHARLES SWINBURNE
(essay date 1866)

[Swinburne, an English poet and critic, was renowned during his lifetime for the technical mastery of his lyrics. In the following excerpt from an 1866 essay, he faults Byron's poetic ear but offers praise for the generally vivid quality of his major works.]

Even at its best, the serious poetry of Byron is often so rough and loose, so weak in the screws and joints which hold together the framework of verse, that it is not easy to praise it enough without seeming to condone or to extenuate such faults as should not be overlooked or forgiven. No poet is so badly represented by a book of selections. It must show something of his weakness; it cannot show all of his strength. Often, after a noble overture, the last note struck is either dissonant or ineffectual. His magnificent masterpiece, which must endure for ever among the precious relics of the world, will not bear dissection or extraction. The merit of *Don Juan* does not lie in any part, but in the whole. There is in that great poem an especial and exquisite balance and sustenance of alternate tones which cannot be expressed or explained by the utmost ingenuity of selection. . . . Much of the poet's earlier work is or seems unconsciously dishonest; this, if not always or wholly unaffected, is as honest as the sunlight, as frank as the seawind. Here, and here alone, the student of his work may recognize and enjoy the ebb and flow of actual life. Here the pulse of vital blood may be felt in tangible flesh. Here for the first time the style of Byron is beyond all praise or blame: a style at once swift and supple, light and strong, various and radiant. Between *Childe Harold* and *Don Juan* the same difference exists which a swimmer feels between lake-water and seawater: the one is fluent, yielding, invariable; the other has in it a life and pulse, a sting and a swell, which touch and excite the nerves like fire or like music. Across the stanzas of *Don Juan* we swim forward as over "the broad backs of the sea"; they break and glitter, hiss and laugh, murmur and move, like waves that sound or that subside. There is in them a delicious resistance, an elastic motion, which salt water has and fresh water has not. . . . Here, as at sea, there is enough and too much of fluctuation and intermission; the ripple flags and falls in loose and lazy lines: the foam flies wide of any mark, and the breakers collapse here and there in sudden ruin and violent failure. But the violence and weakness of the sea are preferable to the smooth sound and equable security of a lake: its buoyant and progressive impulse sustains and propels those who would sink through weariness in the flat and placid shallows. (pp. 242-43)

No poet of equal or inferior rank ever had so bad an ear. His smoother cadences are often vulgar and facile; his fresher notes are often incomplete and inharmonious. His verse stumbles and jingles, stammers and halts, where there is most need for a swift and even pace of musical sound. The rough sonorous changes of the songs in the *Deformed Transformed* rise far higher in harmony and strike far deeper into the memory than the lax easy lines in which he at first indulged; but they slip too readily into notes as rude and weak as the rhymeless tuneless verse in which they are so loosely set, as in a cheap and casual frame. (p. 246)

Except in the lighter and briefer scenes of *Don Juan,* [Byron] was never able to bring two speakers face to face and supply them with the right words. In structure as in metre his elaborate tragedies are wholly condemnable; filled as they are in spirit with the overflow of his fiery energy. *Cain* and *Manfred* are properly monologues decorated and set off by some slight appendage of ornament or explanation. In the later and loftier poem there is no difference perceptible, except in strength and knowledge, between Lucifer and Cain. Thus incompetent to handle the mysteries and varieties of character, Byron turns always with a fresh delight and a fresh confidence thither where he feels himself safe and strong. No part of his nature was more profound and sincere than the vigorous love of such inanimate things as were in tune with his own spirit and senses. . . . [When] once clear of men and confronted with elements, he casts the shell of pretence and drops the veil of habit; then, as in the last and highest passage of a poem which has suffered more from praise than any other from dispraise, his scorn of men caught in the nets of nature and necessity has no alloy of untruth; his spirit is mingled with the sea's, and overlooks with a superb delight the ruins and the prayers of men.

This loftiest passage in *Childe Harold* has been so often mouthed and mauled by vulgar admiration that it now can scarcely be relished. Like a royal robe worn out, or a royal wine grown sour, it seems the worse for having been so good. But in fact, allowing for one or two slips and blots, we must after all replace it among the choice and high possessions of poetry. After the first there is hardly a weak line; many have a wonderful vigour and melody; and the deep and glad disdain of the sea for men and the works of men passes into the verse in music and fills it with a weighty and sonorous harmony grave and sweet as the measured voice of heavy remote waves. No other passage in the fourth canto will bear to be torn out from the text; and this one suffers by extraction. The other three cantos are more loosely built and less compact of fabric; but in the first two there is little to remember or to praise. Much of the poem is written throughout in falsetto; there is a savour in many places as of something false and histrionic. (pp. 247-49)

His few sonnets, unlike Shelley's, are all good; the best is that on Bonnivard, one of his noblest and completest poems. The versified narratives which in their day were so admirable and famous have yielded hardly a stray sheaf to the gleaner. They have enough of vigour and elasticity to keep life in them yet; but once chipped or broken their fabric would crumble and collapse. The finest among them is certainly either the *Giaour* or the *Siege of Corinth;* the weakest is probably either *Parisina* or the *Bride of Abydos.* But in none of these is there even a glimpse of Byron's higher and rare faculty. All that can be said for them is that they gave tokens of a talent singularly fertile, rapid and vivid; a certain power of action and motion which redeems them from the complete stagnation of dead verses; a command over words and rhymes never of the best and never of the worst. In the *Giaour,* indeed, there is something of a fiery sincerity which in its successors appears diluted and debased.

The change began in Byron when he first found out his comic power, and rose at once beyond sight or shot of any rival. His early satires are wholly devoid of humour, wit, or grace; the verse of *Beppo,* bright and soft and fluent, is full at once of all. The sweet light music of its few and low notes was perfect as a prelude to the higher harmonies of laughter and tears, of scorn and passion, which as yet lay silent in the future. It is mere folly to seek in English or Italian verse a precedent or a parallel. The scheme of metre is Byron's alone; no weaker hand than his could ever bend that bow, or ever will. . . . Before the appearance of *Beppo* no one could foresee what a master's hand might make of the instrument; and no one could predict its further use and its dormant powers before the advent of *Don Juan.* In the *Vision of Judgment* it appears finally perfected; the metre fits the sense as with close and pliant armour, the perfect panoply of Achilles. A poem so short and hasty, based on a matter so worthy of brief contempt and long oblivion as the funeral and the fate of George III., bears about it at first sight no great sign or likelihood of life. But this poem which we have by us stands alone, not in Byron's work only, but in the work of the world. Satire in earlier times had changed her rags for robes; Juvenal had clothed with fire, and Dryden with majesty, that wandering and bastard Muse. Byron gave her wings to fly with, above the reach even of these. (pp. 250-52)

Side by side with the growth of his comic and satiric power, the graver genius of Byron increased and flourished. As the tree grew higher it grew shapelier; the branches it put forth on all sides were fairer of leaf and fuller of fruit than its earlier offshoots had promised. But from these hardly a stray bud or twig can be plucked off by way of sample. No detached morsel of *Don Juan,* no dismembered fragment of *Cain,* will serve to show or to suggest the excellence of either. These poems are coherent and complete as trees or flowers; they cannot be split up and parcelled out like a mosaic of artificial jewellery, which might be taken to pieces by the same artisan who put it together. (p. 254)

It would be waste of words and time here to enlarge at all upon the excellence of the pure comedy of *Don Juan.* From the first canto to the sixteenth; from the defence of Julia, which is worthy of Congreve or Molière, to the study of Adeline, which is worthy of Laclos or Balzac; the elastic energy of humour never falters or flags. (pp. 255-56)

As a poet, Byron was surpassed, beyond all question and all comparison, by three men at least of his own time; and matched, if not now and then overmatched, by one or two others. The verse of Wordsworth, at its highest, went higher than his; the verse of Landor flowed clearer. But his own ground, where none but he could set foot, was lofty enough, fertile and various. Nothing in Byron is so worthy of wonder and admiration as the scope and range of his power. New fields and ways of work, had he lived, might have given room for exercise and matter for triumph to [the man Shelley called] "that most fiery spirit." (pp. 257-58)

Algernon Charles Swinburne, "Byron," in his *Essays and Studies,* second edition, Chatto and Windus, 1876, pp. 238-58.

MATTHEW ARNOLD
(essay date 1881)

[Arnold was one of the most important English critics of the nineteenth century. In the following excerpt from an 1881 introduction to a collection of Byron's poems, he admits that Byron lacks the philosophical vision of a great artist but nonetheless declares him to be one of the nineteenth century's best poets.]

[Although] there may be little in Byron's poetry which can be pronounced either worthless or faultless, there are portions of it which are far higher in worth and far more free from fault than others. And although, again, the abundance and variety of his production is undoubtedly a proof of his power, yet I question whether by reading everything which he gives us we are so likely to acquire an admiring sense even of his variety and abundance, as by reading what he gives us at his happier moments. Varied and abundant he amply proves himself even by this taken alone. Receive him absolutely without omission or compression, follow his whole outpouring stanza by stanza and line by line from the very commencement to the very end, and he is capable of being tiresome.

Byron has told us himself that the *Giaour* "is but a string of passages'. He has made full confession of his own negligence. 'No one', says he, 'has done more through negligence to corrupt the language.' This accusation brought by himself against his poems is not just. . . . 'Lara', he declares, 'I wrote while undressing after coming home from balls and masquerades, in the year of revelry, 1814. The *Bride* was written in four, the *Corsair* in ten days.' He calls this 'a humiliating confession, as it proves my own want of judgment in publishing, and the public's in reading, things which cannot have stamina for permanence'. Again he does his poems injustice; the producer of such poems could not but publish them, the public could not but read them. Nor could Byron have produced his work in any other fashion; his poetic work could not have first grown and matured in his own mind, and then come forth as an organic whole; Byron had not enough of the artist in him for this, nor enough of self-command. . . . [It] was inevitable that works so produced should be, in general, 'a string of passages', poured out, as he describes them, with rapidity and excitement, and with new passages constantly suggesting themselves, and added while his work was going through the press. It is evident that we have here neither deliberate scientific construction, nor yet the instinctive artistic creation of poetic wholes; and that to take passages from work produced as Byron's was is a very different thing from taking passages out of the *Oedipus* or the *Tempest*, and deprives the poetry far less of its advantage.

Nay, it gives advantage to the poetry, instead of depriving it of any. Byron, I said, has not a great artist's profound and patient skill in combining an action or in developing a character,—a skill which we must watch and follow if we are to do justice to it. But he has a wonderful power of vividly conceiving a single incident, a single situation; of throwing himself upon it, grasping it as if it were real and he saw and felt it, and of making us see and feel it too. The *Giaour* is, as he truly called it, 'a string of passages', not a work moving by a deep internal law of development to a necessary end; and our total impression from it cannot but receive from this, its inherent defect, a certain dimness and indistinctness. But the incidents of the journey and death of Hassan, in that poem, are conceived and presented with a vividness not to be surpassed; and our impression from them is correspondingly clear and powerful. In *Lara*, again, there is no adequate development either of the character of the chief personage or of the action of the poem; our total impression from the work is a confused one. Yet such an incident as the disposal of the slain Ezzelin's body passes before our eyes as if we actually saw it. And in the same way as these bursts of

incident, bursts of sentiment also, living and vigorous, often occur in the midst of poems which must be admitted to be but weakly-conceived and loosely-combined wholes. Byron cannot but be a gainer by having attention concentrated upon what is vivid, powerful, effective in his work, and withdrawn from what is not so. (pp. 314-15)

To the poetry of Byron the world has ardently paid homage; full justice from his contemporaries, perhaps even more than justice, his torrent of poetry received. His poetry was admired, adored, 'with all its imperfections on its head',—in spite of negligence, in spite of diffuseness, in spite of repetitions, in spite of whatever faults it possessed. His name is still great and brilliant. Nevertheless the hour of irresistible vogue has passed away for him; even for Byron it could not but pass away. The time has come for him, as it comes for all poets, when he must take his real and permanent place, no longer depending upon the vogue of his own day and upon the enthusiasm of his contemporaries. Whatever we may think of him, we shall not be subjugated by him as they were; for, as he cannot be for us what he was for them, we cannot admire him so hotly and indiscriminately as they. His faults of negligence, of diffuseness, of repetition, his faults of whatever kind, we shall abundantly feel and unsparingly criticize; the mere interval of time between us and him makes disillusion of this kind inevitable. But how then will Byron stand, if we relieve him too, so far as we can, of the encumbrance of his inferior and weakest work, and if we bring before us his best and strongest work in one body together? (pp. 315-16)

We will take three poets, among the most considerable of our century: Leopardi, Byron, Wordsworth, Giacomo Leopardi was ten years younger than Byron, and he died thirteen years after him; both of them, therefore, died young—Byron at the age of thirty-six, Leopardi at the age of thirty-nine. Both of them were of noble birth, both of them suffered from physical defect, both of them were in revolt against the established facts and beliefs of their age; but here the likeness between them ends. . . . Leopardi has the very qualities which we have found wanting to Byron; he has the sense for form and style, the passion for just expression, the sure and firm touch of the true artist. Nay, more, he has a grave fulness of knowledge, an insight into the real bearings of the questions which as a sceptical poet he raises, a power of seizing the real point, a lucidity, with which the author of *Cain* has nothing to compare. (p. 323)

[Wordsworth's superiority] is in the power with which [he] feels the resources of joy offered to us in nature, offered to us in the primary human affections and duties, and in the power with which, in his moments of inspiration, he renders this joy, and makes us, too, feel it; a force greater than himself seeming to lift him and to prompt his tongue, so that he speaks in a style far above any style of which he has the constant command, and with a truth far beyond any philosophic truth of which he has the conscious and assured possession. (p. 324)

[Like Wordsworth's,] Byron's poetic value is also greater, on the whole, than Leopardi's; and his superiority turns in the same way upon the surpassing worth of something which he had and was, after all deduction has been made for his shortcomings. We talk of Byron's *personality,* 'a personality in eminence such as has never been yet, and is not likely to come again'; and we say that by this personality Byron is 'different from all the rest of English poets, and in the main greater'. (p. 325)

There is the Byron who posed, there is the Byron with his affectations and silliness, the Byron whose weakness Lady Blessington, with a woman's acuteness, so admirably seized: 'His great defect is flippancy and a total want of self-possession.' But when this theatrical and easily criticized personage betook himself to poetry, and when he had fairly warmed to his work, then he became another man; then the theatrical personage passed away; then a higher power took possession of him and filled him; then at last came forth into light that true and puissant personality, with its direct strokes, its ever-welling force, its satire, its energy, and its agony. This is the real Byron; whoever stops at the theatrical preludings does not know him. (pp. 326-27)

[As] a poet, he has no fine and exact sense for word and structure and rhythm; he has not the artist's nature and gifts. Yet a personality of Byron's force counts for so much in life, and a rhetorician of Byron's force counts for so much in literature! . . . Along with his astounding power and passion he had a strong and deep sense for what is beautiful in nature, and for what is beautiful in human action and suffering. When he warms to his work, when he is inspired, Nature herself seems to take the pen from him as she took it from Wordsworth, and to write for him as she wrote for Wordsworth, though in a different fashion, with her own penetrating simplicity. . . . [His] verse then exhibits quite another and a higher quality from the rhetorical quality,—admirable as this also in its own kind of merit is,—of such verse as

> Minions of splendour shrinking from distress,

and of so much more verse of Byron's of that stamp. Nature, I say, takes the pen for him; and then, assured master of a true poetic style though he is not, any more than Wordsworth, yet as from Wordsworth at his best there will come such verse as

> Will no one tell me what she sings?

so from Byron, too, at his best, there will come such verse as

> He heard it, but he heeded not; his eyes
> Were with his heart, and that was far away.

Of verse of this high quality, Byron has much; of verse of a quality lower than this, of a quality rather rhetorical than truly poetic, yet still of extraordinary power and merit, he has still more. To separate, from the mass of poetry which Byron poured forth, all this higher portion, so superior to the mass, and still so considerable in quantity, and to present it in one body by itself, is to do a service, I believe, to Byron's reputation, and to the poetic glory of our country. (pp. 327-28)

Wordsworth's value is of another kind. Wordsworth has an insight into permanent sources of joy and consolation for mankind which Byron has not; his poetry gives us more which we may rest upon than Byron's,—more which we can rest upon now, and which men may rest upon always. I place Wordsworth's poetry, therefore, above Byron's on the whole, although in some points he was greatly Byron's inferior, and although Byron's poetry will always, probably, find more readers than Wordsworth's, and will give pleasure more easily. But these two, Wordsworth and Byron, stand, it seems to me, first and pre-eminent in actual performance, a glorious pair, among the English poets of this century. Keats had probably, indeed, a more consummate poetic gift than either of them; but he died having produced too little and being as yet too immature to rival them. I for my part can never even think of equalling with them any other of their contemporaries;—either Coleridge, poet and philosopher wrecked in a mist of opium; or Shelley, beautiful and ineffectual angel, beating in the void his luminous wings in vain. Wordsworth and Byron stand out by themselves. When the year 1900 is turned, and our nation comes to recount her poetic glories in the century which has then just ended, the first names with her will be these. (pp. 329-30)

Matthew Arnold, "Byron," in his *Essays in Criticism, first and second series,* Dutton, 1964, pp. 312-30.

T. S. ELIOT
(essay date 1937)

[Eliot, a poet and critic, is closely identified with many of the qualities denoted by the term Modernism: experimentation, formal complexity, artistic and intellectual eclecticism, and a classicist's view of the artist working at an emotional distance from his or her creation. In the following excerpt from an essay originally published in 1937, he praises Byron's storytelling skills.]

One reason for the neglect of Byron is, I think, that he

has been admired for what are his most ambitious attempts to be poetic; and these attempts turn out, on examination, to be fake: nothing but sonorous affirmations of the commonplace with no depth of significance. (p. 226)

The qualities of narrative verse which are found in *Don Juan* are no less remarkable in the earlier tales. Before undertaking this essay I had not read these tales since the days of my schoolboy infatuation, and I approached them with apprehension. They are readable. However absurd we find their view of life, they are, as tales, very well told. As a *tale-teller* we must rate Byron very high indeed: I can think of none other since Chaucer who has a greater readability, with the exception of Coleridge whom Byron abused and from whom Byron learned a great deal. And Coleridge never achieved a narrative of such length. Byron's plots, if they deserve that nature, are extremely simple. What makes the tales interesting is first a torrential fluency of verse and a skill in varying it from time to time to avoid monotony; and second a genius for divagation. Digression, indeed, is one of the valuable arts of the storyteller. The effect of Byron's digressions is to keep us interested in the story-teller himself, and through this interest to interest us more in the story. (p. 227)

It is, I think, worth nothing, that Byron developed the verse *conte* considerably beyond [Thomas] Moore and [Sir Walter] Scott, if we are to see his popularity as anything more than public caprice or the attraction of a cleverly exploited personality. These elements enter into it, certainly. But first of all, Byron's verse tales represent a more mature stage of this transient form than Scott's, as Scott's represent a more mature stage than Moore's. Moore's *Lalla Rookh* is a mere sequence of tales joined together by a ponderous prose account of the circumstances of their narration [modelled upon the *Arabian Nights*]. Scott perfected a straight-forward story with the type of plot which he was to employ in his novels. Byron combined exoticism with actuality, and developed most effectively the use of *suspense*. (p. 230)

Childe Harold seems to me inferior to this group of poems [*The Giaour, The Bride of Abydos, The Corsair, Lara,* etc.]. Time and time again, to be sure, Byron awakens fading interest by a purple passage, but Byron's purple passages are never good enough to do the work that is expected of them in *Childe Harold:*

Stop! for thy tread is on an Empire's dust!

is just what is wanted to revive interest, at that point; but the stanza that follows, on the Battle of Waterloo, seems to me quite false; and quite representative of the falsity in which Byron takes refuge whenever he *tries* to write poetry:

Stop! for thy tread is on an Empire's dust!

An Earthquake's spoil is sepulchred below!
Is the spot mark'd with no colossal bust?
Nor column trophied for triumphal show?
None; but the moral's truth tells simpler so,
As the ground was before, so let it be;—
How that red rain hath made the harvest grow!
And is this all the world has gained by thee,
Thou first and last of fields! king-making victory?

It is all the more difficult, in a period which has rather lost the appreciation of the kind of virtues to be found in Byron's poetry, to analyse accurately his faults and vices. Hence we fail to give credit to Byron for the instinctive art by which, in a poem like *Childe Harold,* and still more efficiently in *Beppo* or *Don Juan,* he avoids monotony by a dexterous turn from one subject to another. He has the cardinal virtue of being never dull. But, when we have admitted the existence of forgotten virtues, we still recognize a falsity in most of those passages which were formerly most admired. To what is this falsity due?

Whatever it is, in Byron's poetry, that is 'wrong', we should be mistaken in calling it rhetoric. Too many things have been collected under that name; and if we are going to think that we have accounted for Byron's verse by calling it 'rhetorical', then we are bound to avoid using that adjective about Milton and Dryden, about both of whom [in their very different kinds] we seem to be saying something that has meaning, when we speak of their 'rhetoric'. (pp. 231-32)

Of Byron one can say, as of no other English poet of his eminence, that he added nothing to the language, that he discovered nothing in the sounds, and developed nothing in the meaning, of individual words. I cannot think of any other poet of his distinction who might so easily have been an accomplished foreigner writing English. The ordinary person talks English, but only a few people in every generation can write it; and upon this undeliberate collaboration between a great many people talking a living language and a very few people writing it, the continuance and maintenance of a language depends. Just as an artisan who can talk English beautifully while about his work or in a public bar, may compose a letter painfully written in a dead language bearing some resemblance to a newspaper leader, and decorated with words like 'maelstrom' and 'pandemonium': so does Byron write a dead or dying language.

This imperceptiveness of Byron to the English word—so that he has to use a great many words before we become aware of him—indicates for practical purposes a defective sensibility. I say 'for practical purposes' because I am concerned with the sensibility in his poetry, not with his private life; for if a writer has not the language in which to express feelings they might as well not exist. . . . Byron did for the language very much what the leader writers of our journals are doing day by day. I think that this failure is much more important than the platitude of his intermittent philosophizing. Every poet has uttered platitudes, every poet has said things that have been said before. It is not the weakness of the ideas, but the schoolboy command of the language, that makes his lines seem trite and his thought shallow. . . . (pp. 232-33)

All things worked together to make *Don Juan* the greatest of Byron's poems. The stanza that he borrowed from the Italian was admirably suited to enhance his merits and conceal his defects, just as on a horse or in the water he was more at ease than on foot. His ear was imperfect, and capable only of crude effects. . . . [He] seems always to be reminding us that he is not really trying very hard and yet producing something as good or better than that of the solemn poets who take their verse-making more seriously. And Byron really is at his best when he is not trying too hard to be poetic. . . . (p. 234)

[At] a lower intensity he gets a surprising range of effect. His genius for digression, for wandering away from his subject [usually to talk about himself] and suddenly returning to it, is, in *Don Juan,* at the height of its power. The continual banter and mockery, which his stanza and his Italian model serve to keep constantly in his mind, serve as an admirable antacid to the high-falutin which in the earlier romances tends to upset the reader's stomach; and his social satire helps to keep him to the objective and has a sincerity that is at least plausible if not profound. The portrait of himself comes much nearer to honesty than any that appears in his earlier work. This is worth examining in some detail.

Charles Du Bos, in his admirable *Byron et le besoin de la fatalité* [*Byron and the Need of Fatality*], quotes a long passage of self-portraiture from *Lara.* Du Bos deserves full credit for recognizing its importance; and Byron deserves all the credit that Du Bos gives him for having written it. This passage strikes me also as a masterpiece of self-analysis, but of a self that is largely a deliberate fabrication—a fabrication that is only completed in the actual writing of the lines. . . . Byron made a vocation out of what for most of us is an irregular weakness, and deserves a certain sad admiration for his degree of success. But in *Don Juan,* we get something much nearer to genuine self-revelation. For Juan, in spite of the brilliant qualities with which Byron invests him—so that he may hold his own among the English aristocracy—is not an heroic figure. There is nothing absurd about his presence of mind and courage during the shipwreck, or about his prowess in the Turkish wars: he exhibits a kind of physical courage and capacity for heroism which we are quite willing to attribute to Byron himself. But in the accounts of his relations with women, he is not made to appear heroic or even dignified; and

these impress us as having an ingredient of the genuine as well as of the make-believe (pp. 234-35)

The last four cantos are, unless I am greatly mistaken, the most substantial of the poem. To satirize humanity in general requires either a more genial talent than Byron's, such as that of Rabelais, or else a more profoundly tortured one, such as Swift's. But in the latter part of *Don Juan* Byron is concerned with an English scene, in which there was for him nothing romantic left; he is concerned with a restricted field that he had known well, and for the satirizing of which an acute animosity sharpened his powers of observation. His understanding may remain superficial, but it is precise. . . . Lord Henry and Lady Adeline Amundeville are persons exactly on the level of Byron's capacity for understanding and they have a reality for which their author has perhaps not received due credit.

What puts the last cantos of *Don Juan* at the head of Byron's works is, I think, that the subject matter gave him at last an adequate object for a genuine emotion. The emotion is hatred of hypocrisy; and if it was reinforced by more personal and petty feelings, the feelings of the man who as a boy had known the humiliation of shabby lodgings with an eccentric mother, who at fifteen had been clumsy and unattractive and unable to dance with Mary Chaworth, who remained oddly alien among the society that he knew so well— this mixture of the origin of his attitude towards English society only gives it greater intensity. . . . Byron's satire upon English society, in the latter part of *Don Juan,* is something for which I can find no parallel in English literature. He was right in making the hero of his house-party a Spaniard, for what Byron understands and dislikes about English society is very much what an intelligent foreigner in the same position would understand and dislike.

One cannot leave *Don Juan* without calling attention to another part of it which emphasizes the difference between this poem and any other satire in English: the Dedicatory Verses. The dedication to Southey seems to me one of the most exhilarating pieces of abuse in the language:

Bob Southey! You're a poet—Poet Laureate,
And representative of all the race;
Although 'tis true that you turn'd out a Tory at
Last, yours has lately been a common case:
And now, my Epic Renegade! what are ye at? . . .

kept up without remission to the end of seventeen stanzas. This is not the satire of Dryden, still less of Pope; it is perhaps more like Hall or Marston, but they are bunglers in comparison. This is not indeed English satire at all; it is really a *flyting*. . . . (pp. 237-39)

I do not pretend that Byron is Villon . . . , but I have come to find in him certain qualities, besides his abundance, that are too uncommon in English poetry, as well as the absence of some vices that are too common. And his own vices seem to have twin virtues that closely resemble them. With his charlatanism, he has also an unusual frankness; with his pose, he is also a *poète contumace* is a solemn country; with his humbug and self-deception he has also a reckless raffish honesty; he is at once a vulgar patrician and a dignified toss-pot; with all his bogus diabolism and his vanity of pretending to disreputability, he is genuinely superstitious and disreputable. I am speaking of the qualities and defects visible in his work, and important in estimating his work: not of the private life, with which I am not concerned. (p. 239)

T. S. Eliot, "Byron," in his *On Poetry and Poets,* Farrar, Straus and Cudahy, 1957, pp. 223-39.

NORTHROP FRYE

(essay date 1959)

[Frye exerted a tremendous influence in the field of twentieth-century literary scholarship, chiefly through his study *Anatomy of Criticism* (1957). In this seminal work he claimed that judgment is not inherent in the critical process and asserted that literary criticism can be "scientific" in its methods and results. In the following excerpt from his 1959 essay "George Gordon, Lord Byron," he observes some of the self-contradictions in Byron's poetic persona.]

The main appeal of Byron's poetry is in the fact that it is Byron's. To read Byron's poetry is to hear all about Byron's marital difficulties, flirtations, love for Augusta, friendships, travels, and political and social views. And Byron is a consistently interesting person to hear about, this being why Byron, even at his worst of self-pity and egotism and blither and doggerel, is still so incredibly readable. He proves what many critics declare to be impossible, that a poem can make its primary impact as a historical and biographical document. The critical problem involved here is crucial to our understanding of not only Byron but literature as a whole. Even when Byron's poetry is not objectively very good, it is still important, because it is Byron's. But who was Byron to be so important? certainly not an exceptionally good or wise man. Byron is, strictly, neither a great poet nor a great man who wrote poetry, but something in between: a tremendous cultural force that was life and literature at once. (p. 174)

Byron's lyrical poetry affords a good exercise in critical catholicity, because it contains nothing that "modern" critics look for: no texture, no ambiguities, no intellectualized ironies, no intensity, no vividness of phrasing, the words and images being vague to the point of abstraction. The poetry seems to be a plain man's poetry, making poetic emotion out of the worn and blunted words of ordinary speech. Yet it is not written by a plain man: it is written, as Arnold said, with the careless ease of a man of quality [see excerpt dated 1881], and its most striking and obvious feature is its gentlemanly amateurism. It is, to be sure, in an amateur tradition, being a romantic, subjective, personal development of the kind of Courtly Love poetry that was written by Tudor and Cavalier noblemen in earlier ages. . . . Byron held the view that lyrical poetry was an expression of passion, and that passion was essentially fitful, and he distrusted professional poets, who pretended to be able to summon passion at will and sustain it indefinitely. . . . *Childe Harold* has the stretches of perfunctory, even slapdash writing that one would expect with such a theory.

In Byron's later lyrics, especially the *Hebrew Melodies* . . . , where he was able to add some of his Oriental technicolor to the Old Testament, more positive qualities emerge, particularly in the rhythm. (pp. 174-75)

Byron did not find the Byronic hero as enthralling as his public did, and he made several efforts to detach his own character from Childe Harold and his other heroes, with limited success. He says of Childe Harold that he wanted to make him an objective study of gloomy misanthropy, hence he deliberately cut humor out of the poem in order to preserve a unity of tone. But Byron's most distinctive talents did not have full scope in this part of his work. . . . His sardonic and ribald wit, his sense of the concrete, his almost infallible feeling for the common-sense perspective on every situation, crackles all through his letters and journals, even through his footnotes. But it seems to be locked out of his serious poetry, and only in the very last canto of *Don Juan* did he succeed in uniting fantasy and humor.

Byron's tales are, on the whole, well-told and well-shaped stories. Perhaps he learned something from his own ridicule of Southey, who was also a popular writer of verse tales, sometimes of mammoth proportions. In any case he is well able to exploit the capacity of verse for dramatizing one or two central situations, leaving all the cumbersome apparatus of plot to be ignored or taken for granted. But he seemed unable to bring his various projections of his inner ghost to life: his heroes, like the characters of a detective story, are thin, bloodless, abstract, and popular. (pp. 178-79)

The same inability to combine seriousness and humor is also to be found in the plays, where one would expect more variety of tone. The central character is usually the Byronic hero again, and again he seems to cast a spell over the whole action. Byron recognized this deficiency in his dramas, and to say that his plays were not intended for the stage would be an understatement. Byron had a positive phobia of stage production, and once tried to get an injunction issued to prevent a performance of *Marino Faliero.* . . . [With] the exception of *Werner,* a lively and well-written melodrama based on a plot by somebody else, Byron's plays are so strictly closet dramas that they differ little in structure from the tales.

The establishing of the Byronic hero was a major feat of characterization, but Byron had little power of characterization apart from this figure. Like many brilliant talkers, he had not much ear for the rhythms and nuances of other people's speech. (pp. 179-80)

But if Byron's plays are not practicable stage plays, they are remarkable works. *Manfred,* based on what Byron had heard about Goethe's *Faust,* depicts the Byronic hero as a student of magic whose knowledge has carried him beyond the limits of human society and given him superhuman powers, but who is still held to human desire by his love for his sister (apparently) Astarte. At the moment of his death the demons he has controlled, with a sense of what is customary in stories about magicians, come to demand his soul, but Manfred, in a crisp incisive speech which retains its power to surprise through any number of rereadings, announces that he has made no bargain with them, that whatever he has done, they can go to hell, and he will not go with them. The key to this final scene is the presence of the Abbot. Manfred and the Abbot differ on all points of theory, but the Abbot is no coward and Manfred is no villain: they face the crisis together, linked in a common bond of humanity which enables Manfred to die and to triumph at the same time.

Two of Byron's plays *Cain* and *Heaven and Earth,* are described by Byron as "mysteries," by which he meant Biblical plays like those of the Middle Ages. Wherever we turn in Byron's poetry, we meet the figure of Cain, the first man who never knew Paradise, and whose sexual love was necessarily incestuous. In Byron's "mystery" Cain is Adam's eldest son and heir, but what he really inherits is the memory of a greater dispossession. "Dost thou not live?" asks Adam helplessly. "Must I not die?" retorts Cain. Adam cannot comprehend the mentality of one who has been born with the consciousness of death. . . . And just as Milton tries to show us that we in Adam's place would have committed Adam's sin, so Byron makes us feel that we all have something of Cain in us: everybody has killed something that he wishes he had kept alive, and the fullest of lives is wrapped around the taint of an inner death. As the princess says in [Horace Walpole's] *The Castle of Otranto:* "This can be no evil spirit: it is undoubtedly one of the family."

The other "mystery," *Heaven and Earth,* deals with the theme of the love of angels for human women recorded in some mysterious verses of Genesis, and ends with the coming of Noah's flood. Angels who fall through sexual love are obvious enough subjects for

Byron, but *Heaven and Earth* lacks the clear dramatic outline of *Cain.* (pp. 180-81)

Don Juan is traditionally the incautious amorist, the counterpart in love to Faust in knowledge, whose pursuit of women is so ruthless that he is eventually damned, as in the last scene of Mozart's opera *Don Giovanni.* Consequently he is a logical choice as a mask for Byron, but he is a mask that reveals the whole Byronic personality, instead of concealing the essence of it as Childe Harold does. The extroversion of Byron's temperament has full scope in *Don Juan.* There is hardly any characterization in the poem: even Don Juan never emerges clearly as a character. We see only what happens to him, and the other characters, even Haidée, float past as phantasmagoria of romance and adventure. What one misses in the poem is the sense of engagement or participation. Everything happens to Don Juan, but he is never an active agent, and seems to take no responsibility for his life. He drifts from one thing to the next, appears to find one kind of experience as good as another, makes no judgements and no commitments. As a result the gloom and misanthropy, the secret past sins, the gnawing remorse of the earlier heroes is finally identified as a shoddier but more terrifying evil—boredom, the sense of the inner emptiness of life that is one of Byron's most powerfully compelling moods, and has haunted literature ever since, from the *ennui* of Baudelaire to the *Angst* and *nausée* of our own day. (p. 184)

The Vision of Judgment is Byron's most original poem, and therefore his most conventional one; it is his wittiest poem, and therefore his most serious one. Southey, Byron's favorite target among the Lake poets, had become poet laureate, and his political views, like those of Coleridge and Wordsworth, had shifted from an early liberalism to a remarkably complacent Toryism. On the death of George III in 1820 he was ill-advised enough to compose, in his laureate capacity, a "Vision of Judgment" describing the apotheosis and entry into heaven of the stammering, stupid, obstinate, and finally lunatic and blind monarch whose sixty-year reign had lost America, alienated Ireland, plunged the country into the longest and bloodiest war in its history, and ended in a desolate scene of domestic misery and repression. . . . The apotheosis of a dead monarch, as a literary form, is of classical origin, and so is its parody, Byron's poem being in the tradition of Seneca's brilliant mockery of the entry into heaven of the Emperor Claudius. (p. 185)

We have not yet shaken off our nineteenth-century inhibitions about Byron. A frequent twentieth-century jargon term for him is "immature," which endorses the Carlyle view that Byron is a poet to be outgrown. . . . There is certainly something youthful about the Byronic hero, and for some reason we feel more defensive about youth than about childhood, and

An 1823 caricature of Byron writing *Don Juan*.

more shamefaced about liking a poet who has captured a youthful imagination. If we replace "youthful" with the loaded term "adolescent" we can see how deeply ingrained this feeling is.

Among intellectuals the Southey type, who makes a few liberal gestures in youth to quiet his conscience and then plunges into a rapturous authoritarianism for the rest of his life, is much more common than the Byron type, who continues to be baffled by unanswered questions and simple anomalies, to make irresponsible jokes, to set his face against society, to respect the authority of his own mood—in short, to retain the rebellious or irreverent qualities of youth. Perhaps it is as dangerous to eliminate the adolescent in us as it is to eliminate the child. In any case the kind of poetic experience that Byronism represents should be obtained young, and in Byron. It may later by absorbed into more complex experiences, but to miss or renounce it is to impoverish whatever else we may attain. (pp. 188-89)

Northrop Frye, "Lord Byron," in his *Fables of Identity: Studies in Poetic Mythology*, Harcourt Brace Jovanovich, 1963, pp. 168-89.

W. H. AUDEN

(essay date 1962)

[Often considered the poetic successor of W. B. Yeats and T. S. Eliot, Auden is also highly regarded for his literary criticism. In the following excerpt, he describes Byron's mastery of comedic verse.]

Most of the literary works with which we are acquainted fall into one of two classes, those we have no desire to read a second time—sometimes, we were never able to finish them—and those we are always happy to re-read. There are a few, however, which belong to a third class; we do not feel like reading one of them very often but, when we are in the appropriate mood, it is the only work we feel like reading. Nothing else, however good or great, will do instead.

For me, Byron's *Don Juan* is such a work. In trying

to analyze why this should be so, I find helpful a distinction which, so far as I have been able to discover, can only be made in the English language, the distinction between saying, "So-and-so or such-and-such is *boring*," and saying, "So-and-so or such-and-such is a *bore*." (pp. 386-87)

Perhaps the principle of the distinction can be made clearer by the following definitions:

A. The absolutely boring but absolutely not a bore: the time of day.
B. The absolutely not boring but absolute bore: God.

Don Juan is sometimes boring but pre-eminently an example of a long poem which is not a bore. To enjoy it fully, the reader must be in a mood of distaste for everything which is to any degree a bore, that is, for all forms of passionate attachment, whether to persons, things, actions or beliefs.

This is not a mood in which one can enjoy satire, for satire, however entertaining, has its origin in passion, in anger at what is the case, desire to change what is the case into what ought to be the case, and belief that the change is humanly possible. (p. 387)

In defending his poem against the charge of immorality, Byron said on one occasion: "*Don Juan* will be known bye-a-bye for what it is intended—a Satire on abuses of the present state of Society": but he was not telling the truth. The poem, of course, contains satirical passages. . . .

But, as a whole, *Don Juan* is not a satire but a comedy, and Byron knew it, for in a franker mood he wrote to Murray [see letter dated 1819]:

I have no plan—I had no plan; but I had or have materials; though if, like Tony Lumpkin, I am to be "snubbed so when I am in spirits," the poem will be naught and the poet turn serious again . . . You are too earnest and eager about a work which was never intended to be serious. Do you suppose that I could have any intention but to giggle and make giggle?

Satire and comedy both make use of the comic contradiction, but their aims are different. Satire would arouse in readers the desire to act so that the contradictions disappear; comedy would persuade them to accept the contradictions with good humor as facts of life against which it is useless to rebel. (p. 388)

Byron's choice of the word *giggle* rather than *laugh* to describe his comic intention deserves consideration.

All comic situations show a contradiction between some general or universal principle and an individual or particular person or event. In the case of the situation at which we giggle, the general principles are two:

1) The sphere of the sacred and the sphere of the profane are mutually exclusive.
2) The sacred is that at which we do not laugh.

Now a situation arises in which the profane intrudes upon the sacred but without annulling it. If the sacred were annulled, we should laugh outright, but the sacred is still felt to be present, so that a conflict ensues between the desire to laugh and the feeling that laughter is inappropriate. (pp. 389-90)

The terms "sacred" and "profane" can be used relatively as well as absolutely. Thus, in a culture that puts a spiritual value upon love between the sexes, such a love, however physical, will seem sacred in comparison with physical hunger. When the shipwrecked Juan wakes and sees Haidée bending over him, he sees she is beautiful and is thrilled by her voice, but the first thing he longs for is not her love but a beefsteak. (p. 391)

Cannibalism, on the other hand, is a crime which is regarded with sacred horror. The survivors from the shipwreck in Canto II are not only starving but also have a craving for meat to which their upbringing has conditioned them. Unfortunately, the only kind of meat available is human. . . . The men in Byron's poem pay with their lives for their act, not because it is a sacred crime but for the profane reason that their new diet proves indigestible.

By night chilled, by day scorched, there one by one
They perished until withered to a few,
But chiefly by a species of self-slaughter
In washing down Pedrillo with salt water.

It is the silly mistake of drinking salt water, not the sacred crime of consuming a clergyman, that brings retribution. Most readers will probably agree that the least interesting figure in *Don Juan* is its official hero, and his passivity is all the more surprising when one recalls the legendary monster of depravity after whom he is named. The Don Juan of the myth is not promiscuous by nature but by will; seduction is his vocation. Since the slightest trace of affection will turn a number on his list of victims into a name, his choice of vocation requires the absolute renunciation of love. (pp. 391-92)

When he chose the name Don Juan for his hero, Byron was well aware of the associations it would carry for the public, and he was also aware that he himself was believed by many to be the heartless seducer and atheist of the legend. His poem is, among other things, a self-defense. He is saying to his accusers, as it were: "The Don Juan of the legend does not exist. I will show you what the sort of man who gets the reputation for being a Don Juan is really like." (p. 392)

Far from being a defiant rebel against the laws of God and man, his most conspicuous trait is his gift for social conformity. I cannot understand those critics who have seen in him a kind of Rousseau child of Nature. Whenever chance takes him, to a pirate's lair, a harem in Mohammedan Constantinople, a court in Greek Orthodox Russia, a country house in Protestant England, he immediately adapts himself and is accepted as an agreeable fellow. Had Byron continued the poem as he planned and taken Juan to Italy to be a *cavaliere servente* and to Germany to be a solemn Werther-faced man, one has no doubt that he would have continued to play the roles assigned to him with tact and aplomb. In some respects Juan resembles the Baudelairian dandy but he lacks the air of *insolent* superiority which Baudelaire considered essential to the true dandy; he would never, one feels, say anything outrageous or insulting. (pp. 392-93)

When one compares Don Juan with what we know of his creator, he seems to be a daydream of what Byron would have liked to be himself. Physically he is unblemished and one cannot imagine him having to diet to keep his figure; socially, he is always at his ease and his behavior in perfect taste. (p. 393)

Byron's poetry is the most striking example I know in literary history of the creative role which poetic form can play. . . . He knew Italian well, he had read Casti's *Novelle Galanti* and loved them, but he did not realize the poetic possibilities of the mock-heroic ottava-rima until he read Frere's *The Monks and the Giants.*

Take away the poems he wrote in this style and meter, *Beppo, The Vision of Judgment, Don Juan,* and what is left of lasting value? A few lyrics, though none of them is as good as the best of Moore's, two adequate satires though inferior to Dryden or Pope, **"Darkness,"** a fine piece of blank verse marred by some false sentiment, a few charming occasional pieces, half a dozen stanzas from *Childe Harold,* half a dozen lines from *Cain,* and that is all. (p. 394)

So long as Byron tried to write Poetry with a capital P, to express deep emotions and profound thoughts, his work deserved that epithet he most dreaded, *una seccatura.* As a thinker he was, as Goethe perceived, childish, and he possessed neither the imaginative vision—he could never invent anything, only remember—nor the verbal sensibility such poetry demands. (p. 395)

What had been Byron's defect as a serious poet, his lack of reverence for words, was a virtue for the comic poet. Serious poetry requires that the poet treat words as if they were persons, but comic poetry demands that he treat them as things and few, if any, English poets have rivaled Byron's ability to put words through the hoops. (p. 399)

There have been poets—Keats is the most striking example—whose letters and poems are so different from each other that they might have been written by two different people, and yet both seem equally authentic. But, with Byron, this is not the case. From the beginning, his letters seem authentic but, before *Beppo,* very little of his poetry; and the more closely his poetic *persona* comes to resemble the epistolary *persona* of his letters to his male friends—his love letters are another matter—the more authentic his poetry seems. (p. 401)

[Byron's] visual descriptions of scenery or architecture are not particularly vivid, nor are his portrayal of states of mind particularly profound, but at the description of things in motion or the way in which the mind wanders from one thought to another he is a great master.

Unlike most poets, he must be read very rapidly as if the words were single frames in a movie film; stop on a word or a line and the poetry vanishes—the feeling seems superficial, the rhyme forced, the grammar all over the place—but read at the proper pace, it gives a conviction of watching the real thing which many profounder writers fail to inspire for, though motion is not the only characteristic of life, it is an essential one.

If Byron was sometimes slipshod in his handling of the language, he was a stickler for factual accuracy. . . . (p. 405)

The material of his poems is always drawn from events that actually happened, either to himself or to people he knew, and he took great trouble to get his technical facts, such as sea terms, correct. (p. 406)

W. H. Auden, "Don Juan," in his *The Dyer's Hand and Other Essays,* Random House, Inc., 1962, pp. 386-406.

FREDERICK L. BEATY
(essay date 1985)

[In the following excerpt, Beaty explores the concept of *Don Juan* as "epic satire."]

The form of *Don Juan* is so indeterminate as virtually to defy categorization. Since the classical epic, Roman satire, Italian epic romance, mock-heroic poetry, the picaresque novel, Restoration comedy, the realistic novel, the novel of manners, the pantomime, Gothic romance, the ballad, the lyric, and neoclassical satire have all left their imprint on the poem, it is not surprising that the receptacle containing such varied ingredients should be amorphous. Critics who have felt uneasy about calling *Don Juan* a "hold-all" have resorted to designating it as a metrical novel, a mock-epic, an epic carnival, an epic of negation, epic satire, or merely satire. While excellent cases can be made for all these labels, none is utterly satisfactory for the poem as a whole. One of the few delineations with which no critics would cavil is James R. Thompson's description of *Don Juan* as "a kind of generic explosion produced by the nineteenth-century pressure to redefine form in highly personal terms."

What is undeniable, in any case, is that the form, or formlessness, accurately reflects Byron's view of life and man's disordered, incongruous, and unpredictable world. His concept of artistic form, as McGann has maintained, is not concerned with internal unity but, in the Horatian tradition, with rhetoric and function. Form, either in the classical sense of a preconceived mold or in the Romantic sense of a product of organic development, has little meaning for *Don Juan.* So long as a poetical work was "simple and entire," as Byron translated the Horatian dictum in *Hints from Horace,* and also was organized in such a way as to express most effectively what the poet had to say, form could take care of itself. Byron's repeated assertions that the cantos of *Don Juan,* whether organized around topics or episodic narrative, could go on almost indefinitely suggest a looseness of structure and an open-endedness that challenge conventional notions of form. The shapelessness of *Don Juan,* however, was not a serious problem with regard to satire. Since its Roman inception, satire has been thought of as a hodgepodge (*farrago*), a medley, or a miscellaneous collection. It has tended to be so unstructured that, as Northrop Frye affirmed, "a kind of parody of form seems to run all through its tradition." Acquaintance with the tradition, which included many varieties of satire and different levels of style appropriate to them, had taught Byron that there was actually no prescribed form.

He was sufficiently skilled as a classicist to appreciate what the Romans called formal satire. In Latin *satura* designated only a particular literary genre—a seemingly unordered poem mixing unfavorable criticism with moral observations. In English, however, the term *satire* could be applied to any artistic composition in which the author's intention was to arouse contempt for his subject. More loosely, it might refer to isolated passages in compositions that were not predominantly derogatory, to the temper characterizing such works, or even to the techniques employed to degrade. It is revealing that in letters and conversations Byron most frequently referred to *Don Juan* as a satire. It is also significant that early reviewers saw the poem primarily as satire—on everything, including the epic. And whatever the generic modulations of the poem, its substance is undeniably permeated by the satiric spirit, even in instances when that spirit, as both Ernest J. Lovell and Alvin B. Kernan have observed, is so thoroughly blended with either comedy or tragedy that it can hardly be identified as "serious" satire. Since there was no satiric form adequate to a large composition, a more comprehensive genre, such as the epic, was needed as a carrier—one in which a variety of intentions, including the satiric, could function. Within this matrix

Byron was able to incorporate not only many kinds of satire but in one instance, the Constantinople episode, an illustration of *satura.*

His conscious adaptation of both the form and substance of Roman satire in Canto V suggests that he wished that portion to be seen in the light of a continuing tradition. This imitation was his way of announcing his genre and establishing his pedigree. His two introductory stanzas beginning that canto advertise his intention of forsaking "amorous writing" in favor of an edifying variety that attaches morals to every error and attacks all the passions. Properly interpreted, the narrator's role becomes that of the Roman satirist with Stoic inclinations. Moreover, the dialogue in which Johnson explains his Stoic philosophy to Juan . . . is an authentic replica of the dialogue form in which both Horace and Persius treated Stoic doctrines. Horace actually invented the satiric dialogue and used it with subtle irony to involve prolocutor and adversary in a dramatic skit. Persius, though strongly inclined toward dramatic conversations even when the presence of his opponent in a debate had to be imagined, used the Horatian innovation as framework for only two whole satires, while Juvenal was even less disposed toward dialogue form. It was Pope, in his *Imitations of Horace,* who proved to be most skillful of all in pitting speakers against one another in an evolving discussion. Pope's example probably inspired Byron to attempt a similar feat. (pp. 138-40)

Byron's skill in combining various ingredients drawn from Roman satire into a traditional satiric form deserves special attention. Though the subject of Johnson's discourse derives primarily from Persius, the general tone of the dialogue more closely resembles the Horatian mixture of genial humor and wry cynicism than the earnest didacticism of Persius. Yet it was Byron's originality in readapting classical materials that earned him a place as a contributor to the tradition. His conversion of metaphorical enslavement into physical reality and his use of Constantinople's slave market as a microcosm of mercantile society, where everyone offers himself to the highest bidder, ingeniously and vastly enriched the possibilities for a thematic conflict between freedom and slavery in that episode. Even Stoic philosophy is so modernized as to be assimilable into Robert Walpole's truism on human venality ("all have prices, / . . . according to their vices" . . .) and to be assailable ultimately as a philosophy of insensibility ("To feel for none is the true social art / Of the world's stoics—men without a heart" . . .). And the dialogue between Johnson and Juan is more than an unresolved debate on Stoicism. As a dramatic mode of dialectic, it stimulates each speaker to a revelation of his own perspective, as well as to a deeper perception of the limitations inherent in his own outlook. Through his naive questioning of Johnson's cynical approach,

Juan serves as friendly adversary or *provocateur* in evoking the differences between sentimental youth and disillusioned age. One of Byron's finest achievements in this *sermo* is the unexpected combination of a crescendo suggesting a modified Stoicism as the key to survival and an ironic coda questioning its validity as a guide to life.

Possibly because Byron saw a number of parallels between Constantinople, which he called "Rome transplanted" (V. 86. 8), and Rome under the early caesars, he drew many other suggestions for his fifth canto from Roman satire and thereby emphasized further his connection with that still vital tradition. The narrator's frequent references to the role of capricious fortune in that section are reminiscent of Juvenal and, to a lesser degree, Horace rather than of Moslem belief. It is likely that Byron had mentally assimilated the extensive commentary Madan wrote for Juvenal's tenth satire on the significance of Fortuna in pagan Rome. Certainly Byron was indebted to the substance of two Juvenalian satires (VI and X) for the encounter involving Juan and the lustful sultana Gulbeyaz. For ideas, phraseology, and analogies he also drew on Madan's notes about the nymphomaniac empress Messalina and her determination to force the handsome Gaius Silius to become her husband. Much of the broad sexual jesting in the fifth canto echoes that of Juvenal. Castration, for example, in addition to being an accepted Turkish practice, may have been suggested by hints in Juvenal's tenth that Madan had explicated. While circumcision remained a notable difference between Christian and Moslem in Byron's day, as his earlier letters observed, he would also have recalled the recurrent jests in Horace, Persius, and Juvenal about Jewish circumcision. Juan's transvestism, as well as its sexual overtones, had precedents in Juvenal and in Madan's notes to Satires II and X. But throughout that episode it is not so much the imitation of the model that deserves study as the ingenious transformation of Juvenalian materials in the alembic of Byron's imagination. Byron's achievement, in altering even the "tragic satire" of Juvenal into half-serious comedy dealing with feminine lust, masculine chastity, marital fidelity, and tyranny over all that should be free, shows how completely he could absorb the ingredients of Roman satire into his own creation.

While the imitation of *satura* is evident only in Canto V, the overall randomness of *Don Juan* suggests satiric content. It is primarily through the satiric spirit, especially as it is assimilated into epic form, that Byron's satire functions. Despite the poem's open defiance of epic conventions, the narrator repeatedly claims that *Don Juan* is an epic and that its contents (love, war, shipwreck, and even a "view of hell") qualify it for that designation. There is good reason, furthermore, to believe that Byron took those claims seriously, that he intended something more than another comic epic in the

Italian tradition. It would be easy, especially in the early cantos, to assert that *Don Juan* is a mock-epic since that subgenre not only incorporates satire in its burlesque of epic conventions but also uses the ideals of previous epics to illustrate, by allusion, the contrast between earlier greatness and contemporary pettiness. But as Brian Wilkie has shown, *Don Juan* is not just a mock-epic. Byron was determined that, unlike his "epic brethren gone before," he would write a *true* epic depicting man and his world realistically. On the assumption that *Don Juan* in scope and purpose deserved to be compared to Homer's *Iliad*, Byron told Thomas Medwin in late 1821 or early 1822 that his poem was "an epic as much in the spirit of our day as the Iliad was in Homer's." Evidently he thought it mirrored the religious, political, and social attitudes of his own era as comprehensively and accurately as Homer's epic had reflected his age. Byron's invocation of Homer's aid before the siege of Ismail . . . , his use of language less formal and stylized than Virgil's or Milton's, and his rejection of a providential or teleological design for background of the protagonist's "heroism" indicate that Byron in some ways felt a closer affinity with Homer than with the later epic poets. But fundamental changes in the inherited tradition were necessary to produce a modern epic depicting the ideals—or lack of them—in contemporary society, and satire was essential in sharpening its negative features.

When in 1823 Byron called *Don Juan* an "Epic Satire" . . . , he acknowledged its hybrid nature. His poetic commentary on *Don Quixote* . . . suggests the relationship that Byron apparently saw between satire and epic. Even though Cervantes may have assumed that in our corrupt world only a fool or a madman could champion chivalric values, he was not, in Byron's judgment, ridiculing the noble idealism for which Quixote fights. Cervantes' "hero" is "right" in

Redressing injury, revenging wrong,
To aid the damsel and destroy the caitiff;
Opposing singly the united strong,
From foreign yoke to free the helpless native. . . .

Yet we smile at the spectacle the deluded knight makes of himself, and, reflecting on the folly of defending virtue, we realize the melancholy plight in which Cervantes has involved us. Thus what Cervantes may have begun as satire on the absurdities of knight-errantry resulted in a "real Epic unto all who have thought." . . . By demolishing the traditional concept of heroism, he destroyed the old form of epic romance. In its place he provided a genuine, realistic epic, the only kind viable in a skeptical, disillusioned age.

This reading of *Don Quixote* has implications for Byron's interpretation of epic satire in *Don Juan*. Like Cervantes, Byron strove through satire to banish a false vision of life. In the course of achieving that goal he produced, like Cervantes, a literary form that radically readapted epic traditions, the epic hero, and the very idea of heroism—a form that could integrate other literary genres into itself and accommodate satire as part of its realistic approach. The union of such an epic and satire was more compatible than might have at first appeared, for the traditions of the two genres already met on common ground. Love, war, shipwreck, banquets, and glimpses of Hades, essential ingredients in the epic, were also standard fare in Roman *satura* and neoclassical adaptations. In *Don Juan* epic of a negative thrust could easily exist in symbolic relationship with satire. The epic element, impelled by narrative, was identifiable with the onward momentum of life; the satiric, conversely, with whatever threatened man's progress. True heroism and idealism, however rare, were not to be scorned, though their goals were usually unattainable and their adherents often appeared foolish to a cynical world. This ironic situation, as Byron saw it, represented the dilemma of modern man, and "Epic Satire" was his way of embodying it.

Quite likely the term *epic satire* also had another association for Byron. Although he may have thought of *Don Juan* in its earliest stages as primarily in the *genus tenue* and the casual Horatian mode, as the poem developed more grandiose proportions he acquired a loftier sense of its mission—one comparable to the Juvenalian concept of satire in the *genus grande*. Particularly from careful study of Juvenal's Satires I, VI, X, and XV, Byron learned that true-to-life satire might be as edifying as tragedy or epic. Even though Juvenal respected

the great epics of the past, he had the utmost contempt for poetasters of his day who strained beyond their abilities to attempt the highest genres. Traditional epic and tragedy, with their artificial conventions, impracticable ideals, and hackneyed mythological subjects, seemed no longer viable to Juvenal because they were irrelevant to contemporary life. What was needed, in view of the corruption permeating every stratum of Roman society, was a literature of truth rather than of literary invention—in short, one that depicted reality as Juvenal saw it. If satire was to supersede the outworn genres in the old poetic hierarchy and assume their instructive functions, the satirist was obliged to aspire to a *genus grande* that would approximate, even while radically readapting, epic form. In practice Juvenal substantiated those assumptions through elevated rhetoric, an impassioned style, and a heroic determination to amend society through exposure of wrong-doing. . . . Juvenal's frequent imitation of epic, whether with serious intent or, when style was inappropriate to subject matter, for humorous effect, further showed that he strove for a nobler goal than that ordinarily associated with the satires of Horace and Persius. It may well be that Juvenal's works, to which Byron repeatedly returned over the years, deepened his concept of satire so that it evolved beyond a youthful lashing out at whatever displeased him into a sophisticated view of life encompassing all things human. (pp. 142-46)

Frederick L. Beaty, in his *Byron the Satirist,* Northern Illinois University Press, 1985, 236 p.

SOURCES FOR FURTHER STUDY

Bostetter, Edward E., ed. *Twentieth Century Interpretations of Don Juan: A Collection of Critical Essays.* Englewood Cliffs, N.J.: Prentice-Hall, 1969, 119 p.

Collection of essays on *Don Juan*, focusing on the poem's structure, themes, and style.

Gleckner, Robert F. *Byron and the Ruins of Paradise.* Baltimore: The Johns Hopkins Press, 1967, 365 p.

Explores the recurrent metaphor of the eternal loss of paradise and a continuing hell on earth in Byron's works.

Joseph, M. K. *Byron the Poet.* London: Victor Gollancz Ltd., 1964, 352 p.

A comprehensive view of Byron's poetry that synthesizes previous work and adds new insights. This book has a particularly enlightening section on *Don Juan.*

Lovell, Ernest J., Jr. *Byron: The Record of a Quest: Studies in a Poet's Concept and Treatment of Nature.* Austin: The University of Texas Press, 1949, 270 p.

Examines Byron's quest in terms of religion, psychology, and intellectualism, and relates the poet's various attitudes to his treatment of nature in his work.

Marchand, Leslie A. *Byron: A Biography.* 3 vols. New York: Alfred A. Knopf, 1957.

Comprehensive critical biography considered the definitive modern source for Byron's life.

Trueblood, Paul Graham. *Lord Byron.* Twayne's English Author Series, edited by Sylvia E. Bowman, no. 78. New York: Twayne Publishers, 1969, 177 p.

Biographical and critical discussion of composition, style, structure, and themes in Byron's poetry.

Albert Camus

1913-1960

Algerian-born French novelist, essayist, playwright, short story writer, and journalist.

INTRODUCTION

Camus is one of the most important literary figures of the twentieth century. In his varied career he consistently and passionately explored his major theme: the belief that people can attain happiness in an apparently meaningless world. Throughout his work, Camus defended the dignity and goodness of the individual and asserted that through purposeful action one can overcome nihilism. Camus posited that to resolve the conflict between life in an "absurd universe" and the human desire for rationality—as he demonstrated most clearly in his essay *Le mythe de Sisyphe* (1942; *The Myth of Sisyphus*)—one must recognize that life is "absurd," that is, irrational and meaningless, and then transcend that absurdity. Although this worldview has prompted many commentators to label Camus an existentialist, he rejected that classification. Respected for his style as well as his ideas, Camus is praised as a fierce moralist who expressed an unwavering faith in humankind. He was awarded the Nobel Prize for literature in 1957.

Camus was born into poverty and finished school by earning scholarships and working part-time jobs. He never knew his father, who died in 1914 while fighting in World War I, and his mother was an illiterate who rarely spoke or showed affection for her child. Despite the lack of intellectual stimulation at home, Camus excelled at school. At the Lycée d'Algiers he studied philosophy, but he contracted tuberculosis before having a chance to begin university studies, which prevented him from pursuing a career as an academician. The disease also forced Camus to face the prospect of mortality, a theme that appears in much of his early work. Instead of teaching, Camus became a journalist, editing the resistance newspaper *Combat* and immersing himself in the Algerian intellectual scene. His interest in the theater was already evident, for during this period he helped to found the theater group Théâtre du Travail, adapted works for the stage, and collaborated on an original play. Camus's first two books, *L'envers et l'endroit* (1937), translated as *The Wrong Side and the Right Side,* and *Noces* (1939), translated as *Nuptials,* are collections of lyrical essays written in the mid-1930s that detail his early life of poverty and his travels through Europe. During this time Camus wrote his first novel, *La mort heureuse* (1971; *A Happy Death*). This posthumously published work, though less stylistically developed than his later novels, touches on the themes of absurdity and self-realization that recur throughout his writings. During World War II Camus moved to Paris, where, with Jean-Paul Sartre, he became a major intellectual leader of the French Resistance opposing the German occupation of France.

In both *The Myth of Sisyphus* and *L'étranger* (1942; *The Stranger*), Camus developed his concept of absurdism. He presented the story of Sisyphus, a figure from Greek mythology who was fated to push a rock up a hill only to see it repeatedly roll back down, as a metaphor for the human condition. For Camus, life, like Sisyphus's task, is senseless, but awareness of this absurdity can help humankind to surmount this condition. Meursault, the protagonist of *The Stranger,* shoots an Arab for no apparent reason, but he is convicted not so much for killing the man as for refusing to conform to society's expectations, as illustrated by his emotionless response to his mother's death. Because he seems indifferent to everything except the most basic sensations of life, Meursault is alienated from the society that wants him to show contrition more expressively. Approaching his execution, Meursault accepts life as an imperfect end in itself and resolves to die happily and with dignity. He finds consolation in resigning himself to what Camus calls the "benign indifference of the universe."

Camus's following novel, *La peste* (1947; *The Plague*), deals with the theme of revolt. Complementing his concept of the absurd, Camus believed in the necessity of each person to "revolt" against the common fate of humanity by seeking personal freedom. Dr. Rieux, the protagonist of *The Plague,* narrates the story of several men in the plague-ridden Algerian city of Oran. Throughout the novel, Camus parallels the conflicting philosophies of Rieux and Father Paneloux over how to deal with the plague: Rieux, a compassionate humanist who repudiates conventional religion, maintains that human action can best combat the disease; Paneloux, a Jesuit priest who views the plague as God's retribution on the sinful people of Oran, holds that only through faith and divine intervention can the city be salvaged. Ultimately, the characters overcome their differences and unite to defeat the plague, at least temporarily, through scientific means. Many critics have interpreted *The Plague* as an allegory of the Ger-

man occupation of France during World War II. Camus's emphasis on individual revolt also pervades the long essay *L'homme révolté* (1951; *The Rebel*), which exemplifies his dictum "I revolt, therefore we are." Examining the nature and history of revolution, Camus theorized that each individual must revolt against injustice by refusing to be part of it. Camus opposed mass revolutions because he believed they become nihilistic and their participants accept murder and oppression as necessary means to an end.

Camus's belief in the supremacy of the individual lies at the heart of one of the most publicized events in modern literature—his break with his long-time compatriot Jean-Paul Sartre. These two leading figures of the postwar French intellectual scene had similar literary philosophies, but their political differences led to a quarrel in the early 1950s that ended their friendship as well as their working relationship. Sartre saw the Soviet purges and labor camps of the 1940s as a stage in the Marxian dialectic process that would eventually produce a just society. Camus, however, could not condone what he perceived to be the Communist state's disregard for human rights. Played out in the Paris and international press, the debate was "won" by Sartre, according to many intellectuals and commentators. This affair disheartened Camus, and his subsequent fall into public scorn affected him over the remainder of his career.

In the following years Camus suffered from depression and writer's block. His reputation was further damaged when he took a neutral position on the issue of Arab uprisings in his native Algiers. Both the French government and Arabs denounced him, and the furor extracted an additional toll on his mental health. His next novel, *La chute* (1956; *The Fall*), is a long, enigmatic monologue of a formerly self-satisfied lawyer who suffers from guilt and relentlessly confesses his sins in order to judge others and induce them to confess as well. Some commentators detected a new tone in this work and suggested that Camus had submitted to nihilism by asserting that every person shares the guilt for a violent and corrupt world. Many argued, however, that Camus's essential love and respect for humanity is a major element of *The Fall* and viewed his wish for a common confession as an attempt to reaffirm human solidarity.

Although Camus maintained a lifelong passion for the theater, his plays generally garnered mixed critical reaction. Of his four original dramas, *Caligula* (1945) is often considered his most significant. This work recounts the search of the young Roman emperor for absolute individual freedom. The death of his sister, who is also his lover, shocks him into an awareness of life's absurdity; as a result, he orders and participates in random rapes, murders, and humiliations that alienate him from others. Most scholars view *Caligula* as a parable warning that individual liberty must affirm, not destroy, the bonds of humanity. *Le malentendu* (1944; *The Misunderstanding*), the story of a man's murder by his sister and mother, is often considered Camus's attempt at a modern tragedy in the classical Greek style. *L'état de siège* (1944; *The State of Siege*) has been variously perceived as a satiric attack on totalitarianism and an allegory demonstrating the value of courageous human action. A plague that ravages a town and terrorizes its citizens is stopped only when one character sacrifices his life for the woman he loves. Scholars who view this play as an attack on ruthless governments believe it reflects Camus's experience of living under the Nazi occupation of France. *Les justes* (1949; *The Just Assassins*) portrays a revolutionary who refuses to throw a bomb because his intended victim is accompanied by a young nephew and niece. This work further emphasizes Camus's strong sense of humanity: he reasons that the end does not justify the means if the cost is human lives. Most critics agree that Camus's overriding concern with intellectual and philosophical issues makes his dramas overly formal and lifeless, also contending that his characters function too often as mere representatives of specific ideologies. While Camus is admired as a director and innovator and his scripts are generally well regarded, critical consensus deems his plays inferior to his fiction.

When Camus published his first collection of short stories, *L'exil et le royaume* (1957; *Exile and the Kingdom*), many critics detected a new vitality and optimism in his prose. The energy of the stories, each written in a different style, led many scholars to suggest that Camus had regained direction in his career and established himself as a master of short fiction. In ensuing years Camus worked around political quarrels, family troubles, and poor health to begin work on a new novel, *Le premier homme.* He worked diligently and with great hope, but before the text was completed, he died in an automobile accident.

Despite marked fluctuations in Camus's popularity—his rise to literary fame in the 1940s occurred as rapidly as his fall from popular appeal in the years preceding his death—his literary significance remains largely undisputed. His work has elicited an enormous amount of scholarly attention and he continues to be the subject of much serious study. A defender of political liberty and personal freedom, Camus endures not only as an important contributor to contemporary literature, but also as a figure of hope and possibility.

(For further information about Camus's life and works, see *Contemporary Authors*, Vols. 89-92; *Contemporary Literary Criticism*, Vols. 1, 2, 4, 9, 11, 14, 32, 63; and *Dictionary of Literary Biography*, Vol. 72: *French Novelists, 1930-1960.*)

CRITICAL COMMENTARY

JEAN-PAUL SARTRE

(essay date 1943)

[Sartre was one of the chief contributors to the philosophical movement of Existentialism. In the following excerpt from an essay written in 1943, he discusses the absurd, meaningless nature of the human condition in *The Stranger*.]

In *The Myth of Sisyphus*, . . . Camus provided us with a precise commentary upon [*The Stranger*]. His hero was neither good nor bad, neither moral nor immoral. These categories do not apply to him. He belongs to a very particular species for which the author reserves the word "absurd." But in Camus's work this word takes on two very different meanings. The absurd is both a state of fact and the lucid awareness which certain people acquire of this state of fact. The "absurd" man is the man who does not hesitate to draw the inevitable conclusions from a fundamental absurdity. (pp. 108-09)

Primary absurdity manifests a cleavage, the cleavage between man's aspirations to unity and the insurmountable dualism of mind and nature, between man's drive toward the eternal and the *finite* character of his existence, between the "concern" which constitutes his very essence and the vanity of his efforts. Chance, death, the irreducible pluralism of life and of truth, the unintelligibility of the real—all these are extremes of the absurd.

These are not really very new themes, and Camus does not present them as such. They had been sounded as early as the seventeenth century by a certain kind of dry, plain, contemplative rationalism, which is typically French and they served as the commonplaces of classical pessimism. (p. 109)

By virtue of the cool style of *The Myth of Sisyphus* and the subject of his essays, Albert Camus takes his place in the great tradition of those French moralists

Principal Works

*L'envers et l'endroit (essays) 1937

*Noces (essays) 1939

L'étranger (novel) 1942

   [The Outsider, 1946; also published as The Stranger, 1946]

Le mythe de Sisyphe (essay) 1942

   [The Myth of Sisyphus, and Other Essays, 1955]

Le malentendu (drama) 1944

   [Cross Purpose published in Caligula. Cross Purpose, 1947; also published as The Misunderstanding in Caligula, and Three Other Plays, 1958]

Caligula (drama) 1945

   [Caligula published in Caligula, and Three Other Plays, 1958]

La peste (novel) 1947

   [The Plague, 1948]

L'état de siège (drama) 1948

   [State of Siege published in Caligula, and Three Other Plays, 1958]

Les justes (drama) 1949

   [The Just Assassins published in Caligula, and Three Other Plays, 1958]

L'homme révolté (essays) 1951

[The Rebel, 1953]

La dévotion à la croix [translator] (drama) 1953

Les esprits [adaptor; from the drama Les esprits by Pierre de Larivey] (drama) 1953

*L'été (essays) 1954

Un cas intéressant [adaptor; from the drama Un caso clinico by Dino Buzatti] (drama) 1955

La chute (novel) 1956

   [The Fall, 1956]

Requiem pour une nonne [adaptor; from the novel Requiem for a Nun by William Faulkner] (drama) 1956

L'exil et le royaume (short stories) 1957

   [Exile and the Kingdom, 1958]

Caligula, and Three Other Plays (dramas) 1958

Les possédés [adaptor; from the novel The Possessed by Fyodor Dostoyevsky] (drama) 1959

   [The Possessed, 1960]

Resistance, Rebellion, and Death (essays) 1961

La mort heureuse (novel) 1971

   [A Happy Death, 1972]

*These collections were incorporated in Lyrical and Critical Essays, 1968.

---

whom Andler has rightly termed the precursors of Nietzsche.

As to the doubts raised by Camus about the scope of our reasoning powers, these are in the most recent tradition of French epistemology. . . . Camus shows off a bit by quoting passages from Jaspers, Heidegger and Kierkegaard, whom, by the way, he does not always seem to have quite understood. But his real masters are to be found elsewhere.

The turn of his reasoning, the clarity of his ideas, the cut of his expository style and a certain kind of solar, ceremonious, and sad sombreness, all indicate a classic temperament, a man of the Mediterranean. His very method ("only through a balance of evidence and lyricism shall we attain a combination of emotion and lucidity.") recalls the old "passionate geometries" of Pascal and Rousseau and relate him, for example, not to a German phenomenologist or a Danish existentialist, but rather to Maurras, that other Mediterranean from whom, however, he differs in many respects.

But Camus would probably be willing to grant all this. To him, originality means pursuing one's ideas to the limit; it certainly does not mean making a collection of pessimistic maxims. The absurd, to be sure, resides neither in man nor in the world, if you consider each separately. But since man's dominant characteristic is "being-in-the-world," the absurd is, in the end, an inseparable part of the human condition. Thus, the absurd is not, to begin with, *the object of a mere idea; it is revealed to us in a doleful illumination.* "Getting up, tram, four hours of work, meal, sleep, and Monday, Tuesday, Wednesday, Thursday, Friday, Saturday, in the same routine" (*Sisyphus*), and then, suddenly, "the setting collapses," and we find ourselves in a state of hopeless lucidity.

If we are able to refuse the misleading aid of religion or of existential philosophies, we then possess certain basic, obvious facts: the world is chaos, a "divine equivalence born of anarchy"; tomorrow does not exist, since we all die. "In a universe suddenly deprived of light and illusions, man feels himself a stranger. This exile is irrevocable, since he has no memories of a lost homeland and no hope of a promised land." The reason is that man is *not* the world. . . . This explains, in part, the title of our novel; the stranger is man confronting the world. Camus might as well have chosen the title of one of George Gissing's works, *Born in Exile.* The stranger is also man among men. "There are days when . . . you find that the person you've loved has become a stranger." The stranger is, finally, myself in relation to myself, that is, natural man in relation to mind: "The stranger who, at certain moments, confronts us in a mirror" (*The Myth of Sisyphus*).

But that is not all; there is a *passion* of the absurd. The absurd man will not commit suicide; he wants to live, without relinquishing any of his certainty, without a future, without hope, without illusion, and without resignation either. He stares at death with passionate attention and this fascination liberates him. He experiences the "divine irresponsibility" of the condemned man.

Since God does not exist and man dies, everything is permissible. . . . [The] absurd man, rebellious and irresponsible, has "nothing to justify." He is *innocent,* innocent as Somerset Maugham's savages before the arrival of the clergyman who teaches them Good and Evil, what is lawful and what is forbidden. (pp. 109-11)

And now we fully understand the title of Camus's novel. The stranger he wants to portray is precisely one of those terrible innocents who shock society by not accepting the rules of its game. He lives among outsiders, but to them, too, he is a stranger. . . . And we ourselves, who, on opening the book are not yet familiar with the feeling of the absurd, vainly try to judge him according to our usual standards. For us, too, he is a stranger. . . .

[You] probably hoped that as you progressed your uneasiness would fade, that everything would be slowly clarified, would be given a reasonable justification and explained. Your hopes were disappointed. *The Stranger* is not an explanatory book. The absurd man does not explain; he describes. Nor is it a book which proves anything.

Camus is simply presenting something and is not concerned with a justification of what is fundamentally unjustifiable. (p. 111)

Camus does not require that attentive solicitude that writers who "have sacrificed their lives to art" demand of the reader, *The Stranger* is a leaf from his life. And since the most absurd life is that which is most sterile, his novel aims at being magnificently sterile. Art is an act of unnecessary generosity. We need not be over-disturbed by this; I find, hidden beneath Camus's paradoxes, some of Kant's wise observations on the "endless end" of the beautiful. Such, in any case, is *The Stranger,* a work detached from a life, unjustified and unjustifiable, sterile, momentary, already forsaken by its author, abandoned for other present things. And that is how we must accept it, as a brief communion between two men, the author and the reader, beyond reason, in the realm of the absurd.

This will give us some idea as to how we are to regard the hero of *The Stranger.* If Camus had wanted to write a novel with a purpose, he would have had no difficulty in showing a civil servant lording it over his family, and then suddenly struck with the intuition of the absurd, struggling against it for a while and finally resolving to live out the fundamental absurdity of his condition. The reader would have been convinced along with the character, and for the same reasons.

Or else, he might have related the life of one of those saints of the Absurd, so dear to his heart, of whom he speaks in *The Myth of Sisyphus:* Don Juan, the Actor, the Conqueror, the Creator. But he has not done so, and Meursault, the hero of *The Stranger,* remains ambiguous, even to the reader who is familiar with theories of the absurd. We are, of course, assured that he is absurd, and his dominant characteristic is a pitiless clarity. Besides, he is, in more ways than one, constructed so as to furnish a concerted illustration of the theories expounded in *The Myth of Sisyphus.* For example, in the latter work, Camus writes, "A man's virility lies more in what he keeps to himself than in what he says." And Meursault [is] an example of this virile silence, of this refusal to indulge in words. . . . (pp. 112-13)

[Meursault] has always lived according to Camus's standards. If there were a grace of absurdity, we would have to say that he has grace. He does not seem to pose himself any of the questions explored in *The Myth of Sisyphus.* . . . The character thus retains a real opacity, even to the absurd-conscious observer. He is no Don Juan, no Don Quixote of the absurd; he often even seems like its Sancho Panza. He is there before us, he exists, and we can neither understand nor quite judge him. In a word, he is alive, and all that can justify him to us is his fictional density.

The Stranger is not, however, to be regarded as a completely gratuitous work. Camus distinguishes, as we have mentioned, between the *notion* and the *feeling* of the absurd. He says, in this connection, "Deep feelings, like great works, are always more meaningful than they are aware of being. . . . An intense feeling carries with it its own universe, magnificent or wretched, as the case may be" (*The Myth of Sisyphus*). And he adds, a bit further on, "The feeling of the absurd is not the same as the *idea* of the absurd. The idea is grounded in the feeling, that is all. It does not exhaust it." *The Myth of Sisyphus* might be said to aim at giving us this *idea,* and *The Stranger* at giving us the feeling. (p. 114)

Camus talks a great deal; in *The Myth of Sisyphus* he is even garrulous. And yet, he reveals his love of silence. . . . [In] *The Stranger,* he has attempted *to be silent.* But how is one to be silent with words? How is one to convey through concepts the unthinkable and disorderly succession of present instants? This problem involves resorting to a new technique.

What is this new technique? "It's Kafka written by Hemingway," I was told. I confess that I have found no trace of Kafka in it. Camus's views are entirely of this earth, and Kafka is the novelist of impossible transcendence; for him, the universe is full of signs that we cannot understand; there is a reverse side to the décor. For Camus, on the contrary, the tragedy of human existence lies in the absence of any transcendence. . . . (pp. 115-16)

He is not concerned, then, with so ordering words as to suggest an inhuman, undecipherable order; the inhuman is merely the disorderly, the mechanical. There is nothing ambiguous in his work, nothing disquieting, nothing hinted at. *The Stranger* gives us a succession of luminously clear views. If they bewilder us, it is only because of their number and the absence of any link between them. Camus likes bright mornings, clear evenings, and relentless afternoons. His favorite season is Algiers' eternal summer. Night has hardly any place in his universe.

When he does talk of it, it is in the following terms: "I awakened with stars about my face. Country noises reached my ears. My temples were soothed by odors of night, earth, and salt. The wonderful peace of that sleepy summer invaded me like a tide" (*The Stranger*). The man who wrote these lines is as far removed as possible from the anguish of a Kafka. He is very much at peace within disorder. Nature's obstinate blindness probably irritates him, but it comforts him as well. Its irrationality is only a negative thing. The absurd man is a humanist; he knows only the good things of this world.

The comparison with Hemingway seems more fruitful. The relationship between the two styles is obvious. Both men write in the same short sentences. Each sentence refuses to exploit the momentum accumulated by preceding ones. Each is a new beginning. Each is like a snapshot of a gesture or object. For each new gesture and word there is a new and corresponding sentence. Nevertheless, I am not quite satisfied. The existence of an "American" narrative technique has certainly been of help to Camus. I doubt whether it has, strictly speaking, influenced him. (p. 116)

I catch a glimpse of a poetic prose underneath, which is probably Camus's personal mode of expression. If *The Stranger* exhibits . . . visible traces of the American technique, it was deliberate on Camus's part. He has chosen from among all the instruments at his disposal the one which seemed to serve his purpose best. I doubt whether he will use it again in future works. (p. 117)

Camus's story is analytic and humorous. Like all artists, he *invents*, because he pretends to be reconstituting raw experience and because he slyly eliminates all the significant links which are also part of the experience.

That is what Hume did when he stated that he could find nothing in experience but isolated impressions. That is what the American neo-realists still do when they deny the existence of any but external relations between phenomena. Contemporary philosophy has, however, established the fact that meanings are also part of the immediate data. But this would carry us too far afield. We shall simply indicate that the universe of the absurd man is the analytic world of the neo-realists. In literature, this method has proved its worth. It was Voltaire's method in *L'Ingénu* and *Micromégas,* and Swift's in *Gulliver's Travels.* For the eighteenth century also had its own outsiders, "noble savages," usually, who, transported to a strange civilization, perceived facts before being able to grasp their meaning. The effect of this discrepancy was to arouse in the reader the feeling of the absurd. Camus seems to have this in mind on several occasions, particularly when he shows his hero reflecting on the reasons for his imprisonment. (p. 118)

Where Bergson saw an indestructible organization, [Camus] sees only a series of instants. It is the plurality of incommunicable moments that will finally account for the plurality of beings. What our author borrows from Hemingway is thus the discontinuity between the clipped phrases that imitate the discontinuity of time.

We are now in a better position to understand the form of his narrative. Each sentence is a present instant, but not an indecisive one that spreads like a stain to the following one. The sentence is sharp, distinct, and self-contained. It is separated by a void from the following one, just as Descartes's instant is separated from the one that follows it. The world is destroyed and reborn from sentence to sentence. When the word makes its appearance it is a creation *ex nihilo.* The sentences in *The Stranger* are islands. We bounce from sentence to sentence, from void to void. (pp. 118-19)

The sentences are not, of course, arranged in relation to each other; they are simply juxtaposed. In particular, all causal links are avoided lest they introduce the germ of an explanation and an order other than that of pure succession. (p. 119)

This is what enables Camus to think that in writing *The Stranger* he remains silent. His sentence does not belong to the universe of discourse. It has neither ramifications nor extensions nor internal structure. (p. 120)

[Can] we speak of Camus's novel as something whole? All the sentences of his book are equal to each other, just as all the absurd man's experiences are equal. Each one sets up for itself and sweeps the others into the void. But, as a result, no single one of them detaches itself from the background of the others, except for the rare moments in which the author, abandoning these principles, becomes poetic.

The very dialogues are integrated into the narrative. Dialogue is the moment of explanation, of meaning, and to give it a place of honor would be to admit that meanings exist. Camus irons out the dialogue, summarizes it, renders it frequently as indirect discourse. He denies it any typographic privileges, so that a spoken phrase seems like any other happening. It flashes for an instant and then disappears, like heat lightning. Thus, when you start reading the book you feel as if you were listening to a monotonous, nasal, Arab chant rather than reading a novel. You may think that the novel is going to be like one of those tunes of which Courteline remarked that "they disappear, never to return" and stop all of a sudden. But the work gradually organizes itself before the reader's eyes and reveals its solid substructure.

There is not a single unnecessary detail, not one that is not returned to later on and used in the argument. And when we close the book, we realize that it could not have had any other ending. In this world that has been stripped of its causality and presented as absurd, the smallest incident has weight. There is no single one which does not help to lead the hero to crime and capital punishment. *The Stranger* is a classical work, an orderly work, composed about the absurd and against the absurd. Is this quite what the author was aiming at? I do not know. I am simply presenting the reader's opinion.

How are we to classify this clear, dry work, so carefully composed beneath its seeming disorder, so "human," so open, too, once you have the key? It cannot be called a *récit,* for a *récit* explains and co-ordinates as it narrates. It substitutes the order of causality for chronological sequence. Camus calls it a "novel." The novel, however, requires continuous duration, development and the manifest presence of the irreversibility of time. I would hesitate somewhat to use the term "novel" for this succession of inert present moments which allows us to see, from underneath, the mechanical economy of something deliberately staged. Or, if it is a novel, it is so in the sense that *Zadig* and *Candide* are novels. It might be regarded as a moralist's short novel, one with a discreet touch of satire and a series of ironic portraits (those of the pimp, the judge, the prosecuting attorney, etc.), a novel that, for all the influence of the German existentialists and the American novelists, remains, at bottom, very close to the tales of Voltaire. (pp. 120-21)

Jean-Paul Sartre, "An Explication of 'The Stranger'," in *Camus: A Collection of Critical Essays,* edited by Germaine Breé, Prentice-Hall, Inc., 1962, pp. 108-21.

E. FREEMAN
(essay date 1971)

[In the following excerpt, Freeman appraises Camus's dramas, focusing on the themes and techniques of his major works.]

It was shortly after seeing a performance of *Les possédés* during its provincial tour that Camus was killed. Those close to him believe that at this time he was just emerging from his long and difficult period of sterility and reappraisal—he is known to have been working hard on a novel, *Le premier homme,* for example. As far as the theatre is concerned, he confided to Germaine Brée in 1959 that he was toying with the idea of a play linking Don Juan-Sganarelle and Faust-Mephistopheles which he regarded as 'two aspects of the same dichotomy'. But it seems certain that no fragment of this or any other late work for the theatre by Camus exists. . . . Whether, once the Algerian War was over, and with his own theatre to work in amid the very different theatrical atmosphere of the 1960s, Camus would have gone on to produce a quantity of work of any significance makes interesting speculation, but is in the last resort doubtful. And so what finally is to be our assessment of the Camus whose last completely original work for the theatre was performed in 1949? Few critics, and even fewer theatre people, now believe that Camus's plays will enjoy the viability which seems assured for the work of dramatists such as Shaw, O'Casey, Pirandello, Brecht and Anouilh, although this stature appeared within Camus's grasp after the success of *Les justes.* Two questions must be asked: to what extent has Camus succeeded in creating the modern tragedy with which he was obsessed throughout his career, and how successful is his work as *theatre,* independently of whether it constitutes a convincing form of modern tragedy?

In answer to the first question, it seems to me that Camus does not make a really effective dramatic exploitation of the advantages which his political and philosophical theories would appear to give him. . . . A predilection for the tragic theme of a conflict between a powerful individual (e.g. Antigone) and an invincible order, or representative of order (e.g. Creon), and a passionate concern for the importance of not transcending limits, more or less equating to the classical horror of *hubris*—overweening pride or *démesure*—these would appear to leave Camus just as richly endowed in dramatic theory as Corneille and Racine. And so they do. But Camus's practice is not really a logical extension in dramatic terms of his theory. His theatre has the absurd as its premise, and this fact has far greater dramatic significance than the actions which result from it on the stage. Even if one agrees with Guicharnaud that Camus's plays, like those of Sartre, are 'crammed with action or the expectation of action', the fact remains that his tragedy is one of situation. It is metaphysical not psychological, and as John Cruickshank has observed, does not present 'flawed' heroes in the Elizabethan sense. Camus was convinced—strangely so in an experienced man of the theatre who revered Sophocles and Shakespeare—that metaphysics and psychology were incompatible in tragedy; and for him psychology in fact was anathema in any guise in any sort of play.

Unfortunately this conception of metaphysical tragedy has resulted in an excessively abstract form of expression. One of the best examples of this is Camus's handling of the mask, a favourite theatrical device of French dramatists since the Renaissance. . . . The mask, the instrument of inscrutability, the totally impenetrable screen around the personality, and cause of doubt, misunderstanding and murder, is the perfect metaphor of the absurd. In *Le malentendu,* the blackest of his plays, Camus implies that this is the natural order of the world. (pp. 148-50)

[A] vision of a world in which 'no one is ever recognized' dominates [*Caligula, Le Malentendu, L'État de siège,* and *Les Justes*]. It should be noted that in each one Camus makes a very sparing literal use of the mask—some form of disguise or game of pretence. Caligula disguises himself as Venus; Kaliayev (off stage) as a street-hawker; Jan assumes the name of Karl Hasek; and Diego wears 'le masque des médecins de la peste'. There is, however, a considerable disparity between the brief and functional uses of the mask at a literal level and its application at the metaphorical level to stress the impossibility of communication, understanding and love between human beings. It is not just in *Le malentendu* that Camus presents a despairing picture of a world in which the normal persona of human beings is the mask of tragedy. Once the mask is in place, it stays on. Only once does Camus manage effectively to exteriorize the transformation which has befallen the wearer, and that is in the powerful Act I curtain to *Caligula.* (p. 151)

An awareness of Camus's idea of how the fact of the absurd can affect the human personality is . . . essential for an understanding of the structure of his plays. Every main character from the first, Pèpe, to the last, Stavroguine, has become literally and metaphorically *figé,* fixed, blocked in time. In this respect—and coincidentally and not at all as a result of any 'influence'—Camus is perhaps more fundamentally Pirandellian than the scores of French dramatists who have made such ostentatious use of the Italian's more superficial plotting and characterization techniques since

1923. The trouble is that he hardly ever succeeds in rendering the mask/absurd metaphor concrete on the stage. The skill with which Anouilh, Giraudoux and Sartre manipulate *personae* is lacking in Camus, if not actually repugnant to him. One feels that Camus's commitment to his thesis—that alienation imposes masks of deception and insensitivity upon the real self—was too sincere. He was not dispassionate enough to use this classic device in a way which might legitimately please and intrigue in the theatre. Criticism after criticism of Camus's theatre offers the opinion that it is 'too intellectual', too obviously the work of a desiccated manipulator of ideas. On the contrary, the converse might just as easily be argued. Camus is indeed an intellectual dramatist in the sense that he believed the theatre ought to be a serious and non-commercial affair, a medium for important statements about the human condition, but hardly an intellectual in the matter of form. He does not possess the ability to stand back from his theme and present it objectively by means of illusion, perspective, juxtaposition of details in the classic manner of French dramatists since the seventeenth century. It is significant that two of Camus's plays which are considered to be among the most successful, *Requiem pour une nonne* and *Les possédés,* are adaptations which retain most of the 'popular' elements of the original novels: physical violence, mystery, dramatic irony, flashbacks. Camus could not avoid the action which is a key feature of the scenarios provided by Faulkner and Dostoevsky, although he did, as we have seen, create a very different atmosphere in each case. I doubt whether, if he had lived to begin a new cycle of plays in the 1960s, Camus would have learned the lesson of these successes, namely that his ideal modern tragedy need not be static, totally verbal and interior. For Camus's abhorrence of technical virtuosity, psychological theatre and the well-made play stem from an intellectual disdain on his part which made him equate popular and 'theatrical' elements with inferior theatre. (pp. 153-54)

[Camus defined *Caligula*] as a 'tragedy of the intelligence' but made repeated attempts in the successive versions to make the play more human by modifying and developing the characters of Hélicon and Scipion for example, and making the character of Caligula more sympathetic. And yet, as Albert Sonnenfeld has argued in a detailed discussion of Camus's 'failure' as a dramatist, it is very difficult for the audience to establish contact on any sort of human level with the hero. The problem is . . . that of communicating to an audience the real experience of the absurd, one of the effects of which is the impossibility of communicating anything to anyone. The task is feasible *à la rigueur* in the novel or cinema, but not in the theatre, as Martin Esslin has argued, unless the dramatist adopts a radically 'anti-cartesian' approach to dialogue, characterization and dramatic structure. Although . . . Camus appeared to be on the verge of a breakthrough with the character of 'le Vieux', the problem is one which he did not make any consistent attempt to solve. The highly experimental (and brilliantly successful) prose style of *L'étranger* has no counterpart in the plays. Split asunder by this gulf between form and theme, Camus's theatre constitutes one of the greatest paradoxes of the transitional decade 1940-50. (pp. 155-56)

The time has now come to make a résumé of the main aspects of Camus's dramatic style, making allowance for the difficulty of synthesizing the work of such a highly personal artist who never repeated the exact theme and form of any work, either in the theatre or in any other medium.

Taking theme first, all of Camus's original plays and most of those he adapted or translated are based in some measure on the premiss that our human condition is absurd. Violence and repression are common features. The inevitability of death is a source of unparalleled anguish (*Caligula*), as is the arrogation of the power of life and death over other people (*Les justes, Requiem pour une nonne*). Even when enjoying social and material success, man is haunted by an eternal quest for some physical or metaphysical goal, the exact nature of which is not always clear to him (*Le malentendu*). Chance frequently takes what seems to be almost a malevolent course, thwarting all attempts to achieve happiness (*Le malentendu*) or arbitrarily destroying that which already exists (*Caligula*). The protagonists are generally alienated from their physical background and from those human beings one would expect to be closest to them (*Le malentendu, Un cas intéressant*). The fact of the absurd can strike not merely individuals but whole sections of society. Civilized society is then split asunder in a conflict characterized by cowardice and treachery, and nihilistic collaboration with the absurd (*L'état de siège, Révolte dans les Asturies, Les possédés*).

All of Camus's plays are based on conflict. The manifestations of the absurd constitute one of the terms—the general condition or existing order, against which the heroes of Camus's plays react, or rebel. The heroes, the antithetical term, are animated by a sense of 'revolt'. In *Le mythe de Sisyphe* revolt designated a state of spiritual tension based on a lucid scrutiny of the absurd, and culminated in a curious form of stoic happiness. But in the theatre Camus handles revolt in a much more moralistic manner. Revolt must be creative and relative, not destructive and absolute (revolution). It must be based on a recognition of values, a 'qualitative' ethic, that is to say a scale of ethical priorities involving the totality of mankind. The rebel may not therefore combat the absurd with all the means at his disposal, and must be prepared for the anguish of making value-judgments about other people, whose claims to life are no less great than his own. At all times the rebel must be aware of a *limit*, beyond which he must not pass, on pain of redeeming transgression with his own life. And yet the absurd presents a terrifying paradox. It is in itself a total experience: life is never the same again. People of intelligence and sensitivity are tempted to make a total reaction, since the 'logic' of the absurd in the mind of whoever fully experiences it requires that the whole basis of society be transformed and an awareness of the absurd be universalized. (pp. 156-57)

The form that Camus's plays take is conditioned by these linked themes of the absurd and revolt. At its most profound level of interpretation Camus's theatre is metaphysical tragedy in which a basically noble and sensitive individual is pitted against an invincible and inscrutable order. It is characterized by a state of tension which is frequently independent of what happens during the course of the play. As a representation of human action on the other hand, Camus's theatre is strictly speaking not tragedy in any recognized formal sense so much as melodrama according to his own definition: a simplistic presentation of right and wrong. This explains the heroic and Romantic aura of much of his characterization. Theme dominates form: what the play is saying is more important than the way in which it says it. Camus has no time for theatrical games. He has something to say and he gets on with it. His characteristic plot is therfore linear, situated on the brink of a crisis, and is developed in a straightforward and chronological manner. (p. 157)

In characterization, too, Camus shows the same tendency to stress general rather than particular features. This explains the inescapable impression of rigidity that many of Camus's characters make. Rather than individuals they represent types of social and philosophical positions: revolt (Diego, Pépe, Kaliayev), 'revolution' (Stepan, Caligula, Martha), cynical nihilism (Nada, Skouratov, Hélicon), proletarian indifference (Foka), vile bourgeoisie (the judge, the grocer, the chemist), the eternal feminine (Dora, Maria, Caesonia, Victoria, Pilar), the young idealist making his first contact with reality (Scipion, Voinov), the mature relativist (Cherea, Annenkov) . . . the list could continue until every character in Camus's theatre is categorized.

Camus's dialogue is consistent with this philosophical conception of character and setting. He regarded language as the main problem in modern tragedy, and sought to create a stylized, neutral idiom which would nevertheless be recognizable as the language of the twentieth century and yet at the same time sufficiently 'distanced' and elevated to create what he considered to be the proper aura of tragedy. With the exception of his immature apprentice-piece, *Révolte dans les Asturies,* his dialogue is polished, correct, even literary. In his search for modern tragedy Camus had no

Camus at the offices of the resistance newspaper *Combat*, 1944.

reads far better than it acts. Thus by the standards the author set himself it is unsatisfactory, not to say a failure. (p. 160)

Incommunicable metaphysics, disparity of form and theme, faulty theatrical judgement, philosophical complexity and abstraction, cloying didacticism and failure to develop a sufficiently personal and artistically appropriate language to bear the weight of the play: these are the principal criticisms of Camus's theatre. Yet it would be quite wrong to regard it as a total failure. (p. 163)

The real merit of Camus's theatre lies in the sphere of theme rather than form, in so far as it is possible to separate the success of one from the failure of the other. Camus's theatre constitutes the most sincere attempt in its genre to create philosophical theatre mirroring the metaphysical anguish of our age. At the same time it combats the nihilism to which such speculation can lead, and in this respect the author follows clearly in the tradition of the great French moralists. Camus's theatre is unequalled for the probity and passion with which it defended human values during a decade in France when they had never been more fragile. (p. 164)

E. Freeman, in his *The Theatre of Albert Camus: A Critical Study*, Methuen & Co. Ltd., 1971, 178 p.

time for naturalism, and, much though he was affected by Hemingway and Faulkner in the novel, one feels he would have wished to derive nothing at all from their fellow American Arthur Miller in the theatre. (pp. 158-59)

Camus thus tried to harmonize all the elements of form to accord with his metaphysical and somewhat abstract themes. The universal and symbolic implications of his plays are stressed at the expense of the historical and concrete. With their elevated and unified tone, purity of language, minimization of physical detail, and concentration upon theme to the exclusion of superfluous humour, anecdote and scenic ingenuity, Camus's plays are thus much more authentically classical in form than those of his contemporaries. And yet there is always something lacking too. That vital spark of human warmth, of truly theatrical tension when a dramatist who is the complete master of his effects grips his audience exactly as he wishes through his characters, glows sporadically in *Le malentendu* and *Les justes* and perhaps comes near to being sustained only in *Caligula*. Despite the fact that, given the right production in the right place, these three plays can and occasionally do work well (and even *L'état de siège* appears to have had its moments in German translation), it remains true that in the last resort Camus's theatre

R. BARTON PALMER
(essay date 1980)

[In the excerpt below, Palmer examines the process of self-awareness depicted in *The Myth of Sisyphus* and *The Stranger*.]

I would like to propose here that, in one sense, [*The Stranger* and *The Myth of Sisyphus* are] commentaries on one another. It is that both are concerned with the epistemology of the human condition, with the changes that occur in man's perception of himself, his life, and his world as the individual process of existence runs its course. While *The Myth* presents Camus's development of absurdism as a *raisonnement*, that is, as a line of argument, the novel dramatizes Meursault's journey toward the epiphany which, on the eve of his execution, enables him to see clearly for the first time.

The Myth offers a sudden insight into a life whose only order is mechanical and artificial. This order is imposed by man himself on an experience otherwise gratuitous. To see through it is to begin to live thoughtfully. . . . The essay develops at some length the consequences of this newly conscious existence. One begins, Camus believes, by understanding the world's indifference and also the human desire for reason. If the terms of this dialectic are violated by neither the leap of faith nor by suicide, then man lives in the absurd, that is, in truth. And if he so persists, he is rewarded by a sense of freedom, by the impulse to revolt, by the life force of passion.

For absurd man, then, life has three stages. The theatricality of a daily routine ends with the realization that conventional wisdoms are invalidated by existence's ultimate meaninglessness. The feeling of absurdity which follows responds to the misproportion between the demands of consciousness for order and a confronting reality that offers none. But this misproportion, Camus argues, should not cause despair, but rather liberate man to enjoy the life given him unasked: " . . . completely turned toward death (taken here as the most obvious absurdity), the absurd man feels released from everything outside that passionate attention crystallizing in him." Absurdity thus frees man to grasp the whole of his life as a process completed in itself, since it lies outside any notion of universal justice. Camus in this way derives a new meaning from the familiar irony of *nascentes morimur.* For death, though not in any Christian sense, releases man to live.

The Myth goes on, of course, to explore some patterns of living which exploit most successfully an existence whose value is itself. Camus's concern here for an ethic of quantity finds no substantial reflection in *The Stranger.* Nor does Meursault resemble the conqueror, Don Juan, or the artist, those absurd types to whom the essay pays so much attention. But the epistemology of absurdism developed therein, a process of awareness undoubtedly parallel to Camus's personal experience, gives the novel its peculiar structure.

For all its superficial clarity, the first section of *The Stranger* puzzles and confuses. The events narrated are clear enough, but, presented with a first person narrative, we wonder why and when the narrator is telling his story. The use of present and *passé composé* verbs suggests a diary, but diary style is otherwise absent. The convention of first person narrative generally includes some information about the speaker, his purpose in writing, and the audience he addresses, even when, as in *Notes from Underground,* such indications deny the attempt to communicate itself. In *The Stranger* we are certain about what has happened, but uncertain about why we have been so informed. Why begin with the receipt of the telegram? Why end with the murder of the Arab? Here is a succession of events that lack what Aristotle calls *mythos,* the plot that imparts causality to experience's raw data. What Camus here presents is in fact a slice of the daily routine, devoid of intention and plot as it must be, a procession of events linked only by chronology. Event succeeds event, perception replaces perception, without any values by which the process may be interpreted.

Thus reproducing the daily routine's automatism

has posed two insoluble technical problems for Camus. These are connected with the process of verbalization itself. First, the narrator, as Fitch has labored to show, must be placed in the present, looking back at this sequence of events. This *tranche* of experience, of course, has significance only because of what happened at the trial, where Meursault is convicted more for his mother's death in the asylum than for the Arab's on the beach. The narrator's viewpoint presupposes reflection and analysis. But Part I represents Meursault's apprehension of life *before* he is forced to assign it value and meaning. Second, by translating Meursault's consciousness (preconsciousness?) into language, Camus alters its character. Speech is an act of will, but the Meursault of Part I is someone without the will to speak. Finally, of course, the slicing of Meursault's experience, giving it a beginning and an end, confers a value on those events that destroys their significance as they were lived, without thought about a future that would judge and order them.

At this stage Meursault is hardly a stranger to society. He follows accepted forms, like work and ritual, as closely as he can. He accepts relationships with others. He takes some joy in what life has to offer. He is, as he maintains before the trial, just like everybody else. But Meursault is at this time a stranger in one important sense. Like others, he is a stranger to his own existence. He is more an instrument than an actor. He feels but does not reflect. The daily routine, after all, does not demand otherwise. Much that happens is all the same to him. He shows no capacity for emotion. In this humble acquiescence to what we consider everyday living, Meursault is like most of us. The examined life may well be the only life worth living, but the world seldom calls upon us to penetrate the opacity of our own experience.

Meursault, however, is elected to penetrate that experience by a bizarre and ultimately inexplicable series of events. Why does he pull the trigger? And why then does he fire four more shots into the Arab's lifeless form? The novel offers an unsatisfactory answer to the first of these questions (it is that the sun itself made Meursault fire) and no answer to the second. But these are valid questions only if the hero's portrait is ethically motivated, if he is to be seen as the champion of truth. Camus's disregard for these issues suggests otherwise. The murder figures simply as the given event that permits Meursault to understand himself and the human condition. The process of justice, as Champigny points out, reduces to absurdity the theatricality of society, which attempts to impose the *mythos* of causality on what happens. And so the events of Part I become the elements of a plot. We know there is no connection between Meursault's behavior at his mother's funeral and his shooting of the Arab. But the prosecution's attempt to establish one betrays the very human need for a *my-*

thos, for a connection between character and motive and between motive and action. Upon the unorder of Part I is imposed a misorder that the reader and Meursault as well must reject. Camus thus makes us feel the difference between the world as experienced and the world as men would conceive it. Meursault is jerked from his automatism as he is faced with a human order that is no more than a fatuous theatricality. He begins to live in the absurd. As in *The Myth,* however, it is death that finally liberates him to live.

For Meursault the trial and its consequences reveal death as the central fact of the human condition. Meursault in this way finds his sentence not an exile from human society, but the key to understanding his full involvement in the life of his fellow condemned. Appropriately, it is in prison that Meursault becomes the narrator of his own experience as he feels the need, served by words, of understanding what has happened and also the desire to communicate that understanding to others. He has the right now to speak, for he has become once again like everyone else. He is the representative of a human race sentenced without real cause to die. As he sees it, death orders life, conferring on all actions a perfect equivalence and on disparate destinies the same finale. But he does not despair. In *The Myth* Camus explains his rejection of solutions like the Christian to human life: "they relieve me of the weight of my own life, and yet I must carry it alone." At the end of the novel Meursault grasps the perfected destiny that is his. He discovers what he calls "the benign indifference of the universe," that is the cosmic meaninglessness which enables man to live his life as his own. Like Aeschylus's Cassandra, he recognizes the inevitability of his destiny and opens himself freely to it. Unlike Cassandra, however, he finds in that inevitability a happiness that overcomes all feelings of loss. In the shadow of death, he feels the urge to live, even if life at this point means only the memory of what has been lived. *The Stranger* and *The Myth* both propose a world without meaning in which death ends existence. Both works, the novel perhaps more dramatically, reject suicide as a solution to the dilemma posed by meaninglessness and mortality. Essay and novel trace instead a process of awareness that culminates in a paradoxical truth: that only in the shadow of annihilation can man discover his freedom, his passion, and, most of all, the grandeur of self-possession. (pp. 123-25)

R. Barton Palmer, " 'The Myth of Sisyphus' and 'The Stranger': Two Portraits of the Young Camus," in *The International Fiction Review,* Vol. 7, No. 2, Summer, 1980, pp. 123-25.

STEPHEN MILLER
(essay date 1980)

[In the excerpt below, Miller provides an overview of Camus's literary career and critical reputation.]

At the time of his death, Camus's reputation was certainly inflated, as he himself would have been the first to admit. He claimed to dislike his public persona and complained in an interview a year before his death about those who praised his honesty, conscience, and humanity—"you know, all the modern mouthwashes." He was also dissatisfied with his own work, and said in 1958 that "I still live with the idea that my work has not even begun." Yet the air went out of his reputation even faster than might have been expected. By 1966, H. Stuart Hughes was uttering a commonplace when he said in *The Obstructed Path* that Camus's prose "was already beginning to sound dated." At the end of the decade, a shadow hung over his work; though he still had fervent admirers, the consensus among *bien-pensant* intellectuals was negative: Camus was an uneven novelist and a muddled thinker.

Behind this verdict lay a political judgment: Camus had squandered whatever talents he had in becoming, as Conor Cruise O'Brien argued in 1970, an obsessed cold warrior as well as, indirectly, an apologist for colonialism. These objections were offered more in sorrow than in anger. Camus's choice, O'Brien said, "wrong as we may think it politically, issued out of the depths of his whole life history." David Caute, too, attributed Camus's literary and political confusions to his ancestry and upbringing. Thus, the conqueror of Paris was himself vanquished in the end by followers of that quintessential Parisian intellectual, Jean-Paul Sartre, who detested Camus's politics.

But if, ten years after his death, Camus's reputation was under a cloud, now, twenty years later, the cloud is beginning to lift because of the profound change in French intellectual life wrought by the revelations of Aleksandr Solzhenitsyn. With the reigning Marxist orthodoxy under serious challenge for the first time in thirty years, Camus is once again being taken seriously. . . . Perhaps the time has come for a new look at Camus's work and for an attempt to reassess his achievement in the light of the last two decades. (p. 53)

By 1941, when he was twenty-eight, the first phase of Camus's work was completed. It includes *Caligula,* a play; the extended essay, *The Myth of Sisyphus;* and, of course, the novel, *The Stranger,* indisputably Camus's most popular work. *The Stranger* is an uneven novel—marred, I think, by the shift in tone between its two parts. Part I is full of luminous detail about the daily life of an easygoing and laconic young man dedicated to the joys of physical life, attractive both in his desire to lead an uncomplicated life and to be true to his feelings. Suddenly in Part II, this same easygoing youth, having committed a gratuitous murder, is transformed into a profoundly cryptic individual who stubbornly refuses to save his life by uttering conventional pieties. Camus later explained the actions of Meursault, the protagonist, by saying he "is animated by a passion that is deep because stubborn, a passion for the absolute and the truth." But the Meursault of Part I has no trace of such heroic severity, and, in fact, casually tells a lie to help a passing acquaintance out of a jam. Thus the novel seems disconnected, and also peculiarly dismissive—though this is seldom remarked upon—of the murder itself.

Why has it been so popular? O'Brien is probably right in his view that "the main secret of its appeal lies in its combination of a real and infectious joy of living, with a view of society which appears to be, and is not, uncompromisingly harsh." The novel celebrates life as absurd—that is to say, as having no intrinsic meaning. The only "meaning" to existence is the sensual enjoyment to be derived from it. If this sounds superficial, there is also a tragic dimension, insofar as death hangs over us continually. Camus said in his *Notebooks* at the time he was writing *The Stranger:* "No one who lives in the sunlight makes a failure of his life." So the novel exhorts us to live in the sunlight, and to revolt against those who invoke sentimental pieties in order to make sense out of human existence. The novel is popular with young readers because they are especially apt to resent the pieties of their elders, and also, no doubt, because these rather shallow propositions sound philosophically "deep." Yet in effect, the novel merely tells us in a roundabout way that by invoking the magic word, Absurd, we can tell everyone to go to hell and run off to the beach—a notion which is obviously quite exhilarating, and makes life very simple indeed.

The Myth of Sisyphus, which Camus started soon after he finished *The Stranger,* is a theoretical exposition of these same ideas: the universe may be devoid of meaning, but the recognition of this meaninglessness is inspiring. Man can then "decide to accept such a universe and draw from it his strength, his refusal to hope, and the unyielding evidence of a life without consolation." But whereas *The Stranger* has some fine moments of novelistic detail—especially the opening scenes, when Meursault attends his mother's funeral— *The Myth of Sisyphus* is tedious in its neo-Nietzschean banalities and murky observations which sometimes sound like a Woody Allen parody ("For everything begins with consciousness, and nothing is worth anything except through it"). In any case, by the time Camus fin-

ished *The Myth of Sisyphus* he was ready to jettison the notion of the Absurd, for the German occupation of Paris had suddenly given life meaning. Camus soon came to realize that the Absurd has nothing to teach us about how to conduct ourselves in the face of real danger—the Nazis, for example—and his *Notebooks* make it clear that by 1942 he had abandoned the notion. Ten years later he admitted that "this word 'Absurd' has had an unhappy history and I confess that now it rather annoys me."

The main work of Camus's second phase was *The Plague,* which he began in 1941 and worked on intermittently for the next five years—his time taken up with work in the Resistance and editorial chores at *Combat.* In this phase, Camus was preoccupied with the problem of action in the face of overwhelming odds, action that necessarily required the cultivation of trust among men who had every reason to distrust each other. The Nazis dispatched members of the Resistance summarily, so that a man's life was held in the balance not only by a small circle of friends but also by many others in the Resistance whom he might not even know—men who might betray their compatriots on any number of grounds, torture being the most obvious. One of Camus's most moving essays is the introduction he wrote to the *Poésies Posthumes* of René Leynaud, a friend in the Resistance who had been caught by the Nazis and executed. *The Plague,* a novel that is in many ways about the problem of fraternity, has as a central scene the moment when Rieux and Tarrou go for a swim "for friendship's sake." The swim over, the narrator remarks that "they dressed and started back. Neither had said a word, but they were conscious of being perfectly at one, and the memory of this night would be cherished by them both."

There is, though, something wooden about this fraternal moment, as there is about the entire novel. O'Brien calls *The Plague* "a great allegorical sermon," but the allegory is both too obvious and not obvious enough. The novel is an allegory of France under the Occupation, but it is not clear how a city in the throes of plague can stand for a country controlled by a foreign army. Or, to put it another way: French conduct during the war years raises questions that cannot be dealt with through this metaphor, among other things because infectious organisms behave in a uniform way, whereas the soldiers and administrators of an occupying army do not. As one critic has said, *The Plague* "is neither deeply rooted in the real stuff of life nor in the poetical matter of myth." The novel is inert, its characters little more than walking editorials in favor of courage, common decency, fraternity, and so forth. Camus himself was unhappy with it, calling it a "tract," and writing in his *Notebooks:* "Plague. In my whole life, never such a feeling of failure. I am not even sure of reaching the end." In any case, by 1946, when he raised these doubts, his mind was elsewhere. A new problem was preoccupying him, the problem of liberty. He had already begun notes for a book he would not finish until five years later: *The Rebel.* (pp. 54-5)

The tension between liberty (or freedom) and justice is the subject of *The Rebel.* At first, Camus had believed that the two could be reconciled, but as the Resistance years receded into the past, he became aware that many people he had been close to and to whom he still remained attached were fervent in their desire for social justice but less inclined to defend freedom. They were driven by a concern for the collective rather than for what Camus called "individual fates," and were therefore very susceptible to Maurice Merleau-Ponty's argument, in *Humanism and Terror* (1947), that Stalinist violence, though not to be condoned, should be regarded as a passing phase in a society moving in the direction of social justice. In other words, since the Soviet Union was marching toward social justice, it would be wrong to dwell on the fate of particular individuals who were being mistreated, even killed, along the way. Doing so could only serve to undermine a progressive regime, and indirectly to aid reactionary ones. In the late 40's, it should be noted, Merleau-Ponty, as managing editor of Sartre's *Les Temps Modernes,* was an influential figure, and this line of reasoning became the standard justification on the French Left for suppressing anti-Stalinist criticism. (p. 55)

Camus himself wrote for Sartre's magazine and moved in the same circles as those intellectuals inclined to think well of the Soviet Union. Friendship between Sartre and Camus was still possible, for Sartre's position had not yet hardened, and he had even publicly criticized Stalin's forced-labor camps, for which he was attacked by the French Communists. By 1950, however, after the Korean war broke out, Sartre called the United States the greatest obstacle in the way of "the salvation of mankind," and decided to submit, as an act of self-discipline, to total acceptance of the Soviet viewpoint, though he would still insist at times that he was not a Marxist.

But though Sartre and Camus were political adversaries in the early 1950's, it is a mistake to assume that their positions were antithetical—that if Sartre embraced Marxism-Leninism and defended the Soviet Union, then Camus must have embraced capitalism and defended the United States. In fact, Camus had nothing good to say about capitalism and clearly disliked the United States. His basic sympathies were with the non-Communist Left, especially the Spanish syndicalists and anarchists, among whom he had many friends, but his politics were always inconsistent: though he considered himself a socialist, he also harbored strong anarchist tendencies and tended to distrust all governments.

In one thing, however, he remained constant: he was a passionate defender of liberty, and in 1950 he saw that the greatest danger to liberty came not from the Right but from the Left. In two plays written in the late 1940's—*State of Siege* and *The Just Assassins*—Camus had touched upon the totalitarian mentality often concealed behind what in his *Notebooks* he called a "mania for virtue," but *The Rebel* constitutes his most fully developed attack on those who dream of a society based on absolute justice.

The Rebel is Camus's most ambitious book, and it suffers from its ambitiousness. Attempting to provide a complete anatomy of rebellion in all its aspects, *The Rebel* zooms all over the landscape of European intellectual history, with Camus in the role of tour guide, making sweeping generalizations about entire historical epochs and coming in the end to the lame conclusion that the ultimate good is a sense of limits—a view supposedly characteristic of that "Mediterranean mind" of which Meagher is so enamored. Despite such mystifications, however, there does exist at the core of the book a well-argued essay against the notion that the sins of Russian Communism should be excused because the Soviet Union is on the right historical track. Camus goes even further, arguing that Russian Communism and German fascism have much in common—both despise "bourgeois" democracy, for one thing—but that Russian Communism is even more dangerous to the world since "the German revolution had no hope of a future" while Russian Communism, by contrast, "openly aspires to world empire. That is its strength, its deliberate significance, and its importance in our history."

Camus, it should be stressed, is not arguing here that the idea of social justice should be dismissed altogether, but that the notion of absolute justice advanced by Marxist-Leninists is a formula for tyranny. Two sentences sum up the book: "Absolute freedom mocks at justice. Absolute justice denies freedom."

In the complicated politics of the early 1950's, Camus's book was well received by parts of the French intelligentsia and condemned by other parts. (pp. 55-6)

In 1952 Sartre also had the difficult task of assigning a reviewer for Camus's book. Despite political differences, the two were still on reasonably good terms and Sartre had, in fact, published a chapter of *The Rebel* in his magazine. Nevertheless, the review that finally appeared in *Les Temps Modernes* by Francis Jeanson, one of Sartre's fervent disciples, was scathing; Jeanson accused Camus of accomplishing an "objectively" reactionary task by attacking Marxism-Leninism, and to prove it he cited the favorable reviews Camus had received not only in the bourgeois press but also in a right-wing journal that was an organ of *Action française.* Stung by the review, Camus replied in a long letter that appeared in the August 1952 issue, along with a response from Sartre himself, commenting both on the particular charges made in Camus's letter and on Camus's politics in general.

Thus, the famous break between Camus and Sartre, which was an event not only in France but in the world press as well. (p. 56)

The last eight years of Camus's life, following the break with Sartre, may be said to constitute a fourth and final phase of his career: he was embittered by the break and haunted by the war in Algeria, but despite long periods of depression, he did work through to a freer prose that is less stilted and pompous than his earlier writing. In several short essays and stories, he is more concise and witty than ever before, and his last and best novel, *The Fall,* successfully combines the earlier lyricism with a new and mordant irony. (p. 57)

The Fall is a bleak novel, yet a curiously exhilarating one. Laced with witty observations about the perversities of human conduct, it is very much in the French *moraliste* tradition, a descendant of Montaigne's *Essays,* La Rochefoucauld's *Maxims,* and Diderot's novella, *Rameau's Nephew.* The narrator, Jean-Baptiste Clamence, is a fascinating character, a self-proclaimed "empty prophet for shabby times" who subtly and ingeniously confesses his own moral failings in order to avoid being judged by others. "The more I accuse myself," he says to his silent companion, "the more I have a right to judge you. Even better, I provoke you into judging yourself, and this relieves me of that much of the burden."

Some critics have regarded Clamence as a self-portrait, an attempt by Camus to exorcise the burden of his supposed "sainthood"; others see it as a portrait of Sartre, the man who continually proclaimed his own guilt over belonging to the bourgeoisie. But whoever sat for it, this portrait of a twisted hero of our times, who perverts notions of Christian guilt in order to maintain his own sense of self-esteem and to dominate others, is Camus's masterpiece. It is also a fascinating, extended gloss on Lionel Trilling's observation that "the life of competition for spiritual status is not without its own peculiar sordidness and absurdity."

But in the end, Camus's literary achievement is secondary to his importance as a political intellectual. (pp. 57-8)

In summing up Camus's importance, it is almost enough to say simply that he never joined those "progressive" French intellectuals on their shepherded journeys around the Soviet Union. Camus was not an original philosopher, and it would be foolish to make great claims for the profundity of his work. But he was a perceptive political journalist who was one of the first French intellectuals to recognize that the central debate was not between capitalism and Communism but between liberty and tyranny. And he was one of the first also to question the notion that poor people do not care about freedom. As he said in a seminal essay, **"Bread and Freedom":** "The oppressed want to be liberated not only from their hunger but also from their masters, since they are well aware that they will be effectively freed of hunger only when they hold their masters, all their masters, at bay."

Camus was instrumental in rallying intellectual opinion to the defense of democratic liberties at a time when many Western intellectuals were reluctant to believe anything ill of the Soviet Union. To paraphrase Orwell, he was a man who struggled constantly to see what was in front of his nose—to see what many Western intellectuals tried, and still try, desperately not to see. (p. 58)

Stephen Miller, "The Posthumous Victory of Albert Camus," in *Commentary,* Vol. 70, No. 5, November, 1980, pp. 53-8.

SOURCES FOR FURTHER STUDY

Bloom, Harold, ed. *Albert Camus.* New York: Chelsea House Publishers, 1989, 195 p.

    Collection of critical essays on many aspects of Camus's work. Includes pieces by Paul de Man, Patrick McCarthy, and Donald Lazere.

Fitch, Brian T. *The Narcissistic Text: A Reading of Camus's Fiction.* Toronto: University of Toronto Press, 1982, 125 p.

    Focuses upon the self-consciousness of Camus's writing and uses this quality to identify the author as a precursor of the French new novelists.

McCarthy, Patrick. *Albert Camus: The Stranger.* Cambridge: Cambridge University Press, 1988, 109 p.

    Concise, lucid book-length study of *The Stranger* that places the novel in the context of French-Algerian history and culture.

Rhein, Philip H. *Albert Camus.* Boston: Twayne Publishers, 1969, 148 p.

    Critical study of Camus's works. Rhein comments: "[Camus's] completed work stands as a testimony to a man who was profoundly concerned with his times. His thought progresses from a personal involvement with the universe to an understanding of it that is acceptable on human terms. . . . Those few things that Camus has illuminated for our times have broadened our range of sympathies and our consciousness of what goes on around us.''

Sprintzen, David. *Camus: A Critical Examination.* Philadelphia: Temple University Press, 1988, 310 p.

    Analysis of Camus's entire *oeuvre,* focusing on his concepts of revolt, dialogue, and community.

Thody, Philip. *Albert Camus.* London: Macmillan, 1989, 125 p.

    Biographical and critical study. Includes bibliography.

Karel Čapek

1890-1938

Czech novelist, dramatist, short story writer, journalist, and travel writer.

INTRODUCTION

Čapek is best known for his works of science fiction, primarily the drama *R.U.R.* (1921; *Rossum's Universal Robots*) and the novel *Válka s mloky* (1936; *War with the Newts*). In these works, he warned against the dehumanizing aspects of modern civilization and satirized a plethora of social, economic, and political systems. Underlying much of Čapek's writing is an ardent humanism and a philosophical belief in the plurality and relativity of truth. He explored this doctrine in greatest depth in his trilogy of novels—*Hordubal* (1933), *Povětroň* (1933; *Meteor*), and *Obyčejný život* (1934; *An Ordinary Life*)—which many critics consider Čapek's masterpiece.

Čapek was born in Malé Svatoňovice, a small village in northeastern Bohemia. A frail and sickly child, he was especially close to his older brother, Josef, and as adults the brothers frequently collaborated on short stories and plays. Josef, an artist as well as a writer, also illustrated several of his brother's books. Čapek began writing poetry and fiction in high school; soon after graduation he was publishing stories, written in collaboration with Josef, in Czech newspapers. After studying at universities in Prague, Berlin, and Paris, Čapek earned a doctorate in philosophy at Prague's Charles University in 1915. Two years later, he began a career as a journalist whose articles often championed the cause of Czech nationalism. The creation of the Czechoslovak republic after World War I greatly inspired Čapek, and his enthusiasm for the new democratic government led to a personal friendship with Tomáš Masaryk, Czechoslovakia's first president. Čapek first received literary acclaim in the early 1920s with the dramas *R.U.R.* and *Ze života hmyzu* (1922; *The Insect Play*). During this time he also began to write novels; he continued his success as a fiction writer and dramatist for the rest of his career. As World

War II approached, Čapek and his brother, both outspoken opponents of fascism, were advised to leave Prague, but they chose to remain and continue their opposition to Nazism. Čapek died three months before the Nazis invaded Prague; the secret police, unaware of his death, arrived at his home seeking his arrest. Josef was interned in a concentration camp, where he died shortly before the end of the war.

Among Čapek's dramas, *R.U.R.*, which introduced the word "robot," is considered the most successful. At its premiere, audiences and critics were both fascinated and terrified by its vision of a technically advanced society unable to control its ultimate labor-saving creation, the robot. Čapek, however, was disappointed in *R.U.R.*, believing that the social allegory he intended was overshadowed by the novelty of the robots. In *The Insect Play*, Čapek presented various human vices and weaknesses as species of insects, such as cold efficiency represented by ants. *Věc Makropulos* (1922; *The Makropoulos Secret*) propounded the pessimistic view that boredom would accompany eternal youth, and critics have suggested that it was written as a refutation of Bernard Shaw's positive view of immortality in *Back to Methuselah* (1921).

Čapek's science fiction novels are more highly regarded than his dramas. The common theme of these novels is the potential misuse of technology. While he did not oppose technological innovations, Čapek was deeply disturbed by the fact that human beings could not possibly take into consideration all the adverse possibilities of their inventions and discoveries, regardless of their benign intent. For example, in his novels *Továrna na absolutno* (1922; *The Absolute at Large*) and *Krakatit* (1924), Čapek foresaw the destructive potential of atomic energy while acknowledging that the objective of nuclear scientists is to improve the condition of humankind. While these early novels evince stylistic immaturity, his later novel *War with the Newts* is praised both for its narrative artistry and its power as satire. Aimed at the exploitive and dehumanizing aspects of capitalism, communism, and fascism, *War with the Newts* expresses a view of human nature and politics that is still considered timely. In this novel Čapek departed from his usual allegorical method of characterization and fashioned more psychologically complex characters. The trilogy of novels that includes *Hordubal, Meteor*, and *An Ordinary Life* probes the relativity of truth and reality, examining the ways that personality and experience affect an individual's actions, perceptions, and understanding. Although the plots of the three novels are unrelated, together these works present Čapek's philosophy of pluralism and democracy.

Čapek is considered one of Czechoslovakia's foremost writers. His works are important for their contribution to the literature of his country and to science fiction, and are also esteemed for their expression of profound concern for humanity and its future. William E. Harkins has stated of Čapek: "The tragedy of his homeland and his premature death cut short the philosophical and creative development of a great writer, a profound thinker, and a great human spirit."

(For further information about Čapek's life and works, see *Contemporary Authors*, Vol. 104; *Drama Criticism*, Vol. 1; and *Twentieth-Century Literary Criticism*, Vols. 6, 37.)

CRITICAL COMMENTARY

RENÉ WELLEK
(essay date 1936)

[Wellek is an influential critic and literary historian whose books include *Theory of Literature* (1949), written with Warren Austin, and the monumental *A History of Modern Criticism* (1955-86). In the following excerpt from an essay first published in 1936 in *The Slavonic and East European Review*, he reviews Čapek's oeuvre, remarking that the Czech writer "has achieved real greatness, even measured by the highest standards."]

[Most] English readers do not know that Karel Čapek is an extremely ambitious and subtle practitioner of the craft of fiction, a philosopher-poet passionately interested in the problems of truth and justice, in short, a great artist who has to be reckoned with as one of the major figures of contemporary literature. (p. 46)

Čapek's earliest writings reach back to pre-war times . . . and inevitably bear the traces of the time and the youth of their author. Čapek then wrote in conjunction with his elder brother Joseph, who has since become a distinguished modernist painter. . . . *Krakonoš's Garden* [a collection of their stories] is a curious mixture of little burlesque tales, anecdotes and epigrams, prose-poems and phantasies. Parodies of the style of symbolism clash piquantly with quotations

Principal Works

Lásky hra osudna [with Josef Čapek; first publication]
(drama) 1910

Zářivé hlubiny [with Josef Čapek] (short stories) 1916

R.U.R. (Rossum's Universal Robots) (drama) 1921

[R.U.R. (Rossum's Universal Robots), 1923]

Trapné provídky (short stories) 1921

[Money, and Other Stories, 1929]

Továrna na absolutno (novel) 1922

[The Absolute at Large, 1927]

Věc Makropulos (drama) 1922

[The Makropoulos Secret, 1925]

Ze života hmyzu [with Josef Čapek] (drama) 1922

[And So Ad Infinitum (The Life of the Insects), 1923;
also published as The World We Live In (The Insect
Comedy), 1933, and as The Insect Play in "R.U.R."
and "The Insect Play," 1961]

Anglické listy (travel sketches) 1924

[Letters from England, 1925]

Krakatit (novel) 1924

[Krakatit, 1925]

Adam Stvořitel [with Josef Čapek] (drama) 1927

[Adam the Creator, 1930]

*Povídky z druhé kapsy (short stories) 1929

[Tales from Two Pockets (partial translation), 1932]

†Povídky z jedné kapsy (short stories) 1929

[Tales from Two Pockets (partial translation), 1932]

Hordubal (novel) 1933

[Hordubal, 1934]

Provětroň (novel) 1933

[Meteor, 1935]

Obyčejný život (novel) 1934

[An Ordinary Life, 1936]

Válka s mloky (novel) 1936

[War with the Newts, 1937, 1985]

Bilá nemoc (drama) 1937

[Power and Glory, 1938; also published as The White
Plague, 1988]

Privni parta (novel) 1937

[The First Rescue Party, 1939]

Matka (drama) 1938

[The Mother, 1939]

Život a dílo skladatele Foltýna (unfinished novel) 1939

[The Cheat, 1941]

Kniha apokryfů (short stories) 1945

[Apocryphal Stories, 1949]

*This collection is also rendered in English as Tales from
One Pocket.

†This collection is also rendered in English as Tales from
the Other Pocket.

---

from telegrams and newspapers. Much in the book is crude and naïve: but some numbers present a certain interest as they anticipate later developments, for instance **"System"**, which, in a grotesque fashion, treats the problem of the robots before the name was adopted. (pp. 46-7)

The very early comedy *The Fateful Game of Love* . . . succeeds very much better. There is no denying the artificiality of the trifle, a sort of *commedia dell' arte* with a tragic leading motive in an ironic setting. Gilles, the romantic weakling, is killed in a duel by the bullying ruffian Trivalin, but the lady is carried off by the plotting Brighello. This traditional theme, which is treated in very musical blank verse, is lightened by a series of devices that purposely bridge the gulf between the public and the actors. For instance, the doctor asks the audience why they came at all, Trivalin suddenly refuses to go on acting or challenges anybody in the audience. . . . All this deliberate spoiling of the theatrical illusion is very amusing, though the device is, of course, known since the times of Ludwig Tieck at least. The very same ironic and melancholy setting of the dying "rococo" recurs in the best story of the next collection of tales. *Luminous Depths* . . . contains a story,

"L'Eventail", which also could be called the fateful game of love. The garden-party of Principe Bodoni in 18th century Naples catches the right flavour of the time: the automatic dolls of M.J.L. Droz are worthy of E.T.A. Hoffmann though the Čapeks aim at something more restrained and objective. The preceding **"Red Story"** does not come off so well, possibly because of the inherent improbabilities of the very sanguinary action, or because Čapek does not quite succeed in catching the right matter-of-fact tone which we find in Stendhal's *Chroniques italiennes*. . . . The range of the whole collection is remarkable, the advance compared to *Krakonoš's Garden* quite undeniable. The Čapeks have discovered the charm of sheer story-telling, and they move easily from one style to the other among the most various settings. There was, however, no further development towards the style of the Italian "novelle", though **"L'Eventail"** was a promising piece of work. But the rather awkward and wasteful *Luminous Depths* point to the future: to a new and original mystery-story. (pp. 47-8)

[*Wayside Crosses* is] a collection of "detective stories". But they are very unusual detective or rather mystery stories, without any solution for the mysteries.

The very disappointment of our expectation is their main point: just the most important part of the event told remains behind the scene. The justification of this interesting technical device is, of course, in the view of life the stories are meant to convey. *Krakonoš's Garden* was full of a naïve scepticism and an irreverence which rather enjoyed demonstrating that there are no absolute values. But in the *Wayside Crosses* the joy has turned into bitterness. The world appears as a whirlwind of chance and contingencies without deeper coherence. . . . *Luminous Depths* covers huge stretches of time in a few sentences; *Wayside Crosses* concentrates on single mysterious moments. The following *Painful Stories* [translated into English under the title of *Money and Other Stories*] . . . return to the normal epical form, though they do not imply a substantial change of outlook. Life is again arbitrary and disconnected, brutal and disconcertingly illogical. The stories are "painful", because they are so inconclusive, because they frequently end with a submission after a very unheroic revolt. A husband takes money from his wife which he must know she gets from her lover (**"Three"**); an intelligent girl throws herself suddenly at the mercy of a man who does not care for her and rejects her (**"Helena"**). . . . [These] are some of the themes which contrast a very trivial outward occurrence with an inner drama of painful resignation. The supreme instance is possibly the first story, **"Two Fathers"**. A child dies, and the supposed father breaks down in grief on her grave, while the real father—as everybody knows in the village—is singing lustily in the choir. There is an atmosphere of heavy, melancholy fatality in these stories, which can be very well compared with some of the "painful" stories in Maupassant or Chekhov. (pp. 48-50)

Painful Stories very worthily concludes the extremely interesting period of Čapek's early writings. Then came immediately the success of *R.U.R.* . . . , which shows a complete change of style and outlook. . . . *R.U.R.* took the world by storm, and there were some good reasons for this success. The main idea of the robots (the word, derived from robota, drudgery, was suggested by Joseph Čapek) was timely: the discussion of the whole problem of progress and of man's relation to machines was, so to say, in the air just after the War. The whole tendency of the play, its warning of mankind against the dangers of a machine-civilisation, seemed very healthy, and the final optimism, declaiming belief in the power of love and the survival of life, sounded very reassuring. The play has also considerable theatrical qualities: the men-automatons moving stiffly like dolls, the tension of the great revolt, the striking types of men—all this testifies to Čapek's lively sense for the stage. If we, however, examine the play in cold blood, the fissures in the structure and the gaps in the argument become obvious: the robots which are conceived as men-machines without soul or feeling, are changed during the play by a sleight of hand into real men. There is no revolt of robots, but a revolt of oppressed men: one race of men is simply dethroned by another and the whole story loses its point. It all comes to an attack on human ambition, and a recommendation of simple humanity: of love, laughter and tears. The science displayed with much ingenuity is, after all, pseudo-science: a sort of magic by which men are made artificially with bones, veins, muscles, etc., just as any man, though on some mythical chemical basis other than man's.

The second play in this vein, *The Life of the Insects* . . . , seems to me very much better. Of course, its texture is looser: it is almost a ballet, or review. The breathless speed of the dialogue avoids the mistakes of the rather bookish theorising which vitiates the later plays. (pp. 50-1)

[*The Macropoulos Secret*] is again a play about a scientific invention, the magical character of which is here frankly admitted. . . . This looks like a counterpart to Shaw's *Back to Methuselah*, but Čapek's play was written before he had heard of Shaw's, and his tendency is exactly the opposite one. The heroine has lost all joy in life and all desire for further life. All those around her finally reject the use of the recipe and a sensible young girl burns it. So youth has destroyed the fear of death. A life lived decently for sixty years is more valuable than three hundred. The setting of this moral in a legal comedy is not always convincing, however, and the figures remain puppets. The last of Čapek's dramas, *Adam the Creator*, . . . is rather disappointing. The idea seems a good one: Adam has destroyed the world, and God is asking him to recreate it. But he has no ideas of his own: everything he creates makes an even bigger mess of life, and when there is a chance to destroy the second world, he very properly refuses. It seems to be a little unfair to deprive mankind of any right of criticising because it would not be able to create, and the moral to be drawn seems a little too self-righteous about the present state of affairs: but obviously this quietism suited Čapek at a certain point of his development, and one must understand his impatience with all salvationists and world-reformers. But the execution of the idea is not very successful. (pp. 50-2)

Contemporaneously with the plays Čapek started to write utopian romances. The first is *The Absolute at Large* . . . which again starts with a brilliant idea: an engineer is able to burn matter so completely that only the Absolute remains and is liberated. Though the invention is excellent from the economic point of view as one pound of coal is burning weeks and weeks, the general consequences are disastrous: people become affected with religious mania, start to distribute their belongings, preach sectarian fanaticism, etc. This is very amusing satire on the gulf between theory and practice in religion, but after a few chapters Čapek gives the topic up in despair: the Absolute suddenly begins to work all the machines, and overproduction suffocates all economic life, the religious mania leads to endless wars of sects, ending in complete exhaustion. . . . But though the book contains some brilliant humorous scenes, especially on a barge and on a merry-go-round, its main conception is uncertain and the design becomes very loose towards the end. The "utopian" or rather anti-utopian phase of Čapek's writings finds its fullest expression in *Krakatit* . . . , Čapek's longest book. Again the satire is directed against any titanism, and the moral drawn is the moral of resignation. Prokop, the great specialist in high explosives, invents the deadly Krakatit, capable of blowing up anything. Throughout the whole of the novel he fights for withholding his secret, which, if betrayed, might become the end of civilisation. . . . There are many beautiful and striking scenes in *Krakatit;* especially the idyll in the country, which has obvious autobiographical touches, is in Čapek's best vein. But this solid piece of writing clashes curiously with the latter scenes in Balttin, where Prokop is confined. The love-scenes between him and the Princess Wille suddenly take on a phantastic colour of brutal violence which reminds us of some of the most painful scenes in D. H. Lawrence. The whole setting in a fanciful and grotesque aristocratic society, ingredients of melodrama, sex psychology, technological speculation, feverish dreams are mixed up disconcertingly with curious allegorising. The Princess Wille has an allegorical name, and D'Hémon or Daimon is a figure out of fairyland with burning hands. Many of the fever-hallucinations of Prokop are managed very interestingly, and there is a certain largeness in the whole conception, and a fierce intensity in some of the scenes—however absurd their rational connection: but the book drags on many points and the violent changes of style and technique make it incoherent.

Side by side with the plays and romances the essayist Čapek developed his powers. He settles down, so to say, and writes a number of very pleasant, very sensible and humorous books of sketches, essays, travels which in one way or the other express his deep humanity, his belief in ordinary man, his sense of the bewildering variety and beauty of the world. His optimism is sometimes a shade too cheerful, and does not altogether avoid a certain contempt for all that is greatest is man. (pp. 52-3)

Čapek's deep humanity, his astonishing power of observation, come out best in his travel-sketches. The first were the *Letters from Italy* . . . , full of lively reflections on art and architecture, aggreeably set off by genre-pictures of the life of Italian towns, villages and ports. The book shows Čapek's love for the primitive

painters, his real appreciation of early mediaeval Italy, while he is obviously uneasy before Renaissance and Baroque developments. The book is frankly the diary of a holiday tour, very short and very fully enjoyed, and does not pretend to any full comprehension for Italy's past or present. The *Letters from England* . . . show a very much deeper understanding for the character of the people. They are, it is true, light travelling sketches and the surprised attitude of the provincial and continental, battered by first impressions of London traffic, are sometimes a little too self-conscious. Čapek is rather interested in the daily life around him, the English landscape and the English character, than in history or art or anything out of the way. But inside these limits he manages to convey a great deal of subtle observation, quiet fun and real understanding. (p. 54)

The vivid interest in men, their habits of life and their institutions, is the starting-point of Čapek's political interests. A collection of papers, *On Political Things, or Zoon Politicon* . . . , says many sensible things on Czechoslovak and general problems. Čapek is a genuine democrat and has always advocated a humane, tolerant, and liberal government against extremists both on the right and on the left. (p. 55)

[Čapek] is interested very much in a vital question of modern literature: how can literature again appeal to the masses, while keeping a high artistic standard? The way to this ideal seems to lie in a development of the popular *genres* of literature, which should be exalted by the writer while remaining comprehensible to the common mind. This explains his special interest in the despised forms of "low" literature to which he has devoted a brilliant collection of sociological studies: *Marsyas, or on the Margin of Literature.* . . . There he tells us about journalism, the psychology and typology of anecdotes, writes about popular humour and proverbs, collects a series of extremely funny poems from the suburbs of Prague, has his say on pornography, on stories in calendars, novels read by maid-servants, etc. He is sceptical about consciously "proletarian" art, praises very properly the resources of the Czech language, and devotes much space to an illuminating discussion of two genres: the fairy-tale and the detective-story.

Fairy-tales are Čapek's specialty. . . . [His own *Fairy-Tales*] are a veritable treasure-house of pure aimless story-telling. His fairy-world is a happy one: full of sensible little dogs and cats, forward witches, genial, slangy water-sprites, pigmy postmen, ridiculous detectives, polite brigands. These things may look slight to grave pundits, but they are really very difficult to do without becoming sentimental or crude, and Karel Čapek succeeds because he never loses a sincere understanding of childhood, a sense of humour and the light touch. (p. 56)

The mystery-story has interested Čapek since the

Wayside Crosses. Two new brilliant volumes of tales, [*Tales from One Pocket* and *Tales from the Other Pocket*] . . . develop this popular form along new lines. The stories have become very much more concise, brighter, their point very much more epigrammatic compared to the older volume. If we except a few trivial pieces, they are all genuinely concerned with problems of truth and justice, though they seem to be written only for excitement and amusement. Some of the stories, especially in the first volume, praise the intuition and the instinct of ordinary man in preference to the ways of calculating reason, the sagacity of common sense defeating far-fetched speculation. A police agent finds the man who stole an important military document from the larder where it was hidden, because he is not looking for sinister spies but for simple larder-burglars. . . . The second series, though the stories are hardly different in type, is composed differently: while the first is told in the usual objective manner, the second is composed of tales told to other people. They are associated loosely by verbal links which enhance the illusion of spontaneous reminiscence. But there is never any description of the story-tellers or their setting. The style is more colloquial in accordance with this fiction, and the structure looser. (pp. 56-7)

The poet, the writer of tragedy who seems to have slumbered through the period of very pleasant tales and plays and essays celebrating life's fullness and ordinary humanity, awakes again in [*Hordubal, Meteor,* and *An Ordinary Life*]. . . . Though every one of these novels is completely distinct in theme and method, there is a common conception underlying them all. All of them retell the very same story from different points of view and thereby enhance its variety of meaning, the mysteriousness of ultimate reality. Possibly Karel Čapek has learned directly or indirectly something from the masters of perspective in modern fiction—from Henry James or Joseph Conrad, or even more likely he has himself developed a method in his search for truth which remains always in perspective only. (p. 58)

The very last book by Karel Čapek, *War with the Newts* . . . is a return to the utopian romances of former years. Some of the parallels with the *Absolute at Large,* such as the figure of the Jewish captain of industry, are even deliberate. But in distinction to the earlier book, *War with the Newts* has a much better design, and the main idea is carried out with consistency. . . . The book contains very good genre-pictures in Čapek's best vein and delineates very nice human types, such as Captain Van Toch. . . . There is plenty of good, topical satire on modern science and pseudoscience, on recent politics and a lavish display of Čapek's quite extraordinary power of mimicry of styles: scientific, journalistic, colloquial, dialectical, etc. But one feels that much of this power is wasted on a topic rather too well

worn since [William] Morris and Samuel Butler, Wells and Chesterton and Huxley and scores of others.

We must not forget that Karel Čapek is still a comparatively young man at the height of his powers. But his work as it stands now commands admiration by the very variety of his achievement, by the range of his powers, by its earnest striving after the highest goal. . . . In a few books, Karel Čapek has achieved real greatness, even measured by the highest standards. And obviously he should be judged by his best. (p. 61)

René Wellek, "Karel Čapek," in his *Essays on Czech Literature,* Mouton Publishers, 1963, pp. 46-61.

WILLIAM E. HARKINS
(essay date 1964)

[An American educator and critic, Harkins wrote the first book-length biography of Čapek in English. In the following excerpt, he opposes placing too much importance on Čapek's influence on utopian and science fiction, arguing instead that his most significant legacy is the political philosophy outlined in his works.]

Karel Čapek's world reputation rests today primarily on his utopian dramas and novels and his science fiction. To the ordinary reader he is known only as the author of the play about robots, *R.U.R., The Insect Comedy,* and *The War with the Newts,* but not very much else. His fantastic play, *The Makropulos Secret,* was recently revived in New York with great success. And if Čapek has been influential in world literature, one must admit that it has been primarily as a writer of utopian and science fiction.

We may grant that in fact the themes of Čapek's scientific fantasies are significant and striking. His prophetic anticipation in *Factory for the Absolute* and *Krakatit* of later developments in the field of atomic energy was brilliant. Especially successful was his masterly choice of the robot as a symbol in *R.U.R.* The robot stands as a complex expressionistic symbol of both the power of the machine to free man from toil, thus bringing utopia, and the danger that, in removing the element of conflict from human life, a mechanized civilization may in turn dehumanize man, may "robotize" him. This fusion of two meanings in a single symbol was an inspired act of artistic compression; viewed purely as symbolism, *R.U.R.,* for all its faults, is a masterpiece of the expressionistic drama. Moreover, the symbol is a thoroughly dramatic one: the actors who portrayed robots in the first Prague production were able to express eloquently the idea of a mechanized humanity by their stiffness of movement and gait.

Yet, in spite of all their apparent modernity, the scientific fantasies of Čapek strike us today as dated. The warnings against the dangers of a technological civilization sounded in *R.U.R.* or *Factory for the Absolute* seem almost irrelevant for our own age. For the machine has not freed man from conflict; rather, it has brought new conflicts of its own, not the least of which is that of atomic fission. Nor is our machine paradise free from toil, and perhaps no one is busier than the family which dwells in the modern American suburban utopia.

The question of the value of Čapek's scientific fantasies as art leads us to the more general question of the value of all science fiction as art. . . . Man is first and foremost a creature who loves and hates, who is born and dies, and only secondarily a creature who may fly through outer space or travel to the depth of the oceans. The world of science is ultimately unsuitable subject matter for a great literature, because science has no immediate or compulsive symbolic significance for man's spirit and his fundamental needs. This is true in spite of the fact that science and technology satisfy certain of those needs, such as food and clothing. The link between science and its technological products is a purely rational one which can hardly appeal to the creative imagination. The work of science and its effects on human life are the proper subject matter of philosophy or sociology, but not of literature, which is concerned with less rational symbols. Science is not directly involved with any of what we might call the "eternal themes" of literature: the quest for God, the good, self-realization, love, happiness, freedom, the relation of the individual to society, the revolt of youth against age, etc.

Of course it is true that the world of science may serve as a source of irrational and moving symbols which are capable of appealing to our imagination and becoming art. And so science has actually been used by the surrealists in their painting and literature. One thinks of Nezval's long poem, *Edison,* for example. But this surrealistic use goes beyond science itself, and is not what we usually mean by science fiction.

But are not Čapek's expressionist symbols—robots, newts, insects—just such irrational expressive symbols of eternal literary themes, of man's eternal needs? Čapek wrote of *R.U.R.* that he conceived the play as a eulogy to man, that he wanted to view human life in retrospect and say, as his character Hallemeier does in the play, "It was a great thing to be a man." And Čapek comments: "Technology, progress, ideals, faith—all these were rather only illustrations of humanity than the sense of the play." And to the extent that this idea of man's passing from the earth is realized in *R.U.R.,* the play is great. But one must add that this

note of eulogy is not the principal one and not the final one. *R.U.R.* is a failure, . . . and the author himself once admitted to Dorothy Thompson that it was the worst of all his plays, one which he no longer wished to see on the stage, and did not see again until he was trapped in a small Czech provincial town by the manager of the local theater.

The same is true of *The Makropulos Secret.* This play achieves greatness at those moments when it gives us an insight into the horror and tedium of the life of Elena Makropulos, who has used an elixir to prolong her existence because she is afraid of death. The horror of death is an eternal literary theme. But Čapek, the philosophical relativist, finds death to be a good thing; as he and his brother had remarked rather bathetically in *The Insect Comedy:* "Jeden se narodí a jeden umře, a pořád je lidí dost" (One is born and one dies, and always there are people enough). Čapek fails to see the tragedy of individual death; if society is immortal, still the individual must die, and the immortality of society is no sure compensation for one's own death. In *The Makropulos Secret* Čapek is preoccupied with a philosophical concern lest longer life constitute a burden for man, but he overlooks a gripping, "eternal" theme of literature: the tragedy of individual death.

The finest of Čapek's fantasies is doubtless his novel, *War with the Newts.* But it is hardly a fantasy of science. One must distinguish clearly between science fiction and the classical genre of the utopian novel. In the utopian novel, science may serve to transplant man to a strange world or to travel ahead or backward in time; the journey, however, is no mere flight of fancy, but a means of revealing to the reader the vices of his own world all the more sharply and objectively. This is the classical technique of Swift's great satire, *Gulliver's Travels,* and in fact *The War with the Newts* is far more like Swift than H. G. Wells.

Secondly, Čapek's utopian works are vitiated by that very philosophy of relativism which he preached so ardently in the early 1920's. Unlike Maeterlinck or Pirandello, who perceived that the relativism of each man's isolated truth involved individual man in tragic isolation, Čapek tried to believe that life could be enriched by a multiplicity of truths. Yet metaphysical relativism could only imply ethical relativism: if each man has his own truth, then each man's conduct is also somehow right. Quite this far Čapek was not prepared to go; he was too idealistic and sensitive to moral issues, and such a philosophy would have involved the world in an ethical anarchy as total as the ethical anarchy which he sees resulting from absolutism in *Factory for the Absolute.* Ethical relativism could serve to justify all forms of political expediency; it is perhaps no accident that Čapek abandoned relativism and undertook a new search for absolutes just at the end of his life, at a time when it was necessary to strengthen the Czechoslovak will to resist Nazi aggression. The truth of relativism would imply that fascism was somehow "just as right" as democracy.

Among Čapek's works it is his most ardent defenses of relativism, such as *Factory for the Absolute* or *Adam the Creator*, which are the worst artistic failures. If the search for the Absolute is one of literature's eternal themes, the defense of relativism is not. There is an almost unbelievable bathetic quality in the final scene of *Factory for the Absolute*, in which some of the leading characters gather in a tavern to eat sausages and sauerkraut and drink beer and discuss the triumph of the relativist philosophy. And it was only when Čapek, like his contemporary Pirandello, could grasp the tragedy of relativist existence, the existential anxiety to which it exposed the individual, that he could achieve greatness. This discovery came, almost belatedly, with the first novel of his trilogy, *Hordubal.*

The real legacy of Karel Čapek is political. Such a statement may come as a surprise, for at first sight Čapek's political accomplishments seem rather slight. His articles on political questions, collected in *O věcech obecných, čili ZOON POLITIKON,* are on the whole rather undistinguished and uninteresting; an exception might be made only for the eloquent **"Proč nejsem komunistou" ("Why I Am Not a Communist"),** and for one or two articles such as **"Betlém" ("Bethlehem")** and **"O malých poměrech" ("On a Small Scale"),** in which he finds fault with those of his countrymen who apologize for all Czechoslovak shortcomings by pointing to the small scale of Czechoslovak life. (In a healthy regionalism and localism Čapek sees the roots of a vigorous culture, not a weak one.) If Čapek's political theorizing is mildly interesting, his practical action in the field of politics was to prove less successful. The attempt to found a Czechoslovak Labor Party—Strana práce—in the mid-1920's, an attempt which he actively supported, was a disastrous failure, and his noble efforts to stiffen the resistance of his country against Nazi Germany were rendered futile by the betrayal of Czechoslovakia by her allies.

Čapek's whole relation to politics and political thought was confused and in a sense contradictory, and for this reason, too, it may seem strange to call his real legacy political. In the recently published second part of her reminiscences of her two uncles, the Brothers Čapek, Helena Koželuhová characterizes Karel as rather less interested in them as he was interested in everything. The portrait she gives of the brothers is perhaps oversimplified; in her book they appear as political neutrals for whom neutralism and lack of political identification is something quite normal. This characterization no doubt conforms most closely to Karel in earlier life, but one can hardly reconcile it with his later activity as supporter of the Strana práce, biographer of Masaryk, president of the Czech P.E.N. club, opponent

of Communism, or critic and foe of Nazism. Still one must confess that in fact there was a streak of political neutralism in Čapek, and a generous one; his view of life is deeply esthetic, and he celebrates life as good as much because of its beauty and variety as for its moral perfectibility. Čapek the hobbyist, the gardener, the European traveller, photographer, collector of exotic phonograph records, the patient observer of nature who could spend an entire journey by rail in winter observing the formation of "ice flowers" on the windows of the railroad car—this Čapek was an esthete first and foremost, and political man only second.

Conventionally, Čapek has been celebrated as a great democrat, and such he no doubt was, but his faith in democracy was not unlimited; at times he seems inclined to a degree of individualism which can hardly be reconciled with democracy, and which one might best describe as anarchist. Čapek himself used the latter term to S. K. Neumann when he said, "I think that I am almost an anarchist, that that is only another name for my individualism, and I think that you will understand it in that sense as opposed to collectivism." Critics such as Václav Černý have long ago pointed out the deep-seated conflicts in Čapek between an optimistic and a pessimistic view of life, between faith in the collective and fear lest its power destroy the individual. In none of Čapek's works where destruction threatens man—in *R.U.R., Factory for the Absolute, Krakatit, Adam the Creator,* or *The War with the Newts*—does democracy intervene to save man from destruction. As late as in his drama *The White Plague* (1937), Čapek expresses his distrust of the masses, so easily misled by demagogues. And it is the democratic colossi of the Western World who are a principal target of his satire in *The War with the Newts.* Čapek's democracy may seem in the last analysis to be little more than an acceptance of the least of all possible evils.

Yet in the trilogy of three novels, *Hordubal, Meteor,* and *An Ordinary Life,* Čapek has laid down a philosophical foundation for democracy which is well-nigh unique in modern literature. The trilogy was Čapek's masterpiece, free from the artistic defects and shallow relativism typical of his writing of the 1920's. Professor René Wellek has described the trilogy as "one of the most successful attempts at a philosophical novel in any language", and so indeed it is.

From a philosophical point of view, Čapek's trilogy has been analyzed from two standpoints, first, as a study of how man apprehends truth; in the trilogy, Čapek moves from a relativist epistemology to a more sophisticated perspectivism: he finds that the different views of reality which individual men obtain are analogous to the different perspectives which may be joined together to depict truth. Thus the divergent accounts of the unknown victim of the plane crash in *Meteor* may be combined to produce human truth, if not the truth of one human being's life. This epistemological or noetic theme is joined to a metaphysical one: the analysis of the nature of individual man. Less appreciated in the trilogy is the fact that in dealing with the question of the nature of individual existence, Čapek has also faced the question of the individual's relation to society, for the individual can be defined completely only if his relation to society is also defined. In the trilogy, Čapek has answered this question of the individual's relation to society in a positive, democratic spirit. In doing so he has indicated the possibility of an escape for modern man from the existential prison of individualism, and laid down at least the foundation of an acceptable philosophy of democracy. The success of his achievement is almost unique in an age when literature is largely devoted to the expression of scepticism or despair, particularly in dealing with the individual's relation to the world or to society.

The tripartite division of the trilogy suggests the triad formula of dialectic: thesis, antithesis, and synthesis. The first novel of the trilogy, *Hordubal,* is our thesis: all men are separate and distinct, and no man can know the truth of another man's life. The police and court can convict Hordubal's murderers, but they cannot understand the depth of Hordubal's pathetic love for Polana. Hordubal is a figure of isolation rendered tragic by the incommunicability of his deepest feelings. His friendship with animals is sensitively treated by Čapek in order to underscore the pathos of his inability to communicate his feelings to his fellow men. In this novel Čapek has finally realized that the relativism of truths which he had earlier celebrated as a positive good would in fact doom the individual to the prison of self, and each man's truth would remain forever mute, incommunicable. This pessimistic implication of relativism underlies the tragedy of the novel's leading character, and finds its tragic expression in the closing sentence: "The heart of Juraj Hordubal was lost somewhere and never buried."

Meteor is the antithesis. Granted that the "detectives": of the novel—the two doctors, the nurse, the writer and the clairvoyant—who try to reconstruct the life of the unknown victim of the plane crash can only speculate concerning his past. Still, because they are human, they can understand the essence of humanity, of what it is to be a man. They cannot know what has happened in a man's life, but they can know what a man is capable of experiencing, just because he is a man. The clairvoyant of the novel expresses it in an eloquent image comparing man's life to the cycle which water undergoes in its passage from sea to sky and back via the earth to the sea again. Just so, man's life always remains human, no matter what particular form it may take. Life, then, is simply the totality of what is possible to life, and a single life is the potentiality of experiencing all events which are possible. Thus an individual

man may transcend his isolation and come to a sympathetic understanding of his fellows, for his experience is also theirs.

An Ordinary Life is the synthesis of the trilogy. A retired railway official writes the story of his life. At first it seems a quiet, simple, good, and contented life, in everything, a quite "ordinary life". But then, from some subconscious depth, forgotten voices remind him of suppressed longings and experiences; the "ordinary man" he has become is only one of a diversity of persons which existed within him. He concludes that perhaps each man has the potentiality of becoming all men, but must necessarily restrict himself in development to realizing only certain potentialities. And so the plurality of men in external society corresponds to the plurality of personalities within each man. We are given a basis for understanding the truth of another man's life; we may know other men, for we ourselves are potentially like them. Each man is a microcosm which mirrors all human society. "Have you ever seen anyone, brother, who couldn't be *your brother?*" one of the inner group of voices asks the "ordinary man". And Čapek comments in the epilogue to the novel that "this is just the reason why we can know and understand plurality, because we ourselves are such a plurality".

Thus a firm foundation is laid down for the brotherhood and equality of all men. The individual is no prisoner of existential isolation; within him are resources for bridging the gap which seems to separate him from other men. He can know them as aspects of himself and hence he can accept them.

Perhaps Čapek would have gone on to develop his ideas on social democracy further. But the times were against him. The creative freedom and calm which he had enjoyed while composing the trilogy were cut off by the spectre of the rise of Nazi Germany and the threat of war. Paradoxically, it may have been the need to oppose Nazism which turned his attention from the problem of democracy as such; his energies had to be devoted to the attack on fascism, and the superiority of democracy had in a sense to be taken for granted.

But one more concept was added to Čapek's theory of democracy. In *The First Rescue Party* we have a novel of heroism and the need to defend society in the face of a common danger. The novel is an allegory of democratic society defending itself heroically against aggression. The rescue brigade succeeds because of its democratic cooperation, just as democracy is justified in using the political powers of social organization to defend itself against aggression. As the Czech critic Oldřich Králík has recently pointed out, *The First Rescue Party* makes what is in a sense the obverse of the point of *An Ordinary Life*. In the earlier novel one man proves to contain many different personalities. In *The First Rescue Party* a number of individuals merge together into a single group which has its own spirit and distinct personality. The two novels, taken together, supply a humanistic foundation for a philosophy of democracy.

More than this Čapek was not destined to accomplish. The tragedy of his homeland and his premature death cut short the philosophical and creative development of a great writer, a profound thinker, and a great human spirit. (pp. 60-7)

William E. Harkins, "The Real Legacy of Karel Capek," in *The Czechoslovak Contribution to World Culture,* edited by Miloslav Rechcigl, Jr., Mouton & Co., 1964, pp. 60-7.

GEORGE A. TEST

(essay date 1974)

[In the excerpt below, Test discusses Čapek's *War with the Newts*, comparing it favorably to Aldous Huxley's *Brave New World* and *George Orwell's 1984*.]

War With the Newts presents a more terrifying fantasy world than either [Aldous Huxley's] *Brave New World* or [George Orwell's] *1984,* and in any case complements these works by encompassing the economic sphere of life, an area of little concern for either Huxley or Orwell.

The reasons for the present neglect of Capek's satire are not difficult to establish. Although Capek is one of the three Czech writers of the twentieth century with international reputations (Kafka and Hasek are the others) it is [for] the play *R.U.R.* that Capek is best known . . . *War With the Newts* suffered mixed or indifferent reviews and inevitable comparison with *Brave New World* when translations appeared in England and America. . . . None of the major studies of satire in the last ten years has acknowledged its existence. . . . (pp. 1-2)

Even as satire, *War With the Newts* is unconventional. Episodic in extreme, without a central hero, a grab bag of satiric techniques, Capek's work will not satisfy readers and critics who come to the book with conventional novelistic expectations. To call it episodic is in fact generous. A major portion of the novel is really a mock-historical narrative interspersed with various kinds of documents exhibited in mock-scholarly style. Although *War With the Newts* has several richly realized characters, the scope of Capek's satire would have been undesirably restricted by the convention of a novelistic hero. The action of Capek's satire is concern with the Newts, their discovery, their development, and their conflict with man. Since the

Newts are a multi-faceted metaphor, the action is in effect the creation of that metaphor. . . . Whether a device such as Gulliver or Candide would have served Capek's purpose is impossible to say. On the other hand, the vastness of Capek's concept comments implicitly on the parochial nature of Huxley's and Orwell's satire.

If Capek fails (or chooses not) to provide his readers with a conventional novel-like book, he amply compensates for these features, especially for the reader attuned to the techniques and devices of satire. Moreover Capek's satiric commentary, while grounded in conditions and events of the thirties, has the merit of still seeming prophetic while describing reality more accurately with each passing day. (p. 2)

The Newts are, at the simplest level, Capek's convenient animal metaphor for man and his culture, for from the first time that Van Toch comes upon these writhing, grotesque beasts in their protected backwater habitat, they dominate this Menippean satire despite their being submerged throughout.

Actually the Newts' metaphorical function is far richer than this account suggests. Van Toch, their "liberator," exemplifies a paternalistic racism, despite his generally humane attitude. In developing the concept of the Newts as a new labor force to be exploited, Capek builds in significant parallels with the slave trade of the eighteenth and nineteenth centuries. Later Capek mocks do-gooders who seek to make over educationally and culturally in their own image the emerging Newt population. As a symbol for the non-white races, Capek uses the Newts to comment on racism as it manifests itself in exploitation and in attempts to integrate non-white races into Western society. . . .

But the Newts also symbolize what sociologists have come to call "the mass man." The Newts have a deleterious influence on language. Art and music hold no interests for them. The worship of Moloch is the only religion that takes any extensive hold on the Newts. But above all the Newts are consumers and producers without parallel. (p. 3)

The Newts come ultimately to stand for society itself. Economic development, technological changes, and universal armament are forces set in motion by man's greed and thirst for power. Capek pictures these forces as irreversible and self-destructive. Like all the great satirists, Capek is attacking man's pride, man's failure to impose reasonable limitations on what is and is not proper, man's refusal to come to terms with the limitations imposed by his nature and his environment. . . . He seems to suggest that man can find happiness within these limitations, unhappiness and frustration outside them. To try to be more than a man is to transgress an unchangeable rule of nature at one's own peril.

Capek's arsenal of other satiric techniques is as rich as his major metaphor. Unfettered by the demands made by a conventional plot and hero, Capek tells his story and develops his metaphor in a virtuoso performance of parody, travesty, and burlesque. (p. 4)

One especially delightful travesty exploits the famous controversy over the fossil remains discovered near Oeningen, Switzerland by Johannes Scheuchzer in 1726 which he argued were human remains, "relics of the accursed race that perished with the Flood." . . . The paleontologist Cuvier later identified the remains as those of giant salamanders of the genus *Andrias* and named the species *Scheuchzeri!* Capek reprints a picture of Scheuchzer's fossil as part of a mock-scientific report on the geneology of the Newts and quotes from Scheuchzer's *Homo Diluvi Testis.* Capek's device not only satirizes senseless religious controversy and scientific attempts to establish human geneology, but also establishes the metaphorical connection of the Newts with the "that accursed race" before the Flood. Later Capek uses the Scheuchzer fossil to satirize the German pure Nordic race myth. (p. 5)

Ultimately Capek pictures a society so locked into production and consumption that its fate is irreversible. Business responds to warnings that the Newts threatened human civilization with counterwarnings that an attempt to restrict supplies to the Newts would precipitate a slump in production and a "serious crisis in many branches of human industry." (p. 8)

It may be that Capek's success as a satirist in *War With the Newts* is the most damaging statement one can make about him. Unlike Huxley and Orwell whose fantasies are projected into the future where man and his institutions have changed, Capek takes the world before World War II and injects a device of fantasy, the Newts. Neither time, place nor characters have to be changed. In fact Capek uses real places and the names of actual people. The introduction of the Newts is a simple device, but one that makes Capek's book even more terrifying, ultimately, than Orwell's. For in both *1984* and *Brave New World* the future is given, the reader must willingly suspend his disbelief. Capek's device forces the reader to participate in the coming of the future.

Both *1984* and *Brave New World* deal with dictatorships, . . . one concerned with the price of happiness, the other with the threat of naked power. Capek's concerns are much more mundane, fictionally speaking. His Newts fit into the scheme of things as they are. Life goes on as it always has, only more so. Business prospers, governments govern, education, religion and science flourish. But one day life ends terrifyingly in a watery grave. No one seizes power, no one applies behaviouristic psychology. The forces and institutions of society merely destroy themselves. No hedonistic new society, no pathological coercion of man's mind. Only God's voice over the silent deep. Who is responsible? No one. Everyone. We have met the enemy and he is us.

Capek's global view and his social and economic emphasis are unmatched in either Huxley's or Orwell's books. . . . [Capek] manages to yoke events of a global nature with commonplace simplicity of detail which are perhaps more invidious in their impact than the remote melodrama of either Huxley's or Orwell's works. Brainwashing and test tube babies still make Sunday supplement reading, but the threat of a black man or a foreigner taking one's job, the pollution of streams and oceans, and the artificiality of an economy based largely on military consumption are everyday realities. (p. 9)

As a satiric writer Capek combines the rich comic inventiveness of Huxley with the unnerving desire to see the thing as it really is of Orwell. This is only to say that Capek is an effective satirist. But unlike either of them, Capek does not fraction his view of man so completely as they seem to. . . .

Literary history is filled with examples of neglected works that posterity has raised to the status of classics, and conversely with overvalued works that have sunk into oblivion with the years. Capek's *The War With the Newts* was not overvalued when it was first published; it would be foolhardy to proclaim it as a future classic. It is safe to claim however that it is an undeservedly neglected modern satire and compares more favorably with Orwell's and Huxley's classics than its present reputation would indicate. (p. 10)

George A. Test, "Karel Čapek's 'War with the Newts': A Neglected Modern Satire," in *Studies in Contemporary Satire,* 1974, pp. 1-10.

IVAN KLÍMA

(essay date 1985)

[Klíma is a Czech short story writer, dramatist, and critic whose works include *Ma vesela jitra* (1979; *My Merry Mornings: Stories from Prague,* 1985). In the following excerpt, he examines the underlying philosophy of Čapek's work, focusing on *War with the Newts.*]

In January, 1921, the National Theater in Prague, the foremost theater in the country, performed a Karel Čapek play with the strange title *R.U.R.* The author was known to be a talented young writer who had already written several plays together with his brother and one on his own, a moderately successful if rather traditional piece. The theme of his new play, however, astounded first Czech and then foreign audiences, for it dealt with synthetic people—"robots"—and their revolt against the human race. The play was a hit around the globe and soon brought its thirty-one-year-old author international acclaim (its nonhuman heroes held such fascination for the contemporary world that the word "robot," coined by Čapek, has been assimilated by numerous languages). With his drama about the robots Čapek inaugurated a series of fantastic and utopian works. He continued in this vein with a novel, *The Factory of the Absolute,* and a comedy, *The Makropulos Affair,* on the Shavian theme of longevity, both of which appeared in 1922, and the 1924 novel *Krakatit.* After a long hiatus he returned to utopian themes with the famous novel *War with the Newts* (1936) and, a year before his death, the drama *The White Plague* (1937).

Three of the works I have mentioned develop a fantastic motif in striking detail; even their denouements are almost identical. What impelled Karel Čapek to rework his apocalyptic vision so persistently? Many saw in his work instant utopias that presaged technological discoveries with potentially dangerous consequences; others saw a brilliant satire on contemporary political conditions both at home and abroad.

But Čapek's creative work in science fiction had a different purpose: it attempted to provide a philosophical explanation for the antagonisms that were repeatedly plunging the world into crisis.

I am a writer myself. I know that a work of literature cannot be reduced to some message, argument, or philosophy which can be expressed both concisely and in universal concepts. If I am about to consider Čapek's philosophy in his fundamental works, I am risking this oversimplification only because Čapek himself sets out the same way—almost all his works are accompanied by some kind of theoretical commentary. Although he preferred to conceal the didactic and philosophical element in his work by employing rich and fantastic plots, a wealth of brilliantly observed technical and everyday detail, and a vital, even colloquial language, Čapek was certainly the type of artist who wrote *à la thèse.*

Čapek made a thorough study of philosophy. Among contemporary schools of thought, he was most strongly influenced by Anglo-American pragmatism. Opponents have charged the adherents of pragmatism with intellectual shallowness, inconsistency, and failure to mold a genuine philosophical system—although they could not very well have done so, given their resistance to conventional truths and "great" ideas. It was precisely the pragmatists' unwillingness to generalize (something the political ideologies of the day did readily), their interest in everyday human activity, and the respect they showed every individual's truth that appealed to Čapek.

Čapek had already become familiar with the philosophy of James, Dewey, and Schiller during the war. In the same period he had also written a dedicated and sympathetic study on the subject. In the course of the next few years he published several additional detailed articles in which he attempted to define his philosophical views—especially in the area of noetics—as precisely as possible.

Like other pragmatists, Čapek was a relativist and took a skeptical view of the power of understanding, particularly the speculative understanding which attempts to establish universally valid systems. Even the most universal discoveries about reality will become personal to each individual mind and therefore partial and premature. Accordingly, Čapek considered the predilection for generalizations (especially in the area of social relations) to be one of the least propitious tendencies of human thought. "Please, for a moment, approach 'socialism' and other words now in world currency as moral and personal values, not as party or political values," he wrote shortly after the war. "A great number of people who went into the war as the new generation have come out of it with a terrible, gnawing hyper-consciousness of these values, and with their former certainty about them shaken just as terribly. This uncertainty could not be called disillusionment or skepticism or indifference; rather, it is a dismay which finds good and evil on both sides and rejects viewpoints based on principle. . . . "

Čapek's skepticism was the basis for his humanistic demand that no prejudice, no conventional truth or its concerns, be placed above the value of human life. The function of this skepticism was to remove artificial idea-obstacles between people and to stimulate conciliation, tolerance, and active participation in life. "You don't see two bales of hay, but thousands of straws. Straw by straw you gather what is good and useful in the human world; straw by straw you discard the chaff and the weeds. You don't cry out because of the oppression of thousands but because of the oppression of any individual; you've had to destroy the one truth in order to find thousands of them. . . . Ultimately, for want of anything more perfect, you simply believe in people."

In Čapek's works revolutionaries find themselves side by side with dreamers and explorers, demagogues with people's tribunes and redeemers. All these characters, no matter how different or apparently antagonistic their motives, contemplate changing or improving the world by some momentous act. With their absolute visions and judgments about the world, they run afoul of temperate and usually less interesting conservatives—simple folk or people of learning, but always tolerant, willing to help others, and ready to do anything, even to perform the most insignificant task. They know their own limits and the limits of the reality in which they

A scene from a 1922 American production of *R.U.R.*

live. They understand that everything has its season and its tempo and that the world cannot be changed for the better by upheaval, no matter how well intentioned. This is why they enjoy Čapek's sympathy.

Čapek doubted that anything posed a greater threat to mankind than uncontrolled Faustian desire. A man who feels equal to the creator labors under the delusion that he can and should make the world conform to his own idea. In reality, he simply ceases to perceive its complexity, disturbs one of its subtle, imperceptible structures, and triggers calamity.

In *The Factory of the Absolute* everyone believes he has found the true god and that he will save others by bringing them his god and inculcating his own faith and concept of love. People are filled with messianic idealism, but their ideals are contradictory and lead to disputes; the disputes grow into wars. While professing lofty intentions, they overlook other people and justify their own intolerance. At the end of the book one of the heroes confesses, "A person might think that another belief is the wrong belief, but he musn't think that the fellow who holds it is bad, or common, or stupid." And later, "You know, the greater the thing somebody believes in, the more passionately he despises those who don't believe in it. But the greatest belief would be to believe in people. . . . Everybody's just great at thinking about mankind, but about one single person—no. I'll kill you, but I'll save mankind. . . . It'll be a bad world until people believe in people. . . . "

An equally messianic desire and undisciplined need to transform the world brings on the calamity that befalls mankind in the famous play about the robots. "Alquist, it wasn't a bad dream to want to end the slav-

ery of work," says Domin, the director of the robot factory, shortly before his death. "I didn't want a single soul to have to do idiotic work at someone else's machines, I didn't want any of this damn social mess! Oh, the humiliation, the pain are making me sick, the emptiness is horrible! We wanted a new generation!"

In the play Domin's dream of creation is opposed by the engineer Alquist: "I think it would be better to lay one brick than make too grandiose plans." Elsewhere, he implores, "O God, shed your light on Domin and on all those who err; destroy their creation and help people return to their cares and their work; keep the human race from annihilation. . . . the whole world, entire continents, all humanity, everything is one crazy, brutish orgy. They won't even lift a hand for food; it's stuffed right into their mouths so they don't even have to get up. . . . "

In *R.U.R.* we see the first confrontation—at least on a spiritual level—between the "man of the coming times," the revolutionary, the realizer of momentous plans, and the person who believes that man should, in the interest of preserving his own race, continue slowly on the path of his forebears, preferring what is perhaps a harder and poorer existence to the risk of unleashing demons no one will be able to control. The Domins lead the world to ruin. The Alquists warn against following them.

People need no saviors or redeemers, no robots, miracle drugs, or inexhaustible energy sources, and they need not look for grand designs or earth-shaking solutions. On the contrary, they should learn to live in harmony with the world into which they were born and take personal responsibility for it. This sense of responsibility is born of service and participation in everyday human affairs. Only "straw by straw" can the world and human attitudes be improved.

The standards by which Čapek judged human action as positive or negative were so unusual that many readers missed the point of his works. Others were angered. Radical in their own thinking, they showered Čapek with reproach for idealizing the little man, the average person, and even outright provincialism. They claimed that in denying a person's right to generalization and universal truth, Čapek was also stripping him of the right to action that would bring an end to social injustice. They offered their own, revolutionary solutions, which in that time of protracted economic and political crisis seemed to be the only promising alternatives.

This debate has raged to the present day, some believing that it is appropriate to rectify the state of human affairs by force if necessary, others contending that man must try to influence conditions by changing himself first. The events that have transpired in the very country in which Čapek lived and where I, too, live, a country where, in the half-century since Čapek's death, life has deteriorated into a succession of violent upheavals, support, in my opinion, the side of Čapek's truth in this life-and-death controversy.

The skepticism with which Čapek contemplated mankind's future reflected only one side of his personality. There was also something harmonious, even playful in him that managed to endure from the time of his childhood. He took a child's pleasure in thinking up stories. He placed no limits on his imagination and delighted in the unexpected situations he was creating, the new territory he was entering, as well as in the spiteful scoffing that permeated even the works auguring catastrophe. There was also real wonder in his observation of objects and human craftsmanship. With a boy's fascination he would watch a skilled laborer and then tell about his work in the same amusing way one might talk about an avocation or a hobby. (Čapek himself was a passionate gardener, raised dogs and cats, collected oriental carpets and folk music from around the world, took excellent photographs, and made skillful drawings for a number of his books.) He manages to reveal unexpected forms and qualities, the "soul" of objects that are encountered every day—a vacuum cleaner, a camera, a doorknob, a stove. Thus it was that alongside his apocalyptic visions and work in science fiction, perhaps as a counterbalance, he produced travel sketches, newspaper columns, and short prose fiction (his *Stories from One Pocket* and *Stories from the Other Pocket*, which appeared in 1929, enjoyed extraordinary popularity). In these works Čapek granted to people and things what he did not grant them in his longer science fiction—that they might approach each other in the custom of past centuries rather than in the ways of the present.

Čapek himself tells about the origin of his novel *War with the Newts* (1936): "It was last spring, when the world was looking rather bleak economically, and even worse politically—Apropos of I don't know what, I had written the sentence, 'You mustn't think that the evolution that gave rise to us was the only evolutionary possibility on this planet.' And that was it. That sentence was the reason I wrote *War with the Newts*." "It is quite thinkable," Čapek reasons,

that cultural development could be shaped through the mediation of another animal species. If the biological conditions were favorable, some civilization not inferior to our own could arise in the depths of the sea. . . . If some species other than man were to attain that level we call civilization, what do you think—would it do the same stupid things mankind has done? Would it fight the same wars? Would it invite the same historical calamities? What would we say if some animal other than man declared that its education and its numbers gave it the sole right to occupy the entire world and hold sway over all of creation? It was this confrontation with human his-

tory, and with the most pressing topical history, that forced me to sit down and write *War with the Newts.*

A multitude of political allusions (the figure of the Chief Salamander, whose name was "actually Andreas Schultze" and who "had served someplace during the World War as a line soldier" certainly calls to mind the leader of the Nazi Reich, Adolf Hitler, and the chapter on the book of the royal philosopher paraphrases the Nazi theories of the time) led some contemporary critics to conclude that Čapek had abandoned his relativism to write an anti-Fascist pamphlet. This view, incidentally, has been supported to the present day by official Czech and Soviet literary historiography.

The thinking of many of Čapek's contemporaries was rooted in uncompromising and aggressive ideologies which sought to reduce even the most complex problems and conflicts to the simplistic language of slogans. The world was witnessing increasing confrontations between classes, nations, and systems—communism and capitalism, bourgeoisie and proletariat, democracy and dictatorship (the black-and-white ideological thinking which continues to dominate the world). Ostensibly, everything could be grasped and explained in such language. Its chief effect, however, was to obscure the human side of every problem; conflicts and issues were elevated to an impersonal level governed by power, strength, and abstract interests, where man was not responsible for his behavior or actions, and even less for the fate of society.

A writer can make no more fatal mistake than to adopt the simplistic view and language of ideology. Čapek was undoubtedly among the most resolute opponents of Fascism, Nazism, and communism, but now, as before, he sought the causes of modern crises in areas that could be defined by the experience and capabilities of the individual. He found that his contemporaries were becoming estranged from the values that had guided them for centuries and were adopting false values foisted upon them by technology and a consumerist pseudoculture. They were making gods of achievement, success, and quantity.

Isn't our admiration for machines, that is, for mechanical civilization, such that it suppresses our awareness of man's truly creative abilities? We all believe in human progress; but we seem predisposed to imagine this progress in the form of gasoline engines, electricity, and other technical contrivances. . . . We have made machines, not people, our standard for the human order. . . . There is no conflict between man and machine. . . . But it's another matter entirely when we ask ourselves whether the organization and perfection of human beings is proceeding as surely as the organization and perfection of machines. . . . If we wish to talk about progress, let's not rave about the number of cars or telephones but point instead to the value that we and our civilization attach to human life.

—from the article
"Rule by Machines"

By forcing individuality into the background, technological civilization makes room for mediocrity and a stifling collectivism.

In a critical commentary on Ortega y Gasset's essay *Revolt of the Masses,* Čapek observes: "Our age is distinguished by the fact that the ordinary spirit, aware of its own ordinariness, is bold enough to defend its right to ordinariness, and asserts it everywhere. . . . The mass . . . imposes on the world its own standards and its own taste and strives to give its barroom opinions the force of law. . . . The masses . . . have been imbued with the power and glory of their modern surroundings, but not with spirit." Čapek, however, differs with the Spanish philosopher by stressing that the fortunes of mankind are threatened not so much by the mediocrity of the masses as by wholesale failure among individuals, particularly those responsible for maintaining our cultural values and the level of thought—i.e., the intellectuals.

Culture means "above all, continuity with every human endeavor that has gone before"; its significance lies in the fact that it supports the awareness of values already established by mankind and thus helps us "not to lose them and not to sink below them."

Betrayal by the intellectuals was the worst betrayal Čapek could imagine, for its consequences were immeasurable.

> A culturally leveled intelligentsia ceases to fulfill certain obligations on which most higher values depend. . . . If culture breaks down, the 'average' person—the simple, ordinary man, the farmer, the factory worker, the tradesman, with his normal thoughts and moral code—will not be heard, and will go off in search of something that is far beneath him, a barbaric and violent element. . . . Destroy the hierarchical supremacy of the spirit, and you pave the way for the return of savagery. The abdication of the intelligentsia will make barbarians of us all.

Culture which drops below its own level and loses what it had attained breaks down. Since this is what had just taken place throughout much of Europe, Čapek was convinced that we were witnessing "one of the greatest cultural debacles in world history. . . . What happened was nothing less than a colossal betrayal by the intelligentsia. . . . "

Where ideologues spoke of the crisis of the system, Čapek was more consistent, more skeptical, more personal; he found a crisis in man, his values, his sense of responsibility. The fall of the intelligentsia marked the beginning of the fall of the entire civilization, the beginning of tremendous calamities.

As he always did when he resolved to pursue a great theme, Čapek turned to the sphere of science fiction. Not only did it suit his storytelling preferences, but a fictional world in fictional time gave him more room for movement and enabled him to shape that world and order the action with maximum focus on the factors which, in his view, were leading to ruin.

At the same time, Čapek wanted to evoke a sense of verisimilitude and topicality. He therefore patterned his narrative on the events of the time, the catchwords, the diplomatic maneuvers, and the advertising slogans, and he made allusions to living people and their work. He also reinforced the feeling of real life by including exact imitations of the most diverse genres of nonfiction, from reminiscences and news stories to interviews and statements by famous personalities.

Such efforts to make his science fiction more lifelike and closer to a documentary record of actual events were characteristic of Čapek's "anti-utopias" and set them off sharply from the majority of works in that genre. Zamyatin, Boye, Orwell, and Bradbury thought through to their absurd end the destructive (generally totalitarian) tendencies they saw in contemporary society. They created worlds that were terrifying in their alienation or totalitarian violence, but at the same time so artificial as to be remote from everyday human experience. Čapek depicted those same disastrous social tendencies in more realistic (and usually ironic) terms. He did not invent new world empires—the United State, Oceania, or the World State, the Bureau of Guardians or the Ministry of Love; he did not describe television eyes that would follow a person's every movement, or Kallocain and other drugs that would deprive him of his will. Čapek's Vaduz conference resembles any diplomatic meeting of the time, just as the board meeting of the Pacific Export Company resembles a board meeting of any contemporary enterprise. His people experience the joys and worries of life in the age of the newts much as they did in Čapek's own day. The fantastical newts appear to exist in everyday life. But this everyday life is moving toward disaster, precisely because its everyday quality has taken it in that direction. Čapek's fiction is less horrifying (at the beginning, it is even humorous), but all too reminiscent of the world we all live in; and this lends urgency to its admonitions about where that world may be headed.

However lifelike Čapek's utopia may appear, it remains a fiction, an artistic image that cannot be reduced (as some critics have tried to do) to a mere allegory in which the newts are substituted for one of the forces in the contemporary world conflict. No poetic symbol or allegory can be neatly translated back into reality.

The newts have emerged on the scene, and thus entered history, as an independent factor. Of course, they are not loaded down with prejudices or their own history and culture, and in this they resemble children. Eager learners, they strive to emulate everything they perceive to be more developed or more advanced. Like a mirror, they reflect the image of human values and the contemporary state of culture.

What kind of world is encountered by these creatures whose main strength lies in their being average and in their "successful, even triumphal inferiority"? What does modern civilization offer the huge masses of creatures untouched by culture? As Čapek develops his story of the newts and their history, he also refines his answer, and it is a depressing one. Human civilization is racing blindly in pursuit of profits, success, and material progress. Wealth, amusement, and pleasure have become its ideals, and it deifies everything that helps realize those ideals—industry, technology, science, entrepreneurism. En route to its goals, it has not even noticed the loss of what gave it life: human personality, culture, spirit, soul. Inquiry and reflection have been replaced with journalistic jabber, personal involvement in social affairs with a passive craving for sensation, ideas with slogans and empty phrases. "Your work is your success. He who doesn't work doesn't eat! . . ." All this has led to the world's becoming inundated with masses of people dangerous in their mediocrity and their readiness to accept any belief and adopt any goal. Yes, the masses resemble the newts; and the newts have become assimilated by the masses. "Of course, they don't have their own music or literature, but they'll get along without them just fine; and people are beginning to find that this is terribly modern of those Salamanders. . . . They've learned to use machines and numbers, and that's turned out to be enough to make them masters of their world. They left out of human civilization everything that was inexpedient, playful, imaginative, or old-fashioned, and so they eliminated from it all that had been human. . . ."

Everything that happens to the human race in this "Age of Newts" looks like a natural disaster, not because the newts are a natural phenomenon but because no one anywhere in the world can be found who feels personal responsibility for his creations, his actions, his behavior, and the social enterprise that is civilization. Or, more accurately, there is just one person, a doorkeeper, who meets his responsibility; he is that insignificant "little man." Among the powerful, the chosen, no thought has been given to the long-term consequences of the trend civilization is following. Culture has been leveled, art has been displaced by kitsch, philosophy has declined and taken to celebrating destruction, everything has been overcome by petty, local, and mainly nationalistic considerations.

Human civilization has indeed spread throughout the planet, but people show no evidence of being able to treat anything other than particularized concerns; thus, they have no means of *considering,* let alone *controlling* the consequences of their own actions. Modern civilization is so destructive that no being could come into contact with it and escape unscathed. Even the newts are marked by their encounter with people and their "culture." This is why, with no precautions, they begin to destroy dry land as soon as they find it to be in their interests to do so. People committed to "higher" and "suprapersonal" concerns, people who have long since given up the right to share actively in determining their own future, even when threatened with the extinction of not just one people or state but of mankind, work together with the newts to bring about their own destruction. "All the factories" cooperate, "All the banks. All nations."

In the face of this predicament, what people undertake for their salvation could only be viewed as half-hearted and panoptical. The human race has nothing left with which to fight for its existence. These are people who are about to destroy their own planet.

Čapek was a writer of great metaphors, brilliant fantasies, and apocalyptic visions. He was an author who appeared to focus on the events of the external world, on competing ideas, conflicts between nations, the shortcomings of civilization—in sum, conflicts of an entirely impersonal nature. But can real literature develop from impersonal motives, solely from an intellectual need to address a problem, even a very important one? I doubt it.

An argument between Čapek's typical heroes was not merely an argument intended to shed light on a philosophical problem. It was first and foremost Čapek's personal argument. He had an innate, almost prophetic consciousness of sharing responsibility for the fate of human society. He, too, needed to dream of mankind's happiness, of a more peaceful, more secure world. His need was to think up plans, to bring people a good message. At the same time, he realized that all dreams of lofty spirits, all prophetic visions, change into their opposites, and it is precisely these that lead people into fatal conflicts. So he set himself limits. He was Domin in *The Factory of the Absolute,* Prokop in *Krakatite,* Captain van Toch and the entrepreneurial genius Bondy in *War with the Newts.* In these figures he wanted to "smash [himself] with [his] very power," the transgression of which Prokop stands accused in *Krakatite.* But time and again he offered repentance, calling himself to order in the words of Alquist or the unknown X. He was punishing himself for the damage he could have done.

Čapek's entire work testifies to the contradiction faced by a seeing, knowing creative spirit, a spirit that longs to purify and enlighten the world but fears its own imperfection and limitations, fears what people will do with its visions. This dilemma will undoubtedly haunt mankind forever. Čapek's work illuminates it with the power of personal experience. (pp. ix-xxi)

Ivan Klíma, "Čapek's Modern Apocalypse," translated by Robert Streit, in *War with the Newts* by Karel Čapek, Northwestern University Press, 1985, pp. v-xxi.

SOURCES FOR FURTHER STUDY

Doležel, Lubomir. "Karel Čapek and Vladislav Vančura: An Essay in Comparative Stylistics." In his *Narrative Modes in Czech Literature*, pp. 91-111. Toronto: University of Toronto Press, 1973.

> Studies the ostensibly contrasting styles of Čapek and Vančura to show the underlying similarities resulting from a departure from a "traditional, realistic prose style."

Harkins, William E. "Karel Čapek and the 'Ordinary Life'." *Books Abroad* 36, No. 3 (Summer 1962): 273-76.

> Examines Čapek's epistemological approach to "familiar reality." Harkins focuses on *An Ordinary Life,* finding that its series of paradoxes best exemplify the author's basic philosophy.

———. *Karel Čapek.* New York: Columbia University Press, 1962, 193 p.

> Surveys Čapek's life and writings.

Mann, Erika. "A Last Conversation with Karel Čapek." *The Nation* 148, No. 3 (14 January 1939): 68-9.

> A moving interview, conducted shortly after the 1938 Munich pact. Mann suggests that Čapek's death was brought on by the "white sickness," a malady of the spirit described in one of his last dramas.

Matuška, Alexander. *Karel Čapek: An Essay,* translated by Cathryn Allan. London: George Allen & Unwin, 1964, 425 p.

> An important study of Čapek's themes, characters, method, and vision.

Mukařovsky, Jan. "K. Čapek's Prose as Lyrical Melody and Dialogue." In *A Prague School Reader on Esthetics, Literary Structure, and Style,* edited and translated by Paul L. Garvin, pp. 133-49. Washington, D.C.: Georgetown University Press, 1964.

> A detailed study of the phonetic aspects of Čapek's prose. Mukařovsky identifies a fundamental, unifying principle underlying Čapek's works—despite "their developmental differentiation" in style.

Truman Capote

1924-1984

(Born Truman Streckfus Persons) American novelist, short story and nonfiction writer, dramatist, and script-writer.

INTRODUCTION

Capote was one the most famous and controversial figures in contemporary American literature. The ornate style and dark psychological themes of his early fiction, including the novel *Other Voices, Other Rooms* (1948) and the short stories collected in *A Tree of Night and Other Stories* (1949), caused reviewers to categorize him as a Southern Gothic writer. However, other works, including several stories based on his Southern childhood and the novella *Breakfast at Tiffany's* (1958), display a humorous and sentimental tone. As Capote matured, his works became less mannered in style, partly as a result of his experiments in nonfiction writing. In his best-known work, *In Cold Blood: A True Account of a Multiple Murder and Its Consequences* (1966), he became a leading practitioner of New Journalism, popularizing a genre that he called the nonfiction novel.

Because of his celebrity, virtually every aspect of Capote's life became public knowledge, including the details of his troubled childhood. Born in New Orleans, he seldom saw his father, Archulus Persons, and his memories of his mother, Lillie Mae Faulk, mainly involved emotional neglect. When he was four years old his parents divorced, and afterward Lillie Mae boarded her son with various relatives in the South while she began a new life in New York with her second husband, Cuban businessman Joseph Capote. The young Capote lived with elderly relatives in Monroeville, Alabama, and he later recalled the loneliness and boredom he experienced during this time. His unhappiness was assuaged somewhat by his friendships with his great-aunt Sook Faulk, who appears as Cousin Sook in his stories "A Christmas Memory" and *The Thanksgiving Visitor* (1967), and Harper Lee, a childhood friend who served as the model for Idabel Thompkins in *Other Voices, Other Rooms.* Lee, in turn, paid tribute to Capote by depicting him as the character Dill Harris in her novel, *To Kill a Mockingbird* (1960). When Capote was nine years old, his mother, having failed to conceive a child with her second husband, brought her son to live with them in Manhattan, although she still sent him to the South in the summer. Capote was a poor student, causing his parents and teachers to suspect that he was of subnormal intelligence; a series of psychological tests, however, proved that he possessed an I.Q. well above the genius level. To combat his loneliness and sense of displacement, he developed a flamboyant personality that played a significant role in establishing his celebrity status as an adult.

Capote had begun to write secretly at an early age, and rather than attend college after completing high school, he pursued a literary apprenticeship that included various positions at *The New Yorker* and led to important social contacts in New York City. Renowned for his cunning wit and penchant for gossip, Capote later became a popular guest on television talk shows as well as the frequent focus of feature articles. He befriended many members of high society and was as well known for his eccentric, sometimes scandalous behavior as he was for his writings.

Capote's first short stories, published in national magazines when he was seventeen, eventually led to a contract to write his first book, *Other Voices, Other Rooms.* Set in the South, the novel centers on a young man's search for his father and his loss of innocence as he passes into manhood. The work displays many elements of the grotesque: the boy is introduced to the violence of murder and rape, he witnesses a homosexual encounter, and at the novel's end, his failure to initiate a heterosexual relationship with Idabel Thompkins, his tomboy companion, leads him to accept a homosexual arrangement with his elder cousin Randolph, a lecherous transvestite. Each of these sinister scenes presents a distorted version of reality, resulting in a surreal, nightmarish quality. Despite occasional critical complaints that the novel lacks reference to the real world, *Other Voices, Other Rooms* achieved immediate notoriety. This success was partly due to its strange, lyrical evocation of life in a small Southern town as well as to the author's frank treatment of his thirteen-year-old protagonist's awakening homosexuality. The book's dust jacket featured a photograph of Capote, who was then twenty-three, reclining on a couch. Many critics and readers found the picture erotically suggestive and inferred that the novel was autobiographical.

Many of Capote's early stories, written when he was in his teens and early twenties, are collected in *A Tree of Night and Other Stories.* These pieces show the influence of such writers as Edgar Allan Poe, Nathaniel Hawthorne, William Faulkner, and Eudora Welty, all of whom are associated to some degree with a Gothic tradition in American literature. Like these authors, as well as the Southern Gothic writers Carson McCullers and Flannery O'Connor, with whom critics most often compare him, Capote filled his stories with grotesque incidents and characters who suffer from mental and physical abnormalities. Yet Capote did not always use the South as a setting, and the Gothic elements in some of the tales are offset by Capote's humorous tone in others. Critics often place his early fiction into two categories: light and sinister stories. In the former category are "My Side of the Matter," "Jug of Silver," and "Children on Their Birthdays." Written in an engaging conversational style, these narratives report the amusing activities of eccentric characters. More common among Capote's early fiction, however, are the sinister stories, such as "Miriam," "A Tree of Night," "The Headless Hawk," and "Shut a Final Door." These are heavily symbolic fables that portray characters in nightmarish situations, threatened by evil forces. Frequently in these tales evil is personified as a sinister man, such as the Wizard Man feared by the heroine in "A Tree of Night" or the dream-buyer in "Master Misery." In other instances evil appears as a weird personage who represents the darker, hidden side of the protagonist. The ghostly little girl who haunts an older woman in "Miriam" is the best-known example of this doubling device in Capote's fiction. In later years Capote commented that the Gothic eeriness of these stories reflected the anxiety and feelings of insecurity he experienced as a child.

In *The Grass Harp* (1951), Capote drew on his childhood to create a lyrical, often humorous novel focusing on Collin Fenwick, an eleven-year-old boy who is sent to live in a small Southern town with his father's elderly cousins, Verena and Dolly Talbo. At sixteen years of age, Collin allies himself with the sensitive Dolly and other outcasts from the area by means of an idyllic withdrawal into a tree fort. There, the group achieves solidarity and affirms the value of individuality by comically repelling the onslaughts of the ruthless Verena and other figures of authority. The novel, which achieved moderate success, is generally considered to offer a broader, less subjective view of society and the outer world than Capote's earlier fiction, and was adapted as a Broadway drama in 1952. A light and humorous tone is also evident in such works as the novella *Breakfast at Tiffany's* and the three stories published in the same volume, "House of Flowers," "A Diamond Guitar," and "A Christmas Memory." *Breakfast at Tiffany's* features Capote's most famous character, Holly Golightly, a beautiful, waif-like young woman living on the fringes of New York society. Golightly, like the prostitute heroine in "House of Flowers," is a childlike person who desires love and a permanent home. This sentimental yearning for security is also evident in the nostalgic story "A Christmas Memory," which, like the later *The Thanksgiving Visitor,* dramatizes the loving companionship the young Capote found with his great-aunt Sook.

In some of his works of the 1950s, Capote abandoned the lush style of his early writings for a more austere approach, turning his attention away from traditional fiction. *Local Color* (1950) is a collection of pieces recounting his impressions and experiences while in Europe, and *The Muses Are Heard: An Account* (1956) contains essays written while traveling in Russia with a touring company of *Porgy and Bess.* From these projects Capote developed the idea of creating a work that would combine fact and fiction. The result was *In Cold Blood,* which, according to Capote, signaled "a serious new art form: the 'nonfiction novel,' as I thought of it." Upon publication, *In Cold Blood* elicited among the most extensive critical interest in publishing history. Although several commentators accused Capote of opportunism and of concealing his inability to produce imaginative fiction by working with ready-made material, most responded with overwhelmingly positive reviews. Originally serialized in *The New Yorker* and published in book form in 1965 following nearly six years of research and advance publicity, this book chronicles the murder of Kansas farmer Herbert W. Clutter and his family, who were bound, gagged, robbed, and shot by two ex-convicts in November, 1959. In addition to garnering Capote an Edgar Award from the Mystery Writers of America, *In Cold Blood* became a bestseller and generated several million dollars in royalties and profits related to serialization, paperback, and film rights. Written in an objective and highly innovative prose style that combines the factual accuracy of journalism with the emotive impact of fiction, *In Cold Blood* is particularly noted for Capote's subtle insights into the ambiguities of the American legal system and of capital punishment.

In the late 1960s, Capote began to suffer from writer's block, a frustrating condition that severely curtailed his creative output. Throughout this period he claimed to be working on *Answered Prayers,* a gossip-filled chronicle of the Jet Set that he promised would be his masterpiece. He reported that part of his trouble in completing the project was dissatisfaction with his technique and that he spent most of his time revising or discarding work in progress. During the mid-1970s he attempted to stimulate his creative energies and to belie critics' accusations that he had lost his talent by publishing several chapters of *Answered Prayers* in the magazine *Esquire.* Most critics found the chapters disappointing. More devastating to Capote, however, were the reactions of his society friends, most of whom felt betrayed by his revelations of the intimate details of their lives and refused to have any more contact with him. In addition, Capote's final collection of short prose pieces, *Music for Chameleons* (1983), was less than warmly received by critics. Afterward, Capote succumbed to alcoholism, drug addiction, and poor health, and he died shortly before his sixtieth birthday. According to his friends and editors, the only portions of *Answered Prayers* he had managed to complete were those that had appeared in *Esquire* several years previously.

Critical assessment of Capote's career is highly divided, both in terms of individual works and his overall contribution to literature. In an early review Paul Levine described Capote as a "definitely minor figure in contemporary literature whose reputation has been built less on a facility of style than on an excellent advertising campaign." Ihab Hassan, however, claimed that "whatever the faults of Capote may be, it is certain that his work possesses more range and energy than his detractors allow." Although sometimes faulted for precocious, fanciful plots and for overwriting, Capote is widely praised for his storytelling abilities and the quality of his prose.

(For further information about Capote's life and works, see *Concise Dictionary of American Literary Biography, 1941-1968; Contemporary Authors,* Vols. 5-8, 113 [obituary]; *Contemporary Authors New Revision Series,* Vol. 18; *Contemporary Literary Criticism,* Vols. 1, 3, 8, 13, 19, 34, 38, 58; *Dictionary of Literary Biography,* Vol. 2: *American Novelists Since World War II;* and *Dictionary of Literary Biography Yearbook: 1980, 1984;* and *Short Story Criticism,* Vol. 2.)

CRITICAL COMMENTARY

IHAB HASSAN

(essay date 1961)

[Hassan is an Egyptian-born American critic. His books include *Radical Innocence: The Contemporary American Novel* (1961), *The Dismemberment of Orpheus: Toward a Postmodern Literature* (1971), and *The Right Promethean Fire* (1980). In the following excerpt from the first study, he discusses the contrasting "nocturnal" and "daylight" modes in Capote's short fiction, his novels *Other Voices, Other Rooms* and *The Grass Harp*, and his novella *Breakfast at Tiffany's*.]

Whatever the faults of Capote may be, it is certain that his work possesses more range and energy than his detractors allow—witness the clear ring of *The Muses Are Heard,* the crackling impressions of *Local Color,* the crazy humor of his filmscript, *Beat the Devil*—and it is equally certain that no faddish estimate of his work can suggest his real hold on the contemporary imagination.

Yet it is, of course, as a Southern and gothic writer that we insist on knowing Capote. Southern he is by accident of birth more than natural affinity; he once said, "I have lived in many places besides the South and I don't like to be called a Southern writer." He is right. We are quick to sense that the elemental quality in the fiction of Faulkner, Warren, or McCullers is consciously poeticized in his fiction, and that their loving adherence to the manners of Southern life often vanishes before the surrealist appearance of his reveries. Nor can his work be called gothic in the same sense that makes the idea of spiritual isolation in the novels of Carson McCullers functional and intelligible. Of protest and isolation, as we shall see, Capote has much to say. His broader intentions, however, are more nearly defined by [the tradition of American romance]. . . . Romance, as practiced with ironic intentions by Capote and defined by Henry James, is "experience liberated . . . experience disengaged, disembroiled, disencumbered," and as such it remains open to the gothic impulse which is but one of its elements.

The idea of romance, informed by the modern techniques of dream symbolism and analysis, suggests the general quality of Capote's work. We begin to perceive the specific concerns of Capote's fiction when we note the division between his "daylight" and "nocturnal" styles, and when we understand both as developments of a central, unifying, and self-regarding impulse which Narcissus has traditionally embodied. The im-

pulse brings together dread and humor, dream and reality, "in-sight" and "ex-perience." The differences between **"Miriam,"** 1945, and **"House of Flowers,"** 1951, between *Other Voices, Other Rooms,* 1948, and *The Grass Harp,* 1951, distinguish the two styles of Capote; the chronological development suggests a deepening awareness of the tensions between self and world, a redistribution of love between ego and object, a movement toward light which retains the knowledge of darkness. *Breakfast at Tiffany's,* 1958, carries these developments a step farther, and, though it appears to elude some of the distinctions we make, confirms the emergent pattern of Capote's work.

The nocturnal style of Truman Capote—and it is the style we are likely to identify with his achievement—makes the greater use of uncanny trappings and surreal decors. The sense of underlying dreadfulness compels the style to discover "the instant of petrified violence," the revelation which only the moment of terror can yield. In stories like **"Miriam," "The Headless Hawk," "A Tree of Night,"** or **"Shut a Final Door,"** fear seems to take the characters by their entrails and reduce them to that curious condition of insight and paralysis which is the best expression of their predicament. "All our acts are acts of fear," Capote writes in the last story, and so man is consigned to perpetual solitude, not so much because he cannot love or be loved—these are merely the symptoms—but because his dreams must remain unsharable and his night world must rise continually against his daily actions. It is this recognition of the unconscious, and all that it holds of wish and terror, that specifies the nocturnal mode of Capote's writing. The recognition is impelled by a force which D. H. Lawrence noted in Poe's work: the disintegration of the modern psyche. Like Poe, like Carson McCullers, Truman Capote shows, in his nocturnal mood, that his image of the modern psyche is preeminently isolate and Protestant. Hence Capote's interest in the theme of self-discovery—Narcissus may have been the first Protestant—and in the technique of character doubles or alter egoes—**"Miriam," "Shut a Final Door,"** etc. Hence also the omnipresence of dreams in Capote's fiction. Dreams in the earlier stories do not only constitute a private and self-sufficient world, and do not only contain the destructive element of our psyche ("It is easy to escape daylight," Randolph says in *Other Voices, Other Rooms,* "but night is inevitable, and dreams are the giant cage"); dreams also reveal, in the later stories, the creative element of the un-

Principal Works

Other Voices, Other Rooms (novel) 1948

*A Tree of Night and Other Stories (short stories) 1949

Local Color (nonfiction sketches) 1950

*The Grass Harp (novel) 1951

The Grass Harp [adaptor; from his novel] (drama) 1952

Beat the Devil [with John Huston] (screenplay) 1954

The Muses Are Heard: An Account (nonfiction) 1956; published in England as The Muses Are Heard: An Account of the Porgy and Bess Visit to Leningrad), 1957

Breakfast at Tiffany's: A Short Novel and Three Stories (short fiction collection) 1958; published in England as Breakfast at Tiffany's, 1959

Selected Writings (miscellaneous prose) 1963

A Christmas Memory [adaptor; from his 1956 short story] (television script) 1966

In Cold Blood: A True Account of a Multiple Murder and Its Consequences (nonfiction novel) 1966

The Thanksgiving Visitor (novella) 1967

The Dogs Bark: Public People and Private Places (miscellaneous prose) 1973

Music for Chameleons: New Writing (miscellaneous prose) 1983

Answered Prayers: The Partial Manuscript (novel) 1986

*These works were published together in 1956 as The Grass Harp and A Tree of Night and Other Stories.

conscious, and permit that release of the imagination which, as Capote implies, is the prerequisite of love. "But a man who doesn't dream is like a man who doesn't sweat: he stores up a lot of poison," Judge Cool tells Verena in *The Grass Harp* when the latter derisively calls his marriage proposal to Dolly, his confession of love, a dream. If Capote's darker style seems uncanny, it is because uncanny effects are produced, as Freud knew, "by effacing the distinctions between imagination and reality . . . ," by seeing, as Rimbaud did, a mosque at the bottom of a lake.

But in effacing the distinctions between reality and imagination, the nocturnal style not only evokes the shapeless world of our dreams; it evokes, no less, the fabulous world of myth and fairy tale. In our age, alas, dream, myth, and fairy tale are no longer allowed to drowse in their separate corners. Freud has noted the occurrence of material from fairy tales in dreams, and Geza Roheim has argued that myth, animistic thought, and in fact culture itself, find a common source in oneiric fantasies. In Capote's work, the familiar figure of the Wizard Man partakes both of dream and archetype, and it is there to remind us that our archaic fears must

be forever conquered, our childish past reenacted. Such fabulous evocations must reclaim the universal symbols of human experience. Yet it is wise to remember that Capote once said, "All I want to do is to tell a story and sometimes it is best to choose a symbol. I would not know a Freudian symbol as such if you put it to me." In the end, the nocturnal style of Truman Capote appeals to the qualities which Henry James found essential to all fiction of the supernatural, appeals, that is, "to wonder and terror and curiosity and pity and to the delight of fine recognitions, as well as to the joy, perhaps sharper still, of the mystified state. . . . " Of these qualities, and of the human failings which these qualities silently criticize, the supernatural element in Capote's fiction is a metaphor.

But if the supernatural defines the nocturnal mode of Capote, humor defines his daylight style. The style, evident in **"My Side of the Matter," "Jug of Silver," "Children on Their Birthdays,"** *The Grass Harp*, and *Breakfast at Tiffany's*, assumes the chatty, first-person informality of anecdotes. It also specifies character and admits the busyness of social relations more than its darker counterpart. And the scene which it lights upon is usually the small Southern town—not the big city which witnesses in abstract horror the so-called alienation of man from his environment. (The one notable exception, of course, is *Breakfast at Tiffany's*.) Now it is true that humor, like the supernatural, must finally rise to universal implications. But if one may judge from the differences between Twain and Poe, between the American tall tale and the native ghost story, humor is always more of this earth; it is apt to individualize rather than generalize; and it can rise to universal meanings but gradually. Humor has also a social reference. Humor—which may be called a Catholic if the supernatural can be called a Protestant impulse—binds rather than separates: it is as much a mode of communion as the gothic is a mode of self-isolation. (pp. 230-34)

The contrast between the two styles of Capote can be rapidly observed in his short stories, of which the best are collected in *A Tree of Night and Other Stories*, 1949, a selection that excludes such premature efforts as **"The Walls Are Cold"** and **"The Shape of Things."**

With **"My Side of the Matter"** and **"Miriam"** the divided mood of Capote can already be distinguished. The first is a chatty, whacky story, or rather anecdote, of a youthful bridegroom persecuted by two colorful harridans, his wife's aunts, in a tiny Alabama town. The racy narrative, told in the first person by the bridegroom with yarnlike exaggeration and naïveté, remains nevertheless episodic. **"Miriam"** is a different matter. Set in New York, it is a sinister and surrealistic tale of a child, Miriam, who haunts an elderly widow, Mrs. Miller. But what appears in one perspective as a chilling tale of the supernatural—Miriam can vanish at will—appears in another as the hallucination of a lonely old woman obsessed by a guilty image of her other self, a self bold and adventurous as her own is timid and weary. The theme of the double is not new to literature. Conrad and Dostoyevsky made rich use of it, and both Rank and Freud, acknowledging its uncanny effects, understood it as a stratagem of the ego to preserve itself against the intolerable fact of death, a stratagem, in fact, reverting to an early mental stage in which the narcissistic state of the child protects it against the foreign reality of death and corruption.

The regressive quest for identity, revealed in a moment of terror, is also present in Kay's story, **"A Tree of Night,"** in which a college girl on her way back from her uncle's funeral finds herself cornered, robbed, and even mesmerized, by two grotesque show people on a train whose act it is to perform the macabre story of Lazarus in every tank-town. Taken together, the traveling show-couple summon a force of unspeakable tawdriness and evil which awakens in Kay "a childish memory of terrors that once, long ago, had hovered above her like haunted limbs on a tree of night." It is a memory of black omens and death, and of "the unfailing threat of the wizard man." Kay, under the spell of past and present, slips into the dreadful anonymity of night, finally relaxing into that sublunary sleep for which no identity is requisite. In the story called **"Master Misery,"** it is dreams that define our identity. Hence the agony of Sylvia, the solitary girl who sells her dreams to a mysterious figure, Master Misery, who lives in a great marble mansion off Fifth Avenue. It is as the clown, Sylvia's only friend, says, "Dreams are the mind of the soul and the secret truth about us. Now Master Misery, maybe he hasn't got a soul, so bit by bit he borrows yours, steals it. . . . " We understand Master Misery for what he is when we recognize him not only as a wry image of the psychoanalyst or simply an aspect of the "dehumanized" society in which we live—where Santa Claus is a robot and plaster girls pedal mechanical bicycles in shop windows—but also an extension of the self on which he preys. What saves the symbol—the Wizard Man is not a "character"—from sentimentality is precisely what endows the story with the feeling of improbability: the transposition of myth and actuality. For it is in fabulous, and hence generic, terms that Master Misery is described: "All mothers tell their kids about him; he lives in hollows of trees, he comes down chimneys late at night, he lurks in graveyards and you can hear his step in the attic." (pp. 235-37)

The bald dichotomy set up by these stories is more amply elaborated by Capote's two earlier novels, *Other Voices, Other Rooms,* 1948, and *The Grass Harp,* 1951.

The peculiar mixture of fantasy and reality in Ca-

pote's first novel begs for allegorical interpretation. [In his 1955-56 *American Scholar* article], Carvel Collins has suggested the quest of the Holy Grail as a possible framework for the action, pointing out numerous parallels between the details of Joel Knox's story and those to be found in Jessie Weston's account of the Grail myth. John Aldridge, on the other hand, has seen Joel's story essentially as an archetype of the Boy in Search of a Father [see Sources for Further Study]. Both views correspond to genuine analogues of the narrative. But Joel Knox is not only a miniature Dedalus-Telemachus in Dublin-Ithaca, or Parsifal-Galahad at the Chapel Perilous. He is also a smaller model of Castorp-Tannhäuser at Davos-Venusberg, and Narcissus sitting by his pool. Above all, he is simply Joel Knox who, no matter how much or little he may resemble Capote, is still a character in a work of fiction. (p. 239)

The novel begins with Joel's arrival at Noon City, an oasis in the busy world, less pre-Civil War than legendary, near which is the even more legendary mansion of Skully's Landing, where he expects to meet his father for the first time. He is glad to leave Aunt Ellen's house behind: "It was as if he lived those months wearing a pair of spectacles with green, cracked lenses, and had wax-plugging in his ears, for everything seemed to be something it wasn't, and the days melted into a constant dream." But Joel does not see his father, Mr. Samson, for a long time. He roams the wild, incredible garden of the Landing which, like some lost ruin, is haunted by the enfabled past; and, true to Capote's vision, he perceives in an "instant of petrified violence," the apparition of a strange lady in a window. This is his first glimpse of Randolph, of his own fate. Randolph, prototype of the Evil Magician, of the artist, the teacher, and the criminal, whose eloquence and learning are like echoes of a spectral chorus, is the genius who dominates the Landing. Exquisite in his cultivation and irrelevance, at once languid and sinister, lucid and depraved, Randolph has all the unpredictability and perverted innocence which qualify him for becoming the mentor and lover of Joel. Whether he is exposed to the half-pagan Sabbath ceremonies of Jesus Fever and his daughter Zoo, or the primitive magic of Little Sunshine, the wizened Negro hermit who haunts the Cloud Hotel, or the talcumed world of invalids, lunatics, and perverts who inhabit the Landing, Joel's sense of reality is constantly subverted by his environment. Like Little Sunshine, who acts, together with Randolph, as father-substitute, Joel is drawn to the terrible Cloud Hotel: "For if he [Little Sunshine] went away, as he had once upon a time, other voices, other rooms, voices lost and clouded, strummed his dreams." The progressive attenuation of external reality is evident as Joel moves from Aunt Ellen's to Skully's Landing to the Cloud Hotel; the movement is indeed a descent into Hades, a journey, in various stages, toward the darkest unconscious, or perhaps toward the womb of death. Dreaming of the Cloud Hotel, Joel realizes that it was not and never had been a real hotel: "This was the place folks came when they went off the face of the earth, when they died but were not dead." And dreaming of his journey through its rooms, he sees himself "in the dust of thorns listening for a name, his own, but even here no father claimed him."

The second part of the novel, of the "journey," opens with a climactic incident. Joel finally meets his father, and finds him a paralytic with two glinting eyes, who can only communicate with the world by dropping red tennis balls. Meanwhile, we are apprised in a grotesque tale of love and violence that Randolph is responsible for Samson's condition. Joel's resistance to Randolph, and to all that he stands for, receives its first check when Joel discovers that his real father is nearly a zombie. His resistance is further weakened when his relation to Idabel Tompkins fails to confirm his groping manhood. When Joel attempts to kiss Idabel on a fishing trip, she fights him off viciously and overpowers him; and on their excursion to a decayed mill, it is she who kills the water moccasin with Jesus Fever's old Civil War sword. The snake has the eyes of Joel's father, and the boy fails equally in asserting his manhood with Idabel as in conquering the phantom of his father with the ceremonial symbol of the past. Thus it is in *failing* the traditional ordeals, in overcoming which he might have earned his manhood, that Joel makes himself eligible to the insidious knowledge of the Cloud Hotel. (pp. 240-42)

Part Three opens with the return of Joel to the Landing. He returns in a coma, his world contracted, appearance and reality altogether fused, and when he recovers from his illness, he is finally at peace, fully attuned to the enchantments which await him: "Lo, he was where he's never imagined to find himself again: the secret hideaway room in which, on hot New Orleans afternoons, he'd sat watching snow sift through scorched August trees. . . ." It is with Randolph, not Idabel, that he finally visits the Cloud Hotel, while Aunt Ellen looks for him in vain. But for Joel there is no going back to the old realities; like Randolph, like Little Sunshine, he finds at last his Other Room in the Hotel—with a hanged mule in it for effect. And strangely enough, the last acts of Joel indicate not surrender but liberation. Faithful to the Jungian archetype of the Descent into Hades, Joel reemerges somewhat healed, possessed of a dangerous and ambiguous knowledge. " 'I am me,' Joel whooped. 'I am Joel, we are the same people,' " he shouts exuberantly on his way back from the Cloud Hotel. And he is suddenly wise enough to see "how helpless Randolph was: more paralyzed than Mr. Samson, more childlike than Miss Wisteria, what else could he do, once outside and alone, but describe a circle, the zero of his nothingness?" At the end of the novel, when Zoo overturns the cracked, moss-covered bell with which the old plantation owners used to summon their slaves, ancient symbol of a vanished order, and when Randolph appears in a window, beckoning in his female attire to Joel, we are not sure whether it is in triumph or defeat that Joel responds to this mute appeal. We can only sense that the traditional modes of behavior are no longer in command of life.

Mr. Aldridge has objected to the self-contained quality of evil and guilt in the novel, to the failure of the book to "stand in some meaningful relation to recognizable life," and to the feeling that Capote's world "seems to be a concoction rather than a synthesis," its purity "not the purity of experience forced under pressure into shape" but rather the "sort that can be attained only in the isolation of a mind which life has never really violated. . . ." The objections appear serious; but as usual, the impatience of Mr. Aldridge is not entirely justified. We need to remember that Capote's work is, in its intentions, at least, a novel-romance, and that it attempts to engage reality without being realistic. Evil and guilt in it are self-contained only in the sense that they are defined by the individual consciousness without reference to an accepted social or moral order. Evil, in other words, is mainly poetic and archetypal; its moral issue is confined to the predicament of the victim without visible oppressor, and of the beloved almost without a lover. The result is a sharp focus, a reflexive vision seeking constantly to penetrate the arcana of personality. As Randolph puts it to Joel:

> They can romanticize us so, mirrors, and that is their secret: what a subtle torture it would be to destroy all the mirrors in the world: where then could we look for reassurance of our identities? I tell you, my dear, Narcissus was no egotist . . . he was merely another of us who, in our unshatterable isolation, recognized, on seeing his reflection, the one beautiful comrade, the only inseparable love. . . .

Experience is limited to what a mirror reveals of the beholder, and if the novel sometimes appears to be a "concoction" rather than a "synthesis," it is perhaps because the job of dramatic resolution is surrendered to ambience and verbal magic. Here is the context of Joel's final revelation at the Cloud Hotel:

> (He looked into the fire, longing to see their faces as well, and the flames erupted an embryo; a veined, vacillating shape, its features formed slowly, and even when complete stayed veiled in dazzle; his eyes burned tar-hot as he brought them nearer: tell me, tell me, who are you? are you someone I know? are you dead? are you my friend? do you love me? But the painted disembodied head remained unborn beyond its mask, and gave no clue. Are you someone I am looking for? he asked, not knowing whom he meant, but certain that for him there must be such

a person, just as there was for everybody else: Randolph with his almanac, Miss Wisteria and her search by flashlight; Little Sunshine remembering other voices, other rooms, all of them remembering, or never having known. And Joel drew back. If he recognized the figure in the fire, then what ever would he find to take its place? It was easier not to know, better holding heaven in your hand like a butterfly that is not there at all.)

The recognition of Joel is, to a large extent, the event upon which the dramatic unity of the novel depends. It is characteristic of Capote's nocturnal mode that the event should be presented in the guise of a trance or hallucination, a verbal *tour de force,* and that its moral effect should be muffled by "atmosphere." Though other novels seem to us greater, it is otiose to take their more realistic mode as a judgment of Capote's fiction.

Of his first novel Capote has recently said, in *Writers at Work* [1957; edited by Malcolm Cowley], "I am a stranger to that book; the person who wrote it seems to have little in common with my present self. Our mentalities, our interior temperatures are entirely different." The remark accentuates our transition to Capote's second novel, *The Grass Harp,* which is indeed a different story. That the book contains much autobiography is evident from a later story Capote wrote, **"A Christmas Memory,"** in which the prototypes of Collin and Dolly are shown to be, in words *and* picture, young Capote (then an urchin with a happy, toothless grin) and his elderly female cousin. The narrative, written in the "daylight" style, is told in the first person by young Collin Fenwick. The story is not "strummed in dreams," as in *Other Voices, Other Rooms;* it is strummed by the wind on a field of Indian grass adjoining a cemetery—the Grass Harp. To be sure, the contrast between the two novels is not as striking as if Poe had taken up residence at Walden Pond, but it suggests, nevertheless, a welcome restoration of reality to the surface of things, and an expansion in social awareness. *The Grass Harp,* at any rate, sings the story of all people, as Dolly Talbo says, people alive and dead, and to sing one needs more space than the Cloud Hotel affords.

The "initiation" of Collin Fenwick results less in a regression to the oneiric fastness of childhood than in a nostalgic awareness of past innocence and lost love. Collin is an eleven-year-old orphan when he comes to live with Verena and Dolly Talbo, two elderly cousins of his father. The two women are as dissimilar as cactus and violet. Verena, who represents the ruthless, practical world, is shrewd, grasping, and masterful. Her single weakness, the memory of a liaison with a certain Maudie who leaves Verena to get married, enhances her apparent toughness. Dolly, on the other hand, is shy and retiring—her presence is a delicate happening.

She lives in a tender, wistful world, gathering herbs for her dropsy cures, feeding only on sweets, and extending her sympathy to all created things. Her devout friend, Catherine, an old Negro who claims to be of Indian descent, calls her Dollyheart, and calls Verena, That One—the Heart, the Self, versus the Other, the World. With Dolly and Catherine, Collin enters into a spiritual sisterhood dedicated to preserve everything frail, lovely, and unique.

But the trouble comes when Collin is sixteen. The world, in the person of Verena, decides to ask the unworldly trio to account for itself. Verena bullies Dolly to obtain from her the formula of the dropsy cure which has commercial possibilities. When force and persuasion fail, Verena humiliates Dolly by reminding her of her uselessness and dependency. The trio takes to the road, finding refuge in a tree house, a raft floating in the sea of leaves, up an old chinaberry tree.

The tree house, of course, is the last refuge of innocents abroad. But though it is unlike Huck's raft in that it offers limited opportunities of experience, it is not so much a vehicle of escape, Capote would have us believe, as a harbor of lost values. For Dolly teaches Collin that the tree house is a ship, "that to sit there was to sail along the cloudy coastline of every dream." At peace in the tree, the two women and the boy feel at one with their surroundings: "We belonged there, as the sun-silvered leaves belonged, the dwelling whippoorwills." But most important, they feel at one with one another, and with the two "outcasts" from town whom they attract, Riley Henderson and Judge Cool.

Inspired by the enraged Verena, and led by a brutal sheriff, the representatives of Church and State attack the tree and are repulsed time and again in hilarious scenes of impotent fury and gentle mockery. The spirit of the chinaberry tree, the presence of Dolly, the insight into their separate predicaments, unite our five refugees as the sheriff's posse can never be united. "I sometimes imagine all those whom I've called guilty have passed the real guilt on to me: it's partly that that makes me want once before I die to be right on the right side," the Judge, who is the voice as Dolly is the heart of the group, says. He continues: "But here we are, identified: five fools in a tree. A great piece of luck provided we know how to use it: no longer any need to worry about the picture we present—free to find out who we truly are." As usual, the search for identity in Capote's work precedes the discovery of love. But here, for the first time, both the reflexive and the outgoing impulse are caught in a single vision.

The outgoing impulse, the burden of love, is defined when Judge Cool says to Riley—and his message is identical with that of the hobo in Carson McCullers' "A Tree, A Rock, A Cloud"—"We are speaking of love. A leaf, a handful of seed—begin with these, learn a little what it is to love. . . . No easy process, understand;

it could take a lifetime. . . . " At which Dolly with a sharp intake of breath cries, "Then . . . I've been in love all my life." Yet Dolly is not so out of touch with reality that she can accept the world, like Pollyana, on silly faith. The persecutions of Verena, the fact that her friend Catherine is "captured" and thrown into jail, force her to ask Collin—and how ironic that an old woman should ask an adolescent questions about the world—force her to ask him in pain and perplexity, "Collin, what do you think: is it that after all the world is a bad place?" Collin is wise enough (almost too wise) to reflect: "No matter what passions compose them, all private worlds are good, they are never vulgar places: Dolly had been made too civilized by her own, the one she shared with Catherine and me, to feel the winds of wickedness that circulate elsewhere. . . . "

We are never quite sure whether the novel portrays the disenchantment of an elderly woman or the initiation of a young man. But of this we can be more certain, that Dolly in renewing her powers of universal sympathy by drawing constantly on the resources of her inner world strikes a parable of the artist who, secure in the freedom of his imagination, reaches out to free ours. In this sense, the healing powers of Dolly can be said to extend, through the medium of the Grass Harp, not only to the fictive community of tree-dwellers but also to the real community of book-readers. The idea of the artist as healer is, of course, quite ancient. What makes the idea interesting in the works of such contemporary authors as Salinger and Capote is the particular form it acquires. In both writers the concern with lovelessness seems to have allied itself with a criticism of the new Philistinism, the implication being that the poet and lover, to leave out the lunatic, are of one imagination compact. Hence Salinger's interest in Zen and Haiku poetry, which bring the aesthetic and spiritual to meet at a still point, and Capote's interest in Narcissus whose adoration of beauty may be considered an act both of love and cognition.

The reaction against a grim and unlovely world, which insists that all private worlds are good *and* beautiful, tends to perpetuate the myth of the Noble Unconscious. It may also lead to the myth of the Noble Freak. Of this Dolly is an example, and Sister Ida, with her revivalist tribe of fifteen children all sired by different fathers, is another. Ida's wandering brood, whose slogan is Let Little Homer Honey Lasso Your Soul For the Lord, brings into the novel a good deal of bustle and folksy humor. They also reveal a certain outgoingness, an attitude which, in its vigor and acceptance, qualifies the pathos of Dolly. But the impression remains that though Dolly and Ida have suffered much, their idea of freedom is undoubtedly romantic and the form of their rebellion extravagant.

Nothing is very extravagant about the denouement of the novel. Verena, robbed and deserted by the infamous Dr. Ritz, is utterly broken. In a candle-lit, tree-house scene, while rain pours and thunder rages, Verena, who had actually climbed the chinaberry tree, confesses to Dolly: "Envied you, Dolly. Your pink room. I've only knocked at the doors of such rooms, not often—enough to know that now there is no one but you to let me in."

Dolly's "pink room" is a place for Collin to start from; Joel's "other room" at the Cloud Hotel is a place to which he can and must return. When Dolly dies, it is as if a ceremony of innocence and beauty had come to an end, and behind each character the Garden of Eden had clanged its gates shut. But life continues. Riley Henderson goes on to become a public figure, and Collin journeys North to study law. Reality does not surrender to the dream; it is merely redeemed by it. The childish self-absorption of a Joel yields to the wider horizon of a Collin. Seen in retrospect from Collin's point of view, the novel still appears as a pastoral elegy to irrevocable innocence. But the elegy is also mythicized; it is sung by the field of Indian grass, "a grass harp, gathering, telling, a harp of voices remembering a story." The elegy is present and continuous; it may even affect the future. Yet Collin confesses, as Huck would never confess, that "my own life has seemed to me more a series of closed circles, rings that do not evolve with the freedom of the spiral. . . . "

With *Breakfast at Tiffany's,* 1958, the closed rings begin to evolve into a spiral, some open and continuous motion of the hero's spirit, or rather of the heroine's, the amazing Miss Holiday Golightly, Traveling, as her Tiffany cards insist. But whether the driving motion of a spiral, so endless and implacable, possesses more freedom than a circle affords is a conundrum only Euclid may solve.

Holly, like Capote's other protagonists, is not yet out of her teens: "It was a face beyond childhood, yet this side of belonging to a woman." But her initiation began long ago, before she became the child-bride, at fourteen, of Doc Golightly, a horse doctor in Tulip, Texas; began, probably when she lost father and mother and was dumped with her brother Fred, half-starved, on "various mean people." The process of that initiation remains secret—there are intimations of outrage and misery beyond the limits of a child's endurance—for Holly behaves as if past and future were no more tangible than the air she breathes; but its result is nonetheless permanent: a wild and homeless love of freedom. When we see her during the war years in that New York brownstone of the East Seventies, she is fully nineteen, and she strikes us as an improbable combination of the *picaro,* the courtesan, and the *poète maudit.*

Improbability is indeed the quality she uses to criticize a dreary and truthless round of existence, and artifice—she is an inspired liar—to transform it. "I'll never get used to anything. Anybody who does, they might as well be dead," she cries at one point, and we realize that her rebellion against the *given* in life, the useful and prudential, is one of the sources of her vitality. It is as her dwarfish friend and Hollywood agent puts it, the "kid" is a "*real* phony," and her specialty is presenting "horseshit on a platter." Screwball, phony, or saint—some will find it more convenient simply to say "sick, sick, sick"—it does not take us very long to recognize, to admire, Holly's hold on experience. Her philosophy is quite elementary—and hopelessly at odds with our times. "I don't mean I'd mind being rich and famous," she tells the narrator. "That's very much on my schedule, and someday I'll try to get around to it; but if it happens, I'd like to have my ego tagging along. I want to still be me when I wake up one fine morning and have breakfast at Tiffany's." When Holly's dream comes true—the vision symbolized by the *"ordre, luxe, et volupté"* of Tiffany's which she uses to cure her spells of *angst,* "the mean reds"—she wants to be no other than herself. Implied here is no revulsion against one's identity, no holy surrender or unattachment. Holly is in fact very much attached to this world, and therefore to herself. In this respect, she seems the opposite of Salinger's Holden Caulfield with whom she shares the quixotic gift of truth, and shares the ability to gamble everything on a wayward love for, say, Man O'War—Holden's ducks in Central Park—or her brother Fred—Holden's sister Phoebe. But also unlike Holden, whose stringent idealism limits the scope of his commitments, his joy, Holly's truth refers to no self-transcending concept. As she candidly admits: "Good? Honest is more what I mean. Not low-type honest—I'd rob a grave, I'd steal two-bits off a dead man's eyes if I thought it would contribute to the day's enjoyment—but unto-thyself-type honest. Be anything but a coward, a pretender, an emotional crook, a whore: I'd rather have cancer than a dishonest heart." Her loyalty to others—the inmate Sally Tomato, for instance—is a loyalty to her own feelings for which she is willing to risk all. (pp. 243-52)

Holly Golightly may be what we should all like to become if we could deposit comfort and respectability to an insured bank account; and her breezy excesses of fancy as of intuition may be, again, just what our stuffy age most requires. In her case the misfit hero certainly shows a fitting genius for *living*—rebellion here is secondary, spontaneous. But Capote himself is not entirely taken in by Holly's verve and piercing glitter. His tale, though lovingly told, has wit and sharp precision. As Holly sweeps through her zany adventures, one becomes conscious of a groundswell of gentle criticism. Mildred Grossman, the grind whom the narrator recalls from his schooldays, may be a "top-heavy realist," but Holly by the same token must be considered a "lop-sided romantic"; and antithetical as the two girls

seem, both "walk through life and out of it with the same determined step that took small notice of those cliffs at the left." Even Holly's incorrigible tomcat [which she found abandoned by a river] finds at last a home with potted palms and lace curtains, a home and a name; but for Holly the narrator can only pray that she may be granted, sometime, somewhere, the grace of knowledge and repose. Narcissus found both in a reflected image; Holly, whimsical child of old Faust, looks for them beyond a vanishing horizon. For Holly—sooner or later we must say it—is a child too. She is premature in ways both delightful and regressive. (The latest avatar of Capote's Wizard Man is the "fat woman" who haunts Holly's "red nightmares," threatening to inflict punishment, withhold love, or destroy everything high and rare. But does not childhood itself, to which adults wend such tortuous ways, present a criticism of maturity for which we seldom have a ready answer?)

Criticism, the interplay of views, is sustained by right form. The form of *Breakfast at Tiffany's* approaches perfection. It has pace, narrative excitement, a firm and subtle hold on the sequence of events from the first backward glance to the final salutation. A novelette in scope, it still manages to treat a subject usually accorded the fuller scope of the picaresque novel with marvelous selectivity. The point of view, the tone, the style herald no technical discoveries in the field of fiction: they simply blend to make the subject spring to life. Capote allows the story to be told in the first person by a struggling young writer whose vantage of perception, now in the shadow, now in the light, captures the elusive figure of Holly with the aid of such minor figures as Joe Bell and O. J. Berman. The device is both revealing and discreet, for there is, no doubt, something about Holly's complexion that cannot bear too sharp a light. By establishing the right relation between his narrator and subject, Capote also strikes the right tone. For though the whole story is unfolded backward in one sweeping flashback, the tone is not, like *The Grass Harp's,* elegiac. Elegy, where so much hope is called to question, is out of place. The tone comes closer to that of an invocation, a blessing: hail, Holly, and farewell. Criticism, as we have noted, is implied, patronage never. What keeps the tone from becoming patronizing—look at that wonderful spoiled child!—is the style. The style matches the exotic quality of the subject with its clear-headedness, matches whimsey with wit, though here and there, as in the description of the cat, Capote indulges himself in a superfluous flourish of imagery. Holly's lack of self-criticism is balanced by the searching temper of the narrator. Tension and control are maintained. (pp. 253-54)

The development of Capote's adolescent heroes from Joel Knox to Holly Golightly has both an internal logic and a public interest relevant to the prejudices of literature in our time. Joel's urge for self-definition, pursued under its peculiar circumstances, dreamily evokes the idea of Narcissus. But the essence of narcissism, as Theodore Reik maintains, "lies in seeing oneself with the loving eyes of another. The phenomenon does not mean the expression of self-love but the desire of the self to be loved." That same desire presages the broader view Collin Fenwick takes; for the love of all created things that Verena teaches him presupposes some security in the identity we discover to ourselves, presupposes, that is, an ability to turn the need for love outward. Holly Golightly, though she impresses us by her self-sufficiency—indeed, one is sometimes led to wonder how "permanent" any of her attachments can be—converts her restless love for the world into an active and existential pursuit. The movement, we see, is toward greater involvement, a breaking out.

The three heroes, standing for knowledge through dream, love, and free action, represent also three typical attitudes of recent fiction. Joel Knox reflects the current feeling that our world is now discovered, our life organized, our vision confined to some private room of lost childhood. The only freedom we still possess is the freedom to dream, and to the extent that reality becomes more intractable our dreams become compulsive. Collin Fenwick expresses the need to redeem reality through love, a need to which a great part of contemporary fiction is so intensely dedicated. Holly Golightly approaches the ideal of the new picaresque, the free-wheeling hero who insists on the freedom to experience and to denounce precisely because that freedom is no longer granted with immunity by our society. In all cases, the American hero, equally so much more innocent *and* experienced than of yore, remains an outsider, a fugitive from the central concerns of American life, hiding in secret rooms or up a chinaberry tree, or still "lighting out" for the "territory ahead" which is now situated in Africa. Given our burden of bitter and inexhaustible illusions, our hopeless nostalgias and secret regressions, it is no wonder that romancers of Capote's gifts should speak keenly to our condition. But the growth of his vision and the evolution of his more dramatic style also promise, without foregoing the advantages of romance, to discover a form commensurate with the maturity to which we have so long aspired. (pp. 257-58)

Ihab Hassan, "Truman Capote: The Vanishing Image of Narcissus," in his *Radical Innocence: Studies in the Contemporary American Novel,* Princeton University Press, 1961, pp. 230-58.

WILLIAM L. NANCE
(essay date 1970)

[Nance, an American critic, is the author of *The Worlds of Truman Capote* (1970), the first full-length study of Capote's writings. In the following excerpt from that work, he addresses the apparent disparity between Capote's early writings and his later novel, *In Cold Blood.*]

While Capote can take well-deserved pride in *In Cold Blood* as a genuine enlargement of his artistic scope, his deepest satisfaction probably derives from its being something even more important to him: a vindication of his imagination. In its portrayal of Perry Smith and in its pervasive theme of victimization, the book is a factual echo of Capote's earliest fiction.

That fiction began . . . with a series of "dark" stories in each of which the rather unattractive protagonist was trapped in a cage of childhood fears. Near the end of the dark period, in **"Master Misery,"** there appeared a new tendency to see the protagonist (though doomed, like the others) as a somewhat admirable *dreamer,* together with a concomitant scorn for conventional society. Preference for the unconventional may be seen as a new development of a motif present earlier in the stories: the protagonist's own tendency to escape involvement with troublesome characters by dismissing them as "crazy." Another innovation in **"Master Misery"** is that the ever-present bogeyman becomes slightly ambivalent, a not-completely-threatening father.

Perry Smith closely resembles the protagonists of these early stories, as do the other characters of *In Cold Blood* insofar as they are sufferers and dreamers. Perry's most important deviation from the pattern is the "brain explosion" in which he lashes out at the father figure—an act which serves only to confirm his subjection. If Perry remains a trapped child, however, he can hardly be blamed for it: like Sylvia in **"Master Misery,"** he has been robbed of his dreams. Capote is in these early stories, too, of course, though only a part of him. "They're not about me," he has said. "They're very objective portraits of various states of mind—not necessarily my state of mind at all." But he adds, "Yes, those early works were written at a great sort of pressure. Why do you think they're so riddled with anxiety, so neurotic? . . . You must remember how young I was when I wrote those stories." As Harper Lee suggests, when Capote looked at Perry Smith he saw his own dream-trapped childhood.

He had come a long way from that childhood. By a literary process both instinctive and highly deliberate, he had from the beginning been making his escape from its private world. Not content with skillful patternings of fear and constriction such as **"Miriam,"** he had searched for the proper forms to embody a maturing consciousness and sensibility—and in his first novel he began to find them: if the material of *In Cold Blood* is to some extent a return to Capote's childhood and a real-life confirmation of his earliest imaginative creations, its technique, its artistic and ideological presuppositions—even the very fact of its being written—are the almost predictable consequences of directions that Capote began to take in this second phase of his career.

Other Voices, Other Rooms, which Capote describes as "very important to me . . . in my development as a writer," dramatizes the liberation of the Capote protagonist through confrontation of the father after removal from the protective care of the mother. (Capote writes of Perry Smith that he several times "set out to find his lost father, for he had lost his mother as well." Perry, of course, failed in his search.) The mysterious figure that looms over Joel is still the ambivalent father-bogeyman or protector-destroyer, but now with the two sides more equally balanced. The boy's maturation consists in a gradual emergence from dependence on the one, combined with dependence on the mother figure, and fear of the other.

This maturation pattern is uneasily balanced against the fact that the central figure in Joel's experience ceases to be the threatening and protecting parent only to become Randolph, a social outcast and spiritual cipher, yet on one symbolic level both father and mother to the boy. The novel's implication that both material and moral decay is negated by love and by acceptance of one's proper place, while partially undercut by opposite currents in the book itself, remains its dominant theme and principal weakness. A closely related problem is an inadequately defined narrative point of view—an unreliability of the narrator not adequately compensated for by firm handling of other elements—which finally obscures the book's meaning.

What are we to think of Randolph? He is portrayed as radically defective, yet often seems to speak with authority. I asked Capote about Randolph and received the following reply: "I think he's a cripple who has some very sensitive insights because of his isolation and crippledness. . . . Yes, I believe a lot of the things that he says, but I don't think that Randolph is a whole person, or even sane." In the novel, Joel's sweeping final acceptance passes over such distinctions in a disturbing way.

But whatever may be said of Joel's acquiescence in the life of Skully's Landing, it must be recognized as the first appearance of a tendency that will characterize Capote's work up to and including *In Cold Blood:* acceptance of the unconventional, of the misfit in others and in oneself. I asked Capote if this weren't the dominant thing about the novel and he replied, "That's the point of it, isn't it? It's one of the points. That a rather eccentric, sensitive boy has to make some acceptance in his life one way or the other, about himself sexually, physically, morally." One who has made the choice that Joel makes would never again be inclined to dismiss another human being as "crazy"—or as an "obscene, semiliterate and cold-blooded killer."

The tendency toward acceptance that first appears in *Other Voices, Other Rooms* is part of a broad movement in the author's work that expresses itself in several other recurrent motifs and has, at least implicitly, a rather coherent philosophical foundation. The kind of love Joel is initiated into finds its perfect object in Randolph, a completely dependent, completely receptive individual in whom sexual distinctions are virtually nonexistent. The desire to obliterate such distinctions, along with all the other classifications that society imposes on persons, is apparent in all of Capote's work. Closely related to it is a movement away from morality in the narrow sense toward a more spiritual standard. His heroines—Miriam, Sylvia, Idabel, Miss Bobbit, Dolly Talbo—are always shocking people, and they are always right; their way proves always to be the most practical or at least the most pleasant. When "morality" and convention enter the stories, they enter to be refuted by someone with a vision that transcends them.

There is, indeed, a strain of American transcendentalism in Capote, which reminds us that his "student" Perry Smith developed, in his last days, a strong admiration for Thoreau. Behind transcendentalism is Platonism, which Frank Baldanza has seen as a common heritage of Capote and some of his fellow Southern writers, particularly Carson McCullers. They are, he suggests, "natural" Platonists temperamentally inclined to interpret reality in the Platonic manner, and probably influenced as well by direct or indirect contact with the philosopher's writings. Baldanza describes their works as "parables on the nature of love" and adds, "They share with Plato's *Symposium* and *Phaedrus* in particular that curious tone of purely and absolutely spiritual love which grows out of a diffused and circumambient atmosphere of sexuality that never clearly manifests itself."

Randolph and Judge Cool, Capote's two principal lecturers on the nature of love, certainly reflect the Platonic side of the Western mentality; and Dolly Talbo and his other heroines seem to be both highly committed seekers for and actual representatives of the transcendent realm. The maturing of Joel Knox, which we have seen to be the turning point in Capote's fiction, assumes broad relevance when viewed—as Baldanza views it—as a recapitulation of the "passage from the

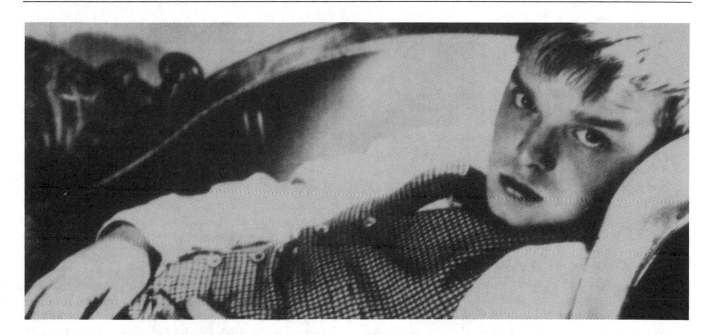

Harold Halma's controversial "erotic" photograph of Capote on the dustjacket of his novel
Other Voices, Other Rooms (1948). Although Capote claimed that the photograph was unposed,
others maintained it was part of a carefully planned publicity stunt.

Heraclitan flux of constant change to the Platonic absolute of love, . . . a momentous achievement of Greek intellectual history."

The spiritual liberation that took place in Capote's work at the time of *Other Voices, Other Rooms* was bound up with another movement that was to reach its ultimate development in *In Cold Blood:* a turning outward to the world of social experience. There are hints of a real world in the neighborhood of Skully's Landing, and the later stories contain more and more realistic treatments of more and more recognizable settings. In style, the stories gradually become less poetic. Their tone becomes less subjective, their atmosphere less thickly crowded with a dreamlike profusion of symbols. Most important, there is a new protagonist at the center of the stories, and this person is usually a woman. Capote had always tended to use feminine protagonists, but in the early work gender did not matter especially, since all the main characters were mirror-images of a single isolated consciousness. The attitude taken toward this captive protagonist ranged from pity to a scorn that was really self-hatred.

Slowly, however, a polarity began to reveal itself. Implicit criticism began to be directed mostly at male characters (Vincent, Walter), and women became the objects of compassion and eventually even of admiration (D.J., Sylvia). Immediately after *Other Voices, Other Rooms,* this heroine achieved a major breakthrough to freedom. Still a sufferer at the hands of life, she was now predominantly a dreamer—an unconventional childlike wanderer whose integrity in the search for an ideal happiness gave her strength to resist the encroachments of society.

While this heroine had obviously been evolving in Capote's imagination, and in fact is, from beginning to end, a projection of himself, a crucial difference from this time on is that her portrayal begins to be based on real girls and women whom Capote has known. Thus the new heroine illustrates most clearly how Capote's liberation is related to a shift—at least partial—from inner to outer experience. *Other Voices, Other Rooms* is the first of his works that has the flavor of factual autobiography, though he describes it as a Gothic dream. While maintaining that the book is not literally true, he says that it is "made of all sorts of things from my childhood." Specifically, it deals with one of his first friendships, that with Harper Lee, and some of the experiences they shared.

In her much more literal way, Miss Lee treated some of the same experiences in *To Kill a Mockingbird.* Capote says that the first part of her book is quite literally true. And, he says, "In my original version of *Other Voices, Other Rooms* I had that same man living in the house that used to leave the things in the trees; and then I took that out. He was a real man, and he lived just down the road from us; we used to go and get those things out of the trees; everything she wrote about it is absolutely true. But you see, I take the same thing and I transfer it into some Gothic thing, a dream, done in an entirely different way."

In Capote's book Harper Lee was transmuted into Idabel Thompkins, whom Joel learns to accept as she is, to pity, and to love. His learning to accept and love his father and Randolph seems much more created and symbolic, and relates most directly to his acceptance of himself. Yet even this seems intimately bound to, or conditioned by, Capote's new extroversion.

From the time of *Other Voices, Other Rooms,* most of Capote's stories are based on his "Platonic" relationships with real women. "I like women. I enjoy their minds," he has said. Age makes no difference, but always his women are to some extent victims and dreamers, and often they share Miss Bobbit's tough unconventionality. **"Children on Their Birthdays,"** published in the same year as the novel, makes use of the young Capote's infatuation for a real girl whom he claims was named June Bug Johnson. **"A Christmas Memory,"** his favorite story, can be taken as the archetype of the relationship. It records his friendship with the elderly cousin who cared for him between the ages of four and ten, and who obviously had a profound formative influence on his imagination. Even in *In Cold Blood* Capote tends to favor the use of women observers.

When I mentioned this similarity, he remarked, "Naturally, I was drawn to them for that reason. It's quite simple to see parallels in the things; I chose what was naturally attractive to me. The postmistress and her mother were two fantastic cases anyway—I couldn't let them go by." I asked him if these various friendships weren't similar to that with the elderly cousin, and he answered:

> Yes, and almost all the girls I've known. I've told you **"Children on Their Birthdays"** was a real little girl; then I had that relationship with Harper Lee. She was a tough little kid that I was stomping on and training and raising up to be something. And then I met the girl who is Holly Golightly, who lived in the building with me. My relationship with them has always been like that. And in this new novel of mine [*In Cold Blood*] it's the same thing, only on a much bigger scale, to put it mildly.

In the stories, Capote usually describes the relationship as one of being "friends," and his usual definition of a friend is "one to whom you can tell everything." In *In Cold Blood* he says of Nancy and Susan, "Thus, the girls were no longer always together, and Nancy deeply felt the daytime absence of her friend, the one person with whom she need be neither brave nor reticent." The tendency in a love relationship of this kind is toward the breaking down of the distinction between self and other—the Platonic identification of the friend as the missing half of the self. Hence, as we see most clearly in Capote's response to Perry Smith, his imaginative breakthrough to others, while real on one level, has—and not surprisingly—been only a partial thing. While *In Cold Blood* is a sort of ultimate extension of that outward-turning that brought Capote his first imaginative liberation, it also remains deeply

personal. It will be recalled that Capote said that liking Perry (and Dick) was the same as liking himself.

It is Capote's highly objective narrative technique that most clearly distinguishes *In Cold Blood* from his fiction and even—as many have remarked—from much journalism. Even this, however, is the completion of a trend that may be observed throughout his work. The early stories portray a world of abnormal, trapped individuals viewed as though from within that world itself: its rules are the only rules; its dreams are realities. There is little or no use of narrative technique to gain an effect of objectivity. In *Other Voices, Other Rooms* we see a similar world, still without clear or consistent distancing through narrative technique or tone; there is, however, a distinction made between the abnormal world and the outside world of society, and, more important, there is the beginning of a division between the central consciousness and this abnormal world through the use of a protagonist who comes from the outside, sees Skully's Landing as distinct from himself, and accepts it freely.

In his later work—as though Capote were coming to identify narrative distance with maturity—the narrative consciousness is more carefully defined and progressively withdrawn from the center of action, which is now dominated by a gently eccentric protagonist wandering through an increasingly realistic world. The first-person narrator of *The Grass Harp* is a boy similar to but slightly older than Joel, and the interest is split between him and his companions, especially the elderly heroine. In *Breakfast at Tiffany's* the narrator is a relatively mature young man more identifiable than ever with Truman Capote (though still ten years younger), and the emphasis has shifted almost completely from him to Holly Golightly. In *In Cold Blood* the narrator is in fact Mr. Capote, and he has virtually refined himself out of the book altogether.

Capote has done in his fiction what Billy Bob did in **"Children on Their Birthdays,"** that first and most delightful expression of Capote's liberation. Having found a heroine who magically embodies the best, most private part of himself, he sadly but determinedly relinquishes her, allowing her to wander free and finally escape him by death. (It is in this story that Capote first employs a dramatized narrator, the young "Mr. C.," whose detachment from the events anticipates the move toward objectivity.) The same relinquishment can be seen taking place near the end of *The Grass Harp,* in a scene that exemplifies Capote's literary strategy more clearly than any other. Collin is seated in the rain-soaked tree house, waiting with Verena and the Judge to hear Dolly's decision about whether to marry: "My impatience equaled theirs, yet I felt exiled from the scene, again a spy peering from the attic, and my sympathies, curiously, were nowhere; or rather, everywhere: a tenderness for all three ran together like raindrops, I could not separate them, they expanded into a human oneness." Objectivity of view blends with universality of sympathy: there could hardly be a better definition of Capote's aim in the nonfiction novel. (Self-effacing in one way, the stance is also god-like in its assumption of unlimited knowledge, power, and benevolence, and accords well with Capote's persistent drive toward a transcendental unity).

Collin's voluntary exile is attended with a strong reluctance to give up the narrower, more childlike identification with Dolly, and it is this reluctance that produces that nostalgic sadness which repeatedly appears as Capote's last word on experience, be it fictional or nonfictional. Standing among graves, listening to a grass harp or gazing at autumn Kansas wheat, he knows that growth is a series of deaths. In a recent interview, Capote gave this feeling a personal expression:

I was terribly bored with my own obsessions. I wanted to forget about my own navel. And now at last I've gotten rid of my own personality. I've gotten rid of the boy with the bangs. He's gone, just gone. I liked that boy. It took an act of will because it was easy to be that person—he was exotic and strange and eccentric. I liked the idea of that person, but he had to go.

Perfect universal sympathy eluded Capote in *In Cold Blood* as surely as did perfect objectivity. Still, his account of the Clutter murders is deeply and broadly compassionate and thus marks a considerable advance along another of the lines Capote has been tracing in his career. Sympathy was almost completely absent in his earliest stories. When, in **"Master Misery,"** he first began to treat his heroine sympathetically as a suffering dreamer, he also began to show a rather sinister tendency to despise everyone who did not share her dream—that is, most of the world. Spite against the townspeople is strong in *Other Voices, Other Rooms,* and the same tendency troubles us in **"A Christmas Memory,"** where the two friends' distaste for the rest of the family seems not quite purified by their childish innocence. While the *Grass Harp* tree-dwellers' uprising against the Establishment is exhilarating, there is something unpleasantly narrow about it. Not only is Capote remote from these people so similar to the Herbert Clutters and the Alvin Deweys; he is positively antagonistic to them. A certain bitchiness in *Breakfast at Tiffany's* may be excused on the grounds that it fits the setting, but a reading of the nonfiction *The Muses Are Heard* suggests that it is still an essential part of Capote's equipment.

In Cold Blood, by bestowing its understanding in every quarter, emerges into a larger world. Here one feels that Capote attributes the sufferings of his victims not to stupid and malicious "other people" but to a more remote and mysterious principle—one closer to the source of genuine tragedy. The closing scene in Valley View Cemetery, while similar to the conclusion of *The Grass Harp,* resonates more widely and hence more deeply.

While Capote's vision of man's fate has grown larger and in that respect come closer to the stature of tragedy, it remains, even in *In Cold Blood,* essentially one of pathos. The tragic world view is an earth-centered one. But Capote's neoplatonists can be only exiles and victims in this world, for they have cast their lot in some other place. Even their power is eccentric, not geocentric. Speaking of the grotesque characters in the fiction of Capote, McCullers, and other Southern writers, Baldanza suggests that "on the philosophical level, the defects of the characters serve symbolically to represent the worthlessness of the material realm." Capote's portrayal of Perry Smith has, finally, the same effect as does the scene in which neighbors burn a pile of the Clutters' belongings and one of the men muses, "How was it possible that such effort, such plain virtue, could overnight be reduced to this—smoke, thinning as it rose and was received by the big, annihilating sky?" It is this strong current of evanescence tugging at a solid fabric of places, facts, and people that gives *In Cold Blood* its deepest intensity.

Dwight Macdonald has attacked *In Cold Blood* as nontragic and hence morally irresponsible and dramatically uninteresting. Though the six major characters are real, he says, none of them is a free agent in the central action and thus there is no significant conflict. We may, I think, agree with him on this last point without accepting his classification of the book as "prurient" in content and comparable in viewpoint to the sadomasochism of Alfred Hitchcock. On its deepest level *In Cold Blood* is not a tragic drama but a meditation on reality. Its immediate dramatic interest lies primarily in the sensational quality of the murders and the pursuit of the criminals, but Capote's approach to the events is not, as has been claimed, voyeuristic. In a *tour de force* deserving of much more respect than Macdonald accords it, Capote has transcended the *True Detective* genre story just as in **"The Duke in His Domain"** he transcended the *Photoplay*-type interview. (pp. 218-28)

William L. Nance, in his *The Worlds of Truman Capote,* Stein and Day, 1970, 256 p.

ALFRED KAZIN
(essay date 1971)

[A highly respected American literary critic, Kazin is best known for his essay collections *The Inmost*

Leaf (1955), *Contemporaries* (1962), and *On Native Grounds* (1942). In the following excerpt from a lecture revision that appeared in the *New York Review of Books* in 1971, he relates his impressions of Capote's "nonfiction novel," *In Cold Blood.*]

When Truman Capote explained, on the publication in 1965 of *In Cold Blood: The True Account of a Multiple Murder and Its Consequences,* that the book was really a "nonfiction novel," it was natural to take his praise of his meticulously factual and extraordinarily industrious record of research as the alibi of a novelist whose last novel, *Breakfast at Tiffany's,* had been slight, and who was evidently between novels. Capote clearly hungered to remain in the big league of novelists, so many of whom are unprofitable to everyone, even if he was now the author of a bestselling true thriller whose success was being arranged through every possible "medium" of American publicity. Capote is a novelist, novelists tend to be discouraged by the many current discourtesies to fiction. Clearly Capote wanted to keep his novelist's prestige but to rise above the novelist's struggle for survival. *In Cold Blood,* before one read it, promised by the nature of the American literary market to be another wow, a trick, a slick transposition from one realm to another, like the inevitable musical to be made out of the Sacco-Vanzetti case.

What struck me most in Capote's labeling his book a "nonfiction novel" was his honoring the profession of novelist. Novels seem more expendable these days than ever, but *novelist* is still any writer's notion of original talent. What interested me most about *In Cold Blood* after two readings—first in *The New Yorker* and then as a book—was that though it *was* journalism and soon gave away all its secrets, it had the ingenuity of fiction and it was fiction except for its ambition to be documentary. *In Cold Blood* brought to focus for me the problem of "fact writing" and its "treatment." There is a lot of "treatment" behind the vast amount of social fact that we get in a time of perpetual crisis. These books dramatize and add to the crisis, and we turn to them because they give a theme to the pervasive social anxiety, the concrete human instance that makes "literature."

In Cold Blood is an extremely stylized book that has a palpable design on our emotions. It works on us as a merely factual account never had to. It is so shapely and its revelations are so well timed that it becomes a "novel" in the form of fact. But how many great novels of crime and punishment are expressly based on fact without lapsing into "history"! *The Possessed* is based on the Nechayev case, *An American Tragedy* on the Chester Gillette case. What makes *In Cold Blood* formally a work of record rather than of invention? Because formally, at least, it is a documentary; based on six years of research and six thousand pages of notes, it retains this research in the text. Victims, murderers, witnesses and law officials appear under their own names and as their attested identities, in an actual or, as we say now, "real" Kansas town.

Why, then, did Capote honor himself by calling the book in any sense a "novel"? Why bring up the word at all? Because Capote depended on the record, was proud of his prodigious research, but was not content to make a work of record. (pp. 209-11)

Fiction as the most intensely selective creation of mood, tone, atmosphere, has always been Capote's natural aim as a writer. In *In Cold Blood* he practices this as a union of Art and Sympathy. His book, like so many "nonfiction" novels of our day, is saturated in sexual emotion. But unlike Mailer's reportage, Capote's "truthful account" is sympathetic to everyone, transparent in its affections to a degree—abstractly loving to Nancy Clutter, that all-American girl; respectfully amazed by Mr. Clutter, the prototype of what Middle America would like to be; helplessly sorry for Mrs. Clutter, a victim of the "square" morality directed at her without her knowing it. None of these people Capote knew—but he thought he did. Capote became extremely involved with the murderers, Perry Smith and Dick Hickock, whom he interviewed in prison endlessly for his book and came to know as we know people who fascinate us. He unconsciously made himself *seem* responsible for them. (pp. 211-12)

This fascinated sympathy with characters whom Capote visited sixty times in jail, whom he interviewed within an inch of their lives, up to the scaffold, is one of many powerful emotions on Capote's part that keeps the book "true" even when it most becomes a "novel." Capote shows himself deeply related to Alvin Dewey of the Kansas Bureau of Investigation, who more than any other agent on the case brought the murderers in. And as a result of *In Cold Blood* Capote, who had so successfully advertised his appearance on the jacket of *Other Voices, Other Rooms* in 1948, had by 1969 become an authority on crime and punishment and an adviser to law-and-order men like Governor Reagan. Capote was a natural celebrity from the moment he published his first book. *In Cold Blood* gave him the chance to instruct his countrymen on the depths of American disorder.

Yet with all these effects of *In Cold Blood* on Capote, the book itself goes back to the strains behind all Capote's work: a home and family destroyed within a context of hidden corruption, alienation and loneliness. Reading *In Cold Blood* one remembers the gypsy children left hungry and homeless in *The Grass Harp,* the orphans in *A Tree of Night, The Thanksgiving Visitor* and *A Christmas Memory,* the wild gropings of Holly Golightly in *Breakfast at Tiffany's* toward the "pastures of the sky." (pp. 212-13)

The victims in *In Cold Blood* were originally the

Clutters, but by the time the crime is traced to the killers and they are imprisoned, all seem equally victims. As in any novel, innocent and guilty require the same mental consideration from the author. In any event, innocence in our America is always tragic and in some sense to blame, as Mr. Clutter is, for incarnating a stability that now seems an "act." Capote is always sympathetic to Nancy Clutter, who laid out her best dress for the morrow just before she got murdered, and Nancy is the fragile incarnation of some distant feminine goodness, of all that might have been, who gets our automatic sympathy. But despite Capote's novelistic interest in building up Mr. Clutter as the archetypal square and Mrs. Clutter as a victim of the rigid lifestyle surrounding her, Capote's more urgent relationship is of course with "Perry and Dick." Almost to the end one feels that they might have been saved and their souls repaired.

This felt interest in "Perry and Dick" as persons whom Capote knew makes the book too personal for fiction but establishes it as a casebook for our time. The background of the tale is entirely one of damaged persons who wreak worse damage on others, but the surface couldn't be more banal. (pp. 213-14)

Terror can break out anywhere. The world is beyond reason but the imagination of fact, the particular detail, alone establishes credibility. It all happened, and it happened only this way. The emotion pervading the book is our helpless fascinated horror; there is a factuality with nothing beyond it in Perry's dwarfish legs, the similar imbalance in Dick's outwardly normal masculinity and his actual destructiveness. On what morsels of unexpected fact, summoned out of seeming nowhere by the author's digging alone, is *our* terror founded! On the way to rob the Clutters, Dick says:

"Let's count on eight, or even twelve. The only sure thing is every one of them has got to go. Ain't that what I promised you, honey—plenty of hair on them-those walls?"

The Clutters are stabbed, shot, strangled, between mawkish first-name American "friendliness" and bouncy identification with one another's weaknesses. Nancy couldn't be sweeter to her killers, Perry worries that Dick may rape her, Kenyon asks Perry not to harm his new chest by putting the knife on it. All this "understanding" between "insecure" people makes the crime all the more terrifying. It is the psychic weakness that removes so many people, taking their "weakness" for themselves, from any sense of justice. So much fluency of self-centered emotion makes crime central to our fear of each other today.

We may all have passing dreams of killing. But here are two who killed perversely, wantonly, pointlessly, yet with a horrid self-reference in the pitiful comforts they offered their victims that establishes their cringing viciousness. And the crime, like the greatest crimes of our time, is on record but remains enigmatic, "purposeless," self-defeating. The will to destroy is founded on what we insist are personal weaknesses, but which we cannot relate to what has been done. Even before the Hitler war was over, there were Nazis who said, "At least we have made others suffer." The fascination of Capote's book, the seeming truthfulness of it all, is that it brings us close, very close, to the victims, to the murderers, to the crime itself, as psychic evidence. Killing becomes the primal scene of our "feelings" that with all the timing of a clever novelist and all the emphatic detail brought in from thousands of interview hours by a prodigious listener, Capote presents to us as a case study of "truth" we can hold, study, understand.

As a novelist, dramatist, travel writer, memoirist, Capote had always been rather a specialist in internal mood, tone, "feeling"; now an action, the most terrible, was the center around which everything in his "truthful account" moved. He was ahead of his usual literary self, and the artfulness of the book is that it gets everyone to realize, possess and dominate this murder as a case of the seemingly psychological malignity behind so many crimes in our day. The book aims to give us this mental control over the frightening example of what is most uncontrolled in human nature.

Technically, this is accomplished by the four-part structure that takes us from the apparently pointless murder of four people to the hanging of the killers in the corner of a warehouse. The book is designed as a suspense story—why did Perry and Dick ever seek out the Clutters at all?—to which the author alone holds the answer. This comes only in Part III, when the book is more than half over. Each of the four sections is divided into cinematically visual scenes. There are eighty-six in the book as a whole; some are "shots" only a few lines long. Each of these scenes is a focusing, movie fashion, designed to put us visually as close as possible now to the Clutters, now to Perry and Dick, until the unexplained juncture between them is explained in Part III. Until then, we are shifted to many different times and places in which we see Perry and Dick suspended, as it were, in a world without meaning, for we are not yet up to the explanation that Capote has reserved in order to keep up novelistic interest. Yet this explanation—in jail a pal had put the future killers on to the Clutters and the supposed wealth in the house—is actually, when it comes, meant to anchor the book all the more firmly in the world of "fact"—of the public world expressed as documented conflict between symbolic individuals. It was the unbelievable squareness of the Clutters as a family that aroused and fascinated the murderers. The book opens on Kansas as home and family, ends on Alvin Dewey at the family graveside,

Then, starting home, he walked toward the trees, and under them leaving behind him the big sky, the whisper of wind voices in the wind-bent wheat.

The circle of illusory stability (which we have *seen* destroyed) has closed in on itself again.

Capote's book raises many questions about its presumption as a whole, for many of the "fact" scenes in it are as vivid as single shots in a movie can be—and that make us wonder about the meaning of so much easy expert coverage by the writer-as-camera. ("A movie pours into us," John Updike has said. "It fills us like milk being poured into a glass.") One of the best bits is when the jurors, looking at photographs of the torn bodies and tortured faces of the Clutters, for the first time come into possession of the horror, find themselves focusing on it in the very courtroom where the boyishness and diffidence of the defendants and the boringly circular protocol of a trial have kept up the jurors' distance from the crime. (pp. 214-17)

The reason for the "nonfiction novel" (and documentary plays, movies, art works) is that it reproduces events that cannot be discharged through one artist's imagination. Tragedy exists in order to be assimilated by us as individual fate, for we can identify with another's death. Death in round numbers is by definition the death of strangers, and that is one of the outrages to the human imagination in the killing after killing which we "know all about," and to which we cannot respond. Capote worked so long on this case—"his" case—because to the "fact writer" reporting is a way of showing that *he knows.* The killing of the Clutter family was not "personal," as even Gatsby could have admitted about *his* murderer's mistake in killing him. History is more and more an example of "accident." The Clutters were there just for their killers to kill them. (pp. 218-19)

Alfred Kazin, "The Imagination of Fact: Capote to Mailer," in his *Bright Book of Life: American Novelists & Storytellers from Hemingway to Mailer,* Atlantic-Little, Brown, 1973, pp. 207-42.

SOURCES FOR FURTHER STUDY

Aldridge, John W. "Capote and Buechner: The Escape into Otherness." In his *After the Lost Generation: A Critical Study of the Writers of Two Wars*, pp. 194-230. New York: McGraw-Hill Book Company, Inc., 1951.

> Early assessment of *Other Voices, Other Rooms* in which Aldridge expresses disappointment with Capote's potential for development as a writer.

Allen, Walter. "War and Post War: American." In his *The Modern Novel in Britain and the United States*, pp. 293-332. New York: E. P. Dutton & Co., Inc., 1964.

> Briefly identifies aspects of the contemporary American novel evident in Capote's fiction prior to *In Cold Blood*.

Capote, Truman. "The Guts of a Butterfly." *Observer* (27 March 1966): 21.

> Angry reply to Kenneth Tynan's accusation that Capote did not do all he could to save Hickock and Smith, the killers portrayed in *In Cold Blood* [see citation below].

Garson, Helen. *Truman Capote.* New York: Frederick Ungar, 1980, 210 p.

> Comprehensive critical survey.

Tompkins, Philip K. "In Cold Fact." *Esquire* LXV, No. 6 (June 1966): 125, 127, 166-68, 170-71.

> While insisting that *In Cold Blood* as a novel is "a work of art," Tompkins identifies several factual inaccuracies he discovered while investigating Capote's claims to documentary accuracy.

Tynan, Kenneth. "The Coldest of Blood." In his *Tynan Right & Left: Plays, Films, People, Places, and Events*, pp. 441-46. Atheneum, 1967.

> Article originally published in the *Observer* attacking Capote for doing "less than he might have" to save Hickock and Smith, the executed killers portrayed in *In Cold Blood* [for Capote's reply, see citation above].

Lewis Carroll

1832-1898

(Pseudonym of Charles Lutwidge Dodgson) English novelist, poet, satirist, and essayist.

INTRODUCTION

A clergyman, mathematician, and logician, the Reverend Charles Lutwidge Dodgson is one of the foremost writers of fantasy in literary history. He is best known as Lewis Carroll, the creator of *Alice's Adventures in Wonderland* (1865) and *Through the Looking-Glass, and What Alice Found There* (1872), works considered among the greatest and most influential children's books ever written in English. Lauded as a genius who fused his eccentric personal characteristics and opinions with a genuine love of children and childhood, he helped liberate juvenile literature from its history of didacticism and overt moralizing. The *Alice* books have a value beyond their appeal to children. They have also been interpreted as political satire and are highly esteemed as sophisticated treatises on mathematics and logic.

Born in Daresbury, Cheshire, Dodgson was the eldest son of a clergyman in the Church of England. He began writing humorous poetry at an early age and displayed a talent for mathematics. He was educated at home and at schools in Richmond and Rugby and began studies at Oxford when he was 18. Two and a half years later he was made a fellow of Christ Church, Oxford, and commenced lecturing in mathematics. In 1856 he began writing humorous pieces for journals under the pen name Lewis Carroll, which was based on Latin translations of his first and second names. He also met Alice Liddell, the daughter of the dean of Christ Church, who later served as the model for the protagonist of the *Alice* books. Four years later his first mathematical treatise was published. He remained at Oxford for the rest of his life, lecturing until 1881 and writing a variety of scholarly works on mathematics and logic as well as humorous fiction for children. He died in 1898.

The *Alice* books grew out of an extemporaneous

story Dodgson told to entertain Alice Liddell and her two sisters on a boating trip in 1862. When Alice pressed Dodgson to write down his tale for her, he transcribed and illustrated it as *Alice's Adventures Under Ground.* He later expanded this text to form *Alice's Adventures in Wonderland* and arranged for John Tenniel, a popular artist who was a political cartoonist for the magazine *Punch,* to illustrate it. The success of *Alice's Adventures in Wonderland* prompted Dodgson to write a sequel, *Through the Looking-Glass,* which Tenniel also illustrated. These two works, which are usually treated as a whole and are loosely structured around a pack of cards and a game of chess, describe how a curious seven-year-old girl enters two dream worlds: one she enters by falling down a rabbit hole, the other by passing through a mirror. Through her experience, which are frustrating as well as wonderful, Alice meets a host of fascinating and unusual characters, both human and anthropomorphic. As Alice meets these creatures, she is drawn into unfamiliar societies that challenge her knowledge and beliefs. She becomes involved in a series of amusing yet often disagreeable events that test her perceptions of time, space, form, and sense. Surprising and terrifying, yet with their own inherent logic, the worlds in which Alice finds herself are revealed through her reactions to them. Each book concludes with Alice ending her dream after becoming disgusted with the insanity, selfishness, and cruelty she has encountered. Critics have noted Dodgson's playful exploration of the paradoxes of thought and language; poet W. H. Auden commented: "[in the *Alice* books], one of the most important and powerful characters is not a person but the English language. Alice, who had hitherto supposed that words were passive objects, discovers that they have a life and will of their own. When she tries to remember poems she has learned, new lines come into her head unbidden and, when she thinks she knows what a word means, it turns out to mean something else."

Many critics believe that Dodgson's later works, with the possible exception of *The Hunting of the Snark: An Agony, in Eight Fits* (1876), lack the merits of the *Alice* books. His mathematical treatises are noted for their occasional humor, but they added little to scholarship, critics have claimed. Aside from his literary accomplishments, Dodgson also developed an interest in photography. His work in this medium is among the most important of the nineteenth century, although his many portraits of nude children, combined with his intimate friendships with young girls, have aroused considerable speculation.

Early reviews of the *Alice* books concentrated on Dodgson's magnificent invention and his skill as a linguist, parodist, and literary stylist. After his death, critics analyzed the stories from many points of view—political, philosophical, metaphysical, and psychoanalytic—often evaluating the tales as products of Dodgson's neuroses and as reactions to Victorian culture. Because of the nightmarish qualities of Alice's adventures and their violent, even sadistic, elements, a few commentators have suggested that the *Alice* books are inappropriate for children; as a result, the stories are not always enjoyed by the audience for whom they were apparently intended. However, Dodgson is consistently applauded as one of the world's foremost writers of nonsense, an author who successfully combined the logical with the illogical in two timeless novels that have fascinated children and adults alike.

(For further information about Dodgson's life and works, see *Children's Literature Review,* Vols. 2, 18; *Dictionary of Literary Biography,* Vol. 18: *Victorian Novelists After 1885;* and *Nineteenth-Century Literature Criticism,* Vol. 2. For related discussion, see the entries on Sir John Tenniel in *Children's Literature Review,* Vol. 18; *Contemporary Authors,* Vol. 111; and *Something about the Author,* Vol. 27.)

CRITICAL COMMENTARY

WILLIAM EMPSON

(essay date 1935)

[Empson was an English critic, poet, and editor. He is best known as the author of *Seven Types of Ambiguity* (1930), a seminal contribution to the formalist school of New Criticism. The following excerpt is from his essay "Alice in Wonderland: The Child as Swain." Here, he examines the *Alice* books from a psychoanalytic perspective. This essay is generally

considered one of the most important examples of twentieth-century Carrollian scholarship.]

It must seem a curious thing that there has been so little serious criticism of the Alices, and that so many critics, with so militant and eager an air of good taste, have explained that they would not think of attempting it. . . . There seems to be a feeling that real criticism would involve psychoanalysis, and that the results would be so improper as to destroy the atmosphere of

Principal Works

A Syllabus of Plane Geometry (essay) 1860

Alice's Adventures in Wonderland [as Lewis Carroll] (novel) 1865

The Dynamics of a Particle (satire) 1865

Phantasmagoria, and Other Poems [as Lewis Carroll] (poetry) 1869

The New Belfry [as D.C.L.] (satire) 1872

*Through the Looking-Glass, and What Alice Found There [as Lewis Carroll] (novel) 1872; also published as Lewis Carroll's Through the Looking-Glass, and What Alice Found There [expanded edition], 1983

The Hunting of the Snark: An Agony, in Eight Fits [as Lewis Carroll] (poetry) 1876

Euclid and His Modern Rivals (essay) 1879

Rhyme? and Reason? [as Lewis Carroll] (poetry) 1883

†Alice's Adventures Under Ground (novel) 1886

Curiosa Mathematica. Part I: A New Theory of Parallels (essay) 1888

Sylvie and Bruno [as Lewis Carroll] (novel) 1889

Curiosa Mathematica. Part II: Pillow Problems Thought Out during Wakeful Hours (essay) 1893

Sylvie and Bruno Concluded [as Lewis Carroll] (novel) 1893

The Collected Verse of Lewis Carroll (poetry) 1929

The Complete Works of Lewis Carroll (novels, poetry, essays, letters, and rules to games) 1936

The Diaries of Lewis Carroll. 2 vols. (diaries) 1953

The Annotated Alice: Alice's Adventures in Wonderland & Through the Looking-Glass (novels) 1960

The Annotated Snark (poetry) 1962

The Letters of Lewis Carroll (letters) 1979

*The expanded edition of this work contains the "Wasp in a Wig" episode not included in the original publication.

†This work is a facsimile of the 1862 manuscript that later became Alice's Adventures in Wonderland.

the books altogether. Dodgson was too conscious a writer to be caught out so easily. . . . The books are so frankly about growing up that there is no great discovery in translating them into Freudian terms; it seems only the proper exegesis of a classic even where it would be a shock to the author. On the whole the results of the analysis, when put into drawing-room language, are his conscious opinions; and if there was no other satisfactory outlet for his feelings but the special one fixed in his books the same is true in a degree of any original artist. I shall use psycho-analysis where it seems relevant, and feel I had better begin by saying what use it is supposed to be. Its business here is not to discover a neurosis peculiar to Dodgson. The essential idea behind the books is a shift onto the child, which Dodgson did not invent, of the obscure tradition of pastoral. The formula is now '*child*-become-judge,' and if Dodgson identifies himself with the child so does the writer of the primary sort of pastoral with his magnified version of the swain. (pp. 253-54)

Pope engraved a couplet 'on the collar of a dog which I gave to His Royal Highness'—a friendly act as from one gentleman to another resident in the neighborhood.

I am his Highness' dog at Kew.
Pray tell me, sir, whose dog are you?

Presumably Frederick himself would be the first to read it. The joke carries a certain praise for the underdog; the point is not that men are slaves but that they find it suits them and remain good-humoured. The dog is proud of being the prince's dog and expects no one to

take offence at the question. There is also a hearty independence in its lack of respect for the inquirer. Pope took this from Sir William Temple, where it is said by a fool: 'I am the Lord Chamberlain's fool. And whose are you?' was his answer to the nobleman. It is a neat case of the slow shift of this sentiment from fool to rogue to child.

Alice, I think, is more of a 'little rogue' than it is usual to say, or than Dodgson himself thought in later years:

loving as a dog . . . and gentle as a fawn; then courteous,—courteous to *all*, high or low, grand or grotesque, King or Caterpillar . . . trustful, with an absolute trust. . . .

and so on. It depends what you expect of a child of seven.

. . . she had quite a long argument with the Lory, who at last turned sulky, and would only say, 'I am older than you, and must know better'; and this Alice would not allow without knowing how old it was, and as the Lory positively refused to tell its age, there was no more to be said.

Alice had to be made to speak up to bring out the points—here the point is a sense of the fundamental oddity of life given by the fact that different animals become grown-up at different ages; but still if you accept the Lory as a grown-up this is rather a pert child. She is often the underdog speaking up for itself.

A quite separate feeling about children . . . may be seen in its clearest form in Wordsworth and Coleridge; it is the whole point of the *Ode to Intimations* and even of *We are Seven*. The child has not yet been put wrong by civilisation, and all grown-ups have been. It may well be true that Dodgson envied the child because it was sexless, and Wordsworth because he knew that he was destroying his native poetry by the smugness of his life, but neither theory explains why this feeling about children arose when it did and became so general. . . . It depends on a feeling, whatever may have caused that in its turn, that no way of building up character, no intellectual system, can bring out all that is inherent in the human spirit, and therefore that there is more in the child than any man has been able to keep. (The child is a microcosm like Donne's world, and Alice too is a stoic.) This runs through all Victorian and Romantic literature; the world of the adult made it hard to be an artist, and they kept a sort of tap-root going down to their experience as children. Artists like Wordsworth and Coleridge, who accepted this fact and used it, naturally come to seem the most interesting and in a way the most sincere writers of the period. Their idea of the child, that it is in the right relation to Nature, not dividing what should be unified, that its intuitive judgment contains what poetry and philosophy must spend their time labouring to recover, was accepted by Dodgson and a main part of his feeling. He quotes Wordsworth on this point in the 'Easter Greeting'—the child feels its life in every limb; Dodgson advises it, with an infelicitous memory of the original poem, to give its attention to death from time to time. That the dream books are

> Like Pilgrim's withered wreaths of flowers
>   Plucked in a far-off land

is a fine expression of Wordsworth's sense both of the poetry of childhood and of his advancing sterility. (pp. 259-61)

Dodgson will only go half-way with the sentiment of the child's unity with nature, and has another purpose for his heroine; she is the free and independent mind. Not that this is contradictory; because she is right about life she is independent from all the other characters who are wrong. But it is important to him because it enables him to clash the Wordsworth sentiments with the other main tradition about children derived from rogue-sentiment. (p. 262)

One might say that the Alices differ from other versions of pastoral in lacking the sense of glory. Normally the idea of including all sorts of men in yourself brings in an idea of reconciling yourself with nature and therefore gaining power over it. The Alices are more self-protective; the dream cuts out the real world and the delicacy of the mood is felt to cut out the lower classes. This is true enough, but when Humpty Dumpty says that glory means a nice knock-down argument he is not far from the central feeling of the book. There

is a real feeling of isolation and yet just that is taken as the source of power. (pp. 262-63)

The talking animal convention and the changes of relative size appear in so different a children's book as *Gulliver;* they evidently make some direct appeal to the child whatever more sophisticated ideas are piled onto them. Children feel at home with animals conceived as human; the animal can be made affectionate without its making serious emotional demands on them, does not want to educate them, is at least unconventional in the sense that it does not impose its conventions, and does not make a secret of the processes of nature. So the talking animals here are a child-world; the rule about them is that they are always friendly though childishly frank to Alice while she is small, and when she is big (suggesting grown-up) always opposed to her, or by her, or both. But talking animals in children's books had been turned to didactic purposes ever since Aesop; the schoolmastering tone in which the animals talk nonsense to Alice is partly a parody of this—they are really childish but try not to look it. On the other hand, this tone is so supported by the way they can order her about, the firm and surprising way their minds work, the abstract topics they work on, the useless rules they accept with so much conviction, that we take them as real grown-ups contrasted with unsophisticated childhood. 'The grown-up world is as odd as the childworld, and both are a dream.' This ambivalence seems to correspond to Dodgson's own attitude to children; he, like Alice, wanted to get the advantages of being childish and grown-up at once. . . . He made a success of the process, and it seems clear that it did none of the little girls any harm, but one cannot help cocking one's eye at it as a way of life. (pp. 265-66)

The changes of size are more complex. In *Gulliver* they are the impersonal eye; to change size and nothing else makes you feel 'this makes one see things as they are in themselves.' It excites Wonder but of a scientific sort. Swift used it for satire on science or from a horrified interest in it, and to give a sort of scientific authority to his deductions, that men seen as small are spiritually petty and seen as large physically loathsome. And it is the small observer, like the child, who does least to alter what he sees and therefore sees most truly. . . . Children like to think of being so small that they could hide from grown-ups and so big that they could control them, and to do this dramatises the great topic of growing up, which both Alices keep to consistently. In the same way the charm of Jabberwocky is that it is a code language, the language with which grown-ups hide things from children or children from grown-ups. Also the words are such good tongue-gestures, in Sir Richard Paget's phrase, that they seem to carry their own meaning; this carries a hint of the paradox that the conventions are natural.

Both books also keep to the topic of death—the

first two jokes about death in *Wonderland* come on pages 3 and 4—and for the child this may be a natural connection; I remember believing I should have to die before I grew up, and thinking the prospect very disagreeable. There seems to be a connection in Dodgson's mind between the death of childhood and the development of sex, which might be pursued into many of the details of the books. Alice will die if the Red King wakes up, partly because she is a dream-product of the author and partly because the pawn is put back in its box at the end of the game. He is the absent husband of the Red Queen who is a governess, and the end of the book comes when Alice defeats the Red Queen and 'mates' the King. Everything seems to break up because she arrives at a piece of *knowledge*, that all the poems are about fish. I should say the idea was somehow at work at the end of *Wonderland* too. The trial is meant to be a mystery; Alice is told to leave the court, as if a child ought not to hear the evidence, and yet they expect her to give evidence herself. . . . I think Dodgson felt it was important that Alice should be innocent of all knowledge of what the Knave of Hearts . . . is likely to have been doing, and also important that she should not be told she is innocent. That is why the king, always a well-intentioned man, is embarrassed. At the same time Dodgson feels that Alice is right in thinking 'it doesn't matter a bit' which word the jury write down; she is too stable in her detachment to be embarrassed, these things will not interest her, and in a way she includes them all in herself. And it is the refusal to let her stay that makes her revolt and break the dream. It is tempting to read an example of this idea into the poem that introduces the *Looking-Glass.*

> Come, hearken then, ere voice of dread,
>   With bitter summons laden,
>   Shall summon to unwelcome bed
>   A melancholy maiden.

After all the marriage-bed was more likely to be the end of the maiden than the grave, and the metaphor firmly implied treats them as identical.

The last example is obviously more a joke against Dodgson than anything else, and though the connection between death and the development of sex is I think at work it is not the main point of the conflict about growing up. Alice is given a magical control over her growth by the traditionally symbolic caterpillar, a creature which has to go through a sort of death to become grown-up, and then seems a more spiritual creature. It refuses to agree with Alice that this process is at all peculiar, and clearly her own life will be somehow like it, but the main idea is not its development of sex. The butterfly implied may be the girl when she is 'out' or her soul when in heaven, to which she is now nearer than she will be when she is 'out'; she must walk to it by walking away from it. Alice knows several reasons

why she should object to growing up, and does not at all like being an obvious angel, a head out of contact with its body that has to come down from the sky, and gets mistaken for the Paradisal serpent of the knowledge of good and evil, and by the pigeon of the Annunciation, too. But she only makes herself smaller for reasons of tact or proportion; the triumphant close of *Wonderland* is that she has outgrown her fancies and can afford to wake and despise them. The *Looking-Glass* is less of a dream-product, less concentrated on the child's situation, and (once started) less full of changes of size; but it has the same end; the governess shrinks to a kitten when Alice has grown from a pawn to a queen, and can shake her. Both these clearly stand for becoming grown-up and yet in part are a revolt against grown-up behaviour; there is the same ambivalence as about the talking animals. Whether children often find this symbolism as interesting as Carroll did is another thing; there are recorded cases of tears at such a betrayal of the reality of the story. I remember feeling that the ends of the books were a sort of necessary assertion that the grown-up world was after all the proper one; one did not object to that in principle, but would no more turn to those parts from preference than to the 'Easter Greeting to Every Child that Loves Alice' (Gothic type).

To make the dream-story from which *Wonderland* was elaborated seem Freudian one has only to tell

Alice peering into the Looking-Glass.

it. A fall through a deep hole into the secrets of Mother Earth produces a new enclosed soul wondering who it is, what will be its position in the world, and how it can get out. It is in a long low hall, part of the palace of the Queen of Hearts (a neat touch), from which it can only get out to the fresh air and the fountains through a hole frighteningly too small. Strange changes, caused by the way it is nourished there, happen to it in this place, but always when it is big it cannot get out and when it is small it is not allowed to; for one thing, being a little girl, it has no key. The nightmare theme of the birth-trauma, that she grows too big for the room and is almost crushed by it, is not only used here but repeated more painfully after she seems to have got out; the rabbit sends her sternly into its house and some food there makes her grow again. In Dodgson's own drawing of Alice when cramped into the room with one foot up the chimney, kicking out the hateful thing that tries to come down (she takes away its pencil when it is a juror), she is much more obviously in the foetus position than in Tenniel's. The White Rabbit is Mr. Spooner to whom the spoonerisms happened, an undergraduate in 1862, but its business here is as a pet for children which they may be allowed to breed. Not that the clearness of the framework makes the interpretation simple; Alice peering through the hole into the garden may be wanting a return to the womb as well as an escape from it; she is fond, we are told, of taking both sides of an argument when talking to herself, and the whole book balances between the luscious nonsense-world of fantasy and the ironic nonsense-world of fact.

I said that the sea of tears she swims in was the amniotic fluid, which is much too simple. You may take it as Lethe in which the souls were bathed before rebirth (and it is their own tears; they forget, as we forget our childhood, through the repression of pain) or as the 'solution' of an intellectual contradiction through Intuition and a return to the Unconscious. Anyway it is a sordid image made pretty; one need not read Dodgson's satirical verses against babies to see how much he would dislike a child wallowing in its tears in real life. (pp. 267-72)

The symbolic completeness of Alice's experience is I think important. She runs the whole gamut; she is a father in getting down the hole, a foetus at the bottom, and can only be born by becoming a mother and producing her own amniotic fluid. Whether his mind played the trick of putting this into the story or not he has the feelings that would correspond to it. A desire to include all sexuality in the girl child, the least obviously sexed of human creatures, the one that keeps its sex in the safest place, was an important part of their fascination for him. He is partly imagining himself as the girl-child (with these comforting characteristics) partly as its father (these together make *it* a father)

partly as its lover—so it might be a mother—but then of course it is clever and detached enough to do everything for itself. . . . So far from its dependence, the child's independence is the important thing, and the theme behind that is the self-centred emotional life imposed by the detached intelligence. (pp. 272-73)

The Gnat gives a . . . touching picture of Dodgson; he treats nowhere more directly of his actual relations with the child. He feels he is liable to nag at it, as a gnat would, and the gnat turns out, as he is, to be alarmingly big as a friend for the child, but at first it sounds tiny because he means so little to her. It tries to amuse her by rather frightening accounts of other dangerous insects, other grown-ups. It is reduced to tears by the melancholy of its own jokes, which it usually can't bear to finish; only if Alice had made them, as it keeps egging her on to do, would they be at all interesting. That at least would show the child had paid some sort of attention, and he could go away and repeat them to other people. The desire to have jokes made all the time, he feels, is a painful and obvious confession of spiritual discomfort, and the freedom of Alice from such a feeling makes her unapproachable. . . . He is afraid that even so innocent a love as his, like all love, may be cruel, and yet it is she who is able to hurt him, if only through his vanity. The implications of these few pages are so painful that the ironical calm of the close, when she kills it, seems delightfully gay and strong. The Gnat is suggesting to her that she would like to remain purely a creature of Nature and stay in the wood where there are no names.

'. . . That's a joke. I wish *you* had made it.'

'Why do you wish *I* had made it?' Alice asked. 'It's a very bad one.'

But the Gnat only sighed deeply, while two large tears came rolling down its cheeks.

'You shouldn't make jokes,' Alice said, 'if it makes you so unhappy.'

Then came another of those melancholy little sighs, and this time the poor Gnat really seemed to have sighed itself away, for, when Alice looked up, there was nothing whatever to be seen on the twig, and, as she was getting quite chilly with sitting so long, she got up and walked on.

The overpunctuation and the flat assonance of 'long—on' add to the effect. There is something charmingly prim and well-meaning about the way she sweeps aside the feelings that she can't deal with. One need not suppose that Dodgson ever performed this scene, which he can imagine so clearly, but there is too much self-knowledge here to make the game of psychoanalysis seem merely good fun.

The scene in which the Duchess has become

friendly to Alice at the garden-party shows Alice no longer separate from her creator; it is clear that Dodgson would be as irritated as she is by the incident, and is putting himself in her place. The obvious way to read it is as the middle-aged woman trying to flirt with the chaste young man. . . . [The] Duchess seems to take the view of the political economists, that the greatest public good is produced by the greatest private selfishness. All this talk about 'morals' makes Alice suspicious; also she is carrying a flamingo, a pink bird with a long neck. 'The chief difficulty Alice found at first was in managing her flamingo . . . it *would* twist itself round and look up in her face.'

> 'I dare say you're wondering why I don't put my arm round your waist,' the Duchess said after a pause: 'the reason is, that I'm doubtful about the temper of your flamingo. Shall I try the experiment?'
>
> 'He might bite,' Alice cautiously replied, not feeling at all anxious to have the experiment tried.
>
> 'Very true,' said the Duchess: 'flamingoes and mustard both bite. And the moral of that is—"Birds of a feather flock together."'

Mustard may be classed with the pepper that made her 'ill-tempered' when she had so much of it in the soup, so that flamingoes and mustard become the desires of the two sexes. No doubt Dodgson would be indignant at having this meaning read into his symbols, but the meaning itself, if he had been intending to talk about the matter, is just what he would have wished to say. (pp. 274-77)

This sort of 'analysis' is a peep at machinery; the question for criticism is what is done with the machine. The purpose of a dream on the Freudian theory is simply to keep you in an undisturbed state so that you can go on sleeping; in the course of this practical work you may produce something of more general value, but not only of one sort. Alice has, I understand, become a patron saint of the Surrealists, but they do not go in for Comic Primness, a sort of reserve of force, which is her chief charm. Wyndham Lewis avoided putting her beside Proust and Lorelei to be danced on as a debilitating child-cult (though she is a bit of pragmatist too); the present-day reader is more likely to complain of her complacence. In this sort of child-cult the child, though a means of imaginative escape, becomes the critic; Alice is the most reasonable and responsible person in the book. This is meant as charmingly pathetic about her as well as satire about her elders, and there is some implication that the sane man can take no other view of the world, even for controlling it, than the child does; but this is kept a good distance from sentimental infantilism. There is always some doubt about the meaning of a man who says he wants to be like a child, because he may want to be like it in having fresh and vivid feel-

ings and senses, in not knowing, expecting, or desiring evil, in not having an analytical mind, in having no sexual desires recognisable as such, or out of a desire to be mothered and evade responsibility. He is usually mixing them up—Christ's praise of children, given perhaps for reasons I have failed to list, has made it a respected thing to say, and it has been said often and loosely— but he can make his own mixture; Lewis's invective hardly shows which he is attacking. The praise of the child in the Alices mainly depends on a distaste not only for sexuality but for all the distortions of vision that go with a rich emotional life; the opposite idea needs to be set against this, that you can only understand people or even things by having such a life in yourself to be their mirror; but the idea itself is very respectable. So far as it is typical of the scientist the books are an expression of the scientific attitude (*e.g.* the bread-and-butter fly) or a sort of satire on it that treats it as inevitable.

The most obvious aspect of the complacence is the snobbery. It is clear that Alice is not only a very well-brought-up but a very well-to-do little girl; if she has grown into Mabel, so that she will have to go and live in that pooky little house and have next to no toys to play with, she will refuse to come out of her rabbit-hole at all. One is only surprised that she is allowed to meet Mabel. All through the books odd objects of luxury are viewed rather as Wordsworth viewed moun-

Alice through the Looking-Glass.

tains; meaningless, but grand and irremovable; objects of myth. The whiting, the talking leg of mutton, the soup-tureen, the tea-tray in the sky, are obvious examples. The shift from the idea of the child's unity with nature is amusingly complete; a mere change in the objects viewed makes it at one with the conventions. But this is still not far from Wordsworth, who made his mountains into symbols of the stable and moral society living among them. In part the joke of this stands for the sincerity of the child that criticises the folly of convention, but Alice is very respectful to conventions and interested to learn new ones; indeed the discussions about the rules of the game of conversation, those stern comments on the isolation of humanity, put the tone so strongly in favour of the conventions that one feels there is nothing else in the world. . . . Dodgson was always shocked to find that his little girls had appetites, because it made them seem less pure. The passage about the bread-and-butter fly brings this out more frankly, with something of the wilful grimness of Webster. It was a creature of such high refinement that it could only live on weak tea with cream in it (tea being the caller's meal, sacred to the fair, with nothing gross about it).

A new difficulty came into Alice's head.

'Supposing it couldn't find any?' she suggested.

'Then it would die, of course.'

'But that must happen very often,' Alice remarked thoughtfully.

'It always happens,' said the Gnat.

After this, Alice was silent for a minute or two, pondering.

There need be no gloating over the child's innocence here, as in Barrie; anybody might ponder. Alice has just suggested that flies burn themselves to death in candles out of a martyr's ambition to become Snapdragon flies. The talk goes on to losing one's name, which is the next stage on her journey, and brings freedom but is like death; the girl may lose her personality by growing up into the life of convention, and her virginity (like her surname) by marriage; or she may lose her 'good name' when she loses the conventions 'in the woods'—the animals, etc., there have no names because they are out of reach of the controlling reason; or when she develops sex she must neither understand nor name her feelings. The Gnat is weeping and Alice is afraid of the wood but determined to go on. 'It always dies of thirst' or 'it always dies in the end, as do we all'; 'the life of highest refinement is the most deathly, yet what else is one to aim at when life is so brief, and when there is so little in it of any value.' A certain ghoulishness in the atmosphere of this, of which the tight-lacing may have been

a product or partial cause, comes out very strongly in Henry James; the decadents pounced on it for their own purposes but could not put more death-wishes into it than these respectables had done already.

The blend of child-cult and snobbery that Alice shares with Oscar Wilde is indeed much more bouncing and cheerful; the theme here is that it is proper for the well-meaning and innocent girl to be worldly, because she, like the world, should know the value of her condition. 'When we were girls we were brought up to know nothing, and very interesting it was'; 'mamma, whose ideas on education are remarkably strict, has brought me up to be extremely short-sighted; so do you mind my looking at you through my glasses?' This joke seems to have come in after the Restoration dramatists as innocence recovered its social value; there are touches in Farquhar and it is strong in the *Beggar's Opera*. . . . [Even] *Wonderland* contains straight satire. The Mock Turtle was taught at school

> Reeling and Writhing, of course, to begin with, and then the different branches of Arithmetic— Ambition, Distraction, Uglification, and Derision . . . Mystery, ancient and modern, with Seaography; then Drawling—the Drawling-master used to come once a week; *he* taught us Drawling, Stretching, and Fainting in Coils.

Children are to enjoy the jokes as against education, grown-ups as against a smart and too expensive education. Alice was not one of the climbers taught like this, and remarks firmly elsewhere that manners are not learnt from lessons. But she willingly receives social advice like 'curtsey while you're thinking what to say, it saves time,' and the doctrine that you must walk away from a queen if you really want to meet her has more point when said of the greed of the climber than of the unselfseeking curiosity of the small girl. Or it applies to both, and allows the climber a sense of purity and simplicity; I think this was a source of charm whether Dodgson meant it or not. Alice's own social assumptions are more subtle and all-pervading; she always seems to raise the tone of the company she enters, and to find this all the easier because the creatures are so rude to her. A central idea here is that the perfect lady can gain all the advantages of contempt without soiling herself by expressing or even feeling it. (pp. 277-83)

[Alice] is almost too sure that she is good and right. The grown-up is egged on to imitate her not as a privileged decadent but as a privileged eccentric, a Victorian figure that we must be sorry to lose. The eccentric though kind and noble would be alarming from the strength of his virtues if he were less funny. . . . (pp. 284-85)

The qualities held in so subtle a suspension in Alice are shown in full blast in the two queens. It is clear that this sort of moral superiority involves a painful isolation, similar to those involved in the intellectual way of life and the life of chastity, which are here associated with it. (p. 285)

Death is never far out of sight in the books. (p. 287)

Once at least in each book a cry of loneliness goes up from Alice at the oddity beyond sympathy or communication of the world she has entered—whether that in which the child is shut by weakness, or the adult by the renunciations necessary both for the ideal and the worldly way of life (the strength of the snobbery is to imply that these are the same). (p. 290)

[About] all the rationalism of Alice and her acquaintances there hangs a suggestion that there are after all questions of pure thought, academic thought whose altruism is recognised and paid for, thought meant only for the upper classes to whom the conventions are in any case natural habit; like that suggestion that the scientist is sure to be a gentleman and has plenty of space which is the fascination of Kew Gardens. (p. 291)

The Queen is a very inclusive figure. 'Looking before and after' with the plaintive tone of universal altruism she lives chiefly backwards, in history; the necessary darkness of growth, the mysteries of self-knowledge, the self-contradictions of the will, the antinomies of philosophy, the very Looking-Glass itself, impose this; nor is it mere weakness to attempt to resolve them only in the direct impulse of the child. Gathering the more dream-rushes her love for man becomes the more universal, herself the more like a porcupine. Knitting with more and more needles she tries to control life by a more and more complex intellectual apparatus—the 'progress' of Herbert Spencer; any one shelf of the shop is empty, but there is always something very interesting—the 'atmosphere' of the place is so interesting—which moves up as you look at it from shelf to shelf; there is jam only in the future and our traditional past, and the test made by Alice, who sent value through the ceiling as if it were quite used to it, shows that progress can never reach value, because its habitation and name is heaven. The Queen's scheme of social reform, which is to punish those who are not respectable before their crimes are committed, seems to be another of these jokes about progress:

'But if you *hadn't* done them,' the Queen said, 'that would have been better still; better, and better, and better!' Her voice went higher with each 'better' till it got to quite a squeak at last.

There is a similar attack in the Walrus and the Carpenter, who are depressed by the spectacle of unimproved nature and engage in charitable work among oysters. The Carpenter is a Castle and the Walrus, who could eat so many more because he was crying behind his handkerchief, was a Bishop, in the scheme at the beginning of the book. But in saying so one must be struck by the depth at which the satire is hidden; the queerness of the incident and the characters takes on a Wordsworthian grandeur and aridity, and the landscape defined by the tricks of facetiousness takes on the remote and staring beauty of the ideas of the insane. It is odd to find that Tenniel went on to illustrate Poe in the same manner; Dodgson is often doing what Poe wanted to do, and can do it the more easily because he can safely introduce the absurd. The Idiot Boy of Wordsworth is too milky a moonlit creature to be at home with Nature as she was deplored by the Carpenter, and much of the technique of the rudeness of the Mad Hatter has been learned from Hamlet. It is the ground-bass of this kinship with insanity, I think, that makes it so clear that the books are not trifling, and the cool courage with which Alice accepts madmen that gives them their strength.

This talk about the snobbery of the Alices may seem a mere attack, but a little acid may help to remove the slime with which they have been encrusted. The two main ideas behind the snobbery, that virtue and intelligence are alike lonely, and that good manners are therefore important though an absurd confession of human limitations, do not depend on a local class system; they would be recognised in a degree by any tolerable society. And if in a degree their opposites must also be recognised, so they are here; there are solid enough statements of the shams of altruism and convention and their horrors when genuine; it is the forces of this conflict that make a clash violent enough to end both the dreams. In *Wonderland* this is mysteriously mixed up with the trial of the Knave of Hearts, the thief of love, but at the end of the second book the symbolism is franker and more simple. She is a grown queen and has acquired the conventional dignities of her insane world; suddenly she admits their insanity, refuses to be a grown queen, and destroys them.

'I can't stand this any longer!' she cried, as she seized the table-cloth in both hands: one good pull, and plates, dishes, guests, and candles came crashing down together in a heap on the floor.

The guests are inanimate and the crawling self-stultifying machinery of luxury has taken on a hideous life of its own. It is the High Table of Christ Church that we must think of here. The gentleman is not the slave of his conventions because at need he could destroy them; and yet, even if he did this, and all the more because he does not, he must adopt while despising it the attitude to them of the child. (pp. 292-94)

William Empson, "Alice in Wonderland: The Child as Swain," in his *Some Versions of Pastoral*, Chatto & Windus, 1935, pp. 253-94.

ROGER W. HOLMES
(essay date 1959)

[In the following excerpt from an essay first published in 1959, Holmes discusses incidents in the *Alice* books as illustrations of logical and philosophical principles.]

Have you ever seen Nobody? What would your world be like if objects had no names? Can you remember what will happen week after next? How many impossible things can you believe before breakfast—*if* you hold your breath and shut your eyes? These questions transport us to the world of Lewis Carroll: to Wonderland, with the White Rabbit and the Mock Turtle. . . . They also transport us to the realm of Philosophy.

Alice's Adventures in Wonderland and *Through the Looking-Glass* belong most obviously and particularly to children whether in nurseries or bomb shelters. . . . [Both] Wonderland and the Looking-Glass country belong to the logician and the philosopher as much as to parents and children. These regions are crowded with the problems and paraphernalia of logic and metaphysics and theory of knowledge and ethics. Here are superbly imaginative treatments of logical principles, the uses and meanings of words, the functions of names, the perplexities connected with time and space, the problem of personal identity, the status of substance in relation to its qualities, the mind-body problem. (pp. 159-60)

Sometimes Carroll finds an unforgettable illustration of a major principle. We know that if all apples are red, it does not follow that all red things are apples: the logician's technical description of this is the nonconvertibility *simpliciter* of universal proportions. (p. 161)

Most often Carroll uses the absurd hilarity of Wonderland to bring difficult technical concepts into sharp focus; and for this gift teachers of logic and philosophy have unmeasured admiration and gratitude. . . . Lewis Carroll reminds us that we often refer to this curious but important logical entity. The White King is waiting for his messengers and asks Alice to look along the road to see if they are coming:

"I see nobody on the road," said Alice.

"I only wish *I* had such eyes," the King remarked in a fretful tone. "To be able to see Nobody! And at that distance too! Why, it's as much as I can do to see real people, by this light."

This is amusing and, without benefit of logic, it is also confusing. When the messenger finally arrives, several pages later, confusion is doubly confounded:

"Who did you pass on the road?" the King went on. . . .

"Nobody," said the Messenger.

"Quite right," said the King; "this young lady saw him too. So of course Nobody walks slower than you."

"I do my best," the Messenger said in a sullen tone. "I'm sure nobody walks much faster than I do!"

"He can't do that," said the King, "or else he'd have been here first."

"Nobody" may stand for no person, but you had better be careful how you talk about him! (pp. 161-62)

[Alice boasts] to the Gnat that she can name the insects:

"Of course they answer to their names?" the Gnat remarked carelessly.

"I never knew them to do that."

"What's the use of their having names," the Gnat said, "if they won't answer to them?"

"No use to *them*," said Alice, "but it's useful to the people that name them, I suppose. If not, why do things have names at all?"

Why, indeed? Medieval philosophers fought bitterly about this. Alice seems to be a Nominalist, suggesting that names are tags by which we can conveniently denote objects without having to point. But a few pages later she comes to the Wood-where-things-have-no-names and quickly discovers what the Medieval Realists knew: that names have a connotation as well as a denotation. . . . [Names] are more than tags: they convey information. Such a wood evokes fascinating philosophic speculation. Suppose we could remember no names. Not only would it be impossible to communicate with anyone about objects except by pointing, but also we should be unable to generalize and should have to rely entirely on conditioned responses. (p. 162)

The most complex discussion of the function of words takes place between Alice and the White Knight when the latter offers to sing Alice a song. This passage is a classic. The Knight announces that the name of the song "is called 'Haddock's Eyes'" and the following famous conversation ensues:

"Oh, that's the name of the song, is it?" Alice said, trying to feel interested.

"No, you don't understand," the Knight said, looking a little vexed. "That's what the name is *called*. The name really *is* 'The Aged Aged Man.'"

"Then I ought to have said 'That's what the song is called'?" Alice corrected herself.

"No, you oughtn't: that's quite another thing! The *song* is called '*Ways and Means*': but that's only what it's *called*, you know!"

"Well, what *is* the song, then?" said Alice, who was by this time completely bewildered.

"I was coming to that," the Knight said. "The song really is '*A-sitting On A Gate*. . . .'"

The issues it raises are technical and abstract, but not without excitement. Pause and analyze the situation which the White Knight describes. There are two things involved, the name of the song and the song itself. Of the name it can be said a) what the name *is*, b) what the name *is called*. And of the song itself it can be said a) what *the song* is, and b) what *the song* is called. (p. 164)

The word "call" is ambiguous. We call a person by name or nickname: if I had known Keats intimately I might *call* him "Jack." In another sense I describe him to someone else; then I *call* him "England's greatest romantic poet" or "one whose name is writ in water." The first illustrates what a name is called, and is the arbitrary assigning of a tag to an individual. The second is an example of what a thing is called, and how information is conveyed. You might say that Keats was so many inches tall; he could then be called a man of such-and-such a stature. You might call a day a period of so many minutes, or a pebble on the beach of Time. Here is essentially the difference between a dictionary and an encyclopedia: the one gives information about names, the other provides data about things. Except, as the White Knight made clear, the items in a dictionary are not properly names at all!

We come, finally, to the thing itself. And here Lewis Carroll was definitely pulling our leg. The White Knight said that the song he was singing *was* "A-sitting On A Gate"—but remember that that was not its name! It was not even what the thing was called—a sad song or a lengthy one. What could it be, if it is neither the name of the song nor a description of the song? It could only be *the thing itself*. . . . To be consistent, the White Knight, when he had said that the song *is* . . . , could only have burst into the song itself. Whether consistent or not, the White Knight is Lewis Carroll's cherished gift to logicians. (p. 165)

The wealth of material which Lewis Carroll presents for the illuminating of philosophy is almost without end. . . . Alice wondered what happens to the flame of a candle when the candle is put out, while she was shutting up like a telescope during her first adventure in Wonderland, wondered whether she would go out altogether—"like a candle." The Pre-Socratics enjoyed that problem. What *does* happen to the flame?

Some of the philosophic problems are perennial. In her bewilderment at the sudden changes in her size and the conversations with a unique rabbit who wore a vest and gloves and carried a watch, Alice asks herself, "Who in the world am I? Ah, *that's* the great puzzle." And it is one of the greatest of philosophic puzzles, the problem of personal identity. (pp. 166-67)

Another passage of major philosophic interest from the *Looking-Glass* book has to do with dreams. Tweedledum and Tweedledee and Alice are watching the Red King, who is sleeping fit to snore his head off, as Tweedledum remarked:

"He's dreaming now," said Tweedledee, "and what do you think he's dreaming about?"

Alice said, "Nobody can guess that."

"Why, about *you*!" Tweedledee explained, clapping his hands triumphantly. "And if he left off dreaming about you, where do you suppose you'd be?"

"Where I am now, of course," said Alice.

"Not you!" Tweedledee retorted contemptuously. "You'd be nowhere. Why, you're only a sort of thing in his dream!"

"If that there King was to wake," added Tweedledum, "you'd go out—bang!—just like a candle."

"I shouldn't!" Alice exclaimed indignantly. "Besides if I'm only a sort of thing in his dream, what are *you*, I should like to know?"

"Ditto," said Tweedledum.

"Ditto, ditto!" cried Tweedledee.

The Red King performs the function of God in the philosophy of Bishop Berkeley, for whom the tree in the forest exists when there are no humans to perceive it. To be is to be perceived, ultimately in the mind of God—or the Red King. (p. 169)

Lewis Carroll is at his best when he considers time. The Looking-Glass country was a place in which time moved backwards. Through a playful reference to memory, he approaches the curious character of Looking-Glass punishment:

"What sort of things do *you* remember best?" Alice ventured to ask.

"Oh, things that happened the week after next," the Queen replied in a careless tone. "For instance, now," she went on, sticking a large piece of plaster on her finger as she spoke, "there's the King's Messenger. He's in prison now, being punished; and the trial doesn't even begin till next Wednesday; and of course the crime comes last of all."

"Suppose he never commits the crime?" said Alice.

"That would be all the better, wouldn't it?" the Queen said, as she bound the plaster around her finger with a bit of ribbon. . . .

Alice was sure there was a mistake somewhere. It reminds one of the story about the irate father who spanked his son for fighting. When the boy insisted he had not been in a fight the father replied, as he continued to apply the hairbrush, that even if he had not been in one that day he was sure to be in one soon. (pp. 170-71)

It just does not make sense. Punishment exists in a Bergsonian time-with-direction. As everyone knows who has seen movies run backwards, most human actions so lose their significance when reversed as to appear hilarious. (p. 171)

One final temporal reference has also to do with the poor disheveled White Queen, who couldn't keep her shawl straight and who had got her brush so tangled in her hair that Alice had to retrieve it for her. Alice said she thought the Queen should have a lady's maid to take care of her:

"I'm sure I'll take *you* with pleasure!" the Queen said. "Twopence a week, and jam every other day."

Alice couldn't help but laughing, as she said, "I don't want you to hire *me*—and I don't care for jam."

"It's very good jam," said the Queen.

"Well, I don't want any *today,* at any rate."

"You couldn't have it if you *did* want it," the Queen said. "The rule is jam tomorrow and jam yesterday—but never jam *today.*"

"It *must* come sometime to 'jam today,' " Alice objected.

"No, it can't," said the Queen. "It's jam every *other* day; today isn't any other day, you know."

"I don't understand you," said Alice. "It's dreadfully confusing!"

And so it is. The difficulty is partly the result of one of Lewis Carroll's favorite devices in entertaining children, the play on words. It is also in part the philosophic problem of knowing when the present becomes the past and the future the present. It is the problem with which James was concerned when he described time as shaped like a saddle. It is the problem that bothers the Idealist when he realizes that he can never know

the present: to know it is to make it an object of our thinking and hence to put it into the past. Can the present ever be known? Can we ever have jam in the todayness of tomorrow? By its nature tomorrow must come; also, by its very definition, it can never come. (p. 173)

The world of Lewis Carroll is more extensive than most travelers in it realize. Less familiar, though unforgettable once visited, is the wild region of the Snark and the Boojum and the Bellman's problem with the bowsprit that got mixed with the rudder sometimes, in *The Hunting of the Snark.* The more conventional land of the story of *Sylvie and Bruno* and the amusing architecture of Lewis Carroll's logic exercises are now seldom included in an itinerary. There is even a vacation spot for students of government, the little-known *The Dynamics of a Particle,* involving plain superficiality, obtuse anger, and acute anger (the inclination of two voters to one another whose views are not in the same direction); a world in which a speaker may digress from one point to another, a controversy be raised about any question and at any distance from that question. . . .

If this essay has any "porpoise" it is to send you, the reader, to the pleasures of philosophy and logic by way of the unique fascination of Lewis Carroll. And do not get caught in the elusiveness of Alice's jam. Do not promise yourself the delights of philosophy tomorrow. Enjoy them now: take Lewis Carroll down from the shelf tonight. (p. 174)

Roger W. Holmes, "The Philosopher's 'Alice in Wonderland'," in *Aspects of Alice: Lewis Caroll's Dreamchild as Seen through the Critics',* edited by Robert Phillips, The Vanguard Press Inc., 1971, pp. 159-74.

MARTIN GARDNER
(essay date 1960)

[An American journalist and writer, Gardner edited *The Annotated Alice: Alice's Adventures in Wonderland & Through the Looking-Glass* and *The Annotated Snark* (1962). In the following excerpt from the introduction to *The Annotated Alice,* he asserts that the *Alice* books cannot be fully appreciated by young children and criticizes psychoanalytic interpretations of Carroll's work.]

The fact is that Carroll's nonsense is not nearly as random and pointless as it seems to a modern American child who tries to read the *Alice* books. One says "tries" because the time is past when a child under fifteen, even in England, can read *Alice* with the same delight as gained from, say, *The Wind in the Willows* or *The Wizard of Oz.* Children today are bewildered and sometimes frightened by the nightmarish atmosphere of

G. K. Chesterton on the changing fortunes of *Alice in Wonderland*:

Any educated Englishman, and especially any educational Englishman (which is worse), will tell you with a certain gravity that *Alice in Wonderland* is a classic. Such is indeed the horrid truth. The original hilarity that was born on that summer afternoon among the children, in the mind of a mathematician on a holiday, has itself hardened into something almost as cold and conscientious as a holiday task. That logician's light inversion of all the standards of logic has itself, I shudder to say, stiffened into a standard work. It is a classic; that is, people praise it who have never read it. It has a secure position side by side with the works of Milton and Dryden. It is a book without which no gentleman's library is complete, and which the gentleman therefore never presumes to take out of his library. I am sorry to say it, but the soap-bubble which poor old Dodgson blew from the pipe of poetry, in a lucid interval of lunacy, and sent floating into the sky, has been robbed by educationists of much of the lightness of the bubble, and retained only the horrible healthiness of the soap.

G. K. Chesterton, in *The New York Times*, 1932.

Alice's dreams. It is only because adults—scientists and mathematicians in particular—continue to relish the *Alice* books that they are assured of immortality. (pp. 7-8)

Like Homer, the Bible, and all other great works of fantasy, the *Alice* books lend themselves readily to any type of symbolic interpretation—political, metaphysical, or Freudian. (p. 8)

In recent years the trend has naturally been toward psychoanalytic interpretations. Alexander Woollcott once expressed relief that the Freudians had left Alice's dreams unexplored; but that was twenty years ago and now, alas, we are all amateur headshrinkers. We do not have to be told what it means to tumble down a rabbit hole or curl up inside a tiny house with one foot up the chimney. The rub is that any work of nonsense abounds with so many inviting symbols that you can start with any assumption you please about the author and easily build up an impressive case for it. Consider, for example, the scene in which Alice seizes the end of the White King's pencil and begins scribbling for him. In five minutes one can invent six different interpretations. Whether Carroll's unconscious had any of them in mind, however, is an altogether dubious matter. More pertinent is the fact that Carroll was interested in psychic phenomena and automatic writing, and the hypothesis must not be ruled out that it is only by accident that a pencil in this scene is shaped the way it is.

We must remember also that many characters and

episodes in *Alice* are a direct result of puns and other linguistic jokes, and would have taken quite different forms if Carroll had been writing, say, in French. One does not need to look for an involved explanation of the Mock Turtle; his melancholy presence is quite adequately explained by mock-turtle soup. Are the many references to eating in *Alice* a sign of Carroll's "oral aggression," or did Carroll recognize that small children are obsessed by eating and like to read about it in their books? A similar question mark applies to the sadistic elements in *Alice,* which are quite mild compared with those of animated cartoons for the past thirty years. It seems unreasonable to suppose that all the makers of animated cartoons are sado-masochists; more reasonable to assume that they all made the same discovery about what children like to see on the screen. Carroll was a skillful storyteller, and we should give him credit for the ability to make a similar discovery. The point here is not that Carroll was not neurotic (we all know he was), but that books of nonsense fantasy for children are not such fruitful sources of psychoanalytic insight as one might suppose them to be. They are much too rich in symbols. The symbols have too many explanations. (pp. 8-9)

It is easy to say that Carroll found an outlet for his repressions in the unrestrained, whimsically violent visions of his *Alice* books. Victorian children no doubt enjoyed similar release. They were delighted to have at last some books without a pious moral, but Carroll grew more and more restive with the thought that he had not yet written a book for youngsters that would convey some sort of evangelistic Christian message. His effort in this direction was *Sylvie and Bruno,* a long, fantastic novel that appeared in two separately published parts. (p. 14)

Ironically, it is Carroll's earlier and pagan nonsense that has, at least for a few modern readers, a more effective religious message than *Sylvie and Bruno.* For nonsense, as Chesterton liked to tell us, is a way of looking at existence that is akin to religious humility and wonder. The Unicorn thought Alice a fabulous monster. It is part of the philosophic dullness of our time that there are millions of rational monsters walking about on their hind legs, observing the world through pairs of flexible little lenses, periodically supplying themselves with energy by pushing organic substances through holes in their faces, who see nothing fabulous whatever about themselves. Occasionally the noses of these creatures are shaken by momentary paroxysms. Kierkegaard once imagined a philosopher sneezing while recording one of his profound sentences. How could such a man, Kierkegaard wondered, take his metaphysics seriously?

The last level of metaphor in the *Alice* books is this: that life, viewed rationally and without illusion, appears to be a nonsense tale told by an idiot mathema-

Alice at the Mad Tea Party with the Marsh Hare, the Dormouse, and the Mad Hatter.

tician. At the heart of things science finds only a mad, never-ending quadrille of Mock Turtle Waves and Gryphon Particles. For a moment the waves and particles dance in grotesque, inconceivably complex patterns capable of reflecting on their own absurdity. We all live slapstick lives, under an inexplicable sentence of death, and when we try to find out what the Castle authorities want us to do, we are shifted from one bumbling bureaucrat to another. We are not even sure that Count West-West, the owner of the Castle, really exists. More than one critic has commented on the similarities between Kafka's *Trial* and the trial of the Jack of Hearts; between Kafka's *Castle* and a chess game in which living pieces are ignorant of the game's plan and cannot tell if they move of their own wills or are being pushed by invisible fingers.

This vision of the monstrous mindlessness of the cosmos ("Off with its head!") can be grim and disturbing, as it is in Kafka and the Book of Job, or lighthearted comedy, as in *Alice* or Chesterton's *The Man Who Was Thursday*. When Sunday, the symbol of God in Chesterton's metaphysical nightmare, flings little messages to his pursuers, they turn out to be nonsense messages.

One of them is even signed Snowdrop, the name of Alice's White Kitten. It is a vision that can lead to despair and suicide, to the laughter that closes Jean Paul Sartre's story "The Wall," to the humanist's resolve to carry on bravely in the face of ultimate darkness. Curiously, it can also suggest the wild hypothesis that there may be a light behind the darkness.

Laughter, declares Reinhold Niebuhr in one of his finest sermons, is a kind of no man's land between faith and despair. We preserve our sanity by laughing at life's surface absurdities, but the laughter turns to bitterness and derision if directed toward the deeper irrationalities of evil and death. "That is why," he concludes, "there is laughter in the vestibule of the temple, the echo of laughter in the temple itself, but only faith and prayer, and no laughter, in the holy of holies."

Lord Dunsany said the same thing this way in *The Gods of Pagana*. The speaker is Limpang-Tung, the god of mirth and melodious minstrels.

I will send jests into the world and a little mirth. And while Death seems to thee as far away as the purple rim of hills, or sorrow as far off as rain in the blue days of summer, then pray to Limpang-Tung. But when thou growest old, or ere thou diest, pray not to Limpang-Tung, for thou becomest part of a scheme that he doth not understand.

"Go out into the starry night, and Limpang-Tung will dance with thee . . . Or offer up a jest to Limpang-Tung; only pray not in they sorrow to Limpang-Tung, for he saith of sorrow: 'It may be very clever of the gods, but he doth not understand.'

Alice's Adventures in Wonderland and *Through the Looking-Glass* are two incomparable jests that the Reverend C. L. Dodgson, on a mental holiday from Christ Church chores, once offered up to Limpang-Tung. (pp. 14-16)

Martin Gardner, in an introduction to *The Annotated Alice: Alice's Adventures in Wonderland & Through the Looking Glass* by Lewis Carroll, Clarkson N. Potter, Inc., 1960, pp. 7-16.

CHARLES FREY AND JOHN GRIFFITH

(essay date 1987)

[In the following excerpt, Frey and Griffith suggest ways of reading *Alice's Adventures in Wonderland* and *Through the Looking-Glass.*]

Alice's Adventures in Wonderland constitutes a perennial enigma for all readers. Is it primarily funny or primarily frightening? Is Alice to be thought of as little, overpolite, easily cowed, too focused on manners, snobbish, often bored, often in tears? Or is she to be thought of as courageous, in love with adventure and fun, indomitably seeking self-understanding and her own maturity? The creatures Alice meets are mostly "mad," yes, but by *mad,* does Carroll mean senseless or angry? What is he saying about the nature of language and logic, reality, and growth and time? In *Alice* what are rules, manners, and social conventions for? What makes the creatures of Wonderland so original and so fascinating? Does Carroll make a case for linking creativity and perverseness? What is the basic human image that emerges from the book? To these and related questions readers will frame divers answers, but there will always be agreement on the central fact: the astounding brilliance of Carroll's tragicomedy.

No parent, teacher, or critic can really "do justice" to *Alice in Wonderland.* The work is far too dense and multivalent to be explicated and interpreted at all satisfactorily, and the work now has become surrounded by so much mystification and hoopla that interested readers must pick their way carefully through a mass of theories and countertheories about Carroll and *Alice* if they wish to guide themselves or any children to sensi-

ble understanding and judgment of the work. It may be best to begin by attempting a "naive" reading of the text. One might usefully chart for oneself what happens in the twelve mock-epic chapters, keeping special track of Alice's changes in size. It is an open question whether the basic sequence of adventures suggests a progression in knowledge and mood. Alice might be seen as moving from a kind of birth trauma—falling down the tunnel, the long low hall, the amniotic pool—through meeting little animals (mouse, rabbit, lizard, caterpillar, pigeon) to meeting larger animals and adult humans. Her adventures intensify in the sense that the Duchess and plight of the baby seem more powerful and threatening than the Caucus Race or Caterpillar, and the tea party picks up the pace of madness while the Queen of Hearts and the Mock-Turtle adventures introduce increased fear and nostalgia ("off with her head," songs of voracious shark and panther). Then comes the final trial, a full social event in which Alice reaches the limit of her frustration and anger, asserts herself aggressively, yet wakes to "dead leaves" and "dull reality." Alice is in one sense "socialized" but with decidedly mixed results (just as in *Through the Looking-Glass* she becomes Queen all right yet finds it is not all "feasting and fun").

Another way to approach the same sequence of adventures is to note that Alice is engaged in a romance quest for her own identity and growth, for some understanding of logic, rules, the games people play, authority, time, and death. How each adventure contributes to or deepens the multiple quest is something each reader may answer variously, yet each time with keen connection to the work. Certainly as children's literature, the adventures are entertaining, but within the playfulness lies another dimension in which Alice repeatedly cries, is treated rudely, fears for her safety or life, and becomes genuinely angry. The book would not have fascinated millions if it were superficial fantasy. When the Caterpillar asks Alice, " 'Who are *you*,' " and Alice can barely stammer out a reply, " 'I—hardly know,' " then Carroll is exposing the quintessential vulnerability of the child whose growth and knowledge of self and the world vary so greatly from day to day that a sense of answerable identity becomes highly precarious if not evanescent.

An obvious and crucial feature of Alice's meetings with the animals is that she, unlike the heroes in tales of the Brothers Grimm or Hans Christian Andersen, is rarely aided by the creatures she meets. Whereas in a tale of Grimms or Andersen or John Ruskin, the protagonist's meeting with a helpful bird or beast would signal his or her charity toward the world or nature, and signal a concomitant abandoning of pure self-interest or pride (often represented in greedy siblings), in the *Alice* story, the animals do not represent nature responsive to innocence, good will, and charity, but rather they are masks for roles and attitudes of humans in a society based upon competitiveness and pride. Alice does not go out into nature but down into dreams and the sub- or un-conscious. No wind, wave, or mountain appears in Wonderland to provide a breath of feeling tone or a sense of living nature. The focus is relentlessly closed, societal, and sophisticated. The animals are chosen largely for incidental associations (mouse with long tail/tale, grinning Cheshire cat, crazy March hare, etc.) that allow for puns or eccentric personalities and behavior. Alice enters a world of intensely insecure but aggressively defensive adults whose narrowness of outlook expresses itself continually in attacks upon the reality or propriety of Alice in her appearance and behavior. Alice's consequent bewilderment is the subject of much mirth, but always ambivalence abounds because of the grotesque disparity in power and politeness between Alice and those she meets. (pp. 116-17)

At the heart of *Alice* may be a simultaneous defense of the dream of childhood's spontaneous, gentle, innocent beauty assailed by adult stuffiness and pride and also a wistful recognition of the imperious nature of the child who demands growth and accepted entry into that very adulthood which will eclipse childish innocence.

Some readers will resist seeing *Alice* not just as silly happy fantasy adventures but also as satire, sometimes hard-driving satire, directed at unruly egos everywhere, at adult attitudes toward children, at the foibles of various social classes, at our pretensions to logic and to manners, and at the child's absorption in self and in the gyrations of its developing personality. Certainly in the very first chapter we are asked to be amused at Alice's opinions and behavior. . . . In the second chapter she mocks "Mabel's" lack of knowledge and her "poky little house" and her few toys in a way that obviously leaves Alice the target of our amusement. But then when she begins meeting the generally rude and eccentric creatures in Wonderland, the equation of satire shifts from bemusement at Alice's ignorant innocence (her unintended insults to the mouse, for example) toward a special combination of laughter at antics of the brusque, logic-chopping creatures and sympathy for the plight of Alice who is forever fearful lest one of the creatures be offended in some way. (p. 118)

Once we recognize that Alice is easily and often dispirited, we may see better the significance of the fact that she is also very resilient and re-buoyant. She consistently comes back for more. In this portrayal of her endurance and comic bounce of spirit, Carroll sides with many writers of children's classics such as Andersen in "The Snow Queen" or Ruskin in *The King of the Golden River* or Robert Louis Stevenson in *Treasure Island,* all of whom reveal youth's incredible capacity to endure the shocks of local defeat and yet keep coming on

for final gain. Children's literature in this sense becomes a recognition that *life is on their side,* and the literature also becomes a celebration of that fact.

One source of Alice's lively resiliency is her curiosity. We are told in the third paragraph of the book that Alice follows the rabbit because she is "burning with curiosity." Soon she finds things becoming "curiouser and curiouser." In Carroll's world, curiosity leads toward that which is curious, and the curious borders on the very strange, and the very strange borders on the mad ("we're all mad here"), and the mad borders on the angry. There is a surprising amount of violence, real and threatened, in *Alice,* and readers owe it to themselves to note its occurrences and to reach some conclusions as to its meanings. Does it appeal to children (who often experience violent emotions and behavior as part of daily life)? Or does it frighten them? Or both? We know from amusement parks that fun and fear are sometimes compatible for children. When is Alice said to be frightened? How does she respond to her fear? How often is she delighted? When does she laugh? Does she ever give in to the nonsense and argument? Enjoy it? " 'It's really dreadful,' she muttered to herself, 'the way all the creatures argue. It's really dreadful,' she muttered to herself, 'the way all the creatures argue. It's enough to drive one crazy!' " The violence of the cook and Duchess produces "an agony of terror" in Alice, but how seriously does she take her own suffering? How seriously do we? Notice how often Alice faces a fear of death, such as by shrinking away to nothing or in threats of headchopping or just growing ever older. There are implicit connections in *Alice* among youth, curiosity, and time. Alice's curiosity is allied to her desire to learn to grow. In *Through the Looking-Glass,* she wants to become and does become a Queen. In *Alice,* she asserts her larger being at the end. But the way of curiosity or growth leads also to eventual extinction, and much of the nonsense seems designed to baffle curiosity and stop time, as if to provide an antidote to death. . . . (p. 119)

Certainly *Alice in Wonderland* fairly bristles with odd characters and conversation fit to fascinate anyone from eight to eighty. The varieties of fascination can be understood partly in terms of the kinds of wit, play, amusement, and nonsense present in the book. Selected examples of puns, parodies, and put-downs should be readily recognizable, such as *non sequiturs* like "It was the *best* butter, you know," and perverse literalisms, such as the Hatter's about "beating time," and capital rude remarks such as the Gryphon's about "uglifying." Then there are the gnomic tags such as the Duchess's "morals," the riddles, and the sheerly inventive wordplay as in the Mock Turtle's account of his school subjects. Once the variety and detail of Carroll's "nonsense" are noted, one is in a much better position to discuss some of the implications of the kaleidoscopic wordplay. Is

Carroll reminding us that language, knowledge, and communication are not the clear, pragmatic, purposeful tools we generally assume? Is he drawing connections between game and bafflement or between play and non-purposiveness? Is he exposing his and our delight in using language to confuse and ridicule others? Is he suggesting that sense is balanced precariously close to nonsense in a highly volatile or "reversible" world of double-meanings and looking-glass effects? Undoubtedly many readers will want to extend such questionings in directions of their own choosing. (p. 120)

Carroll wrote an epilogue poem to *Through the Looking-Glass* and ended it with the lines: "Life, what is it but a dream?" In *Alice,* life is both a dream and a joke. We need, perhaps, to "get" and enjoy the joke but also to realize that Carroll is saying the joke of life is on us (though still funny), just as the joke most of the time is on Alice. Alice offers to readers who are relatively new at the serious study of literature a splendid opportunity to learn respect instead of suspicion for one of the great modes of literature, satire. Satire seems duplicitous and overly sophisticated to some readers who are easily put off by it. But *Alice* provides such genuine delight as well as mystification that such readers may be willing to work with their distrust and modify it. . . .

After being considered "for itself," *Alice* should be brought back into contexts of genre and of historical development in children's literature. Carroll mocks the conventions of quest stories such as the Grimms' tales in which the hero or heroine penetrates strange lands to win a consummate reward. Carroll mocks, furthermore, the tradition of didactic literature for children as in his parodies of supposedly edifying poems. He attacks also the vein of Romantic and Victorian sentimentalism that sees the child as savior of society and nature, Ruskin's Gluck pushed to the extreme. At the end of *Alice,* Alice shouts: "Who cares for you? . . . You're nothing but a pack of cards!" Allowing for a lurking pun in "cards," this finale may sum up part of Carroll's attitude to social organization and "fellowship." A sometimes reclusive bachelor who never married or formed much in the way of close and lasting friendship, Carroll's motto would hardly have been "only connect." Whom should Alice care for and why are questions the book may be asking. It comes up somewhat empty-handed. This is the world of Victorian doubt and isolation in which the little lame Prince must bear his own sufferings in a lonely tower. The fatuous Duchess remarks:

" 'Oh, 'tis love, 'tis love, that makes the world go round!' "

"Somebody said," Alice whispered, "that it's done by everybody minding their own business!"

"Ah well! It means much the same thing," said the Duchess.

Love, then, becomes a matter of minding your own business, a kind of self-love. Alice's adventures tell us why. Yet we may be thankful that Carroll so honestly portrays our universal, if laughable, insistence upon minding each other's business. (p. 121)

Charles Frey and John Griffith, "Lewis Carroll: Alice's Adventures in Wonderland," in their *The Literary Heritage of Childhood: An Appraisal of Children's Classics in the Western Tradition,* Greenwood Press, 1987, pp. 115-22.

SOURCES FOR FURTHER STUDY

Auden, W. H. "Today's Wonder-World Needs Alice." *The New York Times* (1 July 1962): VI, 5.

> Discusses the validity of Alice as a contemporary heroine.

Collingwood, Stuart Dodgson. *The Life and Letters of Lewis Carroll.* New York: The Century Co., 1899, 448 p.

> A sympathetic, often obscure account of Dodgson's life by his nephew, with some valuable primary source material.

Hudson, Derek. *Lewis Carroll.* London: Constable, 1954, 354 p.

> Highly regarded biography of Dodgson.

Kibel, Alvin C. "Logic and Satire in *Alice in Wonderland.*" *The American Scholar* 43, No. 4 (Autumn 1974): 605-29.

> Analyzes Dodgson's use of logical principles for the purpose of satire in *Alice in Wonderland.* This essay contends that the author saw a disjunction between the motives of one character and the purpose of the action as a whole.

Lennon, Florence Becker. *Victoria through the Looking Glass: The Life of Lewis Carroll.* New York: Simon and Schuster, 1945, 387 p.

> Biography of Dodgson, containing analysis of his views of Victorian society.

Taylor, Alexander L. *The White Knight: A Study of C. L. Dodgson (Lewis Carroll).* London: Oliver and Boyd, 1952, 209 p.

> Attempts to debunk both the "split personality" theory and the notion that the *Alice* books are "nonsense." Taylor's book contains logical explanations of what

had previously been thought to be nonsense in Dodgson's work.

Willa Cather

1873-1947

American novelist, short story writer, essayist, poet, and critic.

INTRODUCTION

Cather was an important American author of the early twentieth century. She is best known for such novels as *O Pioneers!* (1913) and *My Ántonia* (1918)—evocative, realistic portrayals of pioneer life that celebrate the courageous endurance of the early midwestern settlers and the natural beauty of the prairie landscape. However, she began her career as a short story writer, and many consider her a master of that form as well. Cather's works often focus on sensitive, alienated individuals and examine their varying degrees of success in resolving conflict. Because she stressed the importance of creativity, imagination, and the many forms of love in transcending adversity, Cather's vision has been described as romantic, while her unadorned and vivid prose style reflects the influence of nineteenth-century Realist author Gustave Flaubert.

Cather was born in Virginia and spent the first decade of her life on her family's farm in Back Creek Valley. In 1884 the Cathers moved to the Great Plains, joining the ethnically diverse group of settlers in Webster County, Nebraska. The family settled in Red Cloud, where Cather began to attend school on a regular basis. Although her primary interest was science, she displayed talent for acting, and she performed plays she had composed for the entertainment of her family, gave recitations, and participated in amateur theatricals staged at the Red Cloud opera house. Planning to become a physician, she also accompanied a local doctor on his house calls, and she was eventually permitted to assist him. Sometime shortly before her thirteenth birthday, Cather adopted a masculine appearance and demeanor and began signing her name "William Cather, Jr." or "William Cather M.D." While biographer James Woodress suggests that this behavior can be construed simply as one aspect of Cather's blanket rejection of the strictures placed upon females in the nineteenth century, others contend that Cather's masculine persona was an authentic reflection of her identity, citing as proof her consistent use of male narrators and her strong attachments to female friends. In either case, Cather was eventually persuaded by friends to return to a more conventional mode of dress, and she later dismissed the episode as juvenile posturing.

Cather entered the University of Nebraska in 1891, and she excelled in studies of language and literature. During her junior year, she assumed the editorship of the college literary journal, in which she published many of her own short stories; by the time she was graduated from the university, she was working as a full-time reporter and critic for the *Nebraska State Journal.* Shortly after graduation, she moved to Pittsburgh to serve as editor of a short-lived women's magazine called the *Home Monthly.* Cather published her first book, *April Twilights,* an undistinguished volume of poetry, in 1903. While she continued to write and publish short stories, she made her living as a journalist and teacher until she moved to New York City in 1906 to assume the managing editorship of the influential *McClure's* magazine.

Cather's affiliation with *McClure's* proved to be pivotal in her life and career: her work for the magazine brought her national recognition, and it was S. S. McClure, the dynamic, iconoclastic publisher of *McClure's,* who arranged for the release of *The Troll Garden,* her first volume of short stories, in 1905. While on assignment in Boston in 1908, Cather met Sarah Orne Jewett, an author whose work she greatly admired; after reading Cather's fiction, Jewett encouraged her to abandon journalism. "I cannot help saying what I think," Jewett wrote to Cather, "about your writing and its being hindered by such incessant, important, responsible work as you have in your hands now." Jewett further advised Cather to "find [her] own quiet centre of life, and write from that to the world." Cather was profoundly influenced by these admonitions, and shortly afterward she relinquished her responsibilities at *McClure's* in order to devote all of her time to writing fiction. After one unsuccessful attempt in the novel *Alexander's Bridge* (1912), Cather found her "quiet centre of life" in childhood memories of the Nebraska prairie, using them and other incidents from her life to create a series of remarkably successful novels between her retirement from *McClure's* in 1912 and her death in 1947.

The influence of Henry James, whom Cather considered "the perfect writer," is apparent in her four short story collections. The themes of these collections, which were written at various stages of her career, reflect her own changing attitudes toward life and art. The stories in *The Troll Garden* deal primarily with the struggles of artists in culturally impoverished envi-

ronments. Often, as in the story "The Sculptor's Funeral," this environment is the Nebraska prairie. The madness, failure, and frustration depicted in this collection reveal the mixture of fascination and fear with which Cather still contemplated midwestern life. In *Youth and the Bright Medusa* (1920), Cather reprinted four of the stories from *The Troll Garden,* along with four of her more recent efforts. In her newer stories she explored a more positive side of the artist's existence by examining the meaning of artistic success. The "bright Medusa" of the title refers to art—"Life's bright challenge"—and the stories portray artists who have chosen either to use art to achieve wealth and popularity or to labor toward the fulfillment of their talents. Cather's passionate idealism and her disdain for materialistic aspiration leave little doubt that, in her view, it was only perfection that should concern the true artist. Cather continued to exalt spiritual over material values in the stories of *Obscure Destinies* (1932). Cather's posthumously published collection of short stories, *The Old Beauty, and Others* (1948), focuses on the theme of remorse and atonement for past wrongs. The doubts and regrets that Cather experienced late in life over the many sacrifices she had made for her career are echoed in the note of irrecoverable loss in these final stories.

As critics have long acknowledged, it is Cather's novels that constitute her major contribution to literature. *Alexander's Bridge,* her first novel, was highly derivative, both in its form and its sophisticated subject matter, due to the author's desire to write in the manner of Henry James. In subsequent works, however, she returned to the Nebraska background that had provided her with the settings and characters for many of her early stories.

Cather combined a regional knowledge of Nebraska with an artistic expertise reminiscent of the nineteenth-century literary masters to create distinguished achievements in twentieth-century American literature. In novels such as *O Pioneers!* and *My Ántonia,* Cather portrayed the lives of Old World immigrants on the American midwestern frontier in a manner that was at once realistic and nobly heroic. For her, the homesteading German, Danish, Bohemian, and Scandinavian settlers of that region were the embodiment of the artistic and cultural tradition she cherished. In her Nebraskan novels, courage and idealism are juxtaposed with modern materialistic values. In other works, such as *The Song of the Lark* (1915), Cather equated the spirit of the artist with that of the pioneer, depicting characters such as Thea Kronberg as a "pioneer of the imagination."

Like many artists after World War I, Cather was disillusioned by the social and political order of the world. With the publication of *One of Ours* (1922), for which she won the Pulitzer Prize in 1922, an underlying mood of hopelessness entered into her novels, as well as a motif stressing the need to escape from contemporary life. Granville Hicks stated that "once [Cather] had created symbols of triumph . . . , but now she concerned herself with symbols of defeat." This pattern appears in such novels as *A Lost Lady* (1923), which chronicles the gradual process of moral degradation in the protagonist Marian Forrester as well as the social decline in America following World War I, and *The Professor's House* (1925), which contrasts the disillusionment of Professor Godfrey St. Peter over his family's materialism with his reminiscences about an idealistic former student who had died in the war. A despairing tone is absent in *Death Comes for the Archbishop* (1927)—an episodic novel fictionalizing the life and achievements of Archbishop Lamy in mid-nineteenth-century New Mexico—and *Shadows on the Rock* (1931)—a tale set in seventeenth-century Quebec—partly because Cather's desire to retreat from the modern world led her, late in her career, to write novels about historic figures to whom she could once again attribute heroic virtues. While some critics, such as Hicks, have condemned Cather's retreat into the past, others have praised her insight and rejection of what she perceived as a materialistic society. Edward and Lillian Bloom have asserted that "looking backward to the fixed values of a satisfying past, [Cather] reaffirmed the moral standards she cherished, thus ultimately denying they could be destroyed by temporary upheavals."

Some recent critics have detected political overtones in much of the negative criticism that accompanied the appearance of Cather's last novels. They argue that Cather's blunt condemnation of materialism in such works as *A Lost Lady* and *The Professor's House* was interpreted as an endorsement of socialism in the politically sensitive decades of the 1930s and 1940s. For this reason they believe that these books may not have been assessed fairly by critics at the time of their publication, and they are now beginning to re-examine them. Cather's willingness to experiment with new forms, her technical mastery, and the superb prose style evident in these works have generally led recent critics to take a more positive view of them than that held by Cather's contemporaries. Thus, Cather's unique stylistic and thematic contribution to American letters and her importance as an early modernist writer are now widely recognized.

(For further information about Cather's life and works, see *Concise Dictionary of American Literary Biography, 1865-1917; Contemporary Authors*, Vols. 104, 128; *Dictionary of Literary Biography*, Vols. 9, 54; *Dictionary of Literary Biography Documentary Series*, Vol. 1; *Short Story Criticism*, Vol. 2; *Something about the Author*, Vol. 30; and *Twentieth-Century Literary Criticism*, Vols. 1, 11, 31.)

CRITICAL COMMENTARY

H. L. MENCKEN
(essay date 1920)

[Mencken, a major figure in American letters during the early twentieth century, is best known for his strongly individualistic, irreverent viewpoint and writing style. In the following excerpt, he discusses the rapid development of Cather's literary talents, noting that *My Ántonia* represents "the best piece of fiction ever done by a woman in America."]

Four or five years ago, though she already had a couple of good books behind her, Willa Cather was scarcely heard of. When she was mentioned at all, it was as a talented but rather inconsequential imitator of Mrs. Wharton. But today even campus-pump critics are more or less aware of her, and one hears no more gabble about imitations. The plain fact is that she is now discovered to be a novelist of original methods and quite extraordinary capacities—penetrating and accurate in

observation, delicate in feeling, brilliant and charming in manner, and full of a high sense of the dignity and importance of her work. Bit by bit, patiently and laboriously, she has mastered the trade of the novelist; in each succeeding book she has shown an unmistakable advance. Now, at last, she has arrived at such a command of all the complex devices and expedients of her art that the use she makes of them is quite concealed. Her style has lost self-consciousness; her grasp of form has become instinctive; her drama is firmly rooted in a sound psychology; her people relate themselves logically to the great race masses that they are parts of. In brief, she knows her business thoroughly, and so one gets out of reading her, not only the facile joy that goes with every good story, but also the vastly higher pleasure that is called forth by first-rate craftsmanship.

I know of no novel that makes the remote folk of the western farmlands more real than *My Ántonia* makes them, and I know of none that makes them seem

Principal Works

April Twilights (poetry) 1903; also published as April Twilights, and Other Poems [enlarged edition], 1923

The Troll Garden (short stories) 1905

Alexander's Bridge (novel) 1912

O Pioneers! (novel) 1913

The Song of the Lark (novel) 1915

My Ántonia (novel) 1918

*Youth and the Bright Medusa (short stories) 1920

One of Ours (novel) 1922

A Lost Lady (novel) 1923

The Professor's House (novel) 1925

My Mortal Enemy (novel) 1926

Death Comes for the Archbishop (novel) 1927

Shadows on the Rock (novel) 1931

Obscure Destinies (short stories) 1932

Lucy Gayheart (novel) 1935

Not under Forty (essays) 1936

The Novels and Stories of Willa Cather. 13 vols. (novels and short stories) 1937-41

Sapphira and the Slave Girl (novel) 1940

The Old Beauty, and Others (short stories) 1948

On Writing: Critical Studies on Writing as an Art (essays) 1949

Uncle Valentine, and Other Stories (short stories) 1973

*This work includes a portion of the earlier The Troll Garden.

table, perhaps, that the author should be plastered with the Wharton label. I myself, asslike, helped to slap it on—though with prudent reservations, now comforting to contemplate. The defect of the story was one of locale and people: somehow one got the feeling that the author was dealing with both at second-hand, that she knew her characters a bit less intimately than she should have known them. This defect, I venture to guess, did not escape her own eye. At all events, she abandoned New England in her next novel for the Middle West, and particularly for the Middle West of the great immigrations—a region nearer at hand, and infinitely better comprehended. The result was *O Pioneers,* a book of very fine achievement and of even finer promise. Then came *The Song of the Lark*—still more competent, more searching and convincing, better in every way. And then, after three years, came *My Ántonia,* and a sudden leap forward. Here, at last, an absolutely sound technique began to show itself. Here was a novel planned with the utmost skill, and executed in truly admirable fashion. Here, unless I err gravely, was the best piece of fiction ever done by a woman in America.

I once protested to Miss Cather that her novels came too far apart—that the reading public, constantly under a pressure of new work, had too much chance to forget her. She was greatly astonished. "How could I do any more?" she asked. "I work all the time. It takes three years to write a novel." The saying somehow clings to me. There is a profound criticism of criticism in it. It throws a bright light upon the difference between such a work as *My Ántonia* and such a work as— . . . But I have wars enough. (pp. 29-31)

H. L. Mencken, "Willa Cather," in *The Borzoi 1920,* edited by Alfred A. Knopf, Knopf, 1920, pp. 28-31.

better worth knowing. Beneath the tawdry surface of Middle Western barbarism—so suggestive, in more than one way, of the vast, impenetrable barbarism of Russia—she discovers human beings bravely embattled against fate and the gods, and into her picture of their dull, endless struggle she gets a spirit that is genuinely heroic, and a pathos that is genuinely moving. It is not as they see themselves that she depicts them, but as they actually are. And to representation she adds something more—something that is quite beyond the reach, and even beyond the comprehension of the average novelist. Her poor peasants are not simply anonymous and negligible hinds, flung by fortune into lonely, inhospitable wilds. They become symbolical, as, say, Robinson Crusoe is symbolical, or Faust, or Lord Jim. They are actors in a play that is far larger than the scene swept by their own pitiful suffering and aspiration. They are actors in the grand farce that is the tragedy of man.

Setting aside certain early experiments in both prose and verse, Miss Cather began with *Alexander's Bridge* in 1912. The book strongly suggested the method and materials of Mrs. Wharton, and so it was inevi-

GRANVILLE HICKS

(essay date 1933)

[Hicks was an American literary critic. His best-known study, *The Great Tradition: An Interpretation of American Literature since the Civil War* (1933), established him as a prominent advocate of Marxist critical thought in Depression-era America. Throughout the 1930s he argued for a more socially responsible brand of literature and censured such writers as Henry James, Mark Twain, and Edith Wharton for failing to confront the bleak realities of human society. In the following excerpt, he finds fault with Cather's writing after *A Lost Lady,* arguing that it retreats into the nostalgic past rather than confronting the realities of contemporary society.]

WORLD LITERATURE CRITICISM

In her first representative book, *O Pioneers!* . . . , Miss Cather clearly indicated the subsequent development of her career. After experiments, some fortunate and some not, in the short story, and after the failure of *Alexander's Bridge,* her one book that betrays the influence of Henry James, she found her distinctive field of literary activity and her characteristic tone. *O Pioneers!* contains all the elements that, in varying proportions, were to enter into her later novels.

We observe first of all that the very basis of *O Pioneers!* is a mystical conception of the frontier. (p. 703)

Miss Cather, too, is concerned with [the] past era, and she looks back at it with nostalgia. "Optima dies. . . . prima fugit" might as well be the motto of *O Pioneers!* as of *My Ántonia.* Alexandra retains to the end the spiritual qualities of the pioneer, but the novel depicts the general disappearance of those virtues after the coming of prosperity. The coarsening of Lou and Oscar Bergson and the confusions of Frank Shabata and Emil are the fruits of change. (p. 704)

Even in little things *O Pioneers!* is prophetic. We find, for example, in her depiction of Amédée's funeral service, the same fondness for the colorful ceremonies of the Catholic church that dictated so many passages in *Death Comes for the Archbishop* and *Shadows on the Rock.* We find, also, in her scorn for the agrarian radicalism of Lou Bergson and Frank Shabata, the political conservatism that is implicit in all her works. And we find the episodic method, the reliance on unity of tone rather than firmness of structure, that is so marked in the later novels.

The two successors of *O Pioneers!*—*The Song of the Lark* and *My Ántonia*—closely resemble it, especially in the qualities we have noted. Both depend upon a mystical conception of the frontier, and both look back longingly to the heroism of earlier days. The more successful portions of *The Song of the Lark* are those portraying Thea's girlhood in Colorado and her visit to the cliff-dwellings. Both of these sections are developed at greater length than the part they play in Thea's life warrants, as if Miss Cather could not resist the temptation to expand upon her favorite theme. *My Ántonia* is exclusively concerned with the frontier, and the heroine retains the pioneer virtues in poverty and hardship, even as Alexandria and Thea do in success. All three women are triumphant products of the pioneering era; in them the mystical essence of a heroic age, now unfortunately passing, is embodied.

But if these three novels were merely mystical and nostalgic we should have less to say about them. After all, Miss Cather saw at first hand the Nebraska of the eighties and nineties, and her accounts of the life there are not without authenticity. However much she emphasizes the heroism and piety of the pioneers, she does not neglect the hardships and sacrifices. And heroism and piety did play their part in the conquest of the frontier. Miss Cather's proportions may be false; she may ignore motives, conditions, and forces that are altogether relevant; but there is nevertheless a basis in reality for the picture she gives.

That is why *O Pioneers!* and *My Ántonia* have their importance in American literature. Although the story of *My Ántonia* is told by Jim Burden, with his concern for "the precious, the incommunicable past," the book does create credible pioneers in the Burdens and Shimerdas and does give convincing details of their life. In the latter part of the book there is a passage in which several daughters of immigrants tell of their homes in the first years in Nebraska, and we realize that Miss Cather can appreciate the bleakness and cruelty of this land for the travelers from across the sea. She can understand their eagerness to escape to the towns, and she knows, too, the monotony and narrowness of the prairie city.

Against this background Miss Cather presents the unforgettable picture of Ántonia, more human than Alexandra because of her weaknesses, more likeable because of her defeats. (pp. 704-05)

From the first, it is clear, the one theme that seemed to Miss Cather worth writing about was heroic idealism, the joyous struggle against nature sustained by a confidence in the ultimate beneficence of that nature against which it fought. In her own childhood she had actually seen such heroic idealism in the lives of Nebraskan pioneers, and in writing of those lives she achieved not only personal satisfaction but also fundamental truth. One may feel that she deals with the unusual rather than the representative, and that what she omits is more important than what she includes. One may be conscious that the haze of regretful retrospection distorts innumerable details. But one cannot deny that here is a beautiful and, as far as it goes, faithful recreation of certain elements in the pioneering experience.

But after *My Ántonia* was written there came a crisis in Miss Cather's career as an artist. She obviously could not go on, painting again and again the Nebraska she had once known. The West was changing, as she had been forced to admit in *O Pioneers!* and the others. Could she learn to depict the new West as she had depicted the old? The story of this new West could scarcely take the form of a simple, poetic idyll. Heroism and romance, if they existed, had changed their appearance. Characters could no longer be isolated from the social movements that were shaping the destiny of the nation and of the world. She would have to recognize that the life she loved was disappearing. Could she become the chronicler of the life that was taking its place?

At first she tried. The earlier chapters of *One of Ours* describe a sensitive Nebraskan boy in the years before the war. Claude Wheeler, who as a youth flinches before the coarseness and materialism of his father, suffers almost as much from the narrow religiosity of his wife. The joy and beauty that are so prominent in the lives of Alexandra and Ántonia have vanished from Claude's Nebraska. Though he seems capable of a heroic idealism, his life is miserable and futile. Then the war comes, and he enlists, goes forth to battle in heroic mood, and dies a hero's death. Thus Miss Cather, thanks to a romantic and naïve conception of the war, was able to approximate her favorite theme. But the second part bears no relation to the issues raised in the account of Claude's unhappiness in Nebraska. For Miss Cather, as for Claude, the war provides an escape from apparently insoluble problems.

Insoluble indeed, Miss Cather found these problems, and as she looked at the life about her, her despair grew. Once she had created symbols of triumph in Alexandra, Thea, and Ántonia, but now she concerned herself with symbols of defeat. Of all the books between *My Ántonia* and *Death Comes for the Archbishop*, *A Lost Lady* is the most moving. Why Marian Forrester is lost Miss Cather never explains, contenting herself with a delicate and pathetic record of that descent. Captain Forrester has in him the stuff of the pioneers, but his wife, though one feels in her capacities for heroism, is the product of changed times, and she abandons her standards, betrays her friends, and encourages medocrity and grossness. She is the symbol of the corruption that had overtaken the age.

But *A Lost Lady* is merely a character study, and Miss Cather felt the need for a more comprehensive record of the phenomena of decay. St. Peter in *The Professor's House* is alienated from his wife and family; he has finished the work that has been absorbing him; he realizes that he must learn to live "without delight, without joy, without passionate griefs." That, Miss Cather seemed to feel at the moment, was what we all must learn. Heroism and beauty and joy had gone. For St. Peter these qualities had been summed up in Tom Outland, dead when the story opens, and perhaps fortunately dead: "St. Peter sometimes wondered what would have happened to him, once the trap of worldly success had been sprung on him." But Tom lives in St. Peter's memory, and his story occupies much of the book. Tom is the pioneer, vital, determined, joyful, sensitive to beauty. In telling his story Miss Cather escapes from her gloom and writes with the vigor and tenderness of her earlier work. But in the end the animation of the Outland narrative only serves to accentuate her melancholy, and she is left, like Professor St. Peter, in a drab and meaningless world. (pp. 705-07)

Her despair increased, and Miss Cather made one more study of defeat, in *My Mortal Enemy.* But obviously she could not continue with these novels of frustration and hopelessness. One may risk the guess that,

while she was writing her studies of despair, she personally was not particularly unhappy. Her reputation and income were both established on a reasonably high level. As a person she could be as contented as anyone else who enjoyed comfort and security, and as indifferent to the woes of the world. But as a writer she had that world as a subject, and the contemplation of it filled her with sadness and regret. It was not a world in which her imagination could be at ease, for her imagination still demanded the heroic idealism of the frontier. She could deal with that world only by portraying, in a few tragic lives, the corruption and defeat of what she held dear. She could not understand why evil had triumphed or how good might be made to prevail. All she could express was her conviction that something of inestimable value had been lost. (pp. 707-08)

Miss Cather has never once tried to see contemporary life as it is; she sees only that it lacks what the past, at least in her idealization of it, had. Thus she has been barred from the task that has occupied most of the world's great artists, the expression of what is central and fundamental in her own age. It was easy for her, therefore, to make the transition from *My Mortal Enemy* to *Death Comes for the Archbishop.* If she could not write as she chose about her own time, she could find a period that gave her what she wanted. The beauty and heroism that she had found in pioneer Nebraska and that seemed so difficult to find in modern life could certainly be attributed to life in mid-nineteenth century New Mexico. And thence she could turn, in *Shadows on the Rock,* to Quebec about 1700. Once more she could show men and women who were neither awed by the savageness of nature nor unappreciative of its beauty. Once more she could deal with "the bright incidents, slight, perhaps, but precious," that are to be found whenever "an adventurer carries his gods with him into a remote and savage country."

Death Comes for the Archbishop, which describes the life of two Catholic missionaries in the Southwest, is highly episodic, and the episodes are so chosen as to make the most of the colorfulness of the country, the heroism of the characters, and the contrast between the crudeness of the frontier and the religious and cultural refinement of the archbishop. As one reads, one seems to be looking at various scenes in a tapestry, rich in material and artful in design. At first one is charmed, but soon questions arise. One asks what unity there is in these various episodes, and one can find none except in Miss Cather's sense that here, in the meeting of old and new, is a process of rare beauty. What significance, one goes on to inquire, has this beauty for us? Does it touch our lives? Is this really the past out of which the present sprang? Did these men and women ever live? Is there anything in their lives to enable us better to understand our own? We ask these questions, and as we try to answer them we realize that we are confronted by the romantic spirit. Miss Cather, we see, has simply projected her own desires into the past: her longing for heroism, her admiration for natural beauty, her desire—intensified by pre-occupation with doubt and despair—for the security of an unquestioned faith.

What is true of *Death Comes for the Archbishop* is also true of *Shadows on the Rock.* Miss Cather has again created her ideal frontier and peopled it with figments of her imagination. The construction is even weaker, the events even more trivial, the style even more elegiac, the characters even less credible. The book has a certain sort of charm, for Miss Cather's dreams have beauty and are not without nobility, and it has brought consolation to many readers who share her unwillingness to face the harshness of our world. But for the reader who is not seeking an opiate *Shadows on the Rock* has little to offer. Compare Cécile with Alexandra and Ántonia; compare Pierre Charron with Tom Outland. What Miss Cather chiefly tries to do is to throw over her Quebec the golden hazen of romance, and she succeeds so well that her characters are, to the reader's vision, obscured and distorted almost beyond recognition.

Apparently it makes little difference what Miss Cather now attempts to do. The three stories in *Obscure Destinies* are more or less reminiscent of her earlier work, but the honesty and enthusiasm have disappeared. As if she were conscious of some lack, she finds it necessary to rely on direct statements. In **"Neighbour Rosicky"** she underlines the harshness and rapacity of the city and exaggerates the security of the country, and she introduces Doctor Ed to point the moral of the tale: "Rosicky's life seemed to him complete and beautiful." **"Old Mrs. Harris"** is so lacking in unity that its point has to be explained in the closing paragraph: "When they are old, they will come closer and closer to Grandma Harris. They will think a great deal about her, and remember things they never noticed: and their lot will be more or less like hers." **"Two Friends,"** concerned with two "successful, large-minded men who had made their way in the world when business was still a personal adventure," teaches that politics is much less important than friendship. Twenty years ago Miss Cather had no need of exposition, for her themes were implicit in her material, but now her romantic dreams involve the distortion of life, and she cannot permit the material to speak for itself.

The case against Willa Cather is, quite simply, that she made the wrong choice. The nostalgic, romantic elements so apparent in her recent work were present in her earlier novels, but they were at least partly justified by the nature of her themes, and they could be introduced without the sacrifice of honesty. But once she had to abandon the material her Nebraskan childhood had so fortunately given her, she had to make her choice. She tried, it is true, to study the life

that had developed out of the life of the frontier, but she took essentially marginal examples of modern life, symbolic of her own distaste rather than representative of significant tendencies. And when time had shown how certainly that path would lead to impotence and ultimately to silence, she frankly abandoned her efforts and surrendered to the longing for the safe and romantic past. (pp. 708-10)

If, to the qualities Miss Cather displayed in *O Pioneers!* and *My Ántonia,* had been added the robustness of a Dreiser or the persistence of an Anderson, not only survival but growth would have been possible. But the sheltered life seldom nurtures such qualities. She has preferred the calm security of her dreams, and she has paid the price. (p. 710)

Granville Hicks, "The Case against Willa Cather," in *English Journal,* Vol. XXII, No. 9, November, 1933, pp. 703-10.

EDWARD A. BLOOM AND LILLIAN D. BLOOM
(essay date 1962)

[In the following excerpt from their book-length study of Cather, *Willa Cather's Gift of Sympathy,* Edward Bloom and Lillian Bloom offer an appraisal of Cather's place in American literature.]

There is a steadiness about Willa Cather's fiction that defies the crosscurrents of the literary age in which she lived and wrote. Like many conscientious American writers, she was profoundly aware of the growing cleavage in her society between moral values and expedient action. Dislocations following the military and economic disasters she witnessed in her lifetime caused her to share a widespread fear that the future was bleakly uncertain, that a spiritual chaos threatened the central purpose of existence. More than most thoughtful Americans, perhaps, she was personally sensitive to devalued conduct and customs. Because she had consciously built her life upon a structure of traditions, and because she had preferred the solid virtues of an inspiriting past to the mercurial shifts of practical reality, she suspiciously resisted change. From time to time she protested against the violation of durable truths, although rarely in the clamorous voice used by many contemporary writers. Looking backward to the fixed values of a satisfying past, she reaffirmed the moral standards she cherished, thus ultimately denying they could be destroyed by temporary upheavals. In so doing, she committed herself to a pattern of continuity and became part of an exclusive but nevertheless great tradition of American writing.

Given fullest expression in the nineteenth century, the tradition is synthesized in the fiction of Cooper, Hawthorne, Melville, and James. Although they differed in their reactions to the convulsions afflicting an America in flux, they are unified by certain connections of personal responsibility. . . . Although all of them drew upon America as the source of their creative purpose, they resembled each other in their awareness of national exigencies rather than in any superficial resort to a common region or even set of circumstances. (pp. 237-38)

In every essential detail, Willa Cather aspired toward the ethical and creative goals of the great tradition, consequently becoming the twentieth-century successor of these four nineteenth-century novelists. Miss Cather's novels are still relatively recent, and historical perspective may not yet permit an ultimate evaluation of her literary position. We do have standards of continuity by which we may measure her achievement, however, and if these standards have any critical validity then Miss Cather is surely in the line of succession. More notably even than Cooper, and with a moral intensity comparable to that of Hawthorne, Melville, and James, Miss Cather has represented the tensions of American existence in the late nineteenth and early twentieth century. Like her predecessors—especially the last three—she is a commentator on the prevailing American condition. Sometimes urgent in her fears but always ardent in her faith, she constantly held before herself the vision of realizable ideals. Out of inspired singleness of conviction grew a distinguished art. To a greater degree than any of the four traditionalists except James, Willa Cather was absorbed in the total identification of an esthetic with moral purpose. Great achievement in the fusion of two inalienable ideals sets her apart from her own contemporaries and fixes her in a continuity of distinguished American writing whose practitioners are few. (pp. 238-39)

At first glance, Miss Cather would appear by virtue of her frequently used frontier subjects to be closest to Cooper. In fact, however, the frontier provides only a superficial resemblance, and Cooper was the writer most distant from her in temperament even as he was in time. That they were alike at all in aim is the result of the fact that they were deeply engrossed in the solution of American crises, each in his own way. Yvor Winters . . . has said of Cooper that his "concern was primarily for public morality; it was the concern of the statesman, or of the historian, first, and of the artist but secondarily." This statement of Cooper's literary interests, acutely defensible, it appears to us, shows the polarity between him and Willa Cather. National morality was, to be sure, intensely part of her fiction of the frontier. But in Cooper's intention we find a reversed image of Miss Cather's. She was the artist, and—more significantly—the moral artist, first. It was only after

she had appeased her esthetic-moral sense that she spoke as the historian, and then but to give fuller definition to her primary intention. Dealing with ethics rather than with manners, dedicated to a personal, non-doctrinal concept of salvation, she drew her characters as moral agents, somewhat as abstractions, if more balanced in physical properties than Hawthorne's. (pp. 240-41)

In her tendency to allegorize her moral searchings, she like Hawthorne never lost sight of her function as a creative artist. Indeed, she devoted herself to the notion that only through the highest expression of art could she give worthy representation to her inner desire. More specifically than Hawthorne, she cherished people as people and incidents as incidents. She softened the lines of her figures and actions, but she never clothed them in such abstractions that they lost verisimilitude. She respected the varieties of human emotions and meant them to be credible aspects of daily, familiar experience.

She was furthermore acutely conscious of artistic techniques, giving her search for esthetic perfection equality with her yearning for inner meaning. With regard to artistic credibility, she was closer to Melville than to Hawthorne, for like the former she sought a more immediate equation between physical reality and spiritual significance. As is true of Melville, she portrayed phenomenal reality and human beings in readily identifiable proportions. She made them agents of an ultimate truth but always invested them with properties which could be accounted for immediately at the conscious level of perception as well as at the somewhat mystic level of moral insight. If she was less visionary than Hawthorne and Melville, and less profound in her moral intensity, she was the more accomplished technician and consequently the more readable novelist.

But among the major writers in the tradition, Henry James undoubtedly bears the closest creative resemblance to Miss Cather. Both as an artist and as a moral realist he was the literary personality who figured most prominently among the influences shaping her artistic development. Greatly respectful of his esthetic achievements, she was attracted to his singularity of purpose, to the manner in which he made an art form cohesive with serious thematic details. James was so evidently the novelist she herself cared to be that she imitated him unsuccessfully in *Alexander's Bridge.* Her blunder, as she realized, was the attempt to capture a style in which meaning was not appropriately related to personal experience. But if James ceased to function as her model for the execution of idea and form, he left a permanent impression upon her because of the purity of aim which she always venerated as the essence of her own practice. Although they dealt with comparable themes somewhat divergently, each drawing upon his particular genius, the subtle likenesses between them make their exterior differences relatively unimportant.

What is important, in the present connection, is the attitude which they took toward their art. It is an attitude of moral sobriety, a deeply serious concern with quintessential American problems. Basic to this commitment is an esthetic sensibility which transfigures ethical responsibility into organic narrative situations. Both Henry James and Willa Cather believed that without appropriately conceived shape the novel fails to represent in true essence the inner experience which is the only justifiable substance of fiction. For each, therefore, a moral sense is powerfully one with an esthetic sense. Concept and form admit of no separation, the two growing simultaneously in the created work, inevitably and rightly. With respect to technical virtuosity, James and Miss Cather progressed beyond the earlier writers. In their fusion of moral idea and physical reality, they acknowledged to a remarkable degree the demands of their art, and then went on to fulfill the obligations to which they had committed themselves.

James and Miss Cather, furthermore, are related in the subjects they chose, although they attacked them from different angles. Yvor Winters . . . has pointed out that James wrote about "the spiritual antagonism which had existed for centuries between the rising provincial civilization and the richer civilization from which it has broken away, an antagonism in which the provincial civilization met the obviously superior cultivation of the parent with a more or less typically provincial assertion of superiority." Whereas for James the antagonism lay between an ancient European culture

Cather at work in 1901 or 1902.

and an upstart American culture, for Miss Cather the rift existed at times as an exclusively American phenomenon. That is, she focused her frontier novels on the divisions existing among native cultural forms. She may be said to have narrowed her view intensively, looking to the frontier first as a reaffirmation of traditional American values, and then to its development as a corruption of those values. As a further point of comparison, however, it must not be forgotten that even in the frontier novels, such as *O Pioneers!* and *My Ántonia,* she often considered with affection the traditions the first-generation pioneers had brought with them from Europe. But whether James and Willa Cather treated American themes as outgrowths of cultural divisions between nations or within the nation, they always did so with a moral responsiveness. Each brought to his novels a personal commitment which wedded feeling with insight, although Miss Cather's sympathies for America were the more immediate and direct.

As a traditionalist in an age which had no reverence for tradition, Miss Cather was a lonely figure. The moral integrity of the individual implied an exaltation of personality, even of egoism, which collided with the mass standardization and rapidly shifting values of mechanistic progress. To resist in a practical sense was, of course, vain. But the convictions of writers such as Miss Cather and James, as well as of Hawthorne and Melville, transcended practicality. Thus, Miss Cather, who formed very few intimate alliances in her lifetime, clung to a somewhat solitary position from which she idealized universal truth and frequently denounced temporization. Like Thoreau she challenged her own society, and like him she demanded a return to good purpose. (pp. 242-45)

Although she considered certain American writers of the 1930's—notably, Hemingway, Wilder, Fitzgerald, and Lewis—to be genuine artists, she thought the fiction of that period was largely without purpose. Yet, if she was hostile to the overt tone of pessimism and cynicism which pervaded much of contemporary fiction, she was closer in spirit to this literature of harsh reality than she herself would have cared to admit. (p. 247)

Throughout her novels . . . , Miss Cather is in the curiously ambivalent position of standing apart from her contemporaries, and yet at the same time of sharing many of the immediate moral problems which they had made their responsibility. Although she directed her vision to a traditional past, as they did not, she was nonetheless able to assess the dilemma of modern times through a conjunction of tradition with present reality. The important thing for her, of course, was that values may never be divorced from art. But it must also be acknowledged that for most serious writers of modern times moral or social responsibility must coincide with esthetic awareness. Willa Cather addresses herself most memorably to a tradition of conscience and hope; in this respect she is in the main stream of great American literary achievement. But she also addresses herself trenchantly, if in a minor key, to affairs of material reality. Eloquently joining past and present, affirmation and censure, she has memorialized herself as an American classic. (p. 250)

Edward A. Bloom and Lillian D. Bloom, in their *Willa Cather's Gift of Sympathy,* Southern Illinois University Press, 1962, 260 p.

DAVID STOUCK

(essay date 1973)

[Stouck, a Canadian educator and critic, is the author of *Willa Cather's Imagination* (1975). In the excerpt below, he examines the novels Cather wrote after *Death Comes for the Archbishop.*]

In her major novels Willa Cather explored the archetypal dimensions of the human imagination: *O Pioneers!,* with its vision of the new land and its heroic settlers, is written in the epic mode; *My Antonia,* with its quest into the author's personal memories, is a pastoral; *The Professor's House,* which chronicles an ugly tale of human greed, is largely satiric, and *Death Comes for the Archbishop,* with its saintly missionary priests, portrays the disciplined, timeless world of the paradisal imagination. But what of those books written after *Death Comes for the Archbishop,* particularly those last four volumes (*Obscure Destinies, Lucy Gayheart, Sapphira and the Slave Girl, The Old Beauty and Others*) which critics agree mark the decline of Miss Cather's art? Can these novels, from a writer of such depth, be as undistinguished and insignificant as has been suggested? The answer is at once affirmative and negative. With the exception of the long story, **"Old Mrs. Harris,"** the later writing lacks the imaginative energy which found consummate expression in the earlier novels. But the vision which underlies these books is precisely one which discounts the urge to expression through art; for it was the author's conviction in later years that not art but only life truly matters in the end. Consequently Willa Cather's last fictions occupy that paradoxical, but not uncommon, position of works of art pointing to their own devaluation.

As a romantic Willa Cather believed in the absoluteness of the artist's vocation. Her major novels were all written as egotistic expressions of an individual consciousness seeking to know and understand itself. Even as apparently selfless and disinterested a book as *Death Comes for the Archbishop* reflects a way of life achieved by the author after she had gone through a nadir of despair over her failure in human relationships. But the last novels and stories posit quite a different relationship between art and human consciousness. No longer driven by the Faustian urge to power through her writing, Miss Cather came to view her lifetime dedication to art as placing selfish and consequently tragic limitations on the demands of life itself. Again Miss Cather was following a path well-worn, to use one of her favorite images, by the "pilgrims" of the imagination. The futility of life's sacrifice to art had been dramatized more emphatically by artists who arrested their work in early or mid-career: by Rimbaud, for example, who went to Abyssinia to make his fortune in the slave trade; by Hardy, who ceased writing fiction after publishing his most powerful novel, *Jude the Obscure;* or by Hart Crane who, in his quest for the ideal, despaired of the mediacy of poetry and committed suicide. For Willa Cather the implications of her vision were never as wholly irrevocable or tragic, yet instinctively she moved toward that same juncture where art terminates in the mute acceptance (or, in Crane's case, hopeful transcendence) of life.

The change is first evident with the publication of *Obscure Destinies.* . . . Willa Cather's achievement of self-mastery with its fictional flowering in *Death Comes for the Archbishop* . . . , her supreme work of art, was irremediably shaken in the following years which brought the disruption of her apartment life in New York and the death of her father in Nebraska. The fictional consequence of this reversal was *Shadows on the Rock* . . . , a book set in seventeenth-century Quebec, but pervaded throughout by a very personal feeling of homesickness and the desire to retreat into a world that never changes. However, it was the illness and death in 1931 of the author's mother which determined the direction of her writing for the remaining years. . . . Where the novels of her middle years had found characters and settings in the world at large, the later fiction returns the author to her personal past once again in Nebraska and Virginia. But what is most significant is that these books are shaped throughout by a desire to see that world, at last, equably and with compassion. The imaginative tension for great art is largely gone, but in its place we have the artist's wisdom, her resolve—her testament to life which is poignantly simple and reassuring.

Miss Cather's last writings are informed throughout by a profound regret that youth in its self-absorption is so often cruel and indifferent, that greatness in any endeavor is achieved at the cost of human sympathy. The most moving expression of this final vision in her art is **"Old Mrs. Harris,"** the second story of *Obscure Destinies.* Here Willa Cather no longer attempts to prove herself in recreating the characters and incidents from her past, nor does she seek in them some way of resolving the tensions in her own private life;

rather her attitude is one of remorse and humility, as though writing were a form of penance and its only objective were to win forgiveness from those remembered persons by means of their sympathetic embodiment in a work of art. In **"Old Mrs. Harris"** Willa Cather recreates the characters and a period in her life (specifically her mother and grandmother as she remembered them from adolescence) which previously she had viewed with little affection. In this story, remembering the past is not an escapist pleasure, but a confrontation with guilty memories evaded for much of a lifetime.

The art and the reprise of **"Old Mrs. Harris"** lie in the subtlety with which point of view is managed. Although the controlling perspective is ultimately the author's—the grown Vickie remembering a sequence from her childhood—the story is narrated so that the three women in the family, while not understanding each other, emerge nonetheless as sympathetic individuals. Miss Cather in effect describes the tragic undertow of this story herself in her essay on Katherine Mansfield when she singles out that author's ability to reveal the many kinds of relations which exist in a happy family: ". . . every individual in that household (even the children) is clinging passionately to his individual soul, is in terror of losing it in the general family flavour. As in most families, the mere struggle to have anything of one's own, to be one's self at all, creates an element of strain which keeps everybody almost at the breaking-point." In **"Old Mrs. Harris"** sympathy at first appears to be reserved for the grandmother alone: the story begins with Mrs. Rosen's visit to Grandma Harris, and from the neighbor's vantage point the old woman appears to be the drudge in her daughter's household and the victim of her son-in-law's ineffectuality in business. But as we are taken inside Mrs. Harris's thoughts we find that as a Southerner she accepts her role in her daughter's kitchen and is grateful to be able to follow her daughter's fortunes in this customary way. Also the picture of her daughter from the neighbor's eyes as haughty and selfish, jealous of any attention paid to her mother, begins to soften as the old woman reflects that while her daughter is indeed proud, she at the same time has a "good heart." The old woman, moreover, admits to herself that, because Victoria had been the prettiest of her children, she had spoiled her. Mrs. Harris could have been wholly idealized if the author had retained only a granddaughter's perspective, but the tension in the family is felt from the daughter Victoria's point of view as well. At the Methodist social we are given a glimpse into her motives and feelings. We see her giving money spontaneously to the children of the poor laundress and know that the gesture is not intended to be patronising; we also feel with her the intended reproach when one of the meddlesome townswomen implies that Victoria exploits her mother in the kitchen. Victoria could have

been a wholly negative character, but sympathy is elicited for her in thus exposing her vulnerability.

The portrait of Vickie, however, is the most complex for hers is the "guilty" perspective; because she is a projection of the author's younger self she is viewed at once most critically and most sympathetically. Vickie's desire to go to college, to escape the cramped existence of an overcrowded family in a small midwestern town, blinds her to the feelings and needs of those around her. The measure of regret the author feels years later is suggested in the homely incident when the family cat dies. Vickie is so absorbed in her studies that she pays little attention to the death of the cat and her grandmother explains to the other children: "Vickie's got her head full of things lately; that makes people kind of heartless." It is a seemingly trivial incident, but it is steeped in the self-recrimination which underlies the story. When Vickie learns that in spite of the scholarship she has won there will not be enough money for her to go to college, she sees everyone as her enemy; she even refuses her grandmother's comfort.

The failure of sympathy and understanding in the family reaches a dramatic crescendo at the end of the story where the members of the family become so engrossed in their personal problems they do not realize the grandmother is dying. Here each of the women gives bitter expression to her frustration and despair as the grandmother looks helplessly on. Victoria asks her mother in an accusing tone if she is sick and says: "You ought to be more careful what you eat, Ma. If you're going to have another bilious spell, when everything is so upset anyhow, I don't know what I'll do." . . . When Vickie hears that her grandmother is ill and her mother lying down in her room she thinks "wasn't it just like them all to go and get sick, when she had now only two weeks to get ready for school, and no trunk and no clothes or anything?" . . . But our sympathies are never onesided: Vickie's selfish indifference is tempered by our knowledge that she is apprehensive and full of self-doubt about going away to school; and we learn that the attractive Victoria is to bring yet another child into the crowded house. The interweaving of multiple viewpoints renders movingly the imaginative tension at the heart of the story: while the memories of hidden longings and isolation are vividly recreated through Vickie's viewpoint, the narrative overview at the same time creates the mother and grandmother with sympathy and compassion. But it is a tragic ambience which surrounds the tale, for the understanding and forgiveness have come too late. The prototypes from life (and it is to life that we are directed in Miss Cather's last writings) are now gone, and compassion can only be expressed in art. The most moving image in the story is that of the poor servant woman, Mandy, washing old Mrs. Harris's feet. The power of this image derives from the Keatsian paradox that the servant's gesture of compassion is momentary but complete, while its artistic recreation must always be compensatory. The homely details of childhood are nowhere in Miss Cather's writing so lovingly described; but that affection is a quietly tragic emotion for art, though timeless, can never replenish life. (pp. 41-5)

The spirit of self-exorcism in which **"Old Mrs. Harris"** was written is pursued even more relentlessly in *Lucy Gayheart*. . . . Of all Willa Cather's novels *Lucy Gayheart* has probably received the greatest amount of negative criticism; the charge is usually that of contrivance and sentimentality. But if one perceives its design, *Lucy Gayheart* appears less contrived. The novel is built around three tales of love, three tales of remorse and reprise. In a letter to a friend Miss Cather suggested that the novel doesn't pull together until one reads the last part. It is in the final section, or Book 3, that we look at the novel through the eyes of a character who is filled with guilt and remorse over his actions in the past. Although Book 3, like the rest of the novel, is written in the third person, it is narrated from the viewpoint of Harry Gordon living on in the small Nebraska town of Haverford, twenty-five years after the heroine's death. Gordon had loved Lucy Gayheart, but he had not understood her. She had gone to Chicago to study piano and there had fallen in love with a singer, Clement Sebastian. Smitten in his pride, Gordon only thought of revenging himself on Lucy, of making her suffer. When Lucy came back to Haverford after Sebastian's death, he refused, in spite of her plea, to help or comfort her, withdrawing into the exclusive confines of his unhappy new marriage and the family bank. On the last day of her life, he had refused to give Lucy a ride in his cutter out of the cold wind. Book 3 takes place following old Mr. Gayheart's death; his winter funeral had made the townspeople feel "almost as if Lucy's grave had been opened." Harry Gordon, now fifty-five, reflects on the years that have elapsed since Lucy's death and admits to himself that he had gone to great lengths in order to make her suffer. The day on which she drowned "he refused Lucy Gayheart a courtesy he wouldn't have refused to the most worthless old loafer in town." . . . Subsequently his sense of guilt over her death has been the preoccupation of his life. He thinks of it (and his marriage) as a "life sentence" and his friendship with Lucy's father as an "act of retribution." He will never leave Haverford, for his home town is the place of his sorrow and his penance. The last section of the novel is a brief but sharply etched account of twenty-five years of remorse; but its mood creates a frame around the whole of *Lucy Gayheart,* for the book opens several years after Lucy's death, recalling the girl's vital presence in the town and mourning her loss. One of the song-cycles that Clement Sebastian performs is Schubert's *Die Winterreise,* the songs of a rejected lover who is psychically resurrected in the dead of winter to expe-

rience again and express the anguish of his loss. Although Gordon is not a singer the musical metaphor applies to him most aptly for his winter memory becomes the controlling perspective in the novel—an extension of the author's lamentation in her remorseful old age.

In **"The Old Beauty,"** written the year after *Lucy Gayheart* was published, Willa Cather touches once again on the major preoccupation of her last writings— her theme of regret and of confronting one's past honestly. Gabrielle Longstreet, the old beauty of the title, was once the rarest flower in London's brilliant society of the nineties. Recalling his acquaintance with her in those years is a very agreeable, nostalgic experience for Seabury, the central consciousness, for those "deep, claret-coloured closing years of Victoria's reign" appear to him from the 1920's as a more noble and more gracious period in human history. But on renewing his friendship with Gabrielle Longstreet, who is living anonymously as Madame de Couçy in France, he finds that her recollections of those years are steeped in regrets. In her youth she had been surrounded by countless unsolicited admirers; they were men of achievement, but she had simply taken them for granted. Now in her old age she has come to recognize their greatness and is filled with remorse that she once held them so lightly. . . . Her chief pleasure now is to read what those men wrote and what has been written about them. In spite of his nostalgia the past has its disagreeable aspect for Seabury as well. Gabrielle recalls to him that the last time they met he had found her in the embraces of a vulgar American businessman. Seabury had gone to China after the incident and had not seen her since. This preoccupation with confronting the past brings the story to its abrupt denouement. The automobile in which Seabury and Gabrielle are riding narrowly misses colliding with a small car driven by two vulgar young American women. Gabrielle dies shortly after this incident and our sympathy for the old beauty is complete. However, that sympathy does not derive, as critics have repeatedly suggested, from a simple juxtaposition of the old order against the new; rather it is extended to a heroine who, in the two American women, has caught a glimpse of herself in her youth. Outward appearances and life styles change but Gabrielle nonetheless marks in them her own thoughtless nature and perhaps her vulgarity too. It is a brutal confrontation, but in this moment of truth the old beauty is pardoned and redeemed.

The quest for some mode of redemption or release runs as a complementary theme throughout the last fiction to the statement of remorse. Earlier, in *The Professor's House,* Willa Cather found that the misery of failure in human relationships could only be transcended by relinquishing the desire for power and possessions in both human and material terms. In the last books the exorcism of man's lust for power still remains the antidote to the futility of ambitions and desires which leave only sorrow and regret in their wake. (pp. 45-7)

Willa Cather's preoccupation with power and possessiveness is nowhere as strikingly in the foreground as in her last novel, *Sapphira and the Slave Girl,* with its focus on the question of slavery. Dramatic conflict in this novel of pre-Civil War Virginia stems from the fact that Sapphira Colbert is a slave owner while her husband and daughter are in essence abolitionists. To Sapphira, an aristocrat, slavery is a natural part of the order to which she was raised, but for her husband and daughter the ownership of a human being is morally wrong. The attitudes to slavery are an essential expression of character in this novel; it is Sapphira, the slave owner, who experiences jealousy (the passion of possession) in relation to her husband whom she suspects of an amorous attachment to the slave girl, Nancy Till. The miller and his daughter, on the other hand, are indulgent and compassionate towards others: Henry Colbert is a gentle, understanding master and Rachel Blake is a Sister of Mercy at the bedsides of the sick. (pp. 47-8)

Much of *Sapphira and the Slave Girl,* with its evocation of a landscape and people, is still told in the loose anecdotal style, but smoldering beneath the descriptions of Virginia and the pre-Civil War way of life is a mordant drama of jealousy and revenge, the action of which is carried forward in fully dramatic scenes. The novel opens at "The Breakfast Table" when Sapphira announces to Henry her intention of sending Nancy to Winchester, and closes with Sapphira's moving repentance and her decision to invite her daughter to come and stay at her house. Such scenes in between as Martin Colbert's sexual pursuit of Nancy and Nancy's flight to Canada, which Miss Cather would formerly have avoided, are dramatized in considerable detail. As a result we see the characters as complex individuals, neither wholly good nor wholly bad, but engagingly and sympathetically human. Sapphira at first appears a malignant force; she is proud and coldly vengeful and sets out to ruin Nancy in order to punish her husband. But we are also made aware that her illness is a heavy burden and that her suspicions of her husband are not without foundation. In contrast we see the miller poring over his Bible down in the mill, striving to be a righteous man. But if Sapphira is too domineering, then her husband is too weak. He is fond of Nancy, as a father of a daughter, but does nothing to protect her from his nephew's advances; his role in helping her escape is a clandestine, noncommittal gesture of leaving some money unguarded in his coat pocket. We see these two characters most equably through the eyes of Rachel Blake. She realizes that by nature she is not equipped to understand her mother, for Sapphira is indeed harsh, often cruel, with her ser-

vants and patronizing towards her husband. But she sees her mother's kindness—her indulgence with Tansy Dave and her affection for Old Jezebel—and realizes that Sapphira genuinely likes to see her servants happy. On the other hand, while Rachel shares her father's quiet, sympathetic nature, she sees clearly his moral cowardice. The full humanity of Sapphira and the miller is disclosed in their last scene together where they recognize their mutual failings and strengths. . . . The full measure of sympathy the author feels for her characters is evident in Sapphira's penitential recognition of her shortcomings; she says contritely to the miller: "We would all do better if we had our lives to live over again." . . . (pp. 50-1)

Critics have discussed the possible directions Miss Cather's imagination would have taken in her new work, which in both time and place represented a significant departure from all her other writing. But in a letter to a friend Miss Cather clearly defines, I believe, that direction herself when she says that she has no more interest in writing since her brother's death, for she realizes nothing in life really matters but the people one loves. . . .

An artist's abandonment or renunciation of his craft, however, does not invalidate his life's work. On the contrary it places it in the more meaningful context of experience achieved, for the artist's path is a circuitous one which returns its pilgrim to life. That Willa Cather, unlike many of her American contemporaries, travelled the full road is not always recognized. But the words of Wallace Stevens are a worthy reminder: " . . . we have nothing better than she is. She takes so much pains to conceal her sophistication that it is easy to miss her quality." (p. 53)

David Stouck, "Willa Cather's Last Four Books," in *Novel: A Forum on Fiction,* Vol. 7, No. 1, Fall, 1973, pp. 41-53.

DEBORAH G. LAMBERT
(essay date 1982)

[In the following excerpt, Lambert examines Cather's treatment of female characters in her novels, noting a transition with *My Ántonia* from delineations of strong, independent women to more conventional portraits.]

My Ántonia (1918), Willa Cather's celebration of the American frontier experience, is marred by many strange flaws and omissions. It is, for instance, difficult to determine who is the novel's central character. If it is Ántonia, as we might reasonably assume, why does she entirely disappear for two of the novel's five books?

If, on the other hand, we decide that Jim Burden, the narrator, is the central figure, we find that the novel explores neither his consciousness nor his development. Similarly, although the narrator overtly claims that the relationship between Ántonia and Jim is the heart of the matter, their friendship actually fades soon after childhood: between these two characters there is only, as E. K. Brown said, "an emptiness where the strongest emotion might have been expected to gather." Other inconsistencies and contradictions pervade the text—Cather's ambivalent treatment of Lena Lingard and Tiny Soderball, for example—and all are in some way related to sex roles and to sexuality.

This emphasis is not surprising: as a writer who was also a woman, Willa Cather faced the difficulties that confronted, and still do confront, accomplished and ambitious women. As a professional writer, Cather began, after a certain point in her career, to see the world and other women, including her own female characters, from a male point of view. Further, Cather was a lesbian who could not, or did not, acknowledge her homosexuality and who, in her fiction, transformed her emotional life and experiences into acceptable, heterosexual forms and guises. In her society it was difficult to be a woman and achieve professionally, and she could certainly not be a woman who loved women; she responded by denying, on the one hand, her womanhood and, on the other, her lesbianism. These painful denials are manifest in her fiction. After certain early work, in which she created strong and achieving women, like herself, she abandoned her female characters to the most conventional and traditional roles;

analogously, she began to deny or distort the sexuality of her principal characters. *My Ántonia,* written at a time of great stress in her life, is a crucial and revealing work, for in it we can discern the consequences of Cather's dilemma as a lesbian writer in a patriarchal society.

Many, if not all, achieving women face the conflict between the traditional idea of what it is to be a woman and what it is to achieve. Achievement in most fields has been reserved for males; passivity—lack of assertiveness and energy, and consequent loss of possibility of achievement—has been traditionally female. When the unusual girl, or woman, rebels, and overcomes the limitations imposed on women, she suffers from the anxiety produced by conflict. Although such a woman is, and knows she is sexually female, in her professional life she is neither female nor male. Finding herself in no-woman's land, she avoids additional anxiety by not identifying herself professionally as a woman or with other women. Carolyn Heilbrun, who diagnoses and prescribes for a variety of women's dilemmas, writes: "Sensing within themselves, as girls, a longing for accomplishment, they have, at great cost, with great pain, become honorary men, adopting at the same time, the general male attitude towards women."

From childhood, Willa Cather was determined to achieve and she perceived, correctly, that achieving in the world was a male prerogative. When she decided as a child to become a doctor, she also began to sign herself "William Cather, MD," or "Willie Cather, MD," and she pursued her vocation seriously, making house calls with two Red Cloud physicians, and on one occasion giving chloroform while one of them amputated a boy's leg. She also demonstrated her clear understanding of nineteenth-century sex roles and her preference for "male" activities when she entered in a friend's album two pages of "The Opinion, Tastes and Fancies of Wm. Cather, MD." In a list that might have been completed by Tom Sawyer, she cites "slicing toads" as a favorite summer occupation; doing fancy work as "real misery"; amputating limbs as "perfect happiness"; and dressing in skirts as "the greatest folly of the Nineteenth Century." At college in Lincoln, her appearance in boyishly short hair and starched shirts rather than the customary frilly blouses—like her desire to play only male roles in college dramatic productions—continued to reflect her "male" ambition. James Woodress, Cather's biographer, speaks of a "strong masculine element" in her personality, a phrase that may obscure what she saw clearly from childhood: that womanhood prohibited the achievement she passionately sought.

After some measure of professional success, Cather began to identify with her male professional peers, rather than with women. Her review of Kate Chopin's novel *The Awakening* (1899) is a poignant example of the troubling consequences of this identification. First, Cather describes Edna Pontellier's struggle towards identity as "trite and sordid" and then, comparing Edna to Emma Bovary, adds contemptuously that Edna and Emma "belong to a class, not large, but forever clamoring in our ears, that demands more out of life than God put into it." In a final irony, Cather writes of Chopin that "an author's choice of themes is frequently as inexplicable as his choice of a wife." Like Flaubert and other male authors with whom she identifies, Cather fails to understand, let alone view sympathetically, the anguish that Chopin brilliantly portrays in Edna's life and death.

Nevertheless, in two novels written before *My Ántonia,* she accomplished what few women authors have: the creation of strong, even heroic, women as protagonists. Cather succeeded in this because she could imagine women achieving identity and defining their own purposes. The woman author, whose struggle toward selfhood and achievement is marked by painful conflict, rarely reproduces her struggle in fiction, perhaps finding its recreation too anxiety-producing, or perhaps simply not being able to imagine the forms that a woman's initiation might take. George Eliot and Edith Wharton, to mention only two familiar examples, never created women characters who possess their own intelligence, ambition, or autonomy. Characteristically, women authors transpose their own strivings to their male characters and portray women in conventional roles. (In this case, the roles ascribed to women in fiction are the same as those ascribed to them in society.) The occasional male author—E. M. Forster, James, and Hawthorne are examples—will create an independent, even heroic, female character, perhaps because male progress toward identity, demanded and supported by society, is generally a less anxious process.

Alexandra Bergson in *O Pioneers!* (1913) and Thea Kronberg in *The Song of the Lark* (1915) are female heroes, women not primarily defined by relationship to men, or children, but by commitment to their own destinies and to their own sense of themselves. Alexandra inherits her father's farm lands and grandfather's intelligence: although her father has two grown sons, he chooses Alexandra to continue his work, because she is the one best-suited by nature to do so. Developing Nebraska farmland becomes Alexandra's mission, and she devotes herself to it unstintingly. She postpones marriage until she is nearly forty years old, and then marries Carl, the gentle and financially unsuccessful friend of her childhood. Ultimately, Alexandra has success, wealthy independence, and a marriage which, unlike passionate unions in Cather's fiction, will be satisfying rather than dangerous. In this portrait of Alexandra, Cather provides a paradigm of the autonomous woman, even while she acknowledges, through the images of Alexandra's fantasy lover, the temptations of self-abnegation and passivity.

Thea Kronberg dedicates herself to music, and her talent defines and directs her life. Born into a large frontier family, she clear-sightedly pursues her goals, selecting as friends those few who support her aspirations. Subordinating personal life to the professional, Thea, like Alexandra, marries late in life, after she has achieved success; and her husband, too, recognizes and accepts her special mission. There is never a question of wooing either of these women away from their destinies to the conventional life of women. Marriage, coming later in life, after identity and achievement, is no threat to the self; moreover, Cather provides her heroes with sensitive, even androgynous, males who are supportive of female ambition. But Alexandra and Thea are unusual, imaginative creations primarily because they embody autonomy and achievement. In these books, Cather does not transpose her struggle for success to male characters, as women authors often have, but instead risks the creation of unusual female protagonists.

What Cather achieved in these two early novels she no longer achieved in her later works. Indeed she stopped portraying strong and successful women and began to depict patriarchal institutions and predominantly male characters. Although she wrote ten more novels, in none of them do we find women like Alexandra and Thea. *Death Comes for the Archbishop* (1927) and *Shadows on the Rock* (1931) are Cather's best-known late novels, and in the former there are virtually no women, while in the latter, women are relegated to minor and entirely traditional roles. Cather's movement toward the past in these novels—toward authority, permanence, and Rome—is also a movement into a world dominated by patriarchy. The writer who could envision an Alexandra and a Thea came to be a celebrant of male activity and institutions.

In this striking transformation, *My Ántonia* is the transitional novel. Given the profound anxieties that beset women authors when they recreate their search for selfhood in female characters, it is not surprising that Cather turned to a male narrative point of view. She rationalized that the omniscient point of view, which she had used in both *O Pioneers!* and *The Song of the Lark,* was not appropriate for her subject matter and continued to ignore the advice of Sarah Orne Jewett, who told her that when a woman tried to write from a man's point of view, she inevitably falsified. Adopting the male persona was, for Cather, as it has been for many other writers, a way out of facing great anxiety. Moreover, it is natural to see the world, and women, from the dominant perspective, when that is what the world reflects and literature records. Thus, in *My Ántonia,* for the first time in her mature work, Cather adopts a male persona, and that change marks her transition to fiction increasingly conventional in its depiction of human experience. (pp. 676-81)

Cather's career illustrates the strain that women writers have endured and to which many besides Cather have succumbed. In order to create independent and heroic women, women who are like herself, the woman writer must avoid male identification, the likelihood of which is enhanced by being a writer who is unmarried, childless, and a lesbian. In the case of *My Ántonia*, Cather had to contend not only with the anxiety of creating a strong woman character, but also with the fear of a homosexual attraction to [the model for Ántonia]

Annie/Ántonia. The novel's defensive narrative structure, the absence of thematic and structural unity that readers have noted, these are the results of such anxieties. Yet, because it has been difficult for readers to recognize the betrayal of female independence and female sexuality in fiction—their absence is customary—it has also been difficult to penetrate the ambiguities of *My Ántonia*, a crucial novel in Cather's long writing career. (p. 690)

Deborah G. Lambert, "The Defeat of a Hero: Autonomy and Sexuality in 'My Antonia'," in *American Literature*, Vol. 53, No. 4, January, 1982, pp. 676-90.

SOURCES FOR FURTHER STUDY

Modern Fiction Studies, Special Issue: Willa Cather 36, No. 1 (Spring 1990): 3-141.
> Includes essays on diverse interpretations of Cather's works.

Murphy, John J., ed. *Five Essays on Willa Cather: The Merrimack Symposium.* North Andover, Mass.: Merrimack College, 1974, 141 p.
> Collection of five essays on Cather's art and technique by such critics as Bernice Slote, John J. Murphy, and Lillian D. Bloom.

O'Brien, Sharon. *Willa Cather: The Emerging Voice.* New York: Oxford University Press, 1987, 464 p.
> Biography that focuses on Cather's life prior to 1915, on the various stages of her gender confusion, and on her search for a personal narrative voice.

Skaggs, Merrill Maguire. *After the World Broke in Two: The Later Novels of Willa Cather.* Charlottesville: University Press of Virginia, 1990, 212 p.
> Traces Cather's literary development from the publication of *One of Ours* in 1922 to her last work, *Sapphira and the Slave Girl,* in 1940.

Slote, Bernice, and Faulkner, Virginia, eds. *The Art of Willa Cather.* Lincoln: University of Nebraska Press, 1974, 267 p.
> Collection of essays on various aspects of Cather's fiction by noted Cather scholars, including James Woodress, James E. Miller, Jr., and Bernice Slote.

Woodress, James. *Willa Cather: A Literary Life.* Lincoln: University of Nebraska Press, 1987, 583 p.
> Comprehensive critical biography.

ISBN 0-8103-8362-4